Mcgraw-Hill Series in Political Science

JOSEPH P. HARRIS, *Consulting Editor*

EUROPEAN AND COMPARATIVE GOVERNMENT

McGraw-Hill Series in Political Science

Joseph P. Harris, *Consulting Editor*

EUROPEAN AND
COMPARATIVE GOVERNMENT

Robert G. Neumann

UNIVERSITY OF CALIFORNIA

LOS ANGELES

SECOND EDITION

New York   Toronto   London

McGRAW-HILL BOOK COMPANY, INC.

1955

To

MARCIA

In Memoriam

PREFACE

This book consists of five parts, four of which deal with the governments of Great Britain, France, Germany, and the Soviet Union, while the fifth attempts a comparative analysis of governments as well as political concepts and institutions which are not confined to the four nations mentioned above. The choice of countries is always a debatable issue, and the author is fully conscious of the possibility of legitimate criticism. Some will feel that Switzerland, with its unusual and highly successful form of government, should have received fuller treatment. Others may be disappointed to see neither Italy nor Scandinavia discussed in independent parts of this book. Others again may wonder why fuller treatment has not been accorded to Latin America or Asia.

All these points are well taken and are not without their justification. However, the author was quite determined not to write an encyclopedia of many volumes, which might have been more admired than read, nor was he going to rush through a dozen or more countries in a few pages. It therefore became necessary to make a narrow choice, in which the author was guided by two principles: (1) the realization that the leading and rival forms of government which put their mark on the rest of the world are to be found primarily in Europe and the United States; (2) the belief that the four states selected represent four different types of outstanding interest: three democratic countries, all very different from one another and from the United States, including now the German Federal Republic (West Germany) with its new and untried parliamentary regime, and the Soviet regime, which of course cannot be absent from any discussion of modern government.

The governments of India, China, and Japan may some day be equally indispensable in a discussion of this kind, but a certain amount of time will have to elapse first. This is in no way intended to diminish the importance of these countries but refers solely to the degree to which their political and constitutional lives will have to jell into a more permanent mold.

The fifth part of the book follows a different pattern. The author has felt for some time that we pay lip service in our classes to the idea of comparative government but actually teach merely individual foreign governments. Obviously a valid comparative approach will achieve little where fundamental knowledge about the institutions and concepts of the most important countries is lacking. But after some knowledge along those lines has been absorbed— and the first four parts are designed to contribute to this goal—it seems desirable to lead the student one step further to the more distant and more difficult planes of comparative analysis, which are capable of producing a better understanding of the phenomena of government itself. Moreover, such an approach makes it possible to bring into the discussion certain important institutions of a great number of countries even though time and space do not permit separate and exhaustive treatment. It is hoped that this small sample will induce the student to proceed to more fully functional or specialized studies.

A word about the general approach: the author has always believed that a purely descriptive treatment, which some confuse with objectivity, is inadequate. Government is not like a rock formation, which is likely to remain unchanged for some time and which can therefore be studied at leisure. Government is a living subject which changes in some respect every minute. To state this is to state the obvious, but what are the consequences? If a living, changeable subject is merely described as it is at a given time, the description is bound to be out of date the moment it leaves the author's hands.

A subject of this kind cannot be presented like a photograph; it must convey the breath of life. But since the author cannot issue daily bulletins to keep his readers abreast of later developments, he can only attempt to show government in motion, as a development and a trend, in order that the reader may easily fit later events into the ever-changing picture. In order to do this, the author must use two tools which are not universally loved and which will probably get him into trouble: history and analysis.

There is, of course, no attempt to rival colleagues in the history departments or to duplicate their efforts. Nor is it intended to give a comprehensive historical treatment. But the author maintains that the present role of Parliament in Great Britain cannot be understood without some knowledge of the gradual development of parliamentary institutions, that France's government will meet only with incomprehension unless one remembers the French Revolution and the fear of "Caesarism," and that Russia's present policies have probably been dictated as much by the direction of its streams and the impact of the Mongols as by the doctrines of Marx and Engels. Therefore the author considers a moderate amount of historical introduction indispensable. This was done in a somewhat elaborate fashion in the first edition of this work. But the greatly expanded political and institutional sections of the second edition have made it necessary to cut the historical parts in order to keep the book within manageable proportions. The essential historical data and information have, however, been retained.

We have spoken of government as living matter. First, one must learn where its institutions and concepts come from; that means history, as has been mentioned. But one must also attempt to see what the government is doing at the moment and what course it takes. In part this is a matter of fact; in part it is a matter of interpretation.

The author believes stubbornly that, contrary to widespread belief, facts do not speak for themselves but speak only when they are properly interpreted and analyzed. To quote Arts. 91–93 of the French Constitution concerning the establishment and operation of a constitutional committee is to quote a fact, but to say that this institution is probably quite meaningless is to state an interpretation. Yet to quote the "fact" without the interpretation is to give a totally erroneous view of the fact.

Interpretation means the analysis of available facts. Such interpretation may at times be tentative and subject to revision as new facts appear. There is always the theoretical and very remote possibility that the French constitutional committee may some day awaken to life, but it has not happened yet and in the light of history and political realities it is not likely to happen; there the interpretation must take its stand.

Interpretation is truth as the author sees it and by such light as he possesses. At times, therefore, it may reflect the author's cultural background, upbringing, and prejudices. However, to dispute this or that interpretation is not to dispute the necessity for interpretation itself. The Weimar Republic of Germany came to a *de facto* end in 1933. That is a fact. It came to an end because the republican parties were too weak or too disunited, or because the civil service was too much opposed to democracy, or because of the depression, or because of Hitler's cleverness, or because of the financial support to the Nazis. All that is interpretation. What is the author to do? Surely he cannot ignore interpretation, nor can he serve every possible interpretation—the likely, the unlikely, and the remote. Such a work, apart from its necessarily huge size, would bewilder the reader, who would need some other book to tell him to which interpretation he should give his attention. The only possible course, therefore, is an honest attempt to consider all available factors and to interpret them in the way which is most likely to be correct. Absolute certainty is not possible in the study of human institutions. Not only the rational, but also the irrational characterizes human beings.

The general plan of the first edition has been maintained in the second. But the vastly increased experience of France and Germany with their new constitutions, the consequences of Stalin's death on the Soviet Union, and governmental changes in Great Britain which permit the results of nationalization to be viewed with some perspective have made it necessary to rewrite a very substantial part of this book. In so doing, the discussions of institutions and political parties have been considerably increased.

In the preparation of the second edition, much use was made of the now considerable supply of primary and secondary French and German sources. The wealth of material on the Soviet Union, produced by a mounting research effort in America and free Europe, was of great help in addition to primary material partly available in translations or translated excerpts. Also the flow of British sources, always more easily available, has increased.

In response to a suggestion by many readers of the first edition, a selected bibliography has been added. However, for practical reasons, only a minimum of foreign-language sources has been included. Some further references may be found in the footnotes.

Several colleagues have suggested that the fifth, comparative section of this book ought to be placed first, to be followed by the individual country parts. This suggestion has received very serious consideration. However, it appears that a considerable majority of those who adopted this book prefer to give students a grounding in the individual countries before undertaking a comparative approach. This would also be the author's inclination, but the comparative part of this book is organized in such a way that it may be taken up first by those inclined to do so.

In his work the author has received help and advice from far too many quarters to mention here. Kind colleagues and students have contributed a great deal. Opportunities to consult with numerous French and German governmental leaders, members of parliament, judges, and other figures of public life have helped to separate theory from practice in those two countries, whose constitutions and political life are of recent nature.

Among several research assistants, the author wishes to express his warm gratitude to Rita Sparks and Abbie Lundgreen and to Peter Toma, as well as to Eva Zimbler Huebscher and Beth Preston Cook, who did spade work on the first edition. A major contribution was again made by the author's wife, whose editorial and critical activities have been indispensable. Sincere thanks go to the author's parents, without whose patient and willing readiness to perform baby-sitter services this edition could never have been finished on time. A heartfelt vote of thanks also to numerous friends, foreign and domestic, who restrained themselves from visiting the author and his wife when the manuscript reached its final stages.

ROBERT G. NEUMANN

CONTENTS

APPENDIXES

Part 1. GREAT BRITAIN

England is not governed by logic, she is governed by Parliament.
BENJAMIN DISRAELI, LORD BEACONSFIELD

A FAMOUS WIT once described Great Britain [1] and the United States as "two countries separated by the same language." This remark bears the obvious stamp of Shavian exaggeration, but it tends to remind us that the many close ties existing between the two countries are not solely, or even primarily, based on the use of a more or less common language. Above and beyond that linguistic kinship there is a vast common heritage in the origin and the practice of many institutions and ideas which are characteristic of free government, although here too misconceptions arise.

Critics of American institutions frequently, though not always correctly, point an envious finger at the supposed excellence of British government. Some, who are exasperated by the recurrent tug of war between President and Congress, extol the British cabinet system and sometimes even advocate its adoption. The critics of certain Congressional investigation committees admire the quietly efficient procedure of the Royal Commissions, while critics of the much-reduced spoils system dream of the British civil service.

Of course such easy comparison often misses the mark, especially when it fails to take into consideration the special problems of a federal state of continental expansion. Also, the advocates of a parliamentary system for America blithely assume that if we adopted it our course would then follow that of Britain and not the less fortunate example of France.

The twentieth century has witnessed the development of increasingly strong British-American relations in the field of international affairs. It is a commonplace to state that Britain is the cornerstone of our military and diplomatic strategy in Europe, while the need for an expanding American market for British exports is and will remain one of the principal concerns of the British government. Such increasing interdependence does not always make for the smoothest of relations, but the fact that our two countries are firmly welded together by innumerable ties is incontestable.

A thorough understanding of British affairs, the nature of her government

[1] The term "Great Britain" as used throughout this book is meant to stand for the United Kingdom, which includes England, Wales, Scotland, and Northern Ireland.

1

and the atmosphere in which it operates, ought therefore to be of great concern to an informed American public. Yet, such understanding is often difficult because of a certain vagueness of institutions and frequent absence of definitions, which a distinguished Englishman has epitomized in these words:

It is a commonplace that the characteristic virtue of Englishmen is their power of sustained practical activity, and their characteristic vice a reluctance to test the quality of that activity by reference to principles. They are incurious to theory, take fundamentals for granted, and are more interested in the state of the roads than in their place on the map.[2]

The apex of this approach is the British "constitution," a generic term covering a multitude of statutes, decisions, customs, and conventions, dealing with the institutions of state and government and the rights of the citizens. Its principal parts are the customs and conventions, *i.e.*, the ideas held at a certain time as to what is or is not done. Customs and conventions, however, are merely another name for practice, and since practice changes continuously, even the most acute and up-to-date description must, of necessity, be outdated and behind the times.[3]

There is a tendency to overlook changes in British public life because the ancient character of many institutions sometimes makes them appear immutable. It is, of course, true that many of the sources of British democracy are venerable with antiquity, but democracy itself is of fairly recent origin. Magna Carta was written in 1215, but at that time it was only the official recognition of feudal privileges. At any rate, one can hardly speak of free or democratic government in England before 1832. Since that time the transformation of British life has never ceased and has in fact been characterized by a more and more accelerated pace.

— The great thing about these transformations has been that they were accomplished peacefully. What greater external change is feasible than the transformation of the British Empire of Disraeli and Joseph Chamberlain into the free association of independent nations, the "Commonwealth," from which the word "British" has now been dropped? What greater internal change is conceivable than the transition from the opulent empire as Queen Victoria knew it to the land of recent austerity and socialist experimentation? In less fortunate countries such changes take place to the accompaniment of protracted bloodshed and in the awful shadow of civil war. In Britain they are announced in a speech from the throne.

These transformations have frequently bewildered foreigners, because they are often hidden behind ancient ritual and immutable façades. The Britisher, who, no matter how radical, is always to some extent a disciple of Burke, values the stability and security which come from accepted and affectionately

---

[2] R. H. Tawney, *The Acquisitive Society,* New York, 1920, p. 1.
[3] Ramsey Muir, *How Britain Is Governed,* Boston, 1935, 3d ed., p. 2.

regarded institutions. But he is also a realist and quite willing to try out some new course of action; consequently, an increasing discrepancy develops between the form of institutions, which remains the same, and the substance, which changes. Now the Britisher understands that perfectly well. He is not greatly troubled by questions involving the purity of a theory or the consistency of an approach; he is primarily interested in successful performance. Therefore he is quite prepared to accept the discrepancy between the form and the substance of institutions and to defend both with equal conviction. To many foreigners, however, especially to Continental Europeans, this seemingly inconsistent attitude smacks of hypocrisy: "perfidious Albion" was once a popular expression.

The continuous growth of constitutional practice has been so peaceful because no single class or group has been permanently excluded from power[4] in contrast to other countries. It has been possible because the fundamental questions of government, the form of the state, the form of government, the relationship between people and government, and the methods of change were fairly well agreed upon before the culmination of the Industrial Revolution. These questions were settled by men who felt secure in the majesty of their country and who were in such fundamental agreement that they could, in the words of Lord Balfour, "safely afford to bicker." Once accepted, this attitude of fundamental agreement prevailed even after security was gone or at least temporarily suspended.

The foreign observer might well ask what marvelous bill of rights, what masterfully constructed institutions and statutes, uphold and maintain this system. The answer will shock him; there are but few. To be sure, there is a bill of rights, and there are various other statutes and institutions, but there is very little *legal* restraint. Theoretically the royal powers are all-inclusive, and Parliament could invest an individual with dictatorial powers or abrogate all civil rights. On the basis of existing statutes, the power of the Home Secretary over public meetings and free speech is extraordinary. Under the famous, or infamous, Sec. 18B of the Defence Regulations, he was able to intern thousands of people, suspending in effect the writ of habeas corpus in the country of its birth. And under the equally famous but now abrogated Control of Engagements Order, the Secretary of Labor could order citizens to accept certain available jobs. The remarkable thing about these statutes and orders is not that they exist, but that they are not used except in rare emergencies. If the King, the Home Secretary, or the Secretary of Labor were to use these theoretical powers indiscriminately, he would immediately and rightfully be accused of unconstitutional conduct. But since there is no constitution in any formal sense, "unconstitutional" means, in effect, only one thing: namely, that it is not proper. This brings us to the core of the British system of government, which is not a constitutional document, nor an elaborate sys-

[4] Harold J. Laski, *Parliamentary Government in England,* New York, 1938, p. 4.

tem of checks and balances, but rather the generally held and clearly understood belief that certain things simply are not done by gentlemen.

Walter Bagehot in his classic work on the English constitution [5] declared that such a system of government was possible in England only because there existed certain prerequisites: mutual confidence among electors, a calm national mind, and the gift of rationality. These qualities all add up to an adult and practical nation. Semibarbarous people, says Bagehot, are marked by "diffused distrust and indiscriminate suspicion."

Some critics of the more radical left have expressed fear that this admirable degree of general consent would disappear if the economic system of capitalism were seriously threatened by a victorious socialist majority. They feared that in the marriage of capitalism and democracy the emphasis might be on capitalism, and that, consequently, vested interests would possibly turn against democracy once a democratic majority threatened their economic power. Recent developments have proved this fear groundless. The Labor government, elected in 1945, had no trouble in obtaining the seals of office, and no insurrection endangered its vast nationalization and planning program. The Opposition fought bitter parliamentary and electoral battles—which was its business—but there was no civil war, no civil disobedience, no underground plotting. Whatever one may think about the merits or demerits of the socialist experiment, it is an impressive fact that these tremendous social and economic changes took place in an atmosphere of peace and due process of law.

The brilliant days of Palmerston, Disraeli, and Gladstone are gone. London is no longer the hub of the universe. But a thoroughgoing restoration of Europe's health and dignity is unthinkable without Britain's leadership, and in her civic discipline as well as in the free association of her Commonwealth the world may find much to admire and emulate. No greater mistake could be made than to write Britain off lightly.

It must always be remembered that Great Britain is a state *sui generis*, and not really a part of Europe, except by an accident of geography. Her ties and interests have always emphasized the Empire and Commonwealth, rather than Continental relations. Britain has been hesitant about getting too closely embroiled in the affairs of Europe for fear of losing her place as the center of the Commonwealth. Common economic, political, and military dangers have driven Britain reluctantly to ever closer cooperation with the Continent, but such action as membership in the Western European Union is still regarded as a *mariage de raison*, not as true love. Bagehot, when seeking comparison or contrast, looked to the United States, not to France or Germany. The student of British government will therefore do well not to fix his eyes on the European character of Britain, but to treat Britain as a world in itself—a world which has by no means been oblivious to its environment, but which has nevertheless retained its own characteristics.

[5] Walter Bagehot, *The English Constitution*, first published in London in 1867.

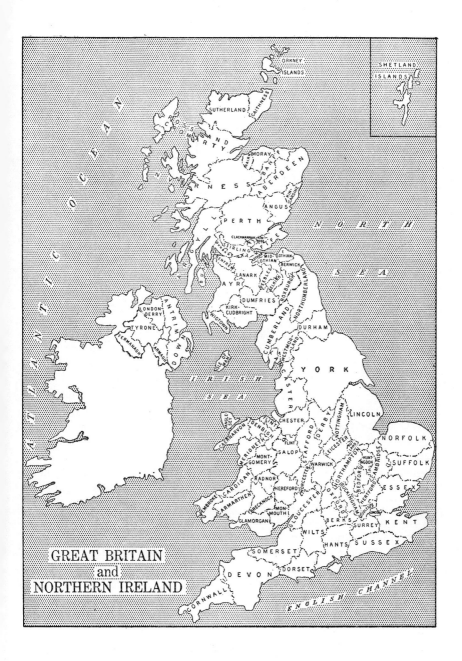

GREAT BRITAIN
and
NORTHERN IRELAND

5

Chapter 1

THE ORIGINS OF THE CONSTITUTION

Celtic (British) and Roman England have left hardly a trace except in literature and in certain place names. Deeply influential as the Roman occupation was in countries like France, it left almost no marks in England although it lasted for 461 years.

The Angles, Saxons, and Danes, who succeeded to the Roman heritage, established seven kingdoms until they were unified under King Alfred (the Great, 849–901). The kingship was an institution known to all Teutonic nations. Customarily the King was elected by the Council of Elders (witenagemot) whose consent was needed on all important questions. This council was known elsewhere as the "thing." In this assembly the King would decide questions of state as well as administer justice, for all these assemblies were courts. There the King would also issue his decrees, the so-called "dooms."

All this is indeed very reminiscent of the later, Norman-Angevin,[1] period. However, what similarity there is can be explained by the fact that both Anglo-Saxon and Norman institutions had their roots in the customs of the Teutonic nations. It is quite possible that the Anglo-Saxons, had they never been conquered, might have developed very much the same forms as are now attributed to the Norman invaders.[2]

The Anglo-Saxon period, which came to an end in 1066, left hardly any mark on the central government of England. But in the field of local government its influence was far more lasting. The townships and especially the shires—later renamed counties—remained. That was also true of the boroughs, especially London. A number of townships formed the *hundreds*, which had their own governmental institutions and courts and were in turn subordinated to the shires. There, the sheriff (*shire-reeve*) became the principal power as the delegate of the King.

[1] Derived from the Anjou dynasty (from Anjou province, France; capital, Angers) which came to power in England with Henry II (1154) and called itself Plantagenet.

[2] George B. Adams, *The Origin of the English Constitution*, New Haven, 1920, 2d ed., pp. 17–18.

6

The Norman-Angevin Period

The constitutional history of England begins, then, with the Norman conquest of 1066. The Normans themselves were of Scandinavian origin, and their own institutions were hardly more sophisticated than those of the Saxons. But the Normans had settled in France in the tenth century and had come in contact with the vastly superior organization of the declining Carolingian monarchy, the Frankish empire. From it they accepted two principal ideas: royal absolutism and feudalism, the two centers of English constitutional developments.

William the Conqueror transplanted these ideas to England—chiefly because he knew them to be the most effective ways of ruling a country. Moreover, so many parallels could be found between Anglo-Saxon and Norman customs that the transition was fairly smooth, especially as the wise Norman rulers ostensibly granted their Anglo-Saxon subjects some of their ancient laws, such as those of Edward the Confessor, but modified—if not to say falsified—sufficiently to make them acceptable to the demands of Norman rule.[3]

As was customary in those days, William declared all English land forfeited to him, which gave him an opportunity to dispossess the native lords and invest his own followers with their holdings. This was the feudal system which was thus transplanted to England. In other countries, especially Germany, it led to the dissolution of the empire because it created mighty lords who challenged the King's power. But in England most of the Norman-Angevin kings retained a high degree of control and thus established a regime which was not only feudal and absolute, but also centralist.

Local customs prevailed in the feudal courts, but the King sent his own royal judges on circuit. These judges—an institution derived from Charlemagne and the Frankish empire—inquired into local customs and law and in their jurisdiction fused them more and more into a unified body of rules. But these judges were usually ecclesiastics who had studied the Church (canon) law, which in turn had taken most of its precepts from the Roman law. Thus, Roman-law ideas and expressions entered into English law. On the whole, the royal law which was established by these itinerant judges was superior and more equitable than the local, feudal rules which it gradually replaced. This was the origin of one of the proudest possessions of the English-speaking nations, the common law, the law which was common to the entire realm, in contrast to local, feudal law.

[3] The cultural development and civilization of the Normans were incomparably higher than those of the Anglo-Saxons. This is attested by the fact that most expressions of the English language which pertain to the professions, arts, and science or otherwise concern a higher type of life are of French origin. The Norman predilection for written records and orderly procedure alone made them superior administrators.

At the same time the jury made its first appearance. Under the Anglo-Saxon rule, the free warriors (*thanes*) had participated in the rendering of the verdict. Now they were called upon to give evidence as to the facts in the case, a combination of witness and jury. This, and the separation of royal from ecclesiastic courts, further strengthened the system of royal justice.

In his role as a ruler, the King was assisted by two bodies, the Grand Council (*Magnum Concilium*) and the King's Court (*Curia Regis*). Both bodies were feudal assemblies to which the nobles were summoned as part of their duties of vassalage to the King. Of the two, the *Curia Regis* was the smaller but more important. Theoretically the two councils were one; every nobleman had a right to sit in the Curia, and the smaller group had all the rights of the larger one. In actuality, however, no vassal appeared at the Curia who was not specifically summoned. Moreover, the assembly of all the vassals, the *Magnum Concilium*, met only three times a year, when the King was in England, and that was not enough to conduct all the business of the state. Hence the growing importance of the *Curia Regis*.

The Norman dynasty declined after the death of the conqueror, but it was succeeded in 1154 by the energetic Henry II of Anjou (Plantagenet). By that time, certain important events had taken place. The royal courts had ceased to be merely temporary makeshifts, and had become permanent features. The common law which they established was recognized, and it was generally assumed that the King was subordinate to the law. Such obligations upon the otherwise absolute King were by no means illogical, since the entire feudal system and the lord-tenant relationship were based on a contract imposing mutual obligations.

Most of the courts of that time were assembly courts, *i.e.*, assemblies like the *Curia Regis* which also discharged judicial functions.[4] But the trend toward more professional courts was already clear in the twelfth century. The *Curia Regis*, which was sometimes difficult to distinguish from the *Magnum Concilium*, had become a permanent, almost professional body. Later it was to be called the Permanent Council. But certain sections of the Curia acquired more and more independent functions until they became separate bodies.[5] This is the origin of the Exchequer (as a court for the settlement of fiscal disputes), of the Court of Common Pleas (for pleas under common law for which the presence of the King was not required),[6] and later of the Court of King's Bench, the Chancery, and the Privy Council. At the same time, criminal justice was improved by the imposition of a permanent jury system

---

[4] See Charles H. McIlwain, *The High Court of Parliament and Its Supremacy*, New Haven, 1910.

[5] D. Pasquet, *An Essay on the Origins of the House of Commons* (trans. by R. D. G. Laffan), Cambridge, 1925, pp. 6–8.

[6] According to Adams, *op. cit.*, pp. 136–143, the Court of Common Pleas did not originate in the *Curia Regis* but had a distinct and separate origin.

whose functions were more reminiscent of our modern grand jury than of the trial jury.

MAGNA CARTA

The institutions just described were not "democratic" as the term was later understood; they were part of the feudal system. But they had become so generally accepted that a lawless king who attempted to do with them as he pleased ran into serious difficulties. This happened to King John, who was forced to accept in 1215 that famous document known as Magna Carta.[7] The Great Charter was not a contract between the King and the nation—there was hardly a nation—nor was it a charter of civil liberties. It was a purely feudal document, in which the King guaranteed to the nobles the rights which, in their opinion and probably correctly, they already possessed. It was not called the "great charter of liberty" (*magna carta libertatis*), but the "great charter of liber*ties*" (*magna carta libertatum*), namely, the liberties of the barons. When the Charter speaks of "free man" (*homo liber*), it refers to the nobles, as it does when referring to the jury trial as "judgment by his peers." [8]

Thus the Charter confirmed primarily the feudal rights of the barons, guaranteeing them their possessions against unlawful interference by the King, and the right to be punished or fined only by the judgment of their peers. It also stopped the arbitrary removal of a case from a baronial court to a royal court and stopped the King from interfering too drastically with the right of inheritance.

However, the Charter's most notable contribution was the provision contained in Sec. 61, which established a machinery for keeping the King under control. The barons realized that a mere promise, extracted from the King when his fortunes were low, could not be relied upon to protect them once he had regained his power. Therefore the Charter established a committee of twenty-five barons to be freely elected by their peers. Any complaint of a violation of the Charter was to be brought to the attention of four of the twenty-five, who would demand that the King or one of his officers redress the wrong. If that were not done within forty days, the four barons were to refer the matter to the rest of the twenty-five, who would review the case. If they agreed that a violation had occurred, they had the right under the Charter to rise in arms, together with the rest of the barons, to seize the King's possessions, or to injure him in any way until redress had been made.

[7] The definitive work on the Great Charter is still M. S. McKechnie's *Magna Carta; A Commentary on the Great Charter of King John*, Glasgow, 1905. See also F. Thompson, *The First Century of Magna Carta: Why It Persisted as a Document*, Minneapolis, 1925.

[8] This term is preserved in the title of "peer," the official designation of the members of the present House of Lords.

Thus was established for the first time in history the principle of a limited monarchy—the first step toward constitutional government. It was contained in two great ideas: that the King was bound by the law, and that his subjects had a right to set up machinery to enforce this obligation, if necessary by civil war. Such an arrangement was quite clumsy, but "considering that the men of 1215 had no precedent to go upon, no model of any such machinery to follow, no literary expression of such ideas, no theorizing about such procedure, they did very well." [9]

The long-range significance of the Charter made its appearance only gradually. However, with every subsequent dispute, the Charter became an increasingly strong weapon for free, constitutional government, which would be quoted by the opponents of arbitrary power as an argument for their cause.[10] This was possible because the Charter bore in the two above-mentioned principles the germ of all future constitutional developments. In this sense one might accept the famous dictum of Bishop Stubbs that the whole of English constitutional history is merely one long commentary on Magna Carta.[11]

Up to the thirteenth century the Great Council and the Curia retained their purely feudal character. It is now generally agreed that in 1254 representatives of the counties were summoned to the Council, for which the term "Parliament" became current.[12] There is no evidence that much was achieved at that time, as the reason for the summons was the chronic need of the King (Henry III) for money, and the nobles were reluctant to grant the requests without the consent of those to whom a part of the burden would be passed on. At any rate, the custom of calling lesser men than the peers of the realm to Parliament was far more significant than the meeting itself, which produced few results.

In subsequent years, the custom of summoning the representatives of the counties grew, especially as the need for financial support increased. Simon of Montfort, after his victory over Henry III, again summoned the knights of the counties in 1264 to meet with the Council the subsequent year. At that time, representatives from the cities appeared as well. However, the reputation of Simon of being the father of the House of Commons appears to be ill founded. There was no House of Commons in 1265 nor for many years thereafter. Everybody met in one assembly, and there is no evidence to show that later meetings were greatly influenced by the gathering of 1265.

[9] Adams, *op. cit.*, pp. 179*f*.

[10] Frederic A. Ogg, *English Government and Politics*, New York, 1936, 2d ed., p. 16.

[11] W. Stubbs, *The Constitutional History of England*, Oxford, 1880, Vol. II, pp. 2*ff*.

[12] First used in the reign of Henry II. See A. F. Pollard, *The Evolution of Parliament*, London, 1920, p. 32. Used more definitely by Matthew Paris, *Historia Anglorum* (1237). Pasquet, *op. cit.*, p. 3.

THE RISE OF PARLIAMENT

The Parliament which King Edward I summoned in 1295 has been termed the "model Parliament." This laudatory expression is acceptable only with considerable caution. Apart from the nobles and the clergy, there were summoned two knights from each county, two citizens from each city, and two burghers from each borough. All this was not new. Each of these groups had been summoned to Parliament before. But the innovation consisted in their being called all to one and the same gathering, and this remained the model for later sessions, though by no means all of them followed it.

There is evidence that the groups deliberated separately at times, but in order to make a decision, they had to meet in one body, which was the rule. There was then as yet no House of Commons, but only one Parliament.

Some doting historians have chosen to present the story of the rise of Parliament as an example of the steady growth of popular demands for self-government. Others have interpreted Edward's statement to the clergy, to the effect that "what touches everyone should be approved by everyone," to mean that the King decided to share the rule of the realm freely with his subjects. Both theories are without foundation. The subjects and nobles were most reluctant to make use of these institutions. The King had to bring great pressure on those whom he summoned in order to make them appear at the session of Parliament. To travel to Oxford, or London, might have taken weeks or longer for some of the delegates. Sometimes the King prorogued Parliament quickly, and summoned it again later, causing great inconvenience. There can therefore be no question of a popular "demand" for parliamentary representation. Nor could as strong-willed a King as Edward I be suspected of wishing to share his power with anyone. The fact was simply that the King desired to strengthen his hand by obtaining the support of the cities and counties, and by imposing a more reliable tax basis on them than was possible if he dealt with the nobles alone. Parliament was therefore largely an institution which the King forced on more or less unwilling subjects for purposes of his own.

The Parliament which was convoked in 1295 was, like its predecessors, above all a court and many writers refer to it as the "High Court of Parliament." There was no idea of legislation. In the Middle Ages, laws were generally not passed but "found" in the customs and conventions of the realm. Deliberations in Parliament had the character of court proceedings, and few acts of Parliament are recorded from those days which would qualify as "legislation" by modern standards. But there were a great many petitions to redress wrongs, and in that manner the King learned a great deal about the state of the realm. With the consent of the urban groups he could also collect taxes more easily.

We cannot fix an exact date when the House of Commons originated. It is certain that it did not exist under Edward I and it is equally certain that it did exist under Edward III. We may surmise that the representatives of the *communes* or *communitates*—from whom the name of the house is derived—appeared before the "bar" of Parliament, of which they were not full-fledged members; that they withdrew, or were urged to withdraw, to deliberate among themselves; and that they appointed a "speaker" who alone had the right to speak in Parliament. Thus they submitted their petitions for the redress of grievances, which were enrolled as statutes. These common pleas required common deliberation and common action on the part of county and city representatives. This habit became an institution, and eventually a house. It grew slowly and imperceptibly, and therein lies its strength.

In the fourteenth century, the clergy generally withdrew from Parliament into their own assemblies. Therefore there remained essentially two bodies, and it is of the utmost significance that, for reasons which are not entirely explored, the lesser nobility joined forces with the "commons," thus giving them both strength and new blood. But it was not until the sixteenth century that the division became official, and we hear officially used the term "House of Lords." Until then, the Commons, although they deliberated separately, were essentially a committee of Parliament. Their power grew immeasurably when the lesser nobility joined and lent their wealth and experience. Gradually, under the guise of "petition" and extreme humility, the Commons established their power, especially in financial matters. By 1407, it was accepted doctrine that financial legislation had to originate in the Commons, and that the two groups, the Lords and the Commons, should confer among themselves and then report to the King upon their full agreement.

The power inherent in Parliament was not quickly realized. The reluctance of members to serve persisted for some time. There was certainly no thought that Parliament was sovereign, for sovereignty as understood by Bodin or Hobbes belongs to a later period. The royal power before the Tudors was of a feudal nature. It emanated from the King as the tenant-in-chief to the magnates of the realm, and from them to their tenants, and so forth down. In this framework, neither Parliament nor any other body of men could claim "sovereignty" for themselves. There was no national ambition for self-government, partly because there was as yet no nation. Moreover, as long as the power of the great lords was overabundant, no national consciousness could arise, for each was lord in his own domain, and their country was Norfolk or Essex or Cornwall, not England. It was only when the cities and counties began to become more interested in sending delegates to Parliament that this situation began to change. What caused the change is impossible to say. Perhaps it was, as one writer put it, "that general stirring of national impulse in English bones of which Wycliffe, Langland, and Chaucer were some of the exponents." Perhaps the close confines of an insular existence emphasized the common weal. The progress of education, which produced some of England's most famous colleges, may have had something to do with it, and the Peasants' Revolt of 1381 would seem to indicate some political consciousness on the part of the lower classes. Whatever the reasons, we notice that after the middle of the fifteenth century more interest was shown in Parliamentary representation. Attendance at meetings picked up, and the representation of a borough or county in Parliament was at last considered an asset rather than a liability. In 1533 a borough member was elected Speaker of the House of Commons for the first time, and only a few years later it is reported that the Speaker had asked for access to the King on behalf of himself and his colleagues. At the same time, even elder sons of peers sought election to the House of Commons.

This increased interest in the House of Commons produced a more careful organization and the keeping of a Journal. Being a member of the House of Commons now brought prestige and public recognition, and men were praised for being great parliamentarians.

The Tudor period was the last great preparatory period which Parliament, especially the House of Commons, had to undergo before facing its crucial test under the Stuarts. A number of writers have dismissed the Tudor period as one in which Parliament was merely a rubber stamp. There is some truth in this, but it misses the point. Henry VIII was the first king who might truly be called a "sovereign." He held in his hand the total power of the realm which was brought to bear upon all subjects, high and low alike. No longer was there a process of delegating power, as was the case under feudalism. But on the other hand, the King sought to dignify his administration by having many of his acts enrolled as acts of Parliament. The King therefore caused Parliament to be in session much more often than before. A common experience and procedure were created, and the House of Commons began to maintain control over its own members. The House did support Henry VIII and Elizabeth in their major actions, but its members were jealous of their right to speak freely, and individual members spoke out in a clear voice against royal acts of which they disapproved.

Although the Tudors generally gained the support of the House of Commons, they were nevertheless aware of its sensibilities. But their successors, the Stuarts, attempted to make an absolute political theory of their supremacy and to relegate the Commons to the lower depths. The House of Commons, which, as we have seen, had gained much in stature and especially in solidarity, was not likely to look kindly upon such endeavors.

The viewpoint of the King was explained in a tract written by himself (James I), entitled *The Trew Law of Free Monarchies*, which was published in 1598. Its thesis was simple to grasp. The King's power derived from God, and it was therefore blasphemy to call him to account. "The state of monarchy is the supremest thing upon earth: for kings are not only God's lieutenants upon earth and sit upon God's throne, but even by God himself they are called Gods." Consequently "kings were the authors and makers of the laws, and not the laws of the kings," and therefore "that which concerns the mystery of the king's power is not lawful to be disputed."

The opposing viewpoint was well stated by the great exponent of the common law, the Chief Justice Sir Edward Coke: ". . . the king cannot change any part of the common law, nor create any offense by his proclamation which was not an offense before, without Parliament. . . ." [13] Now this was an extreme statement, and hardly in accordance with the facts.[14] But while the Commons and Coke might have been short on theory, they were long in the clarity of their political conception. What the King demanded was not a return to the Middle Ages or even to the Tudors, but the establishment of royal absolutism and the abdication of Parliament. Had the Commons elected to surrender, England would have followed the path of France. True, royal absolutism might have been shed later, as in France, but that could have been done only by revolutionary means, which would have deprived English institutions of that steady growth which is their principal strength. Fortunately the Commons chose to fight.

The outcome of this struggle is well known. The Stuart king Charles I lost his head. But the triumphant House of Commons was hardly less arbitrary than the King. Political opponents were eliminated, the House of Lords was abolished, and a Commonwealth (republic) was proclaimed. Oliver Cromwell became the actual ruler, as Lord Protector, but he and the army were scarcely less difficult to bear than the Stuarts. The Commonwealth never became rooted in popular sentiment and did not long survive the death of Cromwell. The rebelling Commons had not really meant to abolish the monarchy when they began their uprising,[15] and the Commonwealth had been the product of the victorious moment, rather than of a carefully conceived plan. The depressing effect of Puritan rule and the excesses of the army quickly made the monarchy popular again, and when General Monk contrived to bring Charles II, the son of Charles I, back to England in 1660 there was general relief. Charles II, although a thoroughly inconsequential and frivolous person, managed to ride the tide, but his brother, James II, burned with the fire of the divine-right-of-kings theory. To make matters worse, he was a Catholic, and Catholics were not popular in England at that time.[16] When the King proceeded to grant far-reaching rights to Catholics and Nonconformists, and to restore the arbitrary Elizabethan Court of High Commission, the House of

[13] The Question of Royal Proclamations (1610), Coke, *Reports*, XII, pp. 74*f*.

[14] Coke's extreme views also sought to restrain Parliament when it interfered with the common law. See Dr. Bonham's case, *ibid.*, XII, p. 75. "It appears in our books, that in many cases, the common law will controul [*sic*] acts of Parliament, and sometimes adjudge them to be utterly void."

[15] See the Grand Remonstrance of 1641.

[16] It should be pointed out, however, that the divine-right-of-kings theory is a Protestant, not a Catholic, concept.

Commons decided to get rid of him. They called upon Prince William of Orange, governor (*stadtholder*) of the United Netherlands and husband of James's daughter Mary, to assume the English throne. James fled the country, and it is perhaps typical that this bloodless shift of power is referred to as the "Glorious Revolution."

The triumphant Commons were in no mood to entrust their liberties to any monarch unprotected. This time their rights were to be put down in black and white. But certain legal difficulties developed.[17] In order to be effective, the new king had to accept certain conditions before his coronation. Yet, without a king, no legal Parliament could be convoked. This dilemma was resolved in the following way: A number of members of Parliament and certain other officers assembled at Westminster, declared the throne vacant on account of James II's flight, and called upon Prince William and Princess Mary to rule the country. Therefore William and Mary, by the advice of the lords spiritual and temporal and "diverse principal persons of the commons," caused a new Parliament to be elected. This Parliament has been called the "Convention Parliament" because it met on January 22, 1689, without being legally convoked. This "Parliament" then drew up a declaration of its rights [18] which was accepted on February 13. Thereupon William and Mary were proclaimed King and Queen. On February 22, the "Convention Parliament" was legalized by royal action, and finally on December 16, the now legal Parliament reenacted its previous declaration with certain additions which became known as the Bill of Rights.[19]

The Bill of Rights of 1689 is one of the fundamental documents of the constitution.[20] It creates no innovations, but it crystallizes the growth and achievements of parliamentarism in England. It provided that Parliament "ought to be free" and held frequently; that Parliament should make laws and that there should be granted no dispensation from them except by act of Parliament; that all ancient rights and liberties be confirmed; and that no Catholic should ever ascend to the throne. These provisions were further broadened in the Toleration Act (1689), which increased the rights of Nonconformists; the Triennial Act (1694), which provided that Parliament should meet at least once every three years; the Trial for Treason Act (1696), which

---

[17] Frederic W. Maitland, *The Constitutional History of England,* London, 1908, pp. 281–288.

[18] Containing a list of grievances against James II, a method which was later adopted in the American Declaration of Independence.

[19] For text see Stephenson and Marcham, *Sources of English Constitutional History,* New York, 1937, pp. 599–605.

[20] Some distinguished authorities have opined that the Bill of Rights is the nearest thing in English history to a written constitution. G. B. Adams, *Constitutional History of England,* New York, 1934, 2d ed., p. 358. This seems to be debatable, as Crowell's *Instrument of Government* (1653) is far more like a constitution and is probably the oldest written constitution.

modified criminal procedure; the Act of Settlement (1701), which established the line of succession to the throne; and finally, under Queen Anne, the Act of Union with Scotland (1707). To these important statutes must be added an earlier one which constitutes one of the proudest possessions of the English-speaking world, the Habeas Corpus Act (1679).

With these acts, but especially in view of its demonstrated strength, the victory of Parliament was achieved. Parliament, however, meant now and henceforth the House of Commons. The House of Lords continued to exist, but the tail now wagged the dog.

Let us pause for a moment and examine what the supremacy of Parliament meant. The King was still, as a medieval writer has stated, "in his court, in his council, in his parliament." [21] The King's powers had greatly declined, while Parliament had become exalted. But while the King had become nearly powerless, the Crown, the symbol of government, had gained immeasurably by the newly found unity of the nation. Yet Parliamentary government, as it emerged in the seventeenth century, had two major flaws: it was not representative, and it was impossible as a government. A large number of seats in Parliament were filled by members who represented no electorate other than a handful of landowners who made and unmade members at will. Those were from the "rotten boroughs," as they came to be called. On the other hand, there were large cities without representation. Much corruption prevailed, and the House of Commons, in sovereign arrogance, declared men elected who had not obtained the necessary number of votes, while duly elected members were not seated. Favors and offices were bought and sold, and political opponents were sometimes persecuted. At the same time, this proud and unrepresentative body could not actually govern the country because it was too large and diversified. Consequently the actual reins of government were often wielded by various cliques of politically ambitious men and women who were essentially responsible to nobody.

The Growth of the Cabinet System

In other countries, such conditions frequently lead to revolution and counterrevolution. In England, this was happily not the case. The fortunate tradition of institutions which grew out of experience and fortuitous accident produced the cabinet system which the leading authority on the subject has described as the "core of the British constitutional system." [22] Parliamentary supremacy had been established in 1689. Nobody could doubt that. But at the same time the King considered himself to be the real executive, and this idea was shared by Parliament, which attempted to check his power by re-

[21] Fleta, II, c. 2, quoted by F. Pollock and F. W. Maitland in *History of English Law to the Times of Edward I,* London, 1911, 2d ed., Vol. I, p. 179.

[22] W. Ivor Jennings, *Cabinet Government,* Cambridge, 1951, 2d ed., p. 1.

affirming its own power of impeachment.[23] The King soon found that he was most likely to get on with Parliament if he selected those men for his advisers who had the confidence of the majority of Parliament. This development really came into its own when the Hanoverian dynasty ascended to the throne in 1714. George I was a German prince who knew no English and cared little for England. He withdrew from the meetings of the cabinet council, leaving the conduct of business to its chairman, who began to be called Prime Minister.[24] There was little change under George II. George III made one last attempt to recover the lost prerogatives of royal power, but Parliament was far too strongly entrenched, and alert to its danger, to permit him to turn the clock back. The loss of the American colonies, the resignation of the Lord North cabinet, and finally the insanity of the King put an end to such endeavors. The prestige of the Crown sank further under the regency and George IV. But William IV and especially Queen Victoria restored its reputation, which increased constantly thereafter. The First and Second World Wars, especially, brought new heights of popularity to the monarchs who shared in the privations of their subjects. But there was no question of giving the King any real power. Queen Victoria had tried to have a hand in the selection of her Prime Ministers and repeatedly attempted to keep the seals of office from the Liberal party leader, William Gladstone. But she was completely unsuccessful, and no subsequent king has dared to make a similar attempt.

It is the English cabinet system which has permitted Britain to become a crowned republic, because it vests the real executive power, not in an untouchable king, but in a responsible cabinet—responsible, that is, to the real sovereign, Parliament, and ultimately to the people.

The cabinet system is one of Britain's outstanding gifts to the science and practice of government. Yet this institution, like so many others, was never "created." It grew imperceptibly, with the result that when it was firmly established, it was already so generally accepted that no serious protests against it were forthcoming. This is generally the advantage of gradually developed institutions over created ones. How unaware even sophisticated contemporaries were of this tremendous innovation is demonstrated by the fact that the wise and well-educated founders of the American Constitution gave little attention to the cabinet problem and none to the concept of a responsible ministry. Likewise, when in 1791 the Pitt government in England framed a government for Canada which was to be based on the English model, no responsible cabinet was created or even proposed.

An essential part of the system of cabinet government is the responsibility

[23] See the Act of Settlement of 1701, 12 & 13 William III, c. 2. Since "the King could do no wrong," the executive power could be curbed only by impeaching the King's ministers.

[24] The first person so called was Sir Robert Walpole.

of the cabinet to the legislature. This too was a feature which emerged gradually. William Pitt still resisted ouster by a hostile majority in the House of Commons, but when Sir Robert Walpole lost his majority in the House in 1742, he resigned as a matter of course. When it was firmly established that a Prime Minister must resign as soon as he has lost the confidence of Parliament, the older remedies of ouster, impeachment, and act of attainder fell into disuse.[25] For a while governments believed it necessary to have the confidence of the Crown as well as of the House of Lords in addition to that of the Commons. As late as 1839 Sir Robert Peel refused office because he felt that he did not possess the confidence of the Crown, and in 1850 a British cabinet (Russell) found it necessary to ask for a special vote of confidence from the House of Commons because it had received a vote of nonconfidence from the House of Lords. But soon thereafter the cabinet's sole responsibility to the House of Commons was fully recognized, and in 1868 Prime Minister Disraeli resigned upon the defeat of his party at the polls, without waiting to meet Parliament as had hitherto been the custom.

Thus it was recognized that the people, in voting ostensibly for members of the House of Commons, actually elect a new government. That has been standing practice ever since. It would be inconceivable for the King to call anyone but the leader of the victorious party to Buckingham Palace to entrust him with the seals of office; nor will the displeasure of the House of Lords ever again endanger the stability of a cabinet. Lord Salisbury was the last Prime Minister (1895–1902) to sit in the House of Lords, rather than the House of Commons. So much importance was attributed to the Prime Minister's ability to represent the government in the House of Commons that, when Prime Minister Bonar Law resigned in 1923 because of ill health, Stanley Baldwin became his successor and not the favored Lord Curzon.

BROADER REPRESENTATION

The close relationship between the cabinet and the House of Commons would not have been possible had the House not become much more broadly representative than it had been in the eighteenth century. We have seen how unrepresentative the House of Commons was before 1832.[26] Large municipal areas were unrepresented, while ruined hamlets "sent" members to Parliament. Worse, rich landowners who themselves may have been members of the House of Lords, the House of Commons, or the cabinet "appointed" members to seats which they controlled and sometimes sold in the most open and shameless manner. More than half the seats in the House of Commons

[25] The last case of impeachment was that of Lord Melville in 1805.

[26] E. Porritt, *The Unreformed House of Commons; Parliamentary Representation before 1832,* Cambridge, 1909, 2d ed., 2 vols., is the most authoritative work.

came from such "rotten" or "pocket" boroughs, a situation which John Locke described in the following terms:

To what gross absurdities the following custom, when reason has left it, may lead, we may be satisfied when we see the bare name of a town of which there remains not so much as the ruins, where scarce so much housing as a sheepcote, or more inhabitants than a shepherd is to be found, send as many representatives to the grand assembly of lawmakers as a whole county numerous in people and powerful in riches.

And one of England's most notable statesmen, himself once the "representative" of a "rotten" borough, William Pitt the younger, declared on the floor of the House of Commons, "This House is not the representative of the people of Great Britain; it is the representative of nominal boroughs, of ruined and exterminated towns, of noble families, of wealthy individuals, of foreign potentates." [27]

After a considerable struggle,[28] the great Reform Bill finally became law in 1832. It did not solve all outstanding problems by any means, but it was a mighty step in the right direction. It abolished the "rotten boroughs" and created new constituencies in hitherto unrepresented or underrepresented areas. Moreover it ended the chaos of conflicting voting qualifications by substituting a single system of property qualifications [29] and by establishing a registration system. The Reform Bill of 1832 did not yet turn England [30] into a fully democratic country in the modern sense. Only 1,000,000 new voters were added to the lists. But it opened up the era of electoral reform which eventually resulted in a fully representative House of Commons. Subsequent acts introduced new classes of people to the polls. The Representation of the People Acts of 1867 and 1884 enfranchised the urban classes, who had not been included in the bill of 1832, and together with the Redistribution of Seats Act of 1885 created a more equitable system of constituencies and created uniform regulations for town and country. At the same time illegal and corrupt election practices were outlawed by a series of statutes, beginning in 1854.

However, inequalities remained, and in fact became more pronounced in certain areas as a result of the passage of time and social change. The First

---

[27] Ogg, *op. cit.*, p. 261.

[28] The bitter opposition of the House of Lords was overcome only after a general election, a second passage of the bill in the House of Commons (after it had once been rejected by the Lords), and the clear understanding that King William IV would, if necessary, create enough Liberal peers to upset the Tory majority in the House of Lords.

[29] Different standards were established for owners and tenants. English tenants, unlike those in some other countries, are on the whole substantial farmers whose tenancy has been handed on in the same family, often for many generations. They cannot be compared to the "poor trash" in certain sections of the United States.

[30] Similar acts were passed for Scotland and Ireland.

World War set a temporary halt to reforms, but it also gave an opportunity for sober reflection. A commission of outstanding persons was called together to consider remedies. The results produced by this "Speaker's Conference on Electoral Reform" [31] culminated in the far-reaching Representation of the People Act of 1918 which wiped out nearly all unreasonable voting qualifications, especially property qualifications in national elections, reorganized the entire electoral procedure, and granted the suffrage to women of thirty years of age or older. The Equal Franchise Act of 1928, known to contemporaries as the "Flapper Bill," finally gave full rights to women by reducing their minimum voting age to twenty-one, the same as for men. The last vestiges of inequality among voters were removed in 1948 when the university constituencies and the business-premises votes, which gave certain groups of people a double vote, were eliminated.

The Reform Bill of 1832 had not only remodeled the House of Commons but had also affected the House of Lords in two ways. By abolishing the "rotten boroughs" it deprived the Lords of much control over the lower house. Secondly, the willingness of the monarch to create enough peers to upset the Tory control of the House of Lords served unmistakable notice that the House of Commons would not be deterred in its course by the opposition of the noble Lords.

However, the problem was kept boiling until 1909 when a predominantly Conservative House of Lords rejected the budget of the Liberal Asquith government, as presented by Lloyd George, the Chancellor of the Exchequer. Although by no means an illegal or unconstitutional action, the attitude of the Lords caused a tremendous upheaval. The government, after receiving a new mandate from the people, was determined to break the power of the House of Lords once and for all, and in 1911 forced the enactment of the Parliament Act. It removed the Lords' influence in financial matters almost entirely by providing that all money bills must receive the consent of the upper house within one month or receive the Royal Assent [32] without it. In all other matters, the Lords could, however, apply a suspensive veto which could delay enactment for two years. Ever since that time, the House of Lords has played in a strictly minor key, but reform movements have nevertheless been active. The Labor party especially, facing a hostile majority in the upper chamber and fearing undue delays in its nationalization program, has been critical of the House of Lords. Although the Lords, mindful of their political weakness and their historical anachronism, cannot be said to have given the Labor government too much trouble, their power has been further

[31] *Letter from Mr. Speaker to the Prime Minister,* Cmd. 8463, London, 1917. Sir W. H. Dickinson, *The Reform Act of 1918,* London, 1918. E. M. Sait and D. P. Barrows, *British Politics in Transition,* Yonkers, 1925, pp. 82–93.

[32] The Royal Assent, a pure formality which cannot be withheld, is the final act which gives a statute the force of law.

curbed by the Parliament Act of 1949, which limits the operation of their suspensive veto to one year. However, it is a foregone conclusion that even this further reduction of the Lords' power will not silence criticism of the institution. A real remedy will emerge only when the composition, rather than the powers, of the upper house is made the principal item of reform.[33]

[33] See especially the *Bryce Report* of 1918, Cmd. 9038; Sait and Barrows, *op. cit.*, p. 175. For a discussion of the nature and function of the House of Lords, see Chap. 4B.

Chapter 2

THE IDEA OF THE CONSTITUTION

Few topics are as easy and at the same time as difficult to explain to a non-British reader as the nature and content of the British constitution.[1] The American or Continental European reader must first of all free himself from nearly all the concepts which he may have derived from the American, French, or German Constitutions. Our American Constitution is a single, written document which is declared to be the "supreme law of the land." Laws or other acts which are in contradiction thereto are declared null and void as soon as a court has an opportunity to review them. To be sure, that is not the whole story; even the most perfunctory student of American government knows that our Constitution grows by means other than formal amendments—by court decisions, by legislative and executive acts, by custom and convention. Yet there is always the written document which cannot be trifled with, and departure from a practice hitherto considered constitutional must be laboriously justified in the courts.

Quite different is the situation in Great Britain. The foreign visitor who enters the British Museum and demands to see the "constitution" cannot be accommodated; if a guide, made wise by past experience with foreigners, wanted to give him a measure of satisfaction, the best he could do would be to hand him two books: a history of England and a treatise on the character of the English people.

The answer is simply that there is no single document which may properly be called "the British constitution." There are many written documents scattered throughout the constitution, but for the most part the constitution is unwritten, *i.e.*, is based on custom and convention. This raises some extraordinary problems. The written sections are occasionally quite misleading, because they sometimes convey powers which could almost certainly not be exercised. Certain powers granted the Home Secretary and the Minister of Labor, as mentioned earlier, lie nearly dormant. Other powers may have been exercised once but have since fallen into disuse. Yet they are rarely actually removed from the statute books, and who can say that they will not, one day, be revived?

---

[1] This part is concerned mainly with the English constitution. Major differences in Scotland or Northern Ireland will be pointed out.

A certain amount of light can be brought into this apparent confusion if one remembers first of all that when we speak, quite properly, of the British "constitution" we mean the sum total of "rules which directly or indirectly affect the distribution or the exercise of the sovereign power in the state." [2] This would include the rules which constitute the organs of government, their branches and divisions, the relationship between these organs, and the relationship between them and the people, as well as the manner in which the functions of government shall be exercised. Understood in that fashion, the British constitution is not quite so unusual, because all other constitutions, too, have their written and unwritten laws, their statutory and conventional rules. What makes the British constitution so unique is the uncommonly large number of its rules which are based solely on convention, and the fact that no act has a higher degree of authority than a simple act of Parliament.

WRITTEN AND UNWRITTEN CONSTITUTION

Lecturers on the subject of the constitution sometimes make a point of distinguishing between the "written" and the "unwritten" rules. Now, it is quite true that large sections of the constitution are written and larger ones unwritten. However, as a great master of the subject has pointed out, this distinction misses the point.[3] Certain rules may be unwritten but have nevertheless the effect of law. Very often such rules are eventually written into the law. For instance the fact that a minister, by countersigning a measure or affixing his seal thereto, becomes responsible for it is certainly constitutional law but is not written law. On the other hand, written law may have long fallen into disuse, like the process of impeachment, or it may not mean what it says, like the legal right of the King to appoint all officers. Everyone knows, of course, that he has ordinarily no choice in the matter.

LAW AND CONVENTION

The important distinction is not between "written" and "unwritten" laws, but between "laws" and "conventions."

Law may take the form either of common law, *i.e.*, the law based on the body of precedents established by judicial decisions, or of statute law, *i.e.*, acts of Parliament. Among all categories of constitutional rules, the latter is the highest ranking and most final type of law, as has been expressed in the famous statement by Bagehot that "Parliament can do anything except make a man a woman, or a woman a man." This means simply in practical terms that Parliament does not submit to any higher law. There is no higher au-

[2] A. V. Dicey, *Introduction to the Study of the Law of the Constitution*, London, 1889, 3d ed., pp. 22*f*.

[3] *Ibid.*, p. 28.

thority than its own acts. Not even past acts of Parliament can preclude contrary later action.[4] Moreover, Britain does not have a doctrine of expressed and enumerated powers. Any field may be invaded by the legislative action of Parliament, and the courts will abide by such laws, although they will try to interpret them wisely and, if possible, in conformity with precedent and international law.[5] It is certainly a fact that Parliament may invade the field of executive discretion (royal prerogative) and impose such limitations as it may see fit.

Nevertheless there are vast and important areas in which statute law does not greatly interfere. For instance, in the important field of civil liberties the English Bill of Rights is not nearly so explicit and comprehensive as its American counterpart. In actuality, the important civil liberties, such as freedom of speech, press, assembly, and religion, are primarily safeguarded by the common law, the great body of court decisions and precedents.[6]

This apparent predominance of statute law and its author, Parliament, must be viewed against the background of British and not of American constitutional life. In the United States the executive and legislative branches of government are largely independent from one another and are presumed to check and balance each other jealously. The British constitution is built on an entirely different principle. The real executive, the cabinet, is a committee and indeed the leader of the legislature. A need for "checks and balances" between the two is inconceivable, since the whole system is based on harmony between the two branches. Without such harmony the cabinet would fall. The supremacy of statute law is therefore merely an expression of the supremacy of the "Crown in Parliament," *i.e.*, of cabinet and Parliament working in concert.

Statute law is not necessarily of a higher order than conventional rules, even though statute may overrule convention. But statute law is usually expressed in more precise terms, and it has the added dignity of extracting unquestioning obedience from everybody. With due deference to Justice Holmes's famous dictum that "the quest for certainty is an illusion," [7] we may state that the existence of a particular law is at least reasonably certain, and a well-trained constitutional lawyer ought to be able to say approximately what the laws of the constitution are at a given moment, although he may differ with his colleagues and the courts as to the interpretation thereof. When it comes to the conventions of the constitution, we are less fortunate. For once, we cannot say with absolute certainty just when a convention is in effect

[4] Ellen Street Estates Ltd. v. Minister of Health, 1 K.B. 590 (1934) ; A. B. Keith, *The Constitution of England from Queen Victoria to George VI*, London, 1940, Vol. I, p. 10.

[5] But if Parliament alters international law, the courts must give it effect no matter what other consequences may arise therefrom. See The Zamora, 2 A.C. 77 (1916).

[6] Hiram M. Stout, *British Government*, New York, 1953, p. 21.

[7] O. W. Holmes, *The Common Law*, Boston, 1881, p. 1.

and when it is not. We may surmise that conventions are based on usage and acquiescence. Their binding force is derived from the willingness of the country—meaning government and Parliament—to be so bound. They are based on the assumption, agreed to by virtually all, that there are things which are or are not done by gentlemen.

So far the difficulty may not seem to be so great, but it increases when a challenge arises. This is especially likely to happen because politicians in England and nearer home are prone to shout "unconstitutional" when in effect they mean to say: "I don't like this." And what one person may call constitutional practice, another might regard as merely an accident of history. Prime Minister Lord Salisbury once wrote to Queen Victoria, "Our constitutional law is based on precedents. If the House of Lords reverses its course, under threats, because a majority of the House of Commons object to their policy, it will, by that very act, become constitutional law that the House of Lords is bound to submit to the House of Commons." [8] This view is doubtless exaggerated. It takes more than one precedent to create a constitutional role. But it is quite impossible to state categorically how many precedents it takes to make a rule. Here again demonstrable acceptance and usage are the key; yet, a government or Parliament may by a single act set aside constitutional conventions. Such an act, if sustained in Parliament, would not necessarily create a new rule, but it would certainly abrogate the old one, or at the very least place it under serious doubt. For instance, it is a constitutional rule that the cabinet bears collective responsibility as well as individual responsibility of its members. But in 1932 the coalition ("National") government was composed of such divergent elements that they "agreed to differ," i.e., permitted ministers of one group to speak against the policy of another group. This has not become a constitutional rule, and at the present time, a minister who felt that he could not go along with the majority of his colleagues would undoubtedly be expected to resign from his post before voicing any criticism.

Despite this flexibility, the conventions of the constitution carry grave weight. Their weight is not derived from any idea that they are the supreme law of the land, but rather from the fact that they are related to the idea of constitutional government and democracy with which nearly all Britishers find themselves in agreement. This remarkable island race simply prefers to retain proven procedures when there is no particularly strong reason to adopt innovations, and has thereby produced a system of time-honored customs and conventions which are observed because they are based not only on precedent but also on reason. One example will suffice. Governmental measures needing royal action are submitted to the King in the form of "advice." It is a constitutional convention that the monarch must abide by the advice of his ministers, especially the Prime Minister. There is no law to compel him to

---

[8] *Letters of Queen Victoria,* 2d Series, Vol. III, pp. 559f., quoted from W. Ivor Jennings, *Cabinet Government,* Cambridge, 1951, 2d ed., p. 6.

do so, but let us consider the consequences of the King's refusal to accept the advice of his Prime Minister. The government would of course have to resign, as it could not be responsible for acts or omissions which are not of its making. The King would have to call on the leader of the Opposition to form a government. If the latter accepted—which is more than doubtful—Parliament would have to be dissolved, since the government formed by the opposition party would not have a majority in the House of Commons and would be defeated on its first appearance. General elections would be held, which would center very much on the constitutional question raised by the King's attitude. If the new government found itself and the King's action sustained by the people, it might get away with it. But if it were defeated, it would constitute a defeat for the King, and his fate as well as that of the monarchical institution itself would be seriously endangered. Win or lose, if the King became a partisan, his role would be materially changed, and the whole-hearted acclaim of the nation, which alone permits a monarchy to endure, would be lost. Consequently the King would seriously endanger and probably destroy his own foundation were he to refuse to take his Prime Minister's advice. It is thus in political reality that the conventions of the constitution are founded.

The conventions of the constitution cover an enormous range. The rules of procedure in both houses of Parliament rest entirely on convention.[9] So does the procedure concerning the dismissal and appointment of governments. In fact the whole cabinet system, the core of the British system of government, is convention.[10]

It has been stated before that acts of Parliament are supreme and must be obeyed by the courts. Acts of Parliament can therefore abrogate convention. Yet such action will not be undertaken lightly unless the convention is clearly outdated or inapplicable. Similarly, a government which possesses a comfortable majority in the House of Commons can set aside convention, but in so doing it may arouse the country and give such strong ammunition to the Opposition that it may face a difficult test at the next elections. Such emotions would be aroused, however, only if the convention is still strongly entrenched and is clearly relevant to existing problems. In the last analysis, therefore, the validity of constitutional conventions will be determined by political realities.

All this would seem to add up to a somewhat uncertain state of affairs. We have seen that the constitution consists of laws and conventions. Of the two categories, law is more dependable than convention, but it is also far from

---

[9] The authoritative reference work on Parliamentary procedure is Sir Thomas Erskine May, *A Treatise on the Law, Privileges, Proceedings and Usage of Parliament*, rev. by Sir G. Campion, London, 1950, 15th ed.

[10] The Ministers of the Crown Act of 1937 does recognize the existence of the cabinet, but only insofar as certain pay raises are concerned.

reliable, for an enormous gulf often exists between legal rights and the actual use or nonuse of those rights. This fact has been clearly expressed by the Judicial Committee of the Privy Council when it interpreted the Statute of Westminster of 1931: "The Imperial Parliament could, as a matter of abstract law, repeal or disregard Section 4 of the Statute. But that is theory and has no relation to realities." [11]

Even greater uncertainty exists in the field of the conventions. Not only can they be set aside, as we have seen, but their exact status and scope are never certain. A former Prime Minister, Stanley Baldwin, has described the situation in the following terms:

The historian can tell you probably perfectly clearly what the constitutional practice was at any given period in the past, but it would be very difficult for a living writer to tell you at any given period in his lifetime what the constitution of the country is in all respects, and for this reason . . . there may be one practice called "constitutional" which is falling into desuetude, and there may be another practice which is creeping into use but is not yet constitutional.[12]

French jurisprudence likes to distinguish between "rigid" and "flexible" constitutions. In actuality no constitution is rigid, or it would stifle the country and would have to be overthrown. But the methods by which flexibility is achieved differ. In Britain the constitution is simply the sum total of the public life of the country, and like life it regulates itself. No act, not even so fundamental a document as the Bill of Rights or the Act of Settlement, is immune from change. Yet such changes appear gradually, peacefully, and with a high degree of consent. That this is so is not guaranteed by any "supreme law of the land" but is solely the result of the devotion to democratic principles in which the British nation excels. There is a firm understanding that there exists a general and loosely defined body of rules and procedures which ought to be observed, and since the British people are, fortunately, not greatly devoted to theoretical perspicacity, they find it quite superfluous to inquire into the precise nature and definition of those rules; where there is general agreement, details may be left to the temporary solutions which spring from the daily unrolling of the governmental process. The British constitution truly "works by a body of understandings which no writer can formulate." [13] This may perhaps also explain why the example of the British form of government, so often emulated elsewhere, has usually failed when applied in countries beyond the British constitutional experience. It also tends to illustrate a point which will be further elaborated later: namely, that the existence of a single written constitution is by no means an absolutely essential criterion of constitutional and democratic government.

[11] British Coal Corporation v. Rex A.C. 500 (1935); Keith, *op. cit.*, p. 10.

[12] Quoted by Jennings, *op. cit.*, p. 12.

[13] Lord Bryce in *Report of the Joint Select Committee on Indian Constitutional Reform,* London, 1934, Vol. I, p. 7.

Chapter 3

THE CROWN

A. THE MONARCH

Walter Bagehot in his memorable and pioneering work on the English constitution distinguished between its *dignified* and *efficient* parts. The first is to appeal to the imagination of the people, while the second does the work. This does not mean that the *dignified* sections of the constitution are pure propaganda. They have their most definite place, and many could not be dislodged without very serious disturbances. An outstanding example of this category is the place which royalty holds in the governance of Britain.

The British monarchy is an institution which is more widely known than understood. It is often fancied that the throne is merely the relic of past greatness, having preserved a fraction of its former popularity. Americans, especially, who are by tradition republicans (but suspiciously fond of aristocracy), often feel that the preservation of the monarchy is just another proof of an alleged British "backwardness" and "quaintness," which must of course eventually give way to a more "modern" concept. A closer examination of history will give little comfort to such misconceptions.

The monarchy was by no means always popular, even if one disregards the fate of Charles I and James II, and under such rulers as George IV it descended to a level of contempt. In fact it might be said that the monarchy, as a popular institution, steadily declined under the Hanoverians in the eighteenth and nineteenth centuries, until Queen Victoria restored and ameliorated its reputation. Genuine popularity came only under her successors. Edward VII, a far more democratic and jovial monarch than his formidable mother, made many friends, but even he was not as close to the people as were George V and especially George VI, as well as the present monarch Elizabeth II.[1] Undoubtedly the two world wars enhanced the reputations of these two kings because of the way in which they shared dangers and privations. George VI, who together with his family remained in London during the entire German blitz bombings and the later attacks by V-1 and V-2

---

[1] The designation Elizabeth II is controversial among Scottish nationalists, who claim that Mary, Queen of Scots, was their rightful monarch and not Elizabeth I. They maintain therefore that the present Queen is the first Elizabeth to reign over England and Scotland.

weapons, added enormously to the people's morale. It is probably not exaggerated to state that the personal popularity of the monarch and the sincere interest of the people in his and his family's doings have never been greater than they are today.

The reputation and the resulting significance of the monarch rest almost entirely on psychological facts, although the belief that monarchy is a form of "father fixation," as has been suggested, might be challenged. But it is certain that the monarch lends flesh and blood to the idea of government, and while to many people the idea of a constitution may be incomprehensible, the existence of a living king is always easily understood. Today, however, this theory which Bagehot suggested eighty years ago has more validity in the colonies than in the British Isles themselves. Therefore a different explanation might be suggested.

In a world of many and frightening changes, in which the quest for security becomes ever more desperate, the British monarchy breathes stability and continuity. The Englishman, bewildered and upset over so many difficulties, confronted by the far-reaching changes which the Empire has undergone, finds a contemplation of the ancient pageantry of monarchy most reassuring. Despite the changes which he has had to endure there is then, after all, one seemingly permanent institution which, despite or perhaps because of the loss of many prerogatives, has stood the test of time. To most Britishers, the monarchy is a symbol of the enduring qualities of their race and living proof that, whatever the future may bring, it will not break too radically with the tried and proven concepts of the past. The tremendous interest in Queen Elizabeth's coronation in 1953 gave most telling proof of this sentiment.

The monarch's position rests on his deportment; it is necessary for him to be close to the people and yet remain on the pedestal of his august position. That is why the abdication crisis of Edward VIII, now the Duke of Windsor, cut so deep. It is idle to speculate now whether the King's conduct and his proposed marriage scandalized the majority of his subjects or not. It certainly divided the country on an issue concerning the royal person, and that is the very opposite of what a monarch ought to do. But the issue was broader than merely the relationship between the King and Mrs. Simpson and their marriage plans. The government stood foursquare against the whole idea, and the Prime Minister, Stanley Baldwin, made it quite clear to the King that even though Mrs. Simpson could never be queen, neither the British Parliament nor the Dominion Parliaments would sanction a morganatic marriage.

Here was a test case to show whether the King must abide by the advice of his Prime Minister even in matters affecting his private life, and it was largely because of this constitutional issue that the leadership of the Labor party, which was then in opposition, rallied to the government. Winston Churchill, perhaps more passionate than prudent at the time, toyed for a moment with the idea of leading a "king's party"; fortunately, nothing came of so wild a plan, which would certainly have done the monarchy irreparable damage, and the will of the government prevailed. Edward extricated himself from his difficulties by resigning the throne—an act which has been condemned as dereliction of duty, but which has given Britain a monarch whose conduct was above reproach. Baldwin's action was naturally condemned by the bobby soxers of all ages and sexes who considered romance more important than constitutional government. If there has ever been any doubt in recent years as to the authority of the Prime Minister's advice over the King, there is no doubt now.

The Act of Settlement of 1701 established with finality the line of succession to the throne, although this act, like any other statute, may be altered by Parliament. Succession may take place in either the male or the female line, but Catholics are ineligible. The coronation oath used to include a rejection of the doctrine of transsubstantiation, but in 1910 this was modified at the coronation of George V.

The position of a reigning Queen is exactly the same as that of a King, but while a King's spouse is called Queen, the husband of a reigning Queen is never called King. Queen Victoria's husband, Prince Albert, received the title Prince Consort during the later years of his life. But the husband of the presently reigning Queen Elizabeth has not received this title and is not likely to because to history-conscious Englishmen this designation is forever tied to the memories of Victoria and Albert. At present Prince Philip, the Queen's husband, is usually addressed by his title as Duke of Edinburgh, but his growing influence is indicated by his appointment as one of the Counsellors of State who would appoint a regent in the case of the death or incapacity of the Queen, during the minority of the Heir Apparent (Prince Charles).

POWER AND INFLUENCE

In abstract theory the powers of the monarch are truly formidable. The Queen, wrote Bagehot in 1872, "could disband the army, she could dismiss all the officers from the General Commanding-in-Chief downward; . . . she could sell off all our ships of war and all our naval stores; she could make a peace by the sacrifice of Cornwall, and begin a war for the conquest of Brittany. . . ." But of course that is pure theory and has no relation whatsoever to fact. In theory all acts of government are acts of the monarch to which he must give his consent, either personally or by proxy. But since the monarch is not responsible to Parliament, the rules of responsible government demand that these acts be countersigned by a minister of the crown, who is responsible. Thus all acts become in effect governmental acts, to which the King or Queen has no choice but to give his or her consent. This does not mean that they are without influence. We know now from the correspondence of Queen Victoria that her influence was considerable and that she attempted many times to have her own way outside constitutional practices. Her desperate attempts to keep Gladstone—whom she loathed and distrusted—from becoming Prime Minister are a matter of history. She even attempted to indulge in intra-party feuds in order to accomplish her aim. We also know that Edward VII's influence was not negligible, although not as great as some historians believed. About more recent events we have only scant information. But there is some evidence that King George V had a hand in the formation of the "National" government of 1931, although the initiative appears to have come from Ramsay MacDonald, and it is rumored that King George VI had some influence in the selection of Ernest Bevin for the post of Foreign Secretary in the Labor government of 1945.

The most important function of the monarch is undoubtedly the selection of the Prime Minister, but usually he has virtually no choice in the matter. Ordinarily each party has its clearly designated leader who, as long as the two-party system exists, will be either Prime Minister or leader of the Opposition. If the government party wins again, there is no question that the Prime Minister will remain in office if he chooses; but if the government loses, he resigns, and the leader of the Opposition is called to Buckingham Palace to receive a commission to form a government. No other course is open to the monarch and the people in voting for a particular party know very well that they are thereby voting for a particular Prime Minister. Englishmen had no doubt that when the Conservative government of Winston Churchill was defeated in 1945, Clement Attlee would be the next Prime Minister.

Queen Victoria attempted to preserve the royal prerogative—already obsolete—of appointing her own candidate, but she was unsuccessful, and it is not likely that any present or future monarch will try to repeat her performance. A certain amount of choice exists when, because of death, illness, or resignation, a vacancy occurs which may not have been foreseen. However, even under such circumstances, the Queen's choice is circumscribed by the fact that whoever is appointed must have a majority in the House of Commons. The choice must therefore be made in close contact with the leadership of the majority party. When William Gladstone retired from public office in 1894, Queen Victoria chose Lord Rosebery from several available candidates. In 1922, when Bonar Law resigned, King George V chose Stanley Baldwin rather than Lord Curzon as his successor, but in so doing he undoubtedly acted in agreement with the Conservative party leadership. The King's action in 1931 is more questionable when he asked Ramsay MacDonald to form a "National" government which was largely based on Conservative support. The initiative very likely came from MacDonald, but the King's failure to consult Arthur Henderson, the leader of the Labor party, after MacDonald's defection, was a highly questionable practice.

We have already seen that the monarch cannot fail to abide by the "advice" of his Prime Minister. This is the very cornerstone of the constitution, and the abdication crisis of 1936 has revealed that it applies even to the most private and personal acts of the King. If the King were to refuse his assent, the resignation of the cabinet would become inevitable, and this would be followed by a general election in which the entire prestige and foundation of the monarchy would be at stake. For the same reason the monarch could not dissolve Parliament against the advice of his government. But there are two recent cases on record in which the government reluctantly agreed to a dissolution and general elections on the urging of the King, who believed that the government ought to receive a new mandate from the people before proceeding to certain far-reaching decisions. Both cases occurred in 1910, when Edward VII urged dissolution over the question of Lloyd George's budget [2] and George V pressed for the same action before the powers of the House of Lords were to be curbed.

It is quite difficult to see how the monarch could refuse dissolution,[3] since any cabinet crisis would be bound to bring about general elections. There is of course absolutely no question about the Royal Assent to acts of Parliament; it cannot be refused.

But there is considerable doubt whether the monarch must "pack" the House of Lords with government supporters if the Lords persist in their frustration of the government's program. The fact that at least two kings, William IV and George V, were reluctantly ready to do so cannot be considered conclusive. However, the King's discretion must be viewed against the probability that a majority of the House of Commons which had been continuously frustrated by the Lords would eventually proceed to drastic reforms, if not abolition, of the upper house.

In order to appraise the position of the British monarch, it is necessary to distinguish between his power and his influence. Theoretically he has great powers; he resides resplendently in his castles, he receives a handsome allowance known as the Civil List,[4] and all acts of government are accomplished in his name. Actually, as we have seen, he has virtually no power at all. But he has a surprising amount of influence. Bagehot was the first to point out that the King has three rights: the right to be consulted, the right to encourage, and the right to warn. To this he adds, "And a king of great sense

[2] Lloyd George was Chancellor of the Exchequer in the Asquith government.

[3] But the King's representative in Canada, Governor-General Lord Byng, did once refuse to grant the Prime Minister, Mackenzie King, a second dissolution, and the Governor-General of South Africa refused a first dissolution to Prime Minister Hertzog.

[4] The Civil List of the present monarch, Queen Elizabeth II, is £475,000, while the Duke of Edinburgh receives £40,000. This includes the salaries and pensions of the household, maintenance and various services, and the privy purse of the Queen. The Crown lands, which are managed by the government, usually yield more than the amount of the Civil List.

and sagacity would want no others." The august position held by the King and the long experience which he is bound to accumulate through the years of his reign give his advice great weight. He is informed about all decisions taken by the cabinet. He is informed about all problems of importance. He is in constant contact with his Prime Minister. An intimate atmosphere of mutual understanding and respect usually develops. It is true that the King can never have his way against a determined Prime Minister who opposes him. But while we do not have too much knowledge of the private conversations between the nominal and the real heads of the country, there is considerable evidence to show that the advice or the warning of the King is not lightly dismissed. The influence of the King will therefore grow in direct proportion to his wisdom and his discretion.

A wise monarch must be well-informed but never partisan. This is sometimes rendered somewhat difficult because of the fact that the King's or Queen's most intimate connection is with the government in power, while more than formal relations with the Opposition would be considered improper and evidence of bias. He is therefore largely dependent on the help and advice which he receives from his staff. It is perhaps not an exaggeration to say that in addition to the native intelligence and experience of the monarch, his staff, especially his secretary, is the keeper of his conscience, and contributes largely to the amount of wisdom and sagacity he displays. It has therefore been suggested that these posts be made regular civil-service appointments. This is not the case at present, but recent appointments have been made with great care and success.

Thus the monarch appears as a symbol of government and state, as a counselor and adviser, and as a reassurance of the application and validity of the British tradition of government. Moreover he is a great convenience. As the official and symbolic link between the mother country and the dominions and colonies, he makes possible an extraordinary flexibility which the best draftsman could not write into any other constitutional form or document. George VI and Elizabeth have emphasized this point through their extensive travels. How widely accepted this notion is may be gleaned from a passage written by an eminent socialist couple, Sidney and Beatrice Webb:

If we pass from the constitutional theory of the text-books to the facts as we see them to-day, what we have to note is that the particular function of the British monarch . . . is not the exercise of governmental powers in any of its aspects, but something quite different, namely, the performance of a whole series of rites and ceremonies which lend the charm of historic continuity to the political institutions of the British race, and which go far, under present conditions, to maintain the bond of union between the races and creeds of the Commonwealth. . . .[5]

[5] Sidney and Beatrice Webb, *A Constitution for a Socialist Commonwealth of Great Britain,* London, 1920, p. 61.

B. THE CABINET

The real executive is not the King but the cabinet, though the cabinet is much more than that. Walter Bagehot, who first pointed to the significance—indeed, the existence—of the cabinet, also demonstrated its peculiar role. The theory expounded by Montesquieu and repeated by others that the genius of English government consists in the separation of powers is completely false. The outstanding characteristic of the English government is the almost complete fusion of legislative and executive functions; and it is the cabinet which effects this fusion and makes it work.

This all-important body of men which we call the cabinet is an oddly informal group. Until 1937 it was unknown to the law of the land, although it had been a living reality for two centuries. Its head, the Prime Minister, still receives his salary as the First Lord of the Treasury, although he leaves the administration of the Treasury to his Chancellor of the Exchequer.[6] Cabinet proceedings have been regularly recorded only since 1916 when the cabinet secretariat was established by Lloyd George, and cabinet decisions take the form either of orders of the Privy Council (Orders in Council) or of advice to the King.

Historically the cabinet emerged as a committee of the Privy Council, and it still retains this fiction as a matter of convenience. Since the Privy Council is composed of every individual who has once held cabinet rank, as well as other persons of note, it is far too big to carry on any governmental business, and meets with its entire membership usually only once in each king's reign and only for ceremonial functions. But the cabinet or even two or three members thereof usually act for the whole Council.

THE PRIME MINISTER

By far the most significant man in any cabinet is its leader, the Prime Minister. If he is strong like Sir Robert Peel, Benjamin Disraeli (later Lord Beaconsfield), William Gladstone, David Lloyd George, or Sir Winston Churchill, he will imprint his stamp on the cabinet. If he is endowed with fewer leadership capacities, like Lord Rosebery or Lord Salisbury, the entire course of his cabinet will be lacking in decisiveness. Other ministers may temporarily overshadow their chief. Joseph Chamberlain outshone Lord Salisbury, and Lloyd George outshone Asquith. Sir Stafford Cripps and Ernest Bevin were more prominent than Attlee. But they can never hope to prevail against the Prime Minister, as Lord Palmerston found out to his peril.

---

[6] Who in turn leaves the administration of the Exchequer proper to the Auditor and Comptroller General.

We have already seen that under ordinary circumstances the choice of the Prime Minister is determined by the electorate. The chosen leaders of both major parties are well known to the people, and those who voted in the general election of 1950 had no doubt that if they voted Conservative they voted for a Churchill government, while those who voted Labor obviously favored an Attlee cabinet. Thus it may be stated that the people of Britain elect their Prime Ministers no less than the American people elect their presidents. This is of course based on the assumption that the two-party system will continue to function, but the entire cabinet system is in fact based on that very same assumption, as we shall see.

Ordinarily, therefore, the Prime Minister is the chosen leader of the party winning a majority at the polls, and if the fortunes of political warfare are reversed, the King or Queen sends for the leader of the Opposition as a matter of course in order to entrust him with the seals of office. However, there are obvious exceptions to the rule. We have already seen that the monarch has a certain amount of choice if the prime ministership becomes vacant as a result of the death or resignation [7] of the incumbent. Even when that choice is a real one—as was the case on the resignations of Gladstone and Bonar Law— the circle of those eligible is necessarily small. Sometimes there is only one possible successor; for instance, there was no doubt that upon the resignation of Stanley Baldwin in 1937 he would be succeeded by Neville Chamberlain. In any case, the appointee must be acceptable to the majority party, because upon his appointment to the premiership he also becomes invariably the leader of the party, not only in form but also very much in fact. But there are exceptions even to that rule. In 1940, Winston Churchill became Prime Minister as a result of overwhelming popular pressure which demanded strong war leadership. Neville Chamberlain reluctantly gave way to the man of "blood, sweat, and tears," and Churchill thus became Prime Minister and automatically leader of the Conservative party. Yet he was by no means the choice of the party, and did not even belong to its principal corps of leaders. In fact he was regarded by the party leaders with suspicion. Had there been no war, Churchill would not have stood the ghost of a chance.

There is also an exception to the rule that the leader of the Opposition must be called to the palace when his party wins at the polls. In 1880, the Liberal party won the election. The leader of the party in the House of Commons was Lord Hartington, and the Queen sent for him. But there was no doubt that the party's leadership in the fight against the preceding government (Beaconsfield) had been in the hands of Gladstone, and he was appointed on Lord Hartington's recommendation. Quite confused was the situation in 1931 when the Labor government headed by Ramsay MacDonald split up. The King reappointed MacDonald, who was for all practical pur-

---

[7] Resignation caused by reasons other than defeat at the polls.

poses a man without a party,[8] and did not consult Arthur Henderson, who, after MacDonald's defection, had become the leader of the party which after all had won the last election before the crisis.

It is important to remember that the Prime Minister and his colleagues in the government are party leaders of long standing and experience. Even in the rare cases where a party does not have a declared leader, the man who will eventually lead the party's destinies will be chosen from among a small group who have stood in the forefront of the political battle—a battle which is carried out in the House of Commons. It follows therefore that no party leader—and consequently no Prime Minister—is ever a "dark horse" in the American sense. To become a party leader he must have proved his mettle in countless Parliamentary skirmishes, and must have won the acclaim and confidence of his followers. To gain distinction in the House of Commons is not an easy thing, for some very keen minds are always to be found there. Undoubtedly not all members are outstanding, but a good many are, since membership in the House of Commons, once called "the world's most exclusive club," is considered a great distinction which is eagerly sought by many bright young men. If a man is able to maintain himself in such company and through the years eventually climbs to the pinnacle of leadership, he has certainly proved that he is a man of considerable ability. Professor Laski was therefore right in saying that "no simple man can ever be Prime Minister of England."

The position of the Prime Minister is a formidable one. He determines the outlines of policy, and all important decisions of the other ministers are cleared with him first. Sir Robert Peel was known to take a detailed interest in the administration of every department, in effect reducing his ministers to virtual under-secretaries. That feat was never repeated thereafter and would be quite impossible now in view of the greatly augmented business of government. Sometimes Prime Ministers have retained control over certain government departments: Lord Salisbury was Prime Minister and Foreign Secretary at the same time; MacDonald performed the same dual function in the first Labor cabinet of 1924. However, the combination of the premiership with the direct administration of a department has always worked to the disadvantage of both offices concerned.

There have also been Prime Ministers who had such a strong hand in the formulation of policy in a particular department that they reduced the status of the responsible minister and undermined cabinet morale. This was the case with Ramsay MacDonald, who left little elbowroom for his Foreign Secretary, Arthur Henderson, and it was true of Neville Chamberlain, who con-

[8] MacDonald and his small band of ex-Labor men called their group "National Labor party," but this term was without reality, and the "party" evaporated at the polls. MacDonald lost his own seat, and a "safe" university constituency had to be found for him.

ducted foreign policy frequently without bothering to consult his Foreign Secretary, Anthony Eden. Sir Winston Churchill's primary interest in foreign affairs also tended to overshadow Foreign Secretary Eden and the Foreign Office until recently.

The relationship between the Prime Minister and his colleagues depends very largely on the personalities involved. The Prime Minister selects the ministers of the crown. This is an exercise of great power, but it is by no means unrestricted. In every party there are men who must obviously be included in any government if the unity and support of the party in the House of Commons is not to be endangered. There are also other members whom the Prime Minister must include in payment of political debts. Conservative governments have found it necessary to divert minor posts to men who had given the party prominent financial or other support while Labor governments have contained deserving former trade-union officials whose loyal support demanded reward.

The distribution of portfolios is very largely in the hands of the Prime Minister, but here again he cannot completely disregard the wishes of prominent party leaders. It is well known, for instance, that MacDonald did not wish to put Henderson in charge of the Foreign Office, but Henderson would not take any other post, and since he could not very well be excluded, the Prime Minister gave in.

Every party which comes to power has a number of leaders who are so obviously important that, as we have seen, they cannot be excluded from the government and the Cabinet without causing such rifts and animosities that the effectiveness of that party's hold on the government would be seriously impaired. This also means that, despite the Prime Minister's preeminent position, government policy is generally the result of constant consultations. Even Sir Winston Churchill, who likes to run things alone, is not exempt from this rule, although his immense prestige allows him a liberty of action which would not easily be granted to lesser men. But even during the important wartime conferences, he was in constant contact with his cabinet colleagues.

Apart from the appointment of important party leaders, other considerations must also play a role in the nomination of ministers of the crown. Both major political parties of Great Britain contain elements who find themselves in some opposition to their party's leadership. Often a Prime Minister finds it useful to appoint one or two of his opponents to cabinet positions, partly in the hope that the burden of responsibilities will have a sobering effect on the appointee, partly because cabinet secrecy and cabinet solidarity will make it more difficult for the men concerned to voice their objections. There is little doubt that Attlee's choice of Aneurin Bevan for the post of Minister of Health did not stem from any high regard for that gentleman. That such action is effective was perhaps clearly enough demonstrated when Aneurin Bevan and the like-minded Harold Wilson resigned from the Attlee cabinet in 1951 in order to regain their freedom of action.[9]

The geographic distribution of cabinet posts is far less important than is the case in the United States. Nevertheless, the Secretary of State for Scotland always comes from that part of the country, and it is generally considered wise not to leave other Scotsmen and perhaps a Welshman entirely out of the government.

The inclusion of some gifted younger men is very important. Failure to do so would not only cause intense dissatisfaction among many Members of Parliament but would also fail to assure the continued supply of leadership material to the party. It is also necessary to appoint several Lords to the cabinet in order to assure the government's leadership in the House of Lords. The Lord Chancellor is of course always a member of the House of Lords, but there must be at least one other member to represent the government, for the Lord Chancellor presides over the upper house and cannot effectively represent the government. The Churchill government of 1952 contained seven Lords, but that is an unusually large number.

The Prime Minister, in appointing ministers and heads of departments, also designates who shall be members of the supreme policy-making body, the cabinet, for not all ministers are cabinet ministers. The selection of cabinet posts has varied from cabinet to cabinet. There are certain departments which are always represented: the Treasury, the Foreign Office, the Ministry of National Defence,[10] the Home Office, the Commonwealth Relations Office, the Colonial Office, the Scottish Office, and the Lord Chancellor. The Lord Privy Seal and the Lord President of the (Privy) Council also rate a seat in the cabinet on grounds of rank alone, but these "sinecure" posts are frequently filled by very important leaders who are thus freed from departmental responsibilities in order to devote themselves to tasks of special importance.[11] The Ministers of Health and Labor are rarely excluded, and the Minister of Agriculture and Fisheries also rates a cabinet seat as a general rule but was excluded from the Churchill government in 1951. The new Ministry of Housing and Local Government is usually also included. The Board of Trade had been excluded from several cabinets in the past, but that has proved impractical in view of the increasing importance of economics and trade in the making of high policy, and it may be assumed that the Board of Trade is now ordinarily found in the cabinet. In addition to the incumbents of these offices, the Prime Minister may also include other

---

[9] The immediate cause was a disagreement over budgetary policies.

[10] In 1946 the three defense departments, the War Office, the Admiralty, and the Air Ministry, were unified under a Ministry of National Defense which became a cabinet office. The three original departments were dropped from cabinet rank.

[11] Recent examples are Clement Attlee in the Churchill coalition government and Herbert Morrison in the Attlee government.

ministers of his choice. Ordinarily a cabinet will be composed of fifteen to twenty people, but some cabinets have been above that number and some below.

Over this body of men, the Prime Minister presides. It is a distinguished group of political leaders, many of whom have held public office before. Some of them may be more brilliant than the Prime Minister; yet he holds their destinies in his hands, and the degree to which he wishes to impose his will upon his colleagues is largely determined by his tact and his capacity for self-restraint. A good Prime Minister is one who gives leadership but does not try to be the whole show. There are always, however, certain fields in which he takes a special interest. He is chairman of the Committee of Imperial Defence, and therefore bears direct responsibility in the field of military preparedness and strategy. In times of crisis he will keep very close to those departments which handle the most crucial issues of the day. At present and undoubtedly for some time to come, these are economic and foreign affairs.

These vast responsibilities of the Prime Minister do not rest on statutory grounds. They rest almost entirely on political considerations. He is the leader of the majority party in the House of Commons. His party has entered the electoral fight under his leadership, and the people who voted for it have thereby unmistakably voted for his premiership. Having achieved a clear majority, the leader of the party and his cabinet are secure against removal by the opposition party unless the margin of seats is very small; ordinarily a leader can be removed only when he loses the support of his own party. That does not occur often. A party which overthrows its leadership in effect confesses failure, and it is only too likely that the electorate will confirm that judgment. Such confirmation is bound to be swift, for if the government falls, general elections are the logical consequence. To be sure, there are exceptions. An intra-party conspiracy overthrew the leadership of Sir Henry Campbell-Bannerman in 1908, and strong internal pressure removed Herbert Asquith in 1916 and Neville Chamberlain in 1940. As a rule, however, the majority party remains intact and rallies to the support of the government. Even if they do not like their leader, they usually like the leader of the Opposition even less, and it is he who may expect to be the beneficiary of a cabinet crisis. It must also be remembered that party discipline is greater in Britain than in the United States, and the government whips usually succeed in corralling the necessary majority of Members of Parliament.

In the exercise of his vast powers, the Prime Minister is therefore reasonably assured of a full term in office between general elections, as small margins, like that after the election of 1950, are unusual. He may expect to remain in office as long as he is able to win elections. He has therefore an indefinite term of office, which tends to strengthen his leadership. If he loses an election, he becomes leader of the Opposition, with good prospects of becoming Prime Minister again when the fortunes of political war are again reversed. But if he loses two or three elections in a row, intra-party pressure is likely to compel his retirement.

For a fuller understanding of the Prime Minister's position it must always be remembered that cabinet and Parliament—or more precisely the House of Commons—are one. The struggle between the legislative and executive branches, so typical in American government, is totally missing in England. The cabinet leads the House, and a serious conflict between the two would only lead to the dissolution of both. As long as the government is in office, it expects to have its legislative program passed by the House of Commons without serious changes or amendments. Yet it is certainly an exaggeration to speak of "cabinet dictatorship." In a democratic state, such as Great Britain, leadership is never a one-sided affair, but can exist only when there is a measure of confidence between the leader and the led. The cabinet does indeed lead Parliament, but it can do so successfully only as long as it remains mindful of the basic need for unity on which the entire cabinet system is based. The cabinet cannot ride roughshod over Parliamentary opposition, but must seek agreement. Naturally such agreement will rarely be unanimous, especially on the Opposition benches. But the government, knowing that close cooperation with the House of Commons is of the essence, always seeks agreement whenever possible, even when it is assured of the necessary votes for victory. So it is receptive to the views of Parliament, and even Opposition views may find their way into legislation. Parliament is not a machinery for checking and balancing the cabinet, but rather a forum for a broad and open discussion of policy—a forum which the ministers can ill afford to ignore.

Power of Dissolution

Some writers, especially French ones, have seen a special significance in the power of the Prime Minister to bring about (by "advice" to the King) the dissolution of the House of Commons. They apparently believe that this is a power which ensures government control in the House. We have seen, however, that government control is based on quite different factors, and that the "threat" of dissolution is a threat to the government in precisely the same proportion as it is a threat to the House of Commons. It is quite true that the Prime Minister uses the power of dissolution; hardly any Parliament remains in session to the very last day of its legal existence. But the power of dissolution serves primarily a tactical purpose; it enables the government to select the moment which it deems most auspicious for a general election. Thus, Prime Minister Attlee resisted strong pressure both within his party and among the Opposition for a general election in the fall of 1949, and postponed it to February 23, 1950, in the hope that a mild winter and the effects of currency devaluation would produce a more favorable situation for the Labor party. Although naturally criticized, the Prime Minister's decision was entirely in agreement with custom and precedent.

There is also another occasion at which dissolution may take place. When a question of great and far-reaching importance has to be decided, the cabinet may wish to assure itself of the people's support by calling for a general election. This is the nearest approach to a plebiscite known to the British system of government, and it has worked very effectively. Most notable have been the two dissolutions of 1910 in which the (Asquith) government was upheld.

When there is no clear majority in the House, the power of dissolution says in fact to the possibly unruly Commons: "Either make government possible, or surrender your seats and entrust yourselves to the vote of the people." The House can thus, by its attitude, decide which it shall be. But in any case a fairly firm government will be the result, usually after a new House has been elected.

It is said that in matters of dissolution the Prime Minister alone determines the issue. This is true only insofar as the Prime Minister bears responsibility for it and the final decision must therefore be his. But it cannot be assumed that he will stake the cabinet's life on an election without consulting his colleagues.[12] This was also true in October, 1949, and January, 1950, when Prime Minister Attlee took the sole responsibility for deciding on dissolution in February, 1950, but did so only after consultation with his colleagues.

The Cabinet System

The British cabinet system has many advantages. Perhaps its most outstanding virtue is the fact that it usually creates clear lines of responsibility. The government has an opportunity to carry out the program on which it has been elected and cannot pass on the blame for its failures and omissions to the legislature or to any other authority. It remains responsible before the people, who thus have a clear choice and will give a clear answer in endorsing or rejecting the government.

The responsibility borne by cabinet members is individual as well as collective. The difference between these two categories depends largely on political circumstances. When a minister is taken to account because of a personal mistake or worse, the responsibility will, as a rule, be confined to

---

[12] The former Prime Minister Asquith wrote: "Such a question as the dissolution of Parliament is always submitted to the Cabinet for ultimate decision." Oxford and Asquith, *Fifty Years of the British Parliament,* Boston, 1926, Vol. II, p. 195; W. Ivor Jennings, *Cabinet Government,* Cambridge, 1951, 2d ed., p. 387. This is possibly a stronger statement than is justified.

him and the stability of the rest of the cabinet may not be affected. When Chancellor of the Exchequer Hugh Dalton imprudently revealed to a favored journalist certain facts about the forthcoming budget message—a gross breach of custom and possibly of law [13]—he resigned in the ensuing storm without shaking in any way the solid foundation of the Attlee government.

A quite different case was the resignation in 1935 of the then Foreign Secretary, Sir Samuel Hoare, over the Hoare-Laval Agreement concerning Abyssinia. At that time, the agreement evoked such a scandal in England that the Prime Minister, Baldwin, had to sacrifice his Foreign Secretary. Yet it is difficult to believe that so important a step as the Hoare-Laval Agreement could have been concluded without the knowledge of the Prime Minister and at least some of the cabinet members. But in this case Sir Samuel was permitted to take sole blame for the act, and the life of the cabinet was spared. We might conclude, then, that in case a cabinet member is blamed for a political, rather than a personal, mistake, the consequences will depend on the depth to which the Prime Minister and the rest of the cabinet are involved, and on the extent to which the commotion dies down after the sacrifice of a minister.

Collective responsibility is feasible only if there is a high degree of cabinet solidarity. Uniformity of opinion cannot be expected, as the cabinet is composed of men of great experience and judgment. Decisions are therefore frequently based on compromise, which can be effected successfully only when ministers may debate their views freely without having to fear political and personal repercussions if they change their minds or concede a point. Cabinet secrecy is therefore vital to a successful conduct of business. This secrecy is technically assured by the Official Secrets Act, the Privy Councillor's oath, and the fact that all cabinet decisions take the form of "advice" to the King, which ought not to be disclosed without his permission. In actuality, however, it is political necessity rather than legal prohibition which protects the confidence of ministers. The violation of confidence would make a useful cooperation of ministers impossible, and the culprit would find it difficult to gain admittance to any future government. Of course, sometimes a minister finds the cabinet position so incompatible with his convictions that he resigns, and in the ensuing debate in the Commons some cabinet facts will invariably be disclosed. But on the whole, official secrecy is preserved, and it is left to later historians and of course to the inevitable memoirs of prominent men to lift an edge of the curtain.

Collective responsibility means, in the words of Lord Salisbury, that "each member [of the cabinet] who does not resign is absolutely and irretrievably responsible, and has no right afterwards to say that he agreed in one case to a

[13] The Official Secrets Act.

compromise, while in another he was persuaded by his colleagues." [14] This has always been a standing rule, except for the strange "agreement to differ" in 1931, which was found quite unworkable because it tended to destroy the idea of party responsibility on which the British system of government is founded.

It must be clear from the foregoing that a government cannot tolerate a minister who opposes government policy but does not resign. This extends not only to cabinet members, but to all ministers, under-secretaries, parliamentary secretaries, junior lords, and other political appointees. How far this can go was demonstrated by Prime Minister Attlee when he caused the dismissal of five private parliamentary secretaries who had voted against the government in connection with a bill regulating Britain's relationship to Eire (Republic of Ireland). This is strong proof of the correctness of Gladstone's saying that a person who enters a government gives up a certain amount of freedom of expression because whatever he says is bound to commit his colleagues. It is obvious, however, that this principle works best when the government is composed of members of one party only. Holding coalition governments together has generally been an unhappy and unsuccessful experience except in times of war.

Until 1917 the secrecy surrounding cabinet meetings was carried so far that there were not even cabinet minutes. The only documentary evidence was the summary of the Prime Minister, which he might have made in support of his own memory or for the purpose of reporting to the sovereign. This "informal" procedure broke down under the weight of decisions which had to be taken in the course of the First World War, and Prime Minister Lloyd George—never a venerator of tradition—established the cabinet secretariat, headed by an uncommonly able man, Colonel (later Sir Maurice) Hankey.[15] This brought order and permanent records into cabinet meetings, and the institution was retained despite some initial opposition.[16]

During the Second World War two further cabinet offices were added: the Economic Section and the Central Statistical Office.

The Haldane Committee of 1918 described the main functions of the cabinet as follows:

[14] Lady Gwendolyn Cecil, *Life of Robert, Marquis of Salisbury,* London, 1921, Vol. II, pp. 219–220. See also Jennings, *op. cit.,* p. 217, and Harold J. Laski, *Parliamentary Government in England,* New York, 1938, pp. 212*f.*

[15] This was originally the secretariat to the Committee of Imperial Defence, of which the Prime Minister is chairman. The secretariat of the Committee became the secretariat of the War Cabinet, and in 1917 the cabinet secretariat.

[16] The Haldane Committee (Ministry of Reconstruction, *Report of the Machinery of Government Committee,* London, 1918, p. 6) recommended the retention of the secretariat. Prime Minister Bonar Law opposed it, but it survived and has become an indispensable fixture.

1. The final determination of the policy to be submitted to the Parliament.

2. The supreme control of the national executive in accordance with the policy prescribed by Parliament.

3. The continuous coordination and delimitation of the activities of the several departments of state.

Among these broad functions, the first is easily the most important. A cabinet may get away with poor administration and would probably be protected from its worst mistakes by the diligent efforts of ubiquitous civil servants, but it can never afford to neglect Parliament. It is no exaggeration to say that the most important function—or at any rate one of the most important functions—of the British executive is primarily legislative in nature. The presentation of policy in Parliament, the answering of questions, and the securing of passage of needed legislation take much of the minister's time.

It is of course true, as we have seen, that a government may usually expect to have its measures passed in Parliament by a comfortable majority, but no matter how conclusive the majority, the government must still subject itself to the scrutiny of the legislature. It has often been stated that the chief function of Parliament is to criticize—a function which makes the Opposition the most important part of Parliament. Now it might perhaps be expected that a government which enjoys a safe and well-disciplined majority need not pay much heed to criticism. Such an attitude, however, would be extremely dangerous for any government to adopt. Members of Parliament are very conscious of the dignity and sovereignty of their House, and a high-handed attitude on the part of the government would be greatly resented. Moreover, it sometimes happens that some issue which is brought up in the House of Commons captures the imagination of the people to such an extent that even a "safe" government finds it prudent to beat a hasty retreat. The Hoare-Laval Agreement and its repercussion is an example of this.

The government finds Parliament a convenient medium through which it can expound its ideas to the country. Attention is always focused on the debates in the House of Commons, and the government has thus a ready-made sounding board of which it makes frequent use. No press conference, no "fireside chat" over the radio, can quite equal the picture of high policy at work which a debate in the House of Commons presents.

All this is true of governments with a comfortable majority in the House. It is even more true of governments with slender leads and of minority governments. That the latter, like the Labor government of 1923–1924, are able to function at all is primarily due to the high sense of responsibility prevailing in the House of Commons, which makes most Members of Parliament realize that there ought to be a government. A minority cabinet may therefore count on a fair degree of tolerance in the House. But naturally its scope of action is seriously restricted, and its life expectancy small.

The preoccupation of ministers with their role in the House of Commons naturally cuts down the time which they can spend on administrative work. Consequently, they must depend on the work of their civil-service staff, a phenomenon common to all modern governments. Some critics have been very unhappy about this and have complained that "the Cabinet has arrogated to itself, half blindly, a series of colossal responsibilities which it cannot meet, which it will not allow Parliament to tackle, and which are not met at all except in so far as they are assumed by the bureaucracy behind the cloak of Cabinet omnipotence." [17] This is indeed a strong indictment, if true. Now it is correct that no mortal man can hope to have expert knowledge of everything that pertains to a government department, but such expert knowledge is neither necessary nor desirable. It is an axiom of democratic government that "the expert should be kept on tap but not on top," because he is too likely to be insensitive to popular sentiment and is apt to have an exaggerated conception of the significance of his special field. That is why policy-making officials ought to be politicians: (1) in order to tell the civil servant, in the famous words of Sir William Harcourt, "what the public won't stand," and (2) in order to coordinate the departmental with the over-all policy for which the government is responsible before Parliament and the electorate.

We have observed that cabinet ministers are not born but are made through experience. Their background ought to enable them to read the one-page memoranda of their permanent staffs, listen to their arguments, and then apply that princely gift of the successful top man, judgment. The amount of judgment which a minister possesses is the measure of his success and of his future. It is this quality which has generally made civilian leadership in war more effective than military leadership. It cannot be pretended that every British minister has been the epitome of wisdom. But the majority of ministers have usually had enough experience and good sense to treat advice from their permanent staff with intelligent detachment. It is not the minister's job to check the technical accuracy of the reports which are placed before him. He must have confidence in his staff, for if there are chronic mistakes and notorious misinformation in their work, that fact will become known soon enough. Generally such confidence will not be misplaced. But where the minister comes in is in his ability to see the broader ramifications of a project and to gauge its effect on government policy. Once he has made up his mind, he always has his way. No civil servant can ever prevail against a minister who has made up his mind on an issue. Moreover, terms of office usually last several years, and the minister has a good chance to learn a great deal about his department. The picture, therefore, of a puppet minister directed by the hands of an anonymous civil servant is a gross exaggeration.

[17] Ramsey Muir, *How Britain Is Governed*, Boston, 1935, 3d ed., p. 105.

The War Cabinet

The cabinet originally emerged from the informal meetings of certain members of the Privy Council when the latter had become too big and cumbersome. During the First World War, even the cabinet seemed to be too large for the big and far-reaching decisions which had to be taken. The result was the creation of a "War Cabinet" in 1916 by Prime Minister Lloyd George. It was composed of five members,[18] only one of whom had any departmental responsibility (Treasury). This group was almost constantly in session and in effect conducted the war and handled the questions arising from it. After the fighting was over, difficulties arose because of the exclusion of the heads of departments whose problems now moved to the forefront of the day. The Machinery of Government (Haldane) Committee recommended a new type of "inner" cabinet, modeled on the War Cabinet, but composed of heads of departments. However, the idea was abandoned; only the Committee on Imperial Defence remained. Its head was the Prime Minister, and its principal task was the coordination of the fighting services.

In the Second World War, Prime Minister Churchill resurrected the idea of the War Cabinet. Again five men were selected, only one of whom bore departmental responsibility (Foreign Office). This War Cabinet was not merely a committee of the cabinet; it was *the* cabinet for the purpose of conducting the war, to which all other matters were subordinate. Churchill describes the situation as follows:

. . . all the responsibility was laid upon the five War Cabinet Ministers. They were the only ones who had the right to have their heads cut off on Tower Hill if we did not win. The rest could suffer for departmental shortcomings, but not on account of the policy of the State. Apart from the War Cabinet no one could say "I cannot take the responsibility for this or that." The burden of policy was borne at a higher level.[19]

The "Inner" Cabinet

Despite the dissolution of the War Cabinet in 1945, the idea of a central nucleus within the cabinet structure has remained. The Labor governments of 1945 and 1950 certainly contained a core of principal leaders with whom the Prime Minister conferred more than with others. Thus something like a hierarchy within the cabinet developed. However, this so-called "inner" cabinet was quite different from the War Cabinet. The latter was, as Churchill reminds us, the official policy-making committee, which consequently bore full and exclusive responsibility for the conduct of affairs. The informal "inner"

[18] In 1918 General Smuts was added.
[19] Winston Churchill, *Their Finest Hour*, Boston, 1949, p. 13.

cabinet was only a group of men who were closer to the Prime Minister and more important than other cabinet members and who helped him to draft policy. But as a group they bore no formal responsibility. Responsibility remains with the cabinet as a whole, and if ministers are expected to bear responsibility, they also expect to have a decisive voice. An informal "inner" cabinet is therefore at best a kind of "general staff"; it can never be a "high command" like the War Cabinet.

COMMITTEES OF THE CABINET

Despite the abandonment of the War Cabinet idea for peacetime purposes, the cabinet works quite efficiently, chiefly because of the frequent use of committees. Some are permanent; others are created for special purposes. Their organization and operation differ widely from cabinet to cabinet depending on the personalities and working methods of the cabinet members and especially of the Prime Minister.

The merit of committees studying specific issues for recommendation to the larger body of the cabinet is obvious. Committees may also keep certain important problems under continuous observation and thus guarantee that the cabinet is kept well informed. Cabinet committees may also call upon non-cabinet members to participate in their work.

Among the Standing Committees, the best known is the Defense Committee, of which the Prime Minister is chairman. Under Churchill's Premiership this committee has been especially significant. Another but less well known committee is the Legislation Committee, which is engaged in reviewing all proposed bills of ministers and recommending the lines of parliamentary procedure to be followed. Other committees deal with economic and many other problems. Their number and structure are subject to periodic changes as circumstances demand.

One of the principal advantages of the cabinet committees is the fact that they provide an opportunity for controversial measures to be thrashed out in an informal exchange of opinion of which no record is kept and to which no publicity is given. Thus, when such measures reach the full cabinet it is likely that a large measure of agreement has already been reached.

THE COMPOSITION OF THE CABINET

The composition of the British cabinet is, as we have noted, decided to a large extent by the Prime Minister. This discretion extends not only to the persons who are to fill the principal offices of government, whether in the cabinet or other ministries (some sixty altogether), but also to the arrangement of the government departments themselves. The Attlee government made an unusual number of changes. The three armed services were unified in 1946, and a Ministry of Defense with cabinet rank was created. The three service departments, the War Office, the Admiralty, and the Air Ministry, were dropped to subordinate status and are no longer in the cabinet. A Ministry of Economics was created, but in the Churchill government the preeminent position of the Treasury was restored, and there is left only a Minister of State for Economic Affairs who is not of cabinet rank.

A number of new ministries have been created, while others have been transformed or dropped. The wartime coalition government already transformed the former Dominion Office into the Office for Commonwealth Relations. The India Office was abolished for obvious reasons. Ministries for Fuel and Power, Supply, Food, National Insurance, Civil Aviation, and Town and Country Planning were added at one time or another, all outside cabinet rank. In 1951 Churchill appointed a Secretary of State for Transport, Fuel, and Power with a seat in the cabinet. This office absorbed the former Ministry of Civil Aviation. In the same year the former Ministry of Town and Country Planning absorbed most of the local government functions of the Ministry of Health and was renamed the Ministry of Housing and Local Government.

At the present time the cabinet is composed of the following officers: the Prime Minister (who is also First Lord of the Treasury and Chairman of the Committee on Imperial Defense), the Foreign Secretary, the Chancellor of the Exchequer, the Lord President of the Council, the Lord Privy Seal, the President of the Board of Trade, the Minister of Defense, the Lord Chancellor, the Home Secretary, the Secretary for Commonwealth Relations, the Colonial Secretary, the Secretary for Transport, Fuel, and Power, the Secretary for Scotland, the Minister of Labor and National Service, the Minister of Health, and the Minister of Housing and Local Government.

Outside the cabinet, but included in that body of heads of government departments often called the "ministry," are the following: the First Lord of the Admiralty, the Secretary for War, the Secretary for Air, the Chancellor of the Duchy of Lancaster, the Minister of Transport and Civil Aviation, the Minister of Supply, the Minister of Food, the Minister of Fuel and Power, the Minister of National Insurance, the Minister of Education, the Minister of Agriculture and Fisheries, the Minister of Works, the Minister of Pensions, the Attorney General, the Solicitor General, the Lord Advocate, and the Solicitor General for Scotland. Outside the cabinet are also the Ministers of State for Economic Affairs and for Scotland, who are essentially subministers. In the same category is the Minister of State, who is actually a subminister and assistant to the Foreign Secretary.

For practical purposes it is possible to distinguish between four distinct ranks in the Ministry, leaving out such junior officials as Parliamentary Secretaries, Under-Secretaries, Junior Lords of the Treasury, etc. At the bottom of the scale are the Minister of Pensions, the Postmaster General, and at times the Chancellor of the Duchy of Lancaster. The next higher group is composed of all other ministers not of cabinet rank. In the cabinet itself there are two groups, the top one being composed of that core of chief advisers to the Prime Minister who are sometimes called the "inner cabinet," while the second highest group is formed of the other cabinet ministers.

The appearance of a "hierarchy within a hierarchy" has been noted with some misgivings. In some instances it has led to jockeying for the support of certain key figures, and it endangers equality of discussion in the cabinet. It may diminish departmental responsibility, it may promote factionalism, and it may narrow down the possible range of choice for future party leadership because of inbreeding. But this, it would seem, is the inevitable result of the growth of governmental functions and the growing complexity of their nature. It is also furthered by the trend toward increasing specialization, which was particularly pronounced under the Labor government. The times when Sir Robert Peel could personally control every department of government now lie in the fabulous past. To some it seems that now even the cabinet is too cumbersome, and they advocate the adoption of the recommendation of the Haldane Committee that a cabinet of not more than ten members be created. This ideal is far from realized today, and the British government finds itself as vexed by the increase of its responsibilities as every other government in the world.

It has attempted, with a measure of success, to streamline its business by the above-mentioned use of cabinet committees. In addition, recent years have produced the institution of the coordinating ministers, called "overlords." [20] Under the Attlee Labor government the Lord President of the Council (Herbert Morrison) supervised the general planning operation of the government and later the noneconomic home problems. The Chancellor of the Exchequer coordinated economic affairs, while the Foreign Secretary also supervised Commonwealth relations. Under the Churchill government the already-mentioned Secretary of State for Transport, Fuel, and Power coordinated the Ministries of Transport and Civil Aviation and the Ministry of Fuel and Power. The Lord President of the Council took on general direction of the British food supply.

THE TREASURY

After the Prime Minister's office, the most important department is the Treasury. During periods when a tense international situation prevails, the Foreign Office may be more in the forefront of public attention, but for purposes of administration and much of the top-level policy, the Treasury is a key post and its chief, the Chancellor of the Exchequer, is not infrequently considered the logical successor to the Prime Minister, should the latter step down. Both Stanley Baldwin and Neville Chamberlain were Chancellors of

[20] Herbert Morrison, *Government and Parliament*, London, 1954.

the Exchequer before they became Prime Ministers upon the withdrawal of their former chiefs.

The importance of the Treasury is emphasized by the fact that the Prime Minister is its nominal head as First Lord of the Treasury. This is a relic from the days when the government maintained itself in office to a large extent by the judicious use of what Americans call the "spoils system," *i.e.*, patronage administered by the Treasury, the office concerned with the payment of salaries. When civil-service reform set in and the Civil Service Commission was created in 1855, it was placed under the Treasury and under the direction of the Prime Minister. As a result, the highest civil-service positions are not necessarily filled from the staff of the department concerned, but transfers are frequent, thereby avoiding narrow compartmentalization on the top level and creating a sense of unity of which the Treasury is the logical hub. Treasury control of the civil service also means the power of general regulation over the entire civil service, which presumes good relations and cooperation between the Treasury and other departments. It has made for a unified service, but it has also created some friction between departments and the Treasury, which is fortunately becoming less frequent.

Treasury control goes far beyond the civil service. Its most important power is its control over fiscal matters in general. The Treasury controls the collection of taxes and other revenues, prepares the budget, supervises the disbursement of funds, exercises considerable borrowing power, and prescribes and supervises the manner in which the public accounts shall be kept. But it is essentially a staff, not an operating agency. The actual operations are performed by such departments as the Board of Inland Revenue and the Board of Customs (which are under Treasury supervision) while the control over the legality of expenditures and the auditing function rest with the Exchequer and Audit Departments headed by the Comptroller and Auditor General.

Many of the Treasury's functions entail a certain amount of regulatory power over other departments, which is increased by the manner in which Parliament appropriates money in large sums, dedicated for certain general purposes, leaving the actual disbursement to the Treasury, which cannot exceed the appropriations but can diminish them. In practice the sanctions at the disposal of the Treasury are sparingly used. What actually happens is that administrative officers of diverse departments, when they seek departure from previous practice—especially when such departure entails increase in expenditures—seek informal contact with their "opposite number" in the Treasury and iron out difficulties in an informal manner before the issue comes to a head.[21]

[21] T. L. Heath, *The Treasury,* London, 1927. This authoritative work is one of the Whitehall Series, which deals with the principal government departments.

It must of course be remembered that the Chancellor of the Exchequer is not an isolated official rendering dictatorial decisions, but a member of the cabinet which settles policy. Treasury control in other than purely technical questions is therefore subject at all times to cabinet control.[22]

Both the "spoils" origin and the key role of the Treasury are reflected in its organization. It is headed, as stated, by the Chancellor of the Exchequer; he is assisted by a Financial Secretary of the Treasury, who is the most important of all junior ministers, is usually a Member of Parliament, and often represents the Treasury there. There is also an Economic Secretary, whose chief function is economic planning. At times there has also been a Minister of Economics, who has always been subordinate to the Chancellor of the Exchequer.

There is also a Parliamentary Secretary of the Treasury. In other government departments, the Parliamentary Secretary is the chief assistant to the minister and fills the role which in the Treasury is played by the Financial Secretary. However, the Parliamentary Secretary of the Treasury has practically nothing to do with the Treasury. He is the government's chief whip in the House of Commons. He is assisted by several Junior Lords of the Treasury who likewise have little to do with the Treasury (and are no Lords) but are assistant whips.

Apart from the various boards, offices, and commissions under the Treasury which carry out its operating functions, there are certain ministries which are subordinate to it. Among them are the Paymaster General's Office (which is often headed by a minister) and the office of the Postmaster General (who is always a minister). The latter has a more independent department whose financial operations are under Treasury control. Also under Treasury control but with a separate budget are a large number of offices and commissions too numerous to mention here.[23]

Some Other Departments

The other departments of government present a picture which looks more confusing than it is. Some are called "Offices," like the Foreign Office, and are headed by Secretaries of State; others are called "Ministries," like the Ministry of Health, and are headed by a minister; others again are called "Boards" and are headed by a "President," as in the case of the Board of

[22] The Treasury also employs a Parliamentary Secretary and Junior Lords of the Treasury. However, they discharge no Treasury business apart from certain formal signatures, but are government whips in Parliament.

[23] Among them are such offices as the Civil Service Commission, the Mint, the Public Record Office, the Historical Manuscript Commission, etc. Their budgets, while separate, appear in the national budget under the Treasury vote. For a list see Jennings, *op. cit.*, p. 526.

Trade, or by a "First Lord," as in the case of the Admiralty. Most of them are, however, organized in a similar manner.[24]

As the Treasury is now primarily responsible for the economic life of the country, so the Foreign Office handles the crucial international problems.

The Home Office is concerned with questions of domestic security. It is in charge of the metropolitan police of greater London and supervises the provincial police systems. During the war, it exercised tremendous power over aliens and Englishmen alike; under Defence Regulation 18B the Home Secretary could intern virtually anybody who was suspect of endangering the security of the state. The Home Office is in charge of naturalization of aliens —largely a discretionary power—and exercises the power of pardon [25] and reprieve. It operates the Extradition Act [26] and wields some influence over local government, although it is not the principal government department in that field. The Home Office has various other miscellaneous functions, such as liquor control, and it provides a channel for all government business for which no other authority is prescribed. As in many other countries, the Home Office is a "catchall" department, to which was added the vast responsibility for civilian defense which it discharged so splendidly during the days of the great blitz and the V-weapon attacks on England during the Second World War.

For Scotland, the Scottish Office exercises many of the functions which in England are carried out by the Home Office,[27] the Ministry of Health, the Ministry of Housing and Local Government, and the Ministry of Agriculture and Fisheries.

The Ministry of Labor and National Service has taken on the aspects of one of the most important government departments. Its general preoccupation is with conditions of labor, unemployment compensation and insurance, and conciliation. During the war it had vast powers over the labor supply, which were used very extensively in order to utilize manpower to best advantage for the purpose of the prosecution of the war. Thus all men and women found themselves directed into either military or civilian occupations which were connected with the war effort. One of the most spectacular incidents of that period was the drafting of men for work in the mines, a service which, while obviously necessary, caused much resentment.

While the Ministry of Labor and National Service possessed until 1950

---

[24] The departments also have deputy ministers called "parliamentary secretaries" (when under ministers) or "under-secretaries" (when under secretaries of state). The political deputy to the Chancellor of the Exchequer is the Financial Secretary; the Parliamentary Secretary is chief government whip.

[25] The prerogative of mercy is exercised in the form of advice to the King. In actuality the Home Secretary is in charge.

[26] However, the decisive element is usually a court.

[27] Except pardon, alien affairs, naturalization, extradition, drug control, workmen's compensations, etc. Control over Northern Ireland reverted to the Home Office in 1920.

vast powers of compulsion over labor under the National Service Act and the Control of Engagement Order, it used them in only 600 cases, preferring to operate by persuasion.

The Ministry of Health has been a more important department than the name would imply. It had considerable powers over two seemingly unconnected fields: health and local government. The connection is historical. The execution of the Poor Laws in the early part of the eighteenth century was a public scandal which led to the appointment of Poor Law Commissioners and later a Poor Law Board with a responsible chief. The connection between the Poor Laws and public health soon became manifest, and in 1848 a Board of Health was created with authority over both. Due to strong resistance, the Board was again dissolved and its functions taken over by the Home Office and the Privy Council. They were again combined under an interdepartmental committee, the Local Government Board, but the vast increase of legislation in that field forced a reconsideration of the problem. The Haldane Committee recommended the establishment of a Ministry of Health, which was created in 1919. This is the Ministry which exercised principal control over local government, though not to the same extent as the Ministry of the Interior in France. But in 1951 the control over local government was taken from the Ministry of Health and given to the Ministry of Town and Country Planning which was renamed Ministry of Housing and Local Government. The Ministry of Health also administers the old-age, widows', and orphans' insurance schemes and, since the National Health Act of 1946, is in charge of the vast machinery of the socialized medical services.

The Board of Trade is theoretically a committee, but it never meets. For all practical purposes it is a ministry like others, with the President of the Board of Trade as the minister. While comparable to the United States Department of Commerce, it is a good deal more important than its American counterpart. Its significance has been greatly increased in view of the directed economy of Britain even under a Conservative government, and the tight control over exports and imports.

A peculiar department in every way is that of the Lord Chancellor. This dignitary, whose office is very ancient and who according to protocol outranks the Prime Minister, is the final refutation of the theory of the separation of powers. He is a cabinet minister, the presiding officer of the House of Lords, and a judge. In addition he performs important functions in the administration of the established Church, for which reason he ought to be a member of the Church of England. He is usually an eminent jurist,[28] as well as a distinguished politician. As a member of the cabinet and its principal legal adviser, he takes part in all its decisions and is sometimes entrusted with special missions. As presiding officer of the upper house, the Lord Chancellor exercises the same functions as the Speaker does in the House of Commons,

[28] Lord Sankey and Lord Maugham were exceptions.

but he possesses less authority. Technically, he need not be a peer himself, but he invariably is one or is created a peer shortly after his appointment.

He is one of the judges in the House of Lords, and he presides over the Judicial Committee of the Privy Council—the two highest judicial offices in the country. He is a member of the High Court of Justice and of the Court of Appeals. He is a member of the rules committee of the Supreme Court of Judicature, which determines the rules of procedure, and he confirms the decisions of the county courts rules committee. He has many administrative duties, especially in connection with appointment of certain judges, and he has certain powers regarding some of the administrative tribunals. He also wields authority over the Land Registry and the Public Trustee's Office.

Other law officers of the Crown are the Attorney General and the Solicitor General. They are both ministers, and some Attorney Generals have been in the cabinet. Their principal duty is to represent the Crown and the departments in court. In some important cases they may prosecute for the Crown, but most prosecutions are still conducted under private direction. The duties of the two ministers have been lightened by the appointment of a Director of Public Prosecution.

In Scotland these duties are carried out by the Lord Advocate and the Solicitor General for Scotland. The law officers, including the Lord Advocate, are almost always members of Parliament, where they are supposed to support the government.

The "Sinecure" Offices

A peculiarity of the British administrative system is the existence of certain so-called "sinecure" offices. Those are offices without many official duties which, nevertheless, because of their historical significance, give the incumbent high rank. There is above all the Lord Privy Seal, who has no departmental duties, and the Chancellor of the Duchy of Lancaster, who has few. The Lord President of the (Privy) Council, although not strictly a sinecure minister, is in a similar category.

The chief advantage of this institution is that it provides an opportunity to appoint a distinguished public servant to a high-ranking office in which he is free to devote himself to such duties as the Prime Minister may assign to him. In the Attlee government Herbert Morrison, one of the principal leaders of the Labor party, became Lord President and leader of the House of Commons. For some time he was also chief planner for the government. Similarly the Lord Privy Seal is usually a very distinguished leader in the government. In 1929 J. H. Thomas was appointed to this office with the special task of finding an answer to the unemployment problem. In 1932 Anthony Eden received this office and was placed in charge of Britain's relationship with the

League of Nations. The Chancellorship of the Duchy of Lancaster has also been used for important assignments and has sometimes found a place in the cabinet. More often, however, the Chancellor of the Duchy of Lancaster has operated under the direction of the Foreign Office. For a while, Chancellor Lord Peckenham was in charge of the occupied areas in Germany and Austria.

C. THE PUBLIC SERVICE

In the preceding section we have seen that cabinet ministers lead very busy lives. They have party duties to perform, they have to spend much time in Parliament and in cabinet meetings, and they cannot easily escape many social functions. Consequently the time which they can devote to the administration of their respective departments is limited. At the close of the nineteenth century Lord Salisbury could boast that he had written all the important dispatches of the Foreign Office himself, but that is hardly practical today. Now the enormously increased burden which rests on each and every government department demands a much greater amount of time and effort as well as expert knowledge, none of which the minister will ordinarily possess. He must therefore rely on having much of his work done or prepared for him in such a way that all pertinent information is carefully digested so that he may familiarize himself speedily with the subject and render a final decision. Even then he will ask for recommendations, although he need not necessarily follow them.

It is clear, therefore, that in order to function properly, the minister must be able to rely on the honesty, efficiency, impartiality, and complete loyalty of the civil service. A civil service which is corrupt, intriguing, or disloyal, which is composed of "empire builders" or of people determined to oppose the minister, would wreck the entire structure of the administration. If the cabinet is the apex of the English system of government, the civil service makes that system possible.

There are people who have many valid objections to all kinds of civil services, but there are few who would deny that the British civil service is one of the best, quite possibly the best, in the world. Before 1853, the government services were inefficient and corrupt. The turn to the better began with the Northcote-Trevelyan report of 1853, which has rightly been called an "epoch-making" document. John Stuart Mill thought that the proposed reforms would constitute the greatest single improvement in the machinery of government. Graham Wallas described it as the greatest British contribution to the practice of politics in a century.[29] Whether this estimate is exaggerated or not, the Northcote-Trevelyan report, the establishment of the Civil Service Commission in 1855, the Superannuation (Retirement) Act of 1859, the Order

[29] H. R. G. Greaves, *The Civil Service in the Changing State*, London, 1947, p. 19.

in Council of 1870 providing for open competition and division into classes, and the Order in Council of 1920 creating the Whitley Council are milestones in the development of the Civil Service.

The high quality of the service is possible because it attracts excellent men and, to an ever-increasing extent, women. The pay is, on the whole, quite good and, in the higher brackets, fairly comfortable. At any rate, it compares not unfavorably with salary rates in equivalent private employment. In addition, there are paid holidays, sick leave, and a noncontributory pension which may amount to two-thirds of one's highest pay. If a civil servant shows great ability, he can go to the top of his class, and although promotions from one class into a higher one are not too plentiful, they are possible. At least one civil servant, Sir Horace Wilson, reached the top position of Permanent Secretary of the Treasury. The knowledge that it is possible to get to the very top inspires men of high ability to enter the service. It must also be remembered that civil servants are highly respected and hold a lofty social rank; at the same time they have not usually become the German type of *Beamter* who is puffed up with his own importance and considers himself a little tin god because he represents the all-powerful "state." It might also be that the qualities which one expects from a civil servant—quiet efficiency, loyalty, a sense of fairness, and a passion for anonymity—are also qualities which one expects to be prominently displayed among Englishmen.

Because the civil servant is permanent and therefore works for governments of changing political texture, it is necessary for him not only to be impartial, but also to refrain from such action and association as might reflect unfavorably on his impartiality. This means that a higher civil servant may not run for public office [30] and that he may not propagate his political views too vigorously. Since the repeal in 1946 of the Trades Disputes Act of 1927, civil servants may again join trade-unions, although strikes are strongly disfavored; but since the civil service has a very effective system for redressing grievances by means of the Whitley Councils, this has not become a question of first-rate importance. Nor do British civil servants high-pressure their government in the manner frequently found in France.

An additional check on improper activities may be seen in the fact that civil servants serve "during the King's pleasure," which means that their tenure rests on custom, rather than on law. This is also true of their retirement benefits, which may be withheld under certain circumstances. These disciplinary measures may be used when the interest of the service requires it. Thus a Permanent Secretary of the Air Ministry was removed because he used his official knowledge for private gain, and an official of the Ministry of Health was once dismissed because he criticized the foreign policy of the government in an anonymous article. Since 1948 membership in the Communist

[30] Exceptions are made for certain civil servants in local offices. A civil servant who is elected to Parliament is presumed to have resigned.

party may lead to transfer or suspension from the service. However, there are some safeguards to guarantee due process.[31]

TREASURY CONTROL

The control of the entire civil service reposes in the Treasury. An order in council [32] describes it as follows: "The Treasury may make regulations for controlling the conduct of His Majesty's civil Establishments, and providing for the classification, remuneration, and other conditions of service of all persons employed therein, whether permanently or temporarily." Chief of the civil service is the Permanent Secretary of the Treasury. Under him is the Establishments department, which is in direct contact with the establishment and organization officer in each department of government. The origin of this system is, of course, the financial responsibility of the Treasury. This has the advantage of uniformity and enables civil servants to move around from department to department, thereby preserving wider visions and acquiring much broad knowledge. On the other hand, Treasury control tends to be restrictive and is sometimes lacking in imagination. According to Gladstone, it is the business of the Treasury to say "No, no, no," but while great care in spending money is the mark of good government, a leading observer points out that "the Treasury should always ask itself whether it is chastity it is defending or an obsession about its chastity." [33]

In order to exercise its extraordinary power, the Treasury must have an intimate knowledge of the working of all departments. Only through such understanding—and, it might be added, sympathy—can the friction between Treasury and the departments, of which the Haldane Committee spoke, be mitigated.

Treasury control has enormous potentialities. It may work as a harmonizer and streamliner. It has unparalleled opportunities for smoothing out differences and for effecting needed coordination. But there is an inherent danger in such over-all control exercised by a fiscal agency. It is inclined to view expenditures from a standpoint of prudent economy rather than of service, and it is understandably suspicious of experimentation. In an age in which the demand for government services is on the increase, such an attitude is in danger of losing touch with political realities.[34]

The Treasury controls the service itself; entry into the service is controlled by the Civil Service Commission. It is made up of three members appointed

---

[31] Especially tribunal procedure.

[32] Order in Council No. 1976 (1920), quoted in H. Finer, *The British Civil Service*, London, 1937, p. 52.

[33] *Ibid.*, p. 61.

[34] This problem was studied by a Royal Commission headed by Lord Tomlin and therefore usually referred to as the Tomlin Commission. It reported in 1931, Cmd. 3909.

by the Crown, *i.e.*, the cabinet. They are completely nonpartisan and independent. Because entry into the civil service is accomplished through competitive examinations, a large number of examiners are employed by the Commission. Most of them are academic personnel, and some are taken from the civil service itself, usually retired persons.

EXAMINATIONS

As in the United States, the use of competitive examinations has marked the transition from patronage to the merit system. But especially in the higher brackets of examinations, the British approach is unlike the one used in America or on the Continent. In America, civil-service examinations contain a fixed set of questions on subjects which presumably have some relationship to the candidate's future work. This is not the case with the British higher civil-service examinations, which are geared to the educational system of the country. A candidate for the top Administrative class, for instance, may choose to be examined in any field or combination of fields. He may choose political science or Sanskrit, ancient history or organic chemistry. This field examination counts for a major portion of the entire test, 700 possible points out of a total of 1,400. The other 700 points may be obtained from five additional tests which are prescribed. There is an essay test (100 points), a paper on the use of English (100), a paper entitled "Present Day," which is a broad current-affairs test (100), a foreign-language test (100), and an oral examination (300). This method, now often referred to as Method I, has been implemented by a simplified Method II open to honors students of the universities. Only 25 per cent of the vacancies in the Administrative class are filled by Method II.[35]

This system might seem rather incredible to foreign observers, but there is some very sound reasoning behind it. First of all, Method I is required only of the highest, numerically smallest, but most important group of civil servants, the Administrative class. It is the British contention that the best preparation for such a career is a broad, sound, and penetrating liberal education. It is felt that, whatever specialized knowledge is needed, the candidate will get it from in-service training and experience, while any vocational training at the university level will invariably encroach on the liberal-arts subjects. This system has many advantages. It favors the broadly educated, highly cultured man over the narrow specialist. This is important because in the course of his lifetime career the civil servant tends to become too narrowly special-

---

[35] For a discussion as seen especially from the universities, see Ernest Barker, "The Home Civil Service," *The British Civil Servant*, edited by W. A. Robson, London, 1937, pp. 29–45. See also Finer, *op. cit.*, pp. 66–108; A. H. M. Hillis, "The British Civil Servant of To-Morrow," *Public Administration Review*, Vol. XI (1951), pp. 173–179.

ized anyway. It is therefore particularly important that he have a broad background before he enters the service. The system minimizes, although it does not eliminate, cramming for the examination, thereby testing the real and permanent knowledge of the candidate. It does not force the educational institutions to make too many concessions in the direction of vocationalism, but allows them to proceed with their proper task.

But there are some disadvantages. This system is geared to the curriculum of the universities, especially to the great institutions of Oxford and Cambridge. It finds its justification in the tutorial system, where the student learns how to appraise and tackle a problem—a knowledge which will be of incalculable value to him in his higher civil-service career. But—and this is a big but—only a small proportion of British youth have an opportunity to study at the universities, and still fewer enroll at Oxford or Cambridge. Despite the increase in the number of scholarships, the group from which higher civil servants are chosen will be found to be a small and select one, which cannot be called representative of the nation and which is also likely to hold social and economic views that may tend to be on the conservative side.[36]

Much criticism has been directed against the oral examination, which counts for a great deal. It does not test specific things but rather general attitude, alertness, etc. Tests have shown great variation in appraising the same candidate, and undue attention may have been paid to nice manners over ability in the raw.

CLASSES

The British civil service is divided into classes. At the top of the pyramid stands the already mentioned Administrative class. It is the smallest in number, having around 4,000 members. Most of them are recruited by competitive examination, as we have seen, and are taken directly from the honor students of the universities. A smaller number enters by promotion from the lower civil-service classes. Below the Administrative class is the Executive class. It fills its ranks by promotion and examination, but promotion is preferred when suitable candidates are available. This class does the higher work in the more specialized branches of the departments, and some of its members become the heads of large units of government engaged in routine operations.

On the lower level there is the Clerical class, divided into a Higher Clerical class, and a Clerical class. The nature of this group's duties is indicated in its name. Most of its members are appointed after examinations, but some are obtained by promotion from the still lower class of Clerical Assistants. There is furthermore a group of Typists, Assessors, Collectors, etc. In addi-

[36] Harvey Walker, *Training Public Employees in Great Britain,* New York, 1935.

tion to these regular classes, there are specialists such as lawyers or physicists, as well as inspectors of various kinds, and others.

All this applies primarily to the national civil service. There are also different services within *the* civil service, such as the Colonial or the Foreign Service. What we have said above applies primarily to the Home Civil Service. The Foreign Service test is now quite similar to the test for the Administrative class, but the grading system differs.

THE WHITLEY COUNCILS

To ensure harmonious relationships between the government and its civil servants, the so-called Whitley Councils [37] were established in 1919.[38] They are more than grievance committees or conciliation boards. In effect, they cover much of the field of public personnel policy. There is a National Whitley Council, composed of 54 members, 27 of whom are appointed by the Chancellor of the Exchequer, representing the employer, the other 27 being appointed by the various Civil Service Associations (unions). There are about 70 departmental councils, and there are a number of district and office committees. The latter groups function in the governmental industries. All councils are composed of employers' and employees' representatives in equal measure.

The councils consider practically all questions of public personnel policy, such as recruitment, promotion, salary, discipline, etc. They are also supposed to improve the service by devising means by which knowledge and training may be better utilized, and by suggesting better training. The decisions of the councils, especially the National Whitley Council, enjoy great prestige and have been at the bottom of many recent reforms. It is of course true that the Whitley Councils cannot definitely commit the Minister, whose decision is final; in practice, however, decisions of this kind are made on the basis of understanding between both sides so that a publicly announced decision of the council in effect constitutes an already-reached agreement.

The National Whitley Council suffers from being very large and cumbersome, and from considering general, rather than specific, problems. This is perhaps why the work in the departmental councils has in many respects been more fruitful, dealing as it does with concrete cases.[39]

Wage disputes, however, are submitted to compulsory arbitration, for which the Civil Service Arbitration Tribunal is the proper forum.[40]

---

[37] Named after J. H. Whitley, chairman of the committee which worked out this plan.

[38] *Report of the National Provisional Joint Committee,* Cmd. 198, 1919. See L. D. White, *Whitley Councils in the British Civil Service,* Chicago, 1933.

[39] For the government industries, the Joint Industrial Councils play the same role. There are also Trade Joint Councils with similar functions.

[40] In the government industries, industrial courts perform the same task.

The Higher Civil Service

It will easily be seen that the key to the entire British civil service system is the Administrative class. Its duties have been well defined by Sir Horace Wilson, then Permanent Secretary of the Ministry of Labor, in his remarks to the Tomlin Commission:

Broadly speaking, the main quality that is required seems to me to be a capacity to take the facts about a particular subject, to put them into shape, to suggest the deductions that might be drawn from them, to propose the lines of policy that might be adopted in relation to them, and generally to apply a constructive analytical mind to what I would call the policy of the Ministry.

The civil servant of the highest (administrative) class needs judgment and general knowledge as well as analytical ability, rather than detailed precise knowledge of technical facts, and universities are relied on to furnish the candidates.

There are obviously some objections to this approach. There is first of all some question whether it is possible to diagnose such qualities with absolute certainty in a young man or (infrequently) woman at the ages of twenty-one to twenty-six. There is also the question whether the establishment of a separate administrative class whose members rotate among departments is not likely to produce men who regard administration as a "talent" or even as some kind of mystery designed for the initiated only, rather than as a science with its own methods and approaches.[41] This disadvantage could be remedied, some critics feel, by staffing the higher civil-service positions by promotion from within the department. There is also some fear that a civil servant of this kind has possibly reached the high mark of his development when he is all keyed up for his examination, and that he is likely to have deteriorated by the time he has accumulated enough seniority to occupy a responsible position. It has also been charged that the cloistered existence of the Administrative class gives its members little opportunity to know the outside "life" which their decisions affect every day. Remedies have been suggested, notably the recruitment of older men, experienced in various social services, into the Administrative class, and an intensive in-service training including sound academic work in the theory of public administration.

Other critics complain that higher civil servants, being the product of the universities, especially of Oxford and Cambridge, are likely to originate from the upper strata of society; that this system may have been of use in the olden days when higher civil servants and their ministers came from the same social class and could confer with one another in an atmosphere of social equality, but that it is quite possibly out of step with the present day; and

[41] Walker, *op. cit.,* p. 13.

that, since a very broad system of scholarships does not exist, this present method of recruitment for the civil service excludes a vast reservoir of man-power, among whom great but unknown talents might be slumbering.

These criticisms may well be exaggerated, but that they are not entirely without foundation may be gleaned from the fact that over half the men appointed to the headship of departments [42] in recent years have not entered the Administrative class through the regular avenue of competitive examina-tions. Since it was necessary to go outside the regular group to seek out men competent enough for great responsibility, it is safe to assume that not all is well among the lower strata of the Administrative class.[43]

The war has brought some relief through a great influx of new blood in the form of many temporary officials. Some have been retained, and the practice of so-called "reconstruction examinations" has allowed persons whose careers were interrupted by the war to gain admission to the civil service. Moreover, specialists of all kinds are used to an ever-increasing extent.[44] Also, informal examinations are more frequently employed.

The objections which have been stated so far are somewhat mitigated by the fact that they can be overcome by a better personnel policy, by the in-fusion of new blood into the machinery, and by devising means through which civil servants may gain knowledge and experience in the broader, "out-side" fields which are affected by their actions. If past experience is any guide, it may be assumed that these weaknesses will be remedied as far as possible, and some progress has already been achieved.

While the higher civil servants are still recruited from the universities, the graduates of these institutions of learning no longer belong exclusively or even predominantly to the social upper classes. The impoverishment of the upper strata of society on the one hand and the increasing use of scholarships for gifted students from impecunious families on the other hand have considerably modified the social composition of university student bodies. Also promotions from one civil-service class to a higher one are now much easier. For instance, 20 per cent of the vacancies arising in the Administrative class are to be filled by candidates from the Executive class who compete successfully in examina-tions especially administered for them. There is also a better system of in-service training now.

There is, however, a further objection which may be directed to all civil services, but which has particular validity in Great Britain in view of the many services which the government has taken over since 1945. It is said that the civil service, as it exists today, was devised for a type of government whose principal administrative duties were control functions. To exercise

[42] Permanent secretaries.

[43] Greaves, *op. cit.*, p. 60.

[44] See *Sixteenth Report from the Select Committee on National Expenditure*, 1941–1942, and *The Scientific Civil Service*, Cmd. 6679, 1945.

efficient control, the necessary virtues are impartiality, discretion, caution, and keeping a jaundiced eye turned toward radical innovations. But under the leadership of the Labor party, Britain has been transformed more and more into a so-called "welfare state" or "service state," which the Conservatives can hardly undo, with the result that the rendering of services, rather than the exercise of control, is becoming more important. The very characteristics which were virtues in a control administration tend to become vices in a service administration. Instead of being impartial, the service-administering official is supposed to believe passionately in what he is doing, thus increasing the efficiency and the scope of the service he is rendering. Instead of being cautious, he is supposed to be a bold innovator and to embark on experiments which, in the last analysis, can alone determine the wisdom or failure of a particular course of action. Instead of saying "No, no, no," to new expenditures, as Gladstone suggested, he is supposed to consider the social aspects of a prospective service, rather than the financial effects on the Treasury. Civil servants are frequently accused, and not entirely without reason, of lacking imagination, of paying excessive devotion to precedent and self-developed rules, and of a plodding and disinterested slowness in the execution of business "through channels." It is certainly no disparagement of the quite excellent British civil service to wonder whether it is really geared to the demands of the new "service state."

THE ADMINISTRATION OF NATIONALIZED INDUSTRY

Because of these considerations, the British government has sought new ways in the administration of its nationalized industries. Experimentation with alternative forms antedates the Labor government by many years, and outstanding examples of earlier public corporations are the British Broadcasting Corporation, the Central Electricity Board, and the London Passenger Transport Board. The forms of organization established for those corporations were perhaps more accident than design, but their semiautonomous character was conceived in order to combine two divergent principles: that of sound business administration, which demands independence from a national bureaucracy, and that of responsibility, to which all sections of governmental activities must ultimately be subjected. Naturally, where there is government responsibility there must be government control.

The newly nationalized industries use a form of organization which was inaugurated in 1947 by the National Coal Board [45] and has spread, with some differences, to the Transport Commission (Railroads) and the British Electricity Authority. The Iron and Steel Corporation, however, had an entirely

[45] The National Coal Board took over on Jan. 1, 1947. Cf. National Coal Board, *Annual Report and Statement of Account*, 1947; William W. Haynes, *Nationalization in Practice, The British Coal Industry*, Boston, 1953.

different setup. The principles by which the nationalized industries are governed can be best shown by the example of the coal industry, the oldest of the recently nationalized industries, which is concerned with the most basic enterprise in Britain. Under private ownership,[46] there had been some larger and some smaller companies, but none of them was excessively large. Only in a few was there any considerable hierarchy.[47] Now there is a formidable machinery. At its top is the National Coal Board itself, a kind of coal "cabinet," whose members used to have departmental responsibilities until 1951 but now have only collective responsibility for the policy of the industry. Below the National Board there are eight divisional boards which are smaller in number of members (six) but largely duplicate the functional division of the National Board. Under the divisional boards there are no less than forty-eight areas, each under an area general manager, under whom are the heads of departments. These departments duplicate the departments on the divisional and national level, and their heads are responsible thereto as well as to the area general manager. Finally there are the many colliery managers. The difficulties of such an arrangement are clear. The lower levels are faced by many confusing lines of authority, and there is a tendency—well known in the civil service—to escape responsibility by passing "the buck" higher up.

The other nationalized industries have not had quite the same problem as the coal industry. The British Electricity Authority, which took over on April 1, 1948, found an already efficiently working system of distribution which had been administered by the Central Electricity Board. A similar arrangement was made for nationalization of gas, which took effect on May 1, 1949. There are twelve area boards and an advisory Central Gas Council. The British Transport Commission took over the railroads on January 1, 1948. It learned much from the experiences of the London Passenger Transport Board, which was created in 1933. The Transport Commission found the railroads already largely consolidated since 1921, when four major companies had been created out of a multitude of others. These railways were now placed under a Railway Executive, under which there are now six "regions," each headed by a chief regional officer and by various functional executives. Just what advantages there are in the "consolidation" of four companies into six regions is not quite clear. A more flexible form of administration has been set up for the Road Haulage Executive which has been in charge of long-distance trucking. Quite different forms of administration have been applied to such special public corporations as the British Broadcasting Corporation, the British Overseas Airways Corporation, the British European Airways, and the Bank of England.

---

[46] One could hardly speak of private *enterprise*. The price cartel agreements of 1930 eliminated all competition, and in 1937 the government acquired all mineral rights.

[47] Charles L. Mowat, "The Anatomy of British Nationalization," *Antioch Review*, 1949, pp. 274*f*.

The Iron and Steel Corporation, which was designed to control the nationalized steel industry, departed from the above system. The various firms remained intact, even under their former names, in order to retain the large amount of good will and reputation attached to certain internationally famous firms. They also remained largely under their former managerial personnel. However, the Churchill government denationalized both the iron and steel industry and the trucking industry. This measure has run into considerable difficulties as there was a great deal of reluctance on the part of private interests to repurchase the stocks of these companies for fear that a possible future Labor government might renationalize them, as the Labor leaders have threatened to do.

These public corporations are subordinate to an appropriate minister who in turn is answerable for their activities in Parliament. However, the exact line between ministerial responsibility and control on the one side, and the corporations' autonomy on the other, has never been entirely determined, and ministers have refused to answer questions in Parliament on matters which they felt lay within the autonomous powers of the corporations.

Another avenue to public control has been sought by means of consumers' councils attached to most public corporations, but they have been generally unsatisfactory and have been accused, rightly or wrongly, of reflecting merely the position of management.

From an administrative standpoint, the nationalized industries have raised many problems. Their cumbersome structure, especially in the coal industry, will have to be streamlined. The National Coal Board admits an increase of 4,799 persons in the administrative and nonindustrial staff as compared to the personnel before nationalization. While some additions were undoubtedly necessary, the situation, as well as other difficulties, would seem to indicate that the administration of a large industry from a central command post is not an easy thing and is certainly not learned overnight.

There are also other problems. There is not as yet a merit system comparable to the civil service in the nationalized industries. Standards are difficult to develop on account of the great diversification of the industries. Moreover, in order to retain the managerial skill of former executives, it has been necessary to pay salaries which are comparable to the top positions in private industry and are substantially higher than comparable civil-service salaries. This has caused considerable criticism and opposition.

There have also appeared new problems of labor relations. Strikes have occurred, but have generally been discouraged by the unions, especially while a Labor government was in office. On the other hand, unions not affiliated with the Trades Union Congress have been squeezed out in some places. In contrast with France, there are no workers' representatives as such on the boards or executives.

It is true some trade-union leaders became members of these boards in their personal capacity, and the close tie between the former Labor government and the unions has forced the latter to urge more production and to discourage certain wage demands—an attitude which runs counter to the fighting tradition of a union. On the other hand, there is no conclusive evidence that nationalization has appreciably affected the workers' morale, and they may perhaps be excused if they find that the new bosses look—and sometimes behave—suspiciously like the old ones. It cannot be assumed that the oft-proven British skill for adaptation will be found wanting; the shortcomings of the nationalized industries are openly discussed and studied, and improvements are undertaken vigorously. But just as the development of the British civil service had to go through many stages, so the administration of the nationalized industries is in its infancy and its definitive analysis must be left to an endeavor which still lies in the distant future.

Nationalization and large-scale governmental planning have apparently raised more questions than they have solved. This is not in itself an argument against the measures undertaken by the Labor government, because a situation of this kind must be expected in any period of transition. However, there are many people who wonder whether the time-honored methods of control still operate today, or whether checks and balances need to be developed in order to keep the enormously growing scope of executive power within the confines of democratic government. In the past, checks and balances have not characterized the British system.

The relatively short time during which nationalized industries have operated in Great Britain does not permit any final conclusions. One thing is certain, however, and that is that nationalization has not fulfilled the expectations of either its protagonists or its opponents. It has not raised production beyond the level achieved in comparable branches of private industry. In some cases the level has remained lower. Nor has greater economy or efficiency prevailed; nor have labor relations markedly improved; and the working man is no happier working for a public corporation than for a private one. In fact, at the annual meeting of the Trade-Union Congress in 1953, several delegates voiced the opinion that it was easier to deal with the old bosses than with the new ones. Certainly in the mining industry, the most ailing before nationalization, higher wages [48] have diminished neither absenteeism nor the ever-growing difficulty of recruiting new labor.

On the other hand nationalization has certainly not ruined the British economy as was widely predicted, and it is unlikely that private management would have done any better either in labor relations or production. In fact, considering the austere days after the war, industrial unrest would probably have been greater under private management, especially in the coal fields, when labor would not have been restrained by its unions.

It is difficult to deny that nationalization has not fulfilled the high expecta-

[48] Miners' wages are among the highest of Britain's industrial workers.

tions of its Labor-party advocates. While some may take satisfaction in the fact that certain private interests have been shorn of their great power, Britain's major economic problem, the increase and greater efficiency of her production, has not been appreciably enhanced by nationalization beyond what has been achieved in the private sector of the economy. As a result, enthusiasm for nationalization has greatly cooled in Labor-party circles, and the annual conference of the party at Margate in 1953 abandoned its demands for further nationalization over the protests of its radical left wing.

Yet the Conservative government has attempted to denationalize only the iron and steel industry and the trucking business. In these two industries an eventual understanding between Labor and Conservative leaders will have to be found if they are not to stagnate and become demoralized between the alternate threats of nationalization and denationalization. As for the rest, what has been nationalized so far is likely to remain so; but further nationalization experiments are not envisaged in the foreseeable future.

ECONOMIC PLANNING AND DIRECTION

There is no country on the face of the earth which does not interfere with its economy in some way. Nor has there ever been a time in modern history when complete noninterference was practiced. Tariff policies, taxation, licensing, currency circulation, fixed rates of interest, etc., exist everywhere. Moreover the well-remembered great depression of the late twenties and early thirties has alerted all governments to keep a finger in the economic pie of their country.

In Great Britain these universal tendencies have been greatly sharpened by the serious economic situation which developed as the result of the Second World War. The near-total loss of Britain's foreign investments, which were largely liquidated when she fought alone, the loss of many of her markets, the destruction of much equipment and shipping, as well as the effects of an overaged industrial machinery, have all made themselves felt. Under the Labor government economic planning took on major proportions. Under the Conservatives it is less prominent, but it is not abolished and resides largely in the Treasury. The Chancellor of the Exchequer, who at the present time is assisted by a Minister of State for Economic Affairs, is in general charge, although economic affairs are so all-pervasive that the entire cabinet has a hand in them and may be called the economic high command. There are a number of agencies concerned with economic planning. Perhaps the most important is the Central Economic Planning Staff, which is in the Treasury; it is headed by a Chief Planning Officer, who is also the chief planning adviser of the Chancellor of the Exchequer.

Other important offices are the Economic Section of the Cabinet Office, and the Central Statistical Office. On a somewhat lower level are committees of

experts drawn from various government departments, often in close cooperation with the above-mentioned offices. An over-all planning agency was perhaps envisaged in the creation in 1947 of the Economic Planning Board,
which was to coordinate the numerous planning boards already in existence.
It has representatives from the already-mentioned planning offices (the Chief
Planning Officer being permanent chairman), from various government departments, and from industry and labor. But its value seems to be limited to
a purely advisory function and it serves primarily as a channel of information.

The striking feature of this arrangement is that there is no real planning
machinery but rather a system of staffs and boards whose actual operation
is not revealed by any table of organization but proceeds through informal
channels of personal contact. R. S. Milne put it succinctly when he wrote:

An intense disregard for rigid organizational arrangements is accompanied by close
personal contacts inside the small circle of individuals who really matter in the
taking of economic decisions. . . . Formally the exchange of relevant information
is assured by means of sending copies of documents to all those likely to be interested; informally, such institutions as clubs allow more general ideas to circulate.
It is the use of these methods which accounts for both the efficiency and the obscurity of the British economic planning machinery.[49]

In the field of agriculture, the wartime needs to grow as much food at home
as possible created patterns of planning and compulsion which have not been
entirely abolished. The Agricultural Act of 1946 not only empowers the
Minister of Agriculture and Fisheries to set practically all prices and, in cooperation with the Minister of Food, to establish marketing policies, but also
places all agricultural production under tight government control. Land which
is not efficiently cultivated may be placed under direct government control,
which includes power to direct the farmer what and how to plant. If that
does not work, the government may forcibly buy the land from its owner and
find a more satisfactory user. The government may also prevent the un-
economic use of good farm land. This comes close to a nationalization of the
land,[50] but it must be emphasized that the County Agricultural Committees
stress advice and aid to the farmer rather than force. As a result there is little
discontent with these powers.

Innumerable statutes exist regulating conditions in various industries. Advisory bodies were set up under the Industrial Organization and Development
Act of 1947, especially for the cotton industry, the most ailing of Britain's
important industries after coal mining. More recently joint Anglo-American
councils have endeavored to study American production methods and to apply
them, where possible, to Britain. The Bank of England has sponsored certain

[49] R. S. Milne, "Britain's Economic Planning Machinery," *American Political Science
Review,* Vol. XLVI (1952), p. 421.

[50] Harold Zink, "The New Role of the Government in Britain," *Western Political
Quarterly,* Vol. I (1948), pp. 413–425.

private development corporations which have as an objective the granting of loans to industry, somewhat comparable to the American Reconstruction Finance Corporation, though of a more restricted and private character.

Unfortunately Great Britain's economic ills come largely from the outside as the result of war and postwar political changes, and both the British government and British industry have only limited opportunities to improve the difficult conditions in which they find themselves. Nevertheless, great progress has been achieved, owing largely to the magnificent discipline and patience of the British people and to the responsible character of the government under both the Labor and Conservative administrations.

PROBLEMS OF BIG GOVERNMENT

As the government has extended its power and influence into many fields, there are pessimistic voices complaining that these powers tend to become arbitrary and unduly free from restraint. Parliament, being overburdened by an ever-increasing legislative load, is increasingly inclined to pass "skeleton" legislation, leaving "details"—often very extensive—to the decision of executive departments, which thus exercise what is sometimes termed "delegated legislation."[51] But then the executive often goes one step further and also establishes ministerial and departmental tribunals or quasi tribunals which decide disputes arising under these orders and regulations. As long as the decision is within the scope of this broad grant of power given by Parliament, it is legal, and the justice or wisdom of the ministerial decision itself cannot be reviewed by a regular court of law.[52] This means that when the law says "the decision of the Minister is final," some anonymous civil servant is in a position to make a nonreviewable final decision which may affect the livelihood and property of individuals very deeply. Moreover, the "minister," or rather the civil servant, is not governed by the rules of judicial procedures which are incumbent upon the courts and may therefore make decisions without a hearing and without giving the affected party an opportunity to submit evidence.[53]

It is a fact that on the whole the British administration leans over back-

[51] The executive orders given as a result of such delegation have many names. They may be called "orders," "rules," "regulations," "warrants," "minutes," "schemes," "bylaws," etc.

[52] In the United States, review by the courts is made possible in such cases by the use of the "due process of law" clause of the United States Constitution. There is no equivalent in Great Britain.

[53] The principal critic was the Lord Chief Justice Lord Hewart of Bury, *The New Despotism*, New York, 1929. See also C. K. Allen, *Law and Orders; Delegated Legislation and Executive Powers in England*, London, 1945; M. A. Sieghart, *Government by Decree*, London, 1950; and W. A. Robson, *Justice and Administrative Law; a Study of the English Constitution*, London, 1947, 2d ed.

ward to be fair and to enable all parties to make their points. Even when the ministers have extraordinary powers, they prefer to rule by persuasion rather than by compulsion. Nor is there any appreciable degree of dishonesty in the wielding of the extraordinary powers and discretions which the civil service frequently possesses. The speed, publicity, and severity with which the Attlee government dealt with a corrupt Parliamentary Secretary of the Board of Trade [54] shows that the government is fully aware of those dangers and is intent upon maintaining the integrity of the administrative machinery. But it is nevertheless true that the increasing number of regulations which economic austerity, planning, and nationalization have brought to England cause many decisions to be made by anonymous civil servants and behind closed doors. This has also the further disadvantage that the civil servant, unlike the judge, is not necessarily bound by precedent, with the result that the citizen remains somewhat uncertain as to the outcome of his case.[55]

On the other hand, the defenders of the present system reply in the following manner to the critics of this form of "delegated legislation" and administrative justice: there is no reason to assume, they say, that a judge is necessarily wiser than a civil servant, although he is of course more independent. Moreover, ministerial decisions frequently involve questions of policy, rather than of abstract justice, and the minister is responsible for that policy before Parliament, and ultimately before the nation. Decisions implementing policy might therefore be said to be quite properly before the minister or his agent, rather than before an independent judge who bears no responsibility for the policy of the government and may even be hostile to it.

The Committee on Ministers' Powers [56] suggested certain remedies such as greater publicity in the performance of quasi-judicial functions. When Parliament is of the opinion that the ordinary courts are not suitable for the determination of certain issues arising out of the administrative work of a department, the disputes should be referred to an independent tribunal and not to the discretionary power of the minister. This would have meant the establishment of an administrative court system on the French model.

Most of these recommendations have not as yet been carried out, although isolated instances of tribunals of the kind envisioned above do exist. While all these dangers and difficulties exist of necessity in an age which demands unprecedented services from its government, and while they ought to be remedied, there is no factual reason as yet to speak of "despotism" or "dicta-

---

[54] This was the Belcher case. Cf. Rebecca West, "The Tribunal That Stirred England," *Harper's Magazine*, Vol. 198 (June, 1949), Part I, pp. 21–33; *ibid.* (July, 1949), Part II, pp. 37–50.

[55] In practice, however, the civil servant is not much less impressed by his own precedents than the judge is, and sometimes more so, even though there is no official rule of *stare decisis* in the civil service.

[56] *Report of the Committee on the Ministers' Powers*, Cmd. 4060, 1932.

torship." It is important to remember that the British civil service is not a "state within the state," as the German civil service used to be, but is part of a democratic and responsible form of government in which large-scale abuse of power would lead to a quick and drastic public reaction which would cause some "heads to roll." On top of the civil servant there is still the responsible minister, whose function it is "to tell the civil service what the public won't stand."

Chapter 4

PARLIAMENT

A. THE HOUSE OF COMMONS

Wherever there is a parliamentary form of government in the world, England is the model, and all comparisons eventually center around the magnificent building on the river Thames which is called the House of Parliament. Indeed this "mother of Parliaments" is a remarkable establishment, but like so many other British institutions it is somewhat different in scope and methods from what the casual observer might expect.

On one thing all are agreed: when we speak of Parliament, we mean the House of Commons. To be sure, there is still the House of Lords, and a later section will show that it is by no means a negligible quantity despite its progressive loss of substantive power. But the sovereignty of Parliament resides in the House of Commons, for it alone is representative of the nation as a whole, and in its chamber are heard the great political debates of the country.

A preceding chapter has demonstrated that the British cabinet and legislature are not separate entities, but one, and that their relationships are based on political realities rather than on any constitutional "checks and balances." Parliament does not rule; no body of more than 600 persons could do that. It actually interferes far less with the administration of government departments than does the United States Congress. Nor does policy emanate from Parliament; that is the business of the cabinet. Yet Parliament stands at the very center of the political stage—is, in fact, the political stage—and if the cabinet is the head of the body politic, then Parliament is its heart.

FUNCTIONS

The Clerk of the House of Commons once defined the functions of the House as follows: "(1) Representation of popular opinion, (2) the control of finance, (3) the formulation and control of policy, (4) legislation." [1] Coming from so authoritative a quarter, this definition might well be accepted, yet it curiously misses the point. For example, the House of Commons is

[1] *Third Report of the Select Committee on Procedure,* October, 1946, p. xxii.

usually representative of popular opinion, although discrepancies between the votes in the country and seats in the House have frequently occurred, but this is not really a function. On the other hand the control of finances is a function, but it is not really exercised by the House. The power, of course, exists, and its existence is well understood by the government. But it is at best negative—the power to object—and it is largely dormant. The budget is actually prepared by the cabinet, presented by the Chancellor of the Exchequer, and, as a rule, passed as it stands. The kind of budget treatment in which the Congress of the United States indulges is totally unknown in Great Britain.

Policy is formulated solely by the cabinet; it may be and very often is announced *in* the House, but not *by* the House. However, there is some control of policy, as will be seen later in this chapter.

The Clerk of the House, as well as the illustrious Bagehot, listed legislation last, and that for very good reasons. The House does not truly legislate in the sense that it originates, formulates, and enacts laws. All legislation of any consequence originates in and is proposed by the cabinet or by a minister. Significant legislation originating in the House is nearly unheard of. The success of a private member, A. P. Herbert, in obtaining passage of some reforms in the divorce laws is still remembered as an outstanding and unusual exception to an otherwise unchallenged practice.

The exercise of legislative initiative on the part of the House of Commons is severely limited by a number of factors. One is that the House does not have the elaborate committee system of the Congress of the United States. The detailed technical examination of bills, the conduct of specialized hearings, is generally impossible, and the House therefore relies mainly on such evidence as is presented by governmental agencies or by special boards of inquiry, as for instance Royal Commissions. The second reason is the government's control over the time of the House, which leaves little room for the consideration of motions by private members.

GOVERNMENT LEADERSHIP

But more important than all preceding reasons for the limitations upon the powers of the House of Commons is the strong control which the Prime Minister and his colleagues exercise in their capacity as party leaders. Both the leaders of the government party and its lesser members, the so-called "backbenchers," understand that serious difficulties to the government are likely to result in dissolution of the House and in general elections under circumstances unfavorable to the majority party. Some of the backbenchers may not like their leaders, but they certainly like the leaders of the Opposition even less. Thus many a reluctant backbencher will fall into line, despite his continued disagreement, because he recognizes the need for party discipline. Of course, some intra-party opposition is always tolerated, for there is a point beyond which Englishmen are not easily pushed, but the party leaders expect obedience in major questions. Recalcitrant members are taken to task by the party leaders, and especially by the "whips," and on occasion expulsion is the punishment of the presumably incorrigible. But since expulsion from the party is likely to set an untimely end to an otherwise promising political career, the very existence of this punishment is usually sufficient, without any need for numerous executions of it. Expelled members may of course run as "independents," but that is rarely successful, as was drastically demonstrated in the 1950 and 1951 elections in which not a single independent was returned to Parliament.

Generally speaking, therefore, it is safe to say that a government which has a solid majority in the House has little to fear until the next election. No government commanding such a majority has been defeated since 1866. A government was defeated in 1885, but it never had a majority on the critical question of home rule for Ireland which caused its downfall, and the Liberal party was split as a result of those events. Later governments which were defeated were minority governments, like the MacDonald regime of 1923–1924. A solid majority is usually considered to be one of at least thirty seats, which makes the government reasonably safe from the chance of illness of members, absenteeism, or other reasons. However, since 1950 no government has enjoyed such a margin. This may perhaps be considered unusual.

While the cabinet thus possesses formidable control over the House of Commons, it does not exercise this control all the time. There are measures on which the government will suffer defeat, but it is for the government to decide when an issue is important enough to require the imposing of party discipline and the staking of the government's life thereon. There are certain questions which are always that important, such as a possible vote of censure or nonconfidence, or defeat on a resolution concerning the major policies of the government, or tampering with the budget. Defeat of the government on such issues will always bring the government to a fall. Consequently, as soon as such questions arise on the Parliamentary horizon, the whips fly into action, and all good men are supposed to come to the aid of their party. An outstanding member of the cabinet, often a Deputy Prime Minister, is designated a "Leader of the House of Commons," and his principal responsibility is for planning the parliamentary debates in cooperation with the leaders of the Opposition. In critical cases the Prime Minister himself may take over this role.

The expression and guidance of public opinion is another function of the House, and in the exercise thereof, the House informs the public how it is being governed. England is a small country. No place is farther than 40 miles from the sea, and every Member of Parliament may visit his constituents easily over the week end—without the use of a plane. Moreover, constituencies are generally not large. Consequently the sentiment back home is usually quite easily discernible, and the members of the House are bound to reflect the views of their constituents when they return to Westminster. Issues which interest the public will quickly find their way to the floor of the House, and the government will be questioned closely. No matter how formidable the majority which the government may control in the House, it can neglect such expressions of sentiment only at its peril. Public opinion must therefore be placated wherever possible, and the government knows very well that the attitude which it takes toward the expression of widely felt grievances will determine the degree to which it may hope to be returned at the next election.

While Parliament thus brings issues and public sentiments to the attention of the government, the government in turn brings its views to the attention of the people. A successful government must lead as well as listen. Weak governments never have found favor with either public or Parliament. The electorate looks upon its representatives and its government as agents who are supposed to use their judgment within the framework of their electoral mandates. Britishers do not regard Members of Parliament as servants whose actions are constantly dictated by demands from their constituents.

Influence on Public Opinion

In telling the public about its policies, the government affects and often changes public opinion. This is what Bagehot called the "teaching function." "A great and open council of considerable men cannot be placed in the middle of a society without altering that society." In the House of Commons, the government finds its best forum. Radio, and now television, may carry the Prime Minister's voice and face into millions of homes, but nothing can equal the atmosphere of the House of Commons. Here are to be found all the symbols of majesty in the use of which the British have no peer. There is the crowded, but intimate, chamber in which the Members and ministers speak quite informally, almost conversationally. There is the formidable figure of the Speaker on his throne with his wig, and there is the mace on the table of the House, the symbol of sovereignty. But at the same time the front-bench speakers may lean on that table and may sometimes even stretch their weary feet on it. Members, whether ministers or private members, speak from their places—a custom which is as practical as it is discouraging to unnecessary oratory; they do not march to a rostrum as they do in France or Germany. The House is not semicircular and amphitheatric, like the French National Assembly, the Weimar and Bonn legislatures, and the United States Congress, but oblong, with the table dividing the government and Opposition benches—a visual manifestation of the two-party system. The

Prime Minister therefore speaks directly to the leader of the Opposition, who sits opposite him and who then rises and attempts to blast his speech.

When there is an important speech or debate, the chamber is crowded. Many members are unable to find seats, and their crowding of the chamber increases the emphasis on the importance of the occasion. That happens only on important occasions, but at such times the attention of the country is focused on the House. The public at large knows that it is witnessing government in action to a far greater degree than could be the case in the United States, where only one branch of the government can usually be observed at a time. When the chamber of the House of Commons was rebuilt after the destruction of the Second World War, it was again constructed with fewer seats than members.

Debate

The debates in the House are noted in the country, and they are continued in every town and village, chiefly in the "public houses" (taverns). Soon it becomes obvious what impression the country has received from the debates, and Parliament feels the implications. Parliament may therefore be said to be the focus of interaction between government and the governed by which each affects and molds the other.

The effectiveness of Parliament is possible because it rests on certain assumptions which all or most members hold in common. It is agreed that there must be a government and that it must be able to govern. It is also agreed that there must be an Opposition which must be given adequate opportunities to oppose. Thus the Opposition fights the government tooth and nail, and when such redoubtable orators as Winston Churchill and Aneurin Bevan step into the arena, strong words fly. But when all is over and done and the majority has had its way, there is rarely an attempt at sabotage. The Opposition is mindful of its political opportunities in creating campaign issues, but it nevertheless often supports the government when, in its opinion, the good of the country requires it. At any rate, when the government carries its program to the floor of the House and the Opposition fights against it, it is understood that both are thereby fulfilling their constitutional functions, and that democratic government would be impossible unless both sides enjoyed considerable freedom. The Prime Minister who debates the leader of the Opposition knows that he is debating his probable successor. The members of the victorious majority party know that so far no party has yet enjoyed a majority in the House for more than ten years and that consequently they will, one day, sit on the Opposition benches. It is therefore necessary for both sides that the rules of the game be observed.

The epitome of this system may be found in the Speaker, who presides over this contest. Once elected by the House, he divests himself of all party connections and rules with absolute impartiality. As a result, he retains his position as long as he chooses and is ordinarily reelected to Parliament. The Speaker used to be reelected, unopposed. But in recent elections there has been ineffective opposition. No Speaker has ever failed to gain reelection although he never campaigns, as that would make him a partisan. In 1945 the Labor party received an overwhelming majority of seats in the House of Commons, but the Speaker, Colonel Clifton Brown, a former member of the Conservative party, was reelected. He was also reelected in 1950.

The spirit of the House of Commons shines in the debates. A leading observer describes it as follows:

> . . . you must remember that here are phlegmatic Englishmen and dour Scots. The "Celtic fringe" is too small to change the atmosphere, especially since the Irish went to enliven their own assembly in Dublin. Scenes are rare. There is no banging of desks; there are no desks to bang; and they would not be banged if there were. The moments of excitement are so rare that they go down in the political annals. . . . The task of the Speaker is easy. A calm word, a humorous comment, usually restores order. He has no bell, no hammer. The Speaker rises, the members sit, and the House is quiet. . . .[2]

Debates may be spirited, but courtesy will usually be observed. New Members and new cabinet ministers are customarily congratulated by the Opposition for their first speeches—after which they may be vigorously attacked. Many Members remain in the House for many years, and have to learn to get along with each other. In America, there are many roads to political leadership, but in Great Britain there is only one—the House of Commons. Thus, this assembly of the great, the nearly great, and the merely dull has acquired an atmosphere of its own which emphasizes the British belief that the most desirable type of humanity is the gentleman.

School for Leadership

In order to become a national figure in the public life of the country, a man has first to make a name for himself in Parliament. He will be listened to if he has something to say, but not otherwise. He will have some pretty sharp debating to do, and the manner in which he conducts himself will make a name for him—or not. A party may get a good many men elected, but it cannot make them leaders. Only after some years in the House do the talents begin to crystallize and the future leadership to emerge. The House is courteous, but not necessarily patient. It does not care much for insincerity or empty oratory. The halting speaker who has something to say is more likely to succeed than the dispenser of glittering generalities. A man who

[2] W. I. Jennings, *Parliament,* London, 1939, p. 20.

gains a reputation in the House of Commons is one who has faced sharp opposition almost daily and has stood his ground. It is after all no small thing to speak knowing that sharp-witted opponents will put every word under a magnifying glass.

What is the result of all this? It is that leadership grows gradually as a man proves his worth in the daily Parliamentary struggle. "Dark horses," as we have noted, have no place in England. Leaders are almost always men who have served fairly long terms in Parliament, who have learned the art of give-and-take, and who have learned to get along with one another. By the time they become "frontbenchers," they have become steeped in Parliamentary tradition and House of Commons lore. " I am a child of the House of Commons," said Winston Churchill, with his inimitable gift for accurately descriptive prose.

This is a most democratic way of attaining leadership. It is not democratic in the perverted sense of ancient Greece, where citizens were held equally capable of holding office to such a degree that they were simply selected by lot, but it is democratic in the modern sense of the idea, which requires that all men should have an equal chance for leadership but that leadership itself be attained by talent and ability. The Conservative party may send the dull sons of famous houses to Parliament, the Labor party may send deserving but equally dull retired trade-union secretaries to the House, but from there on they are on their own. Winston Churchill was once distrusted by the leaders of the Conservative party because he had "crossed the floor" [3] before and was not considered safe. Sir Stafford Cripps had once been expelled from the Labor party. He too was not considered "safe" by the party leadership. Yet later their place was undisputed, even if they continued, like all strong men, to have their opponents on both sides of the House.

GRIEVANCES

Another function of the House is the airing of grievances. When a public official has made an unjust or arbitrary ruling, when negligence or gross inefficiency has been reported to exist in a branch of the public service, when an order or law has been applied unfairly, or when there are other real or imaginary grievances against the government or its agents, a Member of Parliament is bound to hear about it from a constituent. In that case he may bring the matter up in the House. He will question the responsible minister, ask for information on the matter, and demand to know what the minister intends to do about it. Now a minister may have a very comfortable margin of support in the House, but his reputation and leadership are bound to suffer if very many complaints are lodged against the manner in which he administers his department. The minister will therefore usually investigate the case

[3] *I.e.*, changed political parties.

unless the complaint is clearly unfounded, and if it is justified, some redress will usually follow.

This function works well in execution but it works even better by its mere existence. A minister may take pride in improving conditions which have been criticized in Parliament, but he much prefers not to be criticized. Consequently he keeps his eyes open for acts of maladministration, and is likely to press for improvements before the matter has a chance to reach the House. If the shortcomings are of major proportion, the government may appoint an impartial investigating board, sometimes even a Royal Commission whose recommendations usually carry great weight and also prevent the Opposition from making excessive political capital out of the defects found in the government's armor.

This method is not only effective in itself, it is also an excellent and convincing proof of democratic government. Any Member of Parliament, and through him the electorate at large, may put a mighty minister, even the Prime Minister himself, on the stand and demand an explanation. As long as that is possible, all talk of "dictatorship" in England will remain greatly exaggerated.

It must be clear from what has been said that Parliament accomplishes its task primarily by means of debate. Deprecators of democracy have been pleased to speak of it as a "talking shop" or a "debating society." Actually, the House of Commons may take pride in these designations. Debate is the essence of democracy; in the debate, different points of view may come into the open freely and without fear. Only where there is government by debate can decisions be made which are afterward obeyed without recourse to police sticks, concentration camps, or forced labor.

Debate is essential, but it can exist only when there is challenge. The members of the government party are somewhat subdued by considerations of party discipline and the desire not to show up their own leaders. But the Opposition is under no such restraint. The more vigorous its challenge, the better. The importance of the Opposition is now officially recognized, as the leader of the Opposition receives a salary which is charged to the Consolidated Fund and is thus not subject to annual appropriations. In return for this salary, he has no other obligation than to oppose the government. This fulfills two vital tasks: it keeps the government on its toes, and it provides a capable alternative government, should the cabinet in power fail.

Why the System Works

This remarkable system operates on the basis of certain basic assumptions and conditions. In the first place it presupposes a two-party system. Its physical organization, its procedure, the assumption of the basic stability of governments, and the opportunity to carry out a clear electoral mandate are products of the prevailing two-party system. The fact that all previous experiences with coalition governments have been unsatisfactory, except in times of war, further underscores the validity of these stipulations.

Secondly, the British parliamentary system presupposes a close relationship between the Members of Parliament and their constituents. This is necessary because, as we have seen, one of the functions of Parliament is to articulate prevailing public opinion on major issues and to voice grievances encountered by constituents. The fulfillment of this function is all the more vital because, short of elections, there are few other ways in which public opinion may press forcefully upon the government. There is no referendum, and public petitions are of little use.[4] This close relationship between legislator and constituents is made possible by the single-member districts which are customary in the English-speaking world. The introduction of a proportional-representation (PR) system, once hotly debated, might well destroy this relationship as it has done in other countries. However, there appears to be little prospect of a radical change.

A third factor which ought not to be underestimated is the high reputation of Parliament, which causes able men to be attracted by a political career. In Britain the term "politician" does not have to contend with the same disparagement which it suffers in America, and a seat in the House of Commons is considered an outstanding achievement by many businesses and professions. The House of Commons may not be "the world's best club" because, as one writer stated, "there are too many bores in it," but it is still the meeting place of such great or near-great as the current generation possesses.

Perhaps the most important condition of all is that in order to succeed, in order to provide for that common acceptance of the traditions and procedures of Parliament, it is necessary that Parliament be composed of "moderate men," who, in the words of Cardinal Newman, "are hard to be worked up to the dogmatic level." It might be easy to dismiss this by simply referring to an innate quality in the British which makes them moderate, but to be moderate in all cases and under every circumstance might border dangerously on an absence of conviction. Such an accusation cannot legitimately be made against the British people, and it has become quite absurd since their performance in the Second World War, especially when they stood alone. Bagehot and Professor Laski intimate that this moderation springs from a common belief and a common philosophy, which in their view are caused by a common economic basis and similar economic interests. Others feel that this view is somewhat exaggerated and that all which is needed is that there should be no fundamental disagreement over the issue of constitutionalism.[5] Professor

---

[4] The so-called "Peace Ballot" of 1935 was organized by the British League of Nations Union and had the nature of a petition. However, it attained such wide coverage that it is possible to speak of a quasi referendum in this one isolated case.

[5] Carl J. Friedrich, *Constitutional Government and Democracy,* Boston, 1946, p. 161.

Laski wonders whether such "moderation," which he recognizes to be the foundation of British parliamentarism as we know it, could endure if a socialist government were to take over the reins of government.

There is no doubt that this is an important point. Only moderate men can compromise, and freedom in a world of divergent views is hardly possible without compromise. Have the drastic economic changes which have taken place in England shaken the Parliamentary system to its foundations? Obviously not. The victory of the Labor party in 1945 and its aftermath have left the Parliamentary system intact. Perhaps this is a manifestation of an increasing realization that the basic cleavage in the world of today is not between rival economic systems, but between rival political systems, between free government and dictatorship. On that issue, most British are of one mind, and apparently they can therefore still "safely afford to bicker."

THE ELECTION OF MEMBERS

The House of Commons is a large body. At present it is composed of 625 members, 17 of whom are women. They are now all elected from single-member districts. Before the House of Commons (Redistribution of Seats) Act of 1944 and the Representation of the People's Act of 1948, there were several two-member districts in London. There was also the so-called business-premises vote, which permitted a person who occupied an office or land having a rental value of at least £10 to vote in the constituency in which his business premise was located, as well as in the constituency [6] of his residence. Moreover, holders of university degrees could also vote (by mail) in special university constituencies in addition to their regular voting residence. However, after 1918 and before 1950 no person was allowed to cast more than two ballots in any one election. This system of plural voting was of course a residue from an older age when even so enlightened a man as Bagehot could speak of the "rich and wise" on the one hand and the "poor and stupid" on the other. This system benefited the Conservative party, whose members were more likely to hold business premises or country estates, and who also predominated among the university voters.[7] At any rate, few Liberals had been elected from university constituencies, and no regular Labor man. There was little justification in the business-premises vote, but the university constituencies were hotly defended. It was contended that they permitted the election of men who had attained public distinction, but were not prepared to submit to the rough-and-tumble of an electoral campaign. Such exceptional

[6] The English call both the electorate of a district and the electoral district itself "constituency."

[7] In 1945 it was estimated that 200,000 people were qualified to cast a business-premises vote, and 175,000 a university vote. H. Finer, *The Theory and Practice of Modern Government*, New York, 1949, rev. ed., p. 231n.

men were indeed selected at times, though certainly not always, but the same was also true of the former "rotten boroughs" of the days before 1832. At any rate, no really satisfactory answer was found to the Labor party argument "one man, one vote," and plural voting is now a matter of the past. Distinguished men who desire a place in the high councils of the nation but do not wish to stand [8] for a seat in the House of Commons, can now be accommodated only in the House of Lords.

The Parliamentary constituencies are now more or less evenly distributed all over the country, *i.e.*, England and Wales, Scotland, and Northern Ireland.[9] But the United Kingdom has never known the method of periodic redistribution of seats which the United States Constitution provides after each decennial census. By 1944 large movements of population had taken place, which were not reflected in the distribution of constituencies. In 1942 a departmental committee on electoral machinery [10] recommended a permanent boundary commission. This recommendation was endorsed by the Speaker's Conference on Electoral Reforms and Redistribution of Seats in 1944. The Act of 1944 established four separate boundary commissions [11] with the Speaker as chairman of each, but all other members of the House of Commons and of the Parliament of Northern Ireland excluded from membership therein. The commissions effected a considerable redistricting of constituencies. Their principal departure from past practice is that changes in boundaries of constituencies will now be recommended by the commissions and carried out by order in council, rather than by an act of Parliament, although Parliament has an opportunity to intervene.

The elections themselves are fairly simple, though spirited, affairs. When the Prime Minister has decided on the date of the general election, a royal proclamation dissolves Parliament. Writs of election are then dispatched to the election officials all over the country. Eight days after the proclamation (Sundays and holidays not counting), all candidates must have been nominated. This is known as "election day." The formal requirements for candidates are exceedingly simple. All they have to do is to fill out forms giving name, address, and profession as well as the names of voters of the constituency who nominate and second each candidate, and the names of eight more voters who "assent." They must also deposit the sum of £150, which is forfeited unless they manage to poll at least one-eighth of the total vote cast in the constituency. This is a measure designed to discourage hopeless and insincere candidates. It should be noted that there are no residence

---

[8] The different attitude of the two major English-speaking countries is reflected in the use of terms. An American "runs" for Congress, but an Englishman "stands" for Parliament.

[9] Northern Ireland also has a legislature of its own.

[10] Cmd. 6408, December, 1942.

[11] England, Wales, Scotland, and Northern Ireland.

requirements: in other words, a candidate need not be a resident of his constituency. This is very advantageous, because it enables any number of able men to run for office. It also enables political parties to shift their candidates around so that a strong leader may capture a constituency which a less prominent man might have lost. This was demonstrated in 1945 when Herbert Morrison changed constituencies in order to capture a doubtful seat for the Labor party.

Certain persons are, however, ineligible even if they possess other qualifications. Election officials are disqualified, and so are civil servants (who may run but would be deemed to have resigned from the service upon election). United Kingdom peers and Scottish peers are ineligible, but Irish peers who have not been elected representative peers may be candidates. Peeresses are eligible, since they are not permitted to sit in the House of Lords even if they are peeresses in their own right. Likewise, wives of peers may sit in the House of Commons. American-born Lady Astor is a well-known example. Persons convicted of certain crimes, including corrupt practices, may be declared ineligible, and so are lunatics. A residue from the days when religious tests were demanded is the provision that clergymen of the established churches of England and Scotland and priests of the Roman Catholic Church are also ineligible.[12]

Simple as candidacies may be under those rules, it is quite a bit more difficult to be a successful candidate, which now means usually to be officially endorsed by a major political party. The British voters cast their ballots primarily for and against parties, and the independent candidate has only a slim chance of being elected.[13] Since the elimination of the university constituencies, that chance has become even slimmer.

Ordinarily the local party organization, or rather its leadership, picks the "official" candidate. Sometimes advice may be asked from national headquarters. In the Labor party, central control is generally stronger than among Conservatives, as it requires close consultation with headquarters and endorsement of candidates by the national leadership.

The two-party system successfully accomplishes its mission by usually presenting a clear majority and therefore a fully responsible government. But as in the United States, the distribution of votes and of seats in the House of Commons do not always coincide. In 1924 the Conservatives polled 47 per cent of the total vote but obtained 67 per cent of the seats in the House of Commons. The Labor party polled 33 per cent of the vote, but obtained only 25 per cent of the seats. In 1929 the situation was reversed. The Conservatives polled 38 per cent of the total vote and received almost 43 per cent of the seats, while the Labor party polled 37.6 per cent of the

[12] However, since the Church of England was disestablished in Wales in 1914, ministers of that church from Wales may be elected.

[13] In 1945, only fourteen independent candidates were elected; in 1950 and 1951, none.

ELECTIONS TO THE HOUSE OF COMMONS

Year	Conservative		Labor		Liberal		Total
1924	Votes	8,112,811 (49%)	5,470,685 (33%)	2,909,122 (17%)			16,640,279
	Seats	414 (66.8%)	150 (24.8%)	39 (6.5%)			603
1929	Votes	8,669,469 (38%)	8,416,557 (37%)	5,260,050 (23%)			22,657,164
	Seats	260 (42.8%)	287 (47.2%)	59 (9.7%)			607
1931 [a]	Votes	11,907,875 (56.1%)	6,990,503 (33%)	2,320,310 (10.9%)			21,704,000
	Seats	471 (77.5%)	65 (10.7%)	72 (11.8%)			608
1935 [a]	Votes	10,488,626 (48.5%)	8,325,260 (38%)	1,377,962 (6.2%)			22,001,834
	Seats	387 (63.8%)	166 (27.3%)	54 (8.9%)			615
1945	Votes	8,693,858 (35%)	11,985,733 (48%)	2,253,197 (9%)			25,018,393
	Seats	189 (29.5%)	396 (61.8%) [b]	25 (3.9%) [c]			640
1950	Votes	11,518,360 (41.7%)	13,295,736 (46.4%)	2,621,489 (9.1%) [d]			28,769,477
	Seats	298 (47.7%)	315 (50.4%)	9 (1.4%)			625 [f]
1951	Votes	13,718,069 (48.05%)	13,949,105 (48.72%)	730,552 (2.53%)			28,596,695 [e]
	Seats	320 (51.2%)	296 (47.4%)	6 (0.97%)			625 [f]

[a] Combined total of different Labor and Liberal groups.
[b] Including 3 Independent Labor party seats.
[c] 13 Liberal National and 12 Liberal.
[d] There was also a total of 983,630 votes cast for five different categories of National Liberals. None obtained a seat.
[e] There were also cast 94,587 votes for Irish Nationalists, 19,640 for Communists, and other small votes for scattered groups.
[f] The total includes 2 Irish Nationalists (who as a matter of principle never take their seats in the House of Commons) and 1 seat for the Speaker. The Conservative seats include 4 Ulster Unionists.

Source: Whitaker's Almanack, 1954.

vote, less than the Conservatives, but received over 47 per cent of the seats in Parliament. More recently, in 1945, the Labor party obtained 48 per cent of the popular vote but occupied nearly 62 per cent of the seats in the House of Commons. In 1951 the Labor party polled slightly more votes than the Conservatives (48.8 per cent against 48 per cent) but received only 296 seats against the Conservatives' 321.

Election campaigns are short, especially when compared to the American practice. We have seen how candidates must file on "election day," eight days after the proclamation dissolving Parliament. Nine days later, on "polling day," the votes are cast. Of course, it is usually known that an election is impending, and the parties warm up, hold their conferences, and issue their programs, but the actual electoral campaign is over after seventeen to nineteen days. There are no long ballots. Only Members of Parliament are elected on "polling day." Local and other officials are elected at quite different times, and of course there are no referendum questions to answer. The election is therefore simple and straightforward. The British voter merely casts his ballot for one single person.

Party programs, usually adopted on a long-range basis, not merely for electoral purposes, have assumed increasing importance in recent years. The victory of the Labor party in 1945 can certainly be credited in no small degree to the fact that it had a definite program for the solution of the country's problems. But usually the electorate has a few very distinct alternatives before it, and the votes are mostly cast on that basis. The radio and television are not used as extensively as in the United States, but political meetings are more significant. One peculiarity of campaigns is the habit of "heckling," which tests both the stamina and the sense of humor of the candidate. While this habit may seem startling and rude to foreign observers, it forces the candidate to "think on his feet," a habit which will stand him in good stead when he takes his seat in the House of Commons.

CAMPAIGN EXPENSES

Expenditures play a less significant role in Britain than in the United States; the fabulous sums expended in America are not equaled anywhere else in the world. The shortness of the British campaign helps to make it inexpensive; the small size of the constituencies makes it possible for the candidate to travel about in a small car, and Britishers do not expect big shows or barbecues from their candidates. Nevertheless there are some expenses, and they are regulated, chiefly because the eighteenth and early nineteenth-century history of England fairly reeked with political corruption. The Corrupt and Illegal Practices Prevention Act of 1883 and subsequent legislation, including substantial sections of the Representation of the People Act of 1948, regulate the legal scope of electoral campaigns. A significant distinction is made between corrupt practices, involving moral turpitude, and illegal practices, which are merely unfair and therefore outlawed. In the first group are such offenses as bribery, fraud in counting or reporting the results, intimidation, and the publication of false statements concerning a person's character. In the second group are such practices as illegally paying for certain services which may be permitted only when rendered voluntarily, and voting in more than one place.

In addition to the establishment of this "moral code" of elections, these laws also limit the candidate's expenses. The allowable sums used to be very small, but the act of 1948 now permits each candidate a basic expenditure of £450, plus 2d for each registered voter in a rural constituency (county) and 1½d for each voter in an urban area (borough). Each candidate must have a single agent, who is obliged to submit a sworn statement of all receipts and expenditures to the election officials. The expenses of the election itself (polling booths, clerks, etc.) are covered by the government.[14] There is some uneasiness in Britain as to the scope of the 1948 Act. Indications are that not only the expenditures made during the brief election period are included, but also all others. Once a former Attorney General, Sir Hartley Shawcross, threatened to include the campaign of certain firms, notably the sugar industry, against nationalization, but nothing of the sort happened.

Every British subject, male or female, who is of age and not incapacitated mentally or through conviction for a criminal offense, is entitled to vote, provided he is registered as a voter. The registration of voters is undertaken by public authority, not by the voter himself as in the United States. The voter merely reassures himself, if he wishes, that his name is properly listed, and may make representations if he finds that this is not the case. Since the Act of 1948, two registration lists are prepared annually.

Elections may be contested by anyone who has reason to believe that there has been an error in tabulating the vote or in the eligibility of candidates, or that any corrupt or illegal practices have taken place. Judgment is rendered by two judges of the High Court of Justice, or of the Court of Session for cases affecting Scotland. Only the question of legal eligibility is still left to the House of Commons.

Technically a member of either House may not resign his office. This rule is fatal for a peer, as he has absolutely no opportunity to refuse the "writ of summons" which installs him in the upper house, provided he inherits the title. Persons who are to be created peers receive an informal inquiry to determine whether they would accept the honor. Only upon their assent are they then appointed. Brilliant political lights have thus been dimmed by the inheritance of a title, because a top-flight career is possible only in the House of Commons. Resignation from the House of Commons, however, is possible through the use of a fiction. It is customary for a member who wishes to

[14] See James K. Pollock, *Money and Politics Abroad*, New York, 1932, Chaps. 2–10.

resign to ask for appointment to the sinecure office of the Stewardship of the Chiltern Hundreds, since an appointment under the Crown is incompatible with a seat in the House of Commons. This appointment, which has been in use since 1740, results in the automatic vacating of the seat in the House, whereupon the nominal and unpaid office of the stewardship is promptly resigned. Upon the resignation or death of a Member of the House of Commons, or his election to the peerage, a special election known as a "by-election" is held to fill his seat. Apart from replenishing the membership in Parliament, by-elections afford valuable indications of public opinion between general elections. The rules for by-elections are the same as those for general elections. They also often enable an important party leader who has been defeated in a general election to return to the House.

THE SPEAKER

The presiding officer of the House of Commons, and at the same time its official representative before the Lords and the Crown, is the Speaker. He has a number of formal duties, such as reading messages from the King, referring to the proper authorities the bills that are passed, and watching over amendments by the House of Lords to House of Commons bills, lest they infringe upon the financial privileges of the lower house.

His principal function, however, is that of presiding officer, in which capacity he controls the debate. He determines who shall speak, being guided by the consideration that ample time be provided for the presentation of both sides in an issue. Thus if a cabinet minister has made a statement, the Speaker will then call on the principal member of the Opposition who wishes to speak, and start the ball going back and forth. Beyond that, the Speaker wields considerable power in recognizing members. Sometimes such members may ask their whips to let the Speaker know of their desire to address the House, but it has been charged that the Speaker is more likely to recognize a Member whose forensic abilities and sense of humor will hold the interest of the House than one who is deadly dull.

The Speaker rules on points of order, and his powers are extensive. He may refuse a motion for closure or a motion whose purpose is, in his judgment, to cause delay. He may refuse motions which are irregular or improper. For instance, he will refuse a motion creating a tax or fee which has not been recommended by the Crown, or a motion which anticipates matters which have been reserved for later consideration. He may also rule out a bill if it is introduced as a private bill but ought to have been a public one, or if the proper committee stage has not been observed. More often, however, he will call the attention of the House to motions or bills which are out of order and will attempt to secure their voluntary withdrawal.

The Speaker has considerable disciplinary powers to prevent disorder. The most frequently employed device is the custom that no member may stand and speak while the Speaker stands. Thus when the Speaker rises, the member who is on his feet must sit down, and the Speaker must be heard in silence. This is usually sufficient. When it is not, the Speaker may "name" a member for the purpose of disciplinary action by the House, leading to that member's suspension. He may cause the suspension of a member or his withdrawal, by placing a nondebatable motion to that effect before the House. He may also reprimand members and call them to order. None of his rulings on points of order can be challenged when they are issued. To do so would entail disobedience and might result in disciplinary punishment. Challenge is permissible only later and after notice has been given.

The Speaker is also in charge of the administrative department and of officials who perform the "housekeeping" functions. The Clerk of the House is under him, although appointed independently.

Since 1855, the Chairman of Ways and Means has been Deputy Speaker. If he is absent, a Deputy Chairman (of Ways and Means) takes over the chair.

The party whips also play an important role in the maintenance of orderly procedure in the House, because they exercise primary control over their party members and maintain liaison between their Parliamentary party and the chair.

PRIVILEGES OF MEMBERS

Members of Parliament enjoy the customary privileges and immunities of legislators in all democratic countries. It should be noted, however, that their freedom from arrest extends only to civil cases and is therefore virtually extinct, because arrest for civil offenses is no longer in use. Technically the House may itself sentence a member to imprisonment for contempt, but this right is not in use. Members may be arrested and tried for ordinary criminal offenses and the House will not interfere. In fact, during the Second World War, a Member of Parliament, Captain Ramsay, a member of the British Union of Fascists and associate of the notorious Sir Oswald Mosley, was interned without trial for the duration of the war under orders of the Home Secretary (Herbert Morrison) in conformity with Sec. 18B of the Defence of the Realm Regulation. In most other countries, members of parliament are immune from arrest for criminal offenses in order to protect them from political persecution. The British, however, appear to be unworried about such a contingency, which seems remote in view of their attitude and training. It goes without saying, however, that a Member of Parliament is not answerable for criminal words uttered in the House. As to other crimes committed in the House, opinion is divided, especially as it would be difficult to show that such a crime was part of the proceedings of the House.

Members of Parliament (Commons) receive a stipend of £1,000 ($2,800) per year. The Leader of the Opposition receives £2,000. They receive no office space and no assistance for secretarial help.

PROCEDURE

Freedom of debate is assured in the Parliament, but the public may be excluded at any time. It is a privilege of ancient origin that if a member takes notice that "there are strangers in the House" [15] the Speaker is obliged to clear the galleries. This privilege is rarely used, because it is difficult to keep secret a matter which has been revealed to over 600 people. More often the government will simply refuse to discuss a question which bears on the national security. However, during the darkest days of the war, when the Prime Minister wished to fortify national unity by taking the House into his confidence, secret sessions were held very successfully.

Closely connected with the right to exclude strangers is Parliament's control over the publication of its debates and proceedings. They have been published for a long time, and although they have been reported officially ever since 1910, they are still colloquially referred to as "Hansard," after the printer who was first authorized to publish Parliamentary debates in 1809.[16] However, both Houses have retained the privilege to forbid publication of a particular debate.

Most of the rights and privileges of Parliament, which can be found in the formidable volume of Sir Thomas Erskine May (usually quoted by its abbreviated title, *Parliamentary Practice*),[17] are based on convention. So is also the pageantry which surrounds Parliament. The wigged Speaker on his throne is a formidable-looking figure. An air of formality prevailing in the House, even though the tone may be conversational, is revealed in the requirement that all members be "honorable," if they are not "Right Honorable," [18] that all lawyers be "learned" and all officers "gallant." [19] At "division" time, when a vote is to be cast, the members file into the two "division lobbies," and are counted upon their return into the House, whereby a generally reliable and unexcited result is achieved.

The opening of a new session of Parliament provides an exceptional opportunity for pageantry. The government declaration, comparable to the Ameri-

[15] This is merely a formula, as there are always strangers in the House.

[16] There are Parliamentary records considerably antedating Hansard's, but the consistent, complete, and continuous record begins in 1809.

[17] Sir Thomas Erskine May, *A Treatise on the Law, Privileges, Proceedings and Usages of Parliament*, 15th ed. by Sir Gilbert Campion, London, 1950. See also Sir Gilbert Campion, *An Introduction to the Procedure of the House of Commons,* London and New York, 1950, 2d ed.

[18] The title Right Honorable is given to all Privy Councillors.

[19] Jennings, *op. cit.,* p. 19.

can President's "state of the Union" message to Congress, is presented in the form of the "speech from the throne," read by the King, or by the Lord Chancellor in the House of Lords and by the Speaker in the House of Commons.[20] The speech itself is of course drawn up by the government, and the King's private views do not remotely enter into it.

Once a new House has been elected, it is convoked within a few weeks. There is no "lame-duck" session. The House may adjourn at any time, regardless of what the House of Lords does. But only the government (Crown) may prorogue, and both Houses must be prorogued together. Adjournment merely interrupts the session; prorogation terminates all business which cannot be taken up again except *de novo, i.e.,* beginning all over. Thus a bill which has passed its second reading before adjournment may pass on to its ultimate passage, but the same bill whose course has been interrupted by prorogation must be taken up all over again just as if it were an entirely new bill.

The dissolution of Parliament is the prerogative of the Crown, *i.e.,* the government, as we have seen. Usually this takes the form of a prorogation followed by a proclamation of dissolution. If the House is not dissolved or if it has its life prolonged by Act of Parliament, it expires automatically after five years according to the Parliament Act of 1911. However, this is never actually allowed to happen, and the government always makes use of its privilege of determining the date of general election which appears most auspicious for its reelection. But at times of exceptional crisis, especially during war, Parliament has prolonged its life far beyond its ordinary limits. The Parliament of 1910 lasted until 1918; the Parliament of 1935 until 1945.

Until 1867, Parliament was automatically dissolved by the king's death, called "demise of the Crown." Now this is no longer the case, but it is customary that Parliament meet immediately and take the oath once more. This was also the case in 1936 when the abdication of Edward VIII was declared to be a demise of the Crown.

The leadership of the government manifests itself very clearly in the order of business. The House meets at 2:45 P.M. on Monday through Thursday and at 11 A.M. on Friday. Precedence is normally given to government business. Before Easter, Wednesdays are allowed for motions by private members [21] and Fridays for their bills (second reading). After Easter these are allowed only on certain Fridays and not at all on Wednesdays, but even that modest amount of time may be curtailed.

The period from 3 to 3:45 P.M. is set aside for questions. This, as we have seen, is an opportunity to bring up grievances. It is also an opportunity to elicit information on facts and intentions of the government. Sometimes the

[20] To reaffirm their independence, both Houses give a sham bill a first reading before proceeding with the debate on the speech. Nothing further is done about this bill.

[21] A Member of Parliament who is not a member of the government.

questions provide an opportunity for harassing the government, and the number and intensity of questions will increase when there are strong feelings on a subject. Due notice of a question is given in writing so that the minister may prepare himself, but under certain conditions of urgency, verbal notice may be acceptable. However, there ought to be no surprises in the question period, and the questioner is not allowed the elaborate speeches which are associated with interpellations in the French parliament. All elaboration must be left to the time set aside for debate.

Not all questions call for an oral reply, and the minister is not legally bound to answer any question, but of course the House will draw its own conclusion if he does not.

In the question period the British government does not risk its life in the same manner as the French government does when there is an interpellation. Nevertheless, the skill with which this period is handled by the respective ministers will have a strong bearing on their political futures and the regard which the people have for them. The question period is not only a tool in the hands of the Opposition or of private members in order to cause the government embarrassment; it can also become an effective means for the government to make important declarations, defeat whispering campaigns, and generally assert its leadership. On the other hand, the question period serves to remind the government of its ties to the House of Commons and of the limits beyond which it cannot go. Every democratic government needs an occasional reminder of this kind.

As the time of the House of Commons is carefully rationed in order to provide an orderly continuity of business, it becomes clear that some measure for an enforced closure of debate is necessary. Ordinarily an agreement is made "behind the Speaker's chair" between the government and the Opposition with regard to the amount of time allowed for debate, and the Speaker will see to it that the agreement is carried out. If that fails, however, there are several ways in which closure can be brought about. Methods for closure became necessary in 1881 when the Irish Nationalists obstructed the government to such an extent that there was danger of the ordinary procedures of Parliament being destroyed. The result was the adoption of the so-called "simple closure" by which a member moves "that the question be now put." [22] The Speaker is free to allow or disallow the motion, having due deference to the rights of the minority and the demands of a fair and orderly procedure. But if the Speaker does entertain the motion, it must be supported by a majority of members present, or at any rate by not less than 100 members. If adopted, this motion brings the debate to an end.

A more drastic closure method, adopted in 1887, is known as the "guillotine." It presupposes that a motion be made, seconded, and passed by the

---

[22] Not to be confused with the motion "that the previous question now be put," which puts the principal issue up for vote immediately.

House whereby the debate will cease at a certain, specified time, and all issues bearing on the measure or bill in question will be brought to a vote.

A rather unique form of closure is the so-called "kangaroo," first used in 1909, by which the Speaker or Deputy Speaker is empowered to select those clauses and amendments which he thinks most appropriate for discussion, excluding all others. This invests the presiding officer with grave responsibility, but there is virtually no evidence of real abuse. If well administered, this method allows a maximum of useful debate within a minimum of time.

These closure rules have been indispensable, in view of the volume of business. But they also have the disadvantage of sometimes preventing a member from properly informing himself of an issue before the House.

LEGISLATION

The process of legislation which takes up a large portion of Parliament's time is a reasonably simple one. Any member, be he a backbencher or a proud inhabitant of the Treasury bench,[23] has the right to introduce a bill. If he is not a member of the government, his bill will be termed a "private member's bill." It is deposited on the Speaker's table after due notice, but without special permission. The title of the bill is then read, and that action constitutes "first reading," although the bill as first deposited is likely to be merely a dummy. There is no debate at such occasions, but under the "ten-minute rule," the member introducing a bill may make a brief introductory speech in order to dispel possible misconceptions, and an equally short rebuttal statement will follow. Most bills may either be introduced in the House of Commons, or in the House of Lords. Financial bills must originate in the House of Commons, while judiciary bills are first presented to the House of Lords.

The second reading of the bill is its real hurdle. It is fully debated on a specific date. If there is organized opposition to it, its enemies will propose motions designed to destroy it. Such a motion may be either a direct negative, which pigeonholes the bill for the day, or it may be a motion that the bill be read six months later—at which time the House is probably not meeting—thus killing the bill for the session, or it may be a resolution which affects the character of the bill and thus kills it too. Only the general scope and idea of the bill are discussed on second reading, and the Speaker prevents the debate from becoming too technical.

Government bills are likely to pass because of the safe majority which is usually at the disposal of the government, unless the latter takes the whips off and leaves the matter to the individual conscience of the members. Private bills may have tougher sledding, and the casualty rate is considerable.

[23] The front bench on the majority side of the House on the Speaker's right on which the cabinet members sit is called the Treasury bench.

COMMITTEES

After the second reading has been passed successfully, the bill goes to committee. The committee stage is familiar to all bonafide legislatures, but the British approach is in marked contrast to its American, French, and German counterparts. Parliament knows four types of committees: Committees of the Whole House, Select and Sessional Committees, Standing Committees, and Joint Committees.

Much business is transacted in the Committee of the Whole House, which is merely the entire membership of the House deliberating under an informal procedure and under the presidency of the Chairman of Committees, also called Chairman of Ways and Means. When dealing with taxation the Committee of the Whole House is called the Committee of Ways and Means or the House in Ways and Means; when dealing with appropriations it is termed Committee of Supply or the House in Supply.

Ordinarily a bill will go to a Standing Committee unless it is a money bill. The nature of the Standing Committee is derived from its history. Originally all bills were considered by the Committee of the Whole House. In 1882 two committees were created, whose number was raised to four in 1907. In 1919 the number was increased to six, but later diminished, and at present there are just five Standing Committees. One of them is the Scottish Committee, which considers all bills concerned with Scotland. The others are simply called Committees A, B, C, and D. Select Committees are appointed for examining a specific problem and report to the House on their findings. A special form of Select Committees are the Sessional Committees which function during an entire session of the House of Commons, particularly the Committee of Selection (which in America would be called a committee on committees), the Committee on Standing Orders (the American term would be Rules Committee), and the Committee on Public Accounts.

When a bill solely affecting Wales and Monmouthshire is under consideration, all the members from that area must be put on the Committee. The members of the committees are chosen by the Committee of Selection, which is appointed at the beginning of each session and is composed according to the proportional strength of parties in the House.

If the bill is a money bill, it will go to the Committee of the Whole (House), but the House may always rule by motion that any other bill shall also go to that Committee. Private bills go to the Private Bill Committee or to the Committee on Unopposed Bills. Bills to confirm a provisional order are treated like private bills. Certain bills may also go to Select Committees, but they can only report, and the bills must then still be considered in the Committee of the Whole.

The committee system was established to relieve the congestion of business in the House, caused partly by the obstructive tactics of the Irish Nationalists as mentioned above, and consequently the committees are *not* small expert bodies undertaking special studies of the merits of bills, but rather miniature editions of the House, headed by a chairman whose powers and functions are very much like those of the Speaker, including the closure rules.[24] Each committee has a regular membership of twenty, but the Committee of Selection may add as many as thirty for special bills. There are rarely fewer than thirty all told.

The Standing Committees do not have special subjects, as is customary in other democracies, but the Speaker assigns bills to them more or less at will. The purpose of the committees is to put the bill into final shape for adoption after its general character has already been approved at second reading and before it has to be reported out. Public hearings are not conducted by standing committees. Where such hearings seem desirable they are usually held by an extraparliamentary body appointed by the government, such as a Royal Commission, but that is done before the bill is introduced.

The British committee system has worked quite well within its frame of reference, *i.e.*, in doing work which would otherwise have to be accomplished by the entire House with resulting loss of time. But it usually brings no expert scrutiny to bear upon a bill. The House adopts bills on second reading primarily on their general merits, and the Standing Committees are neither capable of screening the technical details nor staffed for the purpose of doing so. There is therefore the danger that Parliament may be abdicating its role and becoming a rubber stamp, since at no time in the procedure does a member find out—except possibly from government sources—just what a technical bill is all about. Small wonder therefore that there has been some agitation for more expert committees. But an expert committee is likely to contradict the government and to burden bills with amendments which were neither proposed nor desired by the government, so all governments to date have preferred the greater docility of the present system.

Eventually the bill is reported out and subjected to a third reading. At this stage debate may again break out, although all viewpoints are likely to have been aired, and the fate of the bill is probably quite certain. Substantial amendments are not accepted at this stage unless the bill is to be referred back to committee. The "division" (vote) is taken, and that is the end as far as the House of Commons is concerned.

The treatment given ordinary bills is not unlike the procedure applied to private bills and the confirmation of provisional orders. The demarcation line between public and private bills is not absolutely fixed, because the House may declare any bill a public bill. But ordinarily a private bill is one which deals with a special local situation. Before a private bill can be introduced,

[24] However, the "guillotine" is not in use.

a petition must be filed with the "examiner of private bills," an officer appointed in each House. It is also demanded that certain preliminary steps be taken in order that all persons affected by the bill may be duly notified. After the second reading, the bill is assigned to a Select Committee of four persons (five in the House of Lords) which conducts such hearings as seem appropriate. If there is no opposition, the bill is assigned to the committee on unopposed bills. From there on it follows the same course as do ordinary bills.

This method of dealing with private bills saves the House a great deal of work, but since hearings are held, witnesses heard, and evidence collected, it takes an inordinate amount of time from the members who are assigned to sit on such committees. Nor are political laurels to be gathered in such hearings, because the treatment of private bills is distinguished by a nonpartisan character.

In order to diminish the number of private bills, government departments have statutory authority to issue orders, which generally need subsequent sanction by Parliamentary act. These orders are usually assembled in groups which may be passed in one act. Such Confirmations of Provisional Orders are handled like private bills. To an ever-increasing extent Parliament vests direct, statutory authority in government departments to issue orders without subsequent confirmation by Parliament. Such "delegated legislation" naturally increases the power of the administrative machinery and has already been touched upon.

Quite different from private bills are "private members' bills." These are simply bills proposed by an ordinary member of the House of Commons, usually a "backbencher," and not by the government or on behalf of the government. Such bills may be introduced during brief periods on two days of the week, and few members avail themselves of this opportunity because their chances of success are virtually nil. The time allotted for the critical second reading is also very brief, and often government business is allowed to cut into it. Moreover, not every private member's bill actually receives a second reading, and if there are more such bills than time allows, lots are drawn in order to determine which one shall receive a second reading. If the government opposes a private member's bill, it has no chance to come to life. If the government acquiesces, it may eventually be enacted. But the government does not care for this invasion of its legislative leadership. Moreover, the passage of a bill requires so many little details which are ordinarily performed by a number of experienced people, but which, in the case of a private member's bill, he must perform himself, that most members find such an effort not very rewarding.

There is one more type of legislation, apart from money bills, which will be dealt with separately. There is an established church in England, which has the right to submit certain measures to Parliament for enactment. Usually this submission is a formality but not always, as was indicated in 1927 and 1928 when the House of Commons refused to accept certain changes in the Book of Common Prayer. When such a step is proposed to Parliament by the National Assembly of the Church of England, Parliament can only accept or reject; it cannot amend.

If the bill has originated in the House of Commons, it goes to the House of Lords after having passed its third reading. There it undergoes very much the same treatment as it received in the House of Commons. There are no regular standing committees in the House of Lords,[25] but select committees are frequently resorted to, and ample use is made of the Committee of the Whole. If the Lords agree, the bill is submitted to the Royal Assent, which makes it final. If the Lords do not agree, attempts are made to compromise the difficulties. Such conference committees, however, deal only in written messages nowadays; a "free" conference, i.e., a really negotiating (oral) committee, is no longer used. More often, informal discussions between party leaders will bring results.

If the Lords refuse to compromise or give in, and if the House remains equally stubborn, the bill (but not a financial bill) becomes law even without the consent of the Lords after one year's delay, as stipulated under the Parliament Act of 1911 as amended in 1949. Private bills and confirmations of provisional orders are not under the protection of the Parliament Act as amended, and the Lords can therefore kill such measures outright. However, such an attitude on the part of the Lords is neither practical—as will be seen later—nor expected.

The final step is the Royal Assent. This is a pure formality, since it must be given and cannot be refused. The refusal formula, *le roy s'avisera* (the King will consider it), has not been employed since 1707. Using the ancient legal formulas in archaic French, the Royal Assent is given in the words of *le roy le veult* (the King desires it) for ordinary bills, *soit fait comme il est desiré* (be that as it is desired) for private bills, and *le roy remercie ses bons sujets, accepte leur bénévolence, et ainsi le veult* (the King thanks his good subjects, accepts their benevolence, and thus desires it) for money bills.

MONEY BILLS

The enactment of money bills is somewhat different from that of others. In the first place they must originate in the House of Commons and in the Committee of the Whole. No appropriation for the public service nor any other drain on the public revenue will be considered by the House unless it has been proposed by the government (Crown). Nor will any taxation measure

---

[25] The so-called "standing" committee for textual revision is formed at the beginning of each session.

be taken up unless recommended by the Crown. The government thus has undivided power of initiative in financial matters.[26]

The burden, responsibility, and power of proposing appropriations, especially the budget (estimates), rests with the Treasury and its chief, the Chancellor of the Exchequer. But insofar as the budget is an expression of cabinet policy, the entire cabinet shares in this responsibility.

Parliament prepares for the budget by appointing the Committee of Supply and the Committee of Ways and Means at the beginning of each session. But this is a formality since both committees are merely the Whole House deliberating under an informal procedure. The budget message itself is invariably presented by the Chancellor of the Exchequer in person, and strict secrecy is preserved until the budget is announced in the House of Commons.[27] The budget bill then goes to committee. The duration of the debate on each item and on the total is strictly regulated and limited; if the allotted time is exceeded, the "guillotine" rule is applied. Revenues and expenditures are discussed during the same period and follow the same procedure. All proposals are handled in groups and passed in the same manner.

All resolutions are then assembled in two statutes, the Appropriation Act and the Finance Act. Earlier in the session, Parliament has passed a Consolidated Fund Bill, in order to make up any deficiency and hold funds on account for the current year. The Appropriation Act now authorizes all necessary expenditures to be made from the general fund (Consolidated Fund) [28] while the Finance Act approves all necessary revenues.

Having passed the House of Commons, the money bills now go to the House of Lords. Since the Parliament Act of 1911, the upper house has lost all control over finance bills. If a bill, duly certified by the Speaker to be a money bill,[29] has been received by the House of Lords at least one month before the end of its session, it receives the Royal Assent and becomes law either upon the approval of the Lords, or a month after it has been submitted to them, whether they have passed or even considered it or not. But even if the House of Lords considers a money bill, it may not amend it under any circumstances.

Opinion is divided on the advantages or demerits of the British system of financial legislation. From the government's standpoint, the British system is nearly ideal. It permits the government to prepare a consolidated budgetary plan with the virtual assurance that it will not be seriously changed. The kind of treatment which the budget usually gets from ax-wielding Congress-

[26] A private member may move that the government ought to spend more or less on certain subjects.

[27] An ill-advised remark on the budget by Chancellor Hugh Dalton led to his resignation on Nov. 13, 1947.

[28] Not all expenditures come from the Consolidated Fund.

[29] The Speaker decides what is a money bill and what is not. His decision cannot be challenged.

men in the United States is unknown in Great Britain. The government is therefore in no position to blame any shortcomings on the failure of Parliament to appropriate the necessary funds. Its responsibility before the public is clear and unequivocal.

On the other hand, it is obvious that the so-called power of the purse which Parliament is alleged to possess is not a reality, even though its theoretical existence might conceivably have a sobering effect on the government. At no time is the budget really scrutinized or seriously debated in either House. "Budget Day," when the Chancellor of the Exchequer makes his great budget speech and presents the document to the House of Commons, is indeed one of the greatest days, if not *the* greatest day, of a Parliamentary session. The speech is long and detailed, invariably lasting several hours, and the ensuing debate is extremely fierce. But the debate may deal only with the general character of the budget, not its details; in effect it is the entire government policy which is at stake, and the Opposition brings out every objection and grievance it can think of. The vote on the budget is then a test of confidence in the government which, in a House where the government has a clear majority, can never be in serious doubt.

Nor can the members of the House and its committees be expected to discharge their alleged responsibilities as "holders of the purse strings." We have seen that all initiative must come from the government as far as financial legislation is concerned, that bills which involve expenditures are not accepted from private members, only from the Crown (government). Parliament may not even increase the appropriations over what the government asks. Theoretically it may decrease them, but that is theoretical to the point of nonexistence. A vote to decrease expenditures below the government figure would be tantamount to a vote of nonconfidence, at the very least in the government department for which the outlay is being asked; at the most it would be a vote of nonconfidence in the government as a whole. That is unthinkable as long as the government has a majority in the House, which is ordinarily the case.

There is not even enough time for an itemized scrutiny of the budget, or enough expert knowledge in the House to evaluate the intricate relationship between the figures in the budget and the inner working of the departments and activities for which they are designed. If there were a great deal of time to study the estimates, some remedy might be found, but the whole bulky document must be whipped through in a mere twenty-six days. Thus an evaluation of the budget would be impossible even if it were contained in a clear and precise statement. But that is by no means the case. In fact, by failing to give an understandable picture of the country's financial situation, the budget hides more than it reveals.

A further handicap is the unwieldy character of the Committee of Ways and Means—which is none other than the Committee of the Whole. A detailed examination of a large technical document would be quite impossible in a body of that size.

This all adds up to one inevitable conclusion: the so-called "power over the purse strings" of Parliament is largely a fiction. It does not exist. Power over the purse rests in the cabinet, especially in the Treasury. This situation is mitigated by the already-discussed need for harmony between government and Parliament, and the resultant desire on the part of the government to compromise—preferably before the situation comes to a head—issues on which strong feelings exist in the House. And if a government were ever to be imprudent enough to try to maintain itself without the basic confidence of the House of Commons, the dormant financial powers of the House could be put to good advantage. As far as the control of the legality and propriety of government spending is concerned, it is adequately exercised by an independent official, the Comptroller and Auditor-General.[30]

Criticism of this situation has naturally been protracted. The Ninth Report of the Select Committee on National Expenditure of 1918 gave the following reasons for a needed reform:

1. Control in Committee of Supply is not in fact a control over the Estimates.
2. Treasury control, invaluable as it is up to a point, is not a substitute for Parliamentary control.
3. Control by ministers is not enough—such a doctrine would convert the responsibility of ministers into irresponsibility.

The result has been the establishment of a Select Committee on Estimates which has functioned with some interruptions since 1920. However, the impact made by that committee has been disappointing. As the estimates still go their customary route, the Committee on Estimates has looked into only a few of the items. It has made some suggestions for possible improvements, which have been quite valuable, but they have in no way restored financial control of Parliament. The Committee on Public Accounts has made even less of an impact.

Criticism of Parliament has often centered on the fact that the House is overworked and is therefore unable to give adequate attention to bills. Various schemes for the devolution of powers have been suggested as possible relief measures. One group of proposals favored regional assemblies, composed of members of the House of Commons for the area concerned, plus a Council of Peers. But these schemes have not proven practical or acceptable. Too

[30] The Exchequer and Audit Departments Act of 1866 (29 & 30 Vict. c. 39), as amended in 1921 and 1939, established the office of the Comptroller and Auditor General who reports directly to the House of Commons, who may be removed only upon Joint Address of Parliament, and who has tenure like a judge of the High Court. He controls the issue of all public money, audits the accounts of all departments, and reports on them to the House of Commons. It is his job to see to it that all pertinent rules are observed, but he has no power over the rules themselves.

much of the business of legislation is national in character, and Parliament derives its great reputation and influence from its role as the single national assembly of political leaders.

The other group of suggestions has attempted to propel the House of Commons in the direction of the American Congressional committee system. Naturally such a possibility is not regarded with favor in government circles, who fear that their well-laid plans might be carved up and rendered unrecognizable by an all-too-independent committee. Opposition members have viewed such proposals usually wtih somewhat more favor than the government. But since opposition parties become government parties sooner or later, nothing has come of such ideas, nor is any far-reaching reform likely to occur in the foreseeable future, especially as many British and other observers prefer the British system by which bills are drafted into final shape by the respective government departments under cabinet control, rather than by legislative committees and their staff as is the practice in the United States.

B. THE HOUSE OF LORDS

Among the many quaint and ancient institutions which exist in the United Kingdom, the House of Lords is one of the most archaic. Its nature, role, and composition are unique in comparison with the second chambers of other countries. The Parliament Acts of 1911 and 1949 have shorn the "other house," as the House of Lords is sometimes called, of much of its former power, but it still leads a vigorous life, and its reform is still a much-debated question. Yet its role is by no means nominal.

Countries which desire a second chamber have been exercised over the problem of how to make the "upper house" representative but at the same time composed in such a way as to prevent it from becoming an exact replica of the "lower house." No such problem confronts the British: the House of Lords is completely unrepresentative, and it is never a replica of the House of Commons.

COMPOSITION

The House of Lords is an all-male assembly. Women are not permitted to sit in it even if they are peeresses in their own rights. It is composed of six classes of peers, two of which are hereditary. The first class consists of the princes of the blood royal, whose membership is largely nominal and who take no part in the consideration of controversial issues. The second class is the largest (nearly 800). It is composed of hereditary peers (barons, viscounts, ears, marquises, and dukes) who are either the descendants of peers (the majority) or newly created lords.

The House has held that a writ of summons created hereditary peerage, but nowadays peerages are always created by letters patent, and a newly created Lord is required to present both his writ of summons and his letters patent to the Lord Chancellor upon taking his seat in the House of Lords for the first time. The difference between the two sources is slight; if the peerage originates through a writ alone, it descends to the general heir at common law, while peerages created by letters patent descend as stipulated in that document, usually to the direct male heir. When a person is due to be created a peer, the intention is made known to him and he may decline, especially when he still has political ambitions which can best be accomplished in the House of Commons. But if he inherits the title, nothing can save him from the "golden sepulchre" of the upper house. He may never take his seat and never hand his papers to the Lord Chancellor, but he is a peer nevertheless and ineligible to sit in the House of Commons.

Peerage may be conferred on or inherited by foreigners, but they may not sit in the House of Lords. Nor may a writ of summons be issued [31] to a bankrupt peer or to a minor. A person who has been found guilty of treason or a felony and imprisoned with hard labor for any term, or with simple imprisonment for twelve months or more, may not sit until sentence is served or until he is pardoned. The Lords may also sentence a person to be disqualified to sit.

Hereditary peers are either English or United Kingdom peers. Scottish and Irish lords do not sit in the House of Lords unless they are designated "representative peers." At the beginning of each session of Parliament, the Scottish lords, about forty, meet at Holyrood Palace in Edinburgh to select sixteen from among them, who are designated "representative peers" and as such comprise the third group of members of the House of Lords. A fourth group are the Irish representative peers. Like their Scottish brothers, they too are designated by the whole body of Irish lords. Originally there were twenty-eight of them, but there are now only six left.[32] There are certain differences between Irish and Scottish peers. The Crown may not create any Scottish peers, but it may technically create one Irish peerage for each three extinct ones. Since the Irish Free State Agreement Act of 1922, no more Irish peerages have been created. Before then, the power to do so had a certain advantage, because Irish peers may sit in the House of Commons (Scottish peers may not), and the Crown thus had an opportunity to honor a man without depriving him of his political future.

A fifth group is formed by the Lords Spiritual. It is a purely English group since the disestablishment of the church in Ireland, Wales, and Monmouth-

---

[31] Writs of summons are issued at every session of Parliament.

[32] The summoning of the Irish lords for the purpose of electing representative peers was accomplished by writ issued by the Lord Chancellor of Ireland. After the demise of that office in 1920, it passed on to the Lord Lieutenant, but that office has also ceased, and there appears to be no legal way in which representative peers may be elected from Ireland.

shire. There is an established church in Scotland, the Presbyterian Church, but it does not send members to the House of Lords. The number of ecclesiastic peers is limited to twenty-six. Five of them, the Archbishops of Canterbury and York, and the bishops of London (Lord Bishop of Lambeth), Durham, and Winchester, maintain their seats in the upper house by virtue of their office, while the other twenty-one are bishops selected on the basis of seniority. All ecclesiastic members hold their seats only during their terms of office as bishops, and the close connection between bishopric and seat in the House of Lords has found its expression in the right of the Crown to appoint bishops which dates back to the days of Henry VIII.

The sixth and last group are the Lords of Appeal in Ordinary, often called "Law Lords." Since the House of Lords is the highest court for the United Kingdom, the inclusion of jurists is desirable. Nine Lords of Appeal in Ordinary are created for that purpose. They hold tenure for life, and receive a salary for their judicial work. They retain their membership in the House of Lords even after resigning their offices as Lords of Appeal, but their seats are vacated upon their death and do not descend to their heirs.

The formidable array of titles and the ancient pageantry which indicates the derivation of the House of Lords from the Grand Council (*Magnum Concilium*) of the Norman and Angevin kings give the impression that the upper house is an aristocratic body. This is not true unless aristocracy were to be understood as a purely formalistic and meaningless term. Not "aristocracy" but "plutocracy" is the word for the House of Lords. The ancient titled families of England form but a very small minority in the House; few titles date back further than the eighteenth century, and half of them were created in the twentieth century. The wealth of the country represented in the House of Lords was originally based primarily on landed property, but the Industrial Revolution shifted the emphasis toward the upper middle classes, the new capitalists.[33] Of course not all men in the House of Lords are wealthy; peerages are also created for "political and public services." In fact, an ever-increasing number of newly created peers are former politicians who, after spending their prime in the House of Commons, are permitted to achieve semi-retirement in the House of Lords. Thus an opportunity is created to retain certain men in public life, when they are no longer willing to submit to the rough-and-tumble of periodic election campaigns. Much of the actual work of the upper house is done by them, and their ranks swell especially when a Liberal or Labor government is in office, attempting to increase its slender representation in the House of Lords.

Finally, appointment to a peerage and a seat in the House of Lords is an excellent opportunity to confer a much-coveted honor on a man who has gained great distinction in the sciences, arts, or other fields.

[33] There is hardly any large corporation which does not have one or several of its directors in the House of Lords.

Because the overwhelming majority of the noble Lords represent wealth or are descendants of wealth, the political composition of the House is overwhelmingly Conservative. About 600 members of the House of Lords are Conservative, less than 100 profess allegiance to the Liberal party, while a little more than 20 belong to the Labor party. Of course there are never that many peers at any one session, but the Conservative majority is still formidable. Also permanent officials and legislators have a well-known tendency to become more conservative, with the result that the majority of the upper house is not only Conservative in party affiliation and sympathy, but actually is even more conservative than the leadership and majority of their party in the House of Commons. They are Conservative not so much out of party loyalty as because they are convinced that the country would go to ruin unless governed by Conservative principles.

Party affiliation is a matter of preference, not of necessity, for peers. Their positions are secure, they need not be concerned about the good graces of a party leadership, and they need not appeal to the country for a vote of confidence. They need not follow the party whip, and they may defeat the government with impunity. In summation, they are responsible to no one—but then no one is responsible to them. The life of the government depends in no way on the wishes of the House of Lords. Were it otherwise, only Conservative governments could exist.

PROCEDURE AND ORGANIZATION

The atmosphere in the House of Lords is quite different from that of the House of Commons. The debate is more leisurely than in the House of Commons, but the daily sessions are not nearly as long. There is a tradition that noble Lords ought to be allowed their dinners at home, and members raising questions dangerously near the dinner hour are regarded with disfavor. There is no pressure on members by their constituents—for they have none. Few of the members hold office in the cabinet. Freedom of speech is virtually unrestricted, because the presiding officer, the Lord Chancellor, has far more limited powers over the debate than are enjoyed by the Speaker in the House of Commons. Moreover the Lords will not hesitate to overrule the Lord Chancellor, who, after all, is a partisan and therefore cannot be regarded as an impartial officer of the type presented by the Speaker.

A visitor to the House of Lords will often find the level of the debate high, and on certain occasions higher than in the House of Commons. This does not mean that there is more talent in the House of Lords—as a matter of fact, a large majority of the Lords are exceedingly and sometimes painfully dull. But most of that type do not attend meetings. It simply means that approximately one-fourth of the Lords are former members of the House of Commons, and a good many are retired statesmen, administrators, professors, etc., all of whom are more likely to attend, especially when an interesting topic is scheduled for debate. It may also be said that since most Lords belong to the same party, they do not have to debate party politics; their discussion may therefore center on the technical problems of the bill or motion under consideration. Many motions will be made and amendments proposed, but most of them are usually withdrawn if the government refuses to accept them.

The organization of the House of Lords closely parallels that of the House of Commons. The presiding officer is, as we have seen, the Lord Chancellor, a member of the cabinet. He presides while sitting on the traditional "wool-sack," which is technically outside the confines of the House of Lords in order that a man who is not a peer may nevertheless be Lord Chancellor. But the point is not important, since Lord Chancellors are invariably peers or are created peers immediately after their appointment.

There is also the Lord Chairman of committees who corresponds to the chairman of ways and means in the lower house and presides over the Committee of the Whole. There is the clerk, called Clerk of the Parliament, and the equivalent to the sergeant-at-arms who bears the more colorful title of "gentleman usher of the black rod."

POWERS

Originally the House of Lord was coequal to the House of Commons. The Lords could not dismiss a government, but they could stop legislation dead in its tracks. This situation came to a head in 1909 when the Lords defeated the budget of the Liberal Asquith government which was presented by Lloyd George, the Chancellor of the Exchequer. By that time the reform of the House of Lords had already been under serious consideration and the speech from the throne in 1907 had alluded thereto. It was therefore with a singularly bad sense of timing that the Lords decided to defeat the budget which suggested a number of social reforms. The argument of the Lords was that a measure of such far-reaching nature should not be passed without a new mandate from the people, although the Liberal party had been put into power in 1906 with the largest majority any party had ever received up to that time. The Lords' action was especially objectionable because it ran counter to the long-standing tradition giving the House of Commons predominance in financial matters.

The election of 1910 sustained the Liberal government, and the House of Lords passed the bill, but the government was determined to prevent a recurrence. Various proposals for reform were made, one even emanating from the House of Lords itself. But while the Liberal government wished to reform the House of Lords and make its membership more representative, it considered a curb on the Lords' powers a more urgent issue. A bill to that effect was carried by the House of Commons, but the outcome in the House of Lords was doubtful, although a second election in the same year (1910), which was fought specifically on that issue, again sustained the government. The decisive factor was the King, George V, who let it be known that he would, on recommendation of the government, create enough Liberal lords to give the government a majority in the House of Lords, if that became necessary. The opposition thereupon collapsed, and the result was the Parliament Act of 1911.

This Act [34] distinguished between money bills and other public bills. If a money bill is passed by the House of Commons, as discussed in a previous section, and sent to the House of Lords at least one month before the end of the session, it may be submitted to the Royal Assent and become law after one month whether passed by the House of Lords or not. A public bill, according to the Parliament Act of 1911, could be passed over the Lords' veto [35] only after it had been passed by the House of Commons in three successive sessions, and after it had been submitted to the House of Lords at least one month before the end of each session and been rejected by the Lords in each case. Upon being passed by the House of Commons a third time, it could be submitted to the Royal Assent and become a law. In the latter case, two years at least had to elapse between the first and third sessions.[36] The Parliament Act of 1949 has reduced this period to one year and has reduced the sessions from three to two.

These two Acts appeared to many people as the end of the House of Lords. But this was by no means the case. It had been clear ever since 1832, when King William IV promised the government then in power to appoint enough Whig lords to pass the Reform Bill, that in a real showdown the Commons would always prevail. It had been the pride of the Duke of Wellington that he preserved the House of Lords by prevailing upon it to yield. Bagehot therefore was able to write in 1867,

Since the Reform Act the House of Lords has become a revising and suspending House. It can alter Bills; it can reject Bills on which the House of Commons is not yet thoroughly in earnest—upon which the nation is not yet determined. Their veto is a sort of hypothetical veto. They say, We reject your bill for this once, or these twice, or even these thrice; but if you keep on sending it up, at last we won't reject it. The House has ceased to be one of latent directors, and has become one of temporary rejectors and palpable alterers.

Does the House of Lords, then, perform a useful function? Or should it be condemned in Winston Churchill's biting words spoken in more radical days— "the House of Lords—unrepresentative, irresponsible, absentee!" To the believers in legislative supremacy, the House of Lords will not be any more acceptable than the entire system of British government. To those who believe that the majority must always have its way without restriction, the

[34] It also fixed the five-year term of Parliament.

[35] Inaction on the part of the Lords is deemed to be rejection.

[36] Technically between the second reading in the first session and final passage in the third session.

House of Lords with its accidental membership and unrepresentative character must seem repugnant. Those who insist that a legislative body must, above all, be representative of the electorate will also reject the House of Lords.

Even if one believes in the desirability of a second chamber to curb the possible exuberance of the House of Commons, it is difficult to be entirely pleased with the House of Lords. It is so obviously, even outrageously unrepresentative and nonresponsible that it cannot dare to stand in the way of the representative part of Parliament, the House of Commons, when the latter is really determined to have its own way, and if it tried to do so, it would be swept away.

Believers in second chambers therefore frequently feel that the House of Lords does not do its job as a true second chamber should and that, even when it tries to act as a curb on the lower house, it does so only when a Liberal or Labor government is in power. A Conservative cabinet need not fear great difficulties from the House of Lords. This does not mean that the peers submit to Conservative party discipline under all circumstances. But on the whole, a Conservative government will find the House of Lords willing to go along, while a Labor government is in a less fortunate position.

With all its serious faults, the House of Lords performs some useful tasks. Its treatment and examination of private bills is recognized as being far superior to that of the busier House of Commons. When the Lords feel that a major measure proposed by the government does not possess the clear support of the country and was not included in the mandate which the electorate gave the government at the last election, they can be very obstreperous and turn down government measures as long as the revised Parliament Act will permit. This is a form of obstruction which is not always designed to defeat measures but rather to force the government to ask the people for a new mandate. Of course the Lords usually believe that the people will sustain them— a belief which has often been erroneous. But again, history records such action on the part of the upper house only when Liberal or Labor governments were in power.

It is not surprising, therefore, that a reform of the House of Lords has frequently been debated in England. Even the Conservatives have realized that some change is necessary, and they gave their support to the far-reaching suggestions of the committee headed by Lord Rosebery in 1911. In 1917 a committee headed by Lord Bryce considered possible reforms,[37] and while it could not agree, it produced a number of alternative suggestions, including election of the members by large constituencies,[38] election by local authorities grouped together into geographic areas, nomination by the King on advice of the cabinet, and election by the House of Commons.

[37] *Report of the Conference on the Reform of the Second Chamber*, Cmd. 9038, 1918.
[38] Similar to the Australian Senate and the New Zealand Legislative Council.

The first suggestion found little favor because there was no intention of making the second chamber an equal companion of the first. Election by local authorities was rejected because local councils are not elected on national issues and the suggested use thereof would introduce an unnecessary and irrelevant element into local elections. There was, however, considerable interest and support for the proposal to have the members of the new second chamber elected by the House of Commons.

Nothing came of it, and numerous other plans followed; all without results. The Conservatives were not eager to lose their stronghold but were willing to agree to a reform of the membership of the House of Lords if it would receive the powers which it possessed before 1911. In the meantime they were in no great hurry to effect a change. The Labor party, on the other hand, was naturally hostile to the upper house, which it could not hope to control. At its annual conference of 1934, the National Executive Committee submitted a report which was adopted by the conference and which read in part as follows: "A Labour Government meeting with sabotage from the House of Lords would take immediate steps to overcome it; and it will, in any event, take steps during its term of office to pass legislation abolishing the House of Lords as a legislative Chamber." [39] A similar provision was put into the election platform of the party in 1935. Earlier, in 1920, the famous work of Sidney and Beatrice Webb on the future socialist Britain declared, "There is, of course, in the Socialist Commonwealth, no place for the House of Lords, which will simply cease to exist as part of the Legislature."

After the Labor party came to power in 1945, it proceeded to bring into operation its vast nationalization and planning program. The Lords, somewhat overwhelmed by the tremendous size of Labor's majority in the House of Commons, made no frontal attack against the first part of the government program. However, they proposed amendments—some good, some less so—which the government frequently accepted rather than face costly delay by having to override the Lords' veto.

There has been some rumbling about drastic reforms of the upper chamber if Labor were to regain a majority,[40] but there is a tendency to go slow. Under the present system, the House of Lords is fairly tame. Occasionally it can still wage a tremendous fight, as evidenced by the debate over the nationalization of the steel industry. But its teeth have been drawn with the imposition of the one-year rule in the Parliament Act of 1949. The government may well prefer the known disadvantages of the present system to the unknown faults of a new scheme. One thing is certain; no British government wants a second chamber which has any remote similarity to the United States Senate or to the Senate of the Third French Republic. Thus the matter stands.

[39] *Report of the Thirty-fourth Annual Conference of the Labour Party*, 1934, p. 263.
[40] None of these reform plans touch the judicial functions of the House of Lords, which are virtually separate. See Chap. 5.

Chapter 5

LAW AND JUSTICE

Many are the achievements of which Englishmen may justly boast. In preceding chapters, Parliament and cabinet government were presented as outstanding English contributions to the political process. Now we may add another pearl to the crown: the English common law, and the idea of the "rule of law."

There are many legal systems in the world, but none has had and still has a more profound effect than the systems of the Roman (civil) law and the English common law. Some writers who affected a kind of "historical nationalism," like Freeman, Froude, and Stubbs, have maintained that the common law is wholly English and Anglo-Saxon in origin. This theory has been definitely exploded: we know that it is of Norman and feudal, rather than of Anglo-Saxon, origin, and we are discovering more and more about significant traces of Roman influence. And yet, while the English law is no more "pure" in its historical development than Englishmen are in racial origin, it is nevertheless very decidedly a specialty of the English-speaking world.

In a preceding chapter we have seen how the Norman kings adopted a method instituted by Charlemagne by which itinerant judges (*missi dominici*) traveled about the country rendering justice in the King's name, and how this kind of justice was preferred over the cruder baronial courts of the feudal period. We have seen that legislation in the modern sense was not the rule; that law had to be "found" in local custom. Yet local custom and Anglo-Saxon law were more often pretense than reality. The Norman kings were appreciative of the need for keeping their Anglo-Saxon subjects in reasonably good humor, yet they preferred their own vastly superior laws. Consequently they presented their subjects with "rediscovered" statutes of Edward the Confessor and of other Anglo-Saxon periods, which in reality contained so many Norman ideas and concepts that one may well speak of falsification.

COMMON LAW

The strong hand of Henry II increased the scope of the royal judges, who in turn sought to discover common elements in their decisions, and who found it convenient to follow their own and each others' precedents in ever-increasing measure. Thus an amorphous and at times ill-defined, but very real, body of law was formed which later became known as the common law. The basis of the law was the rule *stare decisis* (*et quieta non movere*)—(let the decision stand). Under this rule a court decision establishes a precedent which later cases ought to follow when the situation is analogous. This was the law which rose to such proportions that Bracton could write in the thirteenth century that "the king was under God and the [common] law."

These decisions were collected and to some extent systematized by a succession of great legal scholars, beginning with Glanville in the twelfth century, continued by Bracton, Littleton, Fitzherbert, and Coke, and finally culminating in Blackstone's *Commentaries on the Laws of England* in the eighteenth century. From the days of Edward II to Henry VIII, cases were also reported by skilled lawyers in the so-called Year Books.

In the meantime, other developments took place which affected the common law. The jury system which we have already encountered shortly after the arrival of William the Conqueror became more generally adopted, chiefly as a defense against the peculiar system of "witnesses," or rather oath-helpers, through which any rich and noble scoundrel could get exonerated by producing twice as many oath-helpers in court as his opponent.[1] The jury was not an ideal system because the jurors would give their verdict on the basis of what they already knew of the case or had learned about it out of court, and not on the basis of the evidence presented in court. However, it was a great improvement over the method of oath-helpers, which continued to be used for some time.

The prevalence of the jury system profoundly affected the rules of evidence which were developed over the centuries. They were made strict in order not to influence unduly a jury of laymen. They are much laxer in countries in which juries are less frequently employed, because there it is presumed that the learned judge will be able to discern fact from fiction.

EQUITY

At the same time the common law developed a formalism of great strictness which was quite in evidence by the thirteenth century and was considered oppressive. A man might have paid his debt and there might even have been witnesses to his payment, but if he failed to apply certain formalities, such as exchanging certain sealed documents, he could and would be compelled under common law to pay anew. Here a historical process repeated itself. Just as royal justice had once been brought in to mitigate the arbitrariness

---

[1] The oath-helper (witness) would merely swear to the credibility of the party concerned. He was an early form of "character witness," who knew nothing about the case itself and whose testimony, often given out of fear or for love of money, was notoriously unreliable.

and lack of uniformity of the feudal, baronial courts, so now a new type of royal justice was instituted. The king, as the fountainhead of justice, was always entitled to set aside judgments of the common-law courts, and this he did through his principal officer, the Lord High Chancellor. This type of justice was therefore dispensed in chancery—the Lord Chancellor's department—and became known later as "equity." Often it turned out to be a superior type of justice, partly perhaps because the earlier Chancellors were churchmen who knew their Roman law, which often suggested a remedy when the English law did not.[2] Equity is therefore much more influenced by Roman law than is common law.

The Chancellor, who was later replaced by deputies called "masters in chancery," was reasonably free in the rendering of his judgments because he was considered to be the "keeper of the King's conscience." When the common law was manifestly unfair, he could render a contrary decision. As the bulk of equity rules increased and also acquired a certain formalism, the judges who rendered judgments in equity became separated from the Lord Chancellor's office and had their own court, the Court of Chancery. Today there is not a separate court but a division, the Chancery Division in the High Court of Justice, which still applies equity when there is no remedy at common or statute law, or when there is danger of irreparable damage. Actually the application of equity is more or less confined to certain fields of law, and in certain instances is a matter of choice for the parties in a suit.[3]

The Legal Profession

Both common law and equity are forms of law based on precedents. Such precedents can be discovered only after a study of relevant cases; common law and equity are therefore forms of case law. The student of such law must study a great many cases, and it has been the English tradition that he does not study them at law school or at the university, but at the place where the living law daily unrolls itself. These places are called the Inns of Court. Their origin is obscure and very old. Undoubtedly there were law students before there were any Inns of Court. But in the reign of Edward II (1307–1327) a group of students took up quarters in the confiscated former home of the Knights Templars, and as their number grew they divided into an Inner Temple and a Middle Temple. Another group took over Lincoln's Inn. Others again took up residence in the former home of Lord Grey de Wilton, which

---

[2] However, due to the nonexistence of printing and the rarity of manuscripts, Roman law often entered not in its original version but in the way in which the Chancellor remembered it from his ecclesiastical studies.

[3] Equity applies only in civil cases. There is no criminal equity. The sorry distinction of having established a crude system of criminal quasi equity belongs to the Nazis and certain other dictatorships.

was henceforth called Grey's Inn. Students of chancery law took over a number of smaller inns, called Chancery Inns.

Fortescue, one of the greatest legal luminaries, explained in the fifteenth century that law could not be studied at the university, but that far more suitable places were available, near enough to the King's court at Westminster so that the law might be observed in its daily operation.

Full-fledged members of the bar, called "barristers," would instruct and supervise the legal training of the students. To be an instructor (reader) was considered a great honor and the position was avidly sought.

The Courts of Chancery influenced this development in many ways. It was there that a new type of lawyer emerged, the solicitors, whose learning and knowledge were frequently broader than those of the barristers. Moreover, the chancery lawyer, having fewer precedents to go on than his common-law colleague, developed a broader basis of judicial wisdom and philosophy. Yet the connection between common and chancery lawyers was close, and there was much intellectual cross-fertilization.[4]

The administration of justice in contemporary England is profoundly influenced by the experiences of the past. The students still congregate in the Inns of Court. Lawyers still divide into barristers, who alone are permitted to plead in the regular courts, and solicitors, who hire them, prepare the case, and take care of general legal business. Thus, a practical division of labor is accomplished. This is all the more important because the judges are appointed from among the barristers, who have "taken silk" (become members of the bar) at least seven years before becoming judges, or in the case of the High Court, ten years. The English judge, like his American colleague, is therefore a man who has seen the practical side of law and has had opportunity to witness and experience the economic, political, and social effects of judgments. This distinguishes English and American judges from their French or German brethren, who ascend to the bench directly from their theoretical law studies and remain in their career for life, carefully preserved—unless they possess great personal wisdom—from the raw winds of social and economic realities.[5]

[4] Gradually the chancery bar and the common-law bar merged, and both types of lawyers became students at the Inns.

[5] The most extensive and phenomenal study on the history of English law is W. S. Holdsworth, *History of English Law,* London, 1922–1938, 2d ed., 12 vols. A brilliant and standard treatise on the earlier period is F. Pollock and F. W. Maitland's *History of English Law to the Times of Edward I,* Cambridge, 1898, 2 vols. An excellent summary is E. Jenks, *The Book of English Law; As at the End of 1938,* London, 1938, 5th ed. See also W. M. Geldart, *Elements of the English Law,* London, 1912; H. Potter, *A Historical Introduction to English Law and Its Institutions,* London, 1949, 3d ed. On the common law specifically, see O. W. Holmes, *The Common Law,* Boston, 1881; F. Pollock, *The Expansion of the Common Law,* London, 1904, and *The Genius of the Common Law,* New York, 1912; R. Pound, *The Spirit of the Common Law,* Boston, 1921.

STATUTE LAW

Today, common law and equity exist side by side with statute law, *i.e.*, the Acts of Parliament. Acts of Parliament used to confine themselves, more or less, to the field of public law, but an ever-increasing invasion into private law has taken place. Wherever there is statutory law, it is supreme over common law. There is no judicial review in the United Kingdom because there is no written constitutional document like the Constitution of the United States. Acts of Parliament are therefore supreme and must be enforced by the courts. The latter may not declare a statute void because of "unconstitutionality," nor may the clear wording of a law be set aside because it is alleged to be contrary to public policy. However, when the statute is not all-inclusive, the courts exercise wide powers of interpretation, especially in questions involving public policy, and the charge has been made by a brilliant partisan commentator [6] that the judges have exercised their powers in order to restrain certain trade-union and other activities very much along the course of action which the Supreme Court of the United States pursued prior to the Jones and Laughlin case.

For the purpose of evaluating the English legal and judicial system, it is perhaps of little importance to determine the exact line of demarcation which separates statute from common law—if such a thing were possible. What is important, however, is to note that the entire legal fabric, be it statute or common law, is permeated by the common-law system, whose principal genius, in England as in the United States, lies in the rule of precedent, trial by jury, and the doctrine of the rule of law. The significant element of the use of precedent as a source of judicial interpretation is the application of reason to judicial experience. Thus, the judge relies on past decisions in concrete situations, rather than on abstract textual interpretation as is so often done on the Continent. But since no past case is likely to be exactly identical with a later one, there is always some leeway which permits the judge to exercise that infinite quality called wisdom. The common law is the law of the courts, not of the theorists. Therefore Oliver Wendell Holmes could write in his well-known book on the common law: "The life of the law has not been logic, it has been experience."

THE BENCH

In order to exercise these functions properly, it is necessary that the courts be independent of the executive branch of the government. We have seen

---

[6] Laski, *Parliamentary Government in England,* New York, 1938, pp. 303–326. Numerous cases cited there. See also the Taff Vale Case, A.C. 426 (1901), and Osborne v. Amalgamated Society of Railway Servants, A.C. 87 (1910).

above that the courts cannot set aside legislative action on the part of Parliament because of unconstitutionality. But they can invalidate executive action on grounds of illegality. Here the courts enter a twilight zone, because the American doctrine of expressed and enumerated powers in the hands of the national government does not apply to England. There, executive power (prerogative) extends to all fields not specifically limited by statute or by the conventions of the constitution. But the courts have sometimes placed restrictive interpretations on existing prerogative power which has tended to limit the expansion of executive influence.[7] However, as in all other states, there is increasing evidence of "delegated legislation," *i.e.*, rule-making power given by Parliament to government departments who also review grievances and complaints thereunder. In such cases the courts are severely limited because they can only examine whether a department acts *ultra vires, i.e.*, beyond its legal powers. Very often, however, delegated legislation is drafted by Parliament in very general terms, with the result that no act *ultra vires* can be found, and when that is the case the courts are powerless to examine the departmental, quasi-judicial decision on its merits. There are no administrative courts as there are in France.

The personal independence and tenure of judges dates from the Act of Settlement of 1701. Judges are now appointed for good behavior and may be removed only on grounds of misconduct or upon joint address of Parliament. However, the caliber of English judges is such that removal of a judge is virtually unknown. Judges of the county courts are appointed by the government (Crown) upon the recommendation of the Lord Chancellor, and justices of the peace are nominated by local authorities and committees and appointed by the Lord Chancellor. All other judges are appointed by the Prime Minister.

All judges, except the justices of the peace, are chosen from among the most highly qualified and experienced barristers, which means that they are mostly older men because a barrister at the height of his career will often be reluctant to sacrifice his higher earning capacity in private practice. Only the Lord Chancellor is an anomaly. He is really a lawyer, but he is nevertheless selected for his political services rather than for his judicial status, although some Lord Chancellors like Lord Birkenhead have surprised the world by their judicial acumen. As we have seen before, he is a member of the cabinet and combines executive, legislative, and judicial functions in his person.

The independence of judges is furthered by very high salaries, which are much greater than in France or Germany. Moreover there is virtually no promotion, so that a judge need not ingratiate himself with authorities as is the case in some continental countries where the government wields such power

[7] The Zamora, 2 A.C. 77 (1916); Attorney-General v. De Keyser's Royal Hotel, A.C. 508 (1920).

through the Minister of Justice. Proper performance of functions is guaranteed by the rule of publicity which requires all hearings, except for rare exceptions, to be held in open court. The judge is immune, civilly and criminally, for any action performed in court. He is further protected by the rules for contempt of court which shield him from undue attacks, but the right to reasonable and constructive criticism of judicial action has been repeatedly upheld.

We have said before that the jury is one of the essential features of the English system of justice, but today the jury is markedly in decline, and in criminal cases the grand jury has been abolished except for a few unimportant instances.[8]

In civil cases the jury has suffered a similar decline. Since 1933 a party to a lawsuit no longer normally has the right to a jury, although he may make application for jury trial in certain types of cases.[9] Even then the judge may refuse the request if the trial involves prolonged local investigation or documentary or scientific evidence. The judge's discretion is virtually unrestricted in this case. Generally, jury verdicts have met with greater favor of public opinion than judgments rendered by a single judge, but on the other hand the use of a jury in a civil case greatly increases the cost of litigation to the parties.

THE COURT SYSTEM

The United Kingdom has no unified court system. There is one system for England and Wales, there is another for Scotland, and there is still another for Northern Ireland. The Dominions of course have their own. The system with the greatest significance is that of England, and we shall be primarily concerned with it.

There was no judicial unification in England before 1873. Three great common-law courts existed: the Court of King's (Queen's) Bench, the Court of Common Pleas, and the Exchequer. Next to the common-law courts, there were others: the Court of Chancery, which decided equity cases; the Court of Admiralty, which goes back to an act of Richard II; a special Divorce Court; and a Court for the Relief of Insolvent Debtors (Bankruptcy Court). Appeals were a difficult and intricate business, and there was no appeal system from criminal judgments at all, although there were ways in which an error could be brought up to the House of Lords.

The obvious need for reform produced the appointment of a Royal Commission which reported in 1869; as a result the great Judicature Act was

---

[8] 23 & 24 Geo. V, c. 36 (1933). Treason committed overseas, certain offenses against governors, and violations of the Official Secrets Act.

[9] Libel, slander, malicious prosecution, false imprisonment, seduction, breach of promise, and other cases in which a charge of fraud is made against a party and he demands a jury.

finally passed in 1873. This act and subsequent amendments constitute the major portions of the English judiciary system. It created the so-called "Supreme Court of Judicature" which is a somewhat misleading term, because it is neither supreme nor a court. In fact the "Supreme Court of Judicature" is a covering name for a court system which never meets as one court but is composed of parts which are entirely separate. One part is a High Court of Justice which divides into three separate divisions: the Queen's (King's) Bench; Chancery; and Probate, Divorce, and Admiralty. Another is a Court of Appeals which divides into the Court of Appeals proper and the Court of Criminal Appeals.

THE COURT SYSTEM

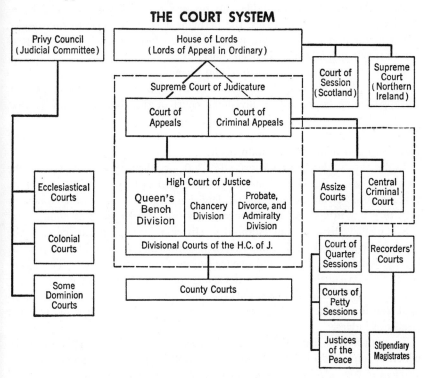

On the lower level, below the "Supreme Court," there are now the county courts. Criminal cases of grave nature are tried in the "assize" courts, which are traveling circuit courts, except the one in London which is called the Central Criminal Court, better known to readers of detective fiction as "Old Bailey." Above the "Supreme Court," there is the House of Lords, whose judicial decisions are rendered by the Lords specifically appointed for that purpose and known as the "Lords of Appeal in Ordinary." The Lord Chancellor presides over them.

There is another "Supreme" court, the Judicial Committee of the Privy

Council, which handles appeals from the ecclesiastic courts, from colonial tribunals, and from the courts of those Dominions which still permit such appeals.

Civil cases—*i.e.*, litigations between private individuals or corporations—are tried before county courts if the sum under dispute is less than £200 ($560). The name "county court" is misleading, because the area covered by each court has no relationship to the county. There are 500 county courts in England and Wales, which are grouped into sixty circuits. To each circuit, the Lord Chancellor assigns one judge who must hold court at least once every month in each of the county courts assigned to him. This volume of work might seem insurmountable, but because of the small sums and issues involved in a majority of cases, the permanent staff assigned to each court, the registrar and his aides, are usually able to settle a great many matters before they reach a hearing in open court.

In the county court the litigants may demand a jury if the sum at issue exceeds £5, but that is quite unusual and would be extremely uneconomical. An appeal may be made to a divisional court of the High Court of Justice, composed of two or more judges taken from the Queen's Bench Division. There the matter ordinarily rests, but the Court of Appeals may allow one more step and take the case unto itself.

If the sum under litigation exceeds £200, or when a party wishes it, the case goes before the High Court of Justice; that is to say, before one of its three divisions, the Queen's Bench Division if it is a trial at common or statutory law in general, the Chancery Division for decisions at equity, and the Probate, Divorce, and Admiralty Division in appropriate cases. The Queen's Bench Division is composed of a Lord Chief Justice—who is not the highest judge in the land—and twenty puisne (associate) judges. The Chancery Division consists of the Lord Chancellor—whose position is nominal—and five judges. The Probate, Divorce, and Admiralty Division has a President and four judges. Trials are handled either by single judges or by small panels of judges.

An appeal from the High Court of Justice goes to the Court of Appeals, which is composed of the "Master of the Rolls" (president) and eight Lord Justices of Appeal. From there a final appeal may be carried to the House of Lords in session composed of the Lord Chancellor and nine Lords of Appeal in Ordinary. In addition the Lord Chief Justice, any former Lord Chancellor, and other peers with high judicial experience may sit. Ordinarily three lords to each case are sufficient, although five is the more frequent number. Technically the "law lords" sit as the House of Lords as a whole; their proceedings are legislative rather than judicial in form and are entered on the journal of the House. In actuality, however, the House of Lords as a judicial body is entirely separate from the House as a legislature, and the separation could easily be made final and practical without harm to anyone. However, with their love for antiquity and time-honored institutions, the people of England prefer to leave well enough alone.

Appeal to the House of Lords can be made in civil cases only upon permission of the Court of Appeals. It is an exceedingly expensive affair and therefore not very frequent. Moreover since 1948 lords are no longer tried "by their peers" as the Magna Carta decreed. A further factor which diminishes the judicial work of the Lords is the extreme rigidity of their reliance on their own previous decisions. But on the other hand, the House of Lords is the only true United Kingdom court, because it accepts appeals from the highest courts of Scotland and Northern Ireland as well as from England and Wales.

Quite outside the regular court hierarchy is the Judicial Committee of the Privy Council. Just as the House of Lords is technically a legislative body but is actually also a judicial one, so the Judiciary Committee of the Privy Council is theoretically an administrative body but is in reality also a court. It is composed of the Lords of Appeal in Ordinary (law lords) with the addition of several judges from the Commonwealth. It is a court of appeals from the colonies and the Dominions. However, Australia, New Zealand, and Ceylon are now the only Dominions left which still permit certain appeals to the Privy Council.[10] Normally only civil cases are appealed, but in exceptional instances an important criminal case may reach the Privy Council.

Criminal cases are handled differently. No indictments are usually rendered by a grand jury, but charges are filed by local officials. There is also a national officer, the Director of Public Prosecutions, who performs this task in cases of exceptional difficulty. The prosecution in court itself may be conducted by a public prosecutor or by a barrister who has been appointed for this purpose by the Crown and given the title of Queen's (King's) Council (Q.C. or K.C.). But whether the prosecution is conducted by a public official or a private person retained for this purpose, it is always in the name of and at the expense of the Crown.

A person who is charged with a criminal offense is taken before a justice of the peace or in large cities before a full-time "stipendiary magistrate" (in London called metropolitan magistrate). Justices of the peace are unpaid officials who perform their duties because of the honor and the prestige involved. Most of them belonged to the class of country squires, but in recent years members of other professions have found access to appointment. Justices of the peace are the only members of the judicial branch who are not learned in the law; they are appointed by the Lord Chancellor upon recommendations by local organizations. They are very numerous [11] and easily

---

[10] The right of a Dominion legislature to abolish appeals to the Privy Council was upheld by the Privy Council itself. Attorney-General for Ontario v. Attorney-General for Canada, A.C. 127 (1947).

[11] Nearly 20,000, less than half of whom exercise juridical functions.

accessible. They have jurisdiction only in minor cases of misdemeanors, such as traffic violations, and they may not impose fines of more than £5 ($14) or imprisonment for more than two weeks. Two justices of the peace sitting together form a Court of Petty Sessions, which may try a wider range of misdemeanors for which maximum punishment does not exceed six months unless the defendant consents. Single justices and petty sessions may concern themselves with cases which are too grave for their jurisdiction, but in those instances the justices of the peace merely exercise the function discharged by the grand jury in the United States or the *juge d'instruction* and *Untersuchungsrichter* in France and Germany respectively. They investigate whether there exists enough prima-facie evidence to commit the accused to trial, and they decide what court shall hear the case, depending on the severity of the transgression. In the cities, stipendiary magistrates exercise the same functions.

Appeals from single justices of the peace or petty sessions may be heard in the assembly of all justices of the peace in each county or important part thereof, known as the Court of Quarter Sessions,[12] which hears all cases *de novo*. In some areas this Court is presided over by a barrister appointed by the Home Secretary and called "the Recorder." Courts of Quarter Sessions may also try more serious crimes but not those for which the death penalty or life imprisonment can be asked. Here the jury is used, and an attempt has been made to make the presiding officer a learned jurist lest he be too much under the thumb of the clerk. Under certain circumstances appeals may be directed to the Court of Criminal Appeals, while in rating and licensing matters the High Court of Justice may be asked to intervene on certiorari. In larger cities, a learned jurist, the recorder, has similar functions.

Grave crimes are brought before the Assizes or, if in London, before the Central Criminal Court. One or two judges of the Queen's Bench [13] are out on circuit and hold court in the more important places. Here, the jury is always used.

The accused has a right to appeal to a higher court, the Court of Criminal Appeals, which is composed of three judges from the Queen's Bench. This appeal may be undertaken on questions of law in any case, but on questions of fact only with the permission of the trial judge or of the Court of Criminal Appeals. Once a case is appealed, however, the Court of Criminal Appeals has great freedom; it may reduce or increase the sentence, or it may quash the entire case, but the possibility of increase keeps the number of appeals down to a minimum.

Ordinarily the Court of Criminal Appeals is the highest court in criminal cases. An appeal to the House of Lords is possible at infrequent instances,

---

[12] Meeting four times each year. For appeal purpose they act through committees.

[13] The "Queen's Bench Division" is not only a court division but also a pool of judges who may be used for various judicial purposes.

provided the Attorney General consents to it, but such an appeal may never come from the prosecution.

One characteristic on which the entire legal world may well look with envy is the English method of creating rules of procedures. In most other countries, these are laid down in the form of legislative acts and codes. These acts may be well organized, or they may be quite confusing, but they are always formidable barriers to simple and speedy trial and are the joy of the lawyer who can save his client only by riding procedural tricks. In England a rules committee does the job. It is composed of the Lord Chancellor, the Master of the Rolls, the Lord Chief Justice, four other judges, two barristers, and two solicitors. This truly "expert" committee, composed of eminently experienced men, has the task of establishing and constantly adjusting the rules of procedure. They have performed exceedingly well, and have produced satisfactory and speedy trials.[14]

No Administrative Courts

The court system described above is the only one existing in England.[15] There are no administrative courts as in France or Germany, and many English judges and lawyers treat the very idea with abject horror, congratulating themselves on having avoided this "monster" in England. But, as we have seen above, there is an increasing tendency toward "delegated legislation" and the power of government departments to make rules, and disputes break out which must be decided in the interests of justice and in order to permit the orderly carrying on of business. Since the courts can, as we have mentioned, examine only the question whether the administrative procedure was *ultra vires* or not, a great number of disputes would remain unresolved unless the government departments themselves took it upon their shoulders to give a fair hearing to people who believe that they have a grievance. Thus, quasi-judicial tribunals, departmental boards, etc., are to be found everywhere, which may be considered "administrative courts" of sorts.

Another question, intimately connected with the problem of administrative justice, is the liability of the government for acts of its agents. If a person incurs damages as a result of the action of a government agent, he has to sue that man, and not the "state" as in France. However, the government stands behind its agents to an increasing degree, and since 1946 it is possible to sue the government for damages incurred as a result of action by an agent which was not necessarily illegal but which caused damages, even though possibly committed in good faith.

[14] H. G. Hanbury, *English Courts of Law*, London, 1944; R. M. Jackson, *The Machinery of Justice in England*, Cambridge, 1940; C. P. Patterson, *The Machinery of Justice in Great Britain*, Austin, 1936. See also S. Amos, *British Justice: An Outline of the Administration of Criminal Justice in England and Wales*, London, 1940.

[15] Ecclesiastic courts and prize courts are not being considered here.

Chapter 6

LOCAL GOVERNMENT

It is a matter of historical experience that national government changes more frequently and more violently than local government. New masters often rewrite the constitution of a country, but leave the structure of local government fairly well alone. England [1] is somewhat of an exception in this development because both local and national governments show a remarkable degree of parallelism; both are deeply rooted in the past, both have institutions of most ancient origin, both have undergone very fundamental changes a little over a century ago, and both have had to make adjustments to fit into the postwar period.

Local government is of great importance and is an interesting and significant indicator of the general relationship between the English people and their government. The many services which the citizen needs for the normal comfort of his daily life are, to a very large extent, provided by local authorities. There is the police for the protection of life, liberty, and property—and the English police is second to none in the world. There are the schools, certain health and welfare functions, the building and maintenance of roads and bridges, and the use of open spaces; Town and Country Planning introduce an even closer relationship, though in a new garb.

Local government is also a school for democracy and the beginning of a political career. While local government is not as independent in England as it is in the United States, it is infinitely more self-reliant than is customary on the European continent. There is a closer tie-in to the national government than in America, but there is no all-powerful Minister of the Interior, as in France, whose hand weighs heavily on the shoulders of local authorities. Under such circumstances, free men may assemble in their councils, pretty much as of yore, and impress the mark of their personalities on their environment. Many leading statesmen began their careers in the councils of local government; most notable among them were Joseph and Neville Chamberlain, both of whom were Lord Mayors of Birmingham before entering the national scene, while one of the outstanding Labor leaders, Herbert Morrison, first became prominent as President of the London County Council.

[1] We are discussing English local government. Insignificant differences exist in Scotland and Northern Ireland.

Development

Modern English local government began in the nineteenth century, but significant elements are discernible much earlier.[2] From the Anglo-Saxon period there remains little that is of great significance except place names. But the feudal society which the Normans brought to England was a different matter. In those days, the basic unit of local government with which the citizen came into contact was the parish. A straight line of authority reached from the King down to the people in the parishes—a system based on the ownership and tenancy of land which was characteristic of feudalism. Above the parishes were the counties. If the parishes were the most important units of local government for the citizens concerned—because they saw to the keeping of the peace—the counties were the most important units from the King's standpoint. It was through the county administration that the King kept the barons in line. This was done through the sheriffs, who were royal proconsuls, and through the royal judges. True, the local lords were permitted to maintain their own baronial courts, but royal justice was so much better that it gained the upper hand, as we have seen in a preceding chapter.

In the thirteenth century an important addition was made to local administration in the form of the justices of the peace. Soon social and economic changes caused their functions to increase steadily. But they found it difficult to discharge them through the existing parish organization, which had a tradition of self-government, while the justices of the peace were appointed by and responsible to the King. Thus a habit of compromise between the two principles, local autonomy and central direction, was established, which marks local government today even though the instrumentalities have greatly changed. At the same time, the King gave special autonomy to certain cities —mostly for political reasons—and exempted them from much of the regular county organization; this was the origin of the later county boroughs.

The Tudor period saw the first integral attempt at a thorough organization of the country along modern lines. The justices of the peace were placed under the close scrutiny of the King's council and the Star Chamber, while a large number of laws regulated many of the functions of local government. The parishes in turn were brought under the justices of the peace, and the overseers of the parishes were put in charge of the administration of the Poor Laws.

[2] The most famous and all-inclusive treatise on the history of local government is the formidable work of Sidney and Beatrice Webb, *English Local Government from the Revolution to the Municipal Corporations Act*, London, 1906–1927, 9 vols. A briefer treatment may be found in W. A. Robson, *The Development of Local Government*, London, 1948, 2d ed., and a detailed historical introduction is contained in J. J. Clarke, *The Local Government of the United Kingdom*, London, 1945, 13th ed. A very useful book has been published in the new Town and County Hall Series by K. B. Smellie, *A History of Local Government*, London, 1947.

The great social and economic changes which accompanied the Industrial Revolution were not at first reflected in the organization of local government. A straight channel of command still led from the King, via the Lord Lieutenant and the Sheriff, to the justice of the peace. In actuality, unwritten changes took place, but no uniformity or system was maintained. In 1832 there existed 15,000 parishes, each a distinct organization which operated a good deal as it pleased. Area, methods of administration, and methods of appointment varied from place to place. Many offices were held by unpaid officials who allowed them to decline. Since the parish vestry was the only assembly (other than Parliament) entitled to impose taxes, there was usually a small group of influential and wealthy people who ran things as they saw fit. Abuse was frequent and corruption abounded.

With the growth of the population and the establishment of many new towns in the North and the Midlands, the local government officials were grossly overworked, and many a prosperous and well-bred citizen exempted himself from a rotating parish office by paying his way out, while those who were unable to do so were determined to make their office pay off. The new towns tended to submerge the parish organization, and additional work was placed on the shoulders of the justice of the peace. In 1765 Blackstone wrote: "Such an infinite variety of business has been heaped upon them, that few care to undertake and fewer understand the office."

In line with the increasingly difficult times, the office of the justice of the peace—once the pride of the country squire—came increasingly under the control of doubtful and rough characters; moreover, politics set in between Whigs and Tories, and between Church of England men and Dissenters, with the result that the whole system was being torn to shreds. The village constable was unable to control the increasing criminality of the industrial age. Nor could the parish and county organization establish effective control over the new industries and the people they brought in. It became increasingly clear that local, piecemeal reform was inadequate, that only comprehensive action from the top down could furnish remedies.

The need for reform was great everywhere, but nowhere was it greater than in the overcrowded industrial cities. There it was inextricably interwoven with the problem of poor relief. Those were the days of the oppressive corn laws and the movement for their repeal.[3] The results were two statutes: the Poor Law Act of 1834 and the Municipal Corporations Act of 1835. Of the two, the Poor Law Act was the more basic.

---

[3] They were laws taxing the import of corn and thus keeping the price high. Repeal became a great political question and was finally successful in 1841. It marked the alliance of worker and manufacturer and became the source of what is sometimes called "Manchester liberalism." See D. G. Barnes, *A History of the English Corn Laws from 1660 to 1846*, London, 1930.

A Poor Law Commission had been set up in 1832 under the chairmanship of Lord Brougham. It employed a large number of investigators and thus began the system of inspectors. The principal recommendation of the Commission was the establishment of a central board to control the administration of the poor law. This board was to be empowered to combine as many parishes and establish as many workhouses as it saw fit. It was to establish standards for the appointment of administrative officers who applied the Poor Laws. This was done in 1834, and thus was established one of the principal tenets of English local government, that of central control. The three Commissioners and the Secretary who were appointed to administer the poor law eventually became the Ministry of Health.

The Municipal Corporations Act of 1835 laid down the broad outlines which all local government eventually followed. It established the municipal corporation as a legal person which expressed itself through an elected council. The rights of the corporation were strictly circumscribed and were not extensive at first. Moreover, while the Poor Law Act went deeply into the question of central control, the Municipal Corporations Act merely touched on it. The permission of the Treasury was required for local government loans as well as alienation of property, and the Privy Council could veto local government bylaws.

Gradually more and more functions were taken on, especially in the field of public health, parks, libraries, sanitation, fire departments, and police. In 1867 Manchester obtained legislation which in effect gave it the first legal basis for slum clearance. Also, a number of commissions were set up for the purpose of controlling public utilities. Eventually, all these functions and more were brought together in the Municipal Corporations Consolidation Act of 1882 and extended to twenty-five more boroughs.[4]

In the meantime the Poor Law Commissioners had not been idle. From pure administrators, they developed into something like social reformers. They began to look into the reasons for poverty and they found terrible health conditions. The secretary to the Poor Law Commission, Edwin Chadwick, was able to show conclusively that poor law expenditures could be reduced only if a drastic improvement of public health were brought about. Epidemics showed the national character of the health menace, and in 1848 a new central authority, the General Board of Health, was established with powers of a large and varied nature. The Board met so much opposition that it was abolished in 1858, but the idea had taken root. Ten years later, a Royal Sanitary Commission was appointed, and its report led to the Public Health Act of 1875, establishing the Local Government Board consisting of the Lord President of the (Privy) Council, the principal secretaries of state,

---

[4] Except for the City of London (the center part of the metropolitan area, in which few people live), the word "city" is not used legally. "Borough" is the official term.

the Chancellor of the Exchequer, a President (of the board), and a secretary who might sit in Parliament.[5] This board inherited the poor relief from the Poor Law Board, the public health functions which the Board of Health had exercised and which had later gone to the Privy Council, and the local government work of the Home Office.

It is not exactly surprising that so much effort was spent on borough (urban) government and so little on county (rural) government. By 1875, approximately two-thirds of all Englishmen lived in towns. Nevertheless, the Municipal Corporations Act of 1835 and subsequent legislation had set the pattern for county government too. When piecemeal reform and the giddy piling up of unrelated boards had made county government nearly unmanageable, the Local Government Act of 1888 and that of 1894 brought relief and carried the counties alongside the boroughs.

The Local Government Act introduced an entirely new system of local units, the so-called "administrative county," which sometimes is identical with the old historical county and sometimes is not. The Act also established councils which followed the pattern established in the boroughs. It transferred nearly all the vast powers of the justices of the peace to the new County Councils. Only petty justice and a certain influence over the police remained in the hands of the justices of the peace. This democratization of local government was carried further down in 1894, when parish councils were established and urban district councils set up in the former Local (Sanitary) Board Districts. On the other hand, many more towns claimed exemption and "county borough" status than had originally been anticipated.

One other innovation might be mentioned: women entered local government before they were admitted to Westminster or Whitehall. In 1894 they became eligible for parish and district councils, and in 1907 they became eligible to the borough and county councils and could become aldermen.[6]

After rural government had caught up with the hitherto more advanced municipal (borough) areas, it was time to undertake the final step in the direction of a better integration at the top. We have seen how a great deal of improvement was achieved by the establishment of the Local Government Board in 1875. But the overlapping and duplication of efforts was still great, especially as Parliament created new commissions for all kinds of purposes; one might wonder for instance why the august Privy Council had to approve the rules of the Central Midwives Board, while the protection of infant life was placed under the Home Office.

The Haldane Commission, which we had occasion to mention before, gained another claim to fame by proposing the creation of a Ministry of Health with

[5] The Poor Law Commissioners had not been allowed to sit in Parliament.

[6] Women's activities in such political associations as the Primrose League (Cons.) and the Women's Liberal Congress helped to obtain these concessions.

very wide powers. This was accomplished a year later, in 1919, and a Parliamentary Secretary was appointed under the Minister, to be in charge of the work of the former Local Government Board and the Insurance Commissions.[7] Subsequent legislation abolished further independent boards and simplified the administration, but the Ministry of Health has remained the major feature in the whole realm of local government.

This relationship, the like of which cannot be found elsewhere, is also unique from another viewpoint. It is a subtle relationship, like many others in the framework of British government. There is central control, but, as we have seen, there is no Minister of the Interior or prefect as in France who may directly interfere with, and indeed run, local government. Local officials are elected locally and have no duty of obedience toward the national government, although most of their powers are regulated by national law. Moreover, local government has its own income resulting from an age-honored system of property taxes, called "rates," but it is not independent financially for it must rely heavily on grants-in-aid of the central government.

THE COUNTIES

Today the system is as follows: there are two types of counties, the historical and the administrative counties. The fifty-two historical counties are relics of former times and are shorn of all important functions. They have no elected council and have only three principal officials, the Lord Lieutenant, the Sheriff, and the justice of the peace. The first two, especially the Sheriff, are election officials for Parliamentary elections. The functions of the justices have been discussed above. All three are appointed by the government.

There are now sixty-two administrative counties superimposed over the historical counties. Their governing authority is an elected council whose chief functions are administrative rather than legislative, especially since most basic local government legislation is accomplished in Parliament. Councilors are elected in single-member districts, very much like Members of Parliament. Before the Second World War the suffrage was restricted by property qualifications, but this was abolished thereafter, and the right to vote in local elections is now exactly like that in national elections.

The county councils are responsible for the policy and the administration of the county and supervise the work of subordinate bodies, such as the district councils. They establish the "rates"[8] and appropriate money. With the

---

[7] However, control over local elections was shifted to the Home Office in 1921.

[8] The rates are property taxes based on an Elizabethan system by which the needs of the local government are determined and then are distributed among property owners, to be paid according to assessed evaluation. This is now the function of the Treasury's Board of Inland Revenue, but collection is done by local government. However, more and

consent of the central government, they may also borrow. Otherwise they maintain the ordinary local services, buildings, and asylums. They also administer the licensing laws except for liquor,[9] and they appoint the regular administrative personnel of the county, most of whom are, however, part of a local civil-service system.

New and very considerable powers and duties have been imposed on the councils as a result of two important national statutes: the Education Act of 1944 and the Town and Country Planning Acts of 1944 and 1947. The Education Act made the county and county borough councils responsible for all primary, secondary, and related education.[10] It also broadened considerably the scope of public education;[11] before 1944 the elementary schools had continued until the student was fourteen, but secondary education had begun at eleven. In fact, 90 per cent of otherwise eligible children were excluded from secondary education, most of which was private. Now, under Sec. 7 of the act, a definite system of education in three progressive steps—primary, secondary, and further education—has been instituted. The act also ordered the establishment of kindergartens, special schools for the handicapped, and for the first time in history, an examination of the desirability of boarding schools, hitherto reserved to the well to do. Private schools are not thereby outlawed. The Act distinguishes between three types of voluntary (private) schools: controlled, aided, and special-agreement schools. But the increasingly heavy financial burden on schools groaning under the ever-increasing demands for higher education is forcing them more and more in the direction of controlled schools. Even the parochial (Roman Catholic) schools are negotiating to enter into a special-agreement category by which the state would pay many of their expenses, but the conditions offered by the Church have been found unacceptable by the Minister of Education.

Town and Country Planning

The Town and Country Planning Acts grew out of the conditions created by war. Devastated areas were to be reconstructed in line with a general plan, rather than haphazardly. Moreover poorly or wrongly developed areas were to be directed toward more useful exploits. General as well as very

---

more money is being received from the central government as block grants-in-aid, especially since land and real property used for agricultural, manufacturing, or transport services have been either exempted altogether (agriculture) or have had their rates drastically reduced.

[9] Liquor licenses are still issued by the justices of the peace.

[10] Under the control of the Minister of Education.

[11] Meaning public education as understood in the United States as well as in Britain. This has nothing whatever to do with the so-called "public schools" (especially Eton, Harrow, Winchester, Westminster, Rugby, Shrewsbury, Charterhouse, St. Paul's, and Merchant Taylor's), which are very exclusive preparatory schools from which the public is excluded.

detailed direction is vested in a new government department, the Ministry of Housing and Local Government. Under it, local authorities are entitled to acquire land which in overcrowded county boroughs may actually be slightly outside the corporation limits. Development on such land remains thus under local and central government control,[12] and even the owner of certain types of property must await the consent of the authorities for certain improvements he might desire to make.

The operation of the Town and Country Planning Acts is a good example of the extent to which local government has absorbed new functions which it exercises under central direction. It is also an example of the attitude of the British government, which desires to have a maximum of consultation before embarking on planning activities and which in this case finds local government a suitable medium for carrying out this design. The act charges local bodies (county and county borough councils) with the drafting of plans for their respective areas. Considerable power of delegation and extensive opportunities for hearing affected interests exist. All such plans had to be approved by the Minister of Town and Country Planning, and local recommendations were sometimes overlooked or forgotten at that stage. New land could be acquired either directly through the local authorities or through the Central Land Board, an agency of the Ministry which only managed land and set certain rates and charges.[13]

An even more ambitious scheme has been the planning of new towns,[14] partly in order to relieve congestion, partly to attract new industries into undeveloped areas, and partly to further the new urban type of "satellite cities."

Success of the latter scheme is doubtful, and outstanding results were not achieved, but the scope of the act was nevertheless enormous. Two types of new towns were planned. One was intended to take population and industry away from overcrowded towns, the other envisaged the satisfaction of immediate industrial needs through expansion and new industries in hitherto undeveloped areas. So far, fourteen new towns have been designated. But this was to be merely a beginning. Eventually 3,000,000 people were to be accommodated in these new communities, which would mean that fifty or sixty of them would have to be built.[15] But performance lags far behind.

[12] Under the 1944 act, a difference was made between war-damaged, "blitzed," areas, and "blighted" areas, *i.e.*, underdeveloped or wrongly developed regions.

[13] It also pockets increments in value accrued by private owners due to government improvements. This is to take speculation out of the business.

[14] The New Towns Act of 1946, 9 & 10 Geo. VI, c. 68. Preparatory to this entire system of town and country planning were two reports, that of the Departmental Committee on the Utilization of Land in Rural Areas (Scott Report), London, 1942, and the Final Report of the Expert Committee on Compensation and Betterment (Uthwatt Report) of the same year. New Towns Committee (Reith), *Final Report*, Cmd. 6876, 1946.

[15] A. E. Telling, "New Towns, Progress and Prospects," in *Town and Country Planning*, Vol. X (1948), p. 80.

The New Towns Act constituted a bold step on the part of the government in the direction of meeting some of Britain's worst needs. But on the other hand a number of critics are disturbed about the manner in which the act has been administered. Since the recommendation of the Reith Commission—that new towns be built where no urban centers existed—was largely ignored by the then Minister of Town and Country Planning, difficulties with property owners and other interested parties arose. These issues illustrate some principal objections raised by opponents of the act. Under the law, which was upheld by the House of Lords,[16] the Minister of Town and Country Planning did not need to "sell" his case to the local citizenry but needed merely to hear objections. Thus a former Minister (Silkin), who was thoroughly committed to the plan, was the one to decide disputes raised by local objections. This made him a judge in his own case, with the result that local opinion found it difficult to make much of an impression.

The operation of the Town and Country Planning Act and of the New Towns Act illustrates the manner in which national and local government functions are interwoven. The Ministry of Housing and Local Government, the successor to the Ministry of Town and Country Planning, is in general charge of planning, but much of the work is carried out by local government and in some instances by joint planning boards of several counties or boroughs.

Another example is education. The counties and county boroughs are local education authorities and are charged with maintaining institutions of primary and secondary education, and frequently various training schools as well. Yet the system is controlled and standardized by the Minister of Education. Similar examples may be found in almost every other field of local government endeavor.

COUNTY COUNCILS AND ALDERMEN

Numerous duties are performed by elected councils in the counties and the county boroughs. Many of them are required by statute. The latter are cities (boroughs) with the quasi status of a county; we may think of them as urban counties.

Since counties vary greatly in size, membership in the county councils varies accordingly. The council elects a number of aldermen, who may be councilors (in which case there is a by-election) or may be chosen from the outside. Their number is one-third of the regular councilors except in the London County Council, where they amount to only one-sixth. Aldermen are elected for a term of six years, half of them being reelected when a new council convenes.

The system of aldermen is unique, for although they are selected on a dif-

[16] Franklin and Others v. Minister of Town and Country Planning, A.C. 87 (1948).

ferent basis than the councilors, they sit with them as one body. However, aldermen are chosen for their wisdom and experience and generally enjoy greater prestige than ordinary councilors.

The county councils are too large to work effectively as administrative bodies. Most of their work is therefore done in committee and in cooperation with their staffs. The organization of the councils, the number of their principal committees, and their general procedure are fixed by the Local Government Act of 1929. But other committees may be established on the council's own initiative. There are also committees in which both the council and other authorities are represented.

The county councils also have limited legislative power to issue "by-laws," which need, however, the approval of the appropriate ministry.

THE STAFF

Because of the steady increase in administrative work, a major portion of the load is actually performed by a staff of permanent officials, among whom the county clerk (in county boroughs, town clerk) is the most important and has the most ancient office. He serves as coordinator and supervisor over the other heads of departments, such as finance officer, surveyor, chief constable, education officer, and health officer. Under each one in turn is a staff the size of which depends of course on the size and character of the county or county borough. The high standards of British local government depend in no small degree on these officials, who are not under a formal civil-service statute but who actually have tenure and look upon their work as a career. Moreover, it is the practice that these officials meet regularly with the appropriate committees of the council, thus helping to blend into a happy and efficient combination the democratic principle of elected officials with the need for expert advice.

DISTRICTS

The rural and urban districts which form the subdivisions of the county are organized very much like their parent bodies, with their own councils, rates, and permanent staffs. At times an urban district may become a borough, but that is not done in a systematic manner. The parishes, however, have deteriorated. In urban centers they merely have ecclesiastic functions, while in the rural parishes very minor administrative duties have been retained.[17]

[17] The parish meeting is the only British institution comparable to the New England town meetings. In English (not Scottish or Northern Irish) parishes, there is also a Parish Council if the parish has more than 300 inhabitants or if it has between 200 and 300 and has made application for the establishment of a council.

The Boroughs

A unit of local government of a special kind is the borough, which is simply a town with a charter. There are two different types of boroughs: the county borough, which, as we have seen, is a county unto itself and exempt from any other county jurisdiction, and the ordinary borough, which forms part of the county in which it is located. County boroughs are usually the more important cities, with inhabitants of 100,000 or more, but no general rule can be applied to the entire system because it is impossible to apply any rational yardstick to determine which town ought to be a borough and which ought to be content with being an urban district.

In order to become a borough, a district must "petition His Majesty in Council" for a charter. No minimum population or ratable value is required in the law, but in practice a minimum population of 20,000 is expected. This applies only to new boroughs; among older ones there is a great discrepancy in size and importance. The Privy Council appoints a committee to report on the matter while an inspector of the Ministry of Health conducts local hearings. If the inspector's report is unfavorable, the petition is dead but may be revived at a future, more opportune date. If the inspector's report is favorable, the charter may be granted either by order in council or by act of Parliament.

The borough is governed by a borough council, constituted similar to a county and district council. Its presiding officer is the mayor or, in more important towns, the Lord Mayor. The term of office for councilors is three years, as in the case of county councilors, with one-third being elected each year. Aldermen are elected as in the county councils. The borough status gives a town a much greater degree of dignity and civic pride; it also means somewhat larger expenses for pomp and circumstance. Much ceremonial attention is paid to the mayor or Lord Mayor, although he actually wields much less power than most American mayors. He heads no special department; apart from being presiding officer of the council, he is merely one of the councilors who casts his vote like other members. In most cases there is no salary, while the duties and expenses may be quite heavy. Often the Lord Mayors must be wealthy men in order to stand the strain, although this tendency is somewhat less emphasized now.

The council is the chief legislature and administration of the borough. In a county borough it also absorbs the functions ordinarily held by the county council. It manages the corporate estate and the borough fund. It establishes the borough rates. It has its own budget and appropriates money. Subject to approval by the central government, it may borrow money. It also administers the municipal services, which are often quite extensive.

Just like the county council, the borough council operates chiefly through committees; however, because of the vast extent of municipal and social services required from a city, the regular staff on quasi civil service looms especially large. Since these officials have tenure, the establishment of a city "machine," which still plagues some American cities, is unlikely in England. However, lack of uniformity in selection and inadequate standards are causing some difficulties which may possibly lead to a more far-reaching reform at some future date.

CENTRAL GOVERNMENT CONTROL

In describing the powers and responsibilities of local government, it has been necessary at various instances to point to the existence of central control. The pivot of this system was the Ministry of Health and is now the Ministry of Housing and Local Government, but other departments, chiefly the Treasury, the Home Office, the Ministry of Transport and Civil Aviation, the Ministry of Education, the Ministry of Agriculture and Fisheries, and the Ministry of National Insurance, are also concerned.

Like all other institutions, local government is of course subject to the supreme authority of Parliament and such laws as it may enact. Beyond that, the various government departments concerned supervise the work of local government and see to it that statutory authority is not exceeded.[18] The Home Office inspects and to a certain extent supervises the police forces, except in the Metropolitan District of London, where the police is directly administered under the Home Office. The latter, logically enough, is also in charge of local civil-defense work, especially the Home Guard. The Treasury must give its consent to borrowing by local government. Of principal interest are the grants-in-aid which enable local government to render its many services, and considerable central control is maintained there. There are two types of grants: allocated grants, which are directed toward certain services, and block grants, which are without specified instructions. The first category has been criticized because it leads to ill-conceived expansion purely for the purpose of earning grants, while block grants, which are gaining in favor, do not show the same tendency. About half of local government expenditures are covered by grants.

Generally speaking, the appropriate central departments supervise the work of local authorities, keep them in line, and establish rules with regard to procedure, organization, qualifications of officials, equipment, and general objectives.

Central departments may invalidate local ordinances which go beyond

[18] In the constitutional theory of the United States, the federal government has only expressed, enumerated, implied, and inherent (see the Curtiss-Wright case) powers, while state powers are inherent and reserved. The opposite is true in England. The powers of local government are not reserved or inherent but solely statutory.

powers granted to the local authorities, and they may compel obedience by recourse to the courts. They, especially the Ministry of Housing and Local Government, audit local government accounts and give appropriate advice. They watch over the efficiency of the local services; for instance, one-half the net expenditures for the police services is refunded if the local force has been found efficient. But under the Local Government Act of 1948, grants given to local governments depend on the extent to which each is above or below a national average of financial strength. This is a process of equalization. National ministries also approve certain appointments and bylaws and, since 1948, participate even in the assessment of property for local tax purposes. Recently the great expansion into the fields of public housing and socialized medicine has broken new ground for central government control, and the end is not yet in sight. Nevertheless, the over-all record of English local government is splendid. The preoccupation of the councils and their committees with administrative matters guarantees that democratic procedures are maintained on all levels and tends to prevent the rise of an all-powerful officialdom. At the same time, the intimate collaboration of councilmen and career officials creates a high level of administrative efficiency and a minimum of friction between elected and appointed officials.

Much can also be said for the exercise of national control over local government, which has generally tended to improve and increase local services without being arbitrary or leading to the unimaginative uniformity of the French system. In particular, national control appears not to have stultified the great vitality of local government or prevented many a pioneering venture.

Despite the generally satisfactory nature of local government and of central-local relationship, there is some uneasiness among certain observers concerning the future of local government.[19] There is a steady invasion of former local government preserves by the national government. The establishment of the National Health Service has relieved local authorities of some responsibilities while creating others, but generally under a greater measure of national control. The nationalization of electricity and gas has deeply affected many local government administrations which used to own and operate their own public utilities—sometimes at lower rates. Local poor relief was made a national matter by the National Assistance Act of 1948.

Another matter for long-standing concern has been the great disparity in size between different counties and county boroughs, which makes local administration unwieldy and encourages central direction. Therefore a great deal of thought has been given to the reform of local government, and the Local Government Boundary Commission has proposed a series of radical

---

[19] Especially since government departments (central and local) are not required to apply court procedures and may therefore decide a dispute against a person without granting him a hearing. Local Government Board v. Arlidge, A.C. 120 (1915).

changes.[20] Private agencies and local government associations have also shown deep concern.[21] But so far these proposals have remained on paper, and until Parliament acts nothing can be done.

Despite these difficulties, local government still constitutes a major part of the British fabric of government and an outstanding school for future statesmen.

POLITICS AND LOCAL GOVERNMENT

Until fairly recently, elections to the numerous local government councils were nonpartisan. But this is now a matter of the past. Spearheaded by the Labor party, local elections are now contested on party lines and usually on the basis of national rather than local issues. In the same manner, many leading national politicians have formerly been active in local government. This has been more frequently the case with Labor-party leaders than with Conservatives because the former often saw in local government an opportunity to carry out some of their ideas in the field of social reform.

As a result, local elections have often been regarded as a barometer of national trends. Such an evaluation, however, must be treated with considerable caution. The voting participation is much smaller in local elections than in national ones. There are a number of candidates who run as independents or as candidates of minor parties and groups. Moreover local issues do sometimes count in certain localities. Consequently voting trends in national and local elections have frequently been quite dissimilar.

THE GOVERNMENT OF LONDON

Many countries have special forms of government in their capital cities. The large size of some has sometimes been the cause. Some governments, especially conservative ones, have wanted to keep a potentially "radical" population of the capital city under control and prevent undue local pressure from trying to influence the central authorities. In many countries, therefore, capital cities possess less self-government than other towns, while only a few have more extensive powers. Examples of the first category are Washington, D. C., and Paris; of the second, Vienna.

But London, like many other British institutions, is in a category by itself. In the first place there are several Londons. There is the so-called "City of London" which comprises only the inner heart of the city, primarily the business and financial center, in which over a million people are active during the

---

[20] *Report of the Local Government Boundary Commission for 1947*, London, 1948.

[21] "Local Government Reorganization," *Public Administration*, Vol. XXXI (1953), pp. 176–188, 285–295.

day but in which few people live at night. Then there is the administrative county of London under the London County Council which consists of twenty-eight metropolitan boroughs. Finally there is the Greater London area, chiefly the Metropolitan Police District with comprises the territory of the administrative county of London plus sections of a number of surrounding counties.[22]

A closer integration of these systems has been advocated for over a century, but has always been defeated, ever since the "city" was able to marshal enough strength to achieve the exclusion of London from the provisions of the Municipal Corporations Act of 1835.

The City of London, properly speaking, is an area of about one square mile, located in the heart of London and divided into twenty-six wards. Its constitution, archaic in every way, is a residue of the guild-dominated city system of the Middle Ages. The City is under the control of three "courts," the Court of Aldermen, the Court of Common Council, and the Court of Common Hall. The Court of Aldermen consists of the Lord Mayor and the Aldermen who are also justices of the peace *ex officio*. It is the only example of a second chamber in British local government. The Court of Common Council, the main legislative chamber, consists of the Lord Mayor, 25 aldermen, and 206 common councilors. The Court of Common Hall consists of the Lord Mayor, the aldermen, the sheriffs, and the "liverymen." The liverymen are the members of the City Livery Companies, the last survivors of the ancient guilds, such as Ironmongers, Fishmongers, Goldsmiths, etc. In reality, however, these are now private societies of wealthy men. The Court of Common Hall annually selects two aldermen, one of whom will be elected Lord Mayor by the Court of Aldermen.

The City of London relies on the county for its municipal services, although it has a small police force and courts. In administers a number of services and extensive trusts. It also controls certain areas outside the city limits. The City of London is the scene of magnificent ceremonies, especially on the annual "Lord Mayor's Day," but it is an anachronism which serves little purpose and only helps to deprive the boroughs of some very lucrative tax property.

The major government of London is carried out by the London County Council. Its structure and that of the twenty-eight metropolitan boroughs are now consolidated in the London Government Act of 1939, which does for London what the Local Government Act of 1929 has done for the counties, but it is peculiar that the largest metropolitan area in the world is governed like a rural county. The London County Council is composed of 124 councilors and 20 aldermen. Its functions, however, differ in many ways from those of ordinary counties. This is also true of the twenty-eight metropolitan boroughs, whose powers are much more extensive than is ordinarily the case in other boroughs. A special feature is the Metropolitan Boroughs Standing Joint

[22] Parts of Kent, Surrey, Middlesex, Herts, and Essex.

Committee, which is composed of representatives of the borough and county councils. It is a coordinating body; its chief functions are the maintenance of London's over-all interest, and the consultation with the county council and ministries concerned with municipal problems.

The administrative county of London is the only county which does not control its own police. The Metropolitan Police is directly administered by the Home Secretary, who appoints commissioners in order to carry out the actual operations. The Metropolitan Police District is larger than the area of the London County Council, and includes also the county boroughs (Croyden, East Ham, West Ham) and the parts of counties which are located outside the control of the London County. The Metropolitan Police District and similar administrative areas, such as the Metropolitan Water District, the Port of London Authority, and the London Passenger Transport Board, also extend beyond the boundaries of the London County.[23]

[23] In addition to the already mentioned works by the Webbs, Robson, and Clarke, see J. Warren, *The English Local Government System*, London, 1946; E. L. Hasluck, *Local Government in England*, London, 1948, 2d ed.; G. D. H. Cole, *Local and Regional Government*, London, 1947; H. Finer, *English Local Government*, London, 1950, 4th ed.; S. E. Finer, *A Primer of Public Administration*, London, 1950; V. D. Lipman, *Local Government Areas, 1834–1945*, Oxford, 1948; C. R. Attlee, *Borough Councils*, London, 1946, 2d ed. (a brochure) ; W. I. Jennings, *Principles of Local Government Law*, London, 1947, 3d ed.; J. A. Hawgood, *The Citizen and Government*, London, 1947; and others. See also E. W. Weidner, "Trends in English Local Government," *American Political Science Review*, Vol. XXXIX (1945), p. 337; W. W. Crouch, "Trends in British Local Government," *Public Administration Review*, Vol. VII (1947), p. 254; W. A. Robson, "Reform of Local Government," *Political Quarterly*, Vol. XIX (1948), p. 254; V. Usill, "Democracy in British Local Government," *National Municipal Review*, Vol. XXXV (1946), p. 620; W. A. Robson, *The Development of Local Government*, London, 1948, 2d ed., and *The Government and Misgovernment of London*, London, 1948, 2d ed.; also E. W. Cohen, *Autonomy and Delegation in County Government*, London, 1953. Among older works, see especially H. J. Laski, W. I. Jennings, and W. A. Robson (eds.), *A Century of Municipal Progress*, London, 1935.

Chapter 7

EMPIRE AND COMMONWEALTH

The special genius of the British nation has long been expressed in its adaptability to regional differences and change. While French and German administration stress uniformity and logic, British administration suggests diversity and experience. As a result, the British Empire and Commonwealth today is an extraordinarily complex organization, which is more easily described than defined. Its expansion is immense; it comprises approximately one-fourth of the land surface of the earth and nearly a quarter of the earth's population. Its parts may be found on every continent and in every ocean. There are few important maps on which a section is not printed red, the traditional color of the British Empire.

This Empire includes areas which are directly governed by colonial administrations, but it also includes completely independent states over which London exercises no control whatsoever and over which its influence is most tenuous.

The most varied manners of acquisition have been used in placing these territories under the British flag. Rudyard Kipling, the bard of imperial glory, summed it up in these words:

> Some we got by purchase,
> And some we got by trade,
> And some we got by courtesy
> Of pike and carronade.

Some lands were acquired by ostensibly private companies, such as the famous East India Company, but were later taken over by the Crown when the abuses and the maladministration of the companies became obvious. Other lands were taken in the name of the Crown when they were either uninhabited or seemed otherwise desirable. Some were acquired from other powers through treaties of cession—often as a result of war. Many were appropriated because of economic or strategic reasons. In some parts of the empire the original inhabitants have become nearly extinct, while in others they constitute the overwhelming majority. Hundreds of different languages and dialects are spoken, all important races of mankind are included, and every possible type of climate is represented, in both the Northern and Southern Hemispheres.

Every stage of cultural development may be found, from the virtual stone-age civilization of the Australian aborigines to the sophisticated culture of the great metropolitan centers of Melbourne, Montreal, or Capetown. Nearly every form of government may be found, from the Governorship of Gibraltar to the self-governing Dominion of Canada or the Republic of India.

The present status and nature of the Empire are the result of evolution, rather than design. A characteristic of British constitutional development has been that men groped more or less blindly for the institutions and legal forms which they considered right, making and formulating their demands which found fulfillment sooner or later. Of course this development was not always peaceful, as exemplified by the secession of the thirteen American colonies and the uprising in Canada in 1837. More recently, the disturbances which heralded India's independence and the separate status of Pakistan, as well as the bloody incidents in Palestine preceding the expiration of the mandate, have been examples of the same sort. Nevertheless, while the British record is certainly not spotless, no other country has found it possible to give complete independence to so many of its former possessions and yet keep them within a broader Commonwealth.

It would be quite impossible to evaluate the British colonial administration within the framework of this book. The infinite variety of the empire alone would make that impossible. Perhaps it might also be said that a successful colonial administration is a contradiction in terms; if the motherland helps its dependent people to obtain a higher standard of living and better education, it also arouses automatically desire for self-government and independence. It is therefore not exaggerated to say that a successful colonial rule rules itself out. But while colonial rule may be on the road to extinction, it has made many contributions to the development of many races and continues to do so. Britishers, at any rate, do not consider the idea of empire to contain any nefarious connotation but regard it rather as a source of justified pride.

The desire for self-government stirred early in the most advanced colonies. In America, demand for home rule and independence was negligible until 1764–1765, when a new system of taxation was imposed. The lesson of the American War of Independence was drawn rather slowly. Three-quarters of a century later, the Canadian colonies raised similar demands. Canada did not leave the Empire, but its progress toward self-government was fairly rapid. In 1867 it received a Constitution—ostensibly in the form of an Act of (the Imperial) Parliament, the British North America Act—and assumed the generic title of "Dominion." [1] Other areas followed, notably Australia in 1900 and South Africa in 1909.

The development toward self-government in these most advanced imperial territories was especially marked in the field of foreign relations. The Do-

[1] Although the term "dominion" was used in the British North America Act of 1867, it came into general use only after the Imperial Conference of 1907.

minions participated in technical conferences and expected to be consulted with regard to commercial treaties and other questions affecting them. A significant step forward was made during and after the First World War. The Dominions had made tremendous contributions to Britain's victory. The fame of the Anzac (Australian and New Zealand Army Corps) troops resounded throughout the Middle East, while the Canadians shed their blood freely at Vimy Ridge, and Indian troops were in evidence in most theaters of war. Imperial leaders, notably General (later Field Marshal) Smuts of South Africa, were consulted on the conduct of the war, and Smuts joined the War Cabinet. The Imperial Conference of 1917 decided to hold a special conference in order to deal with the future constitutional position of the component parts of the Empire. This conference was to recognize the Dominions as "autonomous nations of an Imperial Commonwealth," while India was to become "an important portion of the same." India and all Dominions except Newfoundland participated in the peace conference of 1919, and certain Dominion representatives acted on behalf of the entire Empire in other councils and conferences. The peace treaties were signed and ratified by each Dominion and India, which thereby became original members of the League of Nations. Thus the Dominions, and to a lesser degree India, had gained equality with each other and with the mother country as well as with foreign states.

In 1920 the British government consented to the establishment of a Canadian legation in Washington, and the principles of equality and self-government were specifically recognized in the Constitution of the Irish Free State of 1922 as enacted by Parliament. In 1923, it was agreed that the Dominions were entitled to conclude treaties with foreign states without any participation by United Kingdom representatives.[2]

THE STATUTE OF WESTMINSTER

A milestone of the utmost significance was the Imperial Conference of 1926. A number of questions were in doubt and needed settlement; particularly the role of the King's representative in the Dominions, the Governor-General, and the right of secession as propounded by the nationalist Prime Minister of the Union of South Africa, General Hertzog.

The Imperial Conference of 1926 defined the position and mutual relations of the United Kingdom and the Dominions as follows:

They are autonomous Communities within the British Empire, equal in status, in no way subordinate one to another in any aspect of their domestic or external affairs, though united by a common allegiance to the Crown, and freely associated as mem-

[2] A. J. Toynbee, *Conduct of British Empire Foreign Relations since the Peace Settlement*, London, 1928, pp. 100–104.

bers of the British Commonwealth of Nations. . . . Every self-governing member of the Empire is now master of its destiny. In fact, if not always in form, it is subject to no compulsion whatever. . . . But the principles of equality and similarity, appropriate to *status*, do not universally extend to function.

This definition was undoubtedly premature and, at that time, incorrect. But it clearly foreshadowed changes which were soon enacted.

The legal crystallization of these principles took place in the Statute of Westminster of 1931.[3] It establishes the Crown as the common symbol of the members of the Commonwealth as well as their common allegiance.[4] Most important of all, however, is the provision that no Act of the London Parliament shall extend to any Dominion unless that Dominion has expressly requested it and it is so stated in the Act. The Dominion Parliaments, in turn, are unlimited in their legislative power except insofar as their own constitutions impose limitations. The Dominions may also abolish the power of the Governors-General to "reserve," *i.e.*, veto, bills.

THE COMMONWEALTH TODAY

The true nature of the Commonwealth can hardly be discerned from the Statute of Westminster. The Statute itself is vague enough. It points out some of the things which the members of the Commonwealth may or may not do. But with a full application of the British genius for accepting realities and avoiding definitions, it does not tell us what the Commonwealth is. At the enactment of the Statute of Westminster the "British Commonwealth" consisted of the following Dominions: the Dominion of Canada, the Commonwealth of Australia, the Dominion of New Zealand, the Union of South Africa, the Irish Free State, and Newfoundland. Somewhat of a hybrid status existed in Southern Rhodesia and India.

Since that time the situation has become vastly more complicated. Newfoundland relinquished its independence in 1933, because of financial difficulties, and was administered by a United Kingdom–Newfoundland Commission until 1948, when it elected (by an unimpressive majority and on second try) to join the Dominion of Canada and thus became its tenth province on April 1, 1949.

Ireland, never happy in any form of association with England, rapidly shook off all vestiges of its former bondage. It had become a Free State in 1922. In 1937 it proclaimed a new constitution in which the state, then called Eire, was declared to be "sovereign," "independent," and "democratic." The Governor-General was replaced by a President (Uachtaran nah Eireann) who

---

[3] 22 Geo. V, c. 4. Australia and New Zealand accepted but did not ratify the Statute.

[4] Therefore the Dominions had to be consulted in questions concerning the succession to the throne and similar questions. This point was brought out by Prime Minister Baldwin in the abdication crisis of 1936.

is elected by direct vote of the people and who in turn appoints the Prime Minister (Taoiseach). The Commonwealth was not mentioned at all in the 1937 constitution, but Art. 29 empowered the government to join any group or league of states for certain purposes.

In the Second World War, Ireland chose to remain neutral and thus deprived itself of much sympathy among Allied nations, especially since its neutrality was very helpful to the Germans and tended to render Britain's convoy losses much more serious than they probably would have been had Irish naval and air bases been available. Finally in 1949, exactly thirty-three years after the outbreak of the famous "Easter Rebellion," the last remnants of dominion status were shed, and Eire became officially the Republic of Ireland.

Burma, a former colony, chose to become independent on October 17, 1947 (effective January 6, 1948) and is not a member of the Commonwealth. Another colony, Ceylon, became a Dominion in 1948. But a new status—if that term is appropriate—was assumed by the former Indian empire.

India had first come under British rule through the efforts of a number of adventurers organized in the powerful East India Company. Robert Clive routed the Indians under Siraj-ud-daula at the battle of Plassey in 1757 and established British supremacy. As a result of mismanagement, which had been demonstrated during the long trial of Warren Hastings and in the writings of such famous men as the historian Lord Macaulay, a bloody mutiny broke out in 1857, which was repressed by most cruel means. But a year later, the Crown found it advisable to take over control from the East India Company, and in 1877 Prime Minister Disraeli (Lord Beaconsfield) persuaded Queen Victoria to assume the title of Empress of India.

From 1858 to 1919 India was directly governed by the Crown, *i.e.*, the British government. However, there was a growing amount of representation of Indians in legislative councils. In December, 1919, the Government of India Act was passed by Parliament, establishing partial self-government in the provinces and greatly increasing representation at the top. The Government of India Act of 1935 established virtually complete provincial self-government and greatly increased self-government at the top. The Act of 1935 also envisaged a federation of provinces and princely states, which, however, did not materialize until after independence was won. Until then, these developments toward self-government involved only British India proper, while the states had their own arrangements. This was not an inconsiderable portion, as 24 per cent of India's population of 388,997,955 and 45.3 per cent of its area of 1,581,410 squares miles [5] belonged to the states.[6]

---

[5] Figures based on the 1941 census.

[6] The Indian states ranged all the way from some comprising only a few square miles to Hyderabad, which was as large as Kansas, with 82,000 square miles and 16,000,000 inhabitants.

The agitation for independence had been largely carried by the so-called National Congress party.[7] Its principal guiding spirit was Mohandas Gandhi, who combined the unusual qualities of saint, seer, and shrewd politician.

The outbreak of the Second World War sent India on the home stretch of its road to independence. The provincial ministers who belonged to the Congress party resigned in 1939 in protest against Britain taking India into the war without consulting the Indian people. An extremist group, headed by Subhas Chandra Bose, even went so far as to go over to Britain's enemies and fought on the side of Japan and the Axis powers.

In 1939 and 1940 Britain made two offers to India designed to grant greater self-government and a larger share in the determination of war policies on the part of Indians. Eventual dominion status after the war was envisaged. These proposals culminated in the Cripps Mission of 1942. Sir Stafford Cripps, a member of the War Cabinet and trouble shooter extraordinary, was sent to India to sound out the Indian leaders about their attitude toward a plan adopted by the cabinet. It stated that "the object is the creation of a new Indian Union which shall constitute a Dominion, associated with the United Kingdom and the other Dominions by a common allegiance to the Crown, but equal to them in every respect, in no way subordinate in any aspect of its domestic or external affairs." [8] After dominion status had been achieved, Sir Stafford explained, India would be free to leave the Commonwealth altogether if it wished.

A number of extraordinary difficulties arose. The Cripps proposal envisaged a possibility by which areas not wishing to join the future Indian Dominion could set up their own constituent assemblies or, after having acceded, could later secede from the Indian Union. This was a concession to the Moslem minority [9] powerfully led by the Moslem League under Mohammed Ali Jinnah, who was fearful of the consequences of Hindu domination. But the Congress leadership wanted all of India or nothing and rejected this point, while the Moslem League held that the proposal gave recognition to the principle of one united India and thus allegedly sounded the death knell of their dream of a separate Moslem state, Pakistan.[10] Thus both groups rejected the Cripps proposal.

[7] Contrary to some impressions in America, the National Congress party is a political party, not a congress in the usual sense. It was founded in 1885 by an Englishman, A. O. Hume.

[8] *Draft Declaration for Discussion with Indian Leaders,* Mar. 30, 1942, Cmd. 6350. For a most useful and detailed account of developments up to 1945, see Raleigh Parkin, *India Today,* Montreal, 1945.

[9] The census of 1941 reported 206,117,000 Hindus (53 per cent) plus 48,813,000 Scheduled (depressed, untouchable, etc.) Castes, 94,390,000 Moslems (24.3 per cent), 5,691,000 Sikhs, 6,317,000 Christians, and 27,670,000 others.

[10] Meaning "land of the pure" but its letters stand for the names of the various provinces.

Another part of the Cripps plan which aroused resentment was the suggestion that the Indian Dominion or Dominions should sign special treaties guaranteeing the rights of minorities. This was indignantly rejected by both sides as showing lack of faith in their ability to establish justice. Moreover, the British wished to retain control over the armed forces and foreign affairs for the duration of the war, a view which all Indian groups rejected.

The conference ended in a triangular deadlock between Great Britain, the Congress party, and the Moslem League, and on August 8, 1942, the All-India Congress Committee adopted the famous "Quit India" Resolution.

Further proposals were submitted by Viceroy Lord Wavell in June, 1945, and foundered on conflicting claims of the Congress and the Moslem League.

The defeat of the Conservative government in 1945 had far-reaching consequences for India. L. S. Amery, the Conservative Secretary of State for India, who had been thoroughly detested by the Indian leaders, left office and was replaced by Lord Pethick-Lawrence, of the Labor party. Lord Wavell was directed to renew negotiations, and he appointed an executive council, fifteen of whose twenty-one members were representative Indian leaders. This was accepted.

On February 20, 1947, the British government announced its intention to grant India its freedom, and on June 3 of the same year revealed its decision to partition India into two separate entities, with August 15 to be the new independence day. The Indians had already set up a constituent assembly, and despite enormous difficulties, they and the Moslem League finally accepted the British proposals.

The appropriate bill passed Parliament on July 18, 1947. Everything in India was divided between India and Pakistan, from troops right down to typewriters and paper clips. This process was not smooth, and was followed by bloody riots, termed "communal" because they involved fighting between religious and racial communities.[11] Over 8,000,000 terrified people crossed the border in each direction. Even an age like ours, which had become accustomed to cruelty, found the Indian spectacle a chilling experience. Rioting eventually died down under the shock of Gandhi's assassination in 1948, although later flare-ups occurred, especially in Bengal.

Most princely states declared their accession either to India or to Pakistan and were merged with adjacent provinces or formed various types of combinations, such as the six big "unions" of the larger states. A few of the largest continue to exist as component parts of the Indian Union. Hyderabad was brought into India by force in 1949, while Kashmir is in dispute between India and Pakistan—a dispute which the United Nations is trying to solve.

India was committed to the adoption of a republican form of government. It may be surmised that Jawaharlal Nehru, India's Prime Minister and prin-

[11] The biggest difference is neither religious, nor racial, but cultural.

cipal leader, was quite prepared to accept dominion status, but nationalist pressure and the wording of the new Indian Constitution demanded the proclamation of a republic, which took place in January 26, 1950. Therefore a new formula had to be found if India wished to remain in the Commonwealth. A Commonwealth Conference—the new title for the former Imperial Conferences—was held in London in April, 1949, and adopted the following declaration:

. . . The Governments of the United Kingdom, Canada, Australia, New Zealand, South Africa, India, Pakistan and Ceylon, whose countries are united as members of the British Commonwealth of Nations and owe a common allegiance to the Crown, which is also the symbol of their free association, have considered the impending constitutional changes in India.

The Government of India have informed the other governments of the Commonwealth of the intention of the Indian people that, under the new Constitution which is about to be adopted, India shall become a sovereign independent republic. The Government of India have, however, declared and affirmed India's desire to continue her full membership of the Commonwealth of Nations and her acceptance of the King as the symbol of the free association of its independent member nations and, as such, the head of the Commonwealth.

The governments of the other countries of the Commonwealth, the basis of whose membership of the Commonwealth is not hereby changed, accept and recognize India's continuing membership in accordance with the terms of this declaration.

Accordingly the United Kingdom, Canada, Australia, New Zealand, South Africa, India, Pakistan and Ceylon hereby declare that they remain united as free and equal members of the Commonwealth of Nations, freely cooperating in the pursuit of peace, liberty and progress. . . .

It will be noted that this significant declaration introduces a number of innovations. The section dealing with the past speaks of a "common allegiance to the Crown" and of a "British Commonwealth of Nations." The section dealing with the present, after India has become a republic, speaks only of the "acceptance of the King as the symbol of the free association of its [the Commonwealth's] independent nations." The King (or Queen) is however the "head of the Commonwealth." The word "Dominion" is carefully excluded, and the new association is referred to as the "Commonwealth of Nations," the word "British" having been dropped.

The Commonwealth has thus become a smaller—and, one might add, more successful—United Nations. In the field of legislation, the members of the Commonwealth enact their own laws exclusively. No longer may the Parliament in London legislate with binding effect in the territories of the Commonwealth overseas unless the particular country in question specifically requests it. Even then, the member of the Commonwealth may repeal such a law with regard to its own land at any time. It is also now a "convention" of the constitution that the London Parliament shall not enact laws which affect another member of the Commonwealth without consulting the government concerned.

Although most of the constitutions of the Dominions were originally enacted formally as acts of the British Parliament, like the British North America Act, the Dominions have generally enacted legislation, ratified as a matter of form by the British Parliament, according to which the amendment of those constitutions is solely a matter for the Dominion concerned. In Canada this right extends only to federal matters, and constitutional amendments concerning the provinces and a few other matters would still have to be ratified by the British Parliament. This is a matter of form only. There is no intention on the part of the British Parliament to take sides in a Dominion's constitutional issues. Comparable situations also exist in Australia and New Zealand, but all these residues of past imperial realities have little practical effect today.

Those members of the Commonwealth which have retained dominion status and thus continue to recognize the Monarch as their common sovereign continue to have the Monarch's representative, the Governor-General, in their capitals. In years past, Governors-General have exercised prerogatives which would never be permitted to the Queen in the United Kingdom. In particular, they have, on occasion, vetoed or "reserved" bills. Now this right is in disuse. The Governor-General still gives the assent to all bills, but it is quite impossible for him to refuse. In India, of course, there is no governor-general, since India is a republic. There, the head of state is an elected president.

Governors-General are appointed by the Crown, but in all cases they are nominated by the Commonwealth government concerned. Some Governors-General hail from the United Kingdom, while others are natives of the Dominion in which they serve. The Dominion governments actually select the Governor-General, who is then duly appointed by the Crown.

In their executive functions, the Dominions are as free as in their legislative powers. The fiction of "royal" action is preserved via the Governor-General, but such action takes place only on the advice of responsible ministers, just as in the United Kingdom—but of course these are Dominion, not United Kingdom, ministers. The Monarch therefore may on occasion act technically in contradiction to himself. For instance, during the period of 1939 to 1945 the King was at peace in Eire, then still a Dominion of sorts, but he was at war in all the rest of the Commonwealth and Empire.

Being fully sovereign and independent, all members of the Commonwealth are in full command of their own foreign relations. They receive and send ambassadors, ministers, and lesser diplomatic representatives, and they are all members of the United Nations, several of them having served or serving as members of the Security Council. A special relationship exists between them and the United Kingdom. Although such relations are "foreign relations" for all practical purposes, they are not handled through the usual channels of the Foreign Office and diplomatic representatives but are in the hands of the Secretary of State for Commonwealth Relations in London and of the various Commonwealth ministers for external affairs.[12] Instead of diplomatic agents, High Commissioners act as chief representatives on both sides.

A few tenuous strings between the United Kingdom and the Commonwealth nations are preserved in the field of judicial appeal. The Judicial Committee of the Privy Council is the highest court of appeal for the Empire. However, only Australia, New Zealand, and Ceylon still permit appeal to the Privy Council.[13]

One cannot truly speak of a common policy of the Commonwealth, either in foreign or in domestic affairs. Not only is there no common authority to impose uniformity of action, but the interests of the Commonwealth countries concerned have sometimes been at cross purposes. The sharp antagonism between India and Pakistan came close to open war over the Kashmir question, and relations are still extremely tense. India and the Union of South Africa are also constantly at loggerheads over the treatment of Indians in South Africa. The United Kingdom has shown some unhappiness over the defense agreement between Australia, New Zealand, and the United States.

To iron out some of these and lesser problems, occasional Commonwealth Conferences (formerly called Imperial Conferences) are called, usually at the initiative of the British government. But these conferences constitute neither a common executive nor a common legislature. They are merely diplomatic meetings between the representatives of sovereign states. Yet the relationship between these countries is different from ordinary diplomatic relationships. There is no constitution, no law, no rule to bind them together, but there are often a common history, a similarity of procedures, an unspoken affinity which defies definition. Somehow these countries feel a bond, and this sentiment is stronger than any treaty.

OTHER PARTS OF THE EMPIRE

While the members of the Commonwealth of Nations are without doubt the most important parts of the Empire, they are not the only ones. There are a great many Crown Colonies, which are administered in various fashions by

---

[12] The term "external" rather than "foreign" was adopted because their competence included relations with the United Kingdom, which is not regarded as a foreign nation.

[13] In 1940 the Supreme Court of Canada held that the Parliament of Canada had power to abolish the right of appeal to the Privy Council. This was upheld by the Privy Council [A.C. 127 (1947)]. In 1949 the Canadian Parliament enacted the Supreme Court Act (*The New York Times,* Dec. 23, 1949) making the Supreme Court of Canada the final Court of Appeals.

officials of the Colonial Office, all of which have certain but varying measures of self-government. In some regions this degree of self-government is a very high one: Southern Rhodesia comes very close to dominion status, and its foreign relations are handled through the Commonwealth Relations Office and not the Colonial Office. Malta, distinguished by heroic action during the Second World War, received a new constitution in 1947 which gave it near-dominion status. There are also "condominia," areas held in common with other countries.

Some areas are termed "protectorates" because they are technically not British possessions but are subject to British control, under limitations determined by treaty. Such British control always extends over military matters and foreign affairs, but it also penetrates to varying degrees into the domestic affairs of the protectorate. In actuality, there is little substantive difference between protectorates and Crown Colonies.

A new type of overseas possession was introduced after the First World War in the form of the mandate system, which later, under the United Nations and with significant changes, became the network of trusteeships. Trust territories are former enemy possessions whose relationship to the trustee is determined by treaty between the United Nations and the trustee. However, the conditions imposed by the United Nations Charter and the above-mentioned treaty are not too stringent. Different from the mandate system of the League of Nations, the trusteeship system of the United Nations permits armament of trust territories for purposes of self-defense and related objectives, and a trust territory may be designated a "strategic area," in which case military and naval use is virtually unlimited.

Britain is responsible to the United Nations, especially to the Trusteeship Council, for its stewardship in the trust territories.[14] Unfortunately, however, the Trusteeship Council, together with all other organs of the United Nations, has been made a battleground for East-West controversy. The British feel that much of the criticism which Britain has had to endure has been caused by political maneuvering, unrelated to the facts. They have therefore taken a cool attitude toward the Trusteeship Council and have curtailed the right of the United Nations to send inspectors to trust territories. Since none of Britain's trust territories appears to be capable of immediate independence, it is probably safe to assume that they will soon be indistinguishable from ordinary Crown Colonies.

It is extremely difficult to classify the governmental system of British overseas possessions because of their large variety and the constant change in their status. There is always a governor whose powers may be very large or

[14] That the obligations under the trusteeship system are not empty words may be gathered from the strenuous attempts of the Union of South Africa to incorporate her trust territory, the former German South West Africa, into her territory—an endeavor which has been strongly opposed by the natives.

more limited depending on the advancement of the colony concerned. There is also usually an executive council with advisory function, on which natives may or may not be represented. More advanced colonies have legislative assemblies with varying powers. Local government is usually left to local chieftains with varying degrees of British supervision. There are also colonial courts whose verdicts may be appealed to the Judicial Committee of the Privy Council in London.

The general tenor is constant advancement toward ever greater degrees of self-government. One of the most outstanding pioneering ventures in that respect has been the recently (1950) instituted self-government for the Gold Coast in Africa.[15]

Another trend in British colonial administration has been toward favoring regionalism. Most significant has been the attempt of Southern Rhodesia, Northern Rhodesia, and Nyasaland to form a Central African Federation. Other regional councils have been formed for British East Africa (Uganda, Kenya, and Tanganyika) and the Caribbeans. Still another approach has been the creation of a Commissioner-General for Southeast Asia who does not supersede the existing colonial administrations but helps to coordinate their particularly difficult problems. Closely related is an ambitious regional development scheme known as the Colombo Plan,[16] which envisages a long-range program of rehabilitation, economic improvement, and technical assistance in Southeast Asia through Commonwealth cooperation.

The future of the British Empire [17] is not easily divined. Unrest and desire for independence may be detected in many parts. The spark of nationalism, fanned by the picture of the white man's humiliation by the Japanese, and by growing Communist agitation, is scorching the imperial tree. The need for the British government's intervention in British Guiana in 1953 to remove a locally elected government accused of Communist tendencies is a recent high light. Many observers feel that the age of colonial empires is gone forever, and regard the British Empire as a typically British anachronism. Be that as it may, there is no reason to write off the Empire for a long time to come. Not every nation is capable of immediate self-government, and there are many areas where a British departure would be followed by something worse, as Burma has starkly demonstrated. There may well be some shrinkage, and more nations may graduate from colonial to dominion status, but even today "the sun never sets on the British Empire." Undoubtedly the Empire will continue to play a significant role for a long time to come.

[15] John R. E. Carr-Gregg, *Self-Rule in Africa, Recent Advances in the Gold Coast,* International Conciliation Pamphlet No. 473, New York, 1951.

[16] John R. E. Carr-Gregg, *The Colombo Plan, A Commonwealth Program for Southeast Asia,* International Conciliation Pamphlet 467, New York, 1951.

[17] Whether one can still speak of an empire is debatable, since India does not consider herself in any way "under the King's dominion."

Even more obscure and involved is the future of that part of the Empire which is now officially termed the "Commonwealth of Nations." It is now nothing less than a league of states associating with one another freely for certain purposes. The King, now symbol and head of the Commonwealth, is hardly the factor which causes the survival of that unique combination. Powerful bonds are provided by the common heritage of language and especially legal, governmental, and ideological institutions and concepts. Naturally such a common spirit is less in evidence in South Africa, India, Pakistan, and Ceylon than in the other more English-speaking member states of the Commonwealth. But even in those countries the British past is plainly visible. In an excess of nationalistic exuberance—quite understandable in a nation which has just won its freedom—certain Indian leaders have claimed that 190 years of British rule have scarcely left a trace on their country, but their constitution, their institutions of law and government, and even their lingua franca cast doubt on these assertions.

Other bonds, no less powerful, are provided by common interests. Close economic ties, symbolized by the "sterling bloc," have existed for some time. The United Kingdom used to be the Dominions' chief market and this is still the case.

The Commonwealth is deeply concerned over the near-violent nature of the Soviet-American controversy. Many in Great Britain and in the Commonwealth nations would like to create a kind of "third force" for the purpose of modifying the impact of the struggle. Defense too is a common consideration, although the United States naturally plays a significant role in that picture.[18]

[18] The most useful recent works on the Commonwealth are A. Brady, *Democracy in the Dominions,* Toronto, 1952, 2d ed., and W. I. Jennings, *The British Commonwealth of Nations,* London, 1948. See also Sir Ivar Jennings and C. M. Young, *Constitutional Laws of the Commonwealth,* Oxford, 1952, 2d ed.; A. B. Keith, *The Dominions as Sovereign States: Their Constitutions and Government,* London, 1938; K. C. Wheare, *The Statute of Westminster and Dominion Status,* Oxford, 1949, 4th ed., and *Federal Government,* New York, 1951, 2d ed.; H. V. Evatt, *The King and His Dominions,* Oxford, 1936; Sir E. Barker, *Ideas and Ideals of the British Empire,* London, 1941; W. Y. Elliott, H. Duncan Hall, *et al., The British Commonwealth at War,* New York, 1943; Royal Institute of International Affairs, *The British Empire,* London, 1938, 2d ed.; Sir A. E. Zimmern, *The Third British Empire,* Oxford, 1934, 3d ed.; W. M. C. Hailey, *Britain and Her Dependencies,* London, 1945; and H. V. Hodson, *Twentieth Century Empire,* London, 1948.

Chapter 8

PARTIES AND POLITICS

Preceding chapters have pointed to the fact that the smooth operation of the British constitutional system depends on the existence of two principal, responsible political parties. It is the two-party system which usually creates clear majorities and therefore clear political alternatives between which the people may decide. It is the unity of government and majority party which ordinarily provides a stable government, in contrast to the dismal records of some coalition governments.

It is through the political parties and their network of organizations that the public pulse is constantly being felt, and changes and adjustments are constantly being initiated as a result of the sentiments which reach the surface in such a process. To be sure, each candidate for Parliament is an individual with his own record to defend, but that record is far less important to the voter than the program and the record of the candidate's party. Now it might be argued that these programs are not established by broad masses of people but by small committees, although they may be approved by larger gatherings. This is of course true to a certain extent. No program on earth can ever be written by more than a handful of people. But it is not true to imply that such programs are created in a vacuum. Every political party wants to get its candidates elected. Every political party wants to be in office or be returned to office. This is possible only if it receives a large number of votes; every party is therefore sensitive and receptive to wishes and demands expressed by significant elements among the electorate.

Moderation

This constant process of new intellectual growth from the "grass roots" would, however, have only limited scope if the British parties were strict class parties. In that case, ideas could come only from a relatively narrow section of the population and they would not necessarily have to be heeded, as the members of a specific class would have little choice but to support their class party. Fortunately this is not the case, despite the common belief abroad that British parties are class parties. The Labor party is largely supported by the trade-unions and hence by the workers, and the Conservative party has many

149

of the business and financial interests behind it, but two important factors greatly mitigate this picture. First, not all workers vote Labor, and not all businessmen support the Conservatives. Consequently the Conservatives have to be mindful of the workingman, and Labor cannot completely disregard business. In the second place, there is a vast mass of people between the laboring classes and the moneyed interests. No generic term can cover it; it is the middle class, the white-collar workers, the clerks, the lower to middle civil servants. They owe allegiance to neither party, but they are numerous enough to determine the outcome of elections. No party can hope to receive a majority by ignoring them or by relying solely on one class.

This has important consequences. Party lines are easily and frequently crossed, especially by the middle classes. A party in power may expect to be in opposition a few years hence, while the existing minority party may look forward with some confidence to the day when it will be in office. This has an extremely sobering effect on both. The majority party must remain mindful of the rights of those who occupy the Opposition benches, for sooner or later it will be sitting there. The minority party must guard against extreme, purely propagandistic, slogans without practical value, for some day they would come back to haunt it at an inopportune moment.

Another important result of this situation is that since both major parties must appeal to substantially the same, decisive electorate, their differences of views cannot be too wide. This does not mean that there have not been most bitter contests. The repeal of the corn laws and the issue of Irish home rule divided the country deeply. But the division was not solely between the parties but also within them, and it was not permanent. The landowners who wanted to keep the oppressive corn laws supported the Tories, but it was a Tory leader, Sir Robert Peel, who effected the repeal of the laws. William Gladstone, the great Liberal leader, suffered several defeats over his advocacy of Irish home rule, but the Parliament which gave home rule to Ireland had a Conservative majority. The Conservative party was quite willing in recent years to accept the Labor party's considerable socialization measures, although it would not have gone further in that direction had it been returned to office in the elections of 1950.

Both parties have long been steeped in this tradition.[1] Although precise definitions may not be found in party literature, there is no question but that both political parties and of course the remnants of the nearly defunct Liberal party understand thoroughly the respective roles of government and Opposition. There must be a government or chaos would reign. Therefore the Opposition will make a spirited attack upon the government program, and the government will expect and meet it. The government will not try to shut off debate, for that would imply conceding the Opposition's point. A genuine

[1] For a brief but illuminating discussion, see W. I. Jennings, *The British Constitution*, Cambridge, 1947, pp. 31–36.

parliamentary life depends, therefore, on the existence of a vigorous Opposition.

On the other hand, the Opposition recognizes that the country must have a government which must be able to govern. The Opposition will therefore oppose, but it will not ordinarily obstruct. After the debate has had its course and the minority has spent its maximum effort to influence the course of policy, the division (vote) on the measure finally settles the issue. Obstruction, filibusters, and similar devices by which a minority may try to frustrate the will of the majority are extremely rare in the United Kingdom. They may be brought into play, at unusual and rare instances, when the Opposition feels that the government is taking an unfair advantage of its position. But ordinarily there is quite a sense of fairness and a mutual and profound understanding of proper democratic procedure.

A good example is the story of the bill for the nationalization of the iron and steel industry, which preceded the election campaign of 1950. The Opposition had fought previous nationalization bills but had not seriously attempted to stop the government. However, the nationalization of a complicated, vast, and on the whole successful industry was another matter. The Conservative party felt that the nationalization of steel would affect the entire economy, and to a far greater degree than had been the case by previous nationalization bills. It felt that the government's mandate, received in 1945, did not extend to such actions. It promised a bitter fight, which could have lasted for some time, with the help of the predominantly Conservative House of Lords. The Labor leaders conceded the point in effect, though other reasons entered too. They made an agreement with the Conservative party by which the steel bill was passed, but its execution postponed until after the general election. Thus, the nationalization of the steel industry became an election issue of the first magnitude.

Most of these rules are based on experience and tradition. If all the rules of the Parliamentary game were to be put down in black and white and with the utmost precision, huge loopholes would appear and frightful confusion would ensue. Happily, the British distrust logic and precision, as we have seen, and trust experience. This does not mean, of course, that the party struggle is not spirited, and at times even fierce. But it is never permitted to make orderly government impossible or to suppress the right to oppose.

TWO-PARTY SYSTEM

The existence of a two-party system in Britain is an historical accident which the plurality system of elections and the single-member constituency (district) have helped to preserve.[2] Under the British (and American)

[2] For a different view, see Leslie Lipson, "The Two-Party System in British Politics," *American Political Science Review*, Vol. XLVII (1953), pp. 337–358.

electoral system, third-party candidates are not easily elected because a plurality is sufficient to send a candidate to the House of Commons. Third-party candidates may accumulate a sizable national vote, but they rarely carry many constituencies and consequently a vote for them—unless cast strictly as an act of protest—is largely wasted. The British tend to be pragmatic thinkers rather than doctrinaires, do not generally care to waste anything, and consequently look upon elections as a contest between two possible governments, the incumbents and the hopeful Opposition. The third party, not being a possible government, is thus increasingly ignored. Third parties have an opportunity to arrive in front only if they come upon the scene at a time when one of the major parties begins to disintegrate. This favored the Labor party, which was able to replace the Liberal party as the second party and thereby return to the two-party system.

It must also be remembered that general Parliamentary elections are the sole opportunity by which the mass of the British people may determine policy. There is no popular initiative and referendum, there is no recall, there is nothing like an American presidential election. All issues must be determined in the Parliamentary elections. Consequently, popular attention is focused on a few key issues: whether there should be a return to limited Socialism; whether there should be more or less economic planning; whether the standard of living and general economic security would eventually increase through more austerity and planning, or whether there ought to be some relaxation and confidence in a freer play of economic forces; whether Clement Attlee or Winston Churchill shall be in charge of the country for some crucial four or five years to come. Between these pairs of fairly clear alternatives, a third party, advocating what seem to many to be half measures, is likely to be ground into pulp.

In recent years the shift to an even more pronounced two-party system has become still clearer. The House of Commons of 1945 had some scattered Liberals of different factions, two Communists, two Irish Nationalists, and sixteen Independents. The election of 1950 left only nine Liberals and two Irish Nationalists outside the two big parties. In 1951 the Liberals were reduced to six while the Irish Nationalists maintained themselves. No Independents, no splinter groups, were elected. A closer view of these events produces even more startling conclusions. Of the six Liberals, five were elected without Conservative opposition and with Conservative help. A third Irish Nationalist is a member of the Irish Labor party and may be counted statistically as a Labor member. He won with active Labor support. Thus only three members of Parliament won election independent of one of the major parties.[3]

These events naturally have intensified the desire among Liberals to bring about a change in the electoral system which works so obviously to their disadvantage. A system of proportional representation—that of the single

[3] Ivor Bulmer-Thomas, *The Party System in Great Britain*, London, 1953, pp. 83–91.

transferable vote—and a majority system with an alternative vote [4] have been favored. But while such changes would render fairer results in the distribution of seats in Parliament, it would make the very small Liberal party the decisive element in the government because of the even balance of the two major parties. Such an outcome would certainly not be a just reflection of the will of the British voter. Fortunately, the British, with their political maturity and their preference for proven experience rather than abstract justice, are highly unlikely to change the present electoral system.

The disappearance of splinter groups and Independents and the absorption of their voters by the major parties has furthered the development of a situation in which the two major parties are not only nearly even in national voting strength and in Parliament but in which a large number of electoral contests are won by small margins. This has greatly intensified the energy with which the parties undertake their campaigns. It has also put the British system of government to a severe test because the elections of 1950 and 1951 seem to demonstrate that governments with large majorities may not be expected for some time.

The two major political parties of Britain, the Labor party and the Conservative party, have certain organizational features in common. Both are highly centralized, and direction comes down from the top, although the Labor party is somewhat more sensitive to rank-and-file sentiment, and its organization allows a better opportunity for "ground swells" than does that of the Conservative party.

The Development of the Contemporary Party System

It is hardly possible to speak of a modern party system prior to the Reform Bill of 1832, although its origin lies further back. Jennings suggests that the beginnings of political parties may be seen in the Reformation and the eventual emergence of the Tories as the "Church party." A more common date is the restoration of the Stuarts in 1660. The Tories were the partisans of the King, while the Whigs were the spokesmen of Parliament. But since one party was in Parliament and the other outside, the situation was quite different from the present one. The final victory of Parliament in 1689 made this division obsolete.

The French Revolution profoundly affected English public opinion and

[4] A system by which the voter designates an alternative if the candidate favored by him in first place does not win. Alternate votes are added until a candidate has a majority. The Proportional Representation Society, quoted by Bulmer-Thomas, *op. cit.*, p. 103, figured out that under that system the Conservatives would have received 302, Labor 303, Liberals 15, others 4, while the actual results were 320, 296, 6, and 2. Under proportional representation the Liberals would have been the arbiters of the situation. Such conclusions are, however, inaccurate because a change in the electoral system would also change some voting habits, and the Liberal vote would be likely to increase further.

divided Parliament into those who took a serious view of the French "danger" —men like William Pitt and Edmund Burke—against those who were less concerned, like Charles James Fox. In this may be seen the beginning of a new party division between a more conservative and a more liberal party, the former imperialistic, the latter disinclined toward foreign ventures and stressing reforms at home. However, until 1832 both parties were essentially aristocratic and dominated by a few great families.

The Industrial Revolution brought about both social and political changes. A common front developed between the manufacturers, who were inadequately represented in Parliament and who wanted free trade, and the workers, who wanted free trade and the repeal of the corn laws.

The Reform Bill of 1832 was carried through by the Whigs and a dissident Tory group, but the outstanding spokesmen were outsiders like Richard Cobden and John Bright, powerfully supported by the theories of Adam Smith.

The debate over the Reform Bill was the first true Parliamentary controversy between two rival Parliamentary parties. The King remained neutral and followed the advice of his Prime Minister. Also significant was the fact that the Act of 1832 required the registration of voters, which gave rise to political registration societies. These had the purpose of "getting out the vote" for the parties of their choice and thus were the origins of local party organizations, although the nomination of candidates remained left to chance, the desires of public-spirited men, and the endeavors of men of influence.[5]

Benjamin Disraeli, later Lord Beaconsfield, succeeded in winning the Tory party away from extreme reaction. In that spirit he was responsible for a number of health and welfare measures as well as trade-union and factory acts. It was he who carried to victory the Reform Bill of 1867, which enfranchised a far greater number of people, especially among the working population, than the Act of 1832 had done. The increase in the electorate, as well as the lessons learned by Disraeli from the defeat of his party in 1852, pointed the way toward tighter central party organization. However, it was the Birmingham Liberal Association which, under the leadership of Joseph Chamberlain and his assistant Francis Schnadhorst, became the prototype of an organized political party. It had dues-paying members and ward committees, and it elected delegates to an executive committee which chose the official party candidate for Parliament.

The bitter controversy over the Irish Home Rule Bill caused a certain realignment of political forces. Part of the Liberal party, especially the great Whig families, seceded and joined the Conservatives as "Unionists."[6] Thus

[5] G. M. Trevelyan, *The Two-party System in English Political History,* Oxford, 1926.

[6] As a result, the Conservative party officially bore the name Unionist for many decades. It never became popular and was officially abandoned on Winston Churchill's suggestion.

class lines were more sharply drawn between the two great parties, Liberal and Conservative.

The ambitious social reform program of the Liberal governments of William Gladstone and Lord Rosebery ran into difficulties as a result of the slim majorities those governments maintained. This revealed the need for strengthening party leadership, and an executive committee was set up in 1896 charged with preparing the agenda for the meetings of the representative council (National Convention) and the general committee of the party. To preserve the committee's independence, Members of Parliament were excluded from it. This actually resulted in weakening the committee and strengthening the Parliamentary party leadership, a situation which has been typical of British parties ever since.

The great Liberal victory of 1906 brought a great many social and political reforms which changed the country substantially and which are associated with the names of Sir Henry Campbell-Bannerman and Herbert Asquith, but especially with that of David Lloyd George. The reform of the House of Lords, the Trade Disputes Act, and a vast array of social legislation marked this era.

The First World War put a halt to domestic reforms, and in 1915 an all-party coalition government took over.

The great coalition proved successful in war but disintegrated in peace and broke the back of the Liberal party. Some dissident Liberals, calling themselves Independent Liberals, split off and together with the new Labor party returned to the Opposition benches. The Conservatives and regular Liberals remained united, but in the 1918 election the Conservatives obtained a majority of seats within the coalition as well as in the House of Commons. When the next elections came in 1922 the Conservatives, naturally enough, decided to free themselves from the coalition shackles and by their victory returned the country to the familiar system of responsible party government. The Liberal party never recovered and in 1924 decided to support a minority Labor government, thereby demonstrating that Conservatives and Labor, not Conservatives and Liberals, were the real alternative before the voters. Labor thus became officially the second party, while the remnants of the once-great Liberal party moved steadily toward the outer darkness.

When small segments of the working class rose to political consciousness in the first half of the nineteenth century, they naturally allied themselves with the rising Liberal party. As early as 1868 an attempt was made to elect Labor members to Parliament, but failure resulted. The lessons of this were drawn by the Trade-Union Congress, which had already created a Parliamentary committee for general lobbying purposes. Also individual unions had occasionally been able to elect some of their leaders to Parliament—usually with the help of the friendly neutrality of the Liberal party. One of them received its baptism of fire in the 1874 election, in which it ran thirteen candidates but elected only two. By 1892 fifteen Labor leaders were elected; the number was reduced to twelve in 1895.

While the trade-unions prepared the mass basis of the future Labor party, the intellectual direction and programmatic crystallization came from other sources. They were the Social Democratic Federation,[7] the Fabian Society, and the Independent Labor party. The Social Democratic Federation, led by Henry M. Hyndman, practiced a somewhat unscientific Marxism. It became a victim of factionalism and a major part of it became the British Socialist party, the nucleus of the later British Commonwealth party.[8] The influence of the Social Democratic Federation was negligible among the masses, but it stressed the need for action as a socialist technique when that approach was not generally understood. Moreover many men who later rose to roles of prominence once belonged to the Federation.[9]

Of far greater significance was the so-called Fabian Society.[10] It originated within an ethical and utopian organization called the Fellowship of the New Life. A small group of members broke off and founded the Fabian Society in 1883. In the next few years they were joined by that group of outstanding people who gave the Society its direction, George Bernard Shaw, Sidney Webb, H. G. Wells, Graham Wallas, Annie Besant, and others. The Society first attracted attention through the publication of the Fabian Essays [11] in 1889 which were followed by a large number of tracts designed for popular consumption.

The Fabian Society set the course which was later followed by the Labor party. It established the dominant ideology of the party and thereby set it markedly aside from other Socialist parties on the Continent. The core of Fabianism was the theory of Sidney Webb that the progress from capitalism to socialism was part of a gradual development which already began in the period of capitalist domination. With this theory it set itself in sharp contrast to the Marxist doctrine—then propagated by the Social Democratic Federation—according to which the increasing misery of the working class and the inability of capitalism to solve its inner contradictions were bound to

[7] Founded as the Democratic Federation in 1881, it took the name Social Democratic in 1884, emulating the Socialist parties of other countries, especially Germany.

[8] Hyndman and his close followers rejoined the Labor party.

[9] M. Beer, *A History of British Socialism*, London, 1948; J. Clayton, *The Rise and Decline of Socialism in Great Britain, 1889–1924*, London, 1926; G. D. H. Cole, *A Short History of the British Working Class Movement, 1789–1927*, London, 1932; and T. Rothstein, *From Chartism to Labourism*, London, 1929.

[10] Named after a Roman general, Quintus Fabius Maximus, called Cunctator (the hesitant), who defeated Hannibal's Carthaginian forces by delaying tactics. His name was adopted as a symbol for gradualism.

[11] Newly edited by G. B. Shaw, London, 1931. See also E. R. Pease, *History of the Fabian Society*, London, 1925, 2d ed.; G. B. Shaw, *The Fabian Society, Its Early History*, Fabian Tract No. 41, London, 1892; for a Marxist criticism, see L. D. Trotsky, *Whither England?* New York, 1925.

lead to violent revolution and the radical transformation of society. In contrast to Marx's theory of increased misery, Webb pointed out that the position of the workers had actually improved and was continuing to do so by means of the numerous works of social-reform legislation which marked the end of the nineteenth and the beginning of the twentieth century. After social reform, he envisaged the next step toward socialism through a more equitable distribution of income, brought about by progressive taxation and eventual public ownership of industries. He repudiated the idea of revolution by showing that the rise of capitalism had also led to increasing governmental action on behalf of the worker.[12] Fabianism therefore denied the Marxist concept of the class struggle and relied on persuasion.

It was largely the merit of Beatrice Potter, later Mrs. Sidney Webb,[13] that the Society's attention was directed to the need for effective workers' organization. Her work and that of her husband led them to a reassessment of the importance of political action.[14] Due to their influence, the Fabian Society gave the future Labor party a political ideology and a sense of direction. It never became a mass movement; that was the contribution of the Independent Labor party which was founded by Keir Hardie, a Scottish labor leader, a fiery speaker and an effective journalist although not a profound thinker. In 1893 he was instrumental in founding the Independent Labor party, whose task it was to convince the trade-unions of the necessity for a Socialist program and for separate representation in Parliament.

Increasing dissatisfaction of trade-union leaders with the Liberal party made them receptive to his ideas. The Trade-Union Congress of 1899 adopted a resolution calling for a special congress of cooperative societies, socialist groups, and other labor organizations, in order to devise ways and means for securing the return of an increased number of Labor members to the next Parliament. The Congress met in 1900 and founded the Labor Representation Committee, whose sole task it was to secure the election of Labor representatives to Parliament.[15]

The Committee met with only indifferent success; the cooperative movement and the mineworkers remained outside; and the Social Democratic Federation withdrew. But a decision of the House of Lords holding trade-unions liable for action of their officers in carrying out a strike [16] created great bitterness among labor and caused the trade-unions to redouble their efforts for

[12] The Society also rejected Marx's theory of value—now considered untenable by many Marxists—and followed the marginal utility school of W. S. Jevons, A. Marshall, and others. This fitted well into the generally neoutilitarian philosophy of the Fabians.

[13] Margaret Cole, *Beatrice Webb,* London, 1949.

[14] Sidney and Beatrice Webb, *The History of Trade Unionism,* London, 1894, and *Industrial Democracy,* London, 1897, 2 vols.

[15] For the text of the Resolution, see D. E. McHenry, *His Majesty's Opposition,* Berkeley, 1940, p. 7.

[16] The Taff-Vale case, A.C. 426 (1901). See also Quinn v. Leathem, A.C. 495 (1901).

greater political action. As a result, in 1906, the Labor Representation Committee was renamed Labor party, and that designation has remained.

The new party succeeded in electing twenty-nine of its members to Parliament that same year. It worked in close alliance with the Liberal party and benefited from the wave of reform legislation which the Liberal majority put through the House. Its strength increased steadily despite severe financial difficulties.[17]

The First World War created a crisis in the Labor party between the integral pacifists, led by Ramsay MacDonald and Philip Snowden, and those who, like the trade-union leaders and Arthur Henderson, supported the war effort. But this split was not as serious as in other countries. The Henderson wing of the party retired from the government in 1917, and the electoral campaign of 1918 saw Labor reunited. It obtained only fifty-seven seats and most of its prominent leaders were defeated. But accident would have it that this small party became nevertheless the official opposition in the House of Commons, and this situation remained true after the elections of 1923, which broke up the once mighty Liberal party. The Conservatives had a decided plurality in the House with 258 seats against Labor's 191 and the Liberals' 158. But the Conservative government had called the election and had failed to receive a majority; by British standards, it had been repudiated by the country, and it resigned. Ramsay MacDonald, leader of the Labor party and leader of the Opposition, was called to the palace "to kiss hands" [18] and thus began the unhappy nine months of the first Labor government of Great Britain.

The fall of this minority government in 1924 came as a relief to all because it marked the return to normal majority and party government. Both Labor and the Liberals lost heavily in the 1924 election,[19] the former dropping to 152, the Liberals dropping from 158 to 42. Stanley Baldwin, supported by 415 Conservatives in the House of Commons, returned to 10 Downing Street.[20]

The following years saw increasing economic difficulties. On May 4, 1926, the Trade-Union Congress called a general strike as a countermeasure against conditions in the mining industry. But government and public reacted strongly, which was natural in a country with a tradition which prescribes that political changes should be sought only through the ballot box. The general strike was a complete failure, and after it was broken Parliament enacted the Trade Dis-

---

[17] The trade-unions had supported the party and paid modest salaries to their members in Parliament, who then received no compensation from the government. The House of Lords declared that practice illegal, Osborne v. Amalgamated Society of Railway Servants, A.C. 87 (1910). A partial remedy brought the Trade-Union Act of 1913.

[18] It is a custom that the Prime Minister-designate kiss the hand of the sovereign.

[19] In this election an important role was played by a letter purporting to have been written by G. Zinoviev, Secretary-General of the Communist International.

[20] The official residence of the Prime Minister, located just off Whitehall, the government center.

putes and Trade-Unions Act to prevent the recurrence of such a situation. Numerous restrictions were placed on the unions, especially on their right to call sympathy strikes and to use funds for political purposes. This act and adverse public reaction caused the loss of one million union members to the Labor party.

These events were soon overshadowed by the deepening world depression, and Labor gained again. In 1929 another Labor minority government appeared when the Labor party won 288 seats against the Conservatives' 260. The 59 Liberals were again able to decide the issue.

The second MacDonald government began under auspicious circumstances but suffered under Ramsay MacDonald's inability to work with his colleagues, especially with his Foreign Secretary, Arthur Henderson. Worst of all, the government proved itself utterly incapable of coping with the depression and the fearfully mounting toll of unemployed. The abandonment of the gold standard seemed indicated but was fiercely resisted by the Chancellor of the Exchequer, Philip Snowden, and by MacDonald, who was incapable of understanding fiscal policies and relied completely on Snowden.

The government came under increasing attacks from within and without. The party's left wing held the crisis to be insoluble within the capitalist order and demanded large-scale socialistic measures. The Liberals, whose support was essential, rejected these ideas and favored a policy of economy. One of the Labor ministers, Sir Oswald Mosley, Chancellor of the Duchy of Lancaster, proposed an ambitious program which was only narrowly defeated at the Llandudno conference of the Labor party in October 1930. However, his proposals, which were quite similar to many of the reforms later carried out by the Attlee government, made a deep impression, and he was elected to the party executive. He seemed destined for a top position, perhaps the top one in the Labor party, when, by one of those abrupt and inexplicable decisions which we find in history, he separated from the Labor party and founded his own "New Party." [21] Eventually he came under the influence of totalitarian ideas and founded the British Union of Fascists, was interned during the Second World War, and is of no consequence today.

The Conservative and Liberal pressure for deflationary policies was well received by MacDonald and Snowden, who were conservative at heart. An investigating committee with heavy Conservative predominance, headed by Sir George May, chairman of the Prudential Insurance Company, proposed a policy of heavy retrenchment, including drastic cuts in unemployment benefits.

In the face of this report the government showed an extraordinary incapacity to act, and it was clear that the acceptance of the May report would split the Labor party wide open. Already the Independent Labor party had reaffirmed its independent position at its Birmingham conference in 1930.

[21] Aneurin Bevan, John Strachey, and George Strauss followed Mosley but later returned to the Labor fold.

On August 23, 1931, MacDonald announced in cabinet meeting that he would present the resignation of the entire cabinet to the King. He left everybody with the impression, although it was not clearly stated, that he would be succeeded by Stanley Baldwin heading a Conservative minority government or by a Conservative-Liberal coalition.[22] But he returned from the palace with the surprising announcement that he had been entrusted with the formation of a "national," *i.e.*, coalition, government. It is generally believed that the King induced MacDonald to take this step, though it is certain that he must have found a very willing listener. MacDonald split the Labor party by this move, and only very few followed him and Snowden into the "national" government.

The cabinet of the "national" government had an equal number of Conservative and "national" Labor members (four each) with the Liberals holding two posts. But there was no question as to the men who held the upper hand and determined policy. After the "national" Labor leaders had accomplished the task assigned to them, namely, to destroy their former party, they dropped out in bewilderment or bitterness, depending on character. In the general election of 1931 the Conservatives were pleased to leave the brunt of the battle to MacDonald, Snowden, and their friends, being satisfied with reaping the rewards, which were considerable. The Labor party, disorganized, unable to put up a proper campaign because its leaders had already endorsed most of the policies which were now put into effect by the "national" government, and pursued by the most venomous attacks of its former leaders, made a poor showing and lost 2,000,000 votes. Its Parliamentary defeat was even more catastrophic. It dropped from 289 seats to 46, plus five ILP members and one Independent who went along with Labor. The Liberals lost even more votes, but through fortuitous circumstances were able to increase their representation from 59 to 72. "National" Labor managed to send 13 members into the House of Commons but only because they sailed under the coalition label; they had no following of their own and soon passed into oblivion. Despite the crisis, the Communists did not obtain a single seat.

Nor was this all. Most of Labor's leaders were defeated at the polls. Among them were Henderson, Clynes, Greenwood, Dalton, Shaw, Morrison, Isaacs, Shinwell, Bondfield, Noel Baker, Wilkinson, and Alexander. Of former cabinet members only old George Lansbury returned to take the leadership of a small, demoralized, and inexperienced group of men. His principal aides were Clement Attlee and Sir Stafford Cripps.

We have dwelt on this disaster to such an extent because it helps to explain the subsequent development of Labor and especially of the Labor government which came to power in 1945 and was returned in 1950. The Labor party

[22] For an eyewitness report, see Sidney Webb, *What Happened in 1931: A Record*, Fabian Tract 237, London, 1932, p. 8.

learned from bitter experience that it could hope to achieve little by nibbling reforms. It returned to the doctrine of its left wing, that a future Labor government could hope to accomplish its aims only by bringing about a fundamental change in the social and economic picture of Britain. The Labor party did not then and does not now advocate complete nationalization or integral planning on the Soviet model. Nor has its devotion to democratic measures been affected. But the party realizes that it must be able to influence strongly the entire economy, even the private sector, in order to solve those problems which it believes to be inherent within the capitalistic system. The policies of the Labor government after 1945 reflect these convictions.

Only the Conservative party benefited from the events of 1931. The sorry remnants of "national" labor evaporated. In the 1935 elections, its representation in the House declined to eight, and Ramsay MacDonald was overwhelmingly defeated in his own constituency of Seaham. He was handed the safe Tory seat of the Scottish universities through the intercession of Stanley Baldwin, but died in 1937. He had been obliged to hand the premiership to Baldwin in 1935.

The Liberals also suffered from the splitting disease. At first they had all joined the "national" government, with the exception of a small group around Lloyd George. But soon one section led by Sir Herbert Samuel (later Lord Samuel) went into the Opposition,[23] while another group under Sir John Simon (later Lord Simon) remained in the government and became practically indistinguishable from the Tories.

For the Labor party, troubles were not yet over. The Independent Labor party had long strained at the reins and did not want to submit to party discipline in the form of the standing orders which controlled voting in Parliament. After prolonged and fruitless discussions, the final break eventually came in 1932 when the ILP decided at the Bradford conference to secede from the Labor party. This was accomplished, not without a split in the ILP. A few seats remained under the control of this party, but in 1950 it lost them all and is now a factor of little importance.

For a while the Labor party vegetated under the Parliamentary leadership of George Lansbury, who was seventy-three years old when he became leader of Opposition in 1932. He was beloved by all, a man of the highest moral stature. But he was a convinced pacifist—a creed which was of little help in the years of Hitler's rise to power and Mussolini's increasing aggressiveness. Labor, like its brethren in other countries, had to consider what policy it should adopt in the face of this menace. The Communist agitation for joint action was vigorously opposed by the Labor party, which found little choice between Communism and Fascism. Whatever stand was taken by Socialist

[23] When the government became frankly protectionist, Snowden, by then a viscount and Lord Privy Seal, resigned too.

parties elsewhere, the British Labor party—in its overwhelming majority—always stood foursquare against Communism in all its forms.[24] In 1935 Lansbury, who insisted on his pacifism on grounds of Christian principles, was overruled by the party conference and resigned. He was succeeded by his chief lieutenant, Clement Attlee.

The elections of 1935 produced a Parliament which was to remain in office ten long years. but that could hardly have been foreseen then. The Labor party recovered partially from the 1931 shock and won 154 seats. But the Conservatives still predominated with 387, to which must be added 33 Liberal Nationals who supported the government.

Stanley Baldwin resigned in 1937, at the height of his career, before the consequences of his vacillating foreign and military policy became obvious. His successor was Neville Chamberlain.

A serious split in the Labor party occurred over the possibility of a united front. In January, 1937, the Communist party, the ILP, and the Socialist League had reached an agreement for united action. The Socialist League was part of the Labor party. Its spokesman was Sir Stafford Cripps. Other members included Aneurin Bevan, John Strachey, Harold Laski, and H. N. Brailsford. The Labor party executive condemned any and all common action with the Communists and the ILP and expelled the Socialist League from the Labor party. Then at the party conference at Bournemouth in 1937 Cripps and his group were overwhelmingly defeated. However the "united-front" or "popular-front" agitation continued, and when Sir Stafford Cripps circulated widely a memorandum which had been turned down by the executive, of which he was a member, he was expelled from the Labor party.[25] Also expelled were Aneurin Bevan, Sir Charles Trevelyan, and G. R. Strauss.

The outbreak of the war laid this controversy to rest. The Labor party and the Trade-Union Council supported the war wholeheartedly, although they were still distrustful of the Chamberlain government and refused to enter it. The Soviet-German Nonaggression Pact of August, 1939, and the Soviet Union's subsequent attack on Finland ended, for the time being, all talk of a "united" or "popular" front. Aneurin Bevan and G. R. Strauss returned to the Labor party; Sir Stafford Cripps remained outside for a longer time, as he did not wish to accept the conditions of the party executive. However he cooperated with the party and rejoined it later.

Under the impact of military disaster, the Chamberlain government was

[24] The Labor party issued a manifesto, *Democracy versus Dictatorship* (London, 1933), which placed Nazism and Communism ("reaction of the left") on the same level and condemned them both.

[25] At that time, however, Cripps concentrated more on collaboration with the Liberals than with the Communists. The "Popular Front," different from the earlier "United Front," was to include all parties opposed to the Conservative government with the exception, of course, of the fascists.

overthrown by a rebellion within the Conservative party to which Labor lent active support.[26] On May 12, 1940, Winston Churchill became Prime Minister of a coalition government in which Labor participated.

The coalition government presented a picture of odd bedfellows. Churchill was an imperialist, in many respects a Victorian. In some fields he was quite progressive, but his progressivism was that of Disraeli. To the Labor party, Churchill was the man who had crushed the general strike in 1926, and had sought to destroy them through the Trades Union and Trades Dispute Act. But both sides realized that they needed each other. Since the Conservatives had a majority in the House, the premiership would have been theirs in any case. What was needed in the year of disaster 1940 was a fighting man with indomitable will. That fitted Winston Churchill to a T. And modern warfare necessitated the greatest effort of workingmen, which could be assured only by the Labor party and the trade-unions. Moreover, national unity was imperative in the face of the imminent danger of invasion.

Churchill as Prime Minister also took on the duties of Minister for National Defense which gave him an opportunity to control the war effort effectively. The supreme direction of affairs was taken from the cabinet as a whole and vested in the War Cabinet, which combined supreme military and civil authority. Besides Churchill, it contained Clement Attlee (Lab.) as Lord Privy Seal and later Deputy Prime Minister—a post created for this purpose. There was also Arthur Greenwood (Lab.), Lord Halifax (Cons.), and for a short while Neville Chamberlain (Cons.). By and by the chief men became Winston Churchill (Cons.), Anthony Eden (Cons.), Lord Woolton (Cons.), Lord Beaverbrook (Cons.), Sir James Grigg (Cons.), Clement Attlee (Lab.), Herbert Morrison (Lab.), Ernest Bevin (Lab.), Sir Stafford Cripps (Lab.), A. V. Alexander (Lab.), Sir Archibald Sinclair (Lib.), and Lord Simon (Nat. Lib.). Arthur Greenwood, a member of the first War Cabinet, left in 1942. These men worked together as a team. Churchill gave high praise to the leader of the Opposition who thus became his colleague:

In Clement Attlee I had a colleague of war experience long versed in the House of Commons. Our only differences in outlook were about Socialism, but these were swamped by a war soon to involve the almost complete subordination of the individual to the State. We worked together with perfect ease and confidence during the whole period of the Government. . . . Never did a British Prime Minister receive from Cabinet colleagues the loyal and true aid which I enjoyed during the next five years from these men of all Parties in the State.[27]

[26] Chamberlain was not overthrown by a vote of nonconfidence. On the day of his resignation, May 10, 1939, he still commanded a majority of eighty-one in the House. But he realized that his personality and record were too controversial to provide the kind of leadership that Britain needed. His resignation proved him to be a patriot and earned him more respect than his ineffective and uncomprehending leadership.

[27] Winston S. Churchill, *Their Finest Hour*, Boston, 1949, pp. 13, 26.

The coalition held together until the end of the European war, and the electoral truce was observed. However, when the German armies surrendered unconditionally and victory over Japan was clearly only a matter of time, the Labor party decided to leave the coalition. Churchill had hoped to preserve the coalition for another five years, during reconstruction, or failing that, at least until Japan was conquered. However, the Labor leaders, under increasing pressure from their restive followers, were eager for a contest. That they desired this, after the danger to the nation had passed, is quite understandable. There had been no general election since 1935, and 1935 had not been a good year for Labor. Moreover, the Labor party felt that it had a concrete program for reconstruction on which the electorate was entitled to pass judgment.

THE CONTEMPORARY POLITICAL PICTURE

A general election was held in July, 1945. No greater contrast could be imagined than existed between the two major parties and their campaigns.

The Conservatives were flushed with victory and campaigned almost entirely on the personality of Winston Churchill. Now it was quite true that Churchill was immensely popular. No other man had done so much to carry Britain, and indeed the Western powers, through the war. During the darkest and almost hopeless days, when Britain stood alone and could report nothing but setbacks, his fighting words had given heart and confidence to the free world. No other man embodied in every way the indomitable spirit of that great island race. But now the war was nearly over, and thoughts inevitably turned to postwar problems. A good part of the British electorate did not want to go back to the "good old days," which for many of them had not been good. Vast social problems were bound to loom up, as they always do after great wars, but the record of the Conservative party in solving social problems was not promising. There was also the disturbing presence of American soldiers, whose free-spending ways had perhaps given many Britishers the idea that a higher living standard was attainable for the common man. Moreover, millions of men and women had been in the armed forces and had been repelled by the strong caste system which still prevailed there.

A large share of the responsibility for the Conservative party's defeat must be placed at the doorstep of Churchill. The Conservatives were overconfident and presented no program except in very general terms.[28] Nor did they bother

[28] Full employment in free enterprise, housing through private enterprise but local subsidy, stable market and adequate prices for agriculture, insurance plan of 1944, comprehensive health service, improvement of primary schools, encouragement of overseas trade, stimulation of scientific research, hearings of complaints against monopolies, removal of controls, encouragement of small business, central authority for more efficient fuel and power, better transport, and continued high taxation. "Mr. Churchill's Fourteen Points," *The Manchester Guardian Weekly,* June 15, 1945.

to build up a well-integrated party organization. Their entire campaign was centered around Churchill, the great leader, the indispensable man. By inference, a voter who cast his ballot for a Labor candidate was accused of rank ingratitude to the man of "blood, sweat, and tears."

The Labor party constantly praised Churchill's war leadership, but distinguished it from the Conservative record and the domestic issues on which the election was fought. Many voters resented the necessity for a choice between rejecting the beloved war leader and being saddled with the Tories. Many felt that it was unfair to ask them to make such a heartbreaking decision, and that Winston Churchill should have remained on the high pedestal of a national figure and should not have descended into the mud of a partisan fight. Actually, Churchill berated his former colleagues in the strongest terms though such tactics did not win many votes for the Conservatives and probably lost more than they gained.

The Labor party campaign struck quite a different note. Labor did not expect to win, or at least was far from sure of it, and consequently mapped a careful strategy which was designed to show that Churchill was merely being used by "reactionaries" like Lord Beaverbrook and Brendan Bracken for their own purposes. Thereby the Labor leaders hoped to draw the issue between Labor and Tory, and not between Labor and Churchill.

The Labor party platform was drawn up at the Blackpool conference of May 23, 1945.[29] It contained full employment through government supervision of industry, nationalization of basic industries (including the Bank of England), vigorous Town and Country Planning, and raising the age for compulsory school attendance to sixteen. There was nothing new in the program, which was merely a rewording of earlier platforms. The Labor leaders took pains to explain that nationalization would be gradual and for the time being confined to about 20 per cent of the industrial sector only, with fair compensation for all. To alleviate the fear of socialism, the Labor party pointed out that a number of Dominions had been under socialist governments for some time and had apparently been quite happy.

The Liberals hoped to present a middle-of-the-road choice for those who did not like Conservatives but were distrustful of socialism.

The outcome of the election was a surprise to everyone, including the Labor leaders. In the House of Commons it took on the proportions of a landslide, returning Labor with 394 seats against 202 Conservatives. The Liberals obtained only 25 seats, divided between Independent Liberal (12) and National Liberal (13). ILP and Commonwealth received 5 seats, while the Communists conquered 2. However these figures give a distorted picture of the popular vote. The Labor party polled nearly 12,000,000 votes, the Conservatives nearly 10,000,000, the Liberals 2,500,000, and all others 750,000.

---

[29] "The Labour Program," *The New Statesmen and Nation*, Apr. 28, 1945; "The Labour Party Conference," *The Manchester Guardian Weekly*, June 1, 1945.

The Labor party was thus in a minority of about 1,000,000 as against all other parties, but it is the peculiarity of the British electoral system that it usually overemphasizes the strength of the leading party and thus provides a working majority in Parliament.

The election showed something else. Labor had become a more truly national party. Many of the rural areas, the cathedral towns, the Midlands—all traditionally Conservative strongholds—returned Labor candidates.[30] The class structure of previous elections was broken. To be sure, most working-men voted Labor, and the remaining wealthy voted Conservative, but Labor had made large inroads into the middle class. This was the class which Labor would have to retain in future elections if it wanted to be returned to office. Labor, therefore, would have to concentrate on national, rather than class, policies. This had been the trend for some time, but the elections of 1945 made that point quite clear and the elections of 1950 proved it convincingly.

When Clement Attlee rose to the premiership it became fashionable in many quarters to disparage him. Churchill's unkind quip, "an empty car drove up and out stepped Mr. Attlee," made a quick trip all over the world. Of course, no greater contrast can be imagined than that between Clement Attlee and Winston Churchill. Yet, after two full terms in office, there is no doubt that Clement Attlee is a far stronger man than was generally believed. The wisdom of his policies will forever be a matter of debate, but there can be no doubt that he went about his task with a clear mind and great determination. There is also no doubt that he and no one else was the Prime Minister of the Labor government. Other, reputedly stronger men, cracked under the strain of their office, but Attlee did not.

The life of the two Labor governments (1945–1950, 1950–1951) of Prime Minister Clement Attlee was overshadowed by the extremely difficult economic crisis in which Great Britain found herself as the result of her almost superhuman war effort, the long neglect of her industrial machinery, and the disappearance of some of her markets. Thus, while these governments vigorously went about instituting some of the reforms long urged by them, the emphasis had to be placed on increasing production, which naturally bewildered many of the Labor party's faithful followers. Moreover, because general employment and wages were high, many workers were better off than before the war, despite the continued policy of austerity, and were often unable to comprehend fully the seriousness of the situation which the government tried to get across in the slogan, "We are up against it: we work or we want."

Many of the austerity measures taken by the Labor government were thus the result of the national crisis and not caused by the socialistic program of the administration. In substance, that was conceded by the Opposition. But

[30] See R. B. McCallum and A. Readman, *The British General Election of 1945,* Oxford, 1947.

where the difference of opinion entered was the question as to the most effective means of increasing production and export and thus weathering the crisis. The Conservatives believed that a return to a modified free-enterprise system would provide the necessary incentive, and they pointed to Belgium as a shining example. The Labor party, on the other hand, believed that only careful planning would be successful and that the nationalization of key industries was essential, partly in order to improve their efficiency, partly in order to control the entire economy more effectively. Whatever one might think about this argument, the accusation that Labor placed socialism before the national interest was not justified. To the Labor party, limited socialism and planning were the answers to the crisis.

The economic plan of the first Attlee government may conveniently be divided into four groups:[31]

1. Creation of a central planning organization for the purpose of making an inventory of the national income, manpower, and raw material, and of recommending the most suitable use and distribution thereof.

2. A long-range plan involving the nationalization of basic industries and the direct control of such other industries as service the entire national production mechanism, or are in dire need of reorganization, or have reached such an advanced state of monopoly that private ownership could be considered "socially dangerous." Consequently, coal, the Bank of England, gas, electricity, rail transportation, and long-distance trucking were nationalized, with steel, cement, sugar, and others to follow later. The nationalized industry was to comprise 20 to 25 per cent of all industry.

3. Development plans for industry left under private ownership, in order that it may operate in conformity with the national economic plan.

4. A long-term development of agriculture in order to make the nation less dependent on the import of food.

If nationalization and economic planning constitute the long-range aspects of Labor policy, social services represent immediately realizable goals. The combination of both aspects has long been the essence of the Labor party program, but its own ardent supporters admit that Labor cannot claim full credit for its social-service program.[32] That belongs, to a large extent, to Lord Beveridge, a Liberal, whose famous report on *Social Insurance and Allied Services* was published in 1942 and formed the basis of the Labor government's legislative program in that field. Other important reports on employment policy, national health service, and workmen's compensation were all adopted under the Churchill coalition government. Labor claims, of course, that the Conservatives gave only lukewarm support—a claim which is denied

[31] Francis Williams, *Socialist Britain,* New York, 1949, pp. 86*f.*
[32] Barbara Wootton, "Record of the Labour Government in Social Services," *The Political Quarterly,* Vol. XX (1949), p. 101; Margaret Cole, "Social Services and Personal Life," *Socialism the British Way,* edited by Donald Munro, London, 1947, pp. 89–91.

by their opponents. It is true that two major legislative projects, the National Insurance Act and the Industrial Injuries Act, were passed by the wartime Parliament without dissent, but on the other hand the National Health Service Act was the subject of considerable controversy.

At any rate, the Labor government carried out these ideas with great vigor and added to them. In substance, these are the achievements of the Labor government in the field of social services:

1. The entire population is now covered to a certain extent against the loss of earning power, and a uniform practice has been established.

2. The National Health Service Act which came into operation in July, 1948, provides free medical care, including hospital and dental services, for all. Each citizen contributes a small weekly sum to this program, and all services are free except for a small fee for prescriptions. Other small fees were later added. The contributions have been found completely inadequate and the government discovered that it had to spend much more than it had expected. The opponents of the measure claim that this was caused by a run on medical facilities by people who had no real need for them, while the defenders of the policy, notably former Minister of Health Aneurin Bevan, replied that the miscalculation merely proves that the health of the British people was in even worse shape than had been estimated. Whatever the merits of the program from a fiscal standpoint, there is no doubt that it is enormously popular and will be retained by any future government, especially as abuses are gradually being eliminated.

3. Housing has been a serious problem for many years and no quick or easy solution is feasible. The tightness of the island, the large industrialization, and inadequate progress in the building industry and trades have produced slum conditions. Added to that was the considerable destruction of dwellings by bombing and the V weapons, as well as the deterioration of houses which could not be repaired during the war because of shortages of supplies. A good deal of progress has been achieved, and war damage had been largely repaired by 1947. A number of temporary housing units were produced, and measures were taken to make unused houses available for rent. Long-range solutions were approached through the Town and Country Planning Act and the New Towns Act. However, in that sector progress was not considerable.

4. Educational reforms were already begun under the Churchill coalition government, which caused Parliament to pass the Education Act of 1944. It raised the school-leaving age, prescribed universal secondary education up to the sixteenth year of age, abolished fees in (public) secondary schools, and provided for closer inspection of private schools. Further measures for post-school education were planned. Much remains to be done in this sector, although no substantial disagreement exists between the major parties, and no

insurmountable difficulties have arisen. The main problem is the backwardness of facilities and the omissions of past governments.[33]

CONSERVATIVE GROWTH

The Conservative party, still led by the redoubtable Winston Churchill,[34] reorganized its shattered forces after 1945. Under the keen and quietly efficient direction of Lord Woolton, it rebuilt its organization from the bottom up, paid much attention to the younger element in the party, and girded for the next bout. It accepted and endorsed virtually the entire social-service program of the Labor government, and even pledged itself to broaden it somewhat. It emphasized the fact that it had already endorsed most of those measures during the war, and thereby attempted to demonstrate that their acceptance did not constitute a recent change of heart. Labor opponents, however, pointed to the record of prewar Conservative governments, and Prime Minister Attlee inquired in an election speech why previous Tory governments had not carried out such reforms if the Conservative party was so much in favor of them.

Although the Conservatives had resisted nationalization at every step, they pledged themselves in 1950 and 1951 to maintain what had been achieved, but in 1951 promised to denationalize only the iron and steel industry and road haulage. They pledged themselves to relax austerity by abolishing rationing just as soon as possible and by encouraging production through private enterprise. They promised to cut taxes radically and to effect sizable savings in the bureaucratic machinery of the government. They envisaged more incentive for the investment of risk capital, foreign and domestic.[35]

The Conservatives charged that nationalization had retarded production because of the inevitable confusion accompanying reorganization on such a vast scale. They maintained that the only reasons why the evil effect had not become obvious to all had been the lavish American aid which alone kept Britain above water.

They attacked with special fervor the topic of regimentation and the alleged danger to freedom. While Labor went into the 1950 campaign endorsing a mixed economy [36] of nationalized and private industry, the Conservatives

[33] The quality of British schools, however, is excellent.

[34] He was eighty in 1954. He liked to remind listeners that Gladstone was Prime Minister at eighty-five.

[35] See the Conservative party declaration, *The Right Road for Britain*, London, 1949; R. A. Butler, "Conservative Policy," *Political Quarterly*, Vol. XX (1949), pp. 317–325; Quintin Hogg, *The Left Was Never Right*, London, 1945.

[36] *Labour Believes in Britain*, London, 1949, issued by the National Executive Committee of the Labor Party, pp. 10–13.

maintained that Labor was inevitably committed to eventual total nationalization. The Labor government's plans to control such things as sugar, fruit, and vegetable marketing and to nationalize the wholesale meat business and the government departments' practice of buying what they liked in order to sell it to retailers gave, in the opinion of the Conservatives, some credence to this assumption.

The 1950 Election and Its Consequences

With these records and achievements, the two major parties went into the election of February 23, 1950. The Labor party was in a highly confident mood. It published a self-congratulatory manifesto, called *Let Us Win Through Together,* which suddenly attempted to create an atmosphere of optimism although Sir Stafford Cripps had declared only a few weeks before that Britain was teetering on the brink of economic disaster. The manifesto also managed to give all credit for maintaining the standard of living to the Labor government without mentioning Marshall Plan aid in a single word. These were only natural manifestations of politics in an election year, such as might be expected from any government party, but they did reflect strong confidence that socialist planning would be permitted to have another five years of operation.

The outcome of the election was a shock to such confidence. The Labor party lost 81 seats in the House of Commons, maintaining only 315, two more than a majority. The Conservatives breathed hard on their opponent's neck, obtaining 298 seats. The Liberal party, which had hoped to wax stronger by the votes of those who would turn their backs on Labor but who would not want to endorse the Tories, obtained only 9 seats in the House. The small Communist party lost both its seats in Parliament. The popular vote of 13,295,736 for Labor and 11,518,360 for the Conservatives reflected the same picture as the distribution of seats. The Liberals maintained their vote at 2,621,489 but found it scattered to such an extent as to approximate extinction in the House of Commons. A casual observer might feel that the Liberal vote would have gone to the Conservatives had the Liberal leaders not been so completely mistaken about their prospects, but that is by no means a foregone conclusion, as is indicated by the Liberal party's preelection offer of support to Labor under certain conditions.

The Labor party hoped that the election would give it a mandate for the continuation of its program. Such a mandate was obviously not received. On the other hand, no mandate was given to the Conservative party to lead the country according to its lights. Inasmuch as the election was fought largely for or against socialism, it might be said that there was a socialist defeat. But in a positive sense the elections were inconclusive.

It is not too difficult to see what happened. An analysis of the 1945 election reveals that Labor won because it obtained a large measure of support from the middle classes. These middle classes now began to turn against Labor in 1950. The reason for such fickleness is not difficult to surmise. The Labor regime had done much for the workers. The record of social services was impressive, the export and production drive had created full employment and better wages, housing was improved, medical services were most welcome, and there was cradle-to-grave security. On the other end of the scale, some wealthy men had not done so badly either. Such business as had been retained in private hands was booming. True, taxes took an enormous amount, but something was left. Managers and owners of nationalized enterprises were frequently hired by the various boards at salaries which might not approximate their former earnings but were still greatly above civil-service pay. But the middle class benefited very little and found itself squeezed at both ends.

Middle-class incomes had not kept pace with the rise in prices. The fact that higher income had permitted the workers to bid for scarce goods which the middle classes used to consider their due had driven those prices up or made goods unobtainable. This was especially true because many semiluxuries which middle-class people consider indispensable were not under price control and therefore skyrocketed, if they were obtainable at all. But more serious was the employment situation of the middle class. In the former days it occupied certain layers in the civil service, the professions, and the trades, especially retail and other white-collar positions. This market of opportunities was now threatened from both sides of the social ladder. The so-called "lower classes" were acquiring more education and other opportunities which enabled them to compete for middle-class positions, while the destruction of wealth by taxation forced many members of the so-called "upper classes" into competing for middle-class positions, accommodations, and goods.

Moreover, many middle-class people were sensitive to the growth of bureaucracy and regulations which complicated their lives, and they were more aware of the precarious situation of their country's finances than many workers, who were unaware of the extent to which their livelihood depended on American aid.

THE CONSERVATIVES RETURN TO POWER

The election of 1951 was really a continuation of the 1950 contest.[37] Nationalization of industries became less of an issue because the second Attlee government had too feeble a majority to undertake much beyond forcing through the iron and steel nationalization. Both parties emphasized the con-

[37] H. G. Nicholas, "The British General Election of 1951," *American Political Science Review*, Vol. XLVI (1952), p. 398. For a more complete study see D. E. Butler, *The British General Election of 1951*, London, 1952.

tinuation of the welfare state and promised a better housing program. But greater prominence was given to foreign affairs. This was not so much the result of deep disagreement between Mr. Attlee and Mr. Churchill but was rather due to events and tendencies within the ranks of the Labor party. In April, 1951, Aneurin Bevan, Minister of Health, and Harold Wilson, President of the Board of Trade, resigned from the Attlee government, ostensibly over the size of the government's military effort, but actually over a more and more fundamental disagreement on foreign policy. Bevan became the recognized spokesman of the Labor party's left wing, which is certainly not Communist but which regards the United States with almost as much suspicion.

Although Bevan and his friends certainly did not prevail, their weight helped to focus the campaign on a "peace versus war" issue which tried to pin the "warmonger" label on Churchill. The electorate seemed unimpressed by this artificial issue. Both parties displayed their best organizational efforts. Television was used for the first time, though on a much more limited scale than in the United States.

The outcome was a Conservative success, though far from a landslide. The Conservatives won almost everywhere but with margins only slightly over their 1950 results. But the Liberals dared to run candidates in many fewer constituencies than in 1950, and the majority of their ex-voters seemed to have turned to the Conservatives. Practically all the important leaders of the Liberals were defeated, and the party has apparently reached nearly the end of its road. Of its remaining six members in the House of Commons, five were elected without Conservative opposition and with Conservative help.

Although the Conservatives won a majority in the House of Commons with 321 seats against Labor's 296, their total popular vote of 13,717,538 was smaller than that of the Labor party, 13,948,605. Taking into consideration the fact that four of the Conservative seats from Northern Ireland were unopposed and therefore produced a light vote, it might be said that the two parties are just about even. This means that the country can apparently look forward to a period in which no large majorities can be expected and to elections in which minor changes in a few constituencies may throw the election one way or another. The obliteration of the Liberals has largely contributed to this result, which forces both major parties to concentrate around the center.

PARTY ORGANIZATION IN PARLIAMENT

One of the conditions of an orderly and responsible party system in Parliament is party discipline. This is a difficult and touchy subject. Too much party discipline makes Members of Parliament into mere rubber stamps to "be voted" by their leaders as they see fit. Too little discipline produces unstable governments and irresponsible legislatures. In the British Parliament a good measure of discipline prevails, although dissent is possible and common.

It is said that a Member of Parliament becomes officially a member of a Parliamentary group by accepting its "whip," [38] which means that he accepts the discipline of the party and its parliamentary leadership. Each party has a chief whip and several assistant whips; the chief whip of the government party being, as we have seen, the Parliamentary Secretary of the Treasury, with the Junior Lords of the Treasury as his assistants. The chief whip of the Opposition and his assistants have no such salaried positions, but their authority is also great. The whips of the opposing parties confer frequently with one another and together help to prepare the work of the House.

While it is the general duty of the whips to keep in touch with the members of their parties and to keep them informed of what is expected of them, their most important task comes at "division" (vote) time, when they see to it that everyone is present and doing his duty by the party. While this task has always been important, it has been of special significance since 1950, when the two major parties are separated by such a small margin of votes. In addition the power of the whips has undoubtedly been increased by the facts that Independents have fared very badly in recent elections and that the expulsion of a member from his party would almost certainly terminate his political career as soon as the next election is held. The "whip may be withdrawn" from a member—meaning his expulsion from the Parliamentary group by decision of the leader of the Conservative party or by decision of the Parliamentary party for Labor members.

Of pivotal importance in the operation of the Parliamentary group is the personality of the leader, who is automatically leader of his party in Parliament and in the country, and who is normally designated Prime Minister when his party wins and Leader of the Opposition when it loses. Technically both the Conservative and the Labor leaders are chosen by the members of both the House of Commons and the House of Lords from their respective parties. In reality these gatherings usually merely ratify an obvious choice. This is particularly the case with the Conservatives, among whom real contests have not occurred. When Conservative leader Bonar Law resigned in 1921, Sir Austin Chamberlain succeeded him as a matter of course. The next year when Sir Austin differed with the majority of his party on the question of remaining in the coalition, the King again called upon Bonar Law to become Prime Minister of a Conservative government. When Law retired in 1923, the King called for Stanley Baldwin rather than for Lord Curzon. This was in line with prevailing sentiments in the Conservative-party leadership but without any formal vote being taken. After having become Prime Minister, Baldwin was automatically elected leader of his party. When he

---

[38] Bulmer-Thomas, *op. cit.*, p. 109, reminds us that the expression is derived from "whipper-in," a huntsman's assistant who kept the hounds in line.

retired in 1937, the King appointed the man designated by Baldwin, Neville Chamberlain, who was also automatically elected leader of his party. Chamberlain resigned in 1940 as the result of great pressure inside and outside his party, and the man demanded by all to lead the war effort, Winston Churchill, became Prime Minister. But in this case, for once, and largely in order to spare Chamberlain's feelings, the latter remained leader of his party until his death not long thereafter. Then Churchill was elected as a matter of course.[39] Now that Churchill has resigned his office, there is little doubt that the man whom he designates as his successor, Anthony Eden, will be elected.

The situation in the Labor party is quite similar, although there leadership has been challenged—without success. As long as Ramsay MacDonald remained in the fold, there was no question about who was leader. After his defection, the Labor party went down to defeat in the elections, as we have seen, and all its first-rank leaders failed to gain reelection. In this situation George Lansbury was elected leader and Clement Attlee his deputy. When Lansbury resigned in 1935, Attlee was elected in his stead. This was the only occasion on which there was a real contest, for both Herbert Morrison and Arthur Greenwood were candidates. Nevertheless Attlee was reelected by a large majority. No further serious challenge has developed despite attempts by the left wing of the party. At least since 1945 Clement Attlee has been firmly in the saddle of the Labor party.

These party leaders are not absolute lords and masters; party leadership is a matter of teamwork. Nevertheless their position is extraordinarily strong, particularly that of the leader of the Conservative party, who is all-important. The meetings of the Parliamentary Conservative party are not of great importance: the top leaders do not take an active part therein, and the determination of policy is at any rate the leader's prerogative. Nevertheless the sentiments expressed in party meetings will of course influence the leadership, although the leadership determines how great that influence will be.

In the Labor party, on the other hand, the leaders take a very active part in the meetings of the Parliamentary Labor party.[40] There is a much more formal organization than the Conservatives have, and there is even a kind of executive committee which is called the Parliamentary committee. When the Labor party was in the government this committee had a heavy backbencher note, but since the party has returned to opposition the top leaders have taken it more in hand.

The meetings of the Parliamentary Labor party are much more important than those of the Conservatives because the Labor-party meeting makes policy decisions which are binding on its members, while the Conservative meeting

[39] Many old-line Conservative leaders regarded Churchill, who had twice "crossed the floor" (changed parties), as unreliable and a radical.

[40] Ordinarily the Labor members of both the House of Commons and the House of Lords meet together.

has no such right. The standing orders of the Parliamentary party commit the members to strict obedience to the decisions of the meetings except in certain cases of deeply felt personal and conscientious opinions. In practice the members are held to those rules only within limits, and some opposition has been tolerated, but persistent violators have been expelled. It is one of the attributes of party leadership to know when force or leniency is to be applied.

If one is to summarize the difference between the role of Conservative and Labor backbenchers, one might say that a Conservative has less part in the determination of policy than his Labor colleague but has greater freedom to dissent.

National Party Organization: Conservative

Outside Parliament, the Conservative party is organized on the constituency (electoral district) level. Sometimes these constituencies are subdivided. The Conservative constituency association is a rather loosely organized unit of individual members, most of whom reside in the area although members may merely have their business interests therein. Each constituency organization makes its own rules, usually guided by central headquarters. Such guidance, however, is given only when desired. Sometimes men and women are in the same association; sometimes there is a separate women's branch. There is always a young Conservative organization. Branches are organized around each ward (similar to precincts). Each association elects its own officers. One of its principal functions is the approval of parliamentary candidates whose names are proposed by the executive committee of the association, but no candidate will be endorsed who has not been approved by a (national) advisory committee on candidates. For part of its work the party relies on a string of auxiliary organizations. Especially well known are the Primrose League, the Imperial League (with a junior branch), and the Conservative Workingmen's Clubs.

Each constituency endeavors to have a professional agent, preferably of the full-time variety, who is the professional campaign manager of the party's candidate. These agents belong to a respected profession, and the Conservatives, naturally more affluent than their Labor opponents, have nearly succeeded in having a professional agent in every constituency.

For better organization the Conservatives have established regional groupings whose principal function is the coordination of the work of the various associations. At the national level there is the loosely organized National Union of Conservative and Unionist Associations. It is the purpose of this National Union to promote Conservative party activity all over the country and to work in close cooperation with all affiliated associations, including the Scottish Unionist Association and the Ulster Unionist Council.

The National Union has a central executive committee, a central council, and an annual conference. Its executive committee is reconstituted every year and is composed of the leader of the party, other party officials, the chairmen of the various central advisory committees, five representatives appointed by each provincial area, one representative of Conservative Lords, four representatives of the Conservative Members of Parliament, and various other representatives of Conservative associations.

The central council of the National Union consists of representatives of various groups such as constituency associations, provincial areas, and Conservative peers. It is a larger body than the executive committee but not as large as the annual conference.

Every year a Conservative conference is held. All members of the central councils have the right to attend, and each constituency association and various other groups are entitled to delegates. Approximately ten delegates attend from each constituency as well as representatives of the central council and leadership. Thus between 5,000 and 6,000 persons have a right to attend, and there are as many as 1,000 visitors. Actual attendance has varied between 2,500 and 4,000.

The Conservative conference is a general policy meeting at which the main issues before the party are discussed, but at which party policy is not determined. That is the prerogative of the leader, who does not take part in the work of the conference itself but addresses it when invited (which is usually the case).

The nerve center of the party's organizational effort is the central office (the headquarters of the national party organization). Its officers and staff are salaried and are more or less permanent. The central officers are behind every concentrated publicity campaign and work directly with the constituency election agent. They also conduct a training program, give examinations, and grant certificates. They supply publicity material, bolster the courage of sagging local organizations, and do whatever else may be necessary to keep the organization in full swing (especially at election time). It is generally agreed among Conservatives that the 1945 election was lost largely because of overconfidence and neglect of the party organization. Under the leadership of Lord Woolton, the central office was reorganized and has now reached a very high degree of efficiency.[41]

NATIONAL PARTY ORGANIZATION: LABOR

In contrast to the Conservatives, the Labor party is much more tightly and centrally organized. It is also based on a different organizational principle because it has two types of members, namely, affiliated organizations and in-

[41] Samuel H. Beer, "The Conservative Party of Great Britain," *Journal of Politics*, Vol. XIV (1952), pp. 41–71.

dividual members. The great majority of members are in the affiliated organizations, especially the trade-unions, which means that people join an organization which in turn is a collective member of the Labor party. This somewhat unusual principle is the result of the history of the Labor party, which started out as a roof organization over trade-unions, the Fabian Society, the Independent Labor party, etc.—for the purpose of electing representatives to Parliament.

The Labor party has constituency organizations like the Conservatives, but they must adopt rules which are laid down by the annual (national) party conference. These constituency Labor parties are subdivided into ward organizations to which the individual members are primarily attached. In each ward [42] there is a ward committee consisting of individual members, a women's section, and usually a section of the Labor League of Youth. The ward committees of a constituency together with the affiliated organizations (mostly local branches of trade-unions) form the constituency Labor party. Delegates from the various ward committees form the general committee, which holds an annual meeting at which officers are elected.

The constituent Labor parties do not have as many paid agents as the Conservatives, although their number is increasing. In many places they have part-time agents.

Like the Conservatives, the Labor party has regional councils and federations, but its principal organ is the annual Labor conference. This consists of delegates from the various affiliated organizations.[43] Generally one delegate is appointed for each 5,000 members. Voting is by number of members of affiliated organizations, which means that the trade-unions have the overwhelming power at the annual conference. For instance, the Transport and General Workers Union casts votes for over 800,000 members.

The annual conference hears reports on various aspects of policy, elects the members of the National Executive Committee, and adopts resolutions. Since the Labor conference establishes at least theoretically the policy to be followed by the party in Parliament, debates are exceedingly keen and sometimes heated. When the party is in opposition it has generally been more inclined to follow the guidance of the annual conference than when it bears the burden of office. A casual listener at these conferences may often have a wrong impression about the prevailing sentiment because the representatives of the party's left wing are usually very much in evidence, make fiery speeches, and are hotly applauded, while the more middle-of-the-road element appears less prominent. But when the discussion has ended, and the votes are tabulated, the radicals are usually snowed under by the millions of votes

---

[42] The equivalent to the American precinct is called "ward" in a borough and "polling district" in a county.

[43] Technically the constituency Labor parties are as much affiliated organizations as the trade-unions, Fabian Society, etc.

represented by the trade-unions and cast under the direction of their more conservative leadership.

While the delegates normally vote in a body, election of the members of the National Executive Committee is done by sections (divisions). Twelve members of the "Executive," as the National Executive Committee is commonly called, are nominated by the trade-unions and elected by their delegates. One member is nominated by Socialist, cooperative, and professional organizations and elected by their delegates. Seven members are nominated by constituency Labor parties and their federations and elected by their delegates. Five women members may be nominated by any affiliated organization and are elected by the entire conference. The leader of the party and the Treasurer are ex officio members, bringing the entire membership to twenty-seven. While the Treasurer is elected by the annual conference, the leader of the party is not; the party simply accepts the choice of its Parliamentary group.

The election of the constituency members of the Executive is usually the most heated because it is there that the left wing of the party makes its greatest effort. For a number of years Aneurin Bevan and his friends have dominated this side of the picture, but since the trade-unions are assured of twelve members of the executive, and by their preponderant number can elect the five women members if they so desire, the left wing has absolutely no chance of dominating the party so long as it is unable to conquer the trade-unions—which so far it has failed to do.

Like the Conservatives, the Labor party has a central headquarters, which is commonly known as "Transport House." [44] Its chief full-time official is the General Secretary of the Labor party, and there is a considerable paid staff. Transport House is in close contact with the constituency agents, and the constituency and regional organizations of the party. Like its Conservative counterpart, it provides leadership in the publicity endeavors of the party and supplies the bulk of the publicity material. In contrast to the Conservative party, the national Labor party leadership keeps closer tab over the choice of prospective candidates for Parliament and allows the constituency organization much less leeway. Nobody may run for Parliament as a Labor candidate who does not have the approval of the National Executive. Such endorsement will be given only if the candidate promises to abide by the standing orders of the Parliamentary Labor party, if elected. Very frequently candidates are urged upon local organizations for reasons of national policy.

PARTY PROGRAM AND POLICY: CONSERVATIVE

As the name of their party implies, the Conservatives stand for the essential preservation of the main features of British economic and social life. Tradi-

---

[44] The Labor party shares offices in that building with the Transport and General Workers' Union and the Trade-Union Congress, hence the name.

tionally they have advocated free enterprise and as little government control as possible. In their election publicity they have strongly denounced Socialism and planning.[45] But in actual practice they have had to recognize three salient facts: (1) that Great Britain, as a result of the war and of an overaged, neglected industrial machinery, was confronted by such a serious economic situation that it seemed improbable for private industry to recover unaided and without considerable government direction; (2) that many of the social reforms and services instituted by the Labor government were obviously popular and well liked and that any party which advocated their wholesale abolition would commit political suicide; (3) that it was obviously futile to try to denationalize the nationalized coal industry. What was once scrambled could not again be unscrambled.[46] It might also be added that Britain did not have quite the American type of free-enterprise ideology because for many years much of her economy had been planned and directed by private cartels, not by the government. What the Conservatives object to is not so much planning in itself as the growth of bureaucratic control inherent in state planning. Attacks against an overgrown and unwieldy bureaucracy are usually popular and politically profitable.

The Conservatives have gone to great lengths to prove that they are not opposed to the social reforms and services undertaken by the Labor government. They point out, not without justification, that the major planning and spade work for these reforms and services was undertaken under the wartime coalition government headed by Winston Churchill. This is certainly true with regard to such measures as the National Health Service, the Town and Country Planning Act, the Education Act, and many others. However, one is permitted to suspect that the Conservatives' enthusiasm for these measures was not quite so great as that of their Labor opponents, who had been concerned with these ideas for a long time. At any rate the Conservatives promised to keep these services and reforms but to administer them better.

In foreign and Commonwealth affairs the Conservatives have always been traditionally nationalist and imperialist.[47] For that reason the Labor party tried to pin the "warmonger" label on them in the 1951 elections. This, however, proved unsuccessful, and in view of Sir Winston Churchill's persistent advocacy of a "big-four" conference to undertake the settlement of the East-West conflict, such charges are not likely to be raised again. In actuality there has been very little difference between the foreign policies of

[45] John Boyd-Carpenter, *The Conservative Case: Choice for Britain,* London, 1950; Quintin Hogg, *The Case for Conservatism,* London, 1948; and Bernard Braine, *Tory Democracy,* London, 1948.

[46] The denationalization of the iron and steel industry and of road haulage seemed easier because the companies had remained intact. Even so, denationalization proved a major headache for the Conservative government.

[47] "Imperialist" in the British use of this term means the preservation of the British Empire and Commonwealth rather than its expansion.

the Labor and Conservative parties when they were in office, though which-
ever party is the Opposition tries to make an issue of it. Thus, when Churchill
was in the Opposition, he strongly advocated a united Europe and berated
the Labor government for its negative attitude. But when he became Prime
Minister again he kept Britain out of such a union just as Attlee had. The
Labor party, in turn, had denounced the policy toward Palestine executed
by prewar Conservative governments, but when Attlee became Prime Minister,
and the late Ernest Bevin became Foreign Secretary, little difference could be
seen between their views and those of their Conservative predecessors.

PARTY PROGRAM AND POLICY: LABOR

The British Labor party is a party of democratic socialism and it is proud
of that designation. But at the same time it is not Marxist or revolutionary
in a violent sense. Nor does it believe that all features of life should be
socialized. It has advocated the public ownership of all basic industries as
well as those which are natural monopolies, like public utilities, believing that
these industries can be better run that way and be more dedicated to the
public good—plus the fact that they would be means by which the rest of
the national economy could be controlled.

If Labor leaders have frequently stated, especially at the beginning of the
Labor administration, that they intend to nationalize only 20 per cent of the
industry, this should not be interpreted as a hard and fast rule. It is rather
another instance of British gradualism and a reluctance to plan every step
ahead. Presumably after about 20 per cent of the industry, including all
basic industry, had been nationalized, a second look would be cast and the
situation reviewed. Thus while the general economy would be brought into
line with the over-all economic plan of the government, no attempt would be
made to regulate every facet of individual economic behavior. The Labor
party is as democratic as its Conservative opponents, and there is no thought
of interfering with the freedom of parties, of elections, or of personal
liberties.[48]

Therefore the Labor party has been consistently vigorous in its opposition
to Communism and its program of dictatorship. Whatever the difference may
be between some Americans and some British Laborites with regard to the
place of Communists in the public service, the Labor party has been vigorous
and successful in keeping its own ranks free from Communist infiltration.

It goes without saying that the Labor party considers it the responsibility

[48] Herbert Tracy, *The British Labour Party,* London, 1948, 3 vols.; Donald Munro
(ed.), *Socialism: The British Way,* London, 1948; Francis Williams, *Socialist Britain,*
New York, 1949, and "The Program of the British Labour Party; a Historical Survey,"
Journal of Politics, Vol. XII (1950), pp. 189–210; and Bertrand de Jouvenel, *Problèmes
de l'Angleterre Socialiste,* Paris, 1947.

of the government to ensure an ever-increasing standard of living and personal development to the citizens. Because it is primarily a *labor* party, it has concentrated on increasing the income and purchasing power as well as the general welfare of the working population in order to create greater equality, although the complete equalization of wages is not a Labor policy. Taxation has been used to reduce the status of the remaining upper classes, but generally heavy taxation has been inevitable in Britain since the beginning of the war because of the general economic situation of the country. It is thus difficult to say what part of taxation is social policy and what is economic policy. If the Conservative government was able to grant some tax relief in 1953 it was primarily the result of the improved economic situation and a slight relaxation of world tension after the end of the Korean War.

The health and education programs of the Labor party have been largely fulfilled and have been discussed elsewhere.

The Labor party's foreign policy is not an easy thing to discuss because of the notable discrepancy between the party's policy when in power and when in opposition. Traditionally the party is pacifist, but its coming to power after the war and during the rapid worsening of East-West relations has certainly imprinted the realities of the situation on the party's leadership. Thus the party has had to endorse the continuation of conscription and the heavy military establishments at home and abroad. If Labor feels that America is too extreme in its opposition to the Soviet Union, such sentiments may also be found among Conservatives, and both the Labor and the Conservative governments have on occasion believed it to be their task as America's principal ally to try to slow down a bit their "impetuous cousins" across the water.

There is, however, a segment of the Labor party which differs more profoundly with the Conservatives, with America, and with its own leadership. This group, largely but not entirely composed of intellectuals among whom Aneurin Bevan is the best known but by no means the only spokesman, looks upon America with as much suspicion as the Communists do, though it is certainly not communist. To these men America is the symbol of capitalism—an economic and social order which they dislike and for which they see no future. While they do not find Russia blameless for the existence of world tension, they suspect that America is largely motivated by a desire to destroy the Russian socialist-communist experiment. They therefore advocate that Britain should free herself from all vestiges of American leadership and should endeavor as the leader of a "third force" to negotiate with the Soviet Union. Their statements and resolutions are therefore strongly critical of American policies and personalities.

This is the view of a minority group led by Aneurin Bevan, which is very much in evidence but does not predominate. Its criticism was primarily leveled against the leaders of the party while the Labor party was in power, and its lack of influence was therefore obvious. Since Labor has been in opposition, the party leadership has found it less necessary to put this group under restraint, and the impression has sometimes been created that it is speaking for the Labor party. This, however, is not the case and is not likely to be so in the future.

THE OUTLOOK FOR PARTY POLITICS IN GREAT BRITAIN

We have seen in past discussions that the two major parties, Conservative and Labor, have all but eliminated the Liberal and other "third" parties and are now almost evenly balanced. With this balance there has also come a greater approximation of their policies, which has resulted in strains in both camps.

Among the Conservatives this strain is not excessively great. There are some who hate to see their party approve or at least acquiesce in what they consider to be Socialist policies, although there is no agreement over what constitutes a Socialist policy; in many instances, that is merely a policy to the left of the particular critic. But they are a minority. Somewhat greater has been the strain among those Conservative leaders who felt that Winston Churchill was playing too much "by ear" and was sharing too little of his responsibility with other, younger men. This complaint had some basis when, for a while, Churchill seemed to neglect his Parliamentary duties and kept a somewhat remote, lone hand. However, he has bestirred himself and has again taken full charge. He was inspired to do this by his desire to terminate his long and illustrious career by a supreme gesture toward reconciliation between the East and the West. Nevertheless it cannot be too long before the leadership passes into other hands.

In the Labor party the strain is more profound and has a bearing on the future of British politics. Although the Labor party certainly is predominant among the working population it does not control them all. Moreover, in the social situation of 1954 the term "workingman" may be ascribed to a very large stratum of the British population. In fact both major parties are cross-section parties with a large following in all classes of the population. Winning elections is therefore becoming more and more difficult. The Liberal vote is no longer large enough to decide elections when merged with one or the other party. The contest is therefore heavy for every new voter as well as for those who might be induced to change their allegiance. In this direction the Conservatives seem to have done somewhat better than Labor, and they are gaining some support among trade-unionists who are disillusioned with the performance of the Labor party in office.[49]

This puts it up to the Labor party to decide where to go from here, but it is precisely on this point that differences of opinion and emotions are preva-

[49] Bulmer-Thomas, *op. cit.*, p. 293.

lent. When Labor came to power it was full of enthusiasm and conviction. Its dynamic drive contrasted favorably with the irresolution among Conservatives, who in 1945 could think of nothing better than to run on the record of Winston Churchill's war leadership. Now much of this enthusiasm is gone. Not because the Labor record was a failure; since Labor has done substantially what it set out to do, it would be much fairer to call its record a success. But disillusionment has crept in because, as many Labor people will now privately admit, the successfully instituted Labor measures have not all achieved what they were supposed to. This does not apply to the social services, with which there is general satisfaction, but rather to the program of nationalization and economic planning. The Labor government took over a virtually bankrupt country and its principal problem, as it soon turned out, was not so much the redistribution of wealth as the creation of wealth, or in other words, production. In this field there is no reason to suspect that the Labor government's record is not as good as that of private industry. It may well be better in some of its branches. But a number of fond expectations were not fulfilled. The workers did not work better in the nationalized industries because they were presumably "working for themselves." The workingmen knew very well that the slogan "We are the state" is an illusion. For practical purposes the state is the bureaucracy, the boards, the ministries, and the workingmen could see little difference between the private employer and the state, especially when so many "bosses"—now organs of the state—were the same bosses as before nationalization.

The trade-union leaders, long trained in the school of industrial conflict and used to getting the maximum benefits for the workers out of management, if necessary by means of strikes, were often perplexed when the new management, the Labor government, entreated them to restrain themselves and to help get more work out of the workers. To the pacifists it was disillusioning that no substantial reduction could be made in the British military establishment. And to those who believed that an era of world-wide good will would follow a Labor victory, or that Labor leaders could deal more easily with the Russians than representatives of "capitalist" parties, the political realities of the postwar period provided ground for disillusionment.

The difficulties of the Labor party were and are indeed perplexing. For the party can justly claim that it has given Britain an administration of a high degree of efficiency, and it can certainly say that it has kept its promises. Consequently it seems to many that it was not the Labor performance but the very conception of the Labor program which has been found wanting.[50]

The result of this situation has been a very decided waning of enthusiasm for nationalization among the more conservative leaders of the Labor party

[50] John P. Roche, "The Crisis in British Socialism," *The Antioch Review,* Winter, 1952–1953, p. 393.

and especially among the trade-unions. At both the annual Labor party conferences and the annual meetings of the Trade-Union Congress in 1953 and 1954, nationalization was deemphasized. Especially at the Trade-Union Congresses many voices complained that the private employer was often easier to deal with than the government.

Under these circumstances, the Labor leadership seems to be disinclined to suggest further experimentation, and the exciting period of great changes seems to be over for the foreseeable future, regardless of whether Labor or the Conservatives are in office. This situation does not prevent the Labor party from gaining victory in a future election. But some of the enthusiasm, the *élan* of the past, has gone out of the party, and it seems to be on the way toward being a party of social reform rather than of socialism.

This is a development which is not pleasing to a minority in the party, headed and personified by the able and ambitious Aneurin Bevan. Actually this group is not just one thing. It is composed of a conglomeration of malcontents of different shades. There are the disillusioned enthusiasts for whom the remedy for the shortcomings of partial socialism is more socialism. There are the adherents of a softer policy toward Russia and of a tougher policy toward America, including a sprinkling of "fellow travelers." [51] There are those who think that their party has taken on too much of a "middle-class hue," and they particularly blame Herbert Morrison, who is held primarily responsible for this development. To attack Morrison is a roundabout way of attacking Attlee. There are bearers of other grievances.

In view of the general atmosphere of discontent in the party, this group, which is sometimes for want of a better name called "Bevanite," has grown. At the 1952 Labor-party conference at Morecambe, the Bevanites elected six of the seven constituency representatives on the Executive. At the 1953 conference at Margate they elected all seven but in 1954 Bevan miscalculated when he ran for party treasurer against Morrison and lost. Bevan's role has given rise to alarmist reports in the non-British press. But it must be remembered that the dominant force in the Labor party is and remains the trade-unions, whose leaders would sooner secede from the Labor party than see Aneurin Bevan and his friends installed as leaders. As the trade-unions dominate the National Executive, so the latter in turn keeps tight control over who runs for Parliament under the official Labor-party label. Thus the Parliamentary Labor party cannot be captured by the Bevanites any more than the National Executive.

While the Labor party is in opposition, its leadership maintains loose reins. It would not be useful to create martyrs, and moreover the noisy agitation of the Bevanites is useful in needling the Conservatives. But there is danger that

[51] Outright fellow travelers like Platts-Mills or Koni Ziliacus have been expelled, but they have some friends who have remained in the party.

an unrestrained Bevanism might throw enough of a scare into enough members of the middle classes to push them into the arms of the Conservatives and thus prevent a Labor victory. If that should happen, the struggle for leadership within the Labor party would have to be undertaken in earnest. In such a struggle, the defeat of the Bevanites would be a foregone conclusion. This knowledge probably has a salutary effect on many a "radical" and helps to prevent an open break.

Part II. FRANCE

Plus ça change
Plus c'est la même chose.
(The more it changes,
the more it remains the same.)

MANY ARE the ties of friendship and common cause which exist between the United States and France. Great are the contributions of France to civilization and the arts of government. Yet few Americans have been able to suppress a feeling of impatience, frustration, and exasperation when contemplating the French political and economic scene.

Here is a country which nature has endowed with abundant blessings. Well supplied with natural resources and a fertile soil, France has an ideal balance between rural and urban population. Hers is a people of diligence and many skills. Her educational system is of a high order, producing a well-informed, intelligent, and politically sophisticated population.

Of most outstanding interest for the student of political science is France's lasting and continuing contribution to the realm of political ideas and institutions. Few events, if any, in the entire history of mankind have ever electrified the human race as did the French Revolution of 1789. All Continental European ideas of liberty, of popular sovereignty, and of the republican form of government either are directly derived therefrom or owe France a heavy debt.

The student who considers the nature of parliamentary democracy is inclined to think first of England. But France has given the world a different approach to that same subject, the system of assembly government, which has found many though often involuntary followers.

Less spectacular, but just as significant, is France's leadership in the highly important field of administrative justice, which we in the United States have only recently discovered and where we can learn much from the genius of France's Council of State.

Yet France seems to experience great difficulties in finding herself. Her disunity, her relatively slow rate of recovery, the weakness of her fiscal system, and her difficulty in creating a positive foreign policy have greatly weakened the resonance of her voice in the council of states despite the many factors in her favor.

At the root of the problem stands a fact stated time after time by a galaxy of writers, namely, that Frenchmen are individualists of an extreme kind. French individualism differs substantially from the English and American variety. In the English-speaking world, individualism expresses itself in a reluctance to accept too readily the ministrations of a paternalistic government. At the same time, the members of the Anglo-American family have been by no means adverse to voluntary group action, a habit fostered especially by the growth of Protestantism and anchored in the modalities of the new industrial society.[1] Thus, the English and the Americans, as well as such other nations as the Swiss and the Scandinavians, have that rare gift which makes democratic government a living reality, namely, voluntary discipline. To the Anglo-American peoples, individualism is a modern idea, well suited to the industrial age and its demand for collective action as long as it is the result of a free exchange of ideas and is carried out after a full hearing and under due process of law.

French individualism is essentially a quest for personal independence. "At the end of his day's work the English miner goes to play football; the French miner, who has remained a peasant, goes into his garden." [2] To preserve this precious independence, a Frenchman will toil from dawn till dusk, he will live a most frugal existence, and he will always try to make ends meet. Once he had saved enough, he was likely to retire to live on the interests of his investments, as a *rentier,* though economic developments have now made that quite difficult. He thus becomes the prototype of the French "solid citizen," the *bourgeois.* One of the keenest observers, himself a Frenchman and a patriot, has characterized him thus: "To acquire a little property, a little house, a little business, a little pension is the dream of millions of Frenchmen. It is a precise, limited aim without romanticism: he who pursues it is a realist and may even be called wise, but he borders on the mediocre." [3]

It should be noted that in the preceding quotation the emphasis is on "little." And that is indeed typical of French aspirations. Most business establishments are small, of the family type, and are run like a family, without an urge for expansion, conservatively. There is little desire to make money beyond the immediate needs of the persons concerned. There is little urge for credit expansion, for large construction.[4] It might be said that there is much charm to this attitude. It might even be said that the French viewpoint is more civilized than the American frenzy for dynamic competition and building

[1] On the relations between religion, capitalism, and democracy, see especially Max Weber, *Protestant Ethic and the Spirit of Capitalism,* London, 1930, and R. H. Tawney, *Religion and the Rise of Capitalism,* London, 1926.

[2] Paul Morand, *Paris-Tombouctou,* Paris, 1929, p. 84, quoted by André Siegfried in *Tableau des partis en France,* Paris, 1930, p. 14.

[3] Siegfried, *op. cit.,* pp. 28–29.

[4] David S. Landes, "French Business and the Businessman: A Social and Cultural Analysis," in *Modern France,* ed. by E. M. Earle, Princeton, 1951, pp. 334–353.

for the sake of building. But in this world of ours the French attitude leads to stagnation and makes the nation notoriously unable to cope with the economic and financial problems by which it is constantly confronted.

The French ideal of individualism embodies the idea of life in isolation, economically, socially, and intellectually. The gregarious, frivolous, risqué Frenchman so often portrayed in drama and novels is not typical of his country but represents only a small group which impresses foreigners far more than it impresses Frenchmen. Unfortunately, this French ideal of individualism belongs to a day long gone by when life in isolation was possible. Modern society poses quite different problems: not of individual versus group action, but of voluntary versus enforced group action. The French mode of life—once the most progressive in Europe—is now sometimes a hindrance to progress because time has passed France by. The Frenchman, who is not ordinarily a great traveler, finds it hard to believe that France is no longer the hub of the universe and that French political maxims, such as the French concept of Franco-German relations, are no longer the axis around which the world revolves. This isolation, although self-inflicted, perplexes and irritates him and is inclined to emphasize the stubborn streak inherent in all peasant nations.

His individualism causes the Frenchman to be suspicious of his government and to take a cynical attitude toward it. Yet his intellectual clarity of mind— the mark of an old civilization and of mature reflection—coupled with a Latin temperament, causes him to embrace idealistic schemes which are totally unconnected with his personal interests. He is ready to die for his country, but not to pay its taxes. Even if he is a *bourgeois,* he may fervently embrace the spirit of the French Revolution and cast his vote for a radical candidate— as long as his privacy and his property are not interfered with. "The French carry their heart on the Left and their pocketbook on the Right," is a much-quoted saying.

It is difficult to induce such people to unite except in a dire emergency, and, short of war, it is not easy to convince them that such an emergency exists. To stress the need for unified action has been the endeavor—so far unsuccessful—of every French government since the liberation. "It was imperative then and . . . it is essential now that the French people reacquire the desire and taste for authority, an authority freely accepted. We felt that our main task was to persuade Frenchmen gradually to resume the necessary practice of civic discipline," recently declared a leading French statesman and several times Premier.[5] But that is not easy because the French tradition is one of revolt against authority, which is regarded as tyrannical and as an enemy of the individual.

In the great chess game of international politics the position, the strength,

[5] From a speech by Robert Schuman, then Premier of France, delivered at Poitiers, Apr. 18, 1948. *Le Monde,* Apr. 20, 1948.

and the weakness of France are of the deepest significance. A strong France would make the West predominant and secure beyond its greatest hopes, while a weak France tends to undermine confidence in Europe's future and raises many irksome questions, like that of West German rearmament, which would hardly exist were France to return to her former place as the foremost continental power.

France's weakness and France's strength cannot be measured in military terms. More than in any other major country it is the political stability and cohesion of the French people, their spirit, and the solidity of their institutions which spell the difference between fragility and strength. Frenchmen are not dependent on their environment for their values but carry them within themselves. When conquered, Frenchmen may treat their would-be masters with disdain which stems from an innate and not unjustified feeling of cultural superiority. When free, they may be incapable of settling down to good government. But when they are temporarily vanquished their spirit may ascend to indomitable heights and they may prove quite unmanageable—as the Germans found out to their regret. Domestic "men on horseback" like Boulanger or Laval have encountered similar trouble.

In the few years since her liberation in 1944, France, formidably aided by American resources, has made much headway and sailed successfully around many a dangerous cliff. Yet France is still unsettled in her political course, frequently out of control when governing herself, while at the same time furiously unwilling to be governed by anybody else, somehow surviving even the greatest crises and always coming out on top without ever staying there— a fascinating subject for study, an object of marvel and despair to friend and foe alike.

FRANCE

Chapter 1

EARLY CONSTITUTIONAL AND POLITICAL DEVELOPMENT

In a very real sense France's modern political and constitutional history begins in 1789, the year of the great Revolution. True, earlier developments left their trace, but the Revolution was a break with the past, and there are few modern concepts and problems which cannot be traced back to that epoch.

THE ANCIEN RÉGIME

The prerevolutionary era, known as the *ancien régime,* was characterized by a combination of absolutism and centralism, devised to keep the various feudal lords under control. It reached into every region and was exercised by a well-organized bureaucracy under the leadership of the King's council.

The *ancien régime* did not permit a legislature in which the legitimate complaints of the people could be debated openly. A general assembly, the Estates General, had been known for centuries but had no legislative functions and was usually convoked only in times of great crisis.

Accordingly, public indignation over the severe social inequalities found no outlet until it erupted into violent revolution. The intellectual fathers of the Revolution had no actually existing state of affairs in mind when they described their ideas, with the exception of the American example and a misconception of the British form of government. The idea of the revolution was therefore conceived in the abstract. But this idea had many origins. There was the influence of Rousseau's theories as expressed in the new nationalism of the Revolution. There was the political individualism of the natural-law school and the economic individualism of the physiocrats. The nationalism which the French Revolution engendered led everywhere to a serious intensification of political struggles. Wars which had hitherto been dynastic, almost private affairs, now became the struggle of great masses rising to the new nationalist battle cries. But this nationalism, so disastrous to the stability of the world, also carried with it the new ideas of individual rights, of representative institutions, and of liberalism.

THE DECLARATION OF THE RIGHTS OF MAN

The outstanding expression of the natural-law concept and the resulting belief in individual rights is the "Declaration of the Rights of Man and of the Citizen" of 1789. Several authorities have offered impressive evidence that it was in fact modeled on its American counterpart.[1]

The Declaration asserted the principles of personal freedom and equality, the rights of man to liberty, property, security, and resistance to oppression. It recognized the right of the citizen to participate either directly or through representatives in the legislative process. It recognized the freedom of thought and religion, of speech, press, and assembly. It forbade arrest and indictment except as prescribed by law, and prohibited the taking of private property without just compensation.

The Declaration formed the preamble of the Constitution of 1791 and was repeated or expressly recognized in subsequent documents, including the present Constitution of the French Republic.

The intellectual influence of the Declaration on European thought and practice was enormous. Everywhere men were inspired to think in terms of individual rights. Its specific constitutional significance in France, however, has always remained questionable because it has never been a true constitutional document in the Anglo-American sense; it was rather a syllabus of aims and purposes or, in the words of a distinguished writer, a part of the "social" constitution as distinguished from the political. In other words, it has remained a philosophical call for action which was sometimes heeded and sometimes not. It has never constituted the specific limitations on government which were instituted by the comparable provisions of the United States Constitution.

THE REVOLUTION

The government of France which the Revolution established was as powerful as that which it had overthrown. In contrast to certain British and especially American ideas which emphasize the limitations of governmental power, the French were more concerned with the control of that power than with its extent. According to the concepts of popular sovereignty this control, hitherto in the hands of an all-powerful king, would now be wielded by the

[1] Georg Jellinek, *Die Erklärung der Menschen und Bürgerrechte*, Munich, 1927, 4th ed., pp. 7*ff.*; H. E. Bourne, "American Constitutional Precedents in the French National Assembly," *American Historical Review*, Vol. VIII (1903), pp. 466–486; J. H. Robinson, "The French Declaration of the Rights of Man," *Political Science Quarterly*, Vol. VI (1899), pp. 3–662; Crane Brinton, "Declaration of the Rights of Man," *Encyclopedia of the Social Sciences*, Vol. III, pp. 49–51. Brinton cites a French pamphlet published in 1791 showing connections between the American documents and the French Declaration.

sovereign nation itself. But in a modern, large state, popular sovereignty is always rather theoretical, because the people as a whole cannot rule. From a political and institutional point of view this meant that sovereignty was actually exercised by the legislature, the *convention*. From a sociological standpoint, control was now in the hands of the *bourgeoisie*, the victor of the Revolution. While the Revolution was not able to establish direct rule by the citizens themselves, it made the rise of a strong executive most difficult. Hence, legislative supremacy, also called assembly government or *gouvernement conventionnel*, became identified with the spirit of the Revolution and with those political groups which consider themselves the true custodians of the nation's revolutionary heritage.

The Revolution is tied to the republican tradition of France. An affirmative attitude toward the Republic is supposed to entail an acceptance of the ideas of the Revolution. It is therefore not unusual for otherwise very conservative citizens to give their vote to parties which profess to be revolutionary and hence acting in the true spirit of France.

The Revolution went a long way toward creating a nation. But it also created profound cleavages which are not overcome even today. This is most sharply defined in the now wholly historical struggle over the relationship between state and church in which the parties which consider themselves as belonging to the traditional "left" regard the Catholic Church as antirevolutionary and therefore as an enemy, despite the fact that these terms have lost all meaning today. But in France historical struggles are carried on regardless of the pertinence of the question to contemporary issues. In a way, the entire question about the direction in which "progress" lies has divided and continues to divide the French nation and often prevents it from busying itself with less fundamental, but more practical and urgent tasks. Such fundamental cleavages also make for intransigence which renders most difficult the daily compromises on which all government is based.

THE FIRST CONSTITUTIONS

The National Assembly which drafted the first Constitution of France, that of September 3, 1791, was actually nothing but the so-called Third Estate of the Estates General (*états généraux*), a quasi-legislature of medieval origin. After a history during which the Estates General were sometimes influential, especially when the king needed money, and sometimes not, popular pressure and dire financial strain caused Louis XVI to revive the institution and even to double the representation of the burghers, the Third Estate (*tiers état*).

The Constitution of 1791 was a curious mixture of monarchical and republican principles. It established in most solemn manner the fundamental rights of the citizen. Its references to popular sovereignty were, however, difficult to implement. A number of fruitless attempts were made in a series of Constitutions which followed one another rapidly: the already mentioned one of 1791, that of June 24, 1793, and that of 5 Fructidor, Year III (August 22, 1795).[2] But the Constitution of 22 Frimaire, Year VIII (December 13, 1800), finally abandoned the attempt by proclaiming that "the government is entrusted to three Consuls who are appointed for six years and are reeligible."

These Constitutions were influenced by Jean Jacques Rousseau's doctrine of popular sovereignty, but they failed to respond to his demand that this sovereignty be exercised directly and not through deputies. In actual application, therefore, the legislative branch which, according to prevailing beliefs, most closely represented the will of the people became sovereign rather than the people themselves. Rousseau's demand for direct government was fulfilled only in the form of elections and plebiscites. The latter, however, were frequently abused and do not have a good reputation in France despite their continued existence.

The principle of popular sovereignty was also anchored in the maxim that the people alone could change the Constitution and that they could change it at will. It is true that the manner in which such constitutional changes could be brought about was prescribed in the Constitution, but ever since the Revolution it has been a time-honored tenet that the people cannot be restrained by mere form in the exercise of their sovereign will. Consequently constitutional changes have more often than not been the result of revolutions and of *coups d'état*.[3] For the same reason, judicial review of legislation or any other form of constitutional restraint on legislatures has been generally in disfavor, although the Constitution of the Year VIII did take some wholly theoretical steps in that direction.

NAPOLEON

Despite the Revolution's professed belief in popular sovereignty, there were many instances of short-lived strong executive leadership. Most notable was the revolutionary Committee of Public Safety, which developed into a dictatorship as absolute as any royal government had ever been. The Constitution of the Year III marked a reaction against the broad basis of its predecessors. Voting qualifications were reinstituted, a second chamber, the Council of Elders, was established, and the executive power was vested in the Directory of five members.

The Constitution of the Year III was the last democratic organic act of the revolutionary period. Its successor, the Constitution of the Year VIII, was

[2] The First French Republic attempted to reorganize the calendar. The years were counted from the beginning of the Revolution; the months were renamed and completely rearranged. Fructidor, for instance, lasted from August 18 to September 16.

[3] Jean Brissaud, *A History of French Public Law* (trans. by J. W. Garner), Boston, 1915, p. 545.

strictly authoritarian, and its machinery was placed under the exacting control of the First Consul, Napoleon Bonaparte. Its principal legislative body, the "conservative Senate," was appointed for life and was self-perpetuating. It had power to annul unconstitutional acts, but by decree (*sénatus-consulte*) it amended the Constitution by establishing the Consulate for life in 1802 and the Empire in 1804.

Schoolbooks generally emphasize the belligerent exploits of Napoleon, but far more lasting and significant were his administrative reforms. The judicial system, already streamlined by the Revolution, was made more uniform by Napoleon. Judges, who in the earlier revolutionary period had been elected, were again appointed. In order to satisfy the French concept of the separation of powers, the Council of State (*Conseil d'État*) and prefectual councils were established for the purpose of rendering administrative justice.

Formidable was the work of codification which created the great series of legal codes: the Code of Civil Law (1804), the Code of Civil Procedure (1807), the Code of Criminal Law (1808, supplemented in 1810), and the Code of Commercial Law (1807).

French local government also took its final form under Napoleon. The old territorial divisions of the *ancien régime* had been irregular, inconsistent, and full of enclaves. They were the results of dynastic considerations, acquisition by marriage and conquest, and historical accident. The royal regime used these divisions effectively by imposing on them royal agents designed to keep in check the centrifugal tendencies of the nobles. The Revolution swept all that away and created a unified system of local government composed of departments, districts, cantons, and communes. Some forms of local councils were established, but because of the complete absence of experience with local government, these resulted in chaotic conditions. In order to alleviate them, the central government reverted to the methods of the *ancien régime* by sending delegates-at-large with considerable power to the various regions. Through them, local government quickly became the creature of the central authorities.

Under Napoleon this system was regularized and the government established permanent strict control over local government, even in the most minute detail, through the departmental prefect.

The Restored Bourbons

Upon his first return from long exile, the restored Bourbon monarch Louis XVIII enacted the Constitutional Charter of June 4, 1814, which was full of allusions to divine providence and the other customary formulas of legitimism, but satisfied neither the reactionaries, for whom it did not go far enough, nor the liberals, to whom it smelled of the *ancien régime*. After the death of Louis XVIII in 1824, his brother, Charles X, immediately proceeded to go the *ancien régime* one better; but the cup finally flowed over, and the Revolution of 1830 chased the King out of the country.

CONSTITUTIONAL MONARCHY

The rebellious burghers called to the throne Duke Louis Philippe of Orléans, the son of the man who, under the name of Philippe-Égalité, had been a member of the Revolutionary Convention, had voted for the death sentence against his cousin, Louis XVI, and had finally gone to the guillotine himself as a member of the Girondist party.

The regime of Louis Philippe was that of a constitutional monarchy with reasonably liberal content. Its Constitutional Charter of August 14, 1830, avoided the provocative preamble of the Charter of 1814. But the imagination of the regime was exhausted with these initial reforms. It resisted all further change, which was fatal at a time which knew great advances in human thinking. It gradually lost all support and, at the first show of force against it, it collapsed. On February 24, 1848, Louis Philippe left the country, never to return.

THE SECOND REPUBLIC

If the constitutional monarchy had been lacking in imagination, the Second Republic possessed this fault to an even greater extent. Its sole contribution was the institution of universal suffrage. But the government proved itself incapable of coping with a serious economic condition and met with the bitter resistance of the workers who, under the influence of socialist ideas, rose in arms in June, 1848. After a bloody battle, the workers were defeated and their movement stepped into the background of the political stage, from which it returned only many years later.

The Constitution of November 4, 1848, was modeled on the American example and created a presidency of the Republic in which was vested all executive power. Then, on December 2, the French people went to the polls and by overwhelming majority elected to this all-important post none other than Louis Napoleon Bonaparte, a nephew of the great emperor. The new president attempted from the outset to discredit the legislature, a majority of whom were both antirepublican and anti-Bonapartist. Since the Constitution had made the president ineligible to succeed himself, Louis Napoleon accomplished his aim by the *coup d'état* of December 1–2, 1851. Having seized power and abrogated the offensive presidential election laws, Louis Napoleon demanded that a plebiscite give him power to write a new constitution. The response was overwhelming: 7,439,216 voted "yes," while only 640,757 voted "no," and 36,820 ballots were invalid.

THE SECOND EMPIRE

The Constitution thus sanctioned in advance was promptly promulgated on January 14, 1852, very much in the image of the Constitution of the Year VIII. Like that earlier document, it was merely a stepping stone to the restoration of the Empire. It was established on November 7, 1852, by Senate vote which pronounced Louis Napoleon Bonaparte Emperor of the French under the name of Napoleon III. The Senate resolution was submitted to a plebiscite, which gave its consent to the reestablishment of the Empire by the stupendous majority of 7,824,189 votes against a mere 153,145. Once again it was demonstrated that universal suffrage and free elections are no guarantee against the rise of autocracy.

In the beginning the Second Empire was strictly authoritarian, but after 1860 somewhat more popular government was instituted and greater emphasis was placed on parliamentary government. The Constitution of May 21, 1870, was even more liberal and constituted a real concession to the mounting disaffection among the people.

A new and promising era seemed to dawn over France. But on July 19, 1870, Napoleon III plunged his country into a hasty and ill-considered war against Prussia, and on September 1 the dream of the Second Empire vanished in the disastrous battle of Sedan together with the tarnished crown of the Emperor. When this dreadful news reached Paris, the legislature reinstituted the Republic and set up an emergency government.

A renowned historian and philosopher once remarked that outstanding historical facts and personalities frequently appear twice in the course of history. Another observer commented that he might have added, "once as a tragedy, and once as a farce." If Napoleon I was the tragedy, Napoleon III was the farce.

Chapter 2

THE THIRD REPUBLIC

The period of 1870 to 1875 not only gave rise to the Third Republic but also created the foundations of the Fourth, its nearly identical successor.

The end of the Second Empire brought about various propositions concerning the future course to be followed. For a while they were all brushed aside by the people of Paris, who set up spontaneously a provisional Government of National Defense whose guiding spirit was the fiery Italian-born Léon Gambetta. But despite Gambetta's ardor in raising new armies in the provinces, and despite the diplomatic efforts of such respected men as Thiers and Ferry, the Germans ruled the field, occupied much of France, and besieged Paris, which capitulated on January 28, 1871.

The electoral campaign of 1871 centered on the issue of peace or war. And the victory of the conservative forces who favored peace with Germany was decisive. The majority favored a constitutional monarchy, but this came to naught because they were divided between the "legitimists," adherents of the Bourbon monarchy, whose candidate was the pretender, the Count of Chambord, a grandson of Charles X, and Orléanists, whose candidate was the Count of Paris, a grandson of ex-King Louis Philippe. There was also a small group of "Bonapartists" who remained faithful to Napoleon III and, after his death in 1873, to his son, the Prince Imperial.

Thiers

By a resolution of February 17, 1871, Adolphe Thiers was elected "Chief Executive" rather than President, thus avoiding the creation of a strictly republican institution. He was a man of great prestige, experience, and dignity and got along well with Bismarck, which was important. Although he was to exercise his power under the control of the National Assembly, he dominated it by his enormous prestige and eloquence. But after he had suppressed the uprising of the Paris Commune by force, the National Assembly no longer considered him indispensable.

Undoubtedly he would have been succeeded by a monarch had the monarchist cause not been defeated by the incredible blindness of the principal pretender, the Count of Chambord, who, surrounded by a coterie of faithful followers who were as much out of contact with France as he was, insisted that the French nation must expiate its sins before it could return to the law and order which he proposed to give it. The symbol of his own limited mind was his stubborn insistence that the tricolor flag of France, originally of revolutionary origin, but now accepted by almost all, had to be abandoned and replaced by the white-lily banner, the symbol of the *ancien régime*.

The attitude of the pretender dealt a mortal blow to the monarchist cause. The results of the July, 1871, elections held in forty-six departments showed a decisive shift of public opinion toward republicanism.

As a result, the Rivet law of August 31, 1871, moved a little closer to republicanism. But two years later the growing conflict between President and Assembly resulted in a curtailment of presidential powers and Thiers's downfall.

His successor was Marshal MacMahon, Duke of Magenta, hero of the Crimean and Franco-Austrian Wars, who had been badly defeated and captured at Sedan.

THE CONSTITUTION OF THE THIRD REPUBLIC

Under MacMahon the character of the presidency changed radically and took on the form which it has today. It was a shift which resulted from a difference in personality rather than from the passage of new laws. Thiers had been an extraordinary politician and statesman, a splendid orator, and a renowned historian. MacMahon was brave and dull, personally an honest man, but a convinced monarchist and reactionary. About politics he knew little and cared less. He was quite content to play the role of a formal head of state and leave the actual government of the country to his ministers. Among them the Vice-president became Premier in everything but name.

The National Assembly took due notice of this change and on November 20, 1873, adopted a law removing the President from responsibility to the Assembly and giving him a fixed term of seven years, the so-called *septennat* which is still in effect today.

In subsequent constitutional debates, a number of proposals were submitted, especially by deputies Casimir Périer and Laboulaye, which would have established a clear-cut republican form of government, but which were rejected by the predominantly monarchist Assembly which was prevented from following its natural inclinations only by the intransigent attitude of the pretender.

Finally, amidst general confusion, deputy Wallon proposed an amendment which read as follows: "The President of the Republic is elected by an absolute majority of the Senate and the Chamber of Deputies joined together in the National Assembly." This amendment was designed to separate the Republic from the person of the Marshal and thus make the Republic permanent.

The crucial vote on the Wallon amendment was taken in breathless excitement. The result was adoption by 353 against 352. Thus by indirection and amidst confusion, the Third Republic was created by a majority of one in a predominantly antirepublican Assembly which had no intention of creating anything lasting. Few people in that year of 1875 believed that the Republic was to remain for long. Yet it existed for 65 years and, after the four years of the Vichy régime, found its resurrection in the present Fourth Republic. Never was more justice done to the French saying that nothing lasts as long as the provisional.

After the narrow adoption of the Wallon amendment, the militant opposition against the Republic subsided. Soon a number of constitutional laws followed, "on the organization of the Senate," "on the organization of the public power," and "on the interrelationship of the public power." "The organic law concerning the election of Senators" and "the organic law concerning the election of deputies" completed the constitutional framework of the Third Republic. "Do not search for the principles which guided us," said some of the members of the Assembly, "everything was done without method, without design, blindly, through the imperceptible balance of indecisive minorities; chance was our master." [1]

Subsequent amendments transferred the seat of parliament from Versailles to Paris and "deconstitutionalized" the articles of the Law of 1875 which dealt with the elections to the Senate, thus opening the way for a new electoral law to the Senate to be passed by ordinary legislation.

The government created in 1875 and later was that of a parliamentary democracy. Headed nominally by a President of the Republic, its chief executive was actually the Premier whose official title was, then as now, President of the Council of Ministers.

The legislature was bicameral, consisting of a Chamber of Deputies and a Senate. The Chamber was elected in single-member districts by majority vote and run-off election. The Senate was elected indirectly, each department forming an electoral college similar to the present method of electing members of the Council of the Republic. A minimum age of forty and a term of nine years prescribed for Senators made the Senate a very aged and very independent body which, for practical purposes, was coequal to the Chamber of Deputies. While the Senate did not overthrow cabinets outright, it was known to make their lives so impossible as to force them to resign. This whip was used against both right-wing governments (Tardieu, Laval) and those of the left (Blum). But the general character of the Senate was conservative, whatever the party label, and it was therefore particularly the Socialists and Communists who urged its abolition.

A strange feature in this picture was the fact that in the land of "liberty,

[1] Joseph-Barthélemy and Paul Duez, *Traité élémentaire de droit constitutionnel,* Paris, 1926, p. 33.

equality, and fraternity," women did not possess the suffrage despite the fact that they had always played an important and significant role in the public life of France. It was only after the Second World War that women were given their full political rights.

The Constitution of the Third Republic was characterized by the predominance of parliament. Yet in times of extreme crisis, cabinets were frequently invested with practically unchecked power to rule by decree. That this regime lasted so long and was restored in its major features in 1946 may be credited to the genius of the French people, to their subtle understanding of political realities, and to the long-lasting balance of opposing political forces. Its longevity can hardly be ascribed to the constitutional fabric of 1875, of which the leading French historian of that period has written as follows:

It is not one of those beautiful, straightforward constructions in whose establishment the theoreticians of the last century took pride, comparable to the famous constitutions of 1791, 1793 and 1848, with their majestic pillars of a Declaration of the Rights of Man, the wise order of uniform style and with the ingenious symmetry of three separate and balanced powers. No, this is an incoherent monument whose architect one cannot even find, for the whole world has had its hand in it; masterbuilder and brick-layer alike. A monument? Not even that. At the most it is a piece of masonry, a clump of separate cabins without apparent intercommunication. Less than that, it is a scaffold of chance, a work without name. Not even the word constitution is written on its gable while on its roof sits the menacing amending clause, the permanent stamp of the provisional.[2]

POLITICAL STRUGGLE

At the inception of the Third Republic the principal political division was between monarchists and republicans. This was not merely over the head of state. The monarchists were also, by and large, the economically and socially more conservative element, while the republicans tended to be more progressive and liberal. But this division must be accepted with considerable reservation as all shades of opinions existed in either camp.

The situation was also further complicated by the injection of the so-called "religious question." France is a Catholic country, which does not mean that the majority of the French people are practising Catholics but rather that the Catholic religion is by far the strongest among the religions of France and that a predominantly Catholic cultural pattern permeates the country, even among those who have little to do with the Catholic church. Church questions are therefore sensitive ones.

In the minds of republicans the Catholic Church is identified with antirepublican thought and action. Graduates of Catholic schools are suspected of

[2] Gabriel Hanotaux, *Histoire de la France contemporaine*, Paris, 1903, Vol. III, p. 423.

being automatically antirepublican. Time and again, during the Third Republic, attendance at mass or even the attendance of his wife would retard or even break the career of a soldier or civil servant. Nor was much of the Catholic element less uncompromising, and when Pope Leo XIII [3] and Cardinal Lavigerie recommended acceptance of the Republic, their action was deeply resented by some die-hard groups as practically treasonable.

The religious issue complicated the political picture enormously because a politician who was arch-conservative in economic matters could be regarded as "left" if he also opposed the church, while a Catholic near-Socialist might be labeled as "right."

THE SOCIALISTS

The nineteenth century, which produced the great wave of industrialization in most countries, also brought forth the proletariat and the workers' movement which found its home in the ranks of socialism. It was essentially a movement of protest against intolerable social conditions and the vast cleavage which existed between the workers and other classes. In a way the passing of feudalism had not abolished the feudal system but had only changed the ruling groups and made their methods more subtle. The French worker, in contrast to his American colleague, still has no hope or expectation of individual success. Only as a class can he hope for the improvement of his lot.

French workers' class consciousness antedates Marxism. But in contrast to German socialism, which quickly adopted the Marxist formula and which was forged into a powerful party by the German love for organization and discipline, French socialism was, at first, more individualistic than collectivistic. Neither the theories of Proudhon [4] nor the political action of Auguste Blanqui [5] created a real movement. Eventually Jules Guesde, representing Marxist integralism, and Jean Jaurès, representing the emphasis on humanitarian motives, forged the Socialist party into one (1905).

Because the party professed to be revolutionary, it never was accused of being an "enemy of the state" as was its German counterpart, because the revolutionary tradition is part of the life of France. But because it was French, it never rose to great organizational accomplishment. Jaurès remained the most popular and brilliant of Socialist leaders until his death by assassination on the eve of the First World War.

It was Jaurès's influence over the Socialist party which made it more

---

[3] In the encyclical, *Inter Multiplices Sollicitudines*.

[4] Pierre Joseph Proudhon's principal work, *Système des contradictions économiques, ou philosophie de la misère*, Paris, 1846, 2 vols., was subjected to acid criticism by Marx in his *Misère de la philosophie*, Brussels, 1847.

[5] Blanqui was an old revolutionary who was genuinely popular, but he died in 1881. See Alexandre Zevaès, *Histoire du socialisme et du communisme en France*, Paris, 1947.

humanitarian than Marxist, more gradualist and reformist than revolutionary. But this course was not followed unanimously, and to this day French social-ism is divided on the issue of radicalism versus reformism. At times like the present, when the Socialists are one of the mainstays of a democratic, republi-can regime, this inner cleavage contributes to the weakness not only of the party but also of the regime.

THE COMMUNISTS

The world-wide split within the international socialist movement which followed the First World War also took place in France. At the party conven-tion of Tours (1920) the split between Socialists and Communists became permanent. The majority of the leaders, especially Léon Blum, Marcel Sambat, Pierre Renaudel, and Paul Faure fought the Communist strength vigorously, but the majority of the party was not with them. Had Jaurès still been alive, it might have been different. With the majority going Com-munist, the control over the party's assets, especially its chief newspaper, *L'Humanité*, became Communist. The Socialist remnants established them-selves under great difficulties as the French section of the Second (socialist) International (SFIO).[6]

Until the Second World War the Communists were not successful in taking over the trade-union movement. The General Confederation of Labor (CGT) remained outside their fold and largely Socialist-controlled. The Communists tried to infiltrate various locals and eventually founded a rival movement which they called "Unified" General Confederation of Labor. But this split merely helped the Christian Federation of Labor (CFTC) and sometimes the employers.

THE INTERWAR PERIOD

The First World War left the French nation united and victorious but, by the standards of those days, physically almost destroyed, for France had been the principal battleground and the loss of life had been fearful. Over 1,600,000 were dead—out of a population of 40,000,000—with, at that time, a dangerously declining birthrate. From then on, fear, revulsion against war, any war, remained a dominant element in French political thinking.

The governments between the two wars were usually coalitions either of the left or of the right, but in actuality the difference between them was not so great. While the governments of the right were truly right, those of the left, usually dominated by the Radical Socialist party, which was neither radical nor socialist but actually quite conservative, were little different. On the whole, French politics of the Third Republic were dominated by personalities

[6] *Section française de l'internationale ouvrière.*

such as Raymond Poincaré, André Tardieu, Pierre Laval, Édouard Herriot, and Édouard Daladier far more than by rigid party lines.

But France did not remain immune from fascism. A number of groups appeared, among which the Patriotic Youth (Jeunesses Patriotes), the Action Française, the "hooded men" (Cagoulards), and the Fiery Cross (Croix de Feu) were best known. On February 6, 1934, the pent-up emotions resulted in widespread demonstrations which produced some shooting and swept away the Daladier government.[7] This was the first time that a "left" government had been overthrown by pressure from the "street," and the lesson was not lost. The parties of the left pulled closer together, establishing the so-called "Popular Front." It was composed of the Communists, Socialists, and Radical Socialists. Although such an organization may have seemed logical at the time, it had some serious consequences. Most important of all, it produced a great strengthening of the Communists, and their association with the other parties made them "respectable" and permitted them to infiltrate many organizations, especially the trade-union movement. The common-action program of the Popular Front was announced in 1936, a year of general elections, which also brought to the Communists considerable success. Not that their vote had so greatly increased, but the Popular Front gave them allies and coalition partners for the first time and thus made it possible for many Communist candidates to win runoff elections with Socialist and Radical support.

The Popular Front government, headed by Socialist leader Léon Blum, found itself confronted on the one hand by the profound suspicion of the right and on the other hand constantly pushed into more precipitate action by the Communists. In order to appease the workers, the government had to accept hasty reforms which certainly did much good but also increased the cost of production and weakened output. In order to appease the flight of capital, the government had to adopt halfhearted fiscal measures which satisfied no one. On top of this, the Popular Front governments were confronted by the Spanish Civil War, which produced complex problems of foreign policy, while the Senate constantly sniped at the governments, and made their lives miserable. All this brought confusion to France at a time when Hitler was already in power in Germany and the German rearmament effort was going forward full blast. Léon Blum, now keenly aware of the danger which confronted France, attempted to create a government on a broad national basis but was only partly successful. Faced by Senate refusal to grant him the requested plenary powers, Blum resigned, and on April 13, 1938, he was succeeded by Édouard Daladier, who was supposed to be a strong man but hardly deserved this reputation. The Popular Front experiment had come to an end.

[7] See Alexander Werth, *The Twilight of France*, New York, 1942. Generally the best work on the political parties of the Third Republic days is by François Goguel, *La Politique des partis sous la IIIème République*, Paris, 1946, 2 vols.

Defeat and Vichy

France entered the Second World War without enthusiasm and as a deeply divided nation. Many Frenchmen hated one another more profoundly than they hated the enemy. Marcel Déat, once of the left, wrote his famous article, "Why Die For Danzig?" and scored a smashing hit. The rapid defeat of France was breathtaking and awe-inspiring. When the dazed Frenchmen compared the machinelike efficiency of their conquerors with the spectacle of their own disorganized army retreating in confusion, a feeling of hopelessness and fatalism often overcame them. In this situation, the appearance of Marshal Philippe Pétain was especially significant. He was one of two surviving marshals of France, the hero of Verdun, the symbol of past French glory. Pétain's decision to establish an authoritarian government in order to cope with the extraordinary problems of defeat and reconstruction met with less resistance than might otherwise have been expected, because the supposed superiority of authoritarian regimes had been so tellingly demonstrated by the overwhelming victory of the German Juggernaut. Had Pétain's successors, especially Daladier and Reynaud, possessed the fortitude to hold out against the Armistice and perhaps transfer the seat of the French government to North Africa, a considerable element of public opinion would undoubtedly have rallied around them. But France's collapse was not only military, it was moral as well, and to many Frenchmen further resistance seemed useless.

The transition from the defunct Third Republic to the Vichy regime [8] was effected smoothly and with that strict obedience to legal forms with which authoritarian regimes like to cloak their violation of the legal spirit. An act to call a national assembly for the purpose of amending the Constitution was passed in the Senate by a majority of 225 to 1 and in the Chamber by 385 to 3. The Communists were barred. The National Assembly, which was convened on July 10, 1940, gave full powers to Marshal Pétain by an act passed by a majority of 569 to 80. No one party voted against the act as a solid bloc. The Socialists were the largest group among them, but a majority of Socialist deputies and Senators voted for the act. All the more glory therefore, to the 80 who showed such conspicuous courage, which led most of them to imprisonment and some of them to death.

The debate over Pétain's real motives did not die down with the aged Marshal's imprisonment and death. Some see in him a traitor, others again a misguided patriot who tried to do the best for France in trying days. But whatever Pétain's motives, he was surrounded by men who had gone over to the Germans, lock, stock, and barrel, partly out of convictions and partly out

[8] Paris, being occupied by the Germans, had been abandoned, and a temporary capital of unoccupied France was established at the city of Vichy (Allier), a well-known spa.

of belief in Hitler's ultimate victory. Many of the atrocities committed against patriots in those days were the work of French militiamen who showed that they had learned well the lessons of their German masters.

Fortunately, far more Frenchmen were in the Resistance than supported these shameful acts. The Resistance movement was indeed of such broad nature and covered itself with so much glory that no one has a right to speak of French decadence. The majority of the people, however, merely tried to get by, being neither in the Resistance nor among the fascists. Many of them might have repeated the words of that famous aristocrat who, when asked what he did during the great Revolution, replied simply, "I survived."

Chapter 3

THE REBIRTH OF FRANCE

General Charles de Gaulle

While France lay prostrate before her conqueror and some of her self-appointed leaders tried to ape their goose-stepping masters, the tricolor flag was again unfurled across the Channel. General Charles de Gaulle had not been prominent before the war. He was a professional soldier and a tank specialist whose works were read with far greater attention in Germany than in France. Daladier propelled him into the under-secretaryship of war, and as a field commander he fought one of the few moderately successful engagements with the Germans which French arms could record in 1940.

General de Gaulle became identified with the idea of utmost resistance to Germany and was advised to leave France when all resistance crumbled. He did so on June 17, 1940, and Winston Churchill has given us a graphic description of those memorable events. The same evening De Gaulle addressed the French nation over the network of the British Broadcasting Corporation. "France has lost a battle," he declared, "but she has not lost the war." With these ringing phrases, "Fighting France" was reborn.

The significance of De Gaulle's move was not immediately realized. France was in utter confusion. Her army was, on the whole, loyal to Marshal Pétain, and with its peculiar military logic regarded De Gaulle as a traitor. No political group survived intact, for all of them had some collaborationists in their midst. Moreover the Communists gave at least passive support to the Germans as long as the Soviet-German pact of August, 1939, governed their actions in France as it did all over the world. Their leader, Maurice Thorez, deserted from his regiment early in the war and took up his residence in Moscow. This situation lasted until the invasion of the Soviet Union impelled the Communists to take so active and gallant a part in the Resistance movement that they could claim for themselves, not without reason, the somber title of *"parti des fusillés"* (Party of Executed Men).

The Resistance

The Resistance movements and underground groups which sprang up had little coherence at first, and their effectiveness was small. Moreover Frenchmen had been without dictatorship for so long that conspiratorial habits had not been developed, and Gallic love of intrigue was not enough to counter the Gestapo. In this situation, General de Gaulle fulfilled an extremely useful function by providing both a headquarters beyond German reach and the symbol which French patriots needed. Slowly, gradually, and not without some ugly scenes, the many independent resistance and underground groups coalesced into the Resistance and the French Forces of the Interior. In the meantime, De Gaulle had been able to hold on to a portion of France's overseas empire, and good and reliable communications were established with the French mainland.[1]

The Resistance did more than fight the Germans and give effective aid to allied forces and agents. It gave much thought and attention to the future of France. Criticism of the Third Republic was abundant and sharp; few Resistance fighters wished to return to the system of 1875. Many found the American presidential system attractive and hoped that a reasonable adaptation thereof might solve the chronic and permanent crisis of France.[2] This thinking and planning received further momentum from the creation of a kind of underground government, the National Council of Resistance, which was founded by Jean Moulin in 1943, and whose work was later carried on by Georges Bidault.

At that time very few people had much good to say for the Third Republic, which was saddled with blame for much of the disaster that had befallen France. Only the remnant of the once-mighty Radical Socialist party defended the Third Republic. But its voice was weak, partly because it shared so much of the blame, partly because so many of its leaders had become collaborationists.

Many adherents of right-wing parties joined the Resistance, and many former left-wingers became collaborationists. But on the whole, the overwhelming majority of the Resistance belonged to the left—to the Communists, the Socialists, and a group of Christian Democrats.

There was much talk and writing in the Resistance about the "new France," which would be so different from the old, and about the "dead" political parties of the past. Actually this kind of talk was never too realistic. The Communists, who had stayed out as a body until the invasion of the U.S.S.R., joined as a body and entered the fight with their customary discipline and devotion. Thus, other political groups, especially the Socialists, were forced to look to their own political fences. General de Gaulle himself favored the abandonment of the traditional political party system and supported the idea

[1] Among the many books on the French underground, see especially Rémy (Gilbert Renault-Roulier), *Memoirs of a Secret Agent of Free France* (trans. by L. C. Sheppard), New York, 1948. Charles de Gaulle, *Memoires de Guerre, l'appel 1940–1942*, Paris, 1954.

[2] For an excellent and penetrating account, see Gordon Wright, *The Reshaping of French Democracy*, New York, 1948, pp. 30–40.

of a broad national front. But in 1943 he suddenly sent instructions to encourage the old-line parties and offer them representation on the National Council, by which act he actually recreated artifically certain groups which would otherwise have possessed no right to existence. It is not known for certain just what caused the general to change his mind, but the desire to rid himself of the reputation of fascist tendencies may have been of influence. It may also have been his fear that a single, unified Resistance movement might come under the spell of the Communists. But whatever his motives, it is worthy of note that it was General Charles de Gaulle himself who restored the galaxy of parties of which he complained so much later on.

The liberation of French North Africa brought new vigor to the Gaullist movement, even if its relations with its allies were not always smooth. Now there was again a French government on French soil. Naturally enough, thoughts were directed toward the long-range future, and a study committee (Comité Général d'Études) was formed, which pronounced itself in favor of a strong executive form of government. This, as a matter of fact, was a very current trend of mind within the Resistance movement; even Léon Blum,[3] the socialist doctrinaire of yesteryear, expressed sympathy for that idea. Perhaps it was not so clear then as it became later that, at least in the period immediately following the liberation of France proper, only one strong executive was feasible, and that was Charles de Gaulle. But the Communists did understand this, and in 1944 they vigorously denounced the idea of a strong executive. They also condemned any attempt to return to France with a ready-made constitution; only the people of France had the right to determine their future form of government. This Communist action stopped effectively the incipient trend away from the traditional French course of government by assembly. Moreover, made bold by their success, the Communists developed their ideas further by proposing a system through which legislators could be recalled by the electorate before their term of office was up. On this and other points, unanimity of opinion could not be reached in the Resistance movement or in Algiers, and thus there already was foreshadowed the later constitutional debate.

LIBERATION

With the liberation of France there began a very strange period of French history. General Charles de Gaulle returned to France with unparalleled power and prestige. He had no political party of his own, but a government not headed by him was unthinkable. He was the man of the hour who had restored France's honor, and he alone was enshrined in the hearts of his

---

[3] Blum was imprisoned, first by Pétain, later by the Germans. While in prison he wrote down his thoughts in a book entitled *À l'échelle humaine* (For All Mankind) (New York, 1946).

people. There was no constitution—the Vichy Constitution was, of course, unacceptable—and few people wanted to pick up the remnants of the Third Republic where they had dropped them in 1940. Therefore De Gaulle ruled without any real restraint. A "dictatorship by consent," one writer called it.[4] Yet De Gaulle did not attempt to hold on to power and defy the politicians, nor did he try a *coup d'état* like Louis Bonaparte, nor was a coup constantly in the air as it was during the Boulanger episode.[5]

This strange attitude of De Gaulle's has remained a mystery to many observers. But it is also a key to the man's character. His background is primarily military. Like many general officers and products of military academies, he is used to giving high-level orders with the calm expectation that they will be carried out to the letter by the lower echelon. Whether this is actually true even of a military machine is debatable; but in politics, this is a sure road to failure. Thus the very aloofness which made De Gaulle a symbol of a resurgent France also made him a very poor politician who was often incapable of understanding and shrewdly utilizing existing opportunities. Whether France has reason to mourn or be grateful for the general's shortcomings only the future can tell—and even that is not certain.

THE COMMUNISTS

De Gaulle's policy was that of a broad coalition which was to be representative of France. But in actuality that meant a coalition of the political left. The Communists had established themselves very firmly. Their Resistance record greatly outweighed their inglorious attitude of 1939–1940. Moreover they had been able to achieve virtually absolute domination of the now unified General Confederation of Labor (Confédération Générale du Travail, CGT), and although the old Socialist Léon Jouhaux was still nominal leader, Benoît Frachon, a militant Communist, became general secretary and hence real boss. Thus the workers were more likely to obtain their demands from the Communists than from the Socialists, and the subsequent electoral figures bore that out.

THE SOCIALISTS

The Socialists, now reduced or about to be reduced in strength, were badly split between a left wing headed by Guy Mollet, and a majority of the leadership, dominated by the much-mellowed Léon Blum who, despite advanced age and delicate health, had gained greatly in prestige as a result of his courageous stand before the Vichy-conducted trials of Riom.

[4] Wright, *op. cit.*, p. 51.
[5] General Georges Boulanger was a man of high ambition who played with the idea of a *coup d'état* for a long time without ever carrying it out.

The MRP

Perhaps the greatest phenomenon was the newly created Popular Republican Movement (Mouvement Républicain Populaire, MRP), a genuine child of the Resistance, although a nucleus had existed under the Third Republic. The MRP was one of the several Christian (Catholic) democratic movements which gained prominence after the Second World War. Its principal spokesman was Georges Bidault, diminutive professor at the Lycée Louis-le-Grand and, since 1943, president of the clandestine National Council of Resistance. The movement followed the trend of progressive Catholicism that began with the encyclical *Rerum Novarum* of Leo XIII. On the philosophic and literary side the movement was influenced by such figures as Jacques Maritain, François Mauriac, and Georges Bernanos. Much of its early strength came from the common belief, carefully nurtured by the party itself, that it was the party of De Gaulle. But it also received strength from the record of its leaders, especially Bidault and Maurice Schumann,[6] the youthful editor of the party paper, *L'Aube*, whose voice had become familiar to millions of Frenchmen as the voice of Free France from London. While more conservative than the Communists and Socialists, the party nevertheless was definitely of the left, believing in large-scale social reforms, and quite determined not to be forced to the right.

Other Groups

In the early days of liberated France, these three groups represented France. The Radical Socialist party, the giant of the Third Republic, was tainted with the failure of the regime that had come to such an ignominious end in 1940. The parties of the right were deeply implicated in collaborationism, notwithstanding certain outstanding republican figures such as Louis Marin. Courts of honor were set up in order to eliminate those politicians who had voted in favor of plenary powers for Marshal Pétain in 1940. Only a good Resistance record could reinstate such a man to a place on the ballot or in public office.[7] In that way, many of the political leaders of the Third Republic were excluded, and many of those who remained, like Édouard Herriot who had never compromised with Vichy, were very old and past their prime.

[6] Not to be confused with Robert Schuman, another leader of the MRP and several times Premier and Foreign Minister.

[7] One of those reinstated was Robert Schuman, whose resistance record and imprisonment by the Germans saved him from political extinction. The purge was by no means confined to the right. Over one-half the Socialist deputies voted for Pétain and were purged later for the most part; among them was the party secretary, Paul Faure. Only the Communists, who were not allowed to attend the 1940 session of the legislature, were spared the opportunity to compromise themselves, and their leadership corps therefore remained largely intact, thanks to the "anti-Communism" of the Vichy regime.

Had De Gaulle identified himself with one of those parties, especially the MRP, its victory would have been assured, and while his political basis would have been smaller, it would have been much firmer. But De Gaulle preferred to be a symbol rather than a political leader, and thus he deprived the country of leadership when it was most needed.

Ever since April 21, 1944, it had been established that a future national assembly would decide the form of government.[8] The same ordinance issued by the government (Committee of National Liberation) proclaimed the suffrage of all adult men *and women*, thus ending once and for all the exclusion of women from the polls. But it was not until October 21, 1945, that the return of most French prisoners of war made an election to the National Assembly possible. The political picture was confused. The old parties had not completed their reorganization and were caught off guard. The great Resistance movement was falling to pieces as a political force. For a while De Gaulle had toyed with the idea of placing himself at the head of a Resistance bloc, but the disintegration of the movement was inevitable, because, like all movements with limited objectives, it lost its reason for existence when its objective, the defeat of the Germans, was attained. Perhaps De Gaulle was also motivated by fear of the prominent role of Communists in the Resistance. At any rate he placed himself at the head of the tripartite coalition. Apart from the MRP, the Resistance had produced only two political groups: the French Unified Movement of Reconstruction (Mouvement Unifié de la Renaissance Française, MURF), which was for all practical purposes an appendix to the Communist party, and the Union of Democratic and Socialist Resistance (Union Démocratique et Socialiste de la Résistance, UDSR), which was at first in the socialist camp. Both these groups were of rapidly diminishing significance.

The three principal parties, Communists, Socialists, and MRP, all agreed on the necessity of a new constitution, not merely a revision of the regime of 1875, which the remnants of the Radical Socialists would have preferred. But the MRP disliked the kind of concentration of power in the hands of a unicameral legislature which the Socialists and especially the Communists demanded. They favored the establishment of a second chamber with a suspensive veto. Few people wanted to restore the Senate of the Third Republic with its great powers.

THE FIRST CONSTITUENT ASSEMBLY

Largely under left-wing pressure, France elected the members of the Constituent Assembly under the unfortunate system of proportional representa-

---

[8] *Journal Officiel*, 1944, p. 325. For a good account of the drafting of the Constitution, see *A Constitution for the Fourth Republic*, Washington, D.C., Foundation for Foreign Affairs, 1947.

tion. This system, which had been tried in France before and found wanting, and which had been utilized in Germany with such devastating results, helped establish party discipline and stifled all political independence. Thus, all constitutional issues were settled on strictly a party basis and determined by the nearly sovereign party leaders. One could imagine what kind of instrument, if any, would have been produced in Philadelphia in 1787 had the founding fathers labored under a similar system.

The elections confirmed the preeminence of the three coalition parties. The Communists and affiliates (MURF) received 5,004,121 votes (25.1 per cent), the Socialists and affiliates (UDSR, etc.) 4,491,152 votes (23.4 per cent), and the MRP 4,580,222 (23.9 per cent). The Rasemblement des Gauches Républicains, composed mainly of the Radical Socialists, received only 2,018,665 votes (10.6 per cent). The sensation of the election was the great strength of the MRP and the decline of the Radical Socialists. However, it had to be assumed that much of the electoral strength of the MRP was derived from right-wing voters who wanted to vote against Communism but did not otherwise share the liberal aspirations of the MRP. Another significant event was the considerable representation of overseas France, which proved very influential in the Assembly and foreshadowed possible future consequences of great importance.

DRAFTING THE CONSTITUTION

Under the ordinance which established the Constituent Assembly, a time limit of seven months was set for its labors. Consequently work was undertaken without much delay. A constitutional committee was formed which had the task of drafting the actual instrument. Its chairman was André Philip, a Socialist of great ability who was later succeeded by another Socialist, Guy Mollet. The *rapporteur* [9] was François de Menthon, the most outstanding lawyer of the MRP. Later, De Menthon occupied a cabinet post and was replaced by Pierre Cot, formerly a leader of the Radical Socialists, but now a Communist in everything but name. The right-wing parties were shattered, but they managed to increase their influence by solidifying about half their representatives in the Assembly in a bloc, to which they gave the high-sounding name of "Republican Party of Liberty" (Parti Républicain de la Liberté, PRL).

The Communists were determined to establish what their opponents called a *gouvernement conventionnel,* a government by assembly. They and the Socialists were agreed that the future legislature shold be unicameral, that the Premier should be elected by the assembly, and that the role of the Presi-

---

[9] A *rapporteur* is the principal spokesman of a committee or *commission* on the floor of the legislature.

dent of the Republic should be essentially ornamental. They opposed the doctrine of the separation of powers, and they rejected the use of the popular referendum chiefly because of its unsavory tradition in France. The only check on the all-powerful assembly which they proposed—if it was a check at all—was the right of the electorate to recall a deputy. The MRP fought for a bicameral legislature, for the separation of powers, and for a stronger executive. It also wished to give the President of the Republic, together with the Premier, the right to dissolve the Assembly under certain circumstances. Between the two stood the Socialists, torn between their radical doctrine and their moderate inclinations. They were the advocates of compromise, siding first with the one, then with the other in the process. For a while they voted solidly with the MRP, but by a number of very adroit maneuvers the Communists brought them over to their side in some of the major questions. This proved to be fatal to the constitutional draft, which thus acquired the reputation of being Communist-inspired.

Before the draft was completed, a fateful event took place. The widening split between the left wing and De Gaulle came into the open. The immediate origin of the crisis lay in a number of conflicts, the most drastic of which was De Gaulle's opposition to any cut in the military appropriations. But the actual conflict lay deeper: De Gaulle did not deny the right of the Assembly to overthrow the government, but while he was in office he wanted a fairly free hand. The Socialists and Communists, however, insisted on constant "guidance" of the government by the Assembly, in other words, "assembly government." Embittered by these problems, De Gaulle suddenly resigned on January 20, 1946. No pressure had been put on him. He was still immensely popular and, because of that, held the whip hand over the parties. Had he chosen to carry his case to the people, the position of his opponents would have been very difficult. Instead he decided to sulk. This again illustrates the strange and conflicting character of the man, who gave up power voluntarily but later fought arduously and against much greater odds to reconquer it. Perhaps he fancied himself the indispensable man, who would be quickly recalled to power—in which case his influence would have been without limits. But if that was indeed his dream, he was quickly disabused of it, for the left was much relieved by his political demise and chose Félix Gouin, a Socialist, as his successor.

Much time was spent on the question of civil liberties. After much discussion, a formidable array of rights, civil, economic, and social,[10] were included in the draft. On the other hand, the inhabitants of overseas France were brought into closer relationship to the mother country by the creation of the

---

[10] For instance, Art. 22 of the draft: "Every human being possesses with regard to society rights that guarantee, in the integrity and dignity of his person, his full physical, intellectual and moral development."

French Union, a compromise between extremes which satisfied nobody but which has nevertheless the seed of progress in itself—if properly used.

The Defeat of the Draft Constitution

The break came over the question of the second chamber. The MRP had opposed many of the measures proposed by the Socialists and Communists until some real or imaginary compromise was found. But when the decision in favor of a unicameral legislature was made irrevocable by the Socialist-Communist majority, the MRP went into the opposition. Finally, when the Socialists and Communists refused to accept measures designed to test the constitutionality of laws, François de Menthon resigned as *rapporteur* and declared that the MRP would reject the entire draft.

The draft Constitution was submitted to a referendum. Despite the lack of unanimity, the Socialists and Communists who had adopted the draft were confident of acceptance. The MRP alone bore the main burden of agitating against acceptance. De Gaulle had cloaked himself in dignified silence. Moreover the majority coalition had polled nearly a majority of votes, and the rest would be made up by the voters who in the entire history of France had never defeated a proposition submitted to them by referendum. But the unexpected happened. On June 2, 1946, the draft Constitution was rejected by 10,584,000 (52.9 per cent) votes against 9,454,000 (47.1 per cent).

Few voters had read the Constitution, and fewer had understood the issues. In reality, the views of the Communist-Socialist coalition and the MRP were not very far apart. But the issue of "Communism" was inserted into the referendum and caused the defeat of the draft Constitution. The nearly even division of the electorate illustrated the terrible disunity among the people of France and conjured up evil portents for the future.

The Second Constituent Assembly

At the same time, the elections to the new Constituent Assembly showed what had happened to the votes. The Communists gained 140,000 votes and now constituted nearly 26 per cent of the electorate; the Socialists lost almost 300,000 votes and were reduced to 21.14 per cent of the total; while the MRP gained more than 1,000,000 votes over October, 1945, and with 28.22 per cent of the electorate became the largest party. The Radicals held their own, but the right-wing groups declined.

The second Constituent Assembly was able to produce a final draft within four months. That was possible because relatively few changes were made and some controversial points were avoided. Even the Communists conceded that if the majority which had voted against the first constitutional draft had wanted any specific provision at all, it was that of a second chamber. And

Paul Coste-Floret (MRP), general *rapporteur*, declared that "one of the reasons for which the nation rejected the draft of April 19 by more than a million votes is, rightly or wrongly, its conviction that this text instituted a government by assembly." [11] The acceptance of the second chamber, the Council of the Republic, was thus assured, but it remained a strictly second-ary, advisory body with none of the powers of the former Senate. But on the other hand it was hardly a gain that the bill of rights lost its place in the Constitution proper and was delegated to a legally meaningless place in the preamble. Moreover, the Assembly managed to avoid a repetition of the long and ponderous debates over the philosophical meaning of certain "rights" which, while beautiful from an esthetic viewpoint, had been a waste of time in terms of the drafting process. It did so by failing to spell out many of the rights; instead, it vaguely referred to the Declaration of the Rights of Man and Citizen of 1789, which it "solemnly reaffirms," and even more vaguely to the "fundamental principles recognized by the laws of the (Third) Republic."

The Constitution removed all hope for a self-dissolution of Parliament and only slightly elevated the role of the President of the Republic. The judges were now made officially irremovable except for cause, and a Supreme Council of the Magistrature (Judiciary) was created in order to weaken the notorious hold of the Minister of Justice over the bench. Judicial review in the Ameri-can sense was never accepted in France and has not been instituted in this document either. As an alleged compromise, a constitutional examination committee was created, but it has remained without the slightest significance and will undoubtedly continue this negative role. An Economic Council was created, and the framework of the French Union (the organization of overseas France) was largely retained from the first draft.

The essential character of the second draft is very much like that of the first, and there can be little doubt that it creates nearly as much "government by assembly." Coste-Floret might well speak of "modified unicameralism," while the Council of the Republic has been politely termed a "chamber of reflection."

Neither this Constitution nor the introduction of the proportional system of election has made the appearance of the Fourth Republic very much differ-ent from the Third, and André Philip's assertion that the old form of cabinet instability was "completely eliminated from now on" quickly revealed itself as monstrous nonsense.

While the work of the second Constituent Assembly neared its end, General Charles de Gaulle suddenly emerged from his ivory tower. In no uncertain terms, he condemned the work of the Assembly. His chief concern was the absence of a strong executive in the proposed Constitution, but the remedies

[11] Robert K. Gooch, "Recent Constitution-making in France," *American Political Science Review*, Vol. XLI (1947), p. 438.

he suggested were vague and unrealistic. He apparently favored some combination of the presidential and parliamentary systems without fully comprehending either. He repeated his views in several well-attended speeches, which could not fail to make an impression among many people who were witnessing the rebirth of the system of endless crises which, in their opinion, had been the principal cause of the 1940 disaster.

De Gaulle's fervent attacks against the second draft forced the MRP closer to the Socialists and Communists. Its leaders were not wildly enthusiastic about the Constitution—nobody was, for that matter—but they desired an end of the perpetually provisional. Their break with De Gaulle was not easy on them, especially as they suspected that the redoubtable general would capture many votes from them should he decide to form a party of his own. At any rate, the MRP joined the Socialists and Communists in urging a vote of acceptance for the Constitution, while De Gaulle urged a vote of "no."

ACCEPTANCE OF THE CONSTITUTION

On October 13, 1946, the tired French voters went to the polls again. Out of 25,800,000 voters, 9,257,432 approved the Constitution while 8,125,295 rejected it. Eight million people abstained, an unusually high figure for France. Technically the Constitution was adopted, and it was so proclaimed and promulgated. But the plebiscite nevertheless was an unexpected triumph for De Gaulle. With all three major parties supporting it, the general, who had no party organization, could claim with considerable justification that a decided majority of the French people had withheld their consent from the document. This weakened the prestige of the new Constitution and heralded a new phase in the political development of France, the last of which has not yet been seen. Thus, under doubtful auspices, did the Constitution of September 28, 1946, come into force. Its supporters could perhaps take some comfort from the fact that the fundamental laws of the Third Republic were accepted with even less enthusiasm and yet that regime had endured for seventy years. But this and other similarities between the Third and the Fourth Republics did not augur well for the future.

Chapter 4

CONSTITUTIONAL GOVERNMENT IN FRANCE

A. THE AMENDING [1] PROCESS

It is characteristic of French and Continental jurisprudence that it regards constitutions and constitutional amendments as special forms of legislation.[2] Amendments are therefore not much more difficult to bring about than ordinary acts of legislation. This approach is also strengthened by the belief that the legislature is the highest expression of popular sovereignty, which should not be seriously curbed.

In France, the amending process, which is outlined in Art. 90 of the Constitution, is fairly simple. The first step is a resolution adopted by the National Assembly with absolute majority, outlining the nature and the purpose of the proposed amendment. Absolute majority, sometimes also called "constitutional majority," means a majority of all members of the National Assembly, whether present or not. If the Council of the Republic approves the resolution by absolute majority, the National Assembly draws up the text of the proposed amendment. If the Council does not approve the original resolution, it must be resubmitted to the National Assembly within three months for a second reading. If the Assembly passes the resolution on second reading, it may then proceed to draw up the amendment itself. This proposed amendment is then submitted to parliament like any other piece of legislation. That means it is passed by a simple majority in both houses or, if the Council of the Republic disagrees, by the National Assembly alone on second reading.

Simple, or relative, majority is the same as plurality. In this instance, when there is likely to be only one proposition before the house, simple or relative majority is a majority of those present and voting. Thus the numerical difference between an absolute (constitutional) and a simple (relative) majority is the difference between 313 (when there are no vacancies) and a figure that

---

[1] The word *amendement* is known, but French jurists prefer to speak of a *révision*. This indicates a different method, namely, the rewriting or elimination of sections, rather than the American system by which a new paragraph is added to effect the desired changes.

[2] In the United States the amending process is an act of sovereignty, not legislation. • The President cannot veto Congressional action relative to a constitutional amendment.

may lie in the lower 200's or below. In view of the political atomization of the National Assembly, the difference between absolute and relative majority is frequently the difference between success and failure.

If the amendment has been passed by a three-fifths majority in both houses, or by a two-thirds majority in the National Assembly on second reading, it is promulgated by the President and becomes the law of the land. If it has been passed merely with absolute majority, it must be submitted to popular referendum.

The amending article is very obscurely worded. The text does not make it at all clear whether the original resolution adopted by the National Assembly *must be* submitted to the Council of the Republic, or whether the National Assembly has an option in the matter. The authorities on the subject are completely divided.[3] Nor is it clear whether the resolution must be resubmitted to the National Assembly if the Council of the Republic has not approved it. The wording *dans le délai minimum de trois mois* is bad French and bad draftsmanship. It may mean either "after no more than three months" or "after no less than three months." The debates in the Constituent Assembly make the latter interpretation more plausible but far from certain.

Two instances are removed from the operation of the amending clause. Any amendment relative to the Council of the Republic may be adopted only with the consent of that body or by referendum. On the other hand, the republican form of government may not be the subject of any proposal to amend the Constitution (Art. 95). The value of the second provision is doubtful. The American experience has proven that the term "republican form of government" may be interpreted in different ways, but France's own historical experience has demonstrated that fundamental changes in the form of government are usually accomplished by revolution or *coup d'état*, not by amendment. It is true that the Vichy regime consolidated its power via the amending process, and the framers of the 1946 Constitution were very much aware of this. But the absence of a convenient amending clause would hardly have prevented Pétain and Laval from taking over. The real significance of Art. 95 is therefore that it tends to deprive a future authoritarian regime of a doubtful cloak of "legality."

B. CIVIL RIGHTS

Modern constitutions are frequently compared to the Constitution of the United States, and in that comparison they come off very much the worse.

---

[3] According to J. Laferrière, *Manuel de droit constitutionnel,* Paris, 1947, 2d ed., pp. 948f., and M. Duverger, *Manuel de droit constitutionnel et de science politique,* Paris, 1948, 5th ed., p. 375, the resolution *must be* submitted to the Council of the Republic. According to M. Prélot, *Précis de droit constitutionnel,* Paris, 1950, p. 456, and G. Vedel, *Manuel élémentaire de droit constitutionnel,* Paris, 1948, p. 535, the National Assembly has an option in the matter. The author tends to agree with the latter interpretation.

Even those who regard the work of 1787 as outdated will not deny its coherence, classical simplicity, and comprehensiveness. Nothing of the kind can be claimed for any of the modern documents, and certainly not for the French Constitution of 1946. The reason for this is not hard to find: the men who assembled in Philadelphia in 1787 possessed a remarkable and unparalleled unity of political and especially economic outlook. They differed on methods, but not on fundamental ideology. The members of the French Constituent Assembly of 1946 were not so fortunate. From the Communists and Socialists to the Catholic MRP and the right-wing parties, all colors of the political rainbow were assembled. Had any party alone drafted and enacted the Constitution, it might have shown more coherence, but even if the Socialists and Communists were able to dominate the Assembly, they had to take into account certain taboos of other groups; moreover, these two Marxist parties were frequently at odds. Consequently the Constitution is a compromise, an odd combination of ideas and concepts which are frequently in conflict with one another.

As long as difference of opinion is confined to methods, a compromise may be achieved which, while not wholly desirable from any standpoint, may nevertheless be capable of accomplishing the desired end. But if the difference of opinion is of a sharp ideological nature, a compromise can be achieved only in one of two ways: by leaving out both the opposing ideologies, or by putting them both in. In either case, the only real result is an obscuring of the issue. Thus it may be said that wherever conflicting ideologies have to be appeased in order to arrive at an agreed version of a constitutional provision, the result will be largely meaningless.

There is ample evidence for this in the French Constitution. For instance, it is stipulated that "the right to strike may be exercised within the framework of the laws that govern it," which means that the right to strike may not be exercised if the Assembly legislates against it—which is precisely the situation that would prevail were this paragraph omitted. In the rejected draft of the first Constituent Assembly, civil rights were specifically enumerated. It was stated for instance that "property is an inviolable right," but it was also stated that "the right of property may not be exercised in violation of social purposes . . ."; in other words, property is not inviolable.

The rejected first draft of the Constitution attempted to spell out the civil rights possessed by Frenchmen. It was the most detailed list of rights contained in any constitution, and it bore heavily the mark of the leftist majority. But the draft was rejected by the people, and the second Constituent Assembly did not want to get buried again in the long-drawn-out philosophical discussion which gave birth to the bill of rights of the first draft. Especially the provision concerning the right to property promised to be irksome. In the dilemma, the Assembly ditched the whole problem. It did so, first, by removing the bill of rights from the body of the document and placing it in a preamble, thus depriving it of any hope for legally enforceable validity. Secondly, in order to avoid the spelling out of concrete civil rights, the preamble merely "reaffirms the rights and liberties of man and citizen consecrated by the Declaration of Rights of 1789," and as if that were not already vague enough, it also reaffirms "the fundamental principles recognized by the laws of the (Third) Republic." The Declaration of 1789 was a political document of principles directed against an arbitrary regime. Against royal whims it set up the principle of the rule of law. But modern dictatorship operates by law and decree. In fact, both the Nazi regime in Germany and the Vichy government in France took much pride in their alleged "legality." Declarations like that of 1789, which stipulate that a citizen may speak freely except when otherwise stated in the law, say in effect that the citizen may not necessarily speak freely.

These points are not illuminated by the above-mentioned reference to the "fundamental principles recognized by the laws of the Republic." The Republic existed for seventy years and found itself under many different governments. There is hardly any principle of government for which some justification and precedent could not be found in the laws of the Republic which someone might term a fundamental principle.

The rights actually stated in the preamble go beyond the list of civil liberties in the United States Constitution. But they are stated, not as rights or definite prohibitions, but merely as general principles. After reaffirming the Declaration of 1789 and the principles of the laws of the Republic, the Constitution continues as follows: "It (the French people) further proclaims as particularly necessary in our time the following political, economic, and social principles:" These principles are

1. Equal rights of women and men.

2. The right of asylum to political fugitives.

3. The right and the duty to work.

4. The right to be protected against discrimination on grounds of race or creed.

5. The right to bargain collectively, to engage in trade-union activities, and to strike.

6. Equal access to education.

7. The aspiration of nationalizing (or communizing) all public services and monopolies.

8. Health protection, material security, rest, and leisure, as well as old-age and sick benefits.

9. The solidarity of all Frenchmen in case of national disaster.

10. A Union based upon equality between France and her overseas possessions.

A later discussion will reveal to what extent this last principle has been fulfilled.

The foregoing list is far from all-inclusive. The Declaration of 1789, which is reaffirmed in the preamble to the Constitution, is full of allusions to the doctrines of natural law and of the "general will" current in those days. Apart from a general philosophical discourse, however, it also guarantees the rights of free speech, press, assembly, and religion, except when limited by law, the right to be protected in the enjoyment of one's property except when it is required for public use and then for just compensation, the principle of government through representatives, protection against arbitrary arrest, the prohibition of cruel and unusual punishment, and the right of an accused to be presumed innocent until proven guilty.[4]

The laws of the Republic have added so many provisions that any enumeration would be hopeless. At any rate, this version permitted a compromise in the Constituent Assembly because the left felt satisfied that the secular school was guaranteed, while the MRP was confident that the laws of the Republic had also protected the parochial institutions.

What is then the significance of the French bill of rights? From a strictly legal standpoint it has none. It is part of the preamble and not of the Constitution itself. Its provisions are statements of principle, not legal stipulations, and must be implemented by legislative action and governmental policy. This viewpoint is disputed by some French jurists who point out that the enactment clause preceded the preamble and thus gave the preamble equal status with the rest of the document. It seems, however, that two facts clearly indicate that the framers of the Constitution intended to place the list of civil liberties on a lower level than the rest of the Constitution. (1) While the civil liberties were in the text of the Constitution in the first, rejected, draft, they were relegated to the preamble in the second. What but a desire for their diminution could explain such action? (2) The powers of the Constitutional Committee, which theoretically watches over the constitutionality of the laws, do not extend to the preamble.

France has not adopted the American principle of judicial review, with the result that laws enacted contrary to the Constitution cannot be invalidated except by the legislature which enacted them in the first place. In other words, the French list of civil liberties cannot be compared with the American bill of rights, but rather with our Declaration of Independence, which is also a great charter of principles but not a legal document. In addition, the French bill of rights is also a catalogue of assorted party programs, containing both Marxist-collectivist and more conservative ideas.

Are we then to conclude that France has no civil liberties? By no means. But the French attitude toward them is different from ours. They consider civil liberties to be political rights, and they consider it proper therefore that the political branch of the government should guarantee them. That branch

---

[4] The widely held view that in Roman-law countries like France an accused is deemed guilty until proved innocent is based on a misconception.

is primarily the legislature. Theoretically the legislature is under the Constitution, but there is no sanction against a violation of the Constitution by the legislature, nor is there any means by which obedience can be compelled. The legislature of France is truly sovereign. No civil right could stand up against legislative fiat. On the other hand, executive arbitrariness is effectively dealt with by the formidable administrative courts, especially the Council of State (Conseil d'État), which sees to it that executive organs do not go beyond their legal limits. In a highly centralized country like France, the significance of the Council of State cannot possibly be overestimated.

The law defines in great detail the exercise and limits of the various personal liberties. Their detailed discussion would go far beyond the scope of this book.[5] On the whole this system works in a satisfactory manner, but its greatest weakness lies in the field of police practice. The law attempts to limit the time during which the police can keep a suspect under arrest before bringing him before an examining magistrate, but the police have learned to circumvent this provision by detaining a suspect as a witness rather than as a suspect. Similarly, since the end of the war there is a tendency to be much stricter about releasing a suspect on bail than was the practice before the war. These conditions have frequently been the object of sharp criticism in the French press. They are the results of the war and the unsettled postwar period, and there is reason to hope that they will improve as time passes, but so far they have not.

A threat to the civil liberties of the citizen can quite likely come from the action or inaction of the legislature. In normal times, that possibility may be dismissed, because the disunity among the multitude of political parties and blocs effectively prevents drastic legislation of an undemocratic nature. Moerover, there has always been a sufficiently large number of sincere democrats to defeat authoritarian regimes. But civil liberties are not usually threatened in normal times, but in periods of stress and national emergency. In such periods, a legislature may become a rubber stamp—like the parliament which abjectly adopted the Vichy laws in 1940—or it may become panicky enough to invest the government with awe-inspiring decree-making powers.[6] This is a power for which French governments have always cried in an emergency and which they have often received. In such a case, the government is without restraint. It is of course true that even a supreme court endowed with judicial review, such as the highest tribunal in the United States, is no iron-clad guarantee against rubber-stamping, hysteria, or force. But while it may not be a guarantee, it is nevertheless a formidable obstacle against autocratic

[5] For an excellent and concise presentation of the law and practice of civil liberties, see Claude-Albert Colliard, *Précis de droit public; les libertés publiques,* Paris, 1950.

[6] For a useful study see Otto Kirchheimer, "Decree Powers and Constitutional Law in France under the Third Republic," *American Political Science Review,* Vol. XXXIV (1940), p. 1104.

rule, and it is for that reason that an increasing number of Frenchmen would like to see such a court established in France. For the time being, however, they appear to be very much in the minority.

C. THE EXECUTIVE

The executive power is shared by the President of the Republic, the Premier, and the ministers. Among them, the President of the Republic is the most exalted and the least powerful.

THE PRESIDENT OF THE REPUBLIC

The position of the President of the Republic is very much the same under the Fourth Republic as it was under the Third. He is elected by parliament, *i.e.*, the National Assembly and the Council of the Republic in joint session. His term of office is seven years, and he may be reelected once. He presides over the Council of Ministers and he also appoints Councilors of State, Ambassadors and other envoys, the members of the Superior Council, and the Committee for National Defense. He also presides over the Superior Council of the Judiciary, where he may exercise the right of pardon, and over the High Council of the French Union. But even in those modest rights he is not independent, because the Constitution requires that all his acts be countersigned by the Premier and a minister, which thereby become actually the acts of the cabinet and the Premier.

He does not possess a veto. Ten days after a bill has been passed by the legislature he must promulgate it as law. Even that period of grace may be reduced to five days if the National Assembly declares the bill "urgent." If he does not promulgate the law, the President of the National Assembly (Speaker) will do it in his stead. It is true that the President, instead of promulgating, may return a bill to parliament for reconsideration. But after receiving the bill for reconsideration, the National Assembly may pass it again in the same manner as before, namely, by simple majority. During the Third Republic this right to ask for the reconsideration of a bill was never exercised. Since 1946 it has been used a few times but only in order to repair technical deficiencies and once, under advice of the Constitutional Committee, in order to consolidate different versions of a bill passed by the National Assembly and the Council of the Republic. It has never been used for a political purpose, *i.e.*, in the case of a difference of opinion between President and parliament, and there is little doubt that parliament would visit drastic retributions against a President who would dare to act in this fashion. It is therefore not possible to speak of a presidential veto or even a suspensive veto.

The principal significance of the President lies in his political functions. It is he who selects the new Premier when a cabinet crisis has overthrown the previous government. In Great Britain that power of the King is usually of little significance because he has little choice in the matter; the leader of the majority party is always the Prime Minister–designate. But in France there is no majority party—there are too many parties to permit that. Consequently it depends often on the skill of the President to find a Premier who can marshal a majority in the National Assembly. In his choice, the President is usually motivated by political expediency, but a candidate whom he opposes has little chance of becoming head of the government if an alternative government can be formed. On the other hand, if the President favors a particular candidate his chances are materially improved. This presidential influence has increased as a result of the constitutional reform of 1954 which, as we shall see below, has made the formation of governments somewhat easier.

It would be a mistake to conclude from these facts that the President has complete freedom of choice. Upon outbreak of a cabinet crisis, he must consult with the principal party leaders in order to ascertain what type of political combination would be acceptable to a majority in the Assembly. From such negotiations, the identity of the Premier-designate will usually emerge. Moreover, French political tradition dislikes Presidents who exert political pressure. Alexandre Millerand found this out to his peril in 1924 when a defiant parliament forced him to resign.

Presidential influence, if it is to be exercised at all, must therefore be applied subtly, indirectly, and with great restraint. Outstanding political leaders, like Clemenceau or Briand, have frequently failed of election for this reason. Men of high caliber, like Raymond Poincaré, who were elected to this high position usually chafed at the reins and longed to escape from the "exile of the Elysée."

To be a successful President, it is therefore necessary to have much political experience and to be a man with an outstanding ability to compromise and to act as a mediator. In the past, most Presidents have been ex-ministers and legislators, and several have been ex-presidents of the Senate. The first President of the Fourth Republic, Vincent Auriol, a moderate Socialist, a man with a long and distinguished political career and famed as a compromiser, was a particularly happy choice. He earned much personal respect by his courage in voting against the Pétain decrees in 1940, and his conduct has enhanced the reputation of the presidency. His successor, René Coty, is also a respected former legislator and ex-minister.

President Auriol had occasion to appear as the protector of the French Constitution, reaffirming its validity against its various detractors. On one occasion, when the followers of General de Gaulle raised the cry of dissolution of the Assembly, the President replied in no uncertain terms that the Assembly had been elected under the Constitution and that it would therefore have to serve out its term. In this way he showed more determination than his predecessor, Albert Lebrun, who abdicated ignominiously before Pétain. But it would probably be an exaggeration to term the President a "guarantor of the Constitution." The National Assembly is firmly in the saddle, France has a long tradition of disregarding old constitutions and writing new ones, and the President of the Republic, respected as he is, does not hold the loyalty and affection of the people as the British monarch does. He can therefore hardly expect to become a tremendous rallying point in case the Constitution is threatened. But he can lend it strength, and he can carry out the functions of his office in such a manner that crises are more quickly overcome and that the Republic may achieve a reasonable degree of stability.

President Auriol had several opportunities to exercise a stabilizing influence. On a number of occasions Premiers came to the Elysée Palace to present to him the resignations of their cabinets because the parliamentary situation or an internal conflict among the ministers seemed to render the continuation of the cabinet impossible, but the experienced eyes of President Auriol saw that the crisis was only temporary and he refused to accept the resignations. This gave the cabinet some further time for reconsideration and several times the crisis blew over. But of course when a government is determined to resign, the President cannot stop it, and if it has become the victim of a vote of nonconfidence in the National Assembly the President must accept the situation.

The President of the Republic is therefore far more than a chief clerk or purely an unveiler of monuments. His is a significant and subtle role in the closely woven fabric of French government.

THE PREMIER

The real executive is the Premier, whose official title is President of the Council of Ministers (*président du conseil des ministres*), and his colleagues, the other ministers. Prior to the constitutional reform of December 7, 1954, their appointment took place through a cumbersome and difficult procedure. The President of the Republic, after having explored the political situation and discussed it with all or most of the party leaders, selected a likely candidate for the premiership.[7] This man, called Premier-designate, had to present himself to the National Assembly alone, explain his program even though he did not yet have a cabinet, and then be "invested" by an absolute majority (313) of the Assembly. This procedure made the formation of governments very difficult and prolonged the crisis because such a large majority was not easy to obtain and demanded a very broad coalition government. Yet the fact

---

[7] In difficult situations where it is not clear how the crisis shall be overcome, the President may ask a political leader to undertake a *"mission d'information"* for the purpose of conferring with other party leaders and suggesting a man who might be likely to receive a favorable vote in the Assembly.

that investiture had to be obtained before a cabinet was formed hampered subsequent negotiations because the Premier-designate, once invested, had to make commitments which might be unacceptable to his later cabinet colleagues.

After the formation of the cabinet a second vote of confidence was not required, as is sometimes erroneously stated, but the political situation often produced an interpellation or other question on which this new government had, in effect, to stand another test of confidence. Hence, some observers spoke of a "double investiture."

The constitutional reform of 1954, sometimes called the "reformette," provides for a much more streamlined and more practical method of selecting governments, which goes right back to the habits of the Third Republic. Now the President of the Republic designates the Premier (President of the Council of Ministers), who immediately chooses his cabinet and then presents it and himself to the National Assembly together with an explanation of future government policy. Then the Assembly takes a vote and if confidence is expressed by a plurality the government stands. In view of abstentions and absences, such a plurality may lie somewhere in the two hundreds, in contrast to the previously required vote of 313.

There is little doubt that this reform will allow for quick solutions of government crises, as it is easier than before to find a Premier who is able to win a plurality vote of confidence. This also increases the range of choice at the disposal of the President of the Republic. On the other hand, it may make the Assembly even more ready than before to overthrow a government.

The Premier and the cabinet are collectively and individually responsible to the National Assembly but not to the Council of the Republic. A vote of nonconfidence by the National Assembly forces the government to resign. The issue of confidence in the government may be proposed by the government as well as by members of the Assembly. If the government itself poses the question of confidence in order to reassure itself of a solid political basis in the Assembly, only the Premier himself may raise the question, and only after the issue has been discussed in cabinet meeting.

All officers, civil and military, who are not appointed directly by the President of the Republic are appointed by the Premier. However, the appointment of judges is now reserved to a special body, the Superior Council of the Magistrature (Judiciary), Conseil Supérieur de la Magistrature.

From the foregoing it would seem that the position of the Premier is a strong one: however, as so often in France, constitutional strength is seriously modified by political reality. Because of the large number of parties and parliamentary blocs, only coalition governments are conceivable in France— except in the case of a dictatorship. It is true that Léon Blum once formed an all-Socialist minority government which earned much acclaim, but it was essentially a caretaker government and a rare exception. In a coalition government, the Premier is rarely free to select his ministers and must often accept candidates of the various parties on whose support the life of the government will depend. Once he has appointed his government composed of divergent political forces, he finds that each minister becomes a little tsar in his own department, and he cannot dislodge any of them without incurring the peril of risking the support of a crucial bloc of votes in the Assembly, which may lead to the downfall of the government.

Because of the coalition character of the government, it is usually quite difficult to evolve a clear line of governmental policy. The differences of opinion between the coalition partners are usually too great, and it is therefore politically easier to do nothing, which may explain why a vigorous domestic policy of France is so difficult to achieve. This situation naturally increases the powers of the National Assembly, which is able to utilize the inner difficulties of the cabinets for purposes of its own.

In wartime, coalition governments are the rule, and they usually work effectively under the impact of that one, single goal of all policy—victory in battle. But in peacetime, coalition governments are extremely unstable, and the majority of French cabinets do not resign because of a vote of nonconfidence or censure on the part of the National Assembly, but rather because the inner contradictions within the cabinet became too powerful to be overcome. This practice also serves another purpose: Art. 51 of the Constitution provides that in case the government is forced to resign twice within any eighteen-month period, for reason of a vote of nonconfidence or censure, the National Assembly may be dissolved. This was intended to create stability of government, as members of parliament are customarily not overly anxious to entrust themselves to the tender mercies of the electorate. Unfortunately this expectation was not fulfilled. Governments topple now as frequently as of yore, but instead of being defeated in open roll call on the floor of the National Assembly, they fall apart because the one or the other partner in the coalition finds it impossible to support the government program any longer.

It is customary, in countries where the parliamentary systems prevail, that the various cabinet ministers administer their respective departments with a far greater degree of authority than is allowed to a member of the President's cabinet in the United States. The Premier directs the over-all policy and is primarily responsible for it to the legislature. The actual extent of his leadership depends, however, very largely on his own political strength and support. In Great Britain the Prime Minister derives his greatest source of strength from the fact that he is the leader of the majority party in the House of Commons. In France this is never the case, as there has never been such a thing as a majority party. Consequently the Premier has the difficult and unenviable task of leading a team of very divergent and exceedingly independent men, each representing parties and groups on whose support he is dependent for the life of his cabinet. Each minister administers his department with considerable discretion, as mentioned above, and not too infrequently in opposition to other ministries occupied by rivals.

The Premier bears an immense burden. All interpellations, attacks, and questions are primarily directed at him and he must answer them. Although all policies are essentially the result of compromise, his is the main burden of having to defend and explain them. In a way it might be said that his responsibilities are considerably greater than his powers.

In the exercise of his functions the Premier is assisted by a number of persons and offices. In his political work he has the help of one or several secretaries of state who may also be called upon to share in his administrative responsibilities, and he may also call upon a cabinet minister for help.

From an administrative standpoint the Premier has above all the General Secretariat (Secrétariat Général du Gouvernement) at his disposal.[8] This office was modeled on the British Cabinet Secretariat. Its members assist in the drafting of all government bills and executive orders, follow up on the fate of these bills in the National Assembly, and report to the government on the action taken on them as well as on other bills coming from parliament. Members of the Secretariat also participate in the planning of the parliament's legislative agenda. In general they keep the Premier and the cabinet constantly informed on the state of the legislative picture.

Apart from its legislative work, the Secretariat prepares reports on such topics as may be assigned to it. It keeps the minutes of cabinet meetings and its general secretary helps the Premier to set up the agenda. The Secretariat may also help to iron out differences between the actions of several ministries covering the same subject.

Technically the General Secretariat consists of two services: the Legislative Service and the Administrative and Financial Service. The latter is mainly occupied with housekeeping functions for the Secretariat as a whole, while the Legislative Service performs its real functions. Both are headed by the General Secretary.

Attached to the General Secretariat are the Civil Service Office, which will be discussed later, the Document Center, the Official Journal of the French Republic, and the National School of Administration, as well as the technical services such as the French Broadcasting System and the Postal, Telephone, and Telegraph services.

Also very important is the work of the Council of State, whose principal role as an administrative court will be discussed later.[9] Under the ordinance of July 31, 1945, the Council of State must be consulted with regard to all legislation originated by the government and the more important executive

---

[8] Roy C. Macridis, "The Cabinet Secretariat in France," *The Journal of Politics,* Vol. XIII (1951), pp. 589–603.

[9] See Chap. 4E.

orders, and it may be consulted with regard to other orders. The Council of State may also take other actions within the administration, such as an investigation on behalf of the government, and it may call attention to any need for administrative reform. Moreover it serves as an inspector over all authorities which exercise functions of administrative justice in metropolitan France and overseas. The great usefulness of the Council of State, especially in drafting government-sponsored legislation, lies primarily in the high degree of *expertise* and experience of its members and in the extraordinary respect which they enjoy.

THE CABINET

Because of the great power vested in each ministry—not to speak of the famous "secret funds"—a great deal of juggling precedes the formation of each government. The key ministries are Foreign Affairs, Interior, Finance, and War, and great care is taken lest one party should control too many of them. Under such conditions of rivalry, few governmental programs have ever seen complete fulfillment. The role of a Premier is primarily one of a compromiser and skillful general of intricate maneuvers. The longer he can keep it up, the longer his government will last. But sometimes the incessant political infighting and the patching of parliamentary majorities take up so much time that little is left for governing. Since the country has to be governed, the bureaucracy assumes a great degree of responsibility and discretion. Among postwar Premiers, only General de Gaulle and Pierre Mendès-France have been real leaders who have overshadowed their cabinets and the bureaucracy.

Constitutionally and legally, neither the Premier nor the ministers need to be members of parliament because, as long as they are in office, they may attend and be heard in either house and in all their committees. However, since the role of the cabinet and especially of the Premier is primarily political and parliamentarian, experienced politicians are the rule, and they are almost always members of the National Assembly.

There is a great deal of difference between the British cabinet and its French counterpart. British ministers are usually amateurs in their fields of authority, though some of them have become specialists and near-specialists in a given field during their Opposition period. But specialist or not, a British minister may expect to be in office for some time and has ample opportunity to familiarize himself with his tasks. Not so in France. The average life expectancy of a government is less than six months [10] and is decreasing. The distribution of ministries among available candidates is decided primarily on

[10] Between 1871 and 1914 (43 years) France had 54 cabinets; between 1914 and 1940 (26 years) there were 55 cabinets; and between 1946 (cabinet Gouin) and 1953 (cabinet Mayer) (7 years) there were 16 cabinets. The statistical averages per cabinet are therefore 0.79, 0.47, and 0.44 years respectively.

the basis of party politics. The significant question is usually not which man but which party occupies an office. Consequently the handful of top leaders in each party usually shifts around from ministry to ministry, getting the feel of the entire political keyboard, from agriculture to public health. Only occasionally does a particular man become a fixture in a given department. This was the case with Aristide Briand, the perennial Minister for Foreign Affairs under the Third Republic until his death in 1932. In the governments since the Second World War and until Premier Mendès-France broke many traditions in 1954, the Foreign Office was occupied by two men, Robert Schuman and Georges Bidault (both MRP), and in the Ministry of Agriculture Georges Pfimlin (MRP) held long periods of tenure. Ministers of the Interior were either Socialists or Radicals, and Ministers of Finance were either Radicals or Independents.[11]

Because of this unfamiliarity with the subject matter, the short flicker of life granted to each government, and the preoccupation with party politics, French ministers are virtually incapable of exercising much actual control over their departments. The real administrator and often policy-maker is therefore the permanent civil servant, and usually the best a minister can hope to do is to exercise a certain check and restraint. At the same time he must be ready to answer detailed questions in the Assembly, which makes him all the more dependent on the professionals.

In the day-by-day administration of each department the minister therefore finds that if he hopes to accomplish anything he must do what the civil service decides for him. Nor can he seriously affect the composition of his permanent staff. Although favoritism is not rare in France—especially as regards the intimate assistants of the minister—he cannot make many changes in his own staff quickly enough to matter. Civil-service rules can be amended only by decree of the entire Council of Ministers, and the Council of State renders its advisory opinion on the subject. No wonder that former Premier and long-time Foreign Minister, Robert Schuman, complained bitterly that many of the policies for which a minister receives blame are actually the policies of some civil servant against whom the minister finds himself quite powerless.

Yet, with all this dependence on the permanent, professional staff, nothing can be done without the signature of the minister, and in big matters, in questions of basic policy, he can assert himself when he feels strong and informed enough to do so. But the permanent officials can also try to procrastinate until the inevitable resignation of the cabinet becomes a fact. Then they may try their luck again with the new minister.

The French ministerial system therefore presents a fascinating picture of

[11] Roy C. Macridis, "Cabinet Instability in the Fourth Republic (1946–1951)," *The Journal of Politics*, Vol. XIV (1952), pp. 643–658.

conflicting theory and reality. In theory the Premier is the leader of the government, but in reality he must constantly mend political fences in order to maintain himself. The ministers, whose number varies but is usually between twenty and thirty, nominally wield great power. Their necessary preoccupation with political matters, their short tenure, and the incessant reshuffle usually prevent them from actually administering their departments, but nothing can be done without them. In so highly centralized a country as France, where ministerial decision often determines minute, technical questions of local government, this means that it frequently takes an inordinately long period to accomplish trivia. The minister as a rule may assert his authority in only certain select cases, but nevertheless appointment to office is eagerly sought, in part because of the great social prestige of such a post, which lasts long after it has been vacated.[12] And during all this time the National Assembly does not really accept the government as its leader, but tries through interpellation and political pressure to interfere with the administration, and by skillfully constructed laws constantly keeps the whip hand over the executive branch.

The most notorious fact in any consideration of the French cabinet is its already mentioned short life expectancy, which has become steadily shorter over the last eighty years. This governmental instability is certainly aided by several institutional features, but far more important is the political background of French cabinets. The large number of political parties makes it impossible for any one group to obtain a majority and to give France a stable government on the English or American models. Yet the instability of the French coalition governments is far greater than that of other countries which also have multiparty systems and coalition governments.

The reason for this lies in the peculiar nature of the French party system. Ever since 1849 the division between the parties of the left and of the right has shown an amazing degree of constancy, not only in the over-all vote, but also in its regional distribution. Generally the vote for the left has been a little larger than the vote for the right. But the left is unable to form a coalition government of its own because the Communists form the largest part of the left and no other party can or will collaborate with them. The right is not strong enough to form a purely rightist coalition because its members have too many petty differences ever to be able to pull together. Moreover, for some time the hostility of General de Gaulle's followers split the right as the Communists have split the left. Consequently, no matter what the outcome of any election, the only possible government in France at the present time and in the foreseeable future is a coalition supported by elements of both the left and the

[12] Polite society addresses a man by his title, even if it is long defunct. Thus a man who has once been a minister for three months will probably be addressed as *Monsieur le ministre* as long as he lives.

right—in other words a coalition whose members have nothing in common except that they alone may find a mathematical majority in the National Assembly. Such an odd coalition is naturally full of inner tensions which make it break up at frequent intervals only to force the same groups and usually the same men to try again. Thus we find the peculiar fact that although French cabinets are extremely unstable, the individual ministers are quite stable.[13] As we have seen, in some cabinet offices like Foreign Affairs, there have been fewer changes in France than in the same period in Great Britain or the United States.

Two questions suggest themselves: If the same men return after a cabinet has collapsed, what is the point of the whole crisis? And can it be said that the instability of the French cabinet system is not as great as it seems? The first question should probably be answered in these terms: French cabinets find themselves confronted by an impossible situation. The serious problems which they must face, especially in the field of economics and foreign affairs, demand long-range, often radical solutions. But no such solution is possible because the coalition parties and the other groups which support them in parliament are fundamentally at odds. In this hopeless struggle, the life-energy of the cabinet is quickly exhausted in frustration and it collapses. Léon Blum, a former Premier, said: "Cabinets do not fall, or fall only rarely over questions of general policy. The votes which end their existence have very seldom produced anything which resembles a regroupment of political forces. They [the cabinets] fall because their active strength is exhausted, because they have gasped their last breath, because they have come to the end." [14] In this situation the actual collapse of the cabinet gives a breathing spell to the frustrated energies of its participants and to the Assembly. They have let off steam—they feel better—and they can begin again.

As to the second question, there are indeed many who feel that the relative ministerial stability (in contradistinction to cabinet instability) proves that the system is actually working quite well and that the importance of frequent cabinet changes is exaggerated. However, it is difficult to take such an optimistic viewpoint. The return of the same eligible ministers, the *ministrables*, merely shows the nature of the essentially negative compromises which have to be made in order to obtain yet another cabinet. In other words, the *ministrables* are the men who have learned that they can only agree to do little or nothing. As a result few imaginative, long-range policies have seen the light of day. There is no shortage of brilliant ideas and plans, for France is a country with a superabundance of intelligence, but few such ideas get very far beyond the blueprint stage. The Schuman Plan is the one notable exception.

[13] Maurice Duverger, "Public Opinion and Political Parties in France," *American Political Science Review*, Vol. XLVI (1953), pp. 1069–1078.

[14] Léon Blum, *La réforme gouvernementale*, Paris, 1936.

Internal Organization

The French Constitution does not in any way establish or limit the number of chief government departments (ministries) whose incumbents are members of the cabinet. The standard ministries, such as Foreign Affairs, Interior, Finance, and Defense, are of course always represented. Occasionally special ministries are created, either temporarily or permanently, in order to take charge of a certain problem. For instance, Paul Coste-Floret (MRP) was appointed Minister in Charge of Constitutional Reform in the René Mayer cabinet of 1953. But more often the size of a cabinet is determined by political considerations, *i.e.*, the number of important politicians who must be accommodated. There are usually one or several ministers without specific departments to administer. They used to be called Ministers without Portfolio (Department), but since 1946 the practice has been to call them Ministers of State. Neither the number of ministerial posts nor the distribution of their functions needs parliamentary approval.

In addition to the ministers there are usually a number of secretaries of state and under-secretaries of state. Their positions are not clearly defined, and they differ not only from cabinet to cabinet but also from ministry to ministry. Secretaries of state are in effect junior ministers. They may sign ordinances but only together with a full minister. Their authority is derived from that which the Premier or a minister delegates to them, yet within that framework their functions may be quite substantial.

The status of under-secretaries of state is even more uncertain. Their position lies between those of the minister and secretaries of state on the one hand and the top civil servants of the ministries concerned on the other. If there is no secretary of state their position may approximate that of a secretary of state. Otherwise it is somewhat lower. While ministers and secretaries of state are politicians, under-secretaries may be drawn from the top civil service. More often they are political appointees too. The practice varies so greatly that no general rule can be established. On occasion high commissioners have been appointed. Their rank is below that of an under-secretary but above the regular civil service.

French practice does not know the British type of cabinet which is composed only of the chief ministers. In the French cabinet, every minister has a seat. However, there are two types of cabinet meetings, the Council of Ministers (Conseil des Ministres) and the Cabinet Council (Conseil de Cabinet). Although the official title of the Premier is President of the Council of Ministers, he does not preside over the Council of Ministers; that role is reserved to the President of the Republic, and the Council of Ministers meets at his official residence, the Elysée Palace. In addition to him, the Premier and all the ministers form the Council of Ministers. If its agenda contains questions which concern the responsibilities of certain secretaries of state, they too are invited, but that practice varies greatly. Under exceptional circumstances even under-secretaries may attend.

The Constitution specifies certain problems which must be decided by the Council of Ministers, such as the appointment of certain high officials, the decision to ask the National Assembly for a formal vote of confidence, or the dissolution of the Assembly.[15] Beyond that the Council of Ministers deals theoretically with all questions of high policy, and it receives all government bills either for information or in order to discuss and approve them. If a poll is taken in the Council of Ministers, the minority is supposed either to support the decisions of the majority, once the vote has been cast, or to resign. There can be no "cabinet opposition." In 1947 the Communist ministers attempted to chart a novel course by outwardly supporting the decisions of the cabinet majority, while the Communist deputies in the National Assembly voted against the government. However the Premier, Paul Ramadier (Socialist), declared that a party could not be in the government and oppose it at the same time, and as the Communist ministers refused to resign, a decree of the President of the Republic removed them from office and appointed their successors. There have been no Communists in subsequent cabinets and the incident has not been repeated.

In contradistinction to the Council of Ministers, the Cabinet Council is not mentioned in either the Constitution or the law. It is a more informal session of the cabinet and meets at the Hotel Matignon (the Premier's office) or at one of the ministries. Its presiding officer is the Premier, and it is more generally open to secretaries and under-secretaries of state. It has none of the official functions of the Council of Ministers, but it usually prepares the policy which is then submitted to the latter for formal adoption. Thus the real political decisions are likely to be taken in the informal Cabinet Council, and then merely ratified by the Council of Ministers. The difference between these two types of cabinet meetings is purely the result of historical development.

Either form of cabinet meeting tends to be cumbersome since somewhere around thirty people participate, sometimes even more. Therefore the practice of smaller meetings has become quite current. One form is the Interministerial Council, which is composed of several ministers who have certain common problems to discuss. Such councils may become semipermanent cabinet subcommittees. Another form is called "Supercouncil." It is composed of certain ministers of special eminence whose function is to evolve government policy on specific questions. This institution comes close to an inner cabinet, but the device is infrequently used and only on matters of gravest importance. It was used in 1947 in the controversial questions of the law of the press and the Indochinese problem. Another streamlining device is to place one minister in

[15] See p. 270.

charge and general supervision of several other, lesser, ministries, but this method has not seen much use.[16]

Constitutionally and politically the cabinet is a unit and theoretically presents a united front to the parliament and the public. As we have seen, ministers who cannot go along with government policy resign and thus regain their freedom of action and criticism. Usually the resignation of all the ministers belonging to a certain party will bring down the cabinet; in fact the political reality that agreement can no longer be reached is usually sufficient to cause the Premier to hand in his resignation and that of the cabinet. There are exceptions, of course. When the Communist ministers were dismissed from the Ramadier cabinet in 1947, and when the Socialists resigned from the Bidault cabinet in 1950, the departing ministers were simply replaced. But then it was realized that these two groups had shifted to positions of permanent or at least long-lasting opposition and that it was useless to try to form another cabinet with them. Ordinarily, however, governmental majorities are so fragile that the exodus of a political group is likely to bring down the cabinet.

Because of the difficulty of reaching agreements within the cabinet, it was decided on a few occasions to allow ministers the freedom of their choice and to vote on different sides of a question in the National Assembly. But this is obviously an undesirable situation, and it has been more typical of the Third Republic than of the Fourth. Generally speaking, the burden of obtaining agreement rests on the shoulders of the Premier, and the cabinet stands or falls with his skill in finding ground for compromise and agreement.

THE MINISTRIES

Most of the French ministries' functions are divided in the same manner as those of the chief government departments of other countries. There are of course certain variations. The Foreign Ministry is charged not only with the customary conduct of foreign affairs but also with the heavy burden of dealing with tumultuous Tunisia and Morocco.[17] The French representatives and actual rulers of those two territories, the Residents General, are directly subordinated to the Foreign Minister. Occasionally a question dealing with foreign affairs is placed under the authority of another minister. For instance, in the cabinet of René Pleven (UDSR) of 1950, Minister of State Guy Mollet (Socialist) was placed in charge of affairs concerning the Council of Europe.

France's relations with her overseas empire, except for Tunisia and Morocco, have been vested in the Ministry for Overseas France since the Ministry for the Associated States was abolished in 1953.

The Ministry of the Interior is perhaps the most important key position

[16] Claude-Albert Colliard, *Le travail gouvernemental et ses méthodes*, Paris, 1948.
[17] Tunisia and Morocco are protectorates. They have not become associated states.

because it is in charge of internal security, controls the police, and administers the elections. Through the prefects it maintains tight control over all levels of local government.[18]

Economic affairs have been divided between different ministries in varying fashions. At times Economic Affairs were combined with the Ministry of Finance, as for instance in the Laniel cabinet of 1953. At other times there were Ministries of National Economy separate and distinct from the Ministry of Finance. Usually there was a special Ministry for the Budget, with separate ministries for Industry and Commerce, for Public Works, for Transport and Tourism, and of course for Labor and for Agriculture.

The French Ministry of Finance does not have much influence over the spending policy of other government departments. In that respect it is quite unlike the British Treasury. But on the other hand the economic policy of the country is actually made by the Ministry of Finance and not by any of the economic ministries. This is so because the chief economic problem of France is fiscal: lack of revenue, emptiness of the treasury which forces the government time and time again to get a short-term loan from the Bank of France to tide itself over an emergency period.

The reason for this notorious state of affairs lies in the fact that two important sectors of France's economic life yield little tax money. One of them is business (big and small alike), which is well known for its fraudulent tax-return practices, and the other is the entire farming population, which pays practically no direct taxes at all. This puts the principal burden on the wage earner and produces an emphasis on indirect taxation which is hardest on the lower income groups. The remedies for this unfavorable situation are well known. They would have to include a rigid enforcement machinery and drastic punishment for tax evasion and tax fraud. But these remedies cannot be applied for political reasons. The largest parliamentary support of the government comes from the conservative deputies who would not tolerate strong measures against business, while the majority of the popular vote for the present government parties comes from the rural areas which have never been in the habit of paying taxes.[19] This is not just the fault of the right-wing groups. When the French government was dominated by the left-wing parties no attempts were made to change the situation, for the Socialists get most of their votes from rural areas, and the Communists also have some sizable support among the farm population.

The French ministries are organized on a nearly uniform pattern. One of their peculiar features is a "cabinet" within each ministry. It is headed by a chief (*chef du cabinet*) and is composed of an assistant chief, a secretary,

---

[18] See Chap. 4G.

[19] In all fairness it should be said that few French farmers are rich; a good part of the rural population ekes out a fairly meager existence.

and several attachés. It is no part of the civil service but is composed of strictly political, or more accurately, personal appointees of the minister. Relatives of a minister have frequently been chosen. This "cabinet" is supposed to act as a counterbalance against the top-heavy, overly powerful civil service and is designed to prevent the minister's isolation in his department. It is of course understandable that the minister, whose parliamentary duties and short tenure give him little time to become an expert on technical questions, is somewhat overwhelmed when he finds himself surrounded by permanent officials with a far greater knowledge of the subject matter than he has and who may have views different from his own. In this situation a cabinet of loyal, devoted friends can be of great help. But its value is diminished by the fact that its members are frequently novices with little knowledge of the art of administration in a strongly centralized government. The result is sometimes confusion and demoralization among members of the regular service, who regard the cabinet as the personal espionage service of the minister. In the Third Republic the situation was made worse by the tendency of some ministers to secure high civil-service positions for the members of their cabinets, even by special legislation. This practice is far less frequent in the Fourth Republic, partly as a result of civil-service reform, partly because the constant return to office of a relatively small number of people improves the chances for the cabinet's employment. When the author met Georges Bidault at a time when he was out of office, Bidault introduced his *chef du cabinet* by this title although there was no cabinet at that time. This gentleman was simply standing by and waiting until Bidault would return to office, which occurred for a time in 1953 (Foreign Minister).

ADVISORY AGENCIES

After the First World War a number of economic advisory agencies and councils were established, among them an Economic Council which was formed by law in 1925 and received enlarged power in 1936, but their achievements have been insignificant.

The French Constitution of 1946 provides in Art. 25 for the creation of an Economic Council. Subsequent laws and regulations established the modalities of the Council's organization. It is composed of 45 representatives of non-agricultural wage earners, 20 representatives of industry (6 for the nationalized industries and 14 for private industry), 10 for commerce, 10 for the artisanry, 35 for agriculture, 9 for the cooperatives, 15 for the overseas territories, and 10 for French literature and creative thought. According to an executive order of 1947 these representatives are nominated by their respective professional organizations, labor unions, etc. Only the representatives of French thought are appointed directly by the Council of Ministers. The normal total number of councilors is thus 152, but during the period of reconstruction 2 representatives of war victims were added, bringing the total to 154.

The Economic Council was designed to satisfy a number of diverse ideas and aspirations. It was to appeal to those who wanted some sort of "interest representation," to those who wanted to see the power of the National Assembly checked by other councils, to those who believed in the need for giving experts a high place in the councils of government, to those who resented the preeminence of politics over the economic problems of the country, and to those who had some vague ideas about economic democracy. But none of these aspirations was fulfilled. The Council has only advisory functions and has remained a body of minor significance.

The Economic Council *must* be consulted about any question concerning the establishment of an over-all, national, economic plan. It *must* also be consulted with regard to any executive order or administrative directive which implements a law that has been previously submitted to it for advice. *In all other cases* the government or the parliament have an *option* whether to consult the Council or not. Such consultation may concern any problem of economic or social policy nature with the exception of the budget. Moreover the Council may decide to consider any such question on its own initiative.

The Economic Council has not distinguished itself as an initiator of ideas, nor has its advice had very deep significance. Such economic planning as has been possible under the political circumstances prevailing in France was the work of other agencies. Foremost among them is the General Planning Department (Commissariat Général du Plan) which is the author and custodian of the so-called "Modernization and Equipment Plan," better known by the name of its chief architect, Jean Monnet, as the "Monnet Plan." [20]

The guiding idea at the inception of the plan was the realization that France had been left far behind in the industrial race of the world and that her principal endeavor had to be a rapid modernization of industrial equipment and organization. To this end, a series of most comprehensive studies was made by eighteen task forces, called "modernization commissions." Each task force had a *rapporteur* taken from the staff of the Commissariat, thus contributing to a cohesive, over-all economic plan. In its actual administration, however, the Commissariat concentrates on only six key industries: coal, power, steel, cement, agricultural machinery, and transport. Here the work of the Commissariat is specific, including setting of production goals.

The Monnet Plan has certainly had a considerable measure of success. Production has been greatly increased, considerable funds have been channeled into the sorely needed modernization of equipment, and a general recovery

[20] *Rapport général sur le premier plan de modernisation et d'équipement,* Paris, 1947. Jean Monnet is also the real author of the Schuman Plan and was until 1955 the presiding officer of its High Authority.

since the paralysis of the war is undeniable. A very large amount of credit for that is due to the Marshall Plan and other American aid; yet without very energetic French work the American funds would have accomplished little. But on the debit side of the picture is the fact that modernization and increase in production have been very slow in comparison to other European countries. One explanation is certainly the fact that the Industrial Revolution has not run its course in France as fully as elsewhere, and much of French industry consists of small establishments which are not suitable for modern assembly-line methods. Another factor detrimental to greater productivity is the notoriously antisocial attitude of a substantial part of French industrialists, who dislike competition and believe in high unit profits and low production, while the workers are generally disinterested, regard the "boss" as an enemy, and do not believe in the economic system of the country. There is a general air of stagnation, a reluctance to expand. Detrimental also is the fact that too many people are engaged in commercial activities and not enough in production. Commerce accounts for 16 per cent of the national income as against 8.5 per cent in Germany. The government is weak and unable to take the measures necessary to put its economic house in order, and the treasury is frequently empty as a result of inadequate revenue measures. These are not conditions under which recovery can make very rapid progress, and the gap between wages and prices drives the working population into the arms of extremist parties. However, substantial progress was made for the first time in 1954 and the chances for further improvement are good.

The Nationalized Industries

Nationalization is not a novelty in France. A number of railroads, utilities, and other enterprises have been nationalized for many years. Moreover, the government maintained certain "monopolies," *i.e.*, industries which the government owned and operated and to which it allowed no competition. In 1936 the Popular Front government had introduced further nationalization, notably of the Bank of France and of the munitions and aircraft industries, and had brought all railroads under its control.

During the struggle for liberation, nationalization was a popular topic of discussion among members of the Resistance. In part this was due to the prevalence of leftist elements, but a powerful argument was found in the large degree of collaboration which existed between some of France's largest industries and the hated German enemy.

Consequently nationalization became an item on the agenda of all post-liberation governments. A variety of reasons tended to demand nationalization. Paramount were the political reasons which favored the argument that only nationalization of key industries could free France from the rule of the "trusts." It was felt in certain circles that big, powerful corporations had been able to wield a disproportionate influence through their command of a good part of the press and that they had thus been able to paralyze orderly and constitutional government. It was also known, and revealed from time to time, that certain public officials were not above accepting favors from such sources. Moreover, it was contended that certain corporations, like the steel trust (*comité de forges*), had been notorious for their ties with foreign (German) interests, and it was also remembered that certain financial circles had held the whip hand over the national currency by their constant threat to evacuate their capital from France.

On the economic side of the argument, it was held that only by the direct ownership and administration of key industries could the government hope to control the national economy and direct it into certain well-planned channels. This argument gained many adherents partly because other means of control, such as price and allocation controls, had proven ineffective, partly because of poor administration, partly because of a lack of discipline among the people and their great skill in circumventing the law—a talent developed to a fine art under the German occupation.

Another argument advanced stated that in times of national emergency, during the difficult days of recovery, vital industries should not be in a position to enrich themselves by huge profits. Perhaps it was also hoped that improved morale among the workers would result from nationalization and would produce a higher degree of efficiency.

As a result of these considerations, the most important coal mines, the public-utilities corporations (gas and electricity), and certain aviation and automobile manufacturers [21] were nationalized. More important perhaps than these, the same fate reached the most important banks and a majority of insurance companies. This was an important stroke because it enabled the government to control virtually the entire production process, either directly through the nationalized factories, or indirectly through the nationalized banks and insurance companies. Such loopholes as existed were further plugged when the nationalization rules, already applicable to the Bank of France since 1936, were extended to the Bank of Algiers.

The organizational patterns of the nationalized industries have much in common, even though they differ in certain respects according to their needs. The coal industry, for instance, was organized into nine semiautonomous "*bassins*," each with a full-fledged administrative staff and a board of directors composed of representatives of the government, the consumers, and the workers.[22] These *bassins* are subordinate to the National Coal Authority (Carbonnages de France), which exercises supervisory powers over the administration but controls functions in all financial matters. The other nationalized

[21] The Renault motor works and the Gnôme et Rhône aircraft corporation were nationalized because of the collaborationist activities of their former managers.

[22] The workers' share of seats is proportionally higher than the others'.

industries follow this pattern with some variations. The banking and credit institutions have a National Credit Council, which is headed by the Minister of Finance and is composed of representatives of other ministries, financial institutions, labor, industry, agriculture, commerce, etc. Labor has a large representation on this Council as well as on the board of each of the nationalized banks. Actually, however, the Minister of Finance and the officers designated by him dominate the picture.

The situation in the insurance business is very similar, where a National Insurance Council exists, very much like the National Credit Council but with a more limited representative basis (representing government, policyholders, and employees). The Renault auto works, on the other hand, being a single enterprise, have an appointed president and an advisory board of directors showing the usual interest representation.

Yet all is not plain sailing. On July 24, 1948, André Marie, Premier-designate, declared before the National Assembly: "We want the nationalized industries to become a source of pride for France and to stop being a source of anxiety." Part of the state of affairs to which Marie alluded was caused by the economic difficulties of the postwar period and had no particular connection with the fact of nationalization. But there were and are other factors as well. The tripartite control authority (government, consumers, employees) is composed of elements with very divergent interests. It is sometimes difficult to establish a purposeful business policy. For this reason, a superimposed body, a Special Accounting Office (Chambre de Comptes), whose members are all government-appointed, has wielded much control, thereby rendering somewhat theoretical the principle of decentralization which the law tried to establish.

Later it was replaced by a body with similar functions, the "Commission for the Verification of Accounts in Public Enterprise" (Commission de Vérification des Comptes des Entreprises Publiques), whose members were selected from the staffs of the Ministry of Finance and the General Accounting Office (Cour des Comptes). Like its predecessor, the Commission may remove boards of directors for demonstrated inefficiency. The appointments to the top administrative positions are controlled by the various ministers in charge (commerce and industry, finance, economics, etc.) and are therefore open to political influence. These positions are of key importance because the tripartite board of directors is often unable to agree and consequently the appointed officials in effect often determine policy.

The situation is complicated by the fact that the excessively large representation of the employees on the boards of directors and councils is composed of people appointed by their respective unions, for the workers vote which union shall represent them and not which individuals. This vests control in outsiders most of whom belong to the completely Communist-controlled General Workers Federation (Confédération Générale du Travail). As a result political rather than economic reasons have often motivated the actions of the workers' representatives, especially since the Communists have made an all-out attempt to wreck the Marshall Plan and other American aid programs.

The nationalization of French industry was the result of special circumstances at the end of the war, rather than of over-all planning. It is now an established fact of French life and there are few attempts to denationalize, though some talk is occasionally heard. On the other hand few Frenchmen would point with particular pride to these enterprises, and even fewer would want any more nationalizations. Although it was the political left which once made itself the spokesman of nationalization, it was a coalition regime which brought it about and no single party can claim credit or accept sole blame for it. Consequently as a political issue nationalization plays no role and as an economic and administrative factor it is confined to the sector of the economy which it now occupies.

THE CIVIL SERVICE

French government is characterized by a strongly centralist regime in which most important decisions are made in Paris and executed by a vast bureaucracy. As the political heads of the government departments are faced by the constant instability of their position and the need incessantly to defend their political lives, enormous power is left in the hands of the permanent civil servants. This power is enhanced by the facts that even minute problems of local government must frequently be decided on a central level, and that the central government embraces many functions which in other countries are partly exercised by other levels of government, partly left to private agencies. Thus the centralized machinery not only administers most of local government and the entire educational system but also manages much of the legitimate stage and opera and many other things.

The pay of the French civil servant is not high, but he is better off than many other parts of the population, for the civil-service unions have much power and many political friends and have been able to obtain many concessions. Nor have they refrained from strikes when recourse to this remedy seemed indicated. True, the Council of State has handed down rulings designed to limit certain types of strikes, but this has had little effect. Although civil-service strikes have not been frequent, they have occurred either in an outright fashion, as in the summer of 1953, or indirectly by slowdowns, exaggerated enforcements of minute regulations, or nonenforcement of regulations.

Let us not be too harsh on the French civil servant. While strikes and comparable actions on his part seem obnoxious and improper to the American or Briton, they are merely a reflection of French individualistic society in which the special interest of the person or the group is so often allowed to override the interests of the community. In this respect the civil servants do not differ from other people in France, from parliament, industry, trade, agriculture, labor unions, and the public in general. In this environment, the French civil servant actually exhibits a high order of devotion to duty and principle.

More important than strikes have been the strong political pressures exercised by the civil servants and their unions. Many are candidates for political office and if elected need merely take a leave of absence from their civil-service employment, to which they may return when their term of political office has expired. Between 1944 and 1947 a good number of Communists were able to enter the civil service, especially in the ministries headed by Communists, but most of them have since been eliminated in one way or another, especially those in more important positions. However, the Socialist party (SFIO) is especially strong among civil servants, who, together with teachers, form its organizational backbone. As most recent French governments have taken on a more and more right-wing coloration, the fact that so many civil servants are active partisans of an opposition party raises interesting questions, but presumably not of fundamental loyalty.

Apart from his salary and his family allocations,[23] which are tied to the cost of living, the French civil servant is protected from lawsuits arising from his official functions, for the government is responsible for his acts, except those committed in a strictly personal capacity. At the same time, he may seek redress in the administrative courts (councils) against any superior office seeking to impair his rights under the civil-service laws.

Before 1945 all matters of personnel management, recruitment, promotion, disciplinary action, etc., were in the hands of the personnel boards of the various ministries. Usually there was one board in each ministry, but in the larger ones there were several. These boards were under the fiscal control of the Board of the Budget and under the legal control of the Council of State. This system worked rather badly, lacked uniformity and central control, and often favored the employees of the Ministry of Finance, who were closer to the Board of the Budget.

This was changed in 1945 and formally enacted in the Civil Service Act of October 19, 1946. Without replacing the Board of the Budget, the Act set up a central office directly under the Premier; it is called the Civil Service Office (Direction de la Fonction Publique) [24] and is headed by a director who is assisted by a rather small staff. This office prepares the texts of all laws and executive orders (decrees) concerning the status of civil servants but must

[23] Under the system of family allocations, the French government pays a subsidy to families, which increases with the number of children and constitutes a substantial supplement to the regular salary earned. These family allocations are of course paid to all qualified persons in both public and private employment.

[24] For an excellent discussion on which much of this presentation is based, see Jean Trouvé, "The French Civil Service Office," *Public Administration Review,* Vol. XL (1951), pp. 180–186.

consult the Board of the Budget in financial matters. The office is in charge of classifying civil-service positions, which is for the first time being done in a fairly uniform manner, supervises and approves regulations for recruitment and promotion, and advises on methods to improve the service.

The Civil Service Office is strictly a staff agency, that is, it is solely concerned with planning and advising. The actual operation of the civil service rests with the personnel boards in the various ministries.

Because the Premier is preoccupied with other matters, the practice has emerged by which the supervision of the Civil Service is delegated to a Minister or Secretary of State. This has tied the Director of the Civil Service rather closely to the government, but French governments do not ordinarily interfere with the operation of the service and there is little political influence from the top. There is certainly no spoils system.

The 1946 law established a system of consultative councils, each composed half of supervisors and half of staff employees. There are administrative committees representing one class in a ministry, and there are technical committees representing members of the same service regardless of class. The Minister must consult with the appropriate committee on any decision affecting the status of a civil servant. The same is true in disciplinary cases. The Minister is not bound to follow the committee's advice. There is also a Supreme Civil Service Council of twenty-four members headed by the Minister (or Secretary of State) of the Civil Service. It is a high consulting body on general questions affecting several ministries and a board of appeals in individual cases. The Minister is not obliged to carry out its advice but almost invariably does.

The main civil-service classes follow the British system very closely. The top group is, as in Britain, the Administrative class (*administrateurs civils*). Second in rank and largest in number is the Executive class (*secrétaires d'administration*), which is followed by the Clerical class (*adjoints administratifs*) and the Subordinate Personnel (typists, messengers, etc.)

One may enter the Executive class and the classes below by competitive examinations. These test the desired educational level of the candidate rather than his special preparation for the job. In this respect they follow the British example and are geared to the various levels of (public) education. In contrast to the American practice, a French civil servant who passes his examination successfully enters a so-called "corps of civil servants" of which there are about one thousand. A corps of civil servants comprises a variety of civil-service positions to which one is eligible after passing one particular examination. It also comprises a number of given promotions to which one may be advanced according to regulations and without taking additional examinations.

Recruitment to the highest group, the Administrative class, is handled in a different manner. It is open only to graduates of the National School of Administration (École Nationale d'Administration). The creation of this school had long been a dream in French administrative circles, and the former Premier Léon Blum was a particular advocate thereof. It was realized only in 1945.

Admission to the National School of Administration is possible only through one of two sets of exceedingly difficult examinations. One set is given to young civil servants with a minimum of five years' experience. The other is open to graduates of the various Institutes of Political Science (Instituts d'Études Politiques) attached to the principal universities—Paris, Bordeaux, Strasbourg, Grenoble, etc.[25]

Successful candidates become temporary civil servants and receive a salary while going to school. The course lasts three years and features periodic internships, *i.e.*, work in different branches of the administrative services. The training is divided into four categories between which the student may choose: general administration, economic and financial administration, social administration, and foreign affairs. The rank of each student in each category is determined by examinations which form the basis for later appointment. Rarely do more than 100 students graduate each year.

Special in-service training for high officials is available in three-month courses at the School of Advanced Studies. Both the National School of Administration and the School of Advanced Studies have greatly democratized the civil service and have opened access to the highest positions to all men and women who possess the necessary training and ability.

D. THE LEGISLATURE

The legislature of the Third Republic was supreme but it was divided into two coequal houses, the Chamber of Deputies and the Senate, which balanced one another to some extent or at any rate divided power between themselves. But as we have seen, the leftist majority of the Constituent Assembly of 1945–1946 strongly objected to a revival of the Senate and in fact did not want any balancing factor to limit the power of a single, popularly elected chamber. They did not have their way completely because the unicameral legislature was rejected by the French people in the referendum of May 5, 1946. The second draft, which was adopted on October 13, 1946, did provide for a second chamber, but its powers were very limited, and we have therefore what may be called "legislative supremacy" or, according to a French tradition, "assembly government," which is exercised by the National Assembly.

[25] The principal institute, the one in Paris, is the considerably reorganized former École Libre des Sciences Politiques. The second type of entrance examination to the National School of Administration is open also to students of other university departments, especially law. But the Institutes prepare specially for it.

The entire legislative body of France is called the parliament.[26] It is composed of a larger and more important National Assembly (Assemblée Nationale) of 625 deputies and a smaller and less important Council of the Republic (Conseil de la République) of 320 senators. Which one of them has the upper hand is clearly stated in Art. 13 of the Constitution, which reads: "The National Assembly shall make the laws. It may not delegate this right." And Art. 3 provides that except where the referendum applies, the French people exercise their sovereignty through the deputies of the National Assembly.

Because of the inequality between the two houses, it would be misleading to speak of bicameralism pure and simple. It would be more correct to adopt the characterization of Paul Coste-Floret, who spoke of an "incomplete bicameralism" or a "modified unicameralism."

By law the members of the National Assembly have reserved to themselves the title "deputy" (*député*).[27] By a similar resolution the members of the Council of the Republic later adopted the title "senator" (*sénateur*) for themselves. The latter designation is significant because it denotes a desire on the part of the senators to regain the prerogatives and powers of the Senate of the Third Republic. Toward this goal they have made considerable progress.

THE ELECTORAL PROCESS

While Gallic temperament may lead to occasional fisticuffs and the tearing down or defacing of "enemy" billboards, French elections are usually calm, orderly, and honest. The latter quality is assured by the electoral commissions which control the proceedings and the counting of the ballots. These commissions are composed of regular judges from the courts of first and second instance, a member of the Departmental General Council, a division chief of the prefecture, and optional observers from all political parties.

All French men and women of twenty-one years of age or older have the right to vote unless they are specifically disqualified by such reasons as mental incapacity, preventive arrest, or a court order accompanying a verdict in a criminal trial. Unlike American practice, the voters' lists are prepared by the authorities, and no special registration on the part of the voter is necessary.[28] The lists are open to inspection for a certain period, and a qualified

[26] This is the first time that the legislature is officially called by that name. Colloquially, however, this term was used frequently in the Third Republic.

[27] The purpose of the law was to prevent the members of the Assembly of the French Union from using this time-honored term.

[28] This system is common in Europe. It is made possible by the fact that every person staying in France has to notify the police of his whereabouts. Travelers sign a police registration form at their hotels. French citizens and resident aliens must do the same and also carry identity cards issued by the Ministry of the Interior.

voter whose name has inadvertently been omitted can protest and have his name added.

The situation is a little different for a naturalized French citizen, who has the right to vote only after he has been a citizen for five years. Under the Third Republic the right of the population in the colonial territories to vote was determined by an extraordinarily complex group of laws. The Constitution of 1946 provides for a simpler treatment which seems more equitable than it actually is. Article 80 provides that "All nationals of the Overseas Territories shall have the status of citizens, in the same capacity as French nationals of Metropolitan France or the Overseas Territories." And Art. 4 stipulates that "All French citizens and nationals of both sexes, who are of age and enjoy civil and political rights, may vote under conditions determined by law." This would seem to extend exactly the same rights to the inhabitants of those territories as are enjoyed by the citizens of European France, especially as the overseas territories elect representatives to the National Assembly and the Council of the Republic (Art. 79). However, the last sentence of Art. 80, "Special laws shall determine the conditions under which they may exercise their rights as citizens," has been interpreted to permit legislation which gives the natives of the overseas territories a status very inferior to that of European Frenchmen.

This is done in different ways. In some of the more backward regions, the right to vote is reserved to those citizens who are more advanced than their countrymen. In French East Africa, in French Equatorial Africa, in Togo and Cameroon, in Madagascar and the Comores, the vote is possessed by those who had it under pre–Second World War legislation. For the rest, the following factors are taken into consideration in allocating the right to vote: military service, civil service or other public functions and professions, possession of decorations, ownership of property, and even the possession of a driver's or hunting license.

In the old colonies—those which France had before the Revolution, like Martinique, French Guiana, Guadeloupe and Réunion—everybody of French nationality votes as in any department of France. In Algeria an entirely different system prevails. Here only the men vote—in deference to the Moslem prejudice against equal rights for women—but the voters are divided into two electoral colleges. The First College is composed of Frenchmen and a few Moslems who have received this privilege for individual merit. The Second College is composed of the rest of the native population. Each college sends the same number of deputies (fifteen each) to the National Assembly, and the same number of senators (seven each) to the Council of the Republic in Paris. But when one considers that the native population has a relationship of 8 to 1 to the European settlers, it becomes clear that the natives are numerically greatly underrepresented.

If the right to vote is regulated in a fairly simple fashion, the rules governing eligibility, *i.e.*, the right to be elected, are more complex. The minimum age of eligibility to the National Assembly is twenty-three and to the Council of the Republic thirty-five. In view of the far inferior position of the Council of the Republic this discrepancy between age requirements makes no sense, but it is a tradition that the second chamber has more "reflective" functions than the first and such ability comes, presumably, with age.

Furthermore a candidate must be a French citizen or, if naturalized, must have been a French citizen for at least ten years. He must be a qualified voter, and he must have satisfied the law dealing with military service. This does not mean that he must have served, but he must have either served or been definitely exempted.

French law further decrees certain cases of ineligibility. Among them are the members of the former royal families which have ruled over France in the past. Also ineligible are those who have been condemned by a court to "national indignity" but who have had their right to vote restored to them.[29] A large number of Vichy functionaries are also automatically ineligible, including all those who on July 10, 1940, voted in favor of the enabling act of Marshal Pétain. However, later participation in the Resistance, confirmed by an "honor jury," wiped out this ineligibility.[30]

There are a number of officials who suffer a temporary and relative ineligibility. Their number is kept to a minimum. They are officials whose functions might make it possible for them to influence the outcome of an election: certain judges of the inferior courts, certain administrative officials of the prefecture and comparable services, and military commanders of territories. This kind of "relative ineligibility" comes to an end six months to two years after the official has ceased to exercise the particular function or office.

Finally, deputies or senators who have been unseated by their respective chambers for corrupt practices remain ineligible for two years.

The Constitution has little to say about the method of election. Article 6 leaves the length of the legislative term, the method of election, and the rules of eligibility to both houses of parliament to be determined by ordinary law. It merely states that elections to the National Assembly shall be by direct, universal suffrage,[31] while those to the Council of the Republic shall be by indirect suffrage, by way of the departmental and municipal assemblies.

Under the Third and the Fourth Republics, the method of electing members of the Senate and its successor, the Council of the Republic, has remained

[29] If their right to vote has not been restored, they are automatically ineligible, as the possession of the right to vote is a condition of eligibility.

[30] A well-known case is that of Robert Schuman (MRP), several times Premier and Foreign Minister.

[31] The suffrage is of course equal and secret. Absentee ballots and voting by proxy are permissible only in relatively few cases of military and civil-service personnel on duty, sick persons, and those unable to return because of war.

fairly constant. The same can by no means be said for the Chamber of Deputies and its successor, the National Assembly. The Third Republic knew three systems: the single-member district, the multimember district-list system, and a modified form of proportional representation. Among them the longest lasting and also the simplest was the single-member district system, a majority system with runoff elections (*scrutin d'arrondissement à deux tours*). It operated in this fashion. Any number of people could run in each district (*arrondissement*) for the one seat available. If any candidate obtained a majority (over 50 per cent) of the vote cast, he was elected. However this did not occur very often because the vote was usually split between numerous candidates—on the average there were eight candidates for every seat. Thus if there was no majority, a second, runoff election would be held a week later at which plurality would suffice. The interval between the first and second elections gave an opportunity for certain parties to get together and pool resources by uniting behind the most promising candidate among them. These "blocs" or "cartels" were frequently based on previous arrangements.

This system had the advantage of simplicity and helped to maintain a close relationship between the deputy and his constituents. It gave an advantage to those middle-of-the-road parties who could enter into profitable alliances, but it encouraged the creation of many parties, groups, and independent candidates.

After the liberation of France, the Constituent Assembly instituted the system of proportional representation (PR). Until 1951 it worked in the following manner. Each basic unit of local government (*département*) formed a single constituency with the exception of some larger ones which were subdivided. Each department was assigned a number of seats in the National Assembly (544 for metropolitan France), and each party submitted a list of candidates. For each constituency there had to be as many candidates on each list as the constituency had seats assigned. The political parties alone determined who should be their candidates and the sequence in which they were listed. The voter could vote only for one entire slate. He could not split his ballot among candidates of different parties, nor could he rearrange the order of preference in which the candidates were listed. Nor might any candidate be on more than one list in a given department, although he could be on several lists in different departments. Candidates had to declare their intention to run at least twenty days before election day. At that time each candidate had to deposit with the treasurer of the department the sum of 20,000 francs (about $57), which was forfeited if he failed to obtain at least 3 per cent of the total vote cast.

After the votes were counted, the seats were distributed among the several parties *roughly* in proportion to the votes which they had polled.

The Constituent Assemblies which adopted this electoral law were dominated by the parties of the left who were traditional believers in the system of proportional representation (PR). It was their argument that it reflected with near-fidelity the distribution of the popular vote and was therefore just and truly representative of the popular will. In addition there was the practical, political consideration that the left-wing vote was presumed to be more heavily concentrated in urban areas, which gave an advantage to the more conservative parties under the single-member district system. It must also not be forgotten that many of the new political lights of France came from the clandestine struggle of the Resistance and were of necessity unknown to the public, while the old-style politicians, many of whom had not opposed Vichy, were well known. The single-member district naturally favors the well-established candidate, while the list system of proportional representation makes that much less important.

On the other hand proportional representation has very serious defects. It removes the electoral process very far from the voter who, under the 1946 system, could choose only between lists of candidates presented by the various parties. He could not favor one man or woman over another but had to vote for a given bloc of names. He therefore had no deputy whom he could regard as "his" deputy and to whom he could write, for his district (the *département*) was represented by several people. In choosing for which party to cast his ballot, he had to decide between abstract party programs (none of which can ever be realized as long as coalition governments are the order of the day); he could not give his confidence to personalities. Most serious of all, the system established and strengthened the rule of party bureaucracies which actually decided what candidate should be on what list and in what place,[32] with the result that the candidates were beholden to their party leaders rather than to the voters. At the same time PR encouraged a multiplicity of parties and splinter groups whose existence in the National Assembly made a stable government impossible. It would seem, therefore, that this electoral system had all the vices of its immediate predecessor without any of its virtues.

These considerations, however, did not produce a change. That came rather on purely political grounds. A new National Assembly was to be elected in 1951. The Communists had remained just about as strong as ever, and it was presumed that they would poll at least one-fourth of the vote. And since 1947 General Charles de Gaulle's new party, the Rally of the French People (RPF), had made tremendous gains and demanded a radical change of the form of government. There was no possibility that either Communists or

---

[32] The entire candidate list of a party is hardly ever elected. If a party which has submitted a list of seven names obtains three seats, the first three men on the list are declared elected. It is therefore important not only to be on a list but also to be high on it. Sometimes people are placed on a list out of politeness or to capitalize on their standing in the community without actually giving them a chance for a seat in parliament.

the RPF could obtain a majority, nor could they govern together, but had they obtained more than half of the seats in the National Assembly together no government of France could have prevailed against their negative majority.

There was therefore near-unanimity among the parties (except for the Communists and Gaullists) that the pure PR system had to be replaced by something else. But for a dishearteningly long time that was about as far as agreement would go.[33] The Radicals and the Independents wanted a return to the system of the Third Republic—the single-member district with majority election and runoff. Being old and conservative groups, they expected to profit by their numerous, well-established local connections. But for precisely the same reason the delegates of the Popular Republican Movement (MRP) were dead set against this suggestion. Theirs was a new party, the bulk of whose candidates were not well known locally. Moreover the MRP leaders somewhat disdained that patient but rewarding effort which in America is called "precinct work." They also feared that in any runoff election the traditionally anti-Catholic parties (Socialists and Radicals) would gang up on them and would force the MRP into coalition with the pro-Catholic but extremely conservative Independents and perhaps the Gaullists. The MRP would have preferred the continuation of multimember districts into which the government parties would go as a single bloc with a predetermined distribution of seats among them, but there was no possibility of acceptance of such a plan because it would have given the MRP representation based on its previous strength when everybody knew that it was bound to lose votes heavily—which it did.

With the MRP holding out adamantly against single-member districts and runoff elections, which the country undoubtedly wanted, and with the expiration of the Assembly session coming perilously close, an electoral law was finally adopted on May 7, 1951, which was largely based on an MRP proposal [34] and which constitutes one of the most complicated electoral laws in existence. It operates in the following manner: the basic constituency is the *département*,[35] a multimember district. There is only a single election; no runoff. As under the previous system, each party submits a list of candidates in each department containing as many names as there are seats to be distributed. But at the same time, and this is an innovation, several parties who find their company politically congenial may also register, in addition to their individual lists, an announcement of a list-coupling arrangement called

---

[33] For a more detailed account of this development, the electoral law, and its consequences, see Robert G. Neumann, "The Struggle for Electoral Reform in France," *American Political Science Review*, Vol. XLV (1951), pp. 741–755.

[34] The Roques-Taillade bill.

[35] The following *départements* are divided into several constituencies: Bouches-du-Rhône, Nord, Pas-de-Calais, Rhône, Seine (Paris), Seine-et-Oise, Seine-Inférieure (renamed Seine-Maritime), Gironde.

apparentement. The law provides that only "national" parties may register for an *apparentement*—"national" parties being those which run candidates in at least thirty departments.[36]

Although the candidates' lists are like those of 1946, the voter may now change the preferential listing of the candidates, and he may even strike out the name of a candidate and replace it by a name taken from another party list (*panachage*). This provision actually has little effect on the candidates because their names are reranked only when at least half of the voters express a desire for such a change—which is most unlikely.[37] But votes which a candidate obtains by *panachage* on some list other than his own are added to his party's list.

If a party list obtains a majority (over 50 per cent) of the vote cast, its entire list is declared elected and all other lists lose out completely. This is not a frequent occurrence. If no one party obtains a majority, the *apparentements* come into play. Now the total votes of all the parties having entered into the *apparentement* are counted together, and if the total constitutes a majority the *apparentement* receives all the seats of the department. These seats are then apportioned among the member parties according to the system of proportional representation based on the method of the *strongest average*.

This is done as follows. One seat is given outright to the party with the largest vote—let us call it party A. Then A's vote is divided by two and the resultant figure is compared with the total vote of the next largest party— B. If B's vote is larger than half of A's vote, party B gets a seat. Now half of B's vote is compared to the total vote of the next largest party—C—in the same manner until all qualified parties have received one seat. If any party's total vote is smaller than half the vote of the party before it, it does not receive a seat, and the routine starts again with party A and continues until all seats are filled. This method favors the larger parties, which benefit further by the rule that *apparentement* parties obtaining less than 5 per cent of the total vote are not entitled to a seat.

If the *apparentement* too fails to obtain a majority, then proportional representation according to the strongest average is applied to all parties, and the seats are distributed according to the method described above. However, the members of an *apparentement* again enjoy a small advantage; their votes are counted together, which is beneficial to them because this system favors the larger groups.

Special arrangements are made for the two populous *départements* of the

---

[36] This provision was widely circumvented. Many independent candidates combined into newly formed "parties" in order to qualify as "national." These fly-by-night political creations of course disappeared immediately after the elections.

[37] When less than half of the voters of a party have expressed a preference listing different from the official party sequence, their choice is simply ignored and their votes are counted as if they had simply voted for the official party list.

Seine (Paris) and Seine-et-Oise. Here no *apparentements* are allowed, and only PR prevails. But in this instance proportional representation is applied according to a different method, namely that of the *strongest remainder*. Under this method, the total vote of all parties combined is divided by the number of seats to be apportioned. The resulting figure is the electoral quotient. This quotient is now applied to the votes of each party to determine how many seats each is to receive. But a party whose vote is inferior to the quotient but superior to the remainder of votes of the strongest party after the first determination of seats also receives a seat. Under the method of the strongest average, such a party would have received no seat and the stronger parties would have received more. Since both the Communists and the RPF were strong in that area while the government parties had little success, the reason for this exception is fairly obvious.

Finally, the electoral law of 1951 provided for by-elections to fill seats which become vacant during a legislative term.[38] This is to be done under the system of the *Third Republic, i.e.,* by single-member district, majority election with runoff. This, for once, is quite logical because all the other systems which apply under the 1951 law are designed for multimember districts and could not function for the election of a single candidate.

In 1951, 87 *apparentements* were registered in 95 electoral districts (excluding Seine and Seine-et-Oise). Among them, 13 constituted agreements between the RPF and other parties. The rest were made up largely of government parties, sometimes with the inclusion of right-wing Independents, sometimes without. In 15 *apparentements* of government parties the Socialists did not participate. In 5 the MRP was excluded. Among the 87 *apparentements,* 30 obtained a majority.

The results achieved under this incredible system were indeed bizarre. The Communists and associates polled 26.4 per cent of the vote and received 103 seats. The Socialists had only 14.3 per cent but occupied 104 seats. The RPF polled 21.6 per cent and obtained 119 seats, but the Radicals and associated groups (RGR) secured 93 seats with only 11.3 per cent of the vote.

However inequitable, complicated, and unrepresentative this system is, it has achieved one thing—it has saved France from chaos. The combined total of the votes polled by the RPF and the Communists amounted to the staggering figure of 48 per cent. Under the system of proportional representation applied according to the strongest average, *i.e.,* under the electoral system previously in force, these antigovernmental forces would have had a majority in the National Assembly.[39] Under those circumstances nothing but chaos,

[38] Under the 1946 law, the party to which the departed member belongs would simply have sent the next man on the list to the National Assembly.

[39] It has been figured out that the Communists and the RPF would have obtained 325 seats, a clear majority. Such mathematical deductions are, however, fallacious and inaccurate. Electoral systems not only determine how the vote is to be counted but also

and even civil war, could have been the result. The electoral law of May 7, 1951, saved France. A tenuous victory, perhaps, but a victory nevertheless.

Beyond that the electoral law has had no other lasting effect. The *apparentements* differed from *département* to *département*, not, as some have suggested, because the time was too short to explain the system, but rather because France is a country with very diversified politics. Some *départements* felt strongly about the religious question and some did not. Some bore strong resentment against the agricultural policy carried out when a Socialist was Minister of Agriculture. These factors remain, and therefore future *apparentements* are bound to show the same uneven tendencies. It is certainly too much to expect these casual *apparentements* to lead to more lasting political alliances.

Compared to the method of electing the National Assembly, the electoral system for the Council of the Republic is simple, but only relatively so. The Constitution, as already stated, provides that the Council of the Republic should be elected indirectly, by territorial units. There are now altogether 320 senators—253 from metropolitan France, Guadeloupe, Guiana, Martinique, and Réunion; 14 from Algeria; 44 from other overseas territories and trusteeships; 1 representing the French citizens of Indochina; 5 representing the French citizens of Tunisia and Morocco; and 3 representing French citizens abroad.

In France, Guadeloupe, Guiana, Martinique, and Réunion, each *département* forms an electoral college which is composed of the following persons: (1) all the deputies of the National Assembly elected from that *département*, (2) all the members of the *département's* general council, (3) the delegates of the municipal councils and their alternates. However the numbers of delegates are apportioned in such a manner that the smaller communities are somewhat better represented than the bigger ones. For example:

A community of 100 inhabitants has 1 delegate.

A community of 1,000 inhabitants has 3 delegates.

A community of 10,000 inhabitants has 23 delegates.

A community of 100,000 inhabitants has 48 delegates.[40]

Since 253 out of 320 senators are elected by these colleges, it is not incorrect to refer to the Council of the Republic as representing the small communities of France.

Departments of 154,000 inhabitants or less are entitled to one senator, and

---

influence how it is cast. A number of people, for instance, would have voted for a certain party under PR but disliked the *apparentement* partners and voted for some other party. However, the majority of the CP-RPF under the 1946 system cannot seriously be doubted.

[40] Figures taken from Vedel, *op. cit.*, p. 389. The election of delegates by the municipal councils (who have fewer or more delegates than municipal councilors) follows other, complicated, systems which are omitted here.

all others receive one for every 250,000 additional inhabitants. In those departments which are entitled to four or more senators (654,000 or more), the electoral college elects them under proportional representation according to the strongest average. In departments of lesser size, a majority is required for election or, if no candidate achieves a majority, there is a runoff election. In Algeria there is the already discussed double college system. Each college is composed of the respective deputies to the National Assembly, the members of the Algerian assembly, members of the general council, and the delegates of municipal councils or commissions.

In other overseas territories senators are elected by territorial assemblies according to a variety of systems.

In Tunisia French citizens elect their two representatives by sending their ballots to Paris—similar to our absentee vote. This is done partly because there are no French territorial units in Tunisia as there are in France proper,[41] partly in order to preserve the illusion of a Tunisian sovereignty, which would be impaired by elections to the Paris parliament taking place on Tunisian soil. For Morocco (three) and Indochina (one) the National Assembly itself elects the appropriate senators upon the suggestions of various representative groups and personalities. The same method is applied for the election of the three senators who represent French citizens living abroad.

Under the Constitution (Art. 6) the National Assembly has the right to elect as many as one-sixth of the members of the Council of the Republic, *i.e.*, fifty-three. But under the law of September 23, 1948 (in contrast to the law of October 27, 1946), it uses this right only very sparingly, namely, for the election of the seven representatives of the French citizens of Morocco and Indochina, and for those living abroad. The restrained use of the National Assembly's right of election under Art. 6 is one of the many illustrations of the growing independence of the Council of the Republic.

The Organization of the French Parliament

Most of the bicameral legislatures of the world meet in two chambers of the same large building. Not so in Paris. The National Assembly meets in the sprawling Bourbon Palace, which is situated on the famous Quai d'Orsay, next door to the Ministry of Foreign Affairs, overlooking the Seine River. The Council of the Republic is located approximately $1\frac{1}{2}$ miles away in the smaller but lovelier and far more elegant Luxembourg Palace.

Both chambers are the sole judges of their members' credentials, and both create their own rules of procedure. Nevertheless there is a great deal of similarity between the procedures in each house.

Deputies and senators receive a salary which the Constitution (Art. 23)

[41] Algeria, as indicated before, has a separate and mixed status. It is a Government-General, but it is divided into departments similar to those of France.

has brought into direct relation to that of a civil-service class. The class selected is the highest and most respected: that of Councillors of State.[42] This method assures the members of parliament of a reasonable though hardly excessive rate of compensation and makes it possible for them to increase their salaries without attracting too much attention by simply increasing the civil-service pay rate—which makes for a delicate but not altogether unpleasant relationship between parliament and the civil service.

The immunities of French legislators go beyond those accorded to their American and British colleagues. They may not be prosecuted or held in any way responsible or answerable for the opinions expressed or the votes cast by them in the exercise of their duties. Beyond that, a deputy or senator may not be pursued for a felony except upon the permission of that house of the legislature to which he belongs or, if that house is not in session, upon that of its officers (*Bureau*). He may be arrested *flagrante delicto* (in the very act of committing the crime), but even then the house to which he belongs may order the cessation of all pursuit against him.[43] And if the house has not lifted his immunity within thirty days of the beginning of a session, an arrested member must be freed.

There is a difference between the first-mentioned immunity (*irresponsabilité*) of not being answerable for acts committed in line of duty and the second category (*inviolabilité*) of freedom from criminal pursuit. The former is substantive and the deputy or senator can never be prosecuted for those acts; the second is procedural, which means that he may be prosecuted after his legislative term expires or if his house lifts his immunity.

It is clear that immunities of this kind are necessary for the proper exercise of legislative function. However, they are sometimes abused in France, especially by those members of parliament who are members of the press and who manage to escape the consequences of a violation of the press law or the law of criminal libel. On the whole parliament is disinclined to allow criminal prosecution of its members.

In the life span of the National Assembly three periods may be distinguished. The legislative term (*legislature*) lasts from the first meeting of a newly elected Assembly until its dissolution, which is normally five years.[44] Then there are the session (*session*), which denotes the period during a given

---

[42] Actually the position of the legislators is somewhat more favorable because 42 per cent of their salary is considered to be a reimbursement of expenses and thus both tax-free and nonattachable for debt. They also enjoy nearly free rail transportation, mail franchise, partially free telephone, and retirement pay.

[43] However, a member of parliament may be sued in civil action. If he is a member of the civil service, though on leave, he may be subjected to disciplinary action and may be prosecuted for minor misdemeanors (*contraventions*), which are punishable by not more than ten days' imprisonment.

[44] Legally the prerogatives of a National Assembly expire only when its successor holds its first meeting.

year (not calendar year) when the Assembly is conducting its business, and the meeting (*séance*), which refers to a period of house during which the Assembly is actually, physically meeting.

In the Third Republic the executive had the power within limitations to close or suspend the sessions of the Chamber of Deputies. In 1954 this power was restored to the extent that the Premier may, with the consent of the Council of Ministers, declare closed a session which has lasted at least seven months. The Constitution forbids the interruption of any session to exceed four months in a calendar year. All periods during which no meetings are held for eight clear days are "interruptions" in this sense.

Whether it is convoked or not, the National Assembly meets by virtue of the Constitution for the first time on the third Thursday after its election, and for its annual session on the first Tuesday in October. Otherwise, if the Assembly is not actually meeting, it may be recalled by the collective decision of its president, vice-presidents, and certain other officials (*Bureau*), or upon the request of one-half of the deputies, or upon the demand of the Premier.

No separate rules exist for the meetings of the Council of the Republic because the Constitution provides that it shall be in session at the same time as the National Assembly.[45] In this sense it is completely subordinated to the National Assembly.

The management of the sessions as well as the housekeeping duties are assured in each house by a group of elected officials whose collective name is the *Bureau*. Each *Bureau* is composed of a president (speaker) and several vice-presidents, secretaries, and certain administrators known as questors (*questeurs*). The presidents of both houses are elected by majority vote (usually several ballots must be taken), and the other officers are elected upon an informal agreement reached by the different parties. If no agreement is possible, majority vote prevails here too.

In contrast to the short life span of French governments, the presidencies of the two houses of parliament have been in steady hands. Édouard Herriot, the grand old man of French politics, was president of the National Assembly until 1954. The Council of the Republic has had two presidents, Champetier de Ribes and, since his death, Gaston Monerville. All three men have been superbly able presiding officers.

Under present rules there are six vice-presidents, fourteen secretaries, and three questors, but either house may change the number of officers.[46]

The *Bureau* of each chamber is elected for one session. Consequently when a new session opens it has technically no presiding officers of its own, since the preceding officers' terms have expired. The session is therefore opened by the

---

[45] Of course this does not mean that the two chambers have to meet at precisely the same hours.

[46] For a detailed account of parliamentary procedure see D. W. S. Lidderdale, *The Parliament of France*, London, 1951.

so-called "age bureau" (*Bureau d'age*) which means that the oldest deputy or senator presides and the youngest ones are secretaries. The "age-president" has only two functions to perform: he makes a speech and he presides over the election of the permanent *Bureau.*

In rank of protocol the president of the National Assembly is regarded as the second man of the realm, second only to the President of the Republic. The president of the Council of the Republic ranks third. Each president presides over the meetings of his house unless he asks one of the vice-presidents to replace him temporarily. He watches over the observations of the rules and has some disciplinary power which goes as far as the temporary exclusion of a deputy or senator. But the presidents of the National Assembly and the Council of the Republic have neither the strong control of the Speaker of the British House of Commons nor the political influence of the Speaker of the United States House of Representatives.

In addition to his parliamentary duties the president of the National Assembly also has certain constitutional functions. He may sign a law if the President of the Republic fails to do so. In the unlikely case of a dissolution of the National Assembly under the provision of Art. 52,[47] he becomes Premier and Minister of the Interior, provided the dissolution was preceded by a vote of censure. Both he and the president of the Council of the Republic are consulted by the President of the Republic when a new government is to be formed.

The Committees (*Commissions*)

Both houses of the French parliament have an elaborate committee structure through which all legislation passes, resembling that of the United States and Germany, not that of Great Britain. This committee system became firmly established during the Third Republic, and the Constitution of 1946 actually provides that legislation must first be discussed in the committees of the National Assembly before they can be enacted (Art. 15). The Constitution does not mention the committees of the Council of the Republic, but they function there just the same. In France parliamentary committees are called *commissions.*

The committees are organized, as in the United States, according to the subject matter with which they deal. They are divided into the permanent General Committees (*commissions générales*)[48] and the Special Committees (*commissions spéciales*).

The permanent committees deal with the main topics of legislative concern: economics, foreign affairs, national defense, etc. There are now twenty of

[47] As amended 1954. See p. 270.
[48] But still generally referred to under the name by which they were known in the Third Republic, *grandes commissions permanentes.*

them in both houses. In addition there are two National Assembly committees of smaller size, the Accounts Committee (eleven) and the Committee on Parliamentary Immunity (twenty-two), which are not technically regarded as permanent although they are in fact.

The special committees are set up from time to time in order to study a particular, temporary problem. Some of them are investigating committees (*commissions d'enquête*), often for the purpose of looking into some alleged scandal or a disputed election.

All committees, general or special, may conduct investigations, although generally this is a specialty only of National Assembly committees. If part of this investigation is to take place outside the premises of the National Assembly, a special authorization from the Assembly is needed (*pouvoir d'enquête*). If a committee wishes to subpoena witnesses, it must obtain even more extensive authorization from the Assembly. But in that case it not only can subpoena witnesses but can cause them to be punished for refusing to answer, for refusing to take the oath, for perjury, or for bribing a witness.[49] In France, as in other countries, there is an increasing tendency toward parliamentary investigations, but not on the scale in which they are undertaken in the United States. This is natural because in a parliamentary regime like that of France the legislators can force a minister to divulge facts by using the implied threat of overthrowing the government. This works in France much better than in Great Britain. In the United States, where Congress cannot so threaten the government, Congressional investigations frequently constitute the only way to force out into the open certain facts hidden in the administrative machine.

The permanent (general) committees are very large, being composed of forty-four members in the National Assembly. No one may belong to more than two. Their members are elected according to the proportional representation of party groups. Actually the various parties themselves appoint the respective members of the committees; the leaders (*Bureaux*) of the various parties agree on the number of seats to be allocated to each one and submit to the presiding officer a combined list of nominations which is then put into effect unless at least fifty deputies object; in that case a vote is taken. If a single vacancy occurs on a committee, the party to which the former member belonged simply nominates his successor, who is then duly appointed.

General committees are appointed at the beginning of each legislative term for the following two years and are renominated in each of the following years. Each committee has a *bureau* composed of a president, two vice-presidents, and two secretaries. The Finance Committee of the National Assembly also

---

[49] These rules were first established in 1914 and were reenacted in 1950. See Liddendale, *op. cit.*, p. 170; also, Norman L. Stamps, "A Comparative Study of Legislative Investigations: England, France and Weimar Germany," *Journal of Politics*, Vol. XIV (1952), pp. 592–615.

has a general reporter (*rapporteur général*). Moreover, for each question or bill before a committee, a special reporter (*rapporteur*) is appointed by the committee. All these officers are members of the committee and deputies.

Committee meetings are not generally open to the public, but a cabinet minister may attend any one of them and must be heard. Similarly, other interested persons may be given an opportunity to appear.

Theoretically it is the purpose of the committees, especially the general ones, to discuss legislation and prepare bills for final submission to the full house. However, in addition thereto, the permanent committees keep a close watch over the government departments in their field of specialization. These committees have great power because of the instability of the governments and their small margin of parliamentary majority. Government bills quite often receive a considerable mauling in committee and are sometimes so badly altered that the government finds itself constrained to oppose the bill when it reaches the floor. Since failure to pass an important bill in the National Assembly is sometimes regarded by a cabinet as a vote of nonconfidence, a hostile committee may be instrumental in producing a cabinet crisis. A key role in this and other affairs of committees is played by the reporter who is in charge of guiding the bill through the committee, to report it out to the full National Assembly or Council of the Republic, and to shepherd it through its adoption or rejection on the floor. In the ensuing debate the reporter constitutes a focal point, and his ability, good will, or malevolence have a decisive bearing on the bill's fate. Frequently the personality of the reporter selected for a particularly crucial bill gives a hint about its eventual fate. Thus, close observers found it significant that when the treaty to create the European Defense Community (European army) was submitted to the National Assembly's Committee on National Defense in 1953, the reporter selected was Jules Moch (Socialist), a member of the opposition to the government and a confirmed enemy of the treaty. The treaty was in fact defeated.

LEGISLATION

The right to initiate legislation belongs to the members of the cabinet and to all members of both houses of parliament. Until 1954 all bills had to be first submitted to the National Assembly. Now, most bills may be introduced in either house and are first debated in the house which first receives them.

Bills which have been introduced by a member of the cabinet are known as "law projects" (*projets de loi*), while those introduced by a private member of either house are called "law proposals" (*propositions de loi*). But there is no other difference between them, except that the government has certain means at its disposal to speed up its bills. Of course in all modern states the great bulk of legislation is introduced by the government, directly or indirectly.

A bill is sent to the *Bureau* of the house in which it is introduced; sometimes it is also submitted in the course of a regular meeting. In either case it is immediately referred to the appropriate committee in printed form and consists of a brief explanation of what it is supposed to achieve (*exposé des motifs*) as well as the proposed text itself.

The committee then studies and debates the bill in the manner stated above. It must report to either house within three months of the time that the original bill was distributed to the deputies or senators, in some instances in a shorter period. In appropriate cases bills are referred by the committee to the Economic Council or the Assembly of the French Union [50] for an advisory opinion.

Shortly after the bill is reported out of committee, it is submitted to general discussion on the floor. The bill may be killed at this stage either by moving the previous question or, if the committee has reported negatively, by accepting that report. Bills may also be referred back to committee for further study.

After the general discussion, the Assembly or the Council of the Republic discusses the bill article by article. At this stage articles may be removed or amended. Amendments are often presented directly to the committee but may also come from the floor. An entirely new bill may also be proposed as an amendment, but only if the Assembly or the Council decides to take it into consideration and after committee deliberation.

After this phase there may be reference back to committee for consolidation, and a second deliberation on the floor. Before the bill finally leaves the floor, a vote is taken on it.

This entire procedure is called "first reading." Until the reform of December 7, 1954, the role of the Council of the Republic in the process of legislation was extremely limited. All bills were first taken up in the National Assembly, the Council of the Republic had to operate under a restraining time limit, and any disagreement on the part of the Council with a bill passed by the National Assembly could easily be overridden by the latter by the simple act of repassing the measure. Only if the different version of the Council was passed by absolute majority did the Council have a slightly larger influence, because in that case its version could be overridden only by a vote taken with absolute majority in the Assembly. Otherwise, however, it was clear that the Council of the Republic played a less than secondary role.

The reform of 1954 recognizes the growing importance of the Council of the Republic and gives it near-equal status with the National Assembly. We have already seen that most bills may now be introduced in either house. The only exceptions are bills authorizing the ratification of a treaty and finance and budget bills. These still must be introduced first in the National Assembly, but they may be introduced by either a deputy or a senator. How-

[50] See Chap. 4F.

ever, bills involving the diminution of revenue or the creation of expenditures may be introduced only by deputies of the National Assembly and naturally only in that house.

The bills are considered by both houses with a view toward adopting an identical text. If the bill is introduced first in the Council of the Republic, the Council may take as much time as it wants, or rather as much as its own rules permit. But if the bill has first been passed (in first reading) by the National Assembly, the Council of the Republic must come to a decision within two months of the time of transmission of the bill. When considering budget or finance bills the Council of the Republic may not take up more time than has previously been taken up by the National Assembly. This time may be further cut down if the National Assembly decides to impose urgency rules. But in that case the Council of the Republic may dispose of twice as much time as is permitted to the National Assembly.

If the Council of the Republic makes no decision within the above time limits the law may be considered as passed and will be promulgated by the President of the Republic.

If the Council of the Republic and the National Assembly cannot agree on a common version after the above-mentioned time limits, the bill continues to be deliberated by the two houses, each house being entitled to take as much time as the other house in the preceding reading of the bill. There are no conference committees of the type used in the United States Congress, but the bill may be shunted from house to house and with such amendments as may seem likely to produce agreement. This process is known as "shuttle" (*navette*), and it may go on for one hundred days from the time the bill was transmitted to the Council of the Republic for second reading, or for one month in the case of budget and finance bills, or for fifteen days when urgency procedure has been invoked by the National Assembly. If there is still no agreement, then the National Assembly decides with finality and it may either pass its own last version of the bill or accept any of the amendments proposed by the Council of the Republic.[51] Hence, the National Assembly is still the more important legislative chamber, but the Council of the Republic is not so far behind. The degree to which the Council of the Republic begins to resemble the Senate of the Third Republic has produced the quip that "the Fourth Republic is dead and is being succeeded by the Third!"

Finance Bills

Proposals concerning both revenues and expenditures may be initiated by any deputy. For the most part, however, such proposals originate with the government and find their most important expression in the annual budget.

[51] The National Assembly may extend the above time limits. If it exceeds its own time limit, the time for reaching agreement is correspondingly extended.

This budget is prepared and submitted to the National Assembly by the Minister of Finance. In recent years a separate Minister of the Budget took over primary responsibility for it on occasion, but it is still the far more important Minister of Finance who plays the principal role. This is not easy, not only because of the notorious and chronic financial crisis which has existed through several centuries, but also because the collection and integration of the various budget estimates is of necessity a lengthy process, and, in view of the short life span of French governments, the minister who prepares most of the budget is usually not the one who is in office when the budget is presented to the National Assembly.

The budget is immediately referred to the Finance Committee for consideration. This elevates the Finance Committee over all other committees; while the others are usually concerned with the affairs of a single government department, the Finance Committee is concerned with the appropriations for, and therefore with the management of, all ministries, whose representatives are heard as their respective items come up for consideration. The president and general reporter of the Finance Committee are exceptionally powerful persons who in time often become Ministers of Finance and Premiers themselves.

The budget is reported out by the general reporter of the Finance Committee, who in his initial speech on the floor of the Assembly deals primarily with the general financial situation rather than with specific items. These details are presented afterward by several special reporters appointed by the Finance Committee.

General discussion of the bill begins right after the presentation by the general reporter. Then the budget is discussed ministry by ministry and chapter by chapter. Each chapter is voted on separately. The debate is somewhat curtailed; no deputy may speak more than twice on any one chapter unless replying to a minister. Deputies may propose amendments in the form of separate bills but the Constitution (Art. 17) forbids the moving of amendments to the finance bill itself when such amendments would create new expenditures or increase old ones. In practice, however, such amendments are proposed, but the government and the Finance Committee retain the right to demand the separation of the amendment from the budget, a demand which must be met. In that case the amendment becomes a separate bill which goes to the Finance Committee and the floor in the usual manner. This is to prevent the urgency of passing the budget from being used for the hasty adoption of ill-considered amendments. On the other hand, a deputy who wishes to make an amendment and have it considered together with the budget may transmit it to the Finance Committee before the finance bill is reported out. In that case, it will be discussed by the Committee in connection with the budget. There is no limit on a deputy's right to propose an increase of revenues.

Finally a vote is taken on the whole finance bill, and upon its acceptance the bill is sent to the Council of the Republic, where it is subjected to the same procedure as in the National Assembly, except that the time limit imposed on the Council makes for a more summary procedure.

The final disposition of the finance bill is just like that of any other piece of legislation. However, the provisions for "urgent" bills always prevail, even though this may make little difference to the lengthy procedure in the National Assembly.

DELEGATED LEGISLATION

The history of the Third Republic, especially since the First World War, is replete with instances in which the government did by decree, *i.e.*, executive order, what would ordinarily be done only by law. The manner in which parliament authorized or tolerated these "decree laws" differed; the practice was regarded with suspicion, but it existed and flourished. In fact, any government which found itself confronted by a crisis—and few French governments did not—usually asked for some sort of decree powers and often resigned when they were refused. The parties which were in control of the Constituent Assembly in 1945 and 1946 felt that in some mystical way these decree powers held a measure of responsibility for French defeat, although other observers might have opined that it was not the strength but the weakness of French governments which was to blame. At any rate the new Constitution stipulates in Art. 13 that the National Assembly may not delegate its right to enact legislation.

However, subsequent developments have made it quite clear that delegated legislation and decree laws are not dead in France. French juridical doctrine has always distinguished between the legislative power, which belongs to parliament, and regulatory power, which belongs to the executive. The regulatory power might be called derivative, *i.e.*, derived from law. This derivation may be direct, that is, if the law demands or permits the executive to do certain things. Or it may be indirect and implied in the general obligation incumbent upon the executive to see to it that the laws are faithfully executed and that they attain their objectives. Through this regulatory power the back door (or is it the front door?) is opened to new decree laws which might be called "regulation laws." In two well-known cases in 1948 and 1951, the government received extensive power by means of that delegated legislation which is presumably forbidden by the Constitution. Despite the heavy suspicion of unconstitutionality these laws were not challenged before the Constitutional Committee,[52] and since there is no judicial review of legislative acts, they remain in effect.

[52] See Chap. 4E.

Relationship between Parliament and Government

The National Assembly exercises both direct and indirect control over the Premier and his cabinet. It invests the Premier as described above, and it may remove him and his cabinet. It may, theoretically, even bring about impeachment proceedings before the High Court of Justice, although this is rather unlikely. Beyond that, the National Assembly constantly scrutinizes the acts of the government and subjects them to criticism.

Among the mildest forms of parliamentary influence upon the government is the so-called "question." Any deputy may address a question to the government or one of its members. There are "written" and "oral" questions, but these terms are misleading, for even the "oral" question is written. The written question is printed immediately after presentation, and the minister to whom it is directed has a month's time to reply. He may ask for an extension or he may refuse to answer, but only by claiming that an answer might prejudice the public interest. The question together with the answer are published again in the verbatim report of the National Assembly. Written questions are used a great deal, but it is sometimes difficult to obtain an answer. Moreover most of them deal with matters of special and private interest to the deputy concerned.

The oral question is also presented (to the presiding officer) in writing, but the minister answers orally, in principle within a week. Only five minutes each are allowed to the minister and his questioner, and no other deputy may speak. One day a month is reserved for oral questions. This procedure does not allow for the lively exchange of views associated with the question period in the British Parliament. Moreover in France the oral question is not in great use.

A considerable elaboration of the question and a typically French institution is the interpellation. This is a demand for an explanation directed to a minister by a deputy of the National Assembly. It is started by a deputy's request to the president of the Assembly. If no demand for a specific time is made, the interpellation is scheduled by the conference of presidents,[53] or by agreement between government and interpellating deputy. Upon the written request of the interpellator and fifty deputies present on the floor, an accelerated procedure may take place. But in any case the time for the interpellation must be confirmed by the Assembly, and that may bring about a shorter debate of a political nature in which the subject of the interpellation may already be brought up, rules to the contrary notwithstanding. Sometimes the interpellator may be satisfied by the explanation brought out in this "pre-debate," and the actual debate may never take place. On the other hand the

[53] Presidents of National Assembly and committees.

government may feel so strongly about the date of the interpellation that it may make it a question of confidence.

The debate on the interpellation is opened by the interpellator "developing" his point of inquiry. Then the general debate is opened, in which any deputy may participate, and the government makes its point at the time and in the manner which it chooses. The debate is then closed by a vote to pass on to the next item on the agenda (*passer à l'ordre du jour*). This is a formality of great importance. The motion is either to pass to the next item on the agenda pure and simple—in which case the Assembly indicates that it is satisfied with the explanations of the government—or it is a motivated motion which may expressly manifest confidence in the government or may equally expressly show lack of confidence in the government. Or the criticism of the Assembly may be modified or even be attached to a minor point.

At any rate the wording of the adopted motion is significant, for if it indicates hostility to the government, the latter will almost invariably resign. True, it need not do so under the 1946 Constitution, which has attempted to prescribe precise rules for overthrowing the government. In actual practice, however, a government risks its life in every interpellation—and there are many of them. If the motion is not one of outright hostility but does not give clear-cut support to the government viewpoint either, the government has to decide how to interpret the temper of the Assembly and draw its own conclusions.

Interpellations may be used for clearing up minor points, or they may deal with the most critical points of national policy. They may be brief or they may last several days. They are a useful device for bringing about a debate on government policies, and they provide an opportunity to remind cabinets of the fragility of their existence.

Discussion of the interpellation follows the general rules of debate except that the speeches are briefer. These discussions mark one of the most interesting differences between American and British rules of order on the one hand and French rules on the other. In America and Great Britain, a discussion begins with a motion which helps to give focus to the debate. This is rejected in France, the idea being that the collective minds of the Assembly have not yet crystallized a point of view sufficiently advanced to make a motion. Only after full discussion is a motion entertained. The French viewpoint may be correct theoretically, but in actual practice it lends itself to a diffuse debate and to the exercise of Gallic oratory.

Since the interpellation is a device by which a government may be brought down, and since the government is responsible only to the National Assembly and not to the Council of the Republic, interpellations can exist only in the Assembly and not in the other house. However, the Council of the Republic has a third category of questions (apart from written and oral ones): the "oral question with debate," which is conducted like an interpellation and ends with a proposal for a resolution rather than with a motion to pass on to the next item on the agenda. It provides for useful debates, but since it cannot overthrow a cabinet it does not have the critical significance of an interpellation.

The Constitution of 1946 wanted to regulate in a rigid fashion the relationship between Assembly and cabinet, and it therefore enacted precise rules for votes of confidence and motions of censure. Since these directly affect the life of the government, they are confined to the National Assembly.

Article 50 of the Constitution establishes a procedure for a "motion of censure," which is new in French practice. Any deputy may make such a motion, either at the end of an interpellation or as a separate act. But a vote on the motion can be taken only twenty-four hours or more after it has been made.

The "vote of confidence" under Art. 49 is very similar. While the motion of censure is moved by a private member of the Assembly, the vote of confidence can be proposed only by the Premier. Both can be voted upon in the Assembly but not earlier than a full day after being demanded. This vote is not demanded in the abstract but always in connection with a particular issue. In that way the government says in fact to the National Assembly: "If you do not support this particular policy which we consider vital, we shall resign and you must produce another government."

The demand for a vote of confidence thus constitutes the strongest but also the most critical and double-edged card in the hands of the government, and it is only after consulting with his cabinet that the Premier, and he alone, may pose the question of confidence.

For both the motion of censure and the vote of confidence, the so-called "Constitutional" or "special" majority is required, *i.e.*, a majority of all deputies, present or not, who are entitled to a seat in the Assembly—at the present time, 313. According to the text of Art. 49 and 50 this means that the cabinet *must* resign if a motion of censure is *adopted* by 313 deputies or if a vote of confidence is *rejected* by 313 deputies.

This would seem straightforward enough but actually is not, because the vote of confidence (unlike the motion of censure) is not demanded in isolation but, as has been stated, in connection with a bill or similar measure whose passage is demanded by the government. If such a bill were to be *rejected* by 300 votes against 280, the government would have lost its vital bill but it would not be legally turned out of office, because the vote of confidence would not have been rejected by the required majority. Or a government might raise the question of confidence if a bill which it opposes is passed. If the Assembly passes the bill by 300 to 280 the government has been defeated but is not turned out of office, because the question of confidence, although tied to the bill, is a separate matter and has not been rejected by 313 deputies.

What then does a government do which finds its vital bill rejected or watches the Assembly adopt a law which the cabinet absolutely does not want, as in the examples above? It resigns, of course. In fact no other decent course is open to a government which has just said to the Assembly that it could not govern if such and such a step were taken. But a government which resigns in this fashion is deemed to have resigned "voluntarily" and not to have been forced out by the Assembly. This has political as well as constitutional reasons. Politically the Assembly may think that it can escape the onus of having turned yet another French cabinet out to pasture. Constitutionally the significance lies in the provisions of Art. 51 dealing with the dissolution of the National Assembly.

According to this provision there is only one case in which the National Assembly may be dissolved (and new elections held) before the expiration of its normal five-year term. If two ministerial crises (defeats of government) occur within a period of eighteen months, the National Assembly may be dissolved by decree of the President of the Republic (no option) upon the decision of the cabinet (Council of Ministers). In that case the cabinet remains in office temporarily but, if the dissolution has been preceded by the adoption of a vote of censure, the Premier and the Minister of the Interior resign and are replaced by the president of the National Assembly.

But a "ministerial crisis" within the meaning of Art. 51 takes place *only* if the cabinet has been turned out of office by the formal procedure of Arts. 49 and 50, *i.e.*, by the adoption of a motion of censure or the rejection of a vote of confidence by 313 or more deputies. Therefore the dissolution article of the Constitution has remained without significance and is in effect dead.

For these reasons the formal motion of censure and the vote of confidence are not too frequently used. In fact, as these lines are written, only two governments of the Fourth Republic—the Bidault cabinet (1950) and the Mayer cabinet (1953)—have been forced out of office by a formal vote of this kind. What actually happens far more frequently is that the government, in presenting or opposing an important measure, *lets it be known,* but without using the sacred word "confidence," that if defeated it will resign. This has been called "pseudo vote of confidence," [54] and it avoids the delay, the formalism, and especially the "special" majority. In effect and in parliamentary practice the pseudo vote of confidence has become the real vote of confidence because it recognizes the reality of parliamentary life that a government which does not command a majority cannot remain in office.

The relationship between the National Assembly and the government clearly shows the supremacy of the Assembly. Practical experience has modified some of the extreme rigors of assembly government which the doctrinaire majority of the Constituent Assembly wanted to impose, but the fact of as-

---

[54] The expression was coined in the superb article by Claude-Albert Colliard, *"La pratique de la question de confiance sous la IVᵉ République," Revue du droit public et de la Science Politique,* Vol. LXIV (1948), pp. 220–237. See also Vedel, *op. cit.,* pp. 460–466.

sembly government is essentially unchallengeable. We have seen some of the institutional reforms that have been suggested or created to improve the situation:[55] abandonment of the investiture, a freer delegation of power to the government, etc. Many writers and political leaders insist that much would be achieved by giving the government power to dissolve the National Assembly. But it is difficult to accept that point. In a country of the extreme political division of France, elections do not bring about great changes, and it is unlikely that the well-entrenched politicians would quail before the threat of dissolution which is much more likely to bring down the government than its opponents. At any rate experience with the use of the dissolution power in the German Weimar Republic shows that it has contributed rather to the instability of government.[56] And the stability of the British cabinet regime is certainly not caused by the dissolution power, but, as we have seen, by entirely different factors.[57]

Far beyond institutional handicaps, the weakness of French cabinets is the result of political factors which make lasting governments with a definite policy a virtual impossibility in France. This diversity of parties, groups, and grouplets marks the French parliament. Because there are many political groups, each one is relatively small. To conquer as much as a quarter of the vote is tremendous, and only the Communists have achieved that; none of the government parties have more than 12 per cent. Because their popular basis is so narrow, French parties tend to be particularly forceful in the defense of the special interests or ideas which they represent. Under those circumstances, broad agreement is difficult even for a short time and impossible for a longer period. The Socialists cannot overcome their suspicions of the Catholic character of the MRP. The Radicals are suspicious of Socialist and MRP tendencies to weaken the entrenched privileges of the French in North Africa. The left is suspicious of any motion to take a look at the overgrown social-security system, family allocations, and the overstaffed public services or the heavy pension load. The right will not tolerate any move to collect taxes from business, which the law prescribes, by drastic measures, and the deputies from the rural districts (left or right) will not tolerate any move to collect taxes from the farmers. Deputy Pierre-Henri Teitgen (MRP), several times cabinet minister, has characterized the situation in this lucid indictment:

Since June 17, 1951, the Parliament which France has elected has revealed itself incapable of assuring the stability of a government, incapable of making a decisive choice, incapable of passing a law worthy of that name. . . . It is an even sorrier spectacle, that we see in these debates and discussions many "special representatives"

[55] For a survey of current constitutional reform proposals, some of which have since been executed, see Roy Pierce, "France Reopens the Constitutional Debate," *American Political Science Review*, Vol. XLVI (1952), pp. 422–437.

[56] See Part III, Chap. 5.

[57] See Part I, Chap. 3B.

[*mandataires*] and few deputies: in this Assembly there are representatives of the beet-sugar industry and of the distillers who grow their own raw material, there are the representatives of small business and of big business, there are those who call themselves deputies of the rural areas and those who represent the cities. . . . We sometimes get the impression that there are few men who are simply content with being deputies of France.[58]

E. THE JUDICIARY

The administration of justice in Continental Europe is dominated by the tradition and the system of the Roman law. This is especially true of France, a country which for the most part was once under Roman domination. Gaul was more quickly Romanized than many other provinces. A number of its inhabitants received Roman citizenship early, and the rest were elevated to that state of distinction by the edict of Caracalla in A.D. 212. The old Gallic legal institutions were quickly dropped, and virtually no trace of them remains except in the research work of legal historians.

In the Middle Ages, feudal customs and conventions took their place beside the tradition of the Roman law, sometimes even submerging the latter. Still, Roman law was known and avidly studied, and large parts of it were retained in the canon law, the law of the Roman Catholic Church. As the great divergence of local and customary law created increasing difficulties for the administration of justice, attempts were made to record customary law in codified forms which received royal sanction and were eventually undertaken by royal command. But this did not mean legal unification, as the codified rules of law showed significant variations from region to region.

On top of these various layers of law came an increasing number of royal decrees which were registered by the various regional courts, known as *parlements*. Some bold *parlements*, especially that of Paris, even refused to register certain ordinances.[59] However, as a rule, royal decrees were registered as a matter of course.[60]

The Revolution put an end to this confused and overlapping system. In 1791 and 1795 the first Penal Cole and Code of Criminal Procedure were enacted. But it was only under the rule of Napoleon and under his active furtherance that the crowning edifice, the Civil Code, was finally published in 1804, followed in 1807 by a Code of Civil Procedure. Other codes were

---

[58] *Le Monde*, May 26, 1953.

[59] Sometimes the king forced the *parlement* to register the edict. In that case the *parlement* indicated this fact by adding to the formula the words *de expresso mandato regis, pluries facto.*

[60] But the habit of consulting *parlement* grew over the years and occasionally had a restraining influence on royal absolutism (Jean Brissaud, *A History of French Public Law* [trans. by J. W. Garner], Boston, 1915, p. 447). Needless to say, the French *parlements* never approximated the significance of the English parliament.

enacted subsequently. In all of them, the predominant influence of Roman law is paramount. These codes have of course been revised and amended, yet in their principal structure they still stand today, not only as the living law of France, but also as that of numerous other countries which have since adopted them.[61] The spirit of the great Corsican with whom they are forever identified as the Code Napoléon has found more endurance there than in most of his more glittering military conquests.

THE IMPACT OF ROMAN LAW

The imprint of Roman law is firmly stamped on the whole edifice of French law and justice. Its watchwords are symmetry, unity, and authority. The French codes are well-balanced pieces of jurisprudential art, utterly systematic and conveniently accessible. In each field, the particular code germane to that subject, the amendments thereof, and the commentaries thereto, are the last and reasonably complete word on the subject. The student need not dig his way through tome after tome of cases and decisions. The law, as embodied in the codes, is clear and easily available. Moreover, only one system of law prevails from one corner of the country to the other. But the law so conceived is not the result of gradual social growth. It is the expression of the will of the state, which lays down in final and authoritative manner what the relationships between citizens and between them and the state shall be. This type of paternalism naturally leaves little room for the judge, who becomes merely the expositor of code and statute. It is true that precedent, while officially nonbinding, actually exists, for a judge who is habitually overruled by an appellate authority will find his path to promotion a rocky one. But precedent has a very much smaller scope in the French system than in its English and American counterparts. Moreover, the judge is not regarded as an independent arbiter between the parties to the suit or between the state and the individual; he is a part of the machinery of the state, though protected from direct political interference by the customary privileges and immunities.

Because the knowledge and the administration of the law are not contingent on a long and arduous study of the case material, as is the case in the English-speaking world, judges are not selected from the bar but choose their career from the very beginning of their law studies. This system, which is current in Continental Europe, produces judges who are well trained in the mechanical rules of law and procedure and who can discharge their duties competently and with reasonable dispatch. But the specialist-judge who grows up in this rarefied professional atmosphere is not likely to become a statesman of the bench of the caliber of John Marshall or Lord Coke. He sticks rather narrowly to the interpretation of statutory provisions and never

[61] Some countries, like Egypt, have simply translated the codes for their own use.

assumes the social significance and the majesty of the Anglo-American judge. For these reasons, social and economic changes are not readily reflected in judicial opinions. Such changes must come from the legislature, not from the bench. Consequently the French system is generally a good deal more rigid than the common-law approach. But this is not true of the procedure in court.

Appointment of Judges

During the Third Republic, judges were in actual practice appointed by the Minister of Justice. This interfered with the independence of judges, because unpopular or obstreperous judges could be denied promotion and could, in some cases, be left in some undesirable provincial or overseas spot until they went to seed. The Constitution of 1946 attempts to remedy this by creating the Superior Council of the Judiciary. This Council is composed of the President of the Republic as chairman, the Minister of Justice (called "Keeper of the Seal"), six persons elected by the National Assembly but not from among its members, six alternates elected in the same manner, four judges and four alternates representing all categories of the judiciary, who are elected by their colleagues, and two members of the legal profession who are neither judges nor legislators and who are appointed by the President of the Republic together with two alternates.

The competence of the Superior Council extends to three groups of problems: the appointment of judges, the supervision of the judiciary with regard to administrative discipline and independence, and the exercise of the right of pardon.

According to Art. 84 of the Constitution, the President of the Republic appoints the judges upon nomination by the Superior Council of the Judiciary. This means that he has no choice of his own. Technically he might refuse to appoint someone—but that is most unlikely to happen. However, the normal way to enter the judiciary is by competitive examination, and the Council accepts the results thereof. For the promotion of judges there is an administrative procedure within the judicial machine which is also normally followed, and the Council merely nominates those proposed by this process. This means that much less has changed in the appointment and promotion of judges than might be indicated by the Council's creation. It is undeniable that the Minister of Justice remains in a key position. However, the existence and the prerogatives of the Council tend to prevent abuses and the appointments so far made have been of a high order.

Control over disciplinary infractions among the judiciary and over alleged infringements of judicial independence is exercised directly by the Superior Council. It is not bound by any nominations or proposals emanating from other sources and it decides by majority vote, with the President of the Republic having the right to break a tie vote.

The President of the Republic "exercises the right of pardon in the Superior Council of the Judiciary" (Art. 35). This means that the Council is consulted but that the President alone exercises this right. In practice he consults the members of the Council individually and not collectively.

A presidential pardon releases a prisoner from all or part of his punishment but does not wipe out the crime. An amnesty, on the other hand, removes the criminal character of certain acts. The Constitution (Art. 19) stipulates that an amnesty must be enacted by law according to the usual legislative procedure.

The establishment of the Superior Council of the Judiciary constitutes a compromise between those who wanted to see all judges elected (Communists) and those who wanted to return to the old system of presidential appointment, which was in effect appointment by the Minister of Justice. So far the new system seems to be quite satisfactory.

It has been pointed out that French judges are not appointed from the bar but directly from a brief apprenticeship and after the conclusion of their academic law studies. Newly appointed judges are therefore quite inexperienced, but that is not too serious because the French principle is still *"juge unique, juge inique"* (single judge, unfair judge), and most courts have a panel of judges rather than a single judge. These panels are presided over by an older, more experienced judge. Moreover the ordinary French judges do not have the leeway in interpreting the law which their American and British colleagues enjoy: they stick close to the detailed text of the codes, the laws, and the commentaries. It is frequently argued that a French judge is not burdened by the English common-law rule of *stare decisis* and therefore decides only a single case without setting a precedent for future decisions, but that argument must be regarded with caution. In actual fact the appeals courts see to it that the law is applied with considerable uniformity, and judges whose decisions are erratic will find themselves frequently overruled— which will not help their promotion. In actual practice, therefore, judicial decisions tend to create precedents in fact, if not in theory, though not as much as in the French administrative courts and in the American and British courts. One might perhaps say that the courts of Continental Europe follow precedents more than the Anglo-American lawyers think, while the Anglo-American courts follow precedent somewhat less than the European lawyers believe.

One of the peculiarities of the French judiciary is the fact that it consists of two separate, yet interwoven, groups: the actual judges of the bench, known as the "sitting judiciary" (*magistrature assise*), and the State's Attorney's department, known as the "standing judiciary" (*magistrature debout*). The "sitting" judges have been described. The "standing" ones are more like regular civil servants and form a section of the Ministry of Justice known as the *ministère publique*. They staff the State's Attorney's office, known as the *parquet*, attached to each court. They are not independent but are subject to strict orders of the Ministry of Justice and the advocates-general of their respective (appeals court) districts. They represent the interests of the state in all court actions, but primarily they are prosecutors, filling the functions which in the United States are carried out by district attorneys and equivalent officials. In addition they staff the indictment section (*chambre d'accusation*), which may be compared in function, though not in composition, to the American grand jury.

Although the functions of the "sitting" and "standing" judiciary are widely different by Anglo-American standards, French judges are constantly shifted from one to the other. In many cases this means a promotion. A judge may be transferred to a higher place on the *parquet* and later return to the bench in a superior position. But since members of the *parquet* are not independent but subject to strict instructions from the Ministry of Justice, this system somewhat negates the principle of judicial independence. On the other hand these transfers give members of both sections of the judiciary a varied experience which they would otherwise not have.

This system naturally produces an enormous judiciary, but it is not easy to remedy the situation because the adoption of a single-judge court system would heap responsibilities on the members of the bench for which neither their training nor the legal system has prepared them. On the other hand French courts do fulfill their promise of being easily available and inexpensive. On the whole they function satisfactorily and the judges enjoy a high social prestige which makes up somewhat for their notoriously low pay, especially in the lower brackets.

THE ORDINARY COURT SYSTEM

France is covered with a network of numerous courts in order that justice may be easily accessible to all. In view of the uniformity of the legal system, this is altogether to the good, making it possible for a Frenchman to get justice at far lower cost than his British or American counterpart. The organization of the courts is simple enough. The lowest ranking judicial authority is the justice of the peace (*juge de paix*) who, in contrast to his British counterpart, is a salaried official with some judicial experience, though not ordinarily a law degree. Justices of the peace have jurisdiction over civil suits involving very small sums. In certain cases where the amounts under litigation are minimal, their judgment is final. Otherwise an appeal to the next higher court, the Court of First Instance, is permissible. Justices of the peace also have jurisdiction over small infractions (*contraventions*) and minor misdemeanors (*délits*). The principal reason for the institution of the justice of the peace was originally the intention to make him a conciliator who would spare the regular courts some work. This is still one of his principal roles, and the requirement for parties to submit their dispute first to the justice of the peace still stands. However, this institution has become more and more a formality and has retained its original purpose only in those areas where the judge is able to act as a moderator because of his personal knowledge of the litigants—a condition which is possible only in rural districts.

THE FRENCH COURT SYSTEM

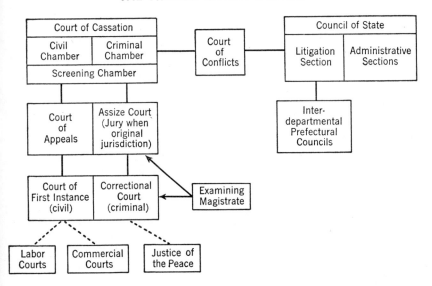

On the same level in the hierarchical order stand two special courts, the Labor Courts (Conseils de Prud'hommes) and the Commercial Courts (Tribunaux de Commerce). Both deal with special subjects (labor disputes and disputes under the Commercial Code), and both have as a specially distinguishing feature a panel of judges, composed of employers and employees in the case of the Labor Courts, or of businessmen in the case of the Commercial Tribunals. In more serious cases, appeal from these courts to the Court of First Instance is possible.

The lowest court of the regular judicial hierarchy is the Court of First Instance (Tribunal de Première Instance) whose criminal section is known as the Correctional Court (Tribunal Correctionnel).[62] Courts of first instance may be found at almost every county (*arrondissement*) seat. In civil cases, these courts have unlimited original judisdiction as well as appellate jurisdic-

---

[62] Although the sections are separated enough to amount to almost separate courts, the judges rotate among them.

tion from the justices of the peace, the Labor Courts, and the Commercial Courts. In criminal cases they deal with misdemeanors and the lesser types of felonies. There are 360 Courts of First Instance in France. Each case is heard by a panel of three judges. Considering the number of trial sections of courts involved, this makes for an astoundingly large number of judges, probably more than are really necessary.

Appeals in civil cases from the Courts of First Instance are brought before the Courts of Appeal (Cours d'Appel), of which there are twenty-seven. These courts engage in an entire rehearing of the case (*de novo*), and their judgments on the facts and the law involved are final as far as the facts are concerned. In civil cases these proceedings may seem rather dull to us as they consist chiefly of filing and counterfiling written statements.

The courts of appeal for criminal cases are the Assize Courts (Cours d'Assises), one of which may be found in session in each of the ninety departments at least once every three months but more frequently in the larger centers. Besides being appeal courts, the Assizes also have original jurisdiction over grave crimes, such as homicide. In the latter case, when the court is sitting as a court of original jurisdiction, it employs a jury. Five or more judges hear each case before the Court of Appeals, and three judges in the Assize Courts. In the latter case, the presiding judge is taken from the Court of Appeals while the other two are taken from the local Court of First Instance or also from the Court of Appeals if the Assizes meet where a Court of Appeals is located.

The apex of the regular judiciary is the Court of Cassation (Cour de Cassation). It is composed of one Chief Justice (First President), four Presidents (of sections) and sixty other judges (counselors, *conseillers*); attached to it is the Chief Prosecutor (Procureur Général) and his staff. Its first section, the screening chamber (Chambre des Requêtes), conducts a preliminary examination and rejects outright those appeals which have no substantial merit. If it is decided to hear the case, it is then referred to either the civil or criminal section of the court.

As the name implies, the court does not technically decide a case, but only quashes (*casser*) it, remanding it to a lower court for retrial. This lower court will be of the same rank as the court from which the appeal was received, but will not be the same court. Should this second lower court again rule contrary to the views of the Court of Cassation, the supreme court may hold a hearing before a panel of not less than thirty-three of its judges, and then remand the case to a third lower court. This court then must execute the will of the Court of Cassation.

The prestige of the Court of Cassation is very high, and while it may not actually decide a case, the reasons for a *cassation* may be tantamount to the same thing. An appeal to the Court of Cassation is relatively easily accomplished in meritorious cases and is fairly inexpensive. However, this fact, together with the litigious nature of the French, burdens the court with a great deal of business and delays its decisions, sometimes for many years.[63]

CRIMINAL PROSECUTION

French judicial procedure is distinguished by a number of characteristics. In criminal cases an accused person is first taken before an examining magistrate, called *juge d'instruction*. He examines the case thoroughly, scrutinizes all the evidence, and then decides whether the case shall go to trial, and if so, whether a correctional court or an assize court should hear the case. Under the Third Republic the *juge d'instruction* could keep the accused in custody while the often lengthy investigation proceeded. This is no longer supposed to be the case, but in practice the old methods are hard to eradicate.

The institution of the examining magistrate, which is by no means confined to France, has been severely criticized for being a secret pretrial at which the accused is at a disadvantage. There is a certain amount of justification to this, although the accusation of "star-chamber proceedings" is greatly exaggerated. However this pretrial procedure has given rise to the oft-heard but totally false idea that in a French court the accused is considered guilty until he proves himself innocent. Actually no civilized country has such a rule in its criminal procedure. However, the fact that a case does not reach the trial court until a *juge d'instruction* has sifted the evidence and found it compelling enough undoubtedly prejudices the court against the defendant from the outset.

British and American observers have been critical of the lax rules of evidence in French courts, the acceptability of hearsay, the inability of witnesses to excuse themselves on grounds of self-incrimination. However, it must be remembered that the Anglo-American rules of evidence have been specifically designed for the jury trial, chiefly to prevent undue bias on the part of the jury. But jury trials are the exception, not the rule, in France, and it is presumed that the learned judges will treat the evidence presented to them with appropriate caution and erudition. This is also borne out by the fact that the judges take an active role in the proceedings and endeavor to get at the facts themselves.

Actually judges often question the accused in a manner which one might associate with the prosecution rather than with a supposedly impartial judge.

[63] Cf. Jean Brissaud, *A History of French Private Law* (trans. by R. Howell), Boston, 1912; Francis Deak and Max Rheinstein, "The Development of French and German Law," *Georgetown Law Journal*, March, 1936; James W. Garner, "The French Judiciary," *Yale Law Journal*, March, 1917; Robert C. K. Enser, *Courts and Judges in France, Germany and England*, Oxford, 1933; A. Grandin, *Bibliographie générale des sciences juridiques, politiques, économiques, et sociales de 1800 à 1926*, Paris, 1926, and annual supplements; A. Esmein, *Histoire de la procédure criminelle en France*, Paris, 1881; A. C. Wright, "French Criminal Procedure," *Law Quarterly Review*, Vol. XLIV (1928), pp. 324–341; Vol. XLV (1929), pp. 92–107.

In these interrogations French judges frequently make comments about such things as the credibility of the accused or of a witness, or about the hideous nature of the crime, which if made in an American or British court would constitute a mistrial. In France both judge and prosecutor are government officials who are interested in their promotion, and sometimes they seek distinction or notoriety by conducting "sharp" trials. In such instances it is often the prosecutor rather than the judge who sees to it that the accused gets a fair trial.

These tendencies on the part of the judge, which must seem rather shocking to an American or British lawyer, are particularly in evidence in trials of a political nature. The judge's eagerness for ferreting out all the facts may involve him in a controversy with the accused in which the judge does not always emerge as the winner. This was particularly in evidence in the trial of Pierre Laval in which the extremely clever and experienced accused proved himself so much the superior of the court that his conviction almost gave the impression of having been decided in advance. Most observers agreed that although Laval may have been justly put to death, the cause of justice was not well served by the trial.

The High Court of Justice

The Constitution of 1946 has added another court in France—the High Court of Justice (*Haute Cour de Justice*). Its composition, procedure, and mode of selection are established by law. It is composed of a president, two vice-presidents, thirty judges, and thirty alternates. President and vice-presidents are elected by the National Assembly by a two-thirds majority. The Constitution does not explicitly state that these men must be members of the National Assembly, but this is clearly implied and was the intention of the framers. Twenty judges and twenty alternates are elected by the National Assembly by proportional representation of political groups from among its members. Ten more judges and ten alternates are elected by the National Assembly from the outside (they can be senators) by two-thirds majority.

The High Court of Justice also has an examining commission (*commission d'instruction*), whose members are partly designated by the Superior Council of the Judiciary (president and two assessors), partly elected by parliament (six judges). The prosecution is in the hands of a procurator-general and two advocates-general elected by the National Assembly.

The High Court of Justice is a court of impeachment which may try only the President of the Republic, cabinet ministers, and their accomplices. The President of the Republic may be tried for high treason and the ministers for other crimes, but all of them only if the offenses were committed in the exercise of their official functions. The indictment of these high officials must be voted by the National Assembly.

The High Court of Justice has not as yet been called upon to try a President or minister, and it is not likely to be confronted by this possibility. Impeachment procedures have little significance in a parliamentary regime in which the parliament may instantly cause the downfall of a minister. The possibility of the President of the Republic committing treason is remote.

The High Court of Justice which was created by the Constitution and organized by law in 1946 should not be confused with a court of *precisely the same name* created by the ordinance of November 18, 1944, and modified by the laws of 1945 and 1948. That court, which had a jury of twelve designated by the National Assembly, is now defunct. It was a purge court which dealt with the higher officials of the Vichy regime. Its trials, especially the earlier ones, were highly emotional affairs, which sometimes reflected little credit on the French administration of justice. Foreign observers were often shocked at the irregularities of procedure, the lax application of the rules of evidence, the way in which everything seemed to be stacked against the defendants. However, one must remember that in all countries which had been under German occupation, the need for the purging of collaborationists caused considerable emotional unheaval in which impartial justice cannot easily triumph. If one considers that in fifty-two trials of major collaborationists, the Court exacted the death penalty in only three cases,[64] its total record must be deemed one of admirable restraint. Belgium, with only one-fifth of France's population, convicted an equal number of collaborationists.

No Judicial Review

None of the aforementioned courts possesses or exercises the right of judicial review as that is known in the United States. The question was raised and laid to rest in 1833, in the case of the newspaper Le National, when the Court of Cassation ruled that a law which had been "deliberated and promulgated according to constitutional forms" could not be attacked as unconstitutional. French jurists, who prefer to analyze questions of this kind on grounds of judicial doctrine rather than of workability, frequently declare that judicial review violates the principle of the separation of power because it allows the judiciary to interfere with the legislative power of parliament. They also argue that it runs counter to the doctrine that law is the expression of the sovereign will.[65] This attitude naturally tends to make the Constitution more of a declaration of principles than a legally binding instrument. It also greatly reduces the status of the judge.

[64] Pierre Laval, prime minister; Fernand de Brinon, chief envoy to the German government; and Joseph Darnand, chief of the militia.

[65] For a refutation of this view see Edward M. Sait, *Government and Politics of France,* Yonkers, 1920, p. 23. The administrative courts do (since 1907) examine the constitutionality of executive acts.

Eminent voices have been heard repeatedly suggesting the introduction of judicial review, but so far to no avail. The majority of the Constituent Assembly found judicial review utterly incompatible with the doctrine of a sovereign legislature. Pierre Cot, the *rapporteur* of the first draft, repeatedly referred to President Franklin D. Roosevelt's difficulties with the Supreme Court as a warning example of a situation which should be avoided in France, and his view carried much weight.

THE CONSTITUTIONAL COMMITTEE

Ostensibly as a concession to the promoters of judicial review, the Constitution created the Constitutional Committee. It is composed of the President of the Republic as chairman, the presidents of the National Assembly and the Council of the Republic, seven members elected by the National Assembly, and three members elected by the Council of the Republic. This committee shall determine whether a law which has been passed but not yet promulgated is constitutional or not.[66] If it is declared unconstitutional, it can be promulgated only after the Constitution has been amended in such a way as to remove this impediment.

Since the members of the committee, other than the three presidents, are elected for each session by the two houses of parliament on the basis of proportional representation of the parties therein, they reflect faithfully the views of the major parties, even though they are not themselves members of the legislature. It is highly unlikely, therefore, that they will declare unconstitutional a law which their parties' representatives have just passed in parliament. Moreover, the effectiveness of review based on general principles rather than on the detailed facts of a concrete case may well be doubted. And even if the committee were inclined to act, it has only fifteen days at best in which to do its work.

It is significant that Arts. 91–93, which deal with the Constitutional Committee, coyly avoid any mention of an "unconstitutional" law, which might reflect on the sovereign Assembly, but speak only of a law which "implies an amendment to the Constitution," which means the same thing. Also these provisions are not in a separate and distinct place in the Constitution but are tucked away in the chapter dealing with amendments. This makes it appear as if an unconstitutional law could only come about by some procedural or drafting error to which the Constitutional Committee might draw attention.[67]

---

[66] It shall do so upon receipt of a joint request of the President of the Republic and of the President of the Council of the Republic. Private citizens may not demand a judgment from the Constitutional Committee.

[67] Cf. Vedel, *op. cit.*, p. 552. The idea of a "constitutional jury" has existed in French legal thinking for some time, having been first proposed during the Revolution by the Abbé Sieyès.

It is also significant that only Titles I to X of the Constitution fall within the province of the committee; the preamble with its reference to civil rights is excluded. And so are the amendment articles, including those dealing with the committee, of Title XI.

The real role which the framers of the Constitution wished to confide to the Constitutional Committee is that of a conciliator, especially between the two houses, but not that of an authority capable of declaring laws unconstitutional. It has played this role of conciliator on nonconstitutional issues a few times, but several laws have been passed whose constitutionality is very much in doubt, to say the least, and they were not submitted to the Constitutional Committee. As an authority of quasi-judicial review, *i.e.*, as an authority capable of preventing the application of unconstitutional laws, the Constitutional Committee plays a role which is purely symbolic, or to put it more bluntly, nonexistent.

This leads us to the following, inescapable, conclusion: in France there is no real difference between Constitution and ordinary law. For all practical purposes the French parliament may enact any law it sees fit whether constitutional or not. In fact such an unconstitutional law amends in actual practice the Constitution, and one would not exaggerate to say that unconstitutional but duly enacted and promulgated laws constitute "informal amendments" to the Constitution. One should not suppose that this is a frequent occurrence, but it occurs.

THE ADMINISTRATIVE COURTS

The ordinary court system which has been discussed above is only one side of the judicial picture, and not even necessarily the most important part at that. Side by side with it there exists another organization: the system of administrative justice. It must be remembered that the French administrative system is characterized by an enormous degree of concentration and centralization, vesting great power in individual officials. At the same time, not all features have really been brought under one roof, and a complicated system has been established which, according to one observer, becomes comprehensible only when one remembers that it was designed to control the overly powerful administrative staff.[68] The French administrative court system, which sees to it that administrative power is not misused, is therefore a necessary part of this approach.

Parallel to this development runs the French doctrine of the separation of powers, which has declared ever since 1789 that the judiciary has no right to interfere with the acts of the legislature or the executive.[69] Thus, while it be-

[68] Carl J. Friedrich, *Constitutional Government and Democracy*, Boston, 1946, pp. 368*f*.
[69] Law of Dec. 22, 1789: ". . . Judicial power should not trouble local administrative agencies in the exercise of their functions." Law of Aug. 16 to 24, 1790: "The judicial

came necessary to have a system by which abuse of power could be checked, such a check could not come from the regular judiciary; it had to come from within the executive machinery itself. The organs of administrative justice form therefore a part of the administration itself. To many an observer such a system appeared to be a mockery. The spectacle of the administration ostensibly judging itself while being exempt from ordinary justice seemed preposterous and a far cry from the "rule of law." [70] In actuality, however, time and custom has given the Council of State, the supreme and principal dispenser of administrative justice, a degree of independence and prestige which is rarely equaled by the ordinary courts. At any rate, the fear expressed by these critics has been found groundless for the most part.

Administrative law is an extremely important field. It covers no less than the whole realm of relationships between the public authorities and the individual.[71] And strangely enough, in France, the country of codified law, administrative law is to a very large extent based on precedent, on judicial decision, with which the legislature does not ordinarily interfere and which the administrative courts themselves alter only gradually. Thus, something like *stare decisis* can be found even in France.[72]

The lowest administrative courts are the Interdepartmental Prefectural Councils (Conseils de Préfecture Interdépartmentaux). Originally they existed in every department and constituted the "consultative" part of the administration, serving the chief official of the department, the prefect. However a decree of July, 1934, reduced the number of councils to twenty-two as an economy measure. Hence the designation "interdepartmental" rather than "departmental." Each council is composed of two or three members (councilors), one of whom acts as president. The others may at any time be delegated to department seats in order to settle minor litigations. The Inter-

---

functions are and will remain forever separate from the administrative functions. The judges will not be allowed, under penalty of forfeiture, to disturb in any manner whatsoever, the activities of the administrative corps, nor to summon before them the administrators concerning their functions." Stephan Riesenfeld, "The French System of Administrative Justice: A Model for American Law?" *Boston University Law Review,* Vol. XVIII (1938), pp. 48–82. William Rohkam and Orville C. Pratt, *Studies in French Administrative Law,* Urbana, 1947, p. 14.

[70] A. V. Dicey, *Law of the Constitution,* London, 1926, 8th ed., Chap. XII.

[71] Marcel Waline, *Traité élémentaire de droit administratif,* Paris, 1951, 6th ed. Gaston Jeze, *Les Principes généraux du droit administratif,* Paris, 1925, p. 283. James W. Garner, "French Administrative Law," *Yale Law Review,* Vol. XXXIII (1924), p. 599. F. M. Marx, "Comparative Administrative Law," *University of Pennsylvania Law Review* (1942), p. 118.

[72] This is a relatively recent development; see the case of Casanova, Canazzi, *et al.,* Council of State, Mar. 29, 1901, Dalloz, *Recueil hebdomadaire de jurisprudence,* Vol. III (1902), p. 34. See also C. S. Lobinger, "Administrative Law and *Droit Administratif,*" *University of Pennsylvania Law Review* (1942), p. 34; C. J. Hamson, "Le Conseil d'État statuant aux contentieux," *Law Quarterly Review,* Vol. LXVIII (1952), pp. 60–87.

departmental Prefectural Councils have limited jurisdiction, usually in minor cases, especially concerning taxation. On the same level is the Prefectural Council of the Seine with jurisdiction over the department of the Seine, in which Paris is located. A similar role is exercised by the Councils for Algeria and the Colonial Litigation Councils (Conseils du Contentieux des Colonies).

In the same category are also certain other authorities with special jurisdiction, such as the Council of Public Instruction (Conseil de l'Instruction Publique), the Draft Review Boards (Conseils Militaires de Révision), and the Departmental Council, a pension-adjustment court. The General Accounting Office (Cour des Comptes) is organized like a court and has certain quasi-judicial functions which also fall in the category of administrative justice. Recently, another court was added, the Court of Budgetary Discipline (Cour de Discipline Budgétaire), which punishes the incurring of unauthorized expenditures.

The apex and by far the most important court in this system is the Council of State (Conseil d'État). The Council of State is not merely a court but has other functions as well; technically, only one section of the Council, the Litigation Section (*section du contentieux*), is an administrative court.

The personnel of the Council of State presents a curious blend of administrative and judicial experiences which add to the excellence of this body. The minister of justice is President of the Council of State, but that position is purely nominal. The actual chairman is a vice-president. Under him serve five presidents of sections, forty-six councilors of the regular civil service who have been promoted from the lower echelons of the Council, twelve councilors who are appointed from the outside, forty-nine masters of petition (*maîtres des requêtes*), and forty-eight junior members (*auditeurs*) of the first and second class. All members of the Council, except the twelve outside councilors and the minister of justice, are appointed on the basis of highly technical, competitive examinations and are then promoted within the hierarchy of the Council. Thus, a preponderance of great experience is assured. The Council of State contains without doubt the cream of the juridical and administrative elite of France.

In order to transact its business, the Litigation Section of the Council of State is divided into nine subsections, each composed of three councilors and several masters of petitions and junior members. Some less important business can be conducted by some of these sections alone (*contentieux spécial*), but for the rest, two sections must deliberate together (*contentieux général*). There are also larger meetings: that of the Litigation Section, which for this purpose is composed of the president of the section, the presidents of the subsections, two councilors from the subsection directly affected, and the *rapporteur;* and then the plenary meeting (*assemblée plenière*), which has the same members as the above meeting of the Section but in addition has the vice-president, the actual head of the Council of State, and instead of the two councilors from one subsection has four councilors from the "administrative" sections (other than the Litigation Section) of the Council.

These enlarged meetings are not appeals sections; rather certain persons (not the parties) have the right to refer certain cases to them. These special people are the vice-president of the Council, the presidents of the Litigation Section and its subsections, and the government commissioner (*commissaire du gouvernement*).

The government commissioners are rather unusual people. There are twelve of them and they are usually recruited from the masters of petitions. Contrary to their title they are *not* the attorneys for the government. If the government wishes to have its viewpoint presented by counsel it must hire one just like any private party. The commissioners represent the public interest; they are not subject to instruction (like the members of the *parquet*) and not dependent on one another. They are men of great knowledge and talent; eventually they are almost certain to be appointed councilors, and the various presidents and vice-presidents are often former commissioners.

The Council of State has original, appellate, and final jurisdiction, but these categories are only vaguely defined by law and rather emerge as the result of past decisions by the Council of State. It is a court of appeals for judgments rendered by the inferior councils and administrative courts. But ordinarily, cases involving the extent of power and discretion of officials are handled by the Council of State in original jurisdiction.

The jurisdiction of the Council is a good deal broader than might be indicated by the above categories. It is the principal purpose of the Council of State to guarantee the "legality and legitimacy" of the administration. It has therefore been called the "guarantor of administrative morality," [73] a role which the Council can exercise all the better because a person who is interested in seeing the law applied properly may take his complaint to the administrative courts without the necessity of violating the decree or regulation whose legality he wishes to attack. Originally, the basis of administrative justice was the plea that a certain administrative act was illegal (*exception d'illégalité*). But soon the Council developed more refined doctrines which permitted a closer examination of administrative acts. The next step was that the Council permitted pleas of *ultra vires* (*recours pour excès de pouvoir*), i.e., the complaint that an official had acted beyond the confines of his legal powers. In the interpretation of this category of pleas, the Council distinguishes between personal liability (*faute personnelle*), for which the guilty official must take personal responsibility, and public liability (*faute de service*), in which case the government will redress the wrong if the judgment goes against it.[74] In addition to these two concepts, illegality and *ultra vires*, the Council of State has added another one, that of abuse of

[73] W. R. Sharp, *The Government of the French Republic*, New York, 1938, p. 317.
[74] *Fautes de service* fall into three categories according to gravity.

power (*détournement de pouvoir*). It is this category which permits the Council to look beyond the question of legality and penetrate the motives of the act. Under the definition of abuse of power, the Council may annul actions and assess damages if an official exercises his authority for purposes for which it was not granted, even though the act itself may be neither illegal nor *ultra vires*.

Among those categories the Council of State has been inclined to restrict the extent of personal liability more and more, while expanding the concept of the public liability. It has even gone so far as to grant damages for accidents or inefficiency.

However, not all *fautes de service* make the government liable for damages. This is generally true only for acts in which the government plays the role of the business manager of the administration (*actes de gestion*).[75] But the government will ordinarily not accept liability concerning acts of authority (*actes d'autorité;* also, *actes de puissance publique*) unless they were either illegal or constituted an abuse of power. Acts of authority concern primarily international relations, but also executive-legislative relationship, national defense, and the "state of siege," [76] as well as certain colonial matters. However, the Council of State has tended to restrict the fields of *actes d'autorité* more and more, except in the field of international relations. A third category, acts of state (*actes de gouvernement*), may not even be the subject of litigation. Such acts concern high-level policy, state security, etc. Their distinction from *actes d'autorité* is not always clear, but the number of cases which may be placed under that category is not large.

Administrative law is the result of practice and precedent. Consequently it is unsystematic and contradictory, and its perimeter is flexible. It is not surprising, therefore, that jurisdictional disputes may arise between the realms of ordinary and administrative justice, but it is surprising that such disputes are few. To decide them, another court has been created, the Court of Conflicts (Tribunal des Conflits), which is composed of the Minister of Justice as chairman (who rarely presides), three councilors of the Council of State, three judges of the Cour de Cassation, and two others nominated by them.

The French system of administrative justice affords an easy and generally inexpensive way of keeping the administrative machine in line. In a highly centralized country in which the bureaucracy is only inadequately checked by rapidly changing political heads, an institution like the Council of State is an absolute necessity, although Anglo-American jurists will contend that

[75] Many *actes de gestion* come from the administrative staff itself, especially complaints against illegal or unfair treatment of civil servants. The drafting of a Civil Service Code, which was largely undertaken by the Council of State itself, has improved this situation.

[76] An act by which civil government is suspended in a certain area, which is thus placed under military control and martial law.

there is no reason why the ordinary courts cannot discharge this function just as well.[77] However, the system of administrative justice would never have worked as well as it did if the executive appointment of members of the bench had not gradually given way to protection of tenure and judicial independence. The practice of the Council of State has disproved the arguments of those critics who feared that the existence of the Council of State within the French administration would produce collusion because the administration would "judge itself." On the contrary, a distinguished observer reports that the system of administrative justice "has been criticized by some Frenchmen for showing an excess of bias against the government and in favor of private individuals; that it has given more consideration to equity and less to law . . . ,"[78] and another famous jurist has even gone so far as to state that "in France the discretionary act no longer exists,"[79] which is perhaps exaggerated.

One major drawback of this system is to be found in the fact that the Council of State is overrun with litigation and is constantly in arrears. Since 1944 more cases have been received every year than have been decided, and in the first five postwar years the arrears amounted to the staggering number of 10,753 cases, which, as Professor Hamson so admirably states, amounts to a denial of justice.[80] This has of course its repercussions in the administrative services. One highly respected and conscientious prefect of a *département* once explained to the author how he had requisitioned housing for his staff knowing full well that his action was of doubtful legality and that the Council of State would overrule him. But he figured that this would take at least two to three years and in the meantime he would find other quarters. And so it was.

A number of proposals have been made for the remedy of this serious shortcoming; the most promising have been those tending to increase the jurisdiction of the interdepartmental prefectural councils, but that is not so easy because the prefectural councils do not possess the high standing and the reputation of the Council of State and it is this reputation which makes it so effective.

In sum total the Council of State is one of the most admirable institutions of France or any country. Far from being an instance in which "the administration judges itself," it is on the contrary a highly effective device of "forbidding the administration to judge its own acts."[81] At a time when the

---

[77] As a matter of fact, regular courts actually deal with a number of administrative questions.

[78] Garner, "French Administrative Law," p. 626.

[79] Léon Duguit, *Law in the Modern State* (trans. by Frieda and Harold Laski), New York, 1919, p. 185.

[80] Hamson, *op. cit.*, p. 84.

[81] Waline, *op. cit.*, Tit. II, Chap. 2, Sec. 1, § 1.

problem of how to control the now tremendous administrative machinery is a serious question in every country, the French Council of State has made an important contribution, or at least one partial answer, thereto.

In conclusion, attention ought to be drawn to the fact that in many respects administrative justice is an aspect of constitutional jurisprudence, the French answer to judicial review (though not its equivalent). It is true that acts of the legislature cannot be challenged. But French legislation frequently leaves much detail and procedure for the administrator to fill in by the use of his regulatory power, and there the Council of State comes into its own. In a way the Court of Conflicts is, according to a leading French authority,[82] a constitutional court par excellence, because it deals with the fundamental question of French constitutional doctrine, the separation of powers.

F. THE OVERSEAS EMPIRE

France's overseas empire is the second largest in the world, exceeded only by Great Britain's. It comprises nearly 5 million square miles, and its population is estimated to be above 70 million. Nine-tenths of this empire is in Africa, where it includes Algeria, Tunisia, Morocco, West Africa, Equatorial Africa, Togo and Cameroun, French Somaliland, and the large island of Madagascar off the east coast of Africa. In Asia France used to control the Indochinese states of Viet-Nam (Annam, Tonkin, Cochin China), Laos, and Cambodia, as well as the island of Réunion in the Indian Ocean. However, the northern part of Viet-Nam was added to the Communist Viet Minh in 1954, and in the rest of Indochina French influence is rapidly declining. Technically, Viet-Nam, Laos, and Cambodia are now independent in the French Union, but that is not yet a reality. France controls a number of islands in the Australian area and Oceania, especially Caledonia and, in condominium with Britain, the New Hebrides. In the Western Hemisphere France rules the islands of St. Pierre and Miquelon just off the coast of Newfoundland, Guadeloupe and Martinique in the Antilles, and French Guiana in South America.

Since Frenchmen believe that there is no place quite like home, the French population of this vast empire is extremely small. Indochina with 25 million inhabitants has only 42,000 Frenchmen; French Equatorial Africa with nearly 3½ million people has only 5,000 French.[83] Only in North Africa are the French more numerous. Algeria, which is closest to France in every respect, has 1 million whites out of a total population of over 8½ million. In Tunisia there are 250,000 Europeans (many of Italian origin) as against 3,200,000

[82] M. Hauriou, *Précis de droit administratif et de droit public*, Paris, 1927, 11th ed., p. 948.

[83] C. A. Julien, "From the French Empire to the French Union," *International Affairs*, Vol. XXVI (1950), p. 487.

natives, while the French population of Morocco (French zone) comprises less than 5 per cent of the population.

In France the French are the staunch advocates of administrative uniformity. But little of that is in evidence in their empire. The protectorates of Morocco and Tunisia fall under the control of the Minister of Foreign Affairs. Algeria, three of whose four departments are governed similarly to departments of France proper, as well as France's prerevolutionary colonies, Guadeloupe, Martinique, Réunion, and Guiana, are under the authority of the Minister of the Interior. Viet-Nam, Laos, and Cambodia were under the authority of the Minister for the Associated States until the Laniel government of 1953 abolished that post. The rest are administered by the Minister for Overseas France. There is no real coordination between these departments. Theoretically the Premier could be the coordinator, but French Premiers remain in power too short a time and are far too preoccupied to assert their leadership in the colonial domain.

In a more real sense, these vast territories are not governed by any of these ministers; their real rulers are the colonial bureaucracies, the anonymous Frenchmen who administer these possessions in their own way, who defy their chiefs and even the minister, and who with the help of various political pressure groups always win out. This deplorable state of affairs was confirmed in an article remarkable for its candor by no less a person than Robert Schuman, long-time Foreign Minister of France, who experienced this situation in Tunisia and Morocco.[84]

The colonial policies of French governments have differed, but on the whole the emphasis has been on assimilation. The colonial bureaucracy and especially the French settlers in the overseas territories, the *colons*, have an abiding belief in the subjugation of the natives. Colonial policies in actual practice have been a combination of the two with the greater weight being on subjugation.

Not all Frenchmen have agreed with this attitude. France's greatest colonial administrator of all times, Marshal Louis Hubert Lyautey, warned against the French centralist tendencies of wishing to control every facet of the governmental structure. He was content to govern indirectly in Morocco, leaving to the Sultan most of the appearance of power, and in many domestic items much of its reality. But his successors have been more inclined to invoke his memory than to carry out his heritage.

The political subjugation of the overseas territories was accompanied by an economic policy which placed its emphasis on the use which France could make of her empire and not vice versa. Also French investments in her possessions were unimpressive and negligible compared to British.

Nevertheless there is no doubt that France did much in her colonies. But

[84] Robert Schuman, "Nécessité d'une politique," *La Nef,* March, 1953, pp. 7–9.

in the opinion of the natives the trouble has been that France did these things *in* rather than *for* her possessions, and that the largest benefits accrued to Frenchmen and not to natives. This accusation is perhaps somewhat exaggerated; much has been done for the health of the natives, though more might have been possible. And although the dreadful *"bidonvilles,"* the slum towns built literally of discarded gasoline cans to house the miserable workers of Morocco, are an undeniable fact, it is also true that the Arabs of French Morocco and Tunisia are better off economically and socially than the Arabs of such independent states as Egypt. As far as education is concerned, the French have established excellent schools, but there the emphasis is on assimilation, the abandonment of native laws and customs, which many natives regard as outright treason. Moreover, in some areas like Morocco the French have used access to their schools as a lever to discriminate against allegedly disloyal families.

The feature of French colonial policy which is most subject to criticism has been the unwillingness of the French to admit any real measure of internal autonomy and to hold out to the natives the promise of eventual self-government and even independence. This is perhaps characteristic of French public opinion, for Frenchmen, who on the whole are not great travelers, find it difficult to believe that anyone would not want to become a Frenchman when he has the chance.

On the other hand French education in the colonies has also backfired. Natives who had an opportunity to benefit by the excellent French schools overseas and in France could not help but notice that the homeland of "liberty, equality, and fraternity" apparently did not regard these things as fit for export, and they contrasted the comparative racial tolerance in France with the intolerance of the French in their overseas empire.[85] It is thus not surprising that most of the leaders of native nationalism have been the products of French education and combine a genuine admiration for French culture with an equally genuine detestation for French rule.

As might have been expected, the Second World War made a profound impression on France's colonial population. Her swift defeat impaired her prestige, and the invasion of North Africa by British and American troops further demonstrated her fall from the ranks of great powers. The more liberal attitude of the American forces toward the natives left ideas which did not disappear with the reembarkation of the GI's.

A reconsideration of the place which overseas France was to occupy was clearly in order. This was inaugurated at the Brazzaville Conference of 1944,

[85] Frenchmen are wont to contrast racial equality in France with conditions in the United States. While race relations in France proper are on the whole good (though not quite so perfect as is generally believed), in her overseas empire France practices a policy of strictest separation and discrimination.

which took place under the propulsion of the great Negro governor of French Equatorial Africa, Félix Eboué,[86] and General de Gaulle's Commissioner for Colonies, René Pleven.

However well-intentioned the Brazzaville Conference was, it illustrated the Achilles heel of French colonial policy. It was an affair of colonial adminis- trators. Representatives of native groups were not invited. The political prin- ciple of the conference was made absolutely clear in the following statement: "The aims of France in her civilizing work in the colonies exclude any idea of self-government, any possibility of development outside the French Empire; the formation of independent governments in the colonies, however distant, cannot be contemplated." [87] And in keeping with these ideas, the statement was made: "We visualize the Empire in the Roman sense of the word, not in the Anglo-Saxon sense." [88] The conference spoke vaguely of federal solutions without daring to face the consequences of such an idea. It condemned forced labor but retained it under another name, and in the field of education it rejected categorically the use of native languages.

Nevertheless, reform was not to be denied. The "old" (prerevolutionary) colonies—Martinique, Guadeloupe, Réunion, and Guiana—became depart- ments of France. This meant assimilation but was demanded by the natives themselves. Assimilist tendencies also prevailed over Algeria and Madagascar, but there they were strongly resented by the natives and their spokesmen. Native deputies from the last-mentioned regions played a considerable role in the two Constituent Assemblies and thereby aided the principle of native representation. But the autonomy which they demanded within the French Union aroused much opposition and was rejected.

Much of the opposition of course came from the French settlers in the colonies, the *colons*, and from the colonial civilian and military officialdom. These groups have powerful political support in France, but in truth French public opinion has little understanding of the true state of affairs in the over- seas empire. On the other hand American critics often fail to recognize the extreme complexity involved in two different cultures living together.

The Third Republic had made a strong distinction between those natives of France's overseas empire who abandoned their native laws and lived more or less like Frenchmen, and those who clung to their accustomed ways. The first group, endowed with what is called "French civil status," enjoyed much greater rights than those members of the *"indigenate"* who preserved their "personal status." The Constitution of 1946 ostensibly does away with that

[86] Félix Eboué was a Senegalese who completely adopted French culture and European customs. He was therefore a Frenchman rather than a native representative. He was one of the first to rally to De Gaulle and thereby helped to preserve a part of Africa for Free France at a time when most other governors of colonies obeyed Vichy. His remains are buried in the Pantheon in Paris, the traditional resting place of France's civilian great.

[87] Julien, *op. cit.*, p. 497.

[88] *Ibid.*

distinction. Article 80 extends full citizenship to all nationals of the overseas territories in the same capacity as nationals of metropolitan France; [89] Art. 82 rules that personal status "may in no case constitute a ground for refusing or restricting the rights and liberties pertaining to the status of French citizens." And Art. 81 extends citizenship in the French Union to all and provides that they shall enjoy the rights guaranteed in the preamble to the Constitution.

A closer examination, however, reveals a somewhat different picture. While Art. 81 guarantees citizenship in the French Union unconditionally, Art. 80 guarantees the far more meaningful equality between citizens of metropolitan France and the overseas territories only with the proviso that "special laws shall determine the conditions under which they may exercise their rights as citizens." In actual practice these "special laws," which must of course be passed by the National Assembly, have determined that the status of citizens of France and of the overseas territories shall be far from equal. A good example is provided by France's most advanced overseas possession, Algeria. Under the Third Republic the three departments of northern Algeria (Alger, Oran, Constantine) elected senators and deputies to the French parliament, but only French citizens could vote. That meant the *colons* and the official-dom, as well as the Algerian Jews who had received full citizenship under the Crémieux decree of 1870. Only a few Moslems were given the right to vote, usually rather assimilated people and men with good war records, etc. Actually it was not too difficult to obtain French citizenship, but in order to do so one had to give up personal status under Moslem law, which in the eyes of fellow Moslems amounted to an act of national betrayal.[90]

After liberation several classes of Moslems were given full citizenship rights and the Algerian Statute of September 20, 1947, established an Algerian Assembly. This is an innovation because the Third Republic knew only small councils, called "financial delegations," with very limited jurisdiction and significance. The Algerian Assembly is composed of 120 members. Sixty are elected by an electoral college of the first class composed of full French citizens and a few others, chiefly veterans, who are permitted to vote in that college in spite of having retained their personal status under Moslem law. The second college, which elects the other sixty members, is composed of all other Algerian voters. Since the voters of the college of the second class are eight times as numerous as those of the college of the first class, and yet elect only the same number of Assembly members, there can be no question of equality, even though the situation has improved. But the Algerian Assembly has only limited legislative power, while executive power is solely vested in a

---

[89] This excludes the citizens of the Associated States (Viet-Nam, Laos, Cambodia) and of the protectorates (Tunisia, Morocco) who have their own citizenship.

[90] H. J. Liebesny, *The Government of French North Africa*, Philadelphia, 1943, and "French North Africa: Empire in Transition," *American Perspective*, Vol. I (1947), pp. 259–285.

Governor-General who is a Frenchman appointed by the government in Paris and solely responsible to it through the French Minister of the Interior.

This pattern of the double college is applied in many other areas. In some other regions, like West Africa, only educated natives can vote and the emphasis is again on assimilation. Everywhere, in one manner or another, the natives are kept in a subordinate position, and local assemblies, where they exist, have either only advisory functions, which are frequently ignored, or only very limited legislative powers. Nowhere outside the Associated States and protectorates do they have executive power.

The Associated States have the dignity of a name which may look like a dominion of the British kind, but in reality they were more like protectorates. At the present time there are only three Associated States, all in Indochina. The largest and most important is Viet-Nam,[91] which is composed of Annam, Tonkin, and Cochin China. The others are Laos and Cambodia. The future of Viet-Nam is more than doubtful and many observers feel that it will fall under Communist domination. The case of Laos and Cambodia is only slightly better. At any rate, French influence appears to have little future in those areas.

The situation of Tunisia and Morocco is quite different. These territories are located in North Africa, quite close to metropolitan France. The distance between Marseilles and Tunis is roughly equivalent to that between New York and Detroit, or between San Francisco and San Diego. It is a 1,000-mile railroad trip from Tunis to Fez or Rabat in Morocco, but this railroad line connects very different areas. Tunisia has been under French control since 1881, while Morocco followed only in 1912. Tunisia is modern and advanced, while Morocco is far more backward. Tunisia had been under Turkish rule before it became a French possession, but Morocco was never conquered before 1912. Both countries are nominally absolute monarchies and all laws are issued by the Bey of Tunis or the Sultan of Morocco,[92] but in actuality the two French Residents-General hold the real power. Repressive measures on the part of the French authorities have resulted in the Tunisian population being almost solidly anti-French. This was not always the case and the Neo-Destour party, the spokesman of sharp nationalism, found much resistance. But since the French arrested the entire Tunisian cabinet in March, 1952, the word has been spread that "even the dogs are Neo-Destourians." In Morocco, on the other hand, the struggle for independence, whose most ex-

[91] Ellen J. Hammer, *The Emergence of Viet Nam,* New York, 1947.

[92] Morocco is officially referred to as the Sherifian Empire; the title Sherif is inherited by descendants of the prophet Mohammed, and the Sultan of Morocco holds this title. His political control, such as it is, extends only over the French zone of Morocco; his spiritual authority, however, extends to the Spanish zone as well as to the international zone of Tangier.

treme spokesman is the Istiqlal party, is also tied in with the struggle between the now deposed Sultan Moulay Yousef and certain pashas (governors), especially the Pasha of Marrakesh, who are appointed by France and support the French position. The difference between Berbers and Arabs, on the other hand, is partly artificial and encouraged by the French.[93]

Tunisia and Morocco are still protectorates. Their rulers have refused to accept the status of "Associated States" because they regard that title to be without reality. The *colons* and their friends on the other hand fear that the status of Associated States would encourage independence tendencies.

Apart from Indochina, where the war has now come to an uneasy end, and Madagascar, where a rebellion was sharply repressed, North Africa is the main trouble spot of the French empire. There have now been several years of bloodshed and repression, assassination and counterassassination. More and more Frenchmen are awakening to the seriousness of the problem, and some French governments have taken steps toward reform. But the powerful *colons* and their political friends in France have been able to frustrate even mild steps and have so far been able to obtain the removal of every Resident-General who failed to conform to their standards. The situation is complicated by the fact that the French of Tunisia (250,000 against 3,200,000 natives) are often long-time settlers, often of a second and third generation of "Franco-Africans" who regard Tunisia and not France as their home. They fear Arab domination, while the Arabs want to be masters in their own house.

Self-government thus does not exist anywhere outside metropolitan France. But an attempt was made by the French Constituent Assembly of 1946 to solve the problem on a wider scale. The result of this endeavor was the creation of the French Union, widely hailed as a totally new departure for France.

THE COMPOSITION OF THE FRENCH UNION

According to the Constitution, the French Union is composed of metropolitan France as well as all her possessions and the "Associated Territories and States," *i.e.*, the protectorates. The position of the latter is defined by an act of the French parliament. The President of the Republic is automatically President of the French Union. Next to him, there is a High Council and an Assembly. The High Council is a council of states, comparable with some caution to the German *Reichsrat* or *Bundesrat*, composed of representatives of the French government and of the "Associated States."

The Assembly of the French Union is composed of a maximum of 240 members, who are elected in the following manner: the deputies of the Na-

[93] Rom Landau, *Morocco*, International Conciliation Pamphlet No. 483, New York, 1952. This booklet is strongly pro-Arab.

tional Assembly from Continental France elect 50 representatives; the Continental members of the Council of the Republic elect 25; the general councils (legislatures and quasi legislatures) of the overseas territories and possessions elect 75 members; the "Associated States" may send a maximum of 45 delegates, which is matched by the French parliament. Thus, when all the Associated States are represented, the Continental deputies of the National Assembly elect 30 additional representatives, while the Council of the Republic elects 15. If fewer than 45 delegates are sent by the "Associated States," the representation of the French parliament decreases proportionately.

The functions of both the High Council and the Assembly of the French Union are purely advisory. The constitution stipulates that the High Council shall "assist the (French) government in the general conduct of the affairs of the Union" while the Assembly may express an opinion and submit proposals.

No Real Power

It must be clear from these remarks that the institutions of the French Union have, at present, no real power at all. They are purely advisory in nature and the government may ignore their advice. Nor are any considerable liberties conferred on the various colonies and possessions. The statute of each is drafted and enacted by the parliament in Paris. The right of secession does not exist. Moreover, the Constitution (Art. 72) specifically states that "legislative power with regard to penal law, civil liberties and political and administrative organization in the overseas territories shall rest with Parliament."

The best that can therefore be said about the existing organization of the French Union is that it at least provides a forum in which the voice of the overseas territories may be heard. But even that fact is mitigated because the meetings of the Assembly of the French Union take place in Versailles and are hardly noticed at all by the press and the public. For the purpose of attracting public attention to the grievances of the colonies, the native deputies in the National Assembly are actually in a far better position than the members of the Assembly of the French Union. As for the High Council, it scarcely meets at all.

As it stands today the French Union is a fiction, or at best a hope. The French government and its agents in the overseas territories remain supreme, and the parliament of France remains the only real legislature in the Empire. Is the French Union then at least a step in the right direction? That is far from certain. There can be no doubt of what the natives want: greater internal autonomy and at least the promise of eventual independence. They are not primarily interested in better representation in Paris, but in better representation in Algiers, Tunis, Rabat, and Tananarive. Such autonomist or federalist developments are, however, not promised by the concept of the French Union, even if it were a reality.[94]

In her more advanced possessions—in North Africa, Madagascar, and Indochina—France faces very dark days. Her chance need not be entirely lost, for many of the passionate native opponents of French rule have preserved a high regard for French culture and not all of them are irrevocably committed to a complete break with France. But a peaceful development is feasible only if the French absorb the lessons of their British neighbors on the Gold Coast and in India, and embark on a policy which grants real local autonomy, reverses the French trend toward administrative centralization, and holds out a promise of eventual independence or near independence. There are some Frenchmen who would go along with such a policy, and on the whole the French of Paris have been somewhat more understanding than the French of the colonies. But such a radical reversal of policy can be undertaken only by a strong and courageous government which can defy the violent opposition that it would face, and which would stay in office long enough to ride out the storm and establish these reforms on a firm basis. Unfortunately, no such government exists or is in the offing in France.

G. LOCAL GOVERNMENT

It is a well-known fact that systems of local government usually outlive systems of national administration. Wars, revolutions, and *coups d'état* put their marks far more on the national than on the local level. France is no exception to that rule. Yet gradual changes have occurred to which the present Fourth Republic has made a small contribution.

Under the *ancien régime* a royal official, the intendant, ruled the principal unit of local administration, the so-called *généralité*. The Revolution of 1789 quickly did away with this institution and replaced it by a totally new system of departments, *arrondissements*, and communes. Departments and communes now elected their councils, which in turn elected their officers.[95] This enlightened system lasted only until 1800, when Napoleon placed local government under rigid central control and created the pivotal position of the prefect. With some modifications, this has remained the system to this day, justifying the famous statement by a former President that "we have the Republic on top and the Empire underneath." [96] This situation has often been termed

[94] In the Constituent Assembly, Ferhat Abbas, leader of the Algerian nationalist party, *Amis du manifeste*, called that part of the Constitution which establishes the French Union the "codification of neo-colonialism." *Assemblée Constituente*, Sept. 28, 1946, p. 4230; *A Constitution for the Fourth Republic*, Foundation for Foreign Affairs, Washington, 1947, p. 72.

[95] See V. D. Lipman, "Recent Trends in French Local Administration," *Public Administration,* Vol. XXV (1947), p. 29.

[96] Paul Deschanel, *La Décentralisation,* Paris, 1895, p. 6.

paradoxical by foreign observers, but the very paradoxicality of the system has created, over the years, a curious blend of authoritarian and democratic threads which is not always apparent to those who confine themselves to a study of the channels of command.

The Third Republic achieved some gradual reforms by a certain amount of democratization and by an increasing tendency to delegate additional functions to units of local government. The Vichy regime, aping its German master, abolished much of this and attempted to reintroduce some features of regionalism. Regionalism has been a frequent discussion topic in France,[97] but its use by the Vichy regime largely discredited it, and the Constituent Assembly of 1946 was not inclined to retain it, although there was no general love for retention without change of the rigid system of the Third Republic. The result was a compromise which made no real changes but referred somewhat vaguely to future organic laws yet to be passed by parliament. That nothing very drastic is contemplated is, however, amply demonstrated by a closer examination of the constitutional text. Title X, dealing with local government, is headed, innocuously enough, "Des Collectivités Territoriales" (territorial units). It "recognizes the existence" of communes, the departments, and the overseas territories, but in the same article it refers to the French Republic as "one and indivisible," an expression which has been traditionally used in favor of a strongly unitary and centralist government and against "home-rule" movements. A development approximating British or even American ideas of local government can therefore hardly be expected.

Territorial Organization

The territorial subdivisions of France are called departments, *arrondissements*, cantons, and communes. There are 90 departments (not counting the seven North African and overseas departments), 281 *arrondissements*, 3,028 cantons, and 38,014 communes. Among them only the departments and the communes are of importance.

While the communes are the product of natural growth, many of them going back to most ancient times, the departments are the artificial creation of the French Revolution. Originally the departments were founded as new areas of self-government. Within a few years of their creation, the departments lost that character completely and became the principal instrument through which the central authorities in Paris controlled the provinces. With some modifications, the Third Republic maintained this institution. Under it, the prefect who was appointed and controlled by the Minister of the Interior was both the representative of the central government and the chief executive officer of the department. After 1833, there existed elected general councils

[97] Charles Brun, *Le Regionalisme*, Paris, 1911; R. K. Gooch, *Regionalism in France*, New York, 1931.

in the departments (with some interruptions), although they were still dependent on the prefect for the execution of their orders. Moreover, the prefect had strong control, called "administrative guardianship" (*tutelle administrative*), over the council and the local administration, through which he could see to it that the councilors acted "wisely."

CHANGES UNDER THE FOURTH REPUBLIC

The "founding fathers" of the Fourth Republic unanimously voted for a change of the prefectural system. They were prompted in this by the lessons of the war, which reminded them how easily the Vichy regime had gained control over the prefects and hence over the country. Yet the well-known statement that those in power always like the prefectural system, because it is so convenient for the effective maintenance of control, tended to neutralize the desire to place local government on a completely democratic and "home-rule" basis. The result was a compromise which attempted to separate the two principal functions of the prefect. He was to retain his role as the representative of the national government but was to yield his place as chief executive of the department to the department's own elected officials. Thus, the president of each department's general council became theoretically the chief executive for the departments, very much in the same manner as the mayors had been chief executives of the communes.

However, the innovation is more apparent than real. Only a few relatively unimportant functions are carried out by the general council: the upkeep of public buildings, the maintenance of certain secondary roads, and similar housekeeping duties. And many of those functions are circumscribed by national law. In effect the constitutional provision dividing power between the prefect and the general council has remained a dead letter because the National Assembly never passed the necessary implementing legislation and, according to one Minister of the Interior, never will do so.

The mayors and municipal councils have somewhat larger functions, chiefly because of their administration of public welfare and communally owned public utilities. All these functions are hamstrung by the very limited right of taxation possessed by all units of local government. Their main income is derived from a small percentage of certain national taxes which are placed at their disposal, income from communal industries, and grants-in-aid. But even these limited budgets are not within the sole province of local government. Over three-fourths of all communal outlays are the result of mandatory national legislation which gives the commune no choice. Problems of education, police, fire, health, etc., are largely removed from the competence of mayor and council, and even in the few areas where they retain functions, as in public welfare, many duties are prescribed for them. This system does not permit or encourage local initiative to any large extent. Postwar disorganization and physical destruction have inspired many mayors and city councils to accomplish heroic acts of reconstruction, proving thereby that the lethargy for which French local government is renowned is not caused by lack of ability on the part of the French people. A remedy is, however, not in sight as long as "unity," or rather uniformity, of administration is considered a virtue [98] and as long as the idea prevails that "France cannot be abandoned to the whims of ninety general councils and 38,000 communes." [99]

THE PREFECTS

Under the Third Republic, prefects were appointed by the President of the Republic upon recommendation by the Minister of the Interior. Now, they are appointed by decree of the Council of Ministers, but in either case they are for all practical purposes the appointees of the Minister of the Interior who is their immediate chief.

Prefects are a curious blend of political and civil-service officers. They are usually appointed from among the civil service, yet they are not required to meet any special standards of professional competence. An outstanding expert [100] has described them as being "essentially political agents whose business it is to support and spread the opinions and wishes of the government throughout the whole administration." This implies that while prefects are not necessarily partisans, they are nevertheless chosen for their obedience to the government. Prefects are rarely dismissed; more frequent is the so-called "movement of prefects," *i.e.*, they are shifted around as a new administration takes office. Obedient prefects will be shifted to more important posts, while less pliable ones may be sent to "exile" in the provinces or even to overseas departments. In some cases, prefects are promoted or "kicked upstairs" to the General Accounting Office or even the Council of State.

Within his department the prefect represents the total power of the national government. As such he not only supervises and controls the local administration, but he carries out directly a number of functions and appoints a considerable number of officers.[101] Especially in the fields of education, public works, road construction, and police, his powers are extensive. He plays a particularly important role in the field of public safety, which is strongly centralized in France. The Minister of the Interior controls all the police forces of France—a method which is common on the European conti-

---

[98] With the exception of Paris and the department (Seine) in which it is located, all French communes and departments have identical organization.

[99] Joseph-Barthélemy, *The Government of France* (trans. by J. B. Morris), New York, 1924, p. 153. (Figures have been adjusted).

[100] *Ibid.*, p. 134.

[101] Technically the prefect may even act as an examining magistrate (*juge d'instruction*) (Art. 10, *code d'instruction criminelle*), but such cases are now virtually nonexistent.

nent, with the result that ministries of the interior are of outstanding importance in the political picture—especially in troubled times. The Ministry of the Interior has the Sûreté Nationale, a plain-clothes force which operates in secret, under its immediate control. A uniformed guard, known as the *gendarmerie*,[102] is stationed in each department and is under the control of the Minister of War. However, both national and local security agencies may call on them for help.

The ordinary police forces are directly administered by the municipal governments, subject to the control of the prefect. In certain key cities, however, the police is under direct national control. In the department of the Seine, in which Paris is located, there are two prefects, and one, the prefect of police, is in direct charge of that important security force.

The original concept of the prefect as created by Napoleon was that of the nearly omnipotent arm of the central authorities. With the improvement of communications and the growth of a democratic spirit, the power of the prefect deteriorated as the central authorities issued more and more detailed directives and increased the scope of their direct intervention. However, there are enough important functions which remain under his jurisdiction as the "delegate of the government."

This conflict between the traditional tendency toward strictest centralism and the modern trend toward decentralization may in time revive the idea of regionalism which has been the subject of much argument in the past. The Vichy regime created regional administrations, and the French Committee of National Liberation decided to maintain them. As a result, eighteen administrative regions were created. But after consolidation, the government decided to return to the purely prefectural regime. However, the danger of public disorder caused by the repercussions of the East-West controversy prompted the government to impose a tighter security control in 1948 by creating eight superprefectures.[103] The superprefects have largely a coordinating function, primarily in cases of widespread emergency. In such cases they act like regional ministers of the interior. However, the superprefects have no staffs and exercise only the functions which are specifically delegated to them —functions which are ordinarily reserved to the Minister of the Interior and not to the prefect. Consequently the superprefect does not diminish the role of the prefect. At times prefects of important departments have been appointed superprefects in addition to their prefectural duties. Superprefects,

[102] It is an American tendency to regard all French policemen as gendarmes. This is quite incorrect. Most French policemen are municipal officers. Gendarmes are vaguely comparable to American state policemen.

[103] The official title is *Inspecteurs Généraux de l'Administration en Mission Extraordinaire*; R. S. Abbott and R. Sicard, "A Postwar Development in French Regional Government: The 'Super Préfet,'" *American Political Science Review*, Vol. XLIV (1950), pp. 426–431.

even when stationed in the provinces, attend regular monthly conferences at the Ministry of the Interior, where they have an opportunity to brief the government on important over-all developments in the country.

A recent example of the use which the government is making of the super-prefects occurred on June 28, 1953, when Premier Joseph Laniel, Minister of the Interior Martinaud-Deplat, and Minister of Finance and Economics Edgar Faure directed them to take energetic measures against unjustified price rises.

Great as the power of the prefect may be, it is nevertheless circumscribed very considerably by a number of important factors. The rapid extension of the civil-service system has curtailed his power of appointment. At the same time his politically ambiguous role has remained. On the one hand he is supposed to lay down the law to the department over which he "rules"; on the other hand he must maintain good relations with the members of parliament from his department, who can make trouble for him in the National Assembly, especially when they belong to a party whose support is important to the Minister of the Interior. The deputy in turn has an attentive ear cocked toward the demands of his constituents, with the result that complaints or requests which ought to be directed to the prefect are actually presented to the deputy from the area concerned, who then intercedes with his considerable influence. To walk the straight and narrow path between pressure from below and possible displeasure from above, the prefect must indeed be a man of remarkable qualities and political talents. He must also be a man of discretion for, insofar as civil service and other regulations permit, he has a certain amount of patronage to dispense, and there are also certain funds at his disposal which may be used prudently in order to strengthen the position of his minister. People imbued with the Anglo-American concept of local government will be unable to see anything good in the prefect, but in a country which believes in centralization he constitutes an essential element of coordination.

THE DEPARTMENTAL GENERAL COUNCIL

While the prefect represents the national government in the department, the local functions are carried out by a General Council (Conseil Général), whose chairman is called president. The general councils are important bodies because of their composition, not because of their functions. In order to maintain or build up local strength, virtually all leading politicians are active members of general and often of municipal councils in which they are joined by men of local and often national distinction. General councils have very few functions except for discussion, as the prefect is the real kingpin of the *département*. However they watch the prefect, and the political role of the council's members makes this an important performance. The General Council has a standing committee which often carries on the functions of the entire council. Where it has an auditing function, it is primarily concerned with the supervision of financial affairs.

THE ARRONDISSEMENT AND ITS SUBDIVISIONS

The department's subdivision, called *arrondissement*, is of little significance. It is primarily an administrative subsection of the department, is headed by a subprefect, and is without an independent life of its own. Under the Third Republic it derived a certain amount of importance from the fact that it was an electoral district. The electoral systems of the Fourth Republic, however, are based on the department, not the *arrondissement* except for by-elections. The latter could easily be abolished, but civic and local pride have been able to prolong its existence.

This has also been said of a further territorial subdivision, the canton, which has no civic life of its own. Yet, it fulfills an unofficial mission by giving a center and cohesion to communities which would otherwise lack them. The canton is grouped around the most important town in the area, which is the seat of a number of necessary officials, especially notaries and court clerks (*huissiers*). Small communities are thereby able to effect a certain amount of consolidation which is otherwise prevented by a senseless uniformity which imposes precisely the same type of municipal government on all towns other than Paris, regardless of size or significance.

MUNICIPAL GOVERNMENT

Each city elects a city council, which in turn elects a mayor who presides over it. In communities of 500 inhabitants or less, eleven councilors are elected. In bigger cities their number is proportionately larger, but the maximum number of councilmen is reached by cities of 60,000 inhabitants, which have thirty-seven members. All larger cities, except Paris, have the same number.

The rules of order, the jurisdiction, and the organization of the city councils are strictly determined by law. The councilors themselves are elected on the basis of a proportional-list system combined with preferential voting, which permits the voter to indicate preferences among the candidates of his party. However, he may not split his vote between different party lists. Municipal elections usually have a partisan character and are often dominated by national, rather than local, issues.

The mayor and his principal assistants (*adjoints*) head the executive departments of the city, which may be simple or complex depending on the size of the community. He prepares and executes the budget, is responsible for public safety and order, administers local licensing and inspection regulations, and maintains housekeeping functions. While the mayor's importance increases with the size of his city, it is nevertheless a fact that he finds himself under stricter control by the prefect when the city is large. Thus, in cities of more than 5,000 inhabitants, the chief of police is appointed by the Minister of the Interior, not the mayor, and in certain larger cities the police is even more strongly controlled by Paris. In addition, the prefect, in exercising his power of *tutelle administrative,* may dissolve city councils or set aside mayors' ordinances if they are deemed illegal. He may also suspend or dismiss mayors for "improper activities." Although it is the prefect who takes such drastic actions, they are almost invariably ordered by the Minister of the Interior. Political considerations as well as fear of being overruled by the Council of State have greatly limited extreme measures of this kind. However, dismissals of mayors have happened repeatedly in recent years in cases of Communist mayors who fused their public and party functions too closely.

Mayors hold a double position. On the one hand, they are the chief executives of their communities; on the other hand, they are agents of the prefect with regard to functions under national law, such as the maintenance of voting lists. Many mayors occupy a special place because of their national, rather than local, importance. What has been true of the departmental general council, namely that nationally prominent politicians seek membership there, is even more so in the case of the mayors of France. Many, if not most, leading statesmen of France have sought to be mayors of their home city and have maintained that office concurrently with their national posts. The dean of France's statesmen-mayors is of course Édouard Herriot, many times Premier and cabinet member and until recently President of the National Assembly, who was mayor of Lyons for over fifty years. Only the Vichy interlude caused a short interruption of this extraordinary record.

The fact that mayors of important towns can afford to be absent for long parliamentary sessions or for terms in cabinet office is made possible by the first *adjoint,* who does the work in the mayor's absence. On the other hand, the national importance of a mayor-deputy or even cabinet minister can do much for a city.[104]

PARIS

A separate case is presented by the city of Paris. In many countries a special status is given the capital city; the nonvoting inhabitants of Washington, D.C., are well aware of that fact. But in other respects Paris cannot be compared with Washington. As a city, Paris is by all odds the most important place of France. The "city of lights" is the political, intellectual, and

---

[104] The permanent town clerk (*secrétaire de la ville*; in larger cities, *secrétaire général de la mairie*) is in charge of the entire staff. In very small communes the schoolmaster may act as clerk.

economic leader of the country. "Who holds Paris, holds France," is a well-known expression. Moreover, all revolutions, of which France has had more than her share, commenced and were decided in Paris. In order to make sure that local issues will not prevail over national ones, Paris has been organized in a special way, as determined by the law of July 24, 1867.

Paris has no mayor but is governed by two prefects for the department of the Seine, one of whom is the regular departmental prefect, while the other is the prefect of police. Paris is divided into twenty *arrondissements,* each headed by a so-called "mayor." But as this official is appointed by the council of ministers, upon recommendation of the Minister of the Interior, he is in fact nothing but a subprefect. If any one official comes close to being the mayor of Paris, it is the president of the city council, but the prefect of the Seine department actually carries most of the functions which are now ordinarily associated with the position of mayor.

Paris has a city council composed of ninety members who are elected by the *arrondissements,* or rather their subdivisions, known as "quarters" (*quartiers*). All city councilors are automatically general councilors of the department of the Seine as well. Fifty additional members are elected by the non-incorporated suburbs. The members of the Paris city council receive a salary, which is unusual in France, but in return they find that theirs is nearly a full-time job because of the almost constant sessions of the council.

In its functions, the Paris city council is even more restricted than French city councils ordinarily are. The authority of the prefects and the need for ministerial approval for some of its most important acts transform the Paris city council into something that is largely decorative. Nevertheless, elections to the council are carried out with much of the gusto which characterizes parliamentary contests.

Debatable Merit

A wide difference of opinion exists between American and French experts on the relative merits of their respective systems. In the belief that "home rule" is the best road to democracy and representative government, the absence of real local self-government as the term is understood in the Anglo-American countries is surprising to us. Movements for "home rule" exist in France, but they have produced no powerful ground swell and the government has been able to ignore them with impunity.

This divergence in concepts illustrates the vast difference of approach between the English and French-speaking worlds. The Anglo-American approach to problems has traditionally been inductive and pragmatic. The French approach is deductive and systematic. America especially has generally been content to let local units of government find their own way and has benefited from their experience. Progress in local and municipal government has often been the result of successful experiments by individual states, counties, and municipalities. From those experiences more general rules have been derived. In France, such an approach would be condemned as unsystematic and wasteful—if not worse. The merit of an innovation must first be proved on the basis of theoretical logic and in conformity with accepted doctrines. If such proof is successful, then the innovation must logically be adopted everywhere; a partial adoption would make no sense. Such general adoption, however, can be accomplished only by the national government. Progress, as understood in France, is therefore tied to centralism and uniformity. "Home rule" is suspected of being capable of becoming the stronghold of reaction; it is feared to be the road to disorder and anarchy, and it is certain to be wasteful.

As this system appears to be acceptable to most Frenchmen, the foreign observer may well remain at ease. It is a system specially adapted to the enforcement of national policy on all levels. In disturbed times such as these, the French system has certain definite advantages and has undoubtedly contributed to the survival of the middle-of-the-road course which the present government is trying to steer.[105]

[105] For a recent comprehensive treatment see Brian Chapman, *Introduction to French Local Government,* London, 1953.

Chapter 5

PARTIES AND POLITICS

To a Frenchman the political party system of France seems entirely clear and simple while the American equivalent appears confused and incomprehensible. Americans, on the other hand, have exactly the opposite impression. Is this merely a case of mutual misinformation? No, the difference lies rather in divergent concepts and definitions of political parties. Americans are inclined to look upon political parties from the standpoint of their purpose, namely, the struggle for control. Frenchmen look primarily for the political philosophy which the parties embrace. Thus Benjamin Constant defined a political party simply as "an assembly of men who profess the same political doctrine." [1]

To a Frenchman, therefore, the galaxy of French parties is utterly clear because each one stands, or at least professes to stand, for a particular philosophy, whereas he is utterly confused by the two big parties of America which he sometimes cannot distinguish from one another. When he learns that some "right" Democrats are farther to the "right" than some "left" Republicans, his confusion is complete. An American, however, cannot understand why the French parties remain separate and thus condemn themselves to a relatively small-scale existence, nor can he easily comprehend what the constant formation and destruction of coalitions is all about.

In order to arrive at a better understanding of the French party system, we will do well to keep both the American and the French concepts in mind, for both doctrinal differences, which Frenchmen take very seriously, and the struggle for power, which everybody takes very seriously, are much in evidence. Unfortunately, these things are not so neatly arranged in practice as they might be in theory, for in politics words are frequently used to obscure meaning rather than to illuminate it. Thus a passionate appeal to an idea may hide a determined quest for power, while an opportunistic action may have been engaged to further the victory of an idea.

The French attention to political ideas makes for stirring debates and beautiful writing. But it also has an atomizing effect, making cooperation difficult

[1] Benjamin Constant de Rebecque, *De la doctrine politique qui peut réunir les partis en France*, Paris, 1822.

for political factions. Compromise over practical issues is obviously easier than over philosophical differences.

These centrifugal tendencies in the French political tradition have undoubtedly received much fuel from the electoral systems in use under the Third and Fourth Republics. Both the majority-single-member-district system with runoff elections (*scrutin d'arrondissement à deux tours*) and proportional representation with or without *apparentement* greatly encourage the existence of a multiplicity of parties.

We have already seen that such political fractionalization makes for weak government. But this is not a uniquely French situation. What is unique is the fact that these parties regroup themselves in different blocs or loose coalitions according to several distinct dividing factors. In most countries the most important factor is the attitude toward social and economic questions; thus groups of parties align themselves on opposite fronts according to their degree of liberal or conservative convictions.[2] In France, however, the most important dividing line is still the religious question, although this is a purely historical problem which has very little basis in reality; unfortunately French memories are extremely long.[3] Next in intensity is the division over social and economic questions, and finally there is the division over the great East-West schism.

The picture which emerges is this: over "religious" questions (such as the important issue of state support to private schools), the Communists, Socialists, and the otherwise very conservative Radicals make common cause against the otherwise leftist MRP, the right-wing Independents, and parts of the Gaullists (ex-RPF, now called Social Republicans). In the broad area of social and economic questions the Communists, the Socialists, and the Catholic MRP face the Radicals, Independents, and most Gaullists. On the question of East-West orientation, the Communists and a handful of "progressives" fight it out against all the rest. There are of course shades in between. The over-all importance of the religious question is shown by the fact that the Socialists are far more ready to make an electoral coalition with the conservative but anti-Church Radicals than with the moderately left-wing but Catholic MRP.

In the relatively short period since liberation, France has seen quite considerable political shifts. At first the political horizon was dominated by the

---

[2] Words are tricky. The terms "liberal" and "conservative" may take many meanings, but they are used here as commonly and colloquially understood in America. Let it be noted, however, that in Continental Europe the word "liberal" stands for opposition to government regulation and planning and for something approaching *laissez faire*. Hence the European use of the term "liberal" corresponds closely to the American concept of "conservative." French newspapers would refer to men like Antoine Pinay, Joseph Laniel, or Paul Reynaud as "liberals," while American papers would call them "conservatives."

[3] Maurice Duverger, "Public Opinion and Political Parties in France," *American Political Science Review*, Vol. XLVI (1952), pp. 1069–1078.

three big parties of the left; Communists, Socialists, and MRP. The Radicals and the right were powerless, discredited partly by collaboration with the Vichy and occupation regimes, partly by too close identification with the then disparaged Third Republic. The increasing East-West tension and the primary loyalty of the Communists to every twist of the Russian political line gradually drove a wedge into the left and separated the Communists from their erstwhile allies. Meanwhile, beginning in 1947, conservative tendencies became strengthened, producing the peculiar and somewhat nebulous Gaullist movement, Rally of the French People (RPF), which achieved great, but not dominant, strength for a time. At its head General Charles de Gaulle appeared for a while within inches of recapturing the reins of power which he had so abruptly cast aside in 1945. But beginning in 1951 Gaullism began to fade, and a part of its remnants has now joined the traditional right. After the election of 1951 the distribution of party strength in popular votes and seats in the National Assembly was as shown in the accompanying table.

Parties	Votes	Percentage of total vote cast in 1951	Seats in National Assembly 1951	Seats in 1946
Communists and associates	5,056,605	26.43	106*	181*
Socialists (SFIO)	2,744,842	14.35	104	102
Various left Independents	38,393	0.20	1 †	2 †
MRP	2,369,778	12.39	85	164
RGR	2,110,992	11.04	93	63
Right and Independents	2,433,586	12.32	110	98
RPF ‡	4,125,492	21.56	119	
Others	87,346	0.46	9	6

* Including the African Democratic Rally (RDA), which habitually votes with the Communists.

† From overseas territories.

‡ Since the election 30 former RPF deputies have broken with the party and have organized themselves as the Groupe Indépendent d'Action Républicaine et Sociale (Independent Group of Republican and Social Action), ARS. The rest of the RPF deputies have relabeled themselves the Union des Républicains d'Action Sociale (Union of Republicans of Social Action), URAS, or Social Republicans.

Source: Ministère de l'Intérieure, Les élections législatives du 17 Juin 1951, Paris, 1953.

POLITICAL IMPACT OF THE TRADE-UNIONS

A new factor has also been introduced into the picture by the power of the trade-unions. The tradition of political trade-unionism in Europe is old, and many strikes have had political, rather than economic, motives. In the period between the First and Second World Wars, there existed three major trade-union federations. The largest was the Socialist-dominated General Confederation of Labor (Confédération Générale du Travail, CGT), the other two being the Communist-dominated Unified General Confederation of Labor (Confédération Générale du Travail Unitaire, CGTU) and the French Confederation of Christian Workers (Confédération Française des Travailleurs Chrétiens, CFTC) which was progressive-Catholic and not tied to any particular party.

The Vichy government dissolved the unions, but they were restored after liberation. The split between the CGT and CGTU had been healed before the outbreak of war. In 1943 the CGT and the CFTC united while they were both working in the underground.

But postwar developments quickly destroyed this unity. The CGT had come under the leadership of the Communists during the period of the underground struggle. Nominally the reemerging CGT was nonpartisan and operated under the joint secretaryship of old Léon Jouhaux (Socialist) and Benoît Frachon (Communist), but Frachon and his Communist friends held all the strings in their hands. This was also apparent in the Communist-sponsored and dominated World Federation of Trade Unions, whose Secretary General is another French Communist, Louis Saillant.

It was not so much the fact of Communist domination itself which broke up the unity of the French labor movement as the use which the Communist leaders made of the unions. This became quite apparent after the Soviet Union denounced the Marshall Plan and Communists all over the world began to sabotage it wherever possible. Hand in hand with this development also came the realization on the part of both Socialists and Catholics that cooperation with the Communists was possible only at the price of surrender. The Christian trade-unions had never been completely integrated into the CGT and their separation was easily effected. The Socialists, however, had to build anew, with great difficulties. In 1943 Léon Jouhaux reluctantly led his followers out of the CGT and formed a new organization called General Federation of Labor—Workers' Force (Confédération Générale du Travail—Force Ouvrière). It is, however, not correct to consider the Workers' Force simply as a Socialist labor union. The Workers' Force is quite independent from the Socialist party and has frequently gone separate ways from it, especially when the Socialists were in the government.

In addition there are a number of independent unions [4] whose membership is larger than one might suppose.

The numerical strength of these unions is subject to considerable speculation, as the figures published by the unions themselves are undoubtedly exaggerated. It was, however, generally conceded that a large majority of workers stood in the ranks of the Communist-dominated CGT, that the Workers'

[4] The Confédération du Travail Indépendente (CTI), formerly the Comité Général du Syndicalisme Indépendent (CGSI), Fédération des Syndicats Autonomes (FSA), Confédération Nationale du Travail (CNT), and various isolated unions.

Force unions were weak,[5] and that the Christian unions had rallied after some setbacks. These estimates received a partial revision in June, 1950, when 5½ million workers went to the polls to elect their representatives on the 234 regional boards of the social-security system. The CGT led with 43.5 per cent, the CFTC received 21.3 per cent, and the Workers' Force received 15.2 per cent. But since the miners, who are supposed to be heavily Communist, have their own social-security system and consequently did not vote in June, 1950, it must be assumed that the Communists still control a majority of the French workers.

Since its heyday of 1945–1946, when the Communist-dominated CGT claimed 6 million members (probably exaggerated), it has lost over half its members. But except for those who participated in the original exodus of the CFTC and the Workers' Force, the other two million workers have simply dropped out of the union movement. And yet the majority of those who have left the CGT because of its Communist-inspired policy continue to vote Communist because they believe that the Communists are the only party which raises its voice for the workers. Reference to the actual conditions in Communist countries is to no avail. The workers feel too bitter over the inaction of the government, the unequally distributed tax burden, the low wages, and the extremely high cost of living to be concerned with conditions in Poland, Czechoslovakia, or the Soviet Union. While the Socialists are in the opposition and the Catholic labor movement is highly restive over the participation of the MRP in predominantly conservative governments, there is little doubt that the working people of France are solidly aligned against the government. The tremendous but abortive near general strike of August, 1953, vividly underscored this point.

The Press and the Parties

The prewar French press was famous for its brilliance but also for its venality. If most papers were not for sale, they most certainly were for rent. However it is not entirely correct to say, as did a famous *bon mot,* that France's prewar press was "in the pay of every government except that of France," because the French government also participated in bribing the press through the famous "secret funds" at the disposal of the ministers.

This merry state of affairs came to an abrupt end upon liberation, when all papers which had continued to appear during the occupation were suppressed. The left attempted to turn the confiscated papers [6] into a state-owned press trust which would lease its facilities at cost to any group wishing

---

[5] For a while they were jokingly referred to as *Faiblesse Ouvrière*—Workers' Weakness.

[6] Only owners who had not collaborated with Vichy or the Germans were compensated, but they too had to give up their property if their papers had appeared during the occupation.

to publish. This extreme suggestion was not carried out, but the confiscated papers were placed under the administration of a National Association of Press Enterprises (Société Nationale des Entreprises de Presse) which was to sell them, with preference and loans to be given to groups and parties having a Resistance record. This system, which was instituted by the Law on the Press Property of 1946 and which was liquidated in 1953, was intended to further the party press over the so-called "press of information"—which comprises both the great nonpartisan journals and the sensational press. It was also expected that the leftist papers would benefit particularly. The independent newspapers complained that they were required to be self-supporting under difficult economic circumstances while the party papers were heavily subsidized by the treasuries of their respective parties.

Actually the situation developed in a radically different manner from these fears and hopes. The party press, despite the law's favoritism, began to lose steadily from the very beginning. This was particularly marked in Paris, which dominates the country intellectually and politically. The Socialist organ *Le Populaire* dropped from 250,000 subscribers to below 40,000 by 1950. Intermittently it had to be published as a single sheet of two pages and was saved from complete extinction only by repeatedly passing the hat among the Socialist parties of other European countries, notably the British Labor party. The chief organ of the MRP, *L'Aube*, also dropped to about 40,000 by 1950, but having nowhere to go to pass a hat, it had to give up the ghost in 1951. There never was a real party press on the right in Paris, and the RPF could not maintain a daily paper.

The Communists, due to their greater party discipline, fared somewhat better. Even so the chief Communist newspaper, *L'Humanité,* lost over half of its readers, and the Communist evening daily, *Ce Soir,* had to suspend publication in 1952. Even the very popular and well-edited Communist agricultural journal, *La Terre,* lost heavily. This picture is not entirely repeated in the provinces, where the party press has done much better. The Communists have lost several papers there but otherwise have held their own, while two Socialist provincial papers, *Nord-Matin* and *Le Provençal,* have circulations of over 200,000, and several others have over 100,000. The Radicals have no proper party press in Paris, but the large daily *L'Aurore* is close to them. They dominate a number of provincial journals, among which the famous *Dépêche de Toulouse* has been resurrected.

The public-opinion field is clearly dominated by the independent press, the "press of information." Its most respected papers are *Le Figaro* and *Le Monde. Le Figaro,* with the much larger circulation of the two, is edited by Gabriel Robineaux and counts some renowned writers, such as François Mauriac, André Siegfried, and Raymond Aron, among its editorialists. *Le Monde,* edited by Hubert Beuve-Méry, has a somewhat neutralist tendency and a younger but also very distinguished group of editorialists.

The reason for the victory of the "press of information" over the party press is undoubtedly due to the fact that the independent press publishes by far the better papers and attracts the better editorialists and writers, most of whom prefer to write without the ideological strait jackets of the party press. On the other hand, these papers seem to have no more influence on political adherence and the casting of the vote than is the case elsewhere. The diminishing fortunes of the party press have not resulted in a corresponding diminution of the party vote. This is most clearly shown in the case of the Communists, who have polled nearly the same percentage of votes at every election despite the steady decline of their party press. While the Socialists and the MRP have lost votes, there seems to be no direct relationship between the numbers of their readers and the numbers of their voters.

PARTY ORGANIZATION

There is a common pattern in the organization of all French parties. Operating in a centralist country, they all show, at least theoretically, centralist characteristics. All parties have an executive committee, known by different names, at their head. This committee is usually elected by an annual congress composed of delegates from the party organizations comprising a *département*. Also elected by the congress is the administrative head of the party, the Secretary-General, and usually the presiding officer, known as president.

The organization on the *département* level is known in all parties as the Federation. This in turn is subdivided into grass-roots organizations at the municipal level, known as sections. In the Communist party this subdivision is more elaborate as we shall see. All parties have various councils, professional organizations, and special-purpose organizations of all kinds. Membership in a party is obtained by a declaration of adherence and formal acceptance by the party organization and is conditioned on the regular payment of membership dues. Party members may be expelled in the manner prescribed by the party statutes.

This near uniformity is, however, more apparent than real. The great majority of Frenchmen are suspicious of formal organizations and discipline and dislike party cards. Much of French party organization is therefore on paper only. The intensity of party organization is greatest on the left and diminishes steadily toward the right. The RPF is an exception; although difficult to classify, it belongs more to the right than anywhere else, but despite declining fortunes it has a strong organizational structure. Otherwise the Radicals have only a very perfunctory organization, preferring to rely on committees of influential men rather than on rank-and-file cadres. And among the Independents, the "classical right," one cannot speak of any party organization at all.

It is a phenomenon to be observed in most countries that the left is more tightly organized than the right, but in few countries is the contrast as sharp as in France. This does not visit such a great disadvantage on the right as might be expected because it is very difficult to find any over-all relationship between the strength of party organization and the size of the party's vote in a given region. Time and again one finds strong organizations and small votes, or weak organizations and a large vote, in any number of *départements*.

Despite membership dues, all parties are dependent on outside sources the nature of which is largely kept secret. But as private contributions to worthy causes are not so common in Europe as they are in America, and as Frenchmen are not great contributors even among Europeans, all parties, with one exception, struggle with a constant financial problem. The one exception is the Communist party, the only one that can always afford to hire the biggest hall, print the largest number of posters and handbills, and unleash an "action" at any time. Their favorable financial situation is the result of several factors: the discipline of their members, the duty of all Communist office-holders to pay two-thirds of their salaries to the party, the secret contributions of businessmen who wish to "reinsure" themselves against all eventualities, and of course funds coming directly or indirectly from behind the Iron Curtain.

French electoral campaigns are a great deal cheaper than are those in the United States, as the business of advertising is far less developed in France. Moreover, during the actual election campaign, the government reimburses the parties for their printing and mailing costs, including the printing of ballots, which is done by the parties along standardized lines. These benefits are available upon the posting of a bond of 20,000 francs ($57) per candidate, which is forfeited if the party list in a given department receives less than 5 per cent of the total vote.

One factor which saves money is that Europeans have fewer cars than Americans and consequently walk more. Many election posters are therefore relatively small and contain a good deal of writing which can easily be absorbed by a passing pedestrian who stops to read the dozens of posters that may be affixed to a single board.

THE COMMUNIST PARTY

The French Communist party (Parti Communiste Français, PCF) is a phenomenon worthy of study.[7] Second only to the Italian Communist party,

[7] There are now a number of excellent studies on the Communist party of France. A. Rossi, *Psychologie du Parti Communiste Français*, Paris, 1948, with an abbreviated English translation; *A Communist Party in Action*, New Haven, 1949; M. Einaudi, J. M. Domenach, and A. Garosci, *Communism in Western Europe*, Ithaca, 1951; and Jules Monnerot, *Sociologie du Communisme*, Paris, 1949.

it is far stronger than any other Communist party outside the iron curtain. In fact, the others are all numerically insignificant in comparison to their French and Italian counterparts.

The French Communist party is not only large; it has a remarkable voters' discipline. Since the liberation, when the Communists emerged from the underground, the party has polled approximately the same vote, roughly between 26 and 28 per cent of the total vote cast, at every election. This is a considerable achievement equaled by no other party; it is even more remarkable when one considers the tremendous political changes which have occurred in that period—from the left domination and De Gaulle's presidency to the resignation of De Gaulle, the breakup of the left coalition, the ouster of the Communists from the government, the intensification of the East-West struggle, the Marshall Plan, and the Korean War. Through all these changes the Communist party has held on to its voters. Moreover, it is the most national party of France in terms of geographic distribution. In no *département* have the Communists polled less than 6 per cent of the total vote in a national election. No other party can make that claim. This voting distribution is also reflected, though not identically, in the party organization; there is no *département* of France in which the Communist party does not have a sizable organization.

The fact of a constant and strong, though isolated and not dominant, Communist party is seemingly permanent in the political life of France. Yet the picture becomes confusing when one remembers that although the Communist vote has remained constant, Communist party membership has steadily declined and so have, even more so, the readers of the Communist press. Even more important, the Communist leadership has been consistently unable to move the bulk of its voters or even the majority of its members to overt political action other than voting for the party. This has been particularly in evidence since 1947. The Communist-led demonstrations against Generals Dwight D. Eisenhower and Matthew Ridgway, when they became NATO commanders, were miserable failures. Political strikes, when not joined by non-Communist organizations, fizzled, and in many other instances the Communist suggestions for action were ignored by the rank and file of the party. The conclusion is therefore inescapable that the majority of people voting the Communist ticket are not believers in Communism but give the party their support for reasons which have nothing to do with Marxism, Communism, or Russia. What are these reasons?

One source of strength is the revolutionary tradition of France which makes a revolutionary ideology an eminently "French" matter, and the Communists have convinced many people, among them many intellectuals, that they are the most revolutionary and left, hence the most "French" party.

Another root lies in the Communist Resistance record. It is true that the Communist leadership collaborated actively with the Germans until the invasion of Russia by the Germans.[8] But after that the Communists threw themselves wholeheartedly into the struggle and contributed a majority of the Resistance martyrs. This is understandable because of the customary discipline of the Communist militants and also because the Communists are always largely an underground organization even when their existence is perfectly legal. Thus they were well prepared for the secret war against Vichy and the Germans.

Perhaps most important of all is the Communist hold over the workers. It is of course not complete. A good many workers are not Communists, nor are all Communists workers. But the Communists have found it possible to identify themselves successfully with the workers' numerous and quite justified grievances: their low wages compared to the high cost of living, the unequal tax burden, the lack of social conscience of a good part of management, inadequate housing, etc. If the workers were to look for other champions, where would they go? Neither the Socialists nor the MRP are workers' parties, although both have workers in their midst. Both, in successive governments, did little for the workers. Some workers tried De Gaulle's RPF, but to most workers it is a party of the right, and a French worker does not vote for the right, which he is wont to consider the "class enemy." Thus the apparent paradox: millions of workers have refused to go into the streets and demonstrate when the Communist leadership demanded it; over 2 million workers have left the Communist-led CGT, in disgust over political misuse of the union movement; yet these same workers, in their majority, continue to vote Communist in election after election because, rightly or wrongly, they believe they have no alternative.

Communism has also made many converts among the rural people, and some purely rural *départements*, like Corrèze, are among the most communized in the country. However, among the rural population Communism is clearly in decline, and although it still is estimated to hold sway over 15 per cent of the rural population, it is more and more confined to the traditionally left (though not traditionally Communist) regions.[9]

Communism also has much appeal for youth and for intellectuals, to whom it offers a "solution" for all problems. Perhaps more important, it offers them a chance for total dedication. The party, says Rossi, is a church, and its militants seem to participate in a retreat. They form a society of their own, with its own principles, hierarchy, and mores. The party is for the militant Communist the picture of the society to come, a society which he is ready, with missionary zeal, to impose on all others.[10] This is the spirit which gives the party its shock troops on whom it can count in any emergency.

---

[8] Documentary proof is presented in A. Rossi, *Les Communistes français pendant la drôle de guerre*, Paris, 1951.

[9] Gordon Wright, "French Farmers in Politics," *South Atlantic Quarterly*, Vol. LI (1952), p. 363.   [10] Rossi, *op. cit.*, pp. 302–303.

These aforementioned factors add to the strength of the Communist party of France. On the reverse side of the medal there is the complete and slavish following of every twist and turn of Russian foreign and domestic policy. There is the familiar joke about Maurice Thorez, the Communist leader: "When Stalin sneezes, Thorez catches a cold." And the same Thorez declared in 1949, ". . . in case of conflict between France and the Soviet Union the French people ought to collaborate with the troops of the Soviet Union." [11] This has caused occasional contortions and disaffections in the party. The thoroughly Moscow-oriented Communist leadership has ruthlessly purged every element that did not depend solely on Russia for each word of revelation. Even so popular a figure as Charles Tillon, a member of the Politburo and wartime commander of the Communist Resistance group, Franc-Tireurs et Partisans (FTP), and the equally popular Resistance leader of the Massif Central, Georges Guingouin, were purged and expelled. Ousted was also one of the oldest top leaders, André Marty, when he failed to toe the line. These expulsions caused arguments, even grumblings; some of the Communist Resistance veterans were reluctant to pour mud on their former idols. But all that blew over, and the basic unity of the Communist party was not shaken. Still, these and other things seemed serious enough to cause ailing party leader Maurice Thorez to return from Moscow after two years of mysterious convalescence.

Although the Communist success in France is primarily the result of domestic considerations, the Communist leadership, following Russian directives as usual, violently opposes America's present role, the North Atlantic Treaty Organization, the European Army, etc. From that they pick up occasional, non-Communist recruits—people who are worried about America's power, German rearmament, or the danger of war.

Communist-party organization begins at the local level, and its smallest and most direct part is called the cell. These cells may be organized in shops and factories, they may cover a few blocks of houses in towns and villages, or they may cover a certain area in rural regions. It is at the cell level that membership is acquired and every member takes part. Even top leaders of the Communist party must not neglect their responsibilities to their local cells.

These cells are grouped together in sections. A section may cover a town or in larger centers part of the town. In these sections too the members take an active and personal part. The sections of a *département* form a Federation, but if there are very many sections, there may be an organization of regions between the sections and the Federation. On the Federation level it is the delegates of the sections rather than the members as a whole who are active.

The delegates of the Federations meet in a national congress which elects a

[11] *The New York Times*, Feb. 25, 1949.

central committee. This in turn elects two other, smaller committees in which the actual leadership of the party is vested: a secretariat, now headed by Maurice Thorez as Secretary-General (despite his return to France, illness has kept him politically inactive), and a political bureau which contains the members of the secretariat and a number of other members. The political bureau meets at least once a week and at every meeting lays down the precise political and propaganda lines to be followed by all segments of the party. In this, it is assisted by a central political control committee, a central cadre committee, and a committee for ideological supervision. Besides the formal party organizations, there are a tremendous number of associations, clubs, and groups, many of them of the camouflaged "front" type.

The serious illness of Thorez raises imperatively the question of his successor. The deputy secretary-general, and leader of the party during Thorez's long absence, is Jacques Duclos, a clever parliamentarian. However, he committed a number of tactical mistakes when he was in charge of the party, and many observers believed that Thorez's eventual successor would be Auguste Lecoeur until the latter fell from grace. Thorez will not be easy to replace as he is genuinely popular among the Communist masses and is an effective speaker without intellectual pretensions.

The tactical line of the Communist party is of course primarily directed toward a fulfillment of the party's major political objectives: defeat of every government, weakening and destruction of the North Atlantic Alliance, prevention of German rearmament, pressure for appeasement of Russia, and the fomenting of every conceivable disaffection in France. To this end the party latches on to every controversy in order to split the other parties or the government coalition. It has been particularly expert and successful in raising the religious and school issue in order to separate the Socialists from the MRP.

Despite the fact that the Communist party is the largest and best organized party of France, and although it has the largest bloc in the National Assembly, it is nevertheless fairly ineffective and unable to make much progress toward its objectives. This is due to its isolation, which condemns it to be consistently outvoted and overruled. There may be a few Socialists who dream vaguely of some "proletarian" unity and common action with the Communists and some former third-string leaders of the MRP who would like to see the same cooperation with the Communists on social and economic issues which existed during and shortly after the Resistance period. But such people are few and ineffective. An overwhelming majority of the Socialists and MRP, as well as of all other parties, have realized that collaboration with the Communists, the "Foreign Nationalist party," as Rossi calls it, is impossible. Except for a small group of "progressists" who scarcely have an independent existence, the Communists are outvoted in Parliament, are at a disadvantage under an electoral system which gives a premium to coalitions, and find themselves equally isolated in municipal and departmental councils.

A forceful uprising by the Communists has become quite impossible since 1947, when an energetic Minister of the Interior purged the police of Communist elements and clamped down on the Communist party. Deprived of an opportunity to change the government by parliamentary or forceful means, the Communist party is largely confined to agitation and propaganda. Nevertheless the fact that one-fifth of the French population (one-fouth of the voters) gives its support to the Communists, and that most of them believe that the social and economic system of France is not viable, constitutes an element of serious weakness in the body politic of France.

THE SOCIALIST PARTY

The Socialist party of France is important but far less so than its British counterpart. The French Socialist party is beset by profound inner contradictions which handicap it in decisive moments and prevent its success. When it was unified in 1905 it was torn between the doctrinaire Marxist viewpoint of Jules Guesde and the humanitarian, reformist attitude of Jean Jaurès. It never solved this contrast but absorbed it. It has retained the Marxist phraseology of Guesde, but it has conducted the reformist policy of Jaurès. The latter makes a mockery of the party program's radical words—and so the party loses the workers who are exasperated by the vacillations and the "immobilism" of the regime and want a radical policy. But the radical phraseology frequently prevents the party from carrying through its responsible, reformist policies—and so the party loses among the more moderate elements. In fact it has steadily declined in voting strength in all national elections since 1945. Between the elections to the first and second Constituent Assemblies in 1945 and 1946 respectively, the Socialists lost nearly 400,000 votes. Between the elections to the second Constituent Assembly in 1946 and the elections to the first National Assembly of the same year, they lost over 700,000 votes; a loss of over 1,100,000 in one year. This is often called the "hemorrhage" of the Socialist party. And then between the National Assembly elections of 1946 and 1951, the party dropped another 700,000 votes. It has probably reached its more permanent level by now and is likely to remain an important political group, but the above figures give the Socialists no cause for cheering.

The Socialist party was handicapped by its association with the declining years of the Third Republic and its inadequate preparation for national defense. But on the other hand its record after the defeat of France did much to restore its reputation. The great majority of Socialist deputies and senators had voted *for* the Pétain enabling act. But thirty-seven of them, the largest group in any party (the Communists had not been "invited" by Pétain), were among the eighty who dared to vote against capitulation to totalitarianism. One year later, André Philip and Henri Ribière tried to reconstitute the Socialist party underground, but its principal leader, Léon Blum, was arrested and together with Édouard Daladier, General Maurice Gamelin, and former Air Minister Guy la Chambre, was tried before the court of Riom. Blum easily outshone his codefendants and the prosecution, and gained much prestige for his party. The party organ, *Le Populaire*, reappeared clandestinely from 1942 onward. Socialist leaders were members of the National Council of Resistance, while André Philip escaped to London and played an important role under General Charles de Gaulle. In North Africa, and later after the liberation of France, several Socialists were members of General de Gaulle's government. It was a Socialist, Félix Gouin, who succeeded De Gaulle as provisional President in January, 1946, and it was another Socialist, Paul Ramadier, who in 1947 as Premier ejected the Communists from the government, to which they were never to return. Yet another veteran Socialist leader, Vincent Auriol, became the first and much respected President of the (Fourth) Republic. A Socialist, Jules Moch, was Minister of the Interior in the critical days of 1947 and stood steadfast in the way of Communist tactics of violence and obstruction. He has earned major credit for having turned Communist violence from a danger to a nuisance.

Nevertheless, the Socialists have suffered from a dearth of leadership. Léon Blum developed from the doctrinaire, even arrogant, leader of Popular Front days into a major statesman without personal ambition, a man of profound humanitarian sentiments, conciliatory, and a realist. But he returned from German internment broken in health, too late to lead the party in the critical days after liberation and never again able to pull his full weight. His death in 1948 constituted an irreparable loss for the party. Other experienced leaders were eliminated by other causes: Vincent Auriol by becoming President of the Republic, Félix Gouin because of a financial affair, Paul Ramadier because he was twice beaten for reelection to the National Assembly. Their place was taken by less distinguished men, among whom the General Secretary of the party, Guy Mollet, ranks first.

"The Socialist party," writes Fauvet,[12] "is the only and the last one which, at least in its title, calls itself international.[13] It is, however, one of the most French of them all. In any case it has most of the good qualities but still more certainly all the faults which one generally attributes to the French." It shares the French national spirit of emphasizing reason and ideas. But it shares the French predilection for failing to check ideas against realities. The Declaration of Principles adopted by the party in 1946 and reprinted as a kind of preamble to the party statute proclaims, "The Socialist Party is an

[12] Jacques Fauvet, *Les forces politiques en France*, Paris, 1951, p. 65.

[13] The official name of the party is still Parti Socialiste, Section Française de l'Internationale Ouvrière (SFIO)—Socialist Party, French Section of the Workers' International. This refers to the Second International of the Socialist parties of the world, which has recently been reestablished.

essentially revolutionary party," and later in the same document, ". . . the Socialist Party has always been and continues to be a party of the class struggle based upon the organization of the working people."

Nothing could be further from the truth. The Socialists are mild and earnest men and women who would not dream of mounting a barricade. As Fauvet rightly stated, "The posters (of the SFIO) don't call for revolution, but for comfort." Moreover the Socialist party, quite different from its British and German prototypes, is not a workers' party. There are some workers in it, and in a very few regions like the departments of Nord and Pas-de-Calais they are represented in fair numbers. But elsewhere and in an over-all analysis, the overwhelming majority of Socialist voters come from small, rural communities, and while often impecunious are not of the working class. As for the active party members, they are mostly recruited among schoolteachers, civil servants, and other white-collar people. It is interesting to note that among the Socialist deputies and senators in parliament there are far fewer men and women of working-class origin than is the case among Communists and the MRP, even though these three parliamentary groups are of similar strength. It is true that a section of the labor movement, called General Confederation of Labor, Workers' Force (CGT, Force Ouvrière), is frequently described as a Socialist union movement. This is, however, a considerable exaggeration. Socialist party and Force Ouvrière very frequently do not see eye to eye with one another and actually have little regard for each other. Force Ouvrière may come closest to the Socialist party as compared to other parties, but it is consciously independent and does not respond to party directives.

The Socialist party (SFIO) thus presents the phenomenon of a party sincerely trying to represent the workers but actually divorced from the main currents of the workers' movement. It is, and is bound to remain, an important party, but it has made practically no dent upon the far stronger Communist party. Since Socialists and Communists compete for the same groups of the electorate in most European countries, a strong Socialist party always means a weak Communist one, or vice versa, as in France.

This situation has become much aggravated since 1947 because of the rise of a strong Gaullist movement on the right while the Communists remained strong on the left. In particular after the election of 1951 it became clear that the parties of the middle had to cooperate in order to support a government. This forced the Socialists, out of a sense of responsibility toward the preservation of the Republic to collaborate with the government. But since the left was split by the Communists, these governments were essentially governments of the right which gradually deepened their conservative tendencies. In such company the position of the Socialists was far from enviable. Their chance of recapturing the workers' vote was hardly improved by their collaboration with forces which the workers regard as their enemies. On the other hand, if the Socialists went into sharp opposition to the government as long as the Gaullists were strong, they risked making democratic government impossible and ensuring a radical change in the French form of government.

The Socialists had another possibility. They could strengthen the left-wing tendencies by adroit and intimate collaboration with the Popular Republican Movement (MRP), whose social and economic ideas are quite close to those of the Socialists. But such an alliance is made virtually impossible by another, peculiarly French, factor. The Socialists still live mentally in the world of their revolutionary phraseology. They regard themselves as the heirs of the men who made the French Revolution. In France this attitude entails a stand of hostility and suspicion toward the Catholic Church. To be left means traditionally to be hostile to or at the very least extremely suspicious of the Church. And the MRP, while not a "church party" in the narrow sense, is without doubt a primarily Catholic party. The Socialist hostility toward the Church is further heightened by the fact that public schoolteachers are the backbone of the Socialist organizations, and these schoolteachers, who are sustained by powerful organizations, regard the Catholic schools as a competition, a menace, and the embodiment of an "anti-Republican" conspiracy. This goes back to the not-so-distant days when "Catholic" and "right wing" were regarded as synonymous, and the product of a Catholic school was automatically regarded as a man of the right. The Socialists, who like most Frenchmen are deeply tied to the past, appear to be unable to free themselves and especially their teacher cadres from these deeply ingrained notions. This explains the curious fact that in all recent elections, national and local, the Socialists have collaborated much more with the very conservative Radical party—which, however, shares with them a now fairly mild version of anti-Catholicism—than with the MRP. In every party congress of the Socialists one can hear several orators intone the now well-known phrase: "Better the worst Radical than the best Popular Republican."

This conflict between Socialists and MRP was heightened by the Barangé Act of 1951,[14] which provides for a small subsidy for education in public and private schools. To throw this law into the fray was actually a Communist and Gaullist maneuver designed to split the Socialists and MRP and thus weaken the government coalition. It succeeded brilliantly. The Socialists fought the law bitterly; the MRP, whose deputies had been elected mostly from the Catholic regions, had to fight just as hard for the law or be finished politically.

The coolness between the Socialists and the MRP prevents both parties

[14] The Barangé Act provided for the extension of a modest scholarship of 1,000 francs ($3) per student and quarter, whether the student attends public or private schools. Thus four-fifths of these funds actually benefit public schools. However, the fight took on a symbolic significance.

from making a more effective fight for their social and economic aspirations. In countries like America or Great Britain, where practical considerations play a major role in politics, such a condition would not be allowed to last long. But in France, where dedication to ideas, even ideas that have few roots in social reality, is almost total, this is quite another matter.

The lowest echelon of the Socialist-party organization is the section which the party strives to establish in every town and village (*commune*). Larger cities are divided into several sections. Executive power in the section is wielded by an elected secretary and a treasurer. But frequently the sections are so weak that they cannot produce a secretary, and in that case the central leadership attempts to persuade someone in the locality to take on the job. Frequently schoolteachers are selected for this often thankless job, which increases their importance in the organization.

A *département* with at least five sections totaling a minimum of 100 dues-paying members is entitled to organize a Federation. The representative organ of the Federation is a federal administrative congress which is composed of the delegates of the sections. The number of delegates which each section is entitled to send to the congress varies according to the number of members in the sections. The Federation has its officers, secretary, treasurer, etc. It in turn elects delegates, proportional to its membership, to a National Congress which meets annually. The National Congress in turn elects an executive committee (Comité Directeur) composed of thirty-one members, no more than ten of whom may be members of parliament. The executive committee elects a general secretary and assistant general secretaries, as well as a treasurer and his assistants. The general secretary is the most important party leader, while the assistant general secretaries do the actual administrative work. The present General Secretary is Guy Mollet.

Since the National Congress meets only once a year, another body, the National Council, has been created to keep the party leaders in touch with the rank and file. It is composed of one delegate from each Federation and meets every three months or more frequently.

The effective direction of the party is supposed to lie in the hands of the executive committee. However, more than once the Socialist members of parliament or at any rate their leaders, who are actually in charge of the day-by-day political decisions, pay little attention to the will of the National Congress or the executive committee. A mixed delegation was set up to coordinate executive committee and parliamentary group—but in reality to impose the preeminence of the executive committee. This led to a great deal of friction and to the resignation of the chairman of the parliamentary group, Charles Lussy. Finally, after a four months' struggle, a compromise solution was reached which vested the more important decisions in a joint meeting of the executive committee and the parliamentary group, which is of course dominated by the deputies and senators because of their vastly larger number.

These conflicts abounded when the Socialist party participated in the government. In 1955 sixteen Socialist deputies were expelled from their party because of repeated votes against German rearmament, in spite of party decisions to the contrary. However, an eventual reintegration of the rebels is expected.

Apart from the regular party organization, the Socialists have also organized factory groups which are to serve as centers of persuasion for other workers. There are also other Socialist organizations like the Socialist Youth Movement, vacation clubs, etc. After the liberation radical elements, many of the Trotskyite variety, found their way into the Socialist Youth Movement, and in 1947 the executive committee found it necessary to dissolve the leadership of the Youth Movement. And although the movement was reorganized, it never recovered from this blow and is leading a meager existence.

While the party has some strong sections, its organization on the whole is weak. But, as has been pointed out previously, there seems to be little connection between its organizational strength and its vote. There are many areas with a small organization and a big vote, others with good organizations and a small vote. This merely emphasizes the reluctance of most Frenchmen to become members of any party.

The party's leadership is less brilliant than that of some other parties. Guy Mollet, the General Secretary, undoubtedly enjoys the greatest prestige in the party, but he is not an electrifying leader. Perhaps the ablest leader is former Minister of the Interior and War, Jules Moch, a son-in-law of the late Léon Blum. But Moch has many personal enemies in the party, and he is too much of a realist to find favor with the party's more doctrinaire wing. Mollet's predecessor, who was also the first General Secretary of the party after liberation, Daniel Mayer, enjoys high prestige as an orator and parliamentarian, but his influence is not of a major order.

But although the party has relatively few men of great national stature, it is solidly entrenched on the local level. Being old, it has many well-liked and respected men in the smaller towns of France who have become mayors, general councilors, etc., and who give a more solid foundation than the weak organization can provide. This is one of the factors which make the Socialist party (SFIO) a permanent force in the political kaleidoscope of France. It polled 14 per cent of the vote in 1951 and has a reliable enough clientele to assure that it is not likely to drop below the 10 per cent mark, and may even slightly increase. Among the galaxy of parties, a group of this kind ranks among the most important.

THE MRP

The Popular Republican Movement (Mouvement Républicain Populaire), generally referred to by its initials, MRP, is a unique phenomenon on the

French political stage. It is essentially a Catholic party although some Protestants, Jews, and even nonbelievers belong to it. But its Catholicism would not make it unique. There are Catholic parties in Belgium, Holland, Italy, and Austria, and Germany's Christian Democratic Union is predominantly Catholic. What distinguishes the MRP is that it is a party of the left in France, where Catholic and "right" have been considered synonyms for years.

The MRP is primarily a product of the underground struggle of the Resistance. However, it has its antecedents in earlier periods in men like the philosopher Lamennais, the Dominican preacher Lacordaire, the Count of Montalembert, and the Count Albert de Mun. Their aim was that the Church should inspire social legislation, but like their more conservative coreligionists, they were distrustful of the Republic. They were, as Goguel has pointed out,[15] social Christians rather than Christian Democrats. To set political forces in motion was left to Marc Sangnier and the movement Le Sillon (the furrow), which he founded in 1897. The aim of Le Sillon was a social democracy based on Christian principles. But the conservative tendencies which permeated the Vatican after the death of Pope Leo XIII caused Pius X to condemn Le Sillon. Marc Sangnier obeyed and dissolved his movement, an act which made it possible for the spirit which he had raised to succeed eventually within French Catholicism rather than outside or against it. Sangnier lived long enough to see the fruits of his endeavor.

In 1911, one year after the condemnation of Le Sillon, he and his friends founded a political movement, La Jeune République (The Young Republic), which advocated social reforms and fought against nationalism and militarism. Particularly significant was their belief in the collective action of the workers, including strikes.

This movement remained small. Only in 1919 was Sangnier elected to parliament together with a handful of others. In 1936 La Jeune République became part of the Popular Front movement.

Politically more significant were the thirteen deputies who, after the elections of 1924, formed a "group of democrats" and later that year were instrumental in founding the Popular Democratic party (Parti Démocrate Populaire). The PDP shared the ideas of the Jeune République but was perhaps a little more cautious. Although definitely a party of the left, its deputies were elected in the Catholic, traditionally conservative provinces of the West and in Alsace and Lorraine.[16] The party's efforts were aided by the Catholic publisher Francisque Gay who founded the newspaper *L'Aube* (dawn), among whose editorialists was the later MRP leader, Georges Bidault.

[15] Mario Einaudi and François Goguel, *Christian Democracy in Italy and France,* Notre Dame, 1952, p. 110.

[16] Except for the party president, Champetier de Ribes, who was elected in the Pyrenees.

Without the defeat of France and German occupation, Christian Democratic thought would probably still be represented by these two small groups. However, the Resistance period caused a complete change. Most of the Popular Democratic deputies, and all those of the Jeune République, voted against emergency powers for Marshal Pétain, percentage-wise the best record of any political party represented in parliament in those fateful days. Immediately afterward practically every Christian Democrat participated in the Resistance movement, and their importance was recognized when one of their foremost leaders, Georges Bidault, became president of the clandestine National Council of the Resistance.

Bidault, François de Menthon, Pierre-Henri Teitgen, and other Christian Democratic Resistance leaders thought in terms of a Christian alliance, but it was a young university student of Lyons, Gilbert Dru, who gave the movement its form and its direction. It was he who converted Georges Bidault and André Colin (later General Secretary of the MRP) to his idea of a large movement which was to fuse the spirit of the Resistance with that of Christianity, democracy, and social progress. In that way Gilbert Dru became the father of the MRP. However, it was not given to him to see the crowning of his work. After returning to his studies and his Resistance work in Lyons, he was arrested by the Germans and executed in 1944 in reprisal for an attack on the Gestapo.[17]

The party which emerged from these endeavors first called itself the Republican Movement of Liberation, but soon changed to Popular Republican Movement (Mouvement Républicain Populaire, MRP).

Being a new party, the MRP has placed particular emphasis on its political philosophy,[18] which it considers as of greater importance than its more concrete program.[19] It is primarily concerned with man's nature, which it conceives in traditional Christian terms as dual, spiritual and temporal, with the spiritual side being eternal and hence more important. In this dual existence man is a rational being and hence capable of being responsible for his actions. This responsibility he can fully discharge only if he is free in his full physical, moral, and mental development. The essence of the MRP philosophy is thus based on an exceedingly strong concept of liberty.

The emphasis on personal liberty is circumscribed and placed in focus by the realization, not shared by other Catholic groups, that man in modern

[17] Jean-Marie Domenach, editor of *Esprit,* has given him a deeply moving monument in his book *Gilbert Dru, celui qui croyait au ciel* (Gilbert Dru, He Who Believed in Heaven), Paris, 1947.

[18] Basic documents are Etienne Gilson, *Notre démocratie,* Paris, 1948, and Albert Gortais, *Démocratie et libération,* Paris, 1947; see also Einaudi and Goguel, *op. cit.,* pp. 123–132.

[19] This is not unusual in Europe but is totally alien to the American concept of political parties. The difference between philosophy and program may be summarized in that philosophy asks, In what do you believe? What is your concept of the world and mankind?, while the program asks, What do you want to achieve? Where do we go from here?

society is incapable of living alone. He lives in a hierarchical system of groups such as family, profession, labor union, and nation. These groups, however, exist for the individual and not the individual for them. Consequently while they are essential to the full development of the individual, they cannot demand that he surrender his essential rights to them. These considerations lead the MRP to a position which is in sharp opposition to both capitalism and socialism. It reproaches capitalism of the French version for preventing the full development of the individual by turning political democracy into a smoke screen behind which a few powerful individuals are actually in control, leaving the workers the illusion without the reality of free choice. It recognizes that in self-defense and exasperation the workers have frequently embraced Marxism, but that Marxism offers no solution and on the contrary aggravates the objectionable features of capitalism. Under the Marxist doctrine, the power of the few is even more marked in a socialist state than in a capitalist one because the various competitive groups and factors of capitalism no longer exist and the men who rule the state hold in their hands the totality of economic and political power. The MRP demands of the state that it be social, that is, mindful of the needs of social improvement, but not that it be socialist because, as Gilson put it, "Personal rights belong to persons, and to take them away from persons under the pretext of making them more secure would be a policy contrary to the very nature of things." The MRP is thus hostile to any form of statism and envisages that such aid as the state must give to the individual for his social improvements should be given through the aforementioned natural groups.

This doctrine places the MRP in opposition to the thinking of both the traditional right and left. It contrasts with the right because of its frank condemnation of capitalism and the attitude which much of French management takes toward the workers. In the eyes of the right, the MRP is simply socialistic. But it is in equal conflict with the left because it opposes the left's belief that social progress can be achieved only by endowing the state with greater power and functions. In addition, the MRP is a Catholic party and in the eyes of the left, therefore, automatically classed with the right.

Because the emphasis of the MRP doctrine is on liberty, the MRP is unreservedly democratic and republican. It wishes to see democracy extended into the economic and social field by giving the workers a share in management and the profits of labor. Management should be in the hands of an elite, but an elite to which all social groups and classes have equal access according to talent and ability. This, the MRP contends, would do away with the class struggle and free man as an individual, in the full enjoyment of his dignity. This is somewhat further spelled out in a plan submitted in the form of a bill by Paul Bacon in 1946. It proposes the creation of a new type of corporation called the Society of Work and Savings, which would be administered by a board of directors composed of representatives of the stockholders, of the workers, and of permanent consultants. Profit sharing would be applied with at least 50 per cent earmarked for the workers.

It should be emphasized that the important thing about this philosophy and program is not so much the concrete proposals, which are vague enough, but rather the endeavor to restore the dignity of the human being by giving him a fuller place in society and by making it possible for him to use his individual talents to the best advantage of himself and of society. In a country like France, where a substantial part of the population no longer believes that it can expect anything from the present political, economic, and social regime, and where even more millions feel that they are regarded as a lower type of humans by the members of a small but rich and frequently arrogant class of economic leaders, the MRP philosophy holds a promise by which the individual could labor toward social improvement without giving up his personality and without violence and revolution. It is this attitude rather than any concrete proposals which is the essential part of the Popular Republican point of view.

The MRP has never been in sole charge of the government nor has it even been its dominant force. Concrete actions to give substantive implementation to its ideas have therefore not been too plentiful. There are, however, areas in which the MRP viewpoint has made a strong impact upon the country. The Popular Republicans have been the spokesmen and spearhead of the complicated system of family allocations, which have imposed a tremendous burden on the treasury but without which a very large number of families would not have reached the existence minimum. The MRP has also been active in the support of all measures to increase and broaden social security while at the same time opposing the absorption of the independent social-security agencies into the state. Together with the Socialists, the MRP has never hesitated to press for higher wages and better working conditions and has wholeheartedly supported the principles of labor unions and of strikes.

In conformity with this attitude is also the MRP stand on the tricky school question. Unlike the traditional right, the MRP is not hostile to public education, but it emphasizes the need for private schools in order to provide a real choice between alternatives. Since the financial situation of private schools is desperate, the MRP has advocated vigorously that the state's aid to schools and schoolchildren should be distributed among both public and private schools alike. To the parties of the traditional left, this is absolutely unacceptable as a matter of principle and constitutes the chief barrier to collaboration between the Socialists and the MRP, despite a high degree of agreement between these two parties on other issues of practical policy.

The tactical situation of the MRP is a difficult one in many ways. It was propelled into national significance almost overnight. In October, 1945, it received 24.8 per cent of the national vote; in June, 1946, it emerged as the strongest party with 28.1 per cent; and in November, 1946, was still formidable with 25.9 per cent. But these results were artificial, and the MRP leadership had few illusions on that score. In 1945 and 1946 the traditional right and even the Radicals led only a shadow existence under the onus of collaborationism or too close association with the failure of the Third Republic. Many voters of the traditional right then voted MRP because that party was relatively the most anti-Communist among the "big three" of the day: Communists, Socialists, and MRP. But as soon as the right began to emerge from the debris of its past, and especially after General Charles de Gaulle organized the Rally of the French People (RPF) in 1947, many of those voters returned in droves to their more natural political habitat. The municipal elections of 1947 were catastrophic for the MRP. In cities of over 9,000 inhabitants the MRP declined from 23.8 per cent to 10.2 per cent. In Paris the party was nearly wiped out. This, however, was the nadir of its political fortunes. The decline was checked, and in the national elections of 1951 the party obtained 12.4 per cent. Since that time the RPF's disintegration and decline have undoubtedly added somewhat to the ranks of MRP sympathizers and voters, although at the time these lines are written no concrete proof of that statement can be given. However, it is quite out of the question that the MRP should return to anywhere near its strength of 1945–1946.

Although the MRP has lost half of its previous electorate, its organization and cadres have remained intact. There has been some criticism of the leadership but there have been no real opposition factions. In fact the party is remarkable for the close relationship between its leaders and the loyalty of its cadres. All this might lead to the conclusion that those voters who have remained with the MRP are strong believers in its philosophy. Their geographical distribution,[20] however, throws some doubt on this assumption. The MRP obtained its largest vote in traditionally Catholic areas. One might therefore suspect that part of the electorate is more conservative than the party itself. But this point should not be carried to extremes, for there were several Catholic groups competing for the vote of the Catholic regions and hence those who voted MRP must have been less conservative than some of their fellows. Moreover the relatively good showing of the MRP in industrial regions would indicate that it does well in areas where people are aware of social problems. Therefore it undoubtedly has a greater degree of voter homogeneity now than it had in 1945–1946, but there are enough who vote for the MRP because of its Catholic character rather than its social program to force it not to be found wanting in the struggle for the Catholic schools, or face the loss of an important segment of its electorate. This is precisely the reason why the collaboration between the otherwise logical partners, Socialists and MRP, is so difficult. The MRP has not sought the fight over the school issue, but once joined, it could not withdraw.

[20] Einaudi and Goguel, *op. cit.*, p. 186. See also François Goguel, *Géographie des élections françaises*, Paris, 1951, pp. 112–113.

Thus the MRP is in an embarrassing position. Because it is sincerely democratic and republican, it cannot usually refuse its participation in the government, for without that participation majorities could be found only by including extremists. But because the Socialists went into the opposition, the MRP was the only left party in an overwhelmingly right government. In this situation it was easily outmaneuvered and had little opportunity to realize any part of its program. It has therefore been the MRP's ambition to enter into a closer working relationship with the Socialists and to persuade the latter to return to the government. But this attempt was interrupted in 1954 when the MRP itself went into the opposition against the foreign policy of the Mendès-France government. This development has underlined the MRP's role as the chief advocate of European unity.

The organization of the MRP follows closely the general French pattern, but it has more discipline and cohesion than any other party except the Communists and, during its better days, the RPF. On the local level there are the sections, which must have at least ten members each. More important is the Federation, the organization on the *département* level, which carries major responsibility for the electoral and generally political activities of the party in the *département*. There is a departmental congress composed of the delegates of the sections, who elect an executive commission which in turn elects an executive committee, as well as specialized federal teams for such groups as women, youth, and workers.

There is an annual meeting of a National Congress composed of delegates of the Federations. The number of delegates is not entirely proportional to the number of members in the Federations in order to prevent certain Federations from dominating the entire Congress. In addition, members of the National Committee and MRP members of parliament may also vote. In order to have more frequent consultation than is possible in the Congress, there is the National Committee which meets every two months. It is composed of the MRP ministers or five former ministers, delegates of the MRP parliamentary group which must compose one-third of the membership of the committee, the delegates of the Assembly of the French Union, representatives from each Federation, representatives of the specialized teams and of the municipal and general councilors, and ten active members chosen because of their individual importance. The National Committee in turn elects a smaller body of approximately fifty persons, the executive commission. However, the president and the general secretary of the party are elected by the National Congress. Georges Bidault served as President for some time, but Art. 39 of the party statute as modified at the Congress of Nantes (1950) does not allow the president to be reelected more than three times consecutively. Bidault was therefore succeeded by Pierre-Henri Teitgen. General Secretary since the creation of the party has been André Colin.

The most significant personality of the MRP is, without doubt, Georges

Bidault, several times Prime Minister and Minister and former President of the National Council of Resistance. He is normally conciliatory, with friends and enjoys respect even among his opponents. A brilliant writer, he is a man of great intelligence, a fact of which he is quite aware. Pierre-Henri Teitgen, law professor and former Resistance leader, is probably next in line, while another law professor, François de Menthon, is now significant chiefly for his parliamentary work, but is no longer an outstanding ministerial candidate. Robert Schuman, former Premier and Foreign Minister, is highly respected but is perhaps less of a power within the party. Maurice Schumann (no relative), on the other hand, is an important party leader. A rising star is also Jean Letourneau, who for a long time occupied the extremely difficult but now abolished position of Minister for the Associated States.

Because of its Resistance work and religious character, the MRP has an abundance of talent, especially among the younger age group. André Colin is a good representative of this section of the party.

THE RADICALS

The party whose official name is Radical and Radical Socialist party (Parti Radical et Radical Socialiste) is in no way "radical" in the American sense. It is rather a conservative party and eminently respectable. Some overenthusiastic historians [21] find its origin in the French Revolution, in the society of Jacobites and the "Mountain" (*La Montagne*) of the Revolutionary convention. Nearer our own time they consider Condorcet and especially Ledru-Rollin, the leader of the Second Republic, as their precursors. However, the Second Empire put an end to this development. Only before the demise of Napoleon the Third's regime did modern radicalism begin to take shape. The declaration of Jules Simon of 1868 and especially the Belleville program of Léon Gambetta in 1869 [22] embodied the basic ideas of "radicalism": universal manhood suffrage, democratic administration, strict separation of state and church, and especially the fighting words "mandatory public, primary education free of charge" (*instruction primaire laïque, gratuite, et obligatoire*).

The Radical party made its debut in 1885 under the propulsion of Georges Clemenceau, but it was only in 1901 that the party, now officially called Radical and Radical Socialist party, organized itself in permanent form. Since then it has held an annual congress (with the exception of the two wars) every year, and it constitutes the oldest among the presently existing organized parties of France.

The Radical party is a French phenomenon which foreigners find hard to classify. First of all it is a party of personalities; it does not have and it does not wish to have a mass basis. It is built around a considerable number of

[21] Jammy Schmidt, *Les grands thèses radicals*, Paris, 1931.
[22] Albert Milhaud, *Histoire du radicalisme*, Paris, 1951, pp. 57–58.

men of high talent and long reputation in both local and national affairs. What these men have in common is not a program nor truly a doctrine but rather an attitude. This attitude may be described as republican and democratic, with no sharp distaste for anyone. Traditionally the Radicals are opposed to the Catholic church, but this opposition is now quite mild and its more militant phases have been taken over by the Socialists. In the social and economic sphere the party officially endorses the principle of reform and progress but denounces revolution. In actuality the Radicals do not believe that their acceptance of the idea of progress obliges them to endorse any particular measure or commits them to any amount of speed. Therefore in the daily parliamentary game they have usually been on the conservative side, and even such measures as the sliding wage scale, which in the United States was instituted by the General Motors Corporation, have met with the violent denunciation of the majority of Radical deputies and senators.

Because the criterion of "radicalism" is a personal attitude and not a definite commitment on program, the party has most heterogeneous elements in its midst, ranging from men who are very close to the Socialists (who are few) to outright reactionaries (of whom there are several). In fact, there is no occasion on record on which all deputies of the Radical party have ever voted on the same side.

This puts the party in a most admirable position. By its philosophy, if that term be applicable, it is a party of the left: rationalistic, humanitarian, antireligious. Consequently during elections in which general principles are primarily at stake, the Radical party forms its most effective coalitions with the Left, especially the Socialists. But in its social and economic policy the party in its great majority belongs clearly to the conservative side, and in the daily alignments of the parliamentary struggle as well as in the operation of government, it works most closely with the right. There are few other countries in which such a situation could long endure. Nothing illustrates better the utter separation between political ideas and political action in France than the success with which the Radical party continues to work both sides of the street. Auguste Maurice Barrès, famed French politician and writer, once said, "France is Radical," by which he meant that the Radical party embodies much of the spirit of France, and indeed he who can understand the Radical party already understands a great deal about France.

The unique position occupied by this party makes it an indispensable partner of any French government. If it associates itself with a government of the left, it gives it respectability by its presence. If it associates itself with a government of the right, it gives it the stamp of "progressivism," even if that is far more theory than practice. This role of the party has become even more essential since 1947, when the Communists left the government and thereby split the left, and when General de Gaulle's RPF menaced a government coalition on the right. The Radical and Radical Socialist party has thus experienced a marvelous renascence from the dark days after liberation when it seemed in hopeless decline. This decline was not so much the result of the ample number of Radicals who had collaborated with Vichy or who had at least not resisted—there were collaborators in every party—but rather because the Radicals appeared as the very symbol of the Third Republic in all its failings. One might say that the Radicals rose again as the Fourth Republic began to look more and more like the Third.

The Radical party is essentially the party of the French countryside, especially in the center and the south. It is particularly well entrenched in smaller communities, where its leaders have important positions in city halls and municipal and general councils, or are otherwise prominent.

While the party is stronger among the commercial and white-collar elements than among the peasants, it seems to be regaining a good part of the peasantry which had given its allegiance temporarily to other parties, especially to the Socialists, RPF, and even Communists. The party has maintained a considerable degree of voters' discipline. In 1951 the Radicals and their associates obtained 11.1 per cent of the vote. Their role in parliament, however, is much larger than that as the result of fortuitous *apparentements* and of their key position. They are not likely to increase or decrease very substantially, but their political power and significance have little relationship to their electoral success.

The Radical party, being a party of notables, has hardly any formal organization. Unlike the Communists, Socialists, and MRP, it has no local sections .but merely a few local committees. Far more important are the Federations, the departmental organizations, which enjoy a great deal of independence. These Federations have few members but often a considerable influence. Candidacies for public office and political combinations on the department level are their exclusive domain, and their relationship to central party headquarters is more administrative than political. The annual congress of the party, which is composed of delegates from the Federations, elects the president and certain members of the executive committee and the executive commission. The party's presidency is a position of great importance which has been held continuously since 1945 by the party's veteran leader Édouard Herriot. The actual administrative direction is in the hands of an administrative president, Léon Martinaud-Deplat, a man of great energy who may be called the real rebuilder of the party.

The executive commission, which is supposed to meet every week, is composed of seventy members. There is also an executive committee, which is actually a larger body although the opposite might be surmised from its name. It is a small congress which meets three or four times a year and is composed of all Radical members of parliament and all the general councils, as well as other members elected by the party congress. The executive committee is composed of several hundred members who, however, do not all come to meetings. For questions of pressing importance there is the Cadillac Committee (named for a town near Bordeaux), which is composed of the members of the executive commission and all Radical members of parliament. It meets only on special occasions, and decisions of the party concerning its attitude during ministerial crises are generally reached in this committee.

There is also an organization of Radical youth, but its importance is very small. The party also has a national council of Radical women, but the Radicals are traditionally reserved toward women's participation in political life, and this council's significance is therefore minor.

The Radical Socialist party has been called the party of presidents. The powerful positions of president of the National Assembly and of the Council of the Republic were for a long time in the hands of Radicals, Édouard Herriot and Gaston Monerville respectively. In addition, the Radicals have had several Premiers, among whom (since 1945) have been Henri Queuille, André Marie, Edgar Faure, René Mayer, and Pierre Mendès-France. Until his retirement in 1954, Édouard Herriot dominated the party. Several times he brought it around to his point of view by threatening to resign. This was especially so in the crisis of 1950, when many Radical deputies wanted to adhere to the principle of double membership in the RPF and the Radical party, which Herriot denounced as "bigamy." That he was proved right by subsequent events has greatly added to his already considerable prestige.

Henri Queuille, several times Premier and an experienced expert at compromise, is also very influential. André Marie and Martinaud-Duplat are other personalities of great influence, while Edgar Faure, one of the few younger. Radicals of first-rate importance, is a rising star. An unusual personality is Pierre Mendès-France, who occupies the left wing of the party. He is highly respected for his great knowledge and scrupulous honesty, but his harsh but realistic views on the remedies for France's permanent financial crisis as well as his somewhat neutralist position in foreign affairs prevented him from obtaining the Premiership until 1954, when he established one of the most controversial regimes in France's recent history. Of all the French parties, the leadership of the Radical Socialists is the most aged, though it would be going too far to speak of an absence of younger leaders. They have emerged more prominently from the roof organization, Rally of the Republican Left (RGR), which is discussed below.

THE RGR

The Rally of the Republican Left (Rassemblement des Gauches Républicaines, RGR) has been described as composed of men of the right sitting in the center.[23] It is a "roof organization" of which the Radical party forms by far the most important section. It was designed originally, in 1946, to con-

[23] Fauvet, *op. cit.*, p. 99.

tribute the youth, as well as the Resistance record, of which the Radicals stood in sore need. However, the RGR has never met with the undivided enthusiasm of the Radical leaders, and relations between the two have been strained at times. This was the result of ill-advised attempts on the part of RGR leaders to form Federations which thus came into direct conflict with the regular Radical organization. When such a Federation was established in the department of the Rhône, the fief of none other than Édouard Herriot himself, a major breakup seemed imminent, but it was avoided.

The RGR is organized along much more elaborate lines than the Radicals, and the coming and going at 7, Place du Palais Bourbon (RGR headquarters) stands in contrast to the placid if not to say mausoleumlike atmosphere of the Rue de Valois (Radical-party headquarters). The RGR undertakes very considerable propaganda activities, and Radical candidates usually run under the RGR label. The occasional tension between the two leaderships is really a controversy between two groups of leaders of the same party because most of the RGR leaders are also Radicals. This is accentuated by the personality of the RGR's president, former Premier Édouard Daladier, whose long-standing running fight with Édouard Herriot has sometimes been called "the war of the Edwards." The spark plug and administrative head of the RGR is its general secretary, Jean-Paul David, a Radical deputy and leader of the anti-Communist propaganda organization Paix-et-Liberté.

Since the RGR does not share the general Radical apprehension about women in politics, the women's section is exceedingly active and successful.

Although the Radical party contributes the bulk of the RGR, there are other groups, among which the most significant is the Democratic and Socialist Union of the Resistance (Union Démocratique et Socialiste de la Résistance, UDSR). This group, which has eleven deputies in the National Assembly, is the product of the Resistance and takes a position generally to the left of the Radicals. The UDSR is not strong nationally but has considerable support in some regions like Brittany because of certain personalities. Its outstanding leader is René Pleven, many times Premier and Minister, while another significant person is François Mitterand, who has also been in several cabinets.

The other groups which compose the RGR have little significance. They are (1) the Republican and Social Party of French Reconciliation (Parti Républicain et Social de la Réconciliation Française), whose members were formerly associated with the Fire Cross and with the French Social party of Colonel de la Rocque; [24] its most significant personality is Pierre de Leotard; (2) the Democratic Alliance of former Premier Pierre-Étienne Flandin, who has long been ineligible to parliament because of collaborationism; (3) the

---

[24] Although the Fire Cross was a fascist group, its members by and large did not collaborate, and many of them took an active part in the Resistance. Colonel de la Rocque himself was arrested by the Germans and died not long after liberation as the result of privation endured during his captivity.

Democratic Socialist party (Parti Socialiste Démocratique), which is composed of former Socialists who had collaborated with the Pétain regime, and whose leader is the former General Secretary of the Socialist party, Paul Faure; and (4) the small remnants of the Republican Socialist party (Parti Républicain Socialiste), a splinter group which finds itself somewhere between Radicals and Socialists.

The last-mentioned four organizations are composed mainly of aging, bitter men who dream of vindication but whom the country largely ignores.

"Moderates" and Independents

It is indicative of the leftist and revolutionary phraseology of France's political life that no party or political group would dare to call itself "conservative." Thus the motley group of right-wing groups and independents are called *les modérés*—the Moderates.

No group is harder to classify. It has no organization, no unified point of view, no recognized leader or leadership committee. Its vote is always split and its members adhere to no discipline. From time to time an abortive attempt is made to bring some organization into this chaos, but soon anarchy reigns again. Yet this is an important group—if it can be called a group—which commands 110 seats in the National Assembly. Without some support from it, no government can stay alive. Fauvet has well characterized it as a "floating mass."

The Moderates are by no means a new phenomenon; they have existed for over half a century. In the Third Republic they possessed a certain amount of parliamentary organization, but certainly not much. There was the Democratic Alliance, perhaps the most significant group, which never could get over the personal and political quarrel between its two most outstanding leaders, Pierre-Étienne Flandin and Paul Reynaud. There was the Republican Federation of Louis Marin. And there was the French Social party, the only one with a definite organization, which emerged from the dissolved Fiery Cross (Croix de Feu) but was more moderate than that near-fascist organization.

The war discredited the Moderates. Not all were collaborationists. Reynaud was imprisoned by Vichy and later by the Germans, Louis Marin escaped to London and joined De Gaulle, Joseph Laniel was a member of the clandestine National Council of Resistance. But the majority collaborated—or at least did not resist. Consequently in the elections of 1945 and 1946 the right had a hard time to find eligible and untainted candidates and did poorly. Many conservatives gave their temporary allegiance to the MRP.

In order to remedy the situation a number of deputies and other rightist leaders founded in 1945 the Republican party of Liberty (Parti Républicain de la Liberté, PRL), which flattered itself as being the "fourth big" (next to Communists, Socialists, and MRP). The PRL defined its aims in terms which were more middle-of-the-road than conservative, but that was in 1945–1946, when it was not the thing to be of the right. "Neither reactionary nor fascist, but strongly attached to the parliamentary regime" were the words of the party's principal spokesman, Joseph Laniel, who as a former member of the National Council of Resistance helped to make the party respectable.

Another group of the Moderates was the Peasant party. What was perhaps most remarkable about it was that it was not prominently composed of or led by peasants. Actually it was a sectional party based mostly on the Massif Central, where there is a tradition of separate political agrarian action, although it did spread somewhat into adjacent areas. Its leader and animator was Paul Antier, but the party split and lost much effectiveness even before the 1951 elections.

Because the electoral law of 1951 favored "national" parties, these moderate groups and independents found it useful to run under common labels, among which the term Union of Independents, Peasants, and National Republicans was the most frequent. Actually, however, there is now no semblance even of party organization among them.

The PRL is a matter of the past, but thirty-five deputies have accepted the label Republicans of Peasant and Social Action (Républicains d'Action Paysanne et Sociale). Other deputies are grouped under such titles as Republican Independents, Independents from Overseas (some of whom are not from overseas), etc. Actually none of these groups is organized, has any cohesion, or recognizes any leadership. They are really composed of independents, men who often have a great personal following in their departments. On the whole they are conservative in economic and social matters, and many of them are "Catholic" in the political tradition of that word in France. But some of them are not Catholic, and others hold more liberal views than some Radicals or the RGR.

The Moderates have a number of outstanding personalities, among whom former Premiers Paul Reynaud, Antoine Pinay, and Joseph Laniel are perhaps the best known.

The Gaullists

The political movement which General Charles de Gaulle created in 1947 is a personal one in every sense of the word. The Rally of the French People (Rassemblement du Peuple Français, RPF) would never have become what it was without Charles de Gaulle, but it never became what it wanted to be because of Charles de Gaulle.

The General's ideas of leadership and authority were already crystallized during his service as an instructor at the general staff college,[25] and he wrote

[25] For a good biography of De Gaulle, see David Thomson, *Two Frenchmen, Pierre Laval and Charles de Gaulle,* London, 1951.

some remarkable books on the army of the future which were avidly and profitably studied in Germany but disregarded in France. His sudden prominence as the leader of the Resistance against Germany and Vichy has already been discussed. As the symbol of France's undying spirit and will to victory, as the savior of France's honor, Charles de Gaulle has already gone into history.

The idea of a great national revival, a great rally, began to take shape during the war. It became more real after De Gaulle's abrupt resignation from his position as Provisional President on January 20, 1946. Then on March 30, 1947, in a speech at Brunval, he launched the idea of a supraparty national rally, and a few days later in Strasbourg he officially inaugurated the Rally of the French People (RPF).[26]

The program of the RPF was at all times expressed in vague and general terms. The very fact that the movement disclaimed a "program" and insisted that it had only "objectives" underlines this point. But of course vagueness of ideas has never been a detriment to a party's success in any country.

The RPF was supposed to be a movement and not a party. This meant originally that people could maintain their previous party affiliations and also belong to the RPF. But this concept never went very far, and the rigid discipline of the RPF itself deprived the principle of double membership of any real future.

The organization of the Rassemblement du Peuple Français is based on two principles, one authoritarian and one democratic. It is headed by a president elected by its National Congress, but the nature of Gaullism is such that the election of anyone other than General de Gaulle was inconceivable. The president *appoints* the executive committee known as the council of directors, and the general secretary, who is always a member of the council. The president in effect establishes the policy of the RPF with such aid from the council of directors as he wishes to obtain.

On the more democratic side of the movement, the RPF has attempted to organize groups in every canton (*groupes*) and every municipality (*section*) of France, as well as in the overseas territories. There are also separate professional organizations with their own headquarters in Paris.

On the departmental level there is a departmental council composed of forty to fifty members elected in equal numbers by the territorial subdivisions and the professional associations. In actuality the decisive element is not this elected departmental council but a departmental delegate who is appointed by the council of directors and who is a kind of party prefect. For an even tighter control the council of directors has appointed regional delegates who, like superprefects, have jurisdiction over several departments.

Once a year a national congress is convoked, which bears the somewhat

[26] Robert G. Neumann, "Formation and Transformation of Gaullism in France," *Western Political Quarterly*, Vol. VI (1953), pp. 250–274.

grandiloquent title of National Assizes. It does not really deliberate but is a demonstration, almost a parade. It elects the National Council composed of 150 members who meet every three months. However, no member of the National Council may belong to the council of directors, and since all real power belongs to the latter, the actual role of the National Council is small.

In this organizational setup it is clear that the authoritarian element far outweighs the democratic, which has added to the suspicion which General de Gaulle's opponents feel toward him and the RPF.

The core of the Gaullist "objectives" is constitutional reform. In almost every speech the General has deplored the weakness of France, the instability of her government, the uncertainty of her policy. These would be remedied by a drastic revision of the Constitution. It envisages the President of the Republic in a key position. He would be elected by an enlarged electoral college composed of members of parliament, representatives of departmental and municipal councils, as well as representatives of the economic and intellectual life of the country. The President in turn would appoint the Premier and the ministers and would play a direct role in the political direction of the country at home and abroad.

According to this plan, he would have a suspensive veto which could be overridden by parliament, but he could appeal to the final decision of the people by ordering a referendum. Whenever President and parliament did not agree and the parliament refused to give the government its confidence, the President could dissolve parliament and order new general elections. Under this plan the exact relationship between President and Premier is obscure, but there is little doubt that the presidency, which the General had obviously reserved for himself, was to be the dominant position.

The present National Assembly would be retained, but its legislative initiative would be curbed, especially in matters of appropriation and budget. The Council of the Republic, on the other hand, would be more drastically changed to be more representative of areas and professions and would be divided into a political council and an economic and social council.

Compared to the pivotal importance of these constitutional ideas, the vague economic and social concepts of the RPF take a much less significant place. In the field of social and economic reform the movement has a project called "Association of Capital and Labor," an idea which originated in the Resistance. Briefly stated, the principal purpose of the association project is the elimination of the traditional forms of the class struggle and the customary European method of collective bargaining between unions and employers' federations. Instead, each plant would constitute one bargaining unit in which employers and employees would deliberate on an equal footing about the division of profits and wages. For this purpose a production council would be established consisting of the elected representatives of the various groups of employers and employees. The net profits would be distributed among employers and employees in the proportion envisaged by the original contract between them which established the association. Management would otherwise be in charge of all managerial functions, but the production council would be kept fully informed about the whole economic picture of the enterprise. This plan was not intended to be compulsory at first but was to be tried out in the form of voluntary pilot projects with a view to establishing associations eventually in every plant.

The vagueness of the RPF "objectives" was the expression of a hope for a broad national front in which men of different political philosophies could unite. There is little doubt that it had much appeal at first among the growing number of people who were weary of governmental instability and inaction. To them must also be added the appeal of De Gaulle's *mystique,* the liberator, and the RPF's vociferous anticommunism which gained many adherents on the right.

So the RPF got off to an excellent start. In the municipal elections of 1947, when it was only half a year old, it obtained 28.1 per cent of the vote in cities over 9,000, and coalition lists which it sponsored won 10.6 per cent more. It won majorities or pluralities in all the larger towns of France, including those of industrial regions like Marseille and St.-Étienne. A comfortable majority was won in Paris. The cantonal elections of 1949 confirmed and broadened this victory.

But these victories were a trifle Pyrrhic. They alarmed the government parties and started them on the way to a reform of the electoral law which was designed to make impossible an RPF or Communist victory. Moreover the rapid rise of the RPF gave little opportunity for integrating the masses and especially the many councilors who had been elected under the RPF label. The headquarters of the movement often tried to reassert discipline, sometimes without too much tact, and some hurt feelings and "alienation of affection" resulted. Some city councilors who had come from the traditional right acted in their accustomed independent ways as if they had never heard of the RPF and its principles.

This situation caused General de Gaulle to decide that no one was to be allowed to enter the 1951 elections under the RPF label who would not be willing to bow to party discipline. As a result, the RPF went into the arena alone in most of France and therefore did not benefit by the electoral law.

The outcome of the elections was a disappointment to the RPF. True, it obtained over 4 million votes (21.5 per cent) and entered the National Assembly with the largest bloc of deputies (119). But it had failed to gain enough to make a government without it impossible. Consequently its leadership set to work to prove that no government could exist in France without it by letting no opportunity pass to oppose and obstruct the government. But this proved the undoing, not of the government, but of the RPF, for after the elections the traditional right had a position of greater importance in parliament, and consequently those RPF deputies who had originally come from the traditional right looked upon these governments with a spirit of affinity and resented De Gaulle's policy of intransigent opposition.

This development came to a head on March 6, 1952, when twenty-seven RPF deputies voted for the investiture of conservative Premier Antoine Pinay. This group enlarged in subsequent votes, and all attempts of the RPF leadership to reassert party discipline failed. When General de Gaulle refused to change his policy, the dissident deputies, among whom were several prominent leaders like Edmond Barrachin and General Bilotte, separated themselves from the RPF and formed their own parliamentary group, which they called "Independent Group of Republican and Social Action" (Groupe Indépendent d'Action Républicaine et Sociale), henceforth to be known as the ARS, which organized itself with thirty deputies. Similar splits occurred in the Council of the Republic and in many city councils, including that of Paris.

The lessons of the split did not seem to be entirely lost on the RPF chiefs. Barring unforeseen events, such as war, the party's road to leadership seemed permanently closed. This led at first to some indecisive moves. The RPF had gained electoral victories in 1951 in many, but not all, of the traditionally "right" departments, but it had also gained much in some of the traditionally left ones, so its claim that it was not merely a party of the right seemed substantiated. Since these defections had occurred mainly on the right, the National Congress held in Paris in November, 1952, had decidedly leftist overtones, and one of the more tempestuous RPF leaders, René Capitant, even went so far as to defend Marx and to attempt a reconciliation between Marxism (but not Leninism-Stalinism) and Gaullism.[27]

While the party Congress veered to the left, the parliamentary group veered to the right. In a hard-fought battle the "participationists" won over the "orthodox" and decided to support (but not to enter) a government, that of Radical René Mayer. However, this decision was not enough to halt the RPF's decline. A party of malcontents which finds itself barred from power cannot long maintain its strength. Several by-elections had shown that the RPF strength was waning. The municipal elections of April, 1953, dealt it a resounding defeat.

It is a curious sidelight on General de Gaulle's character that he saw the disaster coming and did nothing to halt it. He refrained assiduously from endorsing any candidates and chose this crucial time for his party to make an extended pilgrimage to the hallowed grounds of Fighting France in Africa.

After the election, on May 6, 1953, General de Gaulle issued a declaration [28] in which he castigated both right and left for having forsaken him and announced peremptorily that henceforth the RPF would participate in no further elections. Members of the movement could run for office, if they chose,

---

[27] For the text of Capitant's speech see *Le Monde,* Nov. 12, 1952.
[28] For the text see *Le Monde,* May 8, 1953; also Neumann, *op. cit.,* p. 271

but not under the RPF label. Those who were already elected were given their "freedom of action" but were forbidden to continue the RPF designation.

The RPF parliamentary group did not have the slightest idea what to do with this unwelcome "freedom," but, faithful to the General's command, they renamed their group in parliament Union of Republicans of Social Action (Union des Républicains d'Action Sociale), abbreviated by the initials URAS, and later called themselves simply Social Republicans (Républicains Sociaux). But although their leaders urged the deputies to remain united, it seems fairly clear that they will eventually split, one group joining the Independents, another the RGR, with a core of the faithful remaining together and tentatively looking for some ties with the left.

What De Gaulle intended with this startling decision is not easy to determine. Very likely he looked upon himself as a national resource for France in times of need—war (which he anticipates). His luster has been dimmed by the necessary deals and compromises of the parliamentary game. If he is yet to lead a nonpartisan national rally he must not again be embroiled in the factional fights of the legislative assembly. Perhaps if other party leaders did not have RPF candidates to oppose them in their electoral districts, they would be readier to join another national rally. In the meantime, the RPF attempts to make contacts with the non-Communist left, Socialists, MRP, and some Radicals, as well as with the union movements Force Ouvrière and the Catholic CFTC. But these attempts have shown little success, and while the Gaullists are still a powerful group their future is most uncertain and their decline more than probable.[29]

The Future of the French Party System

The French party system presents a peculiar contrast. There is perhaps no other country in whose party councils there is so much intelligence, youth, and real ability. Almost every one of the parties could give the country fairly good leadership. But together they cancel one another out and the result of all their talent comes to nought.

Is this situation likely to undergo a drastic change? Is a two-party system, or at least one of fewer parties, possible? One in which coalitions might be stronger and more permanent, and government longevity greater? Unfortunately the evidence does not point in that direction. True, there are elections and there are slight shifts in the strength of the respective parties. But although they may lose or gain a not insubstantial number of votes, each one of them can count on a certain part of the electorate who will support them in every election, come what may. And the sum total of these "reliable clien-

---

[29] Several minor RPF-URAS deputies entered the Laniel government in 1953, but they were read out of their party. Gaullist participation in the Mendès-France government of 1954 was more official.

teles" embraces so large a section of the electorate that no party may hope for a majority. That the short-lived rise of the RPF was unable to change this fundamental fact is an indication of how firmly this principle is established. The Communists can apparently count on one-fourth to one-fifth of the electorate, which narrows down considerably the range of parties and votes among which a majority may be found.

In order to find solutions for France's numerous and onerous problems, no hope can be placed in the ability of any party, existing or yet to be created, to lead France out of her predicaments. The only solution lies in the willingness of a sufficient number of political leaders and groups to agree on the stern measures necessary to put France on the road to recovery. But such measures might easily lead to the defeat of the parties and leaders advocating these very measures, and self-sacrifice is not a notable political virtue in any country. It is for instance no secret in France that her taxation system is ineffectual and, by placing major emphasis on indirect taxation, unjust. But to adopt an efficient and enforced system of income taxation, as in the United States, would deal a severe blow to the rural population (where virtually no direct taxes are paid) and to people engaged in business, commerce, and the professions (where tax fraud is a recognized fact). Even if such a change were feasible,[30] it would be hard for any coalition to undertake it if that coalition were, as it is now, supported primarily by those groups which would be the first to be hurt. That is why it is possible to say that although France's crisis is economic, social, and military, it is primarily political.

[30] It has been estimated that if France turned to a more vigorous system of income taxation the total revenue would temporarily decline because so many Frenchmen live close to the existence minimum and hence would not be required to pay income taxes.

Part III. GERMANY

Denk ich an Deutschland in der Nacht,
Dann bin ich um den Schlaf gebracht.
(Nights when I think of Germany
Sleep is impossible for me.)
HEINRICH HEINE

THE UNCONDITIONAL surrender of Germany in May, 1945, brought about her temporary demise as a state. The four principal Allies took over all power. Only on the lowest levels of administration did they permit any kind of German government, and that only under rigorous control.

The development of the last five years must have come as a surprise to those who in 1945 believed that Germany could be written off as a powerful nation and a principal factor in international politics. Today Western Germany, the German Federal Republic whose creation is associated with the name of its present capital, Bonn, is the largest state of Continental Europe in terms of inhabitants, outside the Soviet Union. Her industrial potential, "know-how," and organization are unequaled anywhere outside the United States. With her regained strength and her diligent, disciplined—perhaps too disciplined—people, Germany is a powerhouse of the first magnitude for whose favor East and West vie alike.

Everything that happens in Germany has profound repercussions in the world at large, because in the contest between the Soviet world and the Western states, the mastery of Germany is today the principal prize. Under the impact of war and catastrophe the idea of a United Europe has found a great many new adherents, but it is clear to anyone that no such unity is feasible unless Germany, at least Western Germany, plays a decisive role therein. Yet Germany's recent history is a cause for justified discomfort to many, and her internal regime is therefore a major consideration for the assessment of her future role in Europe and the world. It is difficult to forget that Germany, despite her great cultural tradition and her highly developed educational system, threw herself into the arms of one of the most brutal dictatorships that history has ever recorded.

The student of government will notice another item of importance. Germany has become a laboratory of political ideas, plans, and institutions. Here is a country in which a veritable social revolution has been attempted from the outside and by decree. Here is a state in which radically new institutions struggle hard with the customs and prejudices of the past, and here one may study intricate political and constitutional schemes from the blueprint stage up to actual operation and may note the imponderables and problems which emerge in that process. Germany's constitutional fabric, the nature of her parties, and the maturity of her people are problems of world importance.

Much of the recent development of Germany is highly encouraging. Her government has proved the most stable of Europe. Her currency is one of Europe's most reliable. Her economic recovery has been stupendous, and even the tremendous stream of refugees and expellees has been largely absorbed by hard work and sacrifice shared by the entire population. Perhaps most encouraging to the foreign observer is the fact that extremist groups, both Communist and neo-Nazi, have remained so small as to be insignificant. Under the leadership of Chancellor Konrad Adenauer Germany has resolutely taken her place on the side of the West, while the numerous uprisings and revolts in Eastern Germany, especially in 1953, have unmistakably demonstrated where those people would stand if they were only given an opportunity to express themselves.

The late Joseph Stalin is reported to have said: "Without Germany we cannot win, and with Germany we cannot lose." The essential correctness of this analysis remains uncontested.

Chapter 1

HISTORICAL INTRODUCTION: FROM THE HOLY ROMAN EMPIRE TO THE SECOND *REICH*

In the ever-changing maelstrom of human history, mankind has never again seen as long, as glorious, and as relatively stable a period as the 700-odd years of the great Roman Empire. Even after it had passed into history, its memory as the lost "golden age" haunted mankind. It inspired philosophers and theologians, and it soon inspired princes and rulers. And when on Christmas Day, A.D. 800, Charlemagne was crowned emperor by Pope Leo III, it seemed to many contemporaries that the great Roman Empire had been revived with even greater glory. That proved to be an illusion.

The "Holy Roman Empire," as this concoction was to be miscalled,[1] had little in common with its great predecessor, despite periods of undoubted greatness. More than that, the results of the thousand years of this Holy Roman Empire proved generally unfortunate for Germany. The process of national consolidation which must precede the establishment of constitutional government [2] was delayed for centuries; and while the German emperors pursued the elusive myth of the *Reich* [3] in Italy, they lost the reality of the German state to the nobles at home. No truer words were spoken than the indictment that world history has rarely witnessed "a more tragic error in judgment, tenaciously upheld as a tradition fraught with frustration and futility." [4]

[1] It was German rather than Roman, and an aristocratic republic rather than an empire. Its "holiness" may also be doubted.

[2] Carl J. Friedrich, *Constitutional Government and Democracy,* Boston, 1946, p. 8.

[3] The term *Reich* has always confounded the interpreter. Derived from the Latin word *regnum,* it means more than "empire," "commonwealth," or "state." In it is embodied the dream of Germany as the hub and heart of occidental civilization, of a commonwealth which is both of the realm of reality and of the realm of idea. It is a term which embodies essentially an historical myth rather than a constitutional or territorial entity. It is significant that the father of the German Constitution of 1919, the then Minister of the Interior, Hugo Preuss, rejected the suggested term "German Federation" and insisted on the retention of the word *Reich* because of the traditional and emotional value attached to that term in the minds of the German people. The original term *Reich* will therefore be used in this discussion, and no further attempt at translation will be made.

[4] Karl Loewenstein, "Government and Politics of Germany," *Governments of Continental Europe,* edited by James T. Shotwell, New York, 1940, p. 285.

Feudalism

While other less ambitious rulers consolidated their dominions and gradually brought the reluctant nobles under their eventual control, the German medieval emperors chased the elusive dream of a universal empire and neglected their own back yard. Even the greatest and high-minded among them, like Otto the Great, Frederick I (Barbarossa), Henry VI, and the strangely fascinating Frederick II, were essentially dreamers and visionaries. Faced by the alternative of abandoning their Italian campaigns or allowing their chief rivals in Germany, hereditary lords like the Welfs, to consolidate their power, the emperors chose the latter.[5] Thus, while the royal judges in England eliminated feudal justice, the dominant law of Germany was territorial law (*Landrecht*),[6] and the dominant power was that of the barons. In that manner, because of a tragic historical error, constant obstacles were erected to the gradual, natural growth of national unification and the creation of a true state. When unification did come in 1871, it came suddenly, violently, and by government fiat, not by evolution. This peculiar development in German history merits special notice because it embodies the root of many later developments which have so very greatly disturbed the rest of the civilized world.

Because territorial power was dominant, and not imperial power, the holders of the imperial crown frequently sought to increase their power by accumulating lands and wealth for their own family interests. This was the policy of dynastic power (*Hausmacht*) in which the Hapsburgs especially excelled, primarily by means of opportune marriages.

The last official flicker of the Holy Roman Empire's life was extinguished only in 1806, but it came to a virtual end as a result of the Reformation and the Thirty Years' War. This war provided a period of such bloodletting, devastation, and disintegration as the world had never seen before, and with which only the Second World War could be compared. While England and France were reaching new heights of power and consolidation, Germany experienced an age far darker than any medieval mind could have conceived. Above all, Germany emerged weaker and further removed from unity than ever.

The Westphalian peace (1648), which concluded the great war but otherwise settled nothing, restored a semblance of imperial institutions, but they

---

[5] Officially recognized by the "Statute in favor of the Princes" (*statutum in favorem principum*) of 1232 and the *Confoederatio cum principibus ecclesiasticis* of 1220. Cf. Claudius von Schwerin, *Grundzuege der deutschen Rechtsgeschichte*, Berlin, 1941, 2d ed., pp. 141, 200.

[6] Most prominent exposition of both *Landrecht* and the law of feudal relationships (*Lehnrecht*) is the *Saxon's Mirror* (*Sachsenspiegel*) written by Eike von Repgow between 1198 and 1235.

had ceased to exist for all practical purposes, and they evaporated under the hammer blows of Napoleon's victorious armies.

THE RISE OF PRUSSIA

What was significant in the period between 1648 and 1806 was the final decline of Austria, the holder of the imperial crown, and the ascendance of that country which is usually regarded as the embodiment of all that is undesirable in the German character—Prussia.

Prussia was a relative newcomer to German history. Long after the establishment of the Holy Roman Empire, the central and eastern portion of the territory which later became Prussia was inhabited by lawless, pagan tribes of predominantly Slavic origin, called "Pruzzen." [7] They lived mainly from pillage and were a scourge upon their neighbors, especially the far more civilized Poles. Attempts to Christianize them failed. Then the Polish Duke Conrad of Masovia appealed for help to Hermann of Salza, Grand Master of the Order of Teutonic Knights, whose well-trained "elite guard" defeated the aborigines in a series of battles (1226 to 1283) and absorbed their territory. To consolidate it further, they inaugurated a period of forceful "Christianization," and used the pagan character of most of the inhabitants as a convenient excuse for separating them from their possessions. Germanic settlers were also encouraged to acquire homesteads. This was accomplished with particular efficiency in East Prussia, where the Germans became the masters and the original inhabitants became their servants—a process which has characterized all colonizations.

The Order of Teutonic Knights was defeated by an alliance of its neighbors with the Prussian nobles at the battle of Tannenberg (1410) and was saved from total annihilation only by the diplomatic skill of its chief (*Hochmeister*) Henry of Plauen. After a new revolt of the Prussian nobles, who obtained help from Poland, the Order ceded West Prussia and Ermeland to Poland and retained only East Prussia as a Polish fief. Thus was created the "corridor" problem which later plagued German-Polish relations.

Last *Hochmeister* of the Order was Albert of Ansbach, a member of the Hohenzollern family, who renounced his Catholic faith in 1525, became a Protestant, and was created first duke of Prussia by his uncle, the king of Poland. In 1618 the duchy of Prussia and the margravate [8] of Brandenburg were united to form the nucleus of the later Prussian power. Other territory

[7] Even the name of the capital city, Berlin, is of Slavic (Wendish) origin, meaning "dam."

[8] *Mark* was the old Germanic word for frontier. Later it prefixed the name of special frontier counties, especially *Mark Brandenburg;* the rulers thereof were known as *margrave (Markgraf)*; in the latinized form they were called *comes marchae* or *marchisus,* from which the word "marquis" is derived.

was gained in 1648 as a result of the Westphalian Peace, and in 1660, Frederick William, the "Great Elector," [9] forced Poland to renounce its nominal overlordship over Prussia. He also obtained other territory, especially in the Ruhr. His son, Frederick, was the first to become King of Prussia (1701).

Quickly, Prussia shed the remaining vestiges of feudalism. The nobility (*Junkers*) [10] was deprived of its remaining independence but compensated by superior positions in the newly formed professional army. Frederick William I (the "Soldier King") forged the Prussian army, which descended upon an unsuspecting Europe as an instrument of terrible efficiency when led by Frederick II, called by all Germans "the Great." It was this Frederick who began the long power struggle with Austria which eventually ended in Austria's defeat. Casting aside all inconvenient treaties, agreements, or promises, Frederick embarked upon a course of naked power politics which succeeded merely in eliminating whatever unity had remained in Germany. Prussia itself did not gain from the struggle. There is a strange parallel between the Prussia of Frederick II and the Germany of both the Kaiser and Hitler. In order to dominate the scene, he entered into various alliances, especially with France, until both friend and foe suspected his motives with good reason and ganged up on him. As he thus faced an "encirclement" of his own making, Frederick, luckier than his later imitators, was miraculously saved by the death of an enemy (the Empress Elizabeth Petrovna of Russia) and the coming to power of an admirer (Tsar Peter III) at the very moment when his position seemed practically hopeless.[11]

Frederick II was an absolute ruler, a king-dictator. His ministers and generals were merely his secretaries and lieutenants. But it is significant to note that his absolutism was not usually arbitrary. He continued and expanded a most efficient and incorruptible civil service, which, together with the army, was the mainstay of his rule. He alone made the laws, but once made, they were observed by all, including the king. To a more modern generation, the distinction between arbitrariness and law-abiding absolutism may seem ex-

[9] In the Holy Roman Empire the emperors were elected by the principal barons of the realm, who were therefore called "electors" (German, *Kurfürsten*). After 1257 there were seven of them; the Archbishops of Mainz, Trier, and Cologne; the King of Bohemia; the Duke of Saxony; the Margrave of Brandenburg; and the Palatine of the Rhine.

[10] From the Middle High German *junc-herre* (young master). Originally used for the sons of princes and rulers, the name *Junker* (pronounced "yoonker") later covered the Prussian nobility, especially of the agrarian and military type.

[11] The ideas and the deeds of Frederick II have always had a powerful influence on German psychology. Few other historical figures embody the spirit of the German state more than this man who always wrote, and mostly spoke, French and who had a profound contempt for German culture. The last trace of the "Frederick psychosis" occurred in April, 1945, in the final days of the Nazi regime, when Hitler and Goebbels hoped that the death of President Roosevelt might have the same results for them as the death of the Empress Elizabeth had for Frederick II. See H. R. Trevor-Roper, *The Last Days of Hitler*, New York, 1947, p. 100.

ceedingly fine. But in those days, the knowledge of where one stood, and what one's rights were, was a distinct advantage.

The people of Prussia took to this idea of "law and order" which gave the subject few rights but allowed him to sleep peacefully in his bed if he had obeyed all laws and commands. Thus the Prussian state was able to unify into a solid phalanx its army, its civil service, and its people and to create for them the idea of the state as an authority (*Obrigkeitsstaat*) which takes care of all matters and supplies all the answers. In this manner, Prussia was able to preserve its state and crown despite revolution and violent upheaval elsewhere. It protected its citizens from the bloodshed and horror of the French Revolution, but it also prevented them from absorbing any "radical" ideas about popular sovereignty, self-government, and the rights of man. When Napoleon's armies occupied large parts of Germany, the fresh air of French progressivism could not be entirely excluded. But such ideas were confined to intellectuals and some dissident members of the middle and upper classes. The large masses of the people were not affected. Thus the frequently heroic struggle which culminated in the unsuccessful revolution of 1848 was in fact stillborn, and left hardly a dent on the body politic. After making some initial concessions to the revolutionaries, the king had no difficulty in breaking his word and returning to the old ways with a vengeance. Had the revolution been a true popular movement, he could not have afforded to do so, but he gauged the temper of the Prussians more correctly than did the well-meaning intellectuals who gathered at St. Paul's Church in Frankfurt.[12]

Once Prussia had successfully survived numerous defeats at the hand of Napoleon and had overcome the revolutionary wave which swept over Europe, it could now undertake its final task—the conquest of hegemony in Germany. This meant eliminating its archrival, Austria.

THE GERMAN CONFEDERATION

The Congress of Vienna had given some lip service to the idea of German unity by creating the German Confederation in 1815 under the perpetual chairmanship of Austria. The Confederation was equipped with a parliament [13] but found it impossible to provide effective government in the face of a unanimity rule and the necessity for relying upon the individual states for carrying out its decisions. The "revolutionary" assembly of 1848 was a remarkably liberal body, and the federal constitution it drew up was an excellent instrument—on paper. But it had neither the power nor the courage to go beyond a demand for a constitutional monarchy. When Austria objected to the whole idea, the crown was offered to Prussia, only to be con-

[12] The meeting place of the so-called "German National Assembly" on May 18, 1848.
[13] Its members were appointed by the princes.

temptuously refused by Frederick William IV because it was "infected with the malodorous aroma of revolution." Prussia wanted the crown, all right. But its king wanted to be a German Frederick II, not a German Louis Philippe.

BISMARCK

Nevertheless, this development did not leave even Prussia, the fortress of reaction, entirely untouched. Constitutional reforms were grudgingly granted. But when the parliamentary majority refused to sanction the government's military reform, the Prime Minister, Otto von Bismarck, decided to reverse the process of constitutional government by ignoring the will of the legislature and forcing through his entire program. Against the solid opposition of the crown, the army and the civil service, only full-fledged revolution could have changed the course of events. But the Germans had little gumption for that, and thus a weak-kneed, halfhearted liberalism was brought to bay for the second time. Whatever opposition remained was virtually obliterated by Bismarck's victorious wars of aggression against Denmark (1864) and Austria (1866), which apparently proved him right.

The removal of Austria from leadership in Germany opened the way toward the final aim of Prussian hegemony. It closed Germany to the mellowing influence of the old, cosmopolitan, and easygoing Austria and heralded in the development which transformed all Germany into a greater Prussia. Yet, without this development, no unified Germany would have been possible. For Austria, this monstrous conglomeration of discordant lands, languages, and cultures, fused together by a long series of opportune marriages, was visibly decaying; it could not lead itself, let alone lead Germany. The Austrian empire, unable to emulate the development of the British Commonwealth, appeared as a relic of the past which could not long prevail.

THE NORTH GERMAN FEDERATION

After Austria's elimination, a new organization was created under Prussian leadership—the North German Federation. Its constitution came into effect on July 1, 1867. In contrast to the impotent German Confederation, the North German Federation had all the earmarks of a true state. It provided for a Federal Council (*Bundesrat*) composed of delegates from the various state governments and bound by their instructions, as well as a Diet (*Reichstag*) elected by universal manhood suffrage. The executive power was vested in the King of Prussia, whose Prime Minister, Bismarck, was the actual master of the federation.

The scope of Bismarck's domain was soon widened. The south German states were brought into ever closer ties with Prussia, a move which was greatly aided by the approaching conflict with France. Bismarck "edited" the dispatch of Ems relating the conversations between King William of Prussia and the French ambassador, Benedetti, in such a way as to show that an unseemly insult had been inflicted upon the aged sovereign, and he achieved the desired result of solidifying all German public opinion behind the impending Prussian action. In the ensuing war, France was quickly defeated, and the unity of German armed action was soon transformed into permanent political ties. On the basis of previous agreement, King William was crowned German emperor on January 18, 1871, in the magnificent hall of mirrors of Versailles palace, before the princes and military leaders of Germany.

The German Empire

Thus was created the second *Reich*. It was an achievement of Bismarck and his aides, of the nobles, and of the military and civil service. It was not an achievement of the people acting as an independent force. Henceforth the greatness and glory of Germany was forever associated with the throne and the reactionary political and military leaders. The courageous men who fought the forces of absolutism, in order to bring Germany into line with democratic and constitutional developments in other parts of Europe and America, were constantly forced to defend themselves against the accusation of being traitors to the reborn idea of the *Reich*. This proved too great a handicap, and it has never been fully overcome to this very day.

Chapter 2

GOVERNMENT AND POLITICAL LIFE IN IMPERIAL GERMANY

According to the preamble of the imperial Constitution, adopted on April 16, 1871, the new empire was a "permanent federation" established between the King of Prussia in the name of the North German Federation, and the other kings and potentates of the various German states. This federation was to be called the German *Reich*, and the King of Prussia was to be its presiding officer with the title of German Emperor. In reality, however, the Constitution created a true federal state under Prussian hegemony.

PREDOMINANCE OF PRUSSIA

The Emperor derived his real power from his position as King of Prussia. With few exceptions the chief minister of the realm, the *Reich* Chancellor, was usually also Prussian Prime Minister. Prussia dominated the more important upper house of parliament, the *Bundesrat*, and the *Reich* bureaucracy was predominantly Prussian. Despite its vaunted objectivity this bureaucracy knew how to hamstring non-Prussian officials and it was always primarily Prussian and reactionary. During the Weimar Republic it never became truly republican and chose to conceive its "neutrality" as also including neutrality toward the republican form of government.

Nevertheless the imperial regime does not easily fall into any of the current classifications of government. Despite the existence of a freely elected parliament under universal manhood suffrage, it was certainly no democracy. But neither was it a dictatorship, as even so imperious a figure as Bismarck was not unchecked. Nor was it an autocracy in the same sense as Imperial Russia was. Nor was it centralist, for true federalism existed. Imperial Germany was an oligarchic regime ruled by a combination of the Emperor and his court, the high civil service, the nobility, the military, and to a much lesser extent certain economic interests. It operated on a basis of complicated interrelationships which worked fairly well as long as the hands of a virtuoso, Bismarck, guided them, but which broke down increasingly in the fumbling hands of his inferior successors.

Emperor and Chancellor

While the Emperor's prerogatives were modest in his imperial capacity, he was all-powerful as King of Prussia. Through the dominating position of Prussia in the *Bundesrat* he could push or block any legislation, but as Emperor he had no veto. The military organization was entirely in his hands, completely removed from parliamentary control. In the conduct of foreign affairs he had as strong a voice as he cared to make it. His was the dominant influence after the dismissal of Bismarck until the ascendancy of Ludendorff and the Great General Staff in 1916.

The important role of the *Reich* Chancellor is underlined by the fact that no act of the Emperor was valid unless countersigned by the Chancellor. All other ministers were merely department heads and strictly inferior to the Chancellor. No true cabinet existed. But on the other hand the Chancellor was solely responsible to the Emperor, on whose confidence he completely depended. Even as great a statesman as Bismarck could not prevail against the displeasure of the less-than-mediocre Wilhelm II.

The Federal Council

The upper house of parliament, called Federal Council (*Bundesrat*), was composed of the representatives of the various state governments. The representations of the states were unequal: Prussia, by far the largest state, predominated with seventeen votes out of sixty-one, plus the single vote of Waldeck and the three votes of Alsace-Lorraine which Prussia commanded. Moreover Prussia could usually be sure of enough additional votes to have her way. She also presided over the Federal Council, and in that capacity was always able to introduce such legislation as was desired by the *Reich* government.

The members of the Federal Council, although legislators while in the *Bundesrat*, were cabinet ministers or high civil servants in their respective states. Hence, a wealth of experience was assembled there which quickly outshone the lower house of parliament. The cooperation between the *Reich* government and the Federal Council was therefore close, especially as both came essentially from the same social and professional groups and spoke a common language. Since the sessions of the Federal Council were not public and since the members of the Council were solely responsible to the princes and governments of the states, not to the people therein or their representatives, it presented a picture of admirable harmony—from which the people were strictly excluded.

THE REICHSTAG

Article 4 of the Constitution provided that Federal Council and *Reichstag* should be coequal, but that was a conspicuous piece of make-believe. Elections to the *Reichstag* were generally clean and fair, except that the majority system in single-member districts with runoff elections worked against the Socialists, who rarely found coalition partners to help them in the runoff. And of course women could not vote in those days.

The members of the *Reichstag* could question members of the government and of the Federal Council, and they in turn had the right to attend the meetings of the *Reichstag* and its committees and be heard there. But with all this paraphernalia of representative government the *Reichstag* lacked the two things most vital to a true parliament: power and responsibility. The executive branch of the government was in no way responsible to the *Reichstag*. The *Reich* Chancellor and the cabinet were responsible to the Emperor alone, and he to no one. If the government answered questions by deputies it did so condescendingly, as a matter of privilege, not of right. Nor could a vote of nonconfidence or censure oust a government. In the United States too, executive and legislature are separated but they are coequal, and without legislative cooperation no executive can get very far. The German Emperor and his government, however, would tolerate no interference on the part of the *Reichstag*. Even in the field of appropriations the *Reichstag* could not reduce the sums demanded: it could only accept or reject them, and the latter was not seriously attempted. Even in its proper field of legislation the *Reichstag* found itself sidetracked by the Federal Council, in which the government introduced all its legislation. And any legislation proposed by the *Reichstag* could be vetoed by the Federal Council, in which the government, through its command of the Prussian seats, dominated the scene.

Politically the *Reichstag* was a dead-end road. Until 1917 no *Reich* Chancellor was ever selected from the *Reichstag*, nor were any other ministers until the final days of the regime. There was no "government party" and hence no official opposition. When support was needed the government might, on occasion, make certain concessions to certain leaders or groups, but that did not entitle them to a seat in the inner councils of government. Moreover the *Reichstag* knew very well that the government would not hesitate to use force to have its way if it considered it necessary, as it had done on several occasions. And the temporary but unsuccessful suppression of the Social Democratic party on obviously fictitious charges served as an object lesson.

Deprived of any active role, the *Reichstag* could act only in a negative fashion: it could say "No." But even that was difficult because of the disunity which existed in its midst and because of the absence of strong popular support. Deprived of any real role, the *Reichstag* would engage in petty politics and endless debate while the real decisions were taken elsewhere. This gave it that terrible cognomen of "gossip club" (*Schwatzbude*) which accompanied it throughout its history and made it so very difficult for the Germans to understand parliamentary government.

Responsibility for this state of affairs must be shared by the government, which did not wish democratic government, by the *Reichstag* itself, which was incapable of achieving the degree of unity necessary to make a strong stand, and by the German people in general. The Germans, by and large, were not conscious of living under a semiautocratic regime and of lacking many of the political freedoms which were customary in Western Europe. The ingrained acceptance of authority which is so carefully built up in German schools and homes, and which still presents a heroic myth as genuine German history, succeeded in creating not only obedience to authority but also widespread agreement with the idea of the *Obrigkeitsstaat*, the state as a commanding authority. Perhaps this was not entirely surprising. For, undemocratic as the imperial regime was, it was not arbitrary. The laws were known and were scrupulously observed. The courts and the administration were completely free from corruption. Germany bloomed, and its economic power spanned the globe. No unknown dangers lurked in the dark, and the loyal subject who had obeyed all the laws to the letter could then rest peacefully in his home in the secure knowledge that nothing would disturb him. Those were the days before the Gestapo and MVD, and the Germans looked rightfully upon the Russian Ochrana as a sign of Asiatic barbarity from which Germany was mercifully preserved through the wisdom of her rulers and the loftiness of her *Kultur*. In return for those blessings, Germans were willing to leave the power of government in the hands of the authorities, who after all knew much better what was good for the German people.

This *Untertanengeist* (subject spirit) was beautifully captured by Heinrich Heine, Germany's greatest lyric poet, a man who combined a deep love for Germany with a profound understanding of her weaknesses:

> Honor your mayor; it is he
> Who guards the State and zealously
> Decides what's best for old and young.
> So listen well—and hold your tongue.[1]

POLITICAL PARTIES

The major German parties of today have their antecedents in the imperial period. No two-party system—that mainstay of Anglo-American democracy —ever existed in Germany. And German parties were divided on different issues: hence, one might find one type of alignment on social and economic questions, another on colonial problems, another on foreign policy, religion, etc.

---

[1] From Heinrich Heine's "Erinnerung aus Kraehwinkels Schreckenstagen," freely translated by Louis Untermeyer. (L. Untermeyer, *Heinrich Heine, Paradox and Poet*, New York, 1937, pp. 317*f*.)

At the extreme right of the political scale stood the Conservative party, which was strongly Protestant and anti-Catholic, believed in authority, and was opposed to democracy and parliamentarism. Its stronghold was in Prussia, which it dominated. It was also anti-Semitic, but not in the virulent form which characterized the later Nazi regime. Nationalistic in its external policy, it was an adherent of the states' rights school, with emphasis on the predominance of Prussia. A "Free Conservative party" later split off from the parent body in order to deemphasize states' rights and underscore Bismarck's national policy.

A number of parties sailed under the "liberal" banner, but in Europe the term "liberal" means historically a policy of opposition to government intervention, in other words, the opposite of what might now be termed the "welfare state." The National Liberals supported Bismarck strongly until he broke with them in 1878. Another group, calling itself the "German Freeminded party" (*Deutsche Freisinnige Partei*), later split off and made itself independent, perhaps deserving the word "liberal" a little better. But this party split too, and its remnants were absorbed into the "Progressive People's Party" (*Fortschrittliche Volkspartei*) in 1910.

A unique party was the "Center" (*Zentrum*), a Catholic group. In a predominantly Protestant country like Germany, it grew out of opposition to those Conservatives and Liberals who believed in Prussian and Protestant hegemony. Those groups, on the other hand, looked with suspicion upon any party which allegedly was "ultramontane," *i.e.*, which took its orders from "across the mountains," namely, Rome. The recognized leader of the party was Ludwig Windthorst, an opponent of Bismarck from earlier days in the Prussian Diet. Soon the party became the center of most anti-Bismarck campaigns, attracting to its banner numerous other groups, notably the Catholic Poles. All this increased the animosity of Bismarck, who was not one to suffer opposition gladly.

The fateful struggle between the Catholics and the government has entered history under the name of "cultural struggle" (Kulturkampf). It was inaugurated by the Prussian government's refusal to accept the Catholic Church's action of excommunicating certain schismatic elements [2] and the government's insistence that those among them who were teachers of religion in the public schools should continue their instruction.[3] The second action which caused friction was the dissolution of the Catholic division of the Prussian Ministry of Education and Church Affairs, which had upheld Catholic interests, especially in the German-administered part of Poland.

[2] The so-called "Old-style Catholics" (*Altkatholiken*) who refused to accept the doctrine of papal infallibility.

[3] In German public schools religious instruction is part of the curriculum and is given by qualified persons, mostly priests, ministers, and rabbis, but sometimes laymen, nominated by their respective churches and appointed by the government.

A number of most drastic anti-Catholic laws were passed which tended to interfere profoundly with Church discipline and Church organization, even going so far as to decree the election of priests, greater lay control over church property, and an obligatory state examination for priests and teachers of religion.

But the Catholic ranks held firm. Not a single priest, not a single congregation, gave in to the government. The Center party even increased its vote, and the furious anti-Catholic campaign ended as an abject failure. But the long-range consequences of the Kulturkampf have remained in evidence. It inaugurated the habit of the ruling groups to term any attack on their predominance as originating with "enemies of the state," an expression which has been a household word in German politics to this day. The Nazis especially made abundant use of it. It also perpetuated the injection of a religious element into politics and kept alive the mutual suspicion between the Catholic and the Protestant populations in Germany.

Tried by the fire of the Kulturkampf, the Center party continued its opposition in the *Reichstag* and became the chief supporter of the parliamentary idea in Germany. It fought for parliamentary control of appropriations as well as for far-reaching social reforms and political democracy.

At the extreme left stood another group, the Social Democratic party, which was destined to play a dominant role in later German history. Carried upward by the swift tide of industrialization, and influenced from afar by the formidable figure of Karl Marx, its first organized manifestation was the creation of the "German General Workers' Association" by Ferdinand Lassalle in 1863. It went through a number of crises after Lassalle's death, and eventually a separate, Marxist organization was founded, a Social Democratic Workers' party (Eisenach, 1869). In 1875 this party and the remnants of the German General Workers' Association were united at the convention of Gotha.

The government looked upon the unification of the left with great alarm and undertook more and more radical means to suppress it. After some tentative beginnings, a suitable occasion was found in two attempts against the life of the aged monarch, Emperor William I, although they had nothing whatsoever to do with the party. In an atmosphere of increasing agitation and anti-Socialist laws, the Socialists, like the Centrists during the Kulturkampf, closed ranks, and the oppressive measures of the government proved a failure. The anti-Socialist laws expired in 1890, and in the same year the Socialists accumulated the formidable total of 20 per cent of the vote cast. In 1891 they reconstituted themselves as the "Social Democratic Party of Germany" (*Sozialdemokratische Partei Deutschlands,* frequently abbreviated SPD), and gave a new program which has remained basically in force ever since. It is a program of democratic socialism, which rejects both left-wing radicalism and right-wing reformism. In 1912 the Social Democratic party polled 4,238,919 votes and became the largest party in the *Reichstag*, with 110 seats.

Chapter 3

THE COLLAPSE OF THE EMPIRE AND THE ESTABLISHMENT OF THE REPUBLIC

The outbreak of the First World War caught the moderate parties in a dilemma. They, especially the Social Democrats, had favored peace and opposed militarism. They had no part in the declaration of war, but when called upon to vote the necessary military appropriations, they succumbed quickly to the call of patriotism. Only a small minority of the Social Democrats opposed this stand, but they were quickly brought into line. The fear of Russia certainly played a large part in this decision.[1]

THE ARMY IN CHARGE

In the West the Allies fought the war under civilian control which was never seriously challenged. This enabled them to achieve a remarkable measure of national unity and confirmed French Premier Georges Clemenceau's famous expression, "War is too serious a business to be left to the generals." But in Germany a totally different course was taken. The *Reichstag* virtually abdicated by giving the Federal Council tremendous power. In actuality it was the army that took over, and by 1916 the dictatorship of the High Command, which even the Emperor could not challenge, was an accomplished fact. In the lower echelons it was the regional military commanders who took over the control of civil government by proclaiming the "state of siege."

The German soldiers fought with their customary gallantry and discipline, but the military leadership showed little appreciation for the economic requirements of modern war or for the problems of civil government. At first, when victory followed victory, all went well, but when the situation became more difficult, as new opponents came into the fray, and as the economic strangulation of Germany became more apparent, the civilian front showed signs of weakness.

The generals were still certain of winning the war by a military decision. As late as September, 1917, General Erich Ludendorff, Quartermaster-General

[1] S. William Halperin, *Germany Tried Democracy*, New York, 1946, p. 21.

of the army and its real leader, declared that the only acceptable peace was one which would incorporate large parts of Belgium and France as well as Kurland and Lithuania. Belgium, inasmuch as it was not to be incorporated, was to be divided and closely linked with Germany. Ludendorff also demanded a larger colonial empire and naval bases all around the globe.[2] The armistice with Russia of Brest-Litovsk and the subsequent peace treaty of Bucharest demonstrated that these concepts were not just idle dreams.[3]

Some of the civilian leaders, however, had a clearer understanding of Germany's difficult situation. A minority of Social Democrats, led by Hugo Haase, refused to vote the military appropriations and organized themselves into the "Independent Social Democratic party," while a group of extremists, headed by Karl Liebknecht and Rosa Luxemburg, took even more drastic measures and eventually turned completely against the German war effort. In line with these activities was the "peace resolution" passed by the *Reichstag* on July 19, 1917, which was sponsored by the Center party leader, Matthias Erzberger. In Erzberger's speech the German people were told for the first time how dark the situation was, and that victorious battles only prolonged the war but did not lead to victory. The resolution voiced the opinion that now was the time to push a peace of understanding.

The military leaders, however, shunted this resolution aside and strengthened their position by forcing the dismissal of the *Reich* Chancellor, Theodor von Bethmann-Hollweg. They did this by their frequently used trick of offering their resignations in case their will did not prevail. To the German people Hindenburg and Ludendorff were demigods, the guarantors of victory; their dismissal was unthinkable. The German people's peculiar delight in hero worship was ruthlessly utilized by their leaders.

However, the German war effort slowed down. The replacements sent to the front in 1917 and 1918 did not depart in the same spirit as those of 1914. In the fall of 1917 a small-scale mutiny broke out among the sailors stationed at Kiel. Still the discipline of the German people was not seriously shaken, especially as press censorship was able to hide the nature of the slowly unfolding tragedy. As a matter of fact, even as late as July, 1918, Ludendorff was still certain that he could defeat Germany's enemies in one last offensive.

But on August 8, 1918, the "black day" of the German army,[4] British tank forces were able to penetrate the German lines and reveal weaknesses which could no longer be hidden. This, as well as the subsequent collapse of the Balkan front and of the corroded Austrian-Hungarian Empire, belongs to history. Germany's defeat was therefore obviously a military one, as Luden-

[2] Memorandum of General Ludendorff concerning war aims, dated Sept, 14, 1917, quoted in Bernhard Schwertfeger, *Die politischen und militaerischen Verantwortlichkeiten im Verlaufe der Offensive von 1918,* Berlin, 1927, pp. 102–106.

[3] For an excellent account, see John W. Wheeler-Bennett, *The Forgotten Peace,* New York, 1939.

[4] Erich Ludendorff, *Meine Kriegserinnerungen, 1914–1918,* Berlin, 1919, p. 547.

dorff himself admitted in these words: "The situation on the western front was extraordinarily tense, especially with regard to the 17th, 2nd, 18th, and 4th armies. The reserves had been diminished, the troops were exhausted. *The war could no longer be won*." [5]

It was Hindenburg's and Ludendorff's insistence which led to the German request for armistice terms. These were to be demanded by a government which on Ludendorff's suggestion had been broadened and democratized and included leaders of the left-wing parties. In that way he hoped that Germany either would obtain better peace terms or else could fight a last-ditch people's war.

The new Chancellor, Prince Max of Baden, was thus forced to negotiate with the Allies after Hindenburg's and Ludendorff's panicky insistence on an immediate armistice had informed them of Germany's desperate plight and had thus created diplomatically unfavorable conditions for any such negotiation.

THE END OF THE EMPIRE

President Wilson's notes to the German government had made it clear to the German people that any remains of "arbitrary power" were serious impediments to an armistice. And suddenly, now that they realized the true nature of their position, the German people became desperately tired of the futile war. Ludendorff had been dismissed, and a last-minute constitutional revision had taken place; only the emperor remained as a symbol of the old regime. With increasing resonance, voices were now heard demanding his abdication. The demands came from all parts of the population, from industrialists and bankers as well as from workers and shopkeepers. Strikes, which had occurred sporadically, became intensified, and revolts broke out in the navy.

The Social Democrats, the strongest political party in the *Reichstag*, were undecided. Their sudden preeminence was not the result of long planning and fighting; it had fallen into their laps. They were not necessarily opposed to the monarchical form of government under a constitutional regime, but they saw clearly that William II had to go. At the same time the Independent Socialists were agitating for a republic and gaining many adherents. So the Social Democrats demanded that Prince Max obtain the immediate abdication of the emperor; failing this, they would resign from the government. But William II misjudged the situation. He refused to abdicate, although shortly thereafter he expressed willingness to abdicate as German emperor but not as King of Prussia.

The actual decision fell in Bavaria. A small-scale revolution took place there. Under the leadership of an Independent Socialist, Kurt Eisner, a crowd of demonstrators deposed the Wittelsbach dynasty during the night of

[5] Quoted by Schwertfeger, *op. cit.*, pp. 362*f*. (The italics are the author's.)

November 7–8, 1918, and proclaimed a republic. The next morning William II fled to Holland and sealed the fate of the imperial throne.

REPUBLIC

Friedrich Ebert, the leader of the Social Democratic party since Bebel's death in 1913, was of the opinion that the abdication of the emperor and his son the crown prince could not in itself determine the constitutional nature of the state. That was to be reserved to a future national assembly. But the Independent Socialists were agitating for a republic; they gained popular support by the hour. Suddenly a report was brought to the Social Democratic leaders that Karl Liebknecht was addressing the people from the balcony of the royal palace and that he intended to proclaim a soviet republic on the Russian model. Thereupon Ebert's chief lieutenant, Philipp Scheidemann, on his own initiative and without authorization from anyone, proclaimed the German Republic from the balcony of the *Reichstag* building.[6] Thus, on November 9, 1918, at 2 P.M., Germany became a republic.

There had been no revolution. Only twenty-four hours had elapsed between the flight of the emperor and Scheidemann's proclamation. True, restive workers, soldiers, and sailors thronged the streets, and some of them were armed. But they did not overthrow the empire. The empire collapsed because nobody would support it any longer. It had never relied on popular support. When the catastrophe of the lost war and the mood of the long-deceived masses frightened the ruling groups into temporary eclipse, the regime collapsed like a house of cards.

THE "STAB IN THE BACK" LEGEND

The generals who had lost the war stood aside, and the legislators took over. On them now fell the burden of the impoverished country and the onus of the armistice and peace treaties. The generals remained associated with victory; the politicians became associated with a defeat in which they had no part. A myth of the most insidious kind was also born in those days: the "stab in the back" legend. The defeated generals proclaimed to the world that they had not failed but that a conspiracy of socialists, democrats, Jews, etc., had undermined the nation's will to fight and thus "betrayed" Germany. "Like Siegfried stricken down by the treacherous spear of Hagen, our weary front collapsed," proclaimed Hindenburg.[7] And despite clear, unquestionable, documentary proof to the contrary, the story was widely believed. For four

[6] Philipp Scheidemann, *Memoiren eines Sozialdemocraten,* Dresden, 1928, Vol. II, pp. 310–312.

[7] Paul von Hindenburg, *Out of My Life* (trans. by F. A. Holt), New York, 1921, Vol. II, p. 275.

years Germany had ostensibly marched from victory to victory. Suddenly she was laid low. What easier explanation could there be than "foul play"? Moreover, this explanation flattered the Germans, for it proclaimed that they had not lost the war in the field but had been struck down from behind. No need, therefore, to hide one's head in shame—but woe to the "traitors" who had brought it all about!

In this way the disappointment, the hatred, and the quest for responsibility were successfully diverted from the guilty militarists and heaped upon the leaders of the Republic, who were perhaps not always brilliant but certainly innocent as far as the military defeat was concerned.

For the politically inexperienced Germans, the "stab in the back" legend was a potent and fateful drug. No presentation of facts and figures could convince them of the true state of affairs.

Thus the German republic came into being without a true revolution, without real preparation, and particularly against the bitter resentment of a large number of Germans who believed they saw in it the symbol of their misery and defeat.

Chapter 4

CONSTITUTIONAL GOVERNMENT UNDER THE WEIMAR REPUBLIC

In form, the new German state which originated on November 9, 1918, was a soviet republic. The *Reichstag* had been shunted aside. Its place was taken by purely revolutionary, self-constituted bodies, the Councils of Workers and Soldiers, which had sprung up everywhere. Their spark plugs were the Independents, who had learned much from the methods of the Russian Revolution. On that same day of November 9, these Councils met in Berlin in plenary session, and, after declaring themselves the "holders of political power" and Germany a "socialist republic," elected an Executive Committee. This Committee in turn designated a cabinet, called "Council of People's Commissars" (*Rat der Volksbeauftragten*), after the Russian model. In their hands was laid the executive power of the state—a very considerable power, as the Councils of Workers and Soldiers were large, unwieldy, and of too discordant purpose to exercise effective control over the executive branch.[1]

Soon the Social Democrats recaptured the initiative which they had temporarily lost to the extreme left. The Independents insisted that all power should remain with the Councils and the Executive Committee and that a soviet republic should be decreed as the permanent constitution of Germany. The Social Democrats insisted that the future constitution of Germany could be settled only by a democratically elected National Assembly, and they prevailed over the bitter opposition of the Independents. The Council of People's Commissars issued a proclamation on November 12, announcing that henceforth all elections were to be carried out by free, equal, direct, and secret ballot of all German men and women above the age of twenty, based on the proportional system of representation. And the cabinet issued a decree on November 30 for the holding of elections to a National Assembly. With this act, the victory of the moderate forces was complete.[2]

---

[1] Theoretically the Executive Committee was the superior of the cabinet; actually however, the Executive Council soon became reduced to insignificance.

[2] The fate of the Independents was actually sealed on Dec. 19, when the General Congress of Workers and Soldiers Councils rejected (334 against 98) a motion proclaiming the retention of the councils system.

Birth of the Weimar Republic

The National Assembly was elected on January 19, 1919. The Social Democrats emerged as the strongest party by far. They obtained 163 seats, or 45 per cent of all votes cast.[3] Next were the Center party with 89 seats and the Democrats [4] with 74. The Independents lagged far behind with only 22 seats. With this election, the revolutionary period came to an end. The Independents resigned from the government. The task of drafting the new constitution was taken over by the three strongest, moderate parties who came to be known henceforth as the "Weimar Coalition."

The National Assembly met at the city of Weimar in order to avoid revolutionary pressure which still abounded in Berlin. Moreover, Weimar, which is associated with Germany's cultural past, served as a reminder that national greatness did not necessarily rest on feats of arms alone.

The new Constitution was adopted by the National Assembly on July 31, 1919, by a vote of 262 against 75, after much debate and painstaking study. It came into effect on August 11. It established a federal regime but with strongly unitary tendencies.[5] The powers of the national government were only those which were expressed and enumerated in the Constitution, but they were far more extensive than the powers of the American national government. This was not so much the case in the functions which belonged exclusively to the national government, but the list of powers held concurrently by the national and the *Länder* governments (in which the national government was supreme if it chose to act) was practically all-inclusive. Even where it did not choose to act directly, it was often empowered to veto *Länder* measures or to set standards for *Länder* legislation in certain important fields. If these extensive powers were not sufficient, it was further stipulated that in case there was "need for uniformity" the national government could legislate concerning the general welfare as well as public order and safety.[6]

In many ways the national government also controlled the administrative machinery of the *Länder*. It dealt with local questions directly only in a few instances, notably in the field of taxation. For all other purposes it used the

---

[3] This is a greater plurality than any German party, including the Nazis, had ever been able to accumulate until 1953, when the Christian Democratic Union obtained 45.2 per cent.

[4] The former Progressives.

[5] René Brunet, *The New German Constitution* (trans. by Joseph Gollomb), New York, 1922, p. 41; Gerhard Anschuetz, *Die Verfassung des deutschen Reichs,* Berlin, 1930, 13th ed., pp. 69*f*; Arnold Brecht, *Federalism and Regionalism in Germany,* New York, 1945, p. 4.

[6] In the drafting committee Hugo Preuss, the father of the Weimar Constitution, justified this section by saying, "It is necessary to have some catchall clause." Quoted in Fritz Poetzsch-Heffter, *Handkommentar der Reichsverfassung,* Berlin, 1928, 3d ed., p. 115.

machinery of the *Länder*, which thereby took on a dual character, *i.e.*, as local (and regional) government and as the lower level of the central administration. Since in this respect the *Länder* administrations were subsidiary organs of the *Reich*, the latter assumed supervision of them as far as their national functions were concerned (*Reichsaufsicht*).

THE EMERGENCY POWER

The Weimar Constitution had a particularly drastic remedy for recalcitrant *Länder* who failed to obey the directives and laws of the national government.

Article 48, Sec. 1, ruled that in such cases the *Reich* President [7] could compel obedience by means of the armed forces (*Reichsexekution*). This emergency power was used three times in the early period of the republican regime,[8] and once more in 1932 when Chancellor Franz von Papen wanted to get rid of the constitutional government of Prussia. The last action was strictly unconstitutional.

German jurists, who spend much time on exact legal definitions and classifications, have been divided on the question of whether republican Germany was a unitary or a federal state. It is probably correct to say that Germany was on the way to being a unitary state and had already become far more unitary than federal; it was left to the Nazis to bring this development to its conclusion.

Yet, political as well as constitutional elements influenced the relationship between the national government and the *Länder*. *Reich* cabinets were rarely strong enough to embark on a decisive campaign for full unitarism, and they preferred to settle disputes by negotiations. This proved to be relatively easy in Prussia, where the dominant Social Democratic party held unitarian views and was therefore willing to follow the lead of the national government, but was not easy in Bavaria, which took an extreme "anti-Berlin" stand that came close to open rebellion at times.

THE PARLIAMENT

The Weimar Republic retained the bicameral legislature of the empire. Again the upper house, now called National Council (*Reichsrat*), was a council of states composed of representatives of the *Länder* governments and subject to their instructions. Only the delegation of Prussia was divided between representatives of the Prussian government and of the Prussian provincial

[7] Article 50 provided that all orders and decrees issued by the President had to be countersigned either by the Chancellor or by the cabinet minister whose department was primarily concerned with the subject matter in question. Thus all acts of the President were in effect those of the government.

[8] March, 1920, against Thuringia; April, 1920, against Gotha; September–October, 1923, against Saxony.

administrations. However, unlike the old *Bundesrat*, the *Reichsrat* had merely a suspensive veto over legislation passed by the lower house, the *Reichstag*, which could be overridden by a two-thirds majority or a referendum ordered by the President of the *Reich*. However, the *Reichsrat* worked closely with the *Reich* government, and because of the large amount of expert knowledge and experience found in its midst, the *Reichsrat* often functioned in effect as a legislative advisory council. But Prussia no longer dominated it, and its presiding officer was not necessarily the representative of Prussia.[9] Nor was the *Reich* Chancellor any longer simultaneously Prime Minister of Prussia.

The *Reichstag*, the lower house, was now far more important. Its members were elected by a very simple system of proportional representation which worked in the following manner. The political parties presented lists of candidates in each fairly large (multimember) district. The composition and the order of listing of the candidates were solely the responsibility of the parties concerned. The voters could cast their ballots only for entire lists, and one candidate was declared elected on each party list (from the top down) for every 60,000 votes his party received. Remaining, unapportioned votes would then be combined with remainders of other districts to help elect further *Reichstag* members, provided a minimum of 30,000 votes was cast.

The proportional-representation system led to the result commonly attributed to it: a galaxy of parties, none of which was strong enough to form a government without a coalition with other groups. The result of the policies of such a government is always inconclusive. In other countries where democracy is more firmly established, this may not be fatal. But in Germany, unaccustomed to this kind of regime and later in the throes of a terrible economic depression, it seemed to an increasing number of people that the redress of their real or imaginary wrongs could be achieved only by extraparliamentary means, namely, by dictatorship.[10]

---

[9] Prussia had only two-fifths of the members of the *Reichsrat* (at the end of the Weimar Republic, 27 out of 67), and the unity of delegation was destroyed since half of it was appointed by the provincial administrations which were frequently at odds with the Prussian *Land* government. Contrary to uninformed opinion, the record of the Prussian government in fighting the rise of Nazism is much more impressive than that of the *Reich* government. The former was dominated by the sharply anti-Nazi Social Democrats, while the latter moved farther and farther to the right until it played into the hands of the Nazis. See Otto Braun, *Von Weimar zu Hitler*, New York, 1940; and Albert Grzesinski, *Inside Germany*, New York, 1939.

[10] The disastrous effect of PR on the fate of Germany has been explored with finality by F. A. Hermens, *Democracy or Anarchy*, Notre Dame University, 1941. Only four or five of the fifteen-odd parties represented in the *Reichstag* could have maintained themselves under an Anglo-American type of electoral system, and among them a coalition of Social Democrats and Centrists, perhaps with some of the liberal element, could have commanded a two-thirds majority in the *Reichstag*. Such a government would have been in a strong position to deal with the rising Nazi menace. See Carl J. Friedrich, *Constitutional Government and Democracy*, Boston, 1946, p. 288; and F. A. Hermens, *P.R., Democracy and Good Government*, Notre Dame University, 1943, pp. 21*f*.

The *Reichstag* possessed supreme legislative power, although the Constitution also allowed for direct popular legislation by means of the initiative (*Volksbegehren*) and the referendum (*Volksentscheid*). However, these devices of popular legislation were not much used for purposes of real enactment. They served rather as an opportunity to various political groups, especially the extremists, to embark on a campaign of agitation.

The record of the *Reichstag* is somewhat less than brilliant. All parties were ruled by their respective bureaucracies. The old and tried men, not always the most brilliant, maintained themselves high on the electoral list, and ambitious youngsters had a very hard time to rise to prominence. All decisions were made by the unimaginative, plodding party bosses, and the debates in the *Reichstag* had an air of unreality. They degenerated into lengthy, "official" party harangues, without spontaneity. No wonder that a well-informed observer could call them "wooden and stereotyped." [11]

Despite all these handicaps, the *Reichstag* managed to hold its own for nearly ten years. But with the rise of extremism on both the right and the left, both governments and legislature became less and less effective, and the pathetic impotence of the *Reichstag* became manifest. It was finally swept aside as an effective force, not by Hitler but by Chancellor Brüning, who, with the helpless connivance of the majority parties, ruled Germany by illegal "emergency" powers and almost without a parliament after 1930.

THE EXECUTIVE

The *Reich* President was elected by the people as a whole in direct election. He appointed and dismissed the *Reich* Chancellor, his cabinet, and all officials. He could dissolve the *Reichstag* and appeal to the electorate. He had extraordinary powers under the provision of Art. 48. As already mentioned, he could use compulsion by armed force against a disobedient *Land*. But Sec. 2 of that same article gave him even more power. It provided that, "in case public safety and order are considerably disturbed or endangered," he could take "all necessary measures for the restitution of safety and order, if necessary by means of the armed forces." For this purpose, the President was specifically empowered to set aside all civil liberties otherwise guaranteed in the Constitution. All such measures had to be brought to the attention of the *Reichstag*, which could order them to be set aside.

This extraordinary power of the *Reich* President was commonly referred to as his "power of dictatorship" (*Diktaturgewalt*). For all practical purposes, the *Reich* President was free to decide just what constituted a "disturbance" or "danger" to public safety and order, and the courts declared it to be beyond their competence to enter into this question.[12]

---

[11] James K. Pollock, *The Government of Greater Germany*, New York, 1938, p. 26.

[12] *Entscheidungen des Reichsgerichts in Strafsachen* (RGSt.), Vol. LVI, pp. 163, 189, 420; Vol. LVII, pp. 284*f*; Vol. LIX, pp. 41*ff*.

The Cabinet

Although these large powers were associated with the person of the President, they were actually executive powers at large. Article 50 of the Constitution ruled that acts of the *Reich* President needed the countersignature either of the *Reich* Chancellor or of a competent minister in order to be valid. Through this act, the Chancellor or minister "assumed responsibility" before the *Reichstag*, for the President, like the emperor, was removed from the power of the legislature.[13] Thus the President was not able to act without the Chancellor and his cabinet, nor was the Chancellor able to act without the President.

It would be quite wrong to deduce from this relationship that the presidency was merely designed to serve as a front whose acts were in reality those of the Chancellor. That this was often, even usually, the case cannot be denied. But it was not necessarily so, as German constitutional law and practice never knew the English doctrine according to which the chief of state (King) must follow the advice of his Prime Minister.

The chief executive of the Weimar Republic was neither the President nor the cabinet, but both. The President was conceived as a leading figure, taking a full interest in the conduct of the government and making his weight felt.

The first President, Friedrich Ebert, remained scrupulously within his constitutional powers. The second President, Paul von Hindenburg, former imperial chief of the High Command, maintained the practices of his predecessor at first. But after 1930 Germany was ruled virtually without a *Reichstag*, and laws were passed by means of the ordinance power of the President under Art. 48, Sec. 2. Rents were regulated and licensing laws for automobiles and agricultural marketing regulations were enacted under the need of "preserving public safety and order."[14] Finally Art. 48 was used to oust the legally constituted government of Prussia.

It is significant to remember the misuse of Art. 48 by Brüning, Schleicher, Papen, and Hitler—of course with the active connivance of the senile Field Marshal and his entourage—because several of the new German *Land* constitutions have again adopted similar measures. It is a fact that a vigorous, determined *Reichstag* could have stopped the use of Art. 48 at any time. The framers apparently felt they had established sufficient safeguards by giving the *Reichstag* power to order the annulment of all emergency decrees under this article. Executive power rarely gets out of hand against a determined legislature; but during the last years of the Weimar agony, the majority

---

[13] Except for the purpose of impeachment (Art. 59). The President could also be removed by a referendum (recall) provided two-thirds of the *Reichstag* supported the motion.

[14] Harlow H. Heneman, *The Growth of Executive Power in Germany,* Minneapolis, 1934, pp. 164–199.

parties did not dare overrule the decrees of the government. Left and especially right radicalism (Nazism) were gaining strength. The majority parties had lost the spirit and strength for a vigorous counterattack and feared elections under such circumstances. The government therefore could easily corral wavering party bureaucrats by the threat of dissolving the *Reichstag* and calling for new elections—a power which the President possessed under Art. 25.

The German executive had little to fear from the courts in the exercise of its extraordinary powers. Germany never knew the practice of judicial review. Her courts never possessed the prestige and majesty that attaches to British and American tribunals.[15] Moreover the German courts have a long and frequently distasteful history of servility to the demands of a strong executive, especially when the government is controlled by reactionary elements.

Thus the emergency powers of the executive branch were of a large and dangerous kind—not because there were no safeguards, but because these safeguards could not be counted upon to work in an emergency. Dr. Cohn's prophetic words that Art. 48 under a democratic president and his advisers was one thing, and under a president advised by antirepublicans was another, have literally come true.

The conduct of the regular activities of executive government was the function of *Reich* Chancellor and *Reich* government. The President appointed the Chancellor and, upon the latter's suggestion, the other members of the cabinet (Art. 53). Technically the President was free in the appointment of the Chancellor, but it was clearly presumed by the framers that he should be limited in fact by Art. 54, which provided that the cabinet had to have the confidence of the *Reichstag*. Thus Hindenburg's appointments of Papen and Schleicher in 1932 were quite obviously a misuse of his prerogative. On the other hand, there was no definite constitutional practice that the leader of the strongest opposition party was necessarily to be nominated Chancellor in case the government had resigned. As far as the other ministers were concerned, the President could appoint them only upon nomination by the Chancellor or Chancellor-designate. This alone set up the Chancellor on a higher plane than the other members of the cabinet, although ordinary cabinet ministers were responsible before the *Reichstag* individually as well as collectively, and their position was definitely higher than that of their predecessors under the empire.

The main weakness in the position of the Chancellor was a political rather

---

[15] With clear perception, Dr. Walter Simons, President of the German Supreme Court (*Reichsgericht*), wrote as follows: "I . . . have come to the conclusion . . . that our republic cannot continue to exist if the power of the judiciary as compared with the legislative and executive powers, is not given a stronger position and greater jurisdiction than heretofore. The fact that . . . the executive resorts to emergency measures, for which, in many cases, there is no foundation in the Constitution, presents a condition which should not be allowed to continue further." Quoted by Frederick F. Blachly and Miriam E. Oatman in *The Government and Administration of Germany*, Baltimore, 1928, p. 92n.

than a legal handicap. The multiparty system, which prevented any one party from achieving a majority and ruling alone, forced a coalition regime on all Chancellors. Under those circumstances, individual ministers were frequently more or less assigned to the government by their parties. The ministers occupied their departments like domains, and the Chancellors were in no position to interfere unless they dared to jeopardize the support of the parties to which those particular ministers belonged. This situation is typical of most coalition regimes, and it is one of their major weaknesses.

In terms of stability, the record of German cabinets is poor. The fourteen years of the Weimar Republic saw fourteen different cabinets, although a certain number of politicians were appointed to cabinet after cabinet. The government was supposed to remain in office until an election changed the political picture of the *Reichstag*, or until a vote of nonconfidence forced its resignation, but the coalition system and the resulting lack of inner stability were the main cause for such frequent government turnovers. Under such circumstances, true leadership had little chance to emerge. In fact, only Dr. Gustav Stresemann stands out as a political personality, and he was literally hounded to death by his unmerciful opponents. The rest were party bureaucrats and minor leaders whose names have sunk into deserved oblivion.

THE COURTS

Compared to the legislative and executive branches, the judiciary occupied a definitely less illustrious position in Germany. Article 103 stipulated that ordinary jurisdiction was to be carried out by the courts of the *Reich* and of the *Länder*. This is not to be interpreted, however, as if two complete and separate hierarchies had existed on all levels as is the case in the United States. The lower and intermediary courts—district court (*Amtsgericht*), regional court (*Landgericht*), superior regional court (*Oberlandesgericht*)— were courts of the *Länder* or of combinations thereof. They were *Land* as well as *Reich* courts. The highest court of the *Land* for ordinary cases was the Supreme Court (*Reichsgericht*), a court of cassation. For disputes between *Reich* and *Länder*, as well as for interpretation of the Constitution, there existed a High Court of State (*Staatsgerichtshof*). It was primarily a court of conflicts and did not possess what an American would call judicial review.[16]

The Weimar Constitution (Arts. 107, 31, 166) envisaged the creation of a supreme administrative court. Actually such a court was never established under the republican regime, and the highest administrative courts of the *Länder* (*Oberverwaltungsgericht*) remained the highest tribunals of general administrative jurisdiction. There were, however, a number of *Reich* courts

---

[16] There is an instance in which the *Reichsgericht* held that it had the right to examine the constitutionality of a law (*Entscheidungen des Reichsgerichts in Zivilsachen*, 1925, Vol. III, p. 320), but no practical consequences followed therefrom.

which handled administrative questions in certain restrictive fields, such as insurance, finance, veteran's disability, and several others. In importance and scope, these courts cannot be compared with the administrative court system in France, and there was no equivalent to the French Council of State.

In addition to the above, there also existed a number of special courts, especially the courts which could be established under the emergency provisions of Art. 48, as well as courts designated to deal with certain subject matters, especially labor courts.

Under the Weimar Republic, German judges were learned and incorruptible. Yet they never possessed, or apparently aspired to possess, that same position of arbiter between the state and the people that is associated with the countries of the common-law tradition. The German judges were "officials" (*Beamte*), a part of the executive machinery, rather than a third branch of government. Thus they offered little resistance to the many illegalities committed by the "presidential" governments, and they were quickly "coordinated" by the Nazis.

Chapter 5

THE POLITICAL STRUGGLE FOR POWER, 1918 TO 1933

The Weimar Republic came into existence almost inadvertently, through the back door. Nobody was really prepared for it, least of all the political leaders who had to shoulder the responsibility of governing it during its first crucial years. Yet at its inception the Republic enjoyed considerable support, and even the military leaders Hindenburg and Groener (Ludendorff's successor) gave it their allegiance. The history of the Weimar Republic is the story of how that support was quickly dissipated.

Republican Germany started as a soviet republic,[1] but in contrast to Russia it was the moderate element which kept the upper hand, partly at any rate because of widespread revulsion against the Russian methods. The Social Democrats, although still technically dedicated to Socialism, had worked long within the established order, and their thinking was geared to it. Above all they were sincerely democratic and did not believe in violent revolution. Only radical splinter groups called for a complete reversal of the social order. The Independent Social Democratic party (*Unabhängige Sozialdemokratische Partei Deutschlands*), led by Hugo Haase and Georg Ledebour, led a short-lived existence, but another more radical group was to persist longer. Headed by Karl Liebknecht and Rosa Luxemburg, it first called itself the Spartacus League [2] and later, in December, 1918, constituted itself as the Communist party of Germany.

The moderate Social Democrats, led by Friedrich Ebert and Philipp Scheidemann, won all along the line and advanced the date of the election for the National Assembly from February 16 to January 19, 1919. Since the radicals could not hope to dominate a popularly elected assembly, they had to act fast if their revolutionary aims were yet to succeed. The Independents with-

[1] Arthur Rosenberg, *A History of the German Republic,* London, 1936, p. 21, points out that the German soviets (*Räte*) were true soviets inasmuch as they wielded actual power, while their Russian counterparts deteriorated into mere window dressing for the Bolshevik party leadership.

[2] Named after a Thracian gladiator in Roman captivity who escaped in 73 B.C. and, together with other slaves, fought the might of Rome successfully for two years until he was finally overcome.

drew from the Central Committee of the Council of Delegates as well as from the government. By so doing they removed themselves from actual influence and never again held it.

The Communists proceeded to more drastic action. Karl Liebknecht and especially Rosa Luxemburg warned against the use of force, but the hot-headed Communists could not be restrained. The subsequent clashes were bloody and pointless, for the government had little trouble in suppressing the rebellion, but the tragedy was not the suppression of the Communist uprising —that was inevitable—but the means used in that necessary action. The Social Democratic Minister of War, Gustav Noske, was forced to call upon the imperial army to suppress the Communists. That it did, with relish and quite unnecessary cruelty. The upheavals also gave rise to the first "Free Corps," armed bands of former officers and soldiers who participated in the fights and set up the first type of private army known in Germany. Their leaders and most of their members later became the nucleus of the armed Nazi formations.[3]

These events made the young Republic beholden to the army and frustrated any plans for the creation of a totally new, republican armed force. Henceforth Germany had a tightly disciplined army whose military chiefs had sole control over it and who made of it a state within the state with more than uncertain loyalty to the Republic.[4]

Separate developments took place in Bavaria. A government headed by the Independent Socialist Kurt Eisner was overthrown and Eisner was murdered. He was succeeded by a short-lived regime of utopian Socialists, who in turn were replaced by outright Communists. The national government moved troops and Free Corps against the Bavarian Soviet Republic and suppressed it rigorously. But the predominantly conservative citizens of Bavaria had had a sample of Communism and the unpleasant taste lingered in their mouths. Ever since then, Bavaria has remained a center of reactionary intrigues. It is no accident that Munich was later proclaimed by Hitler the "capital of the (Nazi) Movement."

THE GALAXY OF PARTIES

The political picture of the Weimar Republic was forever cursed by the presence of a large number of parties. Their numbers varied considerably as new groups emerged and old ones decayed. At one time as many as thirty parties vied for the favors of the electorate. True, many of these were not of national significance, but their existence made a profoundly unfavorable impression on the German people, an impression which was frequently carried

[3] Free Corps officers arrested Karl Liebknecht and Rosa Luxemburg and murdered them in cold blood.

[4] The architect of this system was General Hans von Seeckt.

over into contempt for the democratic system which made such conditions possible.

Before the rise of Nazism the German Nationalist People's party (*Deutschnationale Volkspartei*) occupied the extreme right of the stage. It was dominated by Prussian reactionaries, many of them of the *Junker* type. It was hostile toward the Republic, especially after Alfred Hugenberg, chief of the UFA film corporation, became its leader. Its antirepublican attitude made it the natural ally of the Nazis, with whom it formed an alliance in 1931, the "Harzburg front." Hugenberg joined the first Hitler government but remained a figurehead, was eased out, and ended his days in oblivion.

The party of big business and finance was the German People's party (*Deutsche Volkspartei*), the successor to the old National Liberals. It was a conservative but constitutional party. It is chiefly remembered for having given the Weimar Republic its only statesman of real magnitude, Gustav Stresemann.

The middle of the stage was occupied by the Center party (*Zentrum*). Neither reactionary nor liberal, the party stood on strictly republican and constitutional grounds. As a Catholic party it embraced both conservative and liberal elements, and its center position made it an indispensable coalition partner in any government. It had a superb voting discipline, and its strength remained constant throughout the life span of the Republic.

An offshoot of the Center was the Bavarian People's party (*Bayerische Volkspartei*), which in 1920 constituted itself as a separate party. Following the Bavarian tradition, it was somewhat more conservative than the Center party but usually made common cause with it.[5] It held absolute sway in Bavaria until its life was extinguished by Adolf Hitler in 1933.

The German Democratic party (*Deutsche Demokratische Partei*) was formed in 1918 as the successor to the Progressive party, under the leadership of the famed politician and publicist Friedrich Naumann. Its aim was to become a focal point for the progressive but anti-Socialist middle classes. After the death of Naumann in 1919 the party declined, and in 1930 it vividly illustrated the sorry plight of the Weimar Republic by renaming itself State party (*Staatspartei*),[6] indicating that even the name "democratic" was fraught with disadvantages.

Until 1932 the strongest party in Germany was the Social Democratic party (*Sozialdemokratische Partei Deutschlands*), whose origins and history have been sketched previously. It was sincerely republican and democratic, but it never rose to the task which history had imposed upon it. Its leaders, men like Philipp Scheidemann, Otto Wels, Rudolf Breitscheid, and Hermann

---

[5] One exception was in 1925 when the Bavarian People's party actively supported the presidential candidacy of Field Marshal Hindenburg in opposition to Wilhelm Marx, the candidate of the Center party.

[6] After fusion with a small party of that name.

Müller, were party bureaucrats who had gained their places of eminence by long, faithful service rather than by special brilliance or imagination. Although the party polled 40 per cent of the vote on the average until 1932, it permitted itself to be constantly outmaneuvered and eliminated from active governmental participation for long stretches of time. After 1930 it had virtually no influence on the course of events.

While the Social Democratic party failed the test of leadership, it nevertheless left a strong mark upon Germany. It gave an unequaled amount of political education to its members and followers, especially among the workers, which even the iron fist of the Gestapo and the concentration camps could not entirely break. As late as March, 1933, two months after Hitler had come to power, and under conditions of utmost terror and ruthlessness unleashed by the Nazis, over 7,000,000 Germans dared to vote for the Social Democratic ticket. This discipline and tradition enabled the party to revive almost immediately after the collapse of the Hitler regime.

The Communist party (*Kommunistische Partei Deutschlands*) took from its inception a position of uncompromising hostility toward the Republic. Since it had absolutely no chance of coming to power in Germany, its propaganda carried both nationalistic and socialistic tendencies without being bothered by contradictions. It used every conceivable maneuver to gain advantages, including common actions with the Nazis, especially when directed against the hated Social Democratic government of Prussia. Aided by the mounting depression, the Communist vote steadily increased, but its highest point, over 6,000,000 in 1932, was far from a majority.

Inflation

Perhaps the greatest single blow to the stability of the young Republic, however, was the outbreak of the most fantastic inflation the world had ever known to that day. The German government headed by Wilhelm Cuno wanted to improve German economic conditions before paying reparations. But the Germanophobe French government of Raymond Poincaré proved adamant and occupied the Ruhr Valley in order to force the German government to pay. Since open resistance was out of the question, passive resistance was proclaimed. It was eventually given up, and the Ruhr issue was subsequently solved because of the more conciliatory policy of Poincaré's successor, Édouard Herriot. But in the meantime incalculable harm had been done. In anticipation of possible trouble the German government accepted short-term enlistments of volunteers who turned out to be the worst type of cutthroats, chiefly former Free Corps men. This was the notorious "Black Reichswehr."

In order to finance passive resistance the German government resorted to the printing press, and unchecked inflation set in. When it came to an end, in

November, 1924, a new currency, the rentenmark, was established at the incredible ratio of 1 rentenmark to 1 trillion old marks. Speculators and profiteers had a field day, but the working population was hard hit and the middle classes were financially wiped out. Henceforth embittered members of the middle class became increasingly attracted to right-wing radicalism, which promised them a rise to their former positions of preeminence once the hated "system" had been overthrown. To those radical groups they brought a reservoir of talent and training which stood them in good stead later on.

The national election of May, 1924, pointed to the catastrophe which had occurred. The Nationalists, determined opponents of the Republic, gained heavily, and so did the Communists, who rose to fourth place. The young Nazi party polled nearly 2 million votes only half a year after its unsuccessful Munich *Putsch*. Chief losers were the Social Democrats and the other parties of the Weimar coalition. The extremists of right and left could of course never hope to form a government coalition together. But together they could obstruct the government most effectively. Cabinet followed cabinet, election followed election,[7] but always with inconclusive results. In 1928, when economic conditions were at their best, the middle-of-the-road parties did achieve success and formed a "great coalition." The extremists all lost heavily; the Nazis went down to 800,000 votes. But the "great coalition" broke up over a relatively minor matter in 1930 and was replaced by a cabinet under Centrist Chancellor Heinrich Brüning.

Brüning was a man of energy and dedication, but faced by the mounting obstructionism of the extremists he lent a willing ear to President Hindenburg's suggestion to keep the government somewhat aloof from parliament. As Brüning's coalition became narrower and as he faced increasing opposition, he resolved to use the presidential emergency powers in order to enact by decree what he could not enact by law. When the *Reichstag* demanded the revocation of the decrees, Brüning prevailed upon Hindenburg to dissolve parliament and call for general elections.

These elections were held at the worst possible moment, on September 14, 1930, when the depression had its sharpest impact and after the government had made itself unpopular by taking strictly deflationary measures by decree. The outcome was a mortal blow to the Republic. The Center party held its own, but all the other moderate parties lost heavily. The beneficiaries were the extremists. The Communists increased their vote by 40 per cent, polling over 4½ million votes. The Nazis made the most spectacular gains. From an 800,000 low in 1928 they soared to 6,400,000.

Now parliamentary work became impossible. The extremists shouted and heckled; the Nazi deputies marched in and out in brown-shirt party uniform and showed their contempt for parliamentary procedure in every way. Brün-

[7] In 1924 and in 1932 elections were held twice in the same year.

ing weathered the storm for a while, but government by decree became more and more frequent until March 26, 1931, when the *Reichstag* adjourned and government was carried on entirely by decree.

HINDENBURG'S REELECTION AND THE FALL OF BRÜNING

Presidential elections were held in March, 1932. Chief candidates were Hindenburg, now candidate of the moderate parties, and Hitler. Communists and Nationalists ran candidates of their own. Hindenburg piled up an impressive total of 18,661,736 votes compared to Hitler's 11,338,571, but he failed by less than 1 per cent to carry an absolute majority. A runoff election was held on April 10, boosting Hindenburg to well over 19,000,000 and Hitler to over 13,000,000. Hindenburg was elected, but the Nazi total was impressive.

For Brüning, who had worked hard for Hindenburg's reelection, this was a Pyrrhic victory. He fell victim to the intrigues of the cliques around the ailing and senile president who turned Hindenburg's mind against the Chancellor. Having relied on presidential power rather than on parliament, Brüning, who was never defeated in parliament on a vote of confidence, had to give up his post at the express request of Hindenburg.

He was succeeded by a renegade Centrist, Franz von Papen, who misused the emergency powers in order to remove the constitutional government of Prussia. If this sacrificial offering at the Nazi altar was to save Papen's political life it failed to accomplish its purpose. The Nazis became the strongest party, and the Communists too gained considerably at the expense of the Social Democrats, who paid heavily for having taken Papen's lawless act lying down.

However, internal dissensions within the Nazi party gave the party a temporary setback, and between the two elections in 1932 the Nazis lost 2 million votes. But fate was not kind to Papen either. The real power in the clique around Hindenburg was an ambitious general, Kurt von Schleicher. Papen had been his protégé, but now he had become too independent and the general turned against him. Schleicher replaced Papen on December 3, 1932, and it seemed for a little while as if he were to meet with success. Dissension was rife within the Nazi party, and Schleicher was negotiating with one of the dissident leaders, Gregor Strasser. But at this moment of lowest Nazi morale, Hitler threw himself and his resources into a relatively minor election in Lippe and by succeeding therein was able to overcome the dead point of the party's momentum.

Schleicher's position deteriorated thereafter, and Papen threw his entire influence with Hindenburg against him. When Schleicher tried to bluff his way through by obtaining a presidential decree to dissolve Parliament, he met with refusal and had to resign.

HITLER BECOMES CHANCELLOR

Upon taking his leave Schleicher recommended to Hindenburg that he appoint Hitler as his successor—whether out of spite against Papen is not known. Hindenburg's "kitchen cabinet" also supported this suggestion, and Hitler took office on January 30, 1933. The Weimar Republic had come to an end.

Under the empire, the German citizen had been excluded from the realm of government. This was the prerogative of certain privileged classes. But in return for this, he had been furnished with an ideal: the ideal of a dazzlingly glorious and brilliant Germany forging ahead under a determined leadership.

In 1918, this idea suddenly evaporated. The war was lost, the emperor in ignominious flight, the traditional exponents of power in confusion. The German people were not prepared to rule themselves alone, for they lacked both experience in government and that innate sense of moderation and freely accepted self-discipline that is the essence of democratic government, and has been the genius of the English-speaking peoples. The unimaginative, uninspiring party bureaucrats took over. But they took over without giving the people another ideal. Thus, to most Germans, the Weimar Republic was form but not substance. For the latter, they dreamed either of the past or of the future, but in any case despised the present. Hitler's genius contrived to combine these dreams for his own purpose and to furnish the German people with what they desired. In that sense Hitler was really what he claimed to be—the embodiment of the German soul—not because he was a typical German, for that he was not, but because he shouted from the rooftops what many Germans had secretly dreamed.

Thus the Weimar Republic was in a real sense the age of transition from Bismarck to Hitler—not because of overt acts (of which there were some, but not many), but because of its omissions, its lack of substance, and its inability to imbue the German people with a new ideal.

From this must be learned an obvious lesson. New democratic forms, seemingly democratic party governments, civil liberties, are the forms, not the substance of democracy. Only when all energies are concentrated on the education of the German as an individual, not merely a part of a glorious machine, is there a chance for developing that personal dignity, that sense of balanced moderation, that innate understanding of generally accepted and therefore unspoken values, which are the mark of a free people.

Chapter 6

THE RISE OF NATIONAL SOCIALISM

Now that the Nazi period is over and can be surveyed as a whole, there can no longer be any doubt that it was to an almost complete extent the work of one man, Adolf Hitler. True, economic and political events aided it greatly, and social as well as psychological factors provided a fertile soil. Yet Hitler's successful use of all these factors gives evidence of his evil genius.

HITLER

Adolf Hitler was born in Braunau on the Inn on April 20, 1889. The accident of birth made him an Austrian, and he never bothered to acquire German citizenship until just before he became German Chancellor. But he always considered himself a German and during the First World War chose a German, rather than an Austrian, regiment.

After a youth of flotsam and military service of little distinction he joined a tiny group called the "German Labor Party," an event which he later termed "the most decisive decision of my life." [1]

Munich was the hub of all kinds of antidemocratic activities at that time, and Hitler found many ready adherents. In this atmosphere he staged his famous "beer-hall *Putsch*" of 1923, which ended in dismal failure. Hitler received a short term of imprisonment during which he wrote that famous conglomeration of platitudes, half-baked philosophy, and propagandistic fulmination which, under the name of *Mein Kampf* (My Struggle), became the Bible of the Third *Reich*.

The failure of the *Putsch* taught Hitler the valuable lesson that it was unwise to challenge the authority of the state directly. Henceforth he was determined to come to power by "legal" means, which did not exclude violence, but by which accusations of illegality might be avoided.

THE NAZI PARTY

From 1919 on, Hitler called his party the "National Socialist German Workers party" (*Nationalsozialistische Deutsche Arbeiterpartei*, NSDAP). The only concrete point in its program was anti-Semitism. Otherwise its plat-

[1] Adolf Hitler, *Mein Kampf*, Munich, 1938 (German ed.), p. 244.

form was composed of an assortment of vague, semimystical phrases.[2] The speeches and the propaganda were harangues of little meaning, designed to appeal solely to the emotions.

What accounts for the rise to power of a group of men most of whom, if measured by ordinary standards, would have been considered uncouth and commonplace? One thing is certain: Hitler was never the tool of so-called "special interests," "capitalists," etc., but it was rather the other way around. Some of these people might have had illusions of controlling Hitler, but if so they were quickly brought back to reality. As a matter of fact the Nazis had no real political theory,[3] very much like their Italian fascist cousins. The realistic Italians accepted that situation calmly, but the Germans were in greater need of philosophy, of *Weltanschauung*. Hence the paraphernalia of would-be philosophy and "racial" concept of history.[4]

Nazism directed its most powerful attraction toward the disgruntled and impoverished middle classes. It even attracted some brilliant intellectuals, who may not have believed every word but who were ready enough to serve. Patriotism in its most extreme form was another weapon in the Nazi arsenal. Hitler showed his qualities of leadership by identifying himself more and more with the "spirit of the nation," and his command thus became the command of patriotism. To resist it became a moral wrong, an act of treason against the nation. Patriotism is something which in the opinion of many Germans excuses almost anything, and many Germans are still not quite sure they understand why other nations find certain German actions so reprehensible. Also useful was the "stab in the back" legend which blamed German defeat in the First World War on certain groups which were identified with the Weimar Republic. It was easy to believe in this legend, contrary to the facts though it was, because it made possible the continuation of the belief in German superiority. Moreover the clearly militaristic undertones of all Nazi activities tended to convey the impression that only the Nazis were doing anything for helping Germany to regain a "place in the sun."

The strongest single aid to the Nazi cause was undoubtedly the depression, which created millions of desperate men and women. Without the depression the Nazis would hardly have come to power. Nor would the depression alone have accomplished that without the Nazi leaders' shrewd appraisal of the German character. The vague Nazi creed, its symbolism, its song of hate, gave every German something to believe in and something to fight against. This does not mean that every German was a Nazi, but Hitler cast a spell over them from which few could keep themselves entirely free.

[2] The principal program of the Nazis was to be found, apart from *Mein Kampf*, in Gottfried Feder's "Twenty-five Points," written in 1920.

[3] Franz Neumann, *Behemoth, the Structure and Practice of National Socialism*, New York, 1942, pp. 459–462.

[4] The official exponent of Nazi "philosophy" was Alfred Rosenberg's *Der Mythus des 20. Jahrhunderts*, Munich, 1930.

THE FIRST HITLER GOVERNMENT

The cabinet which Hitler formed upon his assumption of the Chancellery was composed of surprisingly few Nazis; besides Hitler, only two others, Wilhelm Frick (Interior) and Hermann Göring (Air and Prussian Prime Minister). Quite likely, some of the Nationalists thought that Hitler had reached his zenith and that they would control him. But then came the fantastic burning of the *Reichstag*, according to all available evidence engineered by Göring but blamed on the Communists. This "plot" was used as an excuse for Hindenburg to sign emergency decrees suspending all civil liberties and establishing strict central control. Draconic punishments were imposed for all kinds of old and new crimes, and the death penalty was restored. The decrees also furnished the basis for so-called "protective custody," the name given to imprisonment in the notorious concentration camps.[5] Under these decrees the opponents of the Nazis were hunted down and imprisoned or even killed.

Under these conditions of terror the German people went to the polls on March 5, 1933, and it must be considered remarkable that the Nazis obtained only 43.9 per cent of the total vote. Only together with the Nationalists did they poll a bare majority of 51.9 per cent. It was the last German election in which there was anything like a contest until the collapse of the Nazi regime.

The capstone of this development was the Enabling Act of March 24, 1933, which was rushed through the newly elected *Reichstag* and passed quickly against only the votes of those Social Democrats who were still at liberty to come to the session. The Communists had "received no invitation," and most of them were in jail anyhow.

With the Enabling Act the legislative power was transferred from the *Reichstag* to the government, and it was quite justified to call this law the "Law of Leadership" (*Reichsführungsgesetz*). After all power of executive and legislative leadership was thus united in Hitler's hands, the judiciary was quickly brought in line; and after the blood purge of June 30, 1934, Hitler declared himself the "supreme Lord Justice" (*oberster Gerichtsherr*) of the German people.

After legal unification came political unification, and on July 14, 1933, all political parties were declared dissolved. The Nazi party, being presumably a "movement," was excluded from that provision. Finally, the dissident elements within the Nazi party were wiped out in a gigantic purge which killed well over a thousand people. While the killing was going on, accounts with such old enemies as General von Schleicher and Gustav von Kahr (who turned against Hitler in the beer-hall *Putsch*) were also settled in the approved Nazi manner, *i.e.*, by assassination. Hitler's power could no longer be challenged.

[5] Ernst R. Huber, *Verfassungsrecht des grossdeutschen Reichs,* Hamburg, 1937–1939, p. 38.

And when old President Paul von Hindenburg died on August 1, 1934, a "last will," almost certainly forged, was conveniently found, suggesting that Hitler be made the old Marshal's successor. Hitler was only too glad to oblige and combined the two offices in his hand. He was to be called *"Führer* (leader) and *Reich* President." Later, with pseudo simplicity, he caused himself to be "simply" called *Der Führer.*

Führer and Cabinet

No man ever wielded more personal power than Hitler. He was responsible to no one and consulted, if at all, with whom he wished. He did not even have a Politburo like Stalin. Neither the party leadership nor the cabinet filled that role. In the past several writers held that certain personalities like Heinrich Himmler, Hermann Göring, and Joseph Goebbels were the actual "powers behind the throne." Today we know that Hitler and Hitler alone counted. Even when the regime was crumbling around him he had no trouble in disposing of these pillars of National Socialism.[6]

Hitler was "the chosen one," a modern incarnation of the divine-right-of-kings concept; and all kinds of fanciful legal, social, and political theories were woven around this concept by servile intellectuals.

The members of the *Reich* cabinet were administrators, underlings who did Hitler's bidding and usually had little share in policy making. Only the degree to which Hitler chose to consult them gave them influence, if any. Under them, however, a fairly well functioning bureaucracy continued to operate with fair efficiency.

Centralism

Totalitarianism cannot tolerate decentralized power. Hence, Nazism quickly abolished all vestiges of federalism. The *Länder* were "coordinated" by the use of *Reich* governors (*Reichsstatthalter*); and the *Land* governments, where they remained, retained mainly the function of rewarding party leaders with well-paid offices. Prussia, the largest *Land* by far, was, for all practical purposes, abolished as a *Land*. The only thing that remained was the title of Prussian Prime Minister, now devoid of meaning, which Göring, who collected such things, retained for himself.

Centralization was also extended to lower levels. The German Municipal Code of 1935 established a uniform system of local administration. New territories incorporated into Greater Germany, such as Austria and the Sudetenland, were organized into new types of administrative units, *Reichsgaue*, with the regional party leader (*Gauleiter*) as governor in personal union. The

---

[6] A graphic account of those events can be found in H. R. Trevor-Roper, *The Last Days of Hitler*, New York, 1947.

Reichsgaue were obviously the pattern to be imposed eventually on all of Germany had the Hitler regime lasted longer.

PARTY ORGANIZATION

The National Socialist German Workers party (NSDAP) was a most elaborate structure. At the top stood the *Führer* and a central executive committee (*Reichsleiter*) who ranked with cabinet members, which some of them were. Below the national organization was that of the regions (*Gaue*), districts (*Kreis*) and towns and villages (*Ortsgruppen*). Each was headed by an appropriate "chief" (*Leiter*). On the precinct level were subordinate block leaders and cell leaders.

Associated organizations comprised the brown-shirted militia (storm troopers, SA), the black-uniformed elite guard (SS), the motorized corps (NSKK), and the youth organizations for boys (Hitler Youth) and for girls (BDM). Other affiliations existed for most professions and interests.

It was not always easy to keep away from some form of party affiliation. The pressure to join was heavy; certainly promotion and sometimes continuation of business or job depended on it. On the other hand, some convinced Nazis never joined up formally for one reason or another. Membership in the Nazi party or its affiliates was therefore not always an adequate gauge of sentiment, although it might have been a clue.

Above all the party functioned as a superb control mechanism which hovered over every public and private activity of the citizen. Its network was quickly able to spot dangerous tendencies and to take steps toward their neutralization. On the other hand, as the chief "educator," in control of every medium of information, it molded thought and action. Fortunately, in their heavy-handed way, the Nazis overdid it a little and especially with the younger generations were not always as effective as they might been. Still, their control was complete; no effective underground could exist, and only external force finally overcame their regime.

The regime left behind a path of death and destruction that had few equals in the history of the world. Its racial myth was responsible for the mass murder of over 6 million Jews and many more millions of members of other races, supposedly "inferior" to the German. The terror of the Secret State Police (Gestapo) is still recalled in many parts of Europe, especially in Germany itself. Despite the many horrors still abounding in the world today, and in spite of many Nazi methods faithfully copied or improved upon by other dictators, the names of the death camps of Dachau, Buchenwald, Ravensbrueck, Bergen-Belsen, Maidanek, Oświecim, and many others will long be remembered as a horrible proof of the depth of depravity to which a supposedly civilized country may descend.

Chapter 7

THE COLLAPSE OF THE REGIME AND THE OCCUPATION OF GERMANY

The outbreak of the Second World War found the Nazis in firm control of Germany. There was little evidence of disaffection, even though it can hardly be assumed that Hitler had won over the entire half of the population which, as late as 1933, had dared to vote against him. But Germany was prosperous, the vast rearmament program had obliterated unemployment, and her voice was heard loudly in the concert of nations. And while the Germans would perhaps have preferred to be loved, they would rather be feared than ignored. That at least the Hitler regime had achieved.

Most important was the police system, which made any underground work virtually impossible. No anti-Nazi group—and there were a number—could ever dare to go outside its own small circle; otherwise a police agent would slip in, and before long the names of the conspirators would be read on the well-known orange posters which announced the death penalty against the enemies of the regime. In France, Norway, and Poland, the anti-Nazi forces could rely on most of their countrymen to be on their side. But in Germany one never knew who was friend and who was foe.

Such opposition as existed was silenced by the first great victories of German arms, which appeared to vindicate Hitler and his famous "intuition." After Austria and Czechoslovakia had fallen easily without force of arms, Poland, Norway, the Low Countries, and France fell with shocking ease before the German legions. Hitler was at the zenith of his glory.

The turning points in the war were the battles of London, Stalingrad, and El Alamein. Among them, Stalingrad was of particular significance to the Germans. The consequences of the victory of the small Royal Air Force over the hitherto invincible *Luftwaffe* were not immediately obvious to the German people. The reversal of fortunes in Africa which started at the battle of El Alamein and ended with the surrender of the last German and Italian troops on Cape Bon peninsula was not entirely unexpected, nor did the German people feel overly anxious over the fate of the survivors because they knew, despite all Nazi propaganda to the contrary, that their prisoners would be well treated by their British and American captors. But Stalingrad was quite another matter. This was a battle against an opponent whom the overwhelming majority of the Germans really hated and feared. Hitler had already announced the impending fall of the city. It was Hitler who refused the request of the commander of the sixth German army, bottled up at Stalingrad, to give him permission to fight his way out. This was clearly a battle of prestige, and Hitler's loss of prestige was great when Stalingrad fell and the German troops under Field Marshal von Paulus were forced to surrender.

THE PLOT OF JULY 20, 1944

Despite tremendous efforts by Minister of Propaganda Dr. Joseph Goebbels, who tried to copy Winston Churchill's "blood, sweat and tears" motif, the Germans were uneasy, and for the first time victory seemed somewhat less assured. Disaffection was especially great among the top officers' caste, whose counsel was increasingly shunted aside in favor of Hitler's "intuition." The result of this state of affairs was the plot of July 20, 1944. This was not of a grass-roots nature—that would have been impossible under the vigilant eyes of the Gestapo. The conspiracy had to confine itself to military leaders, such as Field Marshal von Witzleben and General von Beck, and a few former political leaders, such as Karl Goerdeler, former Mayor of Leipzig and member of the Nationalist party, and Hermann Leuschner, former Social Democratic leader. Also involved were certain members of the diplomatic service like the former Ambassador Ullrich von Hassel, and a prominent Foreign Office man, Adam von Trot zu Solz.[1] But despite the restricted membership of the inner circle, the conspirators had made contacts in many parts of Germany, and Allied intelligence officers found traces of the conspiracy in virtually every major German town.

The plot failed chiefly because of a number of accidents. The bomb, placed under Hitler's table by one of the conspirators, Colonel Werner von Stauffenberg, exploded as planned, but Hitler had inexplicably transferred the meeting where the explosion occurred from the "bunker" to a wooden shed. In the concrete bunker, concussion would have killed every person there; in the shed, the walls were blown out, and although there were some casualties, Hitler was only slightly hurt. Stauffenberg, hearing the explosion and believing the deed accomplished, set the prearranged machinery in motion. The rebels did take over the offices of the home army in Berlin, and their success was even greater in Vienna and Paris, where the Gestapo was temporarily placed under arrest.

[1] Ernst Bernd Gisevius, *Bis zum bitteren Ende,* Zurich, 1946, 2 vols., translated as *To the Bitter End,* Boston, 1947; Allen W. Dulles, *Germany's Underground,* New York, 1947; Fabian von Schlabrendorff (edited by Gerov S. Gaevernitz), *They Almost Killed Hitler,* New York, 1947; Hans Rothfels, *The German Opposition to Hitler,* Hinsdale, Ill., 1948.

But the conspirators, the generals who had moved vast armies with clocklike precision, went about their business in a most dilettantelike manner. They failed to secure the lines of communication. Being the products of Prussian militarism, they did not consider the possibility that their orders might be questioned. But a young Nazi officer, a Major Rehmer, became suspicious, contacted Dr. Goebbels, and heard the truth, that Hitler was alive. With that the jig was up. And finally, the most influential conspirator, who might have carried the action to success because of his prestige and reputation, Field Marshal Erwin Rommel, had been severely wounded by an Allied flier and was out of the fight.[2]

The members of the conspiracy were seized, placed before a "People's Court" where they received a kind of trial that constituted a mockery, and executed under torture.

The failure of the plot of July 20 was a tragedy for Germany; most of the physical destruction of that country occurred after that date. And since all opposition was crushed, there was no longer anything to stop Hitler from extracting the last drop of blood from the German people. Hitler's famous boast that if he were forced to depart from the scene, he would "shut the door with a bang," was carried out to the letter.

But for the world at large, the failure of the plot may well have been a blessing. Had the plot succeeded, many Germans would have believed that victory was stolen from them by "traitors" and that they could have won had the assassination not occurred. Thus, a new "stab in the back" legend would have been born, with the accompanying desire for a third round. Instead, the war ended with the physical annihilation of German armed might and the total occupation of Germany. This is an object lesson in the futility of aggressive war which will not be entirely lost on the Germans and may make them more cautious, it is hoped, toward the blandishments of a future *Führer*.

THE END OF THE NAZI REGIME

The fall of the Hitler regime was entirely due to the armed might of the Allied armies. No debt of gratitude is owed to any group within Germany. Hitler himself held the reins of government until his own physical destruction. His last act was that of naming the liquidators. Since his faith in Göring—once his designated successor—was gone, and since he also regarded Himmler as a traitor because of the latter's peace feelers, he designated as his

[2] He died in a hospital and was buried with great honors, Hitler himself being present. But it is certain now that he was killed by Gestapo agents; Hans Speidel (Rommel's chief of staff), *Invasion 1944*, Tübingen, 1950; Albert Lidell-Hart (ed.), *The Rommel Papers* (trans. by Paul Findlay), New York, 1953.

successor Grand Admiral Karl Doenitz, who had set up his headquarters in Flensburg, near the Danish frontier. It fell upon Doenitz to bring the war to a close as far as Germany was concerned.

OCCUPATION

The shape of Germany's future was determined by Allied policy, not by German volition. The outlines of Allied policy toward Germany resulted from several basic considerations. It was believed that the fact of Germany's military defeat had to be brought home to the German people lest another "stab in the back" legend were to develop. Therefore unconditional surrender was demanded. It was felt that because of the deep penetration of National Socialism into every aspect of life, existing institutions and available officials could not be trusted. Therefore, not only military occupation but also military government of Germany was called for. Finally it was clear that the occupation of Germany would be a task devolving upon the principal Allied powers acting in concert.

It became clear at an early date that the military occupation and military government of Germany would have to be accomplished primarily on the basis of separate zones of occupation. This was necessary for two reasons: first, because the integration of officers from different nations into one working party had been tested in North Africa and Italy and had been found wanting; secondly, because of the far more important realization that any integration with a Russian staff was quite impossible except on the top level.[3]

YALTA AND POTSDAM

The conference of foreign ministers which met in Moscow during October, 1943, established the European Advisory Commission, which was given the task of preparing plans for the occupation of Germany as far as the tripartite level was concerned. Later, in 1944, the Provisional Government of France was invited to participate in these deliberations. But the Commission was not able to produce agreement, and thus a final decision had to be made on a higher level. This occurred at the Yalta conference, where it was decided that the United States, the U.S.S.R., and Great Britain should each occupy a zone in Germany, and that the French government should be invited to accept a similar zone for administration. It was also decided that the Soviet Union should occupy hitherto Polish land approximately as far as the so-called Curzon line, and that Poland should be compensated by "substantial accessions" of German territory. This latter provision was later implemented by

[3] A graphic and authoritative description of this lack of liaison between the Western Allies and the Soviet Union can be found in the book by Major General J. R. Deane, *Strange Alliance*, New York, 1947.

the Potsdam conference in August, which handed over to Polish administration all Germany east of the rivers Oder and Neisse, plus the city of Stettin, except the northern part of East Prussia including the city of Königsberg (now renamed Kaliningrad) which was definitely ceded to the Soviet Union.[4]

All German authority actually came to an end as a result of the act of unconditional surrender of May 7 and 8, 1945.[5] The Doenitz government was dissolved and its members imprisoned. Despite vague threats about a Nazi underground movement (*Wehrwolf*), implying the possibility of an underground government or a government in exile, no traces of such subterranean authority have been found.

ALLIED CONTROL

The Allied powers took formal possession of Germany on June 5, 1945, declaring that

. . . the Governments of the United States of America, the Union of Soviet Socialist Republics, and the United Kingdom, and the Provisional Government of the French Republic, hereby assume supreme authority with respect to Germany, including all the powers possessed by the German Government, the High Command, and any state, municipal, or local government or authority.

At the same time, the four zones of occupation and the quadripartite regime of the city of Berlin were finally established. There was also constituted the supreme Allied authority for Germany, the Allied Control Council, and a similarly appointed quadripartite body to adminster the city of Berlin, known by the Russian name of *Komandatura*.

The Allied Control Council, the *Komandatura* in Berlin, and the Allied zone commanders were the sole authority in Germany. Such German authorities as existed then existed by sufferance. Military-government law was the supreme law of the land.

[4] *Department of State Bulletin*, Aug. 5, 1945.

[5] *The Axis in Defeat*, Department of State Publication 2423, pp. 23–25. This publication contains many other documents pertaining to the surrender and the establishment of Allied authority.

Chapter 8

ALLIED CONTROL OVER GERMANY

Military occupation and military government of Germany after her defeat were an inevitable, foregone conclusion. There was no anti-Nazi resistance movement nor a recognized German government in exile which could have taken over the control. Since those who had governed Germany under Hitler could obviously not be permitted to continue their task, only military government remained as a workable alternative. To this end, elaborate planning and training took place in the United States and Great Britain.[1] The Russians, on the other hand, thought that they could rely primarily on German Communists, many of whom had long been trained in Moscow and had become Soviet citizens.

The division of Germany into zones, and especially the establishment of a Russian zone in Eastern Germany, have often been criticized. That this presented a tragedy can hardly be denied. However, it is difficult to see what alternative existed. Negotiations over the future occupation of Germany go back as far as 1943 and 1944. Before the invasion of Europe by the American and British forces it was by no means certain that the Russians would not occupy Germany before the Western forces arrived there. They had, after all, no ocean to cross, and their armies were on the march westward after the German defeat at Stalingrad in January, 1943. It seemed therefore imperative to come to some sort of understanding with the Russians. This meant the division of Germany into zones of approximately equal size and importance. No other basis of agreement with Moscow was feasible.

Allied, especially American, policy toward Germany went through a number of phases, some of which were in violent contradiction to one another. During the war and under the growing impact of Nazi brutalities of which the American public was becoming increasingly aware, ideas were current which envisaged the destruction of Germany as a nation. The most prominent ideas in that direction were contained in the famous "Morgenthau Plan,"

---

[1] There is a considerable literature on military government and its problems. Carl J. Friedrich and Associates, *American Experiences in Military Government in World War II*, New York, 1948; Harold Zink, *American Military Government in Germany*, New York, 1947; Hojo Holborn, *Military Government Organization and Politics*, New York, 1947; W. Friedmann, *The Allied Military Government of Germany*, London, 1947.

which proposed permanent division, subjugation, and deindustrialization of Germany.[2] The Morgenthau Plan never became reality, but it had its impact on official American policy as laid down in the directive of the United States Chiefs of Staff of April 26, 1945 (JCS 1067). This directive showed a very stiff attitude toward the Germans, perhaps natural at the end of a protracted war and in view of the universal loathing for the Hitler regime. Its guiding principles were stated in these terms:[3]

It should be brought home to the Germans that Germany's ruthless warfare and the fanatical Nazi resistance have destroyed the German economy and made chaos and suffering inevitable and that the Germans cannot escape responsibility for what they have brought upon themselves.

"Germany will not be occupied for the purpose of liberation but as a defeated enemy nation. . . .

"The principal Allied objective is to prevent Germany from ever again becoming a threat to the peace of the world. . . .

To this end, the following steps were to be taken: (1) nothing was to be done to bring about the economic rehabilitation of Germany except insofar as that was necessary in the interest of military operation; (2) no relief was to be extended to the German people except as far as necessary in order to avoid disease and such disorder as might impede the Allied war effort; (3) denazification and demilitarization were to be carried out under all circumstances.

Whatever treatment one might wish to mete out to the Germans, the one thing which stands out in these directives is their totally negative character. Detailed instructions were given for the destruction of certain organizations and institutions, notably the Nazi party. But no guidance was offered to the harassed military government officials concerning the encouragement of positive political and economic action with a view toward an eventual rehabilitation of Germany. In defense of JCS 1067, it should be stated that this document concerned itself primarily with the immediate postcombat phase and was therefore essentially short-range in nature. The military chiefs expected at that time that the long-range program for an administration of Germany would eventually be taken over by a civilian agency of the government, presumably the Department of State.

The negative attitude soon proved impractical and was finally abandoned in 1947. But it created a frame of mind which was not conducive to strong positive action on the top planning and operational levels. However, it was not so much the recognition that this policy was unwise which effected a change but rather extraneous causes, one of which was Soviet policy.

[2] For the text, see facsimile reproduction in Henry Morgenthau's *Germany Is Our Problem*, New York, 1945.
[3] For the text, see *The Axis in Defeat*, Department of State Publication 2423, p. 40.

SOVIET POLICY

The Soviet forces, being without a military government organization, vested responsibility in their respective commanders of combat units, who had the help—if help it was—of the commissars and the NKVD, later MVD, men attached to their command. But from the very start, the Soviet Military Administration relied heavily on German Communists, many of whom they had brought with them.[4] While this was altogether in line with customary Soviet procedure, it was a less radical step than was expected by many observers.

Of all the belligerents on the Allied side, the Soviets were the only ones who consistently distinguished between the German people and the Nazis.[5] To emphasize this point, two significant organizations were formed in the Soviet Union during the war. One was the "Free Germany Committee," whose chief organizers were Wilhelm Pieck, veteran German Communist leader, and Erich Weinert, a Communist writer. Even more significant and certainly commanding far more prestige was the "Union of German Officers" founded by General Walter von Seydlitz and Lieutenant Count Otto von Einsiedel, and later headed by Field Marshal Friedrich von Paulus. All these were officers of the German sixth army which surrendered at Stalingrad. Von Paulus was its commanding officer, while Von Einsiedel achieved significance chiefly because he was a grandnephew of Prince Otto von Bismarck, the Iron Chancellor.

It was feared by many that the Soviet authorities were grooming the "Free Germany Committee" and the "Union of German Officers" as the future government of Germany, since the latter group especially could have appealed to a resurgent German nationalism, and since defeated nations seem to have a predilection for defeated generals. Contrary to such expectations, the above two groups were not transplanted intact to German soil.

The Soviet authorities managed to turn the absence of a Russian military government machinery into an asset. Being without adequately trained personnel of their own, they relied from the very beginning on German help. And since there were not enough tested Communists around, other Germans were also used. This made the Russian zone appear in a more favorable light, at least in that instance, than the zones in the West. Moreover the Russians opened schools and places of amusement from the very start while they remained closed in the West waiting for the denazification to take place.

[4] Most important were Wilhelm Pieck and Walter Ulbricht.

[5] It is interesting that Dr. Joseph Goebbels, German propaganda minister, considered the failure of the Western Allies to concede such a difference as one of their worst psychological blunders, which greatly aided German propaganda. These remarks appear again and again in *The Goebbels Diaries* (trans. and ed. by Louis P. Lochner), New York, 1948.

But most important of all was the Russian decision to license four political parties in their zone while the Western powers had forbidden all political activities until they could see clearly whom they could trust. There was danger that the Russian attitude might seem more liberal than that of the West, and to counter that danger the Western Allies were quickly forced to liberalize their own policies. Even so, the Russian policy might have gained considerable political success for the Soviet Union if it had not been for the savage conduct of so many Russian soldiers, which quickly nullified any favorable impression which the Soviet leaders might have wanted to create for their policies.

Even before Russian policy forced a different attitude on American military government, a gradual change made itself felt. The military authorities, in their search for reliable Germans to be used in responsible positions, had frequently appointed men who had been prominent in anti-Nazi political parties before Hitler's rise to power. These men of course immediately contacted their friends and quickly rebuilt a measure of political life before it was officially permitted. American military government officers were aware of this but they needed the relatively few reliable people then available and closed their eyes to an inevitable development, if they did not aid it. Thus, at a time when the official policy was still stiff aloofness, cooperation between military government and Germans became more and more intimate. Later, when the need to build up Germany as a bulwark against Russia became official policy, this was very much more accelerated, but that is part of a later development.

Zones of Occupation

After the cessation of hostilities, the Allied Powers moved into their respective zones of occupation, and a separate zone, considerably smaller than the others, was cut out of the British and American areas and handed over to French administration. On June 5, 1945, was created the then supreme authority for Germany, the Allied Control Council, and a similar, quadripartite, authority was established for the city of Berlin, the *Komandatura* mentioned in Chapter 9.

At first military government confined itself to the local level of territorial units, namely municipalities and districts (*Kreise*). As communications were restored, larger units of government were rebuilt. However, the task of re-creating a completely collapsed governmental and administrative structure was tremendous, and American, British, and French military government with all their faults accomplished an almost superhuman task.

As military government was established on higher levels, its problems multiplied since it became increasingly clear that even the *Länder* were not able to exist economically without integration in a larger country. Moreover, relations between the regular military commands and military government with their different organizational principles and overlapping authorities were not always easy.

DENAZIFICATION

A major stumbling block to successful military government was the monstrous problem of denazification. It was primarily inaugurated by the American planners, and it constituted a problem chiefly in the American zone. This does not mean that there were more Nazis in that zone than in the others. But from the very beginning the American authorities took a more idealistic line toward the problems of Nazism than did the other three occupying powers. The issue itself was simple enough. The terrible brutality of the Nazi regime had become obvious to all. Perhaps the stories of concentration camps had not been entirely believed in America before, despite so much corroborating evidence. But the discovery and liberation of such infernos as Dachau, Buchenwald, and Bergen-Belsen left no doubt whatsoever about the nature of the Nazi regime, and consequently determination to eradicate once and for all every vestige of Nazism grew by leaps and bounds.

It was clear from the beginning that the initial momentum had to be furnished by military government. Moreover, it was well remembered how the Germans had been able to frustrate the desire of the Allied Powers in the First World War to punish German leaders accused of war crimes.[6]

The policy of the United States was first established as follows: All holders of a certain rank in Nazi party organizations were to be automatically arrested and made ineligible for office of any kind. Party members were to be purged from all but menial labor if their membership antedated 1937.[7] This policy was established by JCS 1067 and carried out by Military Government Law No. 8. Later, it was further amplified by various directives.

It is easy enough to see objections to this kind of policy. The denazification rules established in effect a presumption of guilt for certain categories of people; this was contrary to the well-established principle of Anglo-American justice by which a person is considered innocent until proved guilty beyond reasonable doubt. It provided for long periods of imprisonment without trial, as a great number of Germans were affected by this rule and the denazification mills ground only slowly; this was contrary to the Anglo-American tradition of habeas corpus, speedy trial, and fair bail. Besides, the denazification laws

[6] Articles 227 and 228 of the Treaty of Versailles provided for the extradition and trial of the ex-Kaiser and certain military leaders. The ex-Kaiser was never extradited because of the refusal of the Netherlands government; the generals received mock trials in Leipzig, if they were tried at all, and went free with some minor exceptions.

[7] In 1937, the German Civil Service Code was promulgated, and from that time on great pressure to join the Nazi party was exerted, especially against public officials.

were clearly ex post facto laws. While certain other offenses committed by
Nazis might have been considered criminal by direct application of law or by
reasonable analogy, membership or the holding of office in the Nazi party
per se were of course absolutely legal at the time. And finally, the denazification laws deprived many of the best trained experts of their chance to participate in the rehabilitation of Germany. While many of them were guilty
and incapable of fitting into a democratic order, many others had joined up
for reasons of opportunism or fear.

But on the other hand, it is difficult to see what other policy military government could have pursued. The Allied forces were committed to the eradi-
cation of Nazism, which had just thrown the world into a holocaust of death
and destruction. For reasons mentioned above, the task of eliminating Nazis
could not be left to the Germans, at least not in the beginning, and the military-government officials, most of whom knew little about Germany and were
only human, could not be permitted very much discretion in the matter. Consequently the directives which they received established a necessarily mechanical approach. It happened therefore that some real Nazis who had played
a major role in the Hitler war machine were exonerated because for some
reason or other they had never bothered to join the Nazi party, while others,
who had joined under pressure or out of regard for their families, found themselves eliminated from all professional careers. On the whole, however, the
denazification system was not intrinsically unfair. What made it so was the
number of cases involved. Over 11,000,000 people had to register. There were
no authorities, American or German, who could have handled such a staggering number with any degree of expedition.

Then, as military government did not have the personnel to accomplish
such a task, it was eventually turned over to the Germans, although this was
not achieved without some initial difficulties. Upon request by the American
military-government authorities, the Council of German Prime Ministers in
the United States zone, the *Länderrat,* submitted a draft law for denazification
and demilitarization. This was rejected by military government. There were
fundamental differences between the German and American approach to the
problem: the Americans wanted to judge former Nazis on the basis of their
former positions in public and economic life, while the Germans wanted to
confine trials to actual offenses committed. Moreover, in fining business
leaders who had profited from their Nazi activities, the Germans wanted to
extract much larger fines than the Americans were willing to grant. Finally
the Germans wanted to enact legislation for the purpose of checking unproven
accusations.[8]

The "Law for the Liberation from National Socialism and Militarism" was

[8] Carl J. Friedrich, "Denazification," in Friedrich *et al., op cit.,* pp. 263–265. W. E.
Griffith, "Denazification in the United States Zone of Germany," *Annals of the American
Academy of Political and Social Science,* January, 1950, pp. 68–76.

finally proclaimed by the Council of Prime Ministers and approved by military government on March 5, 1946. It recognized the supremacy of Military Government Law No. 8 and of the Allied Control Council Directive No. 24,[9] which established the over-all policy for the removal of Nazis from office. But the very fact that the final form of this law was determined to a considerable extent by the directives of American military government kept the Germans from considering it a really "German" law and thus deprived it of some of its psychological effect.

The law [10] established five classes of persons required to register as Nazis: (1) major offenders, (2) offenders, (3) lesser offenders, (4) followers, and (5) exonerated persons who upon investigation proved not to have been Nazis. The offenders were further subdivided into (*a*) activists (Art. 7), (*b*) militarists (Art. 8), and (*c*) profiteers (Art. 9). This portion of the law generally followed the preference of the German leaders for the principle of punishment for acts committed. But, upon insistence of the military-government authorities, there was appended to the law the principle contained in Control Council Directive No. 24, which embodied the American idea of punishment for positions held under the Nazi regime. This appendix referred not only to Nazi leaders of the upper ranks, but to virtually all functionaries, local or national. It also placed in the same category business and professional men of importance, higher ranking judges, all civil servants, and many more. All such persons were to be removed and made ineligible for future appointment.

The Prime Ministers refused to sign the appendix, which fortified the contention that this was an "American" law. They refused to accept the lumping together of Nazi party leaders with high civil servants and business leaders which, they felt, would only exonerate the real Nazis by placing them in one group with generally respected people. One of the keenest American observers has remarked that "no one reading the list . . . can help feeling that the men responsible for it sought a wholesale indictment of the German ruling class in all its branches."

The law established local denazification boards (*Spruchkammern*) and appeal boards, on which was now conferred major responsibility for carrying out the denazification program. This was a jump from one extreme into another. The American denazification authorities had neither the staff nor the detailed knowledge necessary to accomplish this stupendous task. But in many respects it was even worse for the German tribunals. The type of work demanded from the members of the tribunal was not such that leading citizens

---

[9] *Occupation of Germany, Policy and Progress, 1945–46,* Department of State Publication 2783, pp. 20, 113 (excerpts).

[10] For the full text, see James K. Pollock and James H. Meisel, *Germany under Occupation,* Ann Arbor, 1947, p. 179. Excerpts may be found in *Occupation of Germany,* Department of State Publication 2783, p. 119.

or first-line party leaders would willingly indulge in it. Therefore some doubtful elements—a minority, to be sure—found their way to the bench or the prosecutor's table. Secondly, it was a case of neighbors trying and judging neighbors, and consequently strong pressure was brought to bear upon the tribunals. And while the Germans were able to mobilize more staff than the Americans, their number was still quite inadequate. Under the law of March 5, 1946, 11,674,152 persons had been obliged to register. By the end of 1946, only 125,738, that is, a little over 1 per cent, had been tried.

The denazification system created a peculiar situation. A large number of people and their families lived under a shadow. Since they had been obliged to register with the denazification authorities, most of them were barred from their usual employment, and many of them faced financial ruin or a laborer's existence, considered degrading by the white-collar class. Yet most of these people were not deprived of their physical liberty. They were free to go about and spread disaffection. Moreover, the lighter cases were to be tried first, which was meant to favor the lesser offenders and followers, but frequently had the opposite result; the severity of the denazification procedure was eventually modified, and it was thus often the more dangerous cases who benefited from this new attitude, while many of the lesser offenders had already received more substantial punishment under the older system.

The magnitude of the denazification problem and the gradual reconsideration of the whole German issue eventually created a certain amount of relaxation of the law. In July, 1946, military government granted an amnesty to all German youth born between January 1, 1919, and March 5, 1928—the reason being that this generation had been entirely brought up under the Nazi regime and had had no opportunity to acquaint itself with democratic ways. Then on December 24, 1946, General McNarney extended an amnesty to approximately 800,000 lesser offenders and followers whose financial status was conclusive evidence that they had not profited from the Nazi regime.

The real breakdown of the denazification laws actually occurred in the German tribunals, which were far behind in their work and became more and more lenient.[11] Despite all attempts of the so-called "Special Branch" of military government's Public Safety Division, denazification became more and more of a mechanical process, something like delousing—unpleasant, but with clearly foreseeable results. Only prominent Nazis had to fear the tribunals, and even that was not always true, especially with numerous refugees from the East who were unknown in their new environment and frequently managed to hide their former identity.

Another major cause of the breakdown in the denazification procedure was the fact that only in the American zone was there any serious attempt at it. The British had a brief try but on the whole confined themselves to grave

---

[11] On Nov. 5, 1946, General Lucius Clay, the American Commander, felt obliged to rebuke the Germans for this laxity. *New York Times*, Nov. 6, 1946.

cases. They took great pains to investigate and if possible clear quickly those whom they wished to appoint to more important positions. In the French and Soviet zones there never was any denazification to speak of, although some former Nazi leaders were liquidated with or without trial. In July, 1947, Marshal Sokolovsky declared a virtual amnesty for all Nazis in the Soviet zone except for the most serious offenders.[12] Former Nazis who join the Socialist Unity party (SED), the Communist-dominated official favorite of the Soviet authorities, are treated with indulgence and often even with considerable favor, as their bad past record puts them at the mercy of the authorities, who know that they could not afford to be disloyal to their new masters. Thus they are sometimes preferred over less pliable men of proven anti-Nazi convictions.

The isolation of the American denazification effort, the tremendous scope of the task, the inner conflicts over policy within the American element, and German reluctance to enforce a "foreign" denazification law deprived the program of much of its original meaning.

Toward a New German State

More and more responsibility was handed over to Germans, especially after local elections had produced more durable native authorities. Gradually active military government withdrew in stages, first from the local municipal and district level, soon thereafter from the regional and provincial levels, and finally even from those of the *Länder*. On the lower echelon only liaison and security officers were left who generally did not directly interfere in the administration but reported their observations to higher, zonal, headquarters. This process was fastest in the United States and U.S.S.R. zones, considerably slower in the British regions, and slowest in the French. Eventually, however, it was completed everywhere.

In principle the former *Länder* were reconstituted where possible. However, all of them had to submit to some surgery, partly in order to accommodate the carved-up pieces of Prussia, partly to settle within the zonal boundary lines, partly to eliminate enclaves and exclaves. Bavaria lost the Palatinate, and a new state of Hesse was created out of all or parts of the former *Land* Hesse and the provinces of Hesse-Nassau and Kurhesse. The various Saxonies were split between the British and Soviet zones. The former Rhine Province, an administrative part of Prussia, had to be divided when the French zone was carved out of the British and American spheres. The former *Länder* of Baden and Württemberg were split for the same reason: the *Land* Württemberg-Baden was created out of parts of both and placed in the American zone, while the rest was divided into two other *Länder*,

[12] Law No. 201, Soviet Military Administration.

Baden and Württemberg-Hohenzollern, which were placed in the French zone. In 1952 these three states were reunited as a result of a plebiscite, and the combined state is now called Baden-Württemberg.

A similar development took place in the Soviet zone, although there the *Länder* were later abolished in favor of a more centralistic government.

The combined territory of the Eastern and Western zones does not correspond to the area of former Weimar or Nazi Germany. The Saar territory has a government of its own and has close ties with France. It is practically separated from Germany. The province of East Prussia has been absorbed by the Soviet Union and Poland. The vast and important area east of the rivers Oder and Neisse, including the city of Stettin, has been handed over to Polish administration, which considers this area as an integral part of Polish territory, in compensation for former Polish territory in the east ceded to the Soviet Union. The Western Allies have always insisted that Poland merely acts as administrator and that a final settlement is yet to be made at a future peace conference.[13] However, their acquiescence in the wholesale removal of 9,000,000 Germans from that area would indicate that the eastern frontier of Germany is already effectively determined, short of another war. Germany has thus lost about one-third of her former territory as it existed after the Treaty of Versailles. At the same time she has maintained her former population despite this shrunken territory, as her war losses were more than made up by the influx of German refugees from such areas as the Sudetenland and the Balkans. The congestion of people in the remaining territory is therefore all the more serious. Moreover, apart from widespread war damage,[14] there has been considerable dismantling and removal of industrial equipment under the provisions of the Potsdam Agreement. Very serious is the loss of approximately 25 per cent of Germany's food-producing land and 11 per cent of her industrial area to Poland and the U.S.S.R.

When the European Advisory Commission and later the Potsdam conference established the crazy-quilt zone pattern of Germany, it was already apparent that Germany could not be governed through such small units as the *Länder* represented. The Potsdam agreement had stipulated (Item 14) that "during the period of occupation, Germany shall be treated as a single economic unit." It was also envisaged (Item 9, iv) that certain central administrative departments headed by state secretaries were to be created, particularly in the fields of finance, transport, communications, foreign trade, and industry.

It is now a matter of record that this plan did not work. The Soviet Union

---

[13] Potsdam agreement, Item 9. *Occupation of Germany*, Department of State Publication 2783, pp. 74*f.*

[14] See United States Strategic Bombing Survey's *The Effects of Strategic Bombing on German Morale*, Washington, 1947.

never permitted an economic integration of the zones, let alone a political one. The French were actually the first to object to a central German authority, but their reservations were quickly overshadowed by the widening split between Washington and London on the one side, and Washington and Moscow on the other.

Faced by the impossibility of creating larger administrative and economic units because of insurmountable Soviet obstruction, and confronted by a dangerous stagnation and decline of whatever German economy was left, the Western powers undertook such combinations as were available to them. First there was created in the American zone the Council of Prime Ministers, the *Länderrat,* whose chief architect was the noted American political scientist, Professor James K. Pollock. Its experiences were very valuable in later developments. Later, as a result of the London conference of June, 1948, the British and American zones were increasingly combined, and eventually a fusion of all three was accomplished. This conference, in which the United States, Great Britain, France, Belgium, the Netherlands, and Luxembourg participated,[15] provided for (1) eventual fusion of the three Western zones; (2) the establishment of a provisional Western German government; (3) an occupation statute which was to define the powers of the occupying states and of the Germans respectively; (4) an international authority of the Ruhr; and (5) minor territorial adjustments of Germany's western border.

The three military governors of the Western powers notified the German Prime Ministers of the London decisions and outlined to them the procedure which was to be followed in calling a constituent assembly. The initial sailing was a bit rough, because the German party leaders composed their differences and issued a counterresolution to the request of the Allies.[16] They proposed to call the constituent assembly "Parliamentary Council," and they opined that the document to be drafted should not have the status of a full-fledged constitution but should rather be a basic law of provisional nature. The drafting of a permanent document was to be deferred until "the Allies are ready to return their sovereignty to the German people." Other objections were also stated, especially regarding the association of the occupation statute with the constitution.

The objections of the German leaders were a political maneuver caused by confusion. The Germans apparently did not realize that the proposals presented to them constituted the result of agreement between the Western Allies, not merely the policy of the military governors. They were prompted to their action by a fear of becoming vulnerable to the accusation of "splitting Ger-

[15] See the text of the agreement between the United States, the United Kingdom, France, and the Benelux countries (Belgium, Netherlands, Luxembourg), *Department of State Bulletin,* June 20, 1948, pp. 807–813.

[16] For a detailed and revealing exposition of these and other developments leading to the adoption of the new constitution, see C. J. Friedrich, "Rebuilding the German Constitution," *American Political Science Review,* Vol. XLIII (1949), pp. 461–482, 704–720.

many" which was the propaganda line of the Communists and of some nationalist circles.

Reason eventually prevailed, and various face-saving devices were adopted in order to permit the Germans to accept the Allied plan without too much loss of face.

THE OCCUPATION STATUTE

The occupation statute itself brought on another battle. The Germans wanted the powers of the Allies more narrowly defined, wanted to limit Allied interference as much as possible, and wanted to broaden the guarantee of civil rights against Allied police action except when the purpose of the occupation itself was endangered.

Few of the German objections were permitted to survive, and on September 21, 1949, the occupation statute entered into force substantially as agreed upon by the three Western foreign ministers at the Washington conference of April 8, 1949.[17]

The occupation statute stipulates that the German government shall have all powers except those specifically reserved to the Allied powers. These reserved powers may be exercised in the following fields: (1) disarmament and demilitarization; (2) control of the Ruhr, restitution of property taken away by the Nazis, reparations, decartelization, antitrust matters, foreign interests in Germany, and claims against Germany; (3) foreign affairs; (4) protections, prestige, and security of the Allied forces, dependents, employees, and representatives, as well as occupation costs; (5) respect for the Basic Law (Constitution) and the constitutions of the *Länder;* (6) control of foreign trade and exchange; (7) control over internal action to a minimum extent and only insofar as to ensure the use of food, funds, and other supplies in such manner as to reduce to a minimum the need for external assistance to Germany; and (8) authority over prisoners charged or sentenced before courts of the occupation powers or occupation authorities.

Technically these powers could be extended to every other field if conditions warrant. Section 3 of the statute reserves to the occupation authorities the right "to resume in whole or in part the exercise of full authority if they consider that to do so is essential to security or to preserve democratic government in Germany. . . ."

The area of the "reserved powers" is not closed to German legislation. The German Federal Government and the *Länder* may legislate and act after due notification to the occupation authorities. However, such action must not be

---

[17] The text of the occupation statute may be found in the *1st Quarterly Report on Germany,* issued by the Office of the U.S. High Commissioner for Germany, Washington, 1950, Appendix IV. See also Edward H. Litchfield and Associates, *Governing Postwar Germany,* Ithaca, 1953, pp. 616*ff.*

contrary to occupation policy, and the Allied authorities may of course nullify all German action in the "reserved" fields. All amendments to the federal Constitution need the approval of the occupation authorities.

A fair appraisal will show that the Allies have been using these reserved powers moderately and to an ever-decreasing extent. These prerogatives were further limited by the Petersberg Protocol of November 22, 1949.[18] On May 26, 1952, the Foreign Ministers of Britain, France, and the United States, as well as the Chancellor of Germany, signed a treaty on the relations between the three powers and the Federal Republic of Germany. This treaty restored virtually complete sovereignty to Germany, revoked the occupation statute, and abolished the Allied High Commission and Offices of the *Land* Commissioners.[19] However, this treaty, generally called the Bonn Treaty, was tied to the ratification of the treaty to create the European Defense Community which was signed in Paris on May 27, 1952. This treaty was defeated by the French National Assembly in 1954 but a substitute arrangement, known as the Western European Union, narrowly passed. Since France, Germany, and Italy have finally ratified the agreement, and other nations are following their example, for all practical purposes German sovereignty is virtually an accomplished fact. The Allied High Commissioners, who upon the adoption of the German Constitution in 1949 replaced the Military Governors, have in turn been transformed into Ambassadors, in June, 1953. Germany has established embassies and legations abroad as well as consulates, whose existence clearly indicates the *de facto* sovereignty of the German Federal Republic.

Another temporary limitation on German sovereignty was the Allied control over the Ruhr industries, which culminated in the creation of the International Authority for the Ruhr on December 28, 1948. This Authority, however, never achieved full effectiveness. Its power to allocate material in order to prevent discriminatory policies quickly became pointless since coal, coke, and steel were no longer in short supply. With the creation of the European Coal and Steel Community (Schuman Plan), the Ruhr Authority was officially terminated in February, 1953.

[18] *First Quarterly Report on Germany,* Appendix VII. Also Litchfield, *op. cit.,* pp. 619*ff.*

[19] *Ibid.,* pp. 622*ff. Department of State Bulletin,* June 16, 1952, p. 931.

Chapter 9

CONSTITUTIONAL GOVERNMENT IN THE FEDERAL REPUBLIC OF GERMANY

Ever since the German *Länder* governments were reestablished, the American military-government authorities pressed for the drafting and adoption of constitutions. The other occupation nations followed suit with the British trailing behind, partly because their own form of government has no room for a formal single constitutional document, partly because the transfer of governmental authority to the Germans was slowest in the British zone.[1] Certain general principles were drawn up by the occupation authorities, but they were basically what the Germans would have adopted anyhow. But the speed with which the Germans felt obliged to work in the United States zone produced documents some of which fall considerably short of perfection.

In principle the German leaders had no objection to the drafting of *Länder* constitutions as such. There had always been such separate documents even under the Weimar Republic, and nobody believed they were incompatible with the sacred concept of German unity. Article 13 of the Weimar Constitution had provided that *Reichsrecht bricht Landrecht* (national law overrules *Land* law), and *Länder* constitutions paid their respect to the aspiration of an all-German state. The constitutions in the Soviet zone proclaimed themselves "part of a German Democratic Republic" long before such an entity was created, and many constitutions in the West repeated the provision of Art. 13 of the Weimar Constitution with slight variations. Bavaria, always the most "separatist," merely promised to join a future federal state (Art. 178) if certain conditions were fulfilled.[2] Baden stated that its adherence to a federal constitution of Germany would necessitate a constitutional amendment—which is so obvious as to be superfluous.

A. DRAFTING THE NEW CONSTITUTION

While the German leaders readily accepted the principle of establishing *Länder* constitutions, they raised fundamental objections against drafting a

[1] R. G. Neumann, "New Constitutions in Germany," *American Political Science Review,* Vol. XLII (1948), pp. 448–468.

[2] Voluntary adherence and retention of a measure of autonomy (*staatsrechtliches Eigenleben*).

constitution for Western Germany. We have already mentioned that they were reluctant to undertake any action which could be interpreted as accepting or even approving the permanent division of Germany. But this was not all. Many German politicians felt that the *Länder* constitutions had been discredited in the eyes of the public by the occupation authorities and troops who disregarded them at will.[3] Now it was of course understood that the occupation authorities were not legally bound by the German constitutions, but since they had so often affirmed their devotion to democratic ideals, their arbitrary actions added no credit to their words. Where public safety was involved, the direct intervention of military authorities was easily understandable. But it was not so understandable why the American authorities stubbornly refused to permit a party press in their zone or why there were arbitrary arrests, even though some were justified. On these matters Germans and occupation authorities were bound to have different viewpoints, but it should be stressed that the fears of the German leaders were motivated by their desire to see a future constitution firmly established and accepted by their people without being first discredited. It is possible that the Germans were abnormally sensitive on this point, but that too is understandable.

The first difficulty was partly averted by avoiding the term *Verfassung* (constitution) and instead using *Grundgesetz* (basic law), which does not carry quite the same connotation of sovereignty in German usage. Secondly the preamble proclaims that it is the purpose of the Basic Law "to give a new order to political life for a *transitional* period" (author's italics). And the Constitution calls upon the entire German people "to accomplish, by free self-determination, the unity and freedom of Germany." [4]

This pacified the consciences of the German draftsmen, who were then able to undertake the actual task of writing a new constitution. A special commission was appointed by the Prime Ministers of the *Länder* to lay the groundwork for the constitution, drafting those provisions on which there was agreement and presenting alternative suggestions concerning those on which no consensus could be reached. This document was submitted to the Parliamentary Council, which began to work on it on September 1, 1948. Chairman of the Council was the present Federal Chancellor (Prime Minister) Dr. Konrad Adenauer.

---

[3] Friedrich, "Rebuilding the German Constitution," *American Political Science Review,* Vol. XLIII (1949), cites numerous examples, p. 476. It should be said that in the majority of cases there was no intention on the part of the military authorities to flout German authorities; rather, there was lack of coordination and mutual understanding. Frequently the military authorities felt that the German officials did not act vigorously enough, and a good case can be made for that contention.

[4] The term "basic law" was to denote both incompleteness and transitional stage because of Germany's division. The *rapporteur,* Carlo Schmid, called Western Germany a "State-Fragment." Hermann von Mangoldt, *Das Bonner Grundgesetz,* Berlin and Frankfort, 1953, p. 25.

The drafting process was not entirely smooth, not only because of disagreement between the two major political parties, the Christian Democrats and the Social Democrats, but also because military government injected itself. There were questions pertaining to the degree of federalism which the new state was to have. The Americans and French pressed for a federal solution, while the British favored a more centralized form of government. The problems of the emergency powers, the presidency, bicameralism, the stability of the government, the relationship between the *Länder* and the federation—all were the basis of considerable and able discussion.

On February 11, 1949, the executive committee of the Parliamentary Council submitted a draft to the military governors for their comments, prior to the final adoption of the draft. Then fireworks began to fly. The military governors found a long list of objections throughout the entire document. Their justification cannot be examined here, but they provided an unprecedented intervention of military government in the drafting process, and although the military governors later retreated from many of their positions, they nevertheless furnished antidemocratic elements the argument that the constitution was not a "German" document. This accusation is quite unfounded in fact, for a substantial compromise was eventually reached, but it is debatable whether the gain achieved by the military governors' objections was worth the "foreign" shadow thus cast on the Basic Law of the Federal Republic of Germany.[5]

B. CIVIL RIGHTS

The Constitution opens with a declaration of civil rights which manifests considerable improvement over the Weimar and *Länder* constitutions. Article 1 declares the enumerated civil rights to be "directly valid law on legislation, administration, and judiciary." This lays to rest, once and for all, the assertion heard during the Weimar Republic that civil rights were only "declaratory" and did not constitute actual legal obligations. Nevertheless there are some "rights" in the Constitution which, because of their nature, cannot actually be "directly valid law," like the provision that "marriage and family are under the particular protection of the state" (Art. 6, Sec. 1).

There is a long list of rights: political, social, economic, moral, educational, etc. This is in line with other new constitutions, as for instance those of France and Italy. However, the Weimar Constitution's example of including practically every party program and promising every "right" under the sun has happily not been repeated, and the Bonn Constitution is in that respect more streamlined and realistic. Some of its sections are, naturally enough, projected against the experience of the Nazi regime, such as the first section of Art. 1, which declares the dignity of man inviolable.

[5] The word "constitution" will be used henceforth in line with American usage.

There is the customary protection of physical inviolability as well as of free speech, press, and assembly. There is also the equivalent of *habeas corpus*, which is made even more specific than is the case in the United States, for under the German provisions (Art. 104) it is not necessary that the accused apply for a writ of *habeas corpus*. On the day following his arrest he must be taken before a judge, who will then decide. However, under the German practice it is more difficult to be released on bail.

Censorship is specifically prohibited (Art. 5). Equality before the law and the legal equality of the sexes are also guaranteed. The Constitution not only guarantees the free exercise and profession of all faiths but also includes nonreligious ideologies (*Weltanschauungen*) and specifically recognizes the right to conscientious objection (Art. 4).

Property and the right to inheritance are guaranteed, and while the right of the government to take private property for public use with just compensation (eminent domain) is also granted, appeal to the regular courts is permissible in case of dispute.

Emphasis is placed on the right to join labor unions. Agreements not to join unions ("yellow-dog contracts") are declared null and void (Art. 9).

The problem of education is handled with special care because the controversy of private (parochial) versus public schools is well known in Germany's political history. Religious instruction has always been part of the regular curriculum of German schools, private and public. The Constitution guarantees and perpetuates that system (Art. 7) in all state schools except in the so-called "nonconfessional schools." Private schools are also permitted to exist and are placed on an equal level with state schools, provided they meet the same standards. Recognition of private schools is a duty of the governmental authorities unless proper standards are not met, or segregation of students according to their means is encouraged, or the economic or legal status of the teaching staff is not sufficiently assured (Art. 7). Private elementary (grade) schools are permitted only under certain circumstances, when there is a specific need or when the parents of eligible children request it or when a public elementary school of the same type is not available.

The Constitution deems it necessary to declare that "arts and science, research and instruction are free" (Art. 5), but it is of course clear that the freedom of teaching pertains only to the university level, that is, to academic freedom in the generally accepted sense. In Germany as well as everywhere else, teaching on the primary and secondary levels is strictly subject to regulation by competent authority. The German Constitution adds a loyalty provision stating that "freedom of teaching does not absolve from loyalty to the Constitution." This is a provision which shows that the framers remembered the days when the German universities were centers of antirepublican and Nazi agitation.

One of the chief complaints against the Weimar Constitution and the recent constitutions of the *Länder* was the fact that all the civil rights which they contained existed only "within the framework of the law" or, in other words, could be set aside by law. Since civil rights are endangered in exceptional and critical times when legislatures are frequently willing to cloak governments with extraordinary powers and become rubber stamps, this type of "guarantee" seems a slender reed to lean upon. The Bonn Constitution repeats this process but with significant modifications. In the first place we have already seen that it declares all basic rights directly binding upon all courts and authorities. The law on the Federal Constitutional Court of March 12, 1951, also permits individuals whose civil rights have been injured to make a direct plaint (*Verfassungsbeschwerde*) to the Federal Constitutional Court. Secondly it decrees that limitations of basic rights by law must be general and must not apply to specific cases only. The basic nature of a civil right must not be changed. These limitations are somewhat vague because a law can be framed in such a way as to have general application in theory while it pertains only to specific cases or persons in actual practice. There is also a question as to what constitutes the basic nature of a civil right, especially as Art. 18 provides that "whoever abuses the freedom of expression of opinion . . . in order to attack the free, democratic basic order, shall forfeit these basic rights." A corollary to this rule is also the provision of Art. 21 which declares as unconstitutional "parties which, according to their aims and the behavior of their members, seek to impair or abolish the free and democratic basic order or to jeopardize the existence of the Federal Republic of Germany. . . ." The Federal Constitutional Court decides the application of both Arts. 18 and 21. The reason for these sections is easy to see in view of the way in which the Nazis utilized the civil rights and guarantees of the Weimar Constitution to their own advantage.

Whatever the excellence or fault of written constitutional guarantees, the paper on which they are printed alone does not safeguard them. The Bonn Constitution has therefore instituted a special court for this purpose, the Federal Constitutional Court. The abovementioned forfeiture of basic rights because of abuse must be pronounced by the Federal Constitutional Court, which exercises judicial review and thus has the power to invalidate laws which violate the guarantees of civil rights contained in the Constitution. Similar courts had previously been established by the *Länder* constitutions of the Western zones.

It is of course too early to pass judgment on these constitutional courts. The record of the courts in the Weimar Republic certainly was poor. While there was no constitutional court and no judicial review, the Weimar courts nevertheless had much opportunity to deal with problems involving basic rights as well as attacks against the Republic. By and large the Weimar courts were antidemocratic and antirepublican, showing much leniency to the enemies of democracy and utmost severity to its defenders. Many German judges are holdovers from that period, and some courts have delivered judgments in political cases which must be considered objectionable from a democratic point of view. The Federal Constitutional Court, however, has shown itself amazingly courageous and outspoken, and in dissolving the neo-Nazi Socialist Reich party it did not hesitate to condemn sharply all the racist and nationalistic neo-Nazi practices of that group.[6] This constitutes a most encouraging record.

In discussing the chances for the survival and improvement of civil liberties in Germany, one must not lose sight of the fact that in the long run their existence rests on the response of an alert public. Where public opinion is indifferent or hostile to civil liberties, institutional safeguards are powerless to protect them. On the other hand, a watchful public opinion knows how to transmit its sentiments to courts and administrations. At this time recognition of the desirability of debate, inborn respect for other viewpoints, and essential moderation in public affairs are still not widespread German virtues, and the educational system still carries somewhat of an authoritarian note. But a fair and encouraging beginning has been made. Time alone will tell whether these virtues, which in the German past have been rare, will develop and multiply or whether they will die on the vine.

C. FEDERALISM

The new West German state is a federal union. The appropriate sections of the Constitution (Arts. 20–37, 50–53, 70–75, 105–109) are not too different from their counterparts in the Weimar Constitution, but the abolition of Prussia leaves the Federal Republic of Germany as a union of reasonably equal *Länder*. The smallest *Land* in respect to inhabitants, Bremen, has 750,000, while the largest, North Rhine-Westphalia, has 10,000,000. The crazy-quilt pattern of *Länder* created in the southwest corner of Germany by the artificial establishment of the French zone of occupation was greatly improved in 1952 when the former *Länder* of Württemberg-Baden, Württemberg-Hohenzollern, and Baden were united into one *Land* called Baden-Württemberg.

The Constitution establishes the principle of expressed and enumerated powers for the federation, with the *Länder* possessing all other (reserved) powers. The respective fiscal powers are precisely spelled out in Arts. 105–109. Exclusive federal powers extend to foreign affairs, nationality, passports, migration and extradition, currency, customs, border control, railroad and air traffic, post and telegraph, trade mark, copyright, cooperation with the *Länder* in matters of criminal police, protection of the Constitution, vice control, and federal statistics (Art. 73). The field of concurrent powers in which

[6] Decision of the Federal Constitutional Court establishing the unconstitutionality of the Socialist Reich party, *Bundesverfassungsgericht*, 1 BvB 1/51, Oct. 23, 1952.

both the federation and the *Länder* may legislate is far more extensive. It covers the entire economy, all criminal and civil law as well as labor legislation, the control of associations and assemblies, railways, highway and water traffic, and many more subjects too numerous to mention (Art. 74). Of important fields, only education and police remain exclusively in the hands of the *Länder*. However, "in order to avert imminent danger to the existence or the free democratic basic order of the Federation or a *Land*, a *Land* may call for police assistance from other *Länder*." But if the *Land* concerned is not in a position to combat the danger, "the Federal Government may place the police in that *Land*, or the police forces of other *Länder* under its control" (Art. 91). This arrangement must be rescinded after the danger has passed or whenever the *Bundesrat* demands.

In the field of concurrent powers the *Länder* governments are presumably autonomous and may even conclude treaties with foreign countries concerning subjects under their control, although they may be overruled by superior federal law. However, the Constitution attempts to establish limits to federal legislation by the provision (Art. 72) that the federation shall legislate in the area of concurrent powers only under the following conditions: (1) when a matter cannot be effectively regulated by the *Länder*; (2) if the regulations of one *Land* prejudice the rights of another *Land* or *Länder*; or (3) if "the preservation of legal or economic unity demands in particular the preservation of uniformity of living conditions extending beyond the territory of an individual *Land*." The last condition is exceedingly broad and could, if rashly used, nullify all vestiges of federalism.

Considerable power is also wielded by the federal government through the way in which it administers its policies. Just as in the Weimar Republic, the (Bonn) federal government relies on the *Länder* authorities to execute most of the federal regulations.[7] The *Länder* bureaucracies thus have two sets of functions: those which they exercise in their "autonomous" role, and those which devolve upon them as arms of the federal government. But this of course means federal control, and the Constitution provides that the federal government shall exercise supervision over the *Länder* governments to see to it that federal laws are faithfully executed. The federation may also establish certain uniform standards and practices and send supervisory commissioners to the *Länder* governments if the latter approve or, failing that, if the *Bundesrat* does. The federation may also issue specific, detailed orders (*Einzelanweisungen*). Under the Weimar Republic the *Reich* government (technically, the President) had the right to compel the *Länder* to obedience, even by use of armed might (*Reichsexekution*). Under the Bonn Constitution this right (*Bundeszwang*, federal compulsion) is much more circumscribed. Article 37

---

[7] Direct federal administration on all levels is provided for in the following fields: foreign service, finance administration, railways, and postal services, and conditionally for waterways and shipping (Art. 87).

provides that if a *Land* does not fulfill its obligations under the Constitution or a federal law, the federal government may compel obedience by all means at its disposal and may also commandeer or direct the facilities of the *Länder*. However, and this is an important difference from the Weimar system, such action is possible only with the consent of the *Bundesrat*, which thus becomes the deciding authority. A less drastic form of intervention is a complaint of a *Land* or of the federal government to the *Bundesrat* charging a *Land* with the nonfulfillment of its obligations, provided such nonfulfillment has first been demanded directly by the federal government under its right of federal supervision (*Bundesaufsicht*). The *Bundesrat* then decides with finality (Art. 84). In either case, whether it is a case of federal compulsion or federal supervision, the *Land* concerned can appeal to the Federal Constitutional Court. The federal government or any one of the *Länder* may also directly sue a *Land* for the nonfulfillment of its duties, before the Federal Constitutional Court (Art. 93).

Another form of direct federal intervention is envisaged in Art. 91. If a *Land* or the federation is threatened in its existence or its free democratic constitutions, a *Land* may request the police assistance of other *Länder*. If, however, the *Land* which is so threatened is not able or willing to ward off this danger, the federal government may directly intercede by placing the police of that *Land* or of other *Länder* under its command. These measures must be abandoned whenever the *Bundesrat* so orders. This provision, which could be used in case of a neo-Nazi or Communist uprising, was written into the Constitution when the federal government had no police of its own but was solely dependent on that of the *Länder*. Since then, a Federal Border Police has been created, which is trained for just such cases of internal disorder.

Very detailed provisions exist concerning the respective fiscal responsibilities of the federation and the *Länder* (Arts. 105–109). Here the centralist tendencies of the Constitution are very much in evidence. While it is stated that both the federation and the *Länder* should be mutually independent and self-contained, the equalization of financial responsibilities (*Finanzausgleich*) places far greater responsibilities and powers in the hands of the federal government. These responsibilities in turn have been vastly increased by the provisions of Art. 120 which make the federal government responsible for the occupation costs and the "internal and external burden following from the war," involving in particular the care of refugees and expellees. As a result, the *Länder* get no share of the revenues exclusively placed at the disposal of the federal government, but the federation may take a share of the revenues normally assigned exclusively to the *Länder*; such legislation, however, needs the consent of the *Bundesrat*.

There can be little doubt that the text of the Bonn Constitution shows a decided centralist tendency. This is not so much in evidence in the exclusively federal powers, which comprise a bare minimum, but in the concurrent powers in which the federal government is supreme when it wishes to act. These concurrent powers actually take in everything of importance with the exception of education, and the limitations on that power are so generally worded as not to embarrass seriously the federal government.

In actuality the real guarantee of federalism does not lie in the theoretical limitations of the powers of the Constitution, but rather in the practical existence and power of the *Bundesrat* (Federal Council), the upper house of the federal legislature. The *Bundesrat* consists of members of the *Länder* governments who are appointed and recalled at will by these governments. The *Bundesrat* has a veto over legislation which may be overruled by the lower house, the *Bundestag*, but the *Bundesrat's* power is nevertheless substantial because its consent is mandatory in a number of questions. Also constitutional amendments need the consent of a two-thirds majority in both the *Bundestag* and the *Bundesrat* (Art. 79). There is a danger, however, that political considerations may weaken the position of the *Bundesrat* and heighten the centralist trend. Chancellor Konrad Adenauer has sought incessantly to control the *Bundesrat* by pressing hard for an electoral coalition in the *Länder* composed of his own party and its allies against his chief opponents, the Social Democrats. This maneuver was successful in the newly created *Land* of Baden-Württemberg and especially in Bremen. As a result he controlled the *Bundesrat* for a while as much as the *Bundestag* (after his electoral triumph of September 6, 1953), and an effective bar to excessive centralism was weakened. It is true that Adenauer's party, the Christian Democratic Union, was more federalist-minded in theory than its opponents, but since it has been in power theory and practice have shown an increasing gap.

D. THE EXECUTIVE

As in France, the executive power is shared by a federal President (*Bundespräsident*), a federal Chancellor (*Bundeskanzler*), and federal Ministers (*Bundesminister*).

THE PRESIDENT

The nominal head of the Federal Republic of Germany is the federal President. His role is quite unlike that of his Weimar predecessors and similar to that of his French colleague. In the Weimar Constitution the President was elected by the people and was the equal if not the superior of Chancellor and cabinet. His authority was real, not merely nominal. This arrangement has come in for general condemnation and its evil results under Hindenburg are well known. But in all fairness it should be remembered that in the hands of a democratic president these powers might well have played quite a different role. The tragedy was the election and reelection of Hindenburg rather than the dualism of presidency and cabinet. At any rate the fathers of the Bonn Constitution were not going to run a similar risk. The federal President is now elected by a special convention composed of the members of the *Bundestag* and an equal number of members elected by the popular representative bodies (legislatures) of the *Länder* (*Landtage*) according to the principle of proportional representation. The term of the President is five years, one more than that of the *Bundestag*. He is reeligible only once. If the President is incapable of performing his functions, his deputy is the presiding officer of the *Bundesrat*.

The official acts of the federal President require the countersignature of the federal Chancellor (Prime Minister) or of a competent minister and thus become the acts of the cabinet. Under the Constitution no countersignature is required when the President nominates or dismisses the federal Chancellor (Art. 58). However, this power is wholly theoretical. After the President's nomination the Chancellor must still be elected by the *Bundestag* (Art. 63), which means that the President can nominate only a man who can command the confidence of the majority of the legislature. Any other choice is impractical, since the President does not have general and unconditional dissolution power over parliament and he can therefore do nothing to keep in office a favorite who cannot command a majority. Nor can the President dismiss a Chancellor at will, for the *Bundestag* may refuse to accept any candidate other than the one dismissed. The President's function, like that of his French counterpart, is therefore to employ his skill in finding a government which stands a fair chance of being elected by the *Bundestag*. Otherwise his duties are nominal. Shortly after his election, the first federal President of the Bonn Republic, Theodor Heuss, exhibited certain illusions about his office when he attempted to force his federal Chancellor-designate, Konrad Adenauer, to change the proposed cabinet list in order to suit the preferences of the President. Adenauer, however, stood firm and the President had to abandon his plan.[8] It is expected that such illusions will not soon return to the presidential palace.

THE FEDERAL CHANCELLOR AND THE CABINET

The actual executive consists of the federal Chancellor (*Bundeskanzler*, Prime Minister) and the Ministers (Art. 62). The federal Chancellor is nominated, as we have seen, by the federal President and must then be elected without debate by the *Bundestag*. If the person so nominated is not elected, the *Bundestag* may, two weeks later, elect a federal Chancellor without presi-

[8] *The New York Times*, Sept. 15, 1949.

dential nomination, but to be successful a candidate must receive an absolute majority of votes.[9] If there is still no Chancellor, another ballot shall be taken in which plurality is sufficient. In the latter case the federal President may either appoint him or dissolve the *Bundestag* (Art. 63, Sec. 4), in which case new general elections must be held.

It is the principle of a parliamentary democracy that the government is responsible to the legislature. This is also the case in the Federal Republic of Germany, and the government may receive a vote of nonconfidence from the *Bundestag* at any time.[10] However, the government does not automatically fall in that case but only if the *Bundestag* is able to elect a successor to the federal Chancellor by an absolute majority of its members and submits a request to the federal President to appoint the person so elected. The federal President must then comply. This unusual stipulation was adopted from the constitution of Württemberg-Baden (Art. 73),[11] where it has worked exceedingly well despite predictions to the contrary. It is designed to avoid the Weimar and French practice of frequent and sometimes frivolous overthrowals of cabinets.

Still another feature designed to strengthen the Chancellor is a conditional power to bring about the dissolution of the *Bundestag*. This may be accomplished in the following fashion: the Chancellor has the right to ask the *Bundestag* for a vote of confidence. If that is refused, the President may, upon the proposal of the Chancellor, dissolve the *Bundestag*, in which case new elections are held. If, however, the *Bundestag* were to elect a new Chancellor, the right of the old Chancellor to recommend dissolution would automatically lapse. Moreover, the President may presumably refuse the Chancellor's request for dissolution, in which case the latter would probably resign. This constitutes considerable discretion in the hands of the President, and the precedent of the Weimar presidency would seem to indicate that this discretion will be exercised. However, the relations between President and Chancellor will become crystallized only through actual practice, which is as yet of too recent origin to warrant reliable deductions.

There is still another power which strengthens the hands of the Chancellor. In the case envisaged above (Art. 63) in which the Chancellor has asked for a vote of confidence from the *Bundestag* and has failed to receive it, he may, instead of asking for dissolution, request the federal President, with the approval of the *Bundesrat*, to declare a "state of legislative emergency" (Art. 81) whose details will be explained under "The Legislature," page 421.

---

[9] That is, an absolute majority of votes of all members entitled to vote in the *Bundestag*.
[10] The vote of nonconfidence is directed against the federal Chancellor.
[11] The Bavarian constitution attempted to achieve a similar effect by giving the cabinet a definite term (Art. 44, Sec. 1). However this is hedged with such conditions as to be probably unworkable.

Executive Supremacy

In the short time in which the Federal Republic has existed, it has already become perfectly clear that the cabinet and especially the Chancellor dominate the scene and very definitely lead parliament. How difficult it is for a parliament to get rid of a Chancellor is well demonstrated by the fact that although Konrad Adenauer was elected to his post in 1949 by a majority of only one vote over the required minimum, he remained in office undisturbed throughout the legislative term of that *Bundestag*.

Whatever strength the Constitution gives to the head of the cabinet was immeasurably enhanced by the personality of the Federal Republic's first Chancellor, Konrad Adenauer, and by his own conception of the job. Konrad Adenauer, although a firm democrat in principle, and an uncompromising foe of Nazism, is nevertheless something of a personal authoritarian who likes to run things his own way.[12] This has meant that he would brook no interference from his party, let alone other parties, on whom to appoint to ministerial positions or on his policy. Frequent grumblings by parliament also usually have gone unheeded. In effect Adenauer has transformed his position into something approximating the American presidency but without the checks and balances exercised by Congress.[13] If his position was strong prior to September 6, 1953, it soared to even greater heights after his tremendous election victory, which must be interpreted as a personal triumph. For a time his control of the *Bundesrat* as well as the two-thirds majority of his coalition in the *Bundestag* enabled him to amend the Constitution had he deemed it necessary. It would be unfair to call Adenauer a dictator, for there are constitutional and political limits beyond which he definitely cannot go and there are undoubtedly limits drawn by his conscience. But he is without doubt one of the strongest heads of government outside the iron curtain.

It might perhaps be argued that Germany needed a strong leadership personality to get her back on her feet after the utter collapse of 1945. It might also be argued that a strong leader was necessary to make the new democratic regime palatable to the German masses. But this very fact, that the Germans have a tradition of following leadership, could make Adenauer's concept of the Chancellor-leader an unhealthy one if long allowed to persist. However, he is very advanced in years and it is almost inconceivable that his successor, whatever his name, could have the old master's prestige. Some of the forces in the parties, the parliament, and the government, which now cannot assert themselves because of the imperious personality of the Chancellor and his

[12] Among the innumerable jokes surrounding the Chancellor's personality there is the mischievous one about "Konradolph and his Democraship" (*Konradolf und seine Demokratur*).

[13] The Constitutional Court has shown itself less pliable to the Chancellor's wishes.

immense popularity, are bound to attempt a somewhat more independent role under his successor.

THE CIVIL SERVICE

The German professional civil service has always played a significant role in the governmental system. Under the empire and the Weimar Republic it had an enviable reputation for incorruptibility and efficiency which became mitigated by an attitude of increasing indifference, and often hostility, to the Republic. Hitler did away with both incorruptibility and efficiency, and heavy Nazi infiltration took place. Thus in the 1933–1945 period the German civil service acquired a well-earned reputation for servility and internal autocracy.

The Allies, especially the Americans, attempted to denazify the civil service, but in its formal aspects their endeavor resulted in almost complete failure. Since membership in the Nazi party was almost mandatory for one's being retained in the service during the Hitler regime, a very large percentage of civil servants joined up for fear of losing their jobs and, what was perhaps even more important, their extensive pension rights. As a result it became extremely difficult to distinguish between real Nazis and mere party members without inner convictions. Also, the extent to which civil servants had joined the Nazi party made it impossible to have a public service of experienced men without getting Nazi party members. As a result, amnesties and lenient tribunals made denazification nearly a farce. Originally 53,000 civil servants were removed for Nazi taint. But only 67 were made permanently ineligible by being classed as major offenders, and only 1,004 were classified as offenders and removed from the service.[14] All others were eligible for reinstatement, and under a law of May 11, 1951, their reinstatement was made nearly mandatory.[15]

Nevertheless it would be unfair to say that the German civil service is permeated with active Nazis. As a matter of fact, the problem does not lie in the danger of Nazi control but in the organizational and psychological pattern of the civil service.

The Civil Service Act of 1953 reestablishes in the main the traditional German system and nullifies most of the reforms introduced under the pressure of military government. Most characteristic is the fact that, as of yore, the higher civil-service career is reserved to people with a legal education. This

[14] Report of the German *Statistische Amt* of June 10, 1950, quoted in the excellent article by Arnold Brecht, "Personnel Management," in Edward H. Litchfield and Associates, *Governing Postwar Germany,* Ithaca, 1953, p. 267.

[15] In all justice it should be made clear that this law deals primarily with the reinstatement of civil servants who had lost their jobs because of expulsion or flight from Communist-dominated territories. Nevertheless many civil servants who had been removed because of Nazi affiliations also benefited. For details see Brecht, *op. cit.*, p. 269.

means that they are recruited from an extremely narrow group whose training emphasizes the letter of the law and legal theories but largely neglects other, broader, aspects of public life. This places control over the public service in the hands of a tightly knit caste which certainly has deep devotion to its task but lacks the broader vision which characterizes the civil service of the United States and Great Britain and even that of France. Moreover the exceptionally tight tenure provisions and the strictly circumscribed, bureaucratic rules of promotion help to close the ranks of this caste against any outsiders who occasionally penetrate into the inner sanctum but always remain interlopers. This makes the German civil service a state within the state whose autocratic nature, separation from public opinion, and illusions of superiority over the public make it a poor instrument for a democratic state.[16]

It should not be denied that the German civil service has many people who honestly serve the regime, and the Civil Service Act demands complete loyalty and dedication to, and defense of, the free democratic order established by the Constitution. But the trouble does not lie so much in the problem of individual loyalty as in that of group attitude and principle of organization. This is a matter about which even otherwise dedicated German democrats are only insufficiently alert. German civil servants frequently hide behind a "nonpolitical" mask. But in Germany "nonpolitical" often does not mean absence of partisan politics, but rather dedication to an abstract "state" and a disdain for public opinion. The insistence on the "nonpolitical" character of the civil service is in reality often a rejection of democratic control over its operations. Improvement is certainly possible, but only by governmental and legislative action, which is unfortunately made very difficult by the fact that German civil servants are permitted to be members of parliament without completely resigning from the service.[17]

The German civil service is divided into four classes: (1) the higher service (*der höhere Dienst*), the top positions, access to which is confined to those equipped with a legal education; (2) the elevated service (*der gehobene Dienst*), covering responsible assistant types of jobs; (3) the middle service (*der mittlere Dienst*) of assistants of a lower level; and (4) the simple service (*der einfache Dienst*) of largely menial and service character. Access to these, especially to the first three, is strictly regulated on the basis of precise educational requirements and examinations. Promotion from one group into a higher one is possible but quite rare.

[16] This is emphasized by an excessive use of titles (such as government councilor, superior government councilor, etc.) for each position. It is also interesting to note that every German civil servant knows the military rank exactly equivalent to his position. Few American, British, or French civil servants could or would think in those terms.

[17] Civil servants may be members of *Länder* and local assemblies without resigning. They may run for a seat in the *Bundestag* without resigning, but they must resign after their election before being seated. However, they have a right to reinstatement when they cease to be members of the *Bundestag*.

The important entrance examinations are under the control of commissions, but the hiring of available candidates who have passed their examinations is left entirely to the government departments concerned. There is a Federal Personnel Commission, but its sole function is to grant exemptions from certain rules and to issue general regulations. Since it is composed of high civil servants, it cannot be expected to act against the customary pattern of the service.

THE MINISTRIES

German ministries are considerably smaller than their American, British, or French counterparts. While American federal departments administer their local duties through their own regional agents and field offices, most German ministries are confined to the supervision of the corresponding ministries of the *Länder* which actually perform this task under the provision of Art. 83 of the Constitution. Only the postal service, the railroads, the customs, the fiscal administration, and the newly organized Federal Border Police are directly administered locally by the federal government. On the *Länder* level in turn much responsibility is further delegated to district and municipal authorities.[18] Much of the work of a federal ministry consists in determining the legal responsibility for the performance of certain acts and a great deal of the distribution of the work load is determined by administrative law. This fits in well with the insistence on the legal education of the top civil-service personnel. Within each ministry there are usually several divisions which in turn are subdivided into individual functions, known as *Referate* and headed by a *Referent* who has a small staff at his disposal. The principal job of these *Referenten* is the legal determination of who in *Länder* administration should do the job. Each division chief is responsible for efficiency within his division, while a chief clerk who bears the overwhelming title of Ministerial Bureau Director (*Ministerialbürodirektor*) is in charge of the internal services of the ministry. A special *Referent* for organizational questions (*Organisationsreferent*) sees to the proper coordination of service functions.

This system obviously leaves the bulk of administrative problems to the *Länder*, where the administrative setup is more elaborate and more centralized. It emphasizes the federal structure of the country, but it also makes tighter the degree of policy-making centralism. From an administrative standpoint this is a very simple system, but the ordinary citizen often does not find it so when he has to approach numerous layers of the administrative machinery in order to get something done. Perhaps one of the greatest weaknesses of this system is its excessive emphasis on a legal distribution of the work, which does not allow for effective functional coordination. In particular,

[18] Kurt Glaser, "Organization and Methods Control," in Litchfield and Associates, *op. cit.*, pp. 294–306.

the use of the budget and the bureau of the budget for more effective co-ordination and executive control is almost totally unknown in Germany. But on the other hand, the relative economy in the use of manpower is worthy of emulation elsewhere.

The functions of the various ministries correspond to those in most other countries. At the present time the head of the government, the federal Chancellor (*Bundeskanzler*), also presides over the Foreign Office,[19] but that is explained by Dr. Adenauer's preoccupation with foreign affairs and is undoubtedly not a permanent affair. One of the ministers is designated Vice-Chancellor, but this is a position which is similar to the British sinecure ministries.[20] Perhaps most powerful of all ministries is that of Finance, which does not approximate the position of the British Treasury but which can nevertheless block certain action, especially if the Minister of Finance finds the Chancellor on his side. Undoubtedly the position of this Ministry has been enhanced by the fact that its present incumbent, Dr. Fritz Schäffer, is the strongest personality in the cabinet after the Chancellor. Great influence is also wielded by the Minister of Economics, who, in the person of Professor Ludwig Erhard, is credited with much of the merit for Germany's spectacular economic reconstruction. As times become more normal, however, this Ministry's preeminent position is likely to diminish.

It is noteworthy that the position of the Minister of the Interior is far less powerful than is the case in most other countries of Continental Europe. His influence over local government is circumscribed by law and is normally confined to supervisory functions. The police are strictly the affair of the *Länder*. The Minister of the Interior watches over standards of training and equipment, especially as the federal government participates fiscally therein, but he can command the *Länder* police only under the exceptional circumstances described earlier in this chapter. He is, however, in full charge of the newly created Federal Border Police, which has a semimilitary organization and appearance.

Since, as these lines are written, Germany is not permitted to have an army, there is no official Ministry of War. In reality, however, there is one, at least in the planning stage. It is headed by State Secretary Theodor Blank and is usually referred to as the "Blank Office." Its activities are quite aboveboard because Germany is to enter the Western European Union of 1954, according to which treaty she would organize approximately twelve divisions.

Because of the special position of Germany, there are some unusual ministries. Perhaps most remarkable has been the work of the Ministry for Refugee Affairs, which has presided over the overwhelming task of integrating

[19] The administrative direction of the Foreign Office is in the hands of a former law professor, Dr. Walter Hallstein. Adenauer, however, keeps tight control.

[20] Vice-Chancellor Franz Blücher was in charge of administering the German side of the American aid program.

over 9 million refugees and expellees into the economic life of the Federal Republic. While this task is certainly far from done, the results already accomplished are stupendous. Millions of refugees and expellees have been settled, and work as well as homes have been created for them and by them.[21]

Largely a propaganda affair is the Ministry for All-German Questions, which is headed by Jakob Kaiser, a former Christian Trade-Union leader. Its chief task is that of keeping alive the thought of eventual German reunification.

E. THE LEGISLATURE

The German parliament consists of two houses, the Federal Assembly (*Bundestag*) and the Federal Council (*Bundesrat*). Of the two, only the *Bundestag* is elected by the people. The *Bundesrat* is really a council of ambassadors of the *Länder*. Its members, as already stated, are delegates of the *Länder* governments who are appointed and removed by them at will and are subject to their instructions.

The terms *Bundesrat* and *Bundestag* are historical, the former going back to imperial Germany, the latter even earlier to the German Confederation of 1815–1866. In this sense the terms are perhaps somewhat misleading because these institutions carry historical memories which are not entirely justified in the light of their present composition and functions.

THE ELECTORAL PROCESS

The Weimar Republic was characterized by a proportional-representation system of the most rigid variety. Its disastrous consequences in encouraging splinter parties and rule by party bureaucracy have already been discussed. The new Federal Republic wanted to modify this system but was not able to abandon proportional representation entirely because of Social Democratic insistence thereon. The reason for that was the heavy concentration of the Social Democratic following in industrial centers, which, under a single-member-district plurality system, would have meant that their urban deputies would have been elected by huge majorities but that the more evenly spread middle-class parties would have obtained a larger number of deputies in the country.

---

[21] This work is not greatly concerned with the so-called displaced persons (DP's), who were non-German and who have been largely settled elsewhere. Refugees are Germans who fled from Communist rule, primarily in Eastern Germany; expellees are Germans who were driven out of former German territories east of the Oder and Neisse Rivers, from the Sudeten area of Czechoslovakia, and from other German settlements in Eastern and Southeastern Europe. See P. J. Bouman, G. Beijer, and J. J. Oudegeest, *The Refugee Problem in Western Germany*, The Hague, 1950.

The outcome of much discussion on the subject was a compromise system, first enacted by the electoral law of May 10, 1949, sometimes known as the "sixty-forty" law. Under its terms, 60 per cent of the seats were filled through elections in single-member constituencies, and 40 per cent by proportional representation of votes cast in each state. This law has been superseded by another electoral law of June 25, 1953, which governed the elections of September 6, 1953. However, it was passed only a few days before the life of the *Bundestag* session expired and constitutes a last-minute compromise, which is illustrated by the fact that it was effective only for the election of September 6, 1953. A more permanent law is to be drafted later; it is, however, expected to follow the same general lines. The law of June 25 increased the number of *Bundestag* members from 400 to 484 [22] plus 22 nonvoting representatives from West Berlin.[23] Fifty per cent of the *Bundestag* members are elected in single-member districts by plurality vote. The other 50 per cent are elected in each of the nine *Länder* on the basis of proportional representation. While the division between the members to be elected under the two systems is exactly 50–50 in the *Bundestag*, the proportions differ slightly from *Land* to *Land* as indicated in the accompanying table.

Land	Plurality seats	PR seats	Total
Baden-Württemberg	33	34	67
Bavaria	47	44	91
Bremen	3	3	6
Hamburg	8	9	17
Hesse	22	22	44
Lower Saxony	34	32	66
North Rhine–Westphalia	66	72	138
Rhineland-Palatinate	15	16	31
Schleswig-Holstein	14	10	24
Total *	242	242	484

* Plus 22 nonvoting seats of West Berlin.

The administration of elections under this new law is relatively simple. Each voter casts *two* ballots: one for a single candidate in his own district, the other for a party list. In order to be elected in a single-member district, plurality suffices as in the United States and Great Britain. The apportion-

[22] Actually the number of members in the 1949 *Bundestag* was 402 because of a peculiarity of the electoral law. In Bremen and Hamburg one party each (CDU and SPD) won more seats by plurality election than they could have been allowed under the combined plurality-PR system. In that case they were allowed to keep the larger number.

[23] It was feared that a formal incorporation of West Berlin into the Federal Republic would give the Russians a pretext for drastic measures.

ment of seats under proportional representation is the same as in France, but without *apparentement* or preferential voting.[24]

Any German citizen who has been a resident of the Federal Republic for at least three months and who is at least twenty-one years of age is entitled to vote. To be eligible for membership in the *Bundestag*, a German citizen must be at least twenty-five. Those declared ineligible by court order can, of course, not be seated.

There are certain complexities to the apportionment of seats: in each *Land* there is first a preliminary apportionment of all seats by proportional representation, as if single-member districts did not exist. Then the number of seats won by each party in single-member districts is *deducted* from the above preliminary PR number of seats. The resulting figure determines how many seats each party receives under PR in addition to the seats won in direct single-member districts.[25] In effect, therefore, a party cannot increase the number of its seats by doing exceptionally well in direct, single-member-district elections. The only thing that changes is the internal ratio between directly elected and PR-elected deputies.

This proves that the German electoral system is still essentially a PR system; had there been proportional representation pure and simple, each party would have received the same number of seats that it has now, but under this law some of each party's deputies have a closer relationship to their voters. On the other hand, had there been only single-member districts and plurality voting, the outcome would have been quite different, as is shown by the following figures: of the 242 seats distributed through single-member districts, the Christian Democrats (CDU/CSU) would have received 172 and the Social Democrats (SPD) only 45. Had the Anglo-American (single-member, plurality) system prevailed, the CDU/CSU would have received approximately [26] 344 seats against the SPD's 90. Under the existing system the CDU/CSU received only 244 against the SPD's 151.

In order to combat the atomization of the political picture by the existence of too many parties—as was the case in the Weimar Republic—the electoral law further states that a party cannot receive a seat in the *Bundestag* unless it meets one of the two following conditions: it must either (1) poll a minimum of 5 per cent of the total vote cast in the Federal Republic, or (2) elect at least one deputy by direct plurality election in a single-member district.

[24] Part II, Chap. 4D. This is essentially the system of metropolitan France except for the *départements* of Seine and Seine-et-Oise.

[25] The names of the candidates finally elected by each party under PR are simply taken from the top of each party list down, in the sequence indicated by the party presenting the list.

[26] If Germany had only voted under a plurality single-member-district system, the number of electoral districts would have had to be doubled and the resulting redistricting might have caused some slight variations.

This measure cuts down very considerably the number of parties represented in the *Bundestag*. Among those eliminated were both the Communist party (2.2 per cent) and the neo-Nazi German Reich party (0.8 per cent). The German party (DP) obtained only 3.3 per cent of the total vote, but by concentrated strength was able to elect ten of its fifteen deputies in single-member districts. The refugee party, All-German Bloc (GB/BHE), did not elect a single deputy in single-member districts but just cleared the line by an over-all vote of 5.9 per cent. The small Center party, which polled only 2.2 per cent of the vote, would normally not have been seated in the *Bundestag*. However, by a preelection agreement, a CDU member, who had already represented the Christian Democrats in the 1949 *Bundestag*, agreed to run in North Rhine–Westphalia under the Center-party label but with CDU support. In exchange the Center party placed one of its men on the CDU proportional state list. Thus, one nominal Center-party member was directly elected in a single-member district and the party was therefore able to make all its votes count and sent three members into the *Bundestag*. By previous agreement, one of them then joined the CDU/CSU group there. Therefore while technically 243 CDU/CSU and 3 Center-party members were declared elected, there are actually 244 CDU/CSU and 2 Center-party members in the *Bundesrat*.

The Organization of the Bundestag

The organization of the *Bundestag* is regulated in general terms by the Constitution (Arts. 40–49) and in detail by the rules (*Geschäftsordnung*) adopted for each session [27] by the *Bundestag* itself. Its presiding officer, the president, is elected by secret ballot and has extensive powers. He is considered similar to the head of a household (*Hausrecht*) and has control over the housekeeping functions of the *Bundestag*. He is also in charge of keeping order. The latter function gives him the right to exclude a deputy for as much as thirty days. The president is also endowed with police powers (*Polizeigewalt*) over which he is the final authority. Normally the local police [28] are not permitted to enter the premises of the *Bundestag*, but the president may call upon them for help if it becomes necessary.

The president is assisted by several vice-presidents and a secretariat who, together with him, form the presidium. There is also a curious institution, the Council of Elders (*Ältestenrat*). It is composed of deputies of all major parties who are selected on the basis of age rather than seniority of service. The Council of Elders fulfills some of the functions of a steering committee [29]

---

[27] But the *Bundestag* may readopt the previous rules by tacit consent by merely continuing to apply them. Cf. Mangoldt, *op. cit.*, p. 239.

[28] This means the police of North Rhine–Westphalia and of the city of Bonn.

[29] Harold M. Dorr and Henry L. Bretton, "Legislation," in Litchfield and Associates, *op. cit.*, p. 213.

by bringing about agreement among the different political groups concerning the distribution of the work load. It is also responsible for the selection of committee chairmanships, a good portion of which go to members of the opposition. This practice is in considerable contrast to the methods applied in the Congress of the United States or in the French parliament.

The *Bundestag* may refuse to seat a prospective member for illegality of election, incompatibility, etc., but the person who is refused his seat may appeal to the Federal Constitutional Court.

The deputies enjoy the customary immunities to which is added an unusual one which was found in the Weimar Republic also, namely, that a deputy cannot be obliged to divulge information or documents which he has received in his capacity as a deputy. On the other hand there is a limitation in Art. 46 which specifically excludes such immunity in cases of "defamatory libel" (*verleumderische Beleidigungen*) even when committed in the *Bundestag*.[30] This is undoubtedly a reaction to the abuse of the excessive immunities permitted under the Weimar Constitution. Otherwise the deputies enjoy immunity for their actions and utterances in the *Bundestag*. Before a deputy can be pursued for a criminal act, the Bundestag must give its consent. This is a right of the *Bundestag* and not of the deputy, who cannot voluntarily divest himself of his immunity, for the decisions of the *Bundestag* are presumably dictated by its concern for the public interest and the dignity of the House. Its consent is not necessary if the offender was arrested in the act of committing a crime or during the following twenty-four hours. However, any legal pursuit, imprisonment, or arrest of a deputy must be halted on the demand of the *Bundestag*.

Fraktionen AND COMMITTEES

Any party whose deputies in the *Bundestag* number fifteen or more has the right to organize a parliamentary group, called *Fraktion*. This is in effect the party caucus, and its power was immense in the Weimar Republic. All decisions were made in the *Fraktionen*, in which the party leaders predominated and in which orders were received from a leadership outside parliament. It was possible to force deputies to toe the line by the imposition of compulsory obedience to caucus orders (*Fraktionszwang*). This was certainly one of the things which made the Weimar parliament appear unreal and consequently diminished its prestige.

[30] "Defamatory libel" is not a vague term to be defined by the *Bundestag* as Dorr and Bretton, *op. cit.*, incorrectly imply. The term is precisely defined in Sec. 187 of the German Criminal Code (StGB) as the assertion of a fact which is capable of making a person appear contemptible or degraded in public opinion, if that assertion is proved to be untrue, and if its untruthfulness was known to the accused. To apply this rule was the unanimous intention of the framers. Cf. Mangoldt, *op. cit.*, p. 253. This rule does not apply to lesser forms of libel under Secs. 185 and 186 StGB.

The framers of the Bonn Constitution did not wish to return to this system. True, *Fraktionen* are again organized under the rules of the *Bundestag*. Their importance is stressed by the fact that only a *Fraktion* is entitled to have members on the committees of the *Bundestag,* including the Council of Elders. This means also that a party with fewer than fifteen deputies has no committee assignments. But Art. 38 stipulates that the deputies "shall be representatives of the whole nation, not bound to orders and instructions and subject only to their conscience." This means that there is now *no legal Fraktionszwang.* Even deputies who are expelled from their parties remain members of the *Bundestag,* and if they had been required to deposit an undated letter of resignation with their party leadership, such "resignation" would not be legal.[31] Even if a party dissolves itself or is prohibited by the decision of the Federal Constitutional Court, its members do not thereby lose their seats in the *Bundestag.*

But words are one thing and deeds frequently another. The reference of Art. 38 to the "unbound deputy" (*freies Mandat*) is unrealistic. The Weimar Constitution had a very similar provision in Art. 21, which did not seem to prevent the imposition of *Fraktionszwang.*

It must of course be admitted that there ought to be a measure of party discipline in parliament, which is even more important when coalitions have to be formed. However, too much obedience defeats the parliamentary idea. It replaces open deliberation by the duly elected representatives of the people with secret decisions reached in the caucus room or even by orders received from the outside. This makes an unfavorable impression on the public, an impression enhanced by the fact that the pressure of work frequently forces the *Bundestag* to accept the recommendation of the Council of Elders and restricts debate on sometimes quite important questions to one hour. This allows ten minutes to the author of the bill and only a few minutes to a single representative from each *Fraktion.* Under these circumstances, the role of the individual deputy is even more curtailed than usual, when he would have at least the opportunity to make an individual speech.[32] It should be admitted that in the committees, where most of the real work is done, the expression of opinion is freer, but contrary to American practice German committee deliberations are not open to the press or the public and they do not therefore dispel the unfavorable impression created by the "debate," which is more like a reading of party dicta than an actual exchange of views.

The situation certainly offers some handicaps to the growth of democratic institutions. It is difficult to remedy because of three factors. First of all is the fact that Germany still has essentially a proportional-representation system of election which makes deputies dependent on the party leadership for being placed on the all-important list. Secondly, obedience to leadership and

---

[31] Mangoldt, *op. cit.,* p. 233.

[32] Normally a deputy may speak for one hour. The rule is liberally interpreted.

Fraktion is a deeply ingrained habit which is hard to shake off. And finally there is the fact of unquestionable executive supremacy over the *Bundestag*.

The committee structure of the *Bundestag* follows the American and French systems, rather than the British. In this group must also be counted the already mentioned powerful steering committee, the Council of Elders. As already stated, it is this council which proposes committee chairmanships and memberships. The number of committee members is determined by the proportional strength of the *Fraktionen* represented in the *Bundestag*.[33] The choice of chairmen and committee members is a matter of informal agreement between the *Fraktionen*.

The committees of the *Bundestag* follow the customary categories of executive functions. Their importance is underlined by the fact that the first *Bundestag* of 1949 created thirty-nine standing committees. Because of the strong position of the respective party leaderships, however, the committees are less independent than those of the United States or France. The work is also hampered by the absence of anything like the legislative reference service in America. On the other hand the presence of many civil servants and university professors provides a reservoir of technical knowledge and experience which is reflected even more in the composition of the *Bundesrat*. Universities, especially the conveniently located universities of Bonn and Cologne, may also be counted upon to give a hand. In Germany as well as in most other countries, the bulk of legislative proposals originate in one of the government departments, although the *Bundestag* has used its right of initiative with increasing frequency. The members of the federal government have the right to attend all committee meetings and must be heard when they request it. They may also be summoned by the committees.

Besides the regular standing committees, the Bonn Constitution, like its Weimar predecessor, allows for investigating committees. These committees have a considerable standing and history in Germany. Perhaps one of the best known was the *Reichstag* committee which investigated the events that led up to the First World War and published its findings in an edition of many volumes.[34] Article 44 of the Bonn Constitution entitles the *Bundestag* to organize investigating committees (*Untersuchungsausschüsse*) at any time. These committees are entitled to hold hearings and investigations on their own authority. They are obliged to proceed with an investigation when one-fourth of the committee's members demand it. Contrary to the American theory (but more like the American practice) these committees can hold investigations even if they have no bearing on any past, present, or future

[33] For this reason several small parties united in one *Fraktion* in the first *Bundestag* of 1949. This was not possible in the second *Bundestag* of 1953 because of the reduced number of parties and the slaughter of the splinter groups. Sometimes small groups become "guests" of *Fraktionen* of other parties in order to obtain a measure of access to the more significant aspects of parliamentary life.

[34] *Die Grosse Politik der Europäischen Kabinette,* 1871–1914, Berlin, 1922, 40 vols.

legislation. Traditionally four groups of cases have attracted the interest of investigating committees: (1) economic and social questions whose study might lead to legislation; (2) alleged mismanagement or misconduct in the administration; (3) contested elections; and (4) unusual criminal cases and instances of corruption. The investigating committees have quasi-judicial status inasmuch as they have a right to compel the rendering of certain evidence, but they may not themselves arrest or conduct searches. Apart from the fact that they cannot, of course, sentence a person, their powers are comparable to those of a criminal court. On the other hand the Constitution prescribes that the rules of criminal procedure in court are to be applied by the investigating committees as far as the nature of their work permits.

Finally there is the so-called permanent committee (*ständiger Ausschuss,* Art. 45). Unlike other committees, this one is not confined to the periods during which the *Bundestag* is in session. Its main task is to exercise the right of parliamentary supervision over the executive when the *Bundestag* is not in session, especially between the dissolution of one legislature and the convocation of its successor. The Permanent Committee has the same rights as all other committees, including that of conducting investigations. It may even interpellate the government, but it cannot cast a vote of nonconfidence against the government and it cannot participate in any administrative decision.

The Organization of the *Bundesrat*

It was not a foregone conclusion that the *Bundesrat* of the Bonn Constitution should follow in the footsteps of the Weimar *Reichsrat* and the *Bundesrat* of the empire, because in this institution there is only a hint of its monarchic past. But the decisive argument for its rebirth in 1949 was that the *Länder* governments participate in the execution of the federal laws and that they should therefore have a part in federal legislation.

As already stated, the members of the *Bundesrat* are not elected, but are appointed by their respective *Länder* governments and are subject to their instructions and to removal by them. They are themselves members of the *Länder* governments. Since the latter are democratic governments responsible to their respective *Landtage,* this is not an undemocratic principle.

The number of seats in the *Bundesrat* assigned to each *Land* varies according to size and population of the *Länder* but is by means proportionate thereto. Bavaria, Baden-Württemberg, Lower Saxony, and North Rhine–Westphalia have five seats each. Hesse, Schleswig-Holstein, and Rhineland-Palatinate have four each, and Bremen and Hamburg have three each. This constitutes then a near-equal representation of the *Länder* in the *Bundesrat,* very much in contrast to the situation in the empire and the Weimar Republic. Of course the reason why this is now possible is the disappearance of the gigantic *Land* of Prussia.

Another peculiarity of the *Bundesrat* is the fact that each *Land* delegation votes as a block. Party affiliations within the delegation are thus not adhered to, since the members often belong to different parties. But this should not lead to the erroneous assumption that party politics play no role. Quite the contrary; party politics play an important and increasing role, but it is the party politics of the respective *Länder* governments and not that of their delegates.

The work of the delegates is largely technical. They represent the cream of the crop of trained *Land* officials, and they are capable of making important contributions to legislation and administration. But their opinions have nothing to do with the way their votes are cast. Consequently party politics enter by the back door. For instance, Chancellor Adenauer's program for the ratification of the treaty to create the European Defense Community was endangered when the Social Democrats gained some success in one *Land* and thus were able to effect a shift in the *Bundesrat* vote. By the same token, Adenauer more than rectified the balance by throwing every support to his party and its allies in another *Land* election, the outcome of which modified the *Bundesrat* vote in the opposite direction. What is interesting to note here is that to an increasing extent the *Länder* governments cast their *Bundesrat* votes not according to *Land* interests but according to the partisan viewpoint of the national parties to which they belong. This political note tends to diminish the "expert" nature of the *Bundesrat*, without, however, nullifying it.

Like the *Bundestag*, the *Bundesrat* elects its president, but only for one year. There is of course no repetition of the imperial practice by which the chairmanship was always in the hands of one particular state (Prussia).

Since the *Bundesrat* is a very small body of 38 members plus 4 observers from West Berlin (in contrast to the Bundestag's 484 plus 22 nonvoting members from Berlin), its organization is simple. It has 14 committees, of which 13 are standing committees and one is a conference committee to deliberate in joint session with the equivalent committee of the *Bundestag*. For the same reason the rules of debate are of course simple and there are no disciplinary problems.

In many respects the functions of the *Bundesrat* are quite different from those of the *Bundestag*. The Chancellor and his cabinet are not responsible to the *Bundesrat* as they are to the *Bundestag*, and there can therefore be no vote of confidence or censure in the *Bundesrat*. But on the other hand the government needs the *Bundesrat*'s consent for certain administrative actions: for example, in order to issue executive orders concerning such matters as railroads, refugees, and the dismissal of certain public officials, or regulating the administration of certain federal matters by the *Länder* governments. We have already seen that the government needs the consent of the *Bundesrat* for the imposition of federal compulsion (*Bundeszwang*) and the emergency use of the *Länder* police forces. It is therefore conceivable that the *Bundesrat*,

by refusing to give its consent to some of these measures which the government deems necessary, might actually force a government out of office. So
far this has not occurred and is not likely to occur in the near future.

In the field of legislation the *Bundesrat* has, as we shall see below, only a
suspensive veto in most issues, although it has an absolute veto in some.

The *Bundesrat* does not fall into any of the patterns of bicameral legislatures. It is not the equal of the *Bundestag,* but it has considerable power. It
is both a legislative and an administrative body. It is part of a parliament,
but it is also a council of ambassadors whose members represent other administrations.

LEGISLATION

Bills may be introduced in the *Bundestag* by the government, by *Bundestag*
members, or by the *Bundesrat.* However, a government bill must first be
introduced in the *Bundesrat,* which has three weeks within which it may
comment on the bill before passing it on to the *Bundestag.* A bill, after being
introduced, is subjected to a so-called "first reading." This is a discussion on
the general principles of the bill and not on its details, although it may serve
to bring some order into a complex subject. After a favorable vote on first
reading, during which amendments cannot be considered, the bill is referred to
committee, sometimes to several committees. Then follows a "second reading"
at which details are again not discussed unless the *Bundestag* itself decides
differently. The discussion follows certain main considerations such as principles, titles, etc. A vote terminates the discussion of each general topic. At
this stage amendments may be introduced before the topic in question is put
to the vote. Only international treaties must be discussed and decided without
amendment.

The "third reading" begins again with the discussion of the general principles of the bill followed by a detailed discussion of the bill's component
parts. Amendments may be considered but must be seconded by ten members.
A vote ends the "third reading" and determines the fate of the bill.

This process can be considerably speeded up by unanimous consent of all
members of the *Bundestag* present, which allows all three readings to be
rushed through in a single day. Other rules may also be adjusted upon
unanimous consent. Otherwise, no member may speak beyond one hour unless
permission for extension is granted by a majority resolution. On the other
hand, as already stated, the debate may be curtailed by decision of the Council of Elders.

Once a bill has passed the *Bundestag,* it is submitted to the *Bundesrat.*[35]
The latter may, within two weeks of its receipt of the bill, demand that a

[35] Even if the bill originated in the *Bundesrat* or was first submitted to it for its views,
as is the case with government bills.

conference committee of representatives of both houses be called in order to iron out differences. This conference committee is the only place where, according to the Constitution (Art. 77, Sec. 2), the members of the *Bundesrat* are not bound by instructions.[36] If this conference committee comes up with a new version of the bill, it is not necessary to start again with three readings thereof, but a single (fourth) reading is sufficient. However it is not always necessary that this formal step of the joint conference committee be taken. The role of the *Bundesrat* is essentially constructive, and since Art. 43, Sec. 2, entitles its members to attend all meetings of the *Bundestag* and its committees with the right to be heard at any time, the *Bundesrat* has an opportunity to inject its views into the deliberation of the bill in the *Bundestag* before the three readings have run their course.

If the *Bundesrat* approves a bill for which the Constitution *does not specifically require its consent,* either it may give its formal consent, in which case the bill becomes law immediately, or it may simply do nothing, in which case the bill becomes law two weeks after being sent to it if no joint conference committee has been demanded, or one week after the conference committee has terminated its deliberations. If the *Bundesrat* does not approve a bill for which the Constitution does not specifically require its consent, it has the right to cast a suspensive veto. Conditions for exercising this right are that (1) a meeting of the joint conference committee has been demanded by the *Bundesrat* within two weeks after receiving the bill from the *Bundestag,* and (2) that the suspensive veto (*Einspruch*) is declared within one week after the deliberations of the conference committee have come to an end. No suspensive veto can be cast unless the conference committee has first considered the matter.

The suspensive veto can be overridden by the *Bundestag* by the simple act of repassing the bill with simple majority. If, however, the *Bundesrat* has cast its suspensive veto with a two-thirds majority of its members, it can be overridden by the *Bundestag* only by a two-thirds majority. However, it is sufficient if the two-thirds majority in the *Bundestag* constitutes two-thirds of the members *present,* provided this number is at least equal to a majority of all *Bundestag* members entitled to a seat in the house.

The *Bundesrat's* suspensive veto is operative only against bills passed by the *Bundestag.* It is not operative against other measures taken by the lower house, such as for instance the establishment of an investigating committee.

There are, however, a number of bills for whose passage the consent of the *Bundesrat* is specifically required by the Constitution. This is especially the case with regard to constitutional amendments,[37] for which two-thirds ma-

---

[36] But that would not protect *Bundesrat* members from being removed or dismissed by their respective *Länder* governments.

[37] As in France, constitutional amendments are regarded as special forms of legislation.

jorities in both houses are required, and for legislation concerning changes in the territory of the *Länder* (Art. 29, Sec. 7), regulation of the execution of federal laws by *Länder* administrations (Arts. 84, Secs. 1 and 5; 85, Sec. 1), the enlargement of the federal administration by the creation of new agencies of direct administration (Art. 87, Sec. 3), a number of cases of fiscal legislation (Arts. 105, Sec. 3; 106, Secs. 3 and 4; 107; 108, Sec. 3), and for the disposition of property belonging to the former *Reich* (Arts. 134, Sec. 4; 135, Sec. 5). In these cases, no bill can become law without the express consent of the *Bundesrat*. Here it has not only an absolute veto, but is coequal with the *Bundestag*. Mere failure to object on the part of the *Bundesrat* would not allow the bill to become law. A positive act of consent is required.

The ratification of treaties follows the same procedure as legislation (Art. 59). This means that treaties concerning subjects in which the *Bundesrat* has an absolute veto can be ratified only with its express consent. In other ratifications it has the same suspensive veto as would apply to ordinary legislation.

If there is a dispute over the question whether a bill or a treaty requires the express consent of the *Bundesrat* or not, only the Federal Constitutional Court can decide.

After a bill has been passed by the legislature in the manner described above, it is certified by the federal President after countersignature by the federal Chancellor and the minister into whose field the bill falls. The President's certification is not an act of consent but a confirmation that the bill has been enacted in the manner prescribed by the Constitution, and that it is identical with the version adopted by the *Bundestag*. If the President finds that these conditions have been met, the law is certified and promulgated in the official journal (*Bundesgesetzblatt*). If the President finds that the bill was not enacted in the manner prescribed or that it is not the correct version, he should refuse certification until the error has been remedied. The cabinet too may refuse its countersignature for these reasons; however, the President, before refusing his own certification, may ask for an advisory opinion of the Federal Constitutional Court.[38]

DISSOLUTION AND LEGISLATIVE EMERGENCY

The *Bundestag* is the only popularly elected national body of the German Federal Republic, and the question of dissolution and reelection pertains therefore only to it. The Weimar Constitution gave the *Reich* President and the Chancellor practically unlimited right of dissolution. Its exercise did not give the German government that stability which some advocates of dissolution expected; quite the contrary, for the right was frequently abused, especially toward the end of the Weimar regime, and served to keep in power minority

[38] Art. 97, Sec. 2, Law on the Federal Constitutional Court, March 12, 1951.

governments that nobody wanted. It contributed considerably to the discredit of the ill-fated Weimar Republic.

The Bonn Constitution knows only a very limited right of dissolution which is not likely to be applied often, if at all. There is a remote possibility of dissolution under Art. 63, Sec. 4. If the *Bundestag* does not elect as Chancellor a man nominated by the federal President, and if it does not elect another man within two weeks thereafter, another ballot is to be taken. If a candidate obtains an absolute majority, he must be appointed, but if a candidate obtains only a plurality, the President has the choice of either appointing him or of dissolving the *Bundestag* within seven days.

Normally the Bundestag is elected for a period of four years. If, however, the federal Chancellor, and he alone, asks the *Bundestag* for a vote of confidence and fails to receive it, he may propose to the federal President that the *Bundestag* be dissolved. The President may do so within twenty-one days. However, there is no dissolution when the *Bundestag* elects a new Chancellor. A few words of interpretation are in order here. It is a condition of dissolution that the Chancellor demand a vote of confidence, either directly or by tying the question of confidence officially to the passage of a given bill or measure. However, a vote of censure moved by a member of the *Bundestag,* even if successful, would not constitute grounds for dissolution. On the other hand, if the *Bundestag* fails to act within a reasonable period on the Chancellor's demand for a vote of confidence, that may be considered tantamount to a refusal. Since the President cannot act without the countersignature of the Chancellor, the President could not order dissolution on his own responsibility. But he is not bound by the Constitution to accede to the Chancellor's request.[39] The *Bundestag* may frustrate dissolution by simply electing a new Chancellor. This "new" Chancellor may of course be the same as the "old" one.

This provision, together with others, would prevent such events as the minority Papen and Schleicher governments. The Chancellor has to have a majority at one time at least because he must be elected by the *Bundestag* (Art. 63). At the same time a government cannot escape a vote of confidence or censure by dissolving the *Bundestag.* The latter is thus placed squarely before its responsibilities. Either it may tolerate a minority government or it can elect a new Chancellor or it can create a situation which leads to dissolution and new elections. In no case, however, will there be a governmental vacuum.

The Weimar Constitution endowed the executive (President and Chancellor) with the exceptional and notorious emergency powers of the famous Art. 48. Little of that is found in the Bonn Constitution. The Bonn government cer-

---

[39] The President's refusal would, however, create a conflict between President and Chancellor which might drag the President into a political controversy and make his position difficult, if not untenable.

tainly has no right to set aside fundamental rights and rule by emergency decree "if the public safety and order . . . are seriously disturbed or endangered" (Art. 48, Weimar Constitution) as its predecessors could and did.

There is, however, a curious and involved residue of this situation in Art. 81 of the Bonn Constitution. If the federal Chancellor has (1) asked for a vote of confidence by the *Bundestag* and has failed, and if (2) the *Bundestag* has elected no new Chancellor, and if (3) the *Bundestag* has refused to pass a bill which the government has declared to be "urgent," [40] the government [41] may, instead of urging dissolution,[42] recommend to the federal President that he proclaim a "state of legislative emergency" (*Gesetzgebungsnotstand*). The federal President may or may not accept this recommendation, but he may proclaim a state of legislative emergency only (4) with the consent of the *Bundesrat*.

After the proclamation of the state of legislative emergency, the *Bundestag* has one more chance to avoid the actual carrying out of the proclamation by passing the bill for which the state of legislative emergency was proclaimed. If, however, it fails to do so, or passes it in a form which the government deems unacceptable, or fails to act within four weeks of the bill's resubmission after the proclamation, the bill will nevertheless be "deemed enacted" if the *Bundesrat* consents thereto. The Constitution itself may not be amended or modified in this way.

The state of legislative emergency can last only six months from the date of its proclamation. During that period other bills may also be enacted in the same manner, but in each case the procedure outlined above must be repeated. It is also understood that the *Bundestag* may not repeal these laws within the six-month period, though it may of course do so afterwards.[43] After the six months have passed, *no second* state of legislative emergency may be proclaimed during the same term of the same Chancellor.

What the framers of this provision had in mind is obviously a situation in which the government finds itself in a minority but the *Bundestag* is so badly divided as to be incapable of producing an alternative government. In that case the minority government which thus remains in office should be able to govern, at least for a time. The frequent governmental paralysis of the Weimar period is thus presumably avoided. At the same time it is clear that the state of legislative emergency can function only when the *Bundestag*

[40] Step (1) and step (3) may be combined if the Chancellor ties the question of confidence to the bill.

[41] While dissolution may be recommended by the Chancellor alone (Art. 68), the state of legislative emergency must be recommended by the entire cabinet.

[42] The Constitution merely demands that there be no dissolution. Theoretically the Chancellor might have recommended dissolution and been refused by the President, after which the government recommended the proclamation of the state of legislative emergency. Politically such an eventuality is difficult to envisage.

[43] Mangoldt, *op. cit.*, p. 439.

meets and not when it is prevented from meeting by violence or other circumstances. Moreover, the time and "once in a term" limitations, but especially the need for the consent of the *Bundesrat,* would seem adequate safeguards against abuse, especially as the political composition of the *Bundesrat* is not likely to be totally different from that of the *Bundestag.* On the other hand, the way in which this right is circumscribed raises the question of whether it can actually operate. Up to now it has not been invoked, and in view of the strong position of the CDU/CSU and the comfortable majority of the Adenauer government, it is at any rate unlikely that it will be in evidence during the legislative term of the *Bundestag* which was elected on September 6, 1953.

The experience with the ill-fated Weimar Constitution reveals that dangers to the democratic order come not only from the emergency decree power of the government, but also from the possibility that a rubber-stamp legislature might pass an enabling act transferring its legislative power to the executive. This is in fact the manner in which the Weimar Republic came to an end. A specific prohibition against delegating legislative power was included in the draft of the new Constitution elaborated by the Council of Experts meeting at Herrenchiemsee. A similar version was incorporated in later drafts, but in the fifty-seventh meeting of the Principal Drafting Committee (*Hauptausschuss*) it was unaccountably omitted without discussion.[44]

Nevertheless it goes too far to say that there are simply no limitations on delegated powers. Article 80 permits decree power to be vested by law in the federal or the *Länder* governments, and these decrees need not be confined to implementing laws but may go beyond that and create legal rules of their own. However, Art. 80 stipulates that content, purpose, and extent of the delegated powers be specified in the law. A general, all-embracing enabling act would thus seem unconstitutional, to which must be added that, as already pointed out, decrees in a number of fields such as fiscal matters need the consent of the *Bundesrat.* Most important of all, the infamous Enabling Act of March 24, 1933 was forced down the throat of a terrorized *Reichstag,* many of whose members were already in prison or concentration camps. Although legal niceties were observed in cases of this kind, this was essentially an act of violence rather than law.

SUMMARY OF EXECUTIVE-LEGISLATIVE RELATIONSHIP

There is no doubt that the constitutional position of the government in relation to the parliament is exceedingly strong. Once a Chancellor has been elected, he is quite difficult to eliminate during the legislative term of the *Bundestag.* Neither a successful vote of censure nor an unsuccessful motion of confidence automatically forces the cabinet to resign. Only when the

[44] Mangoldt, *op. cit.,* p. 380.

Bundestag can elect a new Chancellor must the old one step aside. This is quite difficult because the majority which might be formed against a government is frequently a negative one, which is united merely by a dislike for the incumbent but not by any agreement on a substitute. In a country like France where this rule does not exist, the government is first of all overthrown; then the President of the Republic moves to find some likely candidates for a new cabinet. Eventually, the need to give France a government [45] produces enough pressure to get the National Assembly to invest a new Premier and tolerate a new government. But in Germany, the federal President does not suggest candidates when a vote of confidence has gone against the government because the government has not actually resigned. The *Bundestag* must find a candidate alone. There is not the same pressure for ending the period without government, because the government has not resigned but remains in office. Under these circumstances an effort to overthrow the government is likely to collapse in short order, thereby possibly adding even greater strength to the victorious cabinet. Consequently not too many serious attempts are likely to be made, except by an opposition which has no real expectation of success but hopes to keep things stirred up.

In the last analysis, the real relationship between executive and legislature is determined by the political, rather than by the constitutional, system. If Germany moves toward a greater proliferation of parties, internal dissensions within the coalition government are bound to bring the government down frequently, whatever the Constitution may prescribe. If, on the other hand, Germany moves in the direction of fewer and more important parties, as seems to be the case, perhaps even to a two-party system, then governments are likely to be stable and strong. But whatever a constitution can add to government stability and strength within a parliamentary system, the German Constitution has seemingly done.

The fathers of the Bonn Constitution were haunted by the memories of Weimar. They were also aware of the fact that the German people were doubtful of the ability of a democratic government to govern. They were therefore very much preoccupied with the problem of government stability and were determined to prove that a democratic government can be firm and stable. Their task was greatly aided by the political habits of following party leadership on the part of most legislators.

While some of these features are open to criticism, it may nevertheless be argued that one of the reasons why the Bonn regime seems much more firmly established than that of Weimar, despite the Nazi holocaust in between, is at least in part due to the fact that West Germany has produced governmental

---

[45] Technically there is a government because the resigning cabinet is asked to stay in office until a successor is appointed. Such a caretaker government, however, can make no important decisions and can have no legislative program. It is essentially a nongovernment.

leadership of a very high order. Much of that has been due to the influence of the German Federal Republic's first Chancellor, Konrad Adenauer, whose austere and imperious personality has dominated the formative years of the new Germany. Only after he and several of his successors have passed from the scene will it be entirely clear how much was due to the person and how much to the institution.

F. THE JUDICIARY

The reestablishment of a federal judiciary reflects the attempts to avoid some of the worst malpractices of the Hitler regime. The Nazis had destroyed the independence of judges and had abolished the principle that no one shall be tried except on the basis of law (*nulla poena sine lege*); they had abolished the provision that no one shall be deprived of trial before a competent and regular judge; they had established special courts, not bound by any kind of law; and they had proclaimed the principle that the will of the *Führer* was the supremest of all laws. The Bonn Constitution contains specific safeguards against such contingencies—insofar as any constitution can accomplish such a feat. The principle of punishment solely on the basis of law is restored (Art. 103), and the death penalty is abolished. Procedural safeguards are established to assure a fair hearing, and double jeopardy is excluded. No one may be deprived of a trial before a lawful judge and extraordinary courts are prohibited. No ex post facto laws shall apply.

These are excellent principles, which were already included in the Weimar Constitution. But the record of the Weimar judiciary in living up to these high precepts was poor. Enemies of the Republic could usually count on mild judges, provided the offenders belonged to the right and not the left, and many judges and prosecutors took much pain to demonstrate their hostility to democratic institutions.[46] Such an attitude would be dangerous in any country, but it was particularly disastrous in Germany where the law of criminal procedure permits the judge a great deal of discretion and direct participation in the trial.

In view of these antecedents it is perhaps a little surprising to note that the Bonn Constitution has greatly extended the power of the judiciary; so much so, in fact, that some writers have used the term "judiciary state."[47] The explanation is perhaps that the fathers of the Constitution trusted parliament even less than the courts. This may turn out to be a doubtful judgment.

Some commentaries on German courts have referred to the manner in which denazification was carried out, or failed to be carried out.[48] Actually, the

[46] See the evidence in the Nürnberg trial of the German justices. U. S. Military Government, *Information Bulletin* (1948) Nos. 138–142, quoted by Friedrich, *op. cit.*, p. 717.

[47] For quotations of references, see Mangoldt, *op. cit.*, p. 497.

[48] Karl Loewenstein, "Justice," in Litchfield and Associates, *op. cit.*, pp. 246ff.

problem of German courts is not so much the presence of confirmed Nazis, of whom there are few, but rather an attitude of "neutrality" which in the Weimar Republic frequently became neutrality toward the republican form of government, and in the Hitler era unquestioned submission to any form of legalized violence the regime saw fit to impose.

It is not easy to change this attitude, because the German judge, like his French colleague, is not selected from the bar but spends his entire legal life at the law schools of the universities and at court. He thus lacks the balancing experience of having at one time or another represented all sides, especially that opposed to the state. Nevertheless, there is nothing eternal or "biological" about the attitude of many German judges. It is the product of an education which venerated the "state" in the abstract and which is not easily uprooted. It can be modified in the long run by a greater humanitarian and social conscience on the part of the judges and by a more realistic appraisal of the functions of government and society. For the time being, the record of the ordinary German courts is not inspiring and there have been a number of disquieting decisions by inferior courts concerning such matters as the release of a former political assassin, or an excessively legalistic attitude to exonerate vilifiers of the men who were involved in the 1944 rebellion against Hitler.

THE GERMAN COURT SYSTEM

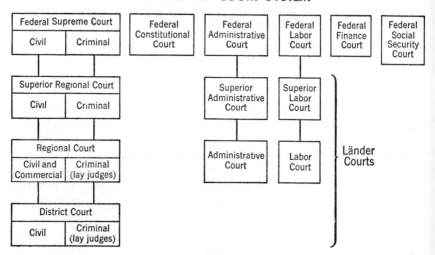

THE ORDINARY COURT SYSTEM

Only the top courts of the three judicial pyramids—ordinary, administrative, and constitutional—are federal courts. The lower echelons, inasmuch as they exist, are courts of the *Länder* and apply both federal and *Land* legislation.

There is no German equivalent to the American, British, or French justice of the peace. The lowest step of the court hierarchy is therefore a regular court known as district court (*Amtsgericht*).[49] District courts are found in every town of any significance. Sometimes a single judge takes care of all business; sometimes in somewhat larger centers there are several judges, each one specializing in different categories of cases. This type of court has jurisdiction in litigation involving sums under 1,000 German marks DM (about $250) as well as probate and similar cases. In criminal cases (other than minor infractions) the trial court is composed of one professional judge and two lay judges (*Schöffen*).

The next higher court, the regional court (*Landgericht*), is both a court of first instance for more important matters and a court of appeals for cases decided by the district court. When engaged in civil cases, either on appeal or in original jurisdiction (amount unlimited), the court is composed of three regular judges. In criminal cases the court's composition is more complicated. If it is concerned with minor offenses on appeal from a single judge's verdict in the district court, it is composed of one regular judge and two lay judges. If concerned with an appeal case from a district court where a judge and two lay judges had decided, the regional court will be composed of three regular judges and two lay judges. The same composition prevails when the regional court holds trial for a more important offense (but not a capital crime) in original jurisdiction. When hearing a case of a grave offense or capital crime in original jurisdiction, the court (*Schwurgericht*) is composed of three professional judges and seven lay judges (*Geschworene*). Despite the difference in name, the smaller group of lay judges (*Schöffen*) and the larger one (*Geschworene*) [50] have the same functions. They are selected by lot from a list of suitable people maintained by the respective city councils.

The distinction between both forms of lay judges (*Schöffen* and *Geschworene*) and the Anglo-American juries is considerable. In America the jury deliberates separately from the judge and usually deals only with questions of fact and not of law, although there are exceptions (as in Illinois). The German lay judges, however, deal with questions of both law and fact and deliberate together with the professional judges. Moreover, while unanimity is often required (or at least a large majority) in America, all German decisions are made by majority.

It is difficult to see much advantage to the German system. While the Anglo-American jury system occasionally leads to abuse, the German system

---

[49] There are no proper translations for *Amtsgericht* and *Landgericht* as neither term is descriptive. The translations "district court" and "regional court" have been chosen as descriptive of the courts' jurisdiction, but there are no agreed translations.

[50] Literally translated, *Geschworene* means "sworn ones" or "jury." Until 1924 the *Geschworenen* were a true jury functioning very much like the American trial jury. Since then, however, they have become lay judges even though they have retained their old title.

leads nowhere. The lay judges, even where they outnumber the professionals, are completely under the thumb of the professional judges by whose learning and superior experience they are greatly impressed. The lay judges therefore can usually be relied upon to ratify the decisions of the professionals.

The lay-judge system does, however, have considerable value and merit in the commercial chambers (*Kammern für Handelssachen*) of the regional courts [51] in which the lay judges are men of commerce and business who are chosen for their expert knowledge.

The next higher court, the superior regional court (*Oberlandesgericht*), is solely an appeals court and ordinarily has no original jurisdiction. It is also the highest ordinary court of the *Länder*. It is composed of a criminal and a civil section (called senates), each made up of three judges. It is the court of final resort for cases which had originally been heard by the district courts. For cases which originated in the regional courts, it is a court of second instance. It does not retry a case but either confirms the verdict of the inferior court or sends the case back for rehearing.

The apex of the ordinary court structure is the Federal Supreme Court (*Bundesgerichtshof*), which resides in Karlsruhe. Its composition is curious because its judges are chosen by an election committee composed of an equal number of people appointed by the *Länder* ministers of justice and elected by the *Bundestag*. The court began its function on October 8, 1950. It has both appellate and original jurisdiction. In civil cases it has only appellate jurisdiction for all cases originating in the regional courts. In its criminal section, the Federal Supreme Court has jurisdiction over cases which originated in the regional courts, but in those capital and other grave cases which were originally tried by the enlarged court of three judges and seven lay judges (*Schwurgericht*) the case goes up on appeal directly from the regional court to the Supreme Federal Court without first being reviewed by the superior regional court.

Strangely enough the Supreme Federal Court has original jurisdiction in the case of treason, which in German law not only comprises acts which aid a foreign power but includes offenses against the internal constitutional order of the state.[52]

The main purpose of the Federal Supreme Court is the unification of law through its jurisdiction. This is a vital task because the period between 1945

---

[51] Commercial chambers, like criminal chambers, may be established in places in which there is no regular regional court.

[52] German law distinguishes between internal treason (*Hochverrat*), which is an attack by force against the internal security and integrity of the country and its constitutional order, and external treason (*Landesverrat*), which comprises aid and comfort to an external enemy or conspiracy to create an external danger to the country, espionage, etc.

and 1950 saw the courts of each *Land* go their own way and create great legal confusion which is still not quite overcome.

THE ADMINISTRATIVE COURTS

Germany's administrative court system follows closely the French pattern from which it was originally adopted. Except for a supreme financial court, neither the German Empire nor the Weimar Republic ever got around to establishing a supreme administrative court on the model of the Council of State in France. The Nazis established such a court in 1941, but due to war conditions and the collapse of the regime it amounted to little.

Under the present constitutional system, administrative courts were first reestablished in the *Länder* in the form of an administrative court (*Verwaltungsgericht*) and, for a court of appeals, a superior administrative court (*Oberverwaltungsgericht*). In 1950 was established the Federal Finance Court (*Bundesfinanzgerichtshof*) with its seat in Munich, and in 1952 the Federal Administrative Court (*Bundesverwaltungsgericht*) was finally organized in West Berlin.

Administrative courts deal with controversies over rights which have been allegedly damaged by an act of public authority. They also very frequently settle jurisdictional disputes between different public authorities. Their impact is not as great as that of the French Council of State, but nevertheless the German administrative courts can claim solid achievements in protecting individuals against administrative arbitrariness. Civil-rights cases, however, fall within the purview of the Federal Constitutional Court.

LABOR COURTS

Special courts for labor questions are known in many European countries. A good system existed under the Weimar Republic. It was abolished by the Nazi regime. With the reestablishment of the free trade-union system, it was again organized in the different *Länder,* all of which have labor courts and superior labor courts. In 1953 a Federal Supreme Court for Labor Affairs (*Bundesarbeitsgericht*) and a Federal Social Security Court (*Bundessozialgericht*) were created.

Labor courts are composed of judges representing both management and trade-unions. They deal with disputes arising out of collective-bargaining agreements or the failure to arrive at such agreements; disputes concerning working conditions, health, and safety; and disputes arising out of agreements between management and shop-steward committees, as well as out of the new "right of codetermination" (*Mitbestimmungsrecht*) which gives labor a part in management.

The Federal Constitutional Court

The summit of the entire German judicial system is a court which is essentially an innovation in the history of Germany although some of its functions were previously exercised by other courts. This is the Federal Constitutional Court (*Bundesverfassungsgericht*), whose seat is in Karlsruhe.

Because its jurisdiction penetrates manifestly into the political field, its composition is markedly different from that of all other tribunals. The Court is composed of two sections, called senates, which divide different categories of cases between them. They are equal and independent from one another and constitute a twin court. The judges are elected to the first or the second senate and do not change. Each senate is composed of twelve judges, one-third of whom (four) are judges of the highest courts (Federal Supreme Court, Federal Administrative Court, Supreme Federal Finance Court, etc.). They are elected for life. The other two-thirds of the judges are elected for eight years in such a way that half of them are elected every four years. Half of all the judges (lifetime and eight-year judges) are elected by the *Bundestag* and the other half by the *Bundesrat*. The *Bundestag* elects them indirectly, through an electoral college of twelve members who in turn elect the judges by a three-fourths majority; the *Bundesrat* elects them directly by a two-thirds majority. The purpose of the large majority required, especially in the *Bundestag*, was to assure that there should be no political domination but a necessity for compromise. In actual practice, the rule led to a great deal of haggling and delayed quite unduly the establishment of the Court.[53]

All judges must be fully trained jurists, and the lifetime judges, although outnumbered, have the task of guarding the legal continuity of the otherwise changing Court.

The jurisdiction of the Federal Constitutional Court is very considerable and extends to five groups of cases:

1. Most important is the right of judicial review. The Federal Constitutional Court decides whether a federal or a *Land* law is compatible with the federal Constitution, or whether *Land* law is compatible with federal law. To bring action in such cases the Constitution requires a motion of the federal government or of a *Land* government, or of one-third of the members of the *Bundestag*. Far more frequently, however, another procedure is followed. In a case pending before some other court, the question of the constitutionality of a law may be invoked by the parties. When that happens, the court must suspend proceedings and refer the question of constitutionality to the Federal Constitutional Court for its decision, which is binding on the original court.

---

[53] Some political influence in the composition of the two senates has been charged, which led to one being popularly called the "Black (Catholic) Senate," and the other the "Red (Socialist) Senate."

The same is true when the question is raised as to whether a rule of international law is part of the law of the land and creates rights and duties for individuals. If the constitutional court of a *Land* intends to interpret the federal Constitution in a manner inconsistent with a past decision of the Federal Constitutional Court or of the constitutional court of another *Land*, it must apply for a decision of the Federal Constitutional Court.

2. The Law on the Federal Constitutional Court (*Bundesverfassungsgerichtsgesetz*) of March 12, 1951, extends the jurisdiction of the Court to the institution of the so-called "constitutional plaint" (*Verfassungsbeschwerde*). According to Art. 90 of that law, an individual who feels deprived of the civil rights granted to him by the Constitution may appeal to the Federal Constitutional Court. Normally this is possible only after all other remedies have been exhausted, but exceptions are possible in case of irreparable damage. The complaint may be directed against any executive, legislative, or judicial act, but it can be raised only if the plaintiff's rights have been directly injured. A mere "taxpayer's suit" is not permissible.

3. The Federal Constitutional Court is responsible for the interpretation of the Constitution regarding disputes between the highest federal organs concerning their respective rights and duties. Obviously the Court does not decide all such disputes, most of which are political or administrative, but only those in which the interpretation of the Constitution is involved.

4. It decides controversies over the rights and duties of the federation and the *Länder* in their mutual relationships, especially with regard to the execution of federal law by *Länder* administrations and the federal supervision thereof.

5. It also has jurisdiction in other federation-*Länder* and inter-*Länder* controversies in public law, and may decide public law disputes even within a *Land* if that *Land* does not have an appropriate judicial authority of its own. The latter is the case in only one *Land*.

Finally the Constitution assigns to the Federal Constitutional Court a number of specific functions, most of which go beyond the usual scope of courts. These are (1) decisions over the loss of fundamental rights because of their misuse (Art. 18); (2) suppression of political parties because of their anticonstitutional attitude (Art. 21); (3) appeal against decisions of the *Bundestag* concerning the validity of an election (Art. 41); (4) impeachment of the federal President (Art. 61); (5) the removal of a federal judge because of offenses against the constitutional order; this can be pronounced only by the Federal Constitutional Court with a two-thirds majority and upon the demand of the *Bundestag* (Art. 98, Secs. 2 and 5); (6) decisions about the continued validity of older law (Art. 126); and (7) decisions of an intra-*Land* controversy concerning the compatibility of *Land* law with that *Land*'s constitution, but only if the law of that *Land* specifically authorizes the Federal Supreme Court to render such a decision (Art. 99).

Despite its recent creation, the Federal Constitutional Court has already achieved an excellent record which greatly exceeds its expectations. It has not hesitated to act vigorously and courageously and has already fully justified its existence. Out of a growing practice, two widely separated decisions might be cited here. In the much discussed Southwest case,[54] the Federal Constitutional Court did not hesitate to declare an executive order unconstitutional because the *Bundestag* in delegating this right to the executive had failed to define the limits and the purpose of such delegation precisely as required by Art. 80 of the Constitution. The Court thus reminded the parliament of its responsibility and helped to curtail sharply any possible return to a Weimar type of rule by decree.

In another case, the Court declared the Socialist Reich party unconstitutional and went into considerable detail in order to demonstrate what kind of political conduct it considers detrimental to the constitutional and democratic order of the state.[55]

These and other decisions have revealed the Federal Constitutional Court as one of the brightest spots in the constitutional fabric of the new Germany.

In view of this multiplicity of "supreme courts" the Constitution envisaged the creation of a "Supremest Federal Court" (*Oberstes Bundesgericht*). However, it was never established and there is some doubt that it ever will be.

G. LÄNDER *GOVERNMENT*

The German system of *Land* and local government has always been basically different from that of the United States. The traditional separation existing in the United States between federal, state, and local governments constitutes a marked contrast to the fundamental unity of the German system. The German national government, both under the Weimar Republic and the Third *Reich,* did not ordinarily employ its own local agents, but used the *Land* and local authorities for that purpose. Thus even where local government was autonomous it always had to act as a local agent of the national authorities in addition to its autonomous functions. So the citizen was usually confronted with only one system of bureaucracy, but on the other hand local government found itself fairly tightly controlled from above. However this control was defined by detailed statutes which tended to prevent arbitrariness. It should also be mentioned that the civil service was thoroughly entrenched on the *Land* and local government level, even including the requirement that the

---

[54] Gerhard Leibholz, "The Federal Constitutional Court in Germany and the 'Southwest Case,'" *American Political Science Review,* Vol. XLVI (1952), pp. 723–731.

[55] Decision of the Federal Constitutional Court of Oct. 23, 1952, concerning the unconstitutionality of the Socialist Reich party, *Entscheidungen des Bundesverfassungsgerichts,* 1 BvB 1/51, Oct. 23, 1952.

mayor was to be a person endowed with high civil-service qualifications. Technical efficiency was therefore of a high order, although the services were frequently more elaborate than economical.

Under the empire the *Länder* had a very great degree of autonomy and considerable "home rule" prevailed in the municipalities. The centralist trend of the Weimar Constitution deprived the *Länder* of much of their autonomy, and while they did not become rubber stamps immediately, they were clearly moving in that direction. The extent to which centralization had taken place during the Weimar Republic can be gathered from the system of taxation. All taxes were collected by the national administration and then apportioned between the *Reich* and the *Länder*. Apportionment among the *Länder* was guided neither by size nor by number of population of the *Länder* but by the amount of income taxes collected in each *Land*.

This type of financial administration interfered with regional and municipal planning to a considerable extent, as taxes were standardized and could not be adjusted to the particular needs of the community. As an experienced observer has pointed out, it was through this type of fiscal management rather than through constitutional or statutory provisions that the last vestiges of German federalism became extinct.[56] This is why the Bonn Constitution spells out in such detail an equitable distribution of fiscal powers between the federation and the *Länder* (Arts. 105–115).

With the arrival of the great depression, German municipal government found itself saddled with staggering burdens which it could not carry, and more and more self-government was lost in the process of receiving additional aid from the national authorities. The poor financial position of the German communities provided the Nazis with a welcome excuse to "reorganize" the entire structure of local government, a task which was accomplished by means of a uniform code for all German municipalities, the German Municipal Act of 1935.

After the collapse of the Nazi regime and under Allied military government, German administrations were first established on the local level before *Länder* governments were reconstituted. This happened at different speeds in the Western zones of Germany. The American zone was the first in that respect; both the British and the French held on much longer to direct administration. Eventually *Länder* constitutions were written and adopted everywhere, with the British zone trailing far behind.

The *Länder* themselves were partly historical, partly artificial units. Bavaria, although it underwent some changes, mentions a one-thousand-year history in its constitution, while Hesse was created out of three former units. The former *Länder* of Baden and Württemberg, after being artificially divided into three units in order to accommodate the creation of a French zone, were

[56] Arnold Brecht, *Federalism and Regionalism in Germany,* New York, 1945, p. 61.

finally reunited in 1952, though with difficulty and much controversy,[57] into one *Land* which bears the name Baden-Württemberg.

The German Federal Republic is thus composed of nine *Länder*: Baden-Württemberg, Bavaria, Bremen, Hamburg, Hesse, Lower Saxony, North Rhine-Westphalia, Rhineland-Palatinate, and Schleswig-Holstein. West Berlin is in a category by itself as will be seen below.

The *Länder* are quite unequal in size although not nearly as much as was the case when Prussia existed. The most populated *Land* is North Rhine–Westphalia, which embraces the Ruhr industrial area and has over 13 million inhabitants. Bavaria is the largest state in area with over 27,000 square miles, but only a little over 9 million inhabitants (whereas North Rhine–Westphalia has a little over 13,000 square miles). The smallest *Land* in both population and area is the city-state of Bremen, which has 558,000 inhabitants and 156 square miles.

All *Länder* are organized on the principle of parliamentary democracy. They have a popularly elected legislature which, except in Bavaria, is unicameral.[58] In most *Länder* it is called *Landtag*, but in Hamburg and Bremen it goes by the name of *Bürgerschaft* (literally translated, citizenry). These legislatures are elected by variously modified proportional-representation systems and their legislative term is usually four years. Despite strong Allied protest, civil servants may be members of the *Landtage* without retiring or even taking a leave of absence. Only the electoral law of North Rhine–Westphalia discourages this practice.

The executives of the *Länder* are cabinets headed by a minister president (*Ministerpräsident*). In Bremen and Hamburg the cabinet is called a senate, and its chairman, the equivalent to the minister president, is called mayor (*Bürgermeister*) and senate president in Bremen, lord mayor (*Oberbürgermeister*) in Hamburg.

Despite the fact that coalition governments are in power in most *Länder*, they have proved themselves very stable. This stability has been enhanced in several states by a provision similar to that in the federal Constitution, stipulating that a government which has received a vote of nonconfidence must resign only when a successor has been elected by the *Landtag*. The constitution of Bavaria has a curious provision in having the minister president elected for four years, but stipulating somewhat vaguely that he must resign when cooperation between him and the legislature has become impossible. This provision has made little difference, and Bavaria is governed like the other *Länder*.[59]

---

[57] The religious conflict between the Catholic population of South Baden and the Protestant one of Württemberg played a significant role here.

[58] The Bavarian Senate is based on a corporative principle and has little significance.

[59] Robert G. Neumann, "New Constitutions in Germany," *American Political Science Review, Vol.* XLII (1948), pp. 448–468; Harold O. Lewis, *New Constitutions in Occupied Germany*, Washington, 1948.

Between the *Land* governmental level and that of local administration there is an intermediary authority in many *Länder* called a government district (*Regierungsbezirk*) and headed by a government president (*Regierungspräsident*) who is appointed by the *Land* government and subject to its direction.

On the whole the *Länder* of the German Federal Republic have more real self-government than they had under the Weimar Republic and of course under the Nazi regime. Contrary to the somewhat naïve and oversimplified assumptions of some Allied military government policy makers, this does not in itself guarantee democracy or bring it necessarily any closer. Democracy and federalism are no more identical than are centralism and dictatorship. The German Empire of the Hohenzollerns was certainly a federal regime but equally certainly not a democracy. France is a unitary, centralist state, but certainly a democracy. Moreover, during the period of the Weimar Republic, the central government and the near-central government of Prussia were frequently more enlightened and democratic than some of the *Länder* governments. One the other hand, since the German people must educate themselves toward a democratic regime, the existence of *Länder* governments, which are much closer to the citizen than is the federal government, may be a good thing.

Germany has shown marked trends toward a more unitary regime. Partly this is political; the Christian Democrats, the chief spokesmen of federalism, are not nearly so keen on it now that they safely dominate the national government. Partly this has been due to the great authority of Chancellor Konrad Adenauer. More important has been the dire economic necessity which confronted the country and made extraordinary measures inevitable. The strong foreign policy and the future, obviously inevitable, rearmament of Germany all strengthen the centralist trend.

What protects the *Länder* from being submerged by the federal government is not so much their reserved powers under the Constitution, which, as we have seen, are few, but rather the important position of the *Bundesrat*. Also the vigorous attitude of the Federal Constitutional Court is likely to play an important role in the defense of "states' rights."

H. LOCAL GOVERNMENT

Just as the federal government exercises its regional functions through the *Länder* governments, so they exercise their local functions through local government. This makes for much streamlining but also for supervision.

Local government was the sector in which former German institutions were relatively satisfactory, at least before 1935. While not uniform, the prevailing system was that of an elected city council which elected a mayor, but the mayor had a very long term of office, certainly much longer than that of the council. In practice this meant that the mayor was a professional who had to blend with the directly elected councilors and did so with generally good results. The Nazis changed this in 1935, but the Allies did not go back to the preceding, generally satisfactory order. They attempted instead to impose the system to which they were accustomed at home. This was far less true of the Americans than of the British and the French. The British insisted on making both the mayor and the *Landrat* (head of the district, *Kreis*) purely political officials, while vesting the actual administration in a civil servant who, in the municipalities, became known as the city director (called, according to the importance of the city, *Gemeindedirektor, Stadtdirektor,* or *Oberstadtdirektor*). For the *Kreis* the British created an elected *Landrat* and a professional *Kreisdirektor*. The results of this reform were on the whole quite unsatisfactory. The Germans did not like the system; the separation between the political and the administrative worked against rather than for a democratic development and on occasion permitted politically doubtful elements to slip into the mayoralty who would have been kept out under the old and tried system.

In the French zone the French attempt to copy the *maire-adjoint* system in a totally foreign environment only raised complete incomprehension. The French system naturally disappeared as soon as the French no longer imposed it. The British system has remained in North Rhine–Westphalia for the time being but has been eliminated elsewhere. The American zone went back to a modified version of the older system without too much difficulty.

Generally speaking, city government is not left to individual charters but is regulated by *Land* law along fairly uniform lines. There are, however, considerable differences between the various *Länder*.[60] Thus in Bavaria and Baden-Württemberg we find what corresponds to a mayor-council type of government, with the mayor in a strong position. He is elected directly by the people and in larger cities is a full-time official with a six-year term. In Hesse the same system prevails on the whole, but the law also permits a commission type of government; normally the *Bürgermeister* is elected by the council. In North Rhine–Westphalia, as already stated, the British type of system still prevails, but it is not likely to be adopted elsewhere and its future is uncertain.

A little more uniformity prevails on the district (*Kreis*) level. These districts are the main units of local government. In the case of more important towns, the town itself becomes a district, called urban district (*Stadtkreis*), in some ways comparable to the British county boroughs, and not subjected to the jurisdiction of the district surrounding the city. The other, ordinary districts are called rural districts (*Landkreis*). There are no uniform rules about when a city is to become a *Stadtkreis*.

Except for North Rhine–Westphalia, the most important official of the *Kreis* is the rural councilor (*Landrat*), whose position is combined with that of the mayor in the *Stadtkreise*. The *Landrat* used to be appointed but is now

[60] Roger H. Wells, "Local Government," Litchfield and Associates, *op. cit.,* pp. 84–116.

elected by the legislative council of the *Kreis*, the *Kreistag*. Only in the area of the former French zone is he still appointed, subject however to confirmation by the *Kreistag*. The *Landrat* is the chief executive of the *Kreis* who appoints all officials. His salary is paid by the *Land*, but that gives the *Land* government only limited control over him, as has been demonstrated by several unsuccessful attempts on the part of *Land* governments to get rid of a *Landrat*.

Unlike the city council, which meets frequently, the *Kreistag* meets only on occasion. In the interim, a committee of the *Kreistag*, the *Kreisausschuss*, carries on much of its business but also serves as something like a commission in a commission type of municipal administration.

Because the municipalities are frequently small and their problems many, they find it useful to undertake certain joint or cooperative operations. Inasmuch as this coordination takes place within the confines of the *Landkreis*, it is regulated by law although additional intermunicipal agreements may be made on a voluntary basis. Such agreements may involve joint handling of certain problems, contracting, purchasing, etc. A more permanent joint authority between municipalities has been established in certain *Länder* under the name of "authority" (*Amt*). These *Ämter* are established for general governmental purposes, but there are also special, intermunicipal authorities for specific purposes, such as joint maintenance of utilities. These are called "common-purposes associations" (*Zweckverbände*).

The functions which local government has to perform are very extensive, especially on the city level. Apart from the usual tasks of planning, safety, health, and welfare, German municipalities usually own and run their utilities and transportation systems and maintain cultural institutions. A truly gigantic task has been added by the influx of refugees and expellees, who by now number well over 12 million people in the German Federal Republic. These unfortunate people arrived with literally nothing to their names. Not only did they have to be housed and clothed but opportunities for work had to be found for them or, as often happened, they were encouraged to create such opportunities for themselves. Social problems of great gravity were created by the very mass of the influx, and these were all the more important as the habits of many of the refugees were quite different from those of the regular residents. There are now many towns and villages in which the refugees outnumber the original inhabitants and constitute the majority of the city administration. It is truly a miracle that under circumstances of this kind there has not been any major explosion.

The immense burden of administration and fiscal outlay which was placed on the shoulders of local government had the disadvantage that it encouraged encroachment by *Land* and federal authorities. This has meant that local government found its own sources of revenue insufficient and had to rely more and more on a share in *Land* and federal revenues. At the same time, local government has become more rigid by the increasing number of mandatory tasks imposed upon it. In view of the emergency situation and the size of the problem, no other development could be expected. However, German local government is aware of these tendencies, watches them carefully, and is by no means in a spirit of submission.

I. THE GOVERNMENT OF WEST BERLIN

It is customary that capital cities of countries are administered differently from other municipalities. This also occurred in Berlin when in 1912 the city was detached, except for certain supervisory functions, from the province of Brandenburg and achieved the status of a province in its own right. The city charter of 1920 established the customary *Magistratsverfassung*, which implies something between a mayor-council and commission type of administration, especially as the position of the mayor was considerably strengthened later on. This city constitution also divided Berlin into twenty districts (*Bezirke*), each one with a charter similar to that of the city, and each with a district mayor and district council.

The Russians, who occupied the city first, revived the pre-Nazi constitution but infiltrated the government heavily with Communists. When the four-power occupation was established, the United States occupied six districts, the British four, the French two, and the Russians eight. Although the city constitution nominally remained in force, considerable divergences existed in the different sectors. This situation continued under the temporary charter of 1946.

The Russians walked out of the Allied Control Council on March 26, 1948, and on June 16, 1948, they left the *Komandatura*. Shortly thereafter the famous Berlin Blockade began, and Communist pressure increased both inside and around the city. On June 23, 1948, a Communist mob stormed the city hall, which was located in the Russian sector; the city council moved to the Western sector, but the councilors of the Communist-controlled Socialist Unity party (SED) refused to go along; and the split into two Berlins became an accomplished fact.

In 1949 the three Western Allied Powers enacted a "little occupation" statute which was the Berlin corollary to the occupation statute for the German Federal Republic, and on August 29, 1950, the permanent constitution for Berlin was adopted.

Berlin is now both a city and a *Land*, somewhat comparable to the constitutions of Hamburg and Bremen. However, for reasons of international politics and out of fear of Russian retaliation, the Allies suspended that part of the constitution which would have incorporated Berlin into the German Federal Republic. Thus Berlin is a *Land* for internal purposes, but it is not a *Land* of the German Federal Republic. However, the German Federal Republic treats Berlin pretty much as if it were one of its *Länder*, and Berlin's hybrid status is underlined by the fact that it sends nonvoting delegates to both the *Bundestag* and the *Bundesrat*.

The constitution of the city-state of Berlin parallels that of other *Länder*. There is a popularly elected house of representatives composed of 200 members, of whom only 127 are actually functioning because 73 seats are reserved for East Berlin as a gesture to demonstrate that the West Berlin city government considers itself a government of the entire city. The House of Representatives is elected by proportional representation for four years. It in turn elects the chief executive, who bears the title governing mayor (*Regierender Bürgermeister*). It also elects a cabinet of nineteen members. Mayor and cabinet must have the confidence of the house of representatives and must resign if that confidence is withdrawn.

Each district elects a district government called *Bezirksamt*, which is headed by a district mayor (*Bezirksbürgermeister*). These district mayors have established a council for mutual consultation and common action.

The people of Berlin have given unmistakable proof of their solidarity with their government, which on December 3, 1950, was elected by an unprecedented vote of 90.4 per cent of the electorate. This has enabled the city to stand firm against Russian and German Communist pressure during the many crises which have marked its recent history.

Chapter 10

POLITICAL LIFE IN GERMANY

In Germany, political life as it is understood in the occidental world came to an abrupt halt on January 30, 1933. Between that date and May 7, 1945, there was only the Nazi one-party state. In other countries occupied by German troops, and even to a certain small extent in Italy under the Fascist regime, some of the former political parties were able to lead a vestige of underground existence. Not so in Germany. There they were obliterated without exception, and only a fast-fading memory remained. The political opulence of party life during the Weimar regime had not equipped any of the parties for the hard realities of a hunted underground life. Nor were they prepared for the ruthlessness of the Nazis. Thus, party records and funds were easily seized by the police, membership lists confiscated, and all more or less prominent leaders imprisoned unless they had been prudent enough to seek exile.

Added to these events were the vigilance of the Gestapo and the heavy punishment meted out to suspected opponents of the regime. Consequently a non-Nazi political life could not exist even in nuclear form. The abortive attempt to overthrow the Nazi regime in June, 1944, was based on a hasty coalition of individuals of widely different political views. It had no grass-root character, which it could not have afforded anyway for fear of discovery by the police, and it did not constitute the beginning of an alternative political movement.

POLITICAL VACUUM

The elimination of the Nazi regime therefore created an absolute political vacuum. The German people were bitter, apathetic, hungry, and tired. For twelve long years their political leadership had told them about the glories of the Third Reich which they were creating for themselves. Now the ruins which surrounded them gave an eloquent commentary to these ambitions. Small wonder, then, that the speeches and promises of Germany's postwar political leaders were received with little enthusiasm, if not with aversion.

And finally there was the sheer effort to keep alive, the standing in line for hours, the necessity of dealing in the black market to avoid starvation, and the interminable jungle of both Allied and German bureaucracies which kept the Germans hopping from *Fragebogen* (questionnaire) to *Fragebogen*. In such an atmosphere, virile political life based on broad popular participation could not grow easily.

There was also a dearth of leadership. The political leaders who did reappear in Germany were for the most part relics of the Weimar period, where most of them had occupied minor posts. Now they came forth and offered themselves to the military-government authorities. They did not represent real parties at first, but rather political clubs which were to form the nucleus for mass parties later on. Some of them had formed so-called "Antifascist Committees" (*Antifa*), most of which were Communist-led. But they had no broad popular basis, and when they were dissolved their disappearance caused hardly a ripple.

Party Life Reborn

Nevertheless political leaders did obtain an early foothold. Military government needed responsible Germans to occupy positions as mayors, district chiefs, and heads of intermediate regions that were known as government districts (*Regierungsbezirke*). These former Weimar politicians and officials were logical choices, and on the whole they served loyally in positions where they had more of the form than the substance of power. However, as these leaders obtained places in the administrative machinery upon appointment by military government, they also began to organize their respective parties in a more or less overt manner.

It had been the plan of the Western occupation powers to make the establishment of political life a gradual, unhurried process. After careful screening, political parties, as well as unions and professional associations, were to be permitted on a local scale. After being tested, they were eventually to be permitted to broaden their basis. By that time, it was hoped, the German people would be a little more alert to their opportunities under a reasonable degree of political freedom, and the increased authority of political leaders would go hand in hand with a process of improved political maturity on the part of the people.

These carefully laid plans came to naught as a result of the policy adopted by the Soviet Military Administration. It has already been stated that the Soviet armies had no regular military-government apparatus and were therefore immediately dependent on native collaborators. The Soviet authorities managed to turn this apparent disadvantage into an advantage by licensing, almost immediately after the cessation of hostilities, four distinct political parties: the Communists, the Social Democrats, the Christian Democrats, and the Liberal Democrats. By this stroke the Russians achieved two things:

they had an opportunity to pose as the most "liberal" occupation power, who gave the Germans political responsibility while the Western powers withheld it; and secondly, by permitting only four parties to organize, they took shrewd cognizance of the strong German aversion against a recurrence of the multitude of parties that marked the Weimar regime.

The creation of those four parties immediately caused such repercussions in Western Germany that military government found it necessary to follow the Russian lead. However, for some time to come, British, French, and United States military-government officials closely controlled the actions of German officeholders, while the Soviet Military Administration was generally content to give greater leeway to officials in its zone, holding them only strictly accountable for their results. As time went on, this process was reversed; the Western powers, especially the Americans, relaxed in their direct interference and gave the Germans a very substantial measure of self-government, while the strong hand of the Russians and their native handmaidens became increasingly evident in the East.

THE PARTY SYSTEM TODAY

In order to appraise the German party system of our days, it is necessary to keep in mind that it has probably not as yet reached its permanent, long-range form, that it is of recent origin, and that it was reborn, after the catastrophe of 1945, under highly unusual circumstances.

It is a peculiar feature of Germany that its political history is not the history of its parties or party leaders. During the formative years of modern Germany—the period of the empire (1871–1918)—the parties were strictly on the sidelines. The government of the country was not in the hands of party leaders but of personalities like Bismarck and his successors, who studiously avoided any partisan tinge. The political parties could talk, and even elect members of parliament, but the administration of the country remained outside their scope.

If the German people felt inclined to look upon their parties in the imperial period with disinterest, they were more likely to regard the Weimar parties with scorn. The galaxy of parties, their splintering tendencies, the frequent crises, the mutual neutralization of the parties, and especially their helplessness in the face of inflation encouraged many people to look for salvation outside the ranks of the traditional parties and to hope for a strong leader. The leader arrived and the party system was destroyed, but the eventual results of this regime, especially its military defeat, discredited even the name "party" because it was so prominently associated with the Nazi party, even though the parties of totalitarian states have little in common with the party system of a democracy.

When parties sprang up again in 1945 and after, they were under the heavy supervision of military government. The business of government, while often entrusted to party leaders, was so strongly controlled and often directed by the Allied authorities that many politicians hesitated to take office for fear of appearing as the executive organs of a foreign state.

It was only after 1949, when Allied control had become nominal and had practically disappeared, that Germany's political profile began to take shape. This is certainly an extremely brief period, too brief to draw definitive conclusions, especially as there are important differences between the present German political-party system and that of Weimar, as will be seen below.

Nevertheless it is quite possible to draw a preliminary balance sheet and to point out several characteristic features of the contemporary German party scene.

1. In sharp contrast to the Weimar experience, the German Federal Republic has not produced the diversity of parties of its unfortunate precursor. After Allied control over the licensing of new parties relaxed its rigidity, there was a flurry of new parties, some special-interest groups, others again formed around specific personalities. But this situation proved short-lived. The newer parties were unable to maintain themselves, and their lack of significance was shown in the elections of September 6, 1953. Only the Refugee party (BHE/GB) has been able to achieve a modest significance, but far less than expected. Moreover, even some of the older parties have declined, with the result that Germany for the first time in her history is confronted by the very real possibility of developing a two-party system. In fact, if Germany had voted solely under the direct-plurality system in single-member districts in 1953, a two-party system would already be an accomplished fact. It must, however, be pointed out that the election of 1953 was overshadowed by an unusually dominating foreign-policy issue and centered on a vote for or against the policy of one man, Konrad Adenauer. It may therefore be hasty to draw definitive conclusions from one election only. Nevertheless, for the time being the decline of all parties except the Christian Democrats (CDU/CSU) and the Social Democrats (SPD) is very much in evidence.

2. The German public, by and large, does not quite understand the connection between political parties and government. It is inclined to look upon government as something impersonal, abstract (the term "state" is preferred to "government"), and to regard political parties as something separate whose place in public life it cannot quite fathom. Parties are more likely to be regarded as a nuisance than as a necessity. The essentiality of political parties for the democratic process is not widely understood. Although Germans are wont to embrace very definite political philosophies, they have, by and large, little regard for political parties, even though these parties may be strong champions of the very same philosophy. The high percentage of German voting participation (in the 1953 election, it was 86 per cent) should be inter-

preted as a dedication to the exercise of a civic duty, rather than enthusiasm for a particular party.

3. The German political parties have strongly oligarchic tendencies. They are controlled by a small group of professional party bureaucrats or individual leaders, whose claim to prominence is more often based on party regularity and seniority than on exceptional qualifications. The CDU is completely dominated by a single individual, Konrad Adenauer, and the same situation prevailed in the Social Democratic party while Schumacher was still alive. These, however, constitute unusual occurrences which are not likely to be repeated so soon. Certainly no single person has been able to step into Schumacher's shoes in the Social Democratic party, and the same situation is probably in store for the CDU after Adenauer ceases to lead it.

These oligarchic tendencies are not the result of any special rules or regulations but are based on habits and traditions. The German deputy, the German party member, are conditioned to follow their leaders without too many questions. Moreover the average German citizen is not conditioned toward the lively participation in civic activities which characterizes American life; even when he joins a party formally (which only a relatively small number of people will do) he does not expect to lay down the law to the party leaders.[1]

4. Although all political parties have youth movements, they have all found it difficult to attract many younger members. This situation has certainly improved since 1951, but the results are still not inspiring and the fact that the average age of members of the *Bundestag* is fifty is significant. In order to improve this situation, time is required so that the young people will be convinced that the democratic order is here to stay and that they will not risk their futures by betting on the wrong horse. Many people, remembering denazification, fear that some day there may come a dedemocratization. Another factor is the reluctance of many older Germans to accept young people as equals. Many young men and women are exaggeratedly sensitive on that point and regard their alleged lack of access to positions of influence with undue pessimism.

5. German parties, like other European parties, are generally associated with certain social classes: the Social Democrats with labor, the CDU with business and farming, etc. These distinctions are not rigid but they prevail to a large extent.

6. Although material for vivid controversy has not been lacking, a certain degree of unity has prevailed on many questions because the huge problems of German reconstruction, care for refugees, and the rebuilding of Germany's international position were considered so important by most parties that no serious disturbance ensued. Especially the workers and their German Trade

---

[1] The classical work on the oligarchic nature of German parties, especially the Social Democrats, is Robert Michels' *Political Parties* (trans. by E. and C. Paul), first published 1915, reprinted 1949.

Union Federation (*Deutscher Gewerkschaftsbund,* DGB), as well as the Social Democrats, generally have refrained from purely demagogic demands upon the government. Only in the bitter controversy over German rearmament did demagogic and undemocratic techniques enter into the political struggle. Repeated attempts by Social Democratic partisans to prevent by force the speeches of some of their opponents were most regrettable. The Social Democrats who had once been themselves the victims of such tactics on the part of the Nazis should have known better.

DISTRIBUTION OF VOTES AND SEATS IN THE *Bundestag* OF THE
GERMAN FEDERAL REPUBLIC ELECTIONS OF SEPTEMBER 6, 1953

		Percentage of total vote		
Parties	Votes	1954	1949	Seats
CDU/CSU	12,444,055	45.2	31	244 + 6 *
Social Democratic party.............	7,944,953	28.8	29.2	151 + 11 *
Free Democratic party..............	2,629,169	9.5	11.9	48 + 5 *
Refugee Bloc, GB/BHE.............	1,616,956	5.9	—	27
German party	896,230	3.3	4.	15
Communist party	607,761	2.2	5.7	
Bavarian party	465,641	1.7	4.2	
All-German People's party..........	318,476	1.2		
German Reich party...............	295,746	1.1		
Center party	217,078	0.8	3.1	2 †
German National Concentration......	70,726	0.3		
South Schleswig Voters League.......	44,585	0.2	0.3	

* Nonvoting delegates from West Berlin.
†Technically the CDU/CSU elected 243 and the Center party 3. But as the latter had "borrowed" one man from the CDU and then returned him to the CDU *Fraktion* as previously explained, the CDU/CSU actually has 244 and the Center party 2 members in the *Bundestag.*
Source: Official election results taken from *The Bulletin*, a weekly survey of German affairs issued by the Press and Information Office of the German Federal Government, Oct. 1, 1953, p. 2.

THE CHRISTIAN DEMOCRATS

The largest and most important German party is the Christian Democratic Union (*Christlich-Demokratische Union,* CDU) which, in conjunction with its Bavarian sister party, the Christian Social Union (*Christlichsoziale Union,* CSU), polled 45.2 per cent of the total vote in the elections of September 6, 1953, the largest percentage ever obtained by a political party in the history of Germany. The CDU/CSU has a bare majority in the *Bundestag* with 244 seats.

The CDU has fallen heir to the position of the Center party of the imperial period and the Weimar Republic. But while the Center party was purely Catholic, the CDU has consciously striven to be nondenominational. In this it has succeeded up to a point. Most of its principal leaders, above all Adenauer himself, are Catholics and former Center men, but there is a sizable Protestant element. Over one-third of the CDU/CSU deputies in the *Bundesrat* are Protestants. Also the fact that the CDU has shown considerable strength in predominantly Protestant areas certifies the fact that it is not simply a Catholic party. If the influence of Catholic leaders predominates, it is mitigated by the fact that it is a lay, and not a clerical, influence. In fact, as far as intra-Catholic relationships are concerned, this is one case in which, in the political field, the lay element definitely predominates over the clergy.

From the Center party the CDU has inherited an intramural quarrel over social policy. The Center party, being a religious rather than a class party, combined many socially and economically heterogeneous groups. In the CDU too a "left" and a "right" group are discernible. When the CDU was first organized it seemed for a while as if the left might prove dominant.[2] However, it failed to take a firm hold of the party organization. Its most significant leader, Jakob Kaiser, was from Eastern Germany and the iron curtain cut off his principal backing. Most decisive, however, was the personal influence of Konrad Adenauer, who is of a more conservative persuasion. The left wing is now led by Karl Arnold, Minister President of Germany's largest *Land*, North Rhine–Westphalia, who is on much better terms with the Social Democrats than is Adenauer, and who has expressed himself in favor of one of their principal social demands, the right of codetermination (*Mitbestimmungsrecht*) of the workers in industry. However, it is Adenauer's and not Arnold's influence which predominates, and the CDU can therefore be designated as a conservative party.

The CDU belongs to the wide circle of Christian Democratic parties of which the French MRP and the Italian Christian Democrats are members,[3] and whose philosophy it basically shares without necessarily drawing the same political conclusions. Its fundamental belief rests in the analysis that the crisis of mankind and of civilization is primarily moral and spiritual and that a regeneration can take place only on a basis of Christian ethics. The same Christian principles lead the party to the profound conviction of human imperfection, and it therefore opposes excessive concentration of power in whatever field, social, economic, political, or administrative. In fact, in an earlier party platform which was contained in the Ahlen program of 1947, a balance between public and private enterprise was advocated. Two factors, however, have turned the course of the party into more conservative waters.

---

[2] Robert G. Neumann, "The New Political Parties of Germany," *American Political Science Review*, Vol. XL (1946), pp. 749–759.

[3] There is a loosely organized international association of Christian Democratic parties called *Nouvelles équipes internationales* (new international teams).

Its economic theory has been dominated by the dynamic Minister of Economics, Ludwig Ehrhard, a former professor of economics, who has vigorously advocated a so-called "social market policy" which is essentially free enterprise plus safeguards under social legislation. This system has been extraordinarily successful and remains the guiding line of the party.[4] In its administrative theory the CDU has been traditionally anticentralist, favoring an emphasis on what Americans would call "states' rights," a heritage from the old Center days when centralism meant northern, Prussian, and Protestant domination over the more Catholic south. However, once in power the CDU has discovered the advantages of centralism and much less is now being said in favor of decentralization.

In recent years the most outstanding feature of the CDU has been its stand on foreign policy, whch is militantly and unreservedly pro-Western and has supported all steps toward a united, federated Europe. The elections of 1953 were primarily fought over this question against the background of the struggle for European integration which Adenauer staunchly defended. The extraordinary electoral victory of the Chancellor guarantees that this issue will be vigorously pressed in the future.[5]

In contrast to the Social Democrats, the CDU does not possess a tight organization. It sprang up in different *Länder* simultaneously and with little coordination. Although an interzonal coordinating committee has existed since 1947, it was only in 1950 that the first real All-German (Federal Republic and West Berlin) Party Congress of the CDU could be held in Goslar.

The CDU's organization lays far less stress on individual membership than does the Social Democratic party. As a result, the CDU must rely on outside funds, which in practice means fairly large donations from a few important financial groups.

The CDU has been, and has remained, the strongest political party of Germany ever since the organization of the Federal Republic in 1949. However, its growth to its present position of preeminence has not been consistent. In 1949 it obtained 31 per cent of the vote (together with the CSU), which constituted somewhat of a decline compared to previous *Länder* elections. In subsequent *Länder* elections the party showed some further, though hardly extraordinary, decline, especially in Hesse, Württemberg-Baden, Bavaria, and Lower Saxony. In contrast, the Social Democrats achieved considerable successes in these *Länder*, except in Lower Saxony.

---

[4] As a result Germany now suffers an embarrassment of riches. She has acquired a substantial surplus in the European Payments Union and is worried, like all creditor nations, about when this money is going to return and how it can be used. Ehrhard therefore has now advocated the adoption of free convertibility of currencies, a thought which appalls some other European nations.

[5] One CDU leader, Heinrich von Brentano, plays a leading role in the Council of Europe.

In Bavaria the CDU's sister party, the CSU, was beset by serious internal difficulties. Like its Weimar predecessor, the Bavarian People's party, the CSU is essentially more conservative than the CDU but has nevertheless maintained a working relationship with the Social Democrats on the basis of a common insistence on "states' rights" and common suspicion of anything coming from north of the Main River. In the person of Josef Müller, former Bavarian Minister of Justice, the CSU has its own "left wing." [6]

The chief difficulty of the CSU has been a serious split in its own ranks. A not inconsiderable section of the party, headed by Josef Baumgartner, seceded from the CSU and formed the Bavarian party (*Bayernpartei*), whose main platform was one of extreme Bavarian nationalism and hostility to the Federal Republic. Much of the conflict was also engendered by personal animosities. At first the Bavarian party obtained considerable success and in the national elections of 1949 gained 20.9 per cent of the Bavarian vote against the CSU's 29.2 per cent. But the Bavarian party has since been beset by internal crises and has declined. In 1953 it polled only half as many votes as it did in 1949 and lost its representation in the *Bundestag,* but it has remained a factor in Bavarian politics.

Largely because of the steadily increasing importance of the foreign political issue, especially the relationship between Germany and the West, the CDU/CSU was able to recover completely from these temporary dips and more than make up for the losses of the past. It should be noted, however, that a great part of the party's extraordinary gains has come from Adenauer's allies. The CDU/CSU has nullified the gains made by the Social Democrats since 1949, but it has not substantially cut into their basic strength. The question therefore arises whether in a future election, when foreign policy may not overshadow all other issues, the CDU will be able to hold on to its present voters. Yet with the voting discipline especially of the Catholic part of its electorate, and its solid following particularly in rural areas, the CDU is almost bound to remain the strongest German party for a long time to come.

THE SOCIAL DEMOCRATIC PARTY

The reestablishment of the Social Democratic party organization had been both prompt and effective. A number of factors contributed to this end. There was the fact that, among the group of survivors of the Weimar regime, the Social Democrats usually had clean records which made them eligible for positions in the German administrative structure under military government. In their ranks there were a number of men who had seen previous service in administrative positions. As experienced and trustworthy civil servants and

[6] Müller has resigned from the Bavarian cabinet and is in perhaps only temporary retirement from public life as a result of his stand in a famous corruption affair which gave his numerous political enemies an opportunity to attack him.

policy-making officials were not easily found, on account of the denazification policy, many of these Social Democratic relics from Weimar days were placed in positions of power and prestige which aided their efforts at reestablishing their party. Moreover, the long rule of the Weimar Social Democrats and the "Free Trade Unions" which they had dominated over the German workers had created a kind of tradition which had often been passed on from father to son and to which the German workers now readily responded.[7]

The Social Democratic program also held considerable appeal. It placed the party squarely behind the democratic form of government. It advocated a democratic and moderate form of socialism, which appeals to many Germans as well as to other Europeans because of the general impoverishment of the population and the obvious need for some sort of state planning and initiative for the gigantic task of reconstruction. On the other hand, concerning questions of the class struggle and the relationship to religion, the party had become very moderate, a development which undoubtedly received its inspiration in the experience of the common suppression of all religions and classes by the defunct Nazi regime.

Because of their clean record as far as the Nazi period is concerned, the Social Democratic leaders were among the first who dared to stand up to such military-government orders as they considered unacceptable. Such criticism was often appreciated by military-government officers in the field, who understood the need for public criticism in a democracy, but it was sometimes resented back home by people whose concept of a loyal democrat was one who walks about draped in the Stars and Stripes, the Union Jack, or the *tricolore*.

Soon after the reestablishment of political parties, the Communists launched their vigorous campaign for a united workers' party. Their overtures were roundly turned down in Western Germany, but they found more receptive ears in the Eastern parts of the country.

The Communist Fusion Propaganda

It is of course easily understandable why the relatively small Communist party would want such a fusion with the much more numerous Social Democrats, especially since experience in the Soviet satellite countries showed that it could easily control its more moderate confreres. No such obvious advantage would seem to be on the side of the Social Democrats. Yet there were peculiar circumstances which exerted pressure in the direction of fusion. The greatest strength of the Social Democratic party in Weimar days had always

---

[7] It must always be remembered that many political parties, but especially the Social Democrats, conducted large-scale programs of education and social affairs for their members. Membership therefore tended to become a way of life and a mold of social contacts which was often retained during the lifetime of the member.

been in those regions which are now the Soviet zone of occupation, including the city of Berlin. Many of the party's leaders feared that, if they refused to make common cause with the Communists, Soviet pressure would sooner or later force them out of office, and perhaps even out of existence, in the regions where they expected to take their strongest hold. They also feared that such renewed elimination would cause many of their followers to go over to the Communists, as that party would then be in a better position to give them what they wanted in the nature of social benefits and improvements of working and living conditions. Perhaps the Social Democratic leaders also dreaded a new period of illegality and suppression after they had emerged from the twelve long years of Nazi rule. Undoubtedly some of them genuinely believed the moderate and seemingly sincere assertions of the Communist leadership, and all of them were deadly afraid of any recurrence of Nazism, and remembered how the advent of Hitler had been made much easier by the fratricidal war between the two leftist parties. Thus, the Social Democratic leaders in Berlin and in the Soviet zone, especially Otto Grotewohl, decided to accept the Communist suggestion. May, 1946, was set as the fusion date.

THE SED

The Social Democrats of Western Germany, led by Kurt Schumacher, protested strongly against this decision. Even more violent opposition came from the membership itself. It was quite clear that this deal was one made by the leaders, not one in which the rank and file concurred. In the Soviet zone, the military-government authorities managed to prevent any plebiscite on the part of the party membership, but in Berlin, where the quadripartite arrangement prevailed, a party convention was held, and the leadership was repudiated by a majority of seven to one. However, the leaders had gone too far to recant, and they went ahead anyway. The Social Democrats of Western Germany and of Berlin repudiated this decision and expelled the renegades. The fusion was accomplished in June, 1946, in Eastern Germany, and the new united party gave itself the name of Socialist Unity party of Germany (*Sozialistische Einheitspartei Deutschlands*) and is commonly referred to as the SED, after its German initials.

THE BERLIN ELECTION, 1946

Since the old-line Social Democratic party (SPD) was outlawed in the Soviet zone, and since no SED existed in the Western zones,[8] the only place where a contest of popular strength was possible was Berlin, where both the SED and SPD were active. The SED went into this contest with high hopes. Not only did it receive the wholehearted support of the Soviet authorities, but

[8] The Communist party continues to operate in the Western zones.

it also counted on the "red" tradition of Berlin, a city in which the Nazis were never able to obtain a majority. But the Berliners went to the polls on October 20, 1946, and handed the now thoroughly Communist-dominated SED a resounding defeat.

Out of 1,945,981 votes cast, the SED obtained only 383,249, or slightly less than 20 per cent. Strongest was the old-line Social Democratic party, which polled 948,851 votes or just under 49 per cent. The Christian Democratic Union, a middle-of-the-road to conservative party, occupied second place with 432,016 votes, or 22 per cent; while the right-wing Liberal Democratic party was last with 181,875 votes, or a little over 9 per cent.[9] Only in the Soviet zone outside Berlin was the SED able to obtain slim majorities and that by means which were far removed from the customary methods of the democratic process.

The Berlin election served as a demonstration for a phenomenon which has now become widely recognized in all other countries as well, namely, that the Communists do not obtain majorities in fair and unfettered elections and that the common people are seldom deceived about the true nature of the Communist program, no matter under what fusion ticket it may sail. In Germany the Berlin election was a turning point insofar as it revealed to the Soviet authorities that Communism had little chance to gain the upper hand through regular elections. Consequently from that time onward the originally fairly mild SED regime in the Soviet zone became much harsher, political opponents were suppressed and even imprisoned in ever-increasing numbers, and the Soviet zone has taken on the appearance of satellite states where government is exercised not by the freely expressed will of the people but by the chosen instrument of the Soviet masters.

The forcible fusion of the Social Democrats and the Communists in the Eastern zone has not hurt the Social Democrats in the West because their strongly anti-Communist stand is well recognized by everyone. In contrast to the Christian Democrats, the Social Democratic party of Germany (*Sozialdemokratische Partei Deutschlands,* SPD) maintains an extremely strong organization. It has about 650,000 members (a decline from a high of 900,000), who are organized in 24 districts and over 9,000 local groups. The financial contributions of the membership make the solicitation of large funds less important for the SPD than it is for the CDU.

The main support for the SPD comes from the working classes, who have a traditional attachment to the party and have remained loyal to it. There is also considerable middle-class support, and for a while it looked as if the

---

[9] Percentages taken from total number of eligible voters. Of these, 89 per cent cast valid ballots. It is significant that the SED was outclassed even in the Soviet sector of Berlin (SED 29.8 per cent, SPD 43.6 per cent). For a detailed breakdown, see Special Report of the Military Governor, United States Zone, *Statistics of Elections in Germany 1946,* rev. ed., Mar. 15, 1947.

party would make large inroads into some rural regions, where in the meantime, however, it has declined. There is also little doubt that the SPD still has considerable support in the Eastern zone, where it can only lead an underground existence. If Germany were to be reunited, the effective strength of the SPD would probably be increased to a considerable extent. This explains in part the party's emphasis on the reunification theme.

In its program, the Social Democratic party is still socialist and Marxist. In actual operation, however, it is more correctly characterized as a left-wing party of social reform. It is in favor of the socialization of heavy industry, especially that of the Ruhr region. But it has not pressed these ideas and has concentrated more on obtaining for the workers the right of codetermination in the business policy of some major industries. According to the Dürckheim program (1950) of the SPD, the party would like to see a planned-credit and raw-material policy, greater equalization of the social burden, federal housing projects, socialization of basic raw materials and key industries, and the reorganization of the social insurance system.

Like the CDU, the SPD emerged after the war under the strong leadership of a remarkable man, Kurt Schumacher, who dominated the party completely. It was largely due to his personal influence that the social and economic policies of the SPD became increasingly overshadowed by questions of international policy. This is perhaps to be explained by the painful memories of the Weimar past in which the SPD was frequently accused of being too international-minded and of "betraying the national interest." Under Schumacher's leadership, the SPD acquired a strongly nationalistic line and concentrated on the problem of German reunification, one of the most popular political issues in Germany. The SPD vigorously rejected any compromise on the Saar question or any recognition of the Oder-Neisse frontier of Eastern Germany. It was very dubious about the Adenauer policy in favor of a "little Europe" composed of the six countries of the Schuman Plan (France, Germany, Italy, Belgium, Netherlands, Luxembourg) because it feared that the political composition of these countries would guarantee the perpetuation of private capitalism. Instead it wanted a larger European Union, especially with the inclusion of Great Britain.

Although the party's anti-Communism cannot be doubted, it has bitterly attacked Adenauer's policy of close political and military collaboration with the West. Its argument is that the reunification of Germany can be the result only of negotiations with Russia and that Russia would never consent to a united Germany if the latter were committed to a completely Western policy.

For a time this attitude produced political results and the SPD steadily increased its votes in a number of *Länder* elections. It is not impossible that this success might have been continued if Schumacher had been able to lead his party with his tremendous dynamic ability and immense popularity. But he died in 1952 and his successor as chairman of the party, the colorless and mediocre Erich Ollenhauer, has proved less successful. The greatest weakness of the party's position, however, lies in the inconclusive character of its central argument. While the SPD's critique of Adenauer's policy of close union with the West was perhaps well taken, its alternative suggestion of negotiating with the Russians carried little conviction since the Germans have had ample experience with the Russians and most of them do not believe that one can be successful in negotiating from a position of weakness.[10]

It was largely the result of the foreign-policy issue which inflicted defeat on the SPD in the national elections of September 6, 1953. The extent of this defeat was, however, greatly exaggerated in the news reports of the time. In comparison to the preceding national election in 1949, the loss of the SPD was negligible, a mere 0.4 per cent of the vote, and an absolute gain of 1 million votes over 1949. Yet compared to the various *Länder* and local elections which have taken place since 1949, the SPD's loss is considerable and means that the entire territory gained since that time has again been lost. In a greatly expanded electorate the absolute gain of 1 million votes is not overwhelming compared to the absolute gain of 5 million by the CDU/CSU. On the other hand there is little doubt that the SPD has retained its hold over the industrial workers. A comparison of the vote in the most highly industrialized region of Germany, the Ruhr, shows a steady increase of the Social Democratic votes from 32.9 per cent in 1947 to 37.6 per cent in 1949, and 40.9 per cent in 1953. But the CDU vote, which showed a slight decrease of 0.1 per cent in that area between 1947 and 1949, took a tremendous increase from 30.3 per cent in 1949 to 41.9 per cent in 1953. Since the Communists decreased in the same period from 10.1 per cent to 4.3 per cent, while the Social Democrats increased from 37.6 per cent to only 40.9 per cent, it would seem obvious that the Social Democrats have picked up only the smaller part of the former Communist vote.

The Social Democrats' place as the second strongest party and the principal opposition is undisputed. With 28.8 per cent of the vote, and 151 seats in the *Bundestag*, the SPD is far ahead of all other parties except the CDU/-CSU. Should economic difficulties appear in Germany, or foreign policy become less of an issue, the Social Democrats are most likely to increase their strength, though it is difficult to see how they can seriously compete with the CDU for first place for a long time to come. While their domination of the workers' vote is assured and the leadership of the unified German Trade-Union Federation (DGB), which is nominally nonpartisan, has shown open sympathy for them, the Social Democrats have had a difficult time making lasting inroads into the rural vote, especially where the Catholic church is strong. The SPD has shown some gains in certain *Länder* elections, but not in all. Nowhere, however, were they spectacular.

[10] Henry L. Bretton, "The German Social Democratic Party and the International Situation," *American Political Science Review*, Vol. XLVII (1953), pp. 980–996.

The indifferent quality of the SPD's leadership since Schumacher's death is no help. West Berlin's mayor Ernst Reuter, who might have had a similarly inspiring influence, died in 1953, but even if he had lived his opposition to the party's foreign policy would probably have kept him from first place. The party's present chairman, Erich Ollenhauer, as mentioned above, is a party bureaucrat without distinction though a personally honest and dedicated man. By far the ablest leader of the SPD is Carlo Schmid. But a personal indiscretion has involved him in a protracted dispute with other party leaders and forced him to remain temporarily on the sidelines. Moreover as a university professor and highly educated man, he has much opposition in a party which has always looked upon intellectuals with some reservations.

THE FREE DEMOCRATIC PARTY

The Free Democratic party (*Freie Demokratische Partei*, FDP) purports to be the heir to the liberal traditions of the Democratic party of the Weimar past.[11] Actually it is not so easily characterized because of its extremely heterogeneous character.

It differs from its Weimar antecedents in that it is, in the main, a party of the right. Yet this is true only in north and central Germany; in south and especially southwest Germany it is more liberal. In the center and the north it is politically right of the CDU and is supported by some business groups. In the south it is left of the CDU/CSU and has its support more among small shopkeepers, artisans, etc. For the same reason, the party collaborates on a national level and in the center and north with the CDU, but in the south and southwest it is closer to the Social Democrats. Everywhere, however, the FDP favors a more centralist regime.

What complicates the picture further is the fact that the FDP is predominantly Protestant and thus offers a refuge to those who agree with CDU policies but resent its alleged Catholic domination. Thus on questions of religious schools, for instance, the FDP would side with the SPD against the CDU/CSU.

At times the FDP—central and northern version—has made strongly nationalist statements, many of which emanated from Thomas Dehler, a Protestant Bavarian, and the *enfant terrible* of the first Adenauer government.[12] These nationalistic gestures were perhaps in part responsible for an infiltration by a former Nazi or perhaps even neo-Nazi element, who grouped themselves around the controversial personality of Friedrich Middelhauve. This gave the FDP much trouble, and it was only shortly before the 1953 elections that the party finally purged this group from its ranks.

---

[11] Actually the FDP appears more comparable to Stresemann's German People's party.

[12] When Adenauer reconstituted his government after the 1953 election, Dehler was quietly dropped and replaced by another FDP leader, Fritz Neumeyer.

Until 1953 the FDP maintained its strength well and made much headway among the younger generation. In the 1953 elections, however, it declined to 9.5 per cent of the total vote against 11.9 per cent in 1949. Its total vote also declined by some 200,000.

The Free Democratic party has participated in the Adenauer government from the beginning and agrees with the Chancellor's foreign policy in general but fears that Adenauer is making too many concessions to France. Its decrease in strength must be viewed as the result of a popular concentration behind the CDU and Adenauer.

The FDP has a number of able leaders, of whom perhaps the most prominent are Theodor Heuss, now President of the Federal Republic, and Franz Bluecher, who is Vice-Chancellor in the Adenauer cabinet. Party Chairman and its strongest personality is Thomas Dehler, who has become a more effective leader since he has left the cabinet.

The party is organized primarily on a *Länder* basis and is only loosely federated on the national level.

The German Party

The German party (*Deutsche Partei*, DP) has its historical origin among the old Hanoverians who objected to the annexation of their kingdom by Prussia in 1866. The destruction of Prussia and the creation of the *Land* of Lower Saxony brought about a revival of the political fortunes of the Hanoverians, sometimes called Welfs or Guelphs,[13] who founded the Lower Saxony *Land* party, which later changed its title to German party.

The German party is in some ways comparable to the Bavarian party inasmuch as it is antifederalist [14] and anti-Prussian. It differs from the Bavarian party, however, in that it does not want to confine itself to one *Land* although most of its strength lies in Lower Saxony.

The German party is decidedly conservative and nationalist. It is a strictly Protestant party but does not object to support for parochial schools because it wants to help build up a Protestant school system. In that stand it differs from the FDP, with which it has otherwise many similarities.

Its foreign political views coincide largely with those of the CDU, and the German party is and has remained a member of Chancellor Adenauer's coalition government. Among its leaders should be mentioned Hans-Christoph Seebohm, Minister of Transport, and Heinrich Hellwege, Minister for *Bundesrat* Affairs. Its principal parliamentary leader is Hans J. von Merkatz.

---

[13] The Welfs (in Italy called Guelphs) were an old German ducal family, one line of which (Brunswick-Lüneburg) changed its name to Hanover. They became kings of Hanover in 1814 but were dethroned in 1866. The pro-Hanoverians and anti-Prussians called themselves Welfs.

[14] Meaning pro–states' rights. In the German usage this term has the opposite meaning.

In size, the German party belongs to the minor league. It polled 4 per cent of the vote in 1949 but declined to only 3.3 per cent in 1953 after dropping an absolute total of 100,000 votes. Although there were indications that it was spreading well beyond Lower Saxony, its progress has been halted and it is not likely to acquire major significance in the future.

THE REFUGEE PARTY

It was not surprising that the tremendous influx of refugees and expellees into Western Germany would make an impact on the political picture of the country. By 1950 over 9 million refugees and expellees had arrived in the Federal Republic; by 1954 they were estimated to have passed the 12 million mark. Most of them came without any possessions to speak of but were in their best working years, as the very young and the very old had died in droves in the fearful conditions under which they had been driven from their former homelands.[15]

Although the German federal government and the *Länder* and local governments made heroic efforts to absorb and settle these masses, a great deal of social and economic tension nevertheless arose. The Allied Powers discouraged separate refugee parties from the beginning for fear that they would become a fertile field for extremists. It was hoped that the refugees and expellees would eventually be absorbed into the regular political parties and that this process would further tie them to their new homes.

But as soon as the Allied injunction was relaxed, a refugee party made its appearance. It called itself the League of the Expellees and Disenfranchised (*Bund der Heimatvertriebenen und Entrechteten*, BHE),[16] and it began operating in the *Land* of Schleswig-Holstein, which has an exceptionally large number of refugees and expellees. In the election to that *Land's* legislature, the BHE obtained 23.4 per cent of the vote. The extent of this victory was not repeated, yet the party won sizable blocks of votes in Hesse, Württemberg-Baden, and Bavaria.

The BHE naturally voices the desire of its members and followers to return to their homelands which have been taken over by Poland, Czechoslovakia, and the Soviet Union. It advocates a greater equalization of the burden of reconstruction and a redistribution of property which is fairer to the refugees and expellees. And it generally supports such issues as may be beneficial to its supporters. Considering the history of these men, it is remarkable that the

---

[15] While the plight of the displaced persons and slave labor deported by the Nazis has been well publicized, the equally hideous treatment of German expellees is not so well known outside Germany.

[16] Literally translated the German title means "league of those driven from their homeland and deprived of their rights."

BHE acts in a restrained and dignified manner. The demands for the return of the lost territories are rarely raised in a belligerent manner, as could so easily be the case. Far from justifying the Allied fears that a refugee party would be the stamping ground of radicalism, the BHE has been rather conservative on the whole.

The earlier hopes of the BHE were not realized in the 1953 elections. Although most refugees and expellees were entitled to vote, the BHE, which entered the elections under the name All-German Bloc (*Gesamtdeutscher Block*, GB), obtained only 1,616,956 votes, or 5.9 per cent of the total. Even in Schleswig-Holstein, the area of its greatest concentration, it was unable to elect its leader, Waldemar Kraft, in a single-member district.[17] This result is encouraging because it indicates that the great majority of refugees and expellees have identified themselves sufficiently with their new homesteads to support the ordinary parties. As this process of integration progresses, the GB/BHE may be expected to decline.

The party has supported the general policy of the Adenauer government, especially its foreign policy. As a result Chancellor Adenauer took it into his cabinet after the 1953 election in order to widen his majority.

The leading man of the GB/BHE is Waldemar Kraft, now Deputy Prime Minister of Schleswig-Holstein. He used to live in that part of the German Empire which was ceded to Poland in 1918 and in fact voted in favor of Poland. Later he became a leader of the German minority in Poland and during the Nazi occupation was president of the German Chamber of Agriculture, in which capacity he received the honorary rank of captain in the Nazi SS. Because of that he was imprisoned by the Allies and remained interned for two years. Despite this past he has not shown any overt neo-Nazi tendencies.

THE COMMUNIST PARTY

The Communist party organized with the greatest vigor in all four zones. Many of its leaders had spent the years of Nazi control in exile, mostly in the Soviet Union, and took firm charge the moment they returned. The party's ostensible head was Wilhelm Pieck, who had already spent a lifetime in the service of the Communist cause and had been one of the principal founders of the party in 1918. Equally—and, to many observers, even more—powerful as a party leader was Walter Ulbricht, a trained Communist agent of the modern, impersonal school. Lesser leaders either came from exile or were found among the survivors of the Nazi concentration camps. As for cadres, the party had to do a substantial rebuilding job, for many of its former leaders

[17] Because the GB/BHE polled over 5 per cent of the vote, it benefited under the PR list system, and Kraft was elected to the *Bundestag* in that fashion.

and adherents had become Nazi victims, many others had become Nazis, and a fair number had turned their backs on the party during the period of Nazi-Soviet collaboration, 1939 to 1941.

The immediate posthostilities phase was marked by the adoption of a propaganda line of "national collaboration" and "antifascist unity" as far as the Communists were concerned. This was the platform adopted at the same time by Communist parties in other countries, thus manifesting the peculiar uniformity in Communist action to which the world at large has now become accustomed. In Germany there were particular reasons which made such a policy appear desirable from a Communist standpoint. The chances of the Communists to win over the large masses of the people never were good in Germany; they became particularly bad after the collapse of Hitlerism. Probably even more important was the conduct of the Russian soldiers in the first few months after their occupation of German territory, which seemed to bear out all the dire warnings with which Joseph Goebbels had tried to hold the Germans together. The Russian atrocities, while generally a result of lack of discipline among Soviet troops rather than of official policy, not only terrorized the population but also managed to antagonize many who might otherwise have shown themselves receptive to Communist ideas. Moreover, the years of anti-Communist propaganda by the Nazis had undoubtedly made an impression, and the absence of a responsible press allowed the grapevine to enlarge and embellish all these events.

Another factor in the notable lack of Communist popularity was the reemergence of former leaders of non-Communist parties, who had had ample opportunity to see the Communists in action during 1918 to 1933 and were naturally doubtful about the sincerity of the new conversion to unity and moderation.

This state of affairs was clear enough to the Communist leaders, who therefore adopted the method of propagating a program which had been exceedingly successful in several of the Eastern European countries. This was the device sometimes called "united front," sometimes "national front," and similar names. This program was not new by any means; but it was hoped by the Communist leadership that it would have greater appeal than had been the case before 1945. This propaganda was directed primarily toward the Social Democrats, because it quickly transpired that the overwhelming majority of the German workers were to be found in the ranks of the moderate Social Democrats and not in those of the Communists. If the latter were to achieve a real mass basis, the absorption of the Social Democrats was imperative.

When this proved impossible in the Western zones, the Communist party of Germany (*Kommunistische Partei Deutschlands*, KPD) turned out to be one of the greatest failures of international Communism. The party was beset by internal difficulties and purges, and one of its most prominent leaders was enticed into the Eastern zone and imprisoned.

The Communist party in Germany naturally follows every turn of the Moscow line, as does every other Communist party, and inveighs vigorously against any pro-Western policy. In a country that has watched the Soviet army in action and where millions of ex-soldiers have seen the reality of life in the Soviet Union, these tactics cannot be expected to obtain good results. Consequently the Communist party has never been able to dent the ranks of the Social Democratic party or to obtain any significant influence over the working classes. Nationally the Communist party has descended from a vote of 1,361,706, or 5.7 per cent, in 1949, to a mere 607,761, or 2.2 per cent in 1953. Especially significant is the party's decline in Germany's biggest industrial area, the Ruhr, where it obtained 22.3 per cent of the vote in 1947, 12.1 per cent in 1949, and 4.3 per cent in 1953. In 1954 the Communist party again participated in the West Berlin election (under the SED label) but barely scraped over the 2 per cent mark.

Since the Communist party polled less than the 5 per cent minimum required by the electoral law and has been unable to elect a deputy through direct plurality election, there are no Communists in the German *Bundestag*. For similar reasons the party has lost its representation in most of the *Landtage* as well. It is now a minor party without significance.

MINOR PARTIES

In this category belong the abovementioned Communist party and the Bavarian party. In addition there is the Center party (*Zentrum*), which is now merely a feeble remnant of the once-great party of that name which flourished during the empire and the Weimar Republic. The real heir of the old Center party is of course the CDU. The contemporary Center party is almost purely Catholic, but its social and economic policy is far to the left of the CDU and is almost identical with that of the Social Democrats. Its strength, such as it is, rests mainly among former Christian Trade-Unionists in the *Land* of North Rhine–Westphalia. It is remarkable in another respect in that its leader for a long time was a highly respected woman, Helene Wessel.

The party's numerical strength has declined from 3.1 per cent in 1949 to 0.8 per cent in 1953. An even greater decline is shown in its former stronghold in the Ruhr, where it polled 9 per cent in 1947, 7.5 per cent in 1949, but only 2.4 per cent in 1953.

Despite the Center's decline, the CDU leadership has always treated it with great care, and it was because of CDU cooperation that it was able to be represented in the *Bundestag*. The CDU leadership evidently hopes that the Center party will some day be incorporated into its own ranks.

A new creation has been the All-German People's party (*Gesammtdeutsche Volks-Partei*, GVP). It was the brain child of a former CDU leader and · Minister of the Interior in the first Adenauer cabinet, Gustav Heinemann.

Heinemann, a prominent Protestant layman, found himself in increasing opposition to Adenauer's foreign policy, largely on pacifist grounds, and left the cabinet. Later he founded the All-German People's party, which adopted a neutralist platform. He was joined by Helene Wessel, former Center-party leader, and allied himself with another neutralist group, the League of Germans (*Bund der Deutschen*), which is headed by former *Reich* Chancellor Joseph Wirth. This group is known to have Communist backing. Before the election of 1953, documents were uncovered which proved that the GVP had received some funds from the Eastern zone, though probably unknown to Heinemann himself. At any rate, the party obtained only 318,476 votes, or 1.2 per cent, and is likely to disappear.

Some time before the 1953 election a frankly neo-Nazi party, called the Socialist Reich party (*Sozialistische Reichspartei*, SRP), made itself heard. Nominally headed by Major Ernst Otto Rehmer,[18] although actually guided by others, it was extremely reminiscent of the Nazi party in the twenties. In the *Land* election of 1951 in Lower Saxony, it alarmed the world by obtaining 11 per cent of the vote. However, it did less well elsewhere and met the determined resistance of the government. The party fell to pieces through internal quarrels and was declared outlawed by the Federal Constitutional Court in 1952.

This verdict had a dampening effect on other would-be neo-Nazi parties. As a result the German Reich party (*Deutsche Reichspartei*, DRP), which many regard as the successor of the SRP and which also has open neo-Nazi tendencies, did not dare to be quite so blatant. It was resoundingly trounced in the 1953 election, obtaining only 295,746 votes, or 1.1 per cent of the total.

None of these minor parties is represented in the *Bundestag*.

OTHER GROUPS

When German labor unions were revived after the war, considerable pressure was brought to bear upon them to amalgamate. In consequence thereof, the three different union groups which had hitherto existed in each of the occupation zones dissolved, and in October, 1949, formed the German Trade-Union Federation (*Deutscher Gewerkschaftsbund*, DGB), which has about 5,000,000 members. Although the DGB is officially nonpartisan, the overwhelming majority of its leaders and members are Social Democrats. The rest belong to the left wing of the CDU. There is virtually no Communist influence.

Under its first chairman, Hans Boeckler, the nonpartisan character of the

---

[18] Rehmer was a major when he was ordered by the temporarily successful plotters of 1944 to arrest Goebbels. The latter, however, convinced him that Hitler was still alive and made him arrest the plotters. For this deed he was promoted to Major General.

German Trade-Union Federation was maintained to a high degree. After his death, however, complaints were heard, and during the 1953 electoral campaign Chancellor Adenauer and the CDU leadership lodged a strong protest against some of the statements made by DGB leaders which seemed to favor the position of the Social Democratic party. There was even a threat made that the Catholic element would withdraw from the Federation and once again organize a separate movement. The DGB leaders rejected the charges as groundless, but some bad feelings have remained. Nothing further, however, has come of this incident.

While the German Trade-Union Federation is not a political party, it nevertheless has legislative demands to make for which it relies mainly on the Social Democratic party. This was made quite clear in the bitter struggle over workers' codetermination resulting in the law of April 10, 1951, which applies to any enterprise in the mining, iron, and steel industries which employs more than 1,000 people. It provides for a board of directors of eleven people, five from management and five from labor (three from the shop-stewards' committees and two from the national unions). The eleventh member is elected by a procedure which is said to favor management.

The enactment of this law created further demands for the enlargement of this system, which resulted in the bitterly contested law of July 19, 1952, which extended the right of workers' representatives on boards of directors but in a manner which maintains management in a two-thirds majority. The Trade-Union Federation is fighting hard for a repeal or amendment to this act, which is not likely to occur in the *Bundestag* that was elected in 1953. In the meantime the codetermination law has worked rather well, and even management has had occasion to express satisfaction. That this is so is largely due to the high degree of responsibility exhibited by German labor leaders. Yet, some industrial circles would like to see the law repealed—an unlikely event.

However restrained the German Trade-Union Federation may have been in the past, its hostility to German rearmament and Chancellor Adenauer's foreign policy has reached near-violent proportions. Together with this development comes the radicalization of its leadership which seems to be bent on converting the DGB into a close ally of the Social Democratic party.

An entirely different type of pressure group has appeared in the form of the various German veterans' organizations. While veterans' organizations tend to be conservative in many countries and in some instances even reactionary, German veterans' organizations have been distinctly different for a number of reasons. In the first place all their leaders have traditionally been former high-ranking officers or staff officers. This makes a German veterans' organization something that is more like an army in civilian clothes than a real veterans' organization. It is often the continuation of the "state within the state" ideology which imbued the army before and after the Second World

War. It also often carries within itself an outspoken or tacit contempt for civilians and an arrogant assumption that the military know best what is good for the state.

In recent years it has been notable that the veterans' organizations have not shown any clear, unified philosophy. On the whole they have been conservative and nationalistic. Some, like the veterans of Field Marshal Erwin Rommel's Africa Corps, have declared themselves strong supporters of democracy, while parachutist General Wilhelm Ramcke makes speeches which could hardly be bettered by an orator of the best Nazi period. Even the former black-shirted SS troopers have their organization, which, out of conviction or strategy, has been rather circumspect in its utterances. Similarly cautious is a veterans' newspaper called the *German Soldier's Journal* (*Deutsche Soldatenzeitung*), which bears the iron cross on its masthead.

These tendencies bear watching, for the history of German veterans' organizations is unsavory. However, only one-tenth (about 800,000 out of approximately 8 million) of Germany's surviving veterans are members of these organizations, and some of the most influential generals like the late former Chief of Staff Heinz Guderian, and General Hasso von Manteuffel, preferred to operate outside these groups.

Outlook

In conclusion, it might be well to return to a point raised in the beginning of this chapter, namely, that the German party system has probably not yet jelled to its final form. On the negative side, the popular incomprehension of a party's function in a democracy remains a handicap and so does the bureaucratic tendency so much in evidence in every party. It is not quite clear whether the strong leadership of an almost authoritarian type exercised by such men as Konrad Adenauer and the late Kurt Schumacher is entirely a liability or an asset. During the period of crisis and inevitable sacrifice which followed the war, strong leadership was undoubtedly necessary. To the German people who were fearful lest democracy prove itself unable to govern effectively, the evidence that democracy too can produce the (to them) most telling proof, the strong leader, undoubtedly made a deep impression. If these autocratic tendencies die out with Schumacher and Adenauer, and thus prove phenomena of the transitional period, they may actually prove to have been assets for having carried Germany gradually from dictatorship to democracy. If, on the other hand, they perpetuate themselves, they would prove serious obstacles to a democratic development.

While some of these negative or doubtful features may provide grounds for legitimate concern and continued observation of the German political scene, it is well to note some significant and encouraging differences between the Weimar and the Bonn regimes. Though a large number of Germans may not as yet be entirely sold on democracy today, the Federal Republic experiences none of the massive, bitter resentment which imbued a large segment of the German population in the tragic years of the Weimar Republic. Although many Germans may not be enthusiastic about democracy today, few are implacably hostile. Moreover the lessons of Weimar and the Nazi cataclysm have not passed unnoticed. The leading men of Bonn are profoundly, even painfully aware of many of the mistakes of the past. Not all have been remedied, but the Bonn government and the Federal Constitutional Court have shown themselves far more alert to the danger of totalitarian activities than were their Weimar predecessors. Among the German people too some transformations are in evidence. There is now a far greater readiness to challenge the authority of the state in the courts or elsewhere than was customary in former days, and while broad civic activities and citizens' participation in public affairs in and out of parties are still the exception rather than the rule, their volume and intensity appear to be on the increase.

Nobody could conclude from this that German democracy is safe forever. But it might be said that never were the chances for a democratic development greater than they are at the present time. Barring war or invasion, the student of German government is entitled to look into the future with some optimism.

Chapter 11

THE GOVERNMENT OF THE SAAR

The Saar [1] territory is entirely separated from the German Federal Republic, which exercises no control or influence over it. It is a relatively small region some 900 square miles in size, with 956,570 inhabitants. Although this makes the Saar a very small country, its population is nevertheless three times that of neighboring Luxembourg. With about 965 people to the square mile, the Saar is the most densely populated country in Europe.

By race, language, culture, tradition, and history, the inhabitants of the Saar are Germans. But economically the area has strong ties with France. The Saar has vast coal fields and an important iron and steel industry which relies on the iron-ore deposits of neighboring Lorraine, a part of France. Ironically it was Germany who forged this economic link between France and the Saar after 1871, when a part of Lorraine was annexed by Germany. In the practice of international politics that meant, after 1918, when all of Lorraine had returned to France, that France together with the Saar could be nearly a match for Germany's steel production, but without the Saar France was heavily outclassed in this key industry.

Cognizant of this fact, France insisted that the Versailles Treaty of 1919 include a special statute for the Saar which separated that territory from Germany and placed it under the administration of a committee appointed by the League of Nations. The application of this statute for the Saar territory, which came into force in 1920, was limited to 15 years. Consequently in 1935 a plebiscite was held in the Saar to determine its future. The choice was between adherence to France, adherence to Germany, or continuation of the international status. The result of this plebiscite, which took place under strict international control, brought an overwhelming victory for Germany; 91.5 per cent of the voters expressed their preference for Germany. While not all of these voters may have favored Hitler's Third *Reich*, they considered it their patriotic duty to take the Saar back to Germany.

At the end of the Second World War the Saar was occupied by American troops who later ceded their place to French forces. The French military government authorities were commanded by Colonel Gilbert Grandval, a very strong-willed man who was determined to do everything in his power to sepa-

[1] The name is derived from the Saar River, a tributary of the Moselle.

rate the Saar from Germany. Under his authority a regime similar to that which existed there between 1920 and 1935 was restored. Part of the administrative responsibilities were later transferred to local Saarlanders.

At the same time political life sprang up in the Saar. As in Germany, four parties made their appearance. The Christian People's party (*Christliche Volkspartei*, CVP) is very much like the German CDU/CSU. The Social Democratic party (*Sozialdemokratische Partei der Saar*, SPS) is the Saar replica of the German Social Democratic party. The Communist party (*Kommunistische Partei der Saar*, KPS) is of course the same as all other Communist parties. The Democratic party (*Demokratische Partei der Saar*, DPS) originally followed the model of the Free Democratic party in Germany, but later it became primarily the spokesman of pro-German tendencies.

The Christian People's party and the Social Democrats declared themselves unreservedly in favor of an eonomic union between France and the Saar and they have steadfastly held on to this view ever since. As a result they have both been "excommunicated" and exorcised by their sister parties in Germany, who regard them as traitors and denounce them with bitter animosity. The Communists have attempted to take an ambiguous, somewhat neutral stand in this all-important question of German-Saar relations.

In order to understand political developments in the Saar it is necessary to take into consideration important economic and social factors. As one of Germany's most important industrial regions, the Saar came under extensive Allied air attacks during the war. The opposing American and German armies which fought over the area took a further toll. Over half of all houses in the Saar were destroyed or damaged. In the capital city, Saarbrücken, 43 per cent of all houses were either destroyed or heavily damaged. In Neunkirchen this was true of 25.1 per cent, and worst of all was Saarlouis, which suffered a loss of 61 per cent.[2] The Saar government, strongly supported and aided by the French, embarked on a vigorous reconstruction policy which netted outstanding results. The French also encouraged the early resumption of industrial activities and extended many benefits to the Saar. French currency became legal tender there. Thus, in 1947, when the economic life of Germany was paralyzed, when Germany went through one of its worst winters, and when German administrations had only a very limited independence of action and decision, the Saar was almost a booming region with a solidly entrenched government and a functioning administration that had considerable internal authority.

The political results of this situation were not surprising. In the 1947 elections to the Saar *Landtag* (legislature), the Christian People's party and the Social Democrats won an overwhelming majority with 51.2 per cent and 32.8 per cent of the vote respectively. The pro-German Democratic party

---

[2] Memorandum of the Saar Government, entitled *The Saar*, Saarbrücken, May 1, 1953, 3rd rev. ed., p. 18*f*.

obtained only 7.6 per cent, and the Communists 8.4 per cent. In this election 95.7 per cent of the voters went to the polls. Similar results were obtained in the municipal elections of 1949, in which the Democratic party obtained only 6.6 per cent, and the Communists 8.6 per cent.

By 1952 the situation was different. While the Saar still had a head start, the German Federal Republic was now quickly catching up, and the presence of an increasingly strong, practically sovereign government with a steadily heightened reputation in the concert of nations did not leave the Saar un-affected. Pro-German groups and political parties in the Saar undertook a campaign designed to reunite their land with Germany. The Saar government on the other hand declared all pro-German parties unconstitutional and sup-pressed them. As a result, in the Saar elections of November 30, 1952, no pro-German party was allowed to run. Yet it is possible to regard these elections as a kind of plebiscite. Although the pro-German parties could not present candidates, their leaders remained free and gave public declarations of prin-ciple which were widely quoted in the Saar and abroad. Moreover almost the entire German press supported the pro-German groups, and the German radio, which is of course widely heard in the Saar, pressed for the same attitude. Consequently the appeal of the pro-German parties to the people of the Saar to abstain from voting or to cast invalid ballots received the widest possible circulation, and no Saarlander could be in doubt about the issue.

The elections, which in themselves were honest and closely scrutinized by some 200 foreign correspondents, produced a participation of 93.1 per cent of the voters. Of those 24.5 per cent cast invalid ballots. This was of course a much greater success for the pro-German parties than they had previously obtained. Nevertheless, even if one were to add to the number of invalid ballots the number of all voters who had failed to go to the polls, obviously an incorrect appraisal, the parties favoring collaboration with France would still have obtained an overwhelming majority. The Christian People's party obtained 54.7 per cent of the valid votes, the Social Democrats 32.4 per cent, the Communists 9.5 per cent, with 3.4 per cent going to others. Viewed dif-ferently, the Christian People's party alone polled 239,405 votes, and the Social Democrats, 141,855, against 141,876 void ballots.

In view of these results, it must be maintained that the great majority of the Saarlanders favored the present regime and its policy of close cooperation with France. This, however, is the situation only at the moment. What attrac-tion the increasing strength of Germany will have on Saar sentiments has yet to be shown, but it is quite probable that in spite of all French efforts, the pro-German sentiment is likely to increase. One of the most disquieting ele-ments in this prognosis is the fact that the element of threat and potential violence is not entirely missing. The leaders of the two "separatist" parties, the Christian People's party and the Social Democrats, have obviously burned all their bridges behind them, and they have been the objects of many threats of violence on the part of pro-German elements.

At the present time the Constitution of the Saar is similar to those of the German *Länder*. There is a unicameral legislature, the *Landtag*, and a cabinet responsible to it. The relationship between the Saar and France is regulated by the Convention of March 3, 1950, which has been progressively revised in 1952, 1953, and 1954. These conventions deal with many economic questions including the management of the Saar coal mines under French influence, work permits to French and Saar nationals, judicial questions, etc. The progressive autonomy of the Saar government was emphasized by the transformation of the French High Commission into an Embassy on January 25, 1952.

It is obvious that the Saar is the last place on earth where the future of the Saar will be determined. This is a controversy between France and Germany which involves not only Franco-German relations but the whole concept of European unity. Unless the question of the Saar is solved, European unity must remain only an ideal that is far removed from reality. While the French government is well content with the continuation of the *status quo*, the German government is irrevocably opposed thereto. In this policy the latter is unconditionally supported by all German political parties; and if the German opposition parties, the German Social Democrats, have any reproach to direct against the federal government, it is that it is not taking a strong enough stand against the Saar government and against France.

By far the brightest hope for a solution of this question lies in the possibility of a European federal union, which alone could make the irksome question of sovereignty over the Saar an irrelevant problem. This is admitted in principle by both sides. But since the French want to make sure that even a European union would not seriously disturb the present close Franco-Saar economic cooperation, while the German government is not willing to write off the Saar in this fashion, the Saar problem, although only soluble through a European union, is in itself one of the major obstacles to that union.

The agreement of October 25, 1954, between France and Germany did not, in itself, bring a final solution to the Saar problem. It was rather designed to change it from a short-run to a long-run problem in order to remove immediate irritation which might impede the ratification of the Western European Union treaty by France and Germany.

This new Saar statute attempts to bypass the irksome, and at present insoluble, question of sovereignty over the Saar region by giving the Saar a "European status" within the Western European Union. To this effect the Council of Ministers of the Western European Union shall appoint a Commissioner, who shall be neither French, nor German, nor Saarlander. However, he cannot be elected against the will of France, Germany, or the Saar. This

Commissioner shall not be the actual governor of the Saar. His functions shall be confined to seeing to it that the Saar statute is observed. However, he shall represent the Saar in matters affecting foreign affairs and defense. In turn, the Saar shall be represented in the various European bodies, notably the Council of Europe, the Coal and Steel Pool (Schuman Plan), and the Western European Union.

Three months after the Saar statute is ratified by France and Germany it shall be submitted to a referendum by the people of the Saar. If the statute is approved (which is not in doubt), its validity may not again be questioned until a peace treaty (which is not in sight) regulates all German questions. Under this statute the pro-German parties and organizations must be re-admitted, but it is clear that the above provision for not questioning the validity of the statute after the plebiscite will curb their activities.

The more difficult questions of the economic relations between France and the Saar are largely left to future Franco-German negotiations. But neither in that sphere nor in that of the internal government of the Saar may any great changes be expected. For all practical purposes the Saar rests completely detached from Germany, with an autonomous government, closely connected with France.

Chapter 12

GOVERNMENT IN EASTERN GERMANY

It is difficult to imagine a greater contrast than that which exists between East and West Germany. While West Germany, the German Federal Republic, is being transformed into a democratic state with the usual accompaniments of such an institution—competing political parties, a press with divergent views, limitations imposed upon government by law and by the courts—Eastern Germany, now called the German Democratic Republic, has become a typical Soviet satellite which in every respect is following the model of the Soviet Union except that certain developments have not yet advanced quite so far.

In the economic sphere the contrast is equally drastic. While the living standard of Western Germany is one of the highest in Europe, while its shops carry every conceivable goods in adequate supply, life in the Eastern zone is drab and impoverished. Only very limited amounts of consumers' goods are available for purchase, and both quality and variety are poor. In this region, which was once one of the chief food producers of Germany, food is now in such short supply that tens of thousands of people from Eastern Germany streamed into the Western sector of Berlin when American and German authorities distributed food parcels there in the summer of 1953. Considering that this mass crossing of the border was accompanied by considerable personal risk for the participants and that many parcels were confiscated by the East German police, the action of these East Germans becomes an even more telling piece of evidence concerning living conditions that exist there.

Eastern Germany is the territory included in the Russian occupation zone. It thus does not include the areas east of the rivers Oder and Neisse, which are now administered as integral parts of Poland and the Soviet Union and from which nearly all German inhabitants have been expelled. As originally constituted, the Eastern zone, later the German Democratic Republic, comprised five *Länder*, Brandenburg, Mecklenburg, Saxony, Saxony-Anhalt, and Thuringia. The Eastern sector of Berlin is also included. The area comprises 30.2 per cent of all German territory east of the Oder and Neisse Rivers. The population is 20 million (in contrast to the 50 million of West Germany).

It has never been and is probably not now Soviet policy to regard the East German state as a final creation. Rather Moscow expected to use it as a stepping stone for the communization of all Germany. But, as has already been pointed out, this policy was a complete failure. Not only did Communism fail to attract West Germany, it failed even to attract strong support in East Germany, and the events of June, 1953, have vividly proved that it requires only a small spark to disclose the real sentiments of the East German population.

This lack of popularity was first brought about by the conduct of the Russian soldiers in the waning months of the war and the initial period of occupation. It tranferred easily to the native Communists and their cohorts, who carried out the orders of their Russian masters.

THE POLITICAL STRUCTURE

Since the Communists could not have their way by persuasion, they set about to obtain it by force. The first avenue to that goal was their use of the political parties. It has already been described how the Communists forced the fusion of the much larger Social Democratic party with them into the Socialist Unity party of Germany (*Sozialistische Einheitspartei Deutschlands*, SED) although the great majority of the Social Democratic rank and file disliked the idea. The SED became the chosen instrument of the Soviet Military Administration and was quickly purged of the majority of Social Democratic holdovers. Even those Social Democratic leaders who had been completely loyal to the Communists in forcing the fusion were eliminated, including men like Max Fechner, who as Minister of Justice did not hesitate to persecute his erstwhile comrades in arms.[1] Only Otto Grotewohl, chief (former) Social Democratic architect of the fusion, holds out in isolated splendor and has even been able to fortify his position, although any prediction of the future and the life expectancy of a Communist leader or satellite is always a highly uncertain proposition.

A different approach was used toward the other parties. When the Soviet Military Administration licensed the Communists and the Social Democrats in 1946 (before the fusion) it also licensed the Christian Democratic Union and the Liberal Democratic party, the latter originally the Eastern version of the Free Democratic party. But beginning in 1946 these parties were subjected to increasing pressure and eventually terror. Registration and Soviet permission to organize were frequently withheld or delayed, paper allocation to non-SED newspapers was curtailed. When these relatively mild methods did not prevail and the non-Communist parties held their own surprisingly well, more drastic methods were used. More and more non-Communist party leaders would disappear. The parties were forced to purge themselves of all officers who failed to do the Soviet or SED bidding. Others again found their salvation in flight. Finally both the CDU and the LDP degenerated into mere instruments of

[1] Fechner was "liquidated" after the June, 1953, anti-Communist uprising.

Communist policy, to be used as the SED leaders saw fit. There is neither similarity nor contact between these shadow groups and their former sister parties in Western Europe. Nor is there any similarity between them and political parties as that term is generally understood. Symbol of total subservience is Otto Nuschke, nominal CDU "leader" in East Germany, whose eventual liquidation despite complete obedience can be safely predicted.

The claim of these nominal "parties" to independent existence eventually became such a farce that the SED found it desirable to found two more parties which were to appeal especially to former Nazis. They were the National Democratic party and the Democratic Peasant party. In both cases the Communist wire pullers did not even bother to go through the motions of a genuine party establishment. The parties were organized from the top down by experienced SED bureaucrats with no more justification than "thousands and thousands of signatures," collected everywhere in the usual manner, "demanding the establishment of these parties." [2]

In addition to these "parties," Eastern Germany has a number of so-called "mass organizations." They are all solidly SED-controlled and are further instruments of Communist policy. There is the Free German Trade-Union Federation (*Freier Deutscher Gewerkschaftsbund*, FDGB). Like all Communist trade-unions in Communist-controlled countries, this is a compulsory organization comparable to the Nazi "Labor Front." It is not a bargaining agent since wages and conditions of work are fixed by the planning agencies. It is a political tool designed to mobilize the workers for special tasks. Another virtually compulsory organization is the Free German Youth (*Freie Deutsche Jugend*, FDJ), the main instrument of the Communist leaders to educate youth in their image. In its intensely political and paramilitary training the FDJ is the spit and image of the Hitler Youth. There is also the Democratic League of Women (*Demokratischer Frauenbund Deutschlands*, DFD) which is the East German branch of a well-known international Communist women's organization whose true nature is often thinly camouflaged in other countries.

The coordination of these parties and mass organizations is the task of the National Front, another SED-dominated organization. Its prototype can or could be found in all the Soviet satellite countries, where it serves as a transition from the multiparty system to the one-party, totalitarian state. Actually, the National Front is merely a control device of the SED.

The SED's organization is very similar to that of the Communist party of the Soviet Union with all decisions being vested in the top. It is generally believed that Moscow-trained Walter Ulbricht is the real leader of the SED and consequently of East Germany. However, as these lines are written, Otto

---

[2] Richard M. Scammon, "Political Parties," in Litchfield and Associates, *op. cit.*, pp. 495–496. The best work on East Germany is J. P. Nettl, *The Eastern Zone and Soviet Policy in Germany, 1945–50*, London, 1951.

Grotewohl, the ex-Social Democrat, has strengthened his position and appears in public as the spokesman of the government more often than Ulbricht. But these things may change rapidly, within the hour, for neither Ulbricht nor Grotewohl nor any other German Communist really directs the SED. That direction lies neither in East Berlin nor in Karlshorst [3] but in Moscow.

THE GOVERNMENTAL STRUCTURE

As early as July 27, 1945, Marshal Zhukov, then chief of the Soviet Military Administration in Germany, established twelve German central agencies. This was obviously an attempt to create Soviet-sponsored and Communist-infiltrated all-German government departments.[4] French opposition to any form of German central government is primarily responsible for frustrating this scheme. On a zone-wide level these central agencies served as planning group3 while orders were actually transmitted directly to the *Länder* administrations by the Soviet Military Administration.

These agencies exercised relatively little control. In 1947, when it became clear that the Western powers were going ahead with the consolidation of their zones regardless of Soviet objection, an Economic Commission was established which was to take tighter control but actually failed to function in that manner. Renamed German Economic Commission in 1948, it took on considerable administrative and legislative power. By the use of the newly drafted Economic Penal Law and the Requisition Law, the German Economic Commission (DWK) undertook the economic communization of the country, the expropriation of private enterprise, and the introduction of measures such as piecework in order to increase production. The expropriated industries and businesses in turn were combined into huge state-owned trusts.

Apart from economic problems, interior administration, justice, and education were administered by other central agencies, which, however, did not possess the vast powers of the German Economic Commission. Yet they held monthly meetings with the *Land* ministers, and their decisions, which actually emanated from the SED leadership, were considered binding under the well-known Communist principle of "democratic centralism" by which the higher level unconditionally imposes its will on the lower one. By this device one-party rule and centralism were actually established while there was still the outward form of a multiparty system and federalism.

While the Council of Foreign Ministers was meeting in London for the purpose of finding a solution for the German problem, the central committee of the SED passed a resolution on November 26, 1947, calling for a "German People's Congress" (*Volkskongress*). It met in Berlin on December 6. Its

---

[3] Headquarters of the Soviet Military Administration.

[4] Kurt Glaser, "Governments of Soviet Germany," in Litchfield and Associates, *op. cit.*, p. 158.

delegates represented the Communist-dominated parties of the East as well as the mass organizations. There were also delegates from the West, but most of them represented either the Communist party or fellow travelers. At any rate the SED possessed absolute control and passed a resolution which was to be presented to the four Foreign Ministers. However, the Western Foreign Ministers refused to receive it.

In the spring of 1948 a second People's Congress met in Berlin and prepared the ground for a popular initiative in which signatures were collected on petitions for German unity.[5] A smaller committee, called People's Council (*Volksrat*), was elected by the Congress and posed as a kind of government, but its chief function was propaganda directed mainly against attempts to establish a government and a constitution for West Germany. The People's Council also proceeded to draft a constitution which was completed the same year. Actually this draft originated in the SED and was presented by Grotewohl. Final action on the constitution was postponed until the establishment of the German Federal (Bonn) Republic in order to place the blame for the split on the West.

Elections for a third People's Congress were held in May, 1949. The single slate of delegates—Soviet style—was presented to the people after a high-pressure propaganda campaign directed against widespread dissatisfaction with the constitutional draft. In spite of the pressure, the removal and arrest of opposition leaders, and the curb on any anti-Communist activities, 40 per cent of the voters dared to reject the slate of delegates. The Congress, nevertheless, convened and ratified the draft constitution.

"Spontaneous" appeals and "demands" broke out all over Eastern Germany on October 2, 1949, which had been proclaimed "World Peace Day," calling for an all-German independent government. The authorities "acceded." The People's Council convened five days later and transformed itself into a People's Chamber (*Volkskammer*) to which the Soviet authorities transferred a number of administrative functions. The People's Chamber then proceeded to enact a number of laws which declared the Constitution to be in force and laid down rules for the appointment of a government as well as of *Länder* governments. Grotewohl was elected Minister President, Ulbricht his deputy. The Soviet Military Administration transferred many of its functions to the German authorities, at least in theory, and on October 12, 1949, the structure of the East German State, now called German Democratic Republic (*Deutsche Demokratische Republik*, DDR) was completed. Wilhelm Pieck, co-founder of the German Communist party in 1918, was elected President of the Republic, while Otto Grotewohl and Walter Ulbricht were elected co-chairmen of the government.

The Constitution of the DDR is centralist rather than federalist. The

[5] H. B. Cox, "Establishment of the Soviet-Sponsored East German Republic," *Department of State Bulletin*, Nov. 21, 1949, pp. 761–764.

national parliament has the power to change *Land* boundaries at will, and the constitutional framework of the *Länder* (now abolished) is prescribed in the DDR Constitution. The national government could work through *Land* administration or establish its own agencies. Where it did the former, it had an unlimited right of control and direction. It could also send its own emissaries into any *Land* agency with the power to give orders.

The parliament of the DDR is composed of the People's Chamber (*Volkskammer*), which has 400 members elected by proportional representation, and a Chamber of States (*Länderkammer*) whose members were elected by the *Landtage* from among their own members. As the *Länder* have now been abolished in the DDR, this system of electing the upper house will have to be changed, but these methods of election are totally without significance since there are no contests in any elections. A single slate of delegates is presented by the *National Front* and then adopted by the people in a Soviet-style polling process. Even under these circumstances the rulers did not feel entirely at ease, and in the *Volkskammer* election of October 15, 1950, the government exerted great pressure on the voters, demanding that they refrain from going into a voting booth and instead hand in their ballots openly. It was made abundantly clear that anyone going into a booth would be suspect of voting against the single slate of candidates and those few who dared to defy the government were later subject to arrest and execution.

As a matter of fact, in most polling places there was no voting booth at all. The vote of 99.6 per cent in favor of the National Front slate is therefore without significance. Most significant was the appeal of the city administration of West Berlin addressed to the people of the Soviet sector urging all those who were opposed to the regime in the East zone to mail the stubs of their September ration books to the West Berlin administration. Although the Eastern government promised a special clothing ration in exchange for the stubs, more than 400,000 of the 600,000 voters of East Berlin sent in their stubs, or letters explaining that the stubs had been destroyed.[6]

The independence and irremovability of judges are not recognized, and there is a specific denial of the right of courts to review the constitutionality of laws.

The Constitution of the German Democratic Republic, like that of the Soviet Union, gives very little idea of how government is actually conducted. The federal structure of the state, which was only nominal to begin with, was made even more problematical by the introduction of central government commissioners (*Inspekteure*) very much on the model of the *Reichstatthalter* of Hitler Germany. Then in the summer of 1952 a law dissolved the five traditional *Länder* and replaced them by fifteen administrative districts. Without the Constitution having been amended in a formal way, the last outward vestige of federalism has thus been removed and complete centralism instituted. This

[6] Glaser, *op. cit.*, p. 182.

is further illustrated by the dissolution of the provincial committees of the East German political parties in favor of a more centralized party administration. The absolute dictatorship of the Communist rulers manifests itself in the customary *modus operandi* of totalitarian regimes: secret political police, imprisonment without trial or with mock trial, and concentration camps. The Minister of State Security, General Wilhelm Zaisser, once known as General Gomez of Spanish Civil War ill fame, built up the paramilitary People's Police (*Volkspolizei*, Vopo), who even by their outward appearance remind one strikingly of the SS Elite Guard of Nazi days. Actually there are two distinct Vopo organizations. There is the blue-uniformed Vopo which carries out regular police duties and the so-called "garrisoned People's Police" (*Kasernierte Volkspolizei*) in Russian-style uniforms, which is a regular army. Although Zaisser was purged after the June, 1953, uprising, the regime has continued its oppressive policies. Indicative thereof is the dreaded law on the Defense of Peace of December 16, 1950,[7] which is so worded as to make any expression critical of the government and its policy punishable by up to life imprisonment and even death.

In spite of the complete paraphernalia of the totalitarian state, the so-called German Democratic Republic is nevertheless weak because it has not a single group of any size on which it can really rely. While the Soviet regime in the U.S.S.R. created an entirely new bureaucracy on which its control is primarily based, the government of the DDR has no equivalent. The bureaucracy of the state, the officers' corps of the police and paramilitary formations, even the staff of the SED itself, are permeated by bourgeois elements who, while not in open opposition, are nevertheless there to worry those in power.[8] The sentiments of the working class, which the regime has so strenuously tried to court, have given drastic evidence of their hostility to the regime in the bitter uprisings of the summer of 1953 which engulfed every industrial center in the entire Eastern zone of Germany. Although drastically repressive measures were taken under the fanatical guidance of the new Minister of Justice, Hilde Benjamin, the regime cannot be under any possible illusion about its lack of popular support. Even in a dictatorship, this is a matter of grave concern. However, the government of the DDR does not exist in its own right but as a satellite of the Soviet Union, by whose support alone it can maintain itself. The future of the DDR is therefore not merely a German problem but one which involves the entire complex of East-West relationships.

[7] For the text of this law see *American Journal of International Law,* Vol. XLVI (1952), supplement, pp. 99–101. Practically identical laws were adopted by the U.S.S.R. and all satellites.

[8] Nettl, *op. cit.,* p. 312.

Part IV. THE UNION OF SOVIET SOCIALIST REPUBLICS

If I do love my land, strangely I love it:
'Tis something reason cannot cure.
Glories of war I do not covet,
But neither peace proud and secure.
MIKHAIL YUREVICH LERMONTOV

IN THESE YEARS which are characterized by the so-called "cold war," it is hardly necessary to emphasize the great importance of the Soviet Union, the colossus of the East and one of the two or three greatest powers in the world. Much if not everything may depend on our ability to understand correctly how the U.S.S.R. operates and what makes it "tick."

Unfortunately such understanding is handicapped by a number of difficulties, even though that vast country is no longer an "enigma" or a "riddle." We have learned much, and we can piece together more. Certainly the pattern of Soviet power and policy can be ascertained with a fair degree of accuracy. But it is extraordinarily difficult to obtain reliable details even on major subjects. We know, for instance, that all policy decisions are made by the leadership of the Communist party assembled in the Politburo, but we do not know for certain how the Politburo arrives at its decisions. Even when Stalin was alive, we were not quite sure to what extent he predominated its deliberations although one may deduce from subsequent changes that his predominance was very great. Now the situation is even more obscure. Georgi Malenkov, Stalin's successor as head of the government, received none of the deification which was heaped upon Stalin during his lifetime. Moreover, the Stalin cult cooled markedly in the Soviet Union and Soviet papers inveighed against "one-man rule." Also the fact that Malenkov did not attempt to hold the office of the General Secretary of the Communist party, which position had been the source of Stalin's rise to power, seemed to indicate that power was distributed among several men. Yet one of the most powerful of these men, Lavrenti Beria, was purged and executed without any apparent difficulty. Georgi Malenkov, Vyacheslav Molotov, and Nikita Khrushchev seemed to occupy the center of the stage. Then on February 9, 1955, at a meeting of the Supreme Soviet, Malenkov abdicated as head of the government and although his place was taken by Nikolai Bulganin, it was clear that Nikita

Khrushchev, first Secretary of the Communist Party, was now in charge. Had "one-man rule" returned? Was the change permanent? Or was this the overture to further power struggles? Among the many difficulties which beset East-West relations and negotiations, not one of the least is this uncertainty about the nature of Soviet leadership.

Accurate and reliable answers to these and many other questions would greatly facilitate a better understanding of the U.S.S.R., because secrecy breeds fear, apprehension, and eventually hatred. The ancient Romans, wise in matters of state, understood this when they coined the phrase *"damnant quod non intelligunt"* (they condemn what they do not understand).

But if we are inadequately informed about the Soviet Union, a major share of responsibility must be placed at the door of the Soviet government itself. A veil of secrecy surrounds even the most commonplace activities. No critical analysis of Soviet institutions or policy ever emerges from the Soviet Union. All studies written by Soviet scholars present every phase of the regime in the most glowing colors, and while individuals may be criticized—after their ouster or reprimand has already been decided by higher authority—the wisdom of policy and the excellence of major institutions have never been questioned. Foreign scholars are given no opportunity to gather detailed on-the-spot information. It is easy enough to gather firsthand information in Great Britain or France; even in Nazi Germany it was possible for a foreign scholar to get about reasonably unmolested and to subject the regime and its governmental machinery to some scrutiny on the spot. But no such opportunities exist in the Soviet Union, where the movements of natives and especially of foreigners are strictly controlled, and where contacts between Soviet citizens and aliens are discouraged by the authorities and punishable by law. That this attitude of excessive secrecy has its origins in the history of tsarist Russia and in the necessarily conspiratorial beginnings of the Communist party is not to be denied. But whether the Soviet government may have good and sufficient reasons for its attitude or not, the fact remains that its official acts and attitude do not facilitate a better understanding of the U.S.S.R.

The foreign scholar and observer must therefore attempt to obtain a picture from three principal sources of information:

1. Official documents and pronouncements. These include published or publicly announced views of individuals, for no Soviet citizen may publish or say in public what is not approved doctrine or what is not in conformity with official policy. The only possibility for divergence exists when an individual has wrongly interpreted the mind of the Politburo, and then he is promptly called to account. These documents and declarations are, of course, invaluable meat for the scholar, but since they rarely admit the possibility of imperfection their usefulness, while great, is limited. Moreover, Soviet publications do not cover the entire ground of government, and the nearer we come to the top of the political pyramid, the rarer becomes the evidence.

2. The "I was there" books written by foreigners. These are of very limited usefulness. In the first place, foreigners are given very little opportunity to leave Moscow or to conduct unescorted investigations.[1] Moreover, most of these writers are foreign correspondents; and few correspondents are trained political scientists or are otherwise equipped to undertake a detailed study of government. They are more likely to give general impressions and revealing personal experiences, which are very valuable for an understanding of the Russian scene but which are necessarily a far cry from a thorough, professional study. Moreover, some of these books contain some fantastic pieces of misinformation, which the author could easily have corrected by checking with his nearest public library and which cast some doubt on his entire work.[2]

3. The increasing number of refugees from the Soviet Union. There have always been some, but the aftermath of the war has supplied them in abundant quantities. This is a very useful source, especially since the large number of fugitives makes careful cross-checking possible. But three factors limit their usefulness: all of them are partisans; the record they paint is done in an unrelieved black, which sometimes fails to render a complete picture; and few of them were in positions where they had an opportunity to study the inner workings of the Soviet government. In fact, in recent years only one high Soviet official has fled to the Western side, and he was not on the policy-making level. Such is the centralization of control in the Soviet Union that an observer has to be very near the top in order to get an over-all picture, and there has as yet been no Russian Rudolf Hess.

Among secondary sources we find a growing number of studies undertaken by research institutions and scholars dedicated to the interpretation and analysis of available information and documents. Under the circumstances these studies often represent the most valuable source of information, but their accuracy and completeness are sometimes difficult to check.

A major difficulty in utilizing these various sources of information lies in the intense partisanship which any discussion about Russia is likely to arouse. The Russian Revolution, like the earlier French Revolution, was not a purely national phenomenon but had and is still having repercussions in every country. Moreover, the ties between the Soviet Union and the Communist parties of all countries carry the controversy right into the discussion of domestic issues; hence the all-pervasiveness of the problem. Sober and balanced observations are even more difficult in such an atmosphere, because there are extremists on both sides. To the Communist and Soviet sympathizers, all critical remarks about their hero are the result either of stupidity or more likely of fiendish design and propaganda. Facts which do not fit into their

---

[1] See, for instance, Robert Magidoff, *In Anger and Pity,* New York, 1949. On this point all foreign correspondents are in agreement.

[2] A most amusing collection of such errors may be found in D. J. Dallin, *The Real Soviet Russia* (trans. by J. Shaplen), New Haven, 1944, pp. 1–9.

concept are simply ignored. Thus, despite the fact that overwhelming and carefully cross-checked information is available about the vast extent of forced labor in the Soviet Union, the "faithful" will declare with a straight face and usually with conviction that such assertions are lies or that forced labor camps are merely educational institutions in which inmates receive excellent treatment. On the other side of the panel there are those to whom nothing but evil can come from the U.S.S.R. and to whom anybody who stated objectively that there had been considerable Soviet successes, as in the nationality question, would immediately fall under a shadow and be quickly suspected of being a card-carrying member of the Communist party. The analyst must therefore expect attacks from both sides unless he confines himself to a purely descriptive role and refrains from any attempt at an explanation.

There is also the difficulty caused by the use of confusing terminology. The decisive element in the government of the Soviet Union is the Communist party, but there is little similarity between the parties which we encountered in the first three parts of this book and the Communist party of the Soviet Union. The former are parties of the masses, while the Communist party of the U.S.S.R. is a relatively small elite organization. Moreover, there are many parties in the West, while the Communist party of the Soviet Union has a complete monopoly.

Even more controversial has been the use of the term "democracy," under which entirely different things are meant in the West and in the Soviet orbit.

Finally there are the theoretical aspects of the regime. Although the political theory of the Soviet Union has proven flexible and adjustable to changing conditions, the Soviet approach to all questions is dominated by the political theory of Marx, Lenin, and Stalin, and no understanding of their country is remotely possible without a thorough comprehension of this theory, its methods, and its language. Unhappily, many Americans are unwilling to accept this point, because they are not theory-minded themselves and have long accepted the highly doubtful conclusion that all people are alike; consequently, since they do not hold by theory, they are prone to dismiss it as "propaganda" or worse and laugh it off as "silly." No greater error could be made.

Last, but not least, it is difficult to regard the U.S.S.R. as merely another country, though an immensely powerful and aggressive one. For the U.S.S.R. is also the center, the head, and the heart of a gigantic secular "world church" whose militant adherents all over the world are dedicated to it with fierce and unflinching devotion. The actions of the Soviet Union and her leaders must therefore be judged not solely in the light of her national interest, though that may predominate, but also in the light of this quasi-religious conviction of and dedication to a mission which encompasses the earth. What we have before us is thus not only a state but also a wider force which a noted writer has, not inaccurately, called "the Islam of the twentieth century." [3]

[3] Jules Monnerot, *Sociologie du Communisme*, Paris, 1949, p. 10.

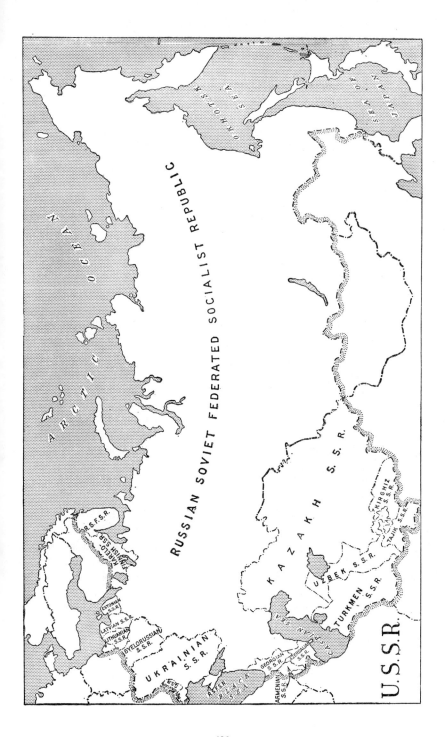

Chapter 1

HISTORICAL ANTECEDENTS

Isolation from the West

The historian Kliuchevsky [1] has stated that three elements dominated the early history of Russia: the steppe with its vast horizon, its dreamy atmosphere, and its constant danger; the great forest, which was home to most of Russia's early population and which forced them to eke out a miserable living at hard labor; and the rivers, the main highways of early days, the scene of constant movement. It is significant that these water roads lead away from Europe, chiefly to the Black Sea. And indeed Russia was unknown and considered to be a country of eternal darkness when ancient Greece and Rome were in bloom, and Russia has therefore no part in the heritage of Greco-Roman culture which is the foundation of Western civilization. There was some contact with the West later, but not until the beginning of the eighteenth century was that contact vital and constant to Russia.

The great forays of Roman generals left Russia alone. Who would have been interested in that bleak, hopeless land with its intemperate climate and its meager resources? Between the sixth and the eighth centuries Slavic tribes founded a number of settlements between the Dnieper and Lake Ladoga, the most important of which was Novgorod. Novgorod was a trading center on the north-south route which connected Scandinavia with Constantinople. This provided an avenue for the Norsemen, one of whose tribes, the Varangians, a Swedish Viking group, established their rule in Novgorod in A.D. 862.

The Norse conquest opened the road to Constantinople and civilization, but a civilization which had adopted distinctive Asiatic features in the Greco-Asiatic tradition of Hellenism. It was thus not European, but a kind of Eurasian influence to which Russia was opened. At the end of the tenth century, the Christian faith was brought to Russia by Greek monks, but by that time the great schism was already in full swing and Russia absorbed Eastern rather than Western thoughts and rites.

[1] Vasily Kliuchevsky, *A History of Russia* (trans. by Hogarth), London, 1911–1931, Vol. I, pp. 2*ff*. See also G. Vernadsky, *Political and Diplomatic History of Russia*, Boston, 1936, pp. 25–36, and *History of Russia*, New Haven, 1951, 3d ed., pp. 1–59; Sir Bernard Pares, *A History of Russia*, New York, 1946, 4th ed., pp. 3–24; and Anatole G. Mazour, *Russia, Past and Present*, New York, 1951, pp. 1–22.

THE MONGOLIANS

The Mongolian conquest, which overwhelmed Russia by the middle of the thirteenth century, was another Eastern influence which profoundly affected Russia. On the one hand the Mongolian rule brought a measure of unity among Russia's ever-quarreling princes, and on the other hand methods of government were introduced which were totally alien to the Western world. It was also due to Mongolian influence that the Russian church, which the Mongolians generally left alone, freed itself from the domination of Constantinople.

The revolt against the Mongols, which succeeded in the fourteenth century and became final 100 years later, was organized and led by the princes of Moscow. Thus Moscow emerged as the center of Russia, and when Constantinople fell to the Turks in 1453, Moscow became the spiritual head of the Greek Orthodox Church—the Third Rome, as it was frequently called. At the same time, the rulers combined spiritual and temporal power in their hands and demonstrated that fact by adopting the title *tsar*.[2]

THE RUSSIAN EMPIRE

Ivan the Terrible is chiefly remembered in history for his great cruelty. But he also gave Russia its first unified code of law and improved local government. He also called consultative assemblies, *sobor*, to hear the views of his subjects. Although he was an autocrat, he permitted the continued existence of a democratic form of village administration, the *mir*, with its elected officers and considerable local autonomy. He broke the power of the aristocracy, the *boyars*, but attempted to institute a new cryptofeudal land-tenure system. Ivan is mostly remembered for having absorbed Siberia into the Russian empire. When he died in 1584, Russia had become a world power but was also faced by formidable enemies and was being bled white in unending wars.

Under Ivan's successors the Russian peasants became serfs. This helped to solve the labor shortage and made the landowners the backbone of Russia. Under these tsars great disorders descended upon Russia, a period of impostors and murder which created seven years of stark anarchy which Russian historians have called the "time of trouble." Poland invaded Russia, occupied Smolensk, and ruled Moscow for two years.

A new stability came in 1613 with the advent of the Romanov dynasty, which mastered the difficulties and in 1686 inaugurated a truly new era for Russia, the era of Peter the Great.

[2] The word came from "Caesar," but in Byzantium the title had second-rate significance, denoting suzerainty. The origin of the term is debated.

Peter effected a transformation which was extraordinary and almost unparalleled. With great energy he embraced a great deal of learning and traveled abroad. On his return, he attempted to Europeanize Russia with gigantic blows almost overnight. This meant politically that Russia was transformed from a feudal state into a European type of autocracy. In this Peter relied on faithful followers and elite regiments rather than on the nobility. He also copied the Prussian administrative system and much of its military organization.

The capstone of Peter's success was his conquest of the Swedish armies, thus proving how much he had learned.

Peter's reforms and conquests were magnificent, but they were also the root of much future trouble. The rapidity with which the reforms were carried out did not permit their integration in the consciousness of the people. The autocratic regime which he established based everything on a thin upper layer of devoted servants. The system of "enlightened absolutism," which was enlightened only in the sense that it brought material achievements of the West to Russia, created a deep social cleavage which nurtured many later revolutions.

REVOLUTIONARY TENDENCIES

A confusion over the line of succession which followed upon the death of Tsar Alexander I in 1825 was utilized by a conspiracy which broke out in December, 1825, and has entered history as the Decembrist Rebellion. It was not the first of its kind, but it went deeper and started a trend. Its leaders were men who knew the West well and wanted to lead Russia toward constitutional government in the image of Western Europe. They also advocated the freeing of serfs and agrarian reforms. It staggers the imagination to reflect what might have become of Russia had the rebellion succeeded. But it was suppressed and thus the kettle boiled underneath while the Tsar created a veritable police state in which the Corps of Gendarmes had power to investigate and arrest without restraint. How great the revolutionary pressure was can be seen from the archives of the Ministry of the Interior which related that there were no less than 547 peasant revolts in Russia between 1828 and 1854.[3] But all these were uncoordinated outbreaks, the result of emotion rather than of revolutionary plans. They all were crushed brutally, and thousands of men, women, and children took to the long road to Siberia. Yet so deep was the despair that the revolts continued as soon as the soldiers had withdrawn.

Conspiratorial organizations also attracted intellectuals, and the growing discontent was reflected in the writings of men like Nikolai Vasilievich Gogol, whose famous comedy, *The Inspector General*, ridiculed the autocratic regime

[3] Otto Rühle, *Die Revolutionen Europas*, Dresden, 1927, Vol. III, p. 202.

and whose tragicomic novel, *Dead Souls,* painted a gripping picture of serf-dom. Among those affected was also Fëdor Mikhailovich Dostoevski, whose writings probed deeply into the Russian soul.

The End of the Tsars

The Crimean War had demonstrated the industrial and administrative inferiority of Russia. Tsar Alexander II (1855–1881) attempted to modernize the country and made the liberation of the serfs a part of his program. But this liberation took place under conditions which visited severe economic difficulties upon the peasants. The result was that no group was satisfied; the conservatives resented what had been done, while the liberal elements were dissatisfied with the results. On the left a new group of terrorists appeared, the so-called "Nihilists," [4] who tried to bring about change by bombs and violence. This brought about counterterror and more bloodshed.

Had the reforms of Alexander II occurred earlier, they might have led the nation into channels of peaceful and gradual modernization. As it happened, they merely whetted the appetite without stilling the hunger for reform, and brought into the open the increasingly bitter struggle which condemned the country to perpetual unrest. This and the oppressive reaction of the tsars plunged Russia into darkest reaction while the rest of Europe experienced great progress on all fronts.

Russia's last tsar, Nicholas II (1894–1917), was more refined than his predecessors but also lacked their will power. At any rate, events had already been set in motion, and the too-easily influenced monarch possessed neither the strength nor the vision to bid them an effective halt.

[4] The term "Nihilist" was derived from the Latin word *nihil* meaning "nothing." It was coined by the great Russian writer Ivan Turgenev in his novel *Fathers and Sons.*

Chapter 2

THE REVOLUTION

The Revolution of 1917 actually began in 1905. At that time the Russo-Japanese War had brought an unbroken series of defeats to Russia. The war was extremely unpopular. The issues were obscure and the people could see no reason for the sacrifices demanded from them. The first demonstration took place in St. Petersburg, led by a priest, Gapon, who was by no means a revolutionary. The demonstrators were met by troops who turned the peaceful march into a terrible blood bath. The news of the massacre spread all over Russia and a wave of strikes and sporadic fighting set in. Peasant revolts were common. Revolts broke out even in the army and a mutiny of the fleet seized the battleship *Potemkin*. The rebellion was suppressed and severe punishments meted out to those responsible. But the regime received a jolt from which it never quite recovered.

THE DUMA

An imperial manifesto of August 19, 1905, granted a Constitution which provided for a consultative assembly, the Duma. Another document followed on October 30, which proclaimed civil liberties, more democratic election laws, and a promise of legislation by representative institutions. Moreover the cabinet system was introduced into Russia and the conservative but not reactionary Count Witte became the first Prime Minister. But these reforms came too late. Witte fell because of his inability to overcome the distrust of both liberals and reactionaries, and he was replaced by the reactionaries Goremykin and Stolypin.

The first Duma lasted only seventy days. After its dissolution, the deputies repaired to Vyborg (Viipuri) in Finland and proclaimed passive resistance against the government.

The second Duma was also dissolved unceremoniously after a few months. The Tsar announced new electoral laws which disenfranchised numbers of people and permitted the manipulation of the election.

Nevertheless the Duma's reputation increased and it even achieved a measure of cooperation with Prime Minister Stolypin. But the latter, who had attempted some belated agrarian reforms, was assassinated, and with him passed the last able leader of imperial Russia. After his death in 1911, the ship of state remained adrift until it foundered in the Revolution of 1917.

THE IMPACT OF MARXISM

The works of Karl Marx and Friedrich Engels were translated into Russian although the complexity of their writing prevented wide circulation. In the chaotic situation created by the incapable tsarist regime, the Marxist solution had much appeal, especially among intellectuals and workers. Marx's principal expositor in Russia was Georgi Plekhanov. He and his colleagues united several revolutionary movements and in 1898 founded the Russian Social Democratic Workers' party. Among the leaders were Georgi Plekhanov, Pavel Axelrod, Vera Zasulitch, L. Martov, and Vladimir Ilich Ulyanov, better known as Lenin.

From the first there were deep-seated differences of opinion. The more moderate wing, led by Plekhanov, Martov, and Axelrod, wanted to concentrate on the struggle for the improvement of the workers' lot and demanded freedom of action for each component part, while Lenin insisted on strictest central authority and organized political action. The moderates wanted a decentralized mass movement; Lenin and the radicals wanted only militants in the party and what they called "democratic centralism," a process by which a decision, once reached at the top policy-making level, is no longer debatable but must be strictly adhered to. At the party congress in London in 1903, Lenin and his followers were temporarily in the majority. Henceforth they called themselves Bolsheviks—from *bolshe*, meaning "greater"—while the moderates were called Mensheviks—from *menshe*, meaning "fewer."

Other parties also existed, notably the Socialist Revolutionary party of agrarian reformist leanings; the Constitutional Democratic party, known as Cadets,[1] a liberal group; and the Octobrists,[2] a moderate monarchist party.

WAR AND COLLAPSE

The First World War brought constant defeat to the Russian armies at the hands of the Germans. Not only were the Russian troops badly led, but the entire supply and production system was in scandalous condition. Although far-seeing elements pressed for reforms and received some concessions, the prevailing sentiment at the court was for more autocracy and suppression. In this policy the neurotic Tsarina, who was long under the influence of the

[1] Named after the Russian pronunciation of the letters K.D., the initials of the Russian words for "constitutional democratic."

[2] Named after the foundation of the "Union of October 30."

evil Rasputin, played a major role. Amidst general restiveness and a feeling of impending doom, the Tsar remained a melancholic fatalist who proved incapable of action.

THE "FEBRUARY" REVOLUTION

When the food supply in St. Petersburg (renamed Petrograd) broke down in February, 1917, because of a faulty distribution system, bread riots commenced and increased despite suppressive measures. Soldiers, even regiments, of the Guards joined the demonstrators. The Duma appointed a provisional committee, composed of all parties except the Social Democrats, to act as the government. One member, the most vigorous one, was a Socialist Revolutionary, Alexander Kerenski. The workers and their delegates had formed revolutionary councils (*soviet* in Russian) and refused to participate in the government, but Kerenski, who was also president of the Soviet, persuaded them to change their minds.

The provisional committee and the army commanders finally convinced the Tsar on March 15, 1917, that only his resignation could remedy the situation. The Tsar at first wanted to resign in favor of his son, but when he learned that his son's illness was incurable, he abdicated in favor of his brother, the Grand Duke Michael. The Grand Duke declared the next day that he would accept the throne only if a constituent assembly invited him to do so. It did not, and with this act, or rather lack of action, the Russian empire and the Romanov dynasty came to an end.

The regime was not really overthrown, it caved in because of its own incapacity and lack of support. The events of March, 1917, have entered history as "the February Revolution" because the Old Style (Julian) calendar was still in force in Russia. If those events could be called "revolution," the Bolsheviks certainly had nothing to do with them. If it can be said at all that the Tsar was overthrown, then he was overthrown by a liberal-conservative government, not by Bolsheviks. When Nicholas II signed the abdication document, Lenin was in Switzerland, Trotsky in New York, and Stalin in Siberia.

The Provisional Government, headed by Prince Lvov and dominated by Kerenski, had a strong majority in the Duma, while the Bolsheviks did not even have a majority in the Soviet. However, revolutions are not made by majorities but, as Lenin pointed out, by energetic minorities led by professional revolutionists.[3]

The Provisional Government never was in full control. All the mainstays of authority crumbled with the end of autocracy. The people were not accustomed to ruling themselves, nor did the government contain experienced ad-

[3] V. I. Lenin, *What Is To Be Done?*, New York, 1929, pp. 116*ff*. (first published in 1902).

ministrators. The dynamics of the situation were supplied by the easily swayed masses who responded to the passionate enthusiasm of the zealots. When the Provisional Government granted the notorious Army Order No. 1, which destroyed the authority of the officers of the armed forces, it was soon swamped by two million deserters and all local authority broke down.

Into this confusion came Lenin and the other Bolshevik leaders, Kamenev, Radek, Lunacharski, and others. Trotsky arrived from Canada a little later. They were able to do so by courtesy of the German High Command, especially General Ludendorff, who considered himself very clever for helping to plant the germ of collapse in the Russian body politic. Lenin and his colleagues quickly organized large demonstrations against those members of the Provisional Government who wanted to continue the war. Amidst rising Bolshevik agitation, Kerenski succeeded Prince Lvov on July 20, 1917, and with his eloquence brought a new fighting spirit to the troops. But the last military offensive collapsed, and many soldiers were won over by the Bolshevik agitation for immediate cessation of hostilities. At the same time, General Kornilov marched against Petrograd but bogged down, and General Krymov tried the same but also with disastrous results.

Lenin pressed for the immediate seizure of power but was opposed in the Bolshevik Central Committee. The more moderate elements carried the day for a while, and the Bolsheviks agreed to enter the constituent assembly which was shortly to be elected. It is interesting to note that these elections, which actually took place after the Bolsheviks had seized power, gave an overwhelming majority to the Socialist Revolutionaries (16,500,000), while the Bolsheviks trailed far behind with 9,000,000. This was the first and only Russian election carried out under conditions of free, equal, and secret suffrage. But in a country which had never known responsible government, such elections were meaningless. The fact that the Bolsheviks did not have the majority of the people behind them by far did not disturb Lenin in the slightest.

The final seizure of power by the Bolsheviks took place on November 7, 1917. The government forces had evaporated. Only a woman's battalion could be found to defend the Winter Palace in Petrograd, the seat of the government. There was a little more fighting in Moscow, but that too was quickly over.

At the same time the Congress of the Soviets was meeting. After learning of the capture of the Winter Palace and the imprisonment of almost the entire Provisional Government, the Congress declared itself to be the repository of all power and advocated immediate peace, the transfer of all land to the peasantry, and control over all production. It also established a government called Council of People's Commissars, composed solely of Bolsheviks. Headed by Lenin, its most important members were Aleksei Ivanovich Rykov, Interior; Leon Trotsky, Foreign Affairs; Joseph Stalin (Iosif Vissarionovich Dzhugashvili), Nationalities; and Anatoli Vasilievich Lunacharski, Education.

The events of November 7, 1917, are known to world history as "the October Revolution" because of the Julian calendar in Russia.[4]

After their victory, the Bolsheviks renamed themselves Communists and thus finalized the separation between themselves and the more moderate Socialists. In a significant and symbolic act, they shifted the seat of government from Petrograd (later renamed Leningrad) to Moscow. Ever since Peter the Great, St. Petersburg–Petrograd had been the foreign city, the "window to the West." Moscow, on the other hand, is a far more Russian city and is imbued with the tradition of the Third Rome, the alternative center of the world. The world would never again be permitted to overlook that fact.

[4] The best and fullest account of the Revolution is W. H. Chamberlin, *The Russian Revolution 1917–1921*, New York, 1935, 2 vols. See also G. Vernadsky, *The Russian Revolution 1917–1931*, New York, 1932; A. Rosenberg, *History of Bolshevism*, Oxford, 1934. For significant partisan accounts, see Leon Trotsky, *History of the Russian Revolution*, New York, 1936, 3 vols.; Alexander Kerenski, *The Catastrophe*, New York, 1927; J. V. Stalin *et al.*, *History of the Communist Party of the Soviet Union*, New York, 1939.

Chapter 3

THE CONSOLIDATION OF THE COMMUNIST REGIME

The Bolshevik Revolution and regime came to Russia as a surprise. Its initial insecurity was demonstrated by the fact that it permitted the Constituent Assembly to meet on January 18, 1918, although the Bolsheviks were heavily outnumbered. But after this single meeting the Assembly dispersed, never to meet again. The Bolsheviks could not possibly have permitted it to consolidate itself, and its destruction came as no surprise. The moderate parties had placed all their hope in the Assembly. When it dispersed, their political influence ceased to exist.

The Communist government consisted of men who had not had any administrative experience, although they made up for that by tremendous energy and devotion to their cause. Their conspiratorial background and their thorough indoctrination with dialectic Marxism was of little help to them. That they were able to conquer years of terrible famine, civil war, and foreign intervention is outstanding proof of the great ability they displayed. Far above them all stood Lenin, perhaps the only one among them endowed with the necessary vision to see the broad picture despite the pressure of many imminent dangers.

Lenin

Like most other Communist leaders, Vladimir Ilich Ulyanov, who called himself Lenin, was not a worker but a middle-class intellectual, the son of a civil servant. He became interested in revolutionary activities early in his life and was deeply influenced by the execution of his older brother Alexander as a result of a Socialist Revolutionary plot against the life of Tsar Alexander III. He became convinced that isolated acts of terrorism were worse than useless, and the oppressive atmosphere of tsarist Russia led him to the unflinching belief that the revolutionary struggle could be won only if the party were dominated by a small, closely knit group of professional revolutionaries.

It is significant that Lenin was forced into exile and remained abroad for seventeen years with brief interruptions. Political leaders who remain in their country, even if underground, are often forced into compromise in order to solve a particular pressing problem. The exiled politician, on the other hand, is free from the moderating influence of responsibility. He is able to conceive his ideas in the abstract and to argue "pure theory." This kind of atmosphere has proved deadly to many an exile who removed himself more and more from reality. It is evidence of Lenin's outstanding ability that he never lost sight of the practical side of the revolution and that he became its foremost tactician. At the same time, being away from Russia and seeing the broader picture, he was a determined opponent of compromise and gradualism. The party, as he saw it, was not to work for piecemeal reform but only for integral revolution. Its principal function was to be a strictly disciplined instrument of revolution. On this issue occurred the split of 1903 which gave Lenin a short-lived majority in the Central Committee and the unchallenged leadership of the ultraradical left.

The crumbling of the foundations of the Russian empire made it clear to him that he could hope to count only on the workers. The *bourgeoisie* would stop the revolution as soon as the autocracy of the tsar was removed, and the peasants would remain united only against the landlords and the tsar. After liberation and land reform they would break up into classes of their own. Lenin derived two conclusions from these theoretical concepts: first, the Bolshevik party had to remain clear of compromises and concessions to other groups in order to prevent the halting of the revolution at the halfway mark; second, the party had to keep its cadres intact in order to wage the inevitable civil war which was sure to follow the overthrowal of tsarism. In that struggle the party with the better leadership and the better discipline was bound to win. During the war he displayed contempt for those socialists who were inclined to cooperate with their governments. He saw in war merely the expression of the inner contradictions of the capitalist society which ought to be turned into a civil war for revolutionary victory.

Lenin was never averse to taking great risks, which on occasion appalled some of his collaborators, but which were never taken in passion but only as part of a well-thought-out plan. For democracy, in the Western sense of the word, he had no use, although he would advocate participation in the formal process of democracy if that gave the party an opportunity for propaganda. Lenin's intellect was flexible but single-minded. He was a man who, by the force of sheer intellect and great learning, knew precisely what he wanted. He had able lieutenants, but Lenin alone carried the Bolshevik revolution to victory and survival. Regardless of whether one agrees or disagrees with his ideas, he stands as one of the outstanding leaders of all times. The Communist regime of the Soviet Union cannot be understood without a comprehension of his person and mind.[1]

[1] There are several collections of Lenin's works in many languages. Of special interest to an understanding of the Revolution and the Communist regime are *What Is To Be*

TROTSKY

A great contrast existed between Lenin and his second in command, Trotsky. Leon (Leib) Davydovich Bronstein, who like many revolutionaries took on a fictitious name and chose that of Trotsky, was an intellectual of dazzling and at times withering brilliance. He was immensely well read on a great number of subjects, but he was arrogantly conscious of his brilliance, which antagonized his associates, and his overconfidence made him an easy target for the far less brilliant but more calculating Stalin. Lenin called Trotsky the ablest man in the Central Committee but criticized him for his overconfidence and his attraction to the purely administrative side of problems. Up to the Revolution, Trotsky was a Menshevik. In 1905 he was vice-president of the first Soviet in St. Petersburg and was deported to Siberia as a result. He lived abroad a good part of his life, was wholly international in outlook, and was at home in a number of languages. He represented Russia brilliantly at the difficult peace conference of Brest-Litovsk, but his single greatest contribution to the victory of the Revolution is his feat as the architect of the Red Army. On August 1, 1918, the Red Army numbered 331,000 men; two years later it had 5,500,000 men, though not all of them were fully equipped. More important than numbers, the army was a striking force which gave a good account of itself in the civil war and the war against Poland. To be sure, these were not wars on the scale of those which were fought on the Western front, but in view of the complete breakdown of the tsarist armies, the rebuilding of any force was a task of no mean proportion.

STALIN

Iosif Vissarionovich Dzhugashvili was a Georgian to whom Lenin gave the name "Stalin," the man of steel. He had an adventurous youth and, unlike Lenin and Trotsky, was almost completely confined to Russia in experience. His early services to his party were undertaken with exceptional daring, and he made the impression of a man of unlimited determination who would remove anything that stood in his path. He had neither Lenin's broad and imminent grasp of great problems nor Trotsky's theoretical brilliance or style. Endowed with a rough and popular sort of humor, he was easily rude and high-handed, although he was able to exercise a certain kind of charm on occasions. Lenin, who thought well of his ability and determination, nevertheless suggested in his political testament that Stalin be removed from the office of

---

Done?, State and Revolution, Imperialism: The Highest Stage of Capitalism, On Dual Power, Left Wing Communism, Letters on Tactics, and *One Step Forward, Two Steps Backward.* There are numerous biographies of Lenin, *e.g.,* D. S. Mirsky, *Lenin,* Boston, 1931; L. Trotsky, *Lenin,* London, 1925; N. K. Krupskaya (Lenin's wife), *Memories of Lenin* (trans. by E. Verney), New York, 1930.

General Secretary of the Communist party and be replaced by a man "more patient, more loyal, more polite and more attentive to comrades, less capricious. . . ." [2] But Stalin was the organizer of the party and eventually of the state. It was he who built the originally secondary position of General Secretary into a powerhouse.

Stalin was patient and steady. Of all the Communist leaders of the first line he appears to be the most Asiatic, more reminiscent of the Great Khan than of Napoleon or Hitler. He was a poor speaker, although his earthy sentences were not without appeal, and he was mediocre as a theorist.[3] Yet there was a tremendous quality of energy, decisiveness, and indomitable will about him which elevated him over his environment and made him one of the outstanding personalities of the century.[4] Trotsky, with his restless energy, cosmopolitanism, and brilliant dialectical ability, was the type of the perpetual revolutionary; Stalin was essentially the man of postrevolutionary consolidation. Lenin, however, belonged to both camps, and it is this which raised him high above the field.

Other Communist Leaders

Compared to this triumvirate, the other Communist leaders of the Revolution belong to a lesser category: Nikolai Bukharin, the brilliant theoretician; Grigori Zinoviev, who became chairman of the Communist International; Lev Borisovich Kamenev, who became President of the Moscow Soviet; Feliks Dzerzhinski, a member of a noble Polish-Lithuanian family who gave the impression of one of the figures painted by El Greco but who became known chiefly as the organizer and head of the dread political police, the Cheka; Mikhail Kalinin, a genuinely popular leader and one of the few men of worker's origin in the party leadership, whose functions as President of the Central Executive Committee and later as President of the Presidium of the Supreme Soviet were primarily formal and ornamental; Anatoli Vasilievich Lunacharski, a close associate of Lenin, an author and dramatist who became People's Commissar for Education; and Karl Radek, the brilliant publicist. There were also Leonid Krasin, Alexandra Kollontai, Nadezhda Krupskaya (Lenin's wife), M. P. Tomski, I. M. Sverdlov, A. I. Rykov, and V. M. Molotov. Of all these people, only Molotov is still in power. Radek is thought to be still in prison, though he may be either released or dead. Trotsky was murdered in Mexico; Zinoviev, Kamenev, Bukharin, and Rykov were executed; Tomski committed suicide; the rest died a natural death.

---

[2] Sir John Maynard, *Russia in Flux* (ed. by S. H. Guest), 1948, p. 201.

[3] J. V. Stalin, *Leninism,* New York, 1928–1933, 2 vols., and *Marxism and the National and Colonial Question,* New York, 1936.

[4] Isaac Deutscher, *Stalin; A Political Biography,* New York, 1949; B. Souvarin, *Stalin,* New York, 1939; I. D. Levine, *Stalin,* New York, 1931; L. Trotsky, *Stalin,* New York, 1946.

CIVIL WAR

The position of the Communist government appeared hopeless in 1917. The whole machinery of distribution had broken down. The radical measures of "war communism," such as the suppression of retail trade and the payment of wages irrespective of work under the slogan, "from everyone according to his ability, to everyone according to his need," and the establishment of factory control by workers' committees, brought the economy down to a low degree of vitality. Moreover, wherever one looked there were enemies. The peace negotiations with the Germans at Brest-Litovsk broke down, and Trotsky walked out of the conference with the formula, "no peace, no war," which left the Germans to do as they pleased—which they did. They occupied the entire Ukraine and the Baltic provinces. The Allied Powers occupied Arkhangelsk, Murmansk, and Vladivostok. A Czech army composed mostly of former prisoners of war was strung along the Trans-Siberian Railroad and knifed through the country at will. Anti-Bolshevik armies known as "Whites" formed on the Don, in the Caucasus, and in Siberia. After the defeat of Germany by the Western powers, the Red Army was able to reconquer the Ukraine from the rule of a native government. In the South, however, the Communists failed after initial successes, and the Whites reached a line running through Tsaritsyn,[5] Voronezh, Orel, Kiev, and Proskurov on the Galician border. In the East the Red Army under Tukhachevski, Frunze, and Kamenev defeated the White army under Admiral Kolchak, and another White army under General Yudenich failed when it reached the outskirts of Petrograd.

That the Communist government was able to survive was primarily due to the extraordinary incapacity of its enemies. The White generals openly championed the cause of the landlords instead of appeasing the peasants. Peasant uprisings were the result. In the fall of 1919 the entire region of the Siberian railway was in open revolt against the White troops of Admiral Kolchak, who was forced to retreat from the Urals. Moreover, the Whites stubbornly demanded a "united and undivided Russia" and could not come to terms with the new states of the Ukraine, Finland, Estonia, Latvia, Lithuania, and Poland. The Ukrainian army could not find common ground with General Denikin's army, and the halfhearted attempt at Allied intervention was abandoned under the pressure of public opinion at home. The Communists had their own hands full, too, but at least, thanks to Lenin's foresight, they possessed perfect discipline and were completely united.

After the retreat of the White armies had turned into a rout, the Poles

[5] Tsaritsyn, the "Red Verdun," was the pivot and was held by Red troops under Voroshilov, despite great pressure from the Whites under General Denikin. Joseph Stalin was political commissar with the Red Army at Tsaritsyn. The city was later renamed Stalingrad.

attacked under Marshal Pilsudski, and in May, 1920, they occupied Kiev. A remaining White army under General Wrangel advanced to the Dnieper and the Don. But the Red Army, brilliantly led by General (later Marshal) Tukhachevski, counterattacked and drove the Poles back to the gates of Lvov and Warsaw. Poland was saved by the fact that Tukhachevski had out-run his supplies and that the other Red Army under General (later Marshal) Budënny did not make contact in time. The Poles, reorganized by the French General Weygand, drove the Red Army back to the Dnieper, but on September 14, 1920, an armistice was concluded between the Polish and Red armies. This rendered hopeless the position of the Whites under General Wrangel in the Crimea; and after extremely stubborn and bloody fighting their remnants were evacuated by ship.

The last White soldier left the soil of Russia on November 16, 1920. From that day on, the Communists were undisputed masters. This was of course highly gratifying to them, but it was not exactly what they had expected. They had hoped that the Russian Revolution would be only the clarion call to world revolution. Now they had been able to maintain themselves against a world of enemies, foreign and domestic, but the world revolution had not materialized. Socialism in one country, surrounded by a hostile world, was now the new problem which led to the deepest division in the ranks of the Communists and promoted the ascendancy of Stalin.

Chapter 4

FROM LENIN TO STALIN

By 1921 military operations were over. They had left Russia in weakened, almost chaotic condition. Large territories were lost; not only the ethnically different regions such as Finland and the Baltic states, but also about ten million Ukrainians and White Russians [1] who came under Polish rule under the Treaty of Peace with Poland, of Riga, March 18, 1921.

The ruin of Russia was indescribable. Most industry was destroyed or had become useless. Transport equipment had worn out, and the civil war had eaten up the country's reserves. The drastic acts of "war communism" had further disrupted the economy, and the black market blossomed because of the suppression of retail trading. The peasants had taken over all the land, but they failed to produce more than they consumed, with the result that famine broke out in the cities. The government sent punitive collection expeditions to the villages, often causing famine there too, without appreciably lessening the burden of the cities.

The NEP

Seeing the danger clearly, Lenin commanded a halt to further extension of the revolution in the economy and on March 21, 1921, inaugurated the New Economic Policy, the NEP. The peasants were now allowed to sell their surplus products after paying a stiff tax, private trade was licensed, factories were permitted in a number of cases to come under restricted private enterprise, and some foreign capitalists were admitted to manage a certain amount of business in Russia. Trade treaties with foreign countries followed, and Russian delegates appeared again at international conferences, culminating in the Treaty of Rapallo of 1922. The NEP marked the abandonment for the time being of plans for imminent world revolution and the retrenchment of the Bolshevik government. It lasted for seven years.

The NEP was a makeshift affair which Lenin called "a strategic retreat." Unlike the "Five-Year Plans" which followed it, the NEP was no plan but rather experimentation and groping in the wilderness.

[1] White Russians are natives of Russia's western section. They are also referred to as "Byelorussians," from the Russian word *byerlui* meaning "white."

In the middle of these events, Lenin died in 1924. He was succeeded by a triumvirate composed of Stalin, Zinoviev, and Kamenev. Trotsky was excluded, and thereby hangs a tale.

THE RISE OF STALIN

There had been opposition within the Communist party almost from its inception. Kamenev and Zinoviev had opposed Lenin on the issue of the revolutionary uprising. Bukharin, Radek, and Smyrnov published for a while a "left" opposition journal. Many Communists were unhappy about the temporary retreat of the NEP. It was Lenin's personality and skill which kept these divergent groups together. When he died, the conflicts came into the open. Trotsky was too sure of himself, too disdainful of lesser minds to build up his own position. He believed that his natural superiority would lay his opponents at his feet. Stalin was handicapped by no such illusion. He entrenched himself in the party as its General Secretary and made it a powerhouse which it had not been before. Together with Zinoviev and Kamenev he dominated the Communist International (Comintern) as well as the government. Lenin was ill for the last two years of his life and was unable to influence the course of events. Trotsky insisted on world revolution. He felt that Germany especially was to be the next battlefield, but Stalin, who bore the responsibility of government, came to the conclusion that the world revolution had temporarily stalled and that it was necessary to concentrate on the reconstruction of Russia and the building up of the Communist state. It should be emphasized that Stalin believed in world revolution as much as Trotsky. No other conclusion was possible for a Marxist-Leninist. But Stalin did not hold with Trotsky's ideas of a "permanent revolution." Like Lenin, he was a realist who knew when it was time to cut one's losses. Everywhere in the world the march of Communism was halted. The German Communist party stagnated, the temporary cooperation between British and Soviet tradeunions proved abortive and came to an end, and in China—always close to Stalin's heart—the Kuomintang under Chiang Kai-shek turned against Russia and its advisers. All these events convinced Stalin that Communism had to be built in one country first before it could engulf the world. Trotsky, on the other hand, bitterly accused Stalin of betraying the cause of the Revolution.[2]

Another issue was intra-party democracy. Trotsky, being out of favor, naturally insisted on freedom of expression within the Communist party, although he believed theoretically in party discipline once a decision was reached. Stalin, however, showed an increasingly strong hand in the management of affairs: what Lenin had achieved by the force of his personality,

[2] Trotsky's views can be found in numerous works, especially *The Real Situation in Russia,* New York, 1928; *My Life,* New York, 1930; *Lessons of October,* New York, 1937, *A History of the Russian Revolution,* New York, 1937, 3 vols.; and *The Revolution Betrayed,* New York, 1937.

Stalin often had to do by force. Of course this debate about "democracy" concerned itself solely with the policy within the party. Neither man had any thought of establishing democracy for the people at large.

There was also the difference over Stalin's emphasis on the peasants and Trotsky's reliance on the international working class.

Stalin proved the stronger. Step by step he overpowered Trotsky and his new associates Kamenev and Zinoviev, who had joined the opposition when they became alarmed over Stalin's entrenched position. Later they retracted and were readmitted to the party for a few years until they were finally extinguished. Trotsky, however, never compromised. He was first deprived of his office as Commissar of War, later of all other official positions, and then was expelled from the party. He was exiled to Soviet Asia in 1927, and in 1929 he was finally expelled from the Soviet Union.[3] In exile he continued the struggle against Stalin until he was killed by a Stalinist agent in 1940. That he had to be pursued even into his Mexican exile is proof of the formidable character of Trotsky's personality, although he never had as numerous a following as Stalin.

Stalin was now undisputed master. In his hands the Communist party had become the central core of the machinery of control. After disposing of the "left" opposition he turned with equal determination against the "right." Men like Rykov and Bukharin, who had supported him against Trotsky, in their turn met ostracism and eventually death.

BUILDING THE NEW COMMUNIST SOCIETY

We have seen that the NEP was a makeshift solution, a necessary but undesirable departure from Communism, a strictly short-term solution. After Stalin had consolidated his position and the country had somewhat recovered from the worst effects of "war communism," he proceeded to direct it again toward its long-term goal, that of being the advance guard of Communism. To this end the country had to be strong, and to be strong meant to be industrialized. This was to be accomplished by a series of Five-Year Plans which emphasized heavy industry and deemphasized light, or consumer-goods, industry. The laxity of the NEP was consigned to the past. More and more rigid controls were applied, sharper and sharper became the measures of punishment and suppression of real or imaginary opposition. The Security Police, the OGPU,[4] later renamed NKVD, MVD, and MGB, became the symbol of the regime. Within the confines of Communist theory this was not without logic. Since industrialization had been decreed as a means of survival in a hostile world, all energy had to be devoted thereto. That meant the imposition of great austerity and the lowering of living standards until that goal was

[3] In 1923 Russia was officially renamed Union of Soviet Socialist Republics.
[4] The initial letters of the Russian words meaning "Unified Political Administration of the State."

accomplished. In the meantime the "fainthearted" who might not wish to travel the long and arduous road to Communism would be given no opportunity to upset the government plan; hence strict control.

For this purpose the face of Russia and of the Russians was to be radically changed. A new generation of civil servants, engineers, workers, etc., was to be created, not in the image of the notoriously slow and inefficient Russian worker, but in an entirely new mold. The League of Communist Youth, the Comsomol, pioneered this development. A new type of administrators and bureaucracy arose, composed of men who had no knowledge of the world outside the Soviet Union and who were single-mindedly devoted to the state.

COLLECTIVIZATION

While enormous plants sprang up all over Russia, Stalin turned his attention to the peasants. New classes had arisen under the NEP. Some peasants, termed *kulaks*, had been able to increase their holdings, although they were still far below Western European peasants in development and prosperity. Much of the surplus of food which went to the cities came from these kulaks. The Central Committee of the Communist Party decided in 1928 to undertake the long-delayed collectivization of the peasants in earnest. Heavy taxation, inability to rent land, and expulsion from the village association, the mir, were used to induce collectivization. Severe resistance by the peasants was the consequence, with much bloodshed. With the utmost force, spearheaded by the OGPU, 55 per cent of the peasantry was driven into collective farming by March, 1933. But the food supply of the country deteriorated, and bread—the staple diet of most of Europe—had to be severely rationed. Finally Stalin called a pause and criticized in a famous article, entitled "Dizzy with Success," the exaggerated zeal shown by his loyal followers.

For a while after that, different types of farms existed concurrently. There were the state farms (*sovkhozi*), the collective farms (*kolkhozi*), and another type of cooperative called *artel* which allowed some degree of private ownership. But the government's goal was clearly the state farm which would transform the peasant into a land laborer and merge him with the proletariat. This type of farming was also considered most suitable for a planned economy. In the early thirties the pressure toward collectivization was again stepped up. This met with bitter resistance, which was suppressed. Wholesale arrests followed, and for the first time large numbers of people were condemned to forced labor, which was used as a cheap working force and helped to undersell the Scandinavian lumber industry. All this was done under the slogan of "liquidation of the kulaks as a class." [5]

[5] Official statistics placed the number of kulaks at 5,859,000 (including family). Most, if not all, of them were deported, Cf. D. J. Dallin, *The Real Soviet Russia* (trans. by J. Shaplen), New Haven, 1944, p. 170.

The repressive measures in the country were accompanied by new control features in the cities. Absenteeism was severely punished, and food distribution and control over the workers' dwellings were transferred to the factories, where they were used to enforce discipline. Moreover, the internal freedom of movement of all citizens was restricted by the introduction of internal passports.

CONSOLIDATION

In 1933 came the end of the first Five-Year Plan and a certain relaxation of repressive measures. One might also speculate whether the coincidence that Hitler came to power in Germany that same year had anything to do with it. At any rate, a little more emphasis was placed on persuasion and good example than before, and the new type of "shock workers," the Stakhanovites,[6] made their appearance. However, the process of strict coordination of all intellectuals was pursued, and large-scale "purges" were conducted among the luminaries and lesser lights of science, art, and letters. Together with this went the increasingly strong propaganda wave against religion, spearheaded by the Union of the Godless, which was under the leadership of Stalin's childhood friend Yaroslavsky.

The period of "relaxation" began in December, 1933, with the permission to certain peasant groups to acquire some privately owned cattle and receive private allotments. The management of cooperatives was also relaxed, and the peasants were given a greater voice in them.

Great improvements were noticed by 1936. "Life is better, life is brighter" was proclaimed from thousands of billboards, and there was some truth to it. Great progress was achieved in the process of industrialization and an increasing quantity of consumers' goods poured from the assembly lines. In foreign affairs Stalin propounded the possibility of peaceful coexistence between capitalistic states and the Soviet Union.[7] Diplomatic relations had been resumed between the Soviet Union and the United States in 1933, and in 1934 the U.S.S.R. had joined the League of Nations. 1935 saw the 1932 nonaggression pact between the Soviet Union and France blossom out into an alliance.

THE 1936 CONSTITUTION

The apex of this development was reached with the Soviet Constitution of 1936, often and quite correctly, as far as we know, referred to as the "Stalin Constitution" because Stalin was its principal architect. On paper this Constitution, which established a federal form of government, was amazingly

[6] Named after a miner named Stakhanov.

[7] Stalin in his report to the 17th Congress of the Communist party of the Soviet Union, quoted in Joseph Stalin, *Leninism,* New York, 1942, pp. 310–313.

liberal, providing for free, equal, universal, and secret suffrage, protection of certain types of private property, independent courts, a bicameral legislature, and many other items which will be discussed later. But no realistic analysis could pretend that all these provisions have become realities, and the life-blood of a Western-type democracy, namely, the rival political parties which present a choice to the voter, is totally missing. Each constituency nominates only one candidate who is then elected on a list of "party and nonparty" candidates. In the beginning there occurred considerable discussion about the candidate's fitness, although this touched only his personal qualifications and had nothing to do with politics as we would understand that term. This impression was confirmed by no less a person than Joseph Stalin himself, who commented on the Constitution as follows:

I must admit that the draft of the new Constitution does preserve the regime of the dictatorship of the working class, just as it also preserves unchanged the present leading position of the Communist Party of the U.S.S.R. If the esteemed critics regard this as a flaw in the Draft Constitution that is only to be regretted. We Bolsheviks regard it as a merit of the Draft Constitution.[8]

The Stalin Constitution of 1936 was discussed in great detail and in innumerable meetings all up and down the country, and it gave rise to much hope for a softening of the regime. Unfortunately these expectations proved unfounded, largely as a result of events which had their origin two years earlier.

KIROV'S ASSASSINATION AND THE GREAT PURGES

S. M. Kirov, Secretary of the Communist party in Leningrad, was assassinated by a Communist in December, 1934. Kirov had been one of Stalin's closest associates. His murder was the first assassination of a major Communist official in sixteen years. Kirov had taken the place of Zinoviev when the latter fell from grace, and Stalin believed he saw a link between the two events. The sense of security which the party leaders had felt, on account of all the progress made, vanished. Their conspiratorial background made them especially sensitive to the possibilities of conspiracy when threatened by others. The increasingly arrogant attitude of the Hitler regime in Germany put them further on edge, and they were also influenced by the pall of heavy suspicion and apprehension toward outside influences which has always existed in Russia and which is understandable in a country that has never known the calm serenity which comes from a habit of freedom.

The perpetrators of the deed and 103 others were executed. Their connection with the murder was doubtful in many cases and not actually proven.

[8] Report delivered at the Extraordinary Eighth Congress of the Soviets of the U.S.S.R., Nov. 25, 1936, quoted in Stalin, *ibid.*, p. 395.

But the NKVD,[9] the OGPU under a new name, was determined to wipe out all possible opposition in the bud.

In 1935 Zinoviev, Kamenev, and ten others were tried for complicity and sentenced to various terms of imprisonment. But it is characteristic of the mounting fear which gripped the regime that they were retried in August, 1936, together with fourteen others, and executed. It was the first time that top Bolshevik leaders had been so treated. In January other distinguished leaders followed: Y. L. Pyatakov, former chairman of the State Bank and Assistant Commissar for Heavy Industry; Karl Radek, editor of *Izvestia* and President of the Chinese (Sun Yat-sen) University in Moscow; Grigori Sokolnikov, Ambassador in London and Assistant Commissar for Foreign Affairs. In June, 1937, the entire high command of the Red Army was liquidated. Among them were Marshal Tukhachevski, Chief of Staff of the Red Army, and Generals Yakir, Uborovich, and Putna, who had all rendered distinguished service to the Soviet Union. They were all shot after a secret trial. Marshal Gamarnik, Assistant Commissar of War and Chief of the Political Department of the Red Army, was said to have committed suicide in prison. The generals were accused of having conspired with Hitler's Germany to overthrow the Soviet regime,[10] and these extraordinary allegations were believed in many quarters in Russia and abroad.[11] However, in the voluminous files of the German government which were found by the Allies after the Second World War no evidence was unearthed to support this contention.

In 1938 another batch of former top Communists was added. Among them were Nikolai Bukharin, leading theoretician and former principal assistant to Stalin in the latter's fight against Trotsky; A. I. Rykov, former chairman of the Council of People's Commissars; N. N. Krestinsky, former Assistant Commissar for Foreign Affairs; and K. G. Rakovski, once chief of the government of the Ukraine and later Soviet Ambassador in London and Paris. They were all shot with the exception of Rakovski, who was sentenced to twenty years' imprisonment.

Similar purges, trials, convictions, and executions were held on lower levels in the various Union Republics, among intellectuals and scientists.

Many different interpretations have been put on these unparalleled events. Some have claimed that Stalin simply forestalled an uprising against him and that he thus made impossible the rise of a fifth column such as plagued other countries.[12] Whatever the reasons may have been, the results were clear. The

[9] Meaning literally People's Commissariat for Internal Affairs.

[10] Quite apart from the absence of any evidence to sustain this point, there is also the fact that three of the executed generals, Gamarnik, Yakir, and Feldmann, were Jews.

[11] Joseph E. Davies, *Mission to Moscow*, New York, 1941. This is a completely uncritical book by the former United States Ambassador to Moscow who swallowed the official Soviet version of the trials without blinking an eyelid.

[12] The story of the absence of fifth columnists is true only to the extent that the Germans were unable to win over top leaders of the Soviet regime, the highest being

"liquidated" leaders had all been leaders of the Bolshevik Revolution. Now Stalin alone remained on lonely heights, the sole living link to the Revolution among top leaders. "The casualties," wrote a noted author, "read like a Communist *Who's Who* of the Twenties." [13] The Communist party was now exclusively the party of Stalin.

THE RUSSO-GERMAN NONAGGRESSION PACT

Many of Stalin's decisions had been influenced, at least in part, by the expectation of war. The Munich agreement of 1938, from which the Soviet Union was excluded, apparently convinced Stalin of a British and French design to let the U.S.S.R. and Nazi Germany fight each other. With greater skill than Neville Chamberlain and Édouard Daladier, he turned the tables, and on August 23, 1939, the world was electrified by the news of the Soviet-German Nonaggression Pact. This was the green light for the Second World War,[14] which broke out a few days later. That Stalin was able to undertake this *volte-face* without any recorded opposition within the U.S.S.R. is proof positive of the absolute control which he had achieved.

The Soviet-German pact was fully obeyed by the Soviet government, and the Communist parties abroad, though weakened by Stalin's policy, promptly fell into line, branded the war as "imperialist" and worked against it wherever they could. During that period the Soviet Union occupied Eastern Poland, the Baltic Republics of Lithuania, Latvia, and Estonia, parts of Eastern Finland, Bessarabia, and Northern Bukovina, all of which were incorporated into the Soviet Union. The native populations, insofar as they remained, were drastically reoriented.

---

merely a general, Vlassov. But German troops were welcomed as the "liberators" in certain parts, especially in southern Russia, until Gestapo and SS methods destroyed whatever good will there was. This fact has been unquestionably established by Allied intelligence work in which the author participated. It was also borne out by the Soviet government, which deprived five Autonomous Republics and Regions of their status and deported their populations because of alleged collaboration with the enemy. They were the German Volga, Kalmyk, Chechen-Ingush, and Crimean Autonomous Soviet Socialist Republics and the Karachaev Autonomous Region. *The New York Times,* Nov. 30, 1945; June 27, 1946.

[13] W. H. Chamberlin, *The Russian Enigma,* New York, 1943, p. 208.

[14] Hitler's decision to attack Poland was made earlier, probably in May, but the Soviet-German Nonaggression Pact removed the last obstacle. It is impossible to believe that Stalin did not know this. The initiative to closer Soviet-German relations came from the U.S.S.R. See the memorandum of the German State Secretary for Foreign Affairs (Weizsäcker) about his conversations with the Soviet Ambassador (Merekalov) on Apr. 17, 1939. Cf. Department of State, *Nazi-Soviet Relations 1939–1941,* Documents from the Archives of the German Foreign Office, Washington, D.C., 1948, pp. 1–2.

WAR

But on June 22, 1941, Germany attacked the Soviet Union, and better relations ensued between Russia and the Western Allies. American lend-lease material arrived in great quantity,[15] although its impact was not felt until later in the war.

The Soviet government, realizing the extreme seriousness of the situation, conducted the war under national rather than Communist propaganda. Stalin called it the "Second Patriotic War."[16] The government relaxed its hitherto strongly antireligious policy and gave some encouragement to the Orthodox Church, which it now controlled. As a means of gaining the confidence of the Western Allies, the Third Communist International was dissolved in 1943.

The U.S.S.R. suffered unprecedented devastation during the war. The German armies encircled Leningrad, took most of Stalingrad, and advanced to within 13 miles of Moscow. Seven million Soviet citizens died in battle or from other consequences of the war; 6,000,000 buildings, 1,700 cities, and 70,000 villages were destroyed.

While the Soviet marshals led the troops, the direction of the war rested securely in the hands of the Communist party leaders, and especially Stalin. A "State Committee of Defense," composed of Stalin (chairman), Molotov (vice-chairman), Beria, Malenkov, and Voroshilov, somewhat reminiscent of the British "War Cabinet," was formed on July 1, 1941, and all internal security agencies were united under Lavrenti Beria.

The Soviet Union emerged from the war with a tremendous increase in power. It had added much new territory: the Petsamo area, the Karelo-Finnish Soviet Socialist Republic, the Estonian, Latvian, and Lithuanian Soviet Socialist Republics, the Moldavian Soviet Socialist Republic, Eastern Poland, Northern East Prussia, Carpatho-Ruthenia,[17] Southern Sakhalin, and the Kurile Islands. Soviet troops occupied Eastern Germany, Eastern Austria, and strategic positions in China.[18] The whole of Eastern Europe was under Russia's sway except for the unexpected defection of Tito's Yugoslavia. Russian armed forces were the largest in the world. Machinery for control of the Communist parties was reestablished in September, 1947, by the creation of the Communist Information Bureau (Cominform). Never in her entire history had Russia wielded such power. Peter the Great would have been pleased with his successors.

[15] Out of a total lend-lease appropriation of $50,000,000,000, the Soviet Union received $11,000,000,000, including 6,800 tanks, 13,300 airplanes, 1,000 locomotives, 406,000 trucks and cars, 2,000,000 tons of steel, and 11,000,000 pairs of shoes. Cf. Edward R. Stettinius, *Lend-Lease: Weapon for Victory*, New York, 1944.

[16] The first was the war against Napoleon in 1812. J. V. Stalin, *The Great Patriotic War of the Soviet Union*, New York, 1945.

[17] Formerly part of Czechoslovakia. Also known as Carpatho-Russia and Carpatho-Ukraine.

[18] Especially Dairen and Port Arthur, as well as the control of the Manchurian Railroad.

Chapter 5

THE U.S.S.R. AFTER STALIN

Joseph Vissarionovich Stalin died on March 5, 1953. But during the year prior to his death there were numerous indications that many changes were in the offing. The nineteenth Congress of the Communist party met in October, 1952, after an interval of thirteen years, and enacted a new statute (rules) of the Communist party of the Soviet Union.[1] Instead of the old Politburo, the new statute provided for a Presidium (of the Central Committee) composed of twenty-five members and eleven candidates—twice as many as had been in the old Politburo. Most of the new members had not previously been close to the chief luminaries of the Politburo.

In December, 1952, an ominous discussion started about Nikolai Voznesensky, a former deputy premier, Politburo member, and chief of the State Planning Commission, who had disappeared years ago. Then in January, 1953, several doctors were arrested on fantastic charges of having killed Georgi Malenkov's great rival, Andrei Zhdanov, in 1948. The accusing finger seemed to point in the direction of police chief Lavrenti Beria, but Malenkov also appeared threatened. In February, 1953, an especially bitter campaign for "vigilance against spies and saboteurs" swept over every corner of the Soviet Union.[2] It was easy to see that a gigantic purge was in the making, perhaps an even bigger one than occurred in the thirties. But when Stalin died in March, his successors lost no time in making their own changes. The Presidium was immediately reduced to the size and the membership of the former Politburo. The accusation against the doctors was dropped and they were reinstated—an almost unheard-of thing—while their accusers were purged, among them N. G. Ignatiev, a candidate for the Presidium and the man Stalin had apparently groomed for Beria's job.

Stalin was of course buried with the customary ceremonies, but soon thereafter the Stalin cult of Byzantinian veneration ceased. After a few weeks little was heard of "the great and wise leader and teacher," the "greatest scientist, artist, linguist, strategist, etc.," who ever walked the face of the earth. In his order of the day of May 9, 1953, Marshal Bulganin declared that the Soviet

[1] For the text of the party statute see James S. Meisel and Edward S. Kozera, *Materials for the Study of the Soviet System,* Ann Arbor, 1953, pp. xliii-lxi.

[2] Klaus Mehnert (K.M.), "In Bewegung Geraten," *Osteuropa,* Vol. III (1953), p. 241.

army had won its victory under the leadership of the "glorious Communist Party"; no mention of the name of Stalin, so common in previous years. On the contrary, there has been a determined campaign against the leadership cult. Thus we read the following words in the Communist party's chief theoretical journal:

Sometimes the acts and the will of outstanding personalities are presented as the determining factor of historical development and are alleged to decide the outcome of class struggles and wars. In the interest of the correct education of cadres, communists, and all toilers, it is necessary to overcome determinedly such errors and distortions of Marxism-Leninism.[3]

And F. B. Konstantinow goes so far as to term the overestimation of strong personalities "one of the most characteristic features of fascism." [4]

The condemnation of the "personality cult" which so characterized the Stalin regime was obviously meant to herald the coming of a collective leadership rather than an individual one. In fact the new rulers of Russia generally avoided the limelight. The new "leader" was supposed to be the Communist party rather than a single individual. This policy was also carried out in the Union Republics and among the lower echelons of the party.

After Stalin's death it appeared that his place had been taken by a "team of three (troika)" composed of Georgi Malenkov, Lavrenti Beria, and Nikita Khrushchev, with Vyacheslav Molotov in an uncertain role.[5] That Khrushchev's star was rising was seen by the fact that he became Stalin's successor as First (General) Secretary of the Communist party. But Beria too fortified his position greatly and worked his MVD (secret police) henchmen into the top administrative positions in such regions as Georgia, Azerbaijan, and Uzbek. At the same time Beria became identified—whether justified or not is not known—with a more permissive policy toward the different non-Russian nationalities and local interests, a policy which appears to have brought him into conflict with Khrushchev, a representative of the Great-Russian claim of preeminence.

It seems likely that Beria's increasing power threatened not only Khrushchev but also Malenkov. It is, however, certain that the decisive element in the situation was the development of the foreign political situation which brought about the fall of Beria, just as it had caused the eclipse of Zhdanov. The policy of the more loosely held reins, associated with Beria, did not lead to positive results favorable to the Soviet Union but instead to an eruption of pent-up feeling in the revolt of the workers of East Berlin and the Soviet zone

---

[3] *Kommunist* (formerly, *Bolshevik*), May 2, 1953.

[4] *Pravda,* June 28, 1953.

[5] Collective leadership was also the aim of Lenin for his succession. See Robert G. Daniels, "The Soviet Succession: Lenin and Stalin," *The Russian Review,* Vol. XII (1953), pp. 153–172.

of Germany on June 17, 1953. Ten days later the Presidium of the Central Committee attended the opening performance of the opera *The Decembrists* at the Bolshoi Theater in Moscow. All members except Beria and M. Bagirov, a candidate and Beria henchman, were present.[6] In other countries such an event would have little significance, but in the Soviet Union the presence or absence of a man at such a function, his place at the center or the side, are all highly significant and duly noted. The removal and arrest of Beria was announced only on July 9,[7] but it is likely that he was already in custody at the time of the opera performance.

The accusations against Beria followed the usual pattern. He was accused of having sought to make himself the sole master of the country, of having wanted to undermine the collective-farm system, of having tried to strengthen bourgeois nationalism, of undertaking illegal administrative acts, and of attempting to replace revolutionary methods with evolutionary ones.[8] The wording of these accusations would indicate that the policy of the looser reins was attributed to Beria and condemned. But this does not exclude its continuation. After all, Stalin too condemned policies of Trotsky's—which he then proceeded to carry out.

It is more important to note that the removal of the seemingly all-powerful master of the police proceeded more easily than might have been expected, and the unconfirmed reports that Beria was lured into a trap may well be correct. It is not clear whether or not the army played a particularly important role in his removal as was reported. It may, however, be important that the presiding officer of the tribunal which tried Beria and condemned him to death was Marshal Ivan Koniev.[9]

The liquidation of Beria left Malenkov and Khrushchev at the top. The secret police, now headed by a relative underling, Sergei Kruglov, was detached from the Ministry of the Interior (MVD) and placed under a Committee for State Security headed by another relative underling, Ivan Serov, who later received ministerial rank. The security services were thus eliminated as a possible independent contender for power.

While the "collective leadership" seemed to continue with Malenkov and Khrushchev at the top, Vyacheslav Molotov and Nikolai Bulganin next in line, and Lazar Kaganovich, the man with the passion for anonymity, farther in the background, some signs of change appeared. Sixteen days after arriving at the top, Malenkov gave up the post of First Secretary of the Communist Party, the position which Stalin had built into a powerhouse. It was taken

[6] *The New York Times,* June 29, 1953.

[7] *Ibid.,* July 9, 1953.

[8] According to the report of *Pravda,* July 10, 1953. See also *The New York Times,* July 10, 1953.

[9] *The New York Times,* Dec. 24, 1953. Beria's trial was held in secret and the accuracy of the reports cannot therefore be tested.

over by Khrushchev. Also, there began a slight revival of the Stalin cult. *Pravda*, the party organ, began to criticize ministries under Malenkov's control, while *Izvestia*, the government organ, passed this campaign over with silence. Khrushchev headed the vital mission to Peking, while Malenkov stayed at home and Molotov went to relatively unimportant East Berlin. To foreign visitors voluble Khrushchev presented himself increasingly as "the boss."

But the outside world learned the facts only on February 9, 1955, when, at a meeting of the Supreme Soviet, its chairman, Alexander Volkov, read a letter from Premier Malenkov asking to be relieved of his job because of "inexperience." In his stead was nominated and elected Nikolai Bulganin, a political marshal who began his work in the Cheka and gained prominence as chairman of the Moscow Soviet (mayor) before and during World War II. Everybody knew that Bulganin was mainly decoration; the real leader was the man who nominated him, Nikita Khrushchev.

If certain new features surrounded this change of command, they were not necessarily significant or permanent. True, Malenkov sat at the rostrum while his letter of resignation was being read, instead of being in prison. Instead of being tried and shot in the approved Stalinist style, he was made Minister of Electric Power Stations. Instead of being denounced in the classical style as a "traitor, saboteur, and foreign hireling," he merely admitted certain errors and shortcomings, including the failure of Soviet agriculture, which was actually in Khrushchev's department. But all that might change overnight. When Trotsky fell from power he too was at first given the same minor ministry before dropping into exile and assassination. The Communist countries recall any number of once prominent leaders who were shifted from top to second-rate positions before being swallowed up by the police cellars and eventually taken in hand by the executioner or the firing squad. Whether this is to be Georgi Malenkov's fate only time will tell. But a regime which could not stand "collective leadership" may not take too kindly to living ex-premiers.

On first impression, Khrushchev's rise to power has much similarity with that of Stalin: his use of the position of party secretary, his emphasis on heavy industry over consumer's goods. However, it is not yet certain that Khrushchev is another Stalin. One of the U.S.S.R.'s chief difficulties in 1955, the year of Khrushchev's coming to the top, is the unsatisfactory condition of her agriculture, and in spite of Malenkov's shouldering the blame, everybody knows that this has been Khrushchev's foremost responsibility.

It is, of course, quite possible that the events of February 9, 1955, may mark the beginning of a long "Khrushchev era" in the Soviet Union. But many believe that it is just another episode in a power struggle which has not yet seen its end.

Chapter 6

MARXISM-LENINISM: THE THEORETICAL FOUNDATIONS OF THE STATE

Every state, every social organism composed of thinking human beings, has a political theory. In fact it is this theory which holds it together. The club, the labor union, the Rotary Club—all have certain ideas which their members hold in common which give them a purpose and make them want to remain in the organization. An association without common concepts would merely be a roomful of people incapable of acting as a group.

Clubs and similar organizations occupy only a limited field in our lives; their purposes are therefore limited, as are the ideas which underlie their existence. But it is different with the state. Aristotle wrote that man was a "political (social) animal," by which he meant that man had to live in organized society in order to be fully himself. Today there are few people in the world who are not subjects or citizens of a state, and the conditions which surround them there determine to a large extent their existence and their aspirations.

Because living in a state is so much more all-pervasive than mere membership in a club, the underlying ideas which all citizens are supposed to hold in common cover a good deal of ground. Some states have been fortunate and have settled their fundamental differences before their people entered into the Industrial Revolution. Other newer states found that their citizens largely agreed on fundamentals when the basic framework of their structure was established. England is an example of the former, and the United States of the latter. The political life of these two countries has therefore evolved around ways and means, rather than fundamentals, for such a long time that their inhabitants have come to regard the controversy over ways and means as the principal, perhaps the sole, basis for political action. Americans are inclined to be distrustful of political theory as a basis for political action, and we sometimes disparage theory as a key to the understanding of other people's political action. We are sometimes wont to consign political theory to the realm of "propaganda"—the useful little word which gives some of us the illusion of shrewdness when we are merely ignorant.

Much of the world has been less fortunate than we were. Questions of fundamental nature still play their tortuous role, and questions are debated on the basis of their agreement with certain doctrines rather than in relation to their practical application. In old Russia there was a time when young intellectuals greeted each other with the words "In what do you believe?"

In a much-debated statement Balfour ascribed the success of the English constitutional system to the fact that the people were basically so much at one that they could safely afford to bicker. Unfortunately the calm security of basic national unity was never granted to the Russian people, and it was therefore never "safe to bicker." Moreover in the insecure environment of tsarist autocracy men could find inner security only in a firm creed, preferably a creed which encompassed every question of man and society, an all-inclusive world philosophy, a *Weltanschauung*.

Those who wish to understand Soviet political philosophy must not think of mere academic theories tentatively proposed from professional ivory towers. Communism is primarily a secular religion which embroils the whole man in its fabric. Like a spiritual religion, it purports to possess the *truth*, although Communism speaks of "scientific accuracy" which amounts to the same thing. Communism, like religion, demands unqualified allegiance to the tenets of the "faith" and stands ever ready to excommunicate the apostate. Like religion it has a kind of "scripture," the writings of the masters, Marx-Engels-Lenin-Stalin, which is subjected to ceaseless exegesis. Like some religions it has a tightly organized quasi church, the body of the elect, the party. Communism also has a hierarchy which demands obedience, and it shows little liking for opposite views which, being "untrue" by definition, cannot be tolerated.

As a quasi religion, Communism provides its followers with an intellectual home in which all questions have an answer—not an inconsiderable attraction in troubled times. It gives them a sense of superiority, because they are supposedly the repositories of the "truth." It gives them a sense of mission, raises them above the confines of their own lives, and imbues them with great courage and devotion. It enables them to justify anything—and there is much to justify. But it also tends to make them peculiarly blind toward the outside world, which they view through their party spectacles and which they believe they understand thoroughly and "scientifically" when in reality they are often woefully ill informed. Such is the frame within which political action originates in the Soviet Union. It is a flexible frame, and much can be seen through it, but like all frames it has its limitations.

Karl Marx

The founder of the school and one of the most creative and original personalities of all time was a German, Karl Marx (1818–1883), who lived in London most of his life. His writings were voluminous and the literature about his work is immense. The following lines are in the nature of a brief survey of Marxism-Leninism-Stalinism which can hope only to scratch the surface.[1]

HISTORICAL MATERIALISM

The foundation of the Marxist system is the concept of historical materialism. Marx contends that human life and aspirations are the result of economic factors, especially the production process, which form them. All spiritual, idealistic, and intellectual processes are the result of economic conditions and therefore molded by them. Marx formulated this thought in the following way:

In the social production which men carry on they enter into definite relationships that are indispensable and independent of their will; these relations of production correspond to a definite stage of development of their material powers of production. The sum total of these relations of production constitutes the economic structure of society—the real foundation on which rise legal and political superstructures and to which correspond definite forms of social consciousness. The mode of production in material life determines the general character of the social, political, and spiritual processes of life. It is not the consciousness of men that determines their existence, but, on the contrary, their social existence determines their consciousness.[2]

The above quotation crystallizes several essential concepts of Marxism. All society is formed by its economic basis, in particular by the production process. Change that and you change society. Historical materialism thus appears in a twin role: it provides a scientific, logical (dialectic) method by which the course of history can be accurately discovered, and it is a tool through which the course of history can be changed by changing the production process.

THE "DICTATORSHIP OF THE PROLETARIAT"

Social history so viewed becomes a dynamic process. Each stage of history is dominated by a class—namely, the class which owns the means of production and thus controls the production process. In modern times, in the era of capitalism, the ruling class which controls the means of production is the *bourgeoisie*. But this class system bears the seed of its own destruction within

---

[1] Among Marx's own works the most important for our purposes is his *Critique of Political Economy;* also *Manifesto of the Communist Party, The Class Struggles in France,* and *Capital* (especially Vol. I), as well as his correspondence. Among Engels' works, note especially *Herr Eugen Dühring's Revolution in Science* (known as the "Anti-Dühring") and his correspondence. Note also G. D. H. Cole, *What Marx Really Meant,* London, 1934; Sydney Hook, *Towards an Understanding of Karl Marx,* New York, 1933, and his *From Hegel to Marx,* New York, 1936; H. J. Laski, *Karl Marx: An Essay,* London, 1922; and Paul M. Sweezy, *Socialism,* New York, 1949.

[2] Karl Marx, *Critique of Political Economy* (trans. by N. I. Stone), New York, 1904, p. 11.

itself, according to Marx, for at a certain stage in its development new production methods conflict with existing property relationships; the result is ever-widening crises and a transformation of the social order. Thus capitalism forges the weapons which destroy it, but it also "calls into existence the men who are to wield those weapons—the modern working class—the proletariat." [3] This is the class which must sell its labor in order to live, but as a result of technological advance there is created an industrial "reserve army" of unemployed which helps to keep wages down to the bare existence level. Because of this condition, the *bourgeoisie* makes greater and greater profits, while the proletariat becomes increasingly impoverished. This development leads to ever-widening crises, which deprive more and more groups of property and force them to merge with the proletariat. But in this way it also strengthens the proletariat, which eventually overthrows the regime and establishes its own dictatorship and a new social order. It should be emphasized that according to this theory the proletariat encompasses the overwhelming majority of the people, and its "dictatorship" may therefore be "democratic." To Marx and Engels the "dictatorship of the proletariat" is more "democratic" than the rule of the *bourgeoisie*, because the former is rule by majority while the latter is rule by a small minority.

The "Withering Away" of the State

The "dictatorship of the proletariat" is not supposed to be the final development. It is still a "state," and a "state" is by definition a machinery for suppression, *i.e.*, suppression of classes.[4] True, according to Marx this is better than "bourgeois democracy," [5] because the former constitutes force exercised by the majority against the minority while the latter means presumably force by the minority against the majority. Yet according to Marx and Engels this is merely a transitory stage.

The proletariat seizes state power, and then transforms the means of production into state property. But in doing this, it puts an end to itself as the proletariat, it puts an end to all class differences and class antagonism, it puts an end to the state as the state. . . . As soon as there is no longer any class of society to be held in subjection; as soon as, along with class domination and the struggle for individual existence based on the former anarchy of production, the collisions and excesses arising from these have also been abolished, there is nothing more to be repressed and a special repressive force, a state, is no longer necessary.[6]

[3] Karl Marx and Friedrich Engels, *Manifesto of the Communist Party* (generally known as the Communist Manifesto), New York, 1932, p. 15 (first published in 1848).

[4] Lenin, *State and Revolution,* New York, 1929, p. 74.

[5] This concept, of course, ignores the fact that majority rule is not the only essence of democracy and that it also includes civil rights for minorities.

[6] Friedrich Engels, *Herr Eugen Dühring's Revolution in Science* (trans. by E. Burns), London, 1935, p. 306.

Thus the state "withers away" because there is no further need for it, and the end of the state ushers in a society without antagonism, without exploitation, in which "people will become gradually accustomed to the observance of the elementary rules of social life . . . without compulsion, without subordination, without the special apparatus for compulsion which is called the state." [7]

This is still the general framework within which Communist political theory develops, but there have been a number of significant modifications. Marx oversimplified society. He presented the picture of a world with two poles called *bourgeoisie* and proletariat. He ignored the peasants and the middle class, whose members he assumed would join the one or the other of the two main classes. In fact, it was the very assumption of the greater part of these two classes joining the proletariat which was to give the latter its overwhelming numerical superiority. Moreover, the proletariat was to become increasingly impoverished and under the theory of economic determinism was to act as a class in accordance with its economic interest. But contrary to these expectations the peasants and the middle class did not cease to exist. In many instances they became stronger. Nor did the proletariat become increasingly impoverished. Social legislation, trade-union activities, adjustments within the capitalistic machinery, and the power of democratic labor parties improved their lot in all industrial countries. The First World War finally revealed that the proletariat did not act in accordance with its alleged interest but proceeded to support its respective bourgeois governments and the war. It became necessary to make adjustments for these events, and this was primarily Lenin's contribution.

LENIN AND THE THEORY OF IMPERIALISM

Lenin stressed the theory that imperialism was the highest stage of capitalism.[8] He maintained that the enormous expansion of the capitalist economy has led to an imperialistic development from which certain parts of the proletariat, especially the skilled workers, profit. This era of imperialism is characterized by the export of finance capital and the control of the banks over industry. It is also characterized by the growth of gigantic monopolies. Again, however, the "inevitable" economic forces throw these monopolies into a savage struggle for markets which culminates in war. Such a war, according to Lenin, is nothing but a war between trusts in which the workers have no stake. The worker must therefore see that he ought not to strive for temporary advantage through the rivalry of one monopolist with another but should realize his opportunity by acting in the ultimate interest of his class, by turning the imperialist war into a civil war.

[7] Lenin, *op. cit.*, p. 74.

[8] Lenin, *Imperialism: The Highest Stage of Capitalism*, New York, 1939.

The Role of the Communist Party

However, it had become obvious to Lenin that the masses of the proletariat were not always aware of their "true" interests. Therefore the proletariat had to be guided by "its most advanced part, the Communist party." This meant in effect that the "dictatorship of the proletariat" became in effect the dictatorship of the Communist party. Lenin justified this as follows:

. . . in the era of capitalism, when the masses of the workers are constantly subjected to exploitation and cannot develop their human faculties, the most characteristic feature of working class political parties is that they can embrace only a minority of their class. . . . That is why we must admit that only this class-conscious minority can guide the broad masses of the workers and lead them.[9]

Stalin later tried to minimize Lenin's frank admission by asserting that Lenin merely meant that the Communist party leads the proletariat and that it does not share that role with any other party. But since the will of the proletariat is clearly established by its leadership and since there is on record no single, solitary instance in which the proletariat or members thereof have expressed themselves in opposition to the party or even differed therefrom, and lived, the difference between Lenin's words as we would ordinarily understand them and Stalin's interpretation thereof is not visible to the naked eye. Under Communist theory there can actually be no such difference between the proletariat and the party. The "dialectical method" according to Communist doctrine is a scientific process by which "correct" policy may be accurately determined.[10] Hence disagreement would only indicate ignorance or worse. In this formulation disagreement becomes "deviation," which is tantamount to mortal sin. It is only natural that the exposition of the "correct" policy must be the task of the "most advanced part" of the proletariat, the Communist party. The position of the party was clearly stated by Stalin:

A party is a part of a class, its most advanced part. Several parties, and consequently, freedom for parties, can exist only in a society in which there are antagonistic classes whose interests are mutually hostile and irreconcilable. . . . But in the U.S.S.R. there are no longer such classes as the capitalists, the landlords, the kulaks, ec. In the U.S.S.R. there are only two classes, workers and peasants, whose interests—far from being mutually hostile—are, on the contrary, friendly. Hence there is no ground in the U.S.S.R. for the existence of several parties, and consequently, for freedom for these parties. In the U.S.S.R. there is ground only for one party, the Communist Party.[11]

The justification of the single-party state is thus based on the contention

[9] Lenin in a speech before the second congress of the Communist International, quoted by Hans Kelsen, *The Political Theory of Bolshevism*, Berkeley, Calif., 1949, p. 52.
[10] Stalin, *Dialectical and Historical Materialism*, New York, 1940.
[11] Stalin, *Leninism*, New York, 1942, p. 395.

that opposing classes have disappeared in the Soviet Union. But did not Engels and Lenin say that when that happens the state "withers away"? No, says Stalin, because the Soviet Union is encircled by capitalist states. According to Stalin, Engels' position can be understood only under two assumptions: (1) by studying the Socialist state solely from the angle of its internal development; or (2) if one assumes that socialism (Communism) has already become victorious in all or the majority of countries and that therefore there is no danger of foreign attack and therefore no need for the state and the army.

But it follows from this that Engels' general formula about the destiny of the Socialist state in general cannot be extended to the partial and specific case of the victory of Socialism in one country alone, a country which is surrounded by a capitalist world, is subject to the menace of foreign military attack, cannot therefore abstract itself from the international situation, and must have at its disposal a well-trained army, well-organized punitive organs, and a strong intelligence service— consequently must have its own state, strong enough to defend the conquests of Socialism from foreign attacks.[12]

Thus, as long as all the world is not dominated by Communism, the Soviet "state" does not "wither away" but on the contrary becomes stronger. This is so because the capitalistic "encirclement" is considered hostile by definition, since the economic interests of capitalist powers require them to fear the alleged attraction of the Soviet Union.

Thus in the theory and the pronouncements of Communism the shape of the Soviet state can already be perceived. It is a state whose leaders believe they possess a "scientific" method for determining "correct" policy. It is a state whose leaders believe in the inevitability of Communist triumph everywhere in the world and who believe that this end can be achieved by an uncompromising revolutionary policy.[13] It is a state which is dominated and guided by a single political party, the Communist party, from which all policy emanates. The Communist party is everything. The institutions of the state are merely tools to be used as the party sees fit, to be picked up or discarded at will. Since the party is presumably the custodian of an inevitable, historical development,[14] it cannot be limited by any institutional or constitutional factors. Consequently in the Soviet Union constitutions and legal documents are as secondary in importance as are the formal institutions of the state. The living constitution, the actual government, is the Communist party. A study of that Communist party must therefore be the first step in the investigation of the institutions of government in the Union of Soviet Socialist Republics.

[12] *Ibid.*, p. 471.

[13] Stalin, *Dialectical and Historical Materialism*, p. 14. Hence, in order not to err in policy, "one must pursue an uncompromising proletarian class policy, not a reformist policy of harmony of the interests of the proletariat and the bourgeoisie."

[14] Waldemar Gurian, *Bolshevism: An Introduction to Soviet Communism,* Notre Dame, 1952, p. 15.

Chapter 7

THE COMMUNIST PARTY

The Communist party of the Soviet Union is not an open mass party like Western political parties but a closed society of the new "elite." No position of any significance can be obtained without membership; only the most rigorous tests will admit a new member, and even after admission he must be constantly prepared to prove his devotion to the "party line" or to face a purge. A party member thus accepts a heavy burden of supervision and uncertainty as a price for the coveted position which party membership confers.

The pivotal and monopoly position of the party is well recognized. "Here in the Soviet Union, in the land of the dictatorship of the proletariat," said Stalin, "the fact that not a single important political or organizational question is decided by our Soviet and other mass organizations without directions from the Party must be regarded as the highest expression of the leading role of the Party. . . . In this sense it could be said that the dictatorship of the proletariat is in essence the dictatorship of its vanguard, the dictatorship of its Party." [1] The Soviet Constitution of 1936 states that

The most active and politically-conscious citizens in the ranks of the working class and other sections of the working people unite in the Communist Party of the Soviet Union (Bolsheviks), which is the vanguard of the working people in their struggle to strengthen and develop the socialist system and is the leading core of all organizations of the working people, both public and state.

And Andrei Vyshinsky, Soviet diplomat and leading jurist of the U.S.S.R., wrote, "The political basis of the USSR comprises—as the most important principle of the working class dictatorship—the leading and directing role of the Communist Party in all fields of economic, social and cultural activity." [2] "The workers themselves," said Lenin, "do not know as yet how to rule and would first have to go through years of schooling. Hence, in order to rule, an army of revolutionaries—Communists hardened in battle, is necessary. We have such; it is the Party." [3] Thus, in the clear words of the Communist

[1] J. V. Stalin, *Problems of Leninism,* New York, 1934, p. 34.
[2] Andrei Y. Vyshinsky, *The Law of the Soviet State* (trans. by H. R. Babb), New York, 1948, p. 159.
[3] J. Towster, *Political Power in the U.S.S.R.,* New York, 1948, p. 120. This is one of the most detailed and authoritative works on the Soviet Union.

leaders themselves, the "dictatorship of the proletariat" is in effect the dictatorship of the Communist party.

THE MONOLITHIC PARTY AND "DEMOCRATIC CENTRALISM"

The monopoly position of the party excludes all possibilities that the formulation of its policy might be challenged by outside forces. Can there be challenge within? The Communist party is a single, unified, and centralized structure, a "monolith." Only one will, one direction may prevail. Factionalism is strictly prohibited. But at the same time Communists claim that their party is endowed with what they are pleased to call "democratic centralism." This term implies a combination between the principle of mass participation at the bottom and the concentration of leadership at the top. According to the party rules, this means:

1. The election of all party bodies, from the lowest to the highest
2. Periodical reports by the party bodies to their party organizations
3. Strict party discipline and subordination of the minority to the majority
4. The absolutely binding character of the decisions of higher bodies upon lower bodies [4]

What is the reality of "democratic centralism"? There will be little dispute about the word "centralism," which means essentially two things in the Communist party: the absolute concentration of power at the top, and the total absence of a federal principle within the party. The term "democratic centralism" implies that there is democracy within each level of the party but that there is no democracy between levels. Thus the upper levels dictate absolutely and without restraint to the lower levels. The area organization dictates to the town organization and is in turn dictated to by the regional organization, and that goes all the way up to the Presidium (formerly Politburo), which dictates the entire policy of the party and thus of the state.

As all power is concentrated at the top, it is clear that no "reserved" powers remain in the hands of the party organizations for the various territorial subdivisions. As far as the Communist party is concerned, the guiding principle is thus clearly unitary and not federal.

Despite this admitted concentration of all power at the top, it is still claimed that there is intra-party democracy because (1) all organs of the party are elected, (2) each organ is accountable to the larger body electing it, and (3) the party practices "self-criticism."

The reality, however, is that the usual way in which party officers are chosen is by cooption, that is, for instance, by members of a committee or presidium deciding who shall fill a given vacancy, or by appointment from high authority.[5] Where there are elections, they are pure formalities, pure

[4] Rule 21, Statute (rules) of the Communist party of the Soviet Union of 1952.
[5] Merle Fainsod, *How Russia Is Ruled,* Cambridge, Mass., 1953, p. 181.

ratification of decisions already made at a higher level. There is not on record a single instance at which a contest developed between rival candidates for office. It is of course impossible to gauge accurately the nature of the informal discussions which precede the formal election of officers. Undoubtedly there are many instances, especially at the lower level, where the qualifications of several people are discussed. However, these discussions concern themselves solely with the personal fitness of a man or woman for a specific task, and never involve differences of policy. The more important the office is, the more evident is the will of the party leadership—a will which is clearly and immediately understood and never disobeyed.

The accountability of officers to larger bodies is purely theoretical and has no relation to reality. Meetings of party congresses and conferences have become more and more irregular and infrequent, despite the provisions of the party rules which demand periodic conferences at given intervals. Nor is there ever feasible, under existing conditions, a ground swell which would oust an officer or committee. The party may give in to popular dissatisfaction against an officer and have him removed, but this occurs only when the bone of contention is the efficiency with which the individual executes official policy. The policy itself may not be questioned. In all such instances the actual ouster is the result of a decision by the party leaders and is always well known to the congress membership before the meeting gets under way. Frequently officials marked for disciplinary action are criticized in the party press, and this serves to give a hint to party members and delegates concerning the attitude and action expected of them. The literature of analysts and eyewitnesses is full of graphic descriptions showing how such "marked men" suddenly find themselves isolated and attacked from all sides.

"Self-criticism"

Most interesting among arguments purporting to show the existence of intra-party democracy is that of self-criticism. Self-criticism undoubtedly exists within the party, sometimes on a fairly large scale, but there are significant limitations to the exercise thereof. The would-be critic must never attempt to organize the supporters for his views, for to do so would make him guilty of "factionalism," [6] a severe breach of discipline and of the principle of party unity. Nor must self-criticism ever attack policy, which as we have seen is laid down to lower bodies by higher ones and originates in the Presidium. To attack the party line constitutes the offense of "deviationism," a most serious error involving great physical danger to the perpetrator.[7]

[6] "Factionalism" has been defined by Stalin as "the rise of groups with special platforms and with the aim of shutting themselves off to a certain extent and creating their own group discipline" (13th Congress of the Communist party).

[7] Stalin, *Leninism*, New York, 1942, pp. 88–133.

What is then the purpose of "self-criticism"? In the first place, it is a method by which broad attention can be focused on the implementation and execution of a policy already decided upon at high levels. Thus a wide array of talent may be brought to bear upon the mechanics of carrying out orders, a process which adds to efficiency and diverts possible criticism from the merits of the policy itself.

Secondly, it is an important means of disciplining inefficient, corrupt, or negligent officials. Of course it would be just as easy to remove them by higher orders, for this "criticism" is never spontaneous but is always ordered and directed by the leadership. However the public indignity of "criticism" serves to keep officials on the alert and provides a constant warning for those who might harbor overly ambitious plans.

Thirdly, it is a method of throwing an official to the wolves in order that pent-up feelings may concentrate on him and be diverted from higher levels.

Fourthly, it serves to demonstrate the all-important and all-powerful character of the party from whose avenging sword no one, not even formerly powerful leaders, is ever exempt.

Fifthly, self-criticism is a peculiar, and to the Western mind, a particularly repulsive part of the Communist ritual. A party member, no matter how high, must, when criticized, immediately confess his errors in a most abject fashion. Since a member, especially a high official, is publicly criticized only when his downfall has already been decided upon by the powers that be, this complete self-debasement is the only way in which the victim can save himself from the worst—and even then he may not succeed. This ritual is typical not only for the Communist party of the Soviet Union but also for all the Communist parties in the world. It serves again to demonstrate the infallibility of the party and the official doctrine. All difficulties are the result of personal error of individuals, of their inability to understand the gospel of Marxism-Leninism "correctly." The party, the doctrine, are never in error.

Thus "self-criticism," far from being an expression of an imagined "intra-party democracy," is only an instrument to help shape the completely obedient party member, who will labor day and night to carry out the party's directives without ever questioning their wisdom or validity, who can be turned in any direction—the perfect human robot.

The question of what constitutes a fit subject for self-criticism lies solely with the Central Committee of the party, which means the Presidium. How limited intra-party democracy is has been clearly stated by Stalin in his reply to the arguments of a certain Lutovinov.

He [Lutovinov] wants real democracy, that all, at least the most important questions should be discussed in all the cells from bottom up, that the whole party should get going on every question and should take part in the consideration of that question. But, comrades, . . . with such an arrangement our party would be transformed into a discussion club of eternally jabbering and never-deciding [people], while our party must, above all, be an acting one, because we are in power.[8]

"Spark Plug"

The functions of the Communist party emerge clearly from its role as the "guide" of state and people. It is the spark plug of all action in the public and sometimes the private sector of Soviet life. All important actions originate in the party and are pressed by the party, but because of the frequent identity of state and party officials, it is not always easy to distinguish between government and party affairs.

Propaganda

The Communist party is also in charge of the ideological education of the people. No regime can get along without a measure of support on the part of the people, and the Soviet leaders are well aware of that. Consequently Marxist-Leninist-Stalinist doctrine is propagated by all organs and sections of the party. Since Communist theory holds that every field of human endeavor is an expression and instrument of class warfare, the party makes use of every available instrument. Thus not only is all political thought strictly streamlined according to the accepted doctrine, but music, art, science, and every other conceivable activity must reflect a proper Communist attitude. At the present time this "proper" attitude has a strongly nationalistic note, which includes the claim that Russians have originated and invented all kinds of things which are ordinarily attributed to such people as Edison, Rutherford, and Marconi. The endeavors to strengthen national pride and to combine it with Communist loyalty may have taken their cue from the experience with patriotic propaganda during the war, and they are undoubtedly quite successful.

The reverse side of the party's teaching function is the duty of exorcising "impurities." Failure to follow the party line may under certain circumstances be considered as "wrecking," and writers who fail to observe the strict confines of Marxism-Leninism as expounded by the party have found themselves termed "enemies of the people." [9]

The Communist party also serves as a device by which the government and the party keep the people informed about their activities. Since the party and the government have a monopoly on all information channels, this is a highly

---

[8] J. Stalin before the 12th Congress of the Russian Communist party, April, 1923; cf. Towster, *op. cit.*, p. 157.

[9] See S. N. Harper and R. Thompson, *The Government of the Soviet Union*, New York, 1949, 2d ed., pp. 76*f*. Article 131 of the Soviet Constitution terms public, socialist property "sacred" and calls persons who commit offenses against it "enemies of the people."

effective means of control. No single organ of information carries as much authority as the chief newspaper of the Communist party, *Pravda* (Truth). Opposing papers, foreign or domestic, are of course prohibited. Apart from underground literature, which probably exists in some measure, foreign radio broadcasts are the only possible source of non-Communist information. Listening to foreign stations is not punishable by law at the present time, though repeating what has been heard is. But short-wave radios are not numerous in the Soviet Union, and recently Soviet stations have been "jamming" such Russian-language programs as the "Voice of America."

As the party carries down to the people what the government does, it also attempts to stimulate them for such action as the government and the party may deem desirable. Meetings are held, speeches heard, and resolutions passed. A special device is the so-called "organized discussion," by far the most frequently heard discussion of public issues in the Soviet Union. This is not an ordinary, free debate exposing different points of view, but rather the exploration and dramatization of the best ways and means by which the given policy may be carried out most efficiently.

LISTENING POST

Not only does the Communist party report to the people about the activities of the government, but it also reports to the government and party leadership about sentiments among the people. Insofar as this is a security function, it is carried out by the Secret Political Police, now the MGB, but it is the duty of the party to report significant changes in public opinion in order that party and government may take the necessary action.

MEMBERSHIP

Among an estimated popultaion of 200,000,000 people, only 6,882,145 (3 per cent) were members of the Communist party on October 1, 1952. Of these, 868,886 were candidate members.[10] Rigorous standards of loyalty, efficiency, and personal conduct must be observed by those who wish to be admitted to the new aristocracy, but once admitted the Communist is by no means safe. He must submit to far greater supervision and control than will be imposed on nonmembers, and in his work as well as his deportment he is supposed to be a model. Failure to live up to these standards as well as any kind of "deviation" or "wrecking" [11] will be met with disciplinary punishment,

---

[10] Quoted by Georgi Malenkov in his keynote address to the 19th Congress of the Communist party on Oct. 5, 1952, J. S. Meisel and E. S. Kozera, *Materials for the Study of the Soviet System,* Ann Arbor, 1953, p. xxiii.

[11] A person who fails to take proper measures against inefficiency and waste, or who fails to report such negligence, may be guilty of "wrecking."

which may include expulsion and worse. Communists are therefore likely to work under considerable strain. Usually they are extremely hard-working, devoted men of unquestioning obedience. Whatever talent and ability the country possesses may be found in the present or former ranks of the Communist party.

Finally, the Communist party exercises a "tutelage" over the people with the avowed purpose of educating them toward the goal of general participation in the processes of government. This is to be achieved by including most Soviet citizens in a great variety of voluntary and compulsory organizations among which the Communist party is the apex. In that way the citizenry is to learn "by doing" the functions of government. In reality, however, little progress appears to have been made in that direction. The Webbs [12] saw in the Soviet Union a pluralistic, multiform society in which all governmental functions are shared by a number of interacting "pyramids," *i.e.*, mass organizations, rising from level to level and culminating in the Kremlin. According to the Webbs, every citizen has a distinctive part in this structure because he participates directly or indirectly on some level or other.

The developments in the Soviet Union and the statements of the Communist leaders themselves have definitely refuted this analysis. The Soviet state, and the all-pervasive Communist party which "leads" it, is monolithic, not pluralistic. The clear and unequivocal expressions of Stalin, Vyshinsky, and other leaders leave no doubt that the Communist party occupies the "leading and directing role" in every field. There are not many "pyramids" but only one. The people who participate in the various mass organizations—and even in the membership of the Communist party below the top level—do not really participate in the process of decision making, of policy, but merely fill an assigned place in a prescribed manner. This kind of "mass participation" does not constitute democracy, but quite on the contrary is the typical mark of totalitarian regimes, which it serves as an effective propaganda device.

Since the Communist party of the Soviet Union is an organization of the governing elite, it is also concerned with the continued supply of future elite material. The party therefore tends more and more to represent the better educated and urban classes.[13] This development was interrupted during and shortly after the war when the doors of the party were thrown open to the members of the armed forces, among whom the rural and less educated elements predominate. But in recent years the long-range elitist trend has been clearly resumed and intensified. This means that workers contribute a decreasing number of party members, while peasant representation is extremely small although it is by far the largest population group in the Soviet Union. In other words, the basis of Communist rule is not the workers, let alone the

---

[12] Sidney and Beatrice Webb, *Soviet Communism: A New Civilization?* New York, 1936, Vol. 1, Introduction.

[13] For an excellent analysis of the party's composition, see Fainsod, *op. cit.*, pp. 209–239.

peasants, as Communist propaganda might indicate, but the managerial personnel, the bureaucracy. This tendency sharpens the gulf between the governors and the governed, and the Soviet rulers find it, therefore, expedient to widen the doors of the party from time to time in order not to lose contact with the masses of the people. But after a while, in order to fulfill its proper role as the directing center the party must return to its elitist tendencies. Thus it constitutes a ruling class more rigid and impenetrable than anything that existed at the time of the tsars. That such a situation produces considerable tensions is clear, but how strong they are is difficult to gauge. Evidence would indicate that they do not threaten the regime seriously, but this might change if the Soviet citizens, including the party members, had continuous contact with countries and civilizations outside the iron curtain. This is why the draconically maintained isolation of the U.S.S.R. from the West is vital to the survival of the Communist regime.

ORGANIZATION

The vast network of functions which the Communist party of the Soviet Union carries out can be put into operation only through well-organized machinery. At the bottom of the ladder stand the primary party organs, formerly known as "cells." They are to be found in every factory, shop, office, school, army, etc., wherever there are at least three party members. Each primary organization elects an executive committee or "bureau" and a secretary who is in reality the chairman and most significant officer. Even at that low level, the exalted position of the Communist party is recognized by the party rules, which provide that the primary organs "have the right of control over the activity of the administration of the enterprise" (rule 58).

If the primary unit is larger, it has a party buro, but in any case its central figure and director is the party secretary. He has his hand in every activity of the unit and gives the orders. He also bears the responsibility for the unit's performance and will be severely taken to task by higher headquarters for any failings.

According to the party statute (rule 57), the responsibility of primary party units comprises agitation and propaganda among the masses, conducting and supervising the political education of party members and candidates, recruiting new members, assisting higher levels of the party, mobilizing all efforts for the fulfillment of production plans, combating negligence, showing proper regard for the improvement of cultural and living conditions of the workers and peasants, developing "criticism" and "self-criticism," and inculcating Communists "in the spirit of an uncompromising attitude toward shortcomings."

Among those functions of particular significance are the recruitment of new members, their screening, and their introduction to their party responsibilities.

As for the party's duty of supervising management, the secretary is not to interfere with the channel of command between the factory management and their technical superiors. But in actuality party secretaries frequently interfere in everything and cause confusion which sometimes meets with criticism from higher levels of command.

It is essential for party control over all enterprise that strictest efficiency and dedication to the task at hand should prevail. Personal influence and cliques are severely condemned. But there are probably few countries in the world where such influences and cliques are more important. Where there is so much power residing in certain positions, people with ambition naturally gravitate thereto. These cliques in turn have their significance in the power struggle which goes on unceasingly. Important party members surround themselves with their "people," and if they fall down, their "people" fall with them. Thus not long after the death of Andrei Zhdanov in 1948, all the Zhdanovites throughout Russia and even in other Communist parties were quickly liquidated. The same happened to the henchmen of Lavrenti Beria after he was executed. Thus to have fair longevity, a party member must not only be unquestioningly obedient, diligent, and efficient, but he must also have learned the art of sensing in good time every change in the power balance of the leadership.

The primary organs elect delegates to the city or district conference of the party. This conference elects a committee which in turn elects a "bureau" and a secretary. This form of organization is then maintained by all other, higher echelons. Above the city or district conference are the organizations for the areas, regions, territories, and Union Republics.[14] They in turn elect delegates to the All-Union Congress of the party on the basis of 1 delegate per 1,000 members. At the sixteenth party Congress there were 2,159 delegates, but at the eighteenth Congress in 1939 there were only 1,574, and at the ninteenth there were 1,359 delegates. Of course none of these elections is contested. Higher party echelons usually let it be known whose election is desired, and the person concerned is then "elected" without fail.

All Union Republics except the Russian Socialist Federated Soviet Republic (R.S.F.S.R.), the largest Republic, which comprises two-thirds of the territory of the U.S.S.R., have their own party organizations which are modeled on the national organization. But the territorial units of the R.S.F.S.R. report directly to the national party organization. The latter is divided into eight territories in the R.S.F.S.R., which in turn are divided into regions and areas. The other Union Republics have only regions and lower units. Below the areas are the city and district organizations, and at the lowest level are the

---

[14] In 1952, at the 19th Congress, the mandate commission reported the existence of 15 central committees (headed by the Central Committee of the Communist party of the Soviet Union), 8 territorial committees, 167 regional committees, 36 area committees, 544 city committees, 4,886 district committees, and 350,304 primary party organizations.

already mentioned primary organizations, whose average membership is twenty.

At the head of each level of the party hierarchy is an executive committee (buro) in which the first secretary plays the key role. In addition a representative of the All-Union Central Committee is attached to each Union Republic in order to supervise the performance of its task. Moreover, party discipline is enforced by a "party Collegium," which is responsible directly to the national party Control Committee.

Sessions of the All-Union Congress are called by the Central Committee. The party rules of 1952 provide that a Congress shall be convoked every four years, though under the rules of 1939 the interval was to be three years. However, party congresses have become most infrequent. The most recent one, the nineteenth, was held in 1952 after an interval of more than thirteen years. Actually only three congresses have been held in the last twenty years. Former party rules also provided for a party Conference to meet more frequently,[15] but the last such Conference met in 1941 and the institution was abolished by the new party statute of 1952.

In the earlier period of the Soviet regime, congresses were held frequently and saw spirited discussions, but this development ended in 1927 after Stalin had consolidated his power. Membership in the Congress increased enormously, and discussion became "organized" as indicated above. Instead of debating and ratifying party policy, the Congress heard a large number of reports which were solemnized by being read to the delegates. Beyond that the sole function of the Congress became the lending of its prestige to government policy. This process was completed at the seventeenth Congress in 1934, when Stalin remarked that "no objections whatever have been raised against the report. Hence it has been revealed that there is extraordinary ideological-political and organizational solidarity in the ranks of our Party."

The Central Committee

By far the most important organism in the Communist party is nominally the Central Committee, within which operates the real ruling force of the Soviet Union, the Presidium, formerly called Political Bureau (Politburo). "Not one important political or organizational question is decided by any one state institution in our republic without guiding instructions of the Central Committee of the Party," said Lenin,[16] and the Communist party rules provide that "the Central Committee directs the work of the central Soviet and public organizations through the Party groups in them." [17]

The Central Committee, as elected in 1952, is composed of 125 members

[15] The party Conference was abolished in 1934 but was reinstated in 1939.
[16] Towster, *op. cit.*, p. 153n.
[17] Party statute of 1952, rule 36.

and 111 candidates. They are elected by the party Congress. All the important leaders of Communism are among them. Meetings take place three or four times a year, and all significant questions are discussed. The proceedings of the Central Committee are not made public, but individual speeches and reports are often published.

For a number of years the Central Committee was the forum within which were carried out the major factional fights within the party. Trotsky called the doctrine that Bolshevism did not tolerate factionalism "a myth of the epoch of decline." [18] He wrote that the "history of Bolshevism is a history of the struggle of factions. . . . The Central Committee relied upon this seething democratic support. From this it derived the audacity to make decisions and give orders."

With the increasingly monolithic and Stalinist character of the Communist party, however, and the revelation that even the heroes of the Revolution were not safe from sudden downfall and execution, factionalism came to an end in the Central Committee.

Very little is known about its actual work. A great number of orders are published as emanating from it, but in view of its infrequent meetings they must come from the Presidium or the Secretariat. All indications point to the correctness of the assumption that the Central Committee has little real significance and that its theoretically enormous powers are wielded, often in its name, by the Presidium of the Central Committee, which was known before 1952 as the Politburo.

THE PRESIDIUM OF THE CENTRAL COMMITTEE

There is a good reason for the decline of the Central Committee. The principle of centralism places a tremendous amount of responsibility and work on the shoulders of those on top. This means a large number of daily decisions on a great variety of subjects. A body like the Central Committee which meets in plenary session only three to four times a year is, of course, quite unable to carry such a load. The overwhelming majority of decisions are therefore made by a smaller, permanent committee of the Central Committee, the Presidium. In the course of years the Central Committee has thus become primarily an organ of ratification for decisions of the Politburo, now called Presidium. When the Central Committee opens its mouth, it is the voice of the Presidium which comes out.

In the entire history of the Soviet Union it has always been this small committee which wielded the decisive power in the state. Under the name of Political Bureau, but better known by its abbreviation as Politburo, it was already established in 1917. The eighth Congress of the Communist party in

[18] L. Trotsky, *The Revolution Betrayed* (trans. by M. Eastman), New York, 1937, p. 95.

1919 established the system which was to last, essentially, until 1952. It placed supreme direction in the Politburo, and organizational work in the Organizational Bureau, better known as Orgburo. The functions of the Secretariat were not clearly defined at that time. It was only through Stalin's use of the Secretariat as a vehicle for his own road to power that it became all-important. In fact, until 1941 Stalin held no official post other than that of General Secretary of the Communist party and member of the Politburo. It was largely due to war exigencies that he assumed officially the post of Premier, whose actual title was Chairman of the Council of People's Commissars, later Council of Ministers.

As early as 1925 Stalin characterized the enormous power of the Politburo as follows: "The Politburo is the highest organ not of the State but of the Party and the Party is the highest directing force of the State." [19]

The nineteenth Congress of the Communist party of the Soviet Union brought certain changes. Both Politburo and Orgburo were abolished. In their stead was created the Presidium of the Central Committee. As elected in October, 1952, it contained twenty-three members, twelve more than the former Politburo, and eleven alternates.

But within twenty-four hours after Stalin's death on March 5, 1953, as already explained, further and abrupt changes were made. The Presidium was reduced to ten members, one less than the number which had comprised the Politburo. Eight of the ten members had also been in the Politburo. Apart from Stalin, Andreyev and Kosygin were dropped, and their places were taken by Saburov and Peruvkhin.

Before the nineteenth Congress of the Communist party in 1952, the party's Secretariat was headed by Stalin as General Secretary assisted by four others, Malenkov, Khrushchev, Suslov, and Ponomarenko. The nineteenth Congress added five new members. After Stalin's death the Secretariat was again reduced to five. Malenkov gave up his post on it and became Chairman of the Presidium as well as Chairman of the Council of Ministers (Premier). Nikita Khrushchev became first secretary, assisted by Suslov, Pespelov, Shatalin, and Ignatiev. Less than a month later, however, Ignatiev was publicly denounced and removed.

Then on July 9, 1953, came the news of Lavrenti Beria's arrest, which reduced the Presidium membership to nine. Beria's place as Minister of the Interior and chief of the secret police was taken by Sergei Kruglov, who is neither a member of the party Presidium nor of membership stature. [20]

At that time, the Presidium was composed of the following persons: Malenkov (Chairman), Khrushchev, Molotov, Voroshilov, Bulganin, Kaganovich, Mikoyan, Saburov, and Peruvkhin. Alternates were Shvernik, Ponomarenko,

---

[19] To the 14th Congress of the Communist party, 1925. Towster, *op. cit.*, p. 160*n*.

[20] Beria became a candidate member of the Politburo one year after his appointment to head the secret police.

and Melnikov. To what extent this line-up changed when Malenkov fell was not announced.

Very little was known about the precise relationship between these men and their relative power or channel of command.[21]

The fall of Malenkov in 1955 brought an end to the period of collective leadership and underlined the position of Khrushchev as top man, at least for the moment. It also underlined the lesson of history that dictatorships find collective leadership most difficult. Another event was equally noteworthy. When Khrushchev proposed the election of Bulganin as chief of government, he declared that the nomination had been decided upon by "the Central Committee and the Council of Elders." That the Presidium was not mentioned as such is not necessarily surprising for it often speaks in the name of the Central Committee. But nobody had ever heard of the "Council of Elders." Was this an "inner cabinet" of the Presidium? Or was it an ad hoc creation of Khrushchev to mask a personal decision? Only time can tell—and it might not.

The Presidium and its predecessor, the Politburo, have always been especially interested in foreign affairs, but Vyacheslav Molotov is the only Foreign Minister who has ever been a member of both; neither Chicherin, Litvinov, nor Vyshinsky were Politburo members. It is even more interesting that not a single professional military man has risen to Politburo-Presidium rank except Marshal Klementi Voroshilov, and he must be classed with the politicians rather than with the generals for he owes his rise to political and not to military achievements. The other marshal on the Presidium, Nikolai Bulganin, is also a political general—even more so than Voroshilov. He distinguished himself as Chairman of the Moscow Soviet during the war and was promoted to a general's rank direct from civilian status. None of the real military leaders of the country has been so elevated, neither Marshal Zhukov, nor Marshals Koniev, Timoshenko, or others.

In order to carry out its vast functions the Presidium, like the Politburo, has a series of well-staffed functional departments which keep its members informed on all developments.[22] This staff is something more than a cabinet secretariat and something less than a supergovernment. It is, as Professor Nemzer points out, only one of the agencies which service the men in command. But it concentrates and channelizes the flow of information on which the members of the Presidium must depend in order to reach their decisions.

Such a concentration of powers is, contrary to a widespread impression, not necessarily a very efficient method. In a country in which error and failure

[21] The book by Nathan Leites, *The Operational Code of the Politburo,* New York, 1951, despite its misleading title, tells us nothing on this subject. It is merely a collection of Communist writings on political tactics and strategy.

[22] Louis Nemzer, "The Kremlin Professional Staff: The 'Apparatus' of the Central Committee, Communist Party of the Soviet Union," *The American Political Science Review,* Vol. XLIV (1950), pp. 64–85.

become treason and sabotage, subordinate levels of the administration are fearful of making decisions and are inclined to refer everything to higher head-quarters, where, as a result, a terrific jam piles up. That this is quite a prob-lem in the Soviet Union is attested by frequent critical remarks in the Soviet press. At the same time there is also an inclination on the part of lower levels and agents abroad to report what corresponds to the official bias rather than objective facts. The desire to please rather than to send unvarnished reports clearly enters into the picture.

THE SECRETARIAT

Even when the Orgburo still existed, it had lost some of its functions to the Secretariat, which had become the real director of party activities. The first secretariat of the Communist party was a small office with an essentially technical and service character. That it developed into something quite dif-ferent is due solely to the personality of Joseph Stalin, who as General Secre-tary transformed it completely. Because many problems concerned both the Politburo and the Orgburo, it was decided at an early period that the General Secretary should be a member of both groups and thus serve as a coordinator. In that and in every other function he was supposed to be solely the executor of the will of the Central Committee and of the Politburo and Orgburo.

Stalin became General Secretary in 1922. He came to this office with a rich experience in organizational matters and a considerable study of nationality problems.[23] His position gave him an exceptional opportunity to be in contact with every branch of party activities, and as the coordinator of Politburo and Orgburo he became the vital center of party and state activities.

As the Secretariat was thus gradually transformed from an executor to an executive, considerable resistance appeared, and Zinoviev submitted plans which would have reduced the Secretariat's status. Stalin was able to thwart this, and when the opposition tried it in 1925 its plans were frustrated.

Today the Secretariat is headed by Nikita Khrushchev as First Secretary and it may or may not have the pivotal significance which it had during Stalin's rise to power. At any rate, it is the gearbox through which all activities of the vast party machine are coordinated and directed.

THE COMMITTEE OF PARTY CONTROL

This is a committee ostensibly elected by the Central Committee, with the chief function of watching over the strict "observance of Party discipline by Party members and candidates, calling to account Communists guilty of vio-lating the program and statute of the Party, Party and State discipline, and

[23] Stalin, *Marxism and the National Question,* New York, 1942 (first published in 1913).

also violators of Party morality (deception of the Party, dishonesty and insincerity before the Party, slander, bureaucratism, dissoluteness in personal life, etc.)." [24]

The Committee of Party Control works with all the security agencies of the government, especially with the secret police. However, the 1952 party rules give it the right and duty to have its own authorized representatives in all Republics, Regions, and Territories. These representatives are independent of all local party organs and responsible only to the Committee of Party Control. That such an organ with such extensive powers is deemed necessary despite the existence of the ordinary organs of state security, above all the secret police, is evidence that the cross-checking and one-watch-the-other attitude which characterizes dictatorships is far from unknown in Russia. The old proverb, "Who watches the watchers?" holds particularly true in a dictatorship.

The Central Auditing Commission is far less important. Its members are formally elected by the party Congress and it is their function to verify the party accounts.

YOUTH ORGANIZATIONS

In addition to the regular cadres of the Communist party, there are certain auxiliaries, among which the youth organizations are by far the most significant. Closest to the party is the All-Union Leninist Communist League of Youth, known by its Russian abbreviation as *Comsomol*, and officially termed "the assistant of the Communist Party of the Soviet Union (Bolsheviks) and its reserve." It is the great organization which connects the youth of the country with the Communist party. Closely patterned on the party, it is nevertheless a mass organization numbering in the neighborhood of 16,000,000 members according to presently available sources. The regime knows well that its future depends on the support of the youth, the coming generation, and much care is spent thereon.[25]

The Communist youths are organized according to age into three groups, Comsomols (fourteen to twenty-six), Pioneers (nine to sixteen), and Little Octobrists (seven to eleven). The aim of the Comsomols and the other youth organizations is both political and nonpolitical. The indoctrination of youth with Marxist ideas and the firm establishment of Bolshevik and Stalinist loyalties are among their foremost goals. The Comsomols also undertake to root out all vestiges of religious feelings.

In order to create an *esprit de corps*, a number of specific tasks were given

[24] Party statute of 1952, rule 35a.
[25] Revealing chapters from Soviet schoolbooks were published by G. S. Counts and N. P. Lodge under the title *I Want To Be Like Stalin,* New York, 1947.

the Comsomols, by command of the party. In the early years of the regime they mobilized thousands of men for war. Later they sent thousands of members to distant places in order to establish factories, railroads, etc., and to help rebuild the shattered economy.

Special emphasis was placed on the role of the Comsomols to give the Soviet Union a new generation of scientists and specialists, and they played a crucial role in the collectivization program. With the advent of war, a great deal of stress was placed on the necessary increase in military strength. The Comsomols took a special interest in the air force, sending many members into its ranks and performing a number of services for it. In return the armed forces furnished instructors for paramilitary training. The Comsomol organization is thus an important conveyer belt for the party, which it furnishes with young activists; it also spearheads those drives which the party considers especially important.

The Pioneers and the Little Octobrists naturally have less ambitious roles to play. For many years the party and the Comsomols made it difficult for sons and daughters of the former *bourgeoisie* and the intelligentsia to join, but the Pioneers always kept their ranks open. The principal task of the Pioneers is education. They are supposed to inculcate their members with a "socialist attitude toward study, labor, and communal activities," [26] and they are supposed to emulate the Comsomols in every respect.

The Little Octobrists engage in constructive supervised play and on occasion help the Pioneers in certain campaigns and work for which they are fitted. Even at that early age military skills are stressed, as are clean and wholesome living habits which will make the young Communist a model to his environment.

All the youth organizations are closely integrated. The Little Octobrists are organized in "links" of five members, each link being led by a Pioneer. Five links are attached to a Pioneer brigade. The Pioneers are also organized in links of ten members each and four links form a brigade. Each brigade is attached to a Comsomol cell and is led by a member of that cell.

The organization of the Comsomols is patterned on the party. Comsomols form cells in factories, shops, offices, schools, etc., which report to district or city committees and from there higher up to provincial and republic committees. A Union Conference is supposed to be held every two years to elect a central committee. Cooperation between party and Comsomols is intimate, and through them the entire youth movement is closely integrated with the party structure.

As in the party, the backbone of the Comsomol organization is the secretaries, who are nominally elected but in actuality are designated by higher

[26] John N. Hazard, "The Socialist State: The Soviet Union and Its Orbit," in F. M. Marx (ed.), *Foreign Governments,* New York, 1949, p. 433.

headquarters. This is confirmed by the fact that almost all Comsomol secretaries are Communist-party members.

The Communist rulers of the Soviet Union obviously lay great stress on the education of youth for the formation of the future cadres of the Soviet regime. For that reason the activities of youth organizations, especially of the Comsomols, concentrate on political indoctrination, military and paramilitary training, and leadership in carrying out the orders and directives of the party. School and youth-organization activities are intimately connected. No subject of instruction is without some political significance. Even the examples in elementary instruction in mathematics carry political symbols. Comsomol members must further instruct the Young Pioneers under their care and serve as models and examples for them in every way. To further these objectives there is also an extensive press especially written for and by these youth groups, among which *Komsomolskaya Pravda* is the best known.

How effective is this system? Many people in the West are inclined to believe that such complete indoctrination is bound to make totally devoted and obedient robots out of the entire Soviet youth. There are many indications, however, that this pessimistic view is greatly exaggerated. In the first place every teacher knows that the degree to which he can influence his students is, after all, limited. Moreover a study of the effects of Nazi indoctrination on the Hitler Youth—a very comparable situation—reveals that excessive indoctrination often leads to a reaction of being overfed with propaganda, and after the young people have seen the contrast between propaganda and reality, to disillusionment.

It is true that these parallels must be drawn with caution as far as the Soviet Union is concerned. The Communists have been in power much longer than the Nazis were, and the geographic situation of Russia has permitted them to isolate their people more effectively than would have been possible in Central or Western Europe. Nevertheless there is impressive testimony to a spirit among Soviet youth which is not totally satisfactory from the standpoint of the Soviet leaders.[27] It has been stated on good authority that children are often bored with their daily dose of propaganda rather than infatuated with it. Those who become inspired at first often become disillusioned at the first contact with reality.[28]

Perhaps the most telling proof of this is the fact that nearly four million Soviet soldiers surrendered to the Germans in the first half year of the war or were easily captured. Of those, many thousands volunteered for service against the Soviet Union. Only when German terrorism began the wholesale

[27] 83d Congress, 1st Session, Senate Document No. 69, *Tensions within the Soviet Union,* July 28, 1953, pp. 10–16.
[28] Merle Fainsod, "Controls and Tensions within the Soviet System," *American Political Science Review,* Vol. XLIV (1950), pp. 275*f.*

slaughter of Russians and the Nazi doctrine of racial superiority was applied in the East did this widespread source of collaboration cease.[29] Other, more recent, indications may be found in numerous complains in the Soviet press and in official speeches about the attitude of youth and the supposedly still strong bourgeois influence in their midst.

The Comsomol is a selective organization, but it is not nearly so selective as the Communist party. During the war, membership in the Comsomols rose to fifteen million, but by 1949 this was down to somewhat more than nine million. This decline was not the result of purges but of nonpayment of dues, nonattendance at meetings, and other evidence of a lack of interest. An intensive campaign waged after the eleventh Congress of the Comsomols in 1949 brought the figure to the presently enrolled sixteen million, but the initial postwar loss remains significant.

It would be foolhardy and unsupported by evidence to regard the Soviet youth as a hotbed of rebellion against Communism. But neither is it that mass of automatons, that "lost" generation which some see. Undoubtedly there are many fanatics in the Communist youth organizations, but the majority join because the Comsomols in particular are a road to the party and hence the almost exclusive avenue to a higher career.

Labor Unions

There was a dispute between Lenin and Trotsky concerning the place of labor unions in the Communist state. Trotsky wanted to integrate them with the organization of the state, while Lenin wanted to keep them separate. During the NEP, when a limited amount of free enterprise was permitted, the unions performed the traditional functions of collective bargaining and general maintenance of the workers' interests. But when that phase was over the role of labor unions had to be redefined. Tomski, the leader of the union movement, advocated continued independence and opposed the idea that labor unions should press the workers for higher production. He was removed and eventually committed suicide during the "purge."

Under a planned socialist economy the setting of wages could no longer be left to the tug of war of collective bargaining but had to be fixed by the state

[29] It has been one of the great tragedies of the war that the Western Allies apparently never realized the depth of this movement and that these Russians acted primarily for reasons of anti-Communist rather than pro-Nazi sentiments. After the war and even as late as 1947 these Russians were handed over to the Soviet authorities, who liquidated them by mass execution and deportation. See George Fischer, *Soviet Opposition to Stalin*, Cambridge, Mass., 1952. He sees the explanation for so much collaboration with the Germans primarily in an inertness of the Russian masses, which according to him made them prone to go with the master of the hour. This interpretation of this otherwise very valuable book is open to considerable dispute.

planners in accordance with the national economy. Higher wages could come only from higher production, and that became the principal goal of the labor unions, which joined forces with the state agencies for that purpose. A leading Soviet book on labor law explains: "The amount of wages and salaries is at the present time fixed by the decisions of the Government (or on the basis of its directives) by means of governmental planned regulation of wages and salaries for separate groups and categories of workers." The author continues that wage fixing is done by negotiation between the labor unions and management only where the regulations provide for a span rather than a precise sum.[30]

Stalin defined the role of labor in these words: "(a) the fight—by means of self-criticism—against bureaucracy, which shackles the labor initiative and labor activities of the masses; (b) the fight—by means of socialist emulation —against the labor shirkers and disrupters of proletarian labor discipline; and finally (c) the fight—by introduction of the uninterrupted week—against routine and inertia in industry." [31]

Labor unions in the Soviet Union are organized industry-wide rather than on the craft principle. The Soviet unions number over thirty million members and in this they are the largest in the world. Their organization follows the well-known principle of "democratic centralism," which means here as in all other respects that all orders emerge from the top. Basic units of the labor unions exist in every factory and elect, at least nominally, their executive committees. In larger factories, shop committees are organized to handle different tasks. There are also "norms and conflicts commissions," but their jurisdiction is limited by the provisions of the law and actually does not extend much beyond the interpretation and application of the law. As to the effectiveness of this grievance machinery, there seems to be a difference of opinion.[32]

Factory unions elect delegates to city and district conferences. They in turn elect delegates to higher level congresses. The pattern of labor-union organization follows closely the pattern of the party organization, and the former is completely dominated by the latter. This is made clear by the by-laws of the labor unions of the U.S.S.R., which state: "Soviet labor unions conduct all their work under the direction of the Communist Party—the organizing and directing force of socialist society. The trade unions of the U.S.S.R. rally the working masses around the party of Lenin and Stalin." [33]

In reality then the Soviet labor unions do not represent the workers, but

---

[30] I. T. Gelyakov (ed.), *Zakonodatel 'stvo o trude,* Moscow, 1947, p. 65, quoted in *Tensions within the Soviet Union,* p. 67n.

[31] Stalin, *Leninism,* p. 135.

[32] Fainsod, *How Russia Is Ruled,* pp. 435f.

[33] *Trud,* May 11, 1949, quoted in *Tensions within the Soviet Union,* p. 67n.

the state and the party. Their task is not the improvement of the worker's lot but the improvement of the worker's labor and the increase of production. In addition they serve as one of the several "mass organizations" which the regime uses from time to time in order to mobilize the people for a given task.

The labor unions function in a number of fields. The wage commission has nothing to do with wages but rather the institution of piecework rates in factories—a practice against which the free labor unions of the world have waged an unceasing battle since the latter part of the nineteenth century. Other commissions look after the observance of safety rules, the most rational use of supplies and labor, cultural enterprise, and housing. In the housing field the commissions have, however, little influence and no funds. The grievance machinery under the norms and conflicts commissions has already been mentioned. Most important of all is, however, the administration of the social-security system. But even that is used for speed-up purposes since it grants markedly higher benefits to labor-union members, people who stay long on their jobs, and Stakhanovites.

If the labor unions do not succeed in increasing the individual performance of the workers, the extremely harsh penalties of the Soviet labor law will. Workers are subjected to extremely severe penalties for absenteeism, for giving up work without permission, and even for laziness.[34] Fines of 25 per cent of six months' wages and six months' imprisonment are provided for absenteeism. Repeated instances of tardiness may involve imprisonment of not less than one year; leaving or changing jobs without permission may result in imprisonment up to three years. The labor law also gives the management of an enterprise the right to transfer workers anywhere in the Soviet Union without regard to their personal preferences. Being tied to the job and under the constant threat of severe penalties for even minor infractions, labor in the Union of Soviet Socialist Republics has reached the state of near serfdom.

FORCED LABOR

In view of the circumstances under which "free" labor exists, it might be said that there is no longer a great deal of difference between that and forced labor. Actually, however, the misery of forced labor is such that it constitutes a considerable degree of deterioration.[35]

It is true that all countries have forced labor as part of their penal systems.

---

[34] Barrington Moore, Jr., *Soviet Politics—The Dilemma of Power*, Cambridge, Mass., 1950, pp. 257*f*.; Vladimir Gsovski, "Elements of Soviet Labor Law," *Monthly Labor Review*, Mar., 1951, p. 258.

[35] In interviews with numerous German prisoners of war (not Germans condemned to forced labor in Russia) lately returned from the U.S.S.R., the author was told repeatedly that there was no great difference between the treatment and food given to prisoners of war and those given to Russian "free" labor.

But in most countries prisoners under sentence of forced (or hard) labor comprise an infinitesimal proportion of the population and are only hardened, common criminals. It remained for the Nazi regime, and to an even larger extent to the Soviet Union, to make an industry thereof. Estimates vary greatly and range somewhere between ten and twenty million men and women engaged in forced labor in the Soviet Union. One of the most careful and reliable studies has stated that the total ranged, in different periods, from seven to twelve million.[36]

Forced labor is not merely a penal measure in the U.S.S.R.; it is also a huge industry which has become so big that the original Commissariat (Ministry) for Internal Affairs (NKVD) had to be split into two organizations: the Ministry for Internal Affairs (MVD) in charge of the administration of forced labor, and the Ministry of State Security (MGB). After Stalin's death they were reunited under the title MVD and again separated in 1955.

The extent of these operations has become clearer from a remarkable document, dated 1941, which eventually came into Western hands.[37] It shows that percentages ranging from 12 to 40 per cent of a large number of construction and industrial projects were to be supplied from forced labor contributed by the NKVD. It has been estimated that an over-all average of 17 per cent of the labor engaged on construction projects in 1941 was to be supplied by the NKVD, *i.e.*, by forced labor.[38] According to this there would have been, very conservatively estimated, three and a half million prisoners in camps under direct NKVD administration and supplied to these projects. This figure does not include other types of prisoners: those held in ordinary prisons, those contracted out to other enterprises, etc. An accurate estimate of forced labor is made difficult not only by the paucity of available information but also by the different categories of such labor, ranging from prisoners in concentration camps to workers compelled to remain at their previous jobs at sharply reduced wages as a penalty for the infraction of labor discipline. The last-mentioned category is already close to "free" labor, and the figure of forced labor will depend partly on the groups included in that term.[39]

[36] David J. Dallin and Boris I. Nicolaevsky, *Forced Labor in the Soviet Union*, New Haven, 1947, p. 86.

[37] Department of State, *Forced Labor in the Soviet Union*, Washington, 1952, p. iv.

[38] Naum Jasny, "Labor and Output in Soviet Concentration Camps," *Journal of Political Economy*, Vol. 59 (1951), pp. 409*f*. For a summary see Fainsod, *op. cit.*, pp. 385*f.*, and *Tensions within the Soviet Union*, p. 80.

[39] Authoritative and richly documented accounts of forced labor and concentration camps in the Soviet Union are now available in considerable quantity. Apart from Dallin and Nicolaevsky, *op. cit.*, see American Federation of Labor, *Slave Labor in Russia*, New York, 1949; Elinor Lipper (a Dutch Communist), *11 Years in Soviet Prison Camps*, Chicago, 1951; Jerzy Gliksman, *Tell the West*, New York, 1948. Many former inmates of Soviet concentration camps also testified in the suit of Victor Kravchenko against the French Communist weekly, *Les Lettres Françaises*, in Paris, 1949.

COLLECTIVE FARMS AND PARTY LEADERSHIP

The first step toward the mass organization of the peasants was the co-operatives, which reached many millions of families. But the older form of consumers' and producers' cooperatives has been superseded among the peasantry by the collective farms, the *kolkhozi*. The kolkhoz is more than a cooperative; it is an entire way of life, embracing every facet of peasant existence. Kolkhoz members pool all their resources, and only very little is left to personal ownership. Through the Machine Tractor Stations (MTS) the state contributes mechanized equipment and exercises control. Theoretically the kolkhoz is self-governing, but that self-government has become increasingly theoretical since the thirties.[40] Unlike the unions, the kolkhozi have no regional or national organization, but each one maintains direct relations with the village Soviet in its area. Through it, the agricultural departments of the state administration exercise direct control over the kolkhoz administrations, whose acts and decisions they may set aside at any time.

Through the tight organization of the kolkhoz, and since the abolition of the older mir, party and state are in a position to reach every peasant and to mobilize him for such purposes as may be necessary. It is also through the kolkhoz organization that the ideological indoctrination of the peasants is accomplished. In this work party members and especially trained Comsomol members are in the forefront, since they fill many posts of kolkhoz chairmen.

Originally it was thought that the state farm, the sovkhoz, was the ideal form of agricultural enterprise from the Communist standpoint. But the performance of the sovkhoz left much to be desired. The peasants shied away from them and the personnel of the state farms were usually of inferior quality and found more land assigned to them than they could handle. Much equipment was mishandled or worn out in the process, and in 1934 Stalin openly acknowledged the failure of the system. Since that time state farms have occupied a relatively small sector of the agricultural economy.

The question of the size of agricultural enterprises is not merely an economic and administrative question in the Soviet Union; to a very considerable extent it is also a political one. Although the great majority of the population is rural, it plays a disproportionately small role in the Communist party and has offered the greatest resistance to communization. In 1947, the last year for which figures are available, only 27 per cent of the total party membership was rural. Actually this figure is probably too large because it includes a considerable number of administrators who are not peasants.[41] Moreover, Com-

[40] See Gregory Bienstock *et al.*, *Management in Russian Industry and Agriculture*, New York, 1944.

[41] Fainsod, *op. cit.*, p. 233.

munist leaders had frequent occasion to complain that there were many collective farms without party organizations in them.

There are a number of factors which contribute to this situation. From the very beginning the Communists have waged a ceaseless war against the peasants, which culminated in the forced collectivization of the thirties and cost approximately five million peasants their lives. Then there were the numerous forays to "liquidate the kulaks as a class," which resulted in mass confiscation and mass deportation, for kulaks were not large landowners—who had long since disappeared—but small holders who had as many as three horses and employed fifty days of labor per year.[42]

From a Communist viewpoint the hostility of the peasants is understandable. In all countries of the world farming is not merely a way to earn a living but a way of life. Farmers and peasants are essentially conservative and have an owner's mentality. To own the land they till is their ambition. In other words, peasants have a capitalistic outlook. Unless their bourgeois inclinations are held under control they may become a menace to the entire system. Just how much they resent collectivization even after so many years of its application was demonstrated during the war when the peasants in the areas occupied by the Germans immediately went about dividing up their collective farms but were prevented by the Nazi administrators who wished to retain the collective farms in order to ensure an uninterrupted food supply. Nevertheless the peasants were able to increase their private garden plots and after the war had to be curbed again.

The stubborn persistence of peasant resentment forced the Communist leadership to reconsider its methods. It came to the conclusion that in view of the sparsity of party organizations on the collectives, the latter themselves would have to be consolidated in order to produce tighter control and to make the available supply of Communist-party manpower cover more ground. Before the war the official line was that work in small groups (*zveno*) of about twenty people to cultivate a given plot was most effective. Politburo member Andrei Andreyev was particularly identified with that system. But in 1950 it was condemned, Andreyev got the axe, at least for the time being, and emphasis was now placed on the much larger brigade. A campaign for the consolidation of collective farms was undertaken in the same year under the leadership of Nikita Khrushchev, Andreyev's successor as the chief agricultural specialist of the Politburo. In October, 1952, Georgi Malenkov reported to the nineteenth Congress of the Communist party of the Soviet Union that the number of collective farms had been reduced from 254,000 to 97,000. Much of that consolidation remained, however, on paper.

While the consolidation campaign was in full swing, Khrushchev proposed

[42] M. K. Bennett, "Food and Agriculture in the Soviet Union, 1947–48," *Journal of Political Economy,* Vol. LVII (1949), pp. 194*f.*

an even more ambitious scheme. He advocated the creation of large agricultural settlements—so-called "agro-cities"—around which the collective farms were to stretch. Private plots were to be diminished and tilled in common. The aim of this plan was clear. It was to transform the peasants into a vast proletariat without the vestige of any independent production. The creation of agro-cities, even more than the consolidation of collective farms, would create an administrative bureaucracy and make possible the organization of strong party units. However, this scheme was soon repudiated and officially condemned. In his speech to the nineteenth Congress, Malenkov strongly criticized it by reminding his listeners that the primary task was the increase of production.

Although Khrushchev's plan of agro-cities was repudiated that time, it does indicate the direction in which Communist thinking goes. Malenkov condemned the scheme because it would have raised havoc with agricultural output, but he did not regard it as permanently or intrinsically bad. That such a plan was proposed in the first place shows the concern of the Russian leaders over the relative weakness of party work and party control in the rural areas. In view of the present preeminence of Nikita Khrushchev, it is not impossible that this fantastic scheme might some day be resurrected.

THE SOVIET ARMY AND THE COMMUNIST PARTY

The control and political loyalty of the armed forces have been matters of primary consideration for the Soviet leaders from the very beginning of the regime. In this they were aided by the fact that the tsarist army went to pieces and that an entirely new instrument had to be forged by the Bolsheviks. It was clear that if the army were to stand aloof from the regime, and show an "unpolitical" or even hostile attitude to it, the very existence of the regime would be in danger. Apart from the general tendency of the regime to permeate all institutions with its spirit, it was of particular importance to do so in the army. As a result the political control and the political education of the soldiers were vested in a system of commissars who, together with the military commanders, bore co-responsibility for their respective units. At the same time care was taken that as many officers and men as possible should be party members and that promotions should be open as far as possible only to party members or to Comsomols.

As the dark clouds of coming war began to form on the horizon, it became necessary to increase the efficiency of the Red Army. Military discipline was heightened, and the social and economic contrast between officers and enlisted men was increased beyond what is customary in the so-called "capitalistic" armies in order to increase the men's desire for promotion.

The institution of the commissars saw its ups and downs. After the great army purge in 1937, which culminated in the execution of Marshal M. N. Tukhachevski and the suicide of Assistant People's Commissar for War, Jan Gamarnik, party control was tightened. Political commissars were made co-equal with the respective commanding officers. But this system worked very badly in the Finnish war and contributed to a great deal of confusion. Hence the commissars were abolished in 1940 and replaced by Assistant Commanders for Political Affairs (*zampolits*). The surrender *en masse* of Red soldiers and officers in the first few months after Russia's invasion by the German army was a danger signal to the party leadership, and it responded by the reinstitution of the commissar system shortly afterward. But when the situation again became consolidated and the large-scale defections ceased, there was again a return to the *zampolits* in October, 1942.

It is noteworthy that the party regards political control of the army as so important that it takes direct responsibility for this task. The army is honey-combed with a system of primary party and Comsomol organizations which are supervised, directed, and advised by the Main Political Administration (MPA). It is interesting to note that the MPA is a department in the U.S.S.R. Ministry of Defense *but at the same time* is also the military department of the Central Committee of the Communist party, or in reality of its Presidium.[43] MPA representatives are attached to every level of command. From the army corps down they work through the *zampolits* and on the company level through the chief party worker, the *politruk*. These different levels of party officers work not only on the improvement of the political education and loyalty of officers and soldiers, but also report periodically to their political superiors on such questions as army morale, the personal reliability of certain officers, the effectiveness of the work of the *zampolits*, etc. In addition the *zampolits* control the clubs and recreation facilities for the soldiers and thus have an opportunity to be doubly effectve. In addition to the party organizations, the primary Comsomol groups in the army reinforce the party's work. These are also under the control of the MPA.

The MPA, the *zampolits*, and *politruks*, as well as the party and Comsomol organizations in the army, may be called the positive instruments of party control. The negative instruments are in the special security organization of the Ministry of Internal Affairs, the MVD. The latter maintains its own chain of command within the army. All levels of command down to the battalion have their attached special sections of MVD men who are in charge of all aspects of security. Files are maintained on every soldier and officer, mail is spot-checked, and denunciations are encouraged.[44] This seems to be the institution most resented, especially by the officers; at any rate that is the

[43] Nemzer, *op. cit.*, pp. 78*f.*
[44] Fainsod, *op. cit.*, p. 415.

story of every officer-escapee from the Soviet Army [45] who has reached sanctuary in the West.[46]

In this system of tensions produced by the party machinery on one side and the MVD on the other, a third factor enters. The soldier, and especially the officer, knows that the road to promotion and thus to a very considerable improvement of both his personal comfort and his social standing goes through the party. Not only will he have to aspire to party or at least to Comsomol membership—and thus submit to further checks and controls—but he must have a good record with his *zampolits* and a clean slate with the MVD. Out of this interlocking system of positive and negative controls, of threats and inducements, it is hard to imagine that the army could emerge as an independent force against the party. Only in an intra-party quarrel could the army lend weight to one side, but even that is not easy to envisage because it presupposes the army as a unit defining its own political line, whereas the above-mentioned system makes that virtually impossible.

Lest the army become a popular symbol for something opposed to the political leadership, the party has consistently played down the famous contemporary military leaders of the country. Marshal Georgi Zhukov was soon after the war shifted to a relatively secondary command. After Stalin's death he became Deputy Minister of Defense under Bulganin. Then Bulganin became head of the government, Zhukov became Minister of Defense, which to many observers indicated the growing importance of the army. But, on the other hand, it is noteworthy that not a single professional soldier has ever been a member of either the Politburo or the Presidium of the Central Committee. It might also be noted in passing that in modern Russian history the army has never played an important political role and has no tradition of so doing. While the army is therefore full of tensions as the result of the tight network of political and security controls which permeate it, there is little to suggest that it could emerge as an alternative or a threat to the present Communist leadership of the country.

THE COMMUNIST PARTY AND RELIGION

The most important religious denomination in the Soviet Union is the Russian Orthodox Church. Complete separation of state and church is ordained (Art. 124). There is also guaranteed "freedom of religious worship and freedom of antireligious propaganda," but persumably not freedom for religious propaganda. The basic attitude of the Soviet government and the Communist party has been dominated by the famous Marxian assertion that "religion is opium for the people." In the earlier periods of the Soviet regime,

---

[45] The Red Army is now officially renamed Soviet Army.

[46] *The Soviet Union as Reported by Former Soviet Citizens,* Department of State, Report No. 3, May 15, 1952, p. 2.

this principle was vigorously pursued. Feelings were mutual, and Patriarch Tikhon in his message to the Orthodox Church on January 18, 1918, warned all believers "not to enter into any kind of association with these monsters of the human race." [47]

The government suppressed the church vigorously; churches were burned or transformed into club homes for the Society of the Godless, altars and icons were desecrated, and other items of worship were carted away. Then followed a relatively quiet period during which the church was pretty much left alone within the confines of the narrow restrictions placed upon it. But the Second World War brought about a spectacular change. The war was fought as a great patriotic adventure, not as a struggle of the Communist party. The church proved itself loyal to the regime, and the sight of masses of worshippers who thronged the cathedrals convinced the government that it had in the church an instrument which could be used for the greater mobilization of the population. This ushered in a reconciliation of church and state in which the former placed itself fully at the disposal of the latter. The government in turn suspended the two principal atheist publications and in 1942 appointed the Metropolitan of Kiev and Galicia, Nicolai, as a member of the "Extraordinary State Commission for the Investigation of German War Crimes."

Since the war this relationship has continued. A new patriarch was elected by a national assembly of the Russian Orthodox Church. The church is under the administration and supervision of the State Council on Affairs of the Orthodox Church, in which the church is not represented, and which is headed by a professed atheist. In return for this relative freedom, the Orthodox Church, inasmuch as it is controlled by Moscow, has become one of the vanguards of the Communist regime, especially outside the Soviet Union.

Communist doctrine is still hostile to religion, and party members are expected not to be believers. One editorial in an official paper claimed that religion was "harmful to the Communist Party and fertilizes the soil for hostile, anti-Soviet elements." [48] At the present time the *modus vivendi* between state and Orthodox Church continues. Other churches, however, are vigorously suppressed, especially the Roman Catholic Church, which the Communists regard as their principal enemy.

If at the present time there is a degree of toleration of the Russian Orthodox Church, it must be emphasized that this toleration extends only to the church as an institution and not to its doctrine as a religion. "Dialectical materialism," wrote an official paper, "the philosophy of Marxism-Leninism and the theoretical foundation of the Communist party, is incompatible with

---

[47] Julius F. Hecker, *Religion and Communism*, New York, 1934, pp. 200*f.*; Paul B. Anderson, *People, Church and State in Modern Russia*, New York, 1944. See also interview with Gyorgy G. Karpov, Chief of the State Council, in *Christian Science Monitor*, Sept. 30, 1944.

[48] Editorial in the official organ of the Byelorussian government, reported in *The New York Times*, Sept. 28, 1948.

religion." [49] The official organ of the Comsomols, *Komsomolskaya Pravda* of October 18, 1947, had this to say: "The party cannot be neutral regarding religion and it conducts antireligious propaganda against all religious prejudices because it stands for science and religious prejudices are opposed to science since any religion is contrary to science." [50]

Although the leadership of the Russian Orthodox Church in the Soviet Union has furthered the Communist objectives in every way and has been particularly active in espousing the Communist "peace" propaganda line, the party has few kind words for it. In a widely distributed official Soviet propaganda pamphlet, the author, P. F. Kolonitsky, writes as follows:

> It is true that, complying with the will of the Soviet churchgoers and also with their duty as citizens, the clergymen of the Orthodox Church stand for the cause of peace. . . . But religion remains religion. . . . Religion itself was and is a reactionary ideology. In that they preach faith in God, the clergy does harm, implants ignorance in believers' minds and, consciously or unconsciously, opposes the cause of the struggle for communism. . . . Therefore, an indivisible part of the communist education of the working people is the exposure and rout of the religious ethic.[51]

All this adds up to the following situation. For the public at large the Russian Orthodox Church is tolerated although religion is discouraged whenever possible. But even the slightest demonstration of religious sentiment on the part of party members is severely criticized and the official party line is that religious belief and party membership are incompatible. Even so slight an act as a local Comsomol secretary's participation in a wedding ceremony in which an icon was held over the bride's head aroused the ire of *Komsomolskaya Pravda*, which condemned the attitude that religion was a private affair. Not so, says that paper. "For the Young Communist League member, just as for the Communist, the attitude to religion can in no way be a 'personal matter,' since religious conceptions are foreign to our communist outlook." [52]

Since all roads to a significant career and promotion lead through membership in the Communist party or at least in the Comsomols, religion is effectively cut off from the more important parts of the Soviet population. It is nevertheless remarkable that so many people are still stubbornly clinging to

[49] *Molodoi Bolshevik,* Nos. 5–6, 1946, p. 58, quoted in *Tensions within the Soviet Union,* p. 33.

[50] *Ibid.*

[51] P. F. Kolonitsky, *Moral Kommunisticheskaya i Moral Religionznaya* (Communist Ethic and Religious Ethic), Moscow, 1952, translated in excerpts in *Current Digest of the Soviet Press,* Vol. IV, Aug. 23, 1952, pp. 5*f.*

[52] *Komsomolskaya Pravda,* Apr. 25, 1951, in *Current Digest of the Soviet Press,* Vol. III, June 2, 1951, p. 8.

their beliefs and that religion is not entirely expunged from the hearts of the young, although few young people can be seen in Russian churches.[53]

Although other religious groups are far less numerous, the Soviet attitude toward them is the same, particularly in the case of the considerable Moslem population, in which the party has run into repeated difficulties which in some respects have been greater than those with the Orthodox Church.

The special ire of the party is reserved for the Roman Catholic Church, not only because of its frankly anti-Communist attitude, but also because its center lies outside the Soviet Union and thus cannot be controlled by Moscow. Today Roman Catholic services are practically extinct in the Soviet Union. For a while foreign Catholic priests could minister to the faithful in one Moscow church; later they were forbidden to do so and were replaced by a Polish priest who had broken with the Vatican; after a while even that practice ceased.

The Roman Catholic Church, as such, never counted a large congregation in the Soviet Union. However, the cession to the U.S.S.R. of former Polish territory brought into the Soviet Union large numbers of members of the Uniate Church, which recognized the spiritual authority of Rome. Immediately after the occupation of those territories the bishops of this church were deported and never seen again. In 1946 the Uniates were forced to break with Rome and reunite with the Russian Orthodox Church, but the assassination in 1948 of Dr. Kostelnik, who was held responsible for this, is evidence of resentment.

The Method of Terror

Secret political police forces are the mark of every dictatorship. Under the tsars the notorious Ochrana became a symbol of the regime, and the rest of the civilized world looked upon it as an example of medieval barbarity. Today a far more callous world, which has experienced two world wars and the horrors of the Nazi Gestapo and concentration camps, may well look back to the Ochrana as a relatively mild form of coercion. The treatment of prisoners, while certainly not good, was usually tolerable. Trials in open court were the rule, not the exception, and the deportations to Siberia, while rigorous, were infinitely more humane than they are today. Deportees were permitted a considerable amount of freedom—which is manifested by the sizable literary output of such men. They were able to keep in touch with their families and could even receive them as visitors or have them accompany them into exile. Escape was not too difficult, as evidenced by those who succeeded. Today a man or woman arrested by the police and sent to a term of forced labor

[53] Alex Inkeles, "Family and Church in the Postwar U.S.S.R.," *Annals of the American Academy of Political and Social Science,* May, 1949, pp. 33–37.

usually disappears without a trace. His family is fortunate if it hears from him at all. Escapes are very rare.[54]

During the Revolution and civil war there was established the Extraordinary Commission to Combat Counter-revolution, Sabotage and Speculation,[55] better known by its abbreviation as the Cheka. The Cheka, sometimes called "the unsheathed punishing sword of the Revolution," had absolute power over life and death, including individual and mass executions without trial. It was renamed Political Administration of the State, abbreviated OGPU, in 1922. The powers of the OGPU were not much less extensive than those of the Cheka. Its beginnings lay in the years of the NEP, but with the institution of the first Five-Year Plan in 1928 the scope of "economic crimes" was greatly enlarged, and the functions of the OGPU enlarged too. At the same time, mounting international tension tightened the administration of internal security in the Soviet Union.

The OGPU was dissolved in 1934, presumably to curb its absolute power, and it became part of the Commissariat of Internal Affairs, NKVD. In this year also occurred the Kirov murder and the beginning of the purge. During the great purge wave of 1937–1938 the NKVD exercised as much absolute power as the Cheka and OGPU ever had. But it overreached itself, and its own leadership was purged twice. A new leadership was established under Lavrenti Beria in 1938, and after that it operated smoothly.

The absorption of new territory, the flood of more or less voluntarily returned prisoners of war and slave laborers (for the Germans), and the tense atmosphere of the "cold war" placed new tasks upon the secret political police, which eventually led, in 1947, to the re-creation of an independent police ministry, the Ministry of State Security, known as the MGB, operating in close conjunction with the Ministry of Internal Affairs, the MVD. In 1953, after Stalin's death, the two agencies were reunited under the title Ministry of Internal Affairs, MVD, only to be divided again after the removal of Beria.

When an accused is brought before a regular court in the Soviet Union, he may usually count on certain basic rights: the rights to counsel, to open trial, to a knowledge of the indictment, and to appeal. This is not always the case; especially in political trials, the defense cannot afford to be vigorous and the outcome is a foregone conclusion. Still, a certain amount of "due process" is observed. But this is not the case when the secret political police is involved. Before the Second World War we had a small number of authoritative reports on the procedure of the secret political police, and since the war, with its displacement of many Russians, the considerable desertions from the Soviet army, and the flight of former Russian diplomats, a great deal of information has come to light. There is really no longer any reason for being ignorant or

[54] One of the few who escaped was V. V. Tchernavin, a professor of ichthyology, who described his experiences in *I Speak for the Silent*, Boston, 1935.

[55] When private trading was prohibited it became "speculation," a criminal offense.

in doubt about this particular question.[56] All testimony agrees that the secret political police is in the habit of arresting people at odd hours of the night; that there are rarely trials, but incessant interrogations at which the accused is frequently pressed to "confess" sins with which he may have no connection; that he rarely has an opportunity to defend himself; and that his verdict is made known to him without opportunity for rebuttal.

Terror as a tool of the regime is not an accidental development but was part thereof from the very beginning. Lenin already said, "We have never rejected terror on principle, nor can we do so. Terror is a form of military operation that may be usefully applied, or may even be essential in certain moments of the battle, under certain conditions, and when the troops are in a certain condition."[57] And Stalin declared, "The GPU or the Cheka is a punitive organ of the Soviet government. It is more or less similar to the Committee of Public Safety which existed during the great French Revolution."[58]

Although terror has existed from the beginning of the Soviet regime, some of its aspects and directions have changed. At first, when the Cheka was created, its efforts were primarily directed against people who were really or potentially hostile to the Communist regime, members of the former privileged classes and the *bourgeoisie*, people carrying on counterrevolutionary activities, speculators, etc. Although the powers of the Cheka were virtually unchecked and large numbers of people were executed without even the pretense of a trial, the masses of the population, inasmuch as they did not belong to the "former people," were relatively unaffected, and so was the Communist party itself. But after the OGPU had replaced the Cheka and during Stalin's ascendancy, the direction of this instrument was increasingly turned inward, against certain elements within the party.

At first a calculated campaign of arrests and show trials was staged against certain classes of the intelligentsia. Engineers especially were arrested in large numbers. Even the Webbs, whose work is more than friendly to the Soviet regime, speak of a "reign of terror against the intelligentsia. Nobody regarded himself as beyond suspicion. Men and women lived in daily dread of arrest.

[56] The outstanding work on NKVD-MVD-MGB procedure as well as forced labor is the survey of evidence submitted to the United Nations by the American Federation of Labor, *Slave Labor in Russia,* New York, 1949. See also P. Pirogov, *Why I Escaped,* New York, 1950, and especially J. Gliksman, *Tell the West,* New York, 1948, a most revealing work. See also T. S. Eliot (ed.), *Dark Side of the Moon,* New York, 1947; L. Fisher, *Thirteen Who Fled,* New York, 1949; V. Kravchenko, *I Chose Freedom,* New York, 1946; R. Magidoff, *In Anger and Pity,* New York, 1949; F. Utley, *The Dream We Lost,* New York, 1940; W. L. White, *Report on the Russians,* New York, 1945; John Scott, *Behind the Urals,* New York, 1942; S. Mora, *Kolyma,* Washington, 1949; D. J. Dallin and B. Nicolaevsky, *Forced Labor in Soviet Russia,* New Haven, 1947; and Tchernavin, *op. cit.*

[57] Lenin, "Where To Begin?" *Selected Works,* Vol. II, p. 17.

[58] Stalin, "Interview with Foreign Workers' Delegations. Answer to the French Delegation, November 5, 1927," *Leninism,* Vol. I, pp. 419*f.*

Thousands were sent on administrative exile to distant parts of the country. Evidence was not necessary. The title of engineer served as sufficient condemnation." [59]

After a while this wave died down. Professor Ramzin, chief defendant in a trial against engineers and convicted as having organized a secret political party, having committed sabotage, and having been an agent of the French secret service, was released and resumed teaching.[60] A few years later another wave of arrests and trials against supposed industrial saboteurs followed.

Again there came a quieter period, which coincided with the concentration of all security functions in the People's Commissariat of Internal Affairs (NKVD). But the murder of Kirov inaugurated the great purge wave in the party itself by which Stalin rid himself of all possible opponents not only by destroying but also by discrediting them. This purge was directed primarily against certain groups in the Communist party itself, and it mounted to an ever higher crescendo terminating with the period in which N. I. Yezhov was head of the NKVD, 1937–1938. This period, generally referred to as the "Yezhovshchina," tore big holes in the party leadership, as well as in that of the NKVD itself.[61] A similar bloodletting was effected in all government departments and in the armed forces. This period closed with Yezhov's disappearance and the emergence of Lavrenti Beria as chief of the NKVD.

During and after the war the efforts of the NKVD, now renamed Ministry of Internal Affairs (MVD), were again turned toward the outside, toward the purge of whole nationalities who were accused of having collaborated with the enemy, like the Volga Germans, the Kalmucks, the Crimean Tatars, etc. Then followed the liquidation of the intelligentsia of Lithuania, Latvia, and Estonia,[62] also the scrutiny and large-scale purge of former Russian prisoners of war and German slave labor.[63] Then followed Beria's "liquidation," but it has not been followed by a general purge except that his associates were of course removed, as is customary in Russia.

The world has asked itself repeatedly the meaning of these incredible waves of terror and the peculiar direction which they take. No authoritative explanation is possible, but most observers agree with certain logical explanations which are further supported by comparisons with the similar but not quite so far-reaching activities of the Nazis. The terror itself makes the

[59] Sydney and Beatrice Webb, *op. cit.*, Vol. II, p. 553.

[60] Fainsod, *How Russia Is Ruled*, p. 364.

[61] Among those executed was Yezhov's predecessor, G. Yagoda.

[62] The massacre of 4,243 Polish officers in the forest of Katyn is now generally "credited" to the NKVD. See *The Katyn Forrest Massacre*, Final Report of the Select Committee to Conduct an Investigation and Study of the Facts, Evidence, and Circumstances of the Katyn Forrest Massacre, 82d Congress, 2d Session, House Report No. 2505, Dec. 22, 1952.

[63] Those who had joined the Vlassov army or other formations fighting with the Germans were executed.

regime infinitely more secure. It frightens potential resisters, it encourages denunciations (often one denounces to save oneself), it sows suspicion everywhere and thus makes it difficult if not impossible for a clandestine opposition movement to get organized. The inward direction of the terror, against the party and its high officers, is designed to underline the fact that nobody is safe and that no leader, however high, should think that he could build a personal machine which might challenge the supreme leadership.

The MVD-MGB has become the Praetorian guard of the Communist-party leadership. Its members receive favored treatment and rapid promotion and their unconditional obedience may be counted upon. To an increasing extent the MVD-MGB is also becoming a training school for future party leaders and an increasing number of important party leaders, among them Bulganin, have an NKVD-MGB-MVD background.

It is important to remember that this system is not a transitory phase but an obviously permanent feature of the regime. Its organization has become constantly more refined, technically more perfect, and its troops more numerous than ever before. The system which the MVD-MGB represents, that of preserving power by keeping everybody in a constant state of fear and uncertainty, demands that it be continued in perpetuity and that it be fed a never-ending stream of new sacrificial lambs. In this the MVD-MGB remains the permanent symbol of the Communist regime.

THE PARTY AND THE BUREAUCRACY

Large and indeed growing bureaucracies are characteristic of all modern states, but this trend is greatly accentuated in totalitarian countries, where hardly any human activity is completely unrelated to the control and the management of the government. There is also another element in the nature of bureaucracy which is particularly typical of modern totalitarian regimes and which has been developed farthest in the Soviet Union. It consists of the fact that there is no such thing as a "neutral" or "unpolitical" civil service, but that on the contrary the primacy of the political element is firm dogma.

This means first of all that there is an increasing degree of personal union between party and governmental leadership. Unlike earlier years when the party leadership, especially Stalin himself, occupied no formal place in the government, although everybody knew where the decisions were actually made, all the members of the Presidium of the Central Committee except two are now cabinet ministers, and except for Bulganin who is Premier (Chairman of the Council of Ministers), they all bear the title of deputy premier. The two Presidium members who are not cabinet ministers are Voroshilov, the nominal head of the state, and Khrushchev, the First Secretary of the Communist party. A similar situation exists on the governmental and top-party levels of the Union Republics.

Secondly, as already mentioned, the road to positions of any significance goes through party membership. This means that the party has a direct hand in the selection of future managerial personnel whom it can test by various assigments, like for instance a period of service in the MVD, before the candidate receives a post in the most sensitive echelons of the governmental hierarchy.

Thirdly, the emphasis on the "political" means that every governmental function, whatever its nature, has to serve a political purpose. It is not sufficient that a given administrative task is carried out in an efficient manner. The official in charge must also be keenly aware of its political significance and unceasingly emphasize it, thus becoming a part of the party propaganda machine.

This total permeation of the atmosphere with political considerations, this never-ending insistence on the political significance of the most minor task, leads inevitably to the conclusion that failure to perform such a task properly is not merely a human error but political sabotage, wrecking, or treason. And in a dictatorship of this kind there are no graver offenses.

The Soviet official is thus subjected to a system of cross pressures of fantastic proportions. His superiors and a long chain of commands and control agencies watch over the proper performance of his task; the party through its multiple channels watches over his political orthodoxy, his party work, and the proper emphasis of the political element in his work. And the MGB watches over everything, not only his deeds and omissions, but also his associations, for to have chosen friends who later turn out to be purged or are friends of those who are purged is to invite speedy perdition.

The experiences of both the Nazi and Soviet regimes suggest that the pressure of such cross tensions is extremely severe and that practically the only way to get a little elbow room is to make deals with those assigned to watch, in other words, corruption, which in the Russian press has received the name "family relationships." But even though corruption is the only way to obtain some freedom of operation, it is also an extremely dangerous method in an atmosphere so heavily loaded wtih denunciations. Consequently, this method, which is designed to relieve tension, produces tension in its turn. Professor Merle Fainsod hardly exaggerates when in a brilliant book he characterizes this network of controls as "a system of power founded on cross-espionage and the institutionalization of mutual suspicion." [64]

CULTURE, SCIENCE, AND THE PARTY

It is a basic tenet of any totalitarian state that there can be nothing outside the control of the state and its leadership. It is a further tenet that mere

[64] Fainsod, *How Russia Is Ruled*, p. 329. See also by the same author, "Recent Developments in Soviet Public Administration," *Journal of Politics*, Vol. XI (1949), pp. 679–714.

obedience is not enough but that everybody must take a positive view of the regime. There can be no "unpolitical" branch of human endeavor.

The logical extension of this doctrine is that there can be no objective science and that there is a party line even in such seemingly unpolitical subjects as physics and horticulture. Thus S. Vavilov, at one time President of the Academy of Science of the U.S.S.R., and an internationally respected physicist, wrote: "The task of Soviet physicists is to exploit unreservedly the dialectical materialism of Marx, Engels, Lenin, and Stalin, as a powerful weapon also in the field of physics." [65]

While these tendencies had been quite noticeable throughout the Soviet regime, they shifted into high gear after the end of the Second World War. Their chief protagonist and spokesman was Andrei Zhdanov, and he began with a purge of Soviet literature in September, 1946, and quickly extended it to all other fields. "Objectivism," "cosmopolitanism," "failure to stress properly Russian achievements," and "lack of ideology" are the accusations directed against those who are to be condemned.

Those who become the victims of this process are by no means open or hidden resisters but rather people who have missed a turn of the party line. The Zhdanov purge reached its heights in 1947 with the condemnation of G. F. Alexsandrov's book on the history of Western European philosophy. Alexsandrov had applied Engels' formula of the jump from the realm of necessity to the realm of freedom in the hitherto conventional form when he found himself condemned by Zhdanov. In the interest of the continuity of the Soviet Union, it was no longer proper to speak of "jumps." Only "continuity" was now officially permitted.

The case most widely publicized was the rise of Trofim Lysenko to leadership in the field of genetics. This man, although of more than doubtful scientific knowledge, and on the basis of experiments which practically all Western scientists regarded as fraudulent, upheld and developed the Michurin theory of environmental transmutation of genes and condemned the traditional Mendelian school of the chromosome theory of heredity. Although the weight of scientific opinion was against him, Lysenko overcame all opposition at the August, 1948, meeting of the Lenin Academy of Agricultural Science by declaring, "The Central Committee of the party has examined my report and has approved it." [66]

As those Soviet geneticists who wished to retain their positions and perhaps even their lives and freedom [67] rushed forward to surrender, one specialist, A. R. Zhebrak, wrote with a frankness which might have been intended

[65] Quoted in *Tensions within the Soviet Union*, p. 18.

[66] Bertram D. Wolfe, "Science Joins the Party," *Antioch Review,* Spring, 1950, pp. 47–60.

[67] Lysenko's predecessor, Professor Vavilov, a world-renowned authority, was sent to a forced-labor camp and died there.

irony: "Now that it has become clear to me that the basic postulates of the Michurin tendency in Soviet genetics have been approved by the Central Committee of the Communist Party, I, as a member of the party, do not consider it possible for me to retain a position that has been recognized as erroneous by the Central Committee." [68]

One of the most recent interventions of the party was carried out by Stalin himself when he condemned the hitherto authoritative (in the U.S.S.R.) school of N. Ya. Marr in linguistics.[69] This and other interventions by Stalin netted him such accolades as these remarks of a military judge in a law journal: "All the most important questions of scientific socialism, political economy, philosophy, law, governmental, economic and cultural construction, military affairs, literature, and art have received the utmost development in the works of Comrade Stalin." [70]

After Stalin's death there was a temporary shift. Criticized composers like Shostakovich and Khachaturian returned and even made some mild snide remarks against "bureaucratic control of creative composition." Michael Sostchenko, one of the victims of Zhdanov's literary purge in 1946, reemerged and started to publish again. And G. F. Alexsandrov, the butt of Zhdanov's ire in 1947, returned to become Minister of Culture. And then the powerful First Secretary of the Communist Party of the Soviet Union, Nikita Khrushchev, launched a sharp attack obviously aimed at Lysenko.

But soon the pendulum swung again the other way. At the Congress of Soviet Writers of 1955 Ilya Ehrenburg, one of the most faithful followers of the party line, was bitterly criticized for a novel which contained some mild satire on the bureaucratic features of Soviet life. The tenor of this Congress seemed to indicate rather clearly that the Khrushchev regime (then not yet official) intends to return to the heavy-handed cultural policies of the Stalin and Zhdanov era.

[68] *Pravda,* Aug. 15, 1948, quoted in *Tensions within the Soviet Union,* p. 21.

[69] *Pravda,* June 20, 1950, quoted in *Current Digest of the Soviet Press,* Vol. II, July 8, 1950, p. 8.

[70] Quoted in *Tensions within the Soviet Union,* p. 27.

Chapter 8

SOVIET FEDERALISM

The existence of over 150 different races and nationalities in the Soviet Union has confronted that country with exceptionally difficult problems. Accidental and often forceful absorption into the Russian empire, as well as a rigorous Russification policy of the tsars, especially harsh under some of them, left a legacy of hate against the "Great Russians." [1]

The nationality problem attracted Stalin's attention at an early time, and Lenin too considered it of prime significance. The views of the founders Marx and Engels were of little help. They regarded nationalism as a possible tactical weapon of the proletariat, but never as a genuine political force per se. For federalism they had no use at all. "The proletariat can use only the form of the one and indivisible republic," wrote Engels.

But Lenin quickly grasped the nature of Russian realities and at an early date embraced the principle of national self-determination. This concept he later enlarged to include the right of individual states to secede from the Union,[2] which is still a full-fledged part of Soviet constitutional theory, although as we shall see it has no place in practice. Lenin attempted to establish certain limitations by his pronouncements against nationalism; while he was for the *right* of secession he was very much opposed to the *reality* of secession.[3] Federalism and the maintenance of national autonomy, political or cultural, was thus in Lenin's eyes a necessary concession to the tactical situation, not a stipulation of deep conviction. But Lenin was aware of the great strength of nationalism and wanted to establish his unitary ideal of the state by voluntary rather than coercive measures, because he believed the former to have more durable results than the latter.

However, every question of national independence was to be studied on the basis of the class angle. In other words, national self-determination which suited Soviet policy was all right, but other types were not.[4]

---

[1] Essentially the people now living in the Russian Soviet Federative Socialist Republic, in contradistinction to the "Little Russians," *i.e.*, the Ukrainians.

[2] V. I. Lenin, *Collected Works*, New York, 1945, Vol. XVI, p. 507.

[3] "We on our part, do not want separation at all. We want as large a state as possible." *Ibid.*, Vol. XXI, p. 316.

[4] Stalin said: "There are instances when the right of self-determination comes into con-

If Lenin and Stalin accepted national self-determination only with reservations, this was even more the case with federalism, which they considered detrimental to the economic development of the socialist state. "Only in individual, exclusive cases can we advance and actively support . . . the replacement of the complete political unity of the state with the weaker, federal unity. . . ."[5]

The federal form of government was established right after the Revolution,[6] however, and has remained a salient feature of government in the Soviet Union. It would be a mistake to see in this development a reversal of earlier policies. The Communist ideal is still one of absolute unity, but the Soviet leaders have learned that this goal can be reached only by indirect means. The idea of unity is condemned to failure without the thorough integration of the non-Russian masses. The federal form of government, together with an emphasis on the preservation of national culture and the economic development of non-Russian areas, is more likely to win over these masses and thus pave the way to a fuller unity. The aim of federalism in the Soviet Union is therefore the establishment of a truly unitary system.

THE UNION REPUBLICS AND THEIR SUBDIVISIONS

Article 13 of the Soviet Constitution of 1936 defines the U.S.S.R. as a "federal state, formed on the basis of a voluntary union of equal Soviet Socialist Republics." These are now the following:

The Russian Soviet Federative Socialist Republic
The Ukrainian Soviet Socialist Republic
The Byelorussian (White Russian) S.S.R.
The Uzbek S.S.R.
The Kazakh S.S.R.
The Georgian S.S.R.
The Azerbaidzhan S.S.R.
The Lithuanian S.S.R.
The Moldavian S.S.R.
The Latvian S.S.R.
The Kirghiz S.S.R.
The Tadzhik S.S.R.
The Armenian S.S.R.
The Turkmen S.S.R.

---

flict with another, higher right—the right of the working class . . . to fortify its power." 12th Congress of the Russian Communist party (1923). J. Towster, *Political Power in the U.S.S.R.*, New York, 1948, p. 61.

[5] Lenin, *op. cit.*, Vol. XVII, pp. 154–156.

[6] See the *Charter of the Nations of Russia*, 1917, signed by Lenin and Stalin. M. W. Graham, *New Governments of Eastern Europe*, New York, 1927, pp. 594*f*.

The Estonian S.S.R.

The Karelo-Finnish S.S.R.

The aforementioned are the so-called "Union Republics." Theirs is the highest form of statehood that nations may obtain in the Union of Soviet Socialist Republics. Theoretically these Republics are equal with one another, but that equality is neither true nor possible. One of them, the Russian S.F.S.R., comprises over three-fourths of the territory of the U.S.S.R., contains more than three-fifths of its population, and extends from the Baltic to the Pacific. To maintain that any real equality can exist between this colossus and, say, the Kirghiz S.S.R. is to state an obvious absurdity.

The Union Republics are subdivided into Territories (6), Regions (124), autonomous republics (15), autonomous regions (9), and national areas (10). These are again subdivided into districts (*raions*) except for the Baltic republics (Lithuanian, Latvian, Estonian S.S.R.'s) which have retained their traditional *uyezds* and *volosts* from the days of the tsars. Not all Union Republics have all of these subdivisions.

The federal relationship extends only from the Union to the Union Republics; all lower units are creatures of the Union Republics.[7]

Each Union Republic has its own constitution, which must be in conformity with the Constitution of the U.S.S.R. Its territory cannot be altered except with its consent (Art. 18), and it has the right "freely to secede from the U.S.S.R." Technically the U.S.S.R. has only expressed and enumerated powers (Art. 14), while all others are reserved to the republics.

FEDERALISM: TRUE OR FALSE?

If one were to confine oneself to the constitutional text one would indeed be forced to conclude that true federalism exists in the Soviet Union, and this impression would be increased by two amendments enacted in 1944 (Arts. 18*a* and 18*b*). One of them grants the Union Republics the right to enter into direct relations with foreign states, to exchange diplomatic and consular representatives with them, and to conclude treaties with them. The other gives the Union Republics control over their own armed forces.[8] These amendments paved the way for the inclusion of the Ukrainian and Byelorussian Soviet Socialist Republics in the United Nations.

Yet a closer examination of the issue will place Soviet federalism in a more debatable category. Federalism, if it is to be real, is based on two conditions: (1) the existence of a constitution, written or unwritten, which actually limits the powers of government, and (2) a substantial division of powers between

---

[7] For an interesting commentary, see V. V. Aspaturian, "The Theory and Practice of Soviet Federalism," *Journal of Politics*, Vol. XII (1950), pp. 20–51.

[8] However, these rights are limited by the powers of the central government as outlined in Art. 14.

central and regional governments, leaving considerable and significant powers to the latter.

All Soviet writers refer to the Constitution as the "fundamental law" to which all other law is subordinate. But another concept proves that this idea can be accepted only with very serious reservations. It is stated that "the dictatorship of the proletariat is authority unlimited by any statutes whatever."[9] It is not the Constitution which lays down the course of the dictatorship of the proletariat, but it is the dictatorship of the proletariat which lays down the legal forms of conduct of which the Constitution is the foremost but by no means the only expression. The Soviet Constitution therefore emerges as a tool of the "dictatorship of the proletariat" or of the political forces which control it, not as a limitation upon that dictatorship. This principle is also borne out by the well-known comment of Stalin that the Constitution (1936) is an expression of what has been achieved, which implies that further changes will, of course, take place and be eventually recorded in the Constitution but that until that is done the Constitution does not prevent those changes. "The forms of our state will again change in conformity with the changes in the situation at home and abroad," said Stalin. But Molotov put it even more clearly when he said that the Communist party was always "subordinating the forms of the state structure to the fundamental interests of socialism and to the task of strengthening the proletarian dictatorship."[10]

THE RELATIONSHIP BETWEEN THE UNION AND THE UNION REPUBLICS

Let us now turn to an examination of the relationship between the Union (central) government and the governments of the Union Republics. The Soviet Constitution distinguishes between All-Union and Union-Republican Ministries. The All-Union Ministries exercise their functions directly throughout the entire territory of the U.S.S.R., while the Union-Republican Ministries "direct the branches of the state administration entrusted to them through corresponding Ministries of the Union Republics" (Constitution, Art. 76). In other words, the power of the Union government is supreme in the fields of both the All-Union and the Union-Republican Ministries, although the form of administration differs. An examination of the pertinent articles in the Constitution (Arts. 77, 78) reveals that every conceivable manifestation of political and especially economic life is controlled by the central government through either All-Union or Union-Republican Ministries, leaving to the authority of the republican governments only limited matters—and those only theoretically.

[9] Andrei Vyshinsky, *The Law of the Soviet State* (trans. by H. R. Babb), New York, 1948, p. 48.

[10] V. Molotov, *The New Soviet Constitution*, New York, 1937, p. 21.

Moreover, a study of the developments in that area since the Bolshevik Revolution shows conclusively that the trend runs unmistakably in the direction of greater centralism. Of the six fields which were once under the exclusive control of the republics, only two, education [11] and social security, have remained. A number of Union-Republican Ministries have become All-Union Ministries.[12] Two Ministries, those for Foreign Affairs and the Armed Forces,[13] went the other way, being transformed from All-Union to Union-Republican rank, but a parallel amendment to Art. 14 gives the Union government the right to the "establishment of general procedure governing the relations of Union Republics with foreign states" and to the "determination of directing principles governing the organization of the military formations of the Union Republics."

In addition there are other manifestations of actual centralism over apparent federalism. The Presidium of the Supreme Soviet has the power to annul decisions and orders of the Councils of Ministers of the Union Republics if they do not conform to law (Art. 49*f*). Also peculiarly centralistic is the position of the Procurator-General of the U.S.S.R., who supervises the strict execution of the laws throughout the entire territory of the Soviet Union.

It also appears that the central authorities have a heavy hand in the incorporation and elimination of lesser units of government. This was evident in the establishment of an autonomous region out of territory ceded by China and other areas taken from Germany and Japan, as well as in the elimination of five units during the war for treasonable activities.[14]

Most important of all, however, is the all-pervasive position of the Communist party, which is strictly centralist and without a spark of federalism. Since all policy emanates from the Communist party, it actually matters little whether there exists a federal form of government or not. The Central Committee or rather the Presidium of the party determines all policy for the entire Union, and this policy is carried out by all state authorities, federal or central. A federal structure, governed by a unitary, monolithic party, provides merely a table of organization of the distribution of the work to be done. Federalism, in order to be real, must reserve to the component parts at least

[11] But not higher education, which is under a Union-Republican Ministry (Art. 78).

[12] In 1936 the Constitution listed eight All-Union and ten Union-Republican Ministries. There are now listed thirty-six and twenty-two respectively, indicating a strong tendency toward specialization. The former Commissariat for Heavy Industry is the parent body for no less than twenty-seven new ministries.

[13] In March, 1950, a new Ministry of the Navy was created.

[14] The Tuva Autonomous Region, the Kaliningrad (formerly Königsberg) Region, etc. Eliminated for treasonable activities were the Kalmyk, Crimean, German Volga, and Chechen-Ingush Autonomous Soviet Socialist Republics and the Karachaev Autonomous Region.

some autonomy in the realm of policy; but that is quite impossible in the one-party state of the Soviet Union.

This is perhaps not unnatural, because the Soviet Union is a state with a strictly and integrally planned economy. The Communists and also most non-Communist socialists have always recognized that federalism and state planning are in fundamental conflict. Because of the close connection between political and economic direction in the Soviet Union, unitarism rather than federalism is the real nature of the regime. When Lenin inaugurated the NEP and the strategic retreat from war communism, federalism, although never a working system, was part of that retreat. Since the return to uncompromising Communism, federalism has steadily lost more and more of whatever ground it had. In fact the supreme, directive function of the state national economic plan is specifically recognized in the Constitution (Art. 11).

CULTURAL AUTONOMY

Any discussion of Soviet federalism will eventually lead to the topic of "cultural autonomy." From the beginning of the regime, the Communist leaders have emphasized the equality of all races and nationalities of the Soviet Union. Much effort has been expended on the furtherance, and at times the revival, of language and culture of the various nationalities. All Soviet languages may be used in the courts and government offices of the U.S.S.R., a tremendous increase in the literature of many Soviet nations has taken place, and the availability of schools in the native language of all citizens has helped to reduce greatly the rate of illiteracy. Compared with the persistent and at times forceful "Russification" attempts by the tsars, this is indeed great progress. But one must never lose sight of the fact that the eventual aim of these cultural activities is unity, not diversity. Stalin felt that national languages and cultures would and should come to an end, but not before the victory of socialism all over the world.[15] Until then cultural diversity is used as a tool for national unity. The form of expression is left to native tongues and cultures, but the meaning and direction of these expressions are as tightly controlled from the top as are all other activities of Soviet citizens. The Politburo lays down the precise line for music, drama, art, etc., and any citizen who disregarded such direction would do so at his dire peril. Moreover an unbridled campaign for nationalism has been unleashed, which has taken on fantastic forms. The repeated claims that all kinds of inventions and other useful contributions have been made by Russians are intended to convey the belief that nothing outside the U.S.S.R. is or can be worth while. Much of this is of course bound to be "Russian" rather than Soviet, but that is only natural in view of the prominent role of the "Great Russians" among the

[15] Stalin, *Marxism and the National and Colonial Question, op. cit.*, pp. 265f.

peoples of the Soviet Union, and it furthers the purpose of uniting all in a common pride.

SECESSION?

The official doctrine still insists that the association of nations, especially of the Union Republics, is free and voluntary and that the right of secession is a reality.[16] In fact Stalin, commenting on the 1936 Constitution, stated that a Union Republic would have to be a border republic "because, since the Union Republics have a right to secede from the U.S.S.R., a republic . . . must be in a position logically and actually to raise the question of secession from the U.S.S.R." But at the same time he admitted that "of course none of our republics would actually raise the question of seceding from the U.S.S.R. But since the right to secede from the U.S.S.R. is reserved to the Union Republics, it must be so aranged that this right does not become a meaningless scrap of paper.[!]" This bit of dialectics fits well into the general pattern. Just how would a Union Republic go about the business of seceding, the policy of the Communist party being clearly against secession? This right is highly theoretical and actually could not be exercised without a breakup of the party.

This emphasis on the unreal right of secession is part of the larger picture which tends to grant the component parts of the Soviet Union more prestige and status while depriving them of substance, thus amassing even greater power and control at the top. That this is a trend which is entirely in conformity with the classical Communist position may be surmised from this statement by Lenin: "In the example of the Russian Soviet Republic we see most graphically that the federation we are introducing will serve now as the surest step to the most solid unification of the different nationalities into a single, democratic, centralized Soviet State." [17]

In another exercise in dialectics Vyshinsky declared,

The Soviet Union State is a federative state. Both by its class essence and by its organizational structure it is sharply distinguished from all existing forms of federation, confederation and unitarism formerly or now existing in the capitalist world. It is a type of state without a precedent in history. It emerges from the problems of the worker class dictatorship in a multinational country. It is the realization and expression of the general will and mutual confidence of the toilers of nations with equal rights.[18]

Trained Leninist-Stalinist dialecticians might perhaps be able to find evi-

[16] Vyshinsky, *op. cit.*, pp. 214–217. The American doctrine of federalism does not recognize the right of secession. Texas v. White, 2 Wall., 700 (1869).

[17] Lenin, *op. cit.*, Vol. XXII, pp. 415*f*.

[18] Vyshinsky, *op. cit.*, pp. 228*f*.

dence of a Soviet federalism, since such dialectics appear to outsiders only too often as the art of declaring that contradictions are not contradictions and that those who see them are blind.. By the generally accepted "Western" standards of political science, Soviet federalism is as real as the Emperor's new clothes in Hans Christian Andersen's famous tale.

Chapter 9

THE SOVIETS

The Soviet Constitution provides that "The political foundation of the U.S.S.R. are the Soviets of Working People's Deputies, which grew and became strong as a result of the overthrow of the power of the landlords and capitalists and the conquest of the dictatorship of the proletariat" (Art. 2).

Literally the Russian word *soviet* means "council," but this form of council which has given the regime its name is the result of historical development in Russia and of the use which the Communist leaders managed to make of it. The first soviets were strike committees which sprang up in the factories during the revolution of 1905. Soon city-wide soviets were formed, composed of factory delegates. Some leaders like Trotsky obtained political fame in those assemblies.

These soviets were revolutionary bodies, composed of activist elements. To what extent they represented the workers might be an interesting though futile topic of discussion, but that they were not elected by standardized, orderly procedure was common knowledge. If they represented the workers it was certainly a small minority of them, but revolutionaries are not easily deterred by such technicalities. There were no such things as labor unions in those days, and the soviets were a makeshift which was possible only amid the confusion of a revolutionary period. There was, however, one significant element in this situation. The authority of the government was wholeheartedly on the side of the employers and against the workers. Consequently the workers' councils, the soviets, directed their activities against the state authorities and were essentially political bodies. When the strike wave became larger, delegates from various factories were elected to a "Soviet of Workers' Deputies." This was a large body, but between sessions a small executive committee took care of current business. This type of organization became best known in St. Petersburg, the capital city, but quickly spread to most other major industrial towns. The left-wing parties were, of course, not slow in seeing possibilities in this development, and they began to organize the soviets for political action. Lenin especially pointed to the soviets as a "government in embryo" and an appropriate tool through which the dictatorship of the proletariat could be achieved.

During the revolutionary period of 1917 there existed a parliament of sorts, the Duma, but simultaneously the soviets were revived, thus creating a picture of "dual power." Soldiers' representatives were sent to the soviets, which became known as "Soviets of Workers' and Soldiers' Representatives." There were also peasants' soviets, but they never acquired the same status as the soviets of workers' and soldiers' representatives mainly because the Bolsheviks saw little chance of dominating them.

THE CONGRESS OF SOVIETS

In June, 1917, an All-Russian Congress of Soviets of Workers' and Soldiers' (later also Peasants' and Cossacks') Representatives was called to St. Petersburg and elected a Central Executive Committee.

The Bolsheviks were able to take control, first of the St. Petersburg and Moscow soviets, later of the second All-Russian Congress of Soviets. Previously Lenin had advanced the slogan "All powers to the Soviets"; now the Congress of Soviets prepared to take all power and appointed a cabinet, the so-called "Council of People's Commissars," which was to be subordinate to the Congress. This was the form of administration which the Communist leaders found eminently suitable and which they have retained with some variations.

The earlier Congresses of Soviets were of enormous size. The last ordinary Congress had 2,562 members, and the last one held, the Extraordinary Eighth Congress of 1936, which enacted the new Constitution, had 2,016 members. Under these circumstances any legislative work was impossible. The Congresses actually became mass meetings. There was also a Central Executive Committee, but it was too numerous (at one time, 757) and met too infrequently. As a result a smaller body, a Union Presidium of twenty-seven members, did most of the work.

THE SUPREME SOVIET

The Central Executive Committee had been a bicameral body. This was essentially the model underlying the Constitution of 1936, which created a Supreme Soviet of the U.S.S.R., described as "the highest organ of state power" (Art. 30). The Supreme Soviet is divided into a Soviet of the Union and a Soviet of Nationalities. The members of the Soviet of the Union are elected on the basis of one deputy for every 300,000 people, while the members of the Soviet of Nationalities are elected by the citizens voting by component parts, with the result that each Union Republic is entitled to twenty-five delegates, each Autonomous Republic to eleven, each Autonomous Region to five, and each National Area to one. Each Union Republic is represented by one deputy chairman on the Presidium of the Supreme Soviet.

The Supreme Soviet is large. In 1946, 1,339 members were elected, 682 to the Soviet of the Union and 657 to the Soviet of Nationalities. Substantially the same numbers appeared in the elections of 1950 and 1954. The Supreme Soviet is elected for a term of four years. In the event of insoluble disagreement between the two houses, the Supreme Soviet is to be dissolved by its Presidium and new elections are to be organized.

Similar soviets exist on all other levels of government, down to the village, but only the Supreme Soviet is bicameral.

ELECTIONS

All Soviet citizens of eighteen or older may vote, and all citizens over twenty-three may be elected. No difference is made as to class, and no group is excluded from the universal, equal, direct, and secret suffrage.[1] Once elected, a deputy may be recalled at any time by a majority of his electors.

For the purpose of elections the country is divided into appropriate election districts, while the local government authorities (executive committees of city and village soviets) compile the voters' lists. Candidates are nominated for their respective electoral districts.

Article 141 of the Constitution provides that the right to nominate candidates on all levels "is secured to public organizations and societies of the working people: Communist Party organizations, trade unions, cooperatives, youth organizations and cultural societies." Election regulations have extended this to general meetings of workers, employees, servicemen, collective farmers, and general rural meetings. Since every Soviet citizen belongs to one of these groups, his right to participate is assured.

The process by which candidates are nominated is quite informal. The exercise of considerable initiative is encouraged because it shows the existence of potential leaders. However, there are also instances in which the party organization makes it quite clear from the beginning whom it wants, and instances have been recorded by (hostile) eyewitnesses in which candidates were presented who were totally unknown to their nominators. More often, however, the party remains in the background at this stage. If and when different candidates are proposed by various organizations, informal conference committees are appointed which narrow down the choice to one single person. It is at that stage that the party exercises its role of leadership and guides the choice which will eventually be made. Not all candidates are Communist

---

[1] Before 1936 certain groups, *bourgeoisie, kulaks,* etc., were disfranchised. In addition workers sent deputies at the rate of one for 25,000 while the rural areas were entitled only to one for each 125,000. The urban population was also directly represented on all levels, while the rural inhabitants were represented only indirectly in the assemblies of the higher levels.

party members, but those who are not must be persons "who are devoted to the cause of Lenin-Stalin." [2] Those nominated are usually distinguished by superior performance in their professions or constitute the elite in some other way. Never is nomination or election a question of policy, as all candidates are supposed to be devoted to the party line and the policy of the government whether they are Communists or not. That an actual opponent of the regime, or even a slightly dissident person, could be nominated is quite out of the question. Not only would such a person be eliminated by the Election Commission (if he had not already been eliminated by the police), but he could hardly get by the scrutiny of the party organization which "guides" the nominations. The extent to which such guidance is effective may be seen from the fact that, although only 3 per cent of the population are members of the Communist party, about three-fourths of all deputies (on all levels) are party members; most deputies are also men who have been the recipients of special honors in the form of decorations, awards, or other distinctions.

Thus on election day the voter has no choice: he has only one candidate on the "List of Communists and Non-party People." He may vote against the bloc, but only an infinitesimal number choose to avail themselves of this opportunity. Despite the Constitution, people vote "openly" in many polling places, thus putting an onus on those who enter the booth. This practice, although not officially sanctioned, helps to discourage the "no" vote. Nevertheless a great deal of propaganda and agitation goes into the campaign. Enormous numbers of propaganda workers are trained and put to work. Meetings are held, some questions are answered, and the attention and excitement could not be much greater if there were a real contest. Actually there is a contest in a way: the problem is that of getting out the vote. A 100 per cent record is the goal, and in Stalin's district in Moscow it was regularly achieved. In the 1954 election to the Supreme Soviet, participation reached an all-time high of 99.98 per cent of all voters.[3]

There is no similarity whatsoever between Soviet and Western elections. All candidates are of one political conviction, only one party exists, and only one candidate is presented at the final election.[4] The idea that a voter decides for or against a policy, for or against a government, is totally absent in the Soviet Union. Actually, Soviet elections have a different function. "The Soviet election system," writes Vyshinsky, "is a mighty instrument for further educating and organizing the masses politically, for further strengthening the bond between the state mechanism and the masses, and for improving the

---

[2] J. Towster, *Political Power in the U.S.S.R.*, New York, 1948, p. 193, quoting A. Gorkin, *The Electoral Law of the Soviet State* (in Russian), Moscow, 1945, p. 32.

[3] Communique of the Central Election Commission for the election of the U.S.S.R. Supreme Soviet on the results of the elections of March 14, 1954, *Pravda,* March 18, 1954, *Current Digest of the Soviet Press,* Vol. 6, Apr. 7, 1954.

[4] On the "List of Communists and Nonparty People."

state mechanism and grubbing out the remnants of bureaucratism." Elections afford the party an opportunity to fill the people with its spirit, to get into direct touch with every layer of the population. Speakers exhort the people to make still greater efforts in production, etc., and things are generally stirred up. Elections are also kinds of "command-post exercises" for the cadres of the Communist party, which have an opportunity to show their organization and agitatorial skill.

For internal and external consumption, Soviet elections are also plebiscites in which the people endorse the regime from time to time. This is another manifestation of the concept of mass participation which the Communists like to call "democracy." [5] Nearly all people have an opportunity to participate in an act of government in which they are the center of attention. At the same time the entire process is carefully organized and controlled by the Communist party, while the outcome of the election is, of course, a foregone conclusion.

This is the manner in which all soviets are elected, but the greatest effort and most persistent agitation are reserved for the election of the Supreme Soviet.

Deputies are men and women from all walks of life, but all of them are people who have gained distinction in their group or profession. The Constitution grants them the customary immunities of members of parliament—to which little attention is paid in practice—and they enjoy a number of other privileges such as free travel. While their legislative duties are light, other obligations burden them considerably. In particular they are supposed to be a link between their electors and the government, and they become therefore the recipients of numerous complaints and other grievances from their constituents, which often give the government an idea where the shoe pinches.

POWER AND ORGANIZATION

Sessions of the Supreme Soviet are regularly convoked twice each year, although extra sessions have been called repeatedly. Each session lasts for about one week. This fact alone, together with the very large number of deputies, demonstrates that the legislative functions of the Supreme Soviet are a myth, even though the Constitution says that "the legislative power of the U.S.S.R. is exercised exclusively by the Supreme Soviet of the U.S.S.R." (Art. 32). The vast amount of laws which a modern state needs could not possibly be ground out by over 1,300 people, meeting twice per year for a week each. Actually most laws, although they may be called decrees, ordi-

[5] "Under the new Stalin Constitution elections to the Supreme Soviet of the USSR . . . have shown that the entire population of the land of the Soviets are completely united in spirit, have demonstrated an unprecedented democracy." Andrei Vyshinsky, *The Law of the Soviet State* (trans. by H. R. Babb), New York, 1948, p. 722.

nances, etc., are issued by the Council of Ministers (government) or the Presidium of the Supreme Soviet, as we shall see.

There are but few committees. Credentials Commissions operate in each house in order to examine the deputies' election papers. There are three committees which work through the bills which fall in their fields of competence: the Legislative Commission, the Budget Commission, and the Foreign Affairs Commission. The Commissions prepare the laws for submission to the two houses which then pass upon them. Consent of both houses is necessary for enactment of laws.

The Supreme Soviet, being the "highest organ of state power in the U.S.S.R.," has power to legislate in all fields over which the Union government as a whole has jurisdiction. This field is outlined in Art. 14 and comprises

a. Representation of the U.S.S.R. in international affairs, including ratification and denunciation of treaties and the establishment of a uniform system for the relations between the Union Republics and foreign nations.

b. War and peace.

c. Admission of new republics.

d. Control over the observance of the Constitution.

e. Confirmation of boundary alterations between Union Republics.

f. Confirmation of the formation of new territories, regions, Autonomous Republics, and Autonomous Regions within Union Republics.

g. Defence of the U.S.S.R. as well as the establishment of uniform standards for the military organizations of the Union Republics.

h. Foreign trade (state monopoly).

i. State security.

j. Economic planning.

k. Budget approval; establishment of a tax and revenue system for all levels of government.

l. Administration of all economic enterprises of all-Union importance.

m. Transport and communication.

n. Money and credit system.

o. (State) insurance.

p. Borrowing and lending money.

q. Establishing principles for the use of land, natural resources, forests, and water.

r. Basic principles for education and public health.

s. Establishment of a unified accounting system.

t. Principles of labor legislation.

u. Establishment of the judicial system and judicial procedure; legislative enactments in civil and criminal law.

v. Nationalization, citizenship, and treatment of aliens.

w. Principles of marriage and family relations law.

x. All-Union acts of amnesty.

Article 31 stipulates that these powers are to be exercised insofar as their execution is not reserved for other authorities such as the Presidium, the Council of Ministers, or the governments of the Union Republics. But in practice the Supreme Soviet may set aside these limitations. This was demonstrated in 1939 and 1942 when the Supreme Soviet and not the duly constituted authority for that purpose, namely, its Presidium (Art. 49), ratified the Soviet-German and Anglo-Soviet treaties—presumably to give them a more solemn character.

AMENDMENTS TO THE CONSTITUTION

In addition to the general Union powers in which the Supreme Soviet may legislate, it also may amend the Constitution (by a two-thirds majority in both houses, Art. 146); elect the Presidium (Art. 48), the Supreme Court (Art. 105), and special courts (for a term of five years); and appoint the Council of Ministers (Art. 560) and the chief law-enforcement and prosecuting officer, the Procurator-General of the U.S.S.R. (for a term of seven years, Art. 114).

THE REALITY OF POWER

On paper these powers are as formidable as those of any Western parliament. In practice the difference could not be greater. We have already seen the striking discrepancy between the vast amount of work a full-fledged national legislature has to do, and the short and infrequent sessions of the Supreme Soviet. In addition to that, there is the fact that all bills originate with the government, and considering the method by which deputies are selected, no differences of opinion are likely to occur. This was not always the case in past Soviet history, but it has been the case since 1936. The regular procedure is that government members make their report or submit their bills,[6] and the deputies shout their approval or signify assent by a show of hands. The formula frequently applied now is to state that the report or proposal of the government was presented with such admirable clarity that no debate was necessary. At the infrequent instances where a bill is debated, all speakers argue in favor of the measure. There are, however, general debates in which deputies bring up shortcomings in performance and tardiness in operation and suggest measures for improvement. Here again, it is never policy that is debated or at stake, but rather the most efficient implementation of a policy already laid down.

[6] Sometimes bills also originate in the commissions.

When it is time for the vote, it is invariably unanimous. There is no instance recorded in which a deputy of the Supreme Soviet failed to vote in favor of a measure introduced or endorsed by the government.

Contrary to official insistence both in the constitutional text and in the opinion of Soviet writers, it is impossible to accept the view that the Supreme Soviet is in fact "the highest organ of state power" or that it exercises legislative power exclusively. An institution which does not determine policy, which in fact has no hand in the determination of policy, cannot easily be held to possess "power." It is also a fact that the overwhelming majority of enactments do not come from the Supreme Soviet, but from its Presidium in the form of "decrees" or from the government in the form of "decisions and ordinances." Soviet writers insist that there is a difference and that statutes enacted by the Supreme Soviet are of a higher order than decrees, decisions, or ordinances, but since such decrees, etc., have never been revoked except on government initiative, and since they come into operation at once without waiting for any Supreme Soviet confirmation, it is difficult to see any practical difference except one of names and totally abstract distinction.

THE PRESIDIUM OF THE SUPREME SOVIET

The Supreme Soviet, at a joint session of both houses, elects the Presidium of the Supreme Soviet of the U.S.S.R. It is composed of a chairman, sixteen vice-chairmen (one for each Union Republic), a secretary, and fifteen other members, thirty-three in all. At the present time, there are only thirty-two, because the chairman of the Presidium, Marshal Klementi Voroshilov, is also chairman of the Presidium of the Supreme Soviet of the Russian Soviet Federative Socialist Republic.

The Presidium is a unique institution, indigenous to the Soviet system and without parallel anywhere else except in the satellite states which have copied the Russian model. The Presidium has a combination of representative, executive, legislative, and even some judicial functions, totally rejecting thereby the concept of the separation of powers.

Stalin described the Presidium as a "collegiate president"—a term which depicts one of its functions quite well. Some of these "presidential" functions are exercised by the chairman of the Presidium, despite the fact that neither the law nor the Constitution gives him any special powers. Nevertheless the statutes enacted by the Supreme Soviet are promulgated with his signature, and he also signs the decrees of the Presidium itself. He receives foreign envoys and ministers, and he exchanges messages with other heads of state as an equal among equals. All his acts, however, are in the name of the Presidium.

The importance of the Presidium goes far beyond these purely formal functions, a fact which is demonstrated by the presence of several members of the Politburo therein. The powers of the Presidium are most extensive, as the following list will indicate. The Presidium

a. Convenes the sessions of the Supreme Soviet.

b. Issues decrees.

c. Interprets the laws of the U.S.S.R.

d. Dissolves the Supreme Soviet under conditions of disagreement between the houses (Art. 47) and designates new elections.

e. Conducts referenda.

f. Annuls decisions and ordinances of the Council of Ministers of the U.S.S.R. and of the Councils of Ministers of the Union Republics in case they do not conform to law.

g. When the Supreme Soviet is not in session, relieves and appoints ministers of the U.S.S.R. at the request of the chairman of the Council of Ministers (Prime Minister). Such appointments must subsequently be confirmed by the Supreme Soviet.

h. Confers decorations and other honors.

i. Institutes decorations, titles, and honors.

j. Exercises the right of pardon.

k. Establishes military and other titles, diplomatic ranks, etc.

l. Appoints and removes the high commands of the armed forces.

m. If the Supreme Soviet is not in session, declares war in the event of an armed attack or whenever necessary to fulfill international treaty obligations concerning mutual defense against aggression.

n. Proclaims general or partial mobilization.

o. Ratifies and denounces international treaties.

p. Appoints and recalls diplomatic representatives of the U.S.S.R.

q. Receives the credentials and letters of recall of foreign diplomatic representatives.

r. Proclaims martial law.

The Presidium has its antecedents and roots in many European institutions: in the nominal presidency of the French type, in the principal standing committee of several European legislatures, in the constitutional review board which the Abbé Sieyès envisaged in the French Revolution and which the French Constitution of 1946 instituted. Nevertheless, it is an original contribution of the Soviet state.

The Presidium never has had occasion to dissolve the Supreme Soviet. Nor has it ever organized a referendum. But it has used all its other prerogatives. In particular a steady stream of decrees, which might just as well be called laws, emanate from it. They are in part based on the Presidium's own jurisdiction, as enumerated in Art. 49, but they also invade freely the sphere which the Constitution reserves to the Supreme Soviet itself.

THE INTERPRETATION OF LAW

Very substantial also is the right of the Presidium to interpret laws, which is accomplished in the form of commentary and directive upon the execution of operative laws.[7] Moreover the Presidium may invalidate executive decrees of the Union and Union-Republican governments if they are not in conformity with the laws (including the Constitution) of the U.S.S.R., but it may not set aside laws passed by the Supreme Soviets of the U.S.S.R. or of the Union Republics, which cannot be vetoed and which go into operation without further ado. The right to annul executive decrees for illegality was shared by the Presidium and the Supreme Court of the U.S.S.R. under the 1924 Constitution, but the 1936 Constitution reserved the right exclusively to the Presidium. There is no judicial review in the Soviet Union.

Soviet writers emphasize the point that the Presidium is responsible to the Supreme Soviet and that it may be removed as a whole or in part at any time. However, if such removals take place the decision, as in every other instance, is not actually taken in the Supreme Soviet but, being a matter of highest policy, emanates from the Politburo.

The Presidium thus emerges as an extremely important and fully occupied [8] administrative device which participates in every branch of the government. Unlike the Supreme Soviet, it is in permanent session and is therefore able to discharge its functions continually.

OTHER SOVIETS

The soviet form of government is not confined to the top but is followed all the way down to the local level. Both the Union Republics and the Autonomous Republics have unicameral Supreme Soviets who elect their Presidia (Arts. 57–63, 89–93), which operate in conformity with the U.S.S.R. Constitution as well as with their own constitutions.[9] On the lower levels— namely, the Territories, Regions, Autonomous Regions, areas, districts, cities, and villages—there are Soviets of Working People's Deputies (Arts. 94–101) which operate in conformity with the Constitution of the Union Republic in which they are located. Actually the most common soviets are for Territories or Regions, districts, cities, and villages.

[7] Continental countries have always known the practice of "authentic interpretation," *i.e.*, interpretation of laws by the legislature. The prerogative of the Presidium is a considerable broadening of that right.

[8] Nine-tenths of the Presidium's publications deal with honors, medals, and decorations.

[9] Union Republic and Autonomous Republic Constitutions must be in conformity with the Constitution of the U.S.S.R. Amendments to the U.S.S.R. Constitution which concern the Union or Autonomous Republics result, therefore, in amendments to those Constitutions as well.

The Union Republics and the Autonomous Republics have Councils of Ministers as their chief executive and administrative organs, but the lower levels have executive committees of their respective soviets composed of a chairman, a vice-chairman, a secretary, and varying numbers of members (Art. 99). In very small localities, the chairman, the vice-chairman, and the secretary of the local soviet are the executive and administrative organs (Art. 100). These executive committees, chairmen, etc., are responsible to their respective soviets and to the soviet of the next higher level (Art. 101).

It is said that the local executives operate under the strict direction of their soviets. But the hand of higher levels is strongly felt, and there is always the ubiquitous secretary of the Communist party in the village, town, or other unit of government, who cannot be ignored. In recent years these men have taken on overt administrative responsibilities to an increasing extent. The soviet form of government, with the strict accountability of lower to higher levels of government, lends itself well to the close integration and control of the country which is deemed necessary in order to assure the success of the political and economic aspirations of the regime.

Chapter 10

THE ADMINISTRATION

"The highest executive and administrative organ of the state power of the Union of Soviet Socialist Republics is the Council of Ministers [1] of the U.S.S.R.," states the Constitution (Art. 64). It stands at the head of a vast and ever-increasing bureaucracy which administers the machinery of the state. In our times, when all states have taken upon themselves many functions and services, all governmental machineries have increased their staffs. But in the Soviet Union, where every economic, social, scientific, or artistic activity is controlled and administered by the state, the bureaucracy is of truly formidable size. This has resulted in a mushrooming of bureaus and agencies bewildering even to the casehardened student of public administration. From time to time new bureaus are created in order to investigate why there are so many bureaus, but old bureaucrats never die and the new bureaus continue to exist more or less peacefully side by side with those which they were designed to eliminate.

These 11,000,000 to 12,000,000 clerks, analysts, planners, and administrators are the new "middle and upper classes" of the Soviet Union. They are far more representative of the modern U.S.S.R. than the old-fashioned revolutionaries.

From time to time attempts are made to put new spirit and soul into the machinery of government. Inefficient bureaucrats are pilloried in such journals as *Pravda, Izvestia, Kommunist, Trud,* etc. Red tape and inefficiency are ridiculed in *Krokodil* and on the stage of the cabarets. At public meetings, party conferences, etc., speakers inveigh against the "soulless bureaucracy." Party members point their accusing fingers at certain flagrant cases, and the offenders are then removed or demoted, but like quicksand the immense machinery quickly fills every hole that removal may have created, and matters stand pretty much as they were before.

While Russians are not generally known as speedy operators, the cause of

---

[1] Until Mar. 19, 1946 the government was known as the Council of People's Commissars, often referred to as Sovnarkom, an abbreviation from the Russian Sovyet Narodnykh Komissarov.

this state of affairs does not lie in national characteristics. The size of the machinery itself virtually excludes a high degree of efficiency, because effective direction and supervision become extremely difficult. Worse, however, is the excessive degree of centralism which deprives the working levels of the administration of sufficient authority and places an intolerable burden upon higher authorities. It also facilitates the habit, known colloquially (in America) as "passing the buck," *i.e.*, of letting others, in this case higher authority, take responsibility even when authority exists on the lower levels. Moreover, there is the stultifying "desire to please" so characteristic of all authoritarian regimes where civil servants report to their superiors frequently "that everything is going according to plan" when in reality nothing of the kind is true. Soviet publications have frequently criticized directors of plants and managers of state enterprise who reported fulfillment of production quotas and other glowing results when the reality of the situation was quite the reverse. But in a country in which a wrong decision or a failure to see deficiencies may easily be interpreted as "wrecking," which would result in long terms of forced labor and imprisonment for those held responsible, civil servants and managerial personnel prefer to be "safe" rather than to strike out boldly and to institute innovations. It cannot be said that the Soviet leaders are not aware of this, but all they can do is to change personnel and to inculcate better morale into their services. Inasmuch as the faults are inherent in the system the leaders are powerless to effect lasting improvements without very substantial alterations in the structure and the concepts of the Soviet regime.

It is therefore not surprising that the role of the Communist party in watching over the efficiency of production and service is exceptionally important and absorbs much of the party's efforts. Other organizations, especially trade-unions, also take part in this work. Since effective control from the inside is difficult and often impossible, as the criticism of a superior may result in worse than dismissal, outside inspection is necessary.

Under the constitutional regime of 1924 the government was regarded as both executive and legislative, having the power to issue decrees which were binding in the entire Soviet Union.[2] The Constitution of 1936 places all legislative power exclusively in the hands of the Supreme Soviet, but the Council of Ministers has the power to issue decisions and orders (Art. 66). However, legal and constitutional doctrine demands that these remain within the confines of the law as set out by the Supreme Soviet, to which the Council of Ministers is responsible. So much for the theory. In practice the Council of Ministers is the foremost legislator of the country. By far most of the rules which guide everybody's conduct and are enforced in the entire territory of the Soviet Union are issued by the Council of Ministers. Especially the economic life of the country is regulated almost exclusively by ordinances and

[2] Constitution of 1924, Art. 38.

decisions of the Council of Ministers.[3] Any subordination of these decisions and ordinances to the will of the Supreme Soviet is wholly theoretical and academic.

THE COUNCIL OF MINISTERS

The authority of the Council of Ministers covers the entire field of executive functions, but a major portion of its activities is taken up by economic affairs. In these it has the aid of certain agencies such as the State Planning Commission, the Bureau of Administrative Affairs, and the Secretariat.[4]

A good part of executive business is performed by the individual ministries, but the Council of Ministers now requires to an increasing degree that ministerial orders and activities be submitted to the whole Council for information, and in a number of instances individual acts have been annulled.[5] If a ministry submits an edict to the Council of Ministers for confirmation prior to issue, it becomes an ordinance or decision of the Council and has greater authority than a purely departmental directive.

Ordinarily the Council of Ministers also coordinates the armed forces and the economic activities pertaining thereto. But after the German invasion the Soviet government adopted the British device of the "War Cabinet," in the form of the State Defense Committee. It is interesting that this agency was created in 1941 by a joint decree of the Presidium of the Supreme Soviet, the Central Committee of the Communist Party, and the Council of People's Commissars (ministers). As in Britain, the entire power of government and especially the conduct of the war were placed in the hands of this group. The original members of the State Defense Committee were Stalin, Molotov, Voroshilov, Malenkov, and Beria. Later Kaganovich, Mikoyan, and Voznesenski were included. Still later, Voroshilov was replaced by the rising Bulganin. Actually all real power was vested in Stalin personally. He combined the chairmanship of the State Defense Committee and of the Council of People's Commissars (ministers) with the Commissariat of War and the position of commander in chief of the armed forces.

The Council of Ministers (cabinet) consists of the Chairman (Premier), the ministers, the chairman of the state planning committee, and the chairman of the state committee of construction. The Chairman of the Council of Min-

---

[3] For a revealing comparison of the number of "laws" issued by the Council of Ministers as compared with other agencies, see J. Towster, *Political Power in the U.S.S.R.*, New York, 1948, p. 260n.

[4] Until recently the Economic Council issued quite a number of orders under its own authority, but there is no evidence that it still functions.

[5] It will be noted that, while the Presidium annuls acts of the Council of Ministers, the Council of Ministers annuls acts of individual Ministers.

isters (Bulganin) and several "first deputy chairmen" are the "presidium" of the Council of Ministers, a kind of "inner" or "war" cabinet.

The ministers are the heads of departments. Until 1947 there occurred an increasing proliferation of ministries, most of them being in charge of an economic sector like the aircrafts industry, machine and instrument making, etc. In that year there were 59 ministries. After that their number was reduced by combining two or more into one. From 1948 to 1951 the number rose again slightly from 48 to 51 but on March 15, 1953, was drastically reduced to 25. The majority (16) are concerned with economic matters.

These ministries are divided into All-Union and Union-Republican ministries. The All-Union ones (12) direct their affairs throughout the entire territory of the Soviet Union through their own agents,[6] while the Union-Republican ones (13) operate through the corresponding ministries of the Union Republics.[7] In addition to the regular ministers, there are also ministers without portfolio—without specific departmental responsibility. Thus, as these lines are written, Lazar Kaganovich, member of the Presidium of the Central Committee of the Communist party, is one of the first deputy premiers and general trouble shooter of the government.

The ministers are department heads like their Western colleagues, but there are substantial differences. Western ministers are almost always politicians and amateurs; Soviet ministers often remain for long terms and become professionals. They are not necessarily party leaders, although they are all party members. Unlike their Western colleagues, however, Soviet ministers do not make policy decisions on the highest level; that is the function of the Presidium of the Central Committee of the Communist party.

Ministers are theoretically appointed by and responsible to the Supreme Soviet, but in actuality they are appointed and removed by the party Presidium, to whose policies they are completely subservient and sensitive. Just how the procedure of removal works in detail is unknown, but from time to time the ministers are suddenly removed or shuffled around. Sometimes they also disappear.

It appears, therefore, that Soviet ministers, especially when they are not members of the party Presidium, are highly placed administrative assistants rather than policy-making chiefs like British or French cabinet members. The party Presidium may decide every detail of policy, or it may merely lay

[6] All-Union ministries are those for the coal industry, light and food industry, metallurgy, oil, chemical industry, machine industry, transport and heavy machinery, electrical power stations and electrical industry, defense industry, construction, railways and overland transport, and river and maritime transport.

[7] Union-Republican ministries are those for internal affairs, foreign affairs, defense, foreign and internal trade, agriculture, culture, construction materials, forestry, timber and paper industry, finance, public health, justice, communications, and state control.

down the outlines, leaving the details to the Council of Ministers, but there is never any question where the final authority lies.

The Pattern of Administration

Within each department the "single-manager principle" is in operation, although there are high councils (collegia), composed of the minister, his deputies, and several others in each department. The single-manager principle makes for clear lines of authority, but it also works swift retribution on the inefficient or disloyal individual once he is discovered.

This pattern of administration is followed in the Union Republics, whose cabinets are composed of Union-Republican and Republican ministers, but as we have seen, very little is now left to purely Republican administration.

The use of advisory councils has been widespread and is designed to promote close relationships between the nerve center and the field operations of the various ministries. Different from them are the collegia of high ministerial officials with whom the minister meets from time to time to seek advice. The minister's decision is final, and although the members of the collegia may theoretically appeal to the Council of Ministers, this may turn out to be an extremely ill-advised act unless the collegia maintain unusually close relations to the party leadership and are satisfied that the minister's liquidation is already under way.

All-Union and Union-Republican ministries are generally organized in nearly the same fashion. The difference, that the former operate their own field services while the latter act through the staff of their opposite numbers in the governments of the Republics, affects the choice of subordinate officials only. The power of final decision, in either group, rests at the top.

In each one of the sixteen Republics of the Soviet Union there is a council of ministers which, like the national government, has two types of ministries: those which correspond to ministries of the national government and are subordinate thereto, and those which are concerned with the "exclusive" powers of the Republican government. Among the latter group of Republican ministries one finds lower education, social security, local industry, and local economy.

A simpler form of administration prevails on lower levels. Below the Union Republics we find the Autonomous Republics [and in the R.S.F.S.R. the Territories (*krai*) as well as the Region (*oblast*) and the city and districts (*raion*)]. Larger cities are divided into several *raions*. Smaller towns are directly under the *oblast* or *krai*, while quite small ones are subordinate to a *raion*. But while degrees of centralization differ in the administration, this extends only to the purely technical carrying out of functions. All decisions emanate from the party, and the party organization on all levels watches over the execution of this policy. And if need be, there is always the MVD to underline heavily the reality of power.

THE MINISTRY OF STATE CONTROL

The Ministry of State Control was created in 1940 as a successor to the Soviet Control Commission. It serves as general administrative watchdog. Together with the Ministry of Finance it has control over expenditures, but its functions also go much farther. It is charged in general with seeing to it that the government's decisions are carried out. Its organization parallels that of all the ministries, and its agents are installed in all important offices and enterprises. In the Union Republics there are ministries of state control which follow the same model as the central ministry. Their chief personnel is appointed by the councils of ministers of the Republics with the consent of the Minister of State Control of the Soviet Union. Thus, despite the Union-Republican form of organization, there is actually strict centralization.

In case an error or worse is found, the Ministry has extensive powers to deal with the situation. It may hand down an administrative decision or hand the culprit over to punishment by the courts or the MVD. It may also direct agencies of the government to remove shortcomings.

The Ministry of State Control has always been regarded as important and the party has taken great interest in it. It is not without significance that the present minister, V. N. Merkulov, was formerly a member of the now-defunct Orgburo, a high secret police official, and a former Minister of State Security (then MGB). This appointment illustrates the close relations between the Ministry of State Control and the MVD-MGB.

THE FIVE-YEAR PLAN

A further factor which tends to limit the scope of activities for most ministries is the need for conformity with the over-all economic plan. In the Soviet Union the socialist aim of taking over the means of production has been fully realized, and they are all administered and owned by the state. Their operation is planned with a view to over-all efficiency rather than to the individual performance of any single industry or branch.

The direction of economic policy lies, of course, within the party Presidium as usual. The chief planning agency is the State Planning Commission (Gosplan), which in 1948 was renamed the State Planning Committee. At the same time there was created a Committee for the Material-Technical Supply of the National Economy (Gossnab), which took over the task of rendering more efficient the allocation and distribution of materials and machinery. Thus Gosplan is confined to its responsibility of planning the national economy. It draws up the Five-Year Plan (now the fifth), as well as the annual and quarterly plans, and supervises their execution. These plans are further broken down by territorial units. They are then carried out by the respective ministries, the coordinating units below the departmental level (glavks), the combines, and the trusts. These in turn have their own planning departments in which the general blueprints are spelled out in greater detail.

Each economic enterprise is part of a state trust. Several trusts are organized into industrial combines, and over them is the ministry in charge of that particular type of production. Further coordination is effected by interdepartmental councils and formerly the now inoperative Economic Council.

The Gosplan organization is very elaborate. The national Gosplan has its counterparts in the various Union Republics, and they in turn have their planning committees in all areas down to the regions, districts, and towns. Although the Gosplan is thus organized on the model of a Union-Republican ministry, it is even more centralized than they usually are. The territorial subdivision is balanced by an elaborate structure of sectional organization which deals directly with every aspect of ministerial and governmental activity, and there is yet another, functional structure of sections designed to coordinate the first and the second subdivisions.

While Gosplan is responsible for the elaboration of the economic plan which determines in detail every economic activity of the country, its policy and objectives emanate from the party Presidium, which decides the general direction and emphasis of the plan. Then Gosplan implements it and works it out in detail, always subject to such revisions or adaptations as the party leadership may decide.

Gosplan was originally intended to be only a planning agency. In the course of time, however, it has developed more and more in the direction of supervising the detailed execution of the plan. The managerial personnel which has to operate under these circumstances is strictly controlled and supervised. And the details of instructions received from above, as well as their lack of freedom in selecting their assistants, delimit their field of operations considerably.

The total emphasis in this gigantic operation is on fulfilling "the plan." By directives, speeches, newspaper articles, factory resolutions, praise of the diligent, and blame for the tardy, an atmosphere of competition is created. Among the workers, the Stakhanovites are to set an example for others to follow, while "socialist competition" is the name for a slightly less stringent speedup system.[8] With these "shock troops" of labor setting the pace, the

---

[8] For an authoritative exposition, see Margaret Miller, *Labour in the U.S.S.R.*, London, 1942. Also G. Bienstock, S. M. Schwarz, and A. Yugov, *Management in Russian Industry and Agriculture*, New York, 1944; A. Baykov, *Development of the Soviet Economic System*, Cambridge, England, 1946; L. E. Hubbard, *Soviet Labor and Industry*, London, 1942. For a Communist view, see M. Dobb, *Soviet Planning and Labor*, New York, 1943,

daily output quota, the "norm," is constantly moved upward. Considerable wage differentials [9] and other advantages for the "elite" strengthen the system.

While it is the obvious intention of this method to improve output and efficiency by creating an artificially competitive system, it also creates its own counterforces. The almost frantic emphasis on the fulfillment and overfulfillment of the plan makes for "paper fulfillment"—attempts by plant managements and other subordinate authorities to juggle figures or worse in order to report a triumph when the truth of the situation is quite different. It also produces mutual-protection relationships between administrative organs designed to watch one another; these are the so-called "family relationships" which have already been mentioned. It makes for overbureaucratization and a great use of papers and forms. It produces constant production breakdowns and acute shortages in all kinds of products. The Soviet press is full of such instances, of tales of fraudulent reporting, of "family relationships," of bureaucratic boondoggling. *Krokodil,* the Soviet humor magazine, has shown the type of manager who storms and rages on the last of the month in order to get his quota fulfilled, only to relax into inactivity on the first. It would seem that Communism too has its "inner contradictions" which Marxists like to ascribe only to capitalism.

It would certainly be a gross error to infer that the Soviet economy is breaking down. The relatively low standard of living and the constant shortages of consumers' goods are caused primarily by a long-asserted emphasis on heavy industry to the detriment of consumers' goods. But the flood of complaints which sweep through the Soviet press indicate that the totally state-owned and planned economy of the Soviet Union is far from achieving the clocklike precision which was expected for it.

On the other hand the complete concentration of the entire Soviet economic machinery on heavy industry and other activities of special strategic importance—to the detriment of consumers' goods—has produced significant results. Especially spectacular are Soviet advances in the field of atomic energy and aviation. In spite of relatively low output per man the total industrial achievement of the Soviet Union is therefore quite impressive and constitutes a real challenge to the democratic world.

---

and N. A. Voznesensky, *Economy of the U.S.S.R. during World War II,* Washington, 1948. For a brief summary, based largely on the above works, see *Communism in Action,* prepared by the Legislative Reference Service of the Library of Congress, Washington, 1946, 79th Congress, 2d Session, House Document No. 754. For a bibliography of books and articles, see Harry Schwarz, *Soviet Economy,* Syracuse, 1949.

[9] A. Bergson, *Structure of Soviet Wages,* Cambridge, Mass., 1944.

Chapter 11

LAW AND JUSTICE

The Soviet concept of law is intimately associated with its idea of the nature of the state. According to Marx, Lenin, and Stalin, the state is, as we have previously seen, a coercive machinery designed to establish and uphold a particular type of social organization. The state of capitalistic society and of the transition to socialism in particular is looked upon as an expression of the domination of one class over others, and the law of that state is therefore considered a tool for the maintenance of that domination.

We have also learned that the form of the state results, according to Marx, from productive relationships and that these economic considerations are the basis on which the "physiological superstructure is erected." Naturally law must follow in the same groove. "Marxism-Leninism," writes Vyshinsky, "gives a clear definition (the only scientific definition) of the essence of law. It teachers that legal relationships (and, consequently, law itself) are rooted in the material conditions of life, and that law is merely the will of the dominant class, elevated into a statute." [1] Soviet legal science therefore utterly rejects the concept of an independent "idea of the law" which may exist separate from the economic and class structure of the state. Law is merely an expression of the will of the state, an expression of the material form of life in that state, and in a class society it is the will of the ruling class.

With the eventual "withering away" of the state, the law too will eventually disappear. But until that happens, the strengthening and intensification of Soviet law is necessary, not in the interest of abstract justice, but as a tool for the accomplishment of the Communist aim. The standards of justice are therefore directly derived from this consideration and are not apart therefrom. Law is in essence that which furthers the aims of the Socialist revolution. Impartiality, due process of law, and similar embellishments of the "bourgeois" types of law are of secondary consideration. "Law is a political measure, law is politics," said Lenin.

The character of Soviet law as a "tool" of the regime also has another facet. In the period of "capitalistic encirclement," the defense of the Soviet state

[1] Andrei Vyshinsky, *The Law of the Soviet State* (trans. by H. R. Babb), New York, 1948, p. 13. See also, Harold J. Berman, *Justice in Russia, an Interpretation of Soviet Law*, Cambridge, Mass., 1950; Vladimir Gsovski, *Soviet Civil Law*, Ann Arbor, 1948–1949, 2 vols.

is a matter of paramount importance. Soviet law, therefore, being a tool of that state, has a special role to play in the wiping out of all enemies of the regime, domestic or foreign. Forced labor and police (MVD) detention are consequently merely continuations of the regular judicial machinery, although they exist quite apart administratively.

THE JUDGES

There are certain principles common to all regular Soviet courts. All judges are elected for a special term. The judges of the Supreme Court and the Special Courts of the U.S.S.R., as well as the Supreme Courts of the various Union and Autonomous Republics, are elected by their respective Supreme Soviets for a term of five years. The courts of lesser territorial units are elected for the same term by their respective soviets, while the judges of the lowest courts, the People's Courts, are elected by the inhabitants of their districts for a term of three years (Arts. 105–109).

The courts consist of both professional and lay judges (assessors). Actually the law does not provide that the regular judge must be learned in the law, but that is the rule. The lay judges, of course, are not so trained. Ordinarily there are two lay judges and one professional judge (chairman) in cases involving original jurisdiction, while a larger number of judges is the rule in appeals cases.

Lay judges are people from every walk of life who continue to pursue their professions but are selected for special court duty. They must not be confused with jurors, who do not exist in the Soviet system. The juries of other systems decide only specific questions of facts specially submitted to them, while questions of law are generally reserved to the judge; also, judge and jury deliberate and decide quite separately from each other. In the Soviet Union, however, the lay judges are full-fledged judges and temporary members of the bench as in Germany, and they deliberate and decide all questions of both law and fact together with the professional judge. Decisions are reached by majority vote, although as a rule the view of the professional judge prevails.

According to the Constitution, all court proceedings are public and all languages are permitted, either directly or through interpreters. The Constitution also guarantees the right of counsel and the independence of the judges. However, an attorney who did his best for a defendant accused of a political offense would be quickly liquidated. The "independence" of judges will be discussed later.

THE COURT SYSTEM

Except for the People's Courts, all Soviet courts have both original and appellate jurisdiction, including the Supreme Court of the U.S.S.R. Appeal is permissible from any court to the next higher court, but except for rare incidents appeals do not go any higher. Only the decisions of the Supreme Court in *original* jurisdiction cannot be appealed to any higher authority. Appeals may originate with either party to a suit, or in criminal cases with both the accused (and his attorneys) and the prosecutor.

THE COURT SYSTEM OF THE USSR

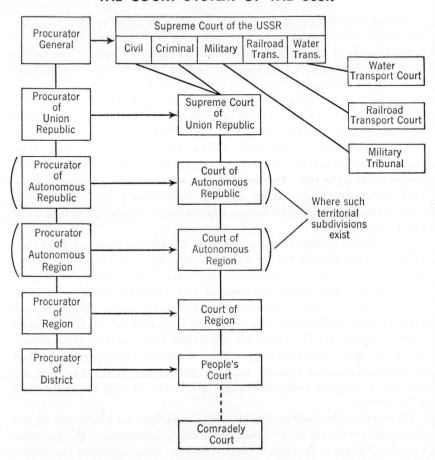

The lowest level of the judicial hierarchy is occupied by the People's Courts. These are exclusively courts of original jurisdiction, and they absorb the great majority of cases, civil and criminal.

A peculiarity are the so-called "comradely courts," which might better be called honor courts. They are organized in factories, farm collectives, and apartment houses to deal with petty theft, libel, etc., and can impose fines and reprimands. They may be elected for each case or consist of all those present at a meeting.[2] The "comradely courts" are under the supervision of the People's Court, which can annul their decisions.

The courts of the areas, Regions, Autonomous Regions, and Autonomous Republics, serve as courts of appeal in cases coming up from the People's Courts of their respective areas. They also have original jurisdiction in cases involving "counterrevolutionary activities, crimes against administrative orders when they involve particular danger to the state, the pillaging of socialist property, and other important economic crimes." Original jurisdiction pertains also to civil cases between state and social institutions, enterprises, and organizations.

The highest judicial authority in each Union Republic is its supreme court. It supervises all inferior courts in the Republic by examining all protests coming from the Procurator-General or Chairman of the Supreme Court of the U.S.S.R., or the procurator or chairman of the supreme court of the Republic. It also examines on appeal the judgments and verdicts of courts which are one step in rank below that of the supreme court.[3] The supreme court may set aside the decision of any inferior court in the Republic. It also has original jurisdiction in cases of exceptional gravity and in crimes involving the top officials of the Republic. But the Presidium of the (Republic's) Supreme Soviet, the Procurator, the Ministry of Internal Affairs, and the full court itself may place other cases directly before the supreme court of the Republic.

The apex of the whole judicial structure is the Supreme Court of the U.S.S.R. (Art. 104). It consists of a Chairman, a Vice-Chairman, a large number of other judges, at present seventy-seven and thirty-five lay judges (people's assessors). It is organized in five divisions or panels, for criminal, civil, military, railroad-transport, and water-transport affairs. The Chairman of the Supreme Court may preside over any case before the court. He may also remove any case from any court in the U.S.S.R. and submit a protest about it to a full session of the Supreme Court.

The Supreme Court is primarily a court of appeals and review, but it also has original jurisdiction in criminal and civil matters of All-Union importance. Its verdicts are final and have the force of law. Its entire plenum convenes not less than once every two months to consider protests against acts of inferior courts and to issue instructions concerning general court practice and procedure which ensure uniformity throughout the country.

No Independence of Judges

The Constitution of 1936 has given the judiciary a higher status and a more independent existence than was the case before. However, the stipulation that

---

[2] Berman, *op. cit.*, pp. 266–269.

[3] Because of the great variety in size among the various Union Republics, the territorial subdivisions thereof differ; some have regional subdivisions which others lack.

judges are "independent and subject only to the law" (Art. 112) must be understood with some qualifications. As we have seen, the Soviet concept of government rejects the notion of an independent law or justice. This principle used to be stated quite frankly. In 1927, the then Commissar of Justice, N. V. Krylenko, wrote,

> The . . . principle is the dependence and removability of our courts. Whereas the basic principle of the bourgeois court is its independence, the irremovability of the judge . . . we say plainly that our judge is both removable and dependent; inasmuch as he is an organ of state power . . . he is, therefore, both removable and dependent upon the proletariat, the state, the toiling class, whom he is called upon to serve.[4]

This principle was officially discarded in the 1936 Constitution. But in the same year when Vyshinsky and others were extolling this complete independence of the judge, the then Commissar of Justice, N. M. Rychkov, stated that the men to be advanced to judicial positions should be party and non-party Bolsheviks, devoted to the cause of socialism, and that all local party and Soviet organs must properly organize the work of the judiciary. Another writer, N. Poliansky, stated even more clearly that "the independence of judges does not at all exclude the duty to follow the general policy of the government. The judiciary is an organ of state power and cannot be outside politics." [5]

It has already been noted that there is, of course, no judicial review in the U.S.S.R. Nor does the judiciary possess the power to annul decisions and decrees of the Presidium of the Supreme Soviet or of the Council of Ministers. On the contrary, the Council of Ministers has established the organization of the courts, including the Law on the Judiciary of 1938 which governs the courts. The Minister of Justice is charged with supervising the administrative part of the Supreme Court's work, and he participates regularly in the deliberations of the Supreme Court when it is meeting in full session.[6]

SPECIAL COURTS

In addition to the regular court hierarchy there are also a number of special courts. These are military tribunals, railroad-transport courts, and water-transport courts. They are subordinate to the Supreme Court of the U.S.S.R., which acts as a court of appeals for them. Their jurisdiction depends on the nature of the crime as well as the status of the accused. Thus military tribunals may also try civilians in certain cases.

---

[4] Quoted by J. Towster, *Political Power in the U.S.S.R.*, New York, 1948, p. 303*n*.

[5] *Ibid.*, pp. 302, 304.

[6] When the Supreme Court meets in full session, the Procurator-General must attend, while the Minister of Justice may also be present.

The Procurator-General

A unique position in the judicial machinery is maintained by the Procurator-General of the U.S.S.R. This officer is appointed by the Supreme Soviet for a term of seven years (Art. 114). His office is a strictly centralized one because he appoints all the procurators of the Republics, Territories, Regions, etc. (Art. 115). The procurators of the lowest units of government, areas, districts, and cities are appointed by the procurators of their respective Union Republics, subject to the approval of the Procurator-General (Art. 116). All members of the procuratorial staff are completely independent from all local organs whatsoever and are subordinate solely to the Procurator-General (Art. 117).

The independence of the Procurator-General does not, of course, mean that he is independent of the Communist party and its Presidium. But his freedom from possible local pressure helps materially in establishing uniform standards of law enforcement through the entire territory of the U.S.S.R.

The powers of the Procurator-General are vast and important. In him is vested supreme supervisory power to ensure the strict observance of the law by all ministries and institutions subordinate to them, as well as by officials and citizens of the U.S.S.R. generally (Art. 113). This is a greater power than that vested in the Supreme Court of the U.S.S.R. which supervises only the judicial activities of subordinate courts. But it is a power which follows strictly the command of the party leadership as evidenced in the numerous purge trials. The Soviet concept of "legality" is thus markedly different from that customary in the West.

In pursuit of his functions the Procurator-General has developed a unique, because official, organization of informers. Vyshinsky, a former Procurator-General, wrote, "All the organs of Soviet Community, the Young Communist League, the trade unions, worker correspondents and peasant correspondents, and so on, take an active part in the work of the Soviet Prosecutor's office, in its struggle to strengthen socialist legality." [7] These groups are well organized and meet regularly under specific leaders. They "signal" cases to the Procurator's office, including cases involving their associates, friends, and parents. Their services have been found most effective by the Soviet authorities.[8]

The regular court system is only one part of the vast organization which controls those who step out of line. In fact, as far as penal justice is concerned, the regular courts are comparable to the visible peaks of an iceberg; much more lies underneath: the secret police, the deportations, and the forced-labor camps.

[7] Vyshinsky, *op. cit.*, p. 528.

[8] S. N. Harper and R. Thompson, *The Government of the Soviet Union*, New York, 1949, 2d ed., p. 237.

Chapter 12

THE POSITION OF THE INDIVIDUAL

The Soviet Constitution establishes and "guarantees" a considerable number of civil rights. The list of liberties (Arts. 118–133) contains all those which are customary in Western democracies and many more. This development emerged in the 1936 Constitution. Previous documents had conferred personal rights only with considerable restrictions and on an unequal basis and had given civil rights only to the workers. The Constitution of 1936 placed everyone on an equal level. Lest the reader should come to the hasty conclusion that Stalin had unfurled the banner of Jeffersonian democracy, let us examine the theory and practice of civil rights in the U.S.S.R.

Soviet theorists assert that in the so-called "bourgeois" states democracy is a sham and an illusion. The people may go through the motions of electing "their" representatives, but in reality they are merely permitted to choose between different representatives of their oppressors. Civil rights, assert the Soviet theorists, are meaningless without economic freedom. They say,

What can be the "personal freedom" of an unemployed person who goes hungry and finds no use for his toil? Only where exploitation is annihilated, where there is no oppression of some by others, no unemployment, no beggary, and no trembling for fear that a man may on the morrow lose his work, his habitation, and his bread— only there is true freedom found.[1]

The Communist concept of personal freedom is thus derived from two principal assumptions: (1) that freedom is possible only when there is complete economic security and abundance; and (2) that only the Communist state can achieve and safeguard this economic goal. Said Stalin, "There neither is nor should be an irreconcilable contrast between the individual and the collective. . . . There should be none forasmuch as collectivism-socialism does not deny individual interests. It amalgamates them with the interests of the collective."[2]

Since a conflict between the state and the individual is "unnatural" under socialism, as that term is understood in the Soviet Union, any such "perver-

---

[1] Stalin in an interview with Roy Howard, 1937.

[2] Quoted by Andrei Vyshinsky, *The Law of the Soviet State* (trans. by H. R. Babb), New York, 1948, p. 540.

sion" can only be the result of criminal tendencies on the part of the individual. Vyshinsky makes this point abundantly clear:

In our state, naturally, there is and can be no place for freedom of speech, press, and so on for the foes of socialism. Every sort of attempt on their part to utilize to the detriment of the state—that is to say, to the detriment of all the toilers— these freedoms granted to the toilers must be classified as a counterrevolutionary crime to which Article 58, Paragraph 10, or one of the corresponding articles of the Criminal Code is applicable.[3]

The Constitution underscores this point. Articles 125 and 126 grant the rights of free speech, press, and assembly, "in conformity with the interests of the working people, and in order to strengthen the socialist system." All other personal rights are granted unconditionally.

The principle that certain economic conditions must precede the establishment of real freedom is graphically demonstrated in Chapter 10 of the Constitution, entitled "Fundamental Rights and Duties of Citizens" (Arts. 118–133), which begins with an enumeration of economic rights, relegating the civil liberties of the Western type to a later, less conspicuous position.

Another characteristic of the Soviet Constitution is the fact that it unites in one section and usually in the same articles both rights and corresponding duties and outlines the machinery through which they may be accomplished. Likewise rights, especially economic rights, call for intervention on the part of the state and the rendering of certain services on the part of the state. All these rights are by Communist doctrine the result of the (socialist) economic and social order. The concept of "natural right" is, of course, rejected.

WORK

The first right (Art. 118) which the Soviet Constitution confers on its citizens is the "right to work." This means that the state furnishes jobs to everybody, and that is only natural because practically all enterprise is owned and operated by the state. The Constitution declares that "the right to work is ensured by the socialist organization of the national economy, the steady growth of the productive forces of Soviet society, the elimination of the possibility of economic crises, and the abolition of unemployment."

What the state gives, the state can take away. The combination of all political and economic power in the hands of the state therefore serves to control the citizen all the more securely, since none of his activities are outside the purview of governmental authority. Unemployment does not exist in the Soviet Union, although a large number of citizens work in forced-labor camps. However, wages in terms of purchasing power are extremely low except in the highest ranks of the hierarchy and the wage differential between execu-

[3] *Ibid.*, p. 617.

tive positions and unskilled labor is as great as in any "capitalistic" country, and frequently greater. This is also reflected in the armed forces, in which a colonel's pay is thirty times that of a private.

The factory or shop in which the Soviet citizen works is a more or less self-contained unit, inasmuch as it satisfies his cultural, medical, and social needs. Often it also furnishes his living accommodation (graded strictly according to rank) and his food and clothing requirements. Exceptionally good work as well as excess profits on the part of the enterprise may lead to bonuses and increase of services. The money which he does not need he may put aside in a state bank. But the government sees to it that these funds are drained off on occasion, thus eliminating the danger of a new capitalistic or "speculator's" class. This drainage is largely accomplished by the "gray market," the state stores which sell goods at prices very much above the controlled prices in other types of stores. Since Soviet citizens may purchase only a limited quantity of rationed goods at controlled prices, the additional expenditure at inflated prices is difficult to avoid. Another method by which money may be drained off is devaluation, which appeared in the Soviet Union as a postwar phenomenon as it has in other countries.

HOUSING

Perhaps the greatest problem of the Soviet worker is that of housing. Not even in the slum areas of the Western capitals is there such a congestion as is commonly found in the industrial centers of the Soviet Union. In many cases one room to a family is a common standard. In view of the continued emphasis on heavy industry in the Five-Year Plan, little relief appears to be in sight, especially as many shoddily built or overage structures become uninhabitable. Private cooperatives for the building of houses and apartments are possible under Soviet law. By decree, a Soviet citizen is now permitted to own or build his own home, although it appears that this is permissible only if he does so for his own use and not for the purpose of resale or renting. However, private construction is not practicable in the larger urban centers, where the greatest shortage exists, and it is difficult to save enough money for the purpose.

HEALTH

Public health services are furnished, and medicine has been largely socialized, yet private medical practice is permissible in view of the shortage of public health facilities. It is interesting to note that Stakhanovites and other shock workers are frequently given permission and compensation for undergoing private treatment as a reward for exceptional merit.

OTHER BENEFITS

The Soviet citizen is insured against the loss of earning power through sick-ness, disability, or old age (Art. 120). But absenteeism or tardiness may lead to severe fines and punishment. He is also entitled to rest and leisure (Art. 119), which means the establishment of the eight-hour day for ordinary work, with reduction to seven or even four hours where labor is especially arduous. He is also entitled to paid vacations and to the use of rest homes and other recreational facilities, all of which the state furnishes. The "parks of culture and rest" and the "workers' clubs" are common in all cities. Vacation spots of great desirability, however, are reserved for especially meritorious cases and for the higher bureaucracy, the new elite of the Soviet society, which is as class-conscious, as superior in deportment, and as removed financially and psychologically as any "upper class" in the despised "bourgeois" states ever was.

In the U.S.S.R. women are accorded equal rights with men in all spheres and levels, but they are not much in evidence now on the highest level of the party. There is no woman member of the party Presidium. Women receive aid for maternity and similar occasions, and the Soviet government has copied the Nazi and Fascist custom of awarding decorations, titles,[4] and monetary com-pensations to women who bear an exceptional number of children.

THE FAMILY

In the beginning of the Soviet regime family ties were taken lightly, and it was assumed that the state would accept much of the burden of rearing children and maintaining households.[5] Marriage with or without official regis-tration was little restrained, since divorce was easy and could be accomplished unilaterally by simple notification on the part of one spouse.

All this has changed very substantially. Marriage must now be registered, and divorce can be obtained only through litigation, which may be quite complicated and costly.[6] In fact, the general Soviet attitude now is one of extolling the virtues of the family and the sanctity of marriage.

---

[4] A woman bearing ten children or more is awarded the title of "Mother Heroine."

[5] Friedrich Engels, The Origin of the Family, Private Property, and the State, New York, 1942; Alexandra Kollontai, Communism and the Family, San Francisco, no date (Russian ed., 1919).

[6] Alex Inkeles, "Family and Church in the Post-war U.S.S.R.," Annals of the American Academy of Political and Social Science, May, 1949, pp. 33–44; John N. Hazard, "Law and the Soviet Family," Wisconsin Law Review (1939), pp. 224–253; Vladimir Gsovski, "Marriage and Divorce in Soviet Law," Georgetown Law Journal, Vol. XXXV (1947), pp. 209–223.

EDUCATION

The Constitution guarantees the right to education (Art. 121). The original version of that article provided for free education, including higher education. In 1947 this was amended to the effect that education is now free only up to the seventh grade. However, tuition fees are not exorbitant, and stipends and scholarships are available for capable students.

The Soviet government fully realizes the importance of education and the need for controlling the minds of the future generation. This is accomplished in the Soviet schools, where the slightest vestige of foreign ideology has been exterminated. The Communist party is forever vigilant in supervising education and research, not as an instrument for the discovery of truth but to further the purposes of the Soviet state. This point of view was well illustrated in an article in the official *Voprosy Istorii* (Questions of History), September, 1948, which finds it alarming that there are still historians who interpret historical problems in the light of "bourgeois objectivism" and not from the party point of view.[7]

The Soviet schools have substantially reduced the illiteracy of prewar days. During the revolutionary period a heavy emphasis was placed on technical instruction to the almost total exclusion of cultural subjects. Later this trend was criticized and reversed. Likewise the equalitarian tendency of earlier days has been modified. There is now recognition of individual and regional differences. Moreover, a compromise is made between the principle of the common secondary level and the need for university preparation. The basis of the school system is compulsory basic instruction lasting seven years (ages seven to fifteen), after which students either complete their education in vocational schools (for four more years) or transfer to specialized technical, medical, or other preparatory schools.[8]

RACE RELATIONS

The Constitution forbids all discrimination on the basis of nationality or race (Art. 123). In this field the Soviet government can claim certain accomplishments in comparison with the situation under the tsars. The vigorous Russification and the virulent anti-Semitism which marked the imperial regime are not so much in evidence today. On the other hand, it cannot be denied that the individual has much less freedom under Communism than even under the tsar, although this system controls all equally without regard to race or color.

[7] Sergius Yakobson, "Post-war Historical Research in the Soviet Union," *Annals of the American Academy of Political and Social Science*, May, 1949, p. 130.

[8] Nicolas Hans, "Recent Trends in Soviet Education," *ibid.*, pp. 114–122.

But even with these qualifications the Soviet claim that there are no racial distinctions and discriminations in the U.S.S.R. cannot be accepted at face value. Although the forceful Russification policy of the tsarist regime has not been repeated, there is little doubt that the Great Russians, essentially the inhabitants of the Western part of the Russian Soviet Federated Socialist Republic (R.S.F.S.R.)—the Russians in the narrow sense of the word—occupy the leading positions in the state and are regarded, in Stalin's own words, as "the leading force of the Soviet Union among all the peoples of our country." [9]

The leading position of the Great Russians was assured even under Stalin, who was not a Russian but a Georgian. In fact, of the nine present members of the party Presidium, seven are Great Russians, one (Mikoyan) is Armenian, and one (Kaganovich) is Jewish. The same is true of the governmental and industrial administrations of the Union Republics, where Great Russians have the lion's share of influential positions.[10] This trend is of course particularly strong among the Asiatic republics because of the greater reservoir of educated and trained manpower which the Russians have at their disposal.

Observers agree in general that Russia's trouble spot is the Ukraine, which has been the target of repeated accusations of "bourgeois nationalism," an accusation which has never been directed against the Great Russians.[11] There is also the fact that the invading German armies found a degree of collaboration in the Ukraine and among other non-Russian people which they did not find among the Great Russians.

The problem of anti-Semitism is one of a different order. It has been latent in Russia for centuries and was frequently encouraged by the tsars. Such sentiments were not tolerated in the earlier period of the Communist regime, especially as many of the Bolshevik leaders were Jews. The Soviet Union had a Jewish Autonomous Region in the R.S.F.S.R. called Birobidzhan, which was not a notable success. It was established in order to offset the attraction of Zionism. During the war anti-Jewish feelings caused some concern to the regime and were officially condemned. However, in 1949 the campaign against intellectuals emphasized the expression "homeless cosmopolitans," which was especially directed against members of the Jewish community. To an increasing extent such people were singled out for their Jewish origin, and the Soviet papers liked to print their Russian names together with their obviously Jewish former names like "G. Yasny (Finkelstein)" [12]—a practice hitherto employed only by Joseph Goebbels and the German Nazi press.

[9] Quoted in *Tensions within the Soviet Union*, p. 43.
[10] *Ibid.*, pp. 43–45.
[11] John S. Reshetar, Jr., "National Deviation in the Soviet Union," *The American Slavic and East European Review*, Vol. 12 (1953), p. 173.
[12] Joseph Newman, "Russia Uncensored: Plight of Jews," *New York Herald Tribune*, Nov. 3, 1949, quoted in *Tensions within the Soviet Union*, p. 40.

Finally in 1952–1953 the Soviet government undertook an openly anti-Semitic campaign in connection with the trial of the Jewish doctors accused of having killed Zhdanov and of having plotted to kill other leaders. The accusation was that they were part of an international Zionist conspiracy hired by the American Joint Distribution Committee, actually a Jewish welfare organization. Although the word "Zionist" rather than "Jewish" was used, the tenor of the campaign was clearly anti-Semitic and so understood by the people of the Soviet Union. This was openly admitted when, on April 4, 1953, after Stalin's death, the Jewish doctors were freed and exonerated. An editorial in *Pravda* declared that the accusation against the doctors constituted an attempt "to inflame in Soviet Society . . . feelings of national antagonism." [13]

Thus ended this particularly virulent anti-Semitic campaign, and diplomatic relations between the U.S.S.R. and Israel, which had been broken off, were restored. The question of motive is still open. Under the tsar, anti-Jewish pogroms usually had the purpose of diverting the people's attention from their real grievances. Perhaps a similar purpose was intended here, but that is conjectural. It is, however, certain that the international dispersion of the Jewish people together with the strong bond of solidarity felt by them has created in them an international spirit and international contacts which are deeply suspect in the Soviet Union.

Speech, Press, Assembly, and Asylum

We have already mentioned the limitations imposed on the rights of free speech, press, and assembly. The corollary to these rights is the statement (Art. 125) that these rights are ensured by placing at the disposal of the working people printing presses, needed supply of paper, and other facilities— over which, however, the state retains complete control, thereby possessing an additional method to prevent the possibility of free speech, press, and assembly from getting out of hand.

The Constitution affords the right of asylum to foreign citizens "persecuted for defending the interests of the working people . . ." (Art. 129), which in practice applies primarily to Communists.

Duties

Finally the section on the fundamental rights and duties of citizens contains an enumeration of duties which appear to be specially significant. Article 130 admonishes every citizen "to abide by the Constitution, to observe the laws, to maintain labor discipline, honestly to perform public duties, and to respect the rules of socialist intercourse." Article 131 instructs every citizen "to safeguard

[13] *The New York Times*, Apr. 12, 1953.

and fortify public, socialist property as the sacred and inviolable foundation of the Soviet system . . ." and declares that all persons "committing offenses against public, Socialist property are enemies of the people."

The Constitution further establishes universal military service, which helps to make the Soviet army by far the largest army of the world, and declares it to be "the sacred duty" to defend the country. "Treason to the motherland —violation of the oath of allegiance, desertion to the enemy, impairing the military power of the state, espionage,—is punishable with all the severity of the law as the most heinous of crimes" (Art. 133).

Behind the façade of civil rights there looms the secret political police, with unrestricted right to arrest any citizen and to confine him in prison or forced-labor camp for any length of time. This is probably the most feared and hated Soviet institution, and many citizens would undoubtedly like to see it modified or abolished. But as far as civil rights in general are concerned, the Soviet citizen who has not lived abroad has never enjoyed civil liberties and therefore has only a dim idea of what he misses. There appears to be little evidence of a "ground swell" in the Soviet Union demanding a bill of rights and the enforcement of real civil liberties.

Chapter 13

THE SOVIET UNION AND THE WORLD

This is not the place to examine the foreign relations of the Soviet Union, to which obviously much more space would have to be devoted than is available here.[1] This chapter merely is to point out certain features of international relations which are peculiar to the Soviet orbit and which are derived directly from the nature of the Communist regime.

Communists believe, as we have seen, in a form of economic determinism. Applied to the field of international relations, this would mean that the cleavage between the capitalistic and the communist worlds is the direct result of their economic differences and is therefore inherent in the era of coexistence of both. Lenin, in emphasizing the role of imperialism as the "highest stage of capitalism," spoke of an "inevitable struggle between the capitalist and the socialist world" and of a "series of frightful clashes" which would result. Stalin echoed these sentiments.[2] Stalin and other Soviet leaders have spoken of the possibility of a "peaceful coexistence" of the "two worlds," but there is not necessarily a contradiction between the two approaches; presumably the struggle—which need not take military forms—is still inevitable and in fact upon us now because of the "inner contradictions" of capitalism and the "predatory nature" of imperialism. The capitalist leaders, we are told, look to the Soviet Union with hatred because of that country's alleged attraction to the workers of the world, and they therefore regard the U.S.S.R. as an enemy. Moreover, they are "warmongers" because they allegedly hope to incite a war in order to divert the masses from domestic difficulties.[3] The very fact of "coexistence" spells danger to the Soviet Union, which must be strong and vigilant in order to avoid disaster. It therefore maintains the largest army and air

[1] See M. Beloff, *Foreign Policy of Soviet Russia*, Oxford, 1947–1949, 2 vols.; D. J. Dallin, *Soviet Russia's Foreign Policy*, New Haven, 1942; L. Fischer, *The Soviets in World Affairs*, New York, 1930, 2 vols.; also his *Trends in Russian Foreign Policy since World War I*, Washington, D.C., 1947, Senate Committee on Foreign Relations, 80th Congress, 1st Session.

[2] N. A. Voznesensky, *The Economy of the U.S.S.R. during World War II* (trans. under the auspices of the American Council of Learned Societies), Washington, D.C., 1948, p. 105.

[3] "X" (George F. Kennan), "The Sources of Soviet Conduct," *Foreign Affairs*, July, 1947.

force in the world and has anchored the system of universal military service in its Constitution.

Despite that fact, the Soviet Union poses as "the camp of peace" while the "capitalistic" countries are, by definition, called "warmongers." Personal and "idealistic" (in contrast to materialistic) factors such as "good will" have little room in Communist thinking. This does not mean that the Soviet government is necessarily and at all times a deceiver. During periods of good diplomatic relations the Soviet government has been found to take great care in its treaty obligations, but otherwise clear violations of treaties are frequent.[4] However, the Communist leaders believe they are "realistic" in utterly rejecting the possibility of "good will" on the part of representatives of countries whose economic interests they believe must be at variance with that of peace with the Soviet Union. The belief in an allegedly hostile environment is fundamental to Soviet foreign policy, but as we have seen it is also a justification for certain domestic measures of the regime.

In one of his last declarations, Stalin spoke of the inevitability of war between capitalist countries and again predicted the downfall of capitalism,[5] but this return to Leninist doctrine would seem to be primarily an attempt to show why capitalism had not yet collapsed. It was a direct slap against those more realistic Soviet economists, like Eugene Varga, who had maintained that capitalism had learned from the past and had adapted itself to the present situation and thus avoided the depression-war cycle, hitherto claimed as inevitable.

INTERNATIONAL LAW

This naturally colors the Soviet government's attitude toward international law. Communist legal science considers international law the law of the dominant states, therefore as "bourgeois international law," as stated by Vyshinsky. The outstanding Soviet authority on the subject, Professor E. A. Korovin, wrote a book to which he gave the revealing title "The International Law of the Period of Transition," [6] namely, of the transition from a capitalistic to a socialist world. This is merely a method of adaptation to the realities in international life, not a matter of conviction or belief in common legal norms. Two more recent works by Professors V. N. Durdenevski and S. B.

---

[4] "Soviet Violations of Treaty Obligations: Document Submitted by the Department of State to the Senate Committee on Foreign Relations," *Department of State Bulletin,* June 6, 1948, pp. 738–744.

[5] J. V. Stalin, "Economic Problems of Socialism in the U.S.S.R.," in *Bolshevik,* Oct. 2, 1952, reprinted in J. S. Meisel and E. S. Kozera, *Materials for the Study of the Soviet System,* Ann Arbor, Mich., 1953, p. xiv.

[6] E. A. Korovin, *Mezhdunarodnoe Pravo Perekhodnovo Vremeni* (International Law of the Age of Transition), Moscow-Petrograd, 1923.

Krylov [7] and by Professor F. I. Kozhevnikov [8] follow a more traditional course by recognizing the existence of international law which, because of the important role of the U.S.S.R., can no longer be considered purely "bourgeois," but their views were roundly denounced by Professor Korovin,[9] who appears to be now again on top. It must be presumed, therefore, that the earlier views of Korovin are dominant and that international law is not accepted in principle except when convenient. This has been stated clearly in a later work by Professor F. I. Kozhevnikov,[10] who accepts only those institutions which serve Soviet policy while he rejects those that do not. In contrast to Korovin, Kozhevnikov had a few kind words to say about arbitration and, with some reservations, about the International Court of Justice. But that was before Korovin's chilling blast, and the present standing of such moderate views must seriously be doubted. This is also in line with the views of Foreign Minister Vyshinsky who, at the occasion of the Belgrade Conference on Navigation on the River Danube, rejected categorically the suggestion that disputes over the treaty should be submitted to the International Court of Justice.[11] Both Korovin and the (reformed) Kozhevnikov agree now that a "new form of international law has emerged from the relationship between the U.S.S.R. and the 'People's Democracies.' " [12]

The above problems belong primarily in the traditional field of foreign policy, which is not our principal concern. There is, however, another side to Moscow's international relations. Ever since its rise to power the Communist party of the Soviet Union—and that means the Soviet government—has been the head and the heart of an international movement with a powerful following in every country.

[7] V. N. Durdenevski and S. B. Krylov, *Mezhdunarodnoe Pravo* (International Law), Moscow, 1946, 3 vols.

[8] F. I. Kozhevnikov, *Uchebnoe Posobie po Mezhdunarodnomy Publichnomu Pravu* (Study Aid for International Public Law), Moscow, 1947.

[9] Review in *Sovetskoe Gosudarstvo i Pravo* (Soviet State and Law), August, 1948. Reprinted in *The American Journal of International Law*, Vol. XLIII (1949), pp. 387–389. The tenor of the criticism is revealed in comments like the following. Kozhevnikov refers to Grotius as the founder of international law. Korovin replies: "It would seem that the title of 'founder' is applicable only to the four great names of Marx, Engels, Lenin and Stalin. They are founders of all contemporary science relating to society and the state." Or: "Those [Soviet contributions] which he has set forth he sometimes treats, not in a militant fashion, but with an objective tone, when they are the very points which should be presented not objectively, but with the full force of Soviet patriotic pathos."

[10] F. I. Kozhevnikov, *Sovetskoe Gosudarstvo i Mezhdunarodnoe Pravo 1917–1947* (The Soviet State and International Law 1917–1947), Moscow, 1948.

[11] Walter A. Radius, "The Issues at Belgrade Were Clearly Drawn," *Department of State Bulletin*, Sept. 19, 1948, pp. 348ff.

[12] For a fuller treatment, see T. A. Taracouzio, *The Soviet Union and International Law*, New York, 1935; E. A. Korovin, "The Contribution of the USSR to International Law," *Soviet Press Translations*, Vol. III (Dec. 1, 1948), pp. 655ff.

THE COMMUNIST INTERNATIONAL

The existence of international political associations is not peculiar to Communism, nor has it originated with them. The forerunner of later Internationals was the Communist League, which was founded in 1836 and for which Marx and Engels wrote the Communist Manifesto in 1848. The so-called First International was founded in London in 1864; it was the first thoroughly organized international organization of socialist parties, and Marx wrote its bylaws. The First International soon disintegrated and was officially dissolved in 1876, but a similar organization was again established in Paris in 1889 as the International Working Men's Association, better known as the Second International.

The Second International was revived after its dormant period in the First World War and retained its status as the international organization of socialist (non-Communist) parties. It disappeared in the Second World War and has now been officially revived. There is also a loose international association of Christian Democratic parties.

But all these organizations were and are free associations of equals. Decisions are taken by majority vote and no one party or country is dominant. The Communist International, however, which was organized in Moscow in 1919 and which became known as the Third International or Comintern (Communist International), as well as its successor the Cominform (Communist Information Bureau), which was founded in 1947, took a different course.

The Bolshevik Revolution had an international character from the very beginning. Its leaders saw it as the first step of the world revolution, and the preamble to the Constitution of 1924 proclaimed that the federation of the Soviet Republics was merely the first step toward a soviet world republic. [13] To this end the Communist International, Comintern, was founded in March, 1919. It is interesting to note that this brain child of Lenin's was not greeted with any great enthusiasm by the Communist parties of Central and Western Europe. The leadership of the German Communists, especially its most outstanding personality, Rosa Luxemburg, opposed this step. They distrusted the Bolshevik (Russian) leaders and wanted to establish strong Communist parties in the West first.[14] However Lenin went ahead and perhaps inadvertently showed his hand by leaving the preparation for the organization of the Comintern in the hands of the Soviet Foreign Office. Because of the dis-

[13] L. H. Laing, M. C. Vernon, S. Eldersveld, J. S. Meisel, J. K. Pollock, *Source Book in European Governments,* New York, 1950, p. 227.

[14] Franz Borkenau, *World Communism,* New York, 1939, p. 161. This is without doubt the most authoritative work on the Communist International.

turbances of the time, few genuine foreign delegations reached Moscow. The delegate of the German Communists, Eberlein, allowed himself to be persuaded to obstain from voting, in direct contradiction to the German Communist leadership, which had instructed him to vote against the formation of the International. The Third (Communist) International was thus from the beginning a Russian creation, dominated completely by the Communist party of the Soviet Union. Its first president was Grigori Zinoviev, and Moscow became its headquarters.

The organization of the Comintern was a replica of the Communist party in the Soviet Union. Nominally, supreme authority was vested in a World Congress, in which all national parties were to be represented and which was to meet every two years. The Congress elected an Executive Committee, which was supposedly responsible to it but which in actuality assumed all the functions of the Congress. There was also elected an International Control Commission. The Executive Committee elected a Presidium (the counterpart of the Politburo) which appointed a Political Secretariat. The Communist party of each country was constituted as a "section" (branch) of the Comintern. Article 13 of the Statute of the Communist International of 1928 provided as follows: "The decisions of the Executive Committee of the Communist International are obligatory for all the sections of the International and must be promptly carried out." And Art. 14 ruled that the Executive Committees of the various Communist parties of the world were responsible to their respective national congresses and to the Executive Committee of the Communist International.[15] No secrecy prevailed concerning the actual leadership of the Executive Committee. Article 8 of the Statute of the Communist International of 1920 read as follows:

The bulk of the work and responsibility in the Executive Committee of the Communist International lies with the Party of that country, where, in keeping with the resolution of the World Congress, the Executive Committee finds its residence for the time being. The Party of the country in question sends to the Executive Committee not less than five members with a decisive vote. In addition to this one representative with a decisive vote is sent to the Executive Committee from each of the other ten to twelve largest Communist Parties. . . .

The country in which the Executive Committee found its residence was, of course, the U.S.S.R.

While the domination of Russian Communism over the Comintern was established from the beginning, it was only under Stalin that the Comintern became the conveyor belt, first of Stalin's domination over Communism at home and abroad, and later of the aspirations of Soviet foreign policy. A former leader of the German Communist party has described graphically and

---

[15] *Blueprint for World Conquest as Outlined by the Communist International,* with an introduction by W. M. Chamberlin, Washington, D.C., 1946.

in detail how the Comintern was employed in order to change the leadership of the party in Germany and to help strengthen Stalin's hand at home,[16] and a former leader of Italian Communism has told how the members of the Executive Committee of the Communist International were once cajoled into issuing a violent protest against a letter by Leon Trotsky—a letter which none of them was permitted to see or read.[17]

The absolute and unquestioned domination of the Comintern by the Soviet leadership became an accomplished fact long before the outbreak of the Second World War. Whenever the Moscow party line changed, the policies of all other Communist parties changed likewise. All of them pursued the ever-increasing hate campaign against the democratic socialists, who were regarded as "social fascists" and the "principal enemy of the workers." All of them suddenly reversed themselves in the thirties when the call went out from Moscow for a united front with the socialists and later for a popular front with all moderate and democratic parties. Similarly it is still well remembered how the Communists of all countries inveighed against the "imperialist war" and how criticism of Nazism and Fascism disappeared from the Communist press—until the German attack against the Soviet Union changed everything, and the same parties which had hitherto condemned the war could hardly get enough of it now and demanded an immediate opening of a second front.

After Russia's entry into the war a period of fairly good relations with other nations ensued, and as a gesture of good will the Comintern was officially dissolved in 1943. However, there is ample proof that the intimate contact between Communist parties did not cease and that they continued to take orders from the same headquarters. In the United States this was most spectacularly revealed when Earl Browder, who had become identified with the policy of good relations between East and West, was criticized during the summer of 1945 by the French Communist leader Jacques Duclos in a French Communist publication, *Les Cahiers du Communisme*. Duclos was generally regarded as a Comintern agent, and his article was reprinted verbatim in the New York edition of the *Daily Worker*, which still carried Browder's name on its masthead as editor in chief. As usual in such cases, Browder suddenly found himself attacked on all sides and was first demoted and then expelled.

The early postwar years showed the Soviet Union in a position of unprecedented power. Not only had it added vast territories to its domain—the only belligerent of the Second World War to reap such a reward—but Communist regimes were set up in Poland, Czechoslovakia, Hungary, Yugoslavia, Bulgaria, Rumania, and Albania. Communist armies fought in Greece, China,

---

[16] Ruth Fischer, *Stalin and German Communism*, Cambridge, Mass., 1948. Ruth Fischer, who together with Paul Maslov was once a principal leader of the German Communist party, is the sister of Gerhard Eisler.

[17] Ignazio Silone, "Farewell to Moscow," *Harper's Magazine*, Nov., 1949, pp. 93–99.

and Indochina. Communist parties of great strength developed elsewhere in Europe, especially in France and Italy.

The Communist Information Bureau

The closer coordination of those forces was effected by the creation in September, 1947, of the Communist Information Bureau, generally known now as the Cominform, whose headquarters were first established in Belgrade and are now in Bucharest. It publishes a journal with the title *For a Lasting Peace, for a People's Democracy.*

The Cominform is even more clearly than the Comintern an instrument of Soviet foreign policy, whose interests it serves without exception. The Cominform has no published statute, and its organization is a good deal looser than was that of the Comintern. Its basis is primarily the Soviet Union and its satellites, while the most powerful Communist parties in the West, especially those of France and Italy, are regularly represented. It was originally designed only "to exchange experiences and coordinate activities," but the expulsion of Tito's Yugoslav Communist party has revealed that it is supposed to have disciplinary power over its members. The strict nature of this conveyor belt of orders from the Kremlin is revealed fully in the exchange of acrimonious notes between the Cominform and the Communist party of Yugoslavia.[18] ". . . the Cominform accepts the process of the Central Committee of the All-Union Communist of Bolsheviks . . .," stated the manifesto which accused Tito of having conducted a "hateful policy in relation to the Soviet Union and the All-Union party of Bolsheviks" and of "an undignified policy of underestimating Soviet military specialists . . ."

The Cominform meets rarely, and when it does it appears to be primarily concerned with some specific issue of Soviet foreign policy [19] and since recently with the struggle against the danger of "Titoism."

The existence of a world-wide system of foreign agents, in the form of the various Communist parties and the Comintern-Cominform, is usually regarded as a great tactical advantage for the Soviet Union. However, this is true only to a limited extent. In war the Communist parties may be counted upon to furnish aid to the U.S.S.R. regardless of their countries' policies—on that we have the word of all the Communist leaders in the world. But on the other hand the existence of these parties isolates Moscow from the rest of the world.

[18] For the text of the Cominform manifesto, see *The New York Times,* June 29, 1948. For the Yugoslav reply, see *Statement of the Central Committee of the Communist Party of Yugoslavia,* Belgrade, 1948. Also Royal Institute of International Affairs, *Soviet-Yugoslav Dispute,* London, 1948, containing the texts.

[19] See the statement by the late Bulgarian Premier Georgi Dimitrov, that internationalism is "international collaboration under Comrade Stalin," speech delivered before the 5th Congress of the Bulgarian Communist party, Dec. 19, 1948, Georgi Dimitrov, *Political Report,* Sofia, 1948.

Every bit of information carried there is seen through the narrow spectacles of party doctrine. A strike in America becomes an expression of the "class struggle"; business difficulties become the beginning of capitalism's inevitable and long-predicted depression. The outside world is consistently misrepresented, and there are many indications that the Soviet leaders, despite an enormous intelligence machinery, are actually poorly informed about the democratic world. The policies of the Cominform have been an unbroken chain of failures. The postwar period has handed Communism spectacular successes, the latest of which is China. But these victories were accomplished through various forms of violence. In Western Europe, where "Action Committees" and similar trappings of impending "People's Democracies" are not tolerated, the Communist parties have suffered considerable reverses as their ties to Moscow become ever more apparent. With complete disregard for the psychology of other nations, the Cominform and other Communist parties have copied the Byzantinian forms of Stalin-worship and chime in with acclamations to the "great leader and teacher," and have with equal alacrity adopted the later Moscow policy against "personal cults."

STRICT OBEDIENCE TO MOSCOW

The numerous gyrations of the party line have caused many Communists outside the Soviet orbit to leave the party, while others have entered afresh. This has led to a very considerable turnover in all these parties, which constitutes an element of weakness. This in turn has forced these parties to hew ever closer to "big brother" in the Soviet Union, whose might gives them strength. The unerring obedience of the Communist parties to Moscow has therefore had a double origin: the will of the Communist party in the Soviet Union and the needs of the Communist organizations elsewhere.

It would follow therefrom that strong Communist parties elsewhere may be in danger of adopting too great an air of independence and must therefore, in the interest of the Soviet Union, be kept under control. The Soviet leadership has been mindful of this danger. On January 28, 1948, an article appeared in *Pravda*, in which Georgi Dimitrov, then Bulgarian Premier and recently Secretary-General of the Comintern, was severely berated for having advocated a Balkan federation. "Not a Balkan Federation is needed," said *Pravda*, "but ever closer adherence to the Soviet Union." The point was not lost, but in June of the same year occurred the great split with Tito's Yugoslavia.

Tito's rebellion points out that powerful Communist parties that possess strength in their own right are not as easily made subservient to Moscow's dictates as are parties whose success depends on Soviet help and on the elevating example of Russia's progress. Titoism has broken out in every country, as demonstrated by the alleged defections of Gomulka (Poland), Rajk (Hungary), Kostov (Bulgaria), and Clementis (Czechoslovakia). But in countries other than Yugoslavia, intensive infiltration by Soviet agents has prevented a recurrence of successful rebellion. Some people feel that Communist China will soon be as great a problem as Tito, but as these lines are written there are no indications that such hopeful predictions will come true. Nevertheless the persistence of "Titoism," or nationalism—a crime permitted only to Russians—denotes a weakness in the political stability of the Soviet satellites and constitutes therefore a considerable problem for the Soviet government.

NATIONALISM

Many observers wonder whether these trappings of internationalism are not really designed to hide a strongly revived Soviet or even Russian nationalism. Nationalism has been condemned by all the official spokesmen of the regime, notably Lenin and Stalin. In the official jargon of the regime and of its satellites, "nationalism" is a crime whose punishment is political and even physical extirpation.[20] Yet it would be difficult to appear more nationalistic than the present Soviet regime. The emphasis on the great contributions of Russia in the past, the belittling of all works done in other countries, past and present, the lore of the "Great Patriotic War" with its conscious reminiscences of 1812, the intense militarism with its emphasis on mass formations, resplendent uniforms, rank, titles, and decorations, are more reminiscent of the tsars than of Karl Marx.

Similarly reminiscent of the tsars is the program of expansion which has now engulfed many lands. Here again the Russians were not merely content with the establishment of their supremacy; although they insist that there are many important differences between the Soviet regime and the so-called "People's Democracies" [21] of the Russian satellites, this difference is steadily narrowed down as the forms of Sovietism are being adopted in the satellite countries, even to purely formal details. So great is now the similarity that the actual absorption of these countries into the U.S.S.R.—which some foresee—could be accomplished without much difficulty.

Is the Soviet government using nationalism as a tool for its internationalist aims? Or is it using the trappings of internationalism for its national aspirations? There are many who feel that the latter is the case, and indeed the various Communist parties, the Comintern, and the Cominform have been consistently employed for the purpose of establishing Stalin's rule and later for furthering, unconditionally, the aims of Soviet national policy.

And yet it is probably a mistake to make a clear and narrow distinction between Soviet nationalism and internationalism. The Stalinist doctrine of

[20] This was the principal charge against Lazlo Rajk (Hungary) and Traicho Kostov (Bulgaria), both of whom were executed.

[21] Hilary Minc, "Concerning the Basis of Planning in the People's Democracies," *For a Lasting Peace, for a People's Democracy,* Nov. 18, 1949.

"Socialism in one country" requires the building up and the strengthening of that country as a bulwark for the eventual world revolution, as a revolutionary headquarters and center of direction and inspiration. A combination of Russian nationalism and Communist internationalism is therefore not impossible and has in fact been achieved.

CONTEMPORARY SOVIET FOREIGN POLICY

The Soviet Union emerged from the Second World War with its power immensely increased and its frontiers greatly extended both in Europe and in Asia. Moreover other Communist regimes had pushed into the heart of the European continent and covered a good part of the Asiatic mainland. But all this was achieved by force. In Europe every Communist victory, except in Czechoslovakia and possibly in Yugoslavia, was achieved by Soviet troops; native Communists merely took over from them. Even in Czechoslovakia and Yugoslavia Communist force was decisive. In Asia, too, Communist expansion was the result of armed might. The Communist hope that the masses would rise and overthrow their own regimes was not realized anywhere in the world. This situation has confirmed the low esteem in which the Russian leaders have often held the Communists of other lands and has made the latter even more dependent on Moscow.

As the hope of turning the masses against their governments with slogans of world revolution was obviously hopeless, Moscow evolved a new and different slogan—of peace. And one must credit its enormous propagandistic skill, that this country which has most consistently disturbed the peace of the postwar world, should succeed in convincing so many people that it was the champion of peace. One of the principal reasons for its success was the fact that the war-ravaged countries of Europe and Asia have a deep longing for peace to which this slogan appeals in a powerful manner. It is doubtful that the slogan and the numerous declarations like the Stockholm declaration or the many "peace congresses" organized by the Communists have actually converted many to Communism, but they have often been able to enlist the services and cooperation of non-Communists who allowed themselves to be convinced of the sincerity of the "peace" aim of the organizers of these meetings. Thus the slogan has received a wider reception than any purely Communist idea could have gained.

To those who feel that the Communists have proved themselves more skillful at propaganda than the West, several facts should be pointed out. In the first place, it must be admitted that the Soviet leaders enjoy one advantage which the West cannot possibly acquire. They have, in every country of the world, an often numerous, but always militant and zealous, totally devoted group of people who will carry out every instruction given them. In other words, the U.S.S.R. has native advocates in every part of the world. The West does not. The idea of an "American," "British," or "French" party in another country, sworn to obedience to the commands of Washington, London, or Paris, is an obvious absurdity and a direct contradiction to the democratic ideals which those countries profess. The West has of course many friends, but friends do not always agree and certainly do not obey orders. As a result, Western ideas and policies sometimes appear as "foreign," especially in countries with a colonial past and an anti-Western sensitivity, while Communist ideas are presented as "native." Yet, despite this enormous advantage, Communism has achieved no new laurels, and since the fall of China to Communism, the East-West fronts have remained in a state of uneasy stability. The Korean War served unmistakable notice that new Communist military aggression would not be tolerated, and in order to prevent a repetition of that affair, America has tried to make it clear that Indochina would not be allowed to fall into Communist hands either.

In the face of this situation Russian defensive policy has largely centered on keeping the Western front from becoming consolidated. The chief aim of U.S.S.R. policy has therefore been to fight the Marshall Plan, the North Atlantic Treaty Organization, and the proposed European Defense Community. This it has done by a well-integrated combination of diplomacy and the use of Communist parties and their numerous "front" groups. Especially in the fight against the European army, Soviet policy has been able to find allies in such bitterly anti-Communist forces as General de Gaulle, who for reasons quite different from those of the Communist wants no part of this plan.

After Stalin's death there were some indications of a "softer" Soviet foreign policy and some excessive expectations were aroused.[22] But although the tone of international conferences become somewhat less acrimonious for a while, both the Berlin Conference of February, 1954, and the Geneva Conference of April–June, 1954, revealed that the Soviet leaders are quite unwilling to give up a single one of their positions or compromise on a single point. This was made particularly clear by Soviet Foreign Minister Molotov's stand on Austria. Here there was no more disagreement left over a treaty returning to that country the independence which the Allied Powers of the Second World War, including Russia, had promised in the Moscow Declaration of 1943. Yet Molotov, while willing for the first time to sign such a treaty, was not willing to withdraw Soviet troops from Austria—thus making all treaty talk pointless. As long as the Soviet Union is unwilling to make a single concession of any significance, no serious credence can be placed in any talk of a changed policy. It must therefore be assumed that both Soviet aspirations and Soviet strategy have remained basically unchanged and that the "new look" was merely tactical and confined to words. The end of the Malenkov regime has removed even the outward trappings of the "new look."

At the same time the Soviet leaders seem to have grasped the immense sig-

[22] Isaac Deutscher, *Russia; What Next?* London, 1954.

nificance of atomic weapons and the universal destruction which would follow the outbreak of a general war. As these lines are written, they seem to have no desire to embark on an ultimate test of strength in the near future. The juxtaposition of the U.S.S.R.'s unwillingness to make concession and of its unwillingness to start a war leaves only one conclusion: the continuation of the so-called cold war, a state of affairs which Lenin and Trotsky once characterized by the words, "No peace, no war."

Chapter 14

CONCLUSIONS

The Bolshevik Revolution is probably the most outstanding event of the twentieth century, comparable in its impact only to the French Revolution of 1789.[1] Since the day when Lenin and his associates took over power in Russia, men of intelligence all over the world have hotly debated the merits or demerits of the Soviet regime. Some see in it the fulfillment of men's highest aspirations, the great hope of mankind, while others regard it as the foulest blot on occidental civilization and the incarnation of all evil. The heat of the debate itself would indicate the importance of the subject, quite apart from the great power which the U.S.S.R. wields in international affairs.

In an atmosphere of this kind, cool analysis is difficult; too many people have already made up their minds, often on purely emotional grounds, and facts presented to them are evaluated on the basis of their agreement or disagreement with preconceived notions, rather than on the basis of intrinsic value. Moreover, the statement made in our preface concerning objectivity is particularly applicable to a discussion of the Soviet regime. A purely factual presentation of the Soviet government is completely meaningless. What is the point of enumerating the powers of the Supreme Soviet or the right of election unless it is also stated what these powers and rights mean? But that gets us into the field of analysis and controversy.

Some extricate themselves from this dilemma of either giving meaningless facts or becoming the target of attacks by escaping into a fairyland in which all facts are equal. Such writers believe it to be "objective" to criticize in equal measure the admittedly reprehensible former Georgia chain gangs in the United States and the forced-labor camps in the Soviet Union as if the two were even remotely comparable in size, scope, and type of inmates. In that fashion a very incorrect and misleading picture is conjured up before the eyes of the reader, who is encouraged to minimize very important differences between his own and certain foreign institutions and approaches.[2]

[1] One viewpoint on the subject has been presented by E. H. Carr in *The Soviet Impact on the Western World*, New York, 1947.

[2] A good illustration of this type of presentation is *The United States and the Soviet Union: Some Quaker Proposals for Peace*, New Haven, 1949. Whether two institutions are similar or different from each other is an important question of fact, the answer to which ought to emerge from the unbiased study of available evidence. This has nothing

There can hardly be any question that the political regime of the U.S.S.R. is that of a dictatorship. It has certain features which are called "democratic," but they are either inoperative or so defined that real freedom of choice and action does not exist concerning any policy question. The policies of state and government are decided on the very highest level of the ruling Communist party by the party Presidium. The slightest contradiction or question of these policies leads to immediate removal, imprisonment, and sometimes death. Nor is there any restriction to the violence which the state authorities may apply to their citizens when they deem it necessary. There is absolutely no free exchange of ideas; the philosophy by which the Soviet citizen is to live is decreed from above and permeates every vestige of his public and private life. Ideas originating beyond the Soviet borders are discouraged, and those even mildly favorable to foreign thoughts or institutions are severely taken to task. The country is hermetically sealed off from the rest of the world, and despite many generous invitations to Soviet students and scholars, to be of the Soviet government's choice, to visit and study abroad, no cultural or personal interchange has been possible for many years.[3] A few foreigners have been permitted to visit the U.S.S.R., but, with the exception of only well-guarded sports teams and theater groups, no similar permission has been granted to Soviet citizens to travel abroad unless on official government business. Of all the features of the present Soviet regime, none is perhaps as frightening as the fact that there is growing up an entire generation in the U.S.S.R. which knows nothing about the outside world beyond the one-sided picture which it receives but which it is not permitted to see for itself.

On the other hand, some progress has been made in the direction of the peaceful coexistence of different races and nationalities in the state. Likewise access to education is general, and illiteracy, while still a problem, is being steadily diminished. Moreover, "mass participation," while a formality from a Western standpoint, is a considerable step forward from the days of the tsars, when the people did not have even a formal part in the government of the country. But on the economic sector the living standard of the people is exceedingly low—in fact, it is one of the lowest in the world—and the assertion that the workers, the most favored class, are much better off than before

---

to do with the moral evaluation of these facts—with the question of good or evil—which the reader is invited to make for himself according to his personal philosophy, but which cannot be considered in a book of this kind.

[3] On Aug. 10, 1949, the Soviet *Teacher's Journal* condemned the education exchange program sponsored by the Institute of International Education in New York and the Carnegie Endowment as a form of "bourgeois cosmopolitanism" aimed at killing patriotism abroad. *The New York Times,* Aug. 11, 1949. For a review of futile American attempts to open cultural relations with the U.S.S.R., see *Cultural Relations between the United States and the Soviet Union,* Department of State, Publication 3480, International Information and Cultural Series 4, Washington, D.C., 1949.

1917 is not easy to substantiate.[4] However, this constitutes not so much a breakdown of the Soviet economy as an expression of the government's determination to transform the U.S.S.R. from an agricultural country into a giant industrial state—a transformation to which one or two generations are consciously sacrificed in the expectation that eventual results will justify the means.

What of the stability of the Soviet regime? The suppression of personal liberty has not followed a consistent path but has gone through waves of ups and downs. The most oppressive periods were those of war communism, of mass collectivization, and of the 1937–1938 purges. In between, some relaxation was apparent, and there is much indication that a relationship exists between the domestic severity of the regime and the international situation. In the present period of the so-called "cold war," an appreciable hardening of public-security measures is in evidence. Thus the feeling of fear and insecurity which permeates the world today has its impact even on the country whose actions, many believe, are responsible for much of it.

The Soviet leaders have promised the millennium if permitted to continue their work in peace and without disturbance. But the absolute dictatorship in the Soviet Union and the existence of a world-wide network of Communist parties, subservient to the commands of the Soviet leadership, are not conducive to the type of peace and stability in which the Communist spokesmen profess to believe.

Despite its nearly 100 per cent votes of endorsement, it is unlikely that the Soviet regime really holds the enthusiastic support of all its citizens. Too many Russians who were taken abroad as the result of the war have done everything possible to remain away from the U.S.S.R., even at the price of remaining in the miserable DP (displaced persons) camps of Germany and Austria. Too many soldiers of the Soviet army have deserted, and too many Soviet officials sent abroad after careful screening have remained there. Moreover, there is ample evidence that the first waves of the German armies were well received in certain areas of the U.S.S.R., especially in regions not inhabited by Great Russians.

Yet there is no evidence of any underground movement to speak of. Most Soviet citizens probably dread the secret political police and the labor camps, but there is no tradition of democracy or personal freedom in Russia and therefore no ideological focus for a possible opposition movement. Moreover, modern technical equipment and principles of police and military organization make it quite possible for relatively small forces to control effectively large numbers of people.

In the absence of concrete evidence to the contrary, it must therefore be concluded that those Russians who dislike the Soviet regime are, on the whole,

<hr>

[4] An interesting tabulation of prices in the Soviet Union compiled on the basis of work-time may be found in *The New York Times*, Dec. 21, 1947.

not conscious of any possible alternatives, and the regime appears to be quite safe. This has been well demonstrated by the smooth transition from the Stalin to the Malenkov and to the Khrushchev-Bulganin regimes, and the ease with which Beria was purged.

Whether the Soviet government will eventually modify its rigor as its stabilization and industrialization increase and as it begins to realize that the non-Communist world is here to stay, all predictions notwithstandng, lies in the laps of the gods.

The Soviet regime demonstrates the feasibility of a completely managed state in which a few men determine, in accordance with a definite political theory, what should or should not be done by all organs of the state down to the lowest branch and by all citizens. It demonstrates a political organism in which every action is designed in some manner to serve the state and the party, and it demonstrates nearly perfect techniques through which the enthusiastic support of the citizens is to be obtained. It also manifests equally perfect methods by which any lack of enthusiasm among the citizens may be rendered harmless to the state and to the party.

It is clear that a political system of this kind gives the U.S.S.R. a certain advantage in the conduct of foreign affairs. No internal opposition has to be appeased. The government may at any time undertake such action as it deems suitable, and it may give its people whatever version thereof it pleases.

But this advantage is not necessarily an unmixed blessing. Lacking an open opposition, the Soviet leaders must rely on their own sense of judgment for a correct assessment of their own and other countries' strength and of the possible consequences of their policies. A major error could have the most devastating consequences.

So far the Soviet leaders have shown themselves shrewd, and while they have committed grave errors, they have taken no really great risks. In this they have proved themselves considerably superior to Hitler. Nevertheless, the magnitude of the Soviet state, the all-pervasive control which its leaders exercise, the skill and persistence with which their policies are carried out, as well as the existence of a world-wide system of Communist parties committed unreservedly to the support of the Soviet Union, are factors which are bound to cause disquiet and which the student must try to evaluate in line with the realities of the internal structure and political concepts of the Soviet Union.

Part V. GOVERNMENT IN COMPARISON

It is evident then, that there must be many forms of government, differing from each other in their particular constitution: for the parts of which they are composed each differ from the other. For government is the ordering of the magistracies of the state; and these the community share between themselves, either as they can attain them by force, or according to some common equality which there is among them . . . And thus in politics, there is the government of the many and the government of the few; or a democracy and an oligarchy.

ARISTOTLE, *Politics*, 1290*a*

THIS IS a study in comparative government, or rather in certain aspects of comparison.[1] As such it is part of the larger field of government. But when we speak about "government" a certain confusion is bound to set in because of the ambiguity of that term and the many uses which have been made of it. In particular, the terms *state* and *government* are frequently intermingled. It is useful to keep them separate as far as possible, because the emphasis on the one or the other determines to a large extent the nature of a study of this kind. The state is essentially a legal abstraction,[2] a politically organized "legal person," while the government is the agency or the sum total of agencies and organizations through which the will and the actions of the state are formulated and executed.[3] The Supreme Court of the United States defines "state" and "government" as follows:

In common speech and common apprehension they are usually regarded as identical; and as, ordinarily, the acts of the government are the acts of the state (because within the limits of its delegation of power), the government of the state is generally confounded with the state itself, and often the former is meant when the latter is mentioned. The state itself is an ideal person, intangible, invisible, immutable. The government is an agent, and within the sphere of the agency, a perfect representative; but outside of that it is a lawless usurpation.[4]

[1] Full treatments of the subject may be found in two excellent works: C. J. Friedrich, *Constitutional Government and Democracy*, Boston, 1950, rev. ed., and H. Finer, *The Theory and Practice of Modern Government*, New York, 1949, rev. ed.

[2] See especially Georg Jellinek, *Allgemeine Staatslehre*, Berlin, 1920, 3d ed., pp. 162–173.

[3] J. W. Garner, *Political Science and Government*, New York, 1932, pp. 48*f*.

[4] Poindexter v. Greenhow, 114 U.S. 270 (1885).

Not only are the two terms confused with one another, but each of them has several meanings. The word *state* is not only used as indicated above; it is also employed as a synonym for "authority." Moreover, in a federal union the members of the federation are frequently called *states*, as for instance in the United States of America and Brazil. The word *government*, on the other hand, may refer to a particular administration as well as to government in general.

Sovereignty, the coercive power, resides in the state but is exercised by the government. The state is surrounded with all the myth [5] and pomp, which often take fantastic and barbaric forms, but it is the human agency, the government, which utilizes this terrestrial mythology for its own ends. At times this separation is useful; the state is presumably unlimited and unrestrained, while its human agents do not enjoy such an exalted position. The government, in speaking for the state and identifying itself with the state, thus often arrogates unto itself power and infallibility which it does not possess. The Germans especially have been past masters in this. Thus, opposition to the government, which is permissible, becomes opposition to the state, which is not permissible because the state is the basis and the framework for all political and social existence.

It is perhaps not untypical that British and American political science has been primarily concerned with the government, while Continental European jurists have been absorbed in the study of the state. This approach has led European scholars to incomparably profound and systematic studies,[6] but it has often caused them to bypass reality. Our purpose, however, is to view the concrete living organism of government, not the theoretical and sometimes dead categories of state forms.

No greater variety could be imagined than that which exists between forms of government. While all existing governments claim to have nothing but the happiness of their respective peoples at heart, there are considerable differences of opinion as to the nature of that happiness. Even among those governments which are more or less agreed on their ends, there is no agreement on means, while those who employ similar means may pursue quite different ends.

Governments are not "scientific" creations; they have not been produced in the laboratories and in test tubes. They are the result of man's groping for solutions, of his growth, his shortcomings, and his frequent irrationality. A purely logical systematic approach therefore has its serious shortcomings. Among several possible methods of studying government, the comparative

---

[5] E. Cassirer, *The Myth of the State*, New York, 1946. See also F. Oppenheimer, *The State*, New York, 1922; G. Jellinek, *Das Recht des modernen Staates*, Berlin, 1905; L. Duguit, *L'État, le droit objectif, et la loi positive*, Paris, 1901; H. Kelsen, *General Theory of Law and State*, Cambridge, Mass., 1946.

[6] See the interesting observations by C. J. Friedrich, "Political Science in the United States in Wartime," *American Political Science Review*, Vol. XLI (1947), pp. 978–989.

approach offers many possibilities. Governmental institutions grow in their own specific economic, political, psychological, and historical climates. When the institutions of one country are transferred lock, stock, and barrel to another soil, serious difficulties arise, as the Germans and the Russians learned recently and are still learning. Nevertheless, few countries remain entirely untouched by other countries' experiences and achievements. The Soviet satellites look to Moscow for their model of government, copying everything from the nominal head of state (Presidium) to the coat of arms. On the other hand all parliamentary forms of government are in one way or another the children of the London Parliament, and all newly created or recreated democracies are trying, though rarely with conspicuous success, to emulate the British cabinet system.

The whole world is now, more than ever, the testing ground of comparative government. The comparative method of study itself is hardly new; it originated, as far as we know, with Aristotle who, together with his students, compiled the constitutions of 158 city-states, of which only the Constitution of Athens has survived. All through history types of government existing in one state have had their impact on other countries: perhaps the most outstanding example has been the ideas of Montesquieu about the nature of English government which, albeit mistaken, made such an impression on the American founding fathers. And in our own time the new constitutions of Germany (East and West), of Italy, of Eastern Europe, of India, and of Japan show the impact of the Western-democratic and Eastern-Communist theories and practices of government.[7]

We can learn much from the practice and problems of other states. The French Council of State, the British cabinet system and civil service, the Scandinavian social services, the Swiss Federal Council system—all have many valuable lessons for us, while our own institutions appear with greater clarity in comparison with different foreign approaches. Moreover, the foreign policy of other nations can be understood only against the background of their internal regimes.

The brief chapters which follow can claim neither finality nor completion. They are a beginning, not an end. It is hoped, however, that they will stimulate more extensive efforts on the part of some of their readers.

[7] In 1947 the Italian Constituent Assembly published a functional comparative analysis of the world's constitutions as an aid to its own drafting work: Assemblea Costituente. *Atti della Commissione per la Costituzione*, Vol. I, "Studi di Legislazione Costituzionale Comparata."

Chapter 1

THE FORM OF GOVERNMENT: CONSTITUTIONAL DEMOCRACY VERSUS DICTATORSHIP

The classification of governments has the purpose of distinguishing between different types according to their most important criteria. If we apply this approach to the principal, traditional methods of classification, we shall probably find that some revision is in order.

TRADITIONAL CLASSIFICATIONS OF GOVERNMENT

The traditional classifications of government usually follow the course set by Aristotle or Machiavelli. Aristotle,[1] himself closely following Plato,[2] distinguishes between the "government of the few" and the "government of the many." He therefore divides them into the three "good" forms of monarchy, aristocracy, and polity—the latter standing for a constitutional, middle-class democracy. Aristotle then describes the perversions of these types into tyranny, oligarchy, and what he calls "democracy," by which he means mob rule. Machiavelli, on the other hand, distinguishes only between monarchy and republic.[3]

The Aristotelian classification has inspired generations of thinkers and has frequently sidetracked them into the futile search for the "best" form of government. Even today this approach has wide appeal and finds its way into some introductory courses in political science. However, it is easy enough to show that this classification is totally meaningless and that it fails the above-mentioned test because it is unable to tell us anything really significant about the governments so classified. The basis of the Aristotelian classification is the number of people who participate in the government. Thus monarchy is the rule of the one, aristocracy the rule of the few, and polity the rule of the many, and that goes also for the perversions of these forms. How-

[1] Aristotle, *Politics*, Book IV, pp. 1289a, b.
[2] Plato, *The Republic*, Books VIII, IX.
[3] Niccolo Machiavelli, *The Prince*, Chap. 1.

ever, modern sociologists have clearly shown that there is no government of the many, that all governments are governments of the few or, in fact, oligarchies.[4] Nowhere in the world do "the people" or even substantial numbers thereof rule. In all states the exercise of government is left to a few hands, while the determination of policy is actually in the hands of minority groups, vested interests, and political leaders.[5] The British cabinet rules the country for all practical purposes, and the same could be said about the party Presidium, the former Politburo in Moscow, yet nobody with any critical faculty would say that these two regimes are alike. Both governments are "aristocratic-oligarchic," but this statement conveys no meaning because it reveals nothing about the real nature of the two countries concerned. Nor do we glean any enlightenment from the answer to the distinction which Machiavelli makes, namely, whether the head of state and government is elected or hereditary.

It would appear that Aristotle was not entirely unaware of that problem. In contemplating the distortion of the "good" forms of government he introduced a moral principle, which thus carries the definition of government beyond the purely descriptive and into the more significant field of investigation into its social purpose.

It is not difficult to find fault with the Aristotelian and Machiavellian systems because they are descriptive rather than analytical. A government could be monarchical and constitutional or monarchical and autocratic, without being a tyranny, as for instance in the period of enlightened absolutism as exemplified by the reign of the German Emperor Joseph II. Government could be a polity (or a democracy, as we would call it today) and yet exclude significant groups from real participation, as was the case in the Greek city-state or in the early years of the United States.

The oversimplification of the Aristotelian system has led early thinkers, such as Cicero, to advocate a "mixed" form,[6] but clarity hardly lies in that direction.

Obviously many different and meaningful classifications of governments are possible. One could, for instance, divide governments by the criteria of economic development in which they operate. Here one might find primitive types, feudal arrangements, and the fashionable division into capitalist and socialist forms, with many steps between them. Similarly the type of community might be accepted as a measuring rod, beginning with tribal government and ending with the dream of world government. Or one could concentrate on the seat and the distribution of sovereignty and consider centralized and federal governments as well as other forms of devolution.

---

[4] Karl Loewenstein, *Political Reconstruction*, New York, 1946, pp. 104–136.
[5] R. M. MacIver, *The Web of Government*, New York, 1949, p. 149.
[6] Marcus Tullius Cicero, *De re publica*, Book I, p. 25.

A Modern Classification

All these classifications are valid, and the principal interest of the observer is likely to determine which he will select. To this author the most significant approach for our times is the one which concerns itself with the manner in which political power is exercised. This is by no means a novel approach. The Greek statesman Alcibiades remarked to his uncle Pericles that a law adopted even by the popular assembly was nothing but an arbitrary act when the majority imposed it on the minority without persuading the latter.[7] Cicero, Thomas Aquinas, and the school of natural law held that government rested on reason and found its limitations in the common good. While natural law, like its modern opponent, legal positivism,[8] could be used to justify autocracy, Thomas Aquinas himself considered the rule of the many safer than the rule of the few, though he demanded reason and moderation from any government. He quoted approvingly the statement of the Roman historian Sallust who remarked, "It is almost incredible if we call to mind how speedily the Roman State grew, when once it had achieved its liberty" (after they had shaken off the shackles of royal rule).[9]

What appears then as the crucial point is the question of liberty, the sensitiveness of the government to divergent thoughts, the degree to which the people may elect or reject a government, not once but periodically, the possibility of organizing public opinion against the government, and the operation of the rule of law. Viewed in this light, we can hardly improve on the system of Kant, who distinguished simply between republicanism (which we would call constitutional democracy) and despotism.[10] Constitutional democracy is essentially limited government, and the limitation is established in the written and especially the unwritten constitution. Constitutional democracy, political democracy, is government under law, and although numerous violations may easily be found and cited, it operates by and large within the confines of the law rather than above it. On the other hand, despotism, autocracy, and dictatorship are characterized by arbitrariness and by the complete subordination of the machinery of government to the unrestrained will of the ruling person or clique. In a democracy, the institutions of government have therefore on the whole a life of their own and keep the administration within certain

[7] Xenophon, *Memorabilia*, Book I, p. 2. See A. Verdross-Drossberg, *Grundlinien der antiken Rechts- und Staatsphilosophie*, Vienna, 1948, 2d ed., p. 60.

[8] Legal positivism regards law as merely a command of a superior to an inferior over whom there is power of punishment; J. Austin, *Lectures on Jurisprudence*, New York, 1875, 2 vols. The rules themselves may have any kind of content. H. Kelsen, *Allgemeine Staatslehre*, Berlin, 1925.

[9] Thomas Aquinas, *De regimine principum* (On Princely Government), Book I, Chap. IV.

[10] Immanuel Kant, *Zum ewigen Frieden, ein philosophischer Entwurf* (Philosophical Essay on Eternal Peace), 1795, Sec. 2.

channels of operation, while a dictatorship uses constitutions, laws, and institutions as mere tools, to be discarded the moment they are no longer useful. This is the issue of our time. Divergent economic forms, varying degrees of advancement in social organization, and the devolution of sovereignty, while interesting, are strictly secondary in importance.

THE RELATIONS BETWEEN INDIVIDUAL AND GOVERNMENT

This simplified classification suggested here should, however, mislead no one into believing that all autocracies are alike and that all forms of democracy are also alike. Actually very considerable differences exist within each type, not only in their respective institutions but also in spirit and emphasis. As far as the democratic countries are concerned, one of the principal differences among them concerns the relationship of the individual to his government. It is the tradition of the English-speaking world to put the individual first and to guarantee his liberties even against his government, while Continental European political thought is more apt to think of the "people" as a collective than as individuals. Consequently Rousseau's general-will theory has found receptiveness on the Continent, with the result that legislative supremacy has found many adherents because the legislature is presumed to be most nearly representative of the broad masses of the people. Under this system the individual has no recourse against the acts of the legislature except through the ballot box, but when small minority groups are concerned, this recourse offers little hope. This is especially true in the case of racial or ethnic minorities, who naturally cannot hope ever to constitute a majority and who consequently can be safely suppressed through the paraphernalia of democratic procedure; in other words their rights are voted away.

The protection of individual rights against legislative encroachments may be vested in the system of judicial review. But it may also rest, as in England, in deeply ingrained respect for human personality. In countries where legislative supremacy and omnipotence prevail, individual rights are often most securely protected by the diversity and multiplicity of political parties, which prevent each other from embarking on oppressive legislation. But this process prevails only when conditions are fairly normal. In times of great strain and danger, governments are apt to demand emergency powers and parliaments often become rubber stamps. This is serious, because civil rights are endangered precisely in troubled times and not when all is well.

Recent experiences have revealed that individual rights may be in danger even in such countries as the United States and Great Britain when unusual danger and public excitement prevail, but the emphasis on individual freedom against government nevertheless makes such aberrations more difficult and infrequent. Perfection is found in no form of government, because they are all human and thus imperfect.

Most intelligent observers will not be surprised to discover many differences between democratic regimes. The emphasis on natural growth, on individualism, and on decision after debate which characterizes democratic government is bound to lead to many variations. But it is often believed that all autocratic, dictatorial regimes are basically alike. Now it cannot be denied that there are certain features which all these regimes have in common, though in varying degrees. But they are no more alike than are democratic governments.

DICTATORSHIP: NAZI-FASCIST

All dictatorships have in common a doctrine by which there exists a "true" or "superior" form of government—namely, their particular dictatorship— which must be accepted on faith and is not open to discussion. They also have in common an administrative principle by which all power rests in the hands of a few men—perhaps of one man—who are responsible to no one or at any rate are never responsible to a body capable of calling them to account. Dictatorships also make much use of tightly organized (rather than necessarily numerous) special troops and police forces which are above and beyond the law and which have as their major function the duty to extirpate all real, potential, or sometimes imaginary opposition to the regime without recourse to the niceties of due process of law.

Yet despite these similarities, there are a number of very different types of dictatorships. The Nazi regime presented one of the extreme forms. Obedience to the leader was declared to be the greatest glory of the German. Leadership was acquired through higher quality which alone gave the right to rule. The leader "elected" himself; "nature" singled him out. Some were made to rule and some to obey.

A philosophy of life [*Weltanschauung*] which by rejecting the democratic concept of the mass-man, endeavors to give this earth to the best nation, the highest type of human beings, must in turn, logically, obey the same aristocratic principle within that nation and must secure leadership and greatest influence for the best brains. It rests on the basis of personality, not on that of majority.[11]

Italian Fascism echoed these sentiments. *"Il Duce ha sempre ragione"* (the Duce is always right), the billboards announced all over Italy, and Mussolini proclaimed in flamboyant phrases, "Fascism is a religious conception in which man is seen in immanent relation to a higher law, an objective will, that transcends the particular individual and raises him to conscious membership in a spiritual society." [12] And this is proclaimed as some sort of higher

[11] Adolf Hitler, *Mein Kampf*, Munich, 1938, p. 493 (first published 1925 and 1927).

[12] Article by Mussolini in the *Enciclopedia Italiana*, Vol. XIV, reprinted as *La Dottrina de fascismo*, Milan, 1933. See H. Finer, *Mussolini's Italy*, London, 1935.

freedom because "always the maximum of liberty coincides with the maximum forces of the state."

This approach to a "natural order" in which men are hierarchically organized by "nature" is not only irrational; it is consciously antirational. It is a myth which is openly presented as such. The leading German exponent on Nazism next to Hitler, Alfred Rosenberg, gave his principal work the title, "The Myth of the Twentieth Century." [13] And Mussolini said, "We have created our myth. The myth is a faith, it is passion. It is not necessary that it shall be a reality. It is reality by the fact that it is a goal, a hope, a faith, that it is courage. Our myth is the nation, our myth is the greatness of the nation." [14]

Why the myth? Hitler explained it with admirable clarity. The myth is the quasi-religious creed of the movement which has the dual function of proselytizing and binding its adherents together. In order to do that it must be more than theory or program; it must be dogma. It is true that the formulation of this dogma may suffer under the test of time and a reformulation may appear to be in order. "But," wrote Hitler, "any such attempt usually ends in disaster. Because, something which ought to be unshakable is opened up to discussion which does not necessarily lead to a newer, better and above all more unified formulation, but results, more likely, in endless debates and general confusion, once a single point has been removed from the quasi-religious dogmatic statement."

Whoever really desires the victory of the racist philosophy must realize that . . . this can be accomplished only through a militant movement, but, secondly, that such a movement can prevail only if it is based on the unshakable security and stability of its program. It must not dare to subject its text to concessions to the passing fancy of time, but must retain the form which has once been found suitable, for all times, or at any rate until it becomes victorious.

The use of the unifying myth dogma is typical of the modern dictatorship in its purest and most totalitarian form. It is not confined to the Nazi-Fascist brotherhood but may easily be observed as an integral part of Communism, although the words used are different. Where Nazis and Fascists were frankly mystical, the Communists claim to be the strongest kind of realists. Where Nazis and Fascists spoke of "creed," the Communists speak of "science." A closer examination of this "science" reveals, however, that it too has the nature of a creed. Its fundamental assertions of the economic basis of man and the class nature of society are no more indisputable than Hitler's and Mussolini's ideas about the hierarchical order of man. Moreover, the unscientific nature of Marxist "science" as interpreted by the Communists

[13] Alfred Rosenberg, *Der Mythus des 20. Jahrhunderts,* Munich, 1939 (first published in 1930).

[14] Speech in Naples, 1922; see Finer, *op. cit.,* p. 218.

is revealed by the Communist insistence on its finality and irrefutability. True scientific theories are always submitted to tests and revised in the light of their results. An alleged science whose veracity may not be assaulted by searching and critical inquiry is not science but a myth or a dogma or both.

The well-known German sociologist Max Weber has given us an elaboration of the term "charisma." Derived from the Greek and originally employed in the earliest period of Christian teaching, it denotes a special, supernatural, or at least definitely unusual quality which a person is supposed to have and for which he is considered to be in a position of leadership. The belief in this charisma assures to the person who is identified with its possession a wide and enthusiastic following. The charismatic community has no fixed laws, no fixed careers, no fixed institutions. All appointments, all administrative decisions, are made by virtue of the charismatic inspiration of the leader. The charisma stands above all law.[15]

Originally the charisma is associated only with certain specific persons who are believed to be personally endowed with special qualities. Later the charisma becomes institutionalized and thus can be transmitted from one person to another by some kind of special procedure.

It is important that the charisma derives its great power from the belief in it. But once believed, obedience, in fact total abandonment of oneself to the charisma, becomes a moral duty. Failure to do so is a sin, a crime, an ignoble act.

It is easy to see that according to this concept, which can be traced throughout all history, the Nazi-Fascist types of dictatorship are clearly charismatic. And so is Communism. Here the charisma lies essentially in the infallible doctrine, in the party. In addition it may also be vested in a person and his inspiration, such as Stalin. But this is not essential, in contradistinction to the Nazi and Fascist regimes, which were inseparably linked to specific charismatic personalities. This is also why succession was difficult to conceive in Fascist Italy and Nazi Germany, while the institutionalized charisma of Communism can be transmitted from person to person.

DICTATORSHIP: COMMUNIST

However, the Nazi-Fascist theory is irrational, an exaggerated appeal to primitive emotions, childishly simple in conception although frequently written in vague and obscure language. Communist theory is different. It lays down premises which it claims are "rational," and once the premises of the creed are accepted, much of the rest follows with formidable logic. Moreover, since Marxism-Leninism is alleged to be the basis of all modern science and knowledge, it needs must be applied to all fields of knowledge and art.

[15] Max Weber, *Wirtschaft und Gesellschaft* (published as part of the series *Grundriss der Sozialökonomik*), Tübingen, 1947, 3d ed., Vol. 1, pp. 140–148.

This naturally brings it into conflict with changing realities of social and economic life. If Marxism-Leninism were primarily a science, this clash would lead to large-scale reinvestigation and revision. But here it reveals itself again as a myth dogma by insisting that all changes have really been foreseen and allowed for in the doctrine. Existing contradictions are then argued away by the use of dialectics, which the Greeks invented as a form of clarifying issues by demonstrating opposing theses but which has since been used to obscure rather than to clarify.

Marxism-Leninism plays the same role for the Communist regime that the Fascist and Nazi myth once played in Germany and Italy; as a mainspring of action and as a unifying dogma and object of worship. But in one respect Communism far outranks Nazism. It is a genuine article of export and world-wide appeal. Nazism and Fascism were always hopelessly tied to Germany and Italy and attractive abroad mainly to nationals and descendants of those two countries. But Communism is made of different stuff. All over the world it has been able to convince millions of people that its regime is a better and freer one than "bourgeois democracy" and it has been able to convince them that it is somehow possible for them to be free and yet have no choice. In this it far outstrips anything Nazism or Fascism was ever able to carry into the field.

SINGLE-PARTY MONOPOLY

Another special feature of full-fledged dictatorships is the existence of a single ruling party whose purpose has been outlined above in the parts dealing with Germany and the Soviet Union. Unlike the democratic concept of parties, the single state parties do not offer the people alternatives but merely implementation and intensification of the official policy line, which descends from above. The state party is an instrument in which close contact between people and political leadership can be maintained, not in order to grant the people any degree of genuine participation in the formulation of policy, but in order to mobilize them for such purposes as the leaders may deem advisable.

Since dictators usually come to power as a result of conspiracy, they are forever alert to the possibility of conspiracy against them. The ruthless extermination of all those who endanger the security of the regime goes without saying. But dictators also find it necessary to break the spirit of those who might be future resisters. Thus seemingly innocent remarks or mere mental reservations may lead to serious consequences. Moreover, dictators find it useful to eliminate entire groups whose presence and inner cohesion are considered dangerous. The campaign against Jews, kulaks, and the churches may be seen in that light. The Roman Catholic Church aroused the special ire of both the Nazis and Communists because, on account of its international character and organization, it could never be completely controlled by a dictator. The Peron regime's action against the Catholic Church in Argentina follows this pattern. The Communists found the Church to be the backbone of the peasant population who resisted collectivization.[16] This was and is one more reason to try and destroy the Church or at least turn it into a national church and obedient tool like the present Russian Orthodox Church. Protestant groups which do not subordinate themselves to the state suffer similar pressure, especially when they have strong national or international ties. This demand for a monopoly of control appears to grow as the dictatorship ages and after a while it becomes apparent that not even the most trusted local party leaders are permitted to retain much autonomous control; central agents and directors move in and take their orders directly from the national capital. This was very clearly the trend in Nazi Germany, where even the completely Nazi-controlled *Länder* governments lost all power to the delegate of the central government (*Reichstatthalter*), while the Soviet Union has allowed only very few functions to remain within the sole jurisdiction of the Union Republics.

COERCION

The apex and most typical symbol of dictatorship are the secret political police and the method of "administrative punishment." There is nothing especially unusual about a "political" police as such. The Federal Bureau of Investigation in the United States and MI–5 in Great Britain are agencies certainly interested in political questions, but what differentiates the FBI and MI–5 on the one hand from the Gestapo, the OVRA,[17] and the MVD (formerly Cheka, OGPU, NKVD, MGB) on the other hand is the fact that the secret police forces of the dictatorships recognize no legal restraint whatsoever, while the security agents of democracies are only one subordinate part of the government, subject to all the limitations of democratic government and compelled to respect due process of law. Violations may occur, but they are the exception, not the rule.

The concept of "administrative penal justice" was originally the right of police agents to impose punishment for minor misdemeanors, but under the dictatorships it has blossomed out into a power over life and death, completely unrestrained by law and subject to no procedural safeguards. Instead of a hearing in open court, prisoners are simply told, if they are lucky, that they are to serve a certain term in a concentration or forced-labor camp. Under the Nazi regime it was customary to leave Gestapo prisoners in the dark as to their fate or the duration of their service. In Russia, however, specific terms of forced labor are the rule, although it is not always observed.

[16] Stephen Kertesz, "Church and State in Hungary," in *Soviet Satellites,* University of Notre Dame, 1949, pp. 37–47.

[17] *Opera Volontaria Repressione Anti-Fascista,* Mussolini's secret police.

"Administrative" punishment fulfills three tasks in a dictatorship. Its unforeseeable character and the uncertainty of one's fate as a prisoner strike terror into the heart of all present or future opponents. Moreover, the manner in which the secret police strikes—in the early morning hours, when a man's will power is at its lowest ebb—tends to increase the widespread belief in its omnipotence and omniscience, and so raises its effectiveness far above its physical potentialities.

A relatively new development is the increasing industrial use of forced labor. In the Soviet Union this development began in the thirties and has reached such proportions that it has been necessary to create two agencies instead of one in order to handle the traffic. In Germany and Italy forced labor was largely unproductive from the standpoint of the national economy until the war. Then concentration-camp labor in Germany became a major, profitable industry, but punishment and extermination remained the principles. Deliberate mass murder was therefore the rule in Germany, while in the Soviet Union the usefulness of forced labor was more fully recognized, and the large death rate was and is usually caused by neglect rather than by deliberate effort.

Other Authoritarian Regimes

Compared with these three giants of totalitarian control, other forms of authoritarianism almost pale into insignificance. The Austrian dictatorship of 1934 to 1938 was established by Engelbert Dollfuss on a technicality and without ever obtaining sufficient popular support. During its brief span of life the Austrian dictatorship, which was continued by Kurt von Schuschnigg after Dollfuss's assassination in 1934, attempted to steer a middle course but failed. For a full-fledged dictatorship it was too humanitarian, and for a democracy it was too dictatorial. It merely succeeded in aligning most of the population against it, and it disappeared without a fight when Hitler raised his voice.

Somewhat similar is the strange dictatorship of Dr. Antonio de Oliveira Salazar in Portugal. Like the Austrian regime of 1934 to 1938, Portugal has a constitution which gives it a "corporative" form of government.[18] Its legislature is composed of a National Assembly whose members are elected by all heads of families, regardless of sex, and a Corporative Chamber whose members are chosen by various guilds in which the various trades and professions are organized. Dr. Salazar, however, rules the country without having to

---

[18] The idea of the corporate state was developed by Karl von Vogelsang (1818–1890), who influenced Pope Leo XIII and the latter's encyclical *Rerum Novarum*. Although by no means a fascist idea in itself, corporatism has been used by fascism in one way or another, but always as a smoke screen, because neither in Italy nor in 1934–1938 Austria nor in Portugal do the corporations have any real influence.

fear a vote of censure from the legislature. Ever since 1934 only one government list of candidates has been presented to the people, although opposition groups have formed and advanced to candidacy only to withdraw under pressure. But on the other hand there is a great deal of difference between the ruthless suppression of opponents under the Nazi, Fascist, or Soviet dictatorships and the Portuguese regime in which opposition exists in the shadow. The Portuguese regime is governed by a high moral purpose, and the rule is more bearable because it is generally not arbitrary.

Again a different type of authoritarian regime is presented by the numerous strong men of Latin America who are known by the designation of *caudillo*. The atmosphere in which a *caudillo* comes to power is quite different from that which is customarily found in European countries. Most Latin-American countries have little concept of democracy. This does not apply to all of them in equal measure, certainly not to Brazil or Uruguay, but it is generally true of most of the rest of Hispano-America that government is habitually in the hands of a few people of exceptional influence, which is often based on either wealth or army position. Between these members of the inner circle there is often strife, and presidents as well as constitutions often change rapidly, with the army playing a decisive, though not always winning, role of "king-maker." Sometimes a man comes to power under such circumstances who has exceptional ability as a leader and acquires greater power and prestige than his more ordinary predecessors. Such a man is usually even less inclined to be patient with parliamentary obstruction, and he represents the type of the "man on horseback."

There are some significant differences between the Latin-American *caudillo* and the European dictator. A *caudillo* may be a strong man but he does not possess the totality of power, and there are several institutions, especially the army, which he must leave alone. Nor do *caudillos* have their single state parties, like the Nazis, or the elaborate system of the secret state police. Political opponents may be hunted down, but they are usually able to seek exile abroad, and there are no Latin-American equivalents of Hitler's Buchenwald, Mussolini's Lipari Islands, or Stalin's Kolyma. The relative ease and frequency with which Latin-American *caudillos* are overthrown demonstrate this point. European dictators are not so easily unseated.

The Perón regime in Argentina is an exception for it has developed into a dictatorship with strong totalitarian tendencies.[19]

The regime of Generalissimo Francisco Franco in Spain was established in a bloody civil war which provided the stage for both Germany and Italy to try intervention and new armaments. Once established in power, Franco surrounded himself with all the paraphernalia of dictatorship. Although Franco calls himself *"caudillo"* and "generalisimo," he does not quite resemble the

[19] See especially George I. Blanksten, *Perón's Argentina,* Chicago, 1953.

current type of Latin-American strong men.[20]   On the other hand the fascist party of Spain, the Falange, is not *the* state party but only one of the forces of the regime, and at the present time not even the dominant one. Franco's regime is a synthesis of various forces, among them the army as well as business and financial interests and the Roman Catholic Church, but the regime faces many opponents not only among its defeated republican enemies but also among powerful monarchist groups.

Of course these groups are all of the political right. The left has been eliminated as an overt force by the civil war. Nevertheless the existence of different groups observing and to a degree checking one another does leave a certain amount of leeway. This, to be sure, is not freedom. It is at best room for maneuver—but that is not without value, for the citizens of an authoritarian country are usually experts at maneuvering. A further consequence is that Spain, while certainly authoritarian, is not totalitarian. In other words, the citizen who does not directly challenge the government is left alone. There is no attempt to permeate every facet of private, cultural, literary, scholarly, etc., life with the doctrine of the regime—always provided that the regime is not directly challenged. In Spain one can openly criticize the regime and its leaders and even if this is done in a public place nothing is likely to happen— in strong contrast to Nazi Germany or the U.S.S.R. But one cannot hold a meeting and condemn the regime, nor can one publish a newspaper which voices open opposition. Nevertheless public criticism is possible to a certain degree, and the existence of different groups produces newspapers which are a far cry from the monotonous uniformity of the Soviet press. The reader will get quite a different slant from reading *Arriba* (Falangist) or *ABC* (monarchist). But as soon as someone attempts to organize opposition to the regime, the latter's authoritarian nature reveals itself in the customary police and penal measures.

In some respects Yugoslavia is in a class by herself. She is of course a Communist dictatorship with no vestige of democracy. But Tito's break with Moscow has created a situation in which the Yugoslav regime attempts strenuously to differentiate between itself and the Soviet Union. At first this was confined to the assertion of Yugoslavia's independence from the U.S.S.R. and of the Communist party of Yugoslavia from that of the Soviet Union and her Cominform satellites. Then came a different course in Tito's foreign policy with the result that good relations with the Western powers ensued and a defensive alliance was concluded. Finally the course of Communism in Yugoslavia also deviated to an increasing extent from the Moscow prototype. This was most clearly shown in the field of collectivization, which was practically abandoned as a failure in Yugoslavia. Also an attempt was made to give more autonomy to local economic enterprise—state-owned enterprise to be

[20] *Caudillo* means "chief," "commander," or "director."

sure. This new direction does not amount to a return to democracy or even to a democratization; nor does it amount to a specific Yugoslav doctrine of Communism; it is frankly a period of experimentation which is designed to produce a specifically Yugoslav form of Communism which is to be without some of the rigors and inefficiencies of the Russian system. Just how well this will succeed is as yet unknown. But while this experimentation continues the state is just a little less monolithic than it was before.

The authoritarian regimes so far discussed in this chapter all have the distinctive characteristics of their respective countries, although foreign influence is of course in evidence. But the regimes of the Soviet satellite countries constitute divorce from their past and complete acceptance of the Russian model. Such indigenous institutions as have been preserved, like the Czech presidency, are clearly temporary in nature. The Soviet doctrine of today, which decrees that the model and the experience of the Soviet Union must be precisely followed, is fully enforced. Whatever has been said about the U.S.S.R. therefore applies in equal measure to the satellites. During the life of the Nazi regime the German satellites like Monsignor Tiso of Slovakia, Tsar Boris of Bulgaria, and Marshal Antonescu of Romania were regularly summoned to Berlin or Berchtesgaden in order to receive instructions, but nothing can compare with the well-oiled Cominform machine as a transmitter of Moscow's policy and direction. This has been glaringly demonstrated by the appointment of a Soviet Marshal, Konstantin Rokossovski, as Minister of War and Commander in Chief of the "independent" Polish Republic.

The discovery that so much of the earth is living under varying forms of authoritarian government is indeed disturbing to those who forget that democracy is a very sophisticated form of government and is therefore unworkable in countries which have not attained a certain amount of political sophistication and education. Democracy requires a sense of responsibility on the part of citizens and their confidence in their own ability to govern themselves. Such confidence, alas, is not too widespread in this world. It has often been stated that man wants to be free, but an unemotional investigation of the world as it exists will subject this brave statement to considerable doubt. It is true that a sense of freedom is widespread today, partly as an aftermath of the war, but only too often this is a negative freedom, the desire to be rid of certain oppressive agencies, like foreign colonial administrators or domestic secret-police forces. The positive virtue of wishing to govern oneself and to make constant decisions on questions of public concern frightens many, who are content to leave their government in the hands of "those who know best." This sentiment is not a monopoly of primitive nations; even inhabitants of successful democracies are sometimes assaulted by a revulsion against the multiplicity of problems which the modern world provides for them and would just as soon "escape" from the heavy burden and strain of freedom.[21] As late

[21] For an interesting analysis, see Eric Fromm, *Escape from Freedom*, New York, 1941.

as 1951 no less than 48 per cent of the French voters supported parties which favored considerable measures of authoritarian government.

As long as this is the case, the coexistence of many different forms of democratic and authoritarian governments must be expected. A change to the better, *i.e.*, toward a fuller realization of democratic government, could be achieved only through a long hard process of education and experience by which the taste and the practice of self-rule may be acquired. Such practice, however, is not encouraged in many parts of the world and is made more difficult by the tremendous differences in cultural levels and achievements in a world which embraces all types of civilizations, from the near-Neanderthal men of the Australian bush to the industrial men of the West.

Chapter 2

CONSTITUTIONS
AND CONSTITUTIONALISM

Every state needs some kind of order, some system by which a reasonably orderly process of government may unroll itself. Without such an order there is anarchy. This order or constitution must lay down certain rules which define the organs of government and how they originate, their mutual relationship, and the relationship between government and individual.

The constitution need not be written, nor is a particular written constitution necessarily the actual living constitution of a certain country. It is not even necessary that constitutional law be a superior type of law which may invalidate other law. The only thing that is required is some sort of legal order which is enforced and which keeps the parts of the state together. The constitution need not be a *superior* law, but it must be *anterior*, the source from which other law emanates.

The Fundamental Order

The concept of the fundamental order, the constitution, was already known to the nations of antiquity; both the Greeks and the Romans distinguished between the fundamental order and the ordinary laws which result therefrom. However, a number of factors contributed to create the modern concept of the constitution. There were the ancient, and especially the medieval, trade guilds who received their charters from their kings, bishops, or other superiors. Many of these medieval charters took the form of contracts, which is not particularly surprising as the contractual or quasi-contractual relationship between superior and inferior was well in conformity with the mode of the feudal society. This emphasized the *written* form of the basic law in contradistinction to ordinary legislation, which was uncommon in those days.

This peculiar combination of the concept of *contract* and the idea of the superior-inferior relationship later produced the notion of the *fundamental law*, which has a higher power than other law and limits even the ruler himself. In the sixteenth century the idea of the fundamental law was already in existence, being evident first among the monarchs. This concept of the fundamental law contract differs from the law of the land to which Bracton referred when he asserted that the king was "under God and the law"—a concept which Lord Coke later utilized to promote his theory that the entire body of common law was, in fact, fundamental law. At any rate, during the Stuart controversy the term "fundamental law" was well known, and in the Act of Attainder of the Earl of Strafford he was accused of having endeavored "to subvert the ancient and fundamental laws and government of his Majesty's realms. . . ."

Another development which entered in was the wide acceptance of the Calvinist idea of the covenant among the members of the congregation as the basis of the church organization—a concept which, especially in America, was transferred from the church to the state, giving rise to the idea that the state was based on a covenant into which all its citizens enter by an act of consent. This solemn covenant was naturally superior to lesser laws and orders which emanated from the fundamental covenant. Here again a written form was desirable, because much depended on the fundamental law; moreover, its dignity was enhanced by the written form. But the contractual nature of the covenant implied that changes could be made, as in all contracts, with the consent of the parties. With a multilateral covenant that meant that changes could be effected only if everybody consented, or at least—as it developed later—if an especially large majority agreed to it.

The unifying force in this development was provided by the school of natural law, which believed in the "inalienable rights" of the citizen, which were not received from state or government but were "inherent." Among those rights was the right to establish government, since all government was based on the consent of the governed.[1]

This means that the citizenry has an unlimited right to establish government and that this "constituent power" (better known under the French term *pouvoir constituent*) belongs to it alone.[2]

As all these ideas merged, there arose the modern concept of the constitution as a covenant agreed upon by the governed, having the characteristics of a superior, fundamental law from which all other law is derived.

Much of this development was English; yet England is the only country without a formal constitution. This was possible because of the gradual nature of English political developments; but when the thirteen British colonies in North America decided to form their own state and break away from English rule, the vacuum created by the destruction of English overlordship had to be filled eventually by a documentary statement of principles, the Constitu-

[1] Declaration of Independence, 1776.
[2] G. Jellinek, *Allgemeine Staatslehre*, Berlin, 1920, 3d ed., p. 507.

tion of the United States. The influence of this American development was decisive,[3] and all other democratic states adopted the American method of the written constitution.

Written and Unwritten Constitutions

Much has been made of the difference between written and unwritten constitutions, but as we have pointed out in another chapter,[4] this distinction is not too significant. In the first place, Great Britain is the only important country without a single, written constitution. Secondly, large parts of all constitutions are unwritten; the system of political parties, for instance, which is a cornerstone of constitutional government, either remains unmentioned or scarcely mentioned in all modern constitutions. Or written provisions may long have fallen into disuse or may never have been applied at all. Or a written rule may not mean what it says when it vests power ostensibly in one official when in reality it is exercised by another. Perhaps the only really significant distinction between written and unwritten constitutions is that in Britain, the classic country of the unwritten constitution, no attempt has been made to systematize and define the entire fabric of government in one authoritative statement. This also means that there is no theory of the above-mentioned *pouvoir constituent* in that country.

It is certainly not true to say that written constitutions are any more permanent, firmer, or more revered than unwritten ones. But the latter are practical only in a country like England where institutions have grown gradually and where there is a firm attachment of the people to certain rules of conduct which are observed without being formulated in legal documents. Wherever there is a new state, or a radical departure from past forms of government, only written documents are feasible. Could anyone imagine the new German Federal Republic (Bonn) without a written constitution?

Rigid and Flexible Constitutions

The right of a nation to give the state which it has created a constitution, this *pouvoir constituent*, which we mentioned above, is an original, sovereign, unrestricted power. But once the constitution is established, it provides for the manner in which it may be amended. With regard to this amending clause, which every such document contains, the classical constitutional doctrine distinguishes between *flexible* and *rigid* constitutions. According to this approach, a *flexible* constitution is one which can be amended by the same agencies which enact laws and in the same manner. Within the purview of this con-

[3] G. Jellinek, *Die Erklaerung der Menschen- und Buergerrecht*, rev. by W. Jellinek, Berlin, 1919, 3d ed.
[4] See Part I, Chap. 2.

cept most constitutions of the world are flexible because they may be amended by the legislature of their countries, but most of them are not completely flexible because there usually is provided a qualified vote, or a combination between a qualified vote and a referendum or other extraneous procedure. Only the British Constitution may be considered completely flexible since ordinary legislative action lays down the supreme law of the land.

By the same definition, the Constitution of the United States would be a prime example of a *rigid* constitution. It provides for four ways in which it can be amended: the amendment may be proposed by two-thirds of both houses of Congress or by a convention called by Congress on the application of two-thirds of the state legislatures, and it must be ratified either by the legislatures of three-fourths of the states or by conventions in three-fourths of the states, the one or the other mode of ratification to be determined by Congress. This is then a method quite different from the legislative process, and it is carried out by different agencies. Even that part of the amending process which is played by Congress is not a legislative act, and the President therefore cannot veto any part thereof.

It may however be questioned whether this difference between rigid and flexible constitutions is very meaningful. Since constitutions provide the legal framework within which the social and political conflicts of a country may operate, it would seem more important to determine how successfully a constitution adapts itself to the changing modalities of these conflicts. A constitution may be rigid in form according to the classical doctrine, but flexible in its adaptability. The Constitution of the United States is both rigid in the classical sense and difficult to amend in the formal sense. This difficulty was created on purpose in order to give it stability and continuity. But the text of the United States Constitution is exceedingly flexible. The terms "due process of law," "interstate commerce" or "freedom of speech," to mention only a few, have undergone vast changes in their interpretation by the Supreme Court of the United States.[5] Constitutions like those of India, Weimar, and Germany (Bonn) may be "flexible" inasmuch as their amending process is a relatively simple one, but their texts go into so many details which might well have been left to ordinary legislation that frequent amendments become a necessity. It is thus a matter of debate which type is the truly *flexible* one, the flexible constitution with the rigid amending clause, or the rigid constitution with the flexible amending provision. However, if the constitution is to be a superior document to which the people are to look up as a symbol and guarantor of their way of life, very frequent changes are likely to defeat that aim. It is certainly a fact that the constitutions of such countries as France

[5] See for instance, Brown v. Mississippi, 297 U.S. 278 (1936); Smith v. Allwright, 321 U.S. 649 (1944); United States v. Darby, 312 U.S. 100 (1941); United States v. South East Underwriters Association, 322 U.S. 533 (1944); Terminiello v. Chicago, 337 U.S. 1 (1949); etc.

or Italy have attained neither the legal significance nor the public attention of the American Constitution.

Since changes are necessary and inevitable, it may be better to have them emerge through the casual and relatively spontaneous ways of America rather than through the formal procedure of constitutional revision. The legal purist and systematizer will not like the American method, nor will the impatient reformer who finds that the Constitution places frequent and formidable obstacles in his path. But of course that is precisely what the founders wanted, and it is a fact that reforms which the people of the United States have really and persistently desired were not prevented permanently, either by the Constitution or by the Supreme Court.

There are different methods by which constitutions may be formally amended. A number of states adopt amendments by a simple legislative process,[6] albeit with a special, qualified majority. This is the case with the Constitutions of the U.S.S.R., South Africa,[7] Egypt, Turkey, Chile, Czechoslovakia, Poland, Hungary, Romania, Yugoslavia, Bulgaria, Austria,[8] and the Federal Republic of Germany (Bonn).

Other countries introduce a certain amount of complication by requiring approval of the amendment in successive sessions. This is the case in France, Sweden, Colombia, Brazil, Norway, Holland, Belgium, Luxembourg, Bolivia, Greece, Nicaragua, Finland, Iraq and Ecuador. Another method provides for the adoption of amendments by the legislature and ratification by special convention. This is stipulated in the Constitutions of Argentina, Paraguay, Guatemala, Cuba, Nicaragua,[9] and the Dominican Republic. The method of ratifying amendments by the individual states of the federal union has been adopted by the United States,[10] Mexico, and Venezuela. Other constitutions require ratification by referendum. Such is the case in Italy,[11] Japan, Denmark, Switzerland, Austria,[12] Uruguay, Portugal,[13] and Haiti.

A number of constitutions also carry provisions by which certain ideas may never be amended. Many federal or semifederal states rule that the federal system, or an aspect thereof, cannot be changed without the consent of that state of the union which is affected thereby. An outstanding example of such a provision is Art. 5 of the United States Constitution, which provides that no state shall be deprived without its consent of its equal repre-

[6] In the United States the amending process is not regarded as a legislative act, and the President cannot veto any part thereof.

[7] With certain exceptions.

[8] Not for total revision.

[9] For partial revision thereof.

[10] By state legislatures or state conventions.

[11] Provided referendum is demanded by one-fifth of either chamber, or by 500,000 voters, or by five regional councils.

[12] Under certain circumstances (Art. 44, Constitution of 1920 as amended).

[13] Under certain circumstances (Arts. 133–135, Constitution of 1933 as amended).

sentation in the Senate. But from time to time constitutions have gone far beyond that. Article 95 of the French Constitution and Art. 139 of the Italian Constitution provide that the republican form of government may not be made the subject of a constitutional amendment. The German (Bonn) Constitution goes even further and forbids amendments which affect the federal organization of the state or the cooperation of the *Länder* in the field of legislation or which violate basic human rights. The intentions of articles declaring inadmissible certain proposals for constitutional revision are of course laudable, and insofar as they increase the dignity and weight of the constitutional order they are all to the good. But in practice movements which would change the republican form of government or the federal system are invariably violent and revolutionary in nature, determined to bring about the desired changes without restraint from a constitutional order which they despise. If they are powerful enough to have their way, constitutional provisions are unlikely to stop them. Constitutional law limits only those who are willing to remain within it. Those who do not feel so bound can be restrained from overthrowing the constitution only by force or by the knowledge of their own impotency to challenge constitutional government effectively.

We have seen that all states have constitutions. But that does not mean that all states observe constitutionalism. Constitutional government is government whose exercise and functions are limited. To constitute is to establish, to establish is to define, to define is to limit.[14] On the other hand, a state in which the plenitude of power is concentrated in a few hands or in the hands of one, where constitutional provisions and institutional arrangements are merely tools to be used as the leadership sees fit and to be discarded at will when they are no longer of service—such a state may have a constitution, but it does not have constitutional government.

CONSTITUTIONAL GOVERNMENT AND DEMOCRACY

Constitutionalism is not identical with democracy. Imperial Germany could hardly be called a democracy, but it had constitutional government; power was generally wielded according to law, not arbitrarily, and the organs of government stayed within their limits generally. On the other hand, all modern democracies have constitutional government; a state in which the majority rules over the minority at will and without restraint could hardly be termed a democracy. In our days all democracies worthy of that name have constitutional government. This is one of the basic errors of Marx, Engels, and Lenin, who believed that the dictatorship of the proletariat would be "democratic" because the proletariat would comprise the great majority of the people. They were certainly no believers in limited government.

[14] The best treatment of this subject is Carl J. Friedrich, *Constitutional Government and Democracy*, Boston, 1950, rev. ed.

Because it is much more difficult to operate successfully under severe limitations than it is to have no restraint, constitutional government demands a high degree of political sophistication. It is not surprising, therefore, that constitutionalism is peculiarly well adapted to the character of the English-speaking nations, because in England sufficient agreement on fundamentals of government was achieved early enough in the country's history to permit the main political struggle to concentrate on means rather than on the fundamental nature of the state. True, England also had her hot battles, but even the controversy over the repeal of the corn laws cannot compare with the deep cleavages of Germany, Italy, or France.

The history of the growth of constitutional government reveals that its development was possible only after national unification had taken place. Nationalism as such was unknown to the Middle Ages, and the cataclysmic struggle between empire and papacy was a clash between two universalist doctrines. It was only after both these forces were weakened in their mutual struggle and gradually died as political powers that the forces tending toward national consciousness were set free. This development was, of course, much more pronounced at the periphery of imperial and papal influence, in England and Sweden, than in the center, in Germany and Italy.

Another historical influence which tended toward constitutionalism was the spread of Christianity, with its doctrine of the limitations of temporal power and its insistence on individual responsibility. Thomas Aquinas already taught that rulers ought to be subject to their laws.[15]

Everywhere the mainstay of the idea of constitutionalism was the middle class. The effects of its increasing power gave it self-confidence, and its world-wide business interests demanded the stability and assurance which come from the rule of law and the right to be left alone. But while the rise of democracy and constitutional government was definitely tied to the rise of the capitalistic middle classes and the new industrial and business groups, there is no evidence that such a tie must continue. In many democratic countries the tradition of constitutionalism is now so firmly anchored in the minds and hearts of the people that other classes can come to the fore without doing away with that precious heritage. On the contrary, the rise of the working people in both economic security and political influence has permeated them in many countries with the democratic traditions prevailing there and has caused them to carry on with the work of the *bourgeoisie* in constitutional matters, no matter how they might differ from it in other respects.

LIMITED GOVERNMENT AND VOLUNTARY CONSENT

We have seen that the essence of constitutionalism rests in the limitations which it imposes on the organs of government, as well as in a certain amount

[15] Thomas Aquinas, *Summa Theologica*, Qu. 96, Art. 5.

of diffusion of power which prevents a dangerous concentration at the top. This limitation may be enforced by a number of means; it may be enforced, in part, by the power of a supreme court to act as the guardian of the constitution and to repel encroachment by any other agency. It may consist of special administrative justice which prevents the executive from exceeding his boundaries or from abusing such power as he has. It may consist of the political constellation of forces which exercise supreme guardianship in the legislature. It may rest on the existence of a federal system which curtails and balances the powers of the central government, or it may rely mainly on a nation's sense of its heritage and on the understanding that certain things are not done and that a certain time-honored procedure is to be followed.

But all these theoretical and legal rules and features of constitutionalism rest on a further "inarticulate major premise," as Justice O. W. Holmes expressed it. It is the expectation that all major factors in a country under constitutional government will agree to be bound by the constitution and will not consciously attempt to go forcefully beyond constitutional limits. In the last analysis this agreement must be basically voluntary. A state in which a very substantial number of citizens is at odds with the essential constitutional fabric either collapses or turns into a dictatorship.

Such voluntary observance of the rules of the game is possible, however, only when the principal political forces in the country concerned are not too far apart from one another. This need not rule out spirited and even heated contests between decidedly different programs. But when divergencies of view concerning the fundamental nature of the state as well as mutual animosity have come to a point where one political party feels that its very life is threatened by the possible victory of another important party, then constitutional barriers are easily brushed aside and the grim struggle for political, and sometimes physical, survival begins.

When the Constitution of the United States was written, America was indeed fortunate to possess draftsmen whose basic political philosophy and economic outlook showed a high degree of harmony. But in our days of more intricate economic systems and greater social cleavages, such ideal conditions cannot be expected to prevail. Modern constitutions, therefore, often appear ambiguous and wordy in their attempts to accommodate different philosophies.

Whatever the method of constitutional change, it is clear that constitutions must not be allowed to become too rigid. Not all wisdom and prescience is given to the framers, and the vast social, political, and economic changes which follow must be accommodated somehow. Observance of constitutional limitations must not become an excuse for the perpetuation of the *status quo*. It may be considered axiomatic that the fundamental cleavages of our day cannot be compromised or put out of the world by some more or less ingenious constitutional formula. The task of modern draftsmanship and modern constitutional government is, therefore, to accommodate the social struggle within the constitutional framework rather than to force it to resort to extra-constitutional means. This also means that social and economic conditions cannot be permitted to deteriorate to such a level that large groups are driven to despair and to a search for violent remedies. The future of constitutional government will depend largely on the degree to which modern constitutional-ism is able to fulfill this task so that the important problems of modern society may be attacked by battalions of legislators and lawyers rather than by regiments of soldiers.[16]

SOME FEATURES OF POSTWAR CONSTITUTIONS

The years after the conclusion of the Second World War saw a veritable flurry of constitution writing. In fact more than fifty such documents have been enacted since 1954. In some parts of the world like Latin America, this was merely the continuation of a seemingly perpetual process.[17] In others, especially in Asia, new constitutions had to be written because of new-found independence. This is especially the case in India, where the diversity of provinces, races, communal and linguistic groups, as well as different cultural developments, have created extraordinary problems which an overly complex constitution is trying to solve. Similar problems in Pakistan and Indonesia have, up to now, prevented the enactment of a permanent constitution.[18] In Burma a long series of interlocking civil wars delayed constitutional life for a long time although a Burmese Constitution was adopted in 1948. The Con-stitutions of Japan, the Republic of Korea, and the Philippines are mainly of foreign inspiration. The Constitution of Japan was largely the result of overt American influence. The Constitutions of Korea and the Philippines are even more clearly based on American models and provide the only ex-amples outside the Western Hemisphere of presidential government. It is not surprising that the Philippines have adopted this model since they were once a territory of the United States to which close ties are still being maintained. In Korea the influence of American institutions is exemplified by President Syngman Rhee, who spent the long years of his exile in the United States. However, in the Philippines the working of the Constitution is still somewhat

[16] Robert H. Jackson, *The Struggle for Judicial Supremacy,* New York, 1941, p. 316.

[17] For a good compilation see Russell H. Fitzgibbon, *The Constitutions of Latin America,* Chicago, 1948. However, Latin American constitutions are amended, set aside, overthrown, replaced by the state of siege or "intervention," or just ignored with such frequency that no collection can long remain up to date.

[18] Pakistan has no constitution and is slowly settling some of the principal issues in-volved. The decision of the Pakistan Constituent Assembly to declare the country an "Islamic Republic" raises the possibility of a "dominant" race—a solution which has had disastrous results in other countries. Indonesia still has a provisional (the second) consti-tution.

on the turbulent side, while the Republic of Korea is characterized by a presidential autocracy with little attention paid to "checks and balances."

In Europe the main effort of constitution writing took place in France, Germany, and Italy, apart from the Eastern European satellites, whose formal constitutional documents have little reality and shall not be considered here.[19]

One of the characteristics which these constitutions have in common is the fact that they were written against the background of past regimes against whose evil features they were to guard. All three documents therefore emphasize the importance of the dignity of man because the Nazi, Fascist, and Pétain-Laval regimes offended particularly in that direction. All kinds of safeguards are to protect the citizen against any repetitions. The German and Italian Constitutions in particular attempt to guard against dangerous delegation of power and the abrogation of civil liberties. Both have provisions for Constitutional Courts endowed with the right to declare laws and executive acts unconstitutional; but only in Germany has that provision become a working reality. In Italy the Court has never been organized, despite the fact that implementing legislation was enacted as late as 1949, and it appears more than doubtful that the Italian Constitutional Court will ever see the light of day. Austria, which already had a Constitutional Court of limited jurisdiction in its 1920 Constitution, has revived the institution.

It is also typical of postwar constitutions, although not entirely a novel feature, that they stress economic and social rights as well as the customary political rights.[20] These, like the right to work and the right to housing, cannot usually be enforced by courts, and it cannot be said that they constitute the law of the land as would be the case in the Constitution of the United States. Rather, they are a profession of faith and principles, comparable to the American Declaration of Independence rather than to the Constitution; in their more practical connotation they are a command to the legislative and executive branches of the government to take appropriate action, although there is no known way in which a constitution can compel a legislature to enact certain laws. Moreover, these rights are often the result of compromises between divergent philosophies and thus are hedged about with limitations and conditions which make their nature and extent unclear. And finally these economic and social rights often reflect the political strength of the left, which in both Germany and France has declined in political influence, in Germany because of an absolute reduction, in France because the existence of the Communist party splits the left and thus assures the domination of the right.

[19] For the character and the functions of Eastern European constitutions, see Robert G. Neumann, "Constitutional Documents of East-Central Europe," in Arnold J. Zurcher (ed), *Constitutions and Constitutional Trends since World War II,* New York, 1951, pp. 175–190.

[20] The Weimar Constitution of 1919 already contained a long list of such rights.

Chapter 3

THE TERRITORIAL DIVISION OF POWER: FEDERALISM

Federal forms of government exist in the United States, Switzerland, Canada, Australia, India, Brazil, Germany (Bonn), and Austria. A much lesser degree thereof exists in the Union of South Africa, while the federalism of the U.S.S.R., Yugoslavia, Mexico, Venezuela, and Argentina is largely theoretical.

Federalism is a method through which power is divided between the central government and the authorities of regional units in a particular country. For true federalism to exist, the power of the federal (central) government must be limited as against the functions of the governments of the individual states (provinces, cantons, etc.) of the union; *i.e.*, true federal government is a form of true constitutional government. If the central authority of a so-called "federal" state is able at the stroke of a pen to destroy or set aside any and all functions of the component states, it is no more possible to regard this as a form of true federalism than it is to regard a government which can remove any and all constitutional limitations as practicing constitutionalism.

We have said that federalism is a form of distributing power. Power, in a constitutional sense, may be regarded as the ability to make decisions and to see that they are carried out. If, therefore, the component parts of a state have no power of policy decision in any field but are confined to carrying out central government directives through the medium of an institutional fabric of federal form, it is not a federal but a unitary state.

FEDERAL GOVERNMENT AND DEMOCRACY

Influenced by the American experience, adherents of federalism sometimes have the tendency to equate federalism with democracy. Other, though far less numerous, observers consider federalism a more progressive system of government. The federal experience proves that these assumptions are not necessarily true, although they may be correct in certain instances. The German empire which came to an end in 1918 was certainly federalist, but it would be difficult to argue that it was democratic. In like manner, the experience of Germany shows that progressivism is not necessarily an element of federalism. In the German empire the federal system, whose cornerstone was the archreactionary government of Prussia, became the last resort of those who resisted change. In the United States, the emphasis on states' rights is sometimes pressed by people who are less interested in the federal system than in the maintenance or recovery of certain interests.

CENTRIPETAL AND CENTRIFUGAL FORCES

Each of the two classic types of federalism, the United States and Switzerland, began as a federation of independent states and eventually turned into a federal union. To them, therefore, federalism denotes a trend toward a more centralized authority. Thus it is not accidental that in the early days of American history the Federalist party stood for a stronger national government. But the contrary development is also in evidence; where unity is endangered by diversity, a combination of the two is necessary in order to avoid serious difficulties and possible disintegration. An extreme case in point is the (formerly British) Commonwealth, in which centrifugal tendencies had to be accommodated increasingly over the years until the present structure was reached, which can no longer be called federalist in any sense but is rather a league of independent states. Likewise the Soviet Union and the Federal People's Republic of Yugoslavia, although not truly federal within the scope of the above definition, were persuaded to adopt the federal form in order to make ostensible concessions to the various nations and races which inhabit those countries. Federal forms of government may thus be the result of both centrifugal and centripetal developments.

Because of these factors, it will be readily understood that federalism is not always easy to determine. The German empire was federalist. The Nazi regime became unitary; between the two the Weimar Republic constituted a transitory stage in which federal paraphernalia were preserved while the central government had such vast powers as to make it virtually unitary. To confuse the picture further, there is the unitary but decentralized state like Great Britain, which is certainly not a federal government but whose decentralized units have considerably more real self-government than do component parts of some alleged federal regimes such as the U.S.S.R. or Argentina.

FEDERAL UNION AND CONFEDERATION

Because federations, confederations, leagues, and alliances are sometimes confused with federalism, it should be pointed out that a federal state is a true, single state, not a combination of states. The component parts of such a federal union may be called "states" as in the United States or in Brazil, or "republics" as in the U.S.S.R. and in Yugoslavia. They may even be called "sovereign" as in Switzerland or sometimes in the United States, but that sovereignty is purely rhetorical, just as is the theoretical right of the Union Republics of the U.S.S.R. to secede. It does not exist,[1] and bloody struggles like the American Civil War and the Swiss *Sonderbundeskrieg* have been fought to prove the point. In this there is a considerable difference between federal unions like the United States and confederations or leagues like the United Nations, where the sovereignty of member states is specifically guaranteed and the right to secession is a foregone conclusion.[2]

The common characteristic of all federal unions is a common executive, a federally constituted (upper) house of the legislature, and some form of judicial authority to decide disputes arising from central-federal relationships. The federal executive may follow either the presidential form or that of parliamentary government. Examples of the former are the United States and Brazil, while Canada and Australia illustrate the latter. When the rights and autonomies of the component parts in a federal union are strongly established, the parliamentary form is often more difficult to administer than the presidential, as has been demonstrated in Australia, where the different composition of the lower and upper houses has been known to raise very considerable problems.

"Reserved" Powers

The distribution of powers between the central and regional governments is also important; in fact, this is the key to the determination of federalism. It matters little whether it is the central or the regional governments which have "reserved" powers. The Constitution of the Weimar Republic granted the national (*Reich*) government only expressed and enumerated powers, leaving all others (reserved powers) to the *Länder*, but the "expressed and enumerated" powers were so extensive as to leave very little that could truly be called "reserved." Similarly the Constitution of the Soviet Union vests only "expressed and enumerated" powers in the Union government, but the enumeration of Union and Union-Republican affairs covers so much that virtually nothing is left to the Union Republics alone. Nor is enumeration of much help when federal (national) intervention may at any time take over or direct the affairs of the "states" or "provinces." Such intervention has made federalism purely theoretical and imaginary in Mexico, Venezuela, and

---

[1] The futility of the search for the seat of sovereignty in a federal union was demonstrated by Carl J. Friedrich, *Constitutional Government and Democracy*, Boston, 1950, rev. ed., p. 190.

[2] The United Nations Charter does not make any provision for withdrawal from membership, but it is nevertheless possible. See Edward E. Stettinius, *Report to the President on the Results of the San Francisco Conference*, Washington, D.C., 1945, pp. 47*ff.*

Argentina, while it has become more of a reality in Brazil since 1945.[3] Somewhat along the same line was the totally illegal use of national executive power (*Reichsexekutionsgewalt*) of the German Papen government in removing the duly constituted government of Prussia in 1932.

Switzerland follows the general model of enumerating federal powers, but this principle is somewhat obviated by the fact that the Swiss Federal Tribunal cannot examine the constitutionality of federal law. Thus, if the Swiss Federal Legislature were to enact laws which invade the sphere reserved to the cantons, the Federal Tribunal could not set them aside.[4] But although there is a noticeable trend toward the increase of federal powers in Switzerland, the Federal Legislature does not operate without restraint. There is, first of all, the second chamber, the Council of States (*Ständerat*, Conseil des États), whose members are elected by the people of the cantons upon electoral laws of the cantons and are paid by the cantons. In contrast to the German *Bundesrat*, the members of the Swiss Council of States are not subject to instructions by any cantonal authority. Nevertheless the coequality of the two houses of the Swiss legislature [5] in the legislative process assures the cantonal point of view a weighty hearing. Moreover the Swiss Constitution provides for a referendum upon the request of 30,000 voters or of eight cantons before a federal law can take effect. This is a condition which is easy to fulfill. Although it does not guarantee the absence of federal encroachment, it places a considerable barrier in its way because it has been the experience of Swiss referenda that they have uniformly operated in the interest of conservative ideas. It is true that the Swiss voters have accepted the majority of the constitutional amendments submitted to them, but it is unlikely that they would approve radical innovations.

A different system prevails in Canada. The Canadian Constitution, *i.e.*, the British North America Act of 1867, as amended, gives both the Dominion and the provinces enumerated powers, but the powers of the Dominion are enumerated, not exhaustively, but only "for greater certainty." [6] This system gives the Dominion rather than the provinces reserved or residual powers. This is also underlined by the power of the Dominion executive to instruct the

[3] However, federal intervention is still provided for in the Brazilian Constitution of 1946, Arts. 7–14.

[4] William E. Rappard, *Le contrôle de la constitutionnalité des lois fédérales par le juge aux États-Unis et en Suisse,* Basel, 1934. However, the constitutionality of cantonal laws may be examined by the Federal Tribunal as well as by the cantonal courts.

[5] Technically both houses, the National Council (*Nationalrat,* Conseil National) and the Council of States, are regarded as two parts of one parliament, the Federal Assembly (*Bundesversammlung,* Assemblée Fédérale), which is emphasized by the fact that both parts frequently deliberate together.

[6] British North America Act of 1867, Art. 91. For the text see Sir Ivor Jennings and C. M. Young, *Constitutional Laws of the Commonwealth,* Oxford, 1952, 2d ed., p. 393, and comments by K. C. Wheare, *Federal Government,* Oxford, 1951, 2d ed., 19*f.* Despite its brevity this is an excellent and useful book.

lieutenant governor of a province to disallow provincial legislation. This right may extend to legislation within the province's own powers if the Dominion government does not approve of it. In practice, however, and that is what counts in the consideration of federal government, the disallowance power is used most sparingly. Moreover, for the last fifty years and until 1949 the Judicial Committee of the Privy Council has interpreted the Constitution in such a way as practically to nullify the residual-power clause in Art. 91 except in times of grave national emergency.[7] In fact the narrow interpretation of Art. 91 and the broad interpretation of Art. 92, enumerating the provincial powers, especially Sec. 13 (Property and Civil Rights in the Provinces), have in effect reversed the Constitution and have actually vested residual rights in the provinces and not, as the Constitution seemed to provide, in the Dominion.

Nevertheless, one might question whether the original Canadian system, namely, that of vesting reserved powers in the central (Dominion) government and expressed and enumerated ones in the provinces, has not much to commend itself for our times. Practical experience reveals the steady growth of central government power in all countries. In federal unions this means that federal powers increase particularly in the field of concurrent powers in which both the central and the regional governments can legislate but in which the federal government is supreme. The result is, as the Weimar experience demonstrates with particular clarity, that the reserved powers of the regional governments become less and less meaningful. One might ask whether the idea of federalism would not be better served by vesting well-defined, specific powers in the regional governments (states, *Länder*, etc.) in order that those at least would be preserved.[8]

Special conditions exist in India, where a federal form of government has been established by a Constitution which came into effect in January, 1950. The federal form of government seemed desirable in view of the vast expanse of the country and the great variety of languages, religions, and cultures. However, the form chosen appears to be practically unmanageable. The Indian Constitution is the longest in the world. It has 395 articles and 8 schedules. In the official version printed by the government of India, it contains 251 pages. It goes into extraordinary detail in the vain attempt to foresee and regulate every conceivable future situation. It is true, as Jennings and Young point out,[9] that the complexity of the Constitution is due to the

---

[7] In 1949 the Supreme Court of Canada became the final judicial authority in constitutional cases of Canada.

[8] See the comment of Professor C. J. Friedrich on this point with regard to the drafting of the new German Constitution: Carl J. Friedrich and Herbert J. Spire, "The Constitution of the German Federal Republic," in Edward H. Litchfield and Associates, *Governing Postwar Germany*, Ithaca, 1953, p. 127.

[9] Jennings and Young, *op. cit.*, p. 364.

complexity of the Government of India Act of 1935, on which it was based to a large extent. But the 1935 Act, being an ordinary law, could be easily amended, while the Constitution is extremely rigid and difficult to amend.

The Indian Constitution goes into minute administrative details which would normally be left to ordinary legislation, executive orders, or departmental directives. In the field of federalism, upon which we can only touch here, the situation is complicated by the existence of different classes of states (A, B, C, D), by the extensive degree to which the parliament of the Union may legislate on matters enumerated in the state list, as well as by the extensive presidential emergency powers. Thus "President's rule" over a state may be imposed in case of war or domestic violence or "if the President is satisfied that there is an imminent danger thereof" (Art. 275, Sec. 3). Or it may be imposed in an even more far-reaching manner upon the receipt of a proclamation issued by a governor of a state and if the President, meaning the government of the Union, "is satisfied that a situation has arisen in which the government of the State cannot be carried on in accordance with the provisions of this Constitution . . ." (Art. 278, Sec. 1). Article 188, which authorizes a state governor to issue such a proclamation, has been interpreted to include a situation in which, due to political strife, no government could be formed. Such an instance of "President's rule" has operated in the state of PEPSU (Patiala and East Punjab States Union) and ended with the formation of a ministry acceptable to the ruling Congress party since it was composed of two Congress ministers holding all the portfolios in the cabinet.

It is already quite clear that the centralist tendencies of the Union government of India are not easily contained by the present Constitution and that here is good reason for dissatisfaction with the operation of this document. Extensive constitutional changes would hardly seem avoidable under these circumstances, and the true nature of Indian federalism will not emerge until this is done and a definite practice is established.

BICAMERALISM

In all these states the foremost expression of federalism is the federally organized chamber in the invariably bicameral legislature. Three different methods for composing this house may be discerned. The first is that of direct election on a regional basis. This is the case in the United States, Australia, and Brazil. Switzerland too uses this system, but not exclusively.[10] The second approach is that of election by state (or provincial) legislatures. This method is applied in Austria, India, and South Africa. A third way is applied

[10] In most cantons and half cantons, members of the Council of States (*Ständerat*) are elected by ballot or by popular meetings called *Landsgemeinde*. In four cantons and half cantons they are elected by the cantonal legislature.

in Germany where the upper house (*Bundesrat*) is actually a council of ambassadors, being composed of representatives of the *Länder* governments who may be recalled and replaced at will.

Quite outside this pattern is the Canadian system. In a sense both houses of Parliament have a federal nature. The British North America Act of 1867 as amended, the basic constitutional document of Canada, provides that the province of Quebec shall have sixty-five members in the House of Commons and the other provinces shall have the same number of members in relation to their population as Quebec has to its own census. The members of the Senate, on the other hand, are appointed by the Governor-General, or in reality by the Dominion government, and due attention is to be given in such appointments to regional representation. But while all regions are in fact represented in the Canadian Senate, they are by no means represented equally.

QUASI FEDERALISM

The U.S.S.R. and the Federal People's Republic of Yugoslavia are both federal in form. Both their constitutions declare their legislatures to be the "highest organ of state power" and "the supreme organ of state authority." However, we have seen in the case of the Soviet Union that this assertion is wholly fictional; in like manner the exclusive legislative power of the Supreme Soviet is also not in line with reality, for we have seen that the overwhelming bulk of Soviet legislation emanates from other organs of government. The same is true of Yugoslavia. The Soviet (Council) of Nationalities, which is composed of members elected by the people of the various component Union Republics, Autonomous Republics (provinces), and Regions, therefore has little significance other than to provide a basis for "mass participation," Soviet style.

A peculiar borderline approach occurs in Czechoslovakia. The history of the Czechoslovak Republic is replete with problems concerning the relationship between Czechs and Slovaks. Differences in language are less important than the gap of culture, industrial development, and educational achievement which separates the two regions, not to speak of the strong hold of the Roman Catholic Church in Slovakia. Even in the first phase of Czechoslovak independence, 1918 to 1938, the designation of the Slovaks as a "second state people" (predominant national group) was considered by many Slovaks to be a polite but empty phrase behind which Czech supremacy could unfold. There were independence movements and a growth of fascist organizations.

During the Second World War an "independent" state of Slovakia held sway, and there is little doubt that this idea was popular among its inhabitants. This "state" disappeared with the downfall of the Nazi regime, but during an abortive uprising against the Germans in the summer of 1944, a

Slovak National Council emerged.[11] Later, when the Red Army marched into Slovakia, the Council was given the task of local administration. The Czech government in exile accepted the situation, and in the Košice agreement of April 5, 1945, the right of the Slovaks to be "masters in their land" as an autonomous nation was recognized.

However, the Czechs found it hard to abandon the form of unitary statehood. The Czechoslovak Constitution of 1948 describes the republic as a "unitary state of two Slav nations possessing equal rights." There is a Slovak National Council, whose few powers are narrowly circumscribed by the Uniform Economic Plan, which is administered by the central government. The Slovak administration lies in the hands of commissioners who are accountable to the central government, which may declare their action null and void.

The Czechoslovak form of government is obviously not federal, and its constitution speaks of "unitary" government as we have seen. Yet the Czech-Slovak situation virtually calls for some sort of federal solution, and it is indicative of the deep distrust between the two nations that not even the wholly theoretical form of federalism instituted in Yugoslavia was adopted in the Czechoslovak Republic, despite the fact that the historic controversy between Serbs, Croats, and Slovenes is in no way smaller than that between Czechs and Slovaks.[12] The Czech refusal to try such a solution must be interpreted as the recognition that even in its most theoretical form federalism carries within itself potentialities for limiting government which the Czech rulers consider intolerable.

The Settlement of Disputes between Federal and Regional Government

Federal forms of government must naturally reckon with the possibility of controversies between the national authorities and the government of component parts. Lest the federal union should break over such difficulties, courts must be instituted in order to arbitrate or settle difficulties of this kind. A supreme judicial authority is therefore essential to federalism, although supreme judicial or arbitral authorities may also exist under a confederation or league rather than federal government.

The settlement of disputes of the above kind would be regarded as an exercise in constitutional law in this country. On the European continent, however, the idea that constitutional law is essentially political sometimes

[11] In Czechoslovakian usage the word "nation" (*národ*) denotes an ethnic group, while the word "people" (*lid*) is used to designate the entire nation.

[12] For a good summary and analysis of the Czech-Slovak controversy and its postwar results, see S. L. Sharp, "The Czechs and the Slovaks: New Aspects of an Old Problem," *American Perspective*, Vol. I (1947), pp. 311–322.

causes disputes to be referred to an administrative tribunal. In the United States it is, of course, the hierarchy of federal courts which is concerned with disputes arising out of state-federal relationships, and in cases in which states are a party the Supreme Court has original jurisdiction. In Canada and Australia there is also a Supreme Court for such purposes, but in Australia, New Zealand, and Ceylon appeals to the Judicial Committee of the Privy Council in London are still possible. In Switzerland the Federal Tribunal has original jurisdiction.[13] In Weimar Germany a special court was created for this purpose, the *Staatsgerichtshof*, but under the new Constitution of the Federal Republic of Germany (Bonn) this function belongs to the Federal Constitutional Court. The same is true of Austria. The republics of India and Brazil, on the other hand, vest original jurisdiction in a Supreme Court.

The Soviet Constitution does not mention the possibility of conflict between Union and Republican levels of authority. In practice, such conflicts can, of course, be ironed out through party channels, although a weighty word from above will be found sufficient. The constitutional provisions concerning the Presidium (Art. 49) give that body the right to annul decrees and orders of the Republic governments, and the Union government (Art. 69) has the right to suspend them. The Procurator-General also sees to it that all laws are observed.

The constitutional situation is slightly different in Yugoslavia. There, the Presidium of the People's Assembly does not have the right to annul orders and decrees issued by the constituent republics,[14] but the Supreme Court may decide issues between administrative organs within each constituent republic. Otherwise the impracticality of serious conflict between federal and republican governments is as great in Yugoslavia as it is in the Soviet Union. The fact that these two constitutions do not consider it necessary to give even theoretical attention to a problem which is regarded as extremely important in Western federal states indicates that the contingency appeared most unlikely to the framers.

Advantages and Disadvantages of Federalism

A survey of constitutional developments over the last few decades shows that the trend toward federalism has somewhat increased in the world. India, a new state, has adopted a full-fledged federal constitution whose validity has yet to undergo the test of time and practice. Pakistan, whose constitution has not been finished as these lines are written, has resolved to constitute

---

[13] The Swiss Federal Tribunal is not a supreme court in the same sense as the Supreme Court of the United States. For most cases the highest courts of the cantons rule with finality.

[14] But it has the right to rule whether a law of a republic is in conformity with the Constitution and the (federal) laws of the F.P.R.Y. (Art. 74, Sec. 4).

itself a federal union.[15] Germany, which drew away from federalism under the Weimar regime and abandoned it entirely under the Nazis, has now returned to it. That is also true of Austria, which became a unitary state in fact under the authoritarian Dollfuss-Schuschnigg regime (1934 to 1938); it has now returned to its previous constitutional principles. Brazil too has given federalism a wider application.

The main reason for federalism is the already mentioned need for a combination of unity and diversity. Such a need exists particularly in countries of great territorial expansion or deep-seated racial, cultural, religious, or linguistic differences. For the solution of such problems it is probably the only possible answer. It staggers the imagination to consider what the state of the world might be like had the rulers of Austria-Hungary granted a full-fledged federal regime and constitutional monarchy to their divergent races prior to 1914.

Countries where such great regional, racial, linguistic, or cultural diversity exists illustrate particularly well the fact that simple majorities are not enough to create general acquiescence and that some form of agreement by majority of regions and not merely by majority of persons must be achieved. In countries of great diversity and perhaps an uneven distribution of population, the application of a simple majority principle might easily lead to the neglect of certain regions; in countries with national minorities this may be even more serious, as under simple majority rule the majority may always outvote the minority and place it in a less favorable position by supposedly "democratic" means. Since national minorities have no chance of becoming majorities, the majority nationality need not fear that it might some day have to change places. The Swiss example has certainly demonstrated that the federal principle is best suited to solve national minority problems.

Although federal constitutions may be *rigid*, the successful operation of a federal system is conditioned on a constant process of adaptation. It is therefore in the actual working relationship between national and regional governments, rather than in any code of laws, that the actual nature of federalism is found. Hence it is primarily a problem of administration, of innumerable, ever-changing, often quite informal intergovernmental relationships.

In order to give these relationships a general direction, court action is required. In performing its role, the court ostensibly applies and interprets the constitution. In a truer sense, however, it may be said that the courts decide in which direction lies the course of wisdom.[16]

---

[15] "Objectives of the Pakistan Constitution," resolution adopted by the Constituent Assembly, Mar. 7, 1949, reprinted in A. J. Peaslee (ed.), *Constitutions of Nations,* Rumford, N.H., 1950, Vol. II, p. 691. This is a three-volume compilation of all constitutions in the world which is useful but unfortunately contains a number of errors and some poor translations.

[16] Wheare, *op. cit.,* pp. 233*f.*

Undoubtedly the American experience has made a deep impression on the draftsmen of Switzerland, Australia, Germany, India, and Pakistan, while the Soviet model was accepted virtually in packaged form by Yugoslavia.

Federal forms of government have thus been adopted largely because of particular conditions prevailing in certain areas and not because it was considered necessarily a superior type of government per se. Neither in India nor in Pakistan was any government other than a federal one feasible, and some overtures toward that goal were required in Yugoslavia in view of the explosive Serb-Croat relationship. Nor did Germany have a real choice. At the constituent assembly of Weimar in 1919 the Social Democrats were predominant, and they were believers in unitary government. Yet "states'-rights" sentiments were too strong to be disregarded. In Bonn, 1948–1949, more conservative tendencies prevailed and states'-rights sentiment ran high, especially in Southern Germany where "Bavarianism" blossomed. Moreover, it is very doubtful that the United States would have given its consent to any German constitution which was not federal.

Despite this command of necessity, other considerable advantages of federalism are clearly in evidence. Abuse of power by the central authority— the most serious and dangerous kind of abuse—is more easily checked by a vigorous federalism than by any other form of government. A mere functional division cannot remotely approach federalism in that respect, as local interests can best be mobilized under federalism against scandalous events on the central government level. Federal structures also afford excellent schools for political education, as each citizen has a full-fledged miniature government relatively near his abode on which he can make his mark far more easily than on the national administration. Moreover, in large countries of territorial expanse, federalism gives the citizen who is so inclined a chance to get acquainted with his government, *i.e.*, state government, while the national administration is of course usually more remote.

These very great advantages are bought at a certain price. There is no denying that federalism makes the constitutional fabric more rigid and changes may at times be difficult to achieve. Uniformity of laws, too—insofar as that is a virtue—is greatly handicapped by federalism except in the federal (national) sphere of legislation. Moreover, the lines of authority and jurisdiction are not always clearly drawn, and twilight zones of administration are common occurrences. Admirers of federalism, however, usually feel that these disadvantages are a small price to pay for the benefits which it bestows, especially on large or divergent countries.

As the British Parliament has been the "mother of Parliaments," so the United States has been the "father of federalism." The history and development of federalism in the United States are therefore of particular significance for analyzing the trends and developments of federalism.

At its inception, federalism was an expression of an age in which political and economic problems were primarily local in character and in which the state was a neutral force, not a salesman. Much has changed since then. Industrialism and the urbanization of large parts of the United States have deprived many problems of their local character, and the federal government has gradually undertaken ever greater tasks. With legislation, constitutional interpretations, and grants-in-aid, the federal scope of influence grew constantly —a trend clearly visible in other federal states regardless of internal political conditions. Now many demand that the state, here and abroad, perform still greater services, and some would like to see it embark on varying degrees of a planned economy. Federalism offers some difficulties to such schemes, and it is hardly equipped for the planned economy, which must be national or international in character. A planned economy is an expression of unity in a most important sector of civil life, while federalism is based on diversity. Integral economic planning and true federalism are therefore presumably incompatible. However, lesser degrees of economic planning may not be entirely impossible in a federal state.

If it be true, as some believe, that greater economic planning and integration is in store for mankind, the task of finding a new synthesis between this economic development and a continued existence of federalism may exercise the minds of scholars and laymen for many years to come.[17]

[17] Among the considerable literature on federalism see especially Sobel Mogi, *The Problem of Federalism,* London, 1931, 2 vols.; Wheare, *op. cit.;* and the many works on the federal regimes of specific countries. For an outstanding bibliographical compilation, see William Anderson, *Federalism and Intergovernmental Relations: A Budget of Suggestions for Research,* Chicago, 1946.

Chapter 4

FUNCTIONAL DIVISION: THE SEPARATION OF POWERS

THE DANGER OF CONCENTRATED POWER

It has already been pointed out that political liberty is possible only when the government is restrained and limited. Montesquieu wrote, in one of his many incomparable passages, "But constant experience shows us that every man invested with power is apt to abuse it, and to carry his authority until he is confronted with limits." [1]

In a preceding chapter we have discussed one form of limitation to authority: federalism, or the division of power between the central government and territorial units. In this chapter we will consider briefly another approach, which may or may not operate in conjunction with the first, the division of power by functions. Montesquieu poses the question clearly enough. Concentrated power is dangerous and leads to despotism. But how is such concentration to be avoided? Montesquieu's answer is that there must be a separation of powers within the structure of government, in order that one power may operate as a balance against another power. "Power halts power" (*le pouvoir arrête le pouvoir*). The great French theorist formulated this thought concretely in what is probably his most famous statement:

When the legislative and executive powers are united in the same person, or in the same body of magistrates, there can be no liberty; because apprehension may arise,

[1] Charles de Secondat, Baron de Montesquieu, *De l'Esprit des Lois*, Book XI, Chap. 4. On the general problem of the separation of powers, see the excellent sections in C. J. Friedrich, *Constitutional Government and Democracy*, Boston, 1950, rev. ed., Chap. X, and H. Finer, *The Theory and Practice of Modern Government*, New York, 1949, rev. ed., Chaps. 6 and 7. See also K. Loewenstein, "The Balance between Legislative and Executive Power: A Study in Comparative Constitutional Law," *University of Chicago Law Review*, Vol. V. (1938), pp. 566–608; A. Esmein, *Éléments de droit constitutionnel français et comparé*, rev. by H. Nézard, Paris, 1927–1928, pp. 493ff; Carré de Malberg, *Contributions à la théorie générale de l'état*, Paris, 1926, pp. 2ff; W. S. Carpenter, "The Separation of Powers in the Eighteenth Century," *American Political Science Review*, Vol. XXII (1928), pp. 32–34. On the history of the idea in America, see B. F. Wright, "The Origins of the Separation of Powers in America," *Economica*, No. 40 (1933), pp. 169–185.

lest the same monarch or senate should enact tyrannical laws, and execute them in a tyrannical manner. Again there is no liberty if the judiciary power be not separated from the legislative and executive. Were it joined with the legislative, the life and liberty of the subject would be exposed to arbitrary control; for the judge would then be legislator. Were it joined to the executive power, the judge might behave with violence and oppression. There would be an end of everything, were the same man or the same body . . . to exercise those three powers, that of enacting laws, that of executing the public resolutions, and of trying the causes of individuals.

Montesquieu thought of limitations to the powers of government in institutional terms. The idea itself was not entirely unknown before him; Aristotle, Polybius, Cicero, Thomas Aquinas, Harrington, and Bolingbroke embraced concepts of "mixed government." Both Cromwell's Instrument of Government, England's first and only written constitution, and John Locke spoke of the separation of powers. Montesquieu elaborated and expanded the theory and formulated it in the concrete terms which were necessary for maximum effectiveness in the France of his days. The theory was developed just at the right time to impress itself deeply on the framers of the United States Constitution, who saw in it the institutional guarantee against tyranny which they sought to establish in America.

THE AUTHORITARIAN OBJECTION TO THE SEPARATION OF POWERS

Two principal objections are frequently heard against the idea of the separation of powers. The first comes from the authoritarian, totalitarian camp; the second, from those who consider the separation of powers outmoded and incapable of guaranteeing the services which they think the state ought to render.

It is not particularly surprising that dictatorships have rejected the concept of separation, because it was instituted precisely for the purpose of preventing despotism. One of the Nazi jurists wrote candidly,

The separation of powers belongs to a political era in which political unity was reduced to a minimum in the interest of an autonomous bourgeois society. However, national and ethnic [völkisch] unity and oneness demand that all political power be gathered in the hand of one leader. The supreme will of the leader [Führer] is contained in the law. But the will of the leader appears also in all individual ordinances of the administration and in all decisions of the courts. The entire political life of the people is determined by the unified and comprehensive will of the leader.[2]

Also the attitude of the Soviet theorists is very similar. Vyshinsky wrote:

. . . from top to bottom the Soviet social order is penetrated by the single general spirit of the oneness of the authority of the toilers. The program of the All-Union

[2] E. R. Huber, *Verfassungsrecht des grossdeutschen Reiches,* Hamburg, 1937–1939, p. 160.

Communist Party (of Bolsheviks) rejects the bourgeois principle of separation of powers.[3]

And in a more recent statement the late Communist Prime Minister of Bulgaria, Vassil Kolarov, declared:

Whoever preaches a division of the people's power, actually places another power next to that of the people. . . . Since two unequally strong powers cannot coexist without struggling for supremacy, the apologists for Montesquieu are in reality working for the domination of the banks and big business.[4]

Thus, with only slightly different expressions, both these systems believe in the "unity" and "oneness" of power. The Nazi concept is quite blunt about it and consigns this unified and absolute power to the Führer. The Soviet writers more subtly assign it to the "people," but obviously the "people" cannot exercise it, and therefore it is exercised for them by the all-powerful assembly. However, as we have demonstrated before, the theoretically all-powerful assembly (Supreme Soviet) has no power whatsoever, and thus the "unity of power" is transferred intact to the real leader, the party Presidium. The astuteness of Montesquieu's observation about the course of unlimited power is thus brilliantly vindicated.

The Democratic Objection to the Separation of Powers

Montesquieu's views were the product of an era which looked upon government itself as something inherently dangerous and possibly despotic. Thomas Jefferson's oft-quoted assertion, "that government is best which governs least," belongs to the same frame of mind, to a political theory which looked upon the desirable state as primarily passive. Initiative was largely the business of the citizen, and the government was to act as an impartial arbiter in case of disputes. Government initiative often appeared as an unwarranted interference with the private domain; a descent of government to the level of quarreling interests. But today even the most conservative person is unable to think of the government in purely passive terms. The intensive integration and complexity of industrial society constantly demand more and more action and services from government. This is a universal development which has no exception in any state in the world.

The increasing amount of service and even planning required of modern government has subjected the idea of the separation of powers to very considerable debate. It is held that planning and active service cannot be the work of separate branches of government which cancel each other out. Man-

[3] Andrei Vyshinsky, *The Law of the Soviet State* (trans. by H. R. Babb), New York, 1948, p. 318.

[4] Speech on the draft Constitution, June 20, 1947, Sofia, Ministry of Information and Arts, 1947, p. 33.

agement must be unified, these critics say, and that also goes for the modern state. Fusion, not separation of functions, is required. They point to England, where the separation into three branches which Montesquieu thought he saw there does not exist. They also point to the development in the United States, where an increasing fusion of powers has taken place as exemplified by the independent regulatory commissions such as the Interstate Commerce Commission, of which Justice Oliver Wendell Holmes said that it performed "legislative, judicial and executive acts, only softened by a *quasi.*" [5]

In the face of such criticism it is worth while to reexamine the doctrine of the separation of powers as Montesquieu proposed it. It is true that he suggested a division of power between the legislative, executive, and judicial branches, but it is necessary to remember that he wrote before the rise of the modern party system, at a time when institutional checks appeared to be the only feasible ones. However, the core of Montesquieu's thinking is not the institutional implementation of his theories, but the moral and ethical code which insists that uncontrolled power is despotic power and which urges that power be distributed among various agencies in order that they may check and balance each other. The particular system of checks and balances between the legislative, executive, and judicial branches, which is the core of the American system, is by no means the only way in which the separation of powers may be applied. For example, in England, which is often presented as an example of unity of power combined with democracy, there are actually checking and balancing factors: there is an independent judiciary, and there is above all the system of two major parties, succeeding each other at fairly regular intervals and thereby checking one another.[6]

The two-party system in a parliamentary democracy thus provides both leadership and checks which help to keep the system efficient and free. But where no leadership can emerge through the prevalence of a galaxy of small, warring parties, an emergency situation may panic the legislature or the people to vest all powers in a certain government or a leader, and then the road to an authoritarian regime is open. France has frequently been in this latter category, despite its proverbial individualism and devotion to liberty.

The separation of powers may at times retard change and reform, especially when applied rigorously. At such times a conflict may arise between those with interests vested in the *status quo* and those whose interests demand change. The first group will then emphasize the separation of powers, while the latter may be inclined to hold the need for reform more important than the retention of checks and balances with which they have lost patience.

We have already stated that there is an indisputable trend toward ever-increasing government services. Even when a government which has been

---

[5] Dissenting opinion in Springer *et al.* v. Government of the Philippine Islands, 277 U.S. 210 (1927).

[6] Friedrich, *op. cit.*, p. 179.

responsible for an increase in administrative functions is defeated at the polls, the opposition which then comes to power rarely relinquishes an iota of what its predecessor has accumulated. When there is pressure for reform and for increasing services of government, violent upheaval eventually follows unless reforms are forthcoming. Recent events in Asia and Africa illuminate that point. But on the other hand when services are rendered without liberty, their extent and nature are determined by an abstract concept of what is "good for the people," which, as experience has abundantly shown, may be very far removed from what the people actually want to have done for them.

The "Public" Interest and the Check to Power

There is no certain manner of ascertaining the "public interest," but it appears that the public has a better idea of what is good for it than any autocrat, be he however wise and learned. The core of the modern problem of government and governmental reform is to find a synthesis combining the answers to two needs—the need for the managerial state and the need for freedom. The managerial state (or the service state, or the welfare state, or whatever other name may be placed on this trend) is characterized by an increasing concentration of power on the executive level and therefore implies the ascendancy of the executive over the legislative branch. This is most clearly revealed in Switzerland, where the Constitution envisages an all-powerful assembly and a subservient government, while constitutional practice—perhaps unconstitutional practice—has definitely established the government (Federal Council) on top.

It is quite possible that many people may be overly alarmed by this development, but unless we ignore all experience and disregard Montesquieu's warning about the frailty of man when in the possession of limitless power, some apprehension is in order. Only if balancing and controlling devices are properly developed to keep pace with the ever-changing face of executive power, may such apprehension be allayed. Far from being less important, the doctrine of the separation of powers is more important today than perhaps at any other time.

Many ways have been developed by which power may be distributed and checked. Montesquieu himself was particularly interested in the judicial power as a check of and arbiter between the other two branches. This concept is most clearly realized in the United States and in the members of the (British) Commonwealth. Under American influence the idea of an independent and coequal judicial branch has spread to Germany and Austria. In France and Italy a supreme administrative court, the Council of State, applies a most effective check on executive power, although it is nominally a part thereof. The Italian Constitutional Court envisaged in Art. 135 of Italy's Constitution has yet to be established, if it ever will be.

Legal, Political, and Administrative Checks

The balance between executive and legislative branches is primarily a *legal* question in countries under the presidential system of government. In such countries the constitution prescribes the rights of both as well as their limitations. But under a parliamentary system their relationship is mainly determined by political considerations. Theoretically there is a unity of both, since the government is constituted as a committee of the legislature and responsible to it. The principal check is, as we have pointed out, the existence of rivaling parties in the legislature, and it works best when there is a two-party or two-bloc system, in order that a periodic change of considerable proportions may be clearly foreseen and in order that the party in power will pay heed to the observations of the opposition. Where there are many parties, not organized into a few blocs which might approximate a two-party system, such change may be long forestalled through parliamentary maneuvers, and the same old crowd may come back, year after year, without having to fear serious or lasting upheavals.

Other attempts at separation have been made by strengthening one branch of government against another. Into this category falls the method of electing a chief of state (president) by popular election, which was the system in Weimar Germany and which is now applied in Finland. Popular elections of presidents of parliamentary republics certainly give them more power and thereby make them a factor in the scheme of the balance of power, but the example of the German presidency under Von Hindenburg shows that such balancing power may be for evil as well as for good. The German Federal Constitution (Bonn), on the other hand, attempts to strengthen the position of the government by decreeing that no vote of nonconfidence may be passed unless a new government is elected at the same time, and the French Constitution makes dissolution of the legislature possible if two governments are removed by the National Assembly within any eighteen-month period, which has little practical effect.

Another approach is provided by Switzerland, where most political parties of importance are represented in the cabinet, thus checking one another directly. It operates successfully even though the largest Swiss party, the Social Democrats, is not represented in the Federal Council at the moment by its own choice. The common work in the Federal Council (cabinet) itself forces everyone to be moderate or the whole system could not endure. It is the most direct form of the balance of power without resort to the three-branch formula.

Another interesting form of separation exists in Sweden, because there it is between the executive and the administrative branches of government. First of all, there are a number of offices outside the purview of the cabinet. There is a National Debt Office whose directors are appointed by parliament (Riksdag). Equally independent from executive administration are the Bank of Sweden and the office of the Attorney General. There are also certain parliamentary, supervising agencies, like the Board of Auditors, and the supervisors of civil affairs (*justitieombudsmannen*) and military matters (*militieombudsmannen*). There is also a joint Committee on Foreign Relations,[7] which serves both as a legislative committee and as an advisory board to the government which must be consulted on all actions in foreign affairs.

The Swedish administrative organization is quite unusual. With the exception of the separate boards and officials already mentioned, the executive machinery is divided into eleven departments (ministries) which are very loosely integrated. They consist of a number of boards, offices, and commissions[8] which are independent within their fields of operation. They are not under the personal jurisdiction of the minister, and they do not need the minister's approval for their action. Over the years a fair amount of cooperation has taken place between the minister and his independent boards and agencies, but such cooperation is revocable and constitutes a constant limitation to the government's authority.

THE SEPARATION OF POWERS CAN GO TOO FAR

The continued and perhaps even increased need for some form of separation of powers should not blind us to the fact that separation, checks and balances, and distribution of power can go too far. When a state is faced by grave and urgent tasks, a close relationship between the branches of government and between the different political parties is necessary. Too much separation may destroy responsibility, immobilize action, and ultimately destroy free government. Government should remain free, but it must ultimately be able to govern. Successful constitutional and democratic government demands that a synthesis be found between the separation of powers and the possibility of concerted governmental action. To find and operate such a synthesis demands all the political genius that a people can muster.

Thus separation of powers is a living force in all democratic countries as a check to unlimited, despotic power. It need not necessarily prevent leadership, for without leadership there would soon be a constitutional crisis and dictatorship, but it endeavors to temper leadership by imposing limitations upon it. The future of the free world will largely depend on the degree to which a happy combination may be found between leadership and constitutional, *i.e.*, limited government.

[7] This committee is specifically mentioned in the Constitution, and its functions are outlined there (Constitution of Sweden of 1809 as amended, Arts. 53, 54).

[8] Except the Ministry of Foreign Affairs.

Chapter 5

THE EXECUTIVE BRANCH OF GOVERNMENT

A. THE HEAD OF STATE[1]

For the purpose of a broad analysis of the positions which heads of state occupy in various countries, it is useful to divide them into two categories: those who are solely heads of state, and those who are both heads of state and heads of government.

This latter category, where heads of state are also heads of government, is confined to certain republican forms of government which are found exclusively in the Western Hemisphere, as well as in the three other countries whose constitutions were modeled on the American pattern, the Philippines, (Southern) Korea, and Liberia. Quite a different form of this type of executive can be found in Spain.

The second category is found in all remaining monarchies, including such royal autocracies as Ethiopia or Saudi Arabia, and in all states which live under some form of parliamentary government, including the Soviet Union and her satellites, where parliamentarism is rather theoretical.

The Presidential System

The presidential form of the executive is relatively simple and straightforward. It is characteristic of presidential forms of government that the president is not merely the *chief* executive: he is *the* executive. The Constitution of the United States says: "The executive power shall be vested in a President of the United States of America." The Brazilian Constitution reads: "The executive power is exercised by the President of the Republic." In the Philippines: "The executive power shall be vested in a president of the Philippines." Nearly identical provisions can be found in the constitutions of all other presidential countries.

Presidential forms of government have a number of features in common.

---

[1] A useful survey of the constitutional role of presidents outside the United States may be found in the article by Karl Loewenstein, "The Presidency outside the United States," *The Journal of Politics*, Vol. XI (1949), pp. 447–496.

The fact that the president is *the* executive makes all cabinet members his assistants and thus denies them the more independent positions of ministers in cabinets of parliamentary-type governments. Under the latter, cabinet ministers are always the most important leaders of the majority party or parties, but under the presidential system the powerful leaders—with the exception of the president—are usually in Congress and sometimes elsewhere but rarely in the cabinet. The president is really secretary of state, treasury, interior, etc., and the position of the secretaries is rather that of under-secretaries. In the United States, for instance, presidents like Harry S. Truman and especially Dwight D. Eisenhower have occasionally given their secretaries a great deal of leeway, but that has not always worked well. On the other hand, there have been presidents like Woodrow Wilson and Franklin D. Roosevelt who kept their secretaries very much in the dark about decisions of which they should have known and confided instead in unofficial advisers like Colonel House and Harry Hopkins.

Checks and Balances

Because of the plenitude of presidential power the president is the equal, not the subordinate, of the legislature, but because of the doctrine of the separation of powers the president ought not to be superior to the legislature. He cannot therefore dissolve or coerce the legislature, but the latter cannot remove him except through the impractical method of impeachment proceedings. President and legislature, being equals, stymie one another, and their equality is heightened by the fact that in all presidential countries the president is popularly elected and thus carries a mandate from the people which is at least as strong as that of the legislative branch. But on the other hand the frequent differences between the executive and the legislative branches of government make for a considerable debate of most public questions and increase the desire of the executive departments to keep the people informed, if only to win their support.

The principal virtue of presidential government is the fact that it creates a stable executive within the framework of a democratic order. But this statement must be accepted with some qualifications. The system creates executive stability as long as the opposition considers the observance of the constitution more desirable than the removal of the president. When such devotion to constitutionalism is not prevalent, the presidential system becomes an invitation to violence, as the dismal history of the presidency in Latin America reveals glaringly.

It is unfortunate that the American presidential system was imitated mostly by countries which had no experience or interest in true constitutional government. With few exceptions, the system has therefore failed to establish democratic government all over Latin America,[2] and its performance in the Philippines and especially Korea shows serious shortcomings. But this constitutes a failure of constitutionalism and political maturity, not of presidentialism. There is no shred of evidence to show that these countries would have operated more successfully under a parliamentary regime. For that matter, the numerous attempts of other nations to copy the British cabinet system have not always been crowned with any greater success.

CRITIQUE OF PRESIDENTIAL GOVERNMENT

It cannot be denied that presidential government has certain disadvantages. Disagreement between president and legislature is unavoidable. Even when relations between them are good, the need to persuade Congress has often meant delay in the American experience. The presidency is so tremendous a plum that it offers, as Lord Bryce remarked, "too great a stimulus to ambition," leading prospective candidates—and what politician is not?—to take equivocating positions in order to placate rather than to lead.

The presidential system has frequently been criticized, at home and abroad, for being unequal to the task of conducting a vigorous foreign policy. It has been charged that the American President's dependence on the cooperation of a frequently recalcitrant Congress makes United States foreign policy an often slow-moving affair, which constantly leaves friend and foe guessing about the degree to which executive actions or commitments will be sustained or repudiated on Capitol Hill. This situation can become particularly aggravating when the President and the majority in either or both houses of Congress do not belong to the same party.

To such critics, the unity of legislature and executive which characterizes cabinet government, as we have seen, appears an enviable model which ought to be emulated. However, such calls for the abandonment of the presidential system ought to be accepted with some caution. It is worth while to remember from our previous discussion of British, French, and German governments that this admirable unity of purpose does not exist under all types of parliamentary systems but only under cabinet government. The other type, assembly government, can claim no such virtue. Now an examination of the American scene reveals that the sharply crystallized class system of Europe, which Marx simplified into a proletariat-*bourgeoisie* equation, is not much in evidence. Instead American society has resolved itself into a great number of social groups. As a result of the still relatively open character of its society, the rapid growth of the American economy, the absorption of masses of immi-

---

[2] Considerable progress has been achieved in Brazil, Uruguay, and (until recently) Guatemala. Uruguay, however, adopted a collegiate form of executive based on the Swiss model in 1951. It went into effect on Mar. 1, 1952.

grants, and a continental expansion of territory, these groups are in constant flux and manifest considerable regional differences. Here, then, is the type of society which is virtually tailor-made for a highly unstable multiparty system, whose actual coming into existence is scarcely prevented by a two-party tradition. Such a tradition would probably count for little under a parliamentary system and could be consigned to history with the same ease with which the once-hallowed two-term "tradition" was broken by Franklin D. Roosevelt. What actually prevents a multiparty system from operating in the United States is the election of *the* executive by the people (disregarding the purely nominal electoral college), hence by a system which makes coalitions impractical and has time and again discouraged the rise of third parties. The two-party system, so important to the proper working of democracy, is thus intimately tied to presidential government in America, and it appears unlikely that one could easily take away one side of this combination without affecting the other. The presidential system thus gives the government of the United States a high degree of stability, which might well be lacking under a parliamentary system were it to be imposed on this country. These considerations, however, in no way detract from the admitted excellence of cabinet government elsewhere.

In a way the American concept of the presidency is the political corollary of the spirit of free enterprise and competition; it is based on the assumption that the citizen is safest when "checks and balances" are provided, especially between the executive and legislative branches. It also assumes that when basic unity is required in an exceptional crisis, statesmanship and patriotism will provide it; so far, the record is good. It is, of course, true that such unity is not achieved overnight, and the history of the late thirties shows that the achievement of such unity may take time, but if President and Congress were at odds over the policy which the United States should have taken toward the Axis powers, or over more recent issues of foreign policy, then this disagreement was merely a reflection of the uncertainty which hung over the country at large.

This often produces what some writers like to call a "great debate." This spectacle astounds, bewilders, or even irritates foreign observers of the American scene. Yet it is part of the vastness and variety of the country, and it illustrates the high degree to which the people believe they have a responsibility for the conduct of their government: not merely for a bare majority approving an important decision, but for a wide measure of approval thereof. Majority rule is merely an accepted convenience.[3] If it were customary for a bare majority to shut off debate and to impose its rule on the minority, a reversal of political fortunes would bring about the repeal of practically all laws

[3] Lord Campion, L. S. Amery, D. W. Brogan, and Others, *Parliament, a Survey*, London, 1952, p. 54.

enacted by the preceding majority. Therefore a "great debate" produces not only wide acceptance but also continuity.

The form in which this great debate is carried out differs widely in the United States and Great Britain. In Britain it is primarily confined to Parliament, which echoes the views of the country. The debate may be carried into the country by a general election being held on that issue. In the United States, with its constitutionally fixed congressional terms, such plebiscitelike general elections are rare, while the extraordinarily intense participation of private citizens all over the country in civic organizations and groups dedicated to discussion of and work for or against issues of public policy lets the great debate take place in every city and county. This makes for a long and frequently intense if not violent debate, which is difficult to control or terminate except by events which may supersede or decide it. But it is a way in which the varied regions, interest groups, and individuals of a vast country crystallize their political will.

However, most other nations, especially those which have had a recent occasion to write new constitutions, have been deeply concerned over the question of unity of action and have accepted the theory that this could be better achieved by a parliamentary regime without checks and balances. They therefore adopted the parliamentary system.

The Latin-American Experience

However successful the presidential system may be in the United States, a glance below the Rio Grande gives food for thought. In the less developed economic and sociological structure of most Latin-American countries, presidential government has degenerated into the rule of small cliques and juntas and especially into *caudillismo,* a native Latin-American type of authoritarianism, but one which differs substantially from the European style of dictatorship and is usually not totalitarian. However, there are marginal cases, such as that of Vargas of Brazil before 1946 and the increasingly dictatorial regime of Juan Domingo Peron in Argentina, which manifest tendencies that go beyond ordinary *caudillismo.*[4]

At one time or another several Latin-American states have attempted to develop some compromise between the presidential and parliamentary systems.[5] This is not easy to accomplish, and the results have been disappointing, but the continuation of such experiments emphasizes a trend of thought which

[4] George I. Blanksten, *Perón's Argentina*, Chicago, 1953; Russell H. Fitzgibbon, "Argentina after Eva Perón," *Yale Review,* Autumn, 1952, pp. 32–45.

[5] For an interesting and comprehensive survey, see W. S. Stokes, "Parliamentary Government in Latin America," *American Political Science Review*. Vol. XXXIX (1945), pp. 522–536.

seeks to make Latin-American institutions more representative and responsible. That is all to the good, but the great diversity among Latin-American countries places such generalizations in need of qualification. Brazil, for instance, has recently made great strides in the direction of constitutionalism, and there is no comparison between the considerable devotion to the rule of law which prevails in Uruguay and the absence thereof in Peron's Argentina. There is an almost total absence of democracy in those countries in which Indians form the majority of the population but are "excluded from national life," [6] as is the case in Bolivia, Ecuador, and Peru. On the other hand conditions have been best in the countries of Uruguay, Costa Rica, and Chile, and in Argentina prior to the Peron regime. Under such circumstances, presidential government can hardly be expected to receive a fair trial in Latin America, and where it has failed its failure had little connection with the particular organization of the executive branch but was rather caused by much deeper historical and economic conditions.[7]

THE GERMAN AND SPANISH EXPERIENCE

Latin America is not the only part of the world in which a compromise between presidential and parliamentary government has been attempted. The Constitution of the German Weimar Republic caused the President to be elected by the people at large. This and the considerable emergency powers under Art. 48 made him a factor to reckon with. Prevailing constitutional theory at that time insisted that the President have a full share in the actual government of the country and not be merely a figurehead. Under Hindenburg that system led to extremely bad results, and the framers of the Bonn Constitution in 1949 were wise to abandon it.

A form of presidentialism has been found useful by a number of recent European dictators. After Hindenburg's death, Adolf Hitler assumed the combined offices of the head of the state and the head of the government, calling himself first *Führer* and Reich Chancellor and later "simply" *der Führer*. Pétain, Tito, Quisling, and Pavelič aped this arrangement in varying degree. In our own day there is still the spectacle of Generalissimo Francisco Franco of Spain who, as "Chief of the Government of the Spanish State" and as *"Caudillo* of the [Falangist] Movement," combines the twin positions, head of state and head of government, with a good deal of quasi-royal pomp. At the same time General Charles de Gaulle, who aspires to the leadership of France, has frequently expressed his preference for the American-type presidential system, but it may be surmised that the General is

---

[6] G. I. Blanksten, *Ecuador: Constitutions and Caudillos,* Berkeley, 1951.

[7] Russell H. Fitzgibbon, "Pathology of Democracy in Latin America, A Political Scientist's Point of View," *American Political Science Review,* Vol. XLIV (1950), pp. 118–129.

selective in his admiration and would like to take the presidential system without the corollary of checks and balances.

THE MONARCH

In countries which have the presidential system, the head of state and government is always a dominant personality who administers this power himself. This is almost never the case in the parliamentary types of government, under which the headship of the state and the actual exercise of executive power are separated from one another. The older type of this kind of head of state may still be found in the remaining constitutional monarchies. In Europe those are Great Britain, Belgium, the Netherlands, Denmark, Norway, and Sweden, as well as the tiny principalities of Luxembourg, Liechtenstein, and Monaco. In the Middle East there are still many monarchies, Iran, Iraq, the Hashemite Kingdom of Jordan (Transjordania), Saudi Arabia, and Yemen. The constitutional character of the Hashemite Kingdom is open to doubt while Saudi Arabia and Yemen are royal and Imamite [8] autocracies. In the Far East the only monarchies worthy of note are those of Japan, Siam, and Afghanistan. Monarchies under colonial or protectorate rule will not be considered here.

CONSTITUTIONAL MONARCHY

It is the mark of a constitutional monarchy that the king does not actively govern. Constitutional government in its modern form is responsible government. The monarch himself is not responsible by definition; consequently responsibility may be imposed only against the ministers who actually govern. These ministers in turn would find it intolerable to be answerable for somebody else's action, namely, the king's; consequently, the idea of a constitutional monarch implies a politically inactive monarch. An active king, as we have pointed out elsewhere, is a king who is headed for trouble. Political activity on his part is bound to lead to partisanship, and partisanship destroys the confidential relations which must exist between monarch and prime minister. In fact a king must be even more careful in that respect than a president of a parliamentary republic, for the president may endanger his position and like Alexandre Millerand in 1924 may be forced to resign, but a partisan king endangers the institution of monarchy above and beyond his personal position. His dereliction inaugurates a constitutional crisis.

Constitutional monarchy is not a rational creation but the result of historical growth, while the position itself is rooted in the "charisma" of which we have already spoken. A rational explanation and analysis can therefore be

[8] The ruler of Yemen is called Imam, combining religious and political functions.

only very moderately successful. Monarchy has the ability to personify the otherwise abstract state. No republican form of government can achieve that feat to any comparable degree. Monarchy also gives an impression, sometimes perhaps an illusion, of stability and continuity. The august position and great prestige of the constitutional monarch have a tendency to somewhat cool political passions; the impoverished middle classes see in the monarchy their last link to pomp and circumstance, while the nation as a whole may see in the medieval splendor of the royal court a reminder of a glorious past.

On the whole a truly constitutional monarchy has few great disadvantages to the establishment and continuation of successful democracy. There are, of course, people who are opposed to monarchy and the hereditary concept in principle and consider it undemocratic that the nominally highest office in the state should be "owned" by a certain family. Objections are also heard with regard to the costs, which are substantially higher than those which the presidency normally incurs, but the amounts concerned are hardly significant enough to warrant an argument. Perhaps the most serious objection against constitutional monarchy is directed at the royal court which perpetuates snobbism and a useless aristocracy. In Great Britain the nobility has received many healthy blood transfusions by the numerous elevations of commoners, but elsewhere an aristocratic element may be observed whose only claim to comfort and privilege is their wisdom in the choice of their parents.

From a point of view of experience rather than logic, the record of constitutional monarchy in Europe is excellent, and there is little likelihood of voluntary change. But this admirable record is not easily repeated elsewhere, because the monarch can fulfill his role effectively only if he does not become a deeply controversial personality. The king who plays politics sows controversy and usually reaps disaster, as previously pointed out. Good examples in recent years have been Tsar Boris of Bulgaria, King Carol of Romania, and to a lesser extent, King Victor Emmanuel III of Italy. In the postwar era a great controversy arose about the person and past activities of King Leopold III of the Belgians. The quarrel, which cannot be discussed here, went deep. It touched on the King's act of surrender to the Germans in 1940 and his subsequent relations with them. It also concerned the King's connections with certain special interests and his close relationship with the Flemings. The truth or falsity of the accusations against the King is of secondary importance. It will probably never be established with absolute clarity. Who has authority to pronounce judgment on the King's surrender in 1940? But what is important is that the King became—perhaps made himself—the center of a controversy, and his usefulness was over. A king who is bitterly opposed by 43 per cent of his country's people cannot fulfill properly the functions of a constitutional monarch. The contrast between Edward VIII, later Duke of Windsor, who understood this, and Leopold III, who did not, and retired only after extreme pressure and riots, is significant. This is a cloud which hangs over Leopold's son, King Baudouin, who has added to his difficulties by his loyalty to his father and the latter's second wife, the controversial Princesse de Réthy.

For the same reason successful constitutional monarchies are probably confined to those countries in which they exist at the present time. The restoration of a dynasty which has long been deprived of the throne, as for instance the Hapsburgs, could be accomplished only over the bitter resistance of substantial parts of the nations which they desire to rule.

KING-AUTOCRATS

The type of the king-autocrat is now rare. The Japanese Emperor has joined the ranks of constitutional monarchs. The Negus of Ethiopia retains authoritarian command. The Kings of the Hashemite Kingdom of Jordan (Transjordania) and of Saudi Arabia, as well as the Imam of Yemen, recognize little restraint upon their authority.

THE PRESIDENCY UNDER PARLIAMENTARY GOVERNMENT

The presidency in parliamentary democracies is in many respects similar to constitutional monarchies, inasmuch as the president has little real power. The prototype of the presidency under a parliamentary type of government is that of France, where a special tradition inveighs against a return of "Caesarism" and where the history of the two Napoleons (I and III), the farce of Boulanger, and the tragedy of Pétain are only too well remembered. The accepted concept of the French presidency is therefore expressly antiauthoritarian to a degree which leaves him without authority. Even attempts by French Presidents to use the powers granted them in the constitution are bitterly resented. Only one President, Millerand, dared to appeal to public opinion and to parliament by sending a message requesting the reconsideration of a law already passed, but that action, though perfectly constitutional, proved his undoing. The new Constitution of 1946 reaffirms that right specifically in Art. 36, but there is little question but that this article is inoperative and a polite fiction which no President desirous of a full term in office would care to disturb.

The presidencies under the three most important post-Second World War constitutions of Europe—France, Germany, and Italy—offer an interesting comparison. All three Presidents operate as part of a parliamentary system, and all three are elected by their respective parliaments in joint session,[9] the French and Italian Presidents for seven years, the German for five. All three require the countersignature of their Prime Ministers or a minister for

[9] The Italian Constitution (Art. 83) provides for additional regional representation when a President is to be elected.

their acts. The French President may be reelected only once, and his German colleague may receive immediate reelection only once but presumably he may be elected again after an interval. No limitation on eligibility for reelection exists in the Italian Constitution. Both the French and German Constitutions allow their Presidents only to designate their Prime Ministers (President of the Council, Federal Chancellor) who may be appointed only after they have received the formal approval of their respective lower houses of the legislature (National Assembly, *Bundestag*); however, the Italian President appoints the Prime Minister and on the latter's proposal appoints the other ministers who need no further confirmation by parliament. The difference between the Franco-German and Italian system of appointing Prime Ministers is not excessive, as the incoming Prime Minister must, of course, have the confidence of parliament.[10] However, the nomination without special ratification gives the new Prime Minister a stronger start and thereby also makes the power of the president more significant. But in one respect the power of the Italian President is greater than that of his German and French counterparts: he has the right to dissolve parliament. The suspensive veto of the French President is entirely theoretical, but the Italian President has actually sent bills back to parliament for reconsideration. It is interesting to note that such bills have not generally been passed over the President's objection. However, it would be hasty to conclude that the Italian President has an actual veto. President Luigi Einaudi is a man of great personal prestige; many leading personalities of Italy's leading party, the Christian Democrats, were once his students; [11] and both his experience and his expert knowledge are treated with respect. It is therefore possible that the great weight of President Einaudi's objections to certain bills is a tribute to his personal influence rather than to the power of the Italian presidency. That, however, is conjectural for the time being and will be proved or disproved only under his successors.

Special Types of Presidencies

Three presidencies are outside the French-type pattern, which is otherwise typical for parliamentary republics. Those exceptions are the presidencies of Switzerland, Turkey, and India.

The executive authority of Switzerland is a cabinet which is called Federal Council (*Bundesrat*). It is composed of seven members and is elected for four years by a combined session (Federal Assembly, *Bundesversammlung*, Assemblée Fédérale) of the two houses of parliament, the National Council

---

[10] He must have the confidence of both houses of parliament (Art. 94), the Chamber of Deputies and the Senate. In this respect the Italian Constitution differs radically from the German and French documents.

[11] Luigi Einaudi is a former professor at the University of Turin and one of the world's foremost economists.

(*Nationalrat*, Conseil National) and the Council of States (*Ständerat*, Conseil des États). In reality the Federal Council is self-perpetuating. One of its members is elected President of the Confederation [12] and another Vice-President. They are elected for one year and may not be immediately reelected. In practice the Vice-President usually follows the President, and the office rotates among the three principal linguistic groups of Switzerland, German, French, and Italian. As president of the Confederation, the nominal chief of state has no special powers other than those which he already possesses as a Federal Councilor. He merely presides over the Council and otherwise discharges the social and formal functions of the headship of the state such as receiving ambassadors, etc.

The Turkish President is elected by Parliament (Grand National Assembly) from among its members for one Assembly term, which is four years. After the foundation of the Turkish Republic and its domination by Kemal Atatürk, the president of the Republic had exercised supreme authority, if not to say dictatorship, despite the fact that the Constitution does not indicate such plenitude of power. Under Kemal's successor İsmet İnönü, the hold of the president over the Grand National Assembly and the country was gradually weakened. The presidential leadership was exercised by means of his control of the Republican People's party, which held undisputed sway over the country until 1950. Similar tendencies developed when the opposition party won overwhelmingly in 1950 and 1954.

The new Constitution of India has created a curiously ambiguous picture of the executive branch of the government. Article 53 declares that "the executive power of the Union shall be vested in the President. . . ." However, despite this American-sounding phrase, there is also a Prime Minister who is appointed by the President and holds office during the latter's pleasure. This would indicate a most extraordinary power of the President, especially as he is elected by both houses of parliament for a specific term of five years and is impervious to a vote of nonconfidence. The reality of the situation is of course different, and the Prime Minister is the real executive, as is the case in all parliamentary republics. But the unclear relationship between the President and the Prime Minister and the possibility of political divergencies between them in a country of hot political tempers may be a source of future trouble.

THE SOVIET-TYPE PRESIDIUM

In the Soviet Union and her satellites there is no formal presidency. Some of the formal and ceremonial duties which are performed by presidents elsewhere are the task of the Presidium of the Supreme Soviet, especially of its chairman. However, he does not have special privileges and may in some ways

[12] The official name of the republic is Swiss Confederation, although Switzerland is really a federation rather than a confederation.

be compared to the president of the Swiss Confederation. Besides the formal and ceremonial functions of the Presidium—a collegiate president, as Stalin termed it—the Presidium has other, more important duties such as the interpretation of laws and the issuance of decrees, both of which have been discussed elsewhere. As a multiple head of state the Presidium exercises few prerogatives and is of little interest. Its chief importance lies in its other functions, as a reviewing and law-making authority. There is actually no particularly good reason why the Presidium could not fulfill its primary task without being the collective head of the state. As a matter of fact, that is accomplished in Czechoslovakia, where there exist both a President of the Republic and a Presidium of the National Assembly.

It appears, however, that the satellite states are destined to follow the Soviet pattern to the smallest details, including even local government and heraldry. It would seem likely, therefore, that the presidencies of Poland and Czechoslovakia are transitory phases which will eventually make way for a soviet-type Presidium. This would also be in line with the Communist constitutional theory of a supposedly all-powerful assembly.

B. THE HEAD OF THE GOVERNMENT AND HIS COLLEAGUES

As we have seen, the head of state and the head of the government are one and the same person under a presidential system, but in a parliamentary type of government they are separate and distinct. The distinction may not be so significant in itself, but it symbolizes a difference in the approach to government. Under a democratic presidential system there is a decisive separation between the executive and the legislative branches which are frequently at odds with each other. The parliamentary system requires a relationship of confidence between those two branches which can be achieved in practice only when the two operate in close conjunction with one another.

The parliamentary form of government is characterized by the fact that the executive branch is responsible to the legislative one and removable by it. Frequently this form of government is presented as one distinct type. Closer examination, however, reveals that there are actually three kinds of parliamentary democracies: one in which the cabinet is the leader, the foremost if not exclusive expositor of policy; one in which the government is under the thumb of the legislature; and one in which the Premier alone dominates. The first type may be called cabinet government; the second, assembly government; the third, Chancellor government.

The differences between these two approaches are primarily political rather than constitutional. Moreover, there are variations on this theme which make a precise line of distinction impossible. We may be certain that Great Britain presents the classic type of cabinet government, and if the term "assembly government" has any meaning at all, it ought to be applied to France. Western Germany is the home of the Chancellor system. But between these extremes there are many less extreme versions of the one or the other which at times defy classification.

Parliamentary Government: Cabinet Government

Cabinet government is characterized by a strong sense of unity. The Prime Minister and his cabinet colleagues are the leaders of the nation and of Parliament. The cabinet will be opposed vigorously by the "outs" who sit on the other side of the house. But even the Opposition expects the government to lead, and Parliament expects to follow in most instances. This does not mean that the legislature becomes a rubber stamp, but it does mean that the Parliament observes its proper role, which is that of a board of review for the broad outlines of government policy and not that of a shadow government which tries to reroute the cabinet's course.

Bagehot was the first to reveal that it was the function of the cabinet to link the executive branch of the government to the legislative. In that capacity it leads the legislature and provides Parliament with the policy upon which decisions are to be made. However, the reason why it is able to accomplish this task is the fact that it is a committee—the leading committee, in fact—of the majority party. And as the leadership and representative of the majority party it carries the immense prestige of a popular mandate received by that party in the most recent election. Because the popular mandate is so important, cabinet governments are usually sensitive to the people's voice and are inclined to demand an expression of preference from the people when especially important issues loom.

This is the system to which most democratic countries aspire. However, there are certain prerequisites without which cabinet government easily turns into something quite different. First and foremost there must be a clear and stable majority in Parliament for which the cabinet is the leader and spokesman. This is best achieved when there is a two-party system, but fairly good results can also be observed where there are two fairly solid party blocs, each consisting of parties who habitually work together and who have enough in common to permit them to evolve a definite political program. Of course the classic example of a two-party system is Great Britain. The situation is similar in the Commonwealth, although in Australia and New Zealand the anti-Laborite groups formed a partnership in order to defeat their Laborite opponents—which they did in 1949. In Scandinavia, on the other hand, there are several important parties in each country. The four larger parties of Denmark, Norway, and Sweden may easily group themselves into two blocs, liberal and conservative, either of which can furnish a government in case one party alone does not possess a solid majority.

There is little doubt that cabinet government is the most efficient form of government under a democratic, parliamentary system, and in the phrase "democratic government" the weightier word is "government"; you may have government without democracy, but you cannot have democracy without a reasonably effective government. No doubt some effectiveness may easily and willingly be sacrificed in order to obtain and preserve democracy, but when government becomes persistently ineffective, chaos and eventual dictatorship of a self-styled "savior" are usual results. It is therefore necessary for a democracy to preserve or create conditions under which effective government is reasonably possible. That means that steps must be taken to avoid the atomization of political power. A country which has perhaps a dozen or more important parties, in which no one group can hope to obtain much more than 25 per cent of the vote, is hardly ever in a position to provide effective leadership and a definite government program. The postwar history of France presents this issue in clear and foreboding terms.

There is no panacea, no institutional or constitutional "sure cure," which may be relied upon to establish effective cabinet government and working government majorities. Undoubtedly the two-party system is most effective, but the Scandinavian countries demonstrate that under certain circumstances this is not absolutely essential. On the other hand, Austria had as much of a two-party system as any other nation of Europe, if not more, yet it can hardly be said that the essential ingredient of cabinet government—unity of cabinet and parliament—was achieved. It has also been said that the disastrous establishment of a myriad of parties is furthered by the proportional system of election; yet PR has created a virtual two-party system in Austria and a simplified multiparty system in Scandinavia. On the other hand, the political picture of France is no more atomized under the present system than it was under the modified majority system of election under the Third Republic. Ordinarily a simple plurality system does reduce the number of parties and tends to present clear majorities most of the time. This is not true of the French system of majority elections in two runs which prevailed under the Third Republic, because it was specifically geared to the multiparty system, allowing parties to form temporary "cartels" for electoral purposes but leaving their individual integrity untouched. Without a second runoff election, mere "cartels" would be insufficient and a consolidation of the political picture might come eventually.

Another essential feature of a successful parliamentary government is a certain degree of moderation among the political parties. Where such moderation prevails, where the parties are not too far apart from one another, stable governments are feasible because the opposition understands and observes the rules of the game as the majority party does. But when one party feels deeply that life and liberty are gravely endangered if a certain other party gains the upper hand, orderly government becomes extremely difficult. Every trick, every method of obstruction and filibuster, is used to effect a certain political result, and if everything else fails, force may eventually be applied. This situation prevails particularly when extremist, antidemocratic forces gain a substantial membership in the legislature, which they proceed to terrorize and ridicule. When that occurs, orderly government often comes to an end and emergency decree takes the place of legislative act. From there it is only a step to dictatorship.

It is not surprising that a good deal of thought has been given to the problem of strengthening the executive in parliamentary governments. One school of thought in particular feels that the power of the executive to effect a dissolution of parliament is all-important. This theory is particularly popular in France, where it has been used to explain why British governments are stable and French are not. In the constitutional crisis of 1934 this was the argument advanced by Premier Doumergue in demanding the dissolution power for his office. Yet evidence does not entirely bear out this point. The power of dissolution is usually an expression of cabinet leadership, not its cause. It is debatable whether this power aids the British cabinet greatly in controlling Parliament. As long as the government has a majority, there is no need for controlling Parliament with the threat "obey, or be dissolved." When the government does not have a clear majority, dissolution and new elections are inevitable anyway. If feelings run high in both parties on a certain issue, a new mandate may be sought by general agreement. Undoubtedly the generally judicious use of the dissolution power has helped to restore clear and responsible government. But that is true because of the underlying agreement among British parties that there ought to be government and leadership and that dissolution may be a way to bring it about.

This is hardly applicable in France and Germany. In Weimar Germany, the dissolution power did not add to the strength of the government; on the contrary, its indiscriminate use detracted therefrom. Nor would the situation in France be materially affected by the adoption of a procedure such as was advocated by Doumergue. The galaxy of parties which characterizes the political picture of that country is such that elections rarely effect a complete reversal of the entire scene. More often, new elections bring about slight shifts, but the postelection coalition governments are often very much like those which preceded them and continue on their disunited course. In that case no notable strengthening of the government is achieved, especially as there is no real readiness on the part of deputies to admit the need for governmental leadership. It is not the power of dissolution per se which strengthens government but the political maturity of the parties.

PARLIAMENTARY GOVERNMENT: ASSEMBLY GOVERNMENT

Assembly government is characterized by the superiority of the legislative over the executive branch of the government. Yet that definition does not tell the entire story. It is clear that a legislative chamber composed of several hundred members of divergent political outlook cannot really govern, but it can prevent the government from governing. Assembly government therefore presents a system which is as much nongovernment as government. It is a government with checks but without balance. It is a system which is particularly incapable of performing the long-range policy and planning functions which are now required of modern governments. Even in France, the homeland of assembly government, *gouvernement conventionnel* is increasingly becoming an object of criticism.

The chief argument in favor of assembly government is its allegedly democratic character. It is held that in a parliamentary democracy the legislature is that branch of the government which is most representative of the popular will. Consequently the doctrine of popular sovereignty demands that the legislature should be supreme.[13] Here is a good example to demonstrate the frequent though baffling discrepancy between logic and experience. The logic of the argument in favor of assembly government as a supposedly most democratic institution is unassailable. In reality, the practical impossibility of government by assembly, the lack of unity and direction which are typical of this system, have made impossible the concentration of power in a small committee which is characteristic of modern cabinet government. Consequently whenever assembly government has been faced by exceptional crisis it has resorted to dictatorial "emergency" powers which it granted the government. In fact assembly government, as one authority has correctly pointed out, has frequently been the façade behind which a strong executive and eventually authoritarianism and dictatorship established themselves. "There is no other form of constitutional government which lends itself so readily to the domination of the state by a strong personality, or group, faction or party."[14]

ASSEMBLY GOVERNMENT IN THE SOVIET ORBIT

It is therefore not surprising that assembly government, legislative supremacy, is the constitutional theory in all Communist-ruled countries, while dictatorship is the reality. According to Communist theory the popular will rules supreme. But this will is conceived as a single, unitary will, not the result of divergent viewpoints. There can be no different "wills." Vassil Kolarov, late

---

[13] The doctrine of legislative supremacy leans heavily on Rousseau's theory of the general will, although the two are by no means identical.

[14] Loewenstein, *op. cit.*, p. 476.

Prime Minister of Bulgaria, explains that "the source of power in a people's democratic system is the people on whom are bestowed the supreme rights, while the fullest and surest expression of the people's will is the National Assembly. . . ." [15]

How is that single will of the people to be expressed? Our previous discussion on the government of the Soviet Union has shown that all policy is formulated by the "vanguard of the working people," the Communist party. Then, through the processes of "democratic centralism" this policy is applied on all levels. In the Soviet Constitution this fact is merely hinted at, while the constitutions of the satellite states generally do not mention it. Only the Hungarian Constitution is more specific by proclaiming that "the leading force . . . is the working class led by its advance guard and supported by the democratic unity of the whole people" (Art. 56). There is, of course, little doubt as to the nature of the "advance guard of the working class."

Thus in the Soviet and Soviet-dominated states, assembly government provides the framework for executive dictatorship, which is nominally vested in the council of ministers but which rests actually in the various Politburos which through the Cominform and other channels are in turn subordinate to the party Presidium in Moscow.

The exercise of dictatorial power with which we are already familiar has taken the form of the so-called "people's democracies" or "people's republics" in the satellite states. This is true even of Yugoslavia, which no longer enjoys membership in the Cominform. If we try to penetrate the dense fog created in the minds of the uninitiated by the Communist vernacular, we come to various definitions among which one by the late Bulgarian leader, Georgi Dimitrov, may be considered fairly typical:

The people's democracy is a state in the transitional period, destined to ensure the development of the state on the path to socialism. This means that although capitalism has been overthrown, the economic roots of capitalism are not yet extirpated. . . . The task of the people's democracy includes . . . consolidation of the key positions held by the working class, headed by the Communist Party, in all spheres of political, economic and cultural life.[16]

The "people's republics" are the crystallization in constitutional form of the "people's democracies." They are interesting subjects of study, because their incompleteness reveals their nature with greater clarity than the more finished product of the Soviet Union. In the latter all opposition groups and tendencies have long been liquidated, but in the "people's democracies" they

[15] Speech on the draft Constitution, June 20, 1947, Sofia, Ministry of Information and Arts, 1947, p. 33.

[16] Georgi Dimitrov, *Political Report,* Sofia, 1948, pp. 52–55. This was a speech delivered before the 5th Congress of the Bulgarian Communist party, Dec. 19, 1948. It was in this same address that Dimitrov defined "internationalism" as "international cooperation under Comrade Stalin."

are still being overcome, and the decisive and commanding role of the Communist party and particularly of its leadership, the party Presidium, is therefore in sharper focus. It is significant that one of the accusations which the Communist Information Bureau (Cominform) leveled against Tito and his associates was the assertion that the Yugoslav Communist party was too far submerged in the People's Front and was not sufficiently out in the open.[17]

There can be little doubt that in the "people's democracies" the real executive, as far as the determination of policy is concerned, is the Communist leadership, the Presidium, while the technical execution of that policy is left to the regular departments. However, in the "people's democracies" the story does not end there. The various Presidia are not the last authority, for they in turn are subject to the commands of the Central Committee of the Communist party in the Soviet Union, or more precisely, of its Presidium. This degree of subordination, of which the Cominform is the outward manifestation, far exceeds the control which Moscow formerly exercised through the Communist International (Comintern). Again the Cominform declaration of "excommunication" of the Titoists reveals the true position:

In Yugoslavia an undignified policy of underestimating Soviet military specialists was allowed. Also members of the Soviet Army were discredited. . . . All these facts prove that the leading persons in the Communist party of Yugoslavia took a standpoint unworthy of Communists, on the line of which they began to identify the foreign policy of the Soviet Union with that of the imperialistic powers, and they treated the Soviet Union in the same manner as they treat the bourgeois states.

This makes it clear that one of the gravest crimes committed by Tito and his friends was to fail in proper subservience to the Soviet proconsuls who were sent to Yugoslavia. But if that declaration still left some doubt as to the real relationship between the U.S.S.R. and her satellites, it must definitely have been dispelled by the announcement of November 7, 1949, which informed the world that a Marshal of the Soviet Army, Konstantin K. Rokossovski, was made Polish Minister of Defense, Marshal of the Polish Armies, and member of the important State Council.

THE CHANCELLOR SYSTEM

The theory and practice of the Constitution of the German Federal Republic have established a new form of parliamentary government, which, for want of a better name, may be called the Chancellor system.

On first impression there seems to be little to distinguish the German system from other types of parliamentary government. There is the confirmation

---

[17] The text of the Cominform declaration against the leadership of the Yugoslav Communist party was first published in the Czech newspaper *Rude Pravo,* June 28, 1948. Reprinted in English translation, *The New York Times,* June 29, 1948.

of the Chancellor by parliament (*Bundestag*), similar to the French method; there is the possibility of removal of the government by a loss of parliamentary confidence; and there is only a remote chance of dissolving parliament. However, there are differences. The Constitution emphasizes the preeminent position of the Chancellor. He "shall determine and assume responsibility for general policy" (Art. 65)—the Chancellor alone, not he and the cabinet. Votes of confidence or censure are cast for or against him, not for or against individual ministers or, for that matter, for or against the cabinet in general. He alone is elected by the *Bundestag* while the other ministers are appointed by the federal President on his suggestion. Moreover, the *Bundestag* cannot overthrow a Chancellor unless it can elect his successor by the required majority. Since, as the French experience shows, the negative coalition which may bring about a Premier's fall can rarely unite on a positive policy or personality, this provision makes the Chancellor virtually irremovable during a legislative term of the *Bundestag*.

This system may be modified by the exigencies of the parliamentary regime; if a Chacellor needs the support of certain parties other than his own in order to have a majority in the *Bundestag*, the ministers who are leaders of the parties concerned will have more influence than the Constitution would indicate. This has, however, not been the practice in Germany up to the present time. On the contrary, the authority of Chancellor Konrad Adenauer was immense even before his electoral triumph in 1953, a remarkable feat when one considers that in 1949 he was elected by a majority of one vote in the *Bundestag*.

The result has been that the Chancellor has been the government, very much like the President of the United States, while the ministers have diminished in power and stature and have become, primarily, his assistants. He dominates the entire government to a degree which is not usual among parliamentary regimes.

The Swiss System

A contrast to both the French and Soviet types of assembly governments is presented by the administration of Switzerland. Theoretically it has a form of assembly government. The bicameral Federal Assembly (*Bundesversammlung*) is declared by the Constitution (Art. 71) to be the "supreme authority" of the Confederation, except for the reserved rights of the cantons and the people. The Federal Assembly elects the cabinet, called Federal Council (*Bundesrat*), for four years. After each general election a new Federal Council has to be designated.

It is the theory of the Swiss Constitution that the Federal Council is an agent of the Federal Assembly, and a subordinate agent at that. The Councilors not only may not be members of the legislature—although they attend all meetings and have the right to be heard—but they also lack the power to dissolve the Federal Assembly or one of its houses. In practice, however, the Federal Council is totally independent of the legislature. Once a man is elected to the Federal Council, he is habitually reelected year after year, as long as he desires to present himself. There is no vote of nonconfidence. The legislature may overrule the Federal Council, but the Council remains in office just the same. This makes for very decided executive leadership and a highly efficient government whose members acquire much experience over the years which they spend in office. Perhaps the most remarkable case was that of the Federal Councilor Giuseppe Motta who was a member from 1911 to 1940. The only disadvantage is the often unrepresentative character of the Federal Council, because powerful but newer parties cannot always gain a seat in the government and have to wait until a vacancy occurs. This has operated especially against the Social Democrats, who had to wait for many years before they obtained a seat on the Federal Council, although they were the largest single party in the lower house (National Council) at intermittent periods. Since the Social Democratic Federal Councilor resigned from the Council because of a disagreement over taxation policies, this party is again unrepresented in the Federal Council.

Swiss Federal Councilors are leading members of parties whose viewpoints are diametrically opposed to one another. However, there is no similarity between the type of coalition government frequently found in France and the Swiss "government by commission." Virtually all parties are represented in the Swiss Federal Council, but most of the work of the Council is administrative and technical, and the members are prone to accept the recommendation of the Councilor in charge of a particular project. From time to time it happens that a Federal Councilor will oppose, on the floor of the legislature, a measure proposed by the Federal Council. In that case the legislature will decide the dispute by its vote. This settles the issue, nobody resigns, and unity is restored.

This unique and remarkable system, which has created a strong executive government in the world's oldest democracy within the framework of an ostensible assembly government, works very well and efficiently. However, its practical applicability in larger states with more complex problems and a different constitutional and political history must be seriously doubted. This also appears to have been the opinion of most draftsmen of later constitutions, for despite great interest in the Swiss system of government, Uruguay is the only country which has made any attempts to copy the Swiss model of the executive.[18]

[18] F. Fleiner, *Schweizerisches Bundesstaatsrecht*, Tuebingen, 1923; R. Brooks, *Government and Politics of Switzerland*, Yonkers, 1918; W. E. Rappard, *L'Individu et l'état dans l'évolution constitutionnelle de la Suisse*, Zurich, 1936; also by the same author, *The Government of Switzerland*, New York, 1936, and *La Constitution fédérale de la Suisse*, Neuchâtel, 1948.

Chapter 6
LEGISLATURES AND THEIR TASK

There is not a single government in the whole world which does not claim that it governs solely "for the people." Most governments also claim to be governments "of the people," and many insist that they are "by the people." So strongly entrenched is the idea of popular government that even the most dictatorial governments have seen fit to establish some kind of agency which they claim to be the representative of the popular will. Even the late unlamented regimes of Hitler and Mussolini had their parliaments, and the Soviet Union as well as her present and former satellites possess legislatures whose members are popularly elected, albeit without contest, and who are declared in their respective constitutions to be "the highest organs of state power."

Legislatures under authoritarian regimes need not concern us here. They do not legislate, except as a matter of form, and that only at infrequent instances. Nor do they fulfill any of the other tasks which democratic legislatures must perform. They are sounding boards and propaganda machines which give people the illusion of "participating" in the governmental process.

ELECTORAL SYSTEMS

In democratic countries the members of the legislative assembly are usually elected on a broad popular basis. Two principal systems of direct election stand out: one based on the majority or plurality in each electoral district, the other being proportional representation (PR). A combination of the two systems is now being tried out in Western Germany.

The study of electoral systems is of great importance, for not only are they merely different ways in which the votes are counted but they also decide to a considerable extent how the votes shall be cast, and they have a profound influence on the party system of the country concerned.[1] It is axiomatic that under a plurality, single-member-district system, the voter is less inclined to vote for third- or fourth-party candidates because their chances of getting elected are obviously slim. Thus the voter, who does not wish to throw away

[1] Maurice Duverger, François Goguel, and Others, *L'Influence des systèmes électoraux sur la vie politique,* Paris, 1949.

689

his vote unless he is primarily motivated by a spirit of protest, is more likely to vote for one of two candidates who have a major chance of being elected. Under proportional representation, on the other hand, there is no reason why such smaller parties should not be supported because they too will gain their share of the seats. The voters are thus more inclined to divide their vote among a larger array of parties.

It is of course true that plurality voting and single-member districts tend to encourage a two-party system only in each electoral district (constituency). A party may be the second or even the first party in certain areas and yet be a third or fourth party nationwide. But it is not likely that such a situation creates parties which can rival the two major groups for first place. Moreover, even allowing that this system does not produce guaranteed two-party systems, it never tolerates the extreme proliferation of parties for which other countries are renowned.

It can hardly be denied that electoral systems also have a profound influence on internal party structures.[2] PR increases party discipline while all kinds of single-member districts tend to weaken it. PR is capable of placing parties under primarily extraparliamentary leadership, which is unlikely in single-member districts, whether under plurality or majority and runoff systems.

There is also a general difference in campaign techniques, as individual candidates for single-member districts have at least some opportunity to bring their personalities and views before the public, while in a multimember district and PR abstract party programs are more in the forefront.

THE PLURALITY SYSTEM

The first approach is typical of the English-speaking world, where it has worked very satisfactorily. Its fundamental nature is simple to grasp. In principle one seat in the legislature is contested in each electoral district. Whoever receives a plurality of votes is elected. A somewhat different version of this system was in use in France during the Third Republic. Instead of plurality, majority was required for election on the first run. If no candidate was able to acquire a majority of all votes cast in the first election, a second, runoff election was held in which plurality was sufficient. This encouraged the political parties to organize "cartels" or "blocs" in which they combined their forces in the runoff election in order to obtain the election of that acceptable candidate who stood the best chance of victory. The simple plurality system has the great advantage of incomparable simplicity. Moreover, small third parties are discouraged because only larger parties stand a chance to elect candidates and most voters eventually tire of throwing their vote away. The plurality system, the single-member district, thus encourages establish-

[2] Maurice Duverger, *Les partis politiques,* Paris, 1951; a significant work.

ment of two major parties through which democratic government usually works best, as experience has shown.

Of course on the other hand it must be admitted that the majority system does not always faithfully reflect every sector of public opinion. This is clearly demonstrated by the fate of the British Liberal party, which received 2,600,000 votes in the 1950 election, representing 9 per cent of the total, but was able to obtain only nine seats in the House of Commons, representing only 1.4 per cent of the entire membership.

Where the votes of one party are heavily concentrated in certain areas, that party may be at a disadvantage. This has been one of the principal objections of the German Social Democrats against the plurality system. Their vote is primarily derived from the working classes, with the result that if the Anglo-American system were applied in Germany they would win in the workers' districts by overwhelming majorities but they would lose out in the rest of the country. Their opponents, on the other hand, would gain by less decisive majorities, but in more districts, thus obtaining a disproportionately larger representation in the legislature. For similar reasons, the Communists also condemn the single-member district. In this they were joined until recently by certain new parties such as the Popular Republican party (MRP) in France, which, for already stated reasons, feared to lose heavily.

PROPORTIONAL REPRESENTATION

Proportional representation (PR) is a name given to various systems of election which aim to distribute seats in the legislature in such a way as to reflect accurately the distribution of votes cast in the election. Its aim is that no vote should be lost and that every minority group as well as the majority should be represented in the legislature in exact proportion to its electoral strength.

There are several methods of PR, but the most widely used varieties follow either the system made popular by the Englishman Thomas Hare, the single-transferable-vote plan, or the approach suggested by the Belgian mathematician Victor d'Hondt which appeals especially to countries with a fixed number of legislators. All these and other systems have a common feature, that the proposed members of parliament are nominated by their parties and presented to the voters in the form of lists. The most widely used method of PR has been the rigid list system [3] which does not permit the voter any choice except between lists. It is exceedingly simple, since the voter need only select the party of his choice; by voting for that party he automatically votes for the list submitted by that party and for the candidates thereon in the

---

[3] All schemes of PR are based on plural-member districts. This system benefits the larger parties when applied by the rule of the largest mean. This is the method employed in most PR countries.

order which the party has determined. This gives the maximum control to the party leaders and the minimum to the electorate, which is one of the reasons why the strict list system has come in for a great deal of criticism. It has therefore been modified in a number of countries in order to allow the voters to rearrange the order of preference. Such a system has recently been adopted in France, in Italy, and in certain parts of Austria. Switzerland had previously given considerable freedom to its voters, permitting them to substitute names on the lists.

In view of the extreme atomization of votes made possible by the proportional system, some states have established an absolute minimum of votes which a party must obtain in order to qualify for any seat in parliament. This system has also been introduced in Germany, where it is primarily directed against the Communists, although it also serves against other groups.

Proponents of the proportional system praise it for its mathematical accuracy in reflecting popular opinion and consider it the most democratic method of election. Political practice, however, has been less favorable to PR in a good many countries. PR emphasizes party regularity and party control and eliminates intimate contact between the voter and his representative, especially when used in its most frequent form of the strict list system. It also causes the election to center on abstract party doctrines rather than on the concrete stand of candidates on given issues.

The plurality system is, of course, deficient in mathematical justice, but it does tend to provide clear majorities, responsible government, and close contact between members of parliament and their constituents. Also one of the most important features of the plurality system is that most candidates have to carry districts with a mixed population, and therefore they cannot be strict class candidates but must appeal to the broader electorate. The two-party system which usually emerges from the plurality system is therefore composed of groups whose differences of opinion are not too violent. But PR permits the parties to appeal to a single class or philosophy and still pick up a sizable vote all over the country. There is no need to appeal to a mixed electorate in each district, and the parties can afford to be sharply different. Such a system, when driven to extremes, may eventually eliminate the marginal voter, with the result that party strength becomes largely frozen. A typical example was the Republic of Austria between 1920 and 1934. The sharply antagonistic Christian Social party (conservative) and the radical Social Democratic party (socialist) [4] virtually commanded the field, as other parties were negligible. The country was very nearly divided between these two political giants, but the Christian Social party, sometimes with the aid of splinter groups, always commanded a small majority. There was no basic

---

[4] The Austrian Social Democratic party of that period was considered one of the most radical (Austromarxist) in Europe.

change in the government in that period, and none was in the offing. This led to mutual frustration, increasing violence, and eventual civil war and fascism.

Political experience, rather than logic, tends to indicate that as far as national elections are concerned, the plurality system tends to produce more acceptable results than PR, and in at least one instance it is generally agreed that PR constituted a major contribution to the downfall of democracy. However, examples are not lacking of countries in which a high type of democracy has been by no means weakened by the existence of PR. This is particularly the case in the Scandinavian countries and Switzerland.[5]

ELECTIONS TO SECOND CHAMBERS

Both major electoral systems, the plurality scheme and proportional representation, attempt to reflect popular opinion through direct elections. Other methods look to indirect voting, especially in those countries which possess two houses in their legislatures. Obviously the second house must somehow be differently composed from the first house, or there would be no point to bicameralism at all. In the United States and a number of other federal states this is achieved by fixing the number of delegates, senators, etc., which each component part is to elect. In the United States, Australia, Brazil, and Switzerland, states (or cantons) [6] have an equal representation in the upper chamber, whether their population is large or small.

In the Soviet Union and Yugoslavia the number of seats allotted to each Republic and other region is graded according to rank, with the Union Republics receiving the most. India has a mixed system which allocates different numbers of seats in the Council of States to the various states but also has appointed members. France and Italy apportion the seats in their upper houses (Council of the Republic and Senate) according to the number of inhabitants, but the French senators are elected indirectly while their Italian colleagues are elected directly. Both systems, however, are quite complicated. The French senators are elected by electoral colleges in each *département* composed of the deputies from the *département*, the members of its General

---

[5] There is a considerable literature on the subject. See especially Duverger and Goguel, *op. cit.*; C. G. Hoag and G. H. Hallett, *Proportional Representation*, New York, 1937; Report of the Royal Commission on Systems of Election, Cmd. 5163, 5352, 1910; J. P. Harris, "The Practical Working of Proportional Representation in the United States and Canada," *National Municipal Review*, Vol. XIX (1930), pp. 335–383; H. F. Gosnell, *Why Europe Votes*, Chicago, 1930; J. H. Humphreys, *Proportional Representation*, London, 1911; F. A. Hermens, *P.R., Democracy and Good Government*, Notre Dame University, 1943; H. Finer, *The Case against Proportional Representation*, Fabian Tract No. 211, London, 1924; J. Hogan, *Election and Representation*, Dublin, 1945.

[6] Each canton elects two members of the Council of States; each half canton one. Half cantons are the two halves of Unterwalden (Nidwalden and Obwalden) and the two halves of Appenzell (Outer Rhodes and Inner Rhodes).

Council, and the delegates from its municipal councils. Italy, on the other hand, is divided into nineteen regions, each of which is entitled to one senator for each 200,000 inhabitants, but each region is entitled to a minimum of six senators except the Valle d'Aosta, which has only one. Each region is then divided into as many electoral districts as it has senators to elect. In each such district each political party may enter only one candidate. A candidate who obtains 65 per cent of the vote in his district is declared elected. If no candidate gains this high figure—the most frequent case in politically split Italy—the votes of all districts of one region which have failed to elect a senator are counted together. The candidates of each party in those districts are placed on a party list with their relative place thereon determined by the size of the vote they polled in their districts. Then the seats are allocated by the application of a system of proportional representation.

The German *Bundesrat* is unique in that its members are appointed by the regional (*Länder*) governments, are subject to their instructions, and are capable of being dismissed by them. Moreover each *Land* delegation must vote as a bloc. The distribution of seats in the *Bundesrat* pays only relatively slight attention to the size of the population. Thus the representation of the *Länder* varies only between three for the smaller ones like Hamburg and Bremen and five for the very large ones like North Rhine–Westphalia or Bavaria.

APPOINTED MEMBERS OF SECOND CHAMBERS AND CORPORATIVISM

A number of states wanted to use their upper house as a place in which distinguished men could be given a voice in public affairs without subjecting them to the rough-and-tumble of an electoral campaign. Their model in part at least is the British House of Lords, although the majority of its members have inherited their titles and the distinction of the newly created peers is based on their political services to the party in power and not indicative of reluctance to enter the political arena.

The Canadian Senate is composed of appointed members. The Irish Constitution has been influenced by the British and Canadian experience but has also been strongly affected by corporative ideas. The upper house (Seanad Eireann) is composed of sixty members, of whom eleven are nominated by the Prime Minister (Taoiseach) and forty-nine are elected. Among those elected three are from the National University of Ireland, three from the University of Dublin, and forty-three from five panels selected as follows: (1) national language and culture, literature, art, education, etc.; (2) agriculture and allied interests, as well as fisheries; (3) labor, organized or unorganized; (4) industry and commerce; and (5) public administration and social services, including voluntary social activities.

The legislatures of Spain and Portugal carry the principle of functional representation (corporativism) even farther than Ireland. The Portuguese Constitution provides for an upper house, called Corporative Chamber, whose members are selected by appropriate functional organizations such as the organization of cultural, economic, and other interests. The Corporative Chamber is only advisory. The Spanish Cortes is composed of both ex-officio and elective members (*procuradores*), such as the cabinet ministers, national councilors, presidents of the supreme judicial, administrative, and military tribunals, representatives of guilds and syndicates, mayors, university presidents, presidents of institutes, and representatives of other organizations and other persons of high rank and station.[7]

The fathers of the Indian Constitution studied the Irish Constitution with some interest, and traces thereof are discernible in the Indian Council of States, which is composed of not more than 238 representatives of the States and twelve members nominated by the President of India from "persons having special knowledge or practical experience in respect of such matters as the following, namely, literature, science, art, and social service." Somewhat similar are the provisions of the Constitution of the Union of South Africa which permit the Governor-General-in-Council, and that means the government, to appoint eight senators in addition to the thirty-two who are elected.[8] The Italian Constitution makes all former presidents of the Republic senators for life and permits the President to appoint as senators for life five other Italian citizens "who have brought renown to the country by merits of the highest order in the social, scientific, artistic or literary fields."

BICAMERALISM

The unusual manner in which some of these upper chambers are selected raises the question of the utility and justification of the whole idea of bicameralism. To some extent bicameralism is based on a distrust of popular opinion and its expression in the lower house.[9] There are four basic reasons for having a second chamber:

1. To represent regional interests and, in corporate states, "estates" and professional groups.

2. To represent wisdom. Upper houses are usually elected for longer terms and under conditions which make for greater conservatism among their members than is true of the lower house. A higher minimum age is one of those

---

[7] Act of 1942 creating the Spanish Cortes, as amended in 1946, Art. 2. The Cortes exercises its legislative right in "cooperation" with the Chief of State (Franco).

[8] Eight from each province.

[9] The term "lower house" is purely historical. In most bicameral countries the "lower" house is the more powerful one.

factors. The Senate of the French Third Republic, with its long term of nine years and its high minimum age of forty, is probably the outstanding example of this kind. Such chambers are obviously created on the assumption that the lower house is capable of rash and unwise action which the more serene and deliberate Senate is to check. To what extent this assumption is correct may be debatable, but legislative history shows that this kind of relationship between the two houses in fact encourages irresponsible action on the part of the lower chamber. The history of the Chamber of Deputies of the French Third Republic contains many examples of the Chamber enacting absurd and ill-considered laws which pleased certain constituents, in the clear expectation that the Senate would quietly eliminate the bill and all would be forgotten. This is not solely a French specialty, as certain acts of the United States House of Representatives have occasionally demonstrated.

3. To placate those who favor bicameralism for the two reasons above, without actually conceding their point. The French people rejected the first constitutional draft in 1946, and their opposition was correctly considered as having been based to a large extent on the unicameral legislature proposed in the draft. The second draft did provide for a second chamber, the Council of the Republic. But since the Constituent Assembly was still dominated by parties committed to unicameralism and the legislative supremacy of the National Assembly, the Council of the Republic which was then proposed was so devoid of power as to be nearly incapable of functioning properly as a chamber of review.

4. In federal unions bicameralism is indispensable. One house represents the proportional principle of the population, the other the regional principle of the states, provinces, cantons, etc.

There is no doubt that genuine bicameralism, if it does its proper job of being a house of review and reconsideration, slows down the legislative machinery and tends to render more difficult radical reforms and changes. Reservations and misgivings are likely to appear when a project is subjected to long scrutiny, and this quite apart from the more conservative composition of upper houses in many countries. But if strong upper houses tend to resist radicalism, it is at least the radicalism of *both* left and right. This emerges clearly from the past history of the French Senate under the Third Republic. The more radical left, which naturally desires more far-reaching changes, is more vocal and frequently speaks of the defeat by the Senate of the popular-front governments under Socialist Léon Blum. But the left frequently neglects to mention that the right-wing Tardieu government suffered an identical fate. This does not mean, of course, that the Senate of the Third Republic was impartial toward left and right; it was not, for it was always somewhat conservative while the Chamber was sometimes more radical. But if second chambers are to do their job, they obviously must not be carbon copies of the lower house and their views must differ.

The Representative Character of Legislatures

It is one of the principal functions of legislative assemblies to be representative. A truly representative parliament therefore must have an opposition in addition to a majority group. A parliament without an opposition is a sham; one-party parliaments wherever they exist are, without exception, mere propaganda devices totally lacking in any power and influence whatsoever, designed merely to provide a suitable sounding board for the leaders and to arouse illusions of mass "participation."

It is easy to demonstrate that one-party assemblies are unrepresentative. But how representative are democratic legislatures? At best, a parliament is representative of its voters on election day. And even then it is not representative of the sometimes numerous nonvoters.[10] After that, new issues come up on which the people have had no opportunity to pass judgment, and yet the representative of the people is supposed to carry on. The frequency of election has therefore been a lively topic of discussion. Too-frequent elections prevent the legislator from doing his job, since his mind and time are absorbed by the constant struggle for reelection. The right to recall deputies before their term of office is up is even worse in many respects. This device not only keeps the political scene in constant turmoil and prevents the legislator from devoting his major attention to legislation, but it also places a tremendous power in the hands of minority groups, who may at any time and almost at will keep public life in a constant state of confusion and uncertainty. They are bound to succeed in the latter even if they fail to obtain the recall of the official in question. It is significant that the Communists have strongly advocated the recall of deputies—and in fact interpreted this as meaning recall by the parties.

The Legislative Term

On the whole there is a fair amount of agreement that legislative terms should be neither too long, in order to prevent the appearance of a legislature divorced from the people, nor too short, in order to permit the legislators to obtain experience and develop a legislative policy. The practice of states indicates that four to five years is often regarded as a happy medium, and many constitutions and electoral laws have adopted such a term.

A related question is that of the fixed term against the right of earlier dissolution. The influence of the power of dissolution on executive-legislative relationship has been discussed earlier with reference to the supposed power which the right of dissolution gives to the executive. But there is another side

[10] Since governments represent at best only a majority of a majority and not a majority of the whole, virtually all governments are minority governments.

to this question. In countries like the United States and France,[11] where there is a fixed term for the legislature and where therefore the end of the legislative term can be clearly foreseen, the legislature rapidly loses its initiative and power as the end of the term approaches. Projects which can be put off— and the interpretation of that term is very liberal—are put off. Congressmen and members of parliament shrink from committing themselves and indulge in the acrobatic feat of sitting on the fence while keeping their ears to the ground. This may go on for months, during which time little direction is given the country, and the world waits breathlessly until the periodic convulsion is over. Such a state of affairs is not excluded where the right of dissolution exists, but if dissolution is applied with dispatch and the election carried out shortly thereafter, as in England, the inevitable period of uncertainty and confusion is at least reduced to a minimum.

THE LEGISLATORS AND THEIR CONSTITUENTS

To what extent should legislators carry out the will of their constituents? This is not a simple question. To be sure, newly elected representatives receive some kind of mandate, but they are also supposed to use their judgment. Legislators ought not to be mere servants but also agents possessing a certain amount of freedom for responsible action. The actual relationship between legislator and constituents is partly influenced by the electoral system. It is, of course, closest under the plurality system and most remote under proportional representation, especially when the latter presents itself in the form of the fixed list. Under the plurality system a candidate must convince a considerable number of voters that he is a personally desirable representative of their interests. True, even in countries of the plurality system most voters cast their ballots for a party and a party leadership, rather than for the local candidate, but there are sufficient marginal voters who are undecided enough to be influenced by personal performance. Attention to such qualities is bound to be greater in a country like the United States, with its great variety of interests, inclinations, economic development, racial composition, etc., than in a country like Great Britain, where issues are more likely to be national and clear cut.

However, it would be a mistake to assume that no contact exists between voters and candidates under a system of PR. The methods of contact vary between the two principal methods of election. Under the plurality system the incumbent or candidate must personally keep in contact with his district. In Great Britain, where distances are short, this is easily accomplished and there is no member of the House of Commons—except possibly those from

[11] Germany too has a fixed term, but its constitutional practice is too recent to warrant a conclusion on this question.

Northern Ireland—who could not easily go home over a weekend. In the United States, where that is obviously not the case, letters, telegrams, etc., play a larger role. Under PR, especially where there is a fixed list system, there is virtually no direct contact. If the candidate or member of parliament is also a local party leader, he probably has some contacts with his local party members but rarely with his general electorate. Since he is only one out of many, he rarely considers himself as *the* representative of a specific district, and the general electorate which has merely voted for a party probably does not even know him or almost certainly does not know what district he represents. Contact, however, is maintained by the party organization. The local cell workers, the equivalents of precinct captains, are bound to hear the low rumbling of disaffection or special pleas and will report them back to higher headquarters. There they will be sifted and analyzed. If they are found to be substantial, they will have their effect on party policy and thus on the actions of the party's members of parliament who, of course, can ill afford to defy party command.

Under either system, plurality or PR, the voters tend to endorse a party rather than a man. This is less pronounced in America, where personal qualifications, attitude, popularity, etc., still play a large role, but in Europe the people tend to vote for parties rather than individuals, a fact which was drastically illustrated in the 1950 and 1951 elections in Great Britain in which not a single independent candidate won a seat in the House of Commons.

In view of these circumstances, one must agree with Professor Finer's view that the legislator receives his mandate from his party,[12] which in turn receives its mandate from the people. This means that the party and its legislators have a mandate to carry out the party's program. A separation of mandates between party and legislator is becoming increasingly theoretical. If this trend is clearly visible in Great Britain, with its plurality system of single-member districts, it is all the more in evidence in countries of PR, where the candidate for office depends solely on the party without whose support he cannot be placed on the all-important "list." The assertion of the German Constitution (Art. 38) that "they [deputies of the *Bundestag*] shall be representatives of the whole people, not bound to orders and instructions and subject only to their conscience," is therefore a pious declaration of something which does not exist, least of all in Germany. However, there is admittedly a difference in degree between the plurality and proportional systems. The former grants at the very least an opportunity to revolt, forces members of the legislature to keep in touch with their constituents, and brings their complaints and wishes to the floor of parliament. The latter makes all legislators party servants.

[12] H. Finer, *The Theory and Practice of Modern Government,* New York, 1949, rev. ed., p. 375.

EXECUTIVE-LEGISLATIVE RELATIONSHIPS

So far we have dealt with the representative character of legislatures. Their main task is obviously deliberative, *i.e.*, the legislative work itself. However, as soon as this topic is broached one thing becomes clear: legislation cannot be placed in a tight compartment all by itself. It is through legislation that modern government performs its operation. Legislation therefore expresses primarily government policy; to the extent that it does that, there is strong government, and insofar as it deviates from it, the weakness of the government becomes more apparent. In other words, wherever there is strong government, there the cabinet—the administration, as it would be called in the United States—is the legislative leader. The power of a legislature can therefore not be viewed in isolation but reveals its true character only within the framework of executive-legislative relationships.

We have already discussed this problem from the executive side. Basically three types of relationships may be discerned among democratic states. They are (1) executive leadership, (2) checks and balances, and (3) legislative supremacy or assembly government.

LEGISLATION UNDER CABINET GOVERNMENT

The first type is best exemplified by Great Britain but is by no means confined to that island kingdom. A view of the organization of the House of Commons shows that it is not actually organized to originate an independent legislative policy. The committees are not specialized and staffed to deal with the technical merits of bills, and the House does not debate bills or even the all-important budget in detail but only in a general way. This clearly demonstrates that the House, majority and minority alike, realizes that it is not really a legislator in the sense that it constructs its own legislative policy, but that its role lies in quite a different field: that of the grand review of government policy. This is true not only in Britain but also in countries like Sweden, where certain important offices are under the direct control of parliament, and Switzerland, where the Federal Assembly has found it repeatedly necessary to overrule certain sectors of the government (Federal Council) in order that a clear policy may prevail. Yet even in Sweden and Switzerland there can be no doubt that executive supremacy has won all along the line.[13]

It is not without interest that this trend has been especially marked in those European countries which are rightly considered among the most democratic, namely, Great Britain, Scandinavia, and Switzerland. This would

---

[13] This trend has been visible for quite some time. See the excellent study by Fritz Fleiner, *Schweizerisches Bundesstaatsrecht*, Tuebingen, 1923.

demonstrate that executive leadership is not necessarily incompatible with democracy provided its powers are carefully controlled and limited. It is not true, however, that such control can be exercised only by the legislature as such.

LEGISLATION UNDER PRESIDENTIAL GOVERNMENT

Under the system of checks and balances the legislature considers itself an equal to the executive. This approach is primarily associated with the presidential system as practiced in the United States. One of its drawbacks may be seen in the relationship which it creates between the executive and legislative branches of the government. Legislation cannot be separated from executive functions, because the latter operates through the former. Under the checks-and-balances method of the presidential system, the legislature frequently turns into a second executive, just as the executive, as everywhere else, tends to become the chief legislator to an ever-increasing extent. The result frequently is deadlock, which a country of the size, power, and wealth of the United States can possibly afford and which has its compensations in the added safeguard of independence and individual liberty. But the possibility of deadlock has not commended itself to the draftsmen of recent European constitutions, who feared the potential inability of their governments to act in a crisis.

LEGISLATION UNDER ASSEMBLY GOVERNMENT

Legislative supremacy requires elaborate organization of parliament and formidable committees. Since the legislature cannot exercise its power to the fullest in a body composed of several hundred members, the nature and strength of its committees become a matter of prime consideration. In the committees of the French National Assembly, the cabinet frequently loses control over its legislative projects and the chairmen of committees and *rapporteurs* take over, often reporting out a bill which has little in common with the original draft. The government may of course oppose the committee version of its draft on the floor of the house as well as in the committees themselves, but its chances for success are not always bright. Thus, the power exercised in the name of the entire legislative body by a few powerful individuals, especially committee chairmen and *rapporteurs*, is a particular feature of assembly government.

COMMITTEES

Nevertheless, legislative committees and especially strong investigating committees have their place and are capable of fulfilling very useful functions.

There are times when certain movements, operations, or persons endanger society and yet their prohibition may not be desirable. In such a situation, exposure to the light of publicity may be sufficient, and thus the harsher and more dangerous step of suppression may be avoided. Or if prohibition is in the cards, the investigations of a legislative committee may be necessary in order to provide a full hearing. Such a task, of course, need not be performed by a legislative committee but may be placed in the hands of an independent and impartial board like the British Royal Commissions. However, not all Royal Commissions have been impartial and not all countries have the tradition of fairness and "playing the game" which impels British governments to start investigations whose outcome may be uncomplimentary to governmental policy or efficiency. Much can therefore be said, in principle, for the independent survey undertaken by legislative committees. That purpose is quickly wasted when the committees become political footballs rather than fact-finding agencies. Especially dangerous is the absence of orderly procedure before certain committees in the United States.

Endeavors by Representative Kenneth B. Keating (Republican, New York) to draft a code of procedure for Congressional committees are therefore particularly laudable and important. In that respect the committees of the German *Reichstag* of the Weimar period and of the *Bundestag* of today may serve as a model because they were and are required to apply, as far as possible or by analogy, the code of criminal procedure of the courts. However, this is not always as simple as it may sound, for the situations before a legislative committee and before a criminal court often differ very widely, and so do their tasks. Moreover the legislature in a parliamentary democracy has, in principle at least, a powerful weapon in its hands to force the government to divulge information, namely, the threat of overthrowing the cabinet. But under the presidential system, the Congress lacks this opportunity, and its ability, through its committees, to force the executive or his agents to produce certain information may be crucial.

It has been said by some observers that the American and French committee systems would be unacceptable in Great Britain because they are incompatible with cabinet government.[14] Legislative, expert committees would become the rivals of the cabinet in leading the House of Commons. If this is valid, then it demonstrates why these committees are indispensable in America and France. In the United States, the separation of powers between the executive and the legislature does not permit the former to be the leader of Congress, and consequently the committees fill that position, including the decision about what shall or shall not be taken up. In France, the executive leads far too brief and uncertain an existence to be the actual leader of the

[14] Lord Campion, L. S. Amery, D. W. Brogan, and Others, *Parliament, a Survey,* London, 1952, pp. 30, 39–40.

National Assembly; the committees (*commissions*) and their chairmen usually have a much longer tenure than the ministers.

Another feature frequently found in assembly or near-assembly governments is the right of interpellation, which is characteristic of France. The right to question a minister or the policy of the government is found in all parliamentary democracies, but in France such interpellation may lead to the downfall of the government. The interpellation thus becomes frequently a question of parliamentary confidence in the government, to which the harassed ministers are constantly subjected.

LEADERSHIP IN PARLIAMENT

The actual position of the legislature is determined by the nature of the leading political parties. The two-party system of Great Britain divides the House into two parts, while the debate and the proceedings are designed to give a more or less even chance to both sides. In the United States the tradition of the two-party system has led to basically similar results, but since the American system is actually a cover for a hidden multiparty system, the two sides on each issue are not always the same, and new political alliances emerge as each problem arises. In this situation the otherwise reprehensible seniority system for committee chairmanships actually helps to avoid acrimonious intra-party battles and thus serves to preserve the framework of a two-party system.

Where there is a multiparty system, the proportional representation of each party on the parliamentary committees is the rule, with the result that the committees become replicas of parliament. Strict party discipline where it prevails is very much in evidence in committee, which sometimes means that issues are decided not in the committee room but at party headquarters.

The party structure becomes particularly evident in the leadership of parliament. In Great Britain the leadership lies unmistakably with the government and especially the Prime Minister. On the other hand, the existence of an "official" opposition clarifies the existing alternatives, while the "official" character of the opposition emphasizes that it supports loyally the same principles of the constitutional system as does the majority. The same situation prevails in the Dominions and in the Scandinavian countries. In the United States the role of leadership is exercised by the majority leaders in the House of Representatives and in the Senate, as well as by the Speaker of the House. Until the power of Speaker Joseph G. ("Uncle Joe") Cannon was broken by a "rebellion" in 1911, the Speaker was the unmistakable leader of the House of Representatives, but after "Uncle Joe's" downfall the Speaker's powers were greatly curtailed. However, a Speaker of great personality and political acumen can still be the most influential member of the House, as has been demonstrated by Speaker Sam Rayburn. On the other hand, the majority leader may find his colleagues reluctant to follow him, especially in the Senate, or there may be more powerful men in the background to whom the senators of the majority party look for leadership. At other times the President has seen fit to entrust specific legislative tasks to men other than the designated majority leader. Leadership in the United States Congress is therefore frequently a diffuse thing; the President, the logical leader, is prevented by the mutual independence of the legislative and executive branches from exercising his leadership to the full, while other men are sometimes not strong enough to wield decisive direction.

In France, parliamentary leadership is even more diffuse than in the United States. The President of the National Assembly is certainly not its leader, although he is usually a highly respected parliamentarian. On occasion he may lend his prestige to speak for or against a certain bill, but he does this merely in his personal capacity. The Assembly will hear him with respect, but if it decides to go against his wishes, his prestige as President is not impaired. Nor can the government be called "leader." As French governments go, the cabinet is usually like a small ship sailing a rough sea. It has a hard enough time to keep afloat without directing the angry parliamentary waves. Whatever legislative direction there is comes from the committees and especially their chairmen.

Legislative leadership is essential for orderly procedure and constructive work. It is not an easy thing, as even experienced democracies have learned, and it comes particularly hard to those states which are trying their hands at self-government and democracy without adequate preparation. India and Germany demonstrate these difficulties, which are essentially problems of adjustment to party government. The Indian majority party, the Congress party, was held together primarily by its united will to resistance against the British raj. When the white man's domination ceased, the same corrosive tendencies appeared in the Congress party as were noticed in the French, Belgian, and Dutch Resistance movements once their objectives were realized. In India these tendencies have not gone nearly as far as in Western Europe, partly as a result of outstanding personalities like Nehru and Patel [15] who were not unmindful of the significance of party discipline. Still, opposing tendencies do appear in the party, and the steering of a decisive legislative course is bound to be made more difficult thereby.

Germany's problems are of a quite different kind. There is no absence of party discipline, although different tendencies are present there as well as elsewhere in the world. Germany's chief problem is the unfamiliarity with the parliamentary process and parliamentary spirit. The present German govern-

---

[15] The late Vallabhbhai Patel did an extraordinary job of disciplining a party which grew in a spirit of revolt. However, his measures were deeply resented by many.

ment has not as yet learned the art of the easy give-and-take which marks a successful executive-legislative relationship, and the leadership of the Social Democratic opposition gives little promise of being better were it to come to power. The government issues its declarations, the opposition makes its attacks, and everything is correct but lifeless. Mutual flexibility and moderation, the art of obeying unwritten rules, must yet be learned by doing.

This is even more the case in Austria, where the peculiar nature of the two dominant parties tends to refer all important decisions to secret conferences between the principal party leaders. As a result, the National Council (*Nationalrat*) merely goes through the motion of set speeches, while the issues have already been decided. It is, of course, true that even in the British House of Commons a speech has moved many but has not changed a single vote; yet the expression of individual, not merely party, viewpoints is possible there and occurs all the time. However, under the strict list system of PR, party discipline usually proves too strong for such individualism.

THE REVIEW OF GOVERNMENT POLICY: DEBATE

The essence of modern democratic legislatures is their function of reviewing government policy. It matters little that the votes are already counted and the issue often "in the bag" before the debate has started. The fact that the government must justify its action and face a vigorous opposition is exceedingly wholesome, since the opposition always has an opportunity to make an impression on the country even though the solid government majority may remain unshaken for the time being. Although the debate may not "change a single vote," debate there must be with all its instructiveness and its information to the electorate. A government which must justify itself and submit to constant challenge is reasonably free. Only when challenge and debate are removed, be it under the disguise of an alleged "unity" or under cover of somebody's self-proclaimed superiority and consequent "right to rule," is free government really defeated.

Debate is thus the core of democracy. This is well understood among those nations which have been fortunate enough to see their institutions develop in the constant light of public discussion. But other nations are not yet so conditioned. Many Germans still fail to see the point of a public debate and are solely interested in the concrete result. Since debate sometimes postpones or even compromises results, they are inclined to call Parliament a "gossip club" (*Schwatzbude*) and see little point in democracy. Such a serious handicap to the growth of genuine democracy may be overcome in time and through practice, but only if a spirit of moderation prevails and if all parties become convinced that opposition is not merely something which must be tolerated but rather something actually desirable.

DEMOCRATIC LEGISLATURES AND ANTIDEMOCRATIC LEGISLATORS

If the core of democracy is debate, then it is the opposition which makes that possible, but only if both the opposition and the majority observe and obey the rules of the game which stipulate that all sides must have a fair chance but that when the issue has been decided the government must be permitted to carry on and the opposition must be free to fight another day. That is not possible where the chasm between the parties is so great that one group will go to almost any length to defeat the other side, including sabotage, violence, and other extraconstitutional means. Thus, when a country is faced with the appearance of a strong group which refuses to play the game and which would bring the parliamentary process to an end if it could, then the country is forced to consider the question of the possible suppression of that group. Of course there are groups like that in any country, but in only a few are they capable of bringing the orderly legislative process to a halt. The actual size of the group is sometimes less important than the determination of the opposition against them. The German *Reichstag* of 1930 to 1932 proved incapable of handling the obstruction of the combined onslaught of the totalitarians (Nazis and Communists), while the French National Assembly of 1951 has learned to outsit and outvote the somewhat less numerous but still formidable Communist opposition. Even more impressive is the record of the young and inexperienced Italian democracy, which has set an effective limit to the obstructionism of the Communist-Socialist (Nenni) alliance without resorting to suppression. The instability of Italian governments after the resignation of Premier Alcide de Gasperi on July 28, 1953, is primarily the result of dissension within the Christian Democratic party.

On general principle, three attitudes have crystallized on this crucial problem of the treatment of undemocratic political movements. One point of view opposes as undemocratic all political suppression under all circumstances. Those are the "conscientious objectors" of democracy. There are others again who would see in any antidemocratic movement a deadly danger and advocate immediate suppression, because they hold that those who will not abide by the rules of democracy cannot be permitted to benefit thereby. Between the two extremes more and more people are accepting a middle ground. They recognize the nature of antidemocratic movements and the possible need for suppressing them, just as the jailing of a burglar under due process of law would not be considered an abridgment of civil liberties. But at the same time they are worried about the inherent danger contained in such measures and wonder just who is qualified to decide who is "subversive" of the democratic process and what degree of adherence to such doctrine should be considered ground for suppression. They are therefore inclined to apply the "clear and present danger" concept to this question and proceed to outlaw political movements only when there is seemingly no other alternative if democracy is to survive.[16] But there is no absolute line at which a "clear and present danger" may be discerned. It is a flexible line which can be staved off indefinitely as long as the democratic majority is united in its determination to use the implements which it possesses and is alert to the existence of those social evils on which totalitarian movements thrive.

However, this theory, if ever fully applied, has come in for considerable revision and rethinking in recent years. Chief Justice Fred Vinson of the United States Supreme Court held that the "clear and present danger" concept of Justices Holmes and Brandeis [17] "cannot mean that before the Government may act, it must wait until the *putsch* is about to be executed, the plans have been laid and the signal is awaited." [18] It was not necessary to wait until an attempt to overthrow the government was made. It was sufficient that there was an organization preparing and willing to make the attempt. The reasoning of the Court was based on the idea announced in the Second Court of Appeals, in the same case, by Judge Learned Hand, who said that "clear and present danger" meant "in every case a comparison between interests which are to be appraised qualitatively." [19] In other words, "clear and present danger" is not a purely objective criteria of measurement but in each situation must be decided on the basis of "whether the gravity of the 'evil,' discounted by its improbability, justifies such invasion of free speech as is necessary to avoid the danger."

These and other attempts to deal with subversion in both a democratic and reasonable manner are far from easy, and abuses are not unknown. But controversial as these methods may be, they prove at the very least that some of the democratic countries are not prepared to take the totalitarian threat from the inside lightly. This is important because no authoritarian group has ever won out over determined and fairly united opposition; authoritarian groups have won and turned legislatures into mockery only when their opponents were weak, uncertain of their purpose, and corroded from within.

[16] Schenck v. United States, 249 U.S. 47 (1919). See the widening of this doctrine in Gitlow v. New York, 268 U.S. 652 (1925). See also Terminiello v. City of Chicago, 337 U.S. 1 (1949), and Winters v. New York, 333 U.S. 507 (1948).

[17] In Gitlow v. New York, *cit.*

[18] Dennis v. United States, 341 U.S. 494 (1951).

[19] United States v. Dennis, 183 F. 2d 201 (2d Cir. 1950). See also Charles R. Nixon, "Vital Issues in Free Speech," *Ethics,* Vol. 42 (1952), pp. 101–120.

Chapter 7

POLITICAL PARTIES

Political parties are the core of the democratic system, its alpha and omega, and their nature and organization determine the success or failure of democratic government. It is easy enough to demonstrate the veracity of this statement. Whatever definition of democracy may be applied, the supremacy of the popular will must inevitably be part of it, although complete and unchecked supremacy is not required. In modern nation-states with their millions of citizens it is, of course, impossible for the popular will to express itself without a crystallization process which results in the formation of groups who act as spokesmen. Now it is true that almost everybody belongs to some professional, religious, avocational, or other group, but these groups are far too numerous to be the carriers of a political will. Moreover, many of them address themselves to purely specialized problems and interests. It is therefore necessary that larger groups be formed which absorb the members of the smaller organizations and which propose some kind of alternative solutions to the principal questions of government; these are the political parties. Without their existence the political process would be atomized and either government would end in chaos or a dictator would take over.

Divergent Political Parties Essential to Democracy

The existence of political parties is thus essential to the reality of democratic government, and consequently there is no democracy when political parties are suppressed. Human nature being what it is, different viewpoints must be expected where there is freedom to draw one's own conclusions. This results in two or more political parties wherever men are free. The pretense, blithely pressed by fascist and communist partisans, that under their dominion men are so basically united as to need only one party cannot be taken seriously. It is belied by the existence of vast concentration and forced-labor camps for political dissenters. The modern one-party state is always and inevitably a dictatorship. However, it is necessary to distinguish between true one-party states, like Nazi Germany or the Soviet Union, and alleged one-party states like the regions of the South of the United States. In the former, the "official" state party has a single doctrine and a monolithic organization.

But the one-party regime of the Southern states in the United States is merely a smoke screen behind which a two-party system may be clearly seen. Electoral fights are no less vigorous in the South than in the North; the only difference is the fact that in the South the real contest is in the primary election. It is a contest between candidates who often present as different policies and personalities as anywhere in the country, but who all have to carry the same party label because of historical developments which have little connection with the issues at hand.

PARTY ORGANIZATION

Although political parties help to crystallize the will of the people, they themselves comprise only a relatively small portion of the people. For only party members or others who have indicated in some manner a more permanent attachment to the party usually have some influence on it. There is no direct relationship between party membership and the vote at the party polls. Generally the parties of the left are better organized than those of the right (except right extremists) and often have a larger membership. This does not prevent the parties of the right from polling formidable totals. Even within well-organized parties it may be found that despite a large party membership in a certain area, a party polls relatively few votes, while the same party obtains more votes in a district in which its organization has left much to be desired. Thus, while all important political parties of democratic countries are mass parties as far as the electorate is concerned, some of them have no mass organization but rest on the shoulders of a few men and committees.[1] This does not necessarily make them less democratic because, as Michels has demonstrated, the tightly organized mass-membership parties are often most easily controlled by an oligarchic leadership.

It may come as a surprise but it is a fact that there were parties in parliament before there were parties in the country. Some of these early parliamentary groups were merely associations of deputies, frequently from the same region. In the French Revolution, for instance, we find such parties as the Girondists—from the Gironde area—and the Breton Club which, after renting the Paris convent of the Jacobin order, assumed the name under which it has gone into history: the Jacobins.

There are still such parties which have no organization to speak of, which are really composed of independent deputies who for reasons of convenience

---

[1] The classical work on party structure, organization, and leadership is Robert Michels, *Political Parties* (trans. by E. and C. Paul), first published 1915, reprinted Chicago, 1949. A worthy modern successor is Maurice Duverger, *Les partis politiques,* Paris, 1951; see also C. W. Cassinelli, "The Law of Oligarchy," *American Political Science Review,* Vol. XLVII (1953), pp. 772–784; Samuel H. Beer, "Les Partis Politiques," *The Western Political Quarterly,* Vol. VI (1953), pp. 512–517.

form loose federations with other deputies in parliament. France especially has had a number of such groups.

Historically the parliamentary groups later branched out into the country and formed electoral committees, a process which was accomplished with different degrees of speed. This was a particularly early development in America because the absence of aristocracy or other traditionally ruling groups made the creation of leadership more imperative. Undoubtedly this development was accelerated in the United States by the large number of elective offices. In other countries, it became increasingly important as the electorate enlarged.

The parliamentary group and the small electoral committees found themselves pressed in the direction of a more proliferated organization when the quest for special favors, for patronage, for spoils, became irresistible. In England, as we have seen, it was largely this demand for spoils which obliged the parties to organize themselves for an orderly dispensation of patronage and for the necessary supervision of the recipients in order to see that whatever promises were made would be carried out. The unashamed manner in which votes were bought in those days accounts for a great deal of modern party organization.

It was the Socialist movement of the nineteenth century, however, which originated the type of the modern mass party with a large, dues-paying membership, a vast bureaucracy, an official party press, and a dominant directorate. Michels's masterly analysis of the Social Democratic party of Germany before the First World War stands as a monument to this type of party.

Such a party is far more than just an association for political action. It has a definite philosophy; it has an extremely proliferated organization. Its local sections hold meetings at least once a week, regardless of whether there is an electoral campaign going on or not. Its headquarters are numerous and fully staffed. Its members are expected to read the official party press and get their inspirations from it. An inactive member, even if he pays his dues faithfully, is looked down upon as a "half member."

The motivation for participation in such a tightly organized party is largely ideological. The hope of building a brave new world inspires many to put up with the endless meetings, the long discussons, and often the narrowness of the doctrine even without the additional propulsion of an impending election. The already powerful trend toward sharp emphasis on political doctrines was greatly augmented by the spread of PR, which concentrates all attention on the parties as entities and consequently on their doctrines. The preeminence of political doctrine in Continental Europe often makes interparty argument a very brilliant affair, in which the intellectuals of both sides have an opportunity to shine. No wonder they sometimes look down their noses at their less theoretically minded British and American colleagues. Such pride is, however, hardly justified. Democratic government is the product of compromise and moderation. Brilliant theorizing rarely adds to the spirit of moderation, and compromise is often possible only when concrete measures rather than abstract theories are discussed.

And what cannot be transformed into "principle"? Party doctrine may start from a few general considerations, but after a while it often spreads to every facet of life. The Socialists and Communists excel in that direction, especially their youth movements. Soon there is a "socialist" (in contradistinction to "bourgeois") way of dressing, cutting one's hair, conducting social relations, etc. This spirit leads to more cleavage and separateness. Socialists must have their own hiking clubs, sport clubs, chess federations, etc. One Central European newspaper, picked at random, announces meetings of the following socialist organizations: the party organizations themselves, the youth groups, socialist students, socialist doctors, workers' (socialist) red cross, workers' radio construction club, socialist educational society, special socialist organizations for commercial employees, recipients of pensions from railroad companies, textile workers, metal workers, railroad employees,[2] small businessmen, socialist hiking club, and various socialist sports organizations.[3] While the Socialists have developed this "state within the state" idea to a fine art, their opponents are little better. It is therefore possible to have one's entire personal and much of one's professional life within the confines of one particular party, reading only the party press [4] and regarding people with other political affiliations as barely human.

This dedication to an all-encompassing idea in connection with a tight and militant party organization can produce the type of party which resembles a monastic or military order whose members adhere to a strict, unquestioning discipline and are prepared to give their all when called upon. These characteristics are in our times associated with the Nazi and Communist parties, and it is not difficult to see that the existence of such parties poses a serious problem for a democratic country in which they may exist.

In contrast to the strongly ideological parties with their communitylike character are the parties which are mere associations designed to further certain common interests.[5] Such parties lack the dedication of the first-dis-

---

[2] These are not trade-unions but party organizations. There are unions besides.

[3] *Arbeiter-Zeitung* (Vienna), Apr. 30, 1950.

[4] Most Continental party organs do not confine their views to the editorial page (which does not exist; there are so-called "leading articles") but editorialize throughout. Accounts of parliamentary debates ignore opposing speakers or mention merely that they spoke. Unfavorable news is suppressed or slanted. At the same time these papers are frequently brilliantly written and edited.

[5] The distinction between the types of group called "community" (German: *Gemeinschaft*) and "association" for special purpose (German: *Gesellschaft*) originated with the German sociologist Ferdinand Tönnies, *Gemeinschaft und Gesellschaft*, Leipzig, 1888, 1st ed.; 1925, 7th ed. See Max Weber, *Wirtschaft und Gesellschaft*, 3d ed., Tuebingen, 1947, Vol. 1, pp. 194–215; and Duverger, *op. cit.*, pp. 149–158.

cussed type; nor do they have their *élan*; nor are their aims as far-reaching or as all-encompassing. They are not dedicated to great changes in the social or political structure of their country. Rather are they designed to further certain programs or preserve certain goods within the established order. Consequently they are not in need of so elaborate an organization as their more ideologically inclined colleagues. They rarely produce as much spirit or as profound a literature, but they often correspond more nearly to the temper of the middle classes and frequently to that of the rural sections. While less inspiring, they are also less upsetting. Their aims are practical and thus capable of compromise, while compromise is much more difficult for a thoroughly indoctrinated party. It is far easier to compromise on the number of post offices to build than over deeply felt philosophical ideas. There is no reason to believe that these two types of parties cannot easily coexist. Their different character may, however, make cooperation somewhat difficult.

PARTY LEADERSHIP

The problem of party leadership presents itself in an entirely different form in the United States than in other countries. One of the unique features of American political life is the primary election system according to which the voters select the official candidates of the political parties.[6] In other countries this is done by the party leadership or by local party committees with central leadership approval, or by conventions or other meetings of party members. In the United States this results in the fact that there is no central party leadership which can hold its members in Congress to any kind of party discipline. Men and women may be nominated and elected for national office as Democrats or Republicans without and even against the will of the party organization. Efforts by party leaders, even by the President himself, to "purge" a recalcitrant Senator or Congressman have not been notable for success. However, local or state-wide control by party organizations is sometimes more effective.

Under other party systems, however, members of parliament and other political officeholders find themselves in varying degrees of dependence on their party leaderships. In countries in which proportional representation prevails as an electoral system, that dependence is very large, as the party leadership usually has a considerable amount of control over the question of whose name is placed on the nomination list and in what order. In countries of

[6] The majority of states in the United States have closed primaries in which a voter must register a party preference in order to vote in the primary election of a party. Most voters register such preferences. Where there are open primaries, no party preference need be disclosed by the voter. Only in the state of Washington can a person vote for candidates of either party in the primary. Only Connecticut has a complete convention system of nomination. Several other states use conventions for some nominations. The direct primary is, however, the rule.

single-member districts this dependence is far less. However, in Great Britain, for instance, central party headquarters must approve the choice of candidates; since the British electorate has shown little willingness in recent years to support candidates who are not endorsed by the major parties, this endorsement carries considerable weight.

There need not be any principal objection to the existence of such a strong party leadership. Some even feel that it makes for a higher degree of party responsibility. However, it raises a number of important questions. The party leadership may not be identical or nearly identical with the party's parliamentary leadership, and a difference may develop between them as the parliamentary leaders are confronted by the daily changing exigencies of the political situation, while the extraparliamentary leadership tends to come under the pressure of the party's militant members whose viewpoint is frequently more doctrinaire, more ideological, less flexible than that of the party's "practitioners" in parliament.

This kind of dispute raises conflicting issues of party responsibility. The advocates of the party leadership's supremacy point out that people vote for party programs rather than for individuals and that it is therefore up to the party leadership to see to it that its members in parliament adhere to the program. In countries in which the proportional-representation system of election (PR) prevails, this point is not without foundation. But the advocates of the parliament member's freedom of action maintain that a member of parliament is responsible to his constituents and that a truly deliberative function of parliament is impossible when its members have to accept dictation from the outside.

In reality these two principles are rarely separated by a neat division; and besides, in parliamentary democracies some of the leaders of the party are bound to be members of parliament. It is rather a matter of emphasis. In Great Britain, for instance, the party leadership is in Parliament, most decidedly among the Conservatives, and to a lesser but still large degree among the Laborites. Both Clement Attlee and his rival Aneurin Bevan are in Parliament. On the other hand in France this is not always the case. The recent history of the French Socialist party (SFIO) is full of conflicts between the parliamentary leadership of the party and the will of the members as represented in resolutions passed at party conventions and incumbent upon the party directorate to carry out. On several occasions the parliamentary leadership of the party ignored these directives, but in other instances it had to carry them out even against its better judgment. Such a directive, for instance, was responsible for the Socialists' departure from the coalition government in 1951 although the parliamentary leadership did not favor this step. A recent prototype of a party represented in parliament but controlled wholly from the outside was General de Gaulle's Rally of the French People (RPF), whose deputies and senators were required to carry out the orders of the general, who himself refused to be a candidate. This situation led to the breakup of the party in its previous form in 1953, but its sizable remnants which are still in parliament continue to adhere to the general's wishes even though the formal tie has been cut.

The Communist party presents a special case in that its national leadership is usually in parliament but its real leadership is in Moscow.

Party leadership is based to a large extent on intangibles. In contrast to the United States, where party leadership, inasmuch as it rests in the White House, is subject to fairly frequent changes, party leadership in parliamentary countries is extremely long-lasting and self-perpetuating. This is not done by an imposition of the leadership on the followers. Quite the contrary, the party becomes symbolized by its leaders, whose replacement becomes inconceivable to the members. Michels expressed it in these words: "Leadership is indefinitely retained, not because it is the tangible expression of the relationships between the forces existing in the party at any given moment, but simply because it is already constituted. It is through gregarious idleness, or, if we may employ the euphemism, it is in virtue of the law of inertia, that the leaders are so often confirmed in their office as long as they like." [7]

This verdict is possibly rather severe. However, the political history of this century knows few instances in which the established leadership of a party was successfully challenged. Neville Chamberlain's replacement by Winston Churchill was the result of the war events and would certainly never have happened in times of peace. The removal of Daniel Mayer from the post of General Secretary of the French Socialist party and his replacement by Guy Mollet in 1946 constituted the settling of the leadership problem rather than the removal of a settled leader. Normally a political leadership, once established, may count on a long tenure.

However oligarchic a party leadership may be, it is important to remember that in a democracy there exists a party organization in the country apart from the party's leadership in parliament and government. Even the most secure party leadership must keep the party members and voters in the country reasonably satisfied and must not prove itself deaf to their wishes and grievances, for there is a point beyond which even the most docile followers cannot be pushed; and such dissatisfaction is bound to transfer itself to parliament, thus threatening the leadership at its nerve center. In fact it is the essence of party leadership to gauge carefully and accurately what the people will not stand. Hence, democratic parties are never entirely unrepresentative. By contrast, in a dictatorship party leadership is identical with the all-powerful government and need cater to hardly any sentiments in the country. There is also no danger that members of bogus parliaments will make themselves the spokesmen of dissatisfaction, for the only people to whom they could tell their grievances would be the members of the secret police. Hence in dictator-

[7] Michels, *op. cit.*, p. 98.

ships we have a perversion of the party system, and legislatures which have lost all significance.

Two-party and Multiparty Systems

Past discussions in this book have endeavored to demonstrate the great advantage of a two-party system when combined with the prevailing spirit of moderation. Such conditions, however, exist only in the English-speaking world, and even there not completely, as indicated by the present coalition regimes of anti-Labor parties in Australia and New Zealand. Austria, the only other country which belongs in this category, suffers an unjustifiable quadri-partite occupation at present, plus exceptional threats to her national independence and security. The two major parties, the People's party (formerly Christian Social) and the Socialists (formerly Social Democrats), have therefore entered into a coalition for the good of the country. Other parties are negligible, like the small League of Independents (VDU), a political catchall specially designed to attract former Nazis, and the still smaller Communist party which was unable to gather more than 5 per cent of the total vote. The League of Independents is now falling apart through internal dissension, and the Communists live solely by the grace of the moral and material support which they receive from the Soviet occupation army. Nevertheless, tension between the major parties is mounting, and it is doubtful that the coalition would survive the departure of the foreign soldiers. Recent elections seem to indicate again, as in the early thirties, that the two major parties have reached a more or less finite electoral size and that great surprises at the polls cannot easily be expected. This situation carries again the danger of frustration and dangerous, forceful experiments.

If two-party systems work well, multiparty systems in which the parties naturally fall into two blocs, each capable of forming a coalition government, work nearly as well. This is particularly the case in the Scandinavian countries, where stable and efficient governments have been a tradition for many decades.

Unlike that of any other country is the political panorama of Switzerland. This alpine republic has a multiparty system which cannot easily be placed in two blocs. But such bloc building is not necessary because of the unique structure of the cabinet (Federal Council), in which most significant parties are represented. Differences of opinion of course exist within the Federal Council, but if they were particularly violent the government could not continue. Consequently it is necessary to conduct the business of government as primarily an administrative problem and to apply moderation and mutual respect. The political parties are also brought closer together by two other factors. While the disagreement between conservative and progressive forces is as great as everywhere else, the conservative groups have recognized the spirit of the times and have warded off integral changes by considerable concessions.[8] Secondly, the Swiss people guard their individual liberty jealously and in referendum after referendum have turned down even moderate encroachments which would hardly stir a ripple in other countries. The lesson of this impressive display of national sentiment has not been lost on the political parties, none of which can afford to deviate greatly from the clearly demonstrated popular will. Authoritarian parties have therefore led a very listless existence in Switzerland, and their prospects are dim.

European Socialism

From the galaxy of European parties two groups stand out because of a higher degree of cohesion than the rest. They are the socialist and the "Christian" (usually Catholic) parties.

European, Continental socialism is plagued by the inner struggle between two principles. There is first of all the doctrine of orthodox Marxism, to which Continental socialist parties usually pay tribute. Marxism implies the recognition of a basic, irreconcilable cleavage in society and the necessity of a relentless class struggle. No matter how far away from Marx these parties have traveled, Marxism gives them their theoretical foundation and their ultimate purpose, and they are understandably reluctant to forgo their heritage. But on the other side there is the other basic element of European socialism, namely, a profound humanitarian sentiment.

The American reader must always remember that, although the general acceptance of the "American way of life" is so widespread in this country, its equivalent is totally missing in Europe. To a very large part of the population there the "good old days" were merely old. To many, the European free-enterprise (capitalistic) system seems neither free nor enterprising, but appears rather as a monopolistic, unimaginative, bureaucratic conspiracy for scarcity rather than for plenty. European capitalism has not produced nearly the high standard of living which its American counterpart has achieved, and there are many millions who feel deeply that the economic order under which they live has withheld their rightful human heritage from them, and some of their human dignity. How widespread is this feeling may be gleaned from the fact that Pope Pius XII and other Vatican sources have seen fit to issue strongly anticapitalistic declarations.

What has invited many Europeans to become Socialists is a profound feeling of rebellion against inhumanity and injustice. Marxism may have given them the road to travel, but humanitarianism is their motive for traveling it. This is the one, all-important issue which divides Communists from Socialists;

---

[8] W. Rappard, *The Government of Switzerland,* New York, 1936, pp. 122*f.*; see also the same author's *L'Individu et l'état dans l'évolution constitutionnelle de la Suisse,* Neuchâtel, 1936.

Communists believe in an allegedly humanitarian aim, but are willing to suppress all humanity in order to achieve it. The Socialists, on the other hand, being primarily humanitarians, are unable and unwilling to adopt inhuman methods of suppression. In the conflict between Marxist aims and humanitarian methods, humanitarianism has clearly won among Socialists.[9] Therefore most free European Socialist parties are democratic. No greater error could be committed than to lump Socialists and Communists together. Their difference is as great as the difference between democracy and dictatorship. In fact, it is greater: both Socialists and Communists are, or are attempting to be, workers' parties. They therefore compete for the same electorate. A strong conservative party makes little inroads into Communist strength—on the contrary, it may solidify the Communist ranks—but a strong Socialist party reduces communism to a minor threat. The evidence is indisputable. Regardless of economic conditions, wherever there is a strong, democratic Socialist party, there the Communist party is a numerically negligible factor. France, which has a relatively weak Socialist party, has a formidable number of Communists. On the other hand, Germany (West) has reduced the Communist party to a little over 2 per cent. Even more impressive is the situation in Austria, where economic conditions are difficult and where the Soviet Army has more soldiers than all the other three occupying powers (United States, Great Britain, France) combined; even there, the Communists have been unable to rise above 5 per cent because of the existence of a strong, democratic Socialist party.

If many Americans still fail to see that Communism in Europe can best be defeated by strong Socialist parties, the Communists are not guilty of a similar mistake. Their principal anger is directed against the Socialists. Immediate liquidation threatens those Socialists who fall into Communist hands without first surrendering to them. But so great is Communist hatred for the Socialists that even surrender does not do them any good; it merely postpones the time of their execution. In Eastern Europe, where some ambitious Socialist leaders have cooperated with the Communists—always against the will of the majority of their party members—they have found themselves shunted aside sooner or later in order to be consigned eventually to oblivion. A recent case is that of Arpad Szakasits of Hungary, who did such yeoman's service for the Communists and who, after driving out the real leaders of his party (people like Karoly Peyer and Anna Kethey), delivered the party up for merger with Communists. After a short term in the meaningless posts of President of the Hungarian Republic and Chairman of the Presidium of the Presidential Council of the Hungarian People's Republic, he finally resigned his position and even his seat in the legislature. His eventual fate can hardly be in doubt.

[9] See the interesting book of the late French Socialist leader Léon Blum, *For All Mankind*, New York, 1946.

While humanitarianism leads the Socialists toward collaboration with "bourgeois" parties, the memory of their Marxist education makes them unhappy about it. Moreover, there is the constant and often justified fear of losing the workers to the Communists if the Socialists are not "activist" enough. Their political actions are therefore given to rather bewildering inconsistencies at times. On the one hand they stress democracy, moderation, and cooperation; on the other hand, their speakers and party papers proclaim that no real improvement can be expected until society is fundamentally reshaped. In their attempts to be on both sides of the fence they sometimes make uncertain coalition partners, as France has demonstrated, and their policy often lacks decisiveness. Even the non-Marxist British Labor party manifested this tendency when it proclaimed its opposition to the Schuman Plan concerning the pooling of industrial resources.

An exception in this picture is the position of the Italian Socialist party. Italian socialism has always been deeply troubled by constant inner dissension.[10] Before Mussolini's "March on Rome" the conservative Turati-Modigliani leadership was at loggerheads with the "Maximalists" and the romantic communism of Angelica Balabanov, while the party secretary, Giacomo Matteotti, attempted to draw the factions together. The long night of exile only strengthened the doctrinaire and uncompromising spirit of the party leaders, especially that of the party's most outstanding leader, Pietro Nenni.

Nenni was not always the unbending pro-Communist that he is today. In 1939 he denounced the Stalin-Hitler pact, which only 100 per cent Stalinists could swallow, and after his return to Italy his mind was apparently not made up. It is always difficult to discover just what influences a man like Nenni, but there can be little doubt that the support which Great Britain and the United States gave the Badoglio government and the House of Savoy helped to propel Nenni in the opposite direction. Despite the loss to the party of several distinguished Socialist leaders and their followers, men like Giuseppe Saragat, Giuseppe Romita, and Ignazio Silone—who have now organized three different groups—the leadership of Pietro Nenni and Lelio Basso (party secretary) still holds sway, directing their party into channels which are still hard to distinguish from orthodox Communism, although Socialist candidates now run on separate lists from the Communists.

The expression of international Socialist solidarity was the Workers' (Socialist) International, commonly called the Second International. Its dream was the assumption that the workers of different nations had more in common with one another than with the "bourgeoisie" in their own countries. This expectation foundered completely on the realities of the First World War. The Second International was recreated thereafter with fewer illusions and with the growing differences between Socialist parties becoming stronger as some of

[10] W. Hilton-Young, *The Italian Left*, London, 1950.

them shouldered governmental responsibility and became advocates of their respective national policies rather than of international Socialism.

The Second International again disappeared in the Second World War and was reestablished some time thereafter, after some tentative efforts had been made in that direction, and not without opposition in the Socialist ranks. But this latest edition of the Second International is quite definitely a weaker copy. In the first place it is no longer as international as it used to be. At an international Socialist conference held in Rangoon, Burma, in January, 1953, the Asiatic Socialist parties decided not to join the Second International as a group (because of its alleged Western domination) but only to maintain liaison with it. Individual Asiatic Socialist parties were permitted to join, though few did.

But what makes the ties between Socialist parties more tentative than they were before is the change in the major problems confronting them. In olden days these were, or were believed to be, primarily economic and social. But now foreign policy looms above everything else. East-West relations, the European army, relations with America, etc.—in these the Socialist parties, many of whom participate in their home cabinets, are more likely to speak the language of their national interests, and these interests do not always coincide.

There is still a bond between Socialist parties: it is the memory of the fighting past. It is also a common theoretical method and approach to problems derived from their Marxist past. It is also a common vocabulary. But it is little more.

CATHOLIC PARTIES

The Catholic parties are made of different fabric. On a continent where most political parties are based on social groups, the Catholic parties are an exception, since their basis is religious rather than economic. Consequently they embrace widely different classes and groups, and they occupy a unique place on the political stage because they face in every direction. At the present time there are Catholic parties in France, Germany, Switzerland, Belgium, the Netherlands, Italy, and Austria. The German Christian Democratic Union/Christian Social Union (CDU/CSU) claims to be interdenominational, but the leadership is predominantly Catholic.

The origin and political programs of the Catholic parties differ widely, although there is a certain fraternal spirit among them and a loosely organized "International" called "New International Team" (Nouvelle Equipe Internationale, NEI). The Catholic Church itself has, of course, the oldest and most complete international organization in the world. In France Catholicism was long associated with conservativism and reaction, chiefly because of the alliance between the Church and the *ancien régime* of the Bourbons. For many years the antagonism between the Church and the Republic was most intense. The Republic was liberal and secular, which meant in the terms of those days that it was anticlerical.

The election of Leo XIII to the papacy introduced a trend toward better relations. At any rate the Church was no longer unconditionally allied with reaction. The encyclicals entitled *Immortale Dei* (1885) and especially *Rerum Novarum* (1891) presented a clearer approach to the state and a far more advanced attitude toward social questions. Still the Church was not popular with progressive and republican forces, and there is hardly a film or play of those days which does not cast a priest, if one is in it, in a slightly ridiculous or nefarious role. The parties of the left, up to and including the Radical Socialists, rejected the Church categorically, except possibly in purely religious matters—and even in those they admitted it reluctantly. Among the parties of the right there were staunch defenders of the Church, but there was no real Church party.

This changed during the war and the long night of German occupation. Catholics, laymen and priests alike, were well represented in the Resistance. The last president of the National Council of Resistance, Georges Bidault, is a prominent Catholic. Out of the experience and soul-searching of the underground and Resistance emerged a Catholic party, the Popular Republican Movement (MRP). The MRP is a party of the left and center. It is well disposed toward many socialistic reforms, and it prefers an alliance on the left to an alliance on the right. It had an opportunity to become *the* anti-Communist party, but it was content to leave that distinction to General de Gaulle's new Rally of the French People (RPF), although this meant great electoral losses. Today the MRP is republican, progressive, and Catholic—a combination which would have been nearly impossible for a significant party under the Third Republic. It is the indispensable center of almost any coalition, not because it is so strong, but rather because it is at the center and therefore in a position to help bridge the gulf between right and left.

The development of Italy follows a somewhat different course, although parallels to the French MRP are clearly discernible. The tradition of the Italian Catholic party, the Christian Democrats, is derived from the Popolari party (*Partito Popolari Italiano*) which was founded in 1919 by the priest Don Luigi Sturzo. The Popolari advocated large-scale economic and social reform, women's suffrage, governmental decentralization, regional self-government, labor reforms, and especially the breakup of the large southern estates (*latifundia*) and their distribution among the landless peasants.[11]

The Popolari were swept away by Mussolini, and Sturzo went into exile. However, the thoughts of the party remained alive, despite the close relations which existed for some time between the Vatican and the Mussolini regime. When Mussolini fell and large-scale partisan activities broke out in the

[11] Luigi Sturzo, *Italy and Fascism* (trans. by B. B. Carter), London, 1926, p. 91.

North,[12] the adherents and heirs of Sturzo immediately entered the stage. After the fall of Marshal Badoglio and the inability of the Resistance to form a stable government under Ferrucio Parri, the renascent Popolari soon became the leading party. They are now called Christian Democrats (*Democristiani*) and were long led by the extremely able Dr. Alcide de Gasperi until his recent, much regretted death. However, they faced a situation which contrasted with that of France. While the MRP was assisted by other strong groups, the Italian Christian Democrats were giants among pygmies. The Actionists, the Republicans, and other small groups contributed outstanding personalities, like Count Carlo Sforza or the celebrated philosopher Benedetto Croce, but they could not command a large electorate. The Socialists were and are organized primarily in the camp of Pietro Nenni, who is firmly committed to a 100 per cent pro-Communist policy, while the anti-Communist Socialist splinter groups of Saragat, Romita, Lombardo, Matteo Matteotti, and Silone have been unable to attract many voters. On the other hand there was in Italy the strongest Communist party outside the Soviet Union, whose destinies were determined by the shrewd and extremely gifted Palmiro Togliatti. Thus the issue Communism–anti-Communism was clearly drawn, and the Christian Democrats became *the* anti-Communist party par excellence. This was a role which it could not decline, for there was no choice except abdication or handing this role to the neofascist Italian Social Movement (*Movimento Sociale Italiano*).

Since Italy appeared to figure prominently on the list of countries selected for Communist conquest, the issue quickly came to a head during the memorable electoral campaign of 1948. After an unprecedented campaign, which saw Italy as a battleground between East and West,[13] the Christian Democrats emerged triumphant, having defeated the Communists and having achieved an absolute majority in the Chamber of Deputies.[14]

In some respects, however, this victory had a Pyrrhic note. The large measure of support which the Christian Democrats received from conservative and reactionary sources has considerably retarded certain imperative reforms, especially the vitally needed reform of the *latifundia* and the narrowing of the revolution-breeding gulf between the ostentatiously rich and the abjectly poor. The situation has strengthened the Communists' hold on the rural population and has enabled them to make up in part their heavy losses among the urban inhabitants. It was only in June, 1950, that three fundamental agricul-

[12] It is often overlooked that the Italian partisan movement fought on a larger scale and often with greater success than the French *maquis*.

[13] The U.S.S.R. gave all possible encouragement to the Communists, while the United States aided the anti-Communists by diplomatic maneuvers (return of Italian warships) and an impressive letter-writing campaign by Americans of Italian descent to their relatives in Italy.

[14] The Christian Democrats obtained 307 out of 574 seats in the Chamber of Deputies and 130 out of 237 elective seats in the Senate.

tural reform bills were passed by the Chamber of Deputies.[15] The elections of 1953 have reduced the party's strength to 40 per cent, a still formidable figure, but serious internal strife has weakened it while the combined Communist-Socialist vote grows.

Again quite different is the course of German political Catholicism. Here the need for political organization arose out of opposition to conservatism and not in alliance with it. The chief opponent of the German Catholics was the militantly Protestant Prussian Conservative party, the representative of darkest reaction. As the Prusso-German monarchy was not parliamentary, the Catholic party, aptly termed Center party (*Zentrum*), emphasized parliamentarism and responsible government. It also attempted to defend the rights of the non-German inhabitants of Germany's border regions, especially in the German part of divided Poland, most of whom were Catholics. Under the shrewd leadership of Ludwig Windhorst, the Center party was the chief opponent of Bismarck.

The rise of the Social Democrats brought about a certain *rapprochement* between the Center and the more conservative groups, but the First World War and its aftermath strengthened the Christian trade-union movement and placed the leadership of the party in the hands of its more progressive wing. During the years of the Weimar Republic, the Center entered into coalitions with both moderate left and right, but its relations were a little easier with the Social Democrats than with the Conservatives. Nazism swept them away, but not until after they had besmirched their record by voting, albeit under terrific pressure and terror, for Hitler's Enabling Act of 1933.

The reemergence of the party in a broader nondenominational frame as the Christian Democratic Union (in Bavaria, Christian Social Union) has placed it in a position in which its chief opponent is the Social Democratic party. The Communists are of negligible strength and worthy of attention only because of the proximity of Russian troops and the stark fact of the completely sovietized Eastern zone. In this political constellation the CDU/CSU has come under decidedly conservative influence as exemplified by its leader, Federal Chancellor Konrad Adenauer. Still, more progressive forces also exist in the party, and the future will undoubtedly see many controversies between these two wings, especially after Adenauer has passed from the scene.

Two trends are discernible among all European Catholic parties; the younger parties, as exemplified by the French MRP and the Italian Christian Democrats, have progressive tendencies, while the older parties are outright conservative. This is generally true of the Catholic parties of Austria, Switzerland, Belgium, Holland, and (with the reservations stated) Germany. Such conservatism has occasionally reached extremes like the authoritarian regime of Engelbert Dollfuss and Kurt von Schuschnigg which was visited on Austria

[15] The bills authorized large-scale public works as well as the seizure and improvement of land in southern Italy and its distribution to landless peasants.

between 1934 and 1938. The short-lived "independent" state of Slovakia, governed through Hitler's grace by Monsignor Tiso, also belongs in this category.

There is little doubt that political Catholicism will continue to play a significant role, especially as long as Communism remains a burning political issue. The Catholic Church and the Catholic parties often gain strength by emphasizing their uncompromising struggle against Communism.[16] But the Catholic Church undertakes this struggle not only as a doctrine but also as a formidably disciplined organization, and it seeks to strengthen this organization by reasserting its claim to a large share in the educational picture of the countries concerned. This claim, however, often rubs the wrong way those who might otherwise be allies, and the Church has sometimes been accused of contributing to the lack of unity in the anti-Communist camp.

ANTIDEMOCRATIC PARTIES

The past discussion has dealt with some of the principles of modern democratic parties. We have disregarded Latin-American parties, most of which are cliques rather than mass organizations, nor have we devoted much space to the discussion of parties under dictatorship. Such parties as the Nazi, Falangist, or Communist parties have nothing in common with democratic parties except the name. Democratic parties are open to all; dictatorship parties are closed except to the elect. In every respect dictatorship parties are parts of the executive machinery of their respective countries, serving to implement and execute the policy of the state. It is interesting that this form of organization is also retained by those parties when they operate in democratic countries. Thus, in the midst of openly operating and freely accessible parties, one finds parties which are closed societies of secret purpose, resembling a conspiracy far more than a political mass organization. However, it is much more difficult to impose upon these parties the iron discipline which applies in a dictatorship when they are forced to operate in a democratic environment. This produces a considerable turnover of members who joined for idealistic purposes and who are appalled by the reality of party life which places the will to power above all other considerations. Many are "purged" for various "deviations," to which the spread of "Titoism" has added a generous portion. Authoritarian parties present an alien pattern in a democracy, to which democratic parties and governments find it difficult to adjust.

[16] The strong views of the Catholic Church with regard to Communism are a matter of common knowledge. See especially the encyclical *Divini Redemptoris*.

Appendix A

CONSTITUTION OF THE FRENCH REPUBLIC
1946

The National Constituent Assembly has adopted,
The French people has approved,
The President of the Provisional Government of
the Republic promulgates the Constitution that follows:

PREAMBLE

On the morrow of the victory of the free peoples over the regimes that attempted to enslave and degrade the human person, the French people proclaims once more that every human being, without distinction of race, religion or belief, possesses inalienable and sacred rights. It solemnly reaffirms the rights and freedoms of man and of the citizen consecrated by the Declaration of Rights of 1789 and the fundamental principles recognized by the laws of the Republic.

It further proclaims as most vital in our time the following political, economic and social principles:

The law guarantees to women equal rights with men in all domains.

Anyone persecuted because of his activities in the cause of freedom has the right of asylum within the territories of the Republic.

Everyone has the duty to work and the right to obtain employment. No one may suffer in his work or his employment because of his origin, his opinions or his beliefs.

Everyone may defend his rights and interests by trade-union action and may join the union of his choice.

The right to strike may be exercised within the framework of the laws that govern it.

Every worker through his delegates may participate in collective bargaining to determine working conditions, as well as in the management of business.

All property and all enterprises that now have or subsequently shall have the character of a national public service or a monopoly in fact must become the property of the community.

The nation ensures to the individual and the family the conditions necessary to their development.

It guarantees to all, and notably to the child, the mother and the aged worker, protection of health, material security, rest and leisure. Every human being who, because of his age, his physical or mental condition, or because of the economic situation, finds himself unable to work, has the right to obtain from the community the means to lead a decent existence.

The nation proclaims the solidarity and equality of all Frenchmen with regard to the burdens resulting from national disasters.

The nation guarantees equal access of children and adults to education, professional training and culture. The establishment of free, secular, public education on all levels is a duty of the State.

The French Republic, faithful to its traditions, abides by the rules of international public law. It will not undertake wars of conquest and will never use its arms against the freedom of any people.

On condition of reciprocity, France accepts the limitations of sovereignty necessary to the organization and defense of peace.

France forms with the people of its overseas territories a Union based upon equality of rights and duties without distinction of race or religion.

The French Union is composed of nations and peoples who wish to place in common or coordinate their resources and their efforts in order to develop their civilization, increase their well-being and ensure their security.

Faithful to her traditional mission, France proposes to guide the peoples for whom she has assumed responsibility toward freedom to govern themselves and democratically to manage their own affairs; putting aside any system of colonization based upon arbitrary power, she guarantees to all equal access to public office and the individual or collective exercise of the rights and liberties proclaimed or confirmed above.

THE INSTITUTIONS OF THE REPUBLIC

TITLE I

SOVEREIGNTY

ART. 1—France is a republic, indivisible, secular, democratic and social.

ART. 2—The national emblem is the tricolor flag—blue, white and red—in three vertical bands of equal dimensions.

The national anthem is the "Marseillaise."

The motto of the Republic is—"Liberty, Equality, Fraternity."

Its principle is: government of the people, for the people and by the people.

ART. 3—National sovereignty belongs to the French people.

No section of the people nor any individual may assume its exercise.

The people shall exercise it in constitutional matters by the vote of their representatives or by the referendum.

In all other matters they shall exercise it through their deputies in the National Assembly, elected by universal, equal, direct and secret suffrage.

ART. 4—All French citizens and nationals of both sexes, who are majors and enjoy civil and political rights, may vote under conditions determined by the law.

TITLE II

THE PARLIAMENT

ART. 5—The Parliament shall be composed of the National Assembly and the Council of the Republic.

ART. 6—The duration of the powers of each Assembly, its mode of election, the conditions of eligibility and the bases of ineligibilities and incompatibilities shall be determined by the law.

However, the two Chambers shall be elected on a territorial basis, the National Assembly by universal, direct suffrage, the Council of the Republic by the communal and departmental bodies by universal, indirect suffrage. The Council of the Republic is renewable one-half at a time.

Nevertheless, the National Assembly may itself elect by proportional representation councillors whose numbers shall not exceed one-sixth of the total number of members of the Council of the Republic.

The number of members of the Council of the Republic may not be less than 250 nor more than 320.

Art. 7—War may not be declared without a vote of the National Assembly and the concurrent opinion of the Council of the Republic.

The State of Siege shall be declared in the manner provided by law.[1]

Art. 8—Each of the two Chambers shall pass upon the eligibility of its members and the regularity of their elections; it alone may receive their resignation.

Art. 9—The National Assembly shall convene by right in *ordinary* session *on the first Tuesday in October.*

When the session has lasted for at least seven months the President of the Council (of Ministers) may declare it closed by decree adopted by the Council of Ministers. In this duration of seven months the interruptions of the sessions are not included. Interruptions of sessions are considered adjournments of more than eight clear days.

The Council of the Republic shall sit at the same time as the National Assembly.

Art. 10—The meetings of the two chambers shall be public. Reports of the debates in extenso, as well as the parliamentary documents, shall be published in the "Journal Officiel."

Each of the two Chambers may convene as a secret committee.

Art. 11—Each of the two Chambers shall elect its *officers* (bureau) every year, at the beginning of the *ordinary* session, *and according to the provisions of its rules of order.*

When the two Chambers meet together to elect the President of the Republic, their officers (bureau) shall be that of the National Assembly.

Art. 12—When the National Assembly is not sitting, its *officers* (bureau) may convoke the Parliament *in special session. The President of the National Assembly must do this at the demand of the President of the Council of Ministers or at that of the majority of the members composing the National Assembly.*

The President of the Council (of Ministers) declares the special session closed in the form provided by Article 9.

If the special session has taken place at the demand of the majority of the National Assembly or of its officers the decree closing it may not be adopted before the Parliament has exhausted the limited agenda for which it has been convoked.

Art. 13—The National Assembly alone shall adopt the laws. It may not delegate this right.

Art. 14—The President of the Council of Ministers and the members of the Parliament shall have the initiative in legislation.

Government bills are filed with the officers (bureau) *of the National Assembly or of the Council of the Republic. However, bills designed to authorize the ratification of treaties under the provisions of Article 27, budget or finance bills, and bills involving the diminution of revenue or the creation of expenditures must be filed with the officers* (bureau) *of the National Assembly.*

Bills submitted by members of Parliament are filed with the officers (bureau) *of the Chamber whose member they are, and, after their adoption, are then transmitted to the other Chamber. Bills submitted by members of the Council of the Republic are not acceptable if they involve a diminution of revenue or the creation of an expenditure.*

Art. 15—The National Assembly shall study the bills and proposed laws submitted to it in its committees, of which it shall determine the number, the composition and the jurisdiction.

Art. 16—The proposed budget shall be submitted to the National Assembly.

---

[1] The changes of the constitution enacted by the National Assembly on November 29, and promulgated December 7, 1954, are italicized.

This bill may include only such provisions as are strictly financial.

An organic law shall regulate the method of presentation of the budget.

ART. 17—The deputies of the National Assembly shall have the right to initiate appropriations.

However, no proposals which would tend to increase appropriations already decided upon or create new ones may be presented during the discussion of the budget and of prospective or supplementary appropriations.

ART. 18—The National Assembly shall regulate the accounts of the nation.

It shall be assisted in this task by the "Cour des Comptes."

The National Assembly may entrust to the "Cour des Comptes" all investigations or studies concerning public revenues and expenditures or the administration of the treasury.

ART. 19—Amnesty may not be granted except by a law.

ART. 20—*All bills are examined in turn by the two Chambers of Parliament with a view towards arriving at the adoption of an identical text.*

Unless the Council of the Republic has already examined the bill in first reading, it must make a decision within two months from the date of transmission of a text passed by the National Assembly in first reading.

With regard to budget and finance laws the time at the disposal of the Council of the Republic must not exceed the time taken up previously by the National Assembly in its deliberation and vote. In case the National Assembly decides on urgency procedure the time limit is twice that allowed by the rules of the National Assembly for its debate.

If the Council of the Republic has not come to a decision within the time limit provided in the preceding paragraphs, the law is ready to be promulgated in the form adopted by the National Assembly.

If no agreement has been reached the examination (of the bill) continues before each Chamber. After two readings by the Council of the Republic each Chamber disposes of as much time for this purpose as has been taken up by the other Chamber in its preceding reading, but this period may not be shorter than seven days, or one day for the bills envisaged in the third paragraph.

If no agreement ensues within one-hundred days from the transmission of the bill to the Council of the Republic for second reading, reduced to one month for budget and finance bills and to fifteen days in case of urgency procedure, the National Assembly may legislate with finality, either by taking up the last version passed by it, or by adopting one or several of the amendments to it proposed by the Council of the Republic.

If the National Assembly exceeds or extends its time limit for the examination of bills, the time limit for reaching agreement between the two Chambers is increased correspondingly.

The time limits provided by this present article are suspended during the interruptions of the session. They may be extended by decision of the National Assembly.

ART. 21—No member of the Parliament may be prosecuted, sought by the police, arrested, detained or tried because of opinions expressed or votes cast by him in the exercise of his function.

ART. 22—No member of Parliament may be prosecuted or arrested during *the duration of a session* for a criminal offense except with the authorization of the Chamber of which he is a member, *unless caught in the act* (flagrant délit). *A member of Parliament arrested out of session may vote by proxy, as long as the Chamber of which he is a member has not decided to lift his parliamentary immunity. If it has not decided within thirty days from the opening of the session, the arrested member shall be freed and his rights restored.*

Except in cases of persons caught in the act (flagrant délit) *and in those of authorized prosecutions or final sentencing, no member of Parliament may be arrested out of session, except with the authorization of the officers* (bureau) *of the Chamber of which he is a member.*

The detention or prosecution of a member of Parliament shall be suspended if the Chamber of which he is a member requests it.

ART. 23—Members of the Parliament shall receive compensation fixed in relation to that of a given grade of civil servants.

ART. 24—No one may be a member both of the National Assembly and of the Council of the Republic. Members of the Parliament may not be members of the Economic Council nor of the Assembly of the French Union.

TITLE III

THE ECONOMIC COUNCIL

ART. 25—An Economic Council whose statutes shall be determined by law, shall examine the bills and proposed laws within its purview in order to give its opinion thereon. The National Assembly shall send such bills to this Council before considering them.

The Economic Council may also be consulted by the Council of Ministers. It must be consulted by that body concerning the establishment of a national economic plan for full employment and the rational utilization of our material resources.

TITLE IV

DIPLOMATIC TREATIES

ART. 26—Diplomatic treaties duly ratified and published shall have the force of law even when they are contrary to internal French legislation; they shall require for their application no legislative acts other than those necessary to ensure their ratification.

ART. 27—Treaties relative to international organization, peace treaties, commercial treaties, treaties that involve national finances, treaties relative to the personal status and property rights of French citizens abroad, and those that modify French internal legislation, as well as those that involve the cession, exchange or addition of territories shall not become final until they have been ratified by a legislative act.

No cession, no exchange and no addition of territory shall be valid without the consent of the populations concerned.

ART. 28—Since diplomatic treaties duly ratified and published have superior authority to that of French internal legislation, their provisions shall not be abrogated, modified or suspended without previous formal denunciation through diplomatic channels. Whenever a treaty such as those mentioned in Article 27 is concerned, such denunciation must be approved by the National Assembly, except in the case of commercial treaties.

TITLE V

THE PRESIDENT OF THE REPUBLIC

ART. 29—The President of the Republic shall be elected by the Parliament.

He shall be elected for seven years. He shall be eligible for reelection only once.

ART. 30—The President of the Republic shall appoint in the Council of Ministers the Councillors of State, the Grand Chancellor of the Legion of Honor, the ambassadors and special envoys, the members of the Superior Council and the Committee for National Defense, the rectors of the universities, the prefects, the chiefs of the central administrative services, the general officers and the Government representatives in the overseas territories.

ART. 31—The President of the Republic shall be kept informed of the progress of international negotiations. He shall sign and ratify all treaties.

The President of the Republic shall accredit ambassadors and special envoys to foreign powers; foreign ambassadors and special envoys shall be accredited to him.

ART. 32—The President of the Republic shall preside over the Council of Ministers. He shall order the minutes of their meetings to be recorded and shall keep them in his possession.

ART. 33—The President of the Republic shall preside in the same capacity over the Superior Council and the Committee for National Defense, and shall have the title of Commander-in-Chief of the armed forces.

ART. 34—The President of the Republic shall preside over the Superior Council of the Judiciary.

ART. 35—The President of the Republic shall have the right of pardon in the Superior Council of the Judiciary.

ART. 36—The President of the Republic shall promulgate the laws within ten days after their text, as finally adopted, has been sent to the Government. This interval may be reduced to five days if the National Assembly declares an emergency.

Within the time limit fixed for promulgation of a law, the President of the Republic, in a message stating his reasons, may ask that it be reconsidered by both Chambers; this reconsideration may not be refused.

If the President of the Republic does not promulgate a law within the time limit fixed by the present Constitution, the President of the National Assembly shall promulgate it.

ART. 37—The President of the Republic shall communicate with the Parliament by means of messages addressed to the National Assembly.

ART. 38—Every act of the President of the Republic must be countersigned by the President of the Council of Ministers and by a Minister.

ART. 39—Not more than thirty and not less than fifteen days before the expiration of the term of office of the President of the Republic, the Parliament shall elect a new President.

ART. 40—If, in the application of the preceding article, the election must take place during the period when the National Assembly is dissolved in conformity with Article 51, the powers of the then President of the Republic shall be extended until such time as a new President is elected. The Parliament shall elect this new President within ten days after the election of the National Assembly.

In this case, the President of the Council of Ministers shall be designated within fifteen days after the election of the new President of the Republic.

ART. 41—If the President of the Republic is not able to exercise his office for reasons duly noted by a vote of the Parliament, or in the event of a vacancy caused by death, resignation or any other circumstance, the President of the National Assembly shall assume the interim functions of the President of the Republic. He shall be replaced in his own duties by a Vice-President.

The new President of the Republic shall be elected within ten days, except under the conditions specified in the preceding article.

ART. 42—The President of the Republic may not be tried except for high treason.

He may be indicted by the National Assembly and arraigned before the High Court of Justice under the conditions set forth in Article 57 below.

ART. 43—The office of President of the Republic is incompatible with any other public office.

ART. 44—Members of families that once reigned over France shall not be eligible for the Presidency of the Republic.

ART. 45—At the opening of each legislative session, the President of the Republic, after the customary consultations, shall designate the President of the Council.

The latter chooses the members of his cabinet and brings the list to the attention of the National Assembly to which he presents himself in order to obtain its confidence for the program and the policy which he intends to pursue, unless circumstances beyond control (force majeure) prevent the meeting of the National Assembly.

The vote is taken by roll call and plurality.

The same procedure shall be followed during a legislative session in the event of a vacancy *in the Presidency of the Council,* except in the case set forth in Article 52.

No ministerial crisis occurring within a fifteen day period after the appointment of the ministers shall require the application of Article 51.

ART. 46—The President of the Council and the Ministers chosen by him shall be formally appointed by a decree of the President of the Republic.

ART. 47—The President of the Council shall ensure the execution of the laws.

He shall appoint all civil and military officials except those specified in Articles 30, 46 and 84.

The President of the Council shall assume the direction of the armed forces and shall coordinate all measures necessary for national defense.

The acts of the President of the Council mentioned in the present article shall be countersigned by the Ministers concerned.

ART. 48—The Ministers shall be collectively responsible to the National Assembly for the general policy of the Cabinet and individually responsible for their personal actions.

They shall not be responsible to the Council of the Republic.

ART. 49—A question of confidence may not be put except after discussion by the Council of Ministers; it can be put only by the President of the Council.

The vote on the question of confidence may not be taken until *twenty-four hours* after it has been put before the Assembly. It shall be taken by a roll call.

The Cabinet is refused a vote of confidence by an absolute majority of the Deputies in the Assembly.

Refusal to give such a vote shall automatically result in the collective resignation of the Cabinet.

ART. 50—Passage of a motion of censure by the National Assembly shall automatically result in the collective resignation of the Cabinet.

The vote on the motion of censure takes place under the same conditions and the same forms as the vote on the question of confidence.

A motion of censure may be adopted only by an absolute majority of the Deputies in the Assembly.

ART. 51—If in the course of an eighteen-month period two ministerial crises occur under the conditions set forth in Articles 49 and 50, the Council of Ministers, after obtaining the opinion of the President of the Assembly, may decide to dissolve the National Assembly. Its dissolution shall be proclaimed by a decree of the President of the Republic in accordance with such decision.

The provisions of the preceding paragraph may not be applied before the expiration of the first eighteen months of the Legislature.

ART. 52—*In case of dissolution the Cabinet remains in office.*

However, if the dissolution has been preceded by the adoption of a motion of censure, the President of the Republic shall appoint the President of the National Assembly President of the Council of Ministers and Minister of the Interior.

General elections shall take place not less than twenty and not more than thirty days after the dissolution.

The National Assembly shall convene by right on the third Thursday after its election.

ART. 53—The Ministers shall have access to the two Chambers and to their Committees. They must be heard when they request it.

In discussions before the Chambers they may be assisted by representatives designated by decree.

ART. 54—The President of the Council of Ministers may delegate his powers to a Minister.

ART. 55—In the event of a vacancy caused by death or any other circumstance, the Council of Ministers shall call upon one of its members to exercise the functions of President of the Council of Ministers temporarily.

TITLE VII

THE LEGAL RESPONSIBILITY OF MINISTERS

ART. 56—The Ministers shall be legally responsible for crimes and misdemeanors committed in the exercise of their functions.

ART. 57—The Ministers may be indicted by the National Assembly and arraigned before the High Court of Justice.

The National Assembly shall vote upon this question by secret ballot and by an absolute majority of its members, with the exception of those who may be called upon to participate in the prosecution, investigation or judgment of the case.

ART. 58—The High Court of Justice shall be elected by the National Assembly at the opening of each legislative session.

ART. 59—The organization of the High Court of Justice and the procedure to be followed before it shall be determined by a special law.

TITLE VIII

THE FRENCH UNION

Section I: Principles

ART. 60—The French Union shall be composed, on the one hand, of the French Republic which comprises Metropolitan France and the overseas departments and territories, and, on the other hand, of the Associated Territories and States.

ART. 61—The position of the Associated States within the French Union shall in each case depend upon the act which defines its relationship with France.

ART. 62—The members of the French Union shall place in common all their resources to guarantee the defense of the whole Union. The Government of the Republic shall coordinate these resources and direct such policies as will prepare and ensure this defense.

Section II: Organization

ART. 63—The central organs of the French Union shall be: the Presidency, the High Council and the Assembly.

ART. 64—The President of the French Republic shall be the President of the French Union whose permanent interests he shall represent.

ART. 65—The High Council of the French Union, under the chairmanship of the President of the Union, shall be composed of a delegation of the French Government and of the representatives that each associated State is permitted to accredit to the President of the Union.

Its function shall be to assist the Government in the general conduct of the affairs of the Union.

ART. 66—The Assembly of the French Union shall be composed half of members representing Metropolitan France and half of members representing the overseas departments and territories and the Associated States.

An organic law shall determine the mode of representation of the different sections of the population.

ART. 67—The members of the Assembly of the Union shall be elected by the regional assemblies for the Overseas departments and Territories; for Metropolitan France, they shall be elected two-thirds by the National Assembly representing the home country and one-third by the Council of the Republic representing the home country.

ART. 68—The Associated States may appoint delegates to the Assembly of the Union within the limitations and conditions determined by a law and an internal legislative act of each State.

ART. 69—The President of the French Union shall convoke the Assembly of the French Union and shall close its sessions. He must convoke it upon the request of half of its members.

The Assembly of the French Union may not sit during interruptions of the sessions of the Parliament.

ART. 70—The rules set forth in Articles 8, 10, 21, 22 and 23 shall be applicable to the Assembly of the French Union under the same conditions as to the Council of the Republic.

ART. 71—The Assembly of the French Union shall examine the bills or proposals submitted to it by the National Assembly or the Government of the French Republic or the Governments of the Associated States in order that it may give its opinion thereon.

The Assembly shall have the power to express its opinion on resolutions submitted to it by one of its members and, if they meet with its approval, to instruct its officers (*bureau*) to send them to the National Assembly. It may submit proposals to the French Government and to the High Council of the French Union.

In order to be admissible, the proposed resolutions referred to in the preceding paragraph must relate to legislation concerning the Overseas Territories.

ART. 72—Legislative power with regard to penal law, civil liberties and political and administrative organization in the Overseas Territories, shall rest with the Parliament.

In all other matters, French laws shall be applicable in the Overseas Territories only by an express provision to this effect or if they have been extended to the Overseas Territories by decree after consultation with the Assembly of the Union.

Moreover, as an exception to Article 13, special provisions for each territory may be enacted by the President of the Republic in the Council of Ministers after consultation with the Assembly of the Union.

Section III: The Overseas Departments and Territories

ART. 73—The legislative regime of the overseas departments shall be the same as that of the metropolitan departments save for exceptions determined by the law.

ART. 74—The Overseas Territories shall be given special status which takes into account their particular interests within the framework of the general interests of the Union.

This status and the internal organization of each overseas territory or group of territories shall be determined by law after the Assembly of the French Union has expressed its opinion thereon and after consultation with the Territorial Assemblies.

ART. 75—The respective status of the members of the French Republic and of the French Union shall be subject to modifications.

Modifications of status and passage from one category to another within the framework established in Article 60 may take place only as the result of a law passed by the Parliament after consultation with the Territorial Assemblies and the Assembly of the Union.

ART. 76—The representative of the Government in each territory or group of territories shall be the repository of the powers of the Republic. He shall be the Administrative head of the territory.

He shall be responsible to the Government for his acts.

ART. 77—An elective Assembly shall be instituted in each territory. The electoral regime, composition and powers of this Assembly shall be determined by law.

ART. 78—In the groups of territories, the management of matters of common interest shall be entrusted to an Assembly composed of members elected by the Territorial Assemblies.

Its composition and its powers shall be determined by law.

ART. 79—The Overseas Territories shall elect representatives to the National Assembly and to the Council of the Republic under the conditions determined by the law.

ART. 80—All nationals of the Overseas Territories shall have the status of citizens, in the same capacity as French nationals of Metropolitan France or the Overseas Territories. Special laws shall determine the conditions under which they may exercise their rights as citizens.

ART. 81—All citizens and nationals of territories within the French Union shall have the status of citizens of the French Union, which ensures them the enjoyments of the rights and liberties guaranteed by the Preamble of the present Constitution.

ART. 82—Those citizens who do not have French civil status shall retain their personal status so long as they do not renounce it.

This status may in no case constitute a ground for refusing or restricting the rights and liberties pertaining to the status of French citizens.

TITLE IX

THE SUPERIOR COUNCIL OF THE JUDICIARY

ART. 83—The Superior Council of the Judiciary shall be composed of fourteen members:

—The President of the Republic, President;

—The Keeper of the Seals or Minister of Justice, Vice-President;

—Six persons elected for six years by the National Assembly, by a two-thirds majority and chosen outside its membership, and six alternates elected under the same conditions;

—Six persons designated as follows:

—Four judges elected for six years under the conditions determined by the law, and representing each category of the judiciary, and four alternates elected under the same conditions;

—Two members appointed for six years by the President of the Republic and chosen outside the membership of the Parliament and the judiciary, but from among the members of the legal profession, two alternates being designated under the same conditions.

The decisions of the Superior Council of the Magistracy shall be taken by majority vote. In case of a tie the President shall cast the deciding vote.

ART. 84—The President of the Republic shall appoint the judges whose names are submitted to him by the Superior Council of the Judiciary with the exception of those in the Office of the Public Prosecutor.

The Superior Council of the Judiciary, according to the law, shall ensure the discipline of these judges, their independence and the administration of the courts.

The presiding judges shall not be removable.

ART. 85—The French Republic, one and indivisible, recognizes the existence of local administrative units.

These units are the communes, the departments and the overseas territories.

ART. 86—The framework, the scope, the eventual regrouping and the organization of the communes, the departments and the overseas territories, shall be determined by law.

ART. 87—The local administrative units shall be governed freely by councils elected by universal suffrage.

The mayor or the president of these councils shall ensure the carrying out of their decisions.

ART. 88—The coordination of the activities of Government officials, the representation of the national interests and the administrative control of these units shall be ensured within the departmental framework by delegates of the Government appointed in the Council of Ministers.

ART. 89—Organic laws will further extend the liberties of the departments and municipalities; for certain large cities they may establish rules of operation and an administrative structure different from those of small towns, and include special provisions for certain departments; they will determine the conditions under which Articles 85 and 88 above are to be applied.

Laws will likewise determine the conditions under which local agencies of central administrations are to function, in order to bring the central administration closer to the people.

ART. 90—Amendment of the Constitution shall take place in the following manner:

Amendment must be decided upon by a resolution adopted by an absolute majority of the members of the National Assembly.

This resolution shall stipulate the purpose of the amendment.

Not less than three months later this resolution shall have a second reading under the same rules of procedure as the first, unless the Council of the Republic, to which the resolution has been referred by the National Assembly, has adopted the same resolution by an absolute majority.

After this second reading, the National Assembly shall draw up a bill to amend the Constitution. This bill shall be submitted to the Parliament and adopted by the same majority and according to the same rules established for any ordinary act of the Legislature.

It shall be submitted to a referendum unless it has been adopted on second reading by a two-thirds majority of the National Assembly or by a three-fifths majority of each of the two assemblies.

The bill shall be promulgated as a constitutional law within eight days after its adoption.

No constitutional amendment relative to the existence of the Council of the Republic may be made without the concurrence of this Council or resort to a referendum.

Art. 91—The Constitutional Committee shall be presided over by the President of the Republic.

It shall include the President of the National Assembly, the President of the Council of the Republic, seven members elected by the National Assembly at the beginning of each annual session by proportional representation of party groups and chosen outside its own membership and three members elected under the same conditions by the Council of the Republic.

The Constitutional Committee shall determine whether the laws passed by the National Assembly imply amendment of the Constitution.

Art. 92—Within the period allowed for the promulgation of the law, the Committee shall receive a joint request that it examine said law from the President of the Republic and the President of the Council of the Republic, the Council having decided the matter by an absolute majority of its members.

The Committee shall examine the law, shall strive to bring about agreement between the National Assembly and the Council of the Republic and, if it does not succeed in this, shall decide the matter within five days after it has received the request. This period may be reduced to two days in case of emergency.

The Committee shall be competent to decide on the possibility of amending only Titles I through X of the present Constitution.

Art. 93—A law which, in the opinion of the Committee, implies amendment of the Constitution shall be sent back to the National Assembly for reconsideration.

If the Parliament adheres to its original vote, the law may not be promulgated until the Constitution has been amended according to the procedure set forth in Article 90.

If the law is considered to be in conformity with Title I through X of the present Constitution, it shall be promulgated within the period specified in Article 36, said period being prolonged by the addition of the period specified in Article 92 above.

Art. 94—In the case of occupation of all or part of the metropolitan territory by foreign forces, no procedure of amendment may be undertaken or continued.

Art. 95—The republican form of government may not be the subject of any proposal to amend the Constitution.

TITLE XII

TEMPORARY PROVISIONS

Art. 96—The secretariat of the National Constituent Assembly shall be responsible for ensuring the continuity of national representation until the meeting of the deputies of the new National Assembly.

Art. 97—In case of exceptional circumstances, the deputies of the National Constituent Assembly may, until the time specified in the preceding article, be called together by the secretariat of the Assembly, either on its own initiative or upon the request of the Government.

Art. 98—The National Assembly will meet automatically on the third Thursday following the general elections.

The Council of the Republic will meet on the third Tuesday following its election. The present Constitution will take effect on that date.

Until the meeting of the Council of the Republic, the organization of public powers will be governed by the law of November 2, 1945, the National Assembly having the attributes conferred by that law on the National Constituent Assembly.

Art. 99—The Provisional Government constituted under the terms of Article 98 will hand its resignation to the President of the Republic as soon as the latter is elected by the Parliament under the conditions set forth in Article 29 above.

Art. 100—The secretariat of the National Constituent Assembly shall be responsible for preparing the meeting of the Assemblies created by the present Constitution and especially for providing, before the meeting of their respective secretariats, the meeting places and administrative facilities necessary to their functioning.

Art. 101—During a period of not more than one year after the meeting of the National Assembly, the Council of the Republic may officially deliberate as soon as two-thirds of its members shall have been proclaimed elected.

Art. 102—The first Council of the Republic will be renewed entirely within the year following the renewal of the municipal councils, which renewal will take place within one year after the promulgation of the Constitution.

Art. 103—Until the organization of the Economic Council and during a maximum period of three months dating from the meeting of the National Assembly the application of Article 25 of the present Constitution will be suspended.

Art. 104—Until the meeting of the Assembly of the French Union and during a maximum period of one year dating from the meeting of the National Assembly, the application of Articles 71 and 72 of the present Constitution will be suspended.

Art. 105—Until the promulgation of the laws provided for in Article 89 of the present Constitution, and without prejudice to the provisions fixing the status of the various departments and overseas territories, the departments and communes of the French Republic will be administered in accordance with the laws now in force, except for Paragraphs 2 and 3 of Article 97 of the law of April 5, 1884, for the enforcement of which the State police shall be placed at the disposal of the mayors.

However, the acts of the prefect in his capacity of representative of the department, will be carried out by him under the permanent supervision of the president of the departmental assembly.

The provisions of the preceding paragraph shall not be applicable to the department of the Seine.

Art. 106—The present Constitution will be promulgated by the President of the Provisional Government of the Republic within two days after the date of the proclamation of the results of the referendum and in the following form:

"The National Constituent Assembly has adopted,

"The French people has approved,

"The President of the Provisional Government of the Republic promulgates the Constitution that follows:

(Text of the Constitution)

The present Constitution, considered and adopted by the National Constituent Assembly and approved by the French people, shall become the law of the land.

Paris, October 27, 1946.

(Journal Officiel, October 28, 1946)

Appendix B

BASIC LAW OF THE FEDERAL REPUBLIC OF GERMANY (BONN)
1949

Conscious of its responsibility before God and mankind, filled with the resolve to preserve its national and political unity and to serve world peace as an equal partner in a united Europe, the German people

in the Laender Baden, Bavaria, Bremen, Hamburg, Hesse, Lower Saxony, North Rhine-Westphalia, Rhineland-Palatinate, Schleswig-Holstein, Wuerttemberg-Baden and Wuerttemberg-Hohenzollern

has, by virtue of its constituent power, enacted this Basic Law of the Federal Republic of Germany to give a new order to political life for a transitional period.

It acted also on behalf of those Germans to whom participation was denied.

The entire German people is called upon to accomplish, by free self-determination, the unity and freedom of Germany.

I

BASIC RIGHTS

ART. 1—(1) The dignity of man shall be inviolable. To respect and protect it shall be the duty of all state authority.

(2) The German people therefore acknowledge inviolable and inalienable human rights as the basis of every human community, of peace and of justice in the world.

(3) The following basic rights shall be binding as directly valid law on legislation, administration and judiciary.

ART. 2—(1) Everyone shall have the right to the free development of his personality, insofar as he does not infringe the rights of others or offend against the constitutional order or the moral code.

(2) Everyone shall have the right to life and physical inviolability. The freedom of the individual shall be inviolable. These rights may be interfered with only on the basis of a law.

ART. 3—(1) All men shall be equal before the law.

(2) Men and women shall have equal rights.

(3) No one may be prejudiced or privileged because of his sex, descent, race, language, homeland and origin, faith or his religious and political opinions.

ART. 4—(1) Freedom of faith and conscience and freedom of religious and ideological (*weltanschauliche*) profession shall be inviolable.

(2) Undisturbed practice of religion shall be guaranteed.

(3) No one may be compelled against his conscience to perform war service as a combatant. Details shall be regulated by a federal law.

ART. 5—(1) Everyone shall have the right freely to express and to disseminate his opinion through speech, writing and illustration and, without hindrance, to instruct himself from generally accessible sources. Freedom of the press and freedom of reporting by radio and motion pictures shall be guaranteed. There shall be no censorship.

(2) These rights shall be limited by the provisions of the general laws, the legal regulations for the protection of juveniles and by the right of personal honour.

(3) Art and science, research and teaching shall be free. Freedom of teaching shall not absolve from loyalty to the constitution.

ART. 6—(1) Marriage and family shall be under the special protection of the state.

(2) The care and upbringing of children shall be the natural right of parents and the supreme duty incumbent upon them. The state shall watch over their activity.

(3) Children may be separated from the family against the will of those entitled to bring them up only on a legal basis if those so entitled fail to do their duty or if, on other grounds, a danger of the children being neglected arises.

(4) Every mother shall have a claim to the protection and care of the community.

(5) Illegitimate children shall, through legislation, be given the same conditions for their physical and spiritual development and their position in society as legitimate children.

ART. 7—(1) The entire educational system shall be under the supervision of the state.

(2) Those entitled to bring up the child shall have the right to decide whether it shall receive religious instruction.

(3) Religious instruction shall form part of the curriculum in the state schools with the exception of non-confessional schools. Religious instruction shall, without prejudice to the state's right of supervision, be given according to the principles of the religious societies. No teacher may be obligated against his will to give religious instruction.

(4) The right to establish private schools shall be guaranteed. Private schools as substitute for state schools shall require the sanction of the state and shall be subject to Land legislation. The sanction must be given if the private schools, in their educational aims and facilities, as well as in the scholarly training of their teaching personnel, are not inferior to the state schools and if a separation of the pupils according to the means of the parents is not encouraged. The sanction must be withheld if the economic and legal status of the teaching personnel is not sufficiently assured.

(5) A private elementary school shall be permitted only if the educational administration recognizes a specific pedagogic interest or, at the request of those entitled to bring up children, if it is to be established as a general community school (*Gemeinschaftsschule*), as a confessional or ideological school or if a state elementary school of this type does not exist in the Gemeinde.

(6) Preparatory schools shall remain abolished.

ART. 8—(1) All Germans shall have the right, without prior notification or permission, to assemble peacefully and unarmed.

(2) For open air meetings this right may be restricted by legislation or on the basis of a law.

ART. 9—(1) All Germans shall have the right to form associations and societies.

(2) Associations, the objects or activities of which conflict with the criminal laws or which are directed against the constitutional order or the concept of international understanding, shall be prohibited.

(3) The right to form associations to safeguard and improve working and economic conditions shall be guaranteed to everyone and to all professions. Agreements which seek to restrict or hinder this right shall be null and void; measures directed to this end shall be illegal.

ART. 10—Secrecy of the mail as well as secrecy of the post and telecommunications shall be inviolable. Restrictions may be ordered only on the basis of a law.

ART. 11—(1) All Germans shall enjoy freedom of movement throughout the federal territory.

(2) This right may be restricted only by legislation and only for the cases in which an adequate basis of existence is absent and, as a result, particular burdens would arise for the general public or in which it is necessary for the protection of juveniles from neglect, for combatting the danger of epidemics or in order to prevent criminal acts.

ART. 12—(1) All Germans shall have the right freely to choose their occupation, place of work and place of training. The practice of an occupation may be regulated by legislation.

(2) No one may be compelled to perform a particular kind of work except within the framework of an established general compulsory public service equally applicable to everybody.

(3) Forced labor shall be admissible only in the event of imprisonment ordered by a court.

ART. 13—(1) The dwelling shall be inviolable.

(2) Searches may be ordered only by a judge or in the event of imminent danger by other authorities provided by law and may be carried out only in the form prescribed therein.

(3) Interventions and restrictions may otherwise be undertaken only to avert a common danger or mortal danger to individuals and, on the basis of a law, also to prevent imminent danger to public safety and order, especially for the relief of the housing shortage, combatting the danger of epidemics or protecting juveniles exposed to dangers.

ART. 14—(1) Property and the right of inheritance shall be guaranteed. The contents and limitations shall be determined by legislation.

(2) Property shall involve obligations. Its use shall simultaneously serve the general welfare.

(3) Expropriation shall be admissible only for the wellbeing of the general public. It may be effected only by legislation or on the basis of a law which shall regulate the nature and extent of compensation. The compensation shall be determined after just consideration of the interests of the general public and the participants. Regarding the extent of compensation, appeal may be made to the ordinary courts in case of dispute.

ART. 15—Land and landed property, natural resources and means of production may, for the purpose of socialization, be transferred to public ownership or other forms of publicly controlled economy by way of a law which shall regulate the nature and extent of compensation. For the compensation, Article 14, paragraph (3), sentences 3 and 4, shall apply appropriately.

ART. 16—(1) No one may be deprived of his German citizenship. The loss of citizenship may occur only on the basis of a law and, against the will of the person concerned, only if the person concerned is not rendered stateless thereby.

(2) No German may be extradited to a foreign country. The politically persecuted shall enjoy the right of asylum.

ART. 17—Everyone shall have the right, individually or jointly with others, to address written requests or complaints to the competent authorities and to the popular representative bodies.

ART. 18—Whoever abuses the freedom of expression of opinion, in particular the freedom of the press (Article 5, paragraph (1)), the freedom of teaching (Article 5, paragraph (3)), the freedom of assembly (Article 8), the freedom of association (Article 9), the secrecy of mail, post and telecommunications (Article 10), property (Article 14), or the right of asylum (Article 16, paragraph (2)), in order to attack the free, democratic basic order, shall forfeit these basic rights. The forfeiture and its extent shall be pronounced by the Federal Constitutional Court.

ART. 19—(1) Insofar as according to this Basic Law a basic right may be restricted by legislation or on the basis of a law, the law must apply in general and not solely to the individual case. Furthermore, the law must name the basic right, indicating the Article.

(2) In no case may a basic right be affected in its basic content.

(3) The basic rights shall also apply to juridical persons within the country insofar as, according to their nature, they may be applied to such persons.

(4) Should any person's rights be infringed by public authority, he may appeal to the courts. Insofar as another authority is not competent, the appeal shall go to the ordinary courts.

II

THE FEDERATION AND THE LAENDER

ART. 20—(1) The Federal Republic of Germany is a democratic and social federal state.

(2) All state authority emanates from the people. It shall be exercised by the people in elections and plebiscites and by means of separate legislative, executive and judicial organs.

(3) Legislation shall be limited by the constitution, the executive and the administration of justice by legislation and the law.

ART. 21—(1) The parties shall participate in forming the political will of the people. They can be freely formed. Their internal organization must conform to democratic principles. They must publicly account for the sources of their funds.

(2) Parties which, according to their aims and the behavior of their members, seek to impair or abolish the free and democratic basic order or to jeopardize the existence of the Federal Republic of Germany, shall be unconstitutional. The Federal Constitutional Court shall decide on the question of unconstitutionality.

(3) Details shall be regulated by federal legislation.

ART. 22—The federal flag shall be black-red-gold.

ART. 23—For the time being, this Basic Law shall apply in the territory of the Laender Baden, Bavaria, Bremen, Greater Berlin, Hamburg, Hesse, Lower Saxony, North Rhine–Westphalia, Rhineland-Palatinate, Schleswig-Holstein, Wuerttemberg-Baden and Wuerttemberg-Hohenzollern. It shall be put into force for other parts of Germany on their accession.

ART. 24—(1) The Federation may, by legislation, transfer sovereign powers to international institutions.

(2) In order to preserve peace, the Federation may join a system of mutual collective security; in doing so it will consent to those limitations of its sovereign powers which will bring about and secure a peaceful and lasting order in Europe and among the nations of the world.

(3) For the settlement of international disputes, the Federation will join a general, comprehensive, obligatory system of international arbitration.

ART. 25—The general rules of international law shall form part of federal law. They shall take precedence over the laws and create rights and duties directly for the inhabitants of the federal territory.

ART. 26—(1) Activities tending to disturb or undertaken with the intention of disturbing the peaceful relations between nations, and especially preparing for aggressive war, shall be unconstitutional. They shall be made subject to punishment.

(2) Weapons designed for warfare may be manufactured, transported or marketed only with the permission of the Federal Government. Details shall be regulated by a federal law.

Art. 27—All German merchantmen shall form a unified merchant marine.

Art. 28—(1) The constitutional order in the Laender must conform to the principles of the republican, democratic and social state based on the rule of law (*Rechtsstaat*) within the meaning of this Basic Law. In the Laender, Kreise and Gemeinden the people must have a representative assembly resulting from universal, direct, free, equal and secret elections. In Gemeinden, the Parish Meeting may take the place of an elected body.

(2) The Gemeinden must be guaranteed the right to regulate under their own responsibility all the affairs of the local community in accordance with the laws. The Gemeindeverbände also shall have the right of self-government within the limits of their legal sphere of functions and in accordance with the laws.

(3) The Federation shall guarantee that the constitutional order of the Laender shall correspond to the basic rights and the provisions of paragraphs (1) and (2).

Art. 29—(1) The federal territory shall. be reorganized by a federal law with due regard to regional unity, historical and cultural connections, economic expediency and social structure. The reorganization shall create Laender which by their size and potentiality are able to fulfil efficiently the functions incumbent upon them.

(2) In areas which, in the reorganization of Laender after 8 May 1945, joined another Land without plebiscite, a certain change in the decision made concerning this subject may be demanded by popular initiative within one year after the coming into force of the Basic Law. The popular initiative shall require the consent of one-tenth of the population qualified to vote in Landtag elections. Should the popular initiative take place, the Federal Government must, in the draft law regarding the reorganization, include a provision determining to which Land the area concerned shall belong.

(3) After adoption of the law, in each area which it is intended should join another Land, that part of the law which concerns this area must be submitted to a referendum. If a popular initiative takes place in accordance with paragraph (2), a referendum must always be carried out in the area concerned.

(4) Insofar as thereby the law is rejected at least in one area, it must be reintroduced in the Bundestag. After re-enactment, it shall require accordingly acceptance by referendum in the entire federal territory.

(5) In a referendum, the majority of the votes cast shall decide.

(6) The procedure shall be regulated by a federal law. The reorganization shall be regulated before the expiry of three years after promulgation of the Basic Law and, should it be necessary in consequence of the accession of another part of Germany, within two years after such accession.

(7) The procedure regarding any other change in the existing territory of the Laender shall be regulated by a federal law, which shall require the approval of the Bundesrat and of the majority of the members of the Bundestag.

Art. 30—The exercise of the powers of the state and the performance of state functions shall be the concern of the Laender, insofar as this Basic Law does not otherwise prescribe or permit.

Art. 31—Federal law shall supersede Land law.

Art. 32—(1) The maintenance of relations with foreign states shall be the affair of the Federation.

(2) Before the conclusion of a treaty affecting the special conditions of a Land, the Land must be consulted sufficiently early.

(3) Insofar as the Laender are competent to legislate, they may, with the approval of the Federal Government, conclude treaties with foreign states.

Art. 33—(1) Every German shall have in each Land the same civil (*staatsbürgerliche*) rights and duties.

(2) Every German shall have equal access to any public office in accordance with his suitability, ability and professional achievements.

(3) Enjoyment of municipal and national civil (*bürgerliche und staatsbürgerliche*) rights, access to public offices, as well as the rights acquired in the public service, shall be independent of religious confession. No one may be prejudiced on account of his adherence or nonadherence to a confession or ideology (*Weltanschauung*).

(4) The exercise of state authority (*hoheitsrechtliche Befugnisse*) shall normally be assigned as permanent functions to members of the public service who are in a status of service and loyalty under public law.

(5) Law regarding the public service shall be regulated with due regard to the established principles concerning the legal status of professional officials (*Berufsbeamtentum*).

ART. 34—If any person, in exercising the duties of a public office entrusted to him, violates his official obligation towards a third party, liability shall in principle rest with the state or his employing authority. In the case of wilful intent or gross negligence, the right of recourse shall be reserved. In respect to the claim for damages and in respect to the right of recourse, appeal to the ordinary courts must not be excluded.

ART. 35—All federal and Land authorities shall render each other mutual legal and official assistance.

ART. 36—In the highest federal authorities civil servants (*Beamte*) from all Laender shall be employed in equitable ratio. Persons employed in the other federal offices shall normally be selected from the Land in which they are employed.

ART. 37—(1) If a Land fails to fulfil its obligations towards the Federation under the Basic Law or any other federal law, the Federal Government may, with the approval of the Bundesrat, take the necessary measures to force the Land by way of federal compulsion to fulfil its duties.

(2) In order to carry out federal compulsion, the Federal Government or its commissioner shall have the right to give orders to all Laender and their authorities.

III

THE BUNDESTAG

ART. 38—(1) The deputies of the German Bundestag shall be elected by the people in universal, free, equal, direct and secret elections. They shall be representatives of the whole people, not bound to orders and instructions and subject only to their conscience.

(2) Any person who has reached the age of 21 years shall be eligible to vote and any person who has reached the age of 25 years shall be eligible for election.

(3) Details shall be determined by a federal law.

ART. 39—(1) The Bundestag shall be elected for a term of four years. Its electoral period shall end four years after its first assembly or with its dissolution. The new election shall take place in the last three months of the electoral period; in the case of its dissolution, at the latest after 60 days.

(2) The Bundestag shall meet not later than thirty days after the election, nevertheless not before the end of the electoral period of the previous Bundestag.

(3) The Bundestag shall determine the closure and resumption of its sessions. The President of the Bundestag may convene it at an earlier date. He shall be obliged to do so if one-third of the members, the Federal President or the Federal Chancellor so demand.

ART. 40—(1) The Bundestag shall elect its President, his deputies and its clerks. It shall draw up its Standing Orders (Rules of Procedure).

(2) The President shall have charge of, and exercise police power in, the Bundestag

building. No search or seizure may take place without his permission in the precincts of the Bundestag.

ART. 41—(1) The review of elections shall be the responsibility of the Bundestag. It shall decide also whether a deputy has lost his membership in the Bundestag.

(2) An appeal to the Federal Constitutional Court against a decision of the Bundestag shall be admissible.

(3) Details shall be regulated by a federal law.

ART. 42—(1) Meetings of the Bundestag shall be public. Upon a motion of one-tenth of its members or upon a motion of the Federal Government the public may, by a two-thirds majority, be excluded. A decision on the motion will be made in a closed meeting.

(2) Decisions of the Bundestag shall require the majority of votes cast insofar as the Basic Law does not determine otherwise. Standing Orders (Rules of Procedure) may admit exceptions in the case of elections to be held by the Bundestag.

(3) Accurate reports of the public meetings of the Bundestag and of its committees shall be privileged.

ART. 43—(1) The Bundestag and its committees may demand the presence of any member of the Federal Government.

(2) The Members of the Bundesrat and of the Federal Government as well as the persons commissioned by them shall have access to all meetings of the Bundestag and its committees. They must be heard at any time.

ART. 44—(1) The Bundestag shall have the right and, upon the motion of one-fourth of its members, the obligation to set up an investigating committee, which shall take the necessary evidence in public proceedings. The public may be excluded.

(2) The provisions relating to criminal procedure shall apply appropriately to the investigations. Secrecy of the mail, post and telecommunications shall remain unaffected.

(3) The courts and administrative authorities shall be obliged to provide legal and official assistance.

(4) The decisions of the investigating committees shall not be subject to judicial review. The courts shall be free to evaluate and judge the facts on which the investigation is based.

ART. 45—(1) The Bundestag shall appoint a Standing Committee which shall safeguard the rights of the Bundestag vis-à-vis the Federal Government in the interval between two electoral periods. The Standing Committee shall also have the rights of an investigating committee.

(2) Wider powers, in particular the right to legislate, to elect the Federal Chancellor and to impeach the Federal President, shall not be within the province of the Standing Committee.

ART. 46—(1) A deputy may at no time be subject to legal or disciplinary action or otherwise be called to account outside the Bundestag because of his vote or any utterance in the Bundestag or in one of its committees. This shall not apply in the case of defamatory insults.

(2) A deputy may be called to account or arrested for a punishable offence only with the permission of the Bundestag, unless he be apprehended while committing the offence or in the course of the following day.

(3) Furthermore, the permission of the Bundestag shall be required in respect of any other restriction of the personal freedom of a deputy or for the initiating of proceedings against a deputy in accordance with Article 18.

(4) Any criminal proceedings and any proceedings in accordance with Article 18 against a deputy, any detention and any other restriction of his personal freedom shall be suspended upon the demand of the Bundestag.

ART. 47—Deputies shall be entitled to refuse to give evidence concerning persons who have entrusted facts to them in their capacity as deputies or to whom they in this capacity have entrusted facts, as well as concerning these facts themselves. Insofar as this right of refusal to give evidence extends, the seizure of documents shall be inadmissible.

ART. 48—(1) Any person seeking election to the Bundestag shall have a claim to the leave necessary for his election campaign.

(2) No one may be prevented from assuming or exercising the office of a deputy. Notice of dismissal or dismissal for this reason shall be inadmissible.

(3) Deputies shall have a claim to adequate remuneration, which shall ensure their independence. They shall have the right to free travel in all publicly owned transport. Details shall be regulated by a federal law.

ART. 49—Articles 46, 47 and 48, paragraphs (2) and (3) shall apply to the members of the Praesidium and the Standing Committee as well as to their chief deputies also in the interval between two electoral periods.

IV

THE BUNDESRAT

ART. 50—The Laender shall participate through the medium of the Bundesrat in the legislation and the administration of the Federation.

ART. 51—(1) The Bundesrat shall consist of members of the Governments of the Laender which shall appoint and recall them. They may be represented by other members of their Governments.

(2) Each Land shall have at least three votes; Laender with more than two million inhabitants shall have four, Laender with more than six million inhabitants shall have five votes.

(3) Every Land may delegate as many members as it has votes. The votes of each Land may be given only as a block vote and only by members present or their representatives.

ART. 52—(1) The Bundesrat shall elect its President for one year.

(2) The President shall convene the Bundesrat. He must convene it if the representatives of at least two Laender or the Federal Government so demand.

(3) The Bundesrat shall take its decisions with at least the majority of its votes. It shall draw up its Standing Orders (Rules of Procedure). It shall meet in public. The public may be excluded.

(4) Other members or representatives of the Governments of the Laender may belong to the committees of the Bundesrat.

ART. 53—The members of the Federal Government shall have the right, and on demand the obligation, to participate in the debates of the Bundesrat and its committees. They must be heard at any time. The Bundesrat must be kept currently informed by the Federal Government on the conduct of federal affairs.

V

THE FEDERAL PRESIDENT

ART. 54—(1) The Federal President shall be elected, without discussion, by the Federal Convention. Every German who is eligible to vote in elections for the Bundestag and has reached the age of 40 years shall be eligible for election.

(2) The term of office of the Federal President shall be five years. Immediate re-election shall be admissible only once.

(3) The Federal Convention shall consist of the members of the Bundestag and an equal number of members elected by the popular representative bodies of the Laender according to the principles of proportional representation.

(4) The Federal Convention shall meet not later than thirty days before the expiry of the term of office of the Federal President, in the case of premature termination not later than thirty days after this date. It shall be convened by the President of the Bundestag.

(5) After the expiry of the electoral period, the time limit of paragraph (4), sentence 1, shall begin with the first meeting of the Bundestag.

(6) The person who has received the votes of the majority of the members of the Federal Convention shall be elected. If such majority is not obtained by any candidate in two ballots, the person who receives most votes in a further ballot shall be elected.

(7) Details shall be regulated by a federal law.

ART. 55—(1) The Federal President may be a member neither of the Government nor of a legislative body of the Federation or a Land.

(2) The Federal President may not hold any other salaried office, carry on a trade or practise a profession or belong to the management or supervisory board of a profit-making enterprise.

ART. 56—On assuming office, the Federal President shall take the following oath in the presence of the assembled members of the Bundestag and the Bundesrat:

"I swear that I shall dedicate my strength to the wellbeing of the German people, enhance what is to its advantage, ward off what might harm it, uphold and defend the Basic Law and the laws of the Federation, fulfil my duties conscientiously and do justice to every man. So help me God."

The oath may also be taken without the religious asseveration.

ART. 57—In the event of the inability of the Federal President to perform the duties of his office or in the event of a premature vacancy in the office, the functions of the Federal President shall be exercised by the President of the Bundesrat.

ART. 58—Orders and instructions of the Federal President shall require for their validity the counter-signature of the Federal Chancellor or the competent Federal Minister. This shall not apply to the appointment and dismissal of the Federal Chancellor, the dissolution of the Bundestag in accordance with Article 63 and a request in accordance with Article 69, paragraph (3).

ART. 59—(1) The Federal President shall represent the Federation in matters concerning international law. He shall conclude treaties with foreign states on behalf of the Federation. He shall accredit and receive the envoys.

(2) Treaties which regulate the political relations of the Federation or refer to matters of federal legislation shall require, in the form of a federal law, the approval or the participation of the corporations competent at the time for federal legislation. For administrative agreements the provisions concerning the federal administration shall apply appropriately.

ART. 60—(1) The Federal President shall appoint and dismiss the federal judges and the federal officials unless otherwise determined by law.

(2) He shall exercise the right of pardon on behalf of the Federation in individual cases.

(3) He may delegate these powers to other authorities.

(4) Article 46, paragraphs (2) to (4), shall apply appropriately to the Federal President.

ART. 61—(1) The Bundestag or the Bundesrat may impeach the Federal President before the Federal Constitutional Court on account of wilful violation of the Basic Law or any other federal law. The motion for impeachment must be brought in by at least one-quarter of the members of the Bundestag or one-quarter of the votes of the Bundesrat. The decision to impeach shall require the majority of two-thirds of the members of the

Bundestag or of two-thirds of the votes of the Bundesrat. The prosecution shall be conducted by a person commissioned by the impeaching body.

(2) If the Federal Constitutional Court finds that the Federal President is guilty of a wilful violation of the Basic Law or of any other federal law, it may declare him to have forfeited his office. After the institution of impeachment proceedings, the Federal Constitutional Court may, by interim order, determine that the Federal President is prevented from performing the duties of his office.

VI

The Federal Government

ART. 62—The Federal Government shall consist of the Federal Chancellor and the Federal Ministers.

ART. 63—(1) The Federal Chancellor shall be elected, without discussion, by the Bundestag on the proposal of the Federal President.

(2) The person who has received the votes of the majority of the members of the Bundestag shall be elected. He shall be appointed by the Federal President.

(3) If the person nominated is not elected, the Bundestag may, within fourteen days after the ballot, elect a Federal Chancellor by more than one half of its members.

(4) If the Federal Chancellor is not elected within this time limit a new ballot shall take place immediately, in which the person who receives most votes shall be elected. If the person elected receives the votes of the majority of the members of the Bundestag the Federal President must, within seven days after the election, appoint him. If the person elected does not obtain this majority the Federal President must, within seven days, either appoint him or dissolve the Bundestag.

ART. 64—(1) The Federal Ministers shall be appointed and dismissed by the Federal President upon the proposal of the Federal Chancellor.

(2) The Federal Chancellor and the Federal Ministers, on assuming office, shall take before the Bundestag the oath provided in Article 56.

ART. 65—The Federal Chancellor shall determine and assume responsibility for general policy. Within the limits of this general policy, each Federal Minister shall direct his department individually and on his own responsibility. The Federal Government shall decide on differences of opinion between the Federal Ministers. The Federal Chancellor shall conduct its business in accordance with Standing Orders (Rules of Procedure) adopted by the Federal Government and approved by the Federal President.

ART. 66.—The Federal Chancellor and the Federal Ministers may not hold any other salaried office, carry on a trade or practise a profession or belong to the management or, without the approval of the Bundestag, to the supervisory board of a profit-making enterprise.

ART. 67—(1) The Bundestag may express its lack of confidence in the Federal Chancellor only by electing a successor with the majority of its members and submitting a request to the Federal President for the dismissal of the Federal Chancellor. The Federal President must comply with the request and appoint the person elected.

(2) There must be an interval of 48 hours between the motion and the election.

ART. 68—(1) If a motion of the Federal Chancellor to receive a vote of confidence does not obtain the support of the majority of the members of the Bundestag, the Federal President may, upon the proposal of the Federal Chancellor, dissolve the Bundestag within 21 days. The right of dissolution shall lapse as soon as the Bundestag, with the majority of its members, elects another Federal Chancellor.

(2) There must be an interval of 48 hours between the introduction of, and the vote on, the motion.

ART. 69—(1) The Federal Chancellor shall appoint a Federal Minister as his deputy.

(2) The office of the Federal Chancellor or of a Federal Minister shall end in any case with the assembly of a new Bundestag, the office of a Federal Minister also with any other termination of the office of the Federal Chancellor.

(3) At the request of the Federal President the Federal Chancellor, at the request of the Federal Chancellor or of the Federal President a Federal Minister, shall be obliged to carry out the duties of his office until the appointment of his successor.

VII

THE LEGISLATION OF THE FEDERATION

ART. 70—(1) The Laender shall have the right of legislation insofar as this Basic Law does not accord legislative powers to the Federation.

(2) The division of competence between the Federation and the Laender shall be determined in accordance with the provisions of this Basic Law concerning exclusive and concurrent legislation.

ART. 71—In the field of exclusive legislation of the Federation, the Laender shall have powers of legislation only if, and so far as, they are expressly so empowered in a federal law.

ART. 72—(1) In the field of concurrent legislation, the Laender shall have powers of legislation so long and so far as the Federation makes no use of its legislative right.

(2) The Federation shall have legislative right in this field insofar as a necessity for regulation by federal law exists because:

1. a matter cannot be effectively regulated by the legislation of individual Laender, or
2. the regulation of a matter by a Land law could prejudice the interests of other Laender or of the Laender as a whole, or
3. the preservation of legal or economic unity demands it, in particular the preservation of uniformity of living conditions extending beyond the territory of an individual Land.

ART. 73.—The Federation shall have exclusive legislation on:

1. foreign affairs;
2. citizenship of the Federation;
3. freedom of movement, passports, immigration and emigration, and emigration and extradition;
4. currency, money and coinage, weights and measures and regulation of time and calendar;
5. the unity of customs and commercial territory, commercial and navigation agreements, the freedom of traffic in goods and the traffic in goods and payments with foreign countries, including customs and frontier protection;
6. federal railways and air traffic;
7. post and telecommunications;
8. the legal status of persons in the employment of the Federation and of public law corporations under direct supervision of the Federal Government;
9. trade marks, copyright and publishing rights;
10. co-operation of the Federation and the Laender in the criminal police and in matters concerning the protection of the constitution, the establishment of a Federal Office of Criminal Police, as well as the combatting of international crime;
11. statistics for federal purposes.

Art. 74—Concurrent legislation shall extend to the following fields:

1. civil law, criminal law and execution of sentences, constitution of courts, court procedure, the bar, notaries and legal advice (*Rechtsberatung*);
2. census and registry matters;
3. associations and assemblies;
4. the right of sojourn and settlement of aliens;
5. the protection of German works of art against removal abroad;
6. matters relating to refugees and expellees;
7. public welfare;
8. citizenship of the Laender;
9. war damages and compensation (*Wiedergutmachung*);
10. provisions for war-disabled persons and surviving dependents, the welfare of former prisoners of war and the care of war graves;
11. law relating to the economy (mining, industry, power supply, crafts, trades, commerce, banking and stock exchanges, private insurances);
12. labor law, including the legal organization of enterprises, protection of workers and provision of employment, as well as social insurance of scientific research;
13. the furtherance of scientific research;
14. the law regarding expropriation insofar as it is concerned with the matters enumerated in Articles 73 and 74;
15. transfer of land and landed property, natural resources and means of production to public ownership or to other forms of publicly controlled economy;
16. prevention of the abuse of economic power;
17. promotion of agricultural and forestry production, safeguarding of food supply, import and export of agricultural and forestry products, deep-sea and coastal fisheries and coastal preservation;
18. transactions in landed property, law concerning land and agricultural lease, housing, settlements and homesteads;
19. measures against epidemic and infectious diseases affecting humans and animals, the licensing for medical and other healing professions and the healing trade and traffic in drugs, medicines, narcotics and poisons;
20. protection relating to traffic in food and stimulants as well as in necessities of life, in fodder, in agricultural and forestry seeds and seedlings, and protection of trees and plants against diseases and pests;
21. ocean and coastal shipping and aids to navigation, inland shipping, meteorological service, ocean channels and inland waterways used for general traffic;
22. road traffic, motor transport and the construction and maintenance of highways used for long-distance transport;
23. railways other than federal railways, except mountain railways.

Art. 75—The Federation shall have the right on the basis of Article 72 to issue general provisions concerning:

1. the legal status of persons employed in the public service of the Laender, Gemeinden and other public law corporations;
2. the general legal status of the press and motion pictures;
3. hunting, protection of nature and care of the countryside;
4. land distribution, regional planning and water conservation;
5. matters relating to registration and identity cards.

Art. 76—(1) Bills shall be introduced in the Bundestag by the Federal Government, by members of the Bundestag or by the Bundesrat.

(2) Federal Government bills shall first be submitted to the Bundesrat. The Bundesrat shall have the right to give its opinion on these bills within three weeks.

(3) Bundesrat bills shall be submitted to the Bundestag by the Federal Government, which must add a statement of its own views.

ART. 77—(1) Federal laws shall be passed by the Bundestag. After their adoption they shall, without delay, be submitted to the Bundesrat by the President of the Bundestag.

(2) The Bundesrat may, within two weeks of the receipt of the adopted bill, demand that a committee composed of members of the Bundestag and Bundesrat be convened to consider the bill jointly. The composition and the procedure of this committee shall be regulated by Standing Orders (Rules of Procedure), which shall be agreed by the Bundestag and shall require the approval of the Bundesrat. The members of the Bundesrat deputed to this committee shall not be bound by instructions. If the approval of the Bundesrat is required for a law, both the Bundestag and the Federal Government may demand that it be convened. Should the committee propose an alteration of the adopted bill, the Bundestag must take a new decision.

(3) Insofar as the approval of the Bundesrat is not required for a law the Bundesrat may, if the procedure in accordance with paragraph (2) is completed, within one week veto a law passed by the Bundestag. The time limit for a veto shall begin in the case of paragraph (2), last sentence, with the receipt of the bill as re-adopted by the Bundestag, in all other cases with the conclusion of the procedure preceding the committee provided for in paragraph (2).

(4) Should the veto be adopted by the majority of the votes of the Bundesrat, it may be rejected by a decision of the majority of the members of the Bundestag. Should the Bundesrat have adopted the veto by a majority of at least two-thirds of its votes, the rejection by the Bundestag shall require a majority of two-thirds, or a least the majority of the members of the Bundestag.

ART. 78—A law passed by the Bundestag shall be enacted if the Bundesrat approves, does not bring in a motion in accordance with Article 77, paragraph (2), does not impose a veto within the time limit of Article 77, paragraph (3), withdraws its veto or if the veto is overridden by the Bundestag.

ART. 79—(1) The Basic Law may be amended only by a law which expressly alters or adds to the text of the Basic Law.

(2) Such a law shall require the approval of two-thirds of the members of the Bundestag and two-thirds of the votes of the Bundesrat.

(3) An amendment to this Basic Law by which the organization of the Federation into Laender, the basic co-operation of the Laender in legislation or the basic principles laid down in Articles 1 and 20 are affected, shall be inadmissible.

ART. 80—(1) By means of a law the Federal Government, a Federal Minister or the Land Governments may be authorized to issue orders (*Rechtsverordnungen*). The contents, purpose and scope of such authorization shall be determined in the law. The legal basis must be cited in the order. If a law provides that an authorization may be further transferred, then the transfer of the authorization shall require an order (*Rechtsverordnung*).

(2) The approval of the Bundesrat shall be required, unless otherwise regulated by federal legislation, for orders (*Rechtsverordnungen*) of the Federal Government or a Federal Minister concerning principles and fees for the use of the facilities of the Federal railways and post and telecommunications, concerning the construction and operation of railways, as well as those issued on the basis of federal laws which require the approval of the Bundesrat or which are executed by the Laender on behalf of the Federation or as their own concern.

ART. 81—(1) Should, in the case of Article 68, the Bundestag not be dissolved, the Federal President may, on the request of the Federal Government with the approval of the Bundesrat, declare a state of legislative emergency for a bill, if the Bundestag rejects it despite the fact that the Federal Government has declared it to be urgent. The same shall apply if a bill has been rejected despite the fact that the Federal Chancellor had combined with it the motion described in Article 68.

(2) If the Bundestag, after the state of legislative emergency has been declared, again rejects the bill or passes it in a version stated by the Federal Government to be unacceptable, the bill shall be deemed adopted insofar as the Bundesrat approves it. The same shall apply if the bill has not been passed by the Bundestag within four weeks after its resubmission.

(3) During the term of office of a Federal Chancellor, any other bill rejected by the Bundestag may be passed within a period of six months after the initial declaration of a state of legislative emergency in accordance with paragraphs (1) and (2). After expiry of the period, a further declaration of a state of legislative emergency shall be inadmissible during the term of office of the same Federal Chancellor.

(4) The Basic Law may neither be amended nor wholly or partially repealed or suspended by a law enacted in accordance with paragraph (2).

ART. 82—(1) Laws enacted according to the provisions of this Basic Law shall be engrossed by the Federal President with countersignature and published in the Federal Legal Gazette. Orders (*Rechtsverordnungen*) shall be signed by the issuing authority and, unless otherwise regulated by law, published in the Federal Legal Gazette.

(2) Each law and each order (*Rechtsverordnung*) shall specify the date of its coming into force. In the absence of such a provision, they shall come into force on the fourteenth day after the end of the day on which the Federal Legal Gazette has been issued.

VIII

The Execution of Federal Laws and the Federal Administration

ART. 83—The Laender shall execute the federal laws as their own concern insofar as this Basic Law does not otherwise determine or permit.

ART. 84—(1) If the Laender execute the federal laws as their own concern they shall regulate the establishment of the authorities and the administrative procedure insofar as federal laws approved by the Bundesrat do not otherwise determine.

(2) The Federal Government may, with the approval of the Bundesrat, issue general administrative provisions.

(3) The Federal Government shall exercise supervision to ensure that the Laender execute the federal laws in accordance with valid law. For this purpose the Federal Government may send commissioners to the highest Land authorities and, with their approval and, in the case of this approval being refused with the approval of the Bundesrat, also to the subordinate authorities.

(4) Should deficiencies established by the Federal Government in the execution of federal laws in the Laender not be overcome then, on application by the Federal Government or the Land concerned, the Bundesrat shall decide whether the Land has infringed law. Against the decision of the Bundesrat, appeal may be made to the Federal Constitutional Court.

(5) For the execution of federal laws the Federal Government may, by federal legislation which shall require the approval of the Bundesrat, be granted in special cases the power to give individual instructions. They shall, except where the Federal Government considers the case urgent, be directed to the highest Land authorities.

ART. 85—(1) Where the execution of federal laws is delegated to the Laender by the Federation, the establishment of the authorities shall remain a concern of the Laender insofar as Federal legislation approved by the Bundesrat does not determine otherwise.

(2) The Federal Government may issue, with the approval of the Bundesrat, general administrative provisions. It may regulate the uniform training of officials and employees. The heads of the authorities at middle level shall be appointed with its agreement.

(3) The Land authorities shall be subject to the instructions of the highest competent federal authorities. Except where the Federal Government considers it urgent, the instructions shall be directed to the highest Land authorities. Execution of the instructions shall be ensured by the highest Land authority.

(4) Federal supervision shall extend to the legality and suitability of the manner of execution. The Federal Government may for this purpose demand submission of reports and documents and send commissioners to all authorities.

ART. 86—If the Federation executes the laws by direct federal administration or by public law corporations or institutions directly supervised by the Federation, the Federal Government shall, insofar as the law does not prescribe details, issue general administrative provisions. It shall regulate, insofar as it is not otherwise determined by the law, the establishment of the authorities.

ART. 87—(1) The foreign service, the federal finance administration, the federal railways, the federal postal services and, in accordance with the provisions of Article 89, the administration of the federal waterways and shipping, shall be conducted by a direct federal administration with its own lower level administrative offices. Federal frontier protection authorities and central offices for police information and communications, for the compilation of data for purposes concerning the protection of the constitution and for the criminal police may be established by federal legislation.

(2) Public law corporations directly supervised by the Federation shall be those carriers of social insurance whose sphere of competence extends beyond the territory of a Land.

(3) In addition, independent central federal authorities and new public law corporations and institutions directly supervised by the Federation may be established by federal legislation for matters on which the Federation has the power to legislate. Should the Federation acquire new functions in matters for which it has legislative competence, federal authorities at middle and lower levels may in case of urgent need be established with the approval of the Bundesrat and of the majority of the Bundestag.

ART. 88—The Federation shall establish a bank of currency and issue as Federal Bank.

ART. 89—(1) The Federation shall be the owner of the former Reich waterways.

(2) The Federation shall administer the federal waterways through its own authorities. It shall exercise those state functions relating to inland shipping extending beyond the territory of a Land and the functions of ocean-going shipping which are conferred on it by legislation. The Federation may delegate the administration of federal waterways, insofar as they lie within the territory of a Land, to this Land, upon request, to act on its behalf (*Auftragsverwaltung*). Should a waterway touch the territories of several Laender, the Federation may delegate (the administration) to the Land agreed upon by the Laender concerned.

ART. 90—(1) The Federation shall be the owner of the former Reich Autobahnen and Reich highways.

(2) The Laender, or such self-governing corporations under public law as are competent in accordance with Land law, shall administer the federal Autobahnen and other federal highways used for long-distance traffic on behalf of the Federation.

(3) At the request of a Land, the Federation may take over into direct federal administration federal Autobahnen and other federal highways used for long-distance traffic, insofar as they lie within the territory of this Land.

Art. 91—(1) In order to avert an imminent danger to the existence or the free democratic basic order of the Federation or a Land, a Land may call in the police forces of other Laender.

(2) If the Land in which the danger is imminent is not itself prepared or in a position to combat the danger, the Federal Government may place the police in that Land or the police forces of other Laender under its instructions. The order (*Anordnung*) shall be rescinded after the danger has been overcome, otherwise at any time on demand from the Bundesrat.

IX

The Administration of Justice

Art. 92—Judicial authority shall be invested in the judges; it shall be exercised by the Federal Constitutional Court, by the Supreme Federal Court, by the federal courts provided for in this Basic Law and by the courts of the Laender.

Art. 93—(1) The Federal Constitutional Court shall decide:

1. on the interpretation of this Basic Law in the event of disputes concerning the extent of the rights and duties of a high federal organ or of other participants accorded independent rights by this Basic Law or in the Standing Orders (Rules of Procedure) of a high federal organ;

2. in cases of differences of opinion or doubts on the formal and material compatibility of federal law or Land law with this Basic Law, on the compatibility of Land law with some other federal law, on the application of the Federal Government, of a Land Government or of one-third of the members of the Bundestag;

3. in cases of differences of opinion on the rights and duties of the Federation and the Laender, particularly in the execution of federal law by the Laender, and in the exercise of federal supervision;

4. on other public law disputes between the Federation and the Laender, between different Laender or within a Land, insofar as appeal to another court is not provided for;

5. in all other cases provided for in this Basic Law.

(2) Furthermore, the Federal Constitutional Court shall act in cases otherwise assigned to it by federal legislation.

Art. 94—(1) The Federal Constitutional Court shall consist of federal judges and other members. The members of the Federal Constitutional Court shall be elected half by the Bundestag and half by the Bundesrat. They may not belong to the Bundestag, the Bundesrat, the Federal Government or corresponding bodies of a Land.

(2) A federal law shall regulate its legal constitution and procedure and determine in which cases its decisions shall have the force of law.

Art. 95—(1) To preserve the unity of federal law, a Supreme Federal Court shall be established.

(2) The Supreme Federal Court shall decide in cases where the decision is of fundamental importance for the uniformity of the administration of justice of the higher federal courts.

(3) The appointment of the judges of the Supreme Federal Court shall be decided jointly by the Federal Minister of Justice and a committee for the election of judges consisting of the Land Ministers of Justice and an equal number of members elected by the Bundestag.

(4) Otherwise the constitution of the Supreme Federal Court and its procedure shall be regulated by federal legislation.

Art. 96—(1) Higher federal courts shall be established for the spheres of ordinary, administrative, finance, labour and social jurisdiction.

(2) Article 95, paragraph (3), shall apply to the judges of the higher federal courts with the proviso that the place of the Federal Minister of Justice and the Land Ministers of Justice be taken by the Ministers competent for the particular matter. Their conditions of service must be regulated by a special federal law.

(3) The Federation may establish federal disciplinary courts for disciplinary proceedings against federal officials and federal judges.

Art. 97—(1) Judges shall be independent and subject only to the law.

*   *   *

Art. 99—By Land legislation the decision on constitutional disputes within a Land may be assigned to the Federal Constitutional Court, and the decision of final instance on matters involving the application of Land law to the higher federal courts.

Art. 100—(1) If a court considers unconstitutional a law the validity of which is pertinent to its decision, proceedings must be stayed and, if a violation of a Land Constitution is involved, the decision of the Land court competent for constitutional disputes shall be obtained and, if a violation of this Basic Law is involved, the decision of the Federal Constitutional Court shall be obtained. This shall also apply if the violation of this Basic Law by Land law or the incompatibility of a Land law with a federal law is involved.

(2) If in litigation it is doubtful whether a rule of international law forms part of federal law and whether it creates direct rights and duties for the individual (Article 25), the court shall obtain the decision of the Federal Constitutional Court.

(3) If the court of a Land, in interpreting the Basic Law, intends to deviate from a decision of the Federal Constitutional Court or the constitutional court of another Land, the said constitutional court must obtain the decision of the Federal Constitutional Court. If, in interpreting other federal law, it intends to deviate from the decision of the Supreme Federal Court or a higher federal court, it must obtain the decision of the Supreme Federal Court.

Art. 101—(1) Extraordinary courts shall be inadmissible. No one may be prevented from appearing before his lawful judge.

(2) Courts for special matters may be established only by law.

Art. 102—The death sentence shall be abolished.

Art. 103—(1) Everyone brought before a court shall have a claim to proper legal hearing.

(2) An act may be punished only if it was punishable by law before the act was committed.

(3) No one may be punished more than once on account of the same act in pursuance of the general criminal laws.

Art. 104—(1) The freedom of the individual may be restricted only on the basis of a formal law and only with the due regard to the forms prescribed therein. Detained persons may be subject neither to physical nor mental ill-treatment.

(2) Only the judge shall decide on the admissibility and continued duration of a deprivation of liberty. If such a deprivation is not based on the order of a judge, a court decision must be obtained without delay. The police may, on its own authority, hold no one in custody beyond the end of the day following the arrest. Details shall be regulated by legislation.

(3) Any person temporarily detained on suspicion of having committed a punishable act must, at the latest on the day following the arrest, be brought before a judge who shall inform him of the reasons for the arrest, interrogate him and give him an opportunity to

raise objections. Without delay, the judge must either issue a warrant of arrest, setting out the reasons therefor, or order his release.

(4) A relative of the person detained or a person enjoying his confidence must be notified forthwith of any judicial decision in respect of the ordering or the continued duration of a deprivation of liberty.

X

FINANCE

ART. 105—(1) The Federation shall have exclusive legislation on customs and financial monopolies.

(2) The Federation shall have concurrent legislation on:
1. excise taxes and taxes on transactions, with the exception of taxes with localized application, in particular the taxes on real estate acquisition, incremental value and on fire protection,
2. the taxes on income, property, inheritance and donations,
3. "Realsteuern" (taxes on real estate and on businesses) with the exception of the fixing of tax rates

if it makes a claim on the taxes in their entirety or in part to cover federal expenditures or if the conditions of Article 72, paragraph (2), apply.

(3) Federal legislation on taxes the yield of which accrues in entirety or in part to the Laender or the Gemeinden (Gemeindeverbände) shall require the approval of the Bundesrat.

ART. 106—(1) Customs, the yield of monopolies, the excise taxes with the exception of the beer tax, the transportation tax, the turnover tax and property dues serving non-recurrent purposes shall accrue to the Federation.

(2) The beer tax, the taxes on transactions with the exception of the transportation tax and turnover tax, the income and corporation taxes, the property tax, the inheritance tax, the "Realsteuern" and the taxes with localized application shall accrue to the Laender and, in accordance with Land legislation, to the Gemeinden (Gemeindeverbände).

(3) The Federation may, by means of a federal law which shall require the approval of the Bundesrat, make a claim to a part of the income and corporation taxes to cover its expenditures not covered by other revenues, in particular to cover grants which are to be made to Laender to meet expenditures in the fields of education, public health and welfare.

(4) In order to ensure the working efficiency also of the Laender with low revenues and to equalize the differing burden of expenditure of the Laender, the Federation may make grants and take the funds necessary for this purpose from specific taxes of those accruing to the Laender. A federal law, which shall require the approval of the Bundesrat, shall determine which taxes shall be utilized for this purpose and in what amounts and on what basis the grants shall be distributed among the Laender entitled to equalization; the grants must be handed directly to the Laender.

ART. 107—The final distribution of the taxes subject to concurrent legislation between the Federation and the Laender shall be effected not later than 31 December 1952 and by means of a federal law which shall require the approval of the Bundesrat. This shall not apply to the "Realsteuern" and the taxes with localized application. In this, both Federation and Laender shall be given a legal claim to certain taxes or shares in taxes corresponding to their functions.

ART. 108—(1) Customs, financial monopolies, the excise taxes subject to concurrent legislation, the transportation tax, the turnover tax and the non-recurrent property dues shall be administered by federal finance authorities. The structure of these authorities and the procedure to be applied by them shall be regulated by federal legislation. The heads of the authorities at middle level shall be appointed by agreement with the Land Governments. The Federation may delegate the administration of the non-recurrent property dues to the Land finance authorities to act on behalf of the Federation (*Auftragsverwaltung*).

(2) Insofar as the Federation makes a claim to a part of the income and corporation taxes it shall have the right to administer them. It may, however, delegate the administration to the Land finance authorities to act on behalf of the Federation.

(3) The remaining taxes shall be administered by Land finance authorities. The Federation may, by means of federal legislation which shall require the approval of the Bundesrat, regulate the structure of these authorities, the procedure to be applied by them and the uniform training of the officials. The heads of the authorities at middle level must be appointed by agreement with the Federal Government. The administration of the taxes accruing to the Gemeinden (Gemeindeverbände) may be transferred by the Laender in entirety or in part to the Gemeinden (Gemeindeverbände).

(4) Insofar as the taxes accrue to the Federation, the Land finance authorities shall act on behalf of the Federation. The Laender shall be liable with their revenues for a regular administration of these taxes; the Federal Minister of Finance may supervise the regular administration through federal plenipotentiaries who shall have the right to give instructions to the authorities at middle and lower level.

(5) Finance jurisdiction shall be uniformly regulated by federal legislation.

(6) The general administrative provisions shall be issued by the Federal Government and, insofar as the administration is incumbent upon the Land finance authorities, with the approval of the Bundesrat.

Art. 109—The Federation and the Laender shall be self-supporting and independent of each other in their budget economy.

*   *   *

Art. 113—Decisions of the Bundestag and Bundesrat which increase the budget expenditure proposed by the Federal Government or include, or imply for the future, new expenditure, shall require the approval of the Federal Government.

Art. 114—The Federal Minister of Finance must present to the Bundestag and the Bundesrat an annual statement of all revenues and expenditures as well as of assets and liabilities. The audit thereof shall be carried out by an Audit Office (*Rechnungshof*) the members of which shall possess judicial independence. In order to secure a discharge for the Federal Government, the general statement of account and a survey of the assets and liabilities shall be submitted to the Bundestag and the Bundesrat in the course of the next fiscal year, together with the observations of the Audit Office. The auditing of accounts shall be regulated by a federal law.

*   *   *

XI

Transitional and Concluding Provisions

Art. 116—(1) Unless otherwise regulated by law, a German within the meaning of this Basic Law is a person who possesses German nationality, or who has been accepted in the territory of the German Reich as of 31 December 1937 as a refugee or expellee of German stock or as the spouse or descendant of such person.

(2) Former German nationals who between 30 January 1933 and 8 May 1945 were

deprived of their nationality for political, racial or religious reasons, and their descendants, shall be regranted citizenship on application. They shall not be considered to have lost citizenship insofar as they took up residence in Germany after 8 May 1945 and have not expressed a wish to the contrary.

ART. 117—(1) Law which conflicts with Article 3, paragraph (2), shall remain in force until it is adjusted to this provision of the Basic Law, but not beyond 31 March 1953.

(2) Laws which restrict the right of freedom of movement in consideration of the present housing shortage shall remain in force until repealed by federal legislation.

ART. 118—The reorganization of the territory comprising the Laender Baden, Wuerttemberg-Baden and Wuerttemberg-Hohenzollern may be accomplished, by agreement between the Laender concerned, in a manner deviating from the provisions of Article 29. Should an agreement not be reached, the reorganization shall be regulated by federal legislation which must provide for a referendum.

* * *

ART. 121—The majority of the members of the Bundestag and of the Federal Convention within the meaning of this Basic Law shall be the majority of their statutory number of members.

ART. 137—(1) The eligibility for election of officials (*Beamte*), employees (*Angestellte*) of the public service and judges of the Federation, of the Laender and the Gemeinden may be restricted by legislation.

(2) For the election of the first Bundestag, of the first Federal Convention and of the first Federal President of the Federal Republic of Germany the Electoral Law to be adopted by the Parliamentary Council shall apply.

(3) The functions of the Federal Constitutional Court pursuant to Article 41, paragraph (2), shall be exercised, pending its establishment, by the German High Court for the Combined Economic Area which shall decide in accordance with its Standing Orders (Rules of Procedure).

* * *

ART. 139—The legal provisions enacted for the liberation of the German people from national socialism and militarism shall not be affected by the provisions of this Basic Law.

ART. 140—The provisions of Articles 136, 137, 139 and 141 of the German Constitution of 11 August 1919 shall be an integral part of this Basic Law.

ART. 141—Article 7, paragraph (3), first sentence, shall not apply in a Land in which on 1 January 1949 another legal Land regulation existed.

ART. 142—Without prejudice to Article 31, provisions of the Land Constitutions shall also remain in force, insofar as they conform to Articles 1 to 18.

ART. 143—(1) Whoever by force or the threat of force changes the constitutional order of the Federation or of a Land, deprives the Federal President of the powers accorded to him by this Basic Law or who by force or the threat of danger compels him to exercise his powers in a specific manner or not at all, or prevents the exercise of his powers, or deprives the Federation or a Land of a territory belonging to them shall be condemned to penal servitude for life or not less than 10 years.

(2) Whoever publicly incites to an action within the meaning of paragraph (1), or plots or otherwise arranges such an action in connivance with another person, shall be condemned to penal servitude up to 10 years.

(3) In less serious cases, a sentence of not less than two years' penal servitude in the cases provided for in paragraph (1), and of not less than one year's imprisonment in the cases provided for in paragraph (2), may be imposed.

(4) Whoever of his own free will gives up his activity or, in case of participation of

several persons, prevents a conspiracy, may not be punished in accordance with the provisions of paragraphs (1) to (3).

(5) Insofar as the action is directed exclusively against the constitutional order of a Land, the highest court of the Land shall, in the absence of any other regulation in Land law, be competent to pass judgment. Otherwise the superior court (*Oberlandesgericht*), in the district of which the first Federal Government chooses its seat, shall be competent.

(6) The aforementioned provisions shall be valid pending another regulation by federal law.

ART. 144—(1) This Basic Law shall require acceptance by the popular representative bodies in two-thirds of the German Laender in which it shall initially be valid.

(2) Insofar as restrictions are imposed on the application of the Basic Law to one of the Laender enumerated in Article 23, paragraph (1), or to a part of one of these Laender, that Land or a part of that Land shall have the right, in accordance with Article 38, to send representatives to the Bundestag and, in accordance with Article 50, to the Bundesrat.

ART. 145—(1) The Parliamentary Council with the participation of the representatives of Greater Berlin shall in a public meeting confirm the adoption of this Basic Law, engross it and promulgate it.

(2) This Basic Law shall come into force at the end of the day of its promulgation.

(3) It shall be published in the Federal Legal Gazette.

ART. 146—This Basic Law shall become invalid on the day when a constitution adopted in a free decision by the German people comes into force.

Appendix C

THE CONSTITUTION OF THE U.S.S.R.
AS AMENDED
1936

CHAPTER I

THE SOCIAL STRUCTURE

ART. 1—The Union of Soviet Socialist Republics is a socialist state of workers and peasants.

ART. 2—The political foundation of the USSR is the Soviets of Working People's Deputies, which grew and became strong as a result of the overthrow of the power of the landlords and capitalists and the conquest of the dictatorship of the proletariat.

ART. 3—All power in the USSR belongs to the working people of town and country as represented by the Soviets of Working People's Deputies.

ART. 4—The economic foundation of the USSR is the socialist system of economy and the socialist ownership of the instruments and means of production, firmly established as a result of the liquidation of the capitalist system of economy, the abolition of private ownership of the instruments and means of production, and the elimination of the exploitation of man by man.

ART. 5—Socialist property in the USSR exists either in the form of state property (belonging to the whole people) or in the form of cooperative and collective farm property (property of collective farms, property of cooperative societies).

ART. 6—The land, its mineral wealth, waters, forests, mills, factories, mines, rail, water and air transport, banks, communications, large state-organized and agricultural enterprises (state farms, machine and tractor stations and the like), as well as municipal enterprises and the bulk of the dwelling houses in the cities and industrial localities, are state property, that is, belong to the whole people.

ART. 7—The common enterprises of collective farms, and cooperative organizations, with their livestock and implements, the products of the collective farms and cooperative organizations, as well as their common buildings, constitute the common, socialist property of the collective farms and cooperative organizations.

Every household in a collective farm, in addition to its basic income from the common collective farm enterprise, has for its personal use a small plot of household land and, as its personal property, a subsidiary husbandry on the plot, a dwelling house, livestock, poultry and minor agricultural implements—in accordance with the rules of the agricultural artel.

ART. 8—The land occupied by collective farms is secured to them for their use free of charge and for an unlimited time, that is, in perpetuity.

ART. 9—Alongside the socialist system of economy, which is the predominant form of economy in the USSR, the law permits the small private economy of individual peasants and handicraftsmen based on their own labor and precluding the exploitation of the labor of others.

ART. 10—The personal property right of citizens in their incomes and savings from work, in their dwelling houses and subsidiary home enterprises, in articles of domestic economy and use and articles of personal use and convenience, as well as the right of citizens to inherit personal property, is protected by law.

ART. 11—The economic life of the USSR is determined and directed by the state national economic plan, with the aim of increasing the public wealth, of steadily raising the material and cultural standards of the working people, of consolidating the independence of the USSR and strengthening its defensive capacity.

ART. 12—Work in the USSR is a duty and a matter of honor for every able-bodied citizen, in accordance with the principle: "He who does not work, neither shall he eat."

The principle applied in the USSR is that of socialism: "From each according to his ability, to each according to his work."

CHAPTER II

THE STATE STRUCTURE

ART. 13—The Union of Soviet Socialist Republics is a federal state, formed on the basis of a voluntary union of equal Soviet Socialist Republics, namely:

The Russian Soviet Federative Socialist Republic
The Ukrainian Soviet Socialist Republic
The Byelorussian Soviet Socialist Republic
The Uzbek Soviet Socialist Republic
The Kazakh Soviet Socialist Republic
The Georgian Soviet Socialist Republic
The Azerbaijan Soviet Socialist Republic
The Lithuanian Soviet Socialist Republic
The Moldavian Soviet Socialist Republic
The Latvian Soviet Socialist Republic
The Kirghiz Soviet Socialist Republic
The Tajik Soviet Socialist Republic
The Armenian Soviet Socialist Republic
The Turkmen Soviet Socialist Republic
The Estonian Soviet Socialist Republic
The Karelo-Finnish Soviet Socialist Republic.

ART. 14—The jurisdiction of the Union of Soviet Socialist Republics, as represented by its higher organs of state power and organs of state administration, embraces:

(a) Representation of the USSR in international relations, conclusion, ratification and denunciation of treaties of the USSR with other states, establishment of general procedure governing the relations of Union Republics with foreign states;

(b) Questions of war and peace;

(c) Admission of new republics into the USSR;

(d) Control over the observance of the Constitution of the USSR, and ensuring conformity of the Constitutions of the Union Republics with the Constitution of the USSR;

(e) Confirmation of alterations of boundaries between Union Republics;

(f) Confirmation of the formation of new Territories and Regions and also of new Autonomous Republics and Autonomous Regions within Union Republics;

(g) Organization of the defense of the USSR, direction of all the Armed Forces of the USSR, determination of directing principles governing the organization of the military formations of the Union Republics;

(h) Foreign trade on the basis of state monopoly;

(i) Safeguarding the security of the state;

(j) Determination of the national economic plans of the USSR;

(k) Approval of the consolidated state budget of the USSR and of the report on its fulfillment; determination of the taxes and revenues which go to the Union, the Republican and the local budgets;

(l) Administration of the banks, industrial and agricultural institutions and enterprises and trading enterprises of All-Union importance;

(m) Administration of transport and communications;

(n) Direction of the monetary and credit system;

(o) Organization of state insurance;

(p) Contracting and granting of loans;

(q) Determination of the basic principles of land tenure and of the use of mineral wealth, forest and waters;

(r) Determination of the basic principles in the spheres of education and public health;

(s) Organization of a uniform system of national economic statistics;

(t) Determination of the principles of labor organization;

(u) Legislation concerning the judicial system and judicial procedure; criminal and civil codes;

(v) Legislation concerning Union citizenship; legislation concerning rights of foreigners;

(w) Determination of the principles of legislation concerning marriage and the family;

(x) Issuing of all-Union acts of amnesty.

ART. 15—The sovereignty of the Union Republics is limited only in the spheres defined in Article 14 of the Constitution of the USSR. Outside of these spheres each Union Republic exercises state authority independently. The USSR protects the sovereign rights of the Union Republics.

ART. 16—Each Union Republic has its own Constitution, which takes account of the specific features of the Republic and is drawn up in full conformity with the Constitution of the USSR.

ART. 17—The right freely to secede from the USSR is reserved to every Union Republic.

ART. 18—The territory of a Union Republic may not be altered without its consent.

ART. 18a—Each Union Republic has the right to enter into direct relations with foreign states and to conclude agreements and exchange diplomatic and consular representatives with them.

ART. 18b—Each Union Republic has its own Republican military formations.

ART. 19—The laws of the USSR have the same force within the territory of every Union Republic.

ART. 20—In the event of divergence between a law of a Union Republic and a law of the Union, the Union law prevails.

ART. 21—Uniform citizenship is established for citizens of the USSR. Every citizen of a Union Republic is a citizen of the USSR.

ART. 22—The Russian Soviet Federative Socialist Republic consists of the Altai, Krasnodar, Krasnoyarsk, Primorye, Stavropol and Khabarovsk Territories;

The Archangelsk, Astrakhan, Bryansk, Velikiye-Luki, Vladimir, Vologda, Voronesh, Gorky, Grozny, Ivanovo, Irkutsk, Kaliningrad, Kaluga, Kemerovo, Kirov, Kostroma, Crimea, Kuibyshev, Kurgan, Kursk, Leningrad, Molotov, Moscow, Murmansk, Novgorod, Novosibirsk, Omsk, Orel, Penza, Pskov, Rostov, Ryazan, Saratov, Sakhalin, Sverdlovsk, Smolensk, Stalingrad, Tambov, Tomsk, Tula, Tyumen, Ulyanovsk, Chelyabinsk, Chita, Chkalov and Yaroslavl Regions;

The Tatar, Bashkir, Daghestan, Buryat-Mongolian, Kabardinian, Komi, Mari, Mordovian, North Ossetian, Udmurt, Chuvash and Yakut Autonomous Soviet Socialist Republics;

And the Adygei, Jewish, Oirot, Tuva, Khakass and Cherkess Autonomous Regions.

Art. 23—The Ukrainian Soviet Socialist Republic consists of the Vinnitsa, Volhynia, Voroshilovgrad, Dniepropetrovsk, Drohobych, Zhitomir, Transcarpathian, Zaporozhye, Ismail, Kamenets-Podolsk, Kiev, Kirovograd, Lvov, Nikolayev, Odessa, Poltava, Rovno, Stalino, Stanislav, Sumi, Ternopol, Kharkov, Kherson, Chernigov and Chernovtsi Regions.

Art. 24—The Azerbaijan Soviet Socialist Republic includes the Nakhichevan Autonomous Soviet Socialist Republic and the Nagorno-Karabakh Autonomous Region.

Art. 25—The Georgian Soviet Socialist Republic includes the Abkhazian Autonomous Soviet Socialist Republic, the Adjar Autonomous Soviet Socialist Republic and the South Ossetian Autonomous Region.

Art. 26—The Uzbek Soviet Socialist Republic consists of the Andizhan, Bukhara, Kashka-Darya, Namangan, Samarkand, Surkhan-Darya, Tashkent, Ferghana and Khorezm Regions and the Kara-Kalpak Autonomous Soviet Socialist Republic.

Art. 27—The Tajik Soviet Socialist Republic consists of the Garm, Kulyab, Leninabad and Stalinabad Regions and the Gorno-Badakhshan Autonomous Region.

Art. 28—The Kazakh Soviet Socialist Republic consists of the Akmolinsk, Aktyubinsk, Alma-Ata, East Kazakhstan, Guriev, Jambul, West Kazakhstan, Karaganda, Kzyl-Orda, Kokchetav, Kustanai, Pavlodar, North Kazakhstan, Semipalatinsk, Taldy-Kurgan and South Kazakhstan Regions.

Art. 29—The Byelorussian Soviet Socialist Republic consists of the Baranovichi, Bobruisk, Brest, Vitebsk, Gomel, Grodno, Minsk, Moghilev, Molodechno, Pinsk, Polessye and Polotsk Regions.

Art. 29a—The Turkmen Soviet Socialist Republic consists of the Ashkhabad, Mari, Tashauz and Chardzhou Regions.

Art. 29b—The Kirghiz Soviet Socialist Republic consists of the Dzhalal-Abad, Issyk-Kul, Osh, Talas, Tien-Shan and Frunze Regions.

Chapter III

The Higher Organs of State Power in the Union of Soviet Socialist Republics

Art. 30—The highest organ of state power in the USSR is the Supreme Soviet of the USSR.

Art. 31—The Supreme Soviet of the USSR exercises all rights vested in the Union of Soviet Socialist Republics in accordance with Article 14 of the Constitution, in so far as they do not, by virtue of the Constitution, come within the jurisdiction of organs of the USSR that are accountable to the Supreme Soviet of the USSR, that is, the Presidium of the Supreme Soviet of the USSR, the Council of Ministers of the USSR, and the Ministries of the USSR.

Art. 32—The legislative power of the USSR is exercised exclusively by the Supreme Soviet of the USSR.

Art. 33—The Supreme Soviet of the USSR consists of two Chambers: the Soviet of the Union and the Soviet of Nationalities.

Art. 34—The Soviet of the Union is elected by the citizens of the USSR voting by election districts on the basis of one deputy for every 300,000 of the population.

Art. 35—The Soviet of Nationalities is elected by the citizens of the USSR voting by Union Republics, Autonomous Republics, Autonomous Regions, and National Areas on the basis of twenty-five deputies from each Union Republic, eleven deputies from each Autonomous Republic, five deputies from each Autonomous Region and one deputy from each National Area.

ART. 36—The Supreme Soviet of the USSR is elected for a term of four years.

ART. 37—The two Chambers of the Supreme Soviet of the USSR, the Soviet of the Union and the Soviet of Nationalities, have equal rights.

ART. 38—The Soviet of the Union and the Soviet of Nationalities have equal powers to initiate legislation.

ART. 39—A law is considered adopted if passed by both Chambers of the Supreme Soviet of the USSR by a simple majority vote in each.

ART. 40—Laws passed by the Supreme Soviet of the USSR are published in the languages of the Union Republics over the signatures of the President and Secretary of the Presidium of the Supreme Soviet of the USSR.

ART. 41—Sessions of the Soviet of the Union and of the Soviet of Nationalities begin and terminate simultaneously.

ART. 42—The Soviet of the Union elects a Chairman of the Soviet of the Union and two Vice-Chairmen.

ART. 43—The Soviet of Nationalities elects a Chairman of the Soviet of Nationalities and two Vice-Chairmen.

ART. 44—The Chairmen of the Soviet of the Union and the Soviet of Nationalities preside at the sittings of the respective Chambers and have charge of the conduct of their business and proceedings.

ART. 45—Joint sittings of the two Chambers of the Supreme Soviet of the USSR are presided over alternately by the Chairman of the Soviet of the Union and the Chairman of the Soviet of Nationalities.

ART. 46—Sessions of the Supreme Soviet of the USSR are convened by the Presidium of the Supreme Soviet of the USSR twice a year.

Extraordinary sessions are convened by the Presidium of the Supreme Soviet of the USSR at its discretion or on the demand of one of the Union Republics.

ART. 47—In the event of disagreement between the Soviet of the Union and the Soviet of Nationalities the question is referred for settlement to a conciliation commission formed on a parity basis. If the conciliation commission fails to arrive at an agreement, or if its decision fails to satisfy one of the Chambers, the question is considered for a second time by the Chambers. Failing agreement between the two Chambers, the Presidium of the Supreme Soviet of the USSR dissolves the Supreme Soviet of the USSR and orders new elections.

ART. 48—The Supreme Soviet of the USSR at a joint sitting of the two Chambers elects the Presidium of the Supreme Soviet of the USSR, consisting of a President of the Presidium of the Supreme Soviet of the USSR, sixteen Vice-Presidents, a Secretary of the Presidium and fifteen members of the Presidium of the Supreme Soviet of the USSR.

The Presidium of the Supreme Soviet of the USSR is accountable to the Supreme Soviet of the USSR for all its activities.

ART. 49—The Presidium of the Supreme Soviet of the USSR:

(a) Convenes the sessions of the Supreme Soviet of the USSR;

(b) Issues decrees;

(c) Gives interpretations of the laws of the USSR in operation;

(d) Dissolves the Supreme Soviet of the USSR in conformity with Article 47 of the Constitution of the USSR and orders new elections;

(e) Conducts nation-wide polls (referendums) on its own initiative or on the demand of one of the Union Republics;

(f) Annuls decisions and orders of the Council of Ministers of the USSR and of the Councils of Ministers of the Union Republics if they do not conform to law;

(g) In the intervals between sessions of the Supreme Soviet of the USSR, releases and appoints Ministers of the USSR on the recommendation of the Chairman of the Council of Ministers of the USSR, subject to subsequent confirmation by the Supreme Soviet of the USSR;

(h) Institutes decorations (orders and medals) and titles of honor of the USSR;

(i) Awards orders and medals and confers titles of honor of the USSR;

(j) Exercises the right of pardon;

(k) Institutes military titles, diplomatic ranks and other special titles;

(l) Appoints and removes the high command of the Armed Forces of the USSR;

(m) In the intervals between sessions of the Supreme Soviet of the USSR, proclaims a state of war in the event of military attack on the USSR, or when necessary to fulfill international treaty obligations concerning mutual defense against aggression;

(n) Orders general or partial mobilization;

(o) Ratifies and denounces international treaties of the USSR;

(p) Appoints and recalls plenipotentiary representatives of the USSR to foreign states;

(q) Receives the letters of credence and recall of diplomatic representatives accredited to it by foreign states;

(r) Proclaims martial law in separate localities or throughout the USSR in the interests of the defense of the USSR or of the maintenance of public order and the security of the state.

ART. 50—The Soviet of the Union and the Soviet of Nationalities elect Credential Committees to verify the credentials of the members of the respective Chambers.

On the report of the Credential Committees, the Chambers decide whether to recognize the credentials of deputies or to annul their election.

ART. 51—The Supreme Soviet of the USSR, when it deems necessary, appoints commissions of investigation and audit on any matter.

It is the duty of all institutions and officials to comply with the demands of such commissions and to submit to them all necessary materials and documents.

ART. 52—A member of the Supreme Soviet of the USSR may not be prosecuted or arrested without the consent of the Supreme Soviet of the USSR, or, when the Supreme Soviet of the USSR is not in session, without the consent of the Presidium of the Supreme Soviet of the USSR.

ART. 53—On the expiration of the term of office of the Supreme Soviet of the USSR, or on its dissolution prior to the expiration of its term of office, the Presidium of the Supreme Soviet of the USSR retains its powers until the newly-elected Supreme Soviet of the USSR shall have formed a new Presidium of the Supreme Soviet of the USSR.

ART. 54—On the expiration of the term of office of the Supreme Soviet of the USSR, or in event of its dissolution prior to the expiration of its term of office, the Presidium of the Supreme Soviet of the USSR orders new elections to be held within a period not exceeding two months from the date of expiration of the term of office or dissolution of the Supreme Soviet of the USSR.

ART. 55—The newly-elected Supreme Soviet of the USSR is convened by the outgoing Presidium of the Supreme Soviet of the USSR not later than three months after the elections.

ART. 56—The Supreme Soviet of the USSR, at a joint sitting of the two Chambers, appoints the Government of the USSR, namely, the Council of Ministers of the USSR.

CHAPTER IV

THE HIGHER ORGANS OF STATE POWER IN THE UNION REPUBLICS

ART. 57—The highest organ of state power in a Union Republic is the Supreme Soviet of the Union Republic.

ART. 58—The Supreme Soviet of a Union Republic is elected by the citizens of the Republic for a term of four years.

The basis of representation is established by the Constitution of the Union Republic.

ART. 59—The Supreme Soviet of a Union Republic is the sole legislative organ of the Republic.

ART. 60—The Supreme Soviet of a Union Republic:

(a) Adopts the Constitution of the Republic and amends it in conformity with Article 16 of the Constitution of the USSR;

(b) Confirms the Constitutions of the Autonomous Republics forming part of it and defines the boundaries of their territories;

(c) Approves the national economic plan and the budget of the Republic;

(d) Exercises the right of amnesty and pardon of citizens sentenced by the judicial organs of the Union Republic;

(e) Decides questions of representation of the Union Republic in its international relations;

(f) Determines the manner of organizing the Republic's military formations.

ART. 61—The Supreme Soviet of a Union Republic elects the Presidium of the Supreme Soviet of a Union Republic, consisting of a President of the Presidium of the Supreme Soviet of the Union Republic, Vice-Presidents, a Secretary of the Presidium and members of the Presidium of the Supreme Soviet of the Union Republic.

The powers of the Presidium of the Supreme Soviet of a Union Republic are defined by the Constitution of the Union Republic.

ART. 62—The Supreme Soviet of a Union Republic elects a Chairman and Vice-Chairmen to conduct its sittings.

ART. 63—The Supreme Soviet of a Union Republic appoints the Government of the Union Republic, namely, the Council of Ministers of the Union Republic.

CHAPTER V

THE ORGANS OF STATE ADMINISTRATION OF THE UNION OF
SOVIET SOCIALIST REPUBLICS

ART. 64—The highest executive and administrative organ of the state power of the Union of Soviet Socialist Republics is the Council of Ministers of the USSR.

ART. 65—The Council of Ministers of the USSR is responsible and accountable to the Supreme Soviet of the USSR, or, in the intervals between sessions of the Supreme Soviet, to the Presidium of the Supreme Soviet of the USSR.

ART. 66—The Council of Ministers of the USSR issues decisions and orders on the basis and in pursuance of the laws in operation, and verifies their execution.

ART. 67—Decisions and orders of the Council of Ministers of the USSR are binding throughout the territory of the USSR.

ART. 68—The Council of Ministers of the USSR:

(a) Coordinates and directs the work of the All-Union and Union-Republican Ministries of the USSR and of other institutions under its jurisdiction;

(b) Adopts measures to carry out the national economic plan and the state budget, and to strengthen the credit and monetary system;

(c) Adopts measures for the maintenance of public order, for the protection of the interests of the state, and for the safeguarding of the rights of the citizens;

(d) Exercises general guidance in the sphere of relations with foreign states;

(e) Fixes the annual contingent of citizens to be called up for military service and directs the general organization of the Armed Forces of the country;

(f) Sets up, whenever necessary, special Committees and Central Administrations under the Council of Ministers of the USSR for economic and cultural affairs and defense.

ART. 69—The Council of Ministers of the USSR has the right, in respect to those branches of administration and economy which come within the jurisdiction of the USSR, to suspend decisions and orders of the Councils of Ministers of the Union Republics and to annul orders and instructions of Ministers of the USSR.

ART. 70—The Council of Ministers of the USSR is appointed by the Supreme Soviet of the USSR and consists of:

The Chairman of the Council of Ministers of the USSR;
The Vice-Chairmen of the Council of Ministers of the USSR;
The Chairman of the State Planning Commission of the USSR;
The Ministers of the USSR;
The Chairman of the Arts Committee.

ART. 71—The Government of the USSR or a Minister of the USSR to whom a question of a member of the Supreme Soviet of the USSR is addressed must give a verbal or written reply in the respective Chamber within a period not exceeding three days.

ART. 72—The Ministers of the USSR direct the branches of state administration which come within the jurisdiction of the USSR.

ART. 73—The Ministers of the USSR, within the limits of the jurisdiction of their respective Ministries, issue orders and instructions on the basis and in pursuance of the laws in operation, and also of decisions and orders of the Council of Ministers of the USSR, and verify their execution.

ART. 74—The Ministries of the USSR are either All-Union or Union-Republican Ministries.

ART. 75—Each All-Union Ministry directs the branch of state administration entrusted to it throughout the territory of the USSR either directly or through bodies appointed by it.

ART. 76—The Union-Republican Ministries, as a rule, direct the branches of state administration entrusted to them through corresponding Ministries of the Union Republics; they administer directly only a definite and limited number of enterprises according to a list confirmed by the Presidium of the Supreme Soviet of the USSR.

ART. 77—The following Ministries are All-Union Ministries:

The Ministry of the Aircraft Industry
The Ministry of the Automobile and Tractor Industry
The Ministry of Foreign Trade
The Ministry of Armaments
The Ministry of Geology [Geological Survey]
The Ministry of State Food and Material Reserves
The Ministry of Procurements [Stocks, State Supplies]
The Ministry of Machine Building and Instrument Construction
The Ministry of the Iron and Steel Industry
The Ministry of the Merchant Marine
The Ministry of the Oil Industry
The Ministry of the Communications Equipment Industry
The Ministry of Railroads
The Ministry of the River Fleet [Inland Water Transport]
The Ministry of Communications
The Ministry of Agricultural Machine Building
The Ministry of Construction and Road Machine Building
The Ministry of Machine-Building Enterprise Construction

The Ministry of the Shipbuilding Industry
The Ministry of Transport Machine Building
The Ministry of Labor Reserves
The Ministry of Heavy Machine Building
The Ministry of the Coal Industry
The Ministry of the Chemical Industry
The Ministry of the Electric Equipment Industry
The Ministry of Electric Power Plants.

ART. 78—The following Ministries are Union-Republican Ministries:
The Ministry of Internal Affairs
The Ministry of the Armed Forces
The Ministry of Higher Education
The Ministry of State [Soviet] Control
The Ministry of State Security
The Ministry of Public Health
The Ministry of Foreign Affairs
The Ministry of Cinematography
The Ministry of Light Industry
The Ministry of Forest Economy
The Ministry of the Lumber and Paper Industry
The Ministry of the Meat and Dairy Industry
The Ministry of the Food Industry
The Ministry of the Buildings Material Industry
The Ministry of the Fishing Industry
The Ministry of Agriculture
The Ministry of State Farms
The Ministry of Trade
The Ministry of Finance
The Ministry of Justice.

CHAPTER VI

THE ORGANS OF STATE ADMINISTRATION OF THE UNION REPUBLICS

ART. 79—The highest executive and administrative organ of the state power of a Union Republic is the Council of Ministers of the Union Republic.

ART. 80—The Council of Ministers of a Union Republic is responsible and accountable to the Supreme Soviet of the Union Republic, or, in the intervals between sessions of the Supreme Soviet of the Union Republic, to the Presidium of the Supreme Soviet of the Union Republic.

ART. 81—The Council of Ministers of a Union Republic issues decisions and orders on the basis and in pursuance of the laws in operation of the USSR and of the Union Republic, and of the decisions and orders of the Council of Ministers of the USSR, and verifies their execution.

ART. 82—The Council of Ministers of a Union Republic has the right to suspend decisions and orders of the Councils of Ministers of its Autonomous Republics, and to annul decisions and orders of the Executive Committees of the Soviets of Working People's Deputies of its Territories, Regions and Autonomous Regions.

ART. 83—The Council of Ministers of a Union Republic is appointed by the Supreme Soviet of the Union Republic and consists of:

The Chairman of the Council of Ministers of the Union Republic;

The Vice-Chairmen of the Council of Ministers;

The Chairman of the State Planning Commission;

The Ministers;

The Chief of the Arts Administration;

The Chairman of the Committee for Cultural and Educational Institutions.

ART. 84—The Ministers of a Union Republic direct the branches of state administration which come within the jurisdiction of the Union Republic.

ART. 85—The Ministers of a Union Republic, within the limits of the jurisdiction of their respective Ministries, issue orders and instructions on the basis and in pursuance of the laws of the USSR and of the Union Republic, or the decisions and orders of the Council of Ministers of the USSR and the Council of Ministers of the Union Republic, and of the orders and instructions of the Union-Republican Ministries of the USSR.

ART. 86—The Ministries of a Union Republic are either Union-Republican or Republican Ministries.

ART. 87—Each Union-Republican Ministry directs the branch of state administration entrusted to it, and is subordinate both to the Council of Ministers of the Union Republic and to the corresponding Union-Republican Ministry of the USSR.

ART. 88—Each Republican Ministry directs the branch of state administration entrusted to it and is directly subordinate to the Council of Ministers of the Union Republic.

CHAPTER VII

THE HIGHER ORGANS OF STATE POWER IN THE AUTONOMOUS SOVIET SOCIALIST REPUBLICS

ART. 89—The highest organ of state power in an Autonomous Soviet Socialist Republic is the Supreme Soviet of the Autonomous Republic.

ART. 90—The Supreme Soviet of an Autonomous Republic is elected by the citizens of the Republic for a term of four years on a basis of representation established by the Constitution of the Autonomous Republic.

ART. 91—The Supreme Soviet of an Autonomous Republic is the sole legislative organ of the Autonomous Republic.

ART. 92—Each Autonomous Republic has its own Constitution, which takes account of the specific features of the Autonomous Republic and is drawn up in full conformity with the Constitution of the Union Republic.

ART. 93—The Supreme Soviet of an Autonomous Republic elects the Presidium of the Supreme Soviet of the Autonomous Republic and appoints the Council of Ministers of the Autonomous Republic, in accordance with its Constitution.

CHAPTER VIII

THE LOCAL ORGANS OF STATE POWER

ART. 94—The organs of state power in territories, regions, autonomous regions, areas, districts, cities and rural localities (stanitsas, villages, hamlets, kishlaks, auls) are the Soviets of Working People's Deputies.

ART. 95—The Soviets of Working People's Deputies of territories, regions, autonomous regions, areas, cities and rural localities (stanitsas, villages, hamlets, kishlaks, auls) are elected by the working people of the respective territories, regions, autonomous regions, areas, districts, cities or rural localities for a term of two years.

ART. 96—The basis of representation for Soviets of Working People's Deputies is determined by the Constitutions of the Union Republics.

ART. 97—The Soviets of Working People's Deputies direct the work of the organs of administration subordinate to them, ensure the maintenance of public order, the observance of the laws and the protection of the rights of citizens, direct local economic and cultural affairs and draw up the local budgets.

ART. 98—The Soviets of Working People's Deputies adopt decisions and issue orders within the limits of the powers vested in them by the laws of the USSR and of the Union Republic.

ART. 99—The executive and administrative organ of the Soviet of Working People's Deputies of a territory, region, autonomous region, area, district, city or rural locality is the Executive Committee elected by it, consisting of a Chairman, Vice-Chairman, a Secretary and members.

ART. 100—The executive and administrative organ of the Soviet of Working People's Deputies in a small locality, in accordance with the Constitution of the Union Republic, is the Chairman, the Vice-Chairman and the Secretary elected by it.

ART. 101—The executive organs of the Soviets of Working People's Deputies are directly accountable both to the Soviets of Working People's Deputies which elected them and to the executive organ of the superior Soviet of Working People's Deputies.

CHAPTER IX

THE COURTS AND THE PROCURATOR'S OFFICE

ART. 102—In the USSR justice is administered by the Supreme Court of the USSR, the Supreme Courts of the Union Republics, the Courts of the Territories, Regions, Autonomous Republics, Autonomous Regions and Areas, the Special Courts of the USSR established by decision of the Supreme Soviet of the USSR, and the People's Courts.

ART. 103—In all Courts cases are tried with the participation of people's assessors, except in cases specially provided for by law.

ART. 104—The Supreme Court of the USSR is the highest judicial organ. The Supreme Court of the USSR is charged with the supervision of the judicial activities of all the judicial organs of the USSR and of the Union Republics.

ART. 105—The Supreme Court of the USSR and the Special Courts of the USSR are elected by the Supreme Soviet of the USSR for a term of five years.

ART. 106—The Supreme Courts of the Union Republics are elected by the Supreme Soviets of the Union Republics for a term of five years.

ART. 107—The Supreme Courts of the Autonomous Republics are elected by the Supreme Soviets of the Autonomous Republics for a term of five years.

ART. 108—The Courts of Territories, Regions, Autonomous Regions and Areas are elected by the Soviets of Working People's Deputies of the respective Territories, Regions, Autonomous Regions or Areas for a term of five years.

ART. 109—People's Courts are elected by the citizens of the districts on the basis of universal, direct and equal suffrage by secret ballot for a term of three years.

ART. 110—Judicial proceedings are conducted in the language of the Union Republic, Autonomous Republic or Autonomous Region, persons not knowing this language being guaranteed the opportunity of fully acquainting themselves with the material of the case through an interpreter and likewise the right to use their own language in court.

ART. 111—In all Courts of the USSR cases are heard in public, unless otherwise provided for by law, and the accused is guaranteed the right of defense.

Art. 112—Judges are independent and subject only to the law.

Art. 113—Supreme supervisory power to ensure the strict observance of the law by all Ministries and institutions subordinated to them, as well as by officials and citizens of the USSR generally, is vested in the Procurator-General of the USSR.

Art. 114—The Procurator-General of the USSR is appointed by the Supreme Soviet of the USSR for a term of seven years.

Art. 115—Procurators of Republics, Territories, Regions, Autonomous Republics and Autonomous Regions are appointed by the Procurator-General of the USSR for a term of five years.

Art. 116—Area, district and city procurators are appointed by the Procurators of the Union Republics, subject to the approval of the Procurator-General of the USSR, for a term of five years.

Art. 117—The organs of the Procurator's Office perform their functions independently of any local organs whatsoever, being subordinate solely to the Procurator-General of the USSR.

Chapter X

Fundamental Rights and Duties of Citizens

Art. 118—Citizens of the USSR have the right to work, that is, the right to guaranteed employment and payment for their work in accordance with its quantity and quality.

The right to work is ensured by the socialist organization of the national economy, the steady growth of the productive forces of Soviet society, the elimination of the possibility of economic crises, and the abolition of unemployment.

Art. 119—Citizens of the USSR have the right to rest and leisure.

The right to rest and leisure is ensured by the establishment of an eight-hour day for factory and office workers, the reduction of the working day to seven or six hours for arduous trades and to four hours in shops where conditions of work are particularly arduous, by the institution of annual vacations with full pay for factory and office workers, and by the provision of a wide network of sanatoria, rest homes and clubs for the accommodation of the working people.

Art. 120—Citizens of the USSR have the right to maintenance in old age and also in case of sickness or disability.

This right is ensured by the extensive development of social insurance of factory and office workers at state expense, free medical service for the working people, and the provision of a wide network of health resorts for the use of the working people.

Art. 121—Citizens of the USSR have the right to education.

This right is ensured by universal and compulsory elementary education; by free education up to and including the seventh grade; by a system of state stipends for students of higher education establishments who excel in their studies; by instruction in schools being conducted in the native language; and by organization in the factories, state farms, machine and tractor stations and collective farms of free vocational, technical and agronomic training for the working people.

Art. 122—Women in the USSR are accorded equal rights with men in all spheres of economic, government, cultural, political and other public activity.

The possibility of exercising these rights is ensured by women being accorded an equal right with men to work, payment for work, rest and leisure, social insurance and education, and by state protection of the interests of mother and child, state aid to mothers of large families and unmarried mothers, maternity leave with full pay, and the provision of a wide network of maternity homes, nurseries and kindergartens.

Art. 123—Equality of rights of citizens of the USSR, irrespective of their nationality or race, in all spheres of economic, government, cultural, political and other public activity, is an indefeasible law.

Any direct or indirect restriction of the rights of, or conversely, the establishment of any direct or indirect privileges for, citizens on account of their race or nationality, as well as any advocacy of racial or national exclusiveness or hatred and contempt, is punishable by law.

Art. 124—In order to ensure to citizens freedom of conscience, the church in the USSR is separated from the state, and the school from the church. Freedom of religious worship and freedom of antireligious propaganda is recognized for all citizens.

Art. 125—In conformity with the interests of the working people, and in order to strengthen the socialist system, the citizens of the USSR are guaranteed by law:

(a) Freedom of speech;

(b) Freedom of the press;

(c) Freedom of assembly, including the holding of mass meetings;

(d) Freedom of street processions and demonstrations.

These civil rights are ensured by placing at the disposal of the working people and their organizations printing presses, stocks of paper, public buildings, the streets, communication facilities, and other material requisites for the exercise of these rights.

Art. 126—In conformity with the interests of the working people, and in order to develop the organizational initiative and political activity of the masses of the people, citizens of the USSR are guaranteed the right to unite in public organizations; trade unions, co-operative societies, youth organizations, sport and defense organizations, cultural, technical and scientific societies; and the most active and political-conscious citizens in the ranks of the working class and other sections of the working people unite in the Communist Party of the Soviet Union (Bolsheviks), which is the vanguard of the working people in their struggle to strengthen and develop the socialist system and is the leading core of all organizations of the working people, both public and state.

Art. 127—Citizens of the USSR are guaranteed inviolability of the person. No person may be placed under arrest except by decision of a court or with the sanction of a procurator.

Art. 128—The inviolability of the homes of citizens and privacy of correspondence are protected by law.

Art. 129—The USSR affords the right of asylum to foreign citizens persecuted for defending the interests of the working people, or for scientific activities, or for struggling for national liberation.

Art. 130—It is the duty of every citizen of the USSR to abide by the Constitution of the Union of Soviet Socialist Republics, to observe the laws, to maintain labor discipline, honestly to perform public duties, and to respect the rules of socialist intercourse.

Art. 131—It is the duty of every citizen of the USSR to safeguard and fortify public, socialist property as the sacred and inviolable foundation of the Soviet system, as the source of the wealth and might of the country, as the source of the prosperity and culture of all the working people.

Persons committing offenses against public, socialist property are enemies of the people.

Art. 132—Universal military service is law.

Military service in the Armed Forces of the USSR is an honorable duty of the citizens of the USSR.

Art. 133—To defend the country is the sacred duty of every citizen of the USSR.

Treason to the motherland—violation of the oath of allegiance, desertion to the enemy, impairing the military power of the state, espionage—is punishable with all the severity of the law as the most heinous of crimes.

CHAPTER XI

THE ELECTORAL SYSTEM

ART. 134—Members of all Soviets of Working People's Deputies—of the Supreme Soviet of the USSR, the Supreme Soviets of the Union Republics, the Soviets of Working People's Deputies of the Territories and Regions, the Supreme Soviets of the Autonomous Republics, the Soviets of Working People's Deputies of the Autonomous Regions, and the area, district, city and rural (stanitsa, village, hamlet, kishlak, aul) Soviets of Working People's Deputies—are chosen by the electors on the basis of universal, equal and direct suffrage by secret ballot.

ART. 135—Elections of deputies are universal: all citizens of the USSR who have reached the age of eighteen, irrespective of race or nationality, sex, religion, education, domicile, social origin, property status or past activities, have the right to vote in the election of deputies, with the exception of insane persons and persons who have been convicted by a court of law and whose sentences include deprivation of electoral rights.

Every citizen of the USSR who has reached the age of twenty-three is eligible for election to the Supreme Soviet of the USSR, irrespective of race or nationality, sex, religion, education, domicile, social origin, property status or past activities.

ART. 136—Elections of deputies are equal: each citizen has one vote; all citizens participate in elections on an equal footing.

ART. 137—Women have the right to elect and be elected on equal terms with men.

ART. 138—Citizens serving in the Armed Forces of the USSR have the right to elect and be elected on equal terms with all other citizens.

ART. 139—Elections of deputies are direct: all Soviets of Working People's Deputies, from rural and city Soviets of Working People's Deputies to the Supreme Soviet of the USSR, are elected by the citizens by direct vote.

ART. 140—Voting at elections of deputies is secret.

ART. 141—Candidates are nominated by election district.

The right to nominate candidates is secured to public organizations and societies of the working people: Communist Party organizations, trade unions, cooperatives, youth organizations and cultural societies.

ART. 142—It is the duty of every deputy to report to his electors on his work and on the work of his Soviet of Working People's Deputies, and he may be recalled at any time upon decision of a majority of the electors in the manner established by law.

CHAPTER XII

ARMS, FLAG, CAPITAL

ART. 143—The arms of the Union of Soviet Republics are sickle and hammer against a globe depicted in the rays of the sun and surrounded by ears of grain, with the inscription "Workers of All Countries, Unite!" in the languages of the Union Republics.

ART. 144—The state flag of the Union of Soviet Socialist Republics is of red cloth with the sickle and hammer depicted in gold in the upper corner near the staff and above them a five-pointed red star bordered in gold. The ratio of the width to the length is 1:2.

ART. 145—The capital of the Union of Soviet Socialist Republics is the City of Moscow.

Chapter XIII

Procedure for Amending the Constitution

Art. 146—The Constitution of the USSR may be amended only by decision of the Supreme Soviet of the USSR adopted by a majority of not less than two thirds of the votes in each of its Chambers.

SELECTED BIBLIOGRAPHY

GREAT BRITAIN

British bibliography is a very rewarding field, not only because of the abundance of material but also because of the analytical effort and the brilliant writing displayed. Bagehot's *The English Constitution*, though outdated in its factual information, will forever remain a classic.

Among recent literature Hiram Stout's *British Government* provides a useful and readable general treatment. Sir Ivor Jennings' *Cabinet Government*, although a contemporary work, has already achieved the stature of a classic. Also very useful are *Parliament* and other works by the same author. Comprehensive treatises on the party system have appeared only very recently. The works of a practitioner, Ivor Bulmer-Thomas, *The Party System in Great Britain*, and of an academician, D. E. Butler, *The Electoral System in Britain*, are particularly useful. There is also a rich literature on legal institutions and on local government. A major effort of British political science has gone into the latter subject.

Great Britain boasts a number of excellent newspapers. Particularly informative are *The Times* and *The Manchester Guardian*, of independent conservative and liberal leanings respectively. Outstanding is the weekly, conservative *Observer*, especially in the foreign-relations field. Among the numerous periodicals and reviews might be mentioned the *Economist, International Affairs, Parliamentary Affairs, Political Quarterly, Public Administration,* and *Quarterly Review.*

HISTORICAL WORKS

Adams, G. B.: *Constitutional History of England*, 2d ed., New York, 1934.

———: *The Origin of the English Constitution*, 2d ed., New Haven, 1920.

Maitland, Frederic W.: *The Constitutional History of England*, London, 1908.

McIlwain, Charles H.: *The High Court of Parliament and Its Supremacy*, New Haven, 1910.

McKechnie, M. S.: *Magna Carta; A Commentary on the Great Charter of King John*, Glasgow, 1905.

Pasquet, D.: *An Essay on the Origins of the House of Commons* (trans. by R. D. G. Laffau), Cambridge, 1925.

Pollard, A. F.: *The Evolution of Parliament*, London, 1920.

Pollock, F., and F. W. Maitland: *History of English Law to the Times of Edward I*, 2d ed., London, 1911.

Porritt, E.: *The Unreformed House of Commons; Parliamentary Representation before 1832*, 2d ed., 2 vols., Cambridge, 1909.

Stubbs, W.: *The Constitutional History of England*, Oxford, 1880.

Thompson, Faith: *The First Century of Magna Carta: Why It Persisted as a Document*, Minneapolis, 1925.

Trevelyan, G. M.: *The Two-party System in English Political History*, Oxford, 1926.

General Works

Amery, Leopold C. M. S.: *Thoughts on the Constitution*, Oxford, 1947.
Anson, Sir William R.: *Law and Custom of the Constitution*, 2 vols., New York, 1922–1935.
Bagehot, Walter: *The English Constitution*, London, 1867.
Campion, Sir Gilbert, and others: *British Government since 1918*, New York, 1950.
Clarke, Charles F.: *Britain Today*, Cambridge, Mass., 1951.
Dicey, A. V.: *Introduction to the Study of the Law of the Constitution*, 9th ed., London, 1939.
Jennings, Sir Ivor: *Cabinet Government*, 2d ed., Cambridge, 1951.
———: *The British Constitution*, 3d ed., Cambridge, 1950.
Keith, Sir Arthur B.: *The Constitution of England from Queen Victoria to George VI*, 2 vols., New York, 1940.
Laski, Harold J.: *Reflections on the Constitution*, New York, 1951.
———: *Parliamentary Government in England*, New York, 1938.
Morrison, Herbert: *Government and Parliament*, London, 1954.
Muir, Ramsey: *How Britain Is Governed*, 4th ed., London, 1940.
Ogg, Frederic A.: *English Government and Politics*, 2d ed., New York, 1936.
Robson, William A.: *The British System of Government*, 3d ed., New York, 1948.
Stout, Hiram M.: *British Government*, New York, 1953.

The Crown and the Executive

Bridges, Sir Edward: *Treasury Control*, London, 1950.
Heath, Sir Thomas: *The Treasury*, London, 1927 (Whitehall Series).
Jennings, Sir Ivor: *Cabinet Government*, 2d ed., Cambridge, 1951.
Keith, Sir Arthur B.: *The British Cabinet System*, 2d ed., London, 1952.
———: *The British Cabinet System, 1830–1938*, London, 1939.
Martin, Kingsley: *The Magic of Monarchy*, New York, 1937.
Schwartz, Bernard: *Law and the Executive in Britain, A Comparative Study*, New York, 1949.

Articles
Einzing, P.: "Treasury Control of Expenditure," *Fortnightly*, Vol. 179 (February, 1953), pp. 81–86.

The Civil Service

Critchley, T. A.: *The Civil Service To-Day*, London, 1951.
Dale, Harold E.: *The Higher Civil Service*, New York, 1941.
Finer, Herman: *The British Civil Service*, 2d ed., London, 1947.
Great Britain, Treasury: *Political Activities of Civil Servants*, Cmd. 8783, London, 1953.
Greaves, Harold R. G.: *The Civil Service in the Changing State: A Survey of Civil Service Reform and the Implications of a Planned Economy on Public Administration in England*, London, 1947.
Monch, Bosworth: *How the Civil Service Works*, London, 1951.
Robson, W. A. (ed.): *The British Civil Servant*, London, 1937.
Stout, Hiram M.: *Public Service in Great Britain*, Chapel Hill, N. C., 1938.
Walker, Harvey: *Training Public Employees in Great Britain*, New York, 1935.
White, L. D.: *Whitley Councils in the British Civil Service*, Chicago, 1933.

Articles

Gladden, Edgar N.: "The British Civil Service in Transition," *American Political Science Review,* Vol. 43 (1949), pp. 333–344.

Hillis, A. H. M.: "The British Civil Servant of To-Morrow," *Public Administration Review,* Vol. 11 (1951), pp. 173–179.

"The Political Activities of Civil Servants," *Public Administration,* Vol. 31 (1953), pp. 163–175.

SOCIAL SERVICES

Marsh, David C.: *National Insurance and Assistance in Great Britain,* London, 1951.

Robson, W. A. (ed.): *Social Security,* 3d ed., London, 1948.

Ross, Sir James: *The National Health Service in Great Britain,* Oxford, 1952.

Articles

Smith, N. A.: "Theory and Practice of the Welfare State," *Political Quarterly,* Vol. 22 (1951), pp. 369–381.

Spenden, S.: "British Intellectuals in the Welfare State: How the New Climate Affects Science and Culture," *Commentary,* Vol. 12 (1951), pp. 425–430.

Wootton, Barbara: "Record of the Labor Government in Social Services," *Political Quarterly,* Vol. 20 (1949), p. 101.

Zink, Harold: "The New Role of the Government in Britain," *Western Political Quarterly,* Vol. 1 (1948), pp. 413–425.

NATIONALIZED ENTERPRISE

Allen, G. C.: *British Industries and Their Organization,* 3d ed., London, 1951.

Brady, Robert A.: *Crisis in Britain: Plans and Achievements of the Labour Government,* Berkeley, 1951.

Chester, D. N.: *The Nationalized Industries: An Analysis of the Statutory Provisions,* 2d ed., London, 1951.

Cole, G. D. H.: *The National Coal Board: Its Tasks, Its Organization and Its Prospects,* London, 1948.

Haynes, William W.: *Nationalization in Practice: The British Coal Industry,* Boston, 1953.

Hutchison, Keith: *The Decline and Fall of British Capitalism,* New York, 1950.

Jewkes, John: *Ordeal by Planning,* New York, 1948.

Palmer, Cecil: *The British Socialist Welfare State: An Examination of Its Political, Social, Moral, and Economic Consequences,* Caldwell, Idaho, 1952.

Robson, W. A. (ed.): *Problems of Nationalized Industry,* London, 1952.

Watkins, Ernest: *The Cautious Revolution,* London, 1951.

Articles

"Denationalization of Iron and Steel," *Public Administration,* Vol. 31 (1953), pp. 277–284.

Dewey, D. J.: "Crisis in Britain: a note on the Stagnation Thesis," *Journal of Political Economics,* Vol. 59 (1951), pp. 348–352.

Haynes, W. W.: "A Test Case from Britain. Does Nationalization Work?" *Harvard Business Review,* Vol. 31, No. 2 (1953), pp. 103–115.

Heldman, Herman: "The Economic Problem of Denationalization," *Political Science Quarterly,* Vol. 45 (1951), pp. 576–597.

Milne, R. S.: "Britain's Economic Planning Machinery," *American Political Science Review,* Vol. 46 (1952), pp. 406–428.

Morrison, Herbert: "Public Control of the Socialized Industries," *Public Administration*, Vol. 28 (1950), pp. 3–9.

Mowat Charles L.: "The Anatomy of British Nationalization," *Antioch Review*, Vol. 9 (1949), pp. 271–285.

Robson, W. A.: "The Administration of Nationalized Industries in Britain," *Public Administration Review*, Vol. 7 (1947), pp. 161–169.

PARLIAMENT

Campion, Sir Gilbert: *An Introduction to the Procedure of the House of Commons*, 2d ed., London and New York, 1950.

Campion, Lord (ed.): *Parliament, A Survey*, London, 1952.

Gordon, Strathearn: *Our Parliament*, 2d ed., London, 1952.

Hemingford, Lord: *What Parliament Is and Does*, New York, 1948.

Herbert, Alan: *Independent Member*, New York, 1951.

Hogg, Quintin: *The Purpose of Parliament*, London, 1946.

Jennings, W. I.: *Parliament*, London, 1939.

May, Sir Thomas Erskine: *A Treatise on the Law, Privileges, and Usage of Parliament*, rev. by Sir G. Campion, 15th ed., London, 1950.

Morrison, Henry: *Parliament, What It Is and How It Works*, London, 1935.

Articles

Aikin, Charles: "The British Bureaucracy and the Origins of Parliamentary Policy," *American Political Science Review*, Vol. 33 (1939), pp. 26–46, 219–233.

Bassett, R.: "British Parliamentary Government To-Day," *Political Quarterly*, Vol. 23 (1952), pp. 380–389.

Chubb, Basil: "Parliamentary Control of the Public Accounts," *Parliamentary Affairs*, Vol. 5 (1950), pp. 344–351, 450–457.

Shearer, J. G. S.: "Standing Committees in the House of Commons, 1945–50," *Parliamentary Affairs*, Vol. 4 (1950), pp. 558–568.

LAW AND JUSTICE

Allen, C. K.: *Law and Orders, An Inquiry into the Nature and Scope of Delegated Legislation and Executive Power in England*, London, 1945.

Amos, S.: *British Justice: An Outline of the Administration of Criminal Justice in England and Wales*, London, 1940.

Ensor, Robert C. K.: *Courts and Judges in France, Germany and England*, New York, 1933.

Friedmann, W.: *Law and Social Change in Contemporary Britain*, London, 1952.

Hanbury, H. G.: *English Courts of Law*, London, 1944.

Hewart, Lord: *The New Despotism*, New York, 1929.

Holdsworth, W. S.: *History of English Law*, 2d ed., 12 vols., London, 1922–1938.

Holmes, O. W.: *The Common Law*, Boston, 1881.

Jackson, R. M.: *The Machinery of Justice in England*, Cambridge, 1940.

Jenks, E.: *The Book of English Law as at the End of 1938*, 5th ed., London, 1938.

Patterson, C. P.: *The Machinery of Justice in Great Britain*, Austin, 1936.

Pollock, F.: *The Genius of the Common Law*, New York, 1912.

———: *The Expansion of the Common Law*, London, 1904.

Potter, H.: *A Historical Introduction to English Law and Its Institutions*, 3d ed., London, 1949.

Pound, Roscoe: *The Spirit of the Common Law*, Boston, 1921.

Radcliffe, C. R. Y., and G. Cross: *The English Legal System*, 2d ed., London, 1946.
Robson, W. A.: *Justice and Administrative Law*, 3d ed., London, 1951.
Sieghart, Marguerite A.: *Government by Decree. A Comparative Study of the Ordinance in English and French Law*, New York, 1950.
Slesser, Sir Henry: *The Administration of the Law*, New York, 1948.

Articles

Harvey, H. J.: "Crown and the Common Law," *International Council*, Vol. 487 (1953), pp. 5–71.

LOCAL GOVERNMENT

Attlee, C. R.: *Borough Councils*, 2d ed., London, 1946.
Clarke, J. J.: *The Local Government of the United Kingdom*, 13th ed., London, 1945.
Cohen, E. W.: *Autonomy and Delegation in County Government*, London, 1953.
Cole, G. D. H.: *Local and Regional Government*, London, 1947.
Finer, Herman: *English Local Government*, 4th ed., London, 1950.
Finer, S. E.: *A Primer of Public Administration*, London, 1950.
Fogarty, M. P.: *Town and Country Planning*, London, 1948.
Haar, Charles M.: *Land Planning Law in a Free Society: A Study of the British Town and Country Planning Act*, Cambridge, Mass., 1951.
Hasbuck, E. L.: *Local Government in England*, 2d ed., London, 1948.
Jennings, W. I.: *Principles of Local Government Law*, 3d ed., London, 1947.
Laski, H. J., W. I. Jennings, and W. A. Robson: *A Century of Municipal Progress*, London, 1935
Lipman, V. D.: *Local Government Areas, 1834–1945*, Oxford, 1948.
Morrison, Herbert: *How London Is Governed*, London, 1949.
Oakes, Sir Cecil, and H. W. Dacey: *Local Government and Local Government Finance*, 9th ed., London, 1950.
Robson, W. A.: *The Development of Local Government*, 2d ed., London, 1948.
———: *The Government and Misgovernment of London*, 2d ed., London, 1948.
Smellie, K. B.: *A History of Local Government*, London, 1947.
Warren, John H.: *Municipal Administration*, London, 1948.
———: *The English Local Government System*, London, 1946.
Webb, Sydney and Beatrice: *English Local Government from the Revolution to the Municipal Corporations Act*, 9 vols., London, 1906–1927.

Articles

Black, Robert B.: "The British Central Land Board," *Public Administration Review*, Vol. 11 (1951), pp. 35–43.
Clark, Keith C.: "The British Labor Government's Town and Country Planning Act: A Study in Conflicting Liberalisms," *Political Science Quarterly*, Vol. 45 (1951), pp. 87–103.
Cohen, Emmeline W.: "Aspects of Local Government in England and Wales," *Public Administration Review*, Vol. 11 (1951), pp. 253–259.
Crouch, Winston W.: "Trends in British Local Government," *Public Administration Review*, Vol. 7 (1947), pp. 254–262.
"Local Government Reorganization," *Public Administration*, Vol. 31 (1953), pp. 176–188, 285–295.
Presthus, R. V.: "British Town and Country Planning: Local Participation," *American Political Science Review*, Vol. 45 (1951), pp. 756–769.
Robson, W. A.: "Reform of Local Government," *Political Quarterly*, Vol. 19 (1948), pp. 254–263.

Telling, A. E.: "New Towns, Progress and Prospects," *Town and Country Planning*, Vol. 16 (1948), pp. 78–97.
Usill, V.: "Democracy in British Local Government," *National Municipal Review*, Vol. 35 (1946), pp. 620–621.
Weidner, E. W.: "Trends in English Local Government," *American Political Science Review*, Vol. 39 (1945), pp. 337–349.

THE COMMONWEALTH

Bailey, Sidney D. (ed.): *Parliamentary Government in the Commonwealth*, London, 1951.
Brady, A.: *Democracy in the Dominions*, 2d ed., Toronto, 1952.
Carr-Gregg, John R. E.: *The Colombo Plan, A Commonwealth Program for Southeast Asia*, International Conciliation Pamphlet No. 467, New York, 1951.
———: *Self-Rule in Africa, Recent Advances in the Gold Coast*, International Conciliation Pamphlet No. 473, New York, 1951.
Carter, Gwendolen M.: *The British Commonwealth and International Security: The Role of the Dominions*, Toronto, 1947.
Crocker, W. R.: *Self-Government for the Colonies*, London, 1949.
Elton, Lord: *Imperial Commonwealth*, New York, 1946.
Evatt, H. V.: *The King and His Dominions*, Oxford, 1936.
Forsey, Eugene A.: *The Royal Power of Dissolution in the British Commonwealth*, New York, 1943.
Hailey, Lord: *Native Administration in British African Territories*, London, 1951.
Hailey, W. M. C.: *Britain and Her Dependencies*, London, 1945.
Hodson, H. V.: *Twentieth Century Empire*, London, 1948.
Jennings, Sir Ivor, and C. M. Young: *Constitutional Laws of the Commonwealth*, 2d ed., Oxford, 1952.
Jennings, W. I.: *The British Commonwealth of Nations*, London, 1948.
Keith, A. B.: *The Dominions as Sovereign States: Their Constitutions and Government*, London, 1938.
MacInnes, C. M. (ed.): *Principles and Methods of Colonial Administration*, London, 1951.
Prim, A. W.: *British Colonies*, New York, 1951.
Simmett, W. E.: *The British Colonial Empire*, 2d ed., London, 1949.
Wheare, K. C.: *Federal Government*, 2d ed., New York, 1951.
———: *The Statute of Westminster and Dominion Status*, 4th ed., Oxford, 1949.

Articles
Hall, M. Duncan, K. C. Wheare, and A. Brady: "The British Commonwealth: A Symposium," *American Political Science Review*, Vol. 47 (1953), pp. 997–1040.
Scott, T. R.: "The End of Dominion Status," *American Journal of International Law*, Vol. 38 (1944), pp. 34–49.
Soward, F. H.: "Commonwealth Countries and World Affairs," *International Affairs*, Vol. 27 (1951), pp. 192–203.
Wheare, K. C.: "Is the British Commonwealth Withering Away?" *American Political Science Review*, Vol. 44 (1950), pp. 545–555.

POLITICAL PARTIES—GENERAL

Bailey, Sydney D. (ed.): *The British Party System*, London, 1952.
Bulmer-Thomas, Ivor: *The Party System in Great Britain*, London, 1953.
Butler, D. E.: *The British General Election of 1950*, London, 1951.
———: *The British General Election of 1951*, London, 1952.

———: *The Electoral System in Britain, 1918–1951*, London, 1953.
McCallum, R. B., and A. Readman: *The British General Election of 1945*, Oxford, 1947.
Pollock, James K., and others: *British Election Studies*, Ann Arbor, 1951.
———: *Money and Politics Abroad*, New York, 1932.

Articles

Clarke, David: "The Organisation of Political Parties," *Political Quarterly*, Vol. 21 (1950), pp. 79–90.
Lewis, Gordon K., "The Present Condition of British Political Parties," *Western Political Quarterly*, Vol. 5 (1952), pp. 231–257.
Lipson, Leslie: "The Two-Party System in British Politics," *American Political Science Review*, Vol. 47 (1953), pp. 337–358.
McKenzie, R. T.: "Party Organization," *Parliamentary Affairs*, Vol. 5 (1951), pp. 116–135.
Nicholas, H. G.: "The British General Election of 1951," *American Political Science Review*, Vol. 46 (1952), pp. 398–405.
———: "The Formation of Party Policy," *Parliamentary Affairs*, Vol. 5 (1951), pp. 142–153.
Potter, Allen: "British Party Organization," *Political Science Quarterly*, Vol. 43 (1949), pp. 65–83.

THE CONSERVATIVES

Birch, N.: *The Conservative Party*, London, 1949.
Boyd-Carpenter, John: *The Conservative Case: Choice for Britain*, London, 1950.
Braine, Bernard: *Tory Democracy*, London, 1948.
Conservative Party: *The Right Road for Britain*, London, 1949.
Conservative Political Centre: *Conservatism, 1945–1950*, London, 1950.
Hogg, Quintin: *The Case for Conservatism*, London, 1948.
———: *The Left Was Never Right*, London, 1945.
White, R. J. (ed.): *The Conservative Tradition*, London, 1950.

Articles

Beer, Samuel H.: "The Conservative Party of Great Britain," *Journal of Politics*, Vol. 14 (1952), pp. 41–71.
Bulmer-Thomas, I.: "How Conservative Policy Is Formed," *Political Quarterly*, Vol. 24 (1953), pp. 190–203.
Butler, R. A.: "Conservative Policy," *Political Quarterly*, Vol. 20 (1949), pp. 317–325.
Salter, Sir Arthur: "British Conservatism Today," *Yale Review*, Vol. 41 (1951), pp. 1–12.
Uthey, T. E.: "Implications of the Conservative Victory," *Fortnightly*, Vol. 177 (1952), pp. 15–19.

THE LABOR PARTY

Attlee, C. R.: *The Labour Party in Perspective; and 12 Years Later*, London, 1949.
Beer, M.: *A History of British Socialism*, London, 1948.
Brockway, Fenner: *Inside the Left*, London, 1947.
Clayton, J.: *The Rise and Decline of Socialism in Great Britain, 1889–1924*, London, 1926.
Cole, G. D. H.: *A History of the Labour Party from 1914*, London, 1948.
———: *A Short History of the British Working Class Movement, 1789–1927*, London, 1932.
Cripps, Sir Stafford: *Toward Christian Democracy*, London, 1946.
Hall, William G.: *The Labour Party*, London, 1949.

Jouvenel, Bertrand de: *Problème de l'Angleterre Socialiste,* Paris, 1947.
Labour Party: National Executive Committee: *Labour Believes in Britain,* London, 1949.
Labour Party: *Party Organization Handbook,* London, 1951.
McHenry, Dean E.: *His Majesty's Opposition,* Berkeley, 1940.
Munro, Donald (ed.): *Socialism: The British Way,* London, 1948.
Rothstein, T.: *From Chartism to Labourism,* London, 1929.
Tracy, Herbert: *The British Labour Party,* 3 vols., London, 1948.
Webb, Sydney and Beatrice: *The History of Trade Unionism,* London, 1894.
Williams, Francis: *Socialist Britain,* New York, 1949.

Articles
Burns, James MacGregor: "The Parliamentary Labor Party in Great Britain," *American
    Political Science Review,* Vol. 44 (1950), pp. 855–871.
Epstein, Leon D.: "Socialism and the British Labour Party," *Political Science Quarterly,*
    Vol. 45 (1951), pp. 507–531.
Roche, John P.: "The Crisis in British Socialism," *Antioch Review,* Vol. 12 (1952–1953),
    pp. 387–398.
Schumacher, E. F.: "In Search of Socialism. Review of New Fabian Essays," *Twentieth
    Century,* Vol. 152 (1952), pp. 33–40.
Williams, Francis: "The Program of the British Labour Party; a Historical Survey,"
    Journal of Politics, Vol. 12 (1950), pp. 189–210.

LIBERALS AND MINOR PARTIES

Cruikshank, R. J.: *The Liberal Party,* London, 1948.
Laski, Harold J.: *The Secret Battalion; An Examination of the Communist Attitude to
    the Labor Party,* London, 1946.
Slesser, Sir Henry: *A History of the Liberal Party,* New York, 1944.

Articles
Fothergill, P.: "The Liberal Predicament," *Political Quarterly,* Vol. 24 (1953), pp. 243–
    249.
Grismond, J.: "The Principles of Liberalism," *Political Quarterly,* Vol. 24 (1953), pp.
    236–242.

FRANCE

To the English-speaking student of France some problems will soon become obvious.
In the first place there is no book in the English language which may be called a general
treatise. Of older and now outdated works, Walter C. Sharp's *The Government of the
French Republic,* though published in 1938, is still useful although it cannot claim the
classic rank possessed by the works of Bagehot or De Tocqueville. Edward M. Earle (ed.),
Modern France, a collection of essays by various authors, is not a comprehensive work but
contains several excellent essays. André Siegfried's *France, a Study in Nationalities,* an
expanded edition of his original classic on the French political parties in the West, retains
its great merit. Joseph Barthélemy's *The Government of France,* although factually outdated, is still of much value.

In the field of historical treatments H. A. Taine's great work, *The Origins of Contemporary France,* is well known. Extremely well written despite great attention to detail
and "asides" is D. W. Brogan's *France under the Republic,* which goes up to the Second
World War but becomes a little thin after the First World War. This book takes some
knowledge of France for granted. Excellent is David Thomson's *Democracy in France;*

the Third and Fourth Republics; and for the establishment of the Fourth Republic, Gordon Wright's *The Reshaping of French Democracy* remains indispensable. O. R. Taylor's *The Fourth Republic of France* gives a brief and useful description of French institutions and parties but is so short, unimaginative, and dry that its value is limited.

In the field of French political parties a promising beginning has been made. François Goguel's *France under the Fourth Republic* contains a lively account of French party politics (but little attention to constitutional or institutional aspects). Jean-Marie Domenach has contributed a brilliant piece on the French Communist party in Einaudi, Domenach, and Garosci's *Communism in Western Europe.* A. Rossi's *A Communist Party in Action,* an abridged translation of the French original, is also excellent. Very useful is also François Goguel's section on the MRP in Einaudi and Goguel's *Christian Democracy in Italy and France.*

This is, however, not a great deal. It is certain that no serious student of France can proceed very far without a good reading knowledge of French. France has a distinguished tradition in the field of political science and political analysis. Apart from constitutional and legal treatises of great brilliance, among which stand the classics of Duguit, Esmain, and Barthélemy, French political science proper has found its focus in the École Libre de Science Politique in Paris, which after the Second World War became the Institut d'Études Politiques of the University of Paris. Similar institutes have been created at several other French universities.

Political analysis thrived under the inspiration of André Siegfried's *Tableau politique de la France de l'Ouest,* Paris, 1913. For the development of the French party system François Goguel's *La Politique des partis sous la IIIe République,* Paris, 1946, has already become a classic. The same author has also enriched our knowledge by a series of articles in *Esprit* dealing with the regional distribution of votes after each election. His findings have been collected in his *Géographie des élections françaises de 1870 à 1951.* A brilliant and amusingly written analysis of the French party system is the work of a journalist, Jacques Fauvet: *Les forces politiques en France,* Paris, 1951. Maurice Duverger's *Les partis politiques,* Paris, 1951, although a general systematic treatise, contains many incisive references to French political parties.

For the interpretation of the Constitution of 1946 there are a number of commentaries: M. Duverger, *Manuel de droit constitutionnel et de science politique,* 5th ed., Paris, 1948, is briefer than the others but written with wit and imagination. Others are the more extensive works by Laférrière, Prelot, Vedel, and Burdeau.

In the field of French parliamentary organization and work, an English work commands the field, D. W. S. Lidderdale's *The Parliament of France.*

Among French newspapers *Le Monde* of conservative and somewhat neutralist tendencies is generally regarded as the most respected and informative. *Le Figaro,* conservative and pro-American, is particularly noteworthy for editorials by some of France's outstanding men of letters. Compared to these papers and others like them (for instance, *Aurore*), the party press has little significance with the exception of the Communist *L'Humanité.* There is also a vigorous provincial press, some of which has national significance.

There is an abundance of reviews, far too numerous to mention. Among them are *Esprit* (left Catholic), *Revue politique et parlémentaire, Revue de Deux Mondes, Escrits de Paris, Politique Etrangère,* etc., etc. Outstanding and extremely useful is *La Nef,* each of whose issues is devoted to one single theme, mostly of a political nature. Students of Communism will not fail to consult the theoretical journal of the party, *Les cahiers du Communisme.*

Among learned journals there is also an abundance. Mention might be made of the *Revue française de science politique* and the *Revue du droit publique et de la science politique.* The National Foundation of Political Science (attached to the Institut d'Études Politiques in Paris) publishes a considerable number of studies in the series *Cahiers de la Fondation Nationale des Sciences Politiques.*

HISTORY

Brogan, D. W.: *France under the Republic,* New York, 1940.
Taine, H. A.: *The Origins of Contemporary France,* London, 1931.
Thomson, David: *Democracy in France: the Third and Fourth Republics,* New York, 1952.
Werth, Alexander: *The Twilight of France,* New York, 1942.
Wright, Gordon: *The Reshaping of French Democracy,* New York, 1948.

GENERAL DISCUSSION

Barthélemy, Joseph: *The Government of France* (trans. by J. B. Morris), New York, 1924.
Earle, E. M. (ed.): *Modern France,* Princeton, 1951.
Goguel, François: *France under the Fourth Republic,* Ithaca, N. Y., 1952.
Poincaré, Raymond: *How France Is Governed* (trans. by B. Miall), New York, 1914.
Sharp, W. R.: *The Government of the French Republic,* New York, 1938.
Siegfried, André: *France, a Study in Nationality,* Yale, 1930.
Taylor, O. R.: *The Fourth Republic of France: Constitution and Political Parties,* New York, 1951.

Articles
Micaud, Charles A.: "The Launching of the Fourth Republic," *Journal of Politics,* Vol. 8 (1946), pp. 292–307.
Ragoff, N.: "Social Stratification in France and in the United States," *American Journal of Sociology,* Vol. 58 (1953), pp. 347–357.

THE CONSTITUTION

Colliard, Claude-Albert: *Précis de droit public: les libertés publiques,* Paris, 1950.
Duguit, Leon: *Traité de droit constitutionnel,* 3d ed., 3 vols., Paris, 1922.
Duverger, Maurice: *Manuel de droit constitutionnel et de science politique,* 5th ed., Paris, 1948.
Esmain, A.: *Elements de droit constitutionnel, français et comparé,* rev. by H. Nézard, 8th ed., 2 vols., Paris, 1927–1928.
Foundation for Foreign Affairs (Otto Kirchheimer): *A Constitution for the Fourth Republic,* Washington, 1947.
Laférrière, J.: *Manuel de droit constitutionnel,* 2d ed., Paris, 1947.
Prélot, M.: *Précis de droit constitutionnel,* Paris, 1950.
Vedel, G.: *Manuel de droit constitutionnel,* Paris, 1949.

Articles
Berlia, G.: "Le Projet de Révision Constitutionnelle adopté par l'Assemblée Nationale le 22 Juillet 1953," *Revue du Droit Public et de la Science Politique,* Vol. 69 (1953), pp. 680–696.
Blamont, E.: "La Révision de la Constitution," *Revue du Droit Public et de la Science Politique,* Vol. 69 (1953), pp. 415–422.
Gooch, Robert K.: "Recent Constitution-making in France," *American Political Science Review,* Vol. 41 (1947), pp. 420–446.

Kirchheimer, Otto: "Decree Powers and Constitutional Law in France under the Third Republic," *American Political Science Review,* Vol. 34 (1940), pp. 1104–1123.
Pierce, Roy: "France Reopens the Constitutional Debate," *American Political Science Review,* Vol. 46 (1952), pp. 422–437.

THE NATIONAL ADMINISTRATION

Blum, Léon: *La réforme gouvernementale,* Paris, 1936.
Colliard, Claude-Albert: *Le travail gouvernemental et ses méthodes,* Paris, 1948.
Sharp, Walter R.: *The French Civil Service: Bureaucracy in Transition,* New York, 1931.

Articles

Campbell, Peter: "The Cabinet and the Constitution in France," *Parliamentary Affairs,* Vol. 5 (1951), pp. 341–361.
Cassin, René: "Recent Reforms in the Government and Administration of France," *Public Administration,* Vol. 28 (1950), pp. 179–187.
Chapman, Brian: "The Organization of the French Police," *Public Administration,* Vol. 29 (1951), pp. 67–75.
Einaudi, Mario: "Nationalization of Industry in Western Europe," *American Political Science Review,* Vol. 44 (1950), pp. 177–191.
Macridis, Roy C.: "Cabinet Instability in the Fourth Republic (1946–1951)," *Journal of Politics,* Vol. 14 (1952), pp. 643–658.
———: "The Cabinet Secretariat in France," *Journal of Politics,* Vol. 13 (1951), pp. 589–603.
Myers, Margaret G.: "Nationalization of Key Industries and Credit in France after Liberation," *Political Science Quarterly,* Vol. 41 (1947), pp. 368–380.
Robson, William A.: "Nationalized Industries in Britain and France," *American Political Science Review,* Vol. 44 (1950), pp. 299–322.
Trouvé, Jean: "The French Civil Service Office," *Public Administration Review,* Vol. 40 (1951), pp. 180–186.

PARLIAMENT

Lidderdale, D. W. S.: *The Parliament of France,* London, 1951.

Articles

Bourne, H. E.: "American Constitutional Precedents in the French National Assembly," *American Historical Review,* Vol. 8 (1903), pp. 466–486.
Cobban, Alfred: "The Second Chamber in France," *Political Quarterly,* Vol. 19 (1948), pp. 223–235.
Plaisant, Marcel: "Le contrôle de la politique extérieure par le Conseil de la République," *Revue politique et parlémentaire,* Vol. 52 (1950), pp. 113–122.
Stamps, Norman L.: "A Comparative Study of Legislative Investigations: England, France and Weimar Germany," *Journal of Politics,* Vol. 14, (1952), pp. 592–615.

LAW AND JUSTICE

Brissaud, Jean: *A History of French Private Law* (trans. by R. Howell), Boston, 1912.
———: *A History of French Public Law* (trans. by J. W. Garner), Boston, 1915.
Ensor, Robert C. K.: *Courts and Judges in France, Germany and England,* Oxford, 1933.
Rohkam, W., and O. C. Pratt: *Studies in French Administrative Law,* Urbana, 1947.
Waline, Marcel: *Traité élémentaire de droit administratif,* 6th ed., Paris, 1951.

Articles

Deak, F., and M. Rheinstein: "The Development of French and German Law," *Georgetown Law Journal,* Vol. 24 (1936), pp. 551–583.

Diamant, Alfred: "The French Council of State. Comparative Observations on the Problem of Controlling the Bureaucracy of the Modern State," *Journal of Politics,* Vol. 13 (1951), pp. 562–588.

Garner, James W.: "French Administrative Law," *Yale Law Journal,* Vol. 33 (1924), pp. 597–627.

————: "The French Judiciary," *Yale Law Journal,* Vol. 26 (1917), pp. 349–387.

Hamson, C. J.: "Le Conseil d'État statuant aux Contentieux" (in English), *Law Quarterly Review,* Vol. 68 (1952), pp. 60–87.

Lobinger, C. S.: "Administrative Law and *Droit Administratif,*" *University of Pennsylvania Law Review,* Vol. 91 (1942), pp. 36–58.

Marx, F. M.: "Comparative Administrative Law," *University of Pennsylvania Law Review,* Vol. 91 (1942), pp. 118–136.

Riesenfeld, Stephan: "The French System of Administrative Justice: A Model for American Law?" *Boston University Law Review,* Vol. 18 (1938), pp. 48–82.

Wright, A. C.: "French Criminal Procedure," *Law Quarterly Review,* Vol. 44 (1928), pp. 324–341 and Vol. 45 (1929), pp. 92–107.

LOCAL GOVERNMENT

Chapman, Brian: *Introduction to French Local Government,* London, 1953.

Articles

Abbott, R. S., and R. Sicard: "A Postwar Development in French Regional Government: The 'Super Prefet,' " *American Political Science Review,* Vol. 44 (1950), pp. 426–431.

Chapman, Brian: "A Development in French Regional Administration," *Public Administration,* Vol. 28 (1950), pp. 327–332.

Hermens, F. A.: "Local Autonomy in France and Italy," in A. J. Zurcher (ed.), *Constitutions and Constitutional Trends since World War II,* New York, 1951, pp. 95–115.

Lipman, V. D.: "Recent Trends in French Local Administration," *Public Administration,* Vol. 25 (1947), pp. 29–38.

Sharp, Walter R.: "France," in William Anderson (ed.), *Local Government in Europe,* New York, 1939, pp. 107–222.

THE OVERSEAS EMPIRE

Catroux, General Georges: *The French Union,* International Conciliation Pamphlet No. 495, New York, 1953.

Hammer, Ellen J.: *The Emergence of Viet Nam,* New York, 1947.

Landau, Rom: *Morocco,* International Conciliation Pamphlet No. 483, New York, 1952.

Royal Institute of International Affairs: *The French Colonial Empire,* New York, 1940.

Articles

Boussenot, G.: "L'Assemblé de l'Union Française, son rôle, l'élargissement de ses pouvoirs," *Revue Politique et Parlémentaire,* Vol. 55 (1953), pp. 29–38.

Julien, C. A.: "From the French Empire to the French Union," *International Affairs,* Vol. 26 (1950), pp. 487–502.

Liebesny, H. J.: "French North Africa: Empire in Transition," *American Perspective,* Vol. 1 (1947), pp. 259–285.

PARTIES AND POLITICS

Blum, Léon: *For All Mankind,* New York, 1946.

Ehrmann, Henry W.: *French Labor from Popular Front to Liberation,* New York, 1947.

Einaudi, M., J. M. Domenach, and A. Garosci: *Communism in Western Europe,* Ithaca, N. Y., 1951.

Einaudi, M., and François Goguel: *Christian Democracy in Italy and France,* Notre Dame, 1952.

Fauvet, Jacques: *Les forces politiques en France,* Paris, 1951.

Goguel, François: *Géographie des élections françaises,* Paris, 1951.

Malraux, André, and J. Burnham: *The Case for De Gaulle,* New York, 1948.

Monnerot, Jules: *Sociology and Psychology of Communism* (trans. by Jane Degras and Richard Rees), Boston, 1953.

Pickles, Dorothy: *French Politics: The First Years of the Fourth Republic,* New York, 1953.

Rossi, A.: *A Communist Party in Action,* New Haven, 1949.

Thomson, David: *Two Frenchmen, Pierre Laval and Charles de Gaulle,* London, 1951.

Articles

Almond, Gabriel A.: "The Christian Parties of Western Europe," *World Politics,* Vol. 1 (1948), pp. 30–58.

———: "Political Ideas of Christian Democracy," *Journal of Politics,* Vol. 10 (1948), pp. 734–763.

Aron, Raymond: "France, Still the Third Republic," *Foreign Affairs,* Vol. 30 (1951), pp. 145–151.

Bouscaren, Anthony T.: "The European Christian Democrats," *Western Political Quarterly,* Vol. 2 (1949), pp. 59–73.

Cook, G. C.: "Charles de Gaulle and the R.P.F.," *Political Science Quarterly,* Vol. 65 (1950), pp. 333–352.

Duroselle, J. B.: "The Turning Point in French Politics: 1947," *Review of Politics,* Vol. 13 (1951), pp. 303–328.

Duverger, Maurice: "Public Opinion and Political Parties in France," *American Political Science Review,* Vol. 46 (1952), pp. 1069–1078.

Ehrmann, Henry W.: "France between East and West," *Western Political Quarterly,* Vol. 2 (1949), pp. 74–88.

———: "French Labor Goes West," *Foreign Affairs,* Vol. 26 (1947), pp. 465–476.

———: "French Views on Communism," *World Politics,* Vol. 3 (1950), pp. 141–151.

Einaudi, Mario: "The Crisis of Politics and Government in France," *World Politics,* Vol. 4 (1951), pp. 64–84.

———: "Western European Communism: A Profile," *American Political Science Review,* Vol. 45 (1951), pp. 185–208.

Katzenbach, Edward L.: "Political Parties and the French Army since Liberation," *World Politics,* Vol. 3 (1950), pp. 533–548.

Le Bras, Gabriel: "Géographie électorale et géographie réligieuse," *Études de Sociologie Électorale* (Cahiers de la Fondation Nationale des Sciences Politiques, No. 1), Paris, 1947.

Neumann, Robert G.: "Formation and Transformation of Gaullism in France," *Western Political Quarterly,* Vol. 6 (1953), pp. 250–274.

———: "The Struggle for Electoral Reform in France," *American Political Science Review,* Vol. 45 (1951), pp. 741–755.

Pickles, Dorothy M.: "The Political Situation in France," *Political Quarterly,* Vol. 18 (1947), pp. 36–47.

Remond, R.: "Les partis catholiques," *La Vie Intellectuelle,* Vol. 24 (1953), pp. 173–189.

Van Dyke, Vernon: "The Position and Prospects of the Communists in France," *Political Science Quarterly,* Vol. 42 (1948), pp. 45–81.

Wright, Gordon: "French Farmers in Politics," *South Atlantic Quarterly,* Vol. 51 (1952), pp. 356–365.

GERMANY

The literature on Germany has suffered from two serious shortcomings: the rapidity with which Germany has changed political regimes in modern times, and the passion which her actions have aroused. Hence political and constitutional studies are available only on individual periods. And the passion aroused makes for a great deal of partisan literature.

Among historical treatises trying to scan the entire course of German history and to chart lasting characteristics, mention might be made of the brief but brilliantly written book by A. J. P. Taylor, *The Course of German History.* Noteworthy are also G. Barraclough, *The Origins of Modern Germany,* and Veit Valentin's *The German People.* A recent outstanding treatment is by J. K. Pollock, M. Thomas, and others, *Germany in Power and Eclipse: the Background of Germany's Development.* There are a great number of studies on individual periods of German history, by both German and foreign scholars.

The Weimar Republic must be studied for parallels and antecedents of the present German Federal Republic. F. F. Blachly and M. R. Oatman's *The Government and Administration of Germany* is truly monumental in its expanse but also in its boredom and total absence of profound penetration. The history of the Weimar Republic has been ably traced by a number of scholars. William S. Halperin's *Germany Tried Democracy* gives a very readable and reliable account. Noteworthy are also *Republican Germany* by H. Quigley and R. T. Clark, and R. T. Clark's *The Fall of the German Republic.* Arthur Rosenberg's *A History of the German Republic* is also very good. G. Scheele's *The Weimar Republic* is an outstanding essay.

On the Constitution of Weimar much material may be found in Herman Finer's *The Theory and Practice of Modern Government.* Special studies are Johannes Mattern, *Principles of Constitutional Jurisprudence of the German National Republic,* H. J. Heneman's *The Growth of Executive Power in Germany,* and A. J. Zurcher's *The Experiment with Democracy in Central Europe.* Much important material can be found in Karl Loewenstein's "Government and Politics in Germany," in J. T. Shotwell's *Governments of Continental Europe* (more extensive in the 1940 than in the 1952 edition).

Among German writers we find the authoritative commentaries by G. Anschütz, *Die Verfassung des deutschen Reichs,* and similar works by Stier-Somlo, Poetzsch-Heffter, and others. Less detailed but more penetrating are the works of two French scholars, R. Brunet, *The New German Constitution,* and E. Vermeil, *La Constitution de Weimar et le principe de la démocratie allemande.* On the German parties of the Weimar period see especially Ludwig Bergsträsser, *Geschichte der politischen Parteien in Deutschland,* and Sigmund Neumann's *Die Deutschen Parteien.*

The literature on the Nazi period is immense. See especially R. D. Butler's *The Roots of National Socialism,* E. Fraenkel's *The Dual State,* Franz Neumann's *Behemoth,* and S. H. Roberts, *The House that Hitler Built.* Konrad Heiden's *Der Fuehrer* is a recognized masterpiece on Hitler. H. R. Trevor-Roper's brilliantly and dramatically written *The Last Days of Hitler* deals only with the fall of Berlin but demonstrates the demoniac hold which Hitler wielded over all near him. For a comprehensive treatment of government under the Nazi regime see J. K. Pollock's *The Government of Greater Germany* and Karl Loewenstein's *Hitler's Germany*. Among the numerous descriptions of Nazi terror, Eugen Kogon's *Der SS-Staat* is particularly impressive.

For the new German Federal Republic the literature is not plentiful. Litchfield and Associates, *Governing Postwar Germany,* is a book of essays by specialists on various aspects of German government. The leading commentary on the German Constitution is Hermann von Mangoldt, *Das Bonner Grundgesetz*. Also see *Kommentar zum Bonner Grundgesetz* (Bonner Kommentar) by numerous authors. Also useful is the publication *Documents on the Creation of the German Federal Constitution* issued by the United States Office of Military Government, as well as the various *Quarterly Reports* issued by the Office of the United States High Commissioner for Germany. For serious students, a study of the growing number of cases decided by the Federal Constitutional Court (*Entscheidungen des Bundesverfassungsgerichts*) is indispensable.

There is as yet no comprehensive treatment of the political parties in the German Federal Republic. Some of the articles dealing therewith are listed below.

Outstanding German newspapers are the *Frankfurter Zeitung, Süddeutsche Zeitung,* and *Die Neue Zeitung* (founded by the United States Military Government). Good weeklies are *Der Rheinische Merkur* and *Die Welt*. Outstanding periodicals are *Die Gegenwart, Die Wandlung, Hochland, Die Welt als Geschichte,* and *Frankfurter Heft*.

There are numerous professional and learned journals. Note especially *Archiv des öffentlichen Rechts, Aussenpolitik, Europa Archiv, Osteuropa, Neue Juristische Wochenschrift, Schmollers Jahrbücher, Zeitschrift für die Gesammte Staatswissenschaft,* and *Internationales Jahrbuch der Politik*. Note also the numerous studies published under the auspices of the various Hochschulen für Politische Wissenschaften (Politik).

Only one book-length study of Eastern Germany is worthy of special note. It is J. P. Nettl's very illuminating *The Eastern Zone and Soviet Policy in Germany 1945–50*.

GENERAL HISTORY

Barraclough, G.: *The Origins of Modern Germany,* 2d ed., Oxford, 1949.
Pollack, J. K., M. Thomas, and others: *Germany in Power and Eclipse: The Background of German Development,* New York, 1952.
Shuster, G. N., and A. Bergsträsser: *Germany, A Short History,* New York, 1944.
Taylor, A. J. P.: *The Course of German History,* New York, 1946
Valentin, Veit: *The German People,* New York, 1946.

Articles
Becker, Howard: "Changes in the Social Stratification of Contemporary Germany," *American Sociological Review,* Vol. 15 (1950), pp. 333–342.

THE WEIMAR REPUBLIC

Blachly, F. F., and M. E. Oatman: *The Government and Administration of Germany,* Baltimore, 1928.
Brecht, Arnold: *Federalism and Regionalism in Germany,* New York, 1945.
Brunet, René: *The New German Constitution* (trans. by Joseph Gollomb), New York, 1922.
Clark, Robert T.: *The Fall of the German Republic,* London, 1935.
Fromm, Erich: *Escape from Freedom,* New York, 1941.
Halperin, William S.: *Germany Tried Democracy,* New York, 1946.

Heneman, Harlow H.: *The Growth of Executive Power in Germany*, Minneapolis, 1934.
Hermens, F. A.: *Democracy or Anarchy*, Notre Dame, 1941.
Quigley, H., and R. T. Clark: *Republican Germany*, New York, 1928.
Rosenberg, Arthur: *A History of the German Republic*, London, 1936.
Scheele, Godfrey: *The Weimar Republic, Overture to the Third Reich*, London, 1946.
Sturmthal, A. F.: *The Tragedy of European Labor 1918–1939*, New York, 1943.

THE NAZI REGIME

Bowen, Ralph: *German Theories of the Corporative State*, New York, 1947.
Butler, R. D.: *The Roots of National Socialism*, New York, 1942.
Dulles, Allen W.: *Germany's Underground*, New York, 1947.
Ebenstein, William: *The German Record*, New York, 1945.
Fraenkel, Ernst: *The Dual State, A Contribution to the Theory of Dictatorship*, New York, 1941.
Gisevius, E. B.: *To the Bitter End*, Boston, 1947.
Heiden, Konrad: *Der Fuehrer*, London, 1944.
Kogon, Eugen: *Der SS-Staat, Das System der deutschen Konzentrationslager*, Munich, 1946.
Kolnai, Aurel: *The War against the West*, New York, 1938.
Neumann, Franz: *Behemoth, the Structure and Practice of National Socialism*, New York, 1942.
Pollock, James K.: *The Government of Greater Germany*, New York, 1938.
Rauschnigg, Hermann: *The Voice of Destruction*, New York, 1940.
Roberts, Stephen H.: *The House that Hitler Built*, New York, 1938.
Rothfels, Hans: *The German Opposition to Hitler*, Hinsdale, Ill., 1948.
Trevor-Roper, H. R.: *The Last Days of Hitler*, New York, 1947.

Articles
Herz, John: "German Administration under the Nazi Regime," *American Political Science Review*, Vol. 40 (1946), pp. 682–702.

THE REESTABLISHMENT OF GERMANY

Almond, Gabriel A. (ed.): *The Struggle for Democracy in Germany*, Chapel Hill, 1949.
Clark, D.: *Again the Goose Step, the Last Fruits of Victory*, Indianapolis, 1949.
Clay, Lucius D.: *Decision in Germany*, New York, 1950.
Friedmann, W.: *The Allied Military Government of Germany*, London, 1947.
Friedrich, C. J., and Associates: *American Experiences in Military Government in World War II*, New York, 1948.
Holborn, Hojo: *Military Government Organization and Politics*, New York, 1947.
Litchfield, E., and Associates: *Governing Postwar Germany*, Ithaca, 1953.
Middleton, Drew: *The Struggle for Germany*, Indianapolis, 1949.
Office of the U. S. High Commissioner for Germany: *Report on Germany, September 21, 1949–July 31, 1952*.
Stolper, Gustav: *German Realities*, New York, 1948.
Utley, Freda: *The High Cost of Vengeance*, Chicago, 1949.
Warburg, James P.: *Germany, Bridge or Battleground*, New York, 1947.
Zink, Harold: *American Military Government in Germany*, New York, 1947.

Articles
Brecht, Arnold: "Re-establishing German Government," *Annals of the American Academy of Political and Social Science* (January, 1950), pp. 28–42.

Griffith, William E.: "Denazification in the U.S. Zone of Germany," *Annals of the American Academy of Political and Social Science* (January, 1950), pp. 68–76.

Guradze, Heinz: "The Länderrat, Landmark of German Reconstruction," *Western Political Quarterly*, Vol. 3 (1950), pp. 190–213.

Herz, John: "The Fiasco of Denazification in Germany," *Political Science Quarterly*, Vol. 63 (1948), pp. 569–594.

Pollock, James K.: "Germany under Military Occupation," *Change and Crisis in European Government*, New York, 1947, pp. 15–61.

Pollock, J. K., J. H. Meisel, and H. L. Bretton: *Germany under Occupation, Illustrative Materials and Documents*, Ann Arbor, 1949.

"Postwar Reconstruction in Western Germany," *Annals of the American Academy of Political and Social Science* (entire issue of November, 1948).

CONSTITUTIONS AND CONSTITUTIONAL LAW

Lewis, Harold O.: *New Constitutions in Occupied Germany*, Washington, 1948.

Mangoldt, Hermann von: *Das Bonner Grundgesetz*, Berlin and Frankfurt, 1953.

Mannz, Theodor: *Deutsches Staatsrecht*, Munich, 1951.

U.S. Office of Military Government, Civil Administration Division: *Documents on the Creation of the German Federal Constitution*, Sept. 1, 1949.

Articles

Bachof, O.: "German Administrative Law," *International and Comparative Law Quarterly*, Vol. 2(3) (1953), pp. 368–382.

Brecht, Arnold: "The New German Constitution," *Social Research*, Vol. 16 (1949), pp. 425–473.

Friedrich, C. J.: "The Constitution of the German Federal Republic," in E. Litchfield and Associates, *Governing postwar Germany*, Ithaca, 1953, pp. 117–151.

————: "Rebuilding the German Constitution," *American Political Science Review*, Vol. 43 (1949), pp. 461–482.

Kalisch, W.: "Grundrechte und Berufsbeamtentum nach dem Bonner Grundgesetz," *Archiv des öffentlichen Rechts*, Vol. 78 (1953), pp. 334–354.

Neumann, Robert G.: "New Constitutions in Germany," *American Political Science Review*, Vol. 42 (1948), pp. 448–468.

Rich, Bennett M.: "Civil Liberties in Germany," *Political Science Quarterly*, Vol. 65 (1950), pp. 68–85.

Simons, Hans: "The Bonn Constitution and Its Government," in Hans Morgenthau (ed.), *Germany and the Future of Europe*, Chicago, 1951.

THE OPERATION OF GERMAN GOVERNMENT

Bonman, P. J., G. Beijar, and J. J. Oudegeest: *The Refugee Problem in West Germany*, The Hague, 1950.

Articles

Brecht, Arnold: "Civil Service Reform in Germany, Problems and Suggestions," *Personnel Administration*, Vol. 9 (1947), pp. 1–8.

————: "Personnel Management," in E. Litchfield and Associates, *Governing Postwar Germany*, Ithaca, 1953, pp. 263–293.

Dorr, Harold M., and H. L. Bretton: "Legislation," in E. Litchfield and Associates, *Governing Postwar Germany*, Ithaca, 1953, pp. 207–235.

Huber, E. R.: "Bundesexekution und Bundesintervention," *Archiv des öffentlichen Rechts*, Vol. 78 (1953), pp. 1–57.

Meyerhoff, Hans: "Reconstruction of Government and Administration," in Gabriel A. Almond (ed.), *The Struggle for Democracy in Germany*, Chapel Hill, 1949.
Wunderlich, F.: "Codetermination in German Industry," *Social Research*, Vol. 20 (1953), pp. 75–90.

LAW AND JUSTICE

Ensor, Robert C. K.: *Courts and Judges in France, Germany and England*, London, 1933.
Wunderlich, Frieda: *German Labor Courts*, Chapel Hill, N. C., 1946.

Articles

Honig, F.: "Criminal Justice in Germany To-Day," *Yearbook of World Affairs*, London, 1951, pp. 131–152.
Leibholz, Gerhard: "The Federal Constitutional Court in Germany and the 'Southwest Case,'" *American Political Science Review*, Vol. 46 (1952), pp. 723–731.
Loewenstein, Karl: "Justice," in Litchfield and Associates, *Governing Postwar Germany*, Ithaca, 1953, pp. 236–262.
———: "Law and the Legislative Process in Occupied Germany," *Yale Law Journal*, Vol. 57 (1948), pp. 724–760, 994–1022.
———: "Reconstruction of the Administration of Justice in American-Occupied Germany," *Harvard Law Review*, Vol. 61 (1948), pp. 419–467.
Rupp, Hans G.: "A Supreme Court in Germany," *Harvard Law School Bulletin*, Vol. 5 (1954), pp. 10–14.

STATE AND LOCAL GOVERNMENT

Gillen, J. F. J.: *State and Local Government in West Germany, 1945–1953, with Special Reference to the U. S. Zone and Bremen*, Berlin, 1953.
Plischke, E.: *Berlin: Development of Its Government and Administration*, Berlin, 1952.
Saar Government: *The Saar*, 3d rev. ed., Saarbrücken, 1953.
U.S. Office of Military Government for Germany, Civil Administration Division: *Land and Local Government in the U. S. Zone of Germany*, 1947.

Articles

Kirchheimer, Otto: "The Decline of Intra-State Federalism in Western Europe," *World Politics*, Vol. 3 (1950–1951), pp. 281–298.
Wells, Roger H.: "Local Government" and "State Government," in Litchfield and Associates, *Governing Postwar Germany*, Ithaca, 1953, pp. 57–83, 84–116.

PARTIES AND POLITICS

Hermens, F. A.: *Europe between Democracy and Anarchy*, Notre Dame, 1951.
Meyer, E. W.: *Political Parties in Western Germany*, Washington, 1951.
Neumann, Franz: *German Democracy 1950*, International Conciliation Pamphlet No. 461, New York, 1950.
Salvin, Marina: *Neutralism in France and Germany*, International Conciliation Pamphlet No. 472, New York, 1951.
Wieck, Hans G.: *Die Entstehung der CDU und die Wiedergründung des Zentrums im Jahre 1945*, Düsseldorf, 1953.

Articles

Almond, Gabriel A.: "The Political Ideas of Christian Democracy," *Journal of Politics*, Vol. 10 (1948), pp. 734–763.

Bretton, Henry L.: "The German Social Democratic Party and the International Situation," *American Political Science Review*, Vol. 47 (1953), pp. 980–996.

Carey, Jane: "Political Organization of the Refugees and Expellees in West Germany," *Political Science Quarterly*, Vol. 45 (1951), pp. 191–215.

Klemperer, Klemens von: "Toward a Fourth Reich? The History of National Bolshevism in Germany," *Review of Politics*, Vol. 13 (1951), pp. 191–210.

Lewis, Harold O.: "The Socialist Unity Party in Germany," *American Perspective*, Vol. 2 (1948–1949), pp. 523–553.

Meyerhoff, Hans: "Parties and Classes in Postwar Germany," *South Atlantic Quarterly*, Vol. 46 (1947), pp. 12–26.

Neumann, Robert G.: "The New Political Parties of Germany," *American Political Science Review*, Vol. 40 (1946), pp. 749–759.

Scammon, Richard M.: "Political Parties" and "Postwar Elections and Electoral Processes," in Litchfield and Associates, *Governing Postwar Germany*, Ithaca, 1953, pp. 471–499, 500–535.

Sturmthal, Adolf: "Democratic Socialism in Europe," *World Politics*, Vol. 3 (1950), pp. 88–112.

U.S. Office of Military Government for Germany, Civil Administration Division, *Political Parties in Western Germany*, 1949.

The Eastern Zone

Department of State Publication 4596: *East Germany under Soviet Control*, Washington, 1952.

Nettl, J. P.: *The Eastern Zone and Soviet Policy in Germany, 1945–50*, London, 1951.

Office of the U.S. High Commissioner for Germany: *Soviet Zone Constitution and Electoral Law*, 1951.

Articles

Cox, H. B.: "Establishment of the Soviet-Sponsored East German Republics," *Department of State Bulletin*, Vol. 21 (1949), pp. 761–764.

Glaser, Kurt: "Governments of Soviet Germany," in Litchfield and Associates, *Governing Postwar Germany*, Ithaca, 1953, pp. 152–183.

Kirchheimer, Otto: "The Government of Eastern Germany," in Hans J. Morgenthau (ed.), *Germany and the Future of Europe*, Chicago, 1951, pp. 131–141.

Kuelz, H. R.: "The Soviet Zone of Germany," *International Affairs*, Vol. 27 (1951), pp. 156–166.

UNION OF SOVIET SOCIALIST REPUBLICS

Bibliography on the U.S.S.R. differs in many significant respects from that on other countries. Primary sources are of course very useful but only up to a point, namely, where information is sought concerning relatively uncontroversial, factual points. Beyond that their usefulness is seriously mitigated by the fact that no Soviet publication is ever critical about anything which occurs in the U.S.S.R. unless it is to attack individuals for their already determined liquidation, or institutions for their already determined abolition or reform. The same is true of Soviet authors of secondary material—only wholly uncritical, often nauseatingly laudatory material about the U.S.S.R. is produced. Much information is to be found even in such works, but their limitations are obvious.

On the other hand, a major effort has been made in recent years by foreign and Russian-exile scholars to throw some light on the government of the Soviet Union, and a vast output of publication has been the result, much of it of high quality. This improves the situation considerably but it has two obvious drawbacks. In the first place, foreign scholars must concentrate on material available abroad, of which there is a great deal, but in which there are some serious lacunae. Little information is available about the more technical level of public administration in the U.S.S.R., and most seriously there is much obscurity about the way in which decisions are made at the very top. The inner workings of the Politburo–party Presidium have remained closed to outsiders.

In view of the vast array of literature on the subject, the works cited below are merely an extract. Among the many useful ones, the author considers as particularly outstanding for general as well as detailed information and excellent readability, Merle Fainsod's *How Russia Is Ruled*. Another excellent book is Barrington Moore's *Soviet Politics—The Dilemma of Power*. Cast in a narrower frame, mainly of a legal and institutional kind, Julian Towster's *Political Power in the U.S.S.R.* (a somewhat misleading title) is unsurpassed in thoroughness, and with its detailed use of not easily available sources it constitutes a major contribution to our knowledge of the U.S.S.R. A very useful source book is J. S. Meisel and E. S. Kozera, *Materials for the Study of the Soviet System*.

Leading Soviet newspapers are *Pravda* and *Isvestia*. Also very important are the periodical *Kommunist* (formerly *Bolshevik*) and the trade-union paper *Trud*. *Nevaya Vremiya* appears in an English edition (*New Times*) and contains many articles on foreign affairs. The organ of the Cominform, *For a Lasting Peace, For a People's Democracy,* also appears in English (published in Bucharest).

Excerpt translations from the Russian press including even the provincial press may be read in English translation in *Current Digest of the Soviet Press* and *Soviet Press Translations,* and for broadcasts in *Soviet Monitor*. All periodicals dedicated to political science, sociology, economics, history, etc., contain occasional articles on the Soviet Union. Especially concerned with the U.S.S.R. are *American Review of the Soviet Union, American Slavic and East European Review, Russian Review, Slavonic and East European Review, Soviet Studies,* and the German periodical *Osteuropa*. The Soviet government issues numerous publications in English, among which might be mentioned the *U.S.S.R. Information Bulletin*.

Some of the best insights into the Soviet totalitarian mind may be found in certain novels, especially Arthur Koestler's *Darkness at Noon,* and *The Yogi and the Commissar,* as well as George Orwell's *1984*.

GENERAL HISTORY

Kliachevsky, Vasily: *A History of Russia* (trans. by Hogarth), 5 vols., London, 1911–1931.
Maynard, Sir John: *Russia in Flux* (ed. by S. M. Guest), New York, 1948.
Mazour, Anatole G.: *Russia, Past and Present,* New York, 1951.
Pares, Sir Bernard: *A History of Russia,* 4th ed., New York, 1946.
Vernadsky, G.: *History of Russia,* 3d ed., New Haven, 1951.
———: *Political and Diplomatic History of Russia,* Boston, 1936.

THE RUSSIAN REVOLUTION

Chamberlin, W. H.: *The Russian Revolution 1917–1921,* 2 vols., New York, 1935.
Kerenski, Alexander: *The Catastrophe,* New York, 1927.
Trotsky, Leon: *History of the Russian Revolution,* 3 vols., New York, 1936.
———: *Lessons of October,* New York, 1937.
———: *My Life,* New York, 1930.
———: *The Revolution Betrayed,* New York, 1937.

Vernadsky, G.: *The Russian Revolution 1917–1931,* New York, 1932.
Wolfe, Bertram D.: *Three Who Made Revolution,* New York, 1948.

LENIN AND STALIN

Deutscher, Isaac: *Stalin: A Political Biography,* New York, 1949.
Krupskaya, N. K.: *Memories of Lenin* (trans. by E. Verney), New York, 1930
Levine, I. D.: *Stalin,* New York, 1931.
Mirsky, D. S.: *Lenin,* Boston, 1931.
Shub, David: *Lenin, a Biography,* New York, 1948.
Souvarin, B.: *Stalin,* New York, 1939.
Trotsky, Leon: *Lenin,* London, 1925.
————: *Stalin,* New York, 1946.

THE THEORY OF COMMUNISM

Berdyaev, Nikolai: *The Origins of Russian Communism,* New York, 1938.
Burns, Emile (ed.): *A Handbook of Marxism,* New York, 1935.
Cole, G. D. H.: *What Marx Really Meant,* London, 1934.
Eastman, Max: *Marxism: Is It a Science?,* London, 1941.
Engels, Friedrich: *Herr Eugen Dühring's Revolution in Science* (trans. by E. Burns),
    London, 1935.
Gurian, Waldemar: *Bolshevism: An Introduction to Soviet Communism,* Notre Dame,
    1952.
Hook, Sydney: *From Hegel to Marx,* New York, 1936.
————: *Towards an Understanding of Karl Marx,* New York, 1933.
Kelsen, Hans: *The Political Theory of Bolshevism,* Berkeley, 1949.
Laski, H. J.: *Karl Marx: An Essay,* London, 1922.
Lenin, V. I.: *Imperialism: the Highest Stage of Capitalism,* New York, 1939.
————: *State and Revolution,* New York, 1929.
————: *What Is to Be Done?,* New York, 1929.
Lindsey, A. D.: *Karl Marx's Capital: An Introductory Essay,* New York, 1947.
Marx, Karl: *Capital*
————: *Class Struggle in France*
————: *Critique of the Political Economy* ⎫ numerous editions.
————: *Manifesto of the Communist Party* ⎭
Sommerville, John: *Soviet Philosophy: A Study of Theory and Practice,* New York,
    1946.
Stalin, J. V.: *Dialectical and Historical Materialism,* New York, 1940.
————: *Leninism,* 2 vols., New York, 1928–1933 (various differing editions).
————: *Marxism and the National and Colonial Question,* New York, 1936.
Sweezy, Paul M.: *Socialism,* New York, 1949.

Articles
Historicus: "Stalin on Revolution," *Foreign Affairs,* Vol. 28 (1949), pp. 175–214.

GENERAL TREATISES, ANALYSES, AND OBSERVATIONS

Barmine, Alexander: *One Who Survived: The Life and Story of a Russian under the
    Soviets,* New York, 1945.
Basily, Nicolas de: *Russia under Soviet Rule,* New York, 1940.
Chamberlin, W. H.: *The Russian Enigma,* New York, 1943.

Crankshaw, Edward: *Cracks in the Kremlin Wall*, New York, 1951.

————: *Russia and the Russians*, New York, 1948.

Dallin, D. J.: *The Real Soviet Russia* (trans. by J. Shaplen), New Haven, 1944.

Deutscher, Isaac: *Russia: What Next?* London, 1954.

Fainsod, Merle: *How Russia Is Ruled*, Cambridge, Mass., 1953.

Fischer, George: *Soviet Opposition to Stalin*, Cambridge, Mass., 1952.

Florinsky, Michael J.: *Towards an Understanding of the U.S.S.R. A Study in Government, Politics, and Economic Planning*, rev. ed., New York, 1951.

Gurian, Waldemar (ed.): *The Soviet Union: Background, Ideology, Reality*, Notre Dame, 1951.

Harper, S. N., and R. Thompson: *The Government of the Soviet Union*, 2d ed., New York, 1949.

Library of Congress, Legislative Reference Service: *Communism in Action*, 79th Congress, 2d Session, House Document No. 754, Washington, 1946.

Magidoff, Robert: *In Anger and Pity*, New York, 1949.

Meisel, J. S., and E. S. Kozera: *Materials for the Study of the Soviet System*, Ann Arbor, 1953.

Moore, Barrington, Jr.: *Soviet Politics—The Dilemma of Power*, Cambridge, Mass., 1950.

————: *Terror and Progress, U.S.S.R.: Some Sources of Change and Stability in the Soviet Dictatorship*, Cambridge, Mass., 1954.

Rosenberg, Arthur: *History of Bolshevism*, Oxford, 1934.

Rostow, W. W. (in collaboration with Alfred Levin): *The Dynamics of Soviet Society*, New York, 1953.

Rothstein, Andrew: *A History of the U.S.S.R.*, New York, 1950.

Schuman, Frederick L.: *Soviet Politics at Home and Abroad*, New York, 1946.

Scott, John: *Behind the Urals*, New York, 1942.

Smith, Walter Bedell: *My Three Years in Moscow*, Philadelphia, 1950.

The Soviet Union as Reported by Former Soviet Citizens, Department of State Report No. 3 (1952).

Stalin, J. V.: *History of the Communist Party of the Soviet Union*, New York, 1939.

83d Congress, 1st session, *Tensions within the Soviet Union*, Senate Document No. 69 (1953).

Timasheff, Nicholas: *The Great Retreat*, New York, 1946.

Towster, J.: *Political Power in the U.S.S.R.*, New York, 1948.

Trotsky, Leon: *The Real Situation in Russia*, New York, 1928.

Utley, Freda: *The Dream We Lost*, New York, 1940.

Webb, Sidney and Beatrice: *Soviet Communism: A New Civilization?* 2 vols., New York, 1936.

White, W. L.: *Report on the Russians*, New York, 1945.

Articles

Fainsod, Merle: "Controls and Tensions within the Soviet System," *American Political Science Review*, Vol. 44 (1950), pp. 266–282.

Mosely, Philip E. (ed.): "The Soviet Union since World War II," *Annals of the American Academy of Political and Social Science*, May, 1949 (entire issue).

THE COMMUNIST PARTY

Central Committee of the Communist Party of the Soviet Union: *History of the Communist Party of the Soviet Union (Bolsheviks), Short Course* (credited to J. V. Stalin), New York, 1939.

Duranty, Walter: *Stalin & Co., The Politburo, The Men Who Run Russia*, New York, 1949.

Kovalyov, S.: *Ideological Conflicts in Soviet Russia*, Washington, 1948.

Leites, Nathan: *The Operational Code of the Politburo*, New York, 1951.

Schneller, George K.: *The Politburo*, Palo Alto, Calif., 1951.

Articles

Daniels, Robert G.: "The Soviet Succession: Lenin and Stalin," *Russian Review*, Vol. 12 (1953), pp. 153–172.

Fainsod, Merle: "The Komsomols—A Study of Youth under Dictatorship," *American Political Science Review*, Vol. 45 (1951), pp. 18–40.

———: "Postwar Role of the Communist Party," *Annals of the American Academy of Political and Social Science* (May, 1949), pp. 20–32.

Leites, Nathan: "Aspects of Politburo Behavior," *World Politics*, Vol. 3 (1950), pp. 549–559.

Mohrenschildt, Dimitri von: "Postwar Party Line of the All-Union Communist Party of the U.S.S.R.," *Russian Review*, Vol. 9 (1950), pp. 171–178.

Moore, Barrington, Jr.: "The Communist Party of the Soviet Union: 1928–1944," *American Sociological Review*, Vol. 9 (1944), pp. 267–278.

Nemzer, Louis: "The Kremlin Professional Staff: The 'Apparatus' of the Control Committee, Communist Party of the Soviet Union," *American Political Science Review*, Vol. 44 (1950), pp. 64–85.

Reshetar, John S., Jr.: "National Deviation in the Soviet Union," *American Slavic and East European Review*, Vol. 12 (1953), pp. 162–174.

Schlesinger, R.: "Notes on the Changing Functions of Party Congresses," *Soviet Studies*, Vol. 4 (1953), pp. 386–402.

Utis, O.: "Generalissimo Stalin and the Art of Government," *Foreign Affairs*, Vol. 31 (1952), pp. 197–214.

FORCED LABOR, COMPULSION, AND TERROR

American Federation of Labor, "Slave Labor in Russia," New York, 1949.

Beck, F., and E. Goodin: *Russian Purge and the Extraction of Confession*, New York, 1951.

Dallin, O. J., and B. I. Nicolaevsky, *Forced Labor in the Soviet Union*, New Haven, 1947.

Eliot, T. S. (ed.): *Dark Side of the Moon*, New York, 1947.

Fisher, L.: *Thirteen Who Fled*, New York, 1949.

Gliksman, Jersy: *Tell the West*, New York, 1948.

Kravchenko, V.: *I Chose Freedom*, New York, 1946.

Lipper, Elinor: *11 Years in Soviet Prison Camps*, Chicago, 1951.

Mora, S.: *Kolyma*, Washington, 1949.

Piragov, P.: *Why I Escaped*, New York, 1950.

Tchernavin, V. V.: *I Speak for the Silent*, Boston, 1935.

U. S. Department of State: *Forced Labor in the Soviet Union*, Washington, 1952.

Weissberg, Alexander: *The Accused*, New York, 1952.

Articles

Jasny, Naum: "Labor and Output in Soviet Concentration Camps," *Journal of Political Economy*, Vol. 59 (1951), pp. 405–419.

CONSTITUTION AND INSTITUTIONS OF GOVERNMENT

Molotov, V.: *The New Soviet Constitution*, New York, 1937.

Vyshinsky, Andrei Y.: *The Law of the Soviet State* (trans. by H. R. Bobb), New York, 1948.

White, D. Fedotoff: *The Growth of the Red Army*, Princeton, 1944.

Articles

Alexeiev, N. M.: "The Evolution of Soviet Constitutional Law," *Review of Politics*, Vol. 2 (1940), pp. 463–476.

Aspaturian, V. V.: "The Theory and Practice of Soviet Federalism," *Journal of Politics*, Vol. 12 (1950), pp. 20–51.

Fainsod, Merle: "Recent Developments in Soviet Public Administration," *Journal of Politics*, Vol. 11 (1949), pp. 679–714.

Guins, George C.: "Soviet Centralism," *American Journal of Economics and Sociology*, Vol. 9 (1950), pp. 335–346.

Hazard, John N.: "Political, Administrative and Judicial Structure in the U.S.S.R.," *Annals of the American Academy of Political and Social Science* (May, 1949), pp. 9–19.

———: "Constitutional Problems in the U.S.S.R.," in James K. Pollock (ed.), *Change and Crisis in European Government*, New York, 1947, pp. 3–16.

———: "Federal Organization of the U.S.S.R.," *Russian Review*, Vol. 3 (1944), pp. 21–29.

Maxwell, Bertram W.: "The Soviet Union," in William Anderson (ed.), *Local Government in Europe*, New York, 1939, pp. 383–447.

Meissner, B.: "Die gesetzgeherische Tätigkeit des Obersten Sowjets der U.S.S.R. und die Entwicklung der Sowietexekutive von 1949–1953," *Europa-Archiv*, Vol. 8 (1953), pp. 5693–5706.

Nove, A.: "Some Aspects of Soviet Constitutional Theory," *Modern Law Review*, Vol. 12 (1949), pp. 12–36.

THE SOVIET ECONOMY

Arakelian, A: *Industrial Management in the U.S.S.R.*, Washington, 1950.

Baykov, A.: *Development of the Soviet Economic System*, Cambridge, 1946.

Bergson, A.: *Structure of Soviet Wages*, Cambridge, Mass., 1944.

Bienstock, Gregory, and others: *Management in Russian Industry and Agriculture*, New York, 1944.

Deutscher, Isaac: *Soviet Trade Unions: Their Place in Soviet Labor Policy*, New York, 1950.

Dobb, M.: *Soviet Planning and Labor*, New York, 1943.

Hubbard, L. E.: *Soviet Labor and Industry*, London, 1942.

Jasny, Naum: *The Soviet Economy during the Plan Era*, Palo Alto, Calif., 1952.

Miller, Margaret: *Labour in the U.S.S.R.*, London, 1942.

Schwartz, Harry: *Russia's Soviet Economy*, New York, 1950.

———: *Soviet Economy*, Syracuse, 1949.

Voznesensky, N. A.: *Economy of the U.S.S.R. during World War II*, Washington, 1948.

Vucinich, Alexander: *Soviet Economic Institutions*, Stanford, 1952.

Articles

Bennet, M. K.: "Food and Agriculture in the Soviet Union, 1947–48," *Journal of Political Economy*, Vol. 57 (1949), pp. 185–198.

Berliner, Joseph S.: "The Informal Organization of the Soviet Firm," *Quarterly Journal of Economics*, Vol. 46 (1952), pp. 342–365.

Gsovski, Vladimir, "Elements of Soviet Labor Law," *Monthly Labor Review*, Vol. 72 (1951), pp. 257–262, 385–390.

Volin, Lazar: "The Turn of the Screw in Soviet Agriculture," *Foreign Affairs*, Vol. 30 (1952), pp. 277–288.

Vucinich, Alexander: "The Kolkhoz, Its Social Structure and Development," *American Slavic and East European Review*, Vol. 8 (1949), pp. 10–24.

LAW AND JUSTICE

Berman, Harold J.: *Justice in Russia, an Interpretation of Soviet Law*, Cambridge, Mass., 1950.

Golyakov, I. T.: *The Role of the Soviet Court*, Washington, 1948.

Gsovski, Vladimir: *Soviet Civil Law*, 2 vols., Ann Arbor, 1948–1949.

Hazard, John N. (ed.): *Soviet Legal Philosophy*, Cambridge, Mass., 1952.

Schlesinger, Rudolf: *Soviet Legal Theory*, New York, 1945.

Articles

Berman, Harold J.: "The Challenge of Soviet Law," *Harvard Law Review*, Vol. 61 (1948), pp. 220–265, and Vol. 62 (1949), pp. 449–466.

Guins, George C.: "Law Does Not Wither Away in the Soviet Union," *Russian Review*, Vol. 9 (1950), pp. 187–204.

————: "Soviet Law—Terror Incognito," *Russian Review*, Vol. 8 (1949), pp. 16–29.

Hazard, John N.: "Socialism, Abuse of Power and Soviet Law," *Columbia Law Review*, Vol. 50 (1950), pp. 448–474.

————: "The Soviet Court as a Source of Law," *Washington Law Review*, Vol. 24 (1949), pp. 80–90.

————: "Soviet Socialism and Due Process of Law," *Michigan Law Review*, Vol. 48 (1950), pp. 1061–1078.

PEOPLE, EDUCATION, AND RELIGION

Anderson, Paul B.: *People, Church and State in Modern Russia*, New York, 1944.

Bauer, Raymond A.: *The New Man in Soviet Psychology*, Cambridge, Mass., 1952.

Counts, G. J., and N. P. Lodge: *The Country of the Blind. The Soviet System of Mind Control* (excerpts from the book by Boris P. Esipov and N. K. Goucharov), Boston, 1950.

Hecker, Julius F.: *Religion and Communism*, New York, 1934.

Inkeles, Alex: *Public Opinion in the Soviet Union*, Cambridge, Mass., 1950.

Kollontai, Alexandra: *Communism and the Family*, San Francisco (no date), Russian ed. 1919.

Schwarz, Solomon M.: *The Jews in the Soviet*, Syracuse, N. Y., 1951.

Timasheff, Nicholas S.: *Religion in Soviet Russia, 1917–1942*, London, 1942.

Articles

Anissimov, O.: "The Soviet System of Education," *Russian Review*, Vol. 9 (1950), pp. 87–97.

Brown, J. A.: "Public Opinion in the Soviet Union," *Russian Review*, Vol. 9 (1950), pp. 37–44.

Gsovski, Vladimir: "Marriage and Divorce in Soviet Law," *Georgetown Law Journal*, Vol. 35 (1947), pp. 209–223.

Hazard, John N.: "Law and the Soviet Family," *Wisconsin Law Review* (1939), pp. 224–253.

Inkeles, Alex: "Family and Church in the Postwar U.S.S.R.," *Annals of the American Academy of Political and Social Science* (May, 1949), pp. 33–44.

Timasheff, Nicholas S.: "Vertical Social Mobility in Communist Society," *American Journal of Sociology*, Vol. 50 (1944), pp. 9–21.

THE SOVIET UNION AND THE WORLD

Barghoorn, Frederick C.: *Soviet Image of the United States; A Study in Distortion*, New York, 1950.
Beloff, M.: *Foreign Policy of Soviet Russia*, 2 vols., Oxford, 1947–1949.
Blueprint for World Conquest as Outlined by the Communist International, Washington, 1946.
Borkenau, Franz: *European Communism*, New York, 1953.
————: *World Communism*, New York, 1939.
Carr, E. H.: *The Soviet Impact on the Western World*, New York, 1947.
Cultural Relations between the United States and the Soviet Union, Department of State Publication 3480, Washington, 1949.
Dallin, David J.: *The New Soviet Empire*, New Haven, 1951.
————: *Soviet Russia's Foreign Policy*, New Haven, 1942.
Ebon, Martin: *World Communism To-Day*, New York, 1948.
Fischer, Louis: *The Soviets in World Affairs*, 2 vols., Princeton, 1951.
————: *Trends in Russian Foreign Policy since World War I*, Senate Committee on Foreign Relations, 80th Congress, 1st Session, Washington, 1947.
Fischer, Ruth: *Stalin and German Communism*, Cambridge, Mass., 1948.
Molotov, V. M.: *Problems of Foreign Policy*, New York, 1949.
Taracouzio, T.: *The Soviet Union and International Law*, New York, 1935.
————: *War and Peace in Soviet Diplomacy*, New York, 1940.

Articles
Korovin, E. A.: "The Contribution of the U.S.S.R. to International Law," *Soviet Press Translations*, Vol. 3 (1949), pp. 655ff.
Silone, Ignazio: "Farewell to Moscow," *Harper's Magazine* (November, 1949), pp. 93–99.
"Soviet Violations of Treaty Obligations: Documents Submitted by the Department of State to the Senate Committee on Foreign Relations," *Department of State Bulletin*, Vol. 18 (1948), pp. 738–744.
"X" (George Kennan): "The Sources of Soviet Conduct," *Foreign Affairs*, Vol. 25 (1947), pp. 566–582.

SOME REMARKS ON COMPARATIVE WORKS

It is of course quite impossible even to attempt a bibliography on "comparative government," for there is no work on any aspect of government anywhere which would not properly belong in this group. Here it is our attention only to point up certain works whose method and content might be considered particularly useful or interesting.

One of the truly great works in this group is Georg Jellinek's *Allgemeine Staatslehre*, 3d ed., Berlin, 1920, of which there is a French, but unfortunately no English, translation. In the same group falls Léon Duguit's *Law in the Modern State* (trans. by Frieda and Harold Laski), New York, 1919; Franz Oppenheimer's *The State*, New York, 1922; and with a different approach and in some distance, R. M. MacIver's *The Web of Government*, New York, 1949. These works are not comparative-government works in the customary sense of the term; rather are they treatises on the nature of the state. But in that capacity they are fundamental to a systematic, comparative approach and may be considered trailblazers.

Comparative government works in the generally accepted sense are two outstanding ones with which every more advanced student must be familiar: Carl J. Friedrich, *Constitutional Government and Democracy*, rev. ed., Boston, 1950; and Hermann Finer, *The*

Theory and Practice of Modern Government, rev. ed., New York, 1949. The comprehensiveness and excellence of these two works have remained unsurpassed. Books of narrower scope are J. A. Corry, *Elements of Democratic Government*, New York, 1951, and G. Lowell Field, *Governments in Modern Society*, New York, 1951.

Among the best in the field of comparative constitutions is J. A. Hawgood, *Modern Constitutions since 1787*, New York, 1939. Of interest also are Daniel Wit, *Comparative Political Institutions: A Study of Modern Democratic and Dictatorial Systems*, New York, 1953; C. F. Strong, *Modern Political Constitutions*, London, 1950; and Manuel Garcia-Pelayo, *Derecho Constitutional Comparado*, Madrid, 1951.

While Robert Michels's classic study, *Political Parties* (trans. by E. and C. Paul), first published in 1915 and reprinted by the Free Press, Glencoe, Ill., 1949, is largely based on one party, the German Social Democratic party, it is nevertheless the first systematic approach to the now abundant bibliography on political parties. A modern and worthy successor to Michels is Maurice Duverger, *Les partis politiques*, Paris, 1951.

The value of brief comparative studies is amply demonstrated by K. Wheare's *Federal Government*, 2d ed., Oxford, 1951, which despite its slender expanse uses the comparative method well in order to give an excellent account of the concept and practice of federalism. Numerous comparable works in other areas could be cited.

The student of comparative government will hardly wish to confine himself to political science in the traditional American sense. Many of the contributions made by the great sociologists Weber, Durkheim, Parett, Tawney, Parsons, etc., are indispensable today. The contributions of modern psychology are also growing as demonstrated by such books as Hanna Ahrendt's *The Origin of Totalitarianism*, New York, 1951; Eric Fromm's *Escape from Freedom*, New York, 1941; Theodor Adorno's *The Authoritarian Personality*, New York, 1950, and many others.

The field has practically no limits and infinite possibilities. It offers much challenge to the able and ambitious student, for there is definitely room for a modern Jellinek or Duguit.

INDEX